Frances Charles Hingeston-Randolph

The Register of Edmund Stafford, (A. D. 1395-1419)

An Index and Abstract of its Contents

Frances Charles Hingeston-Randolph

The Register of Edmund Stafford, (A. D. 1395-1419)
An Index and Abstract of its Contents

ISBN/EAN: 9783742818652

Manufactured in Europe, USA, Canada, Australia, Japa

Cover: Foto ©Thomas Meinert / pixelio.de

Manufactured and distributed by brebook publishing software
(www.brebook.com)

Frances Charles Hingeston-Randolph

The Register of Edmund Stafford, (A. D. 1395-1419)

THE REGISTER

OF

Edmund Stafford,

(A.D. 1395—1419);

AN INDEX AND ABSTRACT OF ITS CONTENTS,

BY THE

REV. F. C. HINGESTON-RANDOLPH, M.A.,

RECTOR OF RINGMORE,
PREBENDARY OF EXETER, AND DEAN-RURAL.

LONDON:
GEORGE BELL & SONS,
YORK STREET, COVENT GARDEN.
EXETER: HENRY S. ELAND, HIGH STREET.
1886.

TO

FREDERICK,

BY DIVINE PERMISSION

LORD BISHOP OF LONDON,

AND SOMETIME

BISHOP OF EXETER,

THIS VOLUME

IS

DEDICATED,

IN GRATEFUL REMEMBRANCE

OF HIS

LORDSHIP'S SANCTION

AND

ENCOURAGEMENT.

PREFACE.

The Register of Bishop Edmund Stafford is comprised in two folio Volumes, written on vellum. They are in excellent preservation and practically perfect, for, although some of the leaves have been injured by damp, the margins are happily so ample that only a few unimportant words have perished.

Vol. I., the "Registrum Commune" or General Record of the Acts of the Bishop, consists, nominally, of 334 folios, but really of only 324: the numbering of the folios, (contemporaneous as far as CCXLVIII), passes from CXLIX to CLX by a clerical error which fortunately occurs in the middle of a sentence, so that it is quite certain that the leaves have not been lost. The General Title is as follows:—"Registrum Venerabilis Patris, Domini Edmundi de Stafforde, Episcopi Exoniensis, qui consecratus fuit in Capella Manerii de Lamhith, Wyntoniensis Diocesis, per Reverendissimum in Christo Patrem et Dominum, Dominum Willelmum Courtenay, Archiepiscopum Cantuariensem, die Dominica videlicet vicesimo die mensis Junii, Anno Domini Millesimo CCC^{mo} Nonagesimo quinto, auctoritate Literarum Apostolicarum subscriptarum, assistentibus eidem Reverendis Patribus, Roberto Londoniensi, et Johanne Sarumensi, Episcopis." The said "Letters Apostolick," eight in number, together with a copy of the Oath taken by the Bishop-Elect, occupy ff. 1—3. The actual Register commences, at fol. 4, with a "licencia absentandi ab ecclesia," in favour of John Hacche, Rector of South Molton, dated at the Bishop's House in London, 14th July, 1395; and it ends on fol. 248, with Letters-Dimissory granted to one Peter Sturte, 3rd September, 1419—followed by the first line of another intended entry:—"Noverint universi quod nos, Edmundus, miseracione Divina Exoniensis Episcopus, ex—; but here the record of the Bishop's work was cut short by his death.

The remainder of the volume is taken up with a complete and valuable Register of all the Ordinations held by Bishop Stafford and by his Suffragans (ff. 249——299), followed by a very interesting series of Wills, sixty in number (ff. 300——334). The back of folio 334 and a fly-leaf at the end are occupied by a rude attempt at an Index,—Notanda in hoc Registro"—written at different times and by several hands, and of no value whatever.

Vol. II. is commonly known as the Register of "Institutions," with which it is mainly concerned; but its contents are of a somewhat miscellaneous character. It comprises 364 folios, nominally, but really there are only 352; and it commences with the Institutions by the Vicars-General of the Diocese, during the Bishop's prolonged residence in London. The first Vicar-General was Ralph Tregrisiou, Dean of Exeter, and his Register occupies ff. 1.——15. Its General Title is as follows: —"Registrum Reverendi Viri Magistri Radulphi Tregrisiou, Legum Doctoris, Decani Exoniensis, Venerabilis in Christo Patris et Domini, Domini Edmundi, Dei Gracia Exoniensis Episcopi, ipso Venerabili Patre in remotis agente Vicarii in Spiritualibus Generalis, de Presentacionibus et Institucionibus, virtute et auctoritate cujusdam Commissionis sibi facte et inferius descripte: xiij die mensis Julii, Anno Domini Millesimo CCC^{mo} nonagesimo quinto, prefatus Magister Radulphus Commissionem dicti Venerabilis Patris recepit, in hec verba." The document referred to is dated London, 5 July; and the first

Institution under its authority was that of John Noble, priest, to the Rectory of Horwood, on the 30th of the same month; the last that of Thomas Prydel, priest, to the Chantry of St. Leonard at Ralegh, 12th March, 1399—1400. "Et sic finiunt Instituciones et Commissiones tempore prefati Magistri Radulphi Tregrisiou, Vicarii-Generalis antedicti." Tregrisiou was succeeded by Robert Rygge, S.T.P., Chancellor of the Cathedral, whose Commission (fol. 15) is dated Crediton, 27th September, 1400, and his Register commences, on the same page, with the Institution of John Lucas, chaplain, to the Vicarage of Tavistock, on the 17th of October in the same year. This is followed by three Institutions; after which this Register becomes a "Registrum Commune," occupying ff. 16—26, and containing Institutions and Exchanges, Dispensations and Letters-Dimissory, arranged in chronological order from 8th October, 1400 to 20th March, 1402. Contemporaneously with this record of the Acts of the Vicars-General, kept at Exeter, a separate Register of Institutions by the Bishop himself was kept in London and elsewhere, and continued throughout his Episcopate. It occupies ff. 27——205; commencing with the collation of John Candlesly, clerk, to a Canonry and Prebend in the Church of Ottery, 5th July, 1395, and ending with the collation of Michael Lercedekne to a Canonry and the Prebend of Karswelle in the Church of Crediton, 3rd September, 1419, (See pp. 161, 2, *infra*).

At this point a gap occurs, more than half of fol. 205 having been cut away, as well as the three following leaves (206—208). It is probable however, that we have *no loss* to lament here; at any rate there is no apparent break except in the numbering of the folios.[1]

[1] This Volume is made up of several distinct groups of MSS., bound together, and then paged throughout; the leaves at the end of each section, which had not been required for use having been apparently left at the time and removed

The next section, extending from fol. 209 to fol. 268 consists of a series of Commissions. They commence with the Commission to Dean Tregrisiou as Vicar-General, dated 20 June, 1395, and end with a Commission of Enquiry as to the vacancy and right of patronage of the Rectory of St. Leonard's, Exeter, issued 24 Aug., 1419. And here again the spare leaves two in number, have been excised since the Book was bound, and the paging passes from 268 to 271.

A miscellaneous collection of Documents follows,—

(1) The Statutes of the Royal Free Chapel of BOSHAM; ff. 271—274.

(2) The "Ordinacio" of the Chapel and Cemetery of KINGSTON in the parish of ERMINGTON; ff. 275—278.

(3) "Ordinacio," by the Bishops of London and Exeter, concerning certain rents and tenements bequeathed to OTTERY Collegiate Church; ff. 278—279.

(4) An "Ordinacio" concerning the right of Sepulture in the Chapel of FUNTINGTON, dependent on Bosham; ff. 280—281.

(5) The "Ordinacio" of the Chantry of Edmund de Stafford, in his Cathedral Church; ff. 281—284.

(6) Copies of Sundry Letters Apostolick [Boniface IX.], touching certain Appropriations, Indulgences, etc.; ff. 284—286.

(7) An "Ordinacio" between the Prior and Monks of COWICK and the Parishioners of ST. THOMAS'S, EXETER; ff. 287—288.

(8) The Appropriation, to SLAPTON COLLEGE, of the Rectory of LODDISWELL; ff. 288—290.

---

subsequently, no doubt by some one who wanted a little vellum. For the same thing, precisely, occurs at the end of other sections, where the pagination indeed is interrupted, but the dates seem to show clearly that nothing had been written upon the missing sheets.

(9) The "Ordinacio" of the Chapel of St. Edmund-the-King in the Town of KINGSBRIDGE; ff. 290—292.

(10) An "Ordinacio" between the Prior and Monks of COWICK, Rectors of Okehampton, and the Vicar of that Parish; ff. 292, 293.

(11) The Dedication of the Chapel and Cemetery of APULDRAM (dependent on Bosham); ff. 293[b]—295.

(12) The "Ordinacio" of the Vicarage of HEAVITREE; ff. 295[b], 296.—At this point another and a more serious gap occurs; for no less than six leaves 297—302 are missing.

(13) A miscellaneous collection of copies of WRITS, etc. (A.D. 1395—1399); ff. 303—309.[b]

(14) "Feodum Archidiaconi Cantuariensis, qui intronizare debet singulos Episcopos Cantuariensis Provincie; fol. 309.[b]

(15) List of Persons who did homage to the Bishop for their Lands, from 28th Jan., 1395, to 30th July, 1419; ff. 310—311.[b]

(16) A continuation of the abovenamed collection of WRITS, etc., (A.D. 1400—1405); ff. 312—318.

(17) "Constitucio Provincialis contra Lollardos," etc., ff. 318—321.

(18) "Statutum Regium contra Lollardos" etc.; ff. 322—323.[b]

(19) "Lez estatuz faiz en parlement tenu a Leycestre le darrein iour davril, lan seconde du regne del Roi Henry V."; ff. 324—330.[b] [written on smaller sheets of vellum: fol. 331 has been cut out, but apparently the leaf was blank].

(20) A further continuation of the collection of WRITS, etc.; (A.D. 1409—1419); ff. 332—364.

At the end of this volume, also, a rough Index has been

attempted on the fly-leaves, which have been much mutilated: it is, however, quite valueless.

It would seem that Richard Tyttesbury was Registrar —"*actorum nostrorum scribam et registrarium* (i, 14^b)—from the beginning of Stafford's Episcopate till some time in May, 1409. His name occurs for the last time on the 2nd of May, and his Will was proved on the 7th of June. Roger Bolter succeeded him, and was holding the Office at the time of the Bishop's death.

The name of Tregrisiou's Registrar does not occur; but John Whyteway, a notary-publick, is twice mentioned by Rygge, his successor in the office of Vicar-General, as serving in that capacity. Both volumes are, with slight exceptions, written with great clearness and precision throughout; and their Latinity is, perhaps, above the average.[1]

Edmund de Stafford—I quote the late Dr. Oliver's "Lives of the Bishops of Exeter"[2]—was descended from a family rivalling the most antient and illustrious within the realm of England." He was the second son of Sir Richard de Stafford Knt. (who was summoned to Parliament as Baron Stafford of Clifton in 1371), by his first wife—Isabel, daughter of Sir Richard de Vernon, of Haddon and Harleston, by Maud eldest

---

[1] There is a curious instance in Vol. I (fol. 219^b), of the trouble taken by the Scribe to secure variety of expression. Eight Letters-Dimissory were issued on the same day (31 March, 1416), and thus the several entries commence,—"Item ultimo die mensis predicti, ibidem"—"Item, *eisdem* die et loco"—Item, *dictis* die et loco"—"Item, *prefatis* &c."—Item, *memoratis* &c."—"Item, *antedictis* &c."—"Item, *sepefatis* &c."—"Item, *prenominatis* &c."—Blank spaces, left, evidently, for the insertion of possible entries, but not required, are always carefully cancelled by the words—"Hic nichil deficit."

[2] The occasional references to *Oliver* are to this Book, or to his "History of the City of Exeter." And I may mention here, that by "*D'Arnis*" is meant the "Recueil de Mots de la Basse Latinité" of W. H. Maigne D'Arnis, published by M. Abbé Migne; and by "Halliwell," his well-known "Dictionary of Archaic and Provincial words."

daughter and coheir of William de Camville, of Clifton, Staffordshire. Entering Holy Orders he was, at an early age, marked out for rapid advancement: from 1369 (in which year he was instituted to the Rectory of Worthen, Salop), to 1377 he was Prebendary of Ufton, and from 1377 to 1395 of Weeford, both in the Cathedral-Church of Lichfield: he was, also, Prebendary of Welton-Paynshall in Lincoln Cathedral, and of Knaresborough *cum* Bickhill in York Minster, as well as Dean of York, at the time of his promotion to the See of Exeter in January, 1395. He was consecrated by Archbishop Courtenay on the 20th of June in that year, the Bishops of London and Salisbury (Robert de Braybroke and John Waltham) assisting. Several years elapsed before the new Bishop visited his Diocese. Appointed Lord Chancellor on the 23rd of October, 1396, he retained that high Office till the abdication of Richard the Second, shortly after which event we find him at Bishop's Clyst on the 23rd of March, 1399—1400. About a month later he commenced his Primary Visitation, which was held almost continuously, and in no less than thirty-eight places in Devon and Cornwall. Returning to London in January, 1400-1, he became Lord Chancellor again in March, and held the Office till February, 1402-3. On the 29th of March we find him at Clyst; and his Register shews that, except on rare occasions, and for a few days only at a time, he never again left his Diocese; and it attests, as his Biographer justly observes, his diligence as an administrator, and his zeal for the good government of all classes of men committed to his charge. His second Visitation commenced in June, 1404, and was held in twenty-one places. The third Visitation was held in twenty-five places, during the months of May and October, 1411. In 1414, he left Clyst at the end of April, proceeding to Ilchester, Bruton, Chipping-Norton, Leicester, Lutterworth, Daventry, Warminster, Chard, and

Honiton, and returning to Clyst on the 14th of June. From this time until his death on the 3rd of September, 1419, the active work of the Diocese at large was committed almost entirely to Suffragans, the Bishop residing in his Manor-Houses of Clyst, Crediton, and Chudleigh, and chiefly at Clyst. His bodily strength had, probably, failed him. But his work at home was incessant until the end, as the record of his acts, in an almost continuous series, amply proves. He died "in harness" at the age of 75, having instituted on the same day a Rector of Blackawton and a Canon of Crediton.[1]

I have compiled an "Itinerary" of the Bishop, after careful collation of all the dated entries in the two volumes of the Register. It will be found, I hope, of much service to Students, affording, as it does, the means of ready reference to the place where every recorded act of the Bishop was performed.

The plan of my Work needs but little explanation. It is no mere "Index," for I have given a full abstract of every important document. The "Institutions"[2] are indexed continuously under one head, for obvious reasons of convenience; and, for the sake, especially, of the Genealogical Student, I have dealt in like manner with the interesting and valuable series of Licences for Domestick Chapels and Oratories. The "Wills" and the "Ordinations" are, also, kept separate, as in the Register itself; and to the latter, as their necessary complement, I have added the numerous "Letters-Dimissory," which are entered

---

[1] His Will, dated 24 July, 1418, and proved 18 Sept., 1419, is preserved in the Register of Archbishop Chicheley (i, 319, 20).

[2] In the case of omitted Parishes, which are very few in number, it should be understood that there was, probably, no change of Incumbents during Stafford's Episcopate. It may, also, be well to note that the name of the Patron is not repeated when the *same* person presented to a Benefice; also, that in all ordinary cases of *collation* the Bishop was, of course, Patron: when he collated *by lapse* the fact is mentioned.

in the order of their dates in the "Registrum Commune." The Index-proper is concerned with everything not included under the above heads, and comprises that great *desideratum* in works of this kind—a series of cross-references, which I have done my best to make complete.[1] I have refrained from burdening my pages by needless repetitions of dates; they will not be found, therefore, in the cross-references; but all the dates are given somewhere, and, as a general rule, under the names of *places*. I may add that I have quoted the *ipsissima verba* of my MS. wherever, for any reason, it seemed desirable to do so.[2] In the case of all Names of Persons I have preserved throughout the variable spelling of the Register; of the Names of Places I have, as a rule, given the modern spelling, adding within brackets every variation of importance.

The pleasing duty remains of thanking the late Bishop of the Diocese and the Deputy Registrar, Mr. Burch, for the ready help and encouragement afforded to this undertaking from the first,[3] as well as the many friends who have enabled it to be accomplished by their generous subscriptions to its cost, or who, as experts, have assisted me in its preparation for the

---

[1] It will be observed that in a considerable number of instances the names of persons and places are simply indexed, without explanation or reference to other parts of this Book. These for the most part,—*all*, indeed, for which the reader is referred to Vol. i, fol. 300 et seqq.—belong to the Series of Wills, wherein the particulars will be found. In the other cases—few in number—there was nothing of importance to notice.

[2] I have done so very freely in the case of the Wills, of which my abstracts are so full as to be virtually translations; nothing is omitted but mere verbiage.

[3] I am, also, largely indebted to Mr. Mugford, of the Principal Registry, for his invariable courtesy and kindness whenever I have had occasion to work in his Office. And a few words must be added *in memoriam*: Mr. Pollard, of North-Street, Exeter, who had undertaken both to print and to publish my Book, was suddenly called away only a few weeks before its completion, from a sphere of manifold usefulness. He took the greatest interest in the Work, and was indefatigable in the personal revision of the proofs.

press. Among the latter I must be permitted to mention, especially, Mr. B. W. Greenfield, of Southampton, (who has read all the sheets as they passed through the press, and to whom I am indebted for many most valuable suggestions); Sir John Maclean; the Rev. C. W. Boase, Fellow of Exeter College, Oxford; the Rev. W. D. Macray, of the Bodleian, and Mr. Robert Dymond, of Exeter.

F.C.H.R.

30th January, 1886.

INDEX, &c.

—

A.

Abbot, John, co-patron of the Rectory of Coates (Dioc. of Ely), ii, 83.

Abbotsbury, i, 320^b.

Abraham, Adam, chantry-priest of St. Thomas-by-the-Bridge, Barnstaple (deceased), ii, 147^b.

Abingdon, John Stapeldon, Prior of, i, 310^b.

Abyngdon, Thomas, R. of Stokeclimsland, i, 78^b, 187^b, 325^b; proxy for Roger Perer on his institution to the Rectory of Powderham, ii, 28^b.

Achard, John, R. of Clayhidon (deceased), ii, 81^b.

Adam, John, clerk, i, 83; collated to the Rectory of St. Stephen's, Exeter, ii, 97.

Adam, Thomas, parishioner of Linkinhorne, i, 116.

Administration to Estates, Mandate of the Archbishop of Canterbury as to (1 July, 1416), i, 223, 224.

Admot, Richard, chantry-priest at Heanton Punchardon (deceased), ii, 149.

Affeton, John, R. of Lustleigh (deceased), ii, 17.

Affeton (or de Affeton) Thomas, patron of Meshaw, ii, 8^b; of East Worlington, ii, 14^b, 95^b; of Affeton,[1] ii, 51^b.

Alberton, William, parish-chaplain of Crediton, i, 314.

Albon, Thomas, R. of St. Endellion, i, 107^b.

Albryghton, Roger, *see* Ottery St. Mary, ii, 278.

Alcobasse, Peter de, R. of St. Mary's, Southampton, exchanges for the Rectory of St. Columb-major, ii, 137^b; resigns, ii, 178^b.

Alcok, Thomas, monk of Tavistock, ii, 59.

Aldebery, Walter, *see* Kentisbeare, ii, 345, 345^b.

---

[1] This parish is now part of the parish of West Worlington, in which it was merged about four centuries ago. In the Taxation of Pope Nicholas (A.D. 1291) we find them entered separately, "Ecclesia de Westwolrington, £1; Ecclesia de Affeton, 10s.," but Affeton does not appear in the *Valor Ecclesiasticus*.

Aldryngton [*alias* Colcombe], Richard, Canon of Crediton, i, 29, 51^{b}; Canon of Exeter, i, 137,^{b} 309^{b}; R. of Lanteglos-by-Camelford, i, 75, 161^{b}; collated to the Archdeaconry of Barnstaple, ii, 50^{b}; and resigns the same, ii, 15^{b}; R. of Stoke-in-Teignhead, ii, 35^{b}, 52, 57; exchanges Lanteglos for St. Mawgan-in-Pyder, ii, 178; R. of St. Columb-Major, ii, 195^{b}, 267^{b}; collated to a Canonry at Crediton, ii, 32; and to a Canonry at Crantock, ii, 45; and at Exeter, ii, 53; exchanges his Canonry at Crediton for a Canonry at Glasney, ii, 134^{b}; and resigns the latter, ii, 134^{b}; R. of Poltimore, ii, 154; resigns Poltimore, ii, 179; resigns his Canonry at Crantock, ii, 196^{b}. *See*, also, ii, 225^{b}, 228^{b}.

Alençon,[1] Philip de, Archdeacon of Exeter, his death; commission to Richard Wykeslond, LL.B., during the vacancy (22 Dec., 1397), ii, 214^{b}.

Alexander V., Pope, Proclamation of the Election of, i, 91; *see*, also, i, 99^{b}, 100, 101^{b}.

Alexander, John, i, 307^{b}.

Aleyn, Geoffrey, chaplain of Brent Tor, i, 161^{b}, 175^{b}.

Aleyn, Nicholas, i, 323.

Aleyn, William, chaplain of St. Endellion, ii, 264^{b}.

Alien Priories [*Breve Regium*]; the King demands a return of the names of all the Priors thereof, instituted since 1 Edw. I (23 April, 1401), ii, 313^{b}.

Alkebarowe,[2] Henry, collated to the R. of St. Stephen's, Exeter, ii, 87^{b}; [resigns, and is] instituted to the V. of Modbury, ii, 93^{b}; exchanges, back again, for St. Stephen's, Exeter, ii, 94^{b}; i, 313^{b}; instituted to the V. of Fremington, i, 141^{b}; ii, 96^{b}; mandate requiring him to appear at Westminster, and shew cause why he should not pay to the Abbot of Hartland 40s., arrears of a yearly rent of 6s. 8d. [*Breve Regium*], 28 Nov., 1412, ii, 346.

Alkebarwe, John, instituted to the V. of Cowick,[3] ii, 85^{b}; his death, ii, 161^{b}. *See*, also, ii, 287 et seq.

Alkebarowe, Robert de, chaplain, i, 305, 313^{b}; ii, 5^{b}; R. of Rackenford (licensed to choose a confessor), i, 5; proxy for Roger Perer, on his collation as Sacrist of Ottery, ii, 28; and for John Neweton, exchanging the R. of Skilgate

[1] In Oliver's List we are merely told that his name "occurs 23 Feb., 1384;" this record of his death having been overlooked.

[2] So, generally; but also Alkebarwe, Alkeberwe, &c.

[3] *i.e.* St. Thomas', Exeter.

(Dioc. of B. & W.), for the Chantry of Ford, ii, 32b; also for Stephen Smyth, exchanging the Chantry of Colcombe for the V. of Stogumber (Dioc. of Bath and Wells), ii, 36; R. of Marhamchurch by exchange for Faringdon (Dioc. of Winchester), ii, 45b; i, 78b; resigns his Canonry at Ottery, ii, 55b; is collated to another Canonry there, ii, 56; resigns the same, ii, 97b; resigns the R. of Marhamchurch, and is collated to the Precentorship at Crediton, ii, 97b; is instituted to the R. of North Huish, ii, 189b; resigns the Precentorship at Crediton, ii, 191.

Alkeburgh, John, R. of Stoke Rivers, (deceased), ii, 66.

Alkebourn, Robert, i, 304b.

Aller, John, R. of Clyst St. George, i, 8, 10b; licensed to choose a confessor (14 Nov., 1395), i, 7; as Warden of the Hospital of St. Gabriel, Clyst, he is directed to appoint John Treveysek, a blind and infirm chaplain, to the vacancy caused by the death of Roger Chambernon (3 May, 1401), i, 56; resigns Clyst St. George and is instituted to the R. of South Pool, ii, 90b; his death, ii, 96b, 97.

Aller, William, R. of St. Olave's, Exeter, commissioned "*ad vendicandum clericos convictos*" (27 Feb., 1395-6), ii, 211; his death, ii, 74.

Allerthorpe, Laurence, instituted to the R. of Charleton "in Southammes," ii, 30; Dean of the Collegiate church of St. Mary at Stafford, ii, 30b; exchanges Charleton for the R. of Brantingham (Dioc. of York), ii, 33.

Allerton, Richard, collated to a Canonry in Exeter Cathedral, ii, 198b.

Allerton, Robert, collated to a canonry at Bosham, ii, 199b.

Alms, collectors of, without authority from the Pope or the Bishop,—*Certificatorium super execucione mandati contra questores elemosinarum* (12 June, 1415), i, 210b.

Almyscumb, John, son of William, i, 318b.

Almyscumb, William, and Joan his wife, i, 318b, 319.

Almysheghys, John, i, 318b.

Alon, William, assaulted in the cemetery of Luppit by John Vyenne, Vicar, ii, 241.

Alphington, Reginald Baron, *alias* Mone,[1] R. of; licence of non-residence (to study at Oxford) for two years from 12 Aug., 1395, i, 4b; and again for one year from 1

[1] Also, "Moun," MS., i, q. Mohun.

Aug., 1398, i, 16b.—John Pleystowe, R. of, having been guilty of irregularity in clandestinely marrying, in his parish church, one Henry Hyrby and Margery his wife, who were not parishioners of his, without either publication of banns or licence obtained, bewails his sin and entreats Pope Gregory XII. to absolve him; the Pope acceding to his prayer, and so directing the Bishop, a dispensation was granted accordingly (7 April, 1408), i, 84b.—Commission of enquiry, on the presentation of Geoffrey Barger, chaplain, to this R. by Edward, Earl of Devon (25 June, 1415), ii, 256b.—Commission of enquiry as to dilapidations, on complaint of the said Geoffrey Barger, Rector (1 Aug., 1415), ii, 257.

Alternon, Chapel of St. Nonna, at Nonnestonys in the parish of, licensed, 18 Sep., 1400, i, 48.

Alvecote, in the parish of Shebbear, i, 92b.

Alvethecote, John, instituted to the V. of St. Mary Church, ii, 165.

Alwington, Chantry in the Church of: Mandamus to admit the nominee of William Hankeford [*Breve Regium*, 24 Nov., 1398]: Richard Colebrygge was, accordingly, admitted by the Bishop's mandate (dated London 2 Dec., 1398) ii, 308b.—Yeo, in the parish of, i, 84.—Thomas [Was], R. of, i, 50, *see* Harri, Henry, i, 72.—John Fayrewode, R. of, i, 124.—John Cokworthy, R. of; licence of non-residence for one year from 28 Feb., 1416-17, i, 231.—Richard and Edith Holemore, of Frithelstock and Alwington, i, 246.

Alyn, William, notary, ii, 174; instituted to the R. of "Chepyngtoryton" [*i.e.* Great Torrington], ii, 196b; licence of non-residence (to study at Oxford) for three years from 2 Aug., 1419, i, 247b. *See*, also, ii, 265b.

Alyn, Roger, R. of Clannaborough, ii, 359.

Amadas, William, patron of Doddiscombsleigh, ii, 3b; proxy for Richard Gabriell on his institution to the R. of Denbury, ii, 108.

Amyct, Robert, R. of Beaford,[1] licensed to celebrate, on the Feasts of Dedication only, in the Chapels of Blymesham and Wollegh in the said parish (23 May, 1400), i, 39; Commission in the matter of his proposed exchange with John Flemmyng, of Pyworthy (18 July, 1401), ii, 228b:

---

[1] Beawford, MS.—Also, Beauford.

see, also, ff. 22 and 24b; [resigns, and is] instituted to the R. of Shirwell, ii, 75b; his death, ii, 96b.

Amyhet, Walter, dispensation[1] in favour of (23 Sep., 1402), i, 61b.

Amys, Richard, Prior of Stoke Courcy,[2] co-patron of the V. of Sidmouth, ii, 22.

Andrew (or Andreu), Henry, clerk, i, 32b; R. of Lympston, i, 81; resigns Lympston, ii, 96.

Andrew, John, licensed to celebrate in the Chapel of St. James in the parish of St. Perran [Zabulo], (12 Sept., 1400), i, 47b.

Andrew, John, R. of Ashprington, i, 99.

Andrew, John, R. of Newton Ferrers, i, 74, 80, 171b; ii, 195b; his institution, ii, 12b; his death, ii, 197. *See* Derlyng, Thomas, i, 229.

Andrw, William, clerk, i, 140b.

Aneray,[3] John, Prior of St. German's (deceased), ii, 78b.

Anslade, Richard, i, 302b.

Anstyswille, Andrew, clerk (*Dispensacio super defectu natalium*—12 August, 1412), i, 163b; instituted to the V. of Linkinhorne, ii, 201b.

Anstyswylle, Simon, Canon of St. Stephen's, Launceston, ii, 117.

Anstyswill, or Ansteswyll, Stephen, V. of Hurstbourne Priors (Dioc. of Winchester), exchanges with John Snape for a Canonry and Bursal Prebend at Crediton, ii, 95b; R. of Bratton [Clovelly], i, 100b, 131b, 138b; his collation thereto, ii, 106; exchanges for the R. of Shobrooke, ii, 186.

Antony, Chapels of the B. V. M. and of SS. Peter and Paul, in the parish of,—William Pyers, V., licensed to celebrate therein on all Festivals of those Saints (31 May, 1408), i, 86.

Appropriate Churches, etc. [*Breve Regium*], the Bishop was to examine the Registers as to the same, and certify (30 Oct., 1416.)

The Bishop certified accordingly, on the 26 of Jan. following:—

He had caused the Registers and other Evidences to be examined, so far as the short time allowed had permitted, and had found (1) that the Abbess of Canonsleigh (alias Monchenleya) held, in the Archdeaconry of Exeter, the Rectories of *Burlescombe* and *Hockworthy* in the Deanery of Tiverton; the Rectory of *Rockbeare* in the Deanery of Aylesbeare; the Rectory of *Dunsford* in the Deanery of Dunsford; and in the Archdeaconry of Barnstaple the Rectory of *Dowland* in the Deanery of Torrington: (2) that the Prioress of Polslo held in the aforesaid Deanery of Aylesbeare the Rectories of *Budleigh* and *Aylesbeare*, and in the Archdeaconry of Totnes

[1] He had been ordained subdeacon *ab alieno episcopo*, without licence.

[2] Stokeursy, MS.

[3] So *Oliver*. Perhaps "Averay."

the Rectory of *Holbeton* in the Deanery of Plympton: (3) that the Prioress of Cornworthy held in the said Archdeaconry of Totnes the Rectory of *Cornworthy* in the Deanery of Totnes, the Rectory of *Clawton* in the Deanery of Holsworthy, and the Rectory of *Marland* in the aforesaid Deanery of Torrington: and (4) that the Hospitallers of St. John within the East-gate, Exeter, held in the aforesaid Deanery of Totnes the Rectory of *Holne*, and in the Archdeaconry and Deanery of Barnstaple the Rectory of *Yarnscombe*. This List is followed by particulars as to the provision made for the several Vicars, and as to the tenths . . . . ii, 359b.

Appuldore (alias Persones), John, i, 306.

Aps, John, who had laid violent hands on Thomas Clyk, clerk; Commission for his absolution (25 Nov., 1410), ii, 236.

Apuldram,[1] Prebend of, in the Collegiate Church of Bosham, ii, 38b, 293b et seqq.

Ardagh,[2] Henry Nony, Bishop of, commissioned to ordain in the Diocese (24 Aug., 1396), ii, 211b; to reconcile Churches and Cemeteries polluted by effusion of blood, etc. (6 Sept., 1397), ii, 213; to confirm, etc. (1398[3]), ii, 220.

Arderne, John, Esquire, commissioned to be supervisor of the Episcopal lands (12 March, 1416-17), ii, 261; mentioned, i, 333, and with Margaret his wife, i, 322b.

Ardyngton, Henry, one of the Vicars at Bosham, ii, 147.

Arthur, Nicholas (of Tintagel), instituted to the V. of St. Madron (13 March, 1309-10), i, 208b. *See* St. Madron.

Arthur, Thomas, scholar (*Dispensacio super defectu natalium*, 21 Sep., 1414), i, 200.

Arundel [Richard Fitz-Alan], Earl of, i, 11.

Arundell, John, instituted to Bodmin Prebend in St. Endellion, ii, 189; ii, 263b[4]; collated to a canonry at Crantock,[4] ii, 196b.

Arundell,[5] Sir John, Knt., presents to the R. of St. Columb-Major, ii, 11b, 76b, 89b, 131b, 137b, 178b, 187, 195b; to the Prebend of Trehaverock in St. Endellion, ii, 46b; to the R. of Phillack, ii, 102b, 106b, 131; to the R. of Whitstone (in Cornwall), ii, 121; to the R. of St. Mawgan-in-Pyder, ii, 121, 139b, 178b; patron (for one out of three turns) of Milton Damerel, ii, 341b; also, *see* Illogan [*Breve Regium*], ii, 314b.

Arundell, John, "domicellus," does homage to the Bishop in London, for his lands in Devon and Cornwall (13 July, 1396), ii, 310; and[6] at Leicester for certain lands in the

[1] Appeldurham, MS.
[2] Ardakan, MS.
[3] The month is omitted.
[4] Described here as "*alias* Hylle."
[5] Aroundell, MS.
[6] Described here as "de Trerya."

village of "Trelong" within the demesne of "Trekeyr" (20 May, 1414), ii, 311; takes the oath as J.P. for Cornwall, ii, 335b; Sheriff of Cornwall, ii, 351.

Arundell, Thomas (of Cornwall), presents to the R. of [Ruan] Lanyhorne, ii, 158b.

Ashburton, William [Hayford], V. of, Penitentiary in the Deanery of Moreton, i, 143, 174, 194b, 207b, 217, 231, 237b, 245.—Geoffrey Attewey of, i, 242; William Geffrey of, i, 240b.

Ashbury, John Milcton, R. of, licensed to celebrate in his manse (16 Feb., 1396-7), i, 11b.

Ashcombe,[1] John and Alice Cade, of, i, 9b.—William, parson of,[2] from whose lands, etc., 52s. had been adjudged to be paid to Robert, Prior of Merton, being arrears of a certain annual payment of 6s. (due at Michaelmas and Easter in equal parts), as well as 6s. 8d. on account of the loss caused by the detention of the money. It had been ascertained that the said William had no land or tenements there, apart from the "Sanctuary;" so the King commanded the Bishop to see that the said moneys were paid from the revenues of his Church [*Breve Regium*, 10 Feb., 1396-7], ii, 304.

Ashling, East and West, *see* Bosham, ii, 280.

Ashprington,[3] Chapel of St. John at Pinford, in the parish of, i, 37.—John Andrew, R. of, licensed to celebrate in the Chapel of St. David at Hamme, in the parish of (26 June, 1419), i, 99; Penitentiary in the Deanery of Totnes, i, 174, 194b, 207b.

Ashreigney,[4] William Smyth, R. of, licence of non-residence for one year from 28 Sept., 1400, i, 49b; also[5] for one year from 25 July, 1410, i, 101.

Ashton,[6] Robert Belet,[7] R. of, licence of non-residence for one year, from 3 Oct., 1405, i, 76b; also, while the Rectory-house, which had been destroyed by fire, was being rebuilt (3 June, 1410), i, 97.

Ashwater,[8] John Tone, R. of, i, 71.—John Jarberd,[9] R. of, licence of non-residence (to study at Oxford), from 23 May, 1413,

[1] Aysschcomb, MS.
[2] Asshcombe, MS.
[3] Ayschpryngton, MS.
[4] Ryngesaysch and Esse Regni, MS.
[5] He was, also, at this time, R. of Nymet Rowland.
[6] Assherton, MS.; "Assereston" in the Taxation of Pope Nicholas.
[7] Robert Belet *or* Balet, MS.
[8] Essewater, MS.
[9] Or Jerberd, MS.

till St. Matthew's Day, i, 180[b]; also, for one year from 30 Sept., 1414, i, 201[b]; also, from 18 Jan., 1415-16, to Michaelmas, 1416, i, 215[b].

Aspe, Alan, proxy for Humphry Bonyour, ii, 146[b].

Asthill, William, collated to a Canonry and Bursal Prebend at Crediton, ii, 38.

Asthorp, William, *see* Exeter, St. George's, ii, 336[b].

Aston, Thomas, Canon of St. Paul's, and Prebendary of "Eeldstrete" therein, ii, 43, 226; Prebendary of Crantock, which he exchanges for the Chapel of St. Helen, Ingelby (Dioc. of Lincoln), ii, 47[b].

Atherington,[1] Walter Bullock, R. of, i, 15, 21.—Thomas Schepey, subdeacon, R. of; dispensation (to study at Oxford) for four years from 17 Feb., 1409-10), i, 94[b]; also, licence of non-residence from 22 Dec., 1414, to Michaelmas, 1415, i, 205[b]; also, for two years, from 28 Aug., 1415, i, 212; also, for two years, from 6 Oct., 1417, i, 235.—Chantry-chapel at Umberleigh[2] in the parish of, ii, 17[b], 96[b]; Commission of enquiry as to the pollution of the Church by two parishioners, Thomas Baudyn and William Juyll (13 Jan., 1414-15), ii, 256.

The Bishop had been informed that the Church had been polluted in an assault committed by Baudyn on Juyll, and was disused in consequence; but finding on enquiry that no blood was shed, he pronounced that there had been no pollution, and that the Church was to be re-opened (21 Jan., 1414-15), i, 207.

atte Forde, Robert, i, 315[b].

atte Haye, John (*alias* Stoke), scholar (*Dispensacio super defectu natalium*—17 Sept., 1406), i, 79.

atte Hulle, Walter, instituted to the R. of Cheldon, ii, 5.

atte Hurn, Adam, V. of Aylesbeare (deceased), ii, 75[b].

atte Hyde, John, R. of Loxbeare (resigns), ii, 20[b].

atte Kyrke, William, V. of Cadeby (Dioc. of Lincoln), exchanges for the R. of Huntshaw, ii, 49[b].

atte Mille, John, V. of Bovey Tracey (deceased), ii, 20.

atte Nywecourte, Thomas, i, 332.

atte Stone, William, i, 304.

atte Wassche, Joan, sister of John Ulveston, V. of Stokenham, i, 330[b].

---

[1] Alderyngton, MS.; also Aderyngton. [2] Wumberley, MS.

atte Water, John, Canon and 7th Prebendary of Ottery, exchanges for a canonry at Glasney, ii, 159; exchanges the latter for a prebend at St. Probus, ii, 182^b; exchanges, again, for the R. of Limpsfield (Dioc. of Winchester), ii, 193^b.

Attewey, Geoffrey, a servant born on the Bishop's Manor of Ashburton—his manumission dated 2 Sep., and signed and sealed by the Dean and Chapter, 3 Sep., 1418, i, 242^b.

atte Wille, John, R. of Clyst St. Laurence (deceased), ii, 2.

atte Wode, Patrick, R. of Lezant[1] (deceased), ii, 155.—*See*, also, ii, 254^b.

atte Wode, Richard, Theobald, and Henry. *See* Sutcombe, i, 233^b; ii, 261^b.

atte Wode, Robert, a proxy for the parishioners of Pancraswyke in the matter of the "Ordinatio," i, 68^b, 69.—*See*, also, i, 332, 332^b.

atte Wylle, John, pollutes the Church of Fremington, ii, 242.

atte Wylle, Robert, clerk, i, 334.

atte Ya, John, instituted to the R. of Satterleigh, ii, 182^b, 261.

atte Yate, Joan, i, 307^b.

atte Yate, Richard, R. of Northlew, ii, 4, 211.

atte ȝeo, Henry, farmer of the revenues of the Prior of Frampton,[2] at Northam, i, 138.

Aubrey, John, instituted to the R. of Bicton, ii, 6; exchanges Bicton for Harpford, ii, 11, 223;[3] exchanges Harpford for the R. of Wambrook (Dioc. of Salisbury), ii, 188, 263.

Auger, Vivian, Precentor of Crediton, ii, 360.

Aumarle (or Amarle), James, co-patron of the R. of Cotleigh, ii, 64, 95^b; of [Clay]hidon R., ii, 81^b; of South Pool R., ii, 90^b, 97; of Dunterton R., ii, 130, 236^b; *see* Cardynham (*Institutions*), ii, 153.

Aumarle, Thomas, R. of Cardynham, resigns, ii, 21.

Aumarle, Luke, i, 312.

Auncell, Richard, Prior of St. Michael's Mount, ii, 124, 338^b, 349.

---

[1] Lansante, MS. —Oliver reads Lansante, "n" and "u" being often ambiguous: but I have found it written Lansante, which settles the question.

[2] "Prioris de Frompton (*sic*) apud Northam." Frampton, near Dorchester (Dorset), was originally a Priory of Black Monks, a cell to the Abbey of St. Stephen, at Caen.

[3] *See*, also, i, 99.

Avenell, John, presents to the R. of Loxbeare, ii, 21, 143^b, 168^b.

Avery, John, R. of St. Laurence, Exeter, i, 59; exchanges for the R. of St. Andrew's, Launcells, ii, 26; exchanges Launcells for the R. of Beaworthy, ii, 69^b.

Aveton-Giffard (now commonly, but not accurately, spelt "Gifford,") John [Juhelȝete], R. of, i, 50; is commissioned to enquire into a case of assault on a priest, *see* Wolhay, John, ii, 226^b.—Thomas Tremayne, R. of, appointed Penitentiary for the Deanery of Woodleigh, i, 94, 115^b, 217, 231, 237^b; *see* Stokenham, ii, 357^b.—John Wytloff's legacy to the church of, i, 306; Isabella Daumarle buried in the church of, i, 308^b.—Mansion of John Bery at, i, 67^b.—The Bridge [over the Avon] at, i, 330^b.

Awliscombe,[1] William [Davy], V. of, appointed a Penitentiary in the Deanery of Dunkeswell, i, 143, 173^b, 194, 207^b, 216^b, 231, 237^b, 245.

Aylesbeare, the R. of, appropriated to Polslo, ii, 359^b.

Aylmere, Richard, instituted to the R. of Luffincott, ii, 12^b.

Aynho, Thomas, i, 300.

Aysch, Joan, (daughter of Giles), ii, 219^b.—*See* Claysch, Thomas.

Aysch, John, instituted to the V. of St. Martin's, Liskeard, ii, 169^b.

Aysch, John, clerk (*Dispensacio super defectu natalium*, dated 6 Feb, 1410-11), i, 114.

Ayscherygh, Nicholas, instituted to the R. of Talaton, ii, 85^b.

Ayschperton, Thomas [V. of Paignton], collated to a Canonry at Bosham, ii, 54; resigns, ii, 92^b; his death, ii, 94^b.

Aysshecote, William, instituted to the V. of Veryan,[2] ii, 23^b.

Axminster, Wyke, in the parish of, i, 82^b; Manor of Weycroft, i, 237.—Mentioned in Sir William Bonevylle's Will, i, 312.—John Whattecomb, V. of, i, 50; ii, 49; his resignation, ii, 17^b.—Henry Pake, chaplain, admitted as his successor (Patrons, Walter Cook and Thomas de Weston, prebendaries,) *ibid.*—John Worthyn, V. of (*see* Worthyn, John), i, 187.—John [Matthu], V. of, appointed a Penitentiary in the Deanery of Honiton, i, 245.—Interdict on the parish-church in consequence of the intrusion of a stranger, without mission, who had preached therein, pretending to be a chaplain (12 Jan., 1411-12), i, 141; the interdict was relaxed on the 23rd of the same month, i, 142.—A "Portio"

[1] Owluscomb, MS. [2] Elerky, MS.

of the Church assigned as part of the endowment of the prebend of Grendale in York Minster, ii, 107; the "Obedientia" of Thomas Grenewode, Canon and Prebendary thereof (31 Oct., 1416), ii, 179b.

Axmouth, William Slade, V. of: his appeal to the Archbishop's Court against Sampson Trigal, Prior of Lodres (Diocese of Sarum), complaining that the Bishop of Exeter had neglected to attend to the proposed augmentation of the said Vicar's portion, is referred to Bishop Stafford, who remits it to the said Court for settlement (9 Dec., 1396),[1] i, 9b.—St. Leonard's Chapel at Dona, in the parish of.

A dispute had existed, for some time, between John Coterel, V. of Axmouth, and the inhabitants of the hamlet of Dona, the latter claiming, and the former refusing to grant occasional services in the said chapel, and the Sacraments and Sacramentals on certain days (the right of burial alone excepted.) The Bishop, desiring to do justice to both parties, made a provisional order—that William Clerk, chaplain, should, for a time, hear confessions there and absolve penitents, except in reserved cases, and celebrate the Eucharist and administer the Holy Communion; but he was to receive no stipend from the Vicar, to whom all oblations, profits, and tithes were to be paid as before (24 March, 1417-18), i, 238b.

B.

Bacheler, Roger, R. of Churchstow, i, 143, 174, 194b, 207b, 217, 231, 237b, 245; ii, 290b et seqq., 357b.

Bachyler (or Bacheler), William, Joan, his wife, Roger (his brother) and Joan and Nichola (his daughters), i, 314b; his Will, *ib.*

Bacon, Adam, proxy for William Pilton, ii, 139.

Bacwylle, Richard, co-patron of the V. of Sidmouth, ii, 22.

Badecok, John, a layman, of Landcross,—

He had complained to the Bishop that certain malicious persons, whose names were unknown, had brought against him an unfounded charge of having stolen four sheep, the property of Richard Scotte of the same parish, to the great injury of his character. He had purged himself of the charge before Archdeacon Hunden, the Chancellor; and the Bishop directed the Deans of Hartland and Torrington to proclaim the excommunication of the offenders in the Churches of those Deaneries (27 July, 1412), i, 163.

Badecok, William, R. of Iddesleigh,—to appear at Westminster within fifteen days from Trinity Sunday,[2] to shew cause why he should not be required to pay to the Abbot of Tewkesbury the sum of fourteen marks, being arrears of an annual payment of 6s. 8d. [*Breve Regium*; 6 May, 1395], ii, 303.

[1] 1390, MS. (clerical error).

[2] 6th June in that year.

Baghedon, John, R. of West Putford (deceased), ii, 82.

Bailly, John, instituted to the R. of Blisland, ii, 124[b]; resigns the same, ii, 138[b].—*See* Blisland, ii, 237.

Baisham, John, co-patron of North Bovey R., ii, 189[b], 264.

Bajazet[1] [I.], Emperor of the Turks, ii, 312[b].

Baker, Andrew, of Ermington, ii, 277.

Baker, Gilbert, admitted (by Commission) to the V. of Buckland [Monachorum], ii, 228; deceased, ii, 88[b].

Baker, John, R. of Martinhoe (deceased), ii, 195.

Baker, Philip (of Cornwall), *see* St. Feock, i, 161.

Baker, Thomas, R. of Kentisbury, i, 327[b]; his institution, ii, 106; licensed to celebrate in the Chapel of St. John Baptist at Patchole[2] in that parish, on the Nativity of St. John Baptist and St. Anne's Day (21 May, 1411), i, 123[b].

Baker (*alias* Meone), Thomas, V. of Tamerton (resigns) ii, 153.

Baker, Thomas, of Ilfracombe, i, 328.

Baker, William, i, 327[b].

Baker, William, an accolite; ordained subdeacon by Bishop Brantingham, at St. Pancras', Exeter (title from the Abbot and Convent of Forde), 23 March, 1385-6; deacon in the Bishop's chapel at Chudleigh, 26 Feb., 1388-9; and priest in his chapel at Crediton, 24 Sep., 1390.—These facts were ascertained by Bishop Stafford on a scrutiny, and published 2 March, 1416-7, i, 231[b].

Ball, Thomas, i, 312.

Ballerd (or Ballard), Robert, instituted to the Chantry at Morthoe, ii, 63[b]; exchanges for the V. of Bridgerule, ii, 100[b].

Balsham, John, instituted (on exchange) to the R. of Blisland, ii, 32; deceased, ii, 124[b]; Commission of enquiry (*see* Blisland), ii, 237.

Bampfylde,[3] John, presents to the R. of Huxham, ii, 115; to the R. of Poltimore, ii, 134, 134[b], 154, 179.

Bampfylde, Thomas de, presents to the R. of Poltimore, ii, 25[b]; to the R. of Huxham, ii, 74[b], 79.

Bampton in Oxfordshire (Diocese of Lincoln), Thomas Plymmes-

---

[1] Bayzetus, MS.
[2] Pacchole, MS.
[3] Also, Baunfilde, MS.

wode, V. of, i, 127ᵇ; *see*, also, the Will of William Poundestoke, i, 322.

Bampton,[1] *see* Waryn, John, i, 138.—[*Breve Regium*], prohibiting the admission of any Clerk to the Benefice, then vacant, pending the settlement of the dispute as to the right of patronage between John, Prior of Bath, the Bishop, Ralph Tregresiow, Dean of Exeter, and Matthew Doune, clerk (30 Nov., 1397), ii, 306ᵇ.—[*Breve Regium*], for the admission of a suitable clerk, the Prior of Bath having established his claim to present against Sir Hugh Courtenay (12 Feb., 1397-8), ii, 307ᵇ.—Edward Dokeworthy, R. of; licence of non-residence, for one year, from 12 Sep., 1410, i, 104; Penitentiary in the Deanery of Tiverton, i, 143, 173ᵇ, 207ᵇ, 216ᵇ, 231, 237ᵇ.

Bampton (*alias* Chapman), John, R. of Bradninch, exchanges with John Wendovere for his Archdeaconry of Lewes (Dioc. of Chichester), ii, 27.

Bard, Robert, a merchant of York, having become surety for one Robert Sauplers of that city, had been imprisoned for a half year, for default. The Bishop grants an Indulgence to all the faithful who should provide Theobalda, his wife, with funds for his relief (30 April, 1398), i, 17ᵇ.

Bardolf, Thomas, R. of Whitstone in Cornwall (deceased), ii, 121; Commission of enquiry as to the dilapidations at Whitstone, ii, 233ᵇ.

Barell, John, chaplain (Dioc. of Bath and Wells), i, 42ᵇ, 313ᵇ, 314; proxy for Simon Lynam (*see* Marhamchurch), ii, 45ᵇ; collated to the R. of Clyst Fomison (Sowton), ii, 54; R. of St. Illogan, i, 88ᵇ, 120ᵇ; ii, 74ᵇ, 76, 125, 314ᵇ; Canon of Glasney, i, 125; ii, 109ᵇ.

Baret, John, a parishioner of Linkinhorne, i, 116.

Baret, John, ii, 362ᵇ.

Baret, Robert, instituted to the R. of Uploman,[2] ii, 136ᵇ.

Baret, Walter, R. of Goodleigh, i, 50, 190ᵇ; ii, 158ᵇ, 252ᵇ.

Barger, Geoffrey, instituted to the R. of Alphington, ii, 166, 256ᵇ; exchanges for the V. of Broad Clyst, ii, 200ᵇ, 267ᵇ.

Barnabe, Simon, patron of Skilgate (Diocese of Bath and Wells), ii, 33.

---

[1] Bawnton or Baunton, MS.

[2] "Wellyngton Lamon," MS.—*See* Uploman (*Institutions*).

Barnard, Thomas,[1] i, 328.

Barnard (or Bernard), Thomas, V. of Davidstow, i, 58ᵇ; (deceased), ii, 101.

Barnet, John, Official of the Court of Arches, i, 29ᵇ; ii, 35.

Barnevyle (or Bernevyle), Simon, co-patron of the R. of Washfield, ii, 108, 142, 168, 259ᵇ, 356ᵇ.

Barnstaple, mansion of John Bydewyll at, i, 62ᵇ.—Walter Lane of, i, 39.—Barnstaple Bridge, i, 302ᵇ.—Lazar-House at, i, 302ᵇ, 303, 306ᵇ, 331ᵇ.

Barnstaple, William [Knyght], V. of, a Penitentiary in the Deanery of Barnstaple, i, 50; John [Lemman], V. of, ditto, i, 194ᵇ, 207ᵇ.—The parish-church, with its cemetery, having been polluted by bloodshed, the Bishop commissions William, Prior of Pilton, to reconcile the same (6 April, 1411), ii, 240ᵇ.—The Bishop, having been informed that the cemetery had been polluted by a quarrel, with bloodshed, between John Jacob and Margery, wife of Thomas Holman, issues a Commission to the Archdeacon, to enquire and certify (10 June, 1411), ii, 241ᵇ. On the 18th June the Bishop published the result of this enquiry, viz. that there had been neither bloodshed nor violence committed, and, consequently, it was not necessary to reconcile the cemetery, ii, 242ᵇ.—Commission of enquiry as to the pollution of the cemetery by John Pytman and John Bryan, with effusion of blood (3 Aug., 1414), and Commission to reconcile the same (dated 5 Aug.), ii, 255; absolution of John Pytman, the assailant, who had given satisfaction to John Bryan (Commission addressed to the said Prior of Pilton, 15 Aug., 1414), i, 198.

Barnstaple Priory presents to the V. of Barnstaple, ii, 71, 139; [Simon],[2] Prior of, in arrears of procurations, due to the Pope's collector, for three years (1408-10), i, 105, 110.

Baron (*alias* Mone), Reginald, deacon, R. of Alphington; i, 4ᵇ.

Baron, Richard, i, 305.

Barstaple, John, of Tiverton, ii, 268ᵇ.

Barton, Richard, proxy for William Barton on his institution to the Archdeaconry of Totnes, ii, 165.

Barton, Simon, R. of Michaelstow; licence of non-residence, for a year, from 10 Dec., 1395, i, 7; for two years from 4 May,

---

[1] "filio meo levato de Sacro Fonte,"—Will of Thomas Barton, Canon of Exeter, q.v.

[2] "*Simon Sele*, alias *Ocle*, alias *Cole*."—*Oliver's Monasticon*.

1397 ("*contemplacione Magistri Thome Southam, Canonici Sarum*"), i, 12; for one year, from 5 Sept., 1399 ("*ab ecclesia sua . . . . et eandem alicui viro ecclesiastico ad firmam dimittendi*), i, 29; for two years, from 14 March, 1402-3, i, 63; deceased, ii, 78[b].

Barton,[1] Thomas, Canon and Prebendary of Bosham, confirmed therein by the Bishop after his Visitation there (1398), i, 22; R. of Ilfracombe,—licence of non-residence for one year, from 6 June, 1410, i, 97; instituted to the R. of Kingsnympton, ii, 96; resigns the same, ii, 100; exchanges his Canonry at Bosham for the prebend of Penylles in the Church of Chulmleigh, ii, 101[b]. He was, also, Canon of Exeter (*see* ii, 226), and Canon and Prebendary of Stowford in the Church of Crediton (*see* ii, 175[b]); his death, ii, 175, 175[b]; his Will, i, 327.—Canon Barton was an executor of the Will of (Canon) Henry Blakbourne, i, 30[b].

Barton, William, Canon and Prebendary of the Holy Cross in Lincoln Cathedral, and R. of Crawley Magna in the Diocese of Lincoln, exchanges for the Archdeaconry of Totnes, ii, 164[b].—*See*, also, i, 325[b].

Basle, William, Bishop of, i, 11[b].

Bassett, John, *see* St. Illogan [*Breve Regium*], ii, 314[b].

Basset, William, Judge, ii, 342.

Bassusstachius, Bishop of Lucerne, his letter to the Bishop of Exeter on behalf of Henry Nansumer, priest (*q.v.*), i, 48[b]; his letter on behalf of Reginald Wellcslegh, i, 54[b].

Bastard, Alice, *see* Rodenay.

Basyngham de Melton, John, V. of Chudleigh, exchanges for the V. of Luppit, ii, 65; and again exchanges for the V. of Westbury (Diocese of Bath and Wells), ii, 71[b].

Bateman, Thomas, i, 304.

Bath, the Prior and Convent of the Cathedral Church of patrons of Bampton, ii, 8, 192, 264; of Uffculme, ii, 44[b].

Bath, St. Michael's, ii, 359.

Batte, Richard, V. of Haslebury (Dioc. of Bath and Wells), exchanges for the R. of Jacobstow (Devon), ii, 157[b]; and again for the V. of Toller-Porcorum (Dioc. of Salisbury), ii, 162.

Battle Abbey,—Patrons of St. Nicholas Priory, Exeter, ii, 5[b] 47, 82, 158[b], 197[b].

---

[1] Also, "Berton," MS.

Batty's Inn,[1] Oxford, the Bishop at, i, 15b.

Batyn (*alias* Toker), John (*see* Beamound, Joan), i, 161b.

Batyn, John, Canon of St. Stephen's, Launceston, ii, 117.

Batyn, John, subdeacon, R. of Denbury, i, 243 ; his institution, ii, 191. *See* also, i, 303b.—On 16 April, 1405, John Batyn exchanged the R. of Stoodleigh, with John Ivery, for the R. of Oake (Dioc. of Bath and Wells), ii, 83b.

Batyn, Roger, a citizen of Exeter, i, 315.

Batyn, Roger, R. of Stockleigh-English (deceased), ii, 6.

Batyn, Walter, instituted to the V. of St. Thomas's, Exeter, ii, 161b, 255b.

Baucomb, John, clerk,—*Dispensacio super defectu natalium* (8 Aug., 1411), i, 130b.

Baudyn, John, instituted to the R. of Broad Nymet,[2] ii, 179 ; resigns, ii, 195b ; is instituted to the R. of Monkokehampton, ii, 192b.

Baudyn, Henry; who had been ordained deacon, without licence, by Johannes, Episcopus Saltoniensis,—dispensation in his favour (10 March, 1402-3), i, 62b.—Henry Baudyn, probably the same person, was instituted to the V. of Buckfastleigh, 22 Dec., 1416, ii, 181b.[3]

Baudyn, Thomas (*see* Atherington), i, 207 ; also ii, 256.

Baunton (or Bampton), William, Canon of Exeter, and Canon and Prebendary of Rigge in the Church of Crediton (deceased), ii, 32.

Baunton, William, chaplain, ii, 125 ; instituted to the V. of Burlescombe, ii, 151b.

Bawcombe (or Bowcombe), manor of James and Isabella Bawcombe, in the parish of Ugborough, i, 43.

Baylebeyn (or Baylyben), John, R. of Cheddon (Dioc. of Bath and Wells) exchanges for the V. of [West] Alvington, ii 49b ; his death, ii, 85.

Bayonne[4] (*see* Bridgewater), i, 96.

Beaford, Robert Amyet, R. of; licence to celebrate (*see* Amyet), i, 39. Commission as to a proposed exchange of this

---

[1] Battysynne, MS.

[2] This Rectory is now united with Bow, *alias* Nymet Tracey.

[3] The name of Henry Bawdyn, also, occurs at ii, 65b, as proxy for William May, q. v. This Bishop (Suffragan) was John Greenlaw — "Episcopus Saltoniensis in Media"—consecrated by Henry Bowet, 8 Sept., 1401. He was Suffragan of Wells, 1401—1408.

[4] Bayne, MS.

benefice, by Robert Amyet with John Flemmyng, for the R. of Pyworthy (18 July, 1401), ii, 228^{b} and 24^{b}.

Beaghe, William, Abbot-Elect of Buckfast, his "Obediencia," (8 Sept., 1415), ii, 169.

Bealde, William, V. of St. Clement's,[1] Truro (deceased), ii, 48^{b}.

Bear, Elias, i, 328.

Beare, Alexander, *See* Exeter *(Collations).*

Beare, John, clerk, i, 306^{b}.

Beare, John, chaplain (*see* Dean Prior), ii, 355.

Beare, John, R. of Roche, i, 61^{b}, 90^{b}, 100^{b}; his institution, ii, 57^{b}.

Beare[2], John de la, patron of the R. of St. Swithin's, Littleham, ii, 13, 22^{b}.

Beare, John, a smith, i, 306^{b}.

Beare, Robert, a parishioner of Linkinhorne, i, 116.

Beare, Walter, does homage to the Bishop, in London, for lands in Tawton (7 Oct., 1398), ii, 310.

Beare, Walter, R. of Zeal Monachorum (q. v.); (deceased), ii, 10.

Beaufys, John, chaplain, i, 310.

Beauchamp, Richard, R. of Whitechapel, London, exchanges for the R. of St. Mawnan, ii, 178.

Beuchamp, Mary, elected Abbess of Canonsleigh, ii, 125; i, 191.

Beaumont[3], Baldwin, R. of Shirwell (deceased) ii, 75^{b}.

Beaumond, Isabella relict of William, presents to the R. of Heanton Punchardon, ii, 247.—*See*, also, ii, 345^{b}.

Beamound, Joan, *v.* Richard Ley (in the Consistory Court),—

It appears that exception had been taken to John Toker, a witness in this case, on behalf of the said Joan, on the ground that, at the time, he was lying under sentence of the Greater Excommunication, on account of his having consented to act as witness at the clandestine marriage of one Robert Martyn with Englisia his own natural daughter, though he knew, and had acknowledged, that it was an uncanonical proceeding. The Bishop, on the 15th of June, 1412, ordered the Register to be searched by the Registrar, Roger Bolter,[4] and it was found therein recorded that the said John Toker, *alias* Batyn, had appeared before the Bishop at Crediton, on the 14th of March, 1411-12, confessing that, although he was well aware that the said Robert Martyn and Alicia Wyllyam, parishioners of Milton Abbot, had been previously married and that Alicia

---

[1] Lamorek, MS.

[2] Also, de la Beer, MS.

[3] Spelt variously in the MS., Beaumond, Beamound, Beaumound, Beaumount, and Beaumont.

[4] Apparently a separate Register, kept at Clyst; the words in the text are "nostrum *in hac parte* Registrarium, et *Registri nostri custodem in manerio nostro de Clyst*, nostre Diocesis." The Bishop refers to his Registers, and with good reason, as "bene et fideliter custoditis."

was still alive, he had, nevertheless, acted as a witness sometime in the month of September, 1411, when one Geoffrey [Aleyn], chaplain, and curate in charge, of the Church of Brent Tor,[1] celebrated the said clandestine marriage in the said Church, without seeking or obtaining permission from the curate of Milton Abbot; also that he had submitted himself to the Bishop's grace and clemency, and prayed to be absolved, i, 161^b. See, also, fol. 175^b, where the account of this business is slightly varied, and it is stated that the ceremony was performed by Geoffrey Aleyn, curate of Brent Tor, but in the Church of Milton Abbot.

Beaumound, John, R. of St. Martin's, Exeter (deceased), ii, 96.

Beaumond, Matilda, daughter of William; *See* Courtenay, Sir Hugh (of Haccombe), i, 235^b.

Beaumont, Roger, R. of Bideford (q. v.) ii, 250.

Beaumont, Thomas, ii, 307^b.

Beaumond, Thomas. *See* Parkham.

Beaumount, Thomas[2], co-patron of the R. of Landcross, ii, 95^b; of Shirwell R., ii, 96^b, 103^b; of Gittisham R., ii, 104; of Stoke Rivers R., ii, 129^b, 180; [*Breve Regium*] for the administration of the oath to him, as Sheriff of Devon (3 Nov., 1412), ii, 345^b.

Beaumont, Thomas (son and heir of William), a minor, *see* Heanton Punchardon *(Institutions)*, ii. 149; patron of Heanton Punchardon [Henry IV, presents, 17 Nov., 1412, during his minority], ii, 146.

Beamound, William, son and heir of Sir John, ii, 8^b; patron of Heanton Punchardon, ii, 7; presents to the R. of Stoke Rivers, ii, 67; to Shirwell R., ii, 75^b; to Beaford R., ii, 76; to Challacombe R., ii, 87^b; to Loxhore R., ii, 90.

Bec [Monasterium de Becco Hellvyng MS.], Abbey of, patrons of Cowick Priory, ii, 37.

Bedeman, *alias* Stevyn (q. v.)

Bedmond,[3] Laurence, S.T.B., R. of Lifton (q. v.); ii, 119^b, 265.

Bedmond,[4] William, R. of Clutton (Dioc. of Wells), exchanges for the R. of Clyst St. Laurence, ii, 102^b, i, 207; his death, ii, 200.

Beef,[5] John, R. of Charlton (Dioc. of Rochester), exchanges for the R. of Clyst Fomison (Sowton), ii, 80^b; promoted to the Wardenship of the Chapel of Clyst St. Gabriel, ii, 96^b.—*See*, also, i, 333.

---

[1] Brentorre, also Brentetorre, MS.

[2] Thomas Beaumont, probably the same, presented Thomas Hendeman to the R. of St. Mabyn, in Cornwall, 13 April, 1415, ii, 164.

[3] Also Bedeman and Bedman, MS.

[4] Also Bedeman, MS.

[5] Also Beeff, Bef, and Befe, MS.

Beff, David, Canon of Frithelstock, i, 53b.

Beer Ferris[1], Richard Monk, Archpriest of, i, 226; licence to farm out the revenues of his benefice (12 Dec., 1410), i, 110b.

Beke, John, R. of Blackborough (deceased), ii, 85.

Bekett, William, instituted as Prior of St. Nicholas Priory, Exeter, ii, 82; deceased, ii, 158b.

Belamyslond, John, R. of Portlemouth (deceased), ii, 13.

Belmyslond, William, R. of Heanton Punchardon, ii, 7.

Belde, John, collated to the V. of Rockbeare, ii, 190b.

Beldegore, William, ii, 346.

Bele, John, i, 333.

Bele,[2] John, chaplain, licensed to serve the Chapel at Holeway in the parish of North Lew (26 Feb., 1404-5), i, 73b; instituted to the R. of Highampton, ii, 94; his death (in 1412), ii, 141.

Bele, John, collated (by lapse) to the Chantry-Chapel of St. Nun in the parish of Pelynt, ii, 106; instituted to the V. of Pelynt (in 1414), ii, 161b.

Belet, Robert, instituted to the R. of St. John in Cornwall, ii, 11; exchanges for the R. of Cheddington[3] (Dioc. of Salisbury), ii, 56b; which he again exchanges for the R. of Ashton (q. v.), ii, 75b.

Belion, Ida, wife of (*sic*), i, 323b.

Bellegh, Stephen. *See* Totnes, i, 245; ii, 267.

Belston, Walter Umfray,[4] R. of, licence of non-residence for one year, from 17 Oct., 1395, i, 6; for one year, from 29 May, 1397, i, 12; from 30 Oct., 1409 to the Feast of the Nativity of St. John Baptist[5], 1410, i, 90b; for one year, from 16 Sept., 1413, i, 183b; also, from 11 Oct., 1414, to Michaelmas, 1415, i, 202b—Adam Hay, R. of, Penitentiary in the Deanery of Okehampton, i, 245b.

Benallack,[6] mansion of James and Isabella Gerveys, i, 36b.

Benet, Alan, R. of Moreleigh (q.v.), instituted to the Third "Portion" (Tydecombe) in the Church of Tiverton, ii, 23b.

Benet, Robert, R. of Thurleston (deceased), ii, 196b.—*See*, also, ii, 357b.

---

[1] Bereferes and Byreferya, MS.
[2] Also Beel, MS.
[3] Chedyngdon, MS.
[4] Also Umfrey, MS.
[5] "contemplacione Comitisse Devonie."
[6] Banadlak MS.

Benet, William, instituted to the R. of Ashton, ii, 14b; exchanges for Coombe-Keynes (Dioc. of Salisbury), ii, 68b.

Bennerton, mansion of John Beauchamp, in the parish of Crowan, i, 209.

Bentley, William, of Plymouth, i, 38.

Benyn, (or Bevyn) Hugh, a parishioner of Cowick (q. v.) ii, 287.

Bere, in the parish of Marhamchurch, i, 43.

Bere, Richard, instituted to the R. of Thornbury, ii, 139.

Bere, Robert, presents to the R. of Huntsham, ii, 195b, 266b.

Bere, William, i, 333b.

Berkeley, Thomas, Lord of Berkeley, presents to "Charleton-in-Southammes," ii, 30, 33, 63b, 103; to North Bovey, ii, 38b.

Berlynch, the Prior and Convent of, present to the V. of Mariansleigh,[1] ii, 5, 56, 105; to Morebath R., ii, 85b.

Bermondsey, the Priory of, ii, 39.

Bernard, Alice (an Anchorite, of Exeter); licence to choose a confessor with power to absolve her "eciam in casibus domino specialiter reservatis," (8 April, 1400), i, 35b.

Bernard, Roger, instituted to the R. of St. Paul's, Exeter,[2] ii, 9; his death, ii, 135b; his Will, i, 314b.

Bernard (or Barnard), Thomas (in the MS. "John," by a clerical error), V. of Davidstow, i, 58b; *See* "Institutions."

Berne, John, instituted to the Chantry of St. Katharine in the Church of Hemyock, ii, 198b, 267b.

Berne, Walter, monk of Tavistock, ii, 59.

Bernevyle, Simon, *see* Barnevyle.

Bernyngham, John, R. of Limpsfield (Dioc. of Winchester), exchanges for a Prebend in St. Probus, ii, 193b.

Berrynarbor,[3] John, R. of, appointed a Penitentiary for the Deanery of Shirwell, i, 94, 115b, 143b, 174, 194b, 207b. 217, 231, 238, 245b.

Berry Pomeroy, Walter Dunnewyll, V. of; Commission to

---

[1] Reginald de Mohun granted the Manor of Mariansleigh, with the advowson of the church, in 1261, to the Priory of St. Nicholas at Barlinch (or Berlynch), in the parish of Brompton-Regis, in the County of Somerset: at ii, 5, we find as patrons "Robert, the Prior, and the Convent of *Belrygge*," but the same place is clearly meant.

[2] He was also a Vicar in the Cathedral (i, 314b.)

[3] Byry, MS.

enquire as to his alleged incapacity through infirmity (22 Nov., 1413) ii, 253. [He died within six months afterwards, ii, 158^{b}.]

Berty, Thomas, V. of St. Gwinear, exchanges for the R. of St. Endellion, ii, 83; exchanges again for the R. of Farringdon, ii, 129^{b}; his death[1], ii, 164^{b}.

Berya, William, *see* Foghel, Gerard.

Beseys, John, i, 312^{b}.

Beston, John, i, 301.

Bethlem Hospital,[2] Indulgence granted by Bishop Stafford to the Faithful contributing to its funds (12 Oct., 1398), i, 21^{b}.

Betty, John, proxy for William Raff, on his institution to the V. of St. Stithians, ii, 153^{b}.

Betty, Otho, collated to the V. of Kea[3], ii, 147^{b}; Commission of enquiry, on his complaint, in the matter of dilapidations (12 Feb., 1412-13), ii, 250^{b}.

Betty, Thomas, R. of Farringdon. *See* Berty.

Beusewyn, Manor of Oliver Wyse, Cornwall, i, 202^{b}.

Bevyle, John, Sheriff of Devon, [*Breve Regium*] to administer the oath (1 Dec., 1415), ii, 354.

Bevyle, Thomas, clerk, *Dispensacio super defectu natalium* (19 Jan., 1402-3), ii, 24.

Bickleigh, John, V. of, appointed a Penitentiary in the Deanery of Tamerton, i, 50.

Bickleigh (East), Chudderleigh in the parish of, i, 85.

Bickleigh, Matilda Latymer's Manor of, i, 329.

Bideford, "the long Bridge;" Indulgence to the Faithful contributing to its repair (5 Dec., 1396), i, 9^{b}, 302^{b}.—Roger Beaumont, R. of,—licence of non-residence for one year, from 29 Jan., 1396-7, i, 11; licence to choose confessors[4] (3 Feb., 1396-7), i, 11^{b}; appointed a Penitentiary in the Deanery of Hartland, i, 50, 94, 115^{b}, 143^{b}, 174, 194^{b}, 207^{b}, 217, 231, 238, 245^{b}; commissioned (together with John Sergeant, R. of Milton Damarel) to investigate a charge

[1] The name is here spelt "Betty," but, I believe, in error: it is elsewhere spelt Berty, and at ii, 129^{b}, the 'r' is written on an erasure.

[2] "Hospitale Beate Marie de Bedlem in suburbiis civitatis Londonie."

[3] Landege, MS.

[4] The licence was in very general terms—"confessorem ydoneum unum et plures, tot et quot, tociens et quociens, sibi placuerit . . . et eciam in casibus a jure vel consuetudine reservatis ad beneplacitum domini."

against one Richard Trengere of having assaulted Thomas Smyth, clerk (1 Aug., 1400), i, 44b.

Bigbury, John Wytloff's legacy to the Church of, i, 306.—Chapel of St. Michael de la Burgh[1] in the parish of, i, 321b; Chapel of St. Milburga the Virgin in the parish of, —licence granted to William Poundestoke, Rector, (18 Oct., 1395), i, 6; to John Bykebury, Rector, 22 June, 1414, i, 197b.—William Poundestoke, R. of, licence of non-residence for one year from 29 April, 1410, provided he continued in residence at Exeter[2] the whole time, i, 95b. his Will, i, 321b.—John Bykebury, R. of,—licence of non-residence for one year from 23 Sep., 1417, i, 234; also, for one year, from 10 Oct., 1418, i, 243.

Bildeston, Nicholas, instituted to the R. of Phillack, ii, 131.

Binegar[3], (Dioc. of Bath and Wells), i, 79.

Birkhede, John, instituted to the R. of Blackawton, ii, 204b.

Bishop's Clyst, *see* Clyst Episcopi.

Bishop's Nympton, Fareby and Rawston in the parish of, ii, 311b.—John Schute, V. of, his appointment as Chaplain to the Bishop (27 Aug., 1406),—

The Bishop refers to a Dispensation by which Pope Innocent VII. granted to his eight chaplains all the revenues of their benefices, notwithstanding their non-residence, and states that he confers the privilege, first, on Shute—*volentes te primum in eodem numero computare, te unum et primum de numero octonario, nobis, ut prefertur, concessu duximus eligendum.* But the Bishop stipulates that suitable vicars be put in charge of his parish and that the cure of souls be in no wise neglected. i, 78b.

Bishopsleigh[4], *see* Burleston, William, ii, 310.

Bishop's Tawton, the Manor of, i, 75.—John Mark, V. of, i, 108b.

[Bishop's] Teignton, *see* Boterell, John, ii, 310b.

Black Torrington,[5] John [Wyndout], R. of, appointed a Penitentiary in the Deanery of Holsworthy, i, 50; David Loueryng, R. of,—licence to celebrate (on the Feast of her Nativity), in the Chapel of the B.V.M., at Witheley in this parish (30 Aug., 1405), i, 76.—*See*, also, i, 330b.

Blackawton, Roger Bolter, R. of,—Dispensation to enable him to study at Oxford for three years, (provided he took

---

[1] On the summit of the island now known as "Burgh Island."

[2] He was Canon of the Cathedral.

[3] Benhauger, MS.: in *Ecton*, Benagre.

[4] Byssbopeslee, MS.

[5] Blaketoryton, MS.

sub-deacon's orders within one year), from 22 Aug., 1401; also, letters dimissory were granted, on the same day, to enable him to be ordained by any English Bishop, i, 58; licence to put out the revenues of his benefice to be farmed, by any ecclesiastical person, for three years (3 Dec., 1414), i, 205.—The Parish church of; *See* Taylor, John, clerk, i, 198^{b}; the Bishop having been informed that the cemetery had been polluted, with violence and effusion of blood, by Guido Coleton and Robert Cole (*alias* Cottebury), so that the said cemetery could not be used for interments, caused enquiry to be made, and decided that it was not a case for a formal Reconciliation, and that the dead might be buried as before (19 July, 1415), i, 215^{b}.

Blackborough, Thomas Toffe, R. of, licence of non-residence for one year, from 5 Nov., 1405, i, 77; for one year, from 7 August, 1410, i, 103— John Forster, R. of, licence of non-residence for one year, from 26 April, 1417, i, 232.

Blakhay, Roger, *presented* to the R. of Clannaborough[1], ii, 259^{b}; proxy for Robert Doget, on his institution to the R. of Ashreigney, ii, 177^{b}; instituted to the R. of Nymet Rowland, ii, 189.

Blagdon[2], John (and Alice) Cade of, i, 6^{b}, 9^{b}.

Blagdon[2] Kyrkham, in the parish of Paignton, i, 115^{b}.

Blake, Eleanora, preferred by the Bishop, by lapse, to be Prioress of Cornworthy, ii, 140.

Blake, Robert, of Kingsbridge, ii, 292^{b}.

Blake, Robert, R. of Heddington (Dioc. of Salisbury) exchanges for the R. of Washfield, ii, 167^{b}; i, 219^{b}; resigns, ii, 180.

Blakebourne[3], Henry, Canon of Exeter and Rector of Stokenham and of Newton Ferrers at the time of his death, ii, 12^{b}, 42^{b}, 91, 358; presents to the Vicarage[4] of Stoken-

---

[1] By the Prior of Taunton (Dioc. of B. and W.); and at the same time, John Rysdon, chaplain, was presented by Philip Boterford. The Bishop (25 July, 1416), issued a Commission to the Archdeacon of Barnstaple to enquire as to the right of patronage in both cases,—*See* ii, 259^{b}. In the end he collated John Thomma, *by lapse*, 23 Jan., 1416-7, ii, 182.

[2] Blakedon MS.

[3] Also, Blakborne, Blakaborn, MS.

[4] This parish is now a Vicarage, and the Rectory is in lay hands. At the time of the Taxation of Pope Nicholas (A.D. 1288-91) it had two Incumbents, a Rector and a Vicar; and this was the case in Bishop Stafford's time and for some time afterwards. When the *Valor Ecclesiasticus* was made, in 1536, the Vicar was the only Incumbent; the Rectorial endowments having been alienated, only a few years before,

ham, ii, 3; mentioned, i, 301, 328, 328b; his executors[1] having neglected to repair the "dilapidations" on the Benefice, the case is referred to the Court of Arches by Thomas de Montacute, his successor (9 Sep., 1399), i, 30b.

Blakelake, John, instituted to the R. of Clyst St. Laurence, ii, 74; exchanges for the R. of Stoodleigh, ii, 85; i, 80b; exchanges for the V. of Pitminster (Dioc. of Bath and Wells), ii, 97; co-patron of the R. of Blackborough, ii, 151b; *see* Kentisbeare, ii, 249, 345, 345b.

Blakemore, Henry, collated to a Canonry and the 6th Prebend at Ottery, ii, 155b.

Blakhalle, Andrew, of Kingsbridge, ii, 292; alleged assault on a priest by, ii, 240b.

Blaunkmonster, Guy, R. of Lansallos (deceased), ii, 82.

Blenche, William, ii, 265b.

Blewe, John, LL.D., R. of Binegar[2] (Dioc. of Bath and Wells) i, 79.

Blisland[3], John Baylly, R. of, complains of the "dilapidations," caused by the neglect of his predecessor, John Balsham; Commission of Enquiry addressed to Thomas Estbroke, LL.B., V. of Duloe (20 Jan., 1410-11), ii, 237. — Commission of Enquiry as to the pollution of the cemetery there, in a quarrel, with effusion of blood, between John Trewynt and John Langston (5 Feb., 1411-12), ii, 245.— Thomas Kardowe, R. of,—licence of non-residence from 12 Jan., 1412-13, to Michaelmas, 1413, i, 173.

---

and bestowed on the Priory of Augustinian Canons at Bisham, in Berkshire, which had been founded, in 1338, by William Montacute, Earl of Salisbury. Tanner states that it was largely endowed 26 Henry VIII (1534-5), surrendered in 1536, was refounded by the King in 1537, (for a mitred Abbot and fifteen Benedictine monks), and finally dissolved in 1539!—The Montacutes were long patrons of this Rectory; and it appears that the Rectors were patrons of the Vicarage, which is now in the gift of Crown.

[1] John Dodyngton, Thomas Barton, Canon of Exeter, John [Ulveston], perpetual V. of Stokenham, and John Dene. The appeal had been first made, in due course, to the Bishop, who, it appears, postponed the hearing *plus debito*, and was accused of practically denying justice to the new Rector. The executors were allowed fifteen days to settle the matter, and, failing a settlement, were to appear on the twentieth day in the Court of Arches. The Bishop was to take all usual and necessary steps, and inform the Court thereof: but he handed over the entire business to the Court, alleging that he was hindered from attending to it *aliis negotiis arduis, multipliciter*; and no wonder, for he had been Lord Chancellor since 23 Oct., 1396, the Diocese being administered by his Vicar-General.

[2] Benhauger, MS.

[3] Blyston, MS.

Blossoms Inn[1], in London, ii, 278.

Bloy, John (senior and junior), i, 315^b.

Blymesham, in the parish of Beaford, i, 39.

Bobawale, John, a parishioner of Linkinhorne, i, 116.

Bocher, John, of Honiton, a blind man, i, 307.

Bochym[2] (in Cury), Chapel of the B. V. M. at, i, 87.

Bockampton, Manor of (in Dorset), ii, 281^b et seq.

Boconnoc, Carmenowe of, i, 12.

Bodde, Henry, i, 315.

Bodellek, in the parish of St. Breoke,[3] i, 45.

Bodeway, Nicholas, R. of Arreton (Dioc. of Winchester), exchanges for the R. of Bridestowe, ii, 34; mentioned i, 18, 26^b, 61^b, 76^b; exchanges for the R. of Bratton [Clovelly], ii, 92^b; exchanges for a Canonry and Prebend in Bosham, ii, 92^b.

Bodinnick[4],—licence granted for a chapel of St. John Baptist, which the inhabitants of the hamlet had built therein, in the parish of Lanteglos "juxta Polrywan[5]" (22 Oct., 1406), i, 80.

[Bodivalgan], in the parish of St. Winnow; *See* Moylys, John, (*Oratories.*)

Bodmin, lands of William Payon and John, his son and heir, in the parish of, i, 45.—Chapels in the parish of, i, 77^b: chapel of St. George in the town of, licensed (24 May, 1405), i, 75; Lazar House of St. Laurence at,—Indulgence of 40 days to the Faithful contributing to its sustentation (11 Oct., 1395), i, 5^b.—"The anchorite at," i, 313; Margaret, an anchorite, dwelling near Bodmin, having asked permission to migrate to the Monastery of St. Bridget-by-Schene, and to join the Order settled there, is licensed by the Bishop accordingly (10 March, 1415-16), i, 218. —John Stephyn, V. of, one of the Commissioners in the matter of the election of a Prior of Bodmin, ii, 72.—[William Carnellow, or Carminow], Prior, and the Convent of, their disputes with William Cornewale, V. of Egloshayle, i, 21.—

St. Petrock's Priory being vacant by the death of the said William Carnellov—

---

[1] Blosmysyn, MS.
[2] Bossim, MS.
[3] Pawton, MS.
[4] Bosdynnek, MS.
[5] "By Polruan," and so called at that time, to distinguish it from Lanteglos-by-Camelford: it is now known as "Lanteglos-by-Fowey."

the Bishop writes to Henry Canterbury, the sub-prior, and to Noel Patreda, Steward of his lands in Cornwall, appointing them guardians of the temporalities of the Priory, and directing that the Sub-Prior should rule in matters spiritual and should order Divine Service. He informs the latter that John Spernon, one of the Brethren, had appeared before him, to tell him of the death of Carnellov on the 10th of November [1403], and that he had issued his licence for the election of a successor (14 Nov., 1403), ii, 71^{b}, 72; Alan Kenegy was elected on the 14th of December following, and John Restaurek, R. of St. Mabyn, and John Stephyn, V. of Bodmin, were commissioned to proclaim the fact, and to certify the Bishop therein, on, or before, the 22nd of December. A copy of John Stephyn's certificate is given, ii, 72. The Confirmation of the Election and the Bishop's Mandate for this new Prior's installation were dated at Chudleigh on the said 22nd of December, ii, 73.

Alan Kenegy, Prior of, ii, 246^{b}; Dispensation (to study at Oxford) for three years, from 24 May, 1405, i, 75; in arrears on account of the procurations due to the Pope's Collector (17 Sept., 1410), i, 105.—The Bishop visits the Priory (15 Sept., 1400), i, 48.—Odo Betty of, i, 26; John Trewyȝthorop, Canon of, i, 50.—The Prior and Convent of, present to the V. of St. Petrock's, Bodmin, ii, 49^{b}, 51^{b}, 183; to the R. of St. Endellion, ii, 26, 83, 129^{b}, 178^{b}, 259^{b}; to the V. of St. Cubert, ii, 41^{b}, 145°; to the R. of Hollacombe[1], ii, 68^{b}, 194^{b}; to Bodmin Prebend in the Collegiate Church of St. Endellion, ii, 189; to the V. of St. Minver, ii, 95^{b}; to the R. of Withiel, ii, 58.—The Friars of, i, 301^{b}.

Bodrigan, Otho, ii, 316.

Bodrygan, William, nominates to the V. of St. Clement's[2], Truro, ii, 15^{b}, 48^{b}.

Bodrygy, Matthew, R. of St. Gerrans, exchanges for the R. of Creed and a Canonry and Prebend in Glasney, ii, 42; mentioned (as R. of Creed), i, 77: resigns the Prebendal Stall of Trehaverock in St. Endellion, ii, 46^{b}; his death, ii, 106.

Bodulget, Stephen, does homage to the Bishop, in London, for lands in the parish of Lawhitton (16 Oct., 1399), ii, 310^{b}.

Body, Simon, V. of Wendron,—licence to celebrate in the chapel of St. Decuman, in that parish, once a year, viz., on the Feast of that Saint[3] (28 May, 1397), i, 12; his death ii, 182.

Body, Thomas, a priest—*see* Holsworthy, i, 99^{b}.

---

[1] St. Petrock's, ii, 194^{b}.
[2] Lamorek, MS.
[3] August 27.

Boghelegh, Philip and John,—the former having resigned the R. of Farway, the latter is instituted to the same, ii, 129[b], and afterwards exchanges for the V. of Widecombe [in-the-Moor], ii, 145[b]; i, 180[b].

Bogheway, Richard, instituted to the V. of Morebath, ii, 85[b].

Bokelly, Nicholas, proxy for Thomas Job, q. v., ii, 188[b].

Bokelond, John, appointed Warden of Ottery (28 Sep., 1399), i, 29; exchanges for the R. of South Wokington, *i.e.*, Ockenden (Dioc. of London), ii, 139[b].

Bokelonde, John, a monk of Dunkeswell Abbey, his Benediction as Abbot, ii, 267[b].

Bokepond (or Bokepound), John, instituted to the V. of Kingsteignton, ii, 57; resigns, ii, 175.

Bokete, Nicholas, chaplain of Sherford[1], ii, 261.

Bokkyng, Thomas, presents to the V. of Stogumber (Dioc. of Bath and Wells), ii, 36.

Bold, Robert, of Kingsbridge, ii, 292.

Bolde, Robert, of Exeter, being excommunicated and contumacious, is handed over by the Bishop to the secular arm (6 Oct., 1418), i, 242[b].

Boldebury, John, i, 303[b].

Bole, Henry, Arch-priest of Haccombe (deceased), ii, 49.

Bole, John, co-patron of the R. of Cotleigh, ii, 64; of [Clay]-hydon, R., ii, 81[b]; of South Pool, R., ii, 90[b], 97.—*See* Cardynham *(Institutions)*, ii, 153.

Bole, Philip, V. of St. Winnow (deceased), ii, 80.

Bole, Robert, R. of Michaelstowe, ii. 99.—*See* Bulle.

Bolham, Nicholas, collated to a Prebend in St. Probus, ii, 102; resigns the same and is instituted to the R. of Landewednack, ii, 175.

Bolham, Richard, V. of Gwennap, exchanges for the R. of Landewednack, ii, 78; collated to a Prebend in St. Probus, ii, 84[b]; resigns the same, ii, 102; resigns Landewednack, ii, 175[2].

[1] A daughter church to Stokenham.

[2] He was R. of Landewednack from 7 Aug., 1404, to 28 Feb., 1415-16. A very interesting font, which has been attributed by some antiquaries to a much earlier period, is preserved here, the true date of which, within the compass of scarcely a dozen years, is determined by these entries. It bears the inscription, "IHC + D[OMINUS] RIC[ARDUS] BOLHAM ME FECIT," carved, in bold relief, on one of its sides.

Bolham, Robert, V. of Mullyon, (deceased), ii, 188^{b}.

Bolle, John, i, 331^{b}.

Bollegh, Benedict, V. of St. Wenn, (q. v.) i, 207^{b}.

Bollok, Walter.—*See* Bullok.

Bolour, Thomas, co-patron of the R. of Cheddington (Dioc. of Salisbury) ii, 75^{b}.

Bolpyth, Margaret, *see* Ruan-Major, i, 181.

Bolter, Roger, (notary-publick, Registrar, &c.)—mentioned, i, 91, 93, 95, 95^{b}, 99^{b}, 102, 114^{b}, 116, 117, 315^{b}, 320, 322, 325, 326^{b}, 332^{b}, 334; instituted to the R. of Blackawton, ii, 19^{b}; i, 58, 205; collated to a Canonry in Exeter Cathedral, ii, 109^{b}; i, 316^{b}; also, to a Prebend in St. Probus, ii, 148; proxy for John Westecote (q.v.), ii, 150^{b}; for John Stevenys (q.v.), ii, 154; collated to a Canonry in the Church of Crediton, ii, 155; proxy for Richard Gabriell (q.v.), ii, 156; collated to a Canonry in Bosham, ii, 176^{b}; 204; collated to the Archdeaconry of Exeter, ii, 182; i, 330; also, to be Treasurer of the Cathedral, ii, 185^{b}; licence of non-residence (as Treasurer), for one year, from 30 Aug.. 1417, i, 233^{b}; resigns the Archdeaconry of Exeter, ii, 187^{b}; also, his Prebend in St. Probus, ii, 189^{b}; is collated to a Canonry in Crantock, ii, 189^{b}; collated to the dignity of Precentor of the Cathedral, ii, 190; licence of non-residence (as Precentor), for one year from 9 Sep., 1418, i, 242^{b}; Precentor Haukyn's bequests to, i, 333; resigns the office of Treasurer, ii, 190, 190^{b}, and his Canonry in Crantock, ii, 191; and in Bosham, ii, 193; presents (as co-patron) to the R. of Poltimore, ii, 197^{b}, 199^{b}; resigns the R. of Blackawton, ii, 198; is instituted to the R. of Ugborough, *ibid.*; with four others, presents to the R. of Huxham, ii, 200. He was appointed Registrar of the Consistory Court, 8 Feb., 1405-6, ii, 230^{b}; and was commissioned by the Bishop, 2 Nov., 1410, "*ad audiendum et terminandum lites in Cancellaria nostra.*" ii, 234^{b}.

Bolworth, Thomas, i, 320.^{b}

Bome, John, R. of North Tawton, ii, 333^{b} et seq.

Bonde, Richard, Prior of Tavistock Abbey, ii, 58^{b}, 59, 59^{b}.

Bondleigh[1], John [Hopere], R. of, appointed a Penitentiary in the Deanery of Chulmleigh, i, 50; Thomas Gambon, R. of

[1] Bonelegh, also Bonlegh and Bonalegh, MS.

licence of non-residence for one year, from 15 Nov., 1403, i, 69; also, for one year, from 30 April, 1407, i, 81; also, for one year, from 1 July, 1410, i, 99b; for one year, from 29 July, 1411, i, 129b; for one year, from 13 Aug., 1412, i, 164; for one year, from 26 Sept., 1413, i, 185; from 13 Dec., 1414, to Michaelmas, 1415, i, 205b; from 20 Nov., 1415, to Michaelmas, 1416, i, 215; from 19 Nov., 1416, to Michaelmas, 1417, i, 228; from 12 Jan., to Michaelmas, 1418, i, 237b; from 27 March to Michaelmas, 1419, i, 246.

Bone, John, instituted to the R. of Feniton, ii, 78b.

Boner, (or, perhaps, Bour) Martin de, V. of St. Feock (q.v.), i, 161.

Bonevile[1], Alice, Lady of the Manor, presents to the R. of Southleigh, ii, 159b, 168; mentioned as wife of Sir William, i, 312.

Bonevyll[1], Anneys, a nun of Wherwell, i, 311b.

Bonevyll, John[2], son of Thomas, i, 312.

Bonevyll, Thomas[3], son of John, i, 311b: a co-patron (in 1417) of the Arch-presbytery of Beerferris, ii, 182, 186, 260b, 261.

Bonevile[1], Sir William, knt., patron of the R. of Churchstanton, ii, 5b; co-patron of the R. of Mamhead, ii, 45b; patron of the R. of Lympston, i, 81b; presents thereto, ii, 96; his mansion in the parish of Holy Trinity, Exeter, i, 70b; his Will, i, 311.—*See*, also, Stoke-Fleming.

Bonevyll, William[4], son of Sir William, i, 311b.

Boniface IX., Pope; his Bull—(1) promoting Edmund Stafford to the vacant See of Exeter, i, 1; (2) to the Clergy of the City and Diocese (on the same subject), i, 1b; (3) to the Lay Folk of the City and Diocese (on the same), i, 1b; also, (4) to the Archbishop of Canterbury, i, 2; (5) to the Chapter of Exeter, i, 2b; (6) to all vassals of the Church of Exeter, *ibid.*—His Bull on behalf of Walter Vyel and Emma his wife, *see* Vyel.—his Bull in favour of Ralph Swayne and Agnes Wyndouth, *see* Swayne, R.—His Letters Apostolick, providing for the government of

---

[1] Spelt thus variously in the MS.

[2] Of Meriet, co. of Somerset, grandson of Sir William.

[3] Of Trelawne, co. of Cornwall, son of John Bonevyll, of Chuton, co. of Somerset, by Elizabeth, dau. and heir of Henry Fitz-Roger.

[4] A witness to the Will of Alice, his step-mother.

Cluniac Priories in England, during the Schism, ii, 39^b. —Dispensation in favour of William Hunden[1] (q.v.), permitting him to hold benefices in plurality (3 Non. Jul. anno tertiodecimo[2]), ii, 101.—Letters Apostolick, as to certain Appropriations, Indulgences, &c. (Dated at St. Peter's, vi Kal. Jan., Anno quartodecimo),[3] ii, 284-286^b; and compare the last entry on fol. 284^b with fol. 288, lines 31 et seqq.

Bonyour, Humphrey[4], instituted to the R. of Okeford, ii, 146^b, 249^b; his death, ii, 179, 259^b.

Bonython in the parish of St. Breage [Cury], i, 237^b.

Bonnok[5], William, V. of Lanlivery,—

He was suspended by the Bishop, at his Visitation in 1400, for one year, (from 27 Sept., then past), on account of guilty conduct which rendered him unworthy to minister at the Altar; and Michael Robert, chaplain, had been appointed to minister in his place, and at a competent stipend. The said William complained to the Bishop that some of the parishioners had retained all that was due to him over and above the said stipend, to his great loss; and he waited personally on the Bishop to seek redress. The Bishop seems to have been satisfied as to the culprit's repentance, for he directed the said Chaplain to collect what was due from the defaulters, and ordered him to allow the Vicar to celebrate on Christmas Day, on Easter Day, and at Pentecost, and for the three days succeeding each Festival. But he was not to be permitted to administer the Sacrament to the parishioners, or to celebrate on any other days whatsoever (20 Nov., 1400), i, 50.

On 18 June, 1416, he resigned the living, ii, 177.

Bordevylle, Richard, i, 315.

Boresleigh, in the parish of Bratton [-Clovelly], Chapel of St. James at, i, 131^b, 138^b.

Bornebury, John, sub-deacon, instituted to the R. of Exbourne, ii, 132^b, 241^b; mentioned, i, 196, 211^b, 221.

Borneslo, John, instituted to the V. of Tavistock, ii, 181.

Boscastle[6],—license granted to the inhabitants for the Chapel of St. James, in the parish of Minster,[7] for *one month* only, (2 June, 1400), i, 39^b; and again, during pleasure (18 Sep., 1400), i, 48.

Bosham,[8] the King's Free Chapel of :—

---

[1] Then Archdeacon of Rochester.
[2] 5 July, 1402.
[3] 27 Dec., 1402.
[4] Boniour at ii, 249^b, and "Bungent" at ii, 179.
[5] Also Bonok, MS.
[6] Boterellescastell, and Botrauxcastell.
[7] Mynstre, MS.
[8] Boseham, MS.—"After the Conquest," says Tanner, "William Warlewast, Bishop of Exeter, obtained of King Henry I. the grant of this place, to himself and successors, who were patrons and visitors of the Secular Canons or Prebendaries founded by that Bishop in the Choir of the parish-

Mandate addressed by the Bishop of Exeter to Peter, the Sacristan, and to John Heynon, one of the Vicars, in the matter of the sequestration of the revenues of the Vicars of Canons Thomas Cook and Richard Courtenay (20 June, 1397), i, 12b.

Mandate addressed by the Bishop to Peter, the Sacristan, for the Visitation of the Chapel. The King had informed the Bishop (2 June, 1398) that it was reported that much disorder prevailed, that the goods of the Church were being wasted, and that the Canons and other ministers were neglecting the Divine Offices and leading a dissolute life: and he commanded him to visit the Community, in person if possible, and to apply a remedy. The Bishop appointed Sept. 15 for his Visitation, when all members of the Community were to appear before him in the choir (8 June, 1398), i, 19.

The Visitation actually commenced on the 18 Sept.; and the Bishop, after consulting the Dean and Chapter of Exeter, and with the approval and consent of the Sacristan and Canons of Bosham, took vigorous measures for the reformation of the Community. His statutes, including minute directions for the conduct of the services, the vestments and the ordinary apparel of the Ministers, and like matters, are set forth at large in a document which was sealed with the Episcopal Seal, at the Bishop's House, in London, 12 June, 1399; with the Seal, also, of the Dean and Chapter of Exeter, in their Chapter-House, 5 Jan. 1399-1400. The Bishop wrote to the Sacristan, on the 25 Jan., requiring the said statutes to be promulgated in the Chapel within fifteen days from the receipt thereof, and once in every quarter, afterwards.—ii, 271-274b.

On 11 Feb., 1398-9, a warrant was applied for, for the arrest of William Maundevyll (late vicar of Nicholas Braybrok, prebendary of Funtington), who had contumaciously refused to appear before the Bishop, i, 25b.

Ralph Waterman, Sacristan, was commissioned 6 May, 1401, to exact, and account for, certain moneys payable to the Bishop, as Ordinary, ii, 228.

The Chapel of the B.V.M. at Funtington was dependent on this Collegiate Church. It appears that William Scardevyle, John Groffham, Thomas Cokwelle, and others, inhabitants of the villages of Funtington and East and West Ashling, represented that the said Chapel was distant two miles or more, from the Mother Church, and had been used, from time immemorial, for all sacraments, services, etc., save only for the burial of the dead, a fit Chaplain being provided there by the Prebendary of Funtington and by the said Collegiate Church; that it sometimes happened that, in consequence of the long and tedious journey and the roughness of the sea, they could not reach Bosham for two or even three days; that, being mostly engaged in agriculture and poor, they could not afford so much time; and, therefore they begged for leave to bury in the said chapel and in its cemetery. The Bishop, after consulting all the parties concerned (viz. the Dean and Chapter of Exeter, John Makworth, William de Langeton, Laurence Haukyn, William Sutton, and Richard Gabriell, Canons of Bosham), and especially John Makworth, the Prebendary of Funtington, John Lamburne, the Sacristan, and John Yonge, the Perpetual Vicar, assented to their petition, with permission to Robert, Bishop of Chichester, or any other English Bishop, to dedicate the same; certain fees, etc., being reserved to the Mother Church, and provision made for preventing all manner of abuse of the concession. Dated at Crediton, 13 Sep.; by the Exeter Chapter, 14 Sep.; by the Canons of Bosham, 21 Sep.; by the Prebendary of Funtington and the Petitioners, 23 Sep, 1408.—ii, 280-281b.

---

church here, which was looked upon as a Royal Free Chapel, dedicated to the Holy Trinity, and exempt from the ordinary jurisdiction of the Bishop of Chichester and his arch-deacon."

Bishop Stafford is described in the Register (ii, 271) as Chaplain Ordinary immediately under the King, sole collator and patron of the Canonries and Prebends therein.

The Chapel of Apuldram was also dependent on the Church of Bosham. It appears that the Bishop of Exeter had received a petition from John Carpenter, Henry Cobay, John Nappe, Thomas Spygernell, William Wrest, Robert Segrom, John Couper, John Wodelond, John Cartere, Richard Coterell, William Shuppe, Roger Pulte, Robert Bury, Walter Cobay, William Cardon (senior and junior), William Idrych, Thomas Tylby, William Goldyng, Thomas Hurst, John Edward, John Nelond, John Burgoun, Thomas Carpenter, and Robert Porter (inhabitants of "Appeldurham *alias* Appeldreham," above-named) setting forth that from time immemorial they had resorted to their Chapel of the B.V.M. for all services except the burial of the dead; that they were three miles from Bosham; and that the road was tedious and dangerous from floods and inundations; that, therefore, they prayed the Bishop to allow them to bury in their Chapel and its cemetery. Their petition was granted, with the usual conditions and reservations. Dated 23 July (by the Bishop), 24 July, by the Exeter Chapter, and by the petitioners (through the President of the Consistorial Court at Exeter, and under his seal), on the same day; by the Canons, etc., of Bosham, 12 Aug., 1417.—ii, 293ᵇ 295ᵇ.[1]

Bosom, Robert, Canon and Chancellor of the Cathedral, i, 10ᵇ:

The Bishop grants him a Dispensation (on account of his distinguished services, his failing sight, and the weak state of his health), in the matter of the Customary Lecture in the Cathedral, founded[2] by Bishop Peter [Quivil]; but requiring him at least to appoint a deputy [16 Oct., 1395), i, 6; his death, ii, 45ᵇ.

Boson, Edmund and Mabel, i, 8ᵇ.

Boson (or Bosyn), Richard, a citizen of Exeter, i, 317; John, his son, i, 315.

Bost, Thomas, Chantry Priest of Charlton Adam (Dioc. of Bath and Wells), exchanged for the V. of Burrington, ii, 133; i, 164.

Bost, Odo, V. of Paul, resigns, ii, 190.

Bostofellek, John, the Bishop's Commissary in the matter of the sequestration of Davidstowe, i, 58ᵇ.

Bosumshele,[3] in the parish of Dittisham, i, 86ᵇ.

Boswithgny, Chapel of St. Mary Magdalen, at; *see* Botreaux (*Oratories*), i, 8ᵇ, 21.

Boswyns (Plymouth), John Beauchamp of, i, 4ᵇ; Roger Beauchamp, of i, 7; *see* Beauchamp (*Oratories*).

Boteler, John, Usher of the King's Chamber, i, 191ᵇ.

Boterel (or Boterell), Geoffrey, i, 301.

---

[1] *See* ii, 314. A *Breve Regium*, dated 14 Dec., 5 Richard II. appears in the midst of similar documents belonging to the reign of Henry IV., without apparent reason. It refers to the intended arrest of certain persons who had infringed the King's rights in his Free Chapel of Bosham, under pretext of certain Papal Provisions made to the King's prejudice.

[2] occasione appropriacionis ecclesie Sancte Neulyne in Cornubia.

[3] Bozonhele, MS.

Boterel, John, chaplain, i, 326.

Boterell, John, does homage to the Bishop, at Chudleigh, for lands in [Bishop's] Teignton (9 May, 1400), ii, 310[b].

Boterell, Walter, cousin of John, i, 326[b].

Boterford, John, and Thomasia his wife, ii, 356.

Boterford, Philip, presents to the R. of Clannaborough, ii, 259[b].

Boterton, John, monk of Tavistock, ii, 58[b], 59.

Botreaux (also, Botriaux), **John**, presents to the R. of Affeton, ii, 107[b], 181[b], 201; to the R. of East Worlington, ii, 198[b].

Botreaux, Sir Ralph, knt., of Linkinhorne, i, 113[b], 116.

Botreaux, Sir William, knt., presents to the R. of St. Pinnock, ii, 268; *see*, also, ii, 351.

Botrigy, Matthew, R. of Creed, *see* Bodrygy, i, 90[b].

Botteburgh, Nicholas, instituted to Bradworthy V., ii, 152[b].

Botuler, John, R. of Chalbury (Dioc. of Salisbury), exchanges for the R. of Jacobstow (Devon), ii, 142[b]; exchanges again for the V. of Haslebury (Dioc. of Bath and Wells), ii, 157.[b]

Boun, John, R. of Cheriton-Bishop, exchanges for the V. of Broad Chalk (Dioc. of Salisbury, ii, 30.

Bouryng (or Bowryng), **John**, elected R. of the Collegiate Chantry of Slapton, ii, 111; i, 317[b]; presents to the office of "Minister" (or P. C. of the Parish Church there), ii, 132; licensed to choose a confessor, and to hear confessions (10 Aug., 1411), i, 131.

Bourgeauuyll,[1] **John**, monk of Bec, instituted to the Priory of Cowick, ii, 37; 287.

Bourne, John, instituted to the R. of Willand, ii, 21; i, 245.

Boure, John, instituted to the R. of North Tawton (*alias* Chepyngtauton), ii, 8; i, 128, 315, ii, 333.[2]—John Boure, perhaps the same, was instituted, 26 April, 1410, to the V. of Monkleigh, ii, 109[b].

Bowryng, Thomas, instituted to the R. of Affeton, ii, 201.

Bovey Tracy, John [atte Mille], V. of, appointed a Penitentiary in the Deanery of Moreton, i, 50.

Bovye, John, *alias* Morton (q.v.), i, 169[b].

Boway, Walter (*see* Burrington), i, 165, 178[b]; ii, 151[b]; made a notary-publick (23 Jan., 1412-13), i, 175[b]; proxy for John

[1] Also, Bourgeauyll, MS.

[2] Not "Bome," as at p. 28: the MS. is very obscure here, but "Boure" was, doubtless, intended.

Speeke,[1] ii, 149b; instituted to the R. of St. Gerrans, ii, 160; exchanges for the R. of St. John in Cornwall, ii, 160; i, 334; proxy for William Knyght, ii, 179; exchanges for the R. of Sutcombe, ii, 181; i, 235b.

Bow, *see* Nymet Tracy.

Bowcombe, *see* Bawcombe.

Bowden,[2] in the parish of Totnes, i, 237.

Bowden, John, instituted to the R. of Dartington, ii, 193, 265b.

Bowode, John, R. of Buckland-Filleigh (q. v.), i, 309b, 314.

Box, Robert, V. of East Coker (Dioc. of Bath and Wells), exchanges for the R. of Combe-Raleigh, ii, 71; i, 78, 82.

Boys, John, R. of Landcross (deceased), ii, 10.

Boys, John, of Halberton, i, 318.

Boyton, Richard (as patron for one turn out of three), presents to the R. of Highampton, ii, 141, 245b.

Bradeford, John, R. of Broad Nymet, i, 331b; (deceased), ii, 179.

Bradelegh, Thomas, instituted to the V. of Buckland [Monachorum], ii, 88b.

Bradenham, William, proxy for William de Humberston, q. v., ii, 52, 79b.

Bradewell,[3] John, R. of [Ruan] Lanyhorne (deceased), ii, 158b.

Bradeworthy, Richard, V. of Townstal, i, 75b; ii, 50b; his death, ii, 92.

Bradford, Roger Langh, R. of; licence of non-residence for one year from 6 June, 1407, i, 82[4]; from 23 Oct., 1408, i, 87; from 3 June, 1410, i, 97[5]; and from 28 May, 1411, i, 123b; Richard Penels, R. of, i, 213, 215; ii, 252; James Carslegh, R. of, i, 246.—Commissions of enquiry as to the patronage,—

(1) When Thomas Deneys had presented Walter Hille, chaplain (15 Nov., 1411); (2) when Isolda Deneys, widow of Walter Deneys, had presented John Chaddesley, chaplain (1 Dec., 1411), ii, 244.

Bradninch,[6] Manor of Hele in the parish of, i, 221b.—Sequestration, on account of the non-residence of John Vendovere (*sic*), R., taken off (2 Dec., 1398), i, 23b; the said John appointed a Penitentiary in the Deanery of Plymtree, i, 50, 94, 115, 143, 173b, 194, 207b, 216b, 231, 237b, 245.

Bradshawe, Nicholas, Esquire,—appointed Supervisor of the

[1] Original proxy for Thomas Speeke.
[2] Bogheden, MS.
[3] Also, Bradevyle and Bradewyll, MS.
[4] *John* Langh in this place—an obvious clerical error.
[5] Roger *Langeman*, MS.
[6] Brathenynche, MS.

Manors, etc., in England which the Bishop had inherited from his father[1] (28 May, 1401), ii, 228^{b}.

Bradstone, Richard Burneman, R. of; licence of non-residence for one year, from 14 Sept., 1395, i, 5^{b}.—*See*, also, ii, 253^{b}.

Bradworthy,—Indulgence to the Faithful contributing to the rebuilding and improvement of the parish Church, which had been destroyed by lightning[2] (16 Dec., 1395), i, 7^{b}.—"Ordinacio" of the Chapelry of Pancraswyke, in this parish, *see* Pancraswyke.—John Dalkyn, V. of; licensed to celebrate, himself, or by some other fit priest, in his parish church (22 May, 1400), i, 38^{b}; 68^{b}.—Isabella Eyer, of (*see* Colyn), i, 93^{b}.—John Forde, a chaplain residing in this parish, i, 244^{b}.

Bragge, Roger, and Agneta, daughter of William Wyburgh,—

They had married in ignorance of all impediment, and had discovered, afterwards, that they were related in the fourth degree of consanguinity: a Dispensation was granted in their favour 25 July, 1416, i, 224^{b}.

Braggher, Andrew, of Honiton (a blind man), i, 307.

Brantingham, Bishop, i, 328; his provision for the repair and completion of the choir of Crediton by the Prebendaries thereof, ii, 226.—Robert, his brother, i, 328.

Brantingham, R. (Dioc. of York), *see* Charleton, ii, 33.

Bratton [Clovelly],[3] Roger, R. of, appointed a Penitentiary in the Deanery of Okehampton, i, 50; Reginald Bryta, R. of, i, 73, 78, 78^{b}, 79^{b}, 313^{b}, 314. Stephen Ansteswyll, R. of; licence of non-residence for one year, from 21 July, 1410, i, 100^{b}; licensed to celebrate in the Chapels of St. James at Boreslegh and St. Margaret at Godescote, in this parish, on the Feasts of those Saints, and, also, in the Chapel of St. Stephen in his own manse[4] (14 Aug., 1411), i, 131^{b}; this licence was renewed, and extended to another parochial Chapel (St. Katherine's), and another private Chapel (St. Anne's) in the manse[5] (4 Nov., 1411), i, 138^{b}.

Bratton, Thomas, co-patron of Cruwys-Morchard R., ii, 194^{b}.

Braunscombe, Dionisia, i, 307^{b}.

---

[1] "post decessum Ricardi, patris nostri, et Matildis uxoris sue."

[2] "ad reedificacionem, construccionem, et emendacionem ecclesie parochialis de Bradeworthy et campanile (*sic*) ejusdem . . . igne fulguris combuste et in favillas funditus converse."

[3] "Bratton" simply in the MS. throughout.

[4] "necnon in Capella Sancti Stephani in manso Rectorie ecclesie sue."

[5] "necnon in Capella Sancte Anne in manso Rectorie sue."

Bray, Elizabeth,[1] relict of William, ii, 46b.

Bray, Henry, V. of St. Hilary (deceased), ii, 74.

Bray, John, R. of St. Columb-major, licensed to hear confessions (9 Nov., 1398), i, 22; ii, 11b; Canon of Glasney (deceased), ii, 41.

Bray, Richard, V. of St. Clether (deceased), ii, 7.

Bray, Richard, Prebendary of St. Probus, exchanges for the Wardenship of St. Margaret's, Chelmsford, ii, 46.

Bray, Richard and William, i, 301b.

Bray, Thomas, V. of Lewannick, i, 26.

Bray, William, instituted to the V. of St. Keverne, ii, 88b.—*See* St. Keverne, ii, 360b.

Braybrok, Sir Gerard (also, Nicholas). *See* Ottery, ii, 278, 278b.

Braybrok,[2] Nicholas, Archdeacon of Cornwall, resigns, ii, 35.

At the time of his death he was Canon and Prebendary of Exeter, and also of Bosham and Crantock, ii, 45.—It appears that he had deposited in the Treasury of the Cathedral a certain chest containing (as was alleged) certain valuable jewels, books, and muniments, of old assigned or bequeathed to the Bishop and to the Diocese. The Dean and Chapter, his executors, were about to open and examine the said chest, when the matter came to the Bishop's ears, who immediately issued a commission to Robert Rygge, the Chancellor, and Canon Richard Aldryngton, requiring them to be present on the occasion and to claim and take custody of the contents (7 June, 1401), ii, 228b.

Bre, Richard. *See* St. Illogan.

Breerlegh,[3] William, instituted to the R. of Woodleigh, ii, 93b; i, 89, 105b, 357b.

Bregg, Robert, Prior of St. Nicholas, Exeter (deceased), ii, 5b.

Bremelcomb, William, LL.B., instituted to the R. of Nymet Tracy (q.v.), ii, 42b; proxy for Thomas Hichecok (q.v.), ii, 40b, and for Walter Dodyngton (q.v.), ii, 41.—*See*, also, ii, 268.

Bremham, Hugh, proxy for John Brent (q.v.), ii, 56b.

Bremmesgrave, John (chaplain), executor to the Will of William Falewell, R. of Ermington, i, 12.—*See*, also, i, 300.

Bremley, Isabella, i, 333b.

---

[1] Hervey Wyket was instituted to a Prebend in St. Endellion, 3 June, 1400, on the presentation of Sir John Aroundell, Knt., the true patron "hac vice . . . jure cujusdam Eliȝabet, Relicte Willelmi Bray, de Treworlas, defuncti; que quodam Eliȝabet advocacionem dicte prebende, sive porcionis prefato domino Johanni Aroundell ista vice dumtaxat per literas suas patentes concessit."

[2] Brabroyk, MS.

[3] Also, Breyrlegh, MS.

Bremour (or Bremor), John, collated to the Archdeaconry of Cornwall, ii, 149; instituted to the R. of St. Columb-major, ii, 187, 267^{b}; his death, ii, 193^{b}, 195^{b}.

Brevannek, in St. Hilary, ii, 348^{b}.

Brendon, William, of Pancraswyke, i, 69.

Brendon, Robert, of Holsworthy (q.v.), i, 99^{b}.

Brendon, Richard Hurde, R. of. *See* Hurde, Richard, i, 202^{b}.

Brent, John, V. of Halse (Dioc. of Wells), exchanges for the R. of Martinhoe, ii, 56.

Brent, *alias* Damesele, Matilda, presents to the R. of East Downe, ii, 108^{b}.

Brent, Benedict Brente, chaplain, M.A., licensed to preach in the parish church of (3 April, 1416), i, 220; licensed as a publick preacher in the Deancries of Woodleigh and Plympton (27 Jan., 1418-9), i, 245.—John Junne, V. of, appointed a Penitentiary for the Deanery of Totnes, i, 94, 115^{b}, 143, 194^{b}, 207^{b}, 217, 231, 237^{b}, 245; licensed as confessor[1] to John Valewyll of Rattery (31 March, 1417), i, 232.

Brentford[2] (Diocese of London), Indulgence to the Faithful contributing to the maintenance of the Hospital of the Holy Trinity at (20 Oct. 1395), i, 6^{b}.

Brent Tor, i, 162, 175^{b}.

Brereton, Hamundus, R. of Marwood (deceased), ii, 70^{b}.

Breton, John (of Devon); *see* St. Feock, i, 161.

Breynyon[3], in Lelant; *see* Mahun, Thomas *(Oratories)*, i, 20^{b}.

Bridestowe, Nicholas Bodeway, R. of, licence of non-residence for one year (at Oxford), from 16 May,[4] 1398, i, 18; for one year (at Oxford), from 1 May, 1399, i, 26^{b}; for three years,[5] from 3 Oct., 1402, i, 61^{b}; for two years[6] (3 Oct., 1405), i, 76^{b}.—Reginald Bryta, R. of, i, 81, 83, 85.—John Prata, R. of, licence of non-residence for one year, from 20 June, 1410, i, 99; also, from 23 Dec., 1411, to Michaelmas, 1412, i, 140^{b}.—John Wykyngston, R. of, ii, 351; licence

---

1 Gynne, MS.

2 Braynford, MS.

3 *hodie* Brannion.

4 Also, the sequestration of his living, on account of non-residence, was taken off.

5 Together with John Redeclyf, R. of Northill, "contemplacione nobilis viri, Edwardi de Courtenay, Comitis Devonie, dummodo in ipsius obsequiis interim steterint."

6 Together with John Godwyn, R. of Sheviocke, "contemplacione, etc.," as before.

of non-residence for one year, from 30 Sept., 1414, i, 201b. —William[1] Weston, R. of, *see* Franke, Robert, i, 214.

Bridford, Chapel of St. Katherine, at Laployd [Lapflote MS.], in the parish of, licensed 6 Nov., 1409, i, 90b.—Richard [Vaysey], Rector of, i, 334.

Bridgewater, for certain captives belonging to—

William Carballa and William Goldsmyth, merchants of Bridgewater, having been seized, together with Robert Wace and John Taunton, in the ship *Mary* of Southampton (Walter Lange, master), had been landed at Harfleur and conveyed thence to Stapyl in Normandy, where they had been thrown into prison and brutally treated. Their ransom had been fixed at twenty pounds sterling; and the Bishop promises an Indulgence to all the Faithful who shall help to raise the money.—25 May, 1410, i, 96.

Bridgewater, Hospital of St. John Baptist at, i, 307b; patrons of the V. of Bovey Tracy, ii, 20; of Davidstow, V., ii, 101, 147; of Lanteglos-by-Fowey, V., ii, 146.—The Friars Minors of, i, 311.

Bristol, the Friars, etc., of, i, 306, 311; St. Michael's in, i, 306.

Bristowe, Robert, proxy for Walter Westney (q. v.) ii, 36b.

Brito, William, his "Liber super vocabula Biblie," i, 324b.

Brittany (*see* Colyn, Robert, and Hals, Richard), i, 198.

Brixham, Elias Penellys and Margaret his wife (*see Oratories*), i, 92b.—Richard Holrygg, V. of, appointed a Penitentiary in the Deanery of Ipplepen, i, 50 (deceased); i, 332b; his Will, i, 329b.—Canon Richard Penels' bequest to the poor of, i, 332b.—Commissions of enquiry as to this Benefice,—

(1.) On the presentation by John, Earl of Huntingdon, of *John Mason*, priest, and by Sir Edward Courtenay, knt., son of Edward, Earl of Devon, of *Walter Wadham*, clerk,—they were joint patrons.—Dated 22 April, 1416.

(2.) On the presentation by Eustace Valdryan, citizen of London, of *Thomas Shordich*, chaplain (same date), ii, 258.b

(3.) As to the pollution of the Cemetery by Adam Blake, John Whyte, and others, with bloodshed.—Dated 8 Oct., 1416, ii, 260.

(4.) For the Reconciliation of the Cemetery.—Dated 14 Oct., 1416, ii, 260b.

[*Breve Regium*]:—Prohibition to admit any Clerk pending the settlement of the dispute, as to the right of patronage, between Eustace Waldryan, citizen of London, and Sir Edward Courtenay, knt., and Sir John Holand, knt.—Dated 29 April, 1416, ii, 355.

[*Breve Regium*]:—Suspension of the Prohibition.[2]—Dated 15 May, 1416, *ibid.*

Broad Clyst, John Mattheu, V. of, i, 327b.

Broadhempston,[3] rebuilding of the parish church of,—

---

[1] John in the MS., an obvious clerical error. *See* ii, 166b, 180.

[2] The result appears at ii, 176b, where it is recorded that Walter Wadham was instituted, 22 May, 1416; Patron, Sir Edward Courtenay.

[3] Hempston Magna, MS.

The parishioners had represented to the Bishop that their Church was in a ruinous condition and notoriously clumsily constructed : they desired to rebuild it on a larger scale, and in a different part of the Cemetery ; and to this the Bishop consented, on condition that they engaged to complete the new church within two years from the pulling down of the old one, and sooner if possible. Moreover, he granted an Indulgence to all the Faithful who should contribute to "so great and pious a work" (28 Dec., 1400), i, 51ᵇ.—On 22 Nov., 1401, scarcely a year later, the new church appears to have been sufficiently advanced for use, as a licence was then granted, for one year, to celebrate Divine Service "in quadam ecclesia, sive basilica, in cimiterio . . . de novo erecta et constructa," i, 58ᵇ; this licence was renewed and for the same period, 4 Nov., 1402, i, 62 ; and again, 4 Nov., 1403, i, 68. After this date there are no further licences recorded ; neither is there any record, apparently, of the consecration of the new church.

Broadwoodwidger,[1] Norton, the manor of Alice Durneford in the parish of, i, 230.—Commission of Enquiry as to the pollution of the Cemetery by Christina, wife of Richard Charde, and John, son of Richard Spryg, parishioners (11 April, 1414), ii, 254.

Brode, John, i, 320ᵇ.

Brode, Nigel, V. of Broad Clyst (deceased), ii, 152.

Brokas, Katherine, widow of Sir Bernard Brokas, knt.,—

On the 14th of January, 1395-6, the Bishop received a Letter from the Bishop of London (dated at Hadham, on the 11th), informing him that the Dame Katherine Brokas, widow, then residing in London, had applied to him for a licence to place herself in the hands of the Bishop of Exeter, that she might take a vow of perpetual chastity, and have some church or chapel assigned to her for her abode.—Accordingly, on the 16th of January, the Bishop received her in the Chapel of his House in London, "juxta Temple barre," and celebrated Pontifical High Mass, during which she took the vow in the terms which follow,—" En le noun de Dieu ieo Katerine Brokas venevowe a Dieu perpetuel chastite en le presence de vous, Reverent Pier in Dieu Esmound, par la grace de Dieu Evesque dexcestre, et promitte establement vivere in chastite, sauuz compaignie de homme, a terme de ma vie."—i, 7ᵇ.

Broke, John, i, 319.

Broke, Nicholas, instituted to the V. of Otterton, ii, 176.

Brokelond, Henry, Canon of Exeter (ii, 212), and Rector of Moreton [Hampstead], his death, ii, 78 ; his Will, i, 303.

Brokhampton, Thomas. *See* Kentisbeare, ii, 345ᵇ.

Bromewych (or Bromwyche), John, does homage to the Bishop, at St. Alban's, for certain lands (10 July, 1399), ii, 310ᵇ; and at Clyst for lands at Fareby, in the parish of Bishop's Nympton (30 July, 1419), ii, 311ᵇ.

Bromford, Nicholas, presents to the R. of Jacobstow (Devon), ii, 86, 142ᵇ, 157ᵇ, 162 ; to Honeychurch, R., ii, 101 ; John

[1] Brodewodwiger *and* Brodewode Wyger, MS.

his son and heir, presents to Jacobstow, ii, 177; Joan, daughter of, i, 315.

He was Escheator in Devon and Cornwall; and the mandate to the Bishop to administer the oath to him is dated 3 Feb., 1411-12 [*Breve Regium*], ii, 344.

Bromley, Richard, Dean of the Collegiate Church of St. Mary, Shrewsbury, ii, 43.

Bromschulf, Thomas, chaplain, ii, 48b.

Brooke, Thomas, i, 312.

Broun, John, of Kingston (parish of Ermington), ii, 277b.

Broun, Richard, M.D. and S.T.B., collated to a Canonry in Exeter Cathedral, ii, 54; his death, ii, 157.

Broun, Thomas, R. of East Buckland (deceased), ii, 4b.

Broun, William, instituted to the V. of Sidbury, ii, 20b; *see*, also, i, 326b, 328b, 329, 331, 333; proxy for William Goldyng (q. v.), ii, 83;—a William Broun was a Priest-Vicar in the Cathedral, ii, 212.

Brounyng, William (chaplain, and a notary-publick), collated, as a sub-deacon, to the R. of St. Stephen's, Exeter, ii, 94; exchanges, as a deacon, for the V. of Modbury, ii, 94b; mentioned, i, 71, 78, 83b, 88b, 89, 91, 93, 94, 313, 313b; ii, 97b; proxy for Walter Galy, ii, 80; for John Cheyne, ii, 84; for Richard Bogheway, ii, 85b; for Laurence Haukyn, ii, 96; for John Dygon, ii, 98; [q. v.]

Brounste (or Bronste), Richard, i, 234b, 308b; co-patron of North Huish, R., ii, 144b, 248b, 189b.

Bruere, David le, *see* Chudleigh, i, 239.

Bruere, Dionisia de la, *see* Exeter, St. George's, ii, 340b.

Bruere, John, of Loddiswell, i, 306.

Brugg, Richard, R. of Ashton (deceased), ii, 14b.

Brugyth, John, i, 301b.

Brunyng, Thomas, exchanges the R. of Willand for that of Halford (Dioc. of Bath and Wells), ii, 31.

Bruter, William, instituted to the R. of Moreton [-Hampstead], ii, 78; exchanges for Paignton, ii, 178b; his death, ii, 189.

Bruton, Richard,[1] Prebendary of Netherhayne in Chulmleigh (ii, 188b), and Prebendary of Bodmin, in St. Endellion, at the time of his death, ii, 189, 263b.

Bruwere, John, instituted to the R. of Bittadon, ii, 12b.

---

[1] Richard Bruton was Chancellor of Wells Cathedral, i, 229b, 230, 236.

Bruyn, Maurice, presents to South Ockenden, R. (Dioc. of London), ii, 139[b].

Bryan, Joan, i, 332.

Bryan, John, i, 198 ; ii, 255.

Brycon, John, senior, i, 319.

Brycon, John, a parishioner of Cowick, ii, 287 et seq.

Bryd, Peter, R. of Halford (Dioc. of Bath and Wells), exchanges for the R. of Willand, ii, 31.

Bryd, Thomas, instituted to Moreton [Hampstead], R., ii, 198.

Brydbrok, William, i, 325.

Brydham, Edward, *see* Kentisbeare, ii, 345[b].

Brydon, William, i, 245 ; ii, 267.

Bryene, Guy de, his Chantry at Slapton (q. v.), ii, 46[b].

Bryghtlegh, Laurence, R. of Great Torrington, i, 35[b] ; his death, ii, 52.

Brympston, John, deputy for William Hulles, Prior of the Order of St. John of Jerusalem, in England, ii, 191[b].

Brynchele, William, Judge ; *see* Smale, John.

Brystow, John, a Canon of St. German's, i, 48.

Brystowe, John, V. of Buckerell (deceased), ii, 20[b].

Bryt, John, collated to the V. of Lelant, ii, 176[b] ; 264.

Bryta, Reginald, R. of Bratton [Clovelly], q. v., ii, 217[b] ; exchanges for the R. of Bridestowe, ii, 92[b] ; i, 81, 83, 85 ; collated to a Canonry in Ottery St. Mary, ii, 97[b] ; exchanges this Canonry for a Prebend in the parish church of Norton (Dioc. of Durham), ii, 100[b] ; collated to a Canonry and the 7th Prebend in Ottery, *ibid.* ; exchanges Bridestowe for the R. of Dittisham, ii, 106[b] ; i, 91, 93, 168[b], 176 ; ii, 164[b] ; licensed as a publick preacher in the Cathedral and City of Exeter (20 June, 1411), i, 127[b] ; collated to a Bursal Prebend at Crediton, ii, 139 ; exchanges it for a Canonry at Wells, ii, 152.

Brythelegh, Thomas, presents to the R. of Talaton, ii, 85[b].

Brythlegh, John (of Chittlehampton) and Emma Pollard (of Horwood),—

Licence, addressed to John [Deyman], R. of Horwood, and Richard Hore, priest, for their marriage in the church of Horwood (9 Jan. 1409-10), i, 93.

Bryton, John, and Joan Langrom,—

Although these persons were aware that one John Wynhaw, related to the said John in the fourth degree of consanguinity, had frequently had illicit intercourse with the said Joan, and the said John Bryton had himself committed fornication and incest with her, and she had borne him children ; yet, as they were anxious to be married, for their children's sake, the Bishop granted a Dispensation (26 March, 1415), i, 209.

Brywer, John, Cantor of Ottery St. Mary (deceased), ii, 104^b.

Bubbewyth,[1] Nicholas, chantry-priest of Sticklepath, resigns, ii, 6; instituted to the Prebend of Heyes, ii, 30^b; collated to a Canonry in Exeter Cathedral, ii, 42^b; resigns the Prebend of Heyes, ii, 67^b.

Buckfast[2] Abbey, i, 306^b, 330^b.—William Paderstow, Abbot of (q. v.), ii, 210^b; commissioned *ad levandam et colligendam secundum medietatem unius decime* (5 May, 1398), ii, 217; William Slade, Abbot of, *see* ii, 290^b et seqq.; *see*, also, Herward, John, ii, 351^b; [William], Abbot of, in arrear of procurations (due to the Pope's collector) for two years (1409-10), i, 105; William Beaghe, Abbot of (q. v.), ii, 169.—John Sturton, monk of, ii, 18.—Abbot and Convent of, patrons of the R. of Zeal Monachorum, ii, 10, 102; of Buckfastleigh, V., ii, 91^b, 160, 173^b, 181^b.

Buckfastleigh (Holy Trinity), John [Fardel], V. of, a Penitentiary in the Deanery of Totnes, i, 50; his Will, i, 306^b; David Hughe, V. of, ii, 355; Roger Goslegh, V. of, *ibid.*,—

Commission of enquiry on the complaint of Roger Goslay *(sic)*, as to dilapidations and waste in the chancel, etc., on the part of his predecessor, David Hughe (30 Oct., 1414), ii, 255^b.

Buckland Abbey [Walter], Abbot of, in arrear of procurations (due to the Pope's collector) for three years (1408-10), i, 105.—The Abbot and Convent of, patrons of the V. of Buckland Monachorum, ii, 40, 88^b; of Walkhampton, V., ii, 88; of Bickleigh, V., ii, 136, 176, 243^b.—*See* Reskimer, Alice, i, 323^b; the Will of Matilda Latymer, i, 329; and of Thomas Reymound, i, 331^b.

Buckland Brewer,[3] John Colyn, of, *see* Colyn, i, 93^b; Manor of Orleigh in, i, 231^b; the parish church of,—

It was represented to the Bishop that the tower had been destroyed by lightning, which had also entered the church and done serious damage,—*sacra vasa, ceteraque ornamenta et bona quam plurima, in eadem existencia mirabiliter igne fulguris . . . . combusta et conversa funditus in favillas.* The parishioners were too poor to rebuild and repair their church without assistance; and the Bishop granted an indulgence to all the Faithful who should help them (25 June, 1399), i, 28.

Buckland-Filleigh, John Castell, R. of; Dispensation (to study at Oxford) for three years, from 11 Dec., 1400, i, 51^b; for four years from 14 Dec., 1403, i, 69^b; *see*, also, i, 84.—John

---

[1] Also Bubbewyt, MS.
[2] Bukfestrie, etc., MS.
[3] Bokelond Brywer, MS.

Bowode, R. of; licence of non-residence for one year, from 12 July, 1410, i, 100ᵇ.

Buckyeth, Nicholas, a chaplain, i, 330ᵇ.

Buddockyssyde (*or* Bottokkyssyde), William, presents to the R. of Dunchideock, ii, 130, 134, 199ᵇ, 267ᵇ.

Bude,—Chapels in the parish of Stratton,—

Licence was granted to Walter Cryk, V. of Stratton (21 Aug., 1400), to celebrate in the Chapels of Holy Trinity and St. Michael, of Bude, and St. Leonard, of Efford, i, 45.

Bulle, Robert, instituted to the R. of Michaelstow, ii, 78ᵇ; his death,[1] ii, 99.

Bullok, Alice, sister of Thomas, i, 314.

Bullok, John, V. of Abbotsham (resigned), ii, 17.

Bullok (or Bollok), Walter, instituted to the Chantry-Chapel of the B.V.M., in the Cemetery of Ermington, ii, 32ᵇ; [resigns,[2] ii, 9ᵇ]; instituted to the R. of Atherington,[3] ii, 36ᵇ; his death,[4] ii, 91ᵇ.

Bullok, Thomas—"*Serviens Domini Episcopi*"—his Will, i, 313ᵇ.

Bunden (or Bondon), John, instituted to the R. of Broadoak, ii, 68; resigns, ii, 157.

Burdett, John, instituted to the V. of St. Madron, ii, 99ᵇ.

Burdon, Richard, co-patron of Inwardleigh, R., ii, 24ᵇ.

Burell, John, instituted to the R. of Clyst St. George, ii, 90ᵇ; resigns, ii, 115.

Burgayn, John, chaplain, i, 202.

Burgbrygg, John, *see* Munford, ii, 106ᵇ.

Burgeawyll, John, Prior of Cowick, q. v.

Burgh, John, chaplain, *see* St. Kew, i, 161ᵇ.

Burgh, John, V. of Townstal, i, 208, 217, 226ᵇ, 231, 237ᵇ, 245; his institution, ii, 158.

Burgh, John, does homage to the Bishop for lands in Burneyre, Cornwall, 21 Oct., 1398, ii, 310.

Burgh, Maurice, of Crediton, i, 304ᵇ.

Burgoun, John, instituted to the R. of St. Olave's, Exeter, ii,

---

[1] Bole, MS., in this place.

[2] Not recorded, but *his successor*, John Sprydell, was instituted 26 July, 1398, and he was himself instituted to Atherington on the 3rd of February preceding (ii, 9ᵇ.)

[3] He was only in subdeacon's orders at the time (3 Feb., 1397-8), and on the day following the Bishop gave him Letters-Dimissory, to be ordained deacon and priest by any English Bishop.

[4] He is here called "John"—a clerical error.

74; Letters Dimissory for his Ordination[1] by any English Bishop, i, 69b; proxy for Richard Mannyng on his institution to St. George's, Exeter, ii, 135; licensed to serve the Chantry in the Palace (2 Dec., 1413), ii 154; commissioned *ad vendicandum clericos convictos coram judicibus secularibus* (17 Feb., 1413-14), ii, 253b; resigns St. Olave's and is collated to the Rectory

"Sancti Ermetis in Cornubia . . . . per mortem domini Johannis Mark, ultimi ejusdem ecclesie Rectoris, vacantem, et ad ipsius Domini collacionem pleno jure spectantem," ii, 166.—*See* St. Erme (*Institutions*). Exchanges for the R. of Lezant, ii, 174b; licensed to celebrate in the Chapel of St. Bridget de Landew, in the parish of Lezant (28 Jan., 1417-18), i, 238; resigns Lezant, ii, 191b; and is instituted to the R. of St. Stephen in Braunel, ii, 190b.

Burgoun, John, of Apuldram, ii, 293b.

Burlegh, John, instituted to the R. of Lustleigh, ii, 93b.—*See* Carslegh, Simon, i, 191; also, i, 315.

Burlescombe,[2] R., appropriated to Canonsleigh, ii, 359b; the parish church, i, 318b.

Burlescombe, Alexander, *see* Dunkeswell Abbey.

Burleston, William, co-patron of the R. of Aveton-Giffard, ii, 67b.

William Burleston, domicellus, did homage to the Bishop, in London, for "Bysschopeslee" (28 Jan., 1395-6), ii, 310.

Burnard, William, i, 331b.

Burnel (or Burnell), John, V. of Collumpton, licensed to celebrate in the Chapel of St. George in that parish (14 July, 1401), i, 57b; his death, ii, 134.

Burnel, Thomas, notary-publick, ii, 139; proxy for Walter Crewys (q. v.), ii, 179b.

Burneman, John, i, 319.

Burneman, Richard, R. of Bradstone[3]; commissioned *ad vendicandum clericos convictos coram judicibus secularibus* in Comitatu Cornubie (24 Feb., 1413-14), ii, 253b.

Burneyre, in Cornwall, *see* Burgh, John, ii, 310.

Burrington, Roger [Cole], V. of,—

[*Breve Regium*]—Requiring him to appear at Westminster within the Octave of St. John Baptist, to shew cause why he should not pay to the Abbot of

---

[1] "Rectori ecclesie parochialis Sancti Olavi, Civitatis Exoniensis, primam tonsuram clericalem habenti."

[2] Burledescomb, MS.

[3] "Bradeston *in Cornubia*," MS.; a curious clerical error, for it is in Devon: Bradstone is on the left bank of the Tamar which divides the counties.

Tavistock the sum of four pounds, arrears of an annual payment of seven shillings (8 June, 1395); ii, 303b:

appointed a Penitentiary in the Deanery of Chulmleigh, i, 50: the repairs required in the chancel, etc.,—

In Sept., 1412, the Bishop commissioned Archdeacon Hunden to investigate the matter; before whom appeared the parties immediately concerned, *viz*: the Abbot and Convent of Tavistock, the Rectors (by their proxy, John Twyford), and Thomas Bost, the Vicar, who disputed the liability, while the Rectors alleged and produced the Letter of Thomas, the late Bishop, duly sealed with his oblong seal, which the Vicar acknowledged to be true and authoritative. This document is given at length; it is dated 24 Sep., 1390, and sets forth that, on searching the Register of Bishop Walter de Stapyldon, it was ascertained that, by the ordination and taxation of the parish, the Sanctuary, and all the land held by the secular Rector, ought to be enjoyed by the Vicars, together with all buildings thereon, as well as all the small tithes, oblations, etc., including the tithe of hay, and all mortuary offerings; they were to pay procurations to the Archdeacon, and also all synodals, etc., and they were to keep the chancel in repair, and the books and ornaments thereof (which the Rectors had been accustomed to maintain), after the same had been put in proper repair, once for all, by the Abbot and Convent of Tavistock. Moreover, they were to pay to the said Religious, every year, at Easter, seven shillings "de fructibus altalagii": but the latter were to defray all extraordinary expenses and burdens. The Abbot and Convent, also, produced witnesses, who were examined on oath; and, both parties assenting and so requiring, the Bishop's Commissary, complying with the terms of their petitions herein, did, on the 19th May, 1412, in the chapel of St. Gabriel, near the Bridge, at Clyst, where the Bishop was, at that time, in residence, decide and decree, in due form of law, as follows:—

"That it was evident that the Abbot and Convent of Tavistock, being Rectors of the parish of Burrington, save and except the pension belonging to the Vicars thereof, were required by Bishop Stapyldon's 'Ordinacio' to put the chancel in proper repair, together with its books and ornaments, once for all, at their own charges. That both sides had been heard; and that it appeared that the liability for such repairs, now and in the future, fell on the Vicar for the time being, and that the said Religious were free from such liability; that they were entitled to demand of the said Vicar the said pension of seven shillings annually, which at Easter last past the said Thomas Bost had failed to pay, and for which default they sought a remedy. That the said Thomas Bost, in order to avoid further proceedings and expense, confessed that the said annual payment was due from him. The Commissary, accordingly, pronounced judgment against him, ordering him to pay the money forthwith, which he consented to do; and, presently, putting his hand into his purse (*marsupium*), he produced and paid over the said seven shillings, and a Deed was duly executed, to give effect to the above provisions, in the presence of John Colkyrk (notary-publick), and Walter Bowhay, clerks, and John Uppecote.

The "Commission" directed to Archdeacon Hunden (27 Jan., 1407-8), is given at length: also, the "Procuratorium" of John Twyford abovenamed (dated 15 Sept., 1402), and the Certificate of Roger Bolter, notary-publick, etc., as to all the proceedings herein and the said decree, i, 164.

Burstede, Robert, inst. to the R. of Marhamchurch, ii, 97b; exchanges for the R. of St. Augustine's "ad portam (Diocese of London), ii, 122.

Bursy, Richard. He is described as "Suffraganeus Decani originalis Decanatus de Schyrewyll," i, 190b.

Burton, Gilbert, presents to the R. of Ideford, ii, 25.

Bury,[1] John, co-patron of the R. of Roseash, ii, 81; of Landcross, R., ii, 95b; of Shirwell, R., ii, 96b, 103b.—*See*, also, St. Pinnock, ii, 351.

Bury, Nicholas, collated to a Canonry in Glasney, ii, 65; his death, ii, 132.

Bury, Robert of Apuldram, ii, 293b.

Bury, Walter, R. of Laȝarton (Dioc. of Salisbury), exchanges for the V. of Harpford, ii, 192b; exchanges for the R. of Poughill, ii, 197.

Buryknoll, John, i, 307.

Buryn, Oger, co-patron of the R. of Bickleigh, ii, 92b.

Busch, John, an executor of the Will of William Falewell, R. of Ermington, i, 12.—*See*, also, i, 300.

Bussh, Luke, of Woodbury, i, 312.

Busshbyry, Lewis, i, 314; collated to the R. of Cheriton-Bishop, ii, 123b.

Butiller, Thomas, Dean of Windsor, i, 33.

Butterford,[2] in the parish of North Huish; licence to the R., Thomas Tremayn, to celebrate on certain days in the Chapel of St. Thomas (15 May, 1400), i, 37; was renewed to the next R., John Combe (6 July, 1403), i, 67b.

Butterton, the Church of (Dioc. of Lichfield), i, 316.

Bycote, John, chaplain of Polslo Priory, ii, 77; instituted to the V. of Aylesbeare, ii, 96b; his death, ii, 121.

Bydelake, John, literate, i, 214.

Bydewille, John, *see* Parkham; also, ii, 307b.

Byke, John, i, 307b.

Bykebury, John, instituted to the R. of Bigbury, ii, 159; 357b.

Bykebury, Sir William de, knt., i, 321b, 322; presents to the R. of Bigbury, ii, 159.

Bykelegh, John de, V. of Doddiscombsleigh, resigns, ii, 3b; instituted to the V. of Veryan,[3] ii, 4.

[1] Also, Byry, MS.

[2] Botforde and Boterford, MS.,—"quarta et sexta feriis per hebdomadam, quum dies festivus in eis non occurrit, et eciam in Festo Sancti Thome Apostoli."

[3] Elerky, MS.

Byldesthorp, Thomas, proxy for Simon Sydenham (q. v.), ii, 81.
Bylker, John, ii, 118.
Bylyngham, William, chaplain, ii, 160b.
Byncombe, John, i, 320b.
Byngham, Robert, R. of Georgenympton (resigns), ii, 99.
Byrde, Roger, chaplain, i, 302.
Byschop,[1] Gilbert, co-patron of the R. of Bickleigh. ii, 92b; of Broad Nymet, ii, 195.
Bisschop, John, instituted to the R. of Uploman,[2] ii, 7b; he had licence of non-residence granted to him for one year, from 12 June, 1401—*dummodo interim orrium*[3] *Rectorie sue competenter faciat reparari*, i, 56b; exchanges for the R. of Bagborough (Dioc. of Bath and Wells), ii, 63b.
Bysschop, Peter, instituted to the R. of [Clay]hydon, ii, 81b.
Byttylsgate, John, R. of Feniton, and Canon of Ottery (deceased), ii, 78b.

C.

Caam, William, instituted to the V. of Mullyon, ii, 188b.
Cabyn, John, i, 332b.
Cade, John, Canon of St. Stephen's, Launceston, ii, 117.
Cade, John, Priest-Vicar in the Cathedral, i, 56.
Cade, Walter, instituted to St. Olave's, Exeter, ii, 166; i, 240.
Cadewell, John, of Littleham, i, 32.
Cadia, Thomasia, daughter of John, i, 200b.
Caermarthen, the Friars Minors of, i, 131b.
Caithness, Bishops of, *see* Catenensi Episcopo.
Calf, Thomas, R. of Cameley (Dioc. of Bath and Wells), exchanges for the V. of Yarcombe, ii, 194; his death, ii, 200b.
Calstock, Thomas Wygetoft, R. of;[3] licence of non-residence for one year, from 19 April, 1396, i, 8b; John Malcsors, R. of,[4] licence of non-residence for one year, from 4 Dec., 1397, i, 14; licence to celebrate in his manse (22 Sept., 1400), i, 49; John Malewayn, R. of,[5] dispensation (to study at

[1] Also, Byshop, Byaschop, Byschope, &c., MS.
[2] Lomen, etc., MS.
[3] Calystok, MS.
[4] His glebe-barn—i. q. "horreum."
[5] Kelstok, MS., and at i, 14, "Chalestokhacche."

Oxford) for two years, from 26 April, 1403, i, 64; also,[1] licence to celebrate in his manse (10 April, 1405), i, 74; also, in the Chapel of St. Cyricus and Julitta, in the parish of (14 June, 1411), i, 125b; appointed[2] a Penitentiary in the Deanery of East, i, 143b, 174, 194b, 207b, 217, 231, 238, 245b.—Peter and Elizabeth Eggecombe, of,[1] i, 123b.—William Flet, a suicide, interred there, contrary to the Canon, ii, 227.

Calwelegh, John, and Joan Nywehous:

They had married in ignorance of the fact, which had come to their knowledge quite recently, that they were related in the fourth degree of affinity, and, dreading the scandal of a divorce, they appealed to Pope Boniface IX. for a Dispensation; which was granted (30 Jan., 1404-5), i, 73.

Camborne,[3] Benedict Canterbury,[4] R. of; licence of non-residence for one year, from 1 July, 1410, i, 99b; 212; appointed to induct Thomas Malesouers to the R. of Calstock, ii, 6b. *See*, also, ii, 233.

Cambridge, Archdeacon Hunden's bequest to the "New Library" in the University of, i, 325.

Camelford, Chapels at,—St. Mary's, licensed 29 Jan., 1396-7, i, 11; St. Thomas-the-Martyr's, licensed 25 May, 1405, i, 75.

Camelford, Roger de, R. of St. George's, Exeter, ii, 340b.

Came (or Camme), John, instituted to the R. of Charleton, ii, 63b; i, 86; his death, ii, 103.

Cammel, Brother John, chaplain, i, 227b.

Campyng, *alias* Lurk, Robert—*Dispensacio super defectu natalium* (14 July, 1413), i, 181b.

Candelesby (*or* Caudelesby), John, collated to a Canonry [and 8th Prebend] at Ottery, ii, 27; to a Prebend at Chulmleigh, ii, 35b; and at St. Probus, ii, 53; resigns his Canonry at Ottery, ii, 151b; his death, 173b.

Canelisy,[5] in Pawton, ii, 311.

Cannington, the Prioress and Convent of, present to the R. of Witheridge, ii, 30.

Canon, John (a baker), i, 323b.

Canonsleigh,[6] "the Abbey of St. John-the-Evangelist and St. Ethelreda-the-Virgin"[7] at, the Bishop's mandate, addressed

---

1 Calestok.
2 Malwyn and Malwen, MS.
3 Cambron, MS.
4 Cauntelbery, MS.
5 The Manor of Pawton is in St. Breoke; "Cannalidgey" is close by, in the adjoining parish of St. Issey.
6 Canonlegh, MS.
7 *See* ii, 125; also, "Ordinis Sancti Augustini," i, 39b.

to [Lucy Warre] the Abbess, for its Visitation on the 19th June (dated 27 May,) 1400, i, 39,—

It appears that this Visitation was postponed to the 25th of June, as on the 24th of that month Chancellor Richard Hals was Commissioned to discharge the duty, on behalf of the Bishop (who states that he was prevented from visiting in person), on that day (ii, 227.) It appears, however, from i, 42ᵇ, that the Bishop had been at the Abbey on June the 20th, on which day he, there, granted a licence for private oratories to Elinor de Fizpayn and to Thomas Horsey and Alice his wife.

Gregory, R. of Raddington (Dioc. of Bath and Wells), appointed Confessor to the Community (17 Feb., 1402-3), i, 62ᵇ; licence to the Abbess (Lucy Warre), for her private Oratory within the Abbey (25 July, 1410), i, 101; in arrear of procurations, due to the Pope's Collector, for three years (1408-10), i, 105, 110.—Election of Abbess,—

The Bishop being at Ottery, William Baunton, a chaplain, appeared before him (4 Dec., 1410), on behalf of Christina Roges (Sub-prioress) and of the whole community, to inform him that they had elected Mary Beuchamp, one of their number; with Baunton were associated John Barel, R. of St. Illogan, and Thomas Gylle, clerk. The Electors were the said Christina Roges, Katharine Tambroke (*cantorissa*), Joan Downes (*sacrista*), Meliora Okinforda (*celeraria*), Joan Laury, Thomasia Tracy, and Elizabeth Fitzwater, Joan More and Margery Cheseldon. Lucy Warre, the last Abbess, had died on 11 Oct., and licence to elect her successor had been granted by Edward, Duke of York (Patron by reason of the minority of Richard, son of Thomas, Lord le Despenser). The election took place on the 24th of November, the Elect with tears (*flebiliter*) demanding time for consideration, and reluctantly consenting thereto on the following day. The Bishop ordered proclamation thereof to be made in due form; his Mandate being addressed to the Dean of Tiverton and Walter Stalworde,[1] chaplain; it it was dated at Clyst, 5 Dec. The Certificate was dated 10 Dec., and set forth that proclamation had been duly made in the Conventual Church and in the parish church of Burlescombe. The election was confirmed by the Bishop at Crediton, 12 Dec., and on the next day he issued his Mandate to the Archdeacon of Exeter for her induction and installation, ii, 125-129.

Mary Beuchamp, Abbess of; licence for her private Oratory within the Monastery (18 Jan., 1413-14), i, 191.—Patrons of Northleigh, R., ii, 17; of Hockworthy, V., ii, 14ᵇ, 44; of Burlescombe, V., ii, 151ᵇ.—Churches appropriated to, ii, 359ᵇ; William Jew, of, i, 319.—*See also* Werthe, Alice, i, 218.

Cantelo, William, R. of Angersleigh (Dioc. of B. & W.), ii, 222.

Canterbury, William Courtenay, Archbishop of, consecrator of Bishop Stafford, i, 1; his sisters, the Ladies Margaret Cobham and Elizabeth Loterell[2] (*sic*),—Indulgence granted

[1] *See* Stalworth, Walter, i, 145ᵇ.

[2] "Archiepiscopi Sorores, viam universe carnis jam pridem, quod dolenter referimus . . . ingresse." The Bishop's Mandate was addressed to Dean Tregrisiou, his Vicar-General, "quod Capitulum Ecclesie nostre Exoniensis predicte, ac omnes et singulos Abbates et Priores, ceterosque Religiosos et Mendicantes, necnon

to the Faithful throughout the Diocese, who should assist at the solemn observance of the exequies of these distinguished Ladies (10 Aug., 1395), i, 4^{b}; Mandate to pray for his soul[1] (3 Aug., 1396), ii, 211^{b}.—Thomas [Arundel], Archbishop of; his Mandate for a general Intercession (at Michaelmas), for the King and the Realm (Dated in the Priory of Dunmow, 24 July, 1397), i, 13; his general Monition against non-residence (14 March, 1409-10), i, 96^{b}.

Canterbury, the Archdeacon of (ii, 309^{b}),—

"Feodum Archidiaconi Cantuariensis, qui introni3are debet singulos Episcopos Cantuariensis Provincie, tam sede Cantuariensi plena, quam eciam ipsa sede vacante.—*In primis*, in descensu Episcopi venientis ad Ecclesiam suam, pro intronisacione sua, Archidiaconus Cantuariensis habebit statim palefridum, cum sella et toto hernesio palefridi, in introitu Civitatis. *Item*, capam suam habebit pluvialem cum capitello[2] et calciamentis ejusdem. *Item*, cupam suam argenteam unde servitur in mensa die introni3ationis sue. *Item*, feoum et prebendam pro xv equis quamdiu moram fecerit pro officio introni3ationis hujusmodi faciendo. *Item*, esculenta et poculenta per tres dies et omni nocte unum Cextarium *(sic)* vini pro collacione sua. *Item*, duos magnos tortices de cera pro tota mora sua, et qualibet nocte duos minores tortices et xxiiij candelas de cera. *Item*, decem marcas sterlingorum in pecunia numerata pro expensis suis eundo et rediundo *(sic)*. *Item*, lectisternia Episcopi peti solebant, ut dicitur, pro feodo camerarii introni3antis hujusmodi; set nescitur si ea solebat habere. Et notandum quod omnia predicta, exceptis lectisterniis, Prior et Capitulum Cantuariensis habuerunt, Sede vacante et Archidiacono carente: Anno Domini millesimo ccc^{mo} nonagesimo tertio."

Canterbury, Benedict, LL.B., [R. of Camborne], i, 323^{b}; ii, 46,

---

ecclesiarum parochialium nostrarum Civitatis et Diocesis Rectores et Vicarios, ac presbiteros curatos et non curatos, clerumque et populum ejusdem universum . . . . moneatis et efficaciter inducatis quatinus prefatarum dominarum exequias quamcicius . . . faciant in eorum ecclesiis solemniter celebrari, ac eciam earum memoriam in eorum missis et aliis orationibus suis, in publicis processionibus et aliis locis privatim factis devote commendent, et pro ipsarum animabus apud Altissimum preces effundant humiles et devotas."

[1] "qui quanto magis" — thus our Bishop writes of the departed Primate—in dignitatis et excellencie sublimitate extiterat constitutus, tanto magis velud arbor in domo Domini fructificans ac sectator omnium bonorum operum aliis relinquens exemplum, conquerentibus videlicet aures benignissimas et humiles exhibendo, de corde multipliciter tribulatos assidue confortando, errores et hereses in Provincia Cantuariensi, inimico humani generis procurante, pullulantes sagaciter extirpando, caritatem et amorem inter regni Anglie proceres ceterasque oves sibi regendas commissas, velud bonus pastor, reformando, ac in necessitatibus quibuslibet constitutis verbo et facto misericorditer subveniendo, devotissime Domino studuit pro viribus complacere, et non solum ad singulares personas, verum etiam ad totum regnum Anglie, sua summa humilitas atque generosa bonitas largissime extendebat.

[2] Not "capucio," as quoted in the *Monasticon Dioc: Exon.* The "Capitellus" is described as "vestis pars superior qua caput tegebatur, vel potius collare; *capuchon*, ou *collet d'habit*."—Acta Sanctorum a Bollando edita *(D'Arnis)*.

46b, 47b, 49, 49b, 50, 50b, 227b, 233, 234; Official Peculiar in Cornwall—Commission dated, 10 Aug., 1395; ii, 210; instituted to a Canonry in Glasney, ii, 2; inducts the R. of Calstock, ii, 6b; *see* also i, 46b, 143b, 174, 194b, 207b, 217, 231, 238; ii, 225.

Canterbury, Henry, sub-prior of Bodmin, ii, 71b, 72.

Caprygg, Walter V. of Otterton (deceased), ii, 176.

Caputgrassis de Sulmona, Paul de, Nuntio and Papal Collector[1] in England,—*Certificatorium pro*, 18 Nov., 1414, i, 206b.

Cara Villa (or Carville), Peter de, instituted to the Priory of St. Michael's Mount, ii, 338b.

Carballa, William, merchant; *see* Bridgewater.

Carden, William (sen. and jun.), of Apuldram, ii, 293b.

Cardynham, Thos. [Aumarle], R. of, a Penitentiary in the Deanery of West, i, 49b.—John Waryn, R. of; licence of non-residence for two years, from 8 Oct., 1416, i, 226b; and for two years, from 18 Oct., 1418, i, 243.

The Bishop issued a Commission (5 March, 1413-14), on Waryn's complaint, in the matter of the "dilapidations" left by John Pole, his predecessor. Pole, however, was not his immediate predecessor; for John Halsanger was instituted (27 Oct., 1413), on Pole's death, and exchanged, almost immediately (2 Jan., 1413-14) with John Waryn, then R. of Grittleton (Dioc. of Salisbury); *see* "Institutions."

Cargaul,[2] the Bishop at, i, 47.

Carkyk, John, of Linkinhorne, i, 113b, 116.

Carleton, William (*see* Oldcastel), i, 192b.

Carmynel, John, R. of Rewe (deceased), ii, 52b.

Carmynow, John. *See* Menhenyot *(Institutions)*, ii, 138.

Carmynow, William, does homage to the Bishop, in London, for lands at Tynten, in Powton,[3] (27 Sep., 1397), ii, 310.

Carnarthur, Ralph and Thomas, *see* St. Illogan.

Carnellou, William, Prior of Bodmin (deceased), ii, 71b.

Carpenter, John and Thomas, of Apuldram, ii, 293b.

Carr, John, ii, 351b.

Carrew, Elizabeth, daughter of Sir William Bonevyll, knt., i, 312.

Carow, Geoffrey, Sacristan of Glasney, i, 65b, 66; his death,[4] ii, 53.

---

[1] A list of defaulters is given, dated 4 Jan., 1414-5.
[2] Cargawell, MS.
[3] i.e. St. Breoke.
[4] Carrev, MS.

Caru, John. *See* Widecombe, i, 180^{b}.

Carrew, Leonard, of the parish of St. Paul's, Exeter, i, 314^{b}.

Carv, Sir Nicholas, knt., i, 26.

Carrew, Thomas, Baron de, presents to the R. of Mamhead, ii, 124; to Stoke Fleming, R., ii, 202.

Carsfield, Peter de, Sacrist of Bosham, exchanges for the V. of Hackington, ii, 41^{b}.

Carslegh (or Carislegh), James, clerk, i, 310; instituted to the R. of Bradford, ii, 191^{b}; exchanges for the Chantry of Forde in the parish of Bampton, and is collated to the R. of Stoke-in-Teignhead, ii, 201^{b}, Official Peculiar in Cornwall (Commission dated 8 April, 1418), ii, 264^{b}; 265^{b}: Commission as Official, the Archdeaconry of Cornwall being vacant (1 Jan., 1418-19), ii, 267.

Carslegh, Simon, of Lustleigh,—

Special licence for his marriage with Beatrix, widow of John Wolf, of Chagford, though their banns had been published irregularly (31 Jan., 1413-14), i, 191.

Carislegh, William, i, 310.

Carswell, the Prior of, in arrear of Procurations, due to the Pope's Collector, for three years (1408-10), i, 105, 110.

Carswyll, Thomas, of Kingston (q. v.), ii, 277^{b}.

Cartaret, Ralph de, instituted to the Priory of St. Michael's Mount, ii, 338^{b}.

Carter, John, instituted to the R. (or Chapel) of St. James in the Castle of Chepyngtoryton,[1] ii, 20; his death, ii, 85.

Carter, William, instituted to the V. of Poughill (St. Olave's), in Cornwall, ii, 186.

Cartere, John, of Apuldram, ii, 293^{b}.

Carwargh,[2] John, instituted to the V. of St. Clether,[3] ii, 7; to South Pool, R. ii, 155^{t}; 357^{b}; resigns the V. of St. Mary Church, ii, 165.

Carvell, John, clerk,—*Dispensacio super defectu natalium* (17 Oct., 1413), i, 186.

Carvell or Carvek,[1] William, R. of Dolton, i, 43^{b}; (deceased), ii, 122^{b}.

---

[1] i.e. Great Torrington.

[2] also Carbargh, Carvagh, and {Carwarch, MS.

[3] He must have resigned St. Clether (though there seems to be no record of the fact), before 18 Nov., 1403 (when his successor, John Hauk, was instituted); and there can be little doubt that he did so on his appointment to St. Mary Church (which he resigned in 1415), but the date of his institution is not recorded.

[4] The name is spelt in both ways (*see Oratories*).

Cary, Sir John, knt., Lord of Puddington, ii, 8; patron of Alphington, R., ii, 10; (for two turns out of three), of Highampton, ii, 141, 245b; co-patron of Bickleigh, R., ii, 92b; of Broad Nymet, ii, 195.

Cary, Robert, Escheator in Devon and Cornwall; Mandate to the Bishop to administer the oath to him (*Breve Regium*, 18 Nov., 1413), ii, 347.—*See*, also, i, 309; ii, 349b.

Cary, Thomasia, relict of William, presents to Clovelly, ii, 133.

Cary, William, patron of Clovelly, ii, 7.

Castelgof, Roger, V. of Kingsteignton, resigns, ii, 57.

Castell, John, collated to the R. of Buckland Filleigh (q. v.), ii, 45.—*See*, also, Wykes, William.

Catenensi[1] Episcopo, Ricardo; Commissions,—

(1) To confirm, etc. in the Diocese (17 Sep., 1417). (2) To ordain to the priesthood (on the 17th of Dec., 1418, in any suitable place in the Diocese), John Knyght, deacon, R. of Cruwys-Morchard (10 Dec., 1418), ii, 266b. (3) To confirm, etc. (18 April, 1419), ii, 267.

Catenensi[1] Episcopo, Willelmo,—Commission for the Benediction of the Abbot of Dunkeswell, ii, 267b.

Catepath, Ralph, *see* Chudleigh, i, 239.

Caudel, Thomas, of Bridgewater, i, 307b.

Caulee, John, i, 308b.

Caurs, Richard, *see* Stafford, ii, 218, 218b.

Caucey, William, instituted to the R. of East Buckland, ii, 4b; resigns, ii, 16.

He appears to have been appointed to the R. of South Perrott (Dioc. of Salisbury); at any rate that benefice was exchanged, in 1417, by William Cavsey (probably the same person) for the R. of Bratton Clovelly.—ii, 186b.

Causton, William, his Chantry in the church of St. Pancras, London, ii, 28, 210b.

Caux, Thomas, R. of Kilve (Dioc. of Bath and Wells), exchanges for the R. of Stoodleigh, ii, 130b.

Cave, William, instituted to the V. of Fowey, ii, 135b, 240; resigns, ii, 143.

Cavendyssh, Walter, citizen and mercer, of London, ii, 278.

Cayllewaye, Edmund, Patron of Cheldon, R., ii, 5.

Caynok, John, V. of Dawlish, i, 122; his death, i, 146b, 177b; ii, 130, 239, 241.

Cergeaux, John (subdeacon), instituted to the R. of St. Martin's by Looe, ii, 35; i, 13b, 14b, 31, 58; an executor of the Will of Michael Cergeaux, ii, 219.

---

[1] i.e. of Caithness.

Cergeaux, Michael,[1] proxy for Ralph Rudruth, on his collation to a Canonry in Glasney, ii, 29^{b}; exchanges his R. of St. Martin-by-Looe for the Prebend of Merston, in the Collegiate Church of St. Mary, Stafford, ii, 30^{b}; collated to a Canonry in Exeter Cathedral, ii, 32; resigns the V. of "Sutton-juxta-Plymmouth," ii, 35; his death, *ibid.*

In the matter of his Will, John Cergeaux and John Sloley, clerks, and Roger Honyngton, domicellus, his executors, made complaint to the Archbishop's Court of delay on the part of the Bishop in causing certain parties to appear before him, viz., Richard Rowe, John Syrlyng, John Mey (butcher), Richard Crowlond, William Noyter, Robert Hoper, Robert Soper, John Hayman, senior, Robert Judde, Haukyn Cokk, and John Holman, all of Plymouth. Accordingly a Mandate, addressed to the Bishop, was issued 4 Kalend. Maii (28 April), 1398. He received it on the 2nd of June, and immediately referred the matter back to the Archbishop's Court for settlement, alleging that he could not attend to it within the time limited (twenty days), "propter quamplura negocia Dominum nostrum Regem ac Regnum Anglie concernencia indiesque emergencia."—ii, 219.

Cergeaux, William, Prebendary of St. Teath, ii, 98.

Cerne Abbey, i, 320^{b}.

Cervyngton, Oliver (*see* Talaton), ii, 315^{b}.

Chaddesley, John, presented, *but not admitted,* to the R. of St. George's, Exeter, ii, 234^{b}; presented, *but not admitted,* to the R. of Bradford, ii, 244.

Chagford, John Prouz, of, ii, 130, 236^{b}.

Challacombe,—Commission of Enquiry on the presentation of John Parles, chaplain, by John Chechester (31 May, 1418), ii, 265^{b}.

Challonsleigh,[2] in the parish of Plympton, i, 112, 195^{b}.

Chalons, Sir Robert, knt., presents to the R. of Great Torrington, ii, 52, 153^{b}, 173^{b}, 190^{b}, 196^{b}, 265, to the R., or Chapel, of St. James in the Castle there, ii, 85.

Chambe, Thomas de la, i, 305.

Chamberlen, Roger, i, 314.

Chamberleyn, John, R. of Exminster (deceased), ii, 6^{b}.

Chamberleyn, Robert, presented (ii, 259), instituted (ii, 177), to the V. of Lanlivery.

[Chambers ?] "Johannes dictus de Camera de Broghton," priest, instituted to the R. of Clannaborough, ii, 359.

Chamburlayn, Robert, *see* Oldcastel, i, 192^{b}.

Chamburleyn,[3] John, R. of St. Michael's, Bristol, exchanges for

[1] Michael Cergeaux, Dean of Arches, ii, 27^{b}, 28.

[2] Cholounslegh, MS.

[3] also Chamberleyn, MS.

Cotleigh, R., ii, 64; and again[1] for the R. of Knyghteslegh (?) Dioc. of Bath and Wells, ii, 95b.—*See* also, i, 326b.

Champernoun, Alexander, esquire, presents to the R. of Newton-Ferrers, ii, 197, 266b, 363b; co-patron of Beer-ferris, ii, 182, 186, 260b, 261.

Champernoun, Otho (and his wife), i, 301; presents to the R. of Clyst Hydon, ii, 41, 104b.

Champernoun,[2] Sir Richard, knt., son and heir of Thomas Champernoun, esquire, lately deceased,—

He makes complaint to the Bishop that certain rogues, names unknown, had carried off charters and muniments affecting his title to his manors of Modbury, Inceworth[3], Millbrook, etc., and craves help from the Bishop, who accordingly issues his Mandate to the four Archdeacons, the Deans Rural, and the Clergy of the Diocese, requiring them to denounce the offenders as excommunicate, in the usual manner (11 March, 1410-11), i, 119.

Patron of Modbury Priory, ii, 10b; and presents thereto, on nomination by the King, ii, 94b, 174b; of Portlemouth, R., ii, 13, 84b; of Bradford, R., ii, 13b; of Dodbrooke, R., ii, 65b, 85, 107b, 124,b 197b, 267; his Will, i, 333b.

Champernoun,[4] Richard, clerk, of Slapton Chantry, ii, 111.

Champernon,[5] Roger, a priest, i, 56.

Champernowne, Thomas, ii, 316.

Champernowne,—"My sister Chambernon" (Will of Matilda Latymer), i, 329.

Champernowne,[6] William, R. of Woodleigh (deceased), ii, 93b.

Chapel, John, instituted to the R. of Mamhead, ii, 45b, his death, ii, 124. *See*, also, ii, 235.

Chapman (or Chepman), Thomas, R. of Hampton-Meisy (Dioc. of Worcester), exchanges for a Canonry in Glasney and the R. of Withiel, ii, 58; i, 77.

Chard, John (junior), and Joan Colyn (junior), daughter of Robert Colyn,—

They had married and had issue, in ignorance of all impediment; but they had since discovered that they were related in the fourth degree of consanguinity. Dispensation granted 30 Sept., 1412, i, 168.

Charde, Christina, wife of Richard, ii, 254.

Charer, Henry, instituted to the R. of Alverdiscott, ii, 54.

Charles, Thomas Passewar, R. of; licence of non-residence for one year, from 14 July, 1400, i, 44.

Charleton,[7] John Syggeston, R. of; licence of non-residence for

[1] Cortelegh, MS.
[2] "*alias* de Campo Arnulphi," MS.
[3] Innyswerk, MS.
[4] Champarnon, MS.
[5] Chambernoun, MS.
[6] Chamburnoun, MS.
[7] Chorleton, MS.

two years, from 13 July, 1397, i, 33.—John Camme, R. of; licence to choose a confessor (7 June 1408), i, 86.—John Wynterbourne, R. of; licence of non-residence from 3 Jan., 1408-9, to Michaelmas, 1409, i, 87ᵇ.—*See*, also, 357ᵇ.

Charleton, Manor of Malston in (*see* Reynald, Walter), i, 173.

Cherleton (*sic*), Nicholas, instituted to the V. of Townstal, ii, 6ᵇ.

Charlton, William, Prior of Pilton (deceased), ii, 147ᵇ.

Chaundeler, John, R. of Quennington (Dioc. of Worcester), exchanges for the V. of St. Cleer, ii, 89; his death, ii, 94.

Chaundos, Sir John, knt., presents to Torbrian, R., ii, 84, 95.

Chauntrell, Thomas, Canon and Prebendary of Great St. Martin's, London, exchanges for Marwood, ii, 89, 179.

Chawleigh, Flambertyswyke in, *see* Wyke *(Oratories)*, i, 42ᵇ.—Chevyston, in, *see* Cayleway *(Oratories)*, i, 45ᵇ.—John Poynes, R. of; licence of non-residence, for one year (to study at Oxford), from 27 June, 1406, i, 78.

Chebesey, William, chaplain, see Milton Damarel, ii, 342.

Chedder, William, a parishioner of Cowick, ii, 287.

Chederleigh,[1] manor of, in the parish of Bickleigh (E), i, 85, 147.

Cheldon, Oliver Radysworthy, R. of, his Will, i, 315ᵇ.

Chepman, John, of Honiton, his Will, i, 307.

Chepman, John, of Honiton, junior, i, 307ᵇ.

Chepman, Matthew, excommunicate and impenitent: the Bishop hands him over to the secular arm (7 Aug., 1411), i, 130ᵇ.

[*Breve Regium*]—It appears that he had been imprisoned for contempt, but had frequently offered to make satisfaction, and give sureties for his obedience to the Mandates of the Church for the time to come. The Bishop, however, had refused to restore him, at which the King expresses surprise; and, being unwilling that the said Matthew should remain longer in prison, contrary to justice, he issues his Mandate, requiring the Bishop to accept his sureties and liberate him at once: otherwise the King would take the necessary steps to compel his release (1 Nov., 1411), ii, 343. Chepman was a parishioner of North Tawton, and was absolved on the 30th of December, i, 140ᵇ.

Chepstow, Edith, i, 307ᵇ.

Chepyngtauton, i. e. North Tawton, q. v.

Chepyngtoryton, i. e. Torrington, Great, q. v.

Cheriton Bishop,[2] Lewis Busshbyry (deacon), R. of; Dispensation (to study at Oxford)—for three years, from 17 Sep., 1411, i, 134ᵇ; also, for four years, from 19 April, 1414, i, 196; licence of non-residence for two years, from 15 May, 1419, i, 247ᵇ.—*See*, also, i, 239.

---

[1] Chudderlegh, MS.

[2] Churiton Episcopi, MS.

Cheriton-Fitzpaine,[1] Richard [Weneman], R. of, a Penitentiary in the Deanery of Cadbury, i, 50, 79b, 143, 173b, 194, 207b, 216b, 231, 237b.

Cherrystow,[2] chapel of St. Wenn at, in the parish of Hartland; licensed 21 May, 1400, i, 38b.

Cheselden, John, esquire, Patron of Penne (Dioc. of Bath and Wells), ii, 54b; of Rewe,[3] R., ii, 21b, 52b; of Warkleigh,[3] R., ii, 22b.

Cheselden, Margery, a Canoness of Canonsleigh, ii, 125.

Chesterton, Thomas, i, 325.

Chetescombe Bolham, in Tiverton, Chapel of St. Thomas at, licensed 2 July, 1400, i, 43.

Chevithorne,[4] manor of, in the parish of Tiverton, i, 221b.

Cheyne, John, Canon of Exeter, the Bishop's Commissary and Official General, i, 41; R. of Ugborough, which he exchanges for the R. of Rotherfield (Dioc. of Chichester), ii, 84; his death, ii, 94.

Chichele, Henry, LL.D., Canon of Salisbury and Vicar-General, ii, 37b.

Chichester,[5] John, patron of Challacombe, R., ii, 105b; co-patron of St. Leonard's Chantry, Ralegh, ii, 137b, 182b, 191.

Chichestre, Richard, scholar — *Dispensacio super defectu natalium* (10 Nov., 1415), i, 214b; proxy for Thomas Bryd, ii, 198.—*See*, also, i, 332b.

Chiselet, John, i, 300b.

Chitterne, John, prebendary of Goodworth in the Conventual Church of Wherwell (Dioc. of Winchester), exchanges for a Prebend in St. Probus, ii, 162b; resigns, ii, 168b,

Chittlehampton, John Brythlegh, of, i, 93.

Chivelston,[6] a chapelry in Stokenham, i, 330b; *see* Husy, Nicholas, ii, 261.

Chope, Sarah, of Monkleigh, i, 99b. *See* Holsworthy.

Choulyng, Richard, *see* Helygan, Nicholas (*Oratories*).

Christopolitanus, Episcopus, Nicholas, i, 61b.

Christow, manor and parish of, i, 73b, 80.—

A Commission of enquiry as to the patronage of this Vicarage, issued 18 Nov., 1411, on the presentation of William Gyle, chaplain, by the Queen, ii, 244.

---

[1] Chyryton Fithpayn, MS.
[2] Charstowe, MS.
[3] Chuselden — Chiseldon — Chuseldon, MS.
[4] Chyvethorn, MS.
[5] also Chechester, MS.
[6] also Chevelston, MS.

Chuddelegh, Sir James, knt.; patron of Landcross, R., ii, 10, 12, 20; of Ashton, ii, 14b; presents (in the absence of Sir Thomas Flemmyng, knt.), to Alverdiscott, R., ii, 19b.—*See*, also, Ringmore (*Institutions*).

Chudderleye, John, Escheator in Devon and Cornwall (*Breve Regium*, 19 Nov., 1410), ii, 337b, 338.

Chudham, Prebend of, in Bosham, i, 22.

Chudleigh, the bridge, i, 332b.—Hugh de Hyckelyng's bequests to the poor of, i, 326, 326b.—In the matter of dilapidations in the parish church,—

The Bishop caused Bishop Grandisson's Register to be searched, and ascertained that, 2 Dec., 1338, there appeared before William de Crauthorn and Benedict de Paston (the Bishop's Commissaries), in the said parish church, John de Sharshull, Precentor of Exeter, and Nicholas Coffin, V. of Chudleigh, who were called on to give an account of the dilapidations in the Chancel, &c. (*super defectibus cancelli et cujusdam interticii inter navem et cancellum*), and to shew cause why they should not be required to repair the same. The said Nicholas denied that he was liable; but being asked whether he had any special grounds for saying so, answered "No" (*respondit quod non*). Asked to shew cause why he should not be required to repair *pro rata*, he said that he ought not to be. He was, therefore, ordered to appear for judgment on 11 Dec., Ralph Catepath, David le Bruere, W. Kamok, and many others, being witnesses. On the appointed day the said Precentor and Vicar both appeared before the said Benedict de Paston, who decreed that the Precentor and Vicar should repair and maintain the said Chancel, each *pro rata porcionis*,—the former *pro duabus*, the latter *pro tertia, partibus*,—and should be compelled to do so. Witnesses: William Doun and Alfred Brigg, clerks. Bishop Stafford certified accordingly, 1 April, 1418, i, 239.

Chulmleigh, Chapel of St. Edmund the Bishop, at Coleton, in the parish of; licensed 6 July, 1402, i, 61; and again (for John Rayschelegh, clerk), 29 Sep., 1413, i, 185.—William Haliet (*alias* Hamme), R. of; licence of non-residence for one year, from 28 Aug., 1395, i, 5.—William Lane, R. of, for one year, from 18 Oct., 1407; a Penitentiary in the Deanery of Chulmleigh, i, 217, 231, 238, 245b.

Churchhull, John, i, 312.—*See*, also, St. Pinnock, ii, 351.

Churchstanton, i, 311b.

Churchstow, John Wytloff's bequest to the Church of, i, 306.—Roger Bacheler, R. of, ii, 290b, 357b; a Penitentiary in the Deanery of Woodleigh, i, 143, 194b, 207b, 217, 231, 237b, 245.—Manor of Newton in, *see* Whitelegh (*Oratories*).

Chyterwell, Walter, instituted to Huntsham, R., ii, 195b, 266b.

Chyvarton (or Chiwarton), John, chaplain, i, 120b; instituted to the R. of St. Stephen's-in-Brannel, ii, 159b.

Chivereston, John de, knt., and Joan his wife, i, 318.

Chyverston, Matilda, *see* St. Issey.

Clampit,[1] in the parish of Linkinhorne, i, 136.

Clannaborough,[2] Robert Doget, R. of; licence of non-residence for one year, from 21 July, 1410, i, 100^{b}.—Commissions, etc.,—

(1) On the presentation, by Philip Boterford, of John Rysdon, chaplain (25 July, 1416); (2) On the presentation, by the Prior of Taunton, of Roger Blakhay, chaplain (same date), ii, 259^{b}. (3) [*Breve Regium*] Prohibition to admit any clerk, pending the settlement of the dispute between the Prior of Taunton and John Boterford, esquire, and his wife Thomasia, (4 Aug., 1416), ii, 356. (4) [*Breve Regium*] To search the Registers and make a List of the Rectors from the time of Walter Stapulton (*sic*)—20 Nov., 1416, ii, 356^{b}. (5) The Bishop made the following Return: he had found that 4 Id. Dec. (i.e. Dec. 10), 1310, Bishop Stapledon admitted, at Stockwill, Richard de Sydewyne, clerk, on the presentation of the Prior and Convent of Taunton: that 31 July, 1314, at Norton, he *collated* Robert de Molton, without prejudice to the above named patrons on the next vacancy; that 8 Kal. Jun. (i.e. 25 May), 1330,[3] Bishop Grandisson, at Clyst, admitted William Trendelove, de Grutelyngton, in an exchange for the Church of St. Michael, Bath,—patrons, the Prior and Convent of Taunton; that 2 Oct., 1332, he admitted, at Horslegh, Thomas de Cordyngton, priest,—patrons, the same: that 19 Sept. 1303 (*sic*), he admitted, at Paignton, John "dictus de Camera, de Broghton," priest (on the resignation of Cordyngton, who had exchanged for the V. of Cadbury)—the same patrons; and that 23 April, 1351, at Chudleigh, he collated, by lapse, Roger Alyn, priest. (Dated at Clyst, 12 Jan., 1416-17, ii, 359. (6) [*Breve Regium*] To search the Registers from the time of Simon de Apulia (i.e. A.D. 1214) to the time of Walter de Stapledon, and certify as to the institutions to Clannaborough (1 July, 1417) ii, 360^{b}. (7) Accordingly, on 7 Aug., 1417,[4] the Bishop, at Clyst, certified that he had found it recorded that on the day of St. Roman[5] the Martyr, 1272, Nicholas Blundel, chaplain, was admitted at Gargauel,[6] by Bishop Walter Bronescombe, on the presentation of the Prior and Convent of Taunton, ii, 361.

Clastek, Peter, instituted to the V. of Morval, ii, 74.

Clawton, R., appropriated to Cornworthy Priory, ii, 359^{b}.

[Clay]hydon, Peter Bysschop, R. of; licence of non-residence[7] for one year, from 20 Oct., 1405, i, 76^{b}; a Penitentiary in the Deanery of Dunkeswell, i, 231; of Plymtree, i, 237^{b}, 245.

Claysch, Thomas (plaintiff) and Joan, daughter of Giles Aysch (defendant); Commissions,—

(1) Directed to Dean Tregrisiou, the Archdeacons of Barnstaple and Totnes

[1] Clompyt, MS.

[2] Clonenburgh and Cloneneburgh, MS.

[3] 1030 in the MS.,—an obvious clerical error.

[4] Meanwhile the Bishop had availed himself of these delays (the "Prohibition notwithstanding) to present to the vacant Benefice *by lapse*, *collating* Henry Thomma, "jure devoluto," 23 Jan., 1416-7. It will be observed that he makes no attempt to begin with Simon de Apulia, and is silent as to the Registers of Briwere and Blondy, Quivil and Bytton; he mentions Bronescombe's only, the first now extant. Was Bytton's lost even then?

[5] 9 August.

[6] Cargaul, in Cornwall.

[7] "Contemplacione nobilis viri, domini Johannis Dynham, militis.

and others, in a matrimonial cause between the parties (12 June 1398), ii, 219b. (2) Directed to William Knyght and Walter Robert; to proceed therein (12 June, 1408), ii, 231b.—The particulars of the case are not given.

Clement, Henry, parochial chaplain at Ottery, appointed coadjutor to John Hamond, Sacristan (12 Nov., 1409), i, 90; instituted to Northam, V., ii, 199b. *See*, also, i, 304.

Clement, John (of Cornwall), *see* St. Feock, i, 161.

Clement, Thomas, chaplain, i, 307b.

Clerk, Hugh, instituted to the V. of Milton[-Abbot], ii, 132b, 243; resigns, ii, 180b.

Clerk, John, de Codeford, instituted (in 1407) to the R. of High Bickington, ii, 95.

Clerk, John, instituted to the V. of Ashford (in 1413), ii, 154.

Clerk, John, instituted to the V. of Linkinhorne (in 1411), ii, 132; died in 1419, ii, 201b.

Clerk, John, V. of St. Uny Lelant (ii, 232b), died in 1416, ii, 176b.

Clerk, Ralph, proxy for Robert Wantynge (q. v.), ii, 167b.

Clerk, William, chaplain, *see* Axmouth, i, 238; instituted to the Chantry of St. Edmund's "juxta pontem," at Colyford, ii, 176b.—

William Clerk, R. of Jacobstow (Devon), exchanged for the Chantry of St. Mary in Crewkerne Church in 1405, ii, 86.

Cleve, John, Canon of St. Stephen's, Launceston, ii, 117.

Cleve, William, proxy for William Hawkyn (q. v.), ii, 68b.

Clifford, Chapel of the Holy Cross at, in the parish of Hartland (licensed 21 May, 1400), i, 38b.

Clive, John, i, 333.

Clive St. Mary (Dioc. of Lichfield), i, 306.

Clok, Richard, chaplain of Carhayes,[1] and others,[2] being contumacious in refusing to appear before the Bishop at Exeter are handed over to the secular arm (4 Jan., 1398-9), i, 24.

Cloneburgh, William, instituted to Berry Pomeroy, V., ii, 158b.

Clopton, Richard, patron of the R. of Kentisbeare, ii, 95, 147.

Cloteworthy, Walter (*see* Hacche, Richard), i, 8b.

Clovter, Thomas, does homage, at Clyst, for lands at Ressere[3] in the parish of Lawhitton (10 June, 1416), ii, 311.

Clovelly, Chapel of St. Giles, Abbot, in the parish of; licensed

---

[1] Caryshays, MS.

[2] Namely, John Marchant and Matthew Fryday, chaplains of Devon, John Jul, V. of St. Austell, Henry [Gathell], R. of St. Mewan, and John *Symon Montfort*, a layman of Veryan [Elerky, MS.].

[3] *hodie* Ressair.

(for three years) 15 Feb., 1401-2, i, 60b; and again, for William Penwonam, R. (6 Sept., 1407), i, 82b; and again, for Richard Plenya, R. (1 June, 1417), i, 233.—Walter Jodel, chaplain, licensed to preach in the parish-church of (19 Feb., 1411-12), i, 145.

Clyfford, Alice, sister, and John and William, brothers, of Canon Thomas Clyfford, i, 333b.

Clyfford, Richard, Archdeacon of Canterbury, presents to the V. of Hackington, ii, 41b. *See*, also, i, 333b.

Clyfford, Thomas, R. of Lanteglos-by-Camelford, i, 11, 26; exchanges, with Richard Aldryngton, for the R. of Stoke-in-Teignhead, ii, 57; i, 86b, 134b; 212b (*see Oratories*); exchanges his canonry in Crantock for a canonry in Exeter Cathedral, ii, 161; his death, ii, 196b; his Will,[1] i, 333b.

Clyfforde, William, *see* Peryn, John, i, 221.

Clyfton (Diocese of Lichfield), i, 334.

Clyfton, John, the Bishop's valet, *see* Crediton, i, 244.

Clyfton, William, V. of Stokenham (deceased), ii, 3.

Clyk, Thomas, *see* Aps, John, ii, 236.

Clyst Episcopi, i, 334.

Clyst Fomison (i. q. Sowton and Clyst St. Michael's), John Beeff, R. of, a Penitentiary in the Deanery of Aylesbeare, i, 143, 173b, 194, 207b, 216b, 231, 237b, 245; church of Clyst St. Michael, i, 304b, 305b.

Clyst St. Gabriel, Hospital of; John Aller, Warden, *see* Aller.—John Buef (or Beef), Warden, *see* Gervys, i, 117. —*See*, also, Hayward, Thomas; and i, 308b, 332b.

Clyst St. George, John Aller, R. of, licensed to choose a confessor (14 Nov., 1395), i, 7; to hear confessions (27 Feb., 1395-6), i, 8; to choose a confessor (7 Jan., 1396-7), i, 10b.—John Burell, R. of, i, 80b; licence of non-residence for two years,[2] from 5 July, 1408, i, 86.—Thomas Twyford, R. of; licence of non-residence (to study at Oxford) from 14 Jan., 1411-12 to Michaelmas, 1412, i, 141b.

Clyst St. Laurence, William Bedmond, R. of, i, 207.

Clyst St. Mary, William Grene, licence of non-residence for

---

[1] Another Thomas Clyfford is mentioned in this Will.

[2] Contemplacione Reverendi in Christo Patris et Domini, Domini Henrici, Dei gratia Archiepiscopi Eboracensis, dummodo medio tempore in ipsius steterit obsequiis."

one year, from 5 May, 1405, i, 74b; the Church of, i, 304b, 305b.

Clyston, John, i, 305.

Clyve (i.e. Cleeve), the Chapel of St. Mary at (Dioc. of Bath and Wells), which had been seriously damaged by the sea[1]; Indulgence to the Faithful contributing to its repair (11 Dec., 1398), i, 23b.

Clyve, William, R. of Whitstone, proxy for Thomas Hendeman, ii, 108b, 109; 138b.—*See*, also, i, 301.

Clyvedon, Alexander, *see* Bickleigh, R. (*Institutions*), ii, 8.

Clyverton, John, chaplain, *see* Goodleigh, i, 190b.

Cobay, Henry and Walter, of Apuldram, ii, 293b.

Cobbeham, Katherine, daughter of Sir William Bonevyll, knt., i, 312.

Cobham, Margaret, *see* Canterbury, i, 4b.

Cobbelegh, Nicholas, does homage to the Bishop at Clyst, for lands at Hokeway in Crediton (20 Feb., 1413-14), ii, 311.

Cobleigh, Robert, ii, 213.

Cobbelond, Roger, proxy for Thomas Launcell (q. v.), ii, 64.

Cobbethorne, John, collated to the V. of Paignton, ii, 189; i, 237b; exchanges for St. Ive, R., ii, 191b; collated to a canonry in Exeter Cathedral, ii, 196b; i, 246b, 248; collated to a canonry at Crediton, ii, 201; Commission appointing him President of the Consistory Court (14 Jan., 1418-19), ii, 266b; elected Dean of Exeter,—

The Process and the Official Documents are set forth at length, from which it appears that Stephen Payn died 17 May, 1419, and that his successor was elected 29 July. The Mandate for his induction and installation was issued 2 Sept.—ii, 202—204b.

Codan, Vivian, instituted to the V. of St. Austell, ii, 162b.

Codemore, Thomas, *see* Cornwood, i, 67.

Coffin, Thomas, instituted to Tedburn[-St. Mary], ii, 196b, 267.

Coffyn, Nicholas, V. of Chudleigh, i, 239.

Cofton [Cokton, MS.], Chapel of the B. V. M. at, *see* Dawlish.

Cogan, Walter, V. of Poughill St. Olave's (deceased), ii, 186.

Coggeshale, Sir William, knt.; patron of St. Dominick, R., ii, 7b; of Dittisham, R., ii, 30.

[1] "Super ripas maris ab antiquo posite et fundate, ubi ad laudem Dei et salutem populi multa fulgere solent miracula et causa devocionis populorum peregrinancium concursus non modicus fieri consuevit; que, vi fluctuum inundencium violentissime jam tarde suffossa, reparacione indiget sumptuosa."

Cok, John, instituted to the R. of St. Mewan, ii, 74.

Cok, John, instituted to the V. of Hennock, ii, 14; his death, ii, 149b.

Cok, Robert, collated (by lapse) to the R. of Hittisleigh, ii, 50; his death,[1] ii, 187b.

Cok, William, instituted to the V. of Hennock, ii, 149b.[2]

Coke, John, R. of St. Petrock-minor (deceased), ii, 37; i, 304b.

Coke (or Cook), William, instituted to the R. of Nymet-Rowland, ii, 104; his death, ii, 189.

Cokesden, Robert, i, 312.

Cokeworthy, John, clerk—*Dispensacio super defectu natalium* (18 May, 1400), i, 37b.

Cokworthy, John, R. of Rudbaxton (Dioc. of St. David's), exchanges for the R. of Alwington, ii, 179; i, 231.

Cokwell, Thomas, of Funtington, ii, 280, 281b.

Colard, John, chaplain, *see* Sture, William, i, 126.

Colcomb, *alias* Aldryngton, q. v.

Cole, Isolda and Alice, i, 332.

Cole, James,[3] clerk, the Bishop appoints him his Procurator-General in the Court of Arches (21 Feb., 1399-1400), i, 33.

Cole, John, esquire, presents to the R. of Hittisleigh, ii, 187b.

Cole, John, of North Pool, i, 319.

Cole, John, collated to a canonry in Crantock, ii, 64b.

Cole, John, instituted to Brendon, R., ii, 105b; resigns, ii, 147b.

Cole, John, instituted to the R. of Meavy, ii, 187b.

Cole, Nicholas, V. of Staverton, exchanges for the R. of St. Laurence, Exeter, ii, 70b.

Cole, Roger, V. of Burrington, exchanges for a Chantry in the Church of Charleton-Adam (Dioc. of Bath and Wells), ii, 133.

Cole, Thomas, chaplain, i, 331b.

Colebrooke [Colbrok, MS.], Church of St. Andrew, i, 331b.

Commission as to the alleged pollution of the parish-church by a quarrel therein between William Wythy, chaplain, and John Spyne (18 Nov., 1412), ii, 249b.

Colebrok, in Crediton, *see* Waleys, Richard, ii, 311.

Colebrugg,[4] Richard, instituted to the Chantry in the Church

[1] Coke, MS.

[2] At i, 331, the tomb of "William Cok" in the Cathedral is mentioned.

[3] James Cole, notary-publick, is mentioned at i, 192b.

[4] Also, Colbrygge, MS.

of Alwington, ii, 10b, 221b, 308b; to Roborough, R., ii, 12; resigns the Chantry, ii, 13; Robert Lywer, R. of Drewsteignton appointed his coadjutor, ii, 23; his death, ii, 25.b

Coleton, in the parish of Chulmleigh (q.v.), i, 61, 185.

Coleton, Richard de, Official and Commissary to the Bishop, ii, 358.

Colkyrk, John, *see* Burrington, i, 165.

Collard, John, chaplain, i, 314b.

Colle, John, collated to the V. of St. Teath, ii, 136.

Colle, Walter, instituted to the R. of Milton Damarel, ii, 150b, 257b, 258b; resigns, and is instituted to the R. of Tiverton (1st Portion), ii, 169b; i, 226, 239, 214, ii, 268b,—Walter and William Colle were nephews to Walter Robert, i, 324.

Collumpton, Chapel of St. George at (*see* Burnell, John), i, 57b; Chapel of St. James at (licensed 14 July, 1401), i, 58.—William Sachevyle, V. of, i, 207. *See* Vawtard.

Collurian, Ralph (St. Germoe), ii, 264.

Colman, John, instituted to the V. of South Petherwin, ii, 123b, 155.

Colmpton, William, i, 324. *See*, also, Bickleigh, R.

Colompton, John, Canon of Exeter, ii, 212b,

Colmpton, Walter, R. of Stoke Fleming (deceased), ii, 17. He was also Canon of Exeter, *see* ii, 53.

Colrygg, John, R. of Huntshaw (deceased), ii, 44b.

Colshull, John, co-patron of the V. of Duloe, ii, 40, 49, 141b, 246; *see* also ii, 308b; of Lansallos, R., ii, 82; of Stowford, R., ii, 105, 164b, 169b.

John Colshull did homage, at Clyst, to the Bishop, for lands at "Canelisy" in Pawton (27 April, 1415), ii, 311.—John Colshull and Emma his wife are mentioned at ii, 317b,—[*Breve Regium*]—to administer to Anne, widow of Sir John Coleshull, knt., the oath "de non maritando sine licencia" (3 Dec., 1418), ii, 363b: the said oath was administered, at Clyst, 10 Jan., 1418-19, *ibid.*

Colswayn, John, instituted to the V. of Davidstow, ii, 147.

Colton de Ledes, Wm. [Dioc. Ebor.], ii, 336b.

Colyer, John, instituted R. of the 3rd (or Tydecombe) Portion of Tiverton, ii, 23b; i, 43.

Colyer, Nychol, a baker, i, 312.

Colyford, the Chantry at (17 June, 1411);

Commission to enquire as to the right of presentation; Thomas de Stowforde, Lord of Gatecomb, having presented John Twete, chaplain, ii, 242.

Colyn, Joan (junior), daughter of Robert, i, 168.

Colyn, John, of Buckland Brewer, and Isabella Eyer, of Bradworthy; licence for their marriage (15 Jan., 1409-10), i, 93b.

Colyn, John, instituted to the R. of Mamhead,[1] ii, 124; i, 173, 226b; exchanges for Rattery, V., ii, 189. *See*, also, ii, 234b, 235, 316.

Colyn, John, R. of Landewednack, exchanges for the V. of Gwennap ii, 78: and, again, for Ludgvan, R., ii, 194, 266.

Colyn, John, V. of St. Vepe[2] (Jan., 1410-11), ii, 138b.

Colyn, Ralph, instituted to the R. of Lansallos, ii, 82.

Colyn, Richard, of Torrington, his alms-house there,—

Indulgence to the Faithful contributing "ad sustentacionem cujusdam domus pauperum in Villa de Toryton . . . per Ricardum Colyn, ejusdem ville, de novo constructe, et eorundem pauperum status relevamen."—i, 5.

Colyn, Robert, collated to St. Stephen's, Exeter, ii, 102,—

Licence of non-residence (when Vicar-Choral of Exeter Cathedral) to enable him to go into Brittany with Master Richard Hals, the King's ambassador to those parts (22 July, 1414), i, 198. *See*, also, i, 303b.

Colyn, Thomas, co-patron of the R. of Roseash, ii, 81, 89b. Thomas Colyn "de Hellond" was patron of Helland, R., ii, 174b. *See*, also, 350b, 351, 351b, 352.

Colyn, Walter, i, 332.

Colyns, Thomas, instituted to a Prebend in Chulmleigh, ii, 175b.

Colyton, Manor of Gatcombe in, i, 240.—Richard Wykeslond, V. of, Sir William Bonevyll's Legacy to, i, 312; his death, ii, 130; Commission to prove his Will (7 Jan., 1410-11) ii, 237.—John Hull, V. of, i, 320b.

Colver, William, i, 333b.

Combrygg, Roger, Prior of St. Stephen's, Launceston (deceased), ii, 115.

Combe, in Holbeton, *see* Fortescue (*Oratories*), i, 37, 149b.

Combe, Gervase, V. of Harberton (deceased), ii, 8b.

Combe, John, Minister of Slapton, i, 302b; instituted to the R. of North Huish, ii, 67b, 112b; i, 67b, 76b; his death, ii, 144b; his Will, i, 317b.

A Commission was appointed, 3 Aug., 1412, to enquire as to his goods and chattels, and to sequestrate the same pending a settlement of the "dilapidations," ii, 247b.

---

[1] '*Thomas*' Colyn, R. of Mamhead; licence of non-residence for one year, from 21 Sept., 1411; i, 135.—And, again, from 28 Oct., 1412 to Michaelmas, 1413; i, 171b.—But *John* Colyn was R. of Mamhead from 14 Oct., 1410 to 23 Dec., 1417, and, doubtless, he is here called "Thomas," by an error of the scribes.

[2] Sancti Vepi, MS.

Comb Davy (*hodie* Culm Davy), in the parish of Hemyock, i, 318b.

Combe-in-Teignhead, R,—Commission of Enquiry (1 March, 1417-18), on the presentation of Richard Halswyll, chaplain, by John Prediaux, ii, 264b.

Combmartin, Richard Nores,[1] R. of; licence of non-residence (to study at Oxford) for one year, from 24 Jan., 1395-6.—Philip Pope, R. of, i, 81; licences of non-residence for one year, from 3 July, 1411, i, 128b; for one year, from 14 Feb., 1413-14, i, 193b; for one year, from 6 May, 1415, i, 210.—Robert Wantynge, R. of; from 22 Aug., 1415, to Easter, 1416, i, 212; for one year, from 8 June, 1416, i, 221b.—John Langle, R. of; from 16 Feb., 1416-17, to the Feast of the Purification, 1418, i, 230b.

Combpyne, William [Langerygg], R. of, ii, 49.—John Knowston, R. of, i, 142; a Penitentiary, in the Deanery of Honiton, i, 143, 173b, 194, 207b, 216b, 231, 237b.—Walter Lebet, R. of,—

A Commission of Enquiry as to the "dilapidations" caused by Knowston's neglect, was issued, on the complaint of Walter Lebet (22 July, 1419). A second Commission, addressed to Reginald Peyt (chaplain of the "capella curata" of Shute)[2], and John Hull (chaplain of the perpetual chantry of Whyteford), was issued 1 Aug., 1419, for the sequestration of the late Rector's effects. The "dilapidations" were estimated in more than £26 10s,—ii, 268.

Combe Raleigh, Robert Box, R. of; licence of non-residence (dated 3 Aug., 1406) for one year from the ensuing Michaelmas, i, 78.

Before this licence had expired, being notoriously infirm and quite unfit for work, he applied to the Bishop, by his proctor, William Ryder, for leave to resign, and for a pension. His resignation having been accepted, the patron, Sir Thomas Pomeroy, appointed Gilbert Deneman, chaplain, to succeed him, and, all the parties consenting, a pension of ten marks for life was assigned to him (31 July, 1407), ii, 82.

Come, William, instituted to Teignbrewer R., ii, 157b.

Compton, [Cumtun Pole, MS.], in Paignton, ii, 310.

Compton, John, instituted to Davidstow, V., ii, 101: resigns, ii, 147; is instituted to Lanteglos [-by-Fowey], ii, 146; i, 174, 194b, 207b, 217, 231b, 238, 245b.

Concilio Domini Regis, Procuratorium pro,—in favour of Nicholas, Bishop of Bath and Wells; 6 May, 1412, i, 149.

Constable, John, proxy for Adam de Mottrum, ii, 47b.

Consecrations and Dedications,—*see* Lympston; Upton Hel-

[1] Noreys, elsewhere.

[2] Schete, MS.

lions, and Woodbury; *also*, Bradworthy (under *Institutions*), i, 49.

Constance, the Seventeenth General Council of,—

The Bishop appoints Robert [Hallum], Bishop of Salisbury, Thomas Teyngton, Canon of Exeter, and Maior Parys, R. of Pilluton, to represent him there; *Procuratorium pro Concilio Generali in Civitate Constanciensi*; 20 Sept., 1414, i, 203[b]; subsidy for, i, 204.

Constans, John, Scholar,—*Dispensucio super defectu natalium* (18 Dec., 1400), i, 51[b].

Constantine (or St. Constantine—Sancti Constantini, MS.).—

This Church, having been appropriated to the Dean and Chapter of Exeter, and certain persons resisting the due collection of the tithes thereof, the Bishop referred the matter to the Deans of Kerrier and Penwith, to Benedict Canterbury, R. of Camborne, and [Peter Gerveys] vicar of the said parish, requiring them to cause the offenders to be publickly warned in Constantine Church, during Mass, and threatened with excommunication (28 Aug., 1415), i, 212.

Peter Gerveys, V. of (*see Oratories*), i, 71; a Penitentiary in the Deanery of Kerrier, i, 245[b].

Convocation of the Province of Canterbury,—

Procuratorium Domini pro Convocacione Cleri; in favour of William Langeton, Canon of Exeter, (24 Feb., 1397-8), i, 15.

Mandatum pro Convocacione Cleri (26 Sept., 1399). The Schedule contains the names of the Dean of Exeter, the four Archdeacons, the Abbots of Tavistock, Hartland, Torre, Forde, Dunkeswell and Buckland, and the Priors of Plympton, Launceston, St. German's, Frithelstock, Bodmin, and Pilton; i, 29.

Mandatum pro Convocacione Cleri (4 Jan., 1400-1). The Schedule contains the Dean and the four Archdeacons, the six Abbots named above, and also those of Buckfast and Newenham; the six Priors named above, and also those of St. Michael's Mount, Tywardreath, Totnes, Barnstaple, Modbury, St. Nicholas Exeter, and St. James' "juxta Exoniam"; also Richard Hals and Laurence Haukyn, Canons of Exeter, and proctors for the Chapter, i, 52.

Commission addressed to Dean Tregresiou (26 April, 1398), ii, 216.

Royal Letter under the Privy Seal summoning Convocation (28 April, 1398), ii, 307[b].

Certificatorium pro Convocacione Cleri (23 Nov., 1411). The Schedule contains the names of the Dean and the four Archdeacons; the Abbots of Tavistock, Hartland, Torre, Buckfast, Forde, Newenham, Dunkeswell, and Buckland, and the Priors of Plympton, Launceston, St. German's, Bodmin, Frithelstock, Barnstaple, Pilton, Totnes, and St. Nicholas, Exeter; i, 139.

Certificatorium pro etc. (4 March, 1412-13). The Schedule contains the same names, omitting only the Prior of Pilton; i, 176[b].

Certificatorium pro etc. (14 Nov., 1413). The Schedule contains the same names and the following addition is made at the end:—

"Conventus omnium et singulorum Monasteriorum et Prioratuum predictorum.

"Frater Ricardus de Pylton
"Frater Johannes de Cowyk } Prioratuum Priores, i, 188[b].

Procuratorium Domini pro etc. [in favour of Thomas Hendeman and William Hunden, Canons of Exeter], 14 Nov. 1413, i, 189.

Certificatorium pro etc. (25 Sept., 1414). The Schedule contains the same names, omitting the Priors of Pilton and Cowick, i, 199.

Certificatorium factum Archiepiscopo pro etc. (5 Nov., 1415; there is no Schedule), i, 218[b].

Procuratorium [*Domini*] *pro etc.* [in favour of Richard Gabriell, Canon of Exeter, and Thomas Stevenys, advocate in the Court of Canterbury] 4 Nov. 1415, i, 214^b.

Certificatorium pro etc. (24 March, 1415-16). The Schedule contains the Dean, the four Archdeacons, and the same Abbots and Priors as before, i, 218^b.

Procuratorium Domini pro etc. [in favour of John Wakeryng, Keeper of the Privy Seal, and Thomas Stephyn, advocates etc.], 24 March, 1415-16 ; i, 219.

Certificatorium pro etc. (31 Oct., 1416). The Schedule contains the same names, omitting only the Prior of Barnstaple ; i, 227.

Procuratorium Domini pro etc. [in favour of Richard Gabryell and Thomas Stephyn], 31 Oct., 1416 ; i, 227^b.

Procuratorium Domini pro etc. [in favour of the same], 15 Nov., 1417 ; i, 235^b.

Certificatorium pro etc. (20 Nov., 1417). The Schedule omits the Dean; gives the four Archdeacons, the same Abbots as before, and the Priors of Plympton, Launceston, St. German's, Bodmin, Frithelstock and Tywardreath ; i, 236.

Cook, Andrew and Isabella, i, 306^b.

Cook, John, instituted to Landcross, R., ii, 95^b.

A Clerk of the same name, and probably the same person, was shortly afterwards instituted to the neighbouring R. of East Down, ii, 108^b.

Cook, Thomas, chaplain, licensed to celebrate *in Capella Sancte Electe*, in the parish of St. Endellion (15 Sept., 1400), i, 48 ; 107^b.

The name occurs several times, and identification is not easy. Thomas Cook was Canon of Bosham and Prebendary of Apuldram therein, i, 12^b, 25^b, which preferment he resigned, ii, 38^b. A Thomas Cook appears as proxy for Walter Lambard, ii, 84^b ; and probably the same man was instituted a little later, to St. Kieran's, Exeter, ii, 103.—A Commission of enquiry was issued, 27 Aug., 1413, in the matter of the excommunication of Thomas Cook, of Torre, for an assault on John Dowelton, priest, and monk of Torre Abbey, ii, 252. *See*, also, i, 301, 308^b.

Cook, Walter, Canon of York and Prebendary of Axminster, i, 15 ; ii, 17^b, 19^b ; co-patron of Axminster, V., ii, 187.

This name is of frequent occurrence, and identification is difficult. Walter Cook was collated (1399) to the Archdeaconry of Exeter, ii, 43^b ; but there is no record, apparently, of his death or resignation : his successor, however, died in 1408, ii, 232. A Walter Cook was instituted to Langtree, R., in 1411 ; ii, 132^b, 239^b, i, 171^b. *See*, too, i, 302^b.

Cook, William, of Cornwall, i, 161.

Cook, William, chaplain, (perhaps, the R. of Nymet Rowland), i, 314. *See* Coke, ii, 104.

Coote, William, Sacristan of Slapton Collegiate Chantry, ii, 111.

Copleston [Copelston, MS.], residence of John Copleston, (*see Oratories*), i, 6^b.

This John Copleston and Alice his wife, were licensed to choose confessors (4 Dec., 1396), i, 9^b.

Copleston, John (senior), i, 302, 332 : John (junior), i, 327,^{b} 332^b : Thomas, i, 332.—John (senior), patron of Nymet Rowland, ii, 25^b, 104, 189 ; of Cheriton Fitz-paine, ii, 191 : John (junior), of Great Torrington, ii, 174.

His Commission as Steward for the Bishop in Devonshire is dated 24 Sept., 1417 ; ii, 263.

Copleston, William, instituted to the R. of Stowford, ii, 164b; resigns and is instituted to Milton-Damarel, R., ii, 169b; 257b; his death, ii, 173b.

Coppe, William, of Kingston (q. v.), ii, 277b.

Copshill, John, V. of Buckland Brewer (deceased), ii, 85b.

Corbyn, John, V. of Wittenham-Rowley (Dioc. of Salisbury), exchanges for Stoodleigh, R., ii, 121b; exchanges again for Kilve, R. (Dioc. of Bath and Wells), ii, 130b.

Corbyn, John, V. of Toller Porcorum (Dioc. of Salisbury), exchanges for Jacobstow, R. (Devon), ii, 162; and again for the Chantry of Cheverel Parva (Dioc. of Salisbury), ii, 177.

Cordington, Thomas de, R. of Clannaborough (q. v.), ii, 359.

Cornu, Henry, presents to Thornbury, R. ii, 75.—*See* i, 71b.

Cornu, John, instituted to the R. of Broad Nymet, ii, 195.

Cornu, Sir Robert, knt., presents to Brushford, R. (Dioc. of Bath and Wells), ii, 4.

Cornu, Robert, co-patron of Merton, R., ii, 146b; of Sutcombe, R., ii, 181.

Cornu, Walter, patron of Thornbury, R., ii, 139.

Cornwall, Archdeaconry of, Mandate for the Bishop's Visitation (5 April, 1400), i, 35b.—*See*, also, Carslegh, James, ii, 267.

[*Breve Regium*]—Mandate to the Bishop to receive the oaths of certain men, as Justices of the Peace for the County, viz. John Arundell, John Grenevyll, William Stourton, Richard Reprenne, and Roger Trewethenek (12 Oct., 1410), ii, 335b.

Cornwale, Joan, wife of Thomas, i, 303b.

Cornewale, John, R. of Langtree (deceased), ii, 132b.

Cornewaylle, Sir John, knt., presents to Calstock, R., ii, 25b; to South Molton, R., ii, 94, 123; to Beerferris (Arch-presb.), ii, 182, 186, 260b, 261; to Dartington, R., ii, 155, 193, 265b.—*See*, also, Newton-Ferrers, ii, 363b, 364.

Cornewayl, Richard, presents to King's Nympton, R., ii, 96, 100, 103b[1], 146, 249b.

Cornevayll, Thomas, LL.B., R. of St. Stephen's-in-Brannel, i, 86, 89b, 106, 109b, 135; exchanges for Thornbury, R. (Dioc. of Chichester), ii, 180b.

Cornewale, William, V. of Egloshayle,—

The Bishop dispenses with his residence, on account of the suits and disputes continually going on between him and the Prior of Bodmin, who resisted

---

[1] With Alice his wife.

his claim to cut firewood[1] in the wood at Dunmeer, and to take tithes on account of the profits of the Mill there, and also as to a certain annual pension of 40s., the Vicar complaining of risk even of bodily injury, and the Bishop deciding that it was lawful for him to leave his parish in order to defend the rights of his Vicarage (" *Tolleratio absencie vicarii, prosequentis jura ecclesie sue.*"—The date of this document is omitted; but it appears to have been issued between 15 Sept. and 12 Oct., 1398), i, 21.
he exchanges for the V. of Batheaston, ii, 52ᵇ.

Cornwood, William Pykkeslegh (or Pygeslegh), R. of; licence to choose a confessor (9 June, 1399), i, 27; licence of non-residence for one year,[2] from 11 June, 1399, *ibid*;

The Bishop issued his Mandate, 6 July, 1403, addressed to the Dean of Plympton, Simon Elys, R. of Harford,[3] and John Stybbe, chaplain, forbidding the revenues of this parish to be farmed by a certain layman, Thomas Codemore, who, in defiance of the said Rector, had fraudulently collected the tithes of the said benefice, ordering the parishioners not to pay their Rector, and falsely pretending to a right to farm the same.—i, 67.

licence of non-residence from 28 Nov., 1404, to Michaelmas, 1405, i, 72.—Robert Offecote, R. of (*see* "Oratories"), i, 110ᵇ; licence of non-residence from 21 March, 1417-18 to Michaelmas, 1418, i, 238ᵇ; from 18 May to Michaelmas, 1419, i, 247ᵇ.

Cornworthy, Margery, wife of John Smyth of, i, 330ᵇ.

Cornworthy Priory, i, 303, 308ᵇ, 309, 311ᵇ, 316, 318, 327ᵇ, 329, 329ᵇ, 330ᵇ, 331ᵇ, 332ᵇ.—Churches appropriated to, ii, 359ᵇ.—The Bishop's Mandates—

(1) For the Visitation of the Priory on the 14th of May (dated 10 April), 1400, i, 36ᵇ.
(2) Against certain persons who interfered with the due[4] payment of offerings at weddings, purifications, and funerals, in the parish church of Cornworthy, appropriated to the said Priory: it was addressed to the Dean of Totnes,

---

[1] "Super quibusdam *focalibus* in silva de Dynmre," — "*Focale.* Annona lignaria, vel jus quod quis habet percipiendi ligna in silvis ad suum focum."—*D'Arnis.*

[2] dum tamen tempore quadragesimali, et festis majoribus medio tempore contingentibus, ad dictam tuam ecclesiam personaliter accedas; Proviso quod eidem ecclesie tue dicto tempore deserviatur laudabiliter in Divinis, et animarum cura diligenter exerceatur in eadem, quodque procuratorem ydoneum in eadem constituas et dimittas, qui nobis, et ministris nostris, ac ceteris ordinariis tuis, respondere valeat vice tua; absencieque tue dampnum recompensetur elimosinarum largicione, nostro arbitrio moderanda."

[3] Herford, MS.

[4] "Ad unius denarii vel alterius modice quantitatis valorem restringere sunt conati." And again—"quidam iniquitatis filii, quorum nomina pariter et persone ignorantur, diebus dominicis et festivis ac aliis, mensibus Junii, Julii, Augusti, et Septembris, sub Anno Domini millesimo quadringentesimo duodecimo jam instante contingentibus, devocionem populi ac oblacionem in exequiis mortuorum . . . . juxta morem antiquum offerre volentis, ad hujusmodi modicam quantitatem predictam restringere nequiter molientes, quam plures Christi fideles in exequiis pro tunc existentes, et ibidem juxta morem offerre volentes quominus offerre valebant impedire temere presumpserunt, et ipsis sic offerre volentibus quibusdam occulte ne offerrent, quibusdam palam et publice, vetuerunt."

John [Andrew], R. of Alphington, and Nicholas, chaplain of Cornworthy Church, who were to ascertain the names and descriptions of the malefactors, and cite as many as were found blameworthy to appear before the Bishop at Clyst (7 Oct., 1412), i, 168b.

The Priory having been vacant since the death of Joan Lucy, 3 Oct., 1411, the Subprioress and other members of the Community who were bound to elect a successor having postponed and neglected their duty, so that the right of preferment had lapsed to the Bishop, he exercised it in favour of Eleanor Blake, one of their number (28 Feb., 1411-12), ii, 140.

Cornysche, Geoffrey, instituted to the R. of Bicton, ii, 83.

Corvet, John, instituted to the V. of Sidmouth, ii, 22.

Coryton [Coreton, MS.] John, R. of, a Penitentiary in the Deanery of Tavistock, i, 50.

Cote, William, instituted to be "Minister" of the parish Church of Slapton, ii, 132; and *see* ii, 357b.

Cotell, John, i, 332.

Cotemor,[1] Thomas, *see* Kingston, ii, 276.

Coterel, John, V. of Axmouth, i, 238b,—

He was instituted to Axmouth on resigning the Wardenship of Ottery St. Mary, ii, 212.

Coterell, Richard, of Apuldram, ii, 293b.

Cotesmore, ii, 43.

Cotteford, Thomas, R. of St. Illogan, i, 12; ii, 316.

Cotyn, William (and his wife), i, 304.

Coulyn, William, *see* Luxulyan, i, 160b; ii, 247.

Coulyng, *see* Oldcastel, i, 191b.

Couper, John, of Apuldram, ii, 293b.

Courtenay, Earl of Devon, *see* Devon.

Courtenay, Sir Edward, knt. ([eldest] son of Edw. Earl of Devon), i, 86; co-patron of Bickleigh, R., ii, 92b; patron of Kentisbeare, ii, 166; of Stoke-Damarel, ii, 169; of Brixham,[2] V., ii, 176b. [He died in 1418, *vita patris*].

Courtenay, Sir Edward, son and heir of Hugh, Earl of Devon (ob. vit. patris), ii, 342.

Courtenay, Sir Hugh, knt. (son of Edward, Earl of Devon), presents to the R. of St. John in Cornwall, ii, 160, 181; to Shevioke, ii, 169.—Sir Hugh Courtenay, senior, knt., presents to the Chantry of Forde, in the parish of Bampton, ii, 186b, 201b, to the R. of Bampton, ii, 264, 307b; to the Archpresb. of Haccombe, ii, 107b, 149. The Bishop grants (16 Oct., 1417) his

---

[1] Possibly the same as Thomas Codemore; Cornwood (q. v.) being an adjoining parish.

[2] *See* Brixham, ii, 258b, 355, also, i, 333.

Licence for the marriage of Sir Hugh Courtenay, of Hacombe, with Matilda, daughter of William Beaumond of Heanton Punchardon, in the Chapel within the said William's mansion of Heanton, provided the banns were duly called in their respective parish churches, and leave obtained from the Curates thereof.—i, 235b.

[*Breve Regium*]—Mandate to administer the oath to Sir Hugh Courtenay, senior, as Sheriff of Devon (5 Nov., 1418), ii, 363b.

Courtenay, John, domicellus, presents to the R. of Ashton, ii, 68b, 75b.

Courtenay, Margaret de, i, 301.

Courtenay, Sir Peter, knt., co-patron of the V. of Sidmouth, ii, 22; presents to Alphington, R., ii, 67, 74; to Moreton [Hampstead], R., ii, 78.

Courtenay, Sir Philip, knt., presents to Bradninch, R., ii, 27; to Honiton, R., ii, 45; to Powderham, R., ii, 49; to Bickleigh, R., ii, 87b.

Courtenay, Richard, Canon of Bosham, i, 12b (and Prebendary of Westbroke therein), i, 25b; collated to a Canonry in Exeter Cathedral, ii, 42b, and *see* i, 56b; resigns his Canonry in Bosham, ii, 54; instituted to Alphington, R., ii, 67; to the Prebend of Heyes, ii, 67b; resigns Alphington, ii, 74; presents to the R. of Honiton, ii, 103, 148; to the R. of Cadeleigh, ii, 96b; resigns his Canonry (Exeter) and the Prebend of Heyghes (*sic*), ii, 152; claims to present to the R. of Milton Damarel, ii, 237b,—a mistaken claim, ii, 342b.—*See* Kentisbeare, ii, 249; also, i, 311b.

Courtenay, Archbishop William, *see* Canterbury.

Courteys, Alexander, M.A., instituted to the R. of Instow, ii, 144b, 248b; *see*, also, i, 168b, 197.

Courteys, John, monk of Tavistock, ii, 59, 61; *see* also, i, 315.

Covele, Thomas, *see* St. Pinnock, ii, 350b.

Coventry, i, 305; election of the Prior of St. German's confirmed at, ii, 79.

Covyntre, Richard, V of Hockworthy, exchanges for Batheaston, V., ii, 44; exchanges again for Egloshayle, V., ii, 52b; his death, ii, 68.

Covyan, Richard, instituted to Littleham, St. Swithins, ii, 22b.

Cowley Bridge, i, 302b.

Cowick (*i.e.*, St. Thomas's, Exeter). See *Institutions*.

Cowick Priory, i, 316, 319b, 327, 331b:—

The Bishop's Mandate to the Prior, for his Visitation on 9 July, 1400 (dated 30 June, 1400), i, 43.—Commission as to the Visitation (7 July, 1400), ii, 227.

John Burgeawyll, Prior of (see *Oratories*), i, 73b, 80; in arrear of Procurations due to the Pope's Collector, for three years (1408-10), i, 105, 110.—"Ordinacio" between the Prior and Monks and the parishioners of St. Thomas "ultra pontem," Exeter,—

The Bishop refers to the fact that Holy Scripture requires the ordinances of Religion to be celebrated in buildings dedicated to God, except in cases of necessity, and states that he had received a Petition from John, Prior of Cowick, and the monks there, and also from the parishioners of that place, setting forth that in the Chapel of St. Thomas of Canterbury, situated at the end of Exe-Bridge, the V. for the time being had continued, and from time immemorial, to perform all parochial functions (the burial of the dead only excepted), until it had been swept away by an inundation of the river, whereupon the said Prior and Monks, Patrons of the Vicarage, and the parishioners—the Faithful elsewhere contributing their alms—had built a fair Basilica, in honour of the said glorious Martyr, on a piece of ground called "Pyryhay" (well removed from the river and from all risk of inundations), the property hitherto of the said Priory, and of their church at Cowick. Now monks, *secundum ethimologiam nominis*, ought to serve God apart from the common intercourse of the people, and the said Mother-Church, moreover, was quite at one end of the parish, and the new Basilica in its midst, so that the latter was, in every way, more convenient and suitable for the Parish Church. The Bishop consented to the prayer of the Petition, that he would consecrate the new church and its cemetery, having first consulted, and obtained the consent of, the Dean and Chapter, the said Prior, the Vicar (John Alkebarwe), and the parishioners at large, represented by Richard Holand, John Floyer, John Brycon, John Kyte, John Farthehill, Hugh Benyn,[1] William Chedder, and Peter Hode—the right of continuing to bury in the cemetery of St. Michael's chapel being reserved for those who preferred it. All duties pertaining to the Rector were to be performed by the Prior and monks, except cure of souls, for which the Vicar would continue responsible; the parishioners to fulfil their customary duties, including the maintenance in good order of the said antient cemetery of St. Michael. The Bishop dedicated and consecrated the new Church on Tuesday, 4 Oct, 1412, and the *mensa* and High Altar, together with the cemetery, on the following day, and ordered that the Feast of Dedication should always be solemnly observed, and in the same manner as Christmas Day. This "ordinacio" was sealed by the Bishop, the Dean and Chapter, and the Prior and Convent; also by the Dean of Kenn (within whose Deanery the Church stands), at the request of John the Vicar; and by the Dean of Christianity, at the request of Richard Holand and the seven other parishioners named above, and on their behalf, because they had no common seal of their own."—ii, 287-288.

The "ordinacio" of, *see* Okehampton, ii, 292^b.

Cowlyng, John, scholar,—*Dispensacio super defectu natalium* (29 Jan., 1398-9),[2] i, 24^b; instituted to St. Minver, ii, 95^b.

Cowlyng, Thomas, instituted to St. Dominick, R. ii, 193^b; i, 245^b.

Cowyk, John, instituted to Pyworthy, ii, 101^b; i, 100^b, 232, 327^b.

---

[1] *Or*, perhaps, Bevyn.

[2] "Data et acta sunt hec . . . in quadam camera magna a retro aula majori infra Prioratum Sancte Fritheswide Virginis, municipii Oxoniensis, Ordinis Sancti Augustini, Lincolniensis Diocesis, situatum."

Crabbe, Walter, R. of Clovelly (deceased), ii, 7.

Cracamtallan, in St. Gennys (now, I believe, Crackington), i, 82b.

Craddock (Cradok, MS.—in the parish of St. Cleer), Chapel of St. Wynwalo at, i, 232..

Cradele, Philip, priest, alleged assault on, ii, 240b.

Crauthorn, William de, *see* Chudleigh, i, 239.

Crantock, Collegiate Church of,—

The nave had been greatly damaged by the fall of the tower; and, the Community being too poor to rebuild the same, the Bishop granted an Indulgence to the Faithful who should contribute to the cost (11 Aug., 1412), i, 163b.

John Waryn, Dean of, i, 256b,—

A Commission was issued 27 July, 1417, addressed to Dean Waryn, for the repair of the Choir (or Chancel) there, and at St. Columb-minor (which was appropriated to the College), and for the raising of the moneys required; which moneys Robert Trehage had been deputed to receive and apply. Some of the Canons had been slow to contribute their proper share; so the Bishop ordered the names of the defaulters to be reported to him, and the Dean was to see that payment was enforced.—ii, 262.

Crawley (Dioc. of Lincoln), Nicholas, R. of, i, 310b.—*See*, also, i, 325.

Crede, John, i, 301.

Crediton, Bridge at New Mill, i, 327b.—Esse Boleyn, in the parish of, i, 82; Foleford[1] in, the mansion of Joan Dyrwyn, i, 185. Spencecombe[2] in, i, 212b. *See* Talaton *and* Hull, (Sir John), ii, 310b. The Bishop's Park at, etc.,—

The Bishop, on the 5th of Dec., 1418, granted to his valet, John Clyfton, as the reward of his faithful service, the office of Keeper of his Park at Crediton, and also the office of Bailiff of the Hundred of Crediton, for the term of his life, with all fees, profits, etc., thereto pertaining. This grant was sanctioned, and sealed, by the Dean and Chapter, 10 Dec., 1418.—i, 244.

Chapel of St. Laurence at,—

The Bishop writes to the Dean of the Collegiate Church, and the Dean of Cadbury, stating that John Matthew, chaplain (Custos of the said Chapel), had complained to him that certain iniquitous persons, whose names he did not know, had carried off certain charters and muniments of great value, vestments also and the oblations of the faithful; and he directs that the offenders be denounced publickly, in the accustomed manner (28 Jan., 1410-11), i, 112b.

The Collegiate Church of, i, 326; Sir John Sully's tomb in the north transept there, i, 327b; bequests of Canon Henry Brokeland to, i, 303; of Maurice Burgh, i, 305b; of Thomas Bullok, i, 313b; of Joan Dyrwyn, i, 323; of Canon Richard Penels, i, 332b; of Canon Thomas Barton, i, 327b; of Thomas Reymound, i, 331b.—Commissions, etc.,—

---

[1] Now "Shobrooke Park."

[2] Spenceryscome, MS.

To compel the Prebendaries of Crediton to contribute to the cost of completing the Choir, etc., of their Church,—directed to John Lugans, Thomas Barton, and John Dodyngton, Canons of Exeter, 31 July, 1399 ; ii, 225.

Mandate for the Visitation of the College on 5 June, 1400,—directed to the Precentor, i, 39.

Letter from the Bishop, directed to the Dean, and to the R. of Lapford, touching the complaint of the R. of Morchard-Bishop against certain chaplains, and especially against Elias Lebe, that they could not be induced to serve in his parish Church, even for competent salaries (5 Sept., 1410), i, 105b.

William Trey (or Tray), Dean of, *see* Sture, William, i, 126 ; his Will, i, 316b.—Thomas Estbrok, Dean of, a Penitentiary for the Deanery of Cadbury, i, 231.—William Fylham, Dean of, i, 237, 237b.—The Precentor and Canons of, in arrear of Procurations, due to the Pope's collector, for one year (1410), i, 105.—John Wythewyll, Precentor of, his Will, i, 309 ; Robert Alkebarowe, Precentor of, ii, 97b ; William Querley, Precentor of, a Penitentiary in the Deanery of Cadbury, i, 245 ; John de Dodyngton, Prebendary of, his Will, i, 301 ; Richard Hopere (or Hooper), Canon of, i, 88, 116, 117 ; William Langeton, Canon of, i, 64 ; Major Parys, Canon of, i, 233 ; the Prebend of Prustecombe in, i, 332b ; of Woodland,—

Mandate, directed to the Dean of Exeter, Ralph Tregresiou, on the complaint of John Prophet, Prebendary of Woodland, against the representatives of John Wendlyngburgh (senior), his predecessor, who had left the Prebendal buildings, etc., in a very dilapidated state. A full enquiry was ordered into all the circumstance of the case (16 Sept., 1395), i, 5b.

William Sutton, Canon and Prebendary of,—

Commission for his absolution : it appears that he had committed an assault on John Lyghfote, one of the Vicars of the Church (7 Sept., 1414), ii, 255.

The Guild in the Church of, i, 305b.

Credy, Adam, brother of William, i, 307b, 308 ; co-patron of the R. of Inwardleigh, ii, 108b.

Credy, Agnes, daughter of Thomas, i, 307b.

Credy, Ivo, esquire, co-patron of the R. of Inwardleigh, ii, 108b.

Credy,[1] Joan, daughter of Adam, i. 307b.

Credy,[1] Ralph, i, 308 ; co-patron of Inwardleigh, R. ii, 108b.

Credy,[1] William, R. of High-Bickington ; licence of non-residence for one year, from 15 Oct., 1395, i, 6 ; his death,[2] ii, 91 ; his Will, i, 307b.—*See*, also, 308b.

---

[1] Crydy, MS.

[2] He is here called "Thomas"—a clerical error.

Creed (or St. Creed), the Church of, i, 323, 331.—Chapel of St. Mary at Grampound,[1] in the parish of (licensed 16 Sept., 1400), i, 48.

Cressa, John, clerk—*Dispensacio super defectu natalium* (24 Sept., 1412), i, 167b.

Cressa, Nicholas, R. of St. Mary Arches, Exeter (deceased), ii, 9.

Cressa, Richard, scholar,—*Dispensacio super defectu natalium* (11 April. 1397), i, 12.

Crese, Richard, (part-owner of the ship *Marie* of Exmouth), i, 320.

Cressy, Reymund, proxy for Thomas Loweden, ii, 110b.

Creuwes, Alexander, ii, 150b.

Crewkerne (Dioc. of Bath and Wells), John de Dodyngton, R. of, i, 301.

Criave, Thomas, co-patron of North Bovey, R., ii, 189b, 264.

Crocker, Robert, chaplain, i, 307, 307b.

Croisere, William, co-patron of Chagford R., ii, 33b, 34b, 356.

Crokern, John (de Childehay); *see* Kentisbeare, ii, 248b, 345b.

Crooke,[2] in North Tawton, Chapel of St. Mary there, i, 128.

Crooke, John, instituted to the R. of Rackenford, ii, 5b; i, 138; (deceased), ii, 150b.

Crosse, Henry, i, 308; ii, 307b; co-patron of Gittisham, R., ii, 104; of Stoke-Rivers, R., ii, 129b, 180.—*See*, also, Parkham.

Crowan, (or St. Crowan), Luke Trenewyth, V. of,—

He had complained to the Bishop that Divine Service was being unlawfully celebrated by certain chaplains, without licence, in the Chapel of St. Augustine, within his said parish; the Bishop commissioned Richard Olyver to enquire, and, if the charge were true, to inhibit the offenders (16 Dec., 1396), ii, 222.—*See* Beauchamp, John and Joan *(Oratories)*.

Crugge, John, presented to St. Leonard's, Exeter, ii, 268b.

Crukern, John, instituted to Saltash V.,[3] ii, 36b; resigns, ii, 102.

Cruse, John, instituted to the R. of High Bray, ii, 191b, 265.

Cruwys[4]-Morchard, Walter, R. of, a Penitentiary in the Deanery of Southmolton, i, 50.—Thomas Frist of, i, 324.—John Pratte of, i, 138.—Commission, for the ordination to the priesthood of John Knight, deacon, R. of this parish (10 Dec., 1418), ii, 266b.

---

1 Grampount, MS.
2 Croke, MS.
3 "Vicarius ecclesie parochialis de Saltash," *i.e.*, "St. Stephen's-by-Saltash; at ii, 102, we find "perpetua vicaria ecclesie parochialis Sancti Stephani de Saltasshe."
4 Crewys, *also* Crues, MS.

Cruwes, Robert, instituted to the R. of Rackenford, ii, 150b.—*See*, also, i, 205, 315.

Crewys, Walter (accolite), instituted to Virginstow, R., ii, 179b.

Cryche, William, Prior of Montacute, presents to the V. of Monkleigh, ii, 109b.

Cryk, Walter, V. of Stratton; licence to celebrate in the Chapels of Holy Trinity and St. Michael, Bude, and St. Leonard's, Efford (21 Aug., 1400), i, 45.

Cryour, Thomas (Canon of Plympton),—

He had appeared before the Bishop, complaining that one John Sutton, a servant and cook[1] of the cell of St. Mary-in-the-Marsh,[2] near Exeter, had been accustomed to annoy him, and on one occasion, finding him in a corner of the hall where there was no chance of escape, had foully abused him, and then rushed at him with a dagger,[3] so that, being in fear of his life, and in self-defence, he attacked his assailant with a stick, which he was lucky enough to find in the corner of the hall, striking him once only on his head, and wounding him. The said John, contemptuously refusing to do what the doctor advised, died three days later, and entirely through his own obstinacy. Cryour, by the advice of his friends, had withdrawn himself from the service of the Altar; but the Bishop, after careful enquiry, pronounced him free from all blame in the matter, and restored him to the full exercise of the duties of his office. The Bishop delivered sentence herein, in the Chapel of his Palace at Exeter, 5 Sept., 1409.—i, 89b.

Cryse, Stephen, prebendary of Crediton (deceased), ii, 139.

Crystow, Thomas, instituted to the V. of Pinhoe, ii, 183.

Crystow, William, does homage to the Bishop at Crediton, for lands there (16 Sept., 1400), ii, 310b.

Cullegh (or Cully), John, co-patron of the R. of Inwardleigh, ii, 24b, 108b.

Cullegh, Robert, instituted to the R. of Monkokehampton, ii, 80b; his death, ii, 192b.

Cullyng, Thomas, Abbot of Tavistock (deceased), ii, 62b.

Cullyng, William, Provost of Glasney,—

The Bishop writes to him (24 Jan., 1398-9), informing him of his intention to collate Laurence Walter, priest, to be Vicar to Canon John Rawe (by lapse), i, 24.

He presents to the V. of Mylor, ii, 21; and (in conjunction with Nicholas Herry, Sacristan of Glasney), to the Chantry "de Porte" therein, ii, 111; 163.—*See* Fraunceys, John; also, ii, 225.

Culm Davy[4] (in the parish of Hemyock), the Chapel at, i, 318b.

Culmstock[5], Prescot[6] in, i, 200b; St. Mary's Chapel at, i, 317b, et seqq.—Culmstock Bridge, i, 318.

[1] Cocus.

[2] "Prioratus, sive celle, Sancte Marie in Marisco, juxta Exoniam."

[3] "Cum quodam cultello *dagger* vulgariter nuncupato."

[4] Comb Davy, MS.

[5] Columpstoke, MS.

[6] Prestecote, MS.

Culmyslond, Thomas, an accolite,—

The Bishop certifies that on searching the Register of his immediate predecessor (Thomas Brantingham), he had found that the said Thomas Culmyslond had been admitted to the order of sub-deacon in the Chapel of his Manor of Clyst, 23 March, 1386-7[1], with title from the Abbot and Convent of Forde (16 Sept., 1412), i, 166.

Curteys, Matilda (wife of Thomas, of Pylle, in the parish of Lanlivery[2]), licence to choose a confessor (6 June, 1405), i, 75.—*See Oratories.*

Curvyn, John, i, 327^b.

Cury[3], the Chapel of the Monks of Hales[4] in the parish of,—

Licence to Richard Polmogh, and other fit chaplains, to celebrate in the said chapel on Sundays and other Festivals, until the said parish Chnrch, which had been polluted by effusion of blood, should have been duly reconciled (21 July, 1395), i, 4.

There was a chapel of the B. V. M. in this parish at Boohym[5]; *see* Bryt (*Oratories*), i, 87.

Custa, John, V. of Upottery, exchanges for the Chantry of St. Andrew in the church of St. Mary Magd., Taunton, ii, 69.

Customs, Collectors of, in the Port of Exeter, ii, 351.

Cutmore, Thomas; licence to choose a confessor, for one year (3 Oct., 1401), i, 58^b.—*See* Codemore and Cotcmor, Thomas (*note*).

Cutton[6], the Prebend of, ii, 347^b.

Commission of enquiry as to "dilapidatious," on complaint, by Prebendary Richard Dounscomb, of the neglect of Thomas Kerdyngton, his predecessor (5 Aug., 1419), ii, 268.

Cutynbek [in St. German's—*hodie* Cuddenbeak], the Bishop's Manor of, i, 46^b.

D.

Dabernon, Agnes, *see* Hunne, John, i, 169; ii, 246^b.

Dabernoun, John, and Thomasia (daughter of John Cadia),—

It appears that at the time of their marriage the said John knew, and Thomasia did not, that they were related in the fourth degree of consanguinity. A Dispensation was granted to them: but it was stipulated that if John should outlive his wife, he should not be at liberty to marry again (28 Sept., 1414), i, 200^b.

Dabernoun, John, i, 306^b.—*See* also, ii, 89^b.

---

[1] "MLXXXVI" in the MS.—a clerical error.

[2] Lannyvery, MS. Sancti Corentini, also, in the MS.

[4] Heylys, MS.

[5] Bossim, MS.

[6] Cotton, MS.

Dagfen, William, resigns the Chantry at Morthoe, and is instituted to that of Colcombe, ii, 13.

Daldych, Robert, R. of Corston (Dioc. of Bath and Wells), exchanges for the Chantry in St. Katherine's Chapel, Hemyock, ii, 195b; resigns, ii, 198b.

Dalkyn, John, V. of Bradworthy, i, 38b, 68b; his death, ii, 88b.

Dalyngton, John, instituted to the Priory of St. Nicholas, Exeter, ii, 197.

Dangy, John, i, 324b.

Danyell, Richard, Prebendary of Carssewell, resigns, ii, 193.

Danyel, Roger, V. of Seaton (deceased), ii, 46.

Danyel, Walter, collated to the R. of the Collegiate Chantry of Slapton, ii, 46b; 68; his death, ii, 111b.

Danyell, William, R. of St. George's, Exeter, ii, 336.

Dart[1], the river (at Holne Bridge), i, 183; Bridge at Staverton over, i, 174b; Dart-Bridge, i, 306b.

Dartington[1], Peter [Overton], R. of, a Penitentiary in the Deanery of Totnes, i, 50; 82; licence of non-residence for one year, from 14 June, 1411; i, 125b.—Ralph Walwayn, R. of, licence of non-residence for one year, from 14 Feb., 1413-14, i, 193b; for one year, from 10 April, 1415, i, 209b; for one year, from 3 June, 1416, i, 221b; for one year, from 2 July, 1417, i, 233.—John Bowden (subdeacon), R. of, dispensation (to study at Oxford), for one year, from 6 Feb., 1418-19, i, 245.

Dartmouth[1], *see* Townstal.—The Chapel of St. Mary "de novo constructa," licensed 21 Aug., 1400, i, 45; the "new chapel at Dartmouth," i, 113; the Chapel of the Holy Trinity there, i, 226b.—Edmund and Joan Arnald, of, i, 146; William Clerk, of, i, 10, 86b.—John and Rosa Rede, of, i, 330b.—*See* Gatewell, Richard.

Daubeney, Thomas, i, 329.

Daubryggecourt, Sir John, knt.—*See* Townstal, i, 226b.

Daudeley, Master, of Exeter, i, 311b.

Daumarle, Isabella, relict of Sir John Daumarle, knt., presents to the R. of North Huish, ii, 8b, 67b, 144b, 248b; her Will, i, 308b; Nicholas, Thomas, and James, her sons, Joan and Margaret, her daughters, *ibid.* *See* ii, 55b.

Damarl, Roger, R. of Mary Tavy, i, 175.

---

[1] Derte.—Dertington.—Dertemouth, MS.

Dauney, John (domicellus) and Joan his wife, i, 75b.

Dauntesey, Edward, Archdeacon of Cornwall, i, 30, 66; ii, 57b, 149; his collation, a Prebend in Glasney being annexed, ii, 35. He was R. of Yate (Dioc. of Worcester), but exchanged for a Prebend in St. Probus, ii, 58; resigns, ii, 84b; instituted to the R. of Ashwater, ii, 91b; exchanges for the R. of Roborough, ii, 148; resigns both Roborough and his Archdeaconry on being consecrated Bishop of Meath, ii, 149.—*See* Poundstock, ii, 229.

Davenport, Adam, instituted to the R. of Stokenham, ii, 183; presents to the V. of Stokenham, ii, 192, 265; *See* also, i, 247b; ii, 260b, 261, 357b.

Davidstow[1], Thomas Bernard, V. of,—

[*Breve Regium*]—To appear before the Judges at Westminster and shew cause why he should not pay to Stephen, Prior of Launceston, the sum of 75s., arrears of an annual payment of 5s. (28 June, 1401), ii, 313b; a little later—29 Nov. in the same year—the Bishop relaxed the sequestration of the Vicar's[2] portion, which had been previously imposed by John Boscofellek, the Bishop's Commissary therein—possibly in connection with these very arrears—i, 58b.

Roger Bernard's bequest to the Church of, i, 314b.

Davy, John, instituted to the V. of Yarnscombe, ii, 166.

Davy, Thomas, *see* Hurde, Richard, i, 202b.

Dawe, John, clerk—*Dispensacio super defectu natalium* (22 Jan., 1407-8), i, 83; instituted to the Chantry "de Ponte," Glasney, ii, 111; resigns, ii, 163.

Dawe, William, instituted to the V. of St. Cleer, ii, 148; i, 228, 232.

Dawlish, John Caynok (or Kenok), V. of, i, 122; proxy for John Burell, ii, 90b.—Thomas Fayrforde, V. of,—

Commission (addressed to Richard Penell, advocate in the Consistory Court) in a case of dilapidations on Fayrforde's complaint against Caynok, his predecessor (7 March, 1411), ii, 239; 241.

—Chapel of Cofton[3], in the parish of,—

An action brought against John Caynok, the late V., by the villagers of Cofton as to providing a chaplain to serve the chapel there, having been decided in the said Vicar's favour, they appealed against the decision of the Court, refusing to resort to the Mother Church for the Sacraments, etc., as the new Vicar, Thomas Fayrforde, in like manner declined to serve Cofton chapel. Pending this appeal, the Bishop directs John [Colyn], R. of Mamhead to hear the confessions of the Cofton people, and to celebrate specially for them, in his own parish-church on Easter-day and administer to them the sacrament[4]; but he was to take no stipend for his work, and no part of the

[1] Dewystowe, MS.
[2] He is twice in this document called *John*, by a clerical error, probably, for *Thomas*, which he is called in the Institution and in the *Breve Regium*.
[3] Cokton, MS.
[4] "sacramentum eukaristie."

revenues of the living was to be diverted from the Vicar (2 April, 1411), i, 122.

Referring to the Commission (of the 7th of March, 1411), in the matter of the dilapidations left by John Caynok, the Bishop declares that the said dilapidations had been assessed in not less than £6 11*s*. 11*d*., and that Fayrforde had represented that, unless the amount could be recovered at once, the property of the deceased would probably be made away with. So he directs sequestration thereof till the said sum be paid (17 April, 1411), ii, 241^{b}.

The controversy between this Vicar and his parishioners at Cofton seems to have been patched up, but not settled, soon afterwards; for on the 11th of August, 1411, he was licensed to celebrate in "the Chapel of St. Mary[1]" (on the Feast of her Assumption only), and on the 30th of August "in capella Beate Marie *de Cokton*," on the Feast of her Nativity, i, 131, 133^{b}.—On the 30th of March, however, 1412, Thomas Uppeton, V. of Kenton, was licensed to serve the Chapel, *pendente lite*; i, 146^{b}; and on 6 March, 1412-13, this licence was renewed, also *pendente lite*; i, 177^{b}. On the 8th of August, 1412, the licence for St. Mary's at "Cokton" was renewed, and at the same time a licence was granted for the Chapel of St. Mary at "Lydeswyll."—i, 163.

Dawny, John, R. of Rame, i, 11^{b}.

Dayell, John [*also*, Dayhulle *and* Dayhyll, MS.], instituted to Ashreigny R., ii, 156; resigns, ii, 177^{b}; instituted to Romansleigh R., ii, 176^{b}; 258^{b}.

Dayow, John, instituted to the V. of St. Stithians, ii, 182.

Dean Prior [Dene Pryour, MS.], John Russell, V. of,—

[*Breve Regium, vocatum "venire facias"*].—The said John Russell and William Floyer, V. of Lamerton, executors of the Will of David Hughe, late V. of Buckfastleigh, were to appear at Westminster and shew cause why they should not pay to John Beare, chaplain, and John Shiplegh, Executors of the will of Roger Goslegh, *alias* Gosley, late V. of Holy Trinity, Buckfastleigh, the sums of £20, by the said John, and £20, by the said William, unjustly detained (7 Feb., 1415—16), ii, 355.

Deen, Richard, V. of Hackington (Dioc. of Canterbury) exchanges with the Sacristan of Bosham, ii, 41^{b}, resigns, ii, 48^{b}.

Defence of the Church and Realm,—

Breve Regium—pro arraimento virorum Ecclesiasticorum in Dioceси Exoniensi—on the King's setting out for the war with France—(28 May, 1415), ii, 352.—*Executio Brevis predicti*[2] (12 June, 1415), ii, 352^{b}.—The Bishop's certificate therein[3] (14 July, 1415)—"in numero videlicet virorum armatorum cciiij et sagittariorum M. ccj." *ibid.*

---

[1] Probably the chapel at "Lydeswell," mentioned below."

[2] "Rectores et Vicarii, et alii beneficiati, quorum beneficia in vero valore annuo, omnibus deductis, juxta communem estimacionem ad decem marcas se extendunt, necnon presbiteri stipendiarii, sint armati, vel ad modum sagittariorum cum arcubus et garbis sagittariorum arraiati. Cujus vero beneficium valet annuatim decem libras, sit armatus. Cujus xx marcas, sit armatus cum uno sagittario. Cujus xx libras, sit armatus cum duobus sagittariis. Cujus vero xl libras, habeat duos armatos cum duobus sagittariis. Cujus C marcas, habeat tres armatos et tres sagittarios. Cujus vero C libras, habeat quatuor armatos et sex sagittarios. Religiosi vero Abbates et Priores, tam exempti quam non exempti, sub forma pre-

Delyngton, Richard, co-patron of Washfield R., ii, 108, 142.

Demalt, Henry, collated V. Choral in the Cathedral, i, 173^{b}.

Dename, mansion of Sir John Colshulle, i, 205.

Denbury, [1] William Reeke of, i, 138.—Thomas Loweden, R. of; licence of non-residence for one year, from 19 April, 1412, i, 148; for one year, from 25 Aug., 1413, i, 183.—John Batyn, sub-deacon, R. of; dispensation (to study at Oxford) for three years, from 14 Oct., 1418, i, 243.

Denclyve, John, sub-deacon, who had been ordained, without licence, *ab alieno episcopo*,—Dispensation in his favour (25 March, 1414), i, 195.

Dene, John, parochial chaplain of Sherford, i, 168^{b}.

He was one of the executors of the Will of Henry Blakbourne, R. of Stokenham, q. v. He was specially licensed to celebrate in the Diocese at large (26 Sept., 1413), i, 185.—A John Dene, no doubt the same, is mentioned, as well as the above-named Henry Blakbourne, in the Will of Canon John Dodyngton, i, 301. There was another John Dene, R. of East Down, who died in 1409-10; ii, 108^{b}.

Dene, William, instituted to Thorverton V., ii, 86; proxy for Roger Smyth, ii, 88; exchanges for the R. of Heathfield -Durburgh (Dioc. of Bath and Wells), ii, 165^{b}.

Deneclyf, Stephen[2]; Commission to prove his Will (20 Jan., 1412-13), ii, 250.

Deneman, Gilbert, chaplain, succeeds Robert Box, R. of Combe Raleigh, i, 82; exchanges for Broadhembury V., ii, 161^{b}.

Densel, Richard, ii, 351.

Denyar, Robert, i, 332.

Denys, Isolda, widow of Walter Denys (of Bradford), presents to the R. of Bradford, ii, 139, 191^{b3}, 201^{b}, 244.

Denys, John, presents to the Chantry of Trewen in the parish church of Holsworthy, ii, 51^{b}.

Denys, Matilda, widow, i, 306.

Denys, Robert, clerk—*Dispensacio super defectu natalium* (4 June, 1411), i, 124^{b}.

Denys, Roger, instituted to Duloe V., ii, 40; his death, ii, 49, 308^{b}.

---

dicta armentur prout facultates eorundem patiuntur, ita quod aliquibus certis die et loco . . . . citra vicesimum diem mensis Julii proxime futuri, in armis suis predictis coram vobis [the Commissioners in each of the four Archdeaconries] se exhibeant."

[1] Devenebyry—Devenebury, MS.

[2] "robas dum vixit nostras gerentis."

[3] "per Isoldam Wybbury, quondam uxorem Walteri Denys defuncti."

Deneys, Thomas, presents to Meeth R., ii, 123^{b}, 233^{b}; to Goodleigh R, ii, 158^{b}, 253^{b}, 349; to Bradford R., ii, 244; does homage, at Crediton, for lands at Hokeway and Carforde, in Crediton (3 Sept., 1415), ii, 311. *See*, also, i, 332.

Deneys, Walter, *see* Marhamchurch, i, 107, *and* Wybbury, Isolda, ii, 177^{b}.

Depedale, Richard, R. of St. Mary Arches, London, ii, 305.

Derby, All Saints, i, 300.

Derby, John, i, 305.

Derham, Richard, S.T.P., Dean of Great St. Martin's, London, ii, 89.

Derlyng, Thomas, priest,—

He was guilty of irregularity in marrying two couples clandestinely and without the knowledge of the Clergy-in-charge in either case, viz., John Ragger and Anna Lyndestan in a certain chapel within the parish of Dodbrooke, and John Andreu and Joan Fogheler in the parish church of Woodleigh. He was liable to excommunication, suspension, and interdict; but, on his humble petition and confession, a fitting penance was assigned, and a Dispensation granted (1 Feb., 1416-17), i, 229.

Derneford, *see* Durneford.

Derwent, William, V. of Tenterden, exchanges for Shobrooke R, ii, 79^{b}; i, 84; for Bratton [Clovelly] R., ii, 186; for South Perrott R. (Dioc. of Sarum), ii, 186^{b}.

Despenser, Richard, heir of Thomas le (a minor; by reason whereof Edward, Duke of York, was patron of Canonsleigh Abbey), ii, 125^{b}.

Despenser, Constance le, presents to the R. of Langtree, ii, 132^{b}; *see* also, ii, 239^{b}, 338, 339^{b}.

Devenysch, Thos. V. Choral in the Cathedral, i, 198.

Deverell, in the parish of St. Gwinear (*see* "Oratories"), i, 194.

Devon and Somerset, Sir William Bonevylle's bequests for the repair, etc., of the bridges on his demesnes in, i, 311^{b}.

Devon, Edward de Courtenay, Earl of, i, 61^{b}, 63, 76^{b}; ii, 256^{b}; his chapel in his mansion at Tiverton, i, 67^{b} (and Matilda, his Countess), i, 324^{b}; presents to Alphington, R., ii, 166, 256^{b}; to the Chantry of Brythlegh, ii, 17; to the Prebend of Carssewell, ii, 193; to Chawleigh, R., ii, 155; to Chulmleigh, R., ii, 81; to Prebendal Stalls in Chulmleigh, ii, 5^{b}, 14^{b}, 35^{b}, 101, 101^{b}, 173^{b}, 175^{b}, 188^{b}; to the Chantry at Colcombe, ii, 13; to the Preb. of Cutton, ii, 46^{b}, 90^{b}, 99^{b}; to Dolton, R., ii, 122^{b}; to All-Hallows, Goldsmith-street, Exeter, ii, 100; to St. Leonard's Exeter, ii, 268^{b}; to

Farway, ii, 129^b, 145^b, 164; to the Preb. of Heyes, ii, 67^b, 152; to Milton-Damarel, R., ii, 132^b (and 238), 150^b, 169^b, 173^b, 190, 341, 341^b[1]; to Musbury, R., ii, 67; to Northill, R., ii, 99, 169; to St. John-in-Cornwall, R., ii, 11, 56^b, 68; to Sampford-Courtenay, R., ii, 22^b, 74^b, 114^b, 201^b; to Shevioke, R., ii, 83^b 94; to Stoke Damarel, R., ii, 122^b; to Sticklepath Chapelry, ii, 6, 7; to the R. of Tiverton (1st Portion), ii, 150^b, 169^b; (2nd Portion), ii, 10, 74^b, 90^b, 99^b; (3rd Portion), ii, 24; to the R. of Woodleigh, ii, 93^b.

Dewdon, mansion of Simon Michel, i, 20. *See* "Oratories."

Deynsell, Thomas, *see* Widecombe, i, 180^b.

Deyman, John, chaplain, i, 310; instituted to Horwood R., ii, 79^b.

Dilapidations.—The Bishop's Mandate to the four Archdeacons as to the repair and maintenance of Chancels and Office-Books, houses and other buildings (9 Dec., 1410), i, 110.

Dittisham, Bosumshele in the parish of, i, 86^b.—William Underwoode, R. of; licence of non-residence for two years, from 13 June, 1396, i, 9; for two years[2], from 8 July, 1398, i, 20^b.—Reginald Bryta, R., i, 91, 93; licensed to preach in all Churches, etc., in the Diocese, except the Cathedral (20 June, 1411), i, 127^b; 168^b, 176; a Penitentiary in the Deanery of Totnes, i, 143; proxy for Richard Hoper, ii, 164^b.

Dobbe, Robert, proxy for Henry Hokisylle, ii, 36^b.

Doboner (*or* Boner) Martin de, V. of St. Feock, i, 26, 161.

Dodbrooke, Chapel of St. Mary "atte Wylle," in the parish of, licensed for Divine Service; but the Rector was not to be bound to find a chaplain to serve the same (4 April, 1403), i, 63; Chapel of Our Lady of Langewyll, at, ii, 244^b.—John Thomas, R. of; dispensation (to study at Oxford) for three years, from 5 May, 1403; but he was to take sub-deacon's Orders within a year, i, 64^b.—Richard Tryby, R. of, his resignation, on institution to the R. of Newton Ferrers, i, 245^b; *see*, also, ii, 357^b.—*See* Derlyng, Thomas, i, 229.—Sir Richard Champernoun of, i, 244^b, 333^b; his anchorite at, i, 334.—John Wytloff's bequest to the Church of, i, 306.

Dodyngton, Agnes and Amicia de, i, 301.

Dodyngton, John, Rector of Crewkerne, Canon of Crediton,

[1] It is stated here that he was Patron for two successive turns out of three.

[2] Undurwode, here, in the MS.

etc., i, 301, 320[b]; Canon of Exeter, ii, 212[b], 213, 226; collated Treasurer of Exeter Cathedral, ii, 42[b], having been previously appointed to assist Reginald Bryta in the administration of the affairs of Treasurer William Trevell, who was incapacitated by age (no date; it comes between 5 May and 18 May, 1398), ii, 217[b]; his Will, i, 301.

Dodyngton, Richard, *see* Oldcastel, i, 192[b].

Dodyngton, Walter, exchanges the R. of Clysthydon for that of Clyst St. Laurence, ii, 41; his death, ii, 74.

Doget, John, R. of St. George's, Exeter, ii, 336[b]; his death, ii, 132[b], 135.

Doget, Robert, R. of Clannaborough; licence of non-residence for a year, from 21 July, 1410, i, 100[b]; instituted to Ashreigny R., ii, 177[b]; licensed to celebrate in the House of the Vicars, Crediton (27 April, 1419), i, 246[b].

Dokeworthy, Edward, instituted to the R. of Bampton, ii, 8; his death, ii, 192.

Dollebeare, Ralph, commissioned as Apparitor-general of the Diocese (28 July, 1396), ii, 211; proxy for William Grym (q.v.), and for Stephen Reskyer (q.v.)—*See*, also, i, 141, 142, 306[b]; ii, 275, 336[b], 351.

Dollebeare, Walter, R. of Southill, i, 104, 197[b], ii, 54[b], 211, 227.

Dollynge, Thomas, i, 329[b].

Dolbiry, John, instituted to Landcross, ii, 20; [resigns and is] instituted to Totnes V., ii, 95.

Dolton, William Carvek (*or* Carvell), R. of, i, 43[b].—Stowford in the parish of, i, 207.

Domet, John, of Uffculme, i, 160 ; ii, 247.

Dommewyll, Walter, instituted to the V. of Berry Pomeroy, ii, 12; his death[1], ii, 158[b]; *see*, also[2], ii, 253.

Dona, Chapel of St. Leonard at, in Axmouth, i, 238[b].

Donk (*or* Douk), John, *see* Govys, John.

Donnyng (*or* Dounyng), William, V. of Ashford (deceased), ii, 154.

Donyell, Nicholas, V. of Linkinhorne (q.v.), i, 50.

Dorchester [Dorset], The Friars of, i, 311, 320[b].

Dotton [ecclesia de Dodyngton, in the Deanery of Aylesbeare.—*See* Taxation of Pope Nicholas],—

Commission: Against those who resorted to the Church and Churchyard there,

---

[1] "Dounewell," MS.

[2] "Dunnewyll," MS.

for the purpose of holding fairs and markets therein (directed to the Dean of Aylesbeare and [Walter Caprugg] V. of Otterton, 10 July, 1400), ii, 227.

Doty, Richard, V. of Launcells, i, 38b; exchanges for St. Lawrence, Exeter, ii, 26; and again for Staverton, ii, 70b; 160b.

Doune (or Downe), John, instituted to Abbotsham V., ii, 17; and to the Chantry of Umberleigh [Womberley MS.], ii, 52b.

Downe, Matthew, instituted to Parracombe R., ii, 7b; resigns, ii, 50; collated to a Canonry and Prebend (of Westbrook), in Bosham, ii, 92b; and exchanges immediately for Bratton [Clovelly], *ibid;* resigns, ii, 106; exchanges his R. (or Portion) de la Grene in the Church of Wodensden (Dioc. of Lincoln) and his Wardenship of the free chapelry of Crofton (Dioc. of Salisbury), for Whimple R., ii, 98; instituted to Cruwys-Morchard R., ii, 104b; exchanges Whimple for Bampton, and is collated to a Canonry in Exeter Cathedral, ii, 192; exchanges Cruwys-Morchard for Farringdon R., ii, 194b; co-patron of Georgenympton R., ii, 99; *see*, also, i, 324b, ii, 306b.

Downe, Thomas, i, 332; presented to Highampton R., ii, 245b.

Downe, William, instituted to the R. of Dolton, ii, 122b.

Dounebryge, William, Canon of Exeter, i, 301.

Dounham, James, scholar—*Dispensacio super defectu natalium* (23 Sept., 1413), i, 184b,

Dowelton, John, *see* Cook, Thomas, ii, 252.

Dowland,[1] R., appropriated to Canonsleigh Abbey, ii, 359b.

Down Thomas, in the parish of Plympton, i, 237.

Down St. Mary, the parish church of,—

The Bishop grants an Indulgence to the Faithful contributing to the rebuilding of the nave and tower thereof—"Cum . . . navis ecclesie Sancte Marie de Downe juxta Crediton . . . . . cum ipsius ecclesie campanili fuerat et sic vetustate consumpta quod jam tarde, pro majori parte, ad terram extat ejecta funditus et prostrata, parochianique ipsius ecclesie, ad quos ipsorum navis et campanilis pertinet reparacio et reedificacio, tante paupertatis dispendio subjacere noscantur quod ad eorum reparacionem, quin verius *novam construccionem*, etc." (15 Nov., 1413), i, 189b.

Downes, Joan, *sacrista* of Canonsleigh Abbey, ii, 125.

Doyggel, Richard, a parishioner of Linkinhorne, i, 116.

Drake, John, R. of Whimple, i, 62, 72; exchanges in 1407 for certain preferment in the Dioceses of Lincoln and Salisbury (*see* Downe, Matthew), ii, 98.—A John Drake is recorded to have resigned the V. of St. Stephen's, Saltash (in 1398), ii, 36b.—*See*, also, i, 332.

---

[1] Doughlond, MS.

Drake, Richard, clerk, i 301b.

Drake, Stephen, chaplain, i, 314.

Drayton, John, instituted to Sutcombe R., ii, 82 ; i, 73b, 76b ; exchanges for Kingsbury (Dioc. of B. and W.), ii, 102b.

Drayton, Richard, i, 323b.

Drayton, Robert, and John Chishull, their Chantry in St. Paul's Cathedral, ii, 155b.

Drenck, Henry, proxy for John Osborn, ii, 50.

Drew, Benedict, proxy for William Fylham, ii, 199.

Drew, Henry, i, 334.

Drewe, John, instituted to Landcross R., ii, 10 ; (deceased), ii, 12.

Drewe, William, V. of Littleham, exchanges for the V. of Brimpton Regis (Dioc. of Bath and Wells), ii, 87.

Drewsteignton, Robert, R. of, appointed co-adjutor to Richard Colebrugg, R. of Roborough (26 Sept., 1402), ii, 23 ; appointed a Penitentiary in the Deanery of Dunsford, i, 143, 173b, 194, 207b, 216b, 231, 237b, 245.

Dreyn, Michael, accolite,—Dispensation[1] in his favour (18 Sept., 1399), i, 29.

Drocus, collated by Bishop Walter de Bronescombe to the V. of St. Perran [Zabulo][2], in 1269, i, 195.

Dublin, David Russell, a Dominican Friar of, i, 101b.

Duffelde, John, i, 327b.

Duk (or Duke), Peter, V. of St. Mary Church, exchanges for Ashburton, V., ii, 34 ; exchanges again for Widecombe, ii, 57 ; and again for Harberton, ii, 86 ; i, 94, 115t,143 ; commissioned to prove the Will of Sir John de la Pomeray, knt. (1 Oct., 1416), ii, 260.—*See*, also, ii, 267.

Duloe [Duloo, MS.], the Church of [St. Kyby], i, 323 ; Chapel of St. Mary "atte Hille" in the parish of (*see* Landawarner—*Oratories*), i, 61b.—The Rectory of,—Lanrak, Thomas, sub-deacon, R. ; dispensation (to study at Oxford) for one year, from 30 Aug., 1395, i, 5 ; ditto (from 4 Jan., 1396-7), i, 10b ; letters dimissory to any *English* Bishop, that he might be ordained deacon and priest,

[1] He had been ordained without licence, "ab alieno Episcopo . . . Thoma, Crispolitano Episcopo." The Bishop refers with satisfaction to the fact that, having done this thing ignorantly and inadvertently, Dreyn had abstained from exercising his office, and he speaks of himself as having been specially moved in this case, "fusis a te nobis devotis precibus ob tuorum exuberanciam meritorum paterna pietate inclinati."

[2] He is described as "de eadem [ecclesia] presbitero."

were granted to him (9 May, 1397), i, 12; but he was ordained deacon "ab *alieno* Episcopo," Nicholas, Bishop of Dunkeld, and priest by the Bishop of Winchester; this rendered a dispensation necessary, which was granted 20 April, 1398, i, 17ᵇ; and on the same day a licence of non-residence, that he might reside for two years in Oxford, *ibid;* co-patron of the V. of Duloe, ii, 40, 49, 141ᵇ.—*See*, also, ii, 246, 308ᵇ.—The Vicarage of,—

[*Breve Regium*].—Prohibition to admit any Clerk to the Vicarage, then vacant, pending a settlement of the dispute as to the right of patronage between the Rector (Thomas Lanrak) and John Colshill and Roger Denys, clerk (27 Oct., 1398), ii, 308ᵇ.

Thomas Estbrok, V. of, appointed a Penitentiary in the Deanery of West, i, 93ᵇ, 115ᵇ, 143ᵇ, 174, 194ᵇ, 207ᵇ, 217, 231ᵇ, 238, 245ᵇ.—*See* ii, 82, 237, 333.—

Commission of enquiry as to the right of patronage, John Colshull, domicellus, and the R., Thomas Laurak, having presented Robert Ousthorp, chaplain (17 May, 1412): the result (which was certified by Henry Wynnegode, LL.B., the Bishop's Official-Peculiar in Cornwall (in St. Mary's Chapel at Looe) was that the presentation was good; ii, 246.

Dunchideock, the Rectory House, etc., at,—

Indulgence granted (26 Jan., 1395-6), to the Faithful who should contribute to its rebuilding—"ad reedificacionem domorum mansi Rectorie ecclesie parochialis de Dunschidiok ad humum funditus prostratorum," i, 7ᵇ.—About two years and a half later, Matthew Stoke, priest, made formal complaint to the Bishop, that in a certain case touching the repair or rebuilding of the chancel of the parish church, and of the manse and other houses belonging to the Rectory, which had been heard before Thomas Tredowargh, a pretended commissary or delegate of Ralph Tregrisiou, (Dean of Exeter and Vicar-General), between John Lange, R. of the said parish, plaintiff, and the said Matthew Stoke, defendant, the said pretended Commissary, though he had no jurisdiction in the matter, proceeded, illegally, and favouring the plaintiff more than was right, to deliver a definitive sentence in the said John's favour, and entirely against the other side; which sentence was null and void; yet because he disobeyed it, one John Dawny, a chaplain, calling himself a special commissary of the said Thomas, had caused him to be threatened with suspension *ab ingressu ecclesie*, and with the greater excommunication—*minus canonice*. He had, moreover, at the instance of the said John, caused it to be publickly announced that he had been so suspended and excommunicated, to his great prejudice and injury. The Bishop, accordingly, commissioned Robert Rugge, Archdeacon of Barnstaple, and Walter Gybbes and Walter Levenaunt, Canons of Exeter, to hear the case on its merits and decide the matter (9 Jun., 1398), i, 19ᵇ.

—John Prous, R. of, (*primam tonsuram clericalem habenti*); dispensation (to study at Oxford), for three years, from 25 Nov., 1411, i, 140ᵇ; ditto[1] (sub-deacon), for four years, from 15 Oct., 1414, i, 202ᵇ.—*See*, also, i, 245.

Dunham, John, Canon of Frithelstock, ii, 183ᵇ.

Dunkeld, Nicholas, Bishop of, *see* Duloe.

---

[1] Prouez—Donsshydyoke, MS.

Dunkeswell Abbey, i, 318,—
Commission to Henry Nony, Bishop of Ardagh, for the Benediction of Alexander Burlescombe, as Abbot thereof (25 Aug., 1397), ii, 212b.—Commission to the same Bishop for the Benediction of Richard Lamport[1], Abbot-elect (17 July, 1399), ii, 225b.—Commission to William, Bishop of Caithness, for the Benediction as Abbot of John Bokelond, monk thereof (10 June, 1419), ii, 267b.

Dunmeer (near Bodmin), the wood and mill of, i, 21.

Dunneworth, Agnes, *see* Wyssynton, William, i, 185b.

Dunnyng, Robert (Dioc. of Bath and Wells), a notary-publick, i, 116, 320b, 325b, 326; instituted to the R. of All Hallows-on-the-Walls, Exeter, ii, 135b; 172; resigns, and is instituted to the R. of Holy Trinity, Exeter, ii, 176.

Dunsbeare, [Dynsbeare] Chapel of the Holy Trinity at, in the parish of Merton, i, 71.

Dunscombe, Richard[2], instituted to the R. of Shevioke, ii, 94; resigns, and is instituted to the R. of Northill, ii, 169.—Richard Donscombe (or Dunscombe) was instituted to the Prebend of Cutton in 1419, ii, 201.

Dunscombe or Dounscomb, William, chaplain, commissioned—*ad vendicandum clericos convictos coram Judicibus Secularibus*, in Devon (20[3] June, 1395), ii, 209b.—R. of Poughill; exchanges for St. Merryn, V., ii, 28b; exchanges again for North Bovey, R., ii, 38; his death, ii, 189b.

Dunsford, R., appropriated to Canonsleigh Abbey, ii, 359b.

Dunsford, Thomas Loteby, V. of, appointed a Penitentiary in the Deanery of Dunsford, i, 50, 94, 115, 143, 173b, 194, 207b, 216b, 231, 237b, 245.—*See*, also, i, 135 (*Oratories*).

Dunste, Richard, instituted to Buckland Brewer, V., ii, 85b.

Dunterton, John Halsanger, R. of; licence of non-residence from 12 Jan., 1411-12 to Michaelmas, 1412, i, 141; also, for one year, from 29 Sept., 1413, i, 185.—Clerk, John of, i, 135.

Durburgh, James, *see* Ringmore (*Institutions*).

Durden, John, instituted to the R. of Arlington, ii, 6b.

Durham, Richard (Dean of the Free Chapel of St. Martin, London), John Haget (Canon of Exeter), and Maior

[1] He was one of those found to be in arrear of Procurations due to the Pope's Collector for three years (1408-1410), i, 105.

[2] Called "William," apparently by a clerical error, at i, 173.

[3] "vicesimo . . . . . . die Junii": a blank was left here and never filled in.

Parys (R. of Pillaton), appointed by the Bishop his Proctors "to visit the Threshold of the Apostles" (3 March, 1409-10), i, 94b.

Durke, John, i, 312.

Durneford, Stephen, of Plymouth, patron of the R. of Drewsteignton, ii, 1b; of St. Pancras, Exeter, ii, 2; Sheriff of Devon,—to administer the oath to him (*Breve Regium*, 10 Nov., 1417), ii, 361.

Durneford, William, and Alice his wife, present to the R. of Parkham, ii, 92.—*See*, also, *Oratories*, and ii, 307b.

Durnell, Thomas, instituted to the R. of Okeford, ii, 179, 259b; i, 231b, 241b.

Duyn, John, instituted to the R. of Ideford, ii, 25.

Dyber, William, Warden of the Free Chapel of Kingston Russell (Dioc. of Salisbury), exchanges for the R. of St. Ive, ii, 54; i, 61; exchanges for the V. of Buckland Abbas (Dioc. of Salisbury), ii, 104.—*See*, also, i, 320b.

Dyer, Edward, i, 312.

Dyer, Roger, of Kingston, ii, 292.

Dygher, William, i, 325, 333.

Dyghere, Robert, V. of Morebath, resigns, ii, 85b.

Dyghte, John, clerk, ii, 46, 47, 49, 50, 50b (notary-publick), ii, 60, 60b, 61.—Commission to, as Registrar of the Consistory Court (1 Aug., 1395), ii, 209b; collated to St. Stephen's, Exeter, ii, 80; his death, ii, 87b.—*See*, also, i, 302.

Dygne, John, scholar—*Dispensacio super defectu natalium* (4 Dec., 1396), i, 10.

Dygon, John (Canon of Plympton), instituted to Thornbury, R., ii, 75; i, 71b, 72b, 85b, 100b; instituted to Meavy, R., ii, 98; resigns Meavy, ii, 121; and Thornbury, ii, 139.

Dygson, Nicholas, collated to a Canonry in Bosham, ii, 198.

Dygon, Richard, chaplain, *see* St. Feock, i, 161.

Dygon, Thomas, V. of Kingston (Dioc. of B. and W.), exchanges for Parracombe, R., ii, 79b, i, 73, 83b; resigns, ii, 153b.

Dylyngton Matilda (widow of Richard), *see* Washfield, ii, 259b, 356b.—*See* Dynyngton.

Dymmok, John, of Ermington, ii, 275.

Dyne, Peter, V. of Spreyton, resigns, ii, 88.

Dynham, Sir John, knt.; licence to choose a confessor (19 Feb., 1396-7), i, 11b.—Patron of South Pool, R., ii, 8; of Roche, R., ii, 8b, 12b, 51b; of the Chantry of St. Katherine at

Hemyock, ii, 195^b; presents[1] to St. George's, Exeter, ii, 234^b; does homage to the Bishop, at Clyst, for lands at Kennerleigh, in Crediton (4 Feb., 1406-7), ii, 310^b.

Dynham, Matilda, wife of Sir John; licence to choose a confessor (26 Nov., 1396), i, 9^b.

Dyneham, Oliver de, patron of St. George's, Exeter, ii, 336^b.

Dynyngton, in [Bishop's] Tawton, *see* Holeway, William, ii, 311.

Dynyngton (*sic*), John, co-patron of Washfield, ii, 168.—*See* Dylyngton.

Dypphull, John, *see* Chagford (*Institutions*), ii, 33^b.

Dyre, John, chaplain, V. of St. Anthony in Kerrier, resigns, ii, 164^b,—*See*, also, i, 332.

Dyrehyll, James, instituted to Marhamchurch, ii, 188, 263^b.

Dyrell, Thomas, a chorister of Exeter, i, 326^b.

Dyrwyn, Joan, wife of Robert, her Will, i, 323.

Dyrwyn, Margery, sister, and William, son of Joan, *ibid.*

E.

Ealdstrete[2], Prebend of, in St. Paul's, London, ii, 43, 226.

East Allington, Richard Olyver, R. of, i, 186^b; a Penitentiary in the Deanery of Woodleigh, i, 143, 174, 194^b, 207^b.—*See*, also, ii, 112^b, 357.

East Anstey, the Church of, i, 319^b.

East Bradleigh, in the parish of Tiverton, chapel of St. Katherine at, licensed 2 July, 1400, i, 43.

East Ogwell [MS., Estwogg], Thomas Ferrers, R. of, a Penitentiary in the Deanery of Kenn, i, 50.

East Worlington [Estwolryngton, MS.], John Richard (*alias* Woborn), sub-deacon, R. of; dispensation (to study at Oxford) for three years, from 21 August, 1400, i, 45; licence[3] of non-residence for two years, from 28 Nov., 1404, i, 72.

Edmund, Roger, of Kingston, ii, 277^b.

Edneves, John, V. of Newton St. Cyres, i, 138.

---

[1] But found not to be the true patron.

[2] Also "Eeldstrete," MS.

[3] Called "John Woborn" only, in this place.

Edward, John, of Apuldram, ii, 293^b.

Efford, in the parish of Stratton, Cornwall, *see* Bude, manor[1] of John Arundell at, i, 190.

Egerdon, William, Canon of Exeter, *see* Ekerdon.

Egg-Buckland [Ecbokelond, MS.], John Mottelegh chaplain, appointed co-adjutor to John Tappyng, V. (23 Oct., 1402), ii, 23.

Egloshayle; William Cornewale, V., his dispute with the Prior and Convent of Bodmin (*see* Cornewale, Wm.), i, 21.—Chapel of St. Nicholas, Pendevy, in this parish; licence granted to the Prior of Bodmin (15 Feb., 1403-4), i, 69^b.

Egloscruk, i.e. St. Issey (q. v.); not "Egloskerry," as in Oliver's List of Parishes in the *Monasticon*.

Eglosros, *see* Philleigh.

Ekerdon, John, i, 320.

Ekerdon or Egerdon (also Ekerton, MS.), William, collated to a Canonry in Exeter Cathedral, ii, 80; licensed to celebrate in any suitable place within the Diocese (16 Nov., 1413), i, 189^b; his death, ii, 154; his Will[2], i, 320^b; *see*, also, ii, 237^b, 281^b.

Elerky, *see* Veryan.

Elie, John, R. of Meshaw, resigns, ii, 8^b.

Elmede, John, proxy for John Pyke, ii, 42^b.

Ellomede, Thomas, i, 303^b.

Elston[3], manor of, in the parish of Churchstow, i, 318^b.

Elwel, Thomas R. of St. Pinnock, exchanges for Cold Aston (Dioc. of Worcester), ii, 351, 352.

Elyot, Edmund, clerk, i, 320^b; ii, 281^b.

Elys (*alias* Helys), John; a case of violation of Sanctuary.—

"Item, VI^{to} die mensis predicti, ibidem [in London], emanavit Commissio directa Decano Ecclesie Exoniensis, ad denunciandum, seu denunciari faciendum, omnes illos excommunicatos fuisse et esse in genere, qui extraxerunt Johannem Elys, *alias* Helys, fugientem ad Ecclesiam Cathedralem Exoniensem ex causa immunitatis habende (6 Aug., 1396), i, 9,

An Indulgence was granted by the Bishop, 3 Nov., 1398, to the Faithful who should contribute to the relief of John Elys, of the County of Essex, whose houses and all his property had recently been totally destroyed by fire, so that he was reduced to absolute poverty, and had nothing left to support his wife and children, i, 22.

---

[1] Effard, MS.

[2] From which it appears that he was also Rector of Longbridge (Dioc. of Sarum).

[3] Alwyston, MS.—"Aileston" in Sir William Pole's time; *hodie* "Elston."

Elys, Simon, R. of Harford (q. v.)—*See*, also, i, 67,

Elys, Thomas, Priest of St. Mary's Chantry at Herne, Kent, exchanges for Poughill, R., ii, 65ᵇ; resigns ii, 147ᵇ.

Enachdune[1] Henry, Bp. of—Commission to ordain and confirm, etc., in the Diocese (3 Sept., 1395), ii, 210; also to bless William Paderstow as Abbot of Buckfast (Sept. 1395), ii, 210ᵇ.

Ermington, "Brigg" (i.e. Ivybridge, in the parish of, i, 69ᵇ, 112.—*See* Dymmok (*Oratories*).—" Ordinacio " touching the Chapel and new Cemetery of Kingston in this parish (*see* Kingston), ii, 275.—Manor of Woodland, i, 195ᵇ.—Worthele (*see* Topcliff, Thomas), i, 238.—William Falewell, R. of; licence of non-residence for two years, from 20 April, 1396, i, 8ᵇ; his Will proved, i, 12; 300.—Richard Tyttesbury, R. of (see *Oratories*), i, 36, 37; licence to choose a Confessor (10 April, 1400), *ibid.*—Thomas Redman, R. of, and also of Kenn, licence of non-residence for one year, from 25 July, 1410, i, 100ᵇ.—John Stybbe, chaplain, see *Oratories*, i, 85.—Thomas Rowe, V. of, i, 313.

The Prior of Montacute [in Somerset] is referred to, in 1411, as "Rectorem sive proprietarium ecclesiarum parochialium Sancti Neoti in Cornubia, et Monkelegh, ac medietatis ecclesie de Ermyngton," ii, 339.

Ernam, John, R. of St. Dominick, resigns, ii, 7ᵇ.

Erth [Erte, MS.], in St. Stephen's by Saltash, i, 186.

Esoth, John, clerk,—*Dispensacio super defectu natalium* (13 Sept., 1400), i, 47ᵇ.

Esse Boleyn, in the parish of Crediton, i, 82.

Esse, Giles de, co-patron of the R. of Ashreigny, ii, 156, 177.

Esse, Joan, daughter of Giles, *see* Clayssch, ii, 231ᵇ.

Esse, Thomas de, *see* Exeter, St. George's, ii, 340ᵇ.

Esse, William, clerk—*Dispensacio super defectu natalium* (31, May, 1401), ii, 18ᵇ.—In i, 73ᵇ is the following entry,—

"Item, eisdem die[2] et loco[3], Dominus [dispensavit] cum Willelmo Esse, clerico, Exoniensis Diocesis, ut in prima tonsura clericali, quam tacito, de defectu natalium quem patitur de soluto genito et soluta incaute, aliter tamen canonice, suscepit, injuncta primitus sibi pro excessu hujusmodi penitentia salutari, libere ministrare, necnon ad omnes alios minores ordines licite aspirare et promoveri, ac beneficium ecclesiasticum, cui cura novi iminet (*sic*), animarum, recipere et licite retinere valeat, hujusmodi defectu non obstante."

---

[1] Now a village called Annaghdown, in the Diocese of Tuam.

[2] 14 March, 1404-5.

[3] At Crediton.

Essex, the Archdeaconry of, *see* Prentys, Edward, ii, 357^{b}.

Estebrok, Richard, V. of Okehampton, his Will, i, 321.

Estebrok, Thomas, instituted to Duloe, V., ii, 49, 49^{b}, 82, 55, 237, 333; resigns Duloe, and is collated Dean of Crediton, ii, 141^{b}; i, 231; resigns Crediton, and is collated Sub-Dean of Exeter and Penitentiary, ii, 187.—

Thomas Estbrok, LL.B., was appointed Official Peculiar, etc., in Cornwall, ii, 230^{b}. The date is omitted, but it must have been between Feb. 1405-6 and Feb. 1407-8. He received a Commission as "Examinator in Consistorio Exoniensi generalis," 20 Sept., 1417; ii, 263. As Sub-Dean he complained of the bad condition in which his predecessor, Thomas Noell, had left the manse, garden, etc., and the Bishop (24 Sept., 1417), commissioned Richard Penels, Canon of Exeter, to examine the premises and report, ii, 263.—*See*, also, i, 321.

Estcolmp (or Estcolm), Canon of Glasney and R. of Stoke Damarel (deceased), ii, 122^{b}, 123^{b}.—*See*, also, ii, 248.

Estcot, manor of, in the parish of Morebath, i, 60.

Estyngton, in the parish of North Tawton, ii, 8, 334.

Estmond, Thomas, i, 303^{b}.

Estrepeny, William, Prior of Cowick, resigns, ii, 37.

Esturmy, Sir William, knt., presents to Tedburn St. Mary, ii, 196^{b}, 267; to Heanton Punchardon, ii, 247; (with Joan, his wife) to the Chantry of the B. V. M. at Heanton Punchardon, ii, 251^{b}.—*See*, also, ii, 344^{b}, 345.

Etewell (or Ettewell), John, instituted to Lustleigh, R., ii, 17; resigns, ii, 93^{b}.—John Etvel, a priest (possibly the same), was assaulted in the Cathedral-yard by one William Glyn, ii, 225^{b}.

Eustas, Roger, instituted to the R. of Lew Trenchard, ii, 12.

Everard, William, proxy for Richard Courtenay, ii, 67^{b}.

Eweny, Thomas, instituted to the Chantry in the parish Church of Alwington, ii, 135^{b}.

Ewty, John, ii, 264.

Exbourne, Richard Hurst, R.; his Will, i, 315.—John Bornebury, sub-deacon, R.; dispensation (to study at Oxford) for two years, and not to be bound to proceed to the higher Orders in the interim, from 6 May, 1414, i, 196; licence of non-residence for a year, from 6 May, 1416, i, 315.

Excestre, John, Canon of Exeter, exchanges for the R. of Ipplepen, ii, 31^{b}.—*See*, also, i, 20.

Exebrig, Richard, ii, 213.

Exeter Cathedral,—

"The Bishop writes to the President of the Consistorial Court, the Archdeacons, the Deans Rural, etc., granting an Indulgence to the Faithful who should contribute to the completion, decoration, and maintenance of the Cathedral church, which he describes as "vestra mater et magistra omnium ecclesiarum nostre Diocesis." Collections were to be made every Sunday in Lent and even up to the Octave of Easter, "usque ad consummacionem dicte fabrice et claustri eidem annexi, ac refeccionis eorundum; cum eandem ecclesiam matrem suam saltem semel in anno venerari actualiter teneantur, et absque Christi fidelium elemosinarum largicione facultates ad fabricam ecclesie et claustri prescripti, ut ex testimonio fidedignorum accepimus, non sufficiant." The Bishop orders the collections to be confined to this work—"aliis questoribus quibuscumque pro eodem tempore dumtaxat exclusis." All moneys so raised were to be paid in immediately after Easter every year, under pain of the greater excommunication if any portion thereof were kept back (3 Feb., 1398-9), i, 25.

Letter from the Bishop, addressed to Walter Gybbes and Henry Brokelond, canons, for the correction of an abuse in the case, especially, of William Broun, a Vicar. He interfered with the chaplains appointed to commemorate the Anniversaries of former Bishops and Benefactors, by taking the office and work and the stipends also (2 March, 1396-7), ii, 212.

The Bishop's Mandate (addressed to the Dean or President), for the Visitation of the Cathedral on the Monday next after the Feast of St. Mark Evangelist, (i.e. April 26—a Sunday, in 1400) to correct and reform whatever in the fabrick itself, or in the Ministers of whatsoever Dignity, may stand in need of correction or reformation. All Canons, Prebendaries, Vicars, Annivellars, etc., were to appear in the Chapter-House at the hour of Prime, or thereabout, and they were to produce their Letters of Orders and their Titles to their Benefices. To the Dean the Bishop adds—"Vos etiam, Domine Decane, ad predictos diem et locum, tenore presentium peremptorie citamus, quatenus ad vos attinet ad omnia et singula supra dicta (5 April, 1400), i, 34[b].

Commission, directed to John Schillyngford, D.C.L., and Richard Hals, Licentiate in Laws, "ad procedendum in Visitacione ecclesie Exoniensis (7 July, 1400), ii, 227.

—Bequests to the Cathedral, by John Prestecote, i, 318; by Canon Wm. Poundestoke, i, 321[b]; by Canon Wm. Ekerdon, i, 320[b]; by Canon Wm. Langeton, i, 322; by Dean Tregrisiow, i, 323; by Archdeacon Hunden (for "the new Library"), i, 325; by Canon Baldwin de Schyllyngford (for the fabrick and Treasury), i, 330.

For the List of *Deans, Precentors, Chancellors, Treasurers, Archdeacons, Sub-deans* and *Canons, see* "Institutions, Collations, etc."

List of Canons present at the election of Dean Payne (18 Sep., 1415), ii, 170.

Dean and Chapter of, in arrear of Procurations due to the Pope's Collector, for three years (1408-10), i, 105, 110,—They present to the Benefices of Ashburton, Branscombe, Broadhembury, Buckerell, Colebrook, Colyton, Dawlish; in Exeter,—(1) All Hallows-on-the-Walls, (2) St. Kerrian, (3) St. Martin, (4) St. Paul's, (5) St. Petrock's, (6) Tri-

Exeter Cathedral—continued.
nity,—Gwennap, Harberton, Heavitree, Littleham, V., Morthoe, Mullyon,[1] St. Breward, St. Erth, St. Mary Church, St. Winnow, Salcombe [Regis], Sancreed, Sidbury, Staverton, Thorverton, Trevalga, Upottery, Veryan, Westleigh, West Anstey, Widecombe[-in-the-Moor], Winkleigh (*see* the *Institutions*).

Exeter, Southernhay,[2] i, 319 ; Roger Batyn, citizen of, i, 315 ; Richard Bolde, of, i, 242ᵇ ; foundation of Bonevyll's Alms-Houses in Combe Street, i, 311ᵇ ; Richard Boson, citizen of, i, 317 ; Richard and John Bosyn, of, i, 315 ; the new Conduit (Grendon's Will), i, 316 ; (Wilford's Will), i, 319ᵇ ; Simon Grendon, citizen of, i, 315ᵇ ; Thomas Reymound's house in, i, 332 ; John Spycer, of, i, 318 ; William Wilford, citizen of, i, 319ᵇ.—The Mayor, etc., present to the R. of St. Edmunds, Exeter, ii, 151ᵇ.—The Chantry in the Bishop's Palace, *see* Matheu, John, ii, 44 ; and Burgoun, John, ii, 154.—College of Vicars' Choral, i, 329, 330.

The Friars Minors of, i, 8, 131ᵇ, 301ᵇ, 302ᵇ, 303, 305, 307ᵇ, 308ᵇ, 309, 310ᵇ, 312ᵇ, 314ᵇ, 316, 317, 318, 319ᵇ, 320ᵇ, 321ᵇ, 326, 328ᵇ, 329ᵇ, 330, 331, 331ᵇ.

The Friars Preachers of, i, 302ᵇ, 303, 305, 307ᵇ, 308ᵇ, 310ᵇ 311, 312ᵇ, 314ᵇ, 316, 317, 318, 319ᵇ, 320ᵇ, 321ᵇ, 326, 327, 328ᵇ, 329ᵇ, 330, 330ᵇ, 331, 331ᵇ.—Dominican Convent —the Bishop's dispensation for the incorporation of an Irish Friar, David Russell, of Dublin (4 Aug., 1400), i, 101.

The Hospital of St. John at, i, 95ᵇ, 301, 301ᵇ, 302ᵇ, 303, 305, 309, 310ᵇ, 311, 312ᵇ, 316, 317, 318, 319ᵇ, 321ᵇ, 326, 327, 328, 328ᵇ, 330, 330ᵇ, 331, 331ᵇ, 332ᵇ. John Rowe, a poor Clerk of, i, 313ᵇ.—The Master and Brethren present to the R. of Yarnscombe, ii, 106, 141ᵇ, 166.

The Master and Brethren, having represented to the Bishop that their Church had been dedicated on the Feast of St. Lambert, and that it frequently happened that the Services proper to their Dedication Festival could not be held, the Bishop complied with their request that the day might be changed, and transferred the said Festival to the second Sunday after the Feast of St. Cosmos and St. Damian.—29 July, 1418 ; i, 241ᵇ.

Churches appropriated to, ii, 359ᵇ.—Matilda Latymer—also, Sir John Hulle, knt., buried in their Church, i, 329.

The Hospital (or *Lazar-House*) *of St. Mary Magd.*, i, 302ᵇ, 306ᵇ, 309, 316, 318ᵇ, 319ᵇ, 326, 330, 331, 331ᵇ, 332ᵇ.

---

[1] Now in the Bishop's gift.

[2] Southynghay, MS.

Exeter—continued.

St. Nicholas Priory, i, 316, 318, 327.—The Prior and Convent present to Brampford Speke, V., ii, 75, 188b; to Butterleigh, R., ii, 23; to Collumpton, V., ii, 134, 175b; to Pinhoe, V., ii, 27b, 92, 183; to Poughill, R., ii, 7b, 28b, 66, 147b, 197; to St. Olave's, Exeter, ii, 74, 166b.—

"*Disautenticacio sigilli Domus Sancti Nicholai Exoniensis*":—On the 3rd of December, 1400, the Bishop, being at Chudleigh, wrote to John Westecote, R. of St. Petrock's, Exeter, and to the Dean of Christianity, informing them that, on the 8th of November, some iniquitous persons had stolen a case containing the seal of the Priory, which had been incautiously left lying about in their Chapter-House, contrary to the will of William Mershe, the Prior, who earnestly besought the Bishop to apply a remedy, as they were in danger of loss from forged and fictitious deeds which the thieves might fabricate, and seal with the said seal; which is thus described,—"rotundum fuerat, habens in medio insculptum ad instar et similitudinem castri quadrati habentis in sui medio unam turrim excelsam, et in angulis suis alias turres bassiores et propugnacula, et supra castrum hujusmodi in una parte vetus scutum armorum Regis Anglie videlicet cum tribus leopardis, et in alia parte gladium erectum, et in ejusdem gladii cuspide, sive punctu, coronam regiam, et subtus castrum draconem gradientem, insculpta. In circumferencia vero, sive circulo, ejusdem sigilli scriptum erat sic: S. Ecclie Sancti Nichi Exon." The Bishop's official had decreed, and the Bishop confirms the decree, that the said seal should be regarded as "disautenticatum, dampnatum, et annullatum," and of no force at all, in the case of all deeds sealed therewith since the said 8th of November; and that it was never again to be accounted the authentick seal of the Priory, but that another seal should be at once prepared "cum diversa sculptura et de alia forma." The thieves were to be threatened with excommunication unless, within fifteen days, the seal were restored to the Priory, to be destroyed and broken up[1], i, 51.

The Parishes and Chapelries of,—

St. Clement's, *see* Heavitree.

St. David's, *see* Heavitree.

St. Edmund's, John Potter, of, i, 122b.

St. George's,—

Commissions of enquiry as to the right of presentation, addressed to the Archdeacon of Exeter: (1) 23 Oct., 1410; for William Sechevill, chaplain, presented by John Uffiete, domicellus. (2) 28 Oct., 1410; for John Halsanggere, chaplain, presented by Sir John Dynham, knt. (3) 31 Oct., 1410; for John Chaddesley, chaplain, presented by Joan, relict of John Speke, jun.,

---

[1] Dr. Oliver, in the *Monasticon*, gives an engraving of this seal, from a deed dated 1 April, 1387; it corresponds accurately with the description given above, except that the inscription is in a less abbreviated form than in the text of the MS.—"Sigillum Eccle Sci Nicholai Exonie." He gives another circular seal, of similar design; but in this a second shield of arms occupies the place of the sword and crown, and the dragon becomes a bird: the inscription is—"Sigillum Prioratus Ecclesie Sancti Nicholai Exonie," and this was, probably, the substituted seal. There is yet a third seal, with a similar castle, but no shields, or other like device, and instead of the dragon (or bird) a scroll: the inscription is the same as in the first seal.

Exeter—continued.

and daughter and heir of Martin Fyschakre; ii, 234[b].—(4) 19 Nov., 1410; for Richard Mannyng, presented by King Henry IV., ii, 235. (5) 24 Nov., 1410; for Richard Lyle, chaplain, presented by Margaret, Countess of Somerset, ii, 235[b].

[*Breve Regium*], Mandamus to the Bishop to search the Registers and certify the king as to the names of all persons instituted to this Benefice since 40 Edw. III. (dated 12 Nov., 1410), ii, 335[b].

[*Breve Regium*], Prohibition to admit to this Benefice, pending the settlement of the dispute as to the right of patronage, between the King and John Uffiete and William Sachevyll (dated 12 Nov., 1410), *ibid.*

The Bishop's Certificate as to the result of the search:—In *Grandisson's* Register he had found that William Danyell "de Eton Meisi" was admitted 17 July, 1347; patron, Sir John de Ralegh, of Beaudeport, knt., as proxy for Oliver de Dyneham: also, that on the 3rd of Jan., 1359-60, John Lucas, priest, was collated, by lapse: also, that on the 9th of June, 1363, Simon Squyer, priest, was collated, by lapse. In *Brantyngham's* Register he had found that William Trevellys instituted a Rector in 1381, name and patron not recorded; but on the 15th of June, 1382, John Doget, chaplain, was admitted on the death of Nicholas Terrers, patron, William Asthorp (proxy, William Colton de Ledes, clerk—Dioc. Ebor.) Dated 4 Jan., 1410-11, ii, 336.

[*Breve Regium*], Mandamus to the Bishop to search the Registers, and certify the King as to the names, etc., of all persons instituted to this Benefice from the first year of Edward, son of Henry [*i.e.* 1 Edw. I, 1272] to 20 Edw. III. [1346].—15 May, 1411, ii, 340[b].

On the 13th of June the Bishop certified that he had found in Bishop *Grandisson's* Register that 8 Kal. Dec. (i.e. 24 Nov. 1328) he admitted, at Morchard, Roger de Camelford, priest; the Church having been vacant from the Saturday next before the Feast of St. Luke the Evangelist; patron Thomas de Ease, clerk, representing Dionisia de la Bruere, ii, 340[b].

Meanwhile the Bishop had collated Walter Simon, chaplain, by lapse, on the 2nd of May, 1411 (ii, 132[b]); but, shortly afterwards, the King (at the Assizes held at Exeter in August), recovered his right of presentation against John Uffiete and William Sechevyle, chaplain, and issued his mandate to the Bishop accordingly (*Breve Regium*, 7 Aug., 1411), ii, 341. Walter Symon's collation was held to have been null and void[1]; and Richard Mannyng, clerk, was instituted, 19 Aug., 1411, Patron, King Henry IV., ii, 135.

Richard Mannyng, R. of; dispensation (to study at Oxford) for three years, from 8 June, 1412; i, 161.

This Rector did not long enjoy his Benefice; and on his death, about three years later, a Prohibition to admit was served on the Bishop, pending the settlement of the dispute as to the right to present, between King Henry V. and Richard Uffiete (*Breve Regium*, 24 Oct., 1414), ii, 349[b]. This was shortly followed by a Mandate to admit William Normanton, the King's nominee (*Breve Regium*, 22 Nov., 1414), ii, 350: and he was instituted accordingly, 7 Dec., 1414; ii, 162[b].

William Normanton (sub-deacon), R. of; licence of non-residence for one year, from 10 Dec., 1414, i, 205; dispensation (to study "in Universitate Oxoniensi, *vel alibi ubi viget studium generale*), for three years, and not to

---

[1] It is ignored altogether in the record of Mannyng's institution "ad ecclesiam parochialem Sancti Georgii.... *quam nuper obtinuit dominus Johannes Doget, ultimus ipsius ecclesie Rector, per mortem ejusdem domini Johannis vacantem.*"

Exeter—continued.

be bound to proceed to the higher Orders in the interim (24 May, 1415), i, 210.

St. Giles' [Sancti Egidii], *see* Heavitree.

St. John-de-Arcubus, i, 317.

St. Kerrian's [Sancti Kerani *and* Kierani, MS.], Thomas Cook, R. i, 142b; Walter Trote, R., his Will, i, 302b.

St. Laurence's, John Avery, R., licence of non-residence from 16 Dec., 1401, to the Feast of St. Peter-ad-Vincula (1st August), and relaxation of the sequestration imposed in consequence of previous absence from his benefice, i, 59.

St. Leonard's, Larkbeare, in this parish, i, 223.—The female recluse at, i, 312b, 313, 328;—

The Bishop issued a Commission, 18 May, 1397, directed to John Dodyngton, Canon of Exeter, for the enclosure of Alice . . . . "in quadam domo in cimiterio ecclesie parochialis Sancti Leonardi extra portam australem," ii, 212b.

Commission of Enquiry as to the patronage, on the presentation, by Edward, Earl of Devon, of John Crugge, chaplain (24 Aug., 1419), ii, 268b. (The *last* Commission issued by Bishop Stafford, who died at Clyst, ten days later). He was instituted shortly afterwards, but soon resigned. Matthew Stoke was R. in 1410, *see* i, 106b.

St. Martin's,—Richard Mark, R., licensed as a Publick Preacher (5 Jan., 1409-10), i, 92b.

St. Mary Major, Robert Lyngham, R. of; licence (for one year) to choose confessors (27 Oct., 1395), i, 6b; *see*, also, i, 310, 322, 326b, 328b, 331.

St. Mary Steps[1], David [Loueryng], R., a Penitentiary in the Deanery of Christianity, i, 50.

St. Olave's, John Burgoun, R., ii, 253b; Walter Cade, R. of, i, 240.

St. Pancras, John Holond, R., i, 310, 332; his institution, ii, 2.

St. Paul's, Roger, Bernard, R., his Will, i, 314b; William Nycol, Rector, i, 330.—

Commission (dated 4 March, 1410-11), as to the presentation of Reginald Russell, chaplain, by the Dean and Chapter, ii, 239. See *Institutions*.

St. Petrock's, John [Westecote], R., a Penitentiary in the Deanery of Christianity, i, 50, 51; licensed as a Publick Preacher[2] (5 Jan., 1409-10), 92b; his Will, i, 331; *see* also, i,

---

[1] Sancte Marie de Gradibus, MS.

[2] "officium et exercicium predicacionis et proposicionis Verbi Dei . . . . ac Verbum Dei clero et populo, sermone Latino vel vulgari, publice proponere et predicare."

142^b, 316^b, 319^b; ii, 21, 21^b.—John Rysby (accolite), R. dispensation (to study at Oxford) for three years from 4 Oct., 1418 (also Letters Dimissory), i, 242^b; *see* also, i, 70^b, 203, 319^b.

St. Sidwell's, i, 316, 320; *see* Heavitree.

St. Stephen's, Henry Alkebarowe (accolite), R., i, 77^b, 313^b.

Holy Trinity, John Govys, R. of (*licencia celebrandi in quadam aula*, 17 April, 1404; *see* Bonevyle (*Oratories*), i, 70^b; also (27 Sept., 1404), licence to celebrate Divine Service in the parish Church of the Holy Trinity, "juxta portam Australem," which is described as "de novo erecta et constructa," i, 72; his Will, i, 328^b.

Exmansworthy [Ashmandesworthi, MS.], Chapel at, in the Parish of Hartland (licensed 21 May, 1400), i, 38^b.

Exminster, St. Martin's, i, 301^b.—John Gardiner, R.; licence of non-residence for one year, from 29 Jan., 1396-7, i, 11; his Will, i, 301^b.

Exmouth, in the parish of Littleham; licence granted to the inhabitants for Divine Service in the Chapel of the Holy Trinity there, from 1 June to the Feast of the Nativity of S. John Baptist, 1412, i, 160^b. On the 27th of June this licence[1] was renewed, to last during pleasure, i, 162. —The ship 'Mary' of—'navis, sive bargie, vocate *le Marie de Exemoth*,' i, 320.

Eyer, John, co-patron of Coates, R. (Dioc. of Ely), ii, 83.

Eyr, Agnes, relict of Hervey Eyr, *see* Lansallos, ii, 253^b.

Eyr, Stephen, R. of Uplyme (deceased), ii, 7^b.

F.

Fabyan, Joan and Alice, i, 332.

Fairforde, John, R. of Parkham (deceased), ii, 8^b.

Falewell, Joan, *see* Bosom (*Oratories*), i, 8^b, 86^b.

Falewell, William, R. of Ermington, i, 8^b; his death, ii, 34^b; his Will, i, 12, 300.

---

[1] "Loci distanciam, corporumque vestrorum quorundam debilitatem, et viarum lutosarum discrimina, que vestrum accessum ad ecclesiam parochialem de Lytelham supradictam reddunt plurimum tediosum, vestreque devocionis affectum quem ad Divini Cultus obsequium habere noscimini, propensius advertentes, etc." Nevertheless, they were to attend the Mother Church on Sundays and Festivals, and render to its ministers (*ipsius ministris*) their dues, as aforetime.

Fardell, John Ralegh of, i, 302.

Fardell, John, V. of Buckfastleigh (dec.), ii, 91^b; his Will, i, 306^b.

Fareby, in Bishopsnympton: *see* Bromewych, John, ii, 311^b.

Fareway, John, does homage to the Bishop in London, for lands at Penryn (23 Oct., 1399), ii, 310^b.

Faringdon (Dioc. of Winchester), i, 49^b, 313; ii, 310^b, 311.

Farleigh, in the parish of Tiverton, i, 80.

Farnham (Dioc. of Winchester), i, 64^b.

Farringdon, [Farendon, MS.], Thomas Tredowargh (subdeacon), R.: dispensation (to study at Oxford) for two years, from 3 Nov, 1397; i, 14; also, for two years, from 25 Oct., 1399; i, 33.—Thomas Greyston, R., i, 210, 334.—John Knyght, R., i, 240.

Farthehyll, John, a parishioner of Cowick, ii, 287.

Fauchilon, William, instituted Prior of Modbury (Moddebury, MS.), ii, 174^b.

Favel, Richard, i, 303^b.

Fax, John, i, 324.

Fayreby, John, i, 332.—*See*, also, ii, 37^b.

Fayreste (*also* Fayryste *and* Fayrest), John, chaplain, presented [but not admitted] to Instow, R., ii, 234; instituted to Roborough, R., ii, 149; i, 246.

Fayreford, Thomas, V. of Dawlish, i, 122, 146^b, 131, 133^b, 163, 177^b; his institution, ii, 130.—*See*, also, ii, 239, 241.

Fayrwode, John, LL.B., Warden of St. David's Hospital, Swansea (a deacon), exchanges for Alwington, R., ii, 131; dispensation (to study at Oxford), for three years, from 6 June, 1411, i, 124; exchanges for Rudbaxton, R. (Dioc. of St. David's), ii, 179.

Fecos, John, instituted to St. Columb-major, R., ii, 11^b; exchanges for Creed, R., and a Canonry in Glasney, ii, 42; exchanges for St. Gerrans, R., *ibid.*, his death, ii, 160. *See* "Oratories."

Fedde (*or* Vedde, *see* i, 190^b), William, chaplain, instituted to Loxhore, R., ii, 90.

Feld, Robert, instituted to Mariansleigh, V., ii, 56; [resigns, and is] collated to Coleridge, V., ii, 104^b; resigns, ii, 140.

Felde, William, i, 320^b.

Fen Ottery [Fenotry, MS.], The Chapel at,—

This Chapel and its cemetery had been dedicated on, or about, the Feast of St. Gregory the Pope, and the parishioners there had of old time enjoyed the right of sepulture and other parochial privileges; but, by reason of various hindrances they were frequently unable to hold the proper services on their Feast of Dedication; they, therefore, petitioned the Bishop to change the day to 10 December, which he consented to do, and wrote (1 July, 1410) to John Awbry, V. of Harpford [Herford, MS.], and curate of the said chapel, giving the necessary licence, and promising an Indulgence to the Faithful attending the services on the new Day of Dedication, i, 99.

Feniton [Fynaton, *and* Fyneton, MS.], John [Byttylsgate], R.; a Penitentiary in the Deanery of Plymtree, i, 50: John Bone R., ditto, i, 143, 173b, 194, 207b, 216b, 231, 237b, 245.

Fenton, John, chaplain, instituted (1404), to Huish, R., ii, 80b.

John Fenton, V. of Pitminster (Diec. of Bath and Wells), exchanged in 1407 for Stoodleigh, R., ii, 97; i, 89; which he exchanged for Wittenham Rowley, R. (Dioc. of Salisbury), ii, 121b.

Fereste, John, V. of Barnstaple (deceased), ii, 33.

Feriby, Thomas de, exchanges his Prebend of St. Martin's Altar in Beverley Colleg. Church for the Prebend of Kingsteignton and Yealmpton in Salisbury Cathedral, ii, 37b; presents to Kingsteignton, V., ii, 57, 175: to Yealmpton, V., ii, 167b.

Ferrers, Martin, patron of Newton Ferrers, R, ii, 12b.

Ferrers, Richard, clerk,—admitted by Commission (28 Feb., 1398-9), to be a Proctor in the Consistory Court, ii, 223b.

Ferres, Richard, does homage to the Bishop at Clyst, for lands at Minster, Tremaen [Tremeana, in St. Gennys], Croghtpagem, Trevardregth, and Bosvousek, all within his demesne of Minster (21 March, 1413-14), ii, 311.

Ferrers, Thomas, R. of E. Ogwell, exchanges with the Precentor of Ottery, ii, 135; *see*, also, i, 319.

Ferrers, William (de Churcheton), presents to Thurleston, R., ii, 196b,

Ferrour, Hugh, a parishioner of St. Paul's, Exeter, i, 314b.

Ferrour, Roger, V. of Yarcombe, exchanges for Clysthydon, R., ii, 104b.

Ferrour, Thomas, senior, priest, and Thomas Ferrour, junior, clerk, of Slapton Collegiate Church, ii, 111.

Festivals of certain Saints,—

(1) St. George, St. David, St. Cedde, and St. Wenefride,—*Certificatorium super celebracione Festorum*, Georgii, etc. (28 Feb., 1415-16), i, 216. (2) Of St. John of Beverley, St. Crispin, and St. Crispinian. The Archbishop's Mandate for their observance (8 Jan., 1416-17), i, 229b.—The Bishop's Mandate for the execution of the same (6 Feb., 1416-17), i, 230.

Filham, Chapel of St. Andrew at, in Ugborough, i, 51b.

Fillegh, Isabella de, patron of East Buckland, R., ii, 4b.

Filleigh, John, patron of Filleigh, R., ii, 13; of East Buckland, R., ii, 16.

Filleigh, William [Prydeaux], R., a Penitentiary in the Deanery of Barnstaple, i, 143[b], 174.—Desecration of the Parish Church,—

Robert Rychard[1] appeared before the Bishop at Crediton, craving absolution from the sentence of the greater excommunication, incurred by reason of a murderous assault, committed on one Oliver Lange, in this parish Church, even shedding his blood and polluting the Church, which had to be reconciled at the charges of the parishioners. The Bishop acceded to his petition, and committed the business to his Chancellor, William Hunden, who (having ascertained the amount of the fees paid by the parishioners, and ordered full satisfaction to be made to them), assigned to him the following penance : after the manner of a penitent, stript off all his garments—"braccis et camisia dumtaxat exceptis," he was to undergo, at suitable hours on appointed days, three "fustigaciones corporales" through the market-place at South Molton, and the like number through the church of Filleigh, carrying a wax candle, half a pound in weight, and on the last of the appointed days delivering the said candle into the hands of the priest, who should be saying High Mass in the said Church (22 Dec., 1410), i, 110[b].

On the same day, the Bishop wrote to the Deans of Barnstaple, [South] Molton, and Shirwell, requiring them to cause this sentence to be proclaimed in the usual manner, i, 111.

In vol. ii (fol. 235[b]), is a Copy of the Commission for an investigation of this case directed to Archdeacon Hunden (24 Nov., 1410).

Firebeacon, Chapel of St. Mary at, *see* Hartland, i, 38[b].

Fiton, William, i, 312.

Fitz-Herbert, Nicholas i, 301; presents to Honeychurch, ii, 159.

Fitzhugh, Sir Henry, knt., co-patron of Otterton, V., ii, 176.

Fitzhugh, Robert, M.A., son of Henry, Lord Fitzhugh, collated to the Prebend of Grendale in the Cathedral-church of York, ii, 196.

Fitz-Payn, Elinor, [*also* Alienora de Fypeyn, MS.], presents to Stoodleigh, R., ii, 83[b], 97, 121[b], 130[b].

Fitzwaryn, Sir Ivo, knt., patron of the R. (or chapel) of St. James in the Castle of "Chepyngtoryton," ii, 20; of Sutcombe, R., ii, 82, 102[b]; of Merton, R., ii, 146[b].

Fitzwaryn, Fulk (son of Sir Fulk), a minor, patron of Warkleigh, R., ii, 54[b].

Fitzwaryn, Philip, patron of Parracombe, R., ii, 7[b], 50.

Fitzwater, Elizabeth, a Canoness of Canonsleigh, ii, 125.

Flambertyswyke, in the parish of Chawleigh, i, 42[b].

Flay, William, i, 320[b].

Flemmyng, John, son of Thos., presents to Alverdiscott, ii, 54.

---

[1] Of Chittlehampton, *see* i, 111.

Flemmyng, John, R. of Pyworthy, ii, 22; exchanges for Inwardleigh, R., ii, 24^{b}; i, 74; resigns, ii, 108^{b}.

Flemmyng, Sir Thomas, knt., patron of the Rectories of Alverdiscott, ii, 19^{b}; Bratton Fleming, ii, 109; High Bray, ii, 191^{b}, 265.

Flesshewer, John, instituted to Seaton, V., ii, 193, 265^{b}.

Flet, William, a suicide,—

This person, being (as was alleged) neither insane nor overcome by passion, committed suicide by throwing himself into the river, and had been buried at Calstock, contrary to the Canon. The Bishop, accordingly, issued a Commission directed to Walter Dollebeare, R. of Southill, and John Philip, R. of Menhenyot, for a full enquiry, with a view to the exhumation of the body (23 June, 1400), ii, 227.

Floyer, John, a parishioner of Cowick, ii, 287.

Floyer, William, chaplain, ii, 111; instituted to Lamerton, V., ii, 161; 256, 355; to a Prebend in Chulmleigh, ii, 173^{b}.

Fodryngheye, John, instituted to Farway, R., ii, 164.

John Fodyngheye, probably the same person, was collated (in 1417) to a Canonry and the seventh Prebend in Ottery, ii, 186, and John Fotergay, chaplain, is mentioned at i, 315.

Foghel, Gerard, and William Berya, a chaplain, serving in "the new chapel" at Dartmouth, i, 113.

Fogheler, Joan, *see* Derlyng, Thomas, i, 229.

Foughler, John, proxy for John Ikelyngton, ii, 131^{b}; for Peter de Alcobasse, ii, 137^{b}.

Fokeray, William, co-patron of No. Huish, R., ii, 144^{b}, 189^{b}, 248.^{b}

Foldehay, Richard, *see* Goodleigh, ii, 349.

Foleford (now Shobrooke Park, Crediton), i, 185, 323.

Foleford, Henry, i, 326; co-patron of Aveton Giffard, R., ii, 67^{b}; of the Chantry "de Lyneton" in that Church, ii, 91^{b}; of St. Leonard's Chantry, Raleigh, ii, 137^{b}, 182^{b}, 191.

Folford, William, clerk,—*Dispensacio super defectu natalium* (30 July, 1415), i, 212.

Folle, John, *see* Symon, John, ii, 332^{b}.

Folyet, John, scholar,—*Dispensacio super defectu natalium* (13 March, 1399-1400), i, 33^{b}.

Fontevrault, Abbess and Convent of. *See* Tintagel, V., ii, 46^{b}.

Foot, Edith, i, 324^{b}.

Forchull, Juliana, wife of John, i, 329.

Forde, John, chaplain; *see* Milton-Damarel, i, 244^{b}; 325.

Forde, Robert, *see* atte Forde.

Forde, Robert, R. of Nymet Rowland, exchanges for the Chantry of Umberleigh, ii, 25^b; resigns, and is instituted to East Worlington, R., ii, 95^b; his death, ii, 198^b.

Forde, Thomas, instituted to Tamerton, V., ii, 153;—

This was in October 1418. On 23 Sept., 1412, Thomas Ford (*alias* Row), clerk, obtained a Dispensation *super defectu natalium*, i, 167.

Ford, William, senior, Canon of Frithelstock, ii, 183^b.

Forde Abbey—in arrears of Procurations due to the Pope's Collector for three years (1408-10), i, 105, 110.

Sir William Bonevyll's bequest to, i, 312; Thomas Reymound's, i, 331^b.—The Abbot and Convent of, present to Payhembury, V., ii, 150.—*See* Culmyslond, Thomas, i, 166.

Fordeman, John, co-patron of Inwardleigh, R., ii, 24^b, 108^b.

Forneauxs, Alice, Wife of John, i, 312^b.

Forst, John, instituted to Bishop's Tawton, V., ii, 136.

Forste, Richard, R. of Bagborough (Dioc. of B. and W.), exchanges for Uploman, R., ii, 63^b; for Chardlinch, R., (Dioc. of B. and W.), ii, 93.

Forster, John, collated to Blackborough, R., *by lapse*, ii, 156; i, 232.

Fortesku, John,—Mandate to the Bishop to administer the oath to him as Escheator in Cornwall and Devon (*Breve Regium*, 20 Dec., 1416), ii, 360.

Fosse, John, collated to Bridestowe, R., ii, 180.

Foster, Walter, ii, 351^b.

Foter, Reginald, V. of Treneglos (deceased), ii, 106^b.

Fotyngdon, John, instituted to Colyton, V., ii, 130; his death ii, 147^b.

Fouke, John, instituted to Parkham, R., ii, 12^b: i, 36^b, 62^b; his death, ii, 92; *see*, also, Foke, John, ii, 307^b.

Fountenay, Alexander, clerk,—*Dispensacio super defectu natalium* (23 May, 1404), i, 71.

Fourbour, Robert, and Agnes his wife, i, 319.

Fowey, John [Hemburgh], V. of, i, 49^b.—

Commission of enquiry on the presentation of Richard Udan, chaplain, by the Prior and Convent of Tywardreath (17 June, 1416). ii, 259.

Fowey [Fowy, MS.], John and Thomas Taverner, of, i, 315; the road from Fowey to Plymouth (*see* Looe),—i, 137^b.—Bridge at Treverbyn, over the river Fowey, i, 175.

Fox, Laurence, i, 306^b.

Fox, Nicholas, a poor scholar of Ugborough, i, 313^b.

Foxholes, Thomas, proxy for Richard Fitzhugh, ii, 196.

Frake, John, R. of All-Hallows, Goldsmith St. (deceased), ii, 100.

Franke, John, collated to Peter Tavy, R., ii, 77b; i, 78.

Franke, Robert, a chaplain of Devon,—

He was offered by John Weston, R. of Bridestowe, a competent salary to serve the parish church there; but he refused the work, and the said R. appealed to the Bishop for a remedy. Accordingly, a Commission was issued (31 Oct., 1415) directed to the Dean of Tavistock and to Henry, R. of Lydford, William Hawke, chaplain of Sourton, and John Bydelake, literate, to warn the said Robert, three several times, that he proceed, within ten days, to the work at Bridestowe, on pain of suspension. If he refused to submit, he was to appear in person before the Bishop, at Clyst, i, 214.

Frankcheyne, James, instituted to Tiverton (2nd Portion), ii, 99; i, 87, 171b; *see* Kentisbeare, ii, 249.

Frankecheny, James, instituted to Stokenham, V., ii, 192, 265.

Frankeleyn, Ralph, V. of Mylor (deceased), ii, 21.

Franseys, John, i, 15.

Fraunceys, John,—" literarum Apostolicarum in Romana Curia abbreviatorem "—

With John Tyre, John Bremour, and William Cullyng, appointed by the Bishop his proctor *ad visitandum Limina Apostolorum* (12 March, 1402-3), i, 63.

Fraunceys, Simon, collated to a Canonry at Crantock, ii, 70; also, 159b.

Fraunces, Walter, instituted to St. Clement's [Moresk], ii, 105.

Fraunceys, William, i, 327b.

Fraunkeleyn, William, ii, 314.

Freman, Thomas, chaplain, i, 329.

Afterwards, I think, V. of Braunton. *See* Lacy's Reg., ii, 43b.

Fremington, Henry Alkeberwe, chaplain, V. of, ii, 346.

A Licence to celebrate in the Chapel of St. Katherine in the Manor of Fremington, was granted to this V., 17 June, 1411, i, 126b.

A scrutiny of the Register [of Institutions, vol. ii, fol. 96b], having been made, the Bishop ascertained that on the 9th of June, 1407, he had instituted Henry Alkebarwe to this benefice, on the presentation of the Abbot and Convent of Hurtland, and nomination of K. Henry IV., by reason of the minority of the son and heir of Sir John Holond, knt., (15 Jan., 1411—12), i, 141b.

The Bishop having been informed that the Church of Fremington had been polluted in a quarrel, with effusion of blood, between John Haye and John atte Wyll, issues a Commission to the Archdeacon of Barnstaple to enquire and report (17 June, 1411), ii, 242.—The Bishop decided that there had been neither violence nor bloodshed, and, consequently, no pollution, ii, 242b.

Frenche, Robert [probably, of Sharpham], i, 306.

Frend, Henry, V. of Liskeard, his resignation, ii, 222.

Frend, Henry, chaplain,—

He had been ordained Priest three weeks before he had attained the proper age, and a Dispensation was granted to him 8 Oct., 1409, i, 90b.

Frengy, William, Canon of St. Stephen's, Launceston, ii, 117.

Frensch, John, i, 316.

Frensche, R., licence to choose confessors (3 Feb., 1409-10), i, 94.

Frenschton, Blonchia, daughter of Wm. (of Sidbury, i, 229).

Frenssh, Katherine, and John Radener, citizen of London, their divorce (Commission dated 22 Feb., 1397-8), ii, 215, 215b.

Fresell, Walter, of the parish of Southill,—

He was excommunicated at the instance of Walter Dollebeare, R. of Southill, for defamation; and, being contumacious, was handed over by the Bishop to the secular arm, 22 July, 1414; i, 197b.

Fricon, Nicola, *see* Hake, Robert, i, 207b; ii, 255b.

Frist, Thomas, of Cruwys Morchard, i, 324.

Frithelstock Priory,—Mandate for its Visitation on the 22nd of May, 1400 (dated 14 April), i, 36b.

At this Visitation, the Prior, John Pynnok, was found to have grievously wasted the goods of the Priory, reducing it almost to a state of desolation: but, submitting himself to the Bishop,—" pure, sponte, et absolute, alte et basse, solempniter se submisit,"—he was dealt with mercifully. He was punished, however, by suspension from the administration of the temporalities of the Priory, and Thomas Rede, one of the Canons, was entrusted therewith during the Bishop's pleasure, The Bishop required monthly accounts to be kept, and the state of the House reported annually to himself; and he appointed two other Canons to assist in this work, viz., Adam Prode and David Beff, restraining them from interfering in other respects with the Prior, whom he bound to obedience on pain of deprivation. In order to free the Priory from the debts caused by Pynnok's improvidence, and as part of the penance to be imposed on him, the Bishop ordered him not to take his meals in the great Hall—" 'aula Prioris' vulgariter ibidem appellata "—but to resort to the Refectory with the rest, unless honourable and *bona fide* guests should happen to arrive—" tunc enim in camera sua, aut alia camera *Hevytre* nuncupata, cum hospitibus hujusmodi, se reficere, ac prandere, et cenare valeat "—but that was not to be an event of too frequent occurrence, so as to evade the Bishop's order. He made restrictions, also, as to clothing and the number of the servants, allowing but one servant to the Prior, and a quarterly allowance of 40s. for clothes, wine, and other necessaries, to be paid him by the administrator. Also, he ordered an inventory of all the goods of the Priory to be prepared before Christmas, and submitted to the Bishop before Epiphany; and in like manner a list of the Prior's debts, with names and amounts, and stating why they were incurred. Also, he ordered that the Divine offices be duly said by day and by night; and that the Brethren abstain from all idle wandering up and down, from hunting, and the like; observing their rule strictly; and giving attention to reading, etc., in the church, the cloister, and elsewhere; abstaining from festivities publick and private, and from all drinking in improper places or at unsuitable times, especially after compline—matters in which the Prior was bidden to remember that it was his duty to set an example to the rest and to devote himself to the Divine Mysteries, and to his Convent, night and day. None of their land, or other property, was to be put out to farm, or sold, during the administration of the said Thomas, without the Bishop's special licence. And severe punishment was threatened in case of disobedience or rebellion.—The Bishop's mandate was formally communicated to the Prior and Convent, 6 December, 1400; and 4 January, 1400-1, the inventory was sent to the Bishop, together with the Prior's formal undertaking to submit to the Bishop's decrees—"per omnia humiliter et reverenter parui, pareo, et parebo," i, 53. The Prior and Convent were, of course, returned as in heavy arrears on account of the Procurations due to the Pope's Collector, i, 105, 110.—

Election of Prior,—

On the 8th of May, 1417, the Bishop received notice of the election of Thomas Rede. The formal documents are given at length; from which it appears that the late Prior, John Pynnok, died on the 19th of March, and was buried on the 21st; that on the 22nd of April the Convent met in Chapter and fixed May the 4th for the election. The electors were William Ford, senior Canon and President, Thomas Rede, Walter Whytbe, and James Dunham, Canons of Frithelstock; also, Philip Tone, Abbot, and Gentian Mautynghe, Canon, of Hartland (who had a right to attend and to vote). After the usual formalities, the election of Thomas Rede was confirmed; and the Mandate for his installation was issued by the Bishop at Clyst, 18 May, 1417; ii, 183, 185b.

The Prior and Convent present to Ashwater, R., ii, 75b, 91b; and to Broadwoodwidger, V., ii, 95.—Thomas Reymound's bequest to, i, 331b.—Richard and Edith Holemore, of Frithelstock, i, 246.

Frode, John, who had received all the sacred orders, without licence, *ab alieno Episcopo*,—Dispensation in favour of (22 Sept., 1408), i, 86b.

Froden, John, proxy for Michael Lercedekne, ii, 180b.

Frogmer, Stephen, V., of Haselbeare (Dioc. of Wells), exchanges for Pinhoe, V., ii, 92; resigns, ii, 183.

Frome St. Quintin (Dioc. of Salisbury), i, 306.

Frouses, John, a parishioner of Linkinhorne, i, 116.

Frund, John, V. of Maker, resigns, i, 86.

Fry, Robert, proxy for Richard Wynchcombe, ii, 29.

Fryday, Matthew, a chaplain in Devon, being excommunicate and contumacious, is handed over by the Bishop to the secular arm (4 Jan., 1398-9), i, 24.

Frye, William, "de Fyneton," presents to Feniton, R., ii, 78b; to St. Mellion, R., ii, 190, 264b.

Frye, William (proxy—Robert Frye), collated to a Preb. in St. Probus, ii, 193.

Fryngg, John, co-patron of Coates, R. (Dioc. of Ely), ii, 83.

Fulford [Foleford, MS.], Chapel in the Manor of, i, 61b.

Fulford, Henry,—

Mandate to the Bishop to administer the oath to him as Escheator in Devon and Cornwall (*Breve Regium*—3 Nov., 1412), ii, 346.

Mandate to administer the oath to him as Sheriff of Cornwall (*Breve Regium*, 10 Nov., 1417), ii, 361.

Fuller, John, instituted to Fowey, V., ii, 143; his death, ii, 177.

Funtington [Fontiton and Fontyngdon, MS.], *see* Bosham, ii, 45, 280.

Furber, Peter, i, 316b.

Fursdon, of Fursdon, *see Oratories.*

Fyccok, Matilda, wife of William, *see* Ruan-major, i, 181.

Fycon, Ralph, presents to Monkokehampton, R., ii, 192b.

Fyfide, John, Preb. of St. Probus, exchanges for a Canonry and Preb. of Bedford-minor at Lincoln, ii, 56b; 57b.

Fylham, William, M.A., Scholar in Theology, licensed to preach in the Deaneries of Plympton, Woodleigh, and Totnes (20 Sept., 1414), i, 199b; collated Dean of Crediton, ii, 187; licensed to preach in the Cathedral and in all churches in Devon (2 Dec., 1417), i, 237; a Penitentiary in the Deanery of Cadbury, i, 237b; collated Canon of Exeter and R. of Stokeinteignhead, ii, 196b; resigns the Deanery of Crediton, ii, 197; collated to the Archdeaconry of Cornwall, ii, 199; resigns Stokeinteignhead, ii, 201b.

Fynour, Robert, instituted to Shirwell R., ii, 96b; exchanges for Honiton R., ii, 103, 252; his death, ii, 148.

Fysch (Fyschacre and Fysshacre), Edward, V. of Widecombe, exchanges for Honiton R., ii, 45, i, 307; exchanges Honiton for Shirwell, R., ii, 103; exchanges Shirwell for Collumpton, V., ii, 175b.

Fyschacre[1], Joan, daughter of Martin de, co-patron of Moreleigh, R., ii, 159b.

Fyssh, William, i, 305b.

Fyssher, John, R., of the mediety of Danbury (Dioc. of London), exchanges for Affeton, R., ii, 51b.

G.

Gabe, Robert, a parishioner of Linkinhorne, i, 116.

Gabryell, Richard, instituted to St. Mawnan, R.[2], ii, 40; Pyworthy, R., ii, 82b; and to a Preb. in Chulmleigh, ii, 101; resigns Pyworthy, ii, 101b; exchanges his Preb. "of

---

[1] She presented to St. George's, Exeter, but was found not to be the true patron; ii, 234b, where she is described as Joan, relict of John Speke, junior, and daughter and heir of Martin Fyschakre.

[2] In 1398. His resignation is not recorded; but it must have taken place before 1405, in April of which year he acted as proxy for Thomas Pytyngton, *collated, by lapse*, ii, 83b.

Penylles" in Chulmleigh for a Canonry at Bosham, ii, 101b, 280, 281, 294; is instituted to Denbury, R.[1], ii, 108; exchanges his Canonry and Preb. of Warminster (*alias* Luxvyle) in Wells Cathedral for Ipplepen, R., ii, 110b; collated to a Canonry in Exeter Cathedral, ii, 156; resigns Denbury, ii, 191; dies (Canon of Crediton, Bosham, and Exeter), ii, 201, 201b; *See* i, 214b, 226b, 227b, 236, 327b, 328.

Galbrygg, Edward, i, 326b.

Galon de Fayreford, Thomas, instituted to Parracombe, R., ii, 50; exchanges for Kingston, V. (Dioc. of B. & W.), ii, 79b.

Galway, Walter, R. of Bratton Fleming (deceased), ii, 109.

Galy, Walter, inst. to St. Winnow, V., ii, 80; his death, ii, 138.b

Gambon, Thomas, instituted to Bondleigh, R., ii, 69; i, 69, 81, 99b, 129b, 164, 185, 205b, 215, 228, 237b, 246.

Gambon, Walter, presents to Bondleigh, R., ii, 69.

Gaols, at Exeter,—the King's,—the Lord Bishop's, i, 332.

Gardyner, Joan (sister of John), i, 301b, 305.

Gardyner, John, instituted to Exminster, R., ii, 6b; i, 11; proxy for John Wendovere, on his institution to Bradninch, R., ii, 27; his death, ii, 47; his Will, i, 301b.

Gardyner, Henry, instituted to Meavy, R., ii, 5; i, 302; to Exminster, ii, 47; i, 60b; resigns Meavy, ii, 50b; exchanges Exminster for Yate, R. (Dioc. of Worcester), ii, 88; instituted to Blackawton, R., ii, 198; his death, ii, 204b.—Was appointed (4 Oct., 1399), one of the Bishop's Proctors *ad visitandum Limina Apostolorum*, i, 31.

Garton, John de, Canon of Ottery, resigns, ii, 27.

Garton, Robert de, clerk (Dioc. Ebor.), *ibid.*

Gatcombe [Gadcombe, MS.], Manor of, in Colyton, i, 240.

Gatewell, Richard, chaplain, of Dartmouth—

"Seeking his own, not the things which are Jesus Christ's" he had deceived the Faithful, and specially those who belonged to the "new Chapel" at Dartmouth, by falsely pretending to be a Penitentiary (or Confessor) deputed by the Bishop. He even went so far as to deal with cases commonly reserved, taking money from penitents, and to palliate his crime, gave out that the said money was for the Bishop, whose Receiver he falsely pretended to be. Under these circumstances, the Bishop directed the Dean of Totnes, Stephen [Joseph],[2] and Gerard Foghel and William Berya, chaplain of the

---

[1] In 1409. There is no record of his having resigned when Thomas Loweden was instituted to Denbury in 1410, ii, 110b; but, of course, he must have done so. He seems, however, to have kept his hand upon the Benefice, for in 1414, on Loweden's resignation, he was instituted again (ii, 161).

[2] R. of Stoke-Fleming.

"new Chapel" at Dartmouth, on certain Sundays and Festivals in time of Mass (when most people are present), in the said chapel, and in other neighbouring churches and chapels, to denounce the said Richard's proceedings as unauthorized, and such confessions and absolutions as null and void, and to declare that the said moneys had not been sent to the Bishop but kept by the offender for his own purposes (30 Jan., 1410-11), i, 113.

Gathell, Henry, R. of St. Mewan (deceased), ii, 74.—*See*, also, Clok, Richard, i, 24.

Gaunstede, Simon, Keeper of the Rolls, i, 226b.

Gavet, John, i, 321.

Gaylard, John, R. of Petrockstowe (deceased), ii, 151.

Gay, Joan, i, 308b.

Gay, John, chaplain, i, 306b.

Gay, Nicholas, of Devonshire, *see* St. Feock, i, 161.

Gay, Thomas, i, 308b.

Gayne, William, *ibid.*

Gebav, William, *see* St. Kew.

Gedefray, John, R. of Halwell (*see* Godefray, i, 74).

Geffrey, William, born on the Bishop's Manor of Ashburton; his Manumission (6 June, 1418), i, 240b.

Gelow, John, i, 314b.

Gelys, Henry, R. of St. Leonard's, Berwick, proxy for R. Pyttes, ii, 107.

Gentylman, John, instituted to Torbrian, R., ii, 95; i, 88, 105b, 141b, 184, 208b, 215b, 228, 245b.

Georgeham [Haume St. George, MS.], Hole, in this parish, i, 62; also, Pytwyll, i, 69b.

Georgenympton, Robert Hokeway, R. of, a Penitentiary in the Deanery of [South] Molton, i, 143b, 174, 194b, 207b, 217, 231, 238, 245b.

Gerard, Agnes, wife of Alexander; John, Thomas, and Philip, their sons, and Margery, their daughter, i, 330b.

Germansweek, *see* Kelly, Thomas (*Oratories*), i, 128b.

Germyn, Hugh, collated to Rockbeare, V., ii, 88b; his death, ii, 190b.

Germen, John, instituted to Poltimore, R., ii, 179; exchanges for Lawhitton, R., ii, 197b.

Gernon, Geoffrey de, instituted to the Priory of St. Michael's Mount, ii, 338b, 348b.

Gerwes (*sic*), Isabella, relict of James, i, 323b; *see Oratories* (Gerveys), i, 36b, 71. *Also*, Gervays, James, ii, 316.

Gervys, John (chaplain), blind and infirm; the Bishop directs that he be admitted to the Hospital of Clyst St. Gabriel (28 Feb., 1410-11), i, 117.

Gerveys, Peter, priest, i, 15b; V. of Constantine (*see Oratories*), i, 71; also i, 245b; resigns St. Enoder, V., ii, 30b.

Gerveys, Robert, clerk, instituted to Washfield, R., ii, 180, 259b; *see*, also, ii, 356b.

Gerveys, Stephen, instituted to Ruan-major, R., ii, 10; i, 24b; his death, ii, 50.

Gerweys, Thomas, R. of Ludgvan, exchanges for Gwennap, V., ii, 194, 266.

Ghydecote, *see* Denys, John (*Oratories*), i, 38b.

Gidleigh, the parish church of, i, 308b.

Gilbert, John, priest, i, 320b.

Gittisham, Thomas Hert, R. of, his Will, i, 312b.—Walter [Shanke], R. of, a Penitentiary in the Deanery of Honiton, i, 94, 115, 143, 173b, 194, 207b, 216b, 231, 237b, 245.

Glanvyle, Thomas, *see* Sutcombe, i, 233b; ii, 261b.

Glasney, the Collegiate-Church of St. Thomas the Martyr,—

William Cullyng, Provost of, i, 24.

John Hesyll, R. of Jacobstow (Cornwall), licensed to reside therein (26 Oct., 1398), i, 21b (also 7 Oct., 1404), i, 76b.

John Rawe, Canon and Steward of, i, 24; his excommunication for attempting to defraud William Cullyng, the Provost, of the fruits and privileges of his Prebend (8 June, 1385); ii, 215, 217; licensed to celebrate in his manse (3 Feb., 1398-9), i, 25.

Nicholas Stoke, Prebendary of, i, 50b; ii, 43b.

Benedict Canterbury, Canon of, a Penitentiary in the Deanery of Kerrier, i, 50b, 143, 174, 194b, 207b, 217, 231, 238.

Thomas Chamberleyn, Vicar-choral, licensed (7 Aug., 1403), to celebrate in any suitable place "infra clausum dicti Collegii," i, 67b.—Licence granted (17 March, 1404-5), to the Provost, Canons, etc., to celebrate in the Common Hall of the Vicars until Pentecost, unless the Church, which (as was alleged) had been polluted, should in the meantime have been reconciled, i, 74. And on the 29th of the same month the Canons were licensed to celebrate "infra mansiones suas infra clausum," and the others "in communi loco," pending the said Reconciliation, *ibid.*

On the 28th of June, 1403, the Bishop, being at Clyst, was certified by the Provost and Chapter that they had received his Mandate (which they recite at length). The Bishop, at his recent Visitation (4 Sep., 1400), had found certain things requiring correction, and admonished them accordingly; directing (1) That all Vicars and inferior ministers found guilty of neglect or irreverence in saying the Divine offices be punished by the Provost, or (in his absence) by the Sacristan, in open Chapter, "non cameraliter aut privatim." (2) That no Canon should hinder any Vicar from doing his proper duty by imposing upon him "aliquod officium famulare," under penalties to be inflicted on the Canon offending and on the Vicar complying: and whereas the Bishop had ascertained that, through the laxity of the Provost, the Vicars, etc., had been suffered to absent themselves and scandalously neglect their duties, he laid down strict rules as to granting leave of absence. (3) That the Canons, etc., should be present in their proper habit at the Divine offices and at Mass, as the statutes require; the Vicars saying their private masses at such times as not to interfere with the recitation of the Hours in the Choir, which they were themselves bound to attend; and that none of them, whether in their habits or not, presume to walk about the Church, or its precincts, in service-time. (4) That, forasmuch as he only should live of the altar who serves the altar—"cum omnia beneficia ecclesiastica propter officia dentur et fuerint instituta"—the Canons in residence should regularly, in succession, week by week, say High Mass at the High Altar, or, in case of illness or other hindrance, make provision for the same. (5) That the common seal be kept securely under three keys, one in charge of the Provost (or his locum tenens), the others of two of the Canons; the said seal never to be used without the assent of the majority of the (senior) Canons. (6) That the Sacristan, by his clerk, attend carefully to ringing the bells for the services, and to closing the doors in good time, lest damage happen to the Church or scandal to its ministers; that he provide bread and wine ("purum, non acetosum"), daily, for Mass, and cleanse the vessels used at the Altar; the said Clerk, in case of negligence herein thrice repeated, to be dismissed (after a month's notice) by the Sacristan, and a successor to be forthwith appointed, or the appointment to lapse to the Provost. It had been represented, moreover, to the Bishop, at his said Visitation, that the Church wanted repair, and that it was still incomplete—"super restauranda et sustinenda fabrica ipsius ecclesie, ac novo opere complendo, et precipue de choro ipsius et ejus alis arcuandis et voltandis"—and that the sum of 26s. per annum contributed (according to antient custom) by all the prebendaries was insufficient for the purpose: but it appeared that all were anxious to help forward the work, and had agreed to devote to it the whole of their stipends for one year, from Michaelmas next ensuing; the stipends of Geoffrey Carow (the Sacristan), and John Raff, one of the Canons, alone excepted, because they alone of the Community enjoyed no benefices outside the College, while the former was bound to perpetual residence and to take the place of the Provost in his absence, and dispense hospitality; but the said Sacristan would be content to receive for the year, instead of his prebend, £20 in quarterly payments, and the said John Raff was ready to take ten marks, to be paid in like manner. These and other like arrangements, made for so good a purpose, the Bishop approved and sanctioned, and appointed to be Receivers Alan Treles, "Rectorem de Ponte[1]," and Thomas Trefuthon, one of the Vicars-choral, who were to lay out the money with the advice and help of Edward Dauntesey, Archdeacon of Cornwall, and Canon Matthew Bodrigi. To all which the Provost, etc., promised obedience (17 May, 1403), i, 64ᵇ.

Thomas Chapman, R. of Withiel, William Somerford, R. of Lanreath, William Tregoe, R. of Eglosros (i.e. Philleigh), and Matthew Bodrigy, R. of Creed, Canons of Glasney; licence of non-residence for one year, to reside in the College (13 Nov., 1404), i, 77.

Nicholas Harry, Sacristan, a Penitentiary in the Deanery of Kerrier, i, 93ᵇ, 115ᵇ, Indulgence to the Faithful who should contribute to the maintenance and enrichment of the High Altar in the Collegiate Church, and visit the same on certain great Festivals (7 Aug., 1410), i, 102ᵇ.

William Tregos, a Canon, having neglected to appoint a Vicar, the Bishop collates, by lapse (7 Aug., 1410), i, 102ᵇ.

The Provost and Chapter complained to the Bishop that, whereas in the case of temporal estates, all who prohibit their servants and tenants from buying from or selling to the Clergy, so defrauding the Church of her rights, are liable to excommunication, certain heinous offenders, parishioners of St. Just in Penwith (appropriated to their Collegiate Church), had shamelessly interfered with the collection, etc., of the revenues of the said parish.

[1] A Chantry at Glasney.

Whereupon the Bishop commissioned the Dean of Penwith, the Vicars of St. Just and Zennor, &c. to make due enquiry, to publish the excommunication of the offenders and their abettors, and to cite them to appear before him at Crediton (9 Aug., 1410), i, 103.

The College in arrear of Procurations due to the Pope's Collector, for three years (1408-10), i, 105, 110.

William Noe, Canon of Glasney, licensed as Publick Preacher throughout the Diocese (27 March, 1413), i, 178[b].

Richard Olyver, also Canon, licensed to preach in the Collegiate Church, and in all Churches in the Diocese appropriated thereto (28 Jan., 1417-18), i, 238.

Precentor Hugh de Hyckelyng's bequests i, 326; Thomas Reymound's bequest, i, 331[b].

The Provost, etc., present to the V. of Lamorek (i.e. St. Clement's, Truro), ii, 15[b] (on the nomination of William Bodrygan), ii, 48[b].

Prebend at, annexed to the Archdeaconry of Cornwall, ii, 35.

Ralph Rudruth, Canon of, and R. of Creed, ii, 42.

John Fecos, Canon of, and R. of St. Gerrans, *ibid.*

Matthew Bodrigy, Canon of, and R. of Creed, *ibid.*

Thomas Welyn, Canon of, ii, 43[b]

Neglect of their Chancel at St. Budock (q. v.), ii, 225.

The Bishop directs an enquiry to be made as to the removal and alienation of certain goods of this Church, viz., a large sum of money (about 500 marks), and certain ornaments and vestments (Commission directed to William Cullyng, Provost, Ralph Rudruth, Benedict Canterbury, and John Hesyll, Canons, 25 June, 1399), ii, 225.

Commission, directed to Robert Rygge, Chancellor, and Richard Hals, Treasurer, as to the provision of Vicars Choral at Glasney (30 July, 1401), ii, 229.

Commission of enquiry, directed to the Official-Peculiar and to Benedict Canterbury, as to the "dilapidations" caused by the neglect of Walter Estcolm, late Canon (6 Oct., 1410), ii, 234.

Walter Robert, Canon of, *see* Robert, Walter.

(*Breve Regium*, 22 Nov., 1397), Mandate to the Bishop to certify who had been presented (and by whom), instituted and inducted as Provosts of Glasney since 7 Ric. II., ii, 306[b].—

See, also, *Institutions*, *Collations*, etc.

Glastonbury, Abbot and Convent of, i, 311[b]; Patrons of Uplyme, R., ii, 7[b], 12, 49; present in a case of exchange to Uplyme and also Milton, R. [Middleton, MS.—Dioc. of Bath and Wells]; ii, 37.

Glemham, John, presents to Stratford-juxta-Glemham, R., (Dioc. of Norwich) ii, 91.

Gloucester, [Thomas], Duke of, i, 8[b].

Glynn, William, of Exeter;

He appeared before the Bishop at Wallingford, and confessed that, having quarrelled with one John Etvel, a priest, he had assaulted him in the Cathedral Yard, and shed his blood; asking the Bishop to absolve him. The Bishop, having regard to the heinous character of the deed, required more particular information, and ordered the polluted cemetery to be reconciled (28 July, 1399) ii, 225[b].

Gobe, John, of Gittisham, i, 312[b].

God (i.e. "Gode" or "Good"), John, instituted to the Prebend of Carssewell (*alias* Cressewell), ii, 193.—John Gode occurs as R. of Washford, i, 9.

Godecherle, John, a baker of Barnstaple, i, 108^b.

Godefray, John, instituted to Luffincott, R., ii. 10; to Halwell, R., ii, 12^b; resigns Luffincott, ii, 12^b; *See* also, i, 74 ("Gedefray"), and 330^b.

Godefray, Richard, i, 315.

Godegrave, John, a Vicar at Glasney, i, 103: instituted to the Chantry "de Ponte" there, ii, 163.

Godecote, Luke, R. of Denbury (deceased), ii, 108.

Godescote, in Bratton [Clovelly], Chapel of St. Margaret at, i, 131^b, 138^b.

Godman, Ralph, V. of St. Erth (deceased) ii, 2.

Godeman, Richard, i, 325.

Godman, Roger, i, 332.

Godolphin [Godolghan, MS.], Manor of, in St. Breage, i, 23^b.

Godwyn, John, instituted to Shevioke, R., ii, 83^b; i, 76^b; his death, ii, 94.

Goff, Geoffrey, *see* Ruan-major, i, 181.

Goldeney, John, R. of North Tidworth (Dioc. of Salisbury), exchanges with the "Minister," at Ottery, ii, 136^b.

Goldsmyth, Arnulph, ii, 213.

Goldsmyth, William, a merchant; *see* Bridgewater.

Goldyng, William, R. of Coates (Dioc. of Ely), exchanges for Combmartin, R., ii, 82^b; resigns, ii, 87.

Goldyng, William, of Apuldram, ii, 293^b.

Golepyn (*alias* Peryn, q. v.), John, i, 221.

Gome, John, R. of Meeth, ii, 221.

Goodleigh, Walter [Baret], R. of, a Penitentiary in the Deanery of Shirwell, i, 50.

Commission to enquire as to his alleged incapacity, through old age and infirmity (18 Oct., 1413), ii, 252^b.

The result of this enquiry is not recorded; but, probably, he was ordered to procure the help of a chaplain immediately, for shortly afterwards he complained to the Bishop that, although he had made an agreement with one John Clyverton, chaplain, having no cure of souls elsewhere, to serve the church of Goodleigh, for a competent stipend, from Christmas, 1413, to Michaelmas, 1414, and the said John had bound himself so to serve, he had refused to fulfil his agreement. He petitioned the Bishop to interfere; who, accordingly, wrote to the Archdeacon of Barnstaple, to William Vedde, R. of Loxhore, and to Richard Bursy, "suffraganeo Decani originalis Decanatus de Schyrewyll," requiring them, if they found the complaint true, to warn the said John, once, twice, and thrice, peremptorily, to return, within fifteen days, to his duty at Goodleigh, on pain of suspension. If contumacious, he was to be ordered to appear before the Bishop at Clyst, and shew cause why the sentence of suspension should not take effect (12 Jan., 1413-14), i,

190^{b},—Baret (who told the Bishop that he was *blind* as well as infirm), did not long survive this trouble, for the question of patronage was in dispute 6 March, and his successor was instituted 30 May following.

[*Breve Regium*—6 March, 1413-14],—Prohibition to admit any clerk to this Rectory, pending the settlement of the dispute as to the patronage between Richard Foldebay and Thomas Denys and Walter Hulle[1], clerk, ii, 349.—Suspension of the Prohibition, 22 May, 1414; *ibid.*

Commissions of Enquiry (1) on the presentation of John Rysdon, chaplain, by Thomas Denys (28 May, 1418); and (2) on the presentation of Nicholas Toker, chaplain, by Roger Waye (31 May, 1418), ii, 265^{b}.

—Nicholas Toker, R. of, licence of non-residence from 26 Jan., 1418-19, to Michaelmas, 1419, i, 245.

Goof, Stephen, V. of Tintagel (deceased), ii, 46^{b}.

Goorde, John, inst. to Hittisleigh, R., ii, 187^{b}; *see*, also, i, 122^{b}.

Gore, William, resigns Bridford, and is instituted to Portlemouth, R., ii, 13; his death, ii, 84^{b}.

Gore, William, citizen of London and *foundour*, ii, 278.

Gordray, John, V. of [West] Alvington, exchanges for Sutton, R. (Dioc. of Chichester), ii, 29^{b}.

Gorewyll, John, LL.D., i, 310; Canon of Exeter, ii, 237^{b}; licensed as Publick Preacher in the Diocese (13 June, 1410), i, 97^{b}.

Gorewyll (*or* Gorewell), John, junior, LL.B., instituted to Roborough, R., ii, 25^{b}; i, 69^{b}; [resigns and] is instituted to Wyke St. Mary, R., ii, 90^{b}; i, 45, 82^{b}.—John Gorwell, junior, became Canon and Prebendary of Pratum min., in the Cathedral Church of Hereford, 9 June, 1401; ii, 53^{b}.

Gorewell, William, proxy for William Hals, ii, 78; for John Gorewell, junior, ii, 90^{b}.

Gorteboos, William, instituted to St. Endellion, R., ii, 178^{b}; *see*, also, i, 226^{b}; ii, 259^{b}.

Gosley [*also* "Goslay" *and* "Goslegh," MS.], Roger, chaplain, i, 306^{b}; instituted to Buckfastleigh, V., ii, 160; his death, ii, 173^{b}.—*See*, also, ii, 255^{b}, 355.

Gourney (or Gorney), Sir Matthew, knt., i, 26^{b}, 57^{b}, 76^{b},—*see* Gurney *and* Silverton.

Gove, John, does homage at Clyst for lands at Clyst (20 April, 1400), ii, 310^{b}.

Govys, Agnes, relict of John, i, 90^{b}; 168^{b}.

Govys (*alias* Donk), John, i, 310, 311; instituted to Holy Trinity, Exeter, ii, 23; i, 72; his death, ii, 176; his Will, i, 328^{b}.

Gra, Thomas, of York, patron of St. Helen's, Ingelby, ii, 48.

---

[1] Decided in favour of Denys and Hulle; but in the next case against Denys, and in favour of Waye and Toker (*see Institutions*").

Grampound, Chapel of St. Mary at, in Creed, i, 48.

Grandisson, John de, Bishop of Exeter, Founder of Ottery St. Mary, i, 29 ; his Chantry in Exeter Cathedral, ii, 65.

Granger, Alice, wife of Thomas, i, 308b ; John, his son, *ibid.*

Granger, Thomas, his Will, i, 308b.

Grantebrygg, John, proxy for John Syggeston, ii, 33.

Grantelond (*alias* Portey), William, i, 305.

Graunt, William, and Margaret, his wife, i, 145 ; *see Oratories.*

Grede, John, instituted to Poughill, R., ii, 147b ; i, 213 ; exchanges for Harpford V., ii, 197.

Grendon, the Church of (Dioc. of Lichfield), i, 316.

Grendon, Ricarda, wife of Simon, i, 203 (*see Oratories*) ; 316b.

Grendon, Simon, citizen of Exeter, i, 331 ; his Will, i, 315b ; Commission to prove the same (1 Sep., 1411), ii, 243.

Grendon, Walter (Prior of the Hospital of St. John of Jerusalem in England), presents to the R. of St. Ive, ii, 54, 104 ; to St. Cleer, V., ii, 84b, 89, 94, 148 ; to St. Madron, V., ii, 99b ; to Brendon, R., ii, 105b, 147b.

Grendale, Prebend of, in York Cathedral,—Letter from the Archbishop of York to Bishop Stafford concerning it (received 2 Dec., 1418), ii, 196.

Grene, John, chaplain, i, 301b.

Grene, William, chaplain, M.A.—

Licensed as a Publick Preacher in the Archdeaconry of Totnes (17 June, 1415), i, 210b ; chaplain of the Parish Church of Plymouth, i, 217, 237b, 245 ; licensed to confess the parishioners there (2 April, 1416), i, 220 ; a Penitentiary in the Deanery of Plympton, i, 231.

Grene, William, V. of Honington (Dioc. of Lincoln), exchanges for Clyst St. Mary, R., i, 74b, ii, 53b ; and again for Stratford-juxta-Glemham, R. (in Suffolk), ii, 91.

Grenewode, Thomas, Canon of York and Prebendary of Grendale, ii, 179b.

Grenvyll (or Grenwyll), John, R. of Plymtree, q. v.

Greynevill, Sir John, knt., presents to Kilkhampton, R., ii, 71 ; Commission for proving his Will, ii, 244b. [Justice of the Peace for Cornwall, ii, 335b].

Greynville, Richard, clerk, i, 38 ; ii, 16b ; *Dispensacio super defectu natalium* (25 July, 1400), i, 44 ; 78 ; instituted to Roborough, R., ii, 91b, 108b ; instituted to Parkham, R., ii, 92 ; resigns Roborough, i, 91 ; proxy for John Harry, ii, 100 ; collated to a Canonry in Exeter Cathedral, ii, 197b.

Grenewode, Thomas, co-patron of Axminster, V., ii, 187.

Grey, John, R. of Creed, exchanges for Grittleton, R. (Diocese of Salisbury), ii, 28b; resigns Canonry at Glasney, ii, 29b.

Grey, Robert, i, 320b; ii, 281b.

Greyston, a Manor of Oliver Wyse, in Cornwall, i, 202b.

Greyston, Thomas, chaplain, i, 315; instituted to Stowford, R., ii, 105; i, 90b; resigns Stowford and is collated to Farringdon, R., ii, 164b; i, 210, 334; resigns Farringdon, ii, 189; proxy for Henry Trethewy, ii, 190b. Thomas Greyston exchanged his R. of Thorney (Dioc. of Chichester), in 1418, for St. George's, Exeter, ii, 196.

Groffham, John, of Funtington (Dio. of Chichester), ii, 280, 281b.

Grouse [or Grose], John, chaplain of the Chantry of St. Pancras, London, exchanges for Pinhoe, V., ii, 28, 210b; exchanges again for Haselbeare, V. (Dioc. of Wells), ii, 92; and again for Challacombe, R., ii, 105b.

Grylleston, Robert and William, of Collumpton, i, 207.—*See*, Vawtard.

Grym, John, appointed Penitentiary of Polslo (18 Aug., 1395), i, 4b; instituted to Holbeton, V., ii, 6b.

Grym (or Grim), William, R. of Lamorran, exchanges for Buckland Monachorum, V., ii, 40; resigns, ii, 228.

Grymel, Richard, i, 141.

Grymston (or Grymmeston, &c.), John, V. of Holsworthy, q. v.

Gryndel, Friar John, i, 301.

Grysty, Benedict, R. of Shevioke (deceased), ii, 83b.

Guldesfeld, Thomas, R. of Elingdon (Dioc. of Salisbury), exchanges for Sutton-juxta-Plymouth, V., ii, 105b; i, 138; 145b, 146.

Gulval, bequest to the Church of, i, 314b.

Gunny, Edith, i, 329b.

Gunwardby, Robert (son of John), V. of Stapleford (Dioc. of Ely), exchanges with the Sacristan of Bosham, ii, 109b; his death, ii, 147.

Gurney, Matheu (*or* Maiheu) de, i, 311b.—*see* Gourney.

Gurney, Richard, R. of Tiverton, 2nd Portion (deceased), ii, 10.

Gust, William, co-patron of Chedyngdon, R. (Dioc. of Salisbury), ii, 75b.

Guvan, John, a parishioner of Lelant, i, 133b, ii, 232b.

Guy, Rd., proxy for Canon Walter Gybbes (resigning), ii, 29b.

Gvynov, Thomas, i, 323^{b}.

Gwennap, or St. Gwennap [Sancte Weneppe, MS.], John Colyn, V. of, Penitentiary in the Deanery of Kerrier, i, 143^{b}, 194^{b}, 207^{b}, 217, 231, 238.

Gy, Richard, a Minorite Friar, licensed to hear confessions (13 April, 1401), i, 56—perhaps the same as R. Guy, *supra*.

Gybbys (*or* Gybbe), Gunneta, i, 333^{b}.

Gybbys, Thomas, instituted to Huxham, R., ii, 115; to Poltimore, R., ii, 199^{b}; resigns Huxham, ii, 200; co-patron thereof, *ibid.*

Gybbes, Walter, R. of Tawstock (*see Oratories*), i, 9.

He was collated to a Canonry in Exeter Cathedral, ii, 29^{b}; 212, 212^{b}; i, 19^{b}; and in Ottery St. Mary, ii, 78^{b}. But being insane, and, consequently, unable to manage his own affairs, a Commission was directed (27 Jan., 1410-11), to two other Canons, John Gorewyll and William Egerdon, to take charge and administration thereof, ii, 237^{b}. He died about three years later, ii, 150^{b}.

Gydelegh, Richard, clerk,—*Dispensacio super defectu natalium* . . . . "de presbitero et soluta" (22 Dec., 1408), i, 87^{b}.

Gydelegh, William, clerk,—*Dispensacio super defectu natalium* (16 Dec., 1400), i, 51^{b}.

Gyffard, Alfred, R. of Lanivet; licensed to celebrate in the Chapel of St. Benet in that parish (17 June, 1411), i, 126^{b}.

Gyffard, Andrew de, co-patron of Roseash, R., ii, 81.

Gyffard, John, chaplain, instituted to the Chantry at Umberleigh, ii, 17^{b}; exchanges for Nymet Rowland, R., ii, 25^{b}; collated to Spreyton, V., ii, 88; [resigns Nymet Rowland and] is collated to Buckland Filleigh, R., ii, 103^{b}.

Gyffard, John, deacon, instituted to Buckerell, V., ii, 105.

Gyffard, Robert, R. of Thorne-Coffin (Dioc. of Bath and Wells), exchanges for Meeth, R., ii, 221; his death, ii, 123^{b}, 233^{b}.

Gyffard, Stephen, instituted to West Putford, R., ii, 82; i, 77.

Gylbert, John, i, 305.

Gyldespyn, John, scholar,—*Dispensacio super defectu natalium* (28 April, 1418), i, 239^{b}.

Gyldyfold, Thomas, i.q., Guldesfeld (q. v.), i, 138.

Gyle, William, chaplain, instituted to Christow, V., ii, 138, 244; his death, ii, 176. *See* i; 312.

Gyles, John, Canon and Prebendary of Merston in the Collegiate Church of St. Mary at Stafford, exchanges for St. Martins-by-Looe, R., ii, 30^{b}; i, 9; resigns, ii, 35; instituted to Sutton-juxta-Plymouth, V., *ibid*; exchanges for Elingdon, R., (Dioc. of Salisbury), ii, 105b.

Gylle, John, *see* Lostwithiel, i, 229b; ii, 260b; i, 315; instituted to St. Winnow, V., ii, 144.

Gyst, Alfred, instituted to Virginstow, R., ii, 115; resigns and is instituted to Bickleigh, V., ii, 144; and to Down St Mary, R., ii, 145, 248b; his death, ii, 176.

Gyst, Edward, R. of Okeford (deceased), ii, 108.

Gynne *or* Gunne, John, V. of Brent, *see* Junne, *and* Brent.

H.

Hacche, in the parish of South Molton, i, 91.

Hacche, John, R. of South Molton, i, 332; his death, ii, 94.

Hacche, John (son and heir of Robert), presents to Romansleigh, R., ii, 176b, 258b.

Hacche, John, of Kingston, ii, 277b.

Hacche, John, of Churchstow, ii, 291.

Hacche, Richard (*see Oratories*), i, 8b.

Haccombe, Elizabeth Lercedekne of, her Will, i, 309; the Church of St. Blaise at, *ibid.*—Michael Lercedekne, Archpriest of,—Dispensation (to study at Oxford) for *seven* years, from 29 May, 1401; i, 56b; 147b, 162, 166b, 167b, 172b, 176; resigns Haccombe, having been instituted to Thorney R. (Dioc. of Chichester), 18 March, 1412-13, i, 178b.—Edward [Legh], Archpriest of, Penitentiary in the Deanery of Kenn, i, 245.

Hackworthy [Hakeworthy, MS.], in Tedburn St. Mary, i, 212b.

Hadham, the Bishop of London's Manor of, i, 7b, 57b.

Haget [or Hacket, MS.], John, R. of Kingsnympton, collated to a Canonry in Exeter Cathedral, ii, 91; resigns Kingsnympton, ii, 96; is again instituted thereto, ii, 100; exchanges for Fuggleston, R., with Bemerton (Diocese of Salisbury), ii, 103b; exchanges his Canonry for a Canonry in Salisbury, ii, 150.

Hake, Robert (a layman), and Nicola Fricon,—

Commission to enquire as to certain reports about them (1 Oct., 1414), ii, 255b: they had married, although related in the third and fourth degrees of consanguinity, and a Dispensation was granted in their favour (15 Jan., 1414-15), i, 207b.

Hakeworthy (*or* Hakeworth, MS., *margin*), Roger, a layman,—

Having seriously assaulted Richard Philips, a priest of this Diocese, stabbing

him in the face with a dagger, and shedding his blood freely, he was excommunicated for the crime; but, his victim recovering entirely, he sought absolution. Having a wife and children to support, he could not go to Rome in person, but the Bishop absolved him with the authority of the Pope (5 June, 1410), i, 97b.

Hakket, Walter, i, 332.

Halap, James, i, 323b.

Halberton, Moryston (*hodie* Moorstone) in, i, 77; John Chudderlegh of, i, 147; John Boys of, i, 318.

Hales [Heylys, MS.], the Monks of, *see* Cury, i, 4; the Abbot and Convent of, present to St. Breage, V., ii, 69; to Paul, V., ii, 190, 264; the Abbot of, at Torre Abbey, ii, 142b.

Halle, Thomas, does homage to the Bishop, in London, for lands in Devon (24 May, 1396), ii, 310.

Halle, William, of Beare, in the parish of Tawton—the Bishop's "litera homagii," 6 March, 1410; ii, 310b.

Hallum, Robert, collated to a Canonry in Exeter Cathedral, ii, 49b; his death, ii, 93.

Hals, David[3], and Matilda, his wife, i, 306b.

Hals, John, brother of Richard, i, 330; proxy for Richard Hals on his collation to the Prebend of Carswell, in Crediton, ii, 29; *see* Sherford, i, 168b.

Hals, Matilda, mother of Richard, i, 330.

Hals, Richard, R. of North Bovey, resigns, ii, 5,—

He was Canon and Prebendary (of "Crida") in Crediton, and exchanged for the Prebend of Carswell therein, ii, 29; was collated to a Canonry in Glasney, ii, 41; and in Exeter Cathedral, ii, 45, 48; i, 40, 40b, 44b, 46b, 47, 301b; resigned his Canonry in Glasney, ii, 45b; collated Treasurer of Exeter Cathedral, ii, 50b; 58b, 60, 60b, 229; i, 51b, 128, 208; exchanged his R. of St. Ive for All-Hallows-on-the-Walls, R., Exeter, ii, 50b; and immediately resigned the latter, *ibid*; exchanged his R. of Warbleton (Dioc. of Chichester), for a Canonry in Bosham (which he resigned five days later in favour of William Langeton), ii, 52; proxy for Walter Trote, ii, 53b; his death, ii, 185b; his Will, i, 329b. *See*, also, i, 198, and ii, 209b.—He was employed as an ambassador in Britanny in 1414; i, 198.

Hals, William, Chantry priest in the Church of Alwington, resigns, ii, 36b; is instituted to Wyke St. Mary, R., ii, 78; his death, ii, 90b; his Will, i, 306.

Halsanger (*and* Halsaungre, MS.), **John**, instituted to Dunterton, R., ii, 130, 236b; to Cardynham, R., ii, 153, 252b; resigns Dunterton, and exchanges Cardynham for Grittleton, R. (Dioc. of Salisbury), ii, 154b.—John Halsanggere (*sic*) was presented to St. George's, Exeter, but not admitted, ii, 234b.

---

[3] He is described as a brother of William Hals, R. of Wyke St. Mary.

Halswyll, Joan, i, 307^b.

Halswyll, Richard, presented to Combe-in-Teignhead, R., ii, 264^b; *see*, also, i, 308^b, 309.

Halswyll, Robert and William, i, 307^b.

Halwell [Halewyll, MS.], John Gedefray (*sic*), R. of, appointed by the Bishop "curator" to John Flemmyng, R. of Inwardleigh (7 April, 1405), i, 74, 330^b.

Halwyll, John, i, 307^b.

Halyett [*or* Haliet *alias* Hamme, MS.], Wm., R. of Chulmleigh, exchanges for Roseash, R., ii, 80^b; his death, ii, 89^b; i, 324.

Halys, *alias* Sparwe, John, R. of Brushford (Dioc. of B. & W.), exchanges for Washfield, ii, 108; *see* Say, Agnes, i, 121^b; exchanges for Parley, (Dioc. of Salisbury), ii, 142.

Hamme [i.e. Georgeham], John, Rector of, a Penitentiary in the Deanery of Shirwell, i, 50.

Hamme, Chapel of St. David at, in Ashprington, i, 99.

Hamond, John, collated Sacristan of Ottery, ii, 28; i, 90; resigns Powderham, R., ii, 28^b.

Hamond, Robert, V. of Branscombe, resigns, ii, 18^b.

Hamount, William, notary-publick, i, 51^b.

Hampdene, Edmund, Esquire; *see* Ottery St. Mary, ii, 278.

Hamptefforde, William, and Katherine his wife (sister of Thomas Reymound), i, 332.

Hampton, Joan, relict of Ralph Sachevile, of Bicton, ii, 6.

Hampton, Roger, Warden of the Chapel of St. Helen, Ingelby (Dioc of Lincoln), exchanges for a Prebend in Crantock, ii, 47^b; resigns, ii, 52^b; collated to a Canonry and the 8th Prebend in Ottery St. Mary, ii, 151^b.

Hanecok, Walter, i, 320^b.

Hankeford, family of, their patronage,—

John Hankeford was patron of the Chantry of Tadyport, ii, 5; and of Alvington, R., ii, 100, 131^b, 179.—Richard Hankeford was patron of North Tawton, R., ii, 8, 333^b; of Roborough, R. (in right of his wife Thomasia, daughter and heir of Sir Richard Stapeldon, knight), ii, 12, 25^b, 91^b, 108^b, 148, 149; co-patron of Aveton-Giffard, R., ii, 87^b; and of the Chantry de Lyneton in that church, ii, 91^b; also of the Chantry of St. Leonard's, Raleigh, ii, 137^b, 182^b, 191.—Sir Wm. Hankeford, Judge, i, 20^b, was patron of the Chantry in the church of Alwington, ii, 10^b, 13, 135^b, 221^b, 308^b; co-patron of West Putford, R., ii, 82; (with Richard and John Hankeford) he presented to Instow, R., ii, 89^b, 145, 234, 248^b; presented to Ashwater, R., ii, 148^b.—*See* Parkham.

Hantysforde (or Hautysforde), William, presents to Creacombe, R., ii, 13^b, 68^b.

Harberton, *see* Burleston (*Oratories*), i, 105. Richard Jelle of, ii, 226[b].—Peter Duke, V. of, a Penitentiary in the Deanery of Totnes, i, 94, 115[b], 143.

Harcombe (or Harecombe), John, Chantry-priest of St. Mary's, in the Church of Crewkerne, exchanges for Jacobstowe, R. (Devon), ii, 86; i, 88[b]; exchanges[1] for Chalbury, R. (Dioc. of Salisbury), ii, 142[b].

Hardeby, Walter, *see* Lifton, ii, 265.

Hardy (or Hard), John, inst. to St. Michael's Mount, ii, 338[b].

Harfleur ("Harflet" MS.), i, 96.

Harford [Herford, MS], Simon Elys, R of, licence to celebrate in the chapel of St. Nicholas, Stowford [Stoford, MS.], in that parish, 14 Dec., 1400, i, 51[b]; *see*, also, i, 67.

Harlewyn, John, of Littleham, i, 32.

Harpere, Alice, John, and Richard, i, 306[b].

Harpere, Roger, R. of Holy Trinity, Exeter (deceased), ii, 23

Harpford [Herford and Herpeforde, MS.], John Awbry, V. of, i, 99.

Harri, Henry, chaplain,—

He was appointed, by the Bishop, Curate of Alwington [Alvyngton, MS.], the Rector, Thomas Was, being *senio confractus et mentis discrecione privatus* (2 Jan., 1404-5), i, 72.

Harry, John, i, 326[b]; instituted to Shebbear, V., ii, 20.

John Harry (or Henry), perhaps the same, was a little later instituted to the R. of St. Endellion[2] (ii, 26), which he soon exchanged for St. Gwinear, V. (ii, 83), where he was licensed, 10 Oct., 1411, to celebrate in the chapel [3] of St. Wynnerus in that parish, i, 135[b]. Again, a "John Harry" was instituted to Alwington, R. (ii, 100), and soon exchanged it for the Wardenship of the Hospital of St. David, Swansea, ii, 131. Lastly, a John Harry was collated in 1417 to Stoke Gabriel, V., ii, 187[b].

Harry, John, of Brixham, and Margery, daughter of John Baron, of Paignton—special licence for their marriage (15 Jan., 1417-18), i, 237[b].

Harry (or Herry), Nicholas, proxy for Ralph Rudruth, ii, 29; for John Grey, ii, 29[b]; collated Sacristan of Glasney, ii, 53; i, 93[b], 115[b]; co-patron of the Chantry "de Ponte," ii, 163. [He was V. of St. Just-in-Penwith—institution not recorded—and died in 1427].

---

[1] Here called Harkecomb, MS.

[2] He was proxy for John Arondell on his collation to a Canonry in Crantock, ii, 196[b].

[3] This "Chapel" was dedicated to the same Saint as the Mother Church: the licence was granted "perpetuo Vicario ecclesie parochialis Sancti Wynneri, in Cornubia, divina celebrandi in Capella Sancti Wynneri infra parochiam predictam situata, et in honore ejusdem Sancti consecrata."

Herry, Robert, V. of Pelynt (deceased), ii, 2.

Harry, Thomas, collated to St. Colan, V., ii, 133; resigns, ii, 142b; instituted to St. Stephen-in-Brannel, V., ii, 157; resigns it, ii, 159b; on being instituted to [Ruan-] Lanyhorne, R., ii, 158b; *see*, also, ii, 264b.

Harry, Walter, presents to Trentishoe, R., ii, 188b.

Harston (or Hareston), in Brixton [Plympton], i, 28, 64, 87b.

Hartland, Joan More of, i, 313.

Hartland[1], Abbey, the Bishop at; i, 38,—

Mandate for the Visitation of, on 20 May, 1400, i, 36b; Philip Tone, Abbot of, i, 64; the said Abbot, in arrear of Procurations due to the Pope's Collector for three years (1408-10), i, 105.—The Abbot and Convent present to Launcells, V., ii, 26, 69b; to Fremington, V., i, 141b; ii, 96b. Licence granted to them for the celebration of Divine Service in the Chapels of Holy Cross, Clifford and Southole, St. Mary's, Firebeacon[2], St. James's, Milford, and Exmansworthy[3], St. Wenne's at Cherrystow[4], and St. Martin's at Meddon (21 May, 1400), i, 38b.

Haryngton, Elizabeth, relict of Sir John de,—

Mandate to administer the oath "de non maritando sine licencia (*Breve Regium*, 12 July, 1418), ii, 362b. She presented to Ludgvan, R., ii, 194b, 266.

Haselee, Thomas, proxy for John de Spryngthorp, ii, 51.

Hatherleigh, Roger [Trefrew], V. of, a Penitentiary in the Deanery of Okehampton, i, 50.

Haubert, John, *see* Stafford; ii, 218, 218b.

Hauk, John, instituted to St. Clether, ii, 70; resigns, ii, 156b.

Hawke, William, chaplain, of Sourton, i, 214.

Haukden, Thomas, Monk of Tavistock, ii, 59.

Haukherst or Haukryg, Thomas, instituted to St. Nicholas Priory, Exeter, ii, 5b; resigns, ii, 46b.

Haukyn, Laurence,—

He became R. of Chagford by exchange with John Dypphull, ii, 33b, 34b; was collated to a Canonry in Exeter Cathedral, ii, 35; to a Canonry (and Prebend of Thorney) in Chichester Cathedral, ii, 35b; resigned Chagford, *ibid*; was collated to a Canonry (and Prebend of Crosse), in Crediton, ii, 44b, 58b; to a Canonry in Bosham, ii, 45, 280, 281, 294; *by lapse* to North Molton, R., ii, 50b; which he exchanged for St. Columb-major, R., ii, 80b; i, 102; he resigned his Canonry in Bosham, ii, 96; and was collated to another Canonry (and the Prebend of Waleton) there, ii, 96b; proxy for John Haget, ii, 103b; exchanged his Canonry in Exeter Cathedral for a Canonry in Crantock, ii, 161; was collated to another Canonry in Exeter, ii, 166b; and to be Precentor there, ii, 174b; proxy for Edward Prentys, ii, 179b; also for Henry Portioye, ii, 42b; his death, 190, 190b, 191; his Will, i, 333.—*See*, also, i, 47b, 56, 83, 97, 116, 117, 129, 149, 167, 168b, 175b, 184, 184b, 185, 197, 209b, 229, 234b, 301, 307b, 325, 326, 327b, 328b.

Hawkyn or Haukyn, William, V. of Combe Keynes (Dioc. of

[1] Hertylond, MS.
[2] Fyrbykene, MS.
[3] Ashmandesworthi, MS.
[4] Churstowe, MS.

Salisbury), exchanges for Ashton, R., ii, 68^{a}; for Chedingdon, R. (Dioc. of Salisbury), ii, 75^{b}; for Challacombe, R., ii, 87; for Haselbury, V. (Dioc. of B. and W.), ii, 105^{b}.

Haulghton, John, *fellmonger*, of London, long imprisoned and in great poverty.—Indulgence for his relief (16 July, 1411), i, 128^{b}.

Hawlegh (*or* Hauley), John, patron of St. Keyne, R., ii, 9^{b}; Sir John (senior), presents to the Chantry of Washbourne, ii, 65^{b}; John Hauley presents to the same, ii, 197^{b}; *see* St. Keyne, ii, 303^{b}.

Hawley (or Hawlegh), Thomas, collated, *by lapse*, to St. Keyne, R., ii, 32, 9^{b}; i, 12.

Hay, Adam, instituted to Belston, R., ii, 189.

Haydurer, Walter, chaplain, i, 324.

Haye, John, pollutes the Church of Fremington, ii, 242.

Haye, John, *see* atte Haye.

Haye, William de la, Prior of Tywardreath (deceased), ii, 44^{b}.

Hayford, William, inst. to Ashburton, V., ii, 84: i, 301, 310.

Haynok, Henry, chaplain, i, 315.

Hayward, Thomas, an infirm priest,—Commission as to his admission to Clyst St. Gabriel (6 Dec., 1398), ii. 221^{b}.

Haywode, Thomas, instituted to the Chantry "Sancti Salphini," in the Castle of Barnstaple, ii, 104^{b}; instituted to Stoke-Rivers, ii, 129^{b}; exchanges for Poundstock, ii, 180.

Heanok, John, inst. to Blackborough, ii, 151^{b}; his death, ii, 156.

Heanton Punchardon, *see*, Courtenay, Sir Hugh, i, 235^{b}.

Commissions of enquiry as to the right of presentation: (1) On the presentation of Richard Hore, chaplain, by Sir William Esturmy, knight (8 June, 1412), ii, 247; (2) on the presentation of Richard Knyght, priest, by Isabella, relict of William Beaumond (same date), *ibid.*; (3) on the presentation of the said Richard Knyght by the King (19 June, 1412), *ibid.*

the Chantry of St. Mary at,—

(1) Prohibition to the Bishop to admit a clerk, pending the settlement of the dispute as to the patronage between the King and Sir William Esturmy, knight (*Breve Regium*, 13 June, 1412), ii, 344^{b}.—(2) To the same effect (*Breve Regium*, 12 Oct., 1412), ii, 345.—(3) To admit the nominee of Isabella Beaumont, who had sustained her claim to the patronage against Sir William Esturmy (7 Nov., 1412), ii, 345^{b}.—"Hehaunton," MS., ii, 251.

Commissions of enquiry as to patronage, etc.:—(1) On the presentation of William Scoche, chaplain, by Sir William Esturmy, knight, and Joan, his wife (20 March, 1412-13) ii, 251; (2) On the presentation of John Polsave, chaplain, by the King (same date), ii, 251^{b}; (3) to the same effect as (2),—(24 March, 1412-13), *ibid.*

Heanton Sachville [Heampton Sachevyle, MS.], *see* Petrockstowe, i, 58^{b}.

Heavitree [Hevytre, MS.]; the "Ordinacio" of the Vicarage,—

The Bishop states that, recently, between the Dean and Chapter of Exeter (the appropriators), on the one part, and Thomas Plymmeswode (Vicar), on the other part, certain questions had arisen, touching the "portion" assigned to the said Vicarage; and that both parties were willing to accept the Bishop's decision, viz. (1) That the Vicar and his successors should have all the oblations, etc., at the altars of the said Church, and its dependent chapels of St. Sidwell and St. David, and also of two other chapels in the parish, St. Clement's and St. Eligius', with the tithes of the mills, and all small tithes, "nutrimentis animalium," buildings, gardens, etc., at Heavitree and St. Sidwell's formerly assigned to them; also twelve acres of arable land. (2) That the Vicars should be relieved from the annual payment of four marks and ten shillings to the Dean and Chapter, hitherto made by them. (3) They were to be responsible for all ordinary burdens connected with the parish-church and the Chapels of St. Sidwell and St. David [including the repair, and even rebuilding of the three chancels, and everything, generally, for which the parishioners were not responsible]. (4) They were to have no part of the tithes *feni, bladorum, garbarum*, whencesoever arising, whether in orchards, crofts, gardens, or other closes, not even if such lands should again be brought into agricultural cultivation; nor of the apples in the garden of the Dean and Chapter at St. Sidwell's; save and except the tithes of the lands assigned, above, to the said Vicars. But if any arable land were afterwards devoted to crops *lini, canabi, carduorum, porrorum, allei, separum, vel olerum*, or to pasture, the Vicars were to be entitled to their tithes therefrom, as before described, and not otherwise (28 March, 1401). By the Dean and Chapter, in their Chapter-House, 9 April, 1401.—By the said Vicar, at Exeter, under the seal of the Dean of Christianity, 10 April, 1401; ii, 295b; *see*, also, i, 55b.

Simon Grendon's bequest to the Vicar of, i, 316.—John Wythyslond (or Wydeslond), Vicar of, i, 322, 327b.—Chapel of St. Anne, without the Eastgate, in the parish of (*de novo constructa*), licence to the Dean and Chapter to provide for the celebration of Divine Service therein (2 Nov., 1418), i, 214.

Hederlond, Chapel at, dependent on Washfield, R., i, 121b.

Heghedon, *alias* Vays (q. v.), Robert, i, 126b.

Heghes (or Heyes), the Prebend of, ii, 347b.

Hegneh, John, instituted to South Tawton, V., ii, 177b.

Hele (i.e. Bosumshele in the parish of Dittisham), i, 8b.

Hele, Manor of, in the parish of Bradninch, i, 221b.

Hele, John, instituted to Clyst St. Laurence, R., ii, 2; exchanges for Clysthydon, R., ii, 41; presents to Clyst St. Laurence, R., ii, 74; exchanges Clysthydon for Yarcombe, ii, 104b; a Penitentiary in the Deanery of Dunkeswell, i, 94, 115, 143, 173b, 194; exchanges Yarcombe for Manston, R. (Dioc. of Salisbury), ii, 156b.

Hele, Nicholas, *see* Bickleigh, R.

Hele, William, chaplain, i, 306b; inst. to Umberleigh, ii, 122.

Helland, Robert [Mychel], R., a Penitentiary in the Deanery of Trigg-Minor, i, 49b.—John Wyllet, R.; licence of non-residence for one year, from 2 May, 1418, i, 240.

Hellond, Joan de, i, 323b.

Helston, Hospital of St. Mary Magd., near,—Indulgence to the Faithful contributing to its support (7 Oct., 1411), i, 135.

Helyer, Peter, monk of Tavistock, ii, 59.

Helyer, Richard, clerk of Honiton, i, 307.

Helygan, Manor of, in the parish of St. Mabyn, i, 56.

Helygan, Nicholas, *see* St. Kew, i, 75.

Helys, Thomas, inst. to Dodbrooke, ii, 107b; his death, ii, 124b.

Hembery, John, R. of St. Edmund's, Exeter (deceased), ii, 151b.

Hemburgh, John, V. of Fowey (deceased), ii, 135b.

Hemyock, William Rodewyk, R. of, a Penitentiary in the Deanery of Dunkeswell, i, 207b.

Hendeman, Thomas (Dean of Crantock, etc.), instituted to Tiverton (2nd Portion), ii, 10; resigns, and is instituted to Sampford Courtenay, R., ii, 74b; collated to a Canonry in Exeter, ii, 94; exchanges Crantock for the Chantry of St. Michael in the Cemetery of St. Austell, ii, 108b; and his Canonry and Prebend of Colworth (Dioc. of Chichester), for the Archdeaconry of Exeter, ii, 109; resigns Sampford Courtenay, ii, 114b; and the Chantry at St. Austell, ii, 135; is instituted to St. Winnow, V., ii, 138b; and to Widecombe [-in-the-Moor], V., ii, 143b; exchanges the latter for Farway, R., ii, 145b; is instituted to the Prebend of Heyghes[1], ii, 152; resigns Farway, and is instituted to St. Mabyn, R., ii, 164; collated Chancellor of Exeter Cathedral, ii, 181b; resigns his Archdeaconry, ii, 182; *see*, also, i, 324b.

Hendeston, Hugh, instituted to Winkleigh, V., ii, 153.

Hendour, Thomas, presents to St. Stephen-in-Brannel, V., ii, 157, 159b, 180b, 190b.

Hendre, Thomas, instituted to Treneglos, V., ii, 106b.

Hendre, William, R. of St. Mawgan-in-Pydar (deceased), ii, 121; case of "Dilapidations," ii, 233; *see*, also, ii, 55, 333[2].

Hendy, John, inst. to Highampton, R., ii, 141; *see*, also, ii, 245b.

Hendy, Richard, clerk,—*Dispensacio super defectu natalium* (29 May, 1417), i, 232b.

Hennock [Hanok, MS.], William Cok, V. of, i, 179b.

Henford, Thos., inst. to Buckerell, V., ii, 86b; his death, ii, 105.

---

[1] *See* Kardyngton, Thomas, ii, 347b.

[2] Where he is called R. of St. Mawgan "de Lanherne."

Henry IV,—

Mandate to pray for the King, setting out on his expedition against the Scotch (who had committed great outrages and sacrilege on the Border); also, on account of the pestilence (12 July, 1400), i, 43b.

Mandate to pray for the King and his army, setting out against the Welsh rebels (20 June, 1401), i, 57.

Mandate to pray for the King (8 Feb., 1401-2, i, 59.

Mandate to pray for the King and for the peace of the Realm, during the expedition to recover the Dukedom of Aquitaine, under the Duke of Clarence: the Bishop certified the Archbishop, on the 20th of Oct., 1412, that the same had been duly complied with, i, 170.

Patron of the Chantry at Beaford, ii, 19b, 57b; of Warkleigh, R., ii, 22b, 54b[1]; presents to Pyworthy, R., ii, 25, 82b, 101b; to Stoke Climsland, R., ii, 43b; to Holcombe-Rogus, V., ii, 43; to Huntshaw, R., ii, 44b, 49b; to the Priory of Tywardreath, ii, 44b; to Tintagel[2], V., ii, 46b, 98b; to Charles, R., ii, 48b; to Ipplepen, R., ii, 51, 64b; to the Chantry of Umberleigh, ii, 52b, 96b, 122; to Lanteglos-by-Camelford, R., ii, 57; to Uploman, R., ii, 63b, 93[3], 136b[4]; to Combmartin, R., ii, 64, 83, 87; to St. Clether, V., ii, 70; to Marwood, R., ii, 70b, 89; to St. Hilary[5], V., ii, 74; to St. Illogan, R., ii, 74b; to Tawstock, R., ii, 76; to Stokenham, R., ii, 77b; to Wyke St. Mary, R., ii, 78, 90b; to Cowick, V., ii, 85b; to Antony, V., ii, 87; to Spreyton, V., ii, 88; to Clyst St. Mary, R., ii, 91; to High Bickington, R., ii, 91, 95; to Modbury, V., ii, 93b, 94b: nominates to the Priory of Totnes, ii, 96b; and to Fremington, V., *ibid.*; presents to Whimple, R., ii, 98; to the Chantry at Morthoe, ii, 100b, 137[6]; to St. Pancras-juxta-Axmouth, R., ii, 96, 102, 120; to the Chantry of St. Michael in the Cemetery of St. Austell, ii, 103, 135; to the Chantry "Sancti Salphini," in the Castle of Barnstaple, ii. 104b; to Tywardreath, V., ii, 105; to Ermington, R., ii, 105b, 120b; to Treneglos, V., ii, 106b; to Fowey, V., ii, 135b, 143, 240; to St. George's, Exeter, ii, 135, 235; to Heanton Punchardon, R., ii, 146, 247; to the Chantry of St. Thomas-by-the-Bridge, Barnstaple, ii, 147b; to the Chantry at Heanton Punchardon, ii, 149, 251b; claims to present to Loddiswell, R., ii, 238b; presents to the Priory of St. Michael's Mount (on account of the war with France), ii, 338b, 349.

Henry, Prince of Wales and Duke of Cornwall,—

Presents to Michaelstow, R., ii, 78b. 99; to the Priory of Tywardreath, ii, 93b; to Talkern (i.e. Minster), R., ii, 102; to the Priory of St. Michael's Mount, ii, 124, 233 (and *see* ii, 349); to Blisland, R., ii, 124b, 138b; to Menhenyot, R., (co-patron as guardian of the heir of the late John Carmynow), ii, 138, 244: *see* St. Illogan, ii, 314b.

Henry V,—

Presents to Okehampton, V., ii, 154; to Yarcombe, V., ii, 156b; to St. Pancras de Doune-juxta-Lyme [Rousdon], R., ii. 160; St. Thomas', Exeter, V., ii, 161b, 255b; to St. George's, Exeter, R., ii, 162b, 196; to St. Austell, V., ii, 162b; to St. Anthony-in-Kerrier, V., ii, 164b; to Combmartin, R., ii, 167, 181; nominates to the Priory of Modbury, ii, 174b; presents to Shirwell, R., ii, 175b; to Christow, V., ii, 176; to Lanteglos [-by-Camelford], R., ii, 178b; to Moreton [Hampstead], R., 178b,

---

[1] By reason of the minority of Fulk, heir of Sir Fulk Fitzwaryn, knight, the true patron.

[2] By reason of his possession of the temporalities of the Abbey of Fontevrault, during the war in France.

[3] *See* Wroth, Sir John de.

[4] Where it is called the R. of Wellyngton Lamon.

[5] Part of the temporalities of the alien Priory of St. Michael,—during the war in France.

[6] Where it is called "of St. Katharine and St. Mary Magdalene."

198; to Whimple, R., ii, 192.—Mandate to pray for the King,—for his peace and tranquillity and for the peace of the Realm; for fine weather; for the cessation of pestilence and mortality; for the extirpation of sedition, schism, and heresy, specially of that execrable pest—Lollardy (24 Sep., 1413). Published in the Diocese of Exeter, 8 Nov., 1413; i, 187^{b}.

Heppescotes, Thomas de, Judge, ii, 342.

Herbert (or Herberd), Philip, clerk (who had been irregularly ordained)—*Dispensacio super defectu natalium* (3 April, 1400), i, 34; and again (12 June, 1400), i, 42.

Hereford, Thomas, collated to a Canonry at Ottery, ii, 55^{b}; exchanges for Rodmerton, R. (Dioc. of Worcester), *ibid.*

Heresy,—Mandate of the Archbishop of Canterbury for enquiry as to heretical pravity (3 July, 1416), i, 224, published in the Diocese of Exeter (22 July, 1416), *ibid.*

Herewordeshore, John, ii, 305^{b}.

Herle, Hugh, instituted to Ilfracombe, R., ii, 175^{b}; *see*, also, i, 223, 230^{b}; ii, 260, 258.

Herle, Sir John, knt., patron of Pelynt, V.[1], ii, 2; of Stockleigh-English, R., ii, 6; of Marhamchurch, R., ii, 45^{b}, 97^{b}, 122, 188, 249, 263^{b}; of Ilfracombe, R., ii, 175^{b}, 258.

Herle, William, instituted to Stockleigh-English, R., ii, 6.

Hermandysworthy, Robert, of Pancraswyke, i, 69.

Hermane, John, instituted to Bratton [-Fleming], R., ii, 109.

Hert, Thos. R. of Gittisham (deceased), ii, 104; his Will, i, 312^{b}.

Hertecombe [*also* Hyrtecombe, MS.], Nicholas, instituted to Okeford, R., ii, 108; i, 161; his death, ii, 146^{b}.

Hertyscote [or Hertescote, *also* Hurtyschote and Hurtyscote, MS.], Thomas, co-patron of Roche, R., ii, 57^{b}; of [Clay-]hydon, R., ii, 81^{b}; of South Pool, R., ii, 90^{b}, 97, 155^{b}; of Cotleigh, R., ii, 64, 95^{b}, 157^{b}; of Dunterton, R., ii, 130, 154^{b}, 236^{b}, 253; of Cardynham, R., ii, 153, 154^{b}, 252^{b}; of the Chantry of St. Katherine, Hemyock, ii, 198^{b}, 267^{b}.

Hertscote, Agnes, *see* Hunne, John, i, 169.

Hervy, Henry and Walter, parishioners of Linkinhorne, i, 116.

Hervy, Robert, Canon of St. Stephen's, Launceston, ii, 117.

Herward, John, inst. to Petrockstow, ii, 151, 251^{b}; i, 190, 354.

(*Breve Regium—de venire facias*).—The Parson of Petrockstow to appear at Westminster, and shew cause why he should not pay four marks to the Abbot of Buckfast, arrears of an annual rent of 26s. 8d. (12 Feb., 1414-15), ii, 351^{b}.—Herward became R. of Loxbeare by exchange for his R. of Hope-Mansell (Dioc. of Hereford), ii, 168^{b}.

[1] By virtue of his farming the Manor and the Rectory thereof from Newenham Abbey.

Herward, Robert, instituted to Hatherleigh, V., ii, 186; a Penitentiary in the Deanery of Okehampton, i, 94, 115^b, 143^b, 174, 194^b, 217, 231, 237^b.

Herward (*or* Hereward), Rob., Archdn. of Taunton, i, 310, 310^b.

Herygawde, Richard, chaplain, i, 329^b.

Heryngeston (*or* Hernyngeston), Thomas, R. of Martinhoe, exchanges for Halse, V. (Dioc. of Wells), ii, 56; for Charles, R., ii, 98^b; resigns, ii, 106.

Hesyll, John, R. of Jacobstow (Cornwall), q. v.; Canon of Glasney, ii, 225.

Hethen, John, chaplain, i, 47^b; resigns Clyst Fomison, ii, 54, and is collated to Peter Tavy, ii, 53^b; [resigns and] is collated, *by lapse*, to Talaton, ii, 77^b; i, 73; his death, ii, 85^b.

Hethfeld, John, proxy for the Prior and Convent of Cowick (*see* Okehampton), ii, 292^b.

Hetheway, Joan, *see* Lucas, John, i, 85.

Hexham, John, proxy for Thomas Lavyngton, ii, 57^b.

Heye, in the parish of St. Ive, i, 68.

Heyne, Richard, proxy for parishioners of Pancraswyke, i, 68^b.

Heynon, John, priest-vicar of Bosham, i, 12^b.

Heynstekot, John, proxy for John Tone, ii, 75^b.

Heynys, Hugh, collated to the Chantry of the Holy Ghost, at Warlond, near Totnes, ii, 53.

Heysell, John, i, 331^b.

Hichecok, Thomas, exchanges Broad-Sydelyng, V., (Dioc. of Salisbury), for Combe Raleigh R., ii, 40^b; exchanges again for East Coker, V. (Dioc. of Bath and Wells), ii, 71.

Hicka, Thomas, inst. to Buckerell, V., ii, 20^b (deceased), ii, 86^b.

Hickelyng, Hugh, Precentor of Exeter, i, 4; ii, 79, 213.

He was Canon of Wells, and exchanged for a Canonry in Crediton, ii, 152; he died Canon and Precentor of Exeter, Canon of Crediton, and also of Crantock, ii, 174^b; his Will, i, 325^b; Commission to prove the same (26 March, 1416), ii, 258.

Hyckelyng, Hugh, son of Robert, i, 326^b.

Hyckelyng, John de, son of William, *ibid.*

Hyckelyng, Robert de, Esquire, cousin to Hugh de, i, 326.

Highampton [Heyhamton, MS.],—

Commissions of Enquiry as to the right of patronage: (1) on the presentation of John Hendy, chaplain, by Robert Cary, domicellus (24 March, 1411-12), ii, 245^b. (2) on the presentation of Thomas Doune, clerk, by Richard Boyton (26 March, 1412), *ibid.* (3) on the presentation of the said John Hendy by Richard Boyton (12 April, 1412), *ibid.*—*See* "Institutions."

[High] Bickington [Bukyngton, MS.], William Crydy, R. of; licence of non-residence for one year, from 15 Oct., 1395, i, 6; a Penitentiary in the Deanery of Barnstaple, i, 50; his Will, i, 307[b].—John [Clerk], R. of; relaxation of a sequestration, and licence of non-residence for a year, from 27 Oct., 1410, i, 108[b]; from 21 Dec., 1411, to Michaelmas, 1412, i, 140[b]; from 14 Dec., 1412, to Michaelmas, 1413, i, 173; from 14 Dec., 1413, to Michaelmas, 1414, i, 190; from 15 Nov., 1414, to Michaelmas, 1415, i, 203[b].—Langelegh, *see* Pollard ("Oratories") i, 208[b].

High Bray [Hautysbray, MS.], Thomas [Langrom], R. of, *see* Wembworthy.

Hildesle, Edmund, proxy for Walter Medeford, ii, 81.

Hille, Hylle, or Hulle, *see* Hylle.

Hockworthy [Thomas Whytyng], V. of, i, 329.—Appropriated [Ockeworth in the MS. here] to Canonsleigh, ii, 359[b].

Hode, Peter, a parishioner of Cowick, ii, 287.

Hody, John, collated to a Canonry in Exeter Cath., ii, 165.

Hody, William (deceased), i, 331[b].

Hodysford, Alice, daughter of Thomas, i, 313, 313[b].

Hogge, Thomas, i, 332[b]; collated to Grandisson's Chantry in the Cathedral, ii, 65.

Hoggekyn, John, chaplain, i, 120[b].

Hoggeȝ, Alice, of Thurlbeare, i, 312.

Hoghe, William, R. of Mamhead (deceased), ii, 45[b].

Hoker, Hugh, i, 331.

Hoker, John, R. of Cotleigh, exchanges for St. Michael's, R., Bristol, ii, 64; for Seaton, V., ii, 84[b]; his death, ii, 193; his Will, i, 331[b].

Hokere, Hugh, instituted to Budleigh, V., ii, 21[b].

Hoker, Richard, cousin of John, i, 331[b].

Hoker, William, brother of John, *ibid.*

Hokehyll [*also* Hokeshill and Hokisylle, MS.] Henry, i, 306[b]; instituted to the Chantry of Beaford, ii, 19[b]; collated to the Chantry of St. Andrew, in the Church of Alwington, ii, 36[b]; his death, ii, 57[b].—See also, 308[b].

Hokeway, in Crediton, *see* Cobbelegh, Nicholas, ii, 311.

Hokeway, Robert, instituted to Georgenympton, R., ii, 99.

Hokke (or Holke), Philip, V. of Chittlehampton, exchanges for Ashbrittle, R. (Dioc. of Bath and Wells), ii, 3, 210[b].

Hoky, John, V. of St. Breward (deceased), ii, 197b.

Holand, John (of the Chapelry of Sheepwash) and Margaret Apuldore (of the parish of Dolton).—Special licence for their marriage (18 Jan., 1414-15), i, 207.

Holond, John, Chaplain, i, 315, 327b; instituted to St. Pancras, Exeter, ii, 2; i, 310, 332; proxy for Thomas Shepey, ii, 91b; collated to a Canonry in Exeter Cathedral, ii, 191; his death, ii, 197b.

Holond, Sir John, Knt.—*See* Fremington, V., i, 141b; ii, 96b; also, *see* Brixham V., ii, 355.

Holond, Richard, a parishioner of Cowick, ii, 287.

Holbeton, Combe, in the parish of, i, 37, 149b. The Rectory[1] of, appropriated to Polslo, ii, 359b.—John Grym, V. of,—

He was licensed to celebrate "in Capella Sancti Anecorite"[2] in his said parish (27 Sept., 1400), i, 49; this licence was renewed, 24 Dec., 1402, but limited to the Vigil and Feast of the Ascension, and the Exaltation of the Holy Cross, i, 62b; a Penitentiary in the Deanery of Plympton, i, 94, 115b, 143, 174, 194b, 207b, 217, 231, 237b, 245.—*See*, also, i, 308b, 309.

Holcombe-Rogus [Holecomb Rogys, MS.] Kitton[3] in the parish of, i, 226; Matilda Latymer's bequests to the Vicar, the Church, and the poor, i, 329. *See* Nanseglos, Tho., ii, 332.

Holcot, John, clerk, i, 312; instituted to Lympston, R., ii, 96.

Holdyche, John and Robert, of Churchstow, ii, 291.

Holdych, Peter, instituted to the P.C. of Slapton, ii, 68, 111.

He was instituted to Loddiswell, R., ii, 131b, 238b; and, afterwards, to the *Vicarage* of Loddiswell (on the Appropriation of the *Rectory* to Slapton College), ii, 153. *See*, also, i, 194, and ii, 288b; 357b.

Holecombe, John, chaplain, i, 321b.

Holever, Richard, i, 333b.

Holeway, in the parish of North Lew, i, 73b.

Holeway, William,—

He did homage to the Bishop, at Clyst, for lands at Wadeton, in Paignton, at Dynyngton and Wodelond in [Bishop's] Tawton; and at Raveston (*hodie* Rawston), in [Bishop's]-Nympton, 3 Dec., 1417, ii, 311.

Holewyll, John, of Ermington, ii, 277.

Holford, Peter, R. of Willand (deceased), ii, 21.

Hollacombe, Robert [Pytman], Parson of the Church of, i, 332.

Holland, John, Earl of Huntingdon, Patron of North Lew, R., ii, 4b, 211.

---

[1] Holbogheton, MS.
[2] The site is now called "Anchorist Rock."
[3] Keton MS.

Holle, John, i, 314^b

Holman, Margery (wife of Thomas.) *See* Barnstaple, ii, 241^b.

Holme, William, i, 320^b.

Holne, appropriated to the Hosp. of St. John, Exeter, ii, 360.

Holne Bridge, near Ashburton,—

This important Bridge, on the direct road from Ashburton to Tavistock, having been totally destroyed by a flood, the Bishop directs the four Archdeacons to give Notice of an Indulgence to all the Faithful contributing to its rebuilding (19 Aug., 1413), i, 183.

Holridge, mansion of William Werth, in Ideford, i, 246.

Holrig, John, V. of Bampton (Dioc. of Lincoln), ii, 55^b.

Holrygge, Richard, V. of Brixham, i, 332^b; (deceased), ii, 176^b; his Will, i, 329^b.

Holsworthy Deanery; the Clergy convened by the Archdn. of Totnes, to ascertain the true patronage of Milton Damarel, ii, 341^b.

Holsworthy; Chantry of Trewen in the Church of, ii, 48 (*see* "Institutions.")—Thomas Reymound's bequests to this Church, i, 331^b.—John Grymston, R., licence of non-residence for a year, from 26 July, 1396, i, 9;[1] for a year[2] from 26 Oct., 1397, i, 14[3]; for two years, from 30 Jan., 1398-9, i, 24^b;[4] licence[5] to celebrate on St. James's Day in the Chapel of St. James, in this parish (26 May, 1400), i, 30; licence of non-residence (20 Jan., 1401-2), from the F. of the Purification to the same F. in the following year, i, 54^b; licence[6] to choose a confessor (4 March, 1401-2) i, 55; licence of non-residence from 15 Oct., 1402, to the first Sunday in the following Lent, i, 61^b;[7] a Penitentiary in the Deanery of Holsworthy, i, 94[8]; 115^b, 143, 174, 194^b, 207^b, 217, 231, 237^b, 245^b.—*See*, also, i, 71^b, 244^b,[9] 331^b, 332^b.—Manor of Symeston in the parish of, i, 185^b.—Robert Brendon, a parishioner of—

Thomas Body, priest, and parochial chaplain of Jacobstow [Devon], had solemnized a marriage between the said Robert and one Sarah Chope of the parish of Monkleigh, without permission from the curate of either parish; and, notwithstanding the fact (as was alleged) that, when the banns were published, a lawful impediment was declared against the said Robert; moreover, he took from them a fee of 6s. 8d.; incurring for this irregularity the greater excommunication. He was suspended by the Bishop: but, appeal-

---

1 Holdesworthi, MS.
2 Grymeston, MS.
3 Holdesworthy, MS.
4 Holdysworthy, MS.
5 Grymmeston, MS.
6 He is here called "Grymesby," by an obvious clerical error.
7 Hallesworth, MS.
8 "Hall," MS.
9 "Decano decanatus de *Hall*, ac magistro Johanni, Rectori ecclesie parochialis de *Hall*."

ing to Rome, was absolved, and a Dispensation was, in due course, granted (4 July, 1410), i, 99b.

Holt, Margaret, widow of William,—

Commission for her enclosure as an Anchorite in a house pertaining to the Chapel of our Lady of Langewyll, at Dodbrooke, Kingsbridge (10 Jan., 1411-12), ii, 244b.

Holte, William, presents to Monkokehampton, R., ii, 80b.

Honiton, Deanery of,—

Commission directed (21 March, 1410-11), to the Archd. of Exeter, to make enquiry as to certain intruding priests, presuming to preach therein without authorization, contrary to a Provincial Constitution lately provided and promulgated, ii, 239b.

Honiton [Honynton, MS.] Church of St. Michael, i, 307.—Chapel of All Saints', *ibid*;—

An Indulgence was granted (9 June, 1418) to the Faithful contributing to its repair, i, 240b. The Chapel of St. Thomas is mentioned, i, 307b, and the Lazar-House, i, 318b, 331b.—Edward [Fysch], R., a Penitentiary in the Deanery of Honiton, i, 50.—John Sneynton, R., licence of non-residence for two years, from 22 June, 1413, i, 181b. Commission of Enquiry as to "Dilapidations," on the complaint of John Sneynton as to the neglect of Robert Fynour, his predecessor (13 June, 1413), ii, 252; licence of non-residence for a year, from 22 June, 1415, i, 211b.—John Chepman of, i, 307.

Honeychurch, John [Ramfray], R. of, licence of non-residence for a year, from 21 July, 1410, i, 100b; from 20 March, 1411-12, to Michaelmas, 1412, i, 146.

Honychurch, Robert, *see* Widecombe, i, 180b.

Honylond, John, elected as Prior of Launceston, ii, 115—120.

Honyngton, Roger, proxy for John Gyles, ii, 30b.

Hood, Robert, instituted to Tywardreath, V., ii, 105.

Hoper, John, V. of Lanteglos[-by-Fowey], a Penitentiary in the Deanery of West, i, 143b; his death, ii, 146.

Hoper, John, V. of East Coker (Dioc. of B. & W.), exchanges for Bickleigh, R., ii, 92b; for Dulverton, V., ii, 182.

Hopere, John, R. of Bondleigh (deceased), ii, 69.

Houper, John, instituted to Boconnoc, R., ii, 190, 264.

Hoper, John and Reginald Russell—

Commission of Enquiry, &c., directed to Hugh Hickelyng, Precentor, and Robert Rugge and John Dodyngton, Canons of the Cathedral; it appears that Richard Exebridge (*alias* Ducheyet), John Uscher, Robert Coblegh, and others, had laid violent hands on the above-named John and Reginald, Vicars of the Cathedral, and that John Lake, Arnulph Goldsmyth, and others, had aided and abetted them therein (23 Oct., 1397), ii, 213.—On the 14th Dec. following, a second Commission, in like terms, was directed to Precentor Hugh Hickelyng, ii, 214.

Hopere, Peter, i, 310.

Hopere, Richard, V. of St. Merryn, exchanges for Poughill, R., ii, 28b; resigns, and is collated to Clyst Fomison, R., ii,

31; collated to a Canonry and Bursal Prebend in Crediton, ii, 37; i, 85^{b}, 88, 116, 117; exchanges Clyst Fomison for Theynton, R. (Dioc. of Lincoln), ii, 51; i, 167^{b}, 175^{b}, 187^{b}; collated (*jure devoluto*), to Silverton, R., ii, 164^{b}; 257^{b}.

Hoper, Robert, *see* Kyngysford, Ralph, i, 149^{b}, 171^{b}.

Hoper, Thomas, collated to Coleridge, V., ii, 140.

Hoper, William, instituted to All-Hallows-on-the-Walls, R., Exeter, ii, 67^{b}.

Hopkyn, Richard, V. of Morthoe (deceased), ii, 200^{b}.

Hopkyn, William, instituted to St. Cleer, V., ii, 49; exchanges for Icklesham, R., (Dioc. of Chichester), ii, 51.

Hopkyns, Robert, proxy for John Chaundeler, ii, 89.

Hoppeley, Thomas, R. of Lamorran, i, 38; i. q. Wappelegh, q. v.

Hoppyng, John, of Littleham, i, 32.

Hordelegh, Matthew, patron of Rackenford, R., ii, 5^{b}; and, with Juliana his wife, ii, 150^{b}, 251^{b}.

Hore, Joan and Matilda, daughters of William, i, 321.

Hore, Richard, priest, i, 93; a Penitentiary in the Deanery of Barnstaple, i, 217, 231, 237^{b}, 245^{b}; presented to Heanton Punchardon, R., ii, 247.

Horewell, Roger, instituted to Kingsteignton, V., ii, 175.

Horewode, John, Collector of Customs, Exeter; *see* Smyth, Laurence, ii, 351.

Horlok, Thomas, priest, of Ilfracombe, i, 327^{b}; instituted to Charles, R., ii, 190.

Horncastell, John, chaplain, *see* Milton Damarel, ii, 342.

Horne, Roger, i, 332.

Hornesbogh, *also* Hornesbowe, MS., James, presents to Chedington, R. (Dioc. of Salisbury), ii, 56^{b}, 87.

Horrabridge—Indulgence to the Faithful contributing "ad reparacionem et sustentacionem pontis vocati Horebrygge inter Barum et Plymouth," (2 Feb., 1395-6), i, 7^{b}.

Horshay, Tho., and Alice his wife, present to Stoodleigh, ii, 85.

Horslegh, ii, 359.

Horsman, John, i, 320^{b}.

Horwood [Horewode, MS.], John [Deyman], R. of (*see* Brythlegh, John), i, 93.

Horygg, John, instituted to Down St. Mary, R., ii, 176.

Hospitals, the Statute concerning (2 Henr. V.), ii, 324.

Houche, John, Monk of Tavistock, ii, 58^{b}, 59.

Hough, Geoffrey, collated to Combe-in-Teignhead, R., ii, 193.
Houndslow, Conv. of the Holy Trinity (Dio. of London), ii, 32^{b}.
Huchyn, Henry, instituted to Sampford Courtenay, ii, 201^{b}.
Hude, Andrew, V. of Colebrooke (deceased), ii, 174.
Hugelyng, William, co-patron of Washfield, R., ii, 168.
Hugh, David, instituted to Buckfastleigh, V., ii, 91^{b}; 255^{b}; i, 83 (*see* "Oratories"); his death, ii, 160.
Huish [Hywyssh, MS.], in the parish of Instow, i, 73^{b}.
Huish, Robert [Pytman], R. of, *see* Wembworthy.
Hukeleye, Richard, literate, i, 95^{b}.
Hulles, William, Prior of the Order of St. John of Jerusalem in England, ii, 191^{b}.
Hullyng, John, R. of Sutton-juxta-Bigenhurne (Dioc. of Chichester), exchanges for [West] Alvington, V., ii, 29^{b}; for Cheddon, R.,[1] (Dioc. of Bath and Wells), ii, 49^{b}.
Humberston, William de, R. of the Chapel of Legh, *alias* le Mote (Dioc. of Chichester), exchanges for Shobrooke, R., ii, 52; for Tenterden V. (Dioc. of Canterbury), ii, 79^{b}.
Hunden, John and Joeta, parents of William, i, 324^{b}.
Hunden, John, brother, and Margery, sister, of William, i, 325.
Hunden, William, Archdeacon of Totnes,[2]—

His collation, ii, 99^{b}; i, 85, 85^{b}, 88, 88^{b}, 89, 95^{b}, 102, 111, 127, 128, 185^{b}; collated to a Canonry in Exeter Cathedral, ii, 105^{b}; licensed to choose a Confessor (13 Oct., 1410), i, 108; 121^{b}, 149; with the Bishop at Leicester "in hospicio vocato *Golchesterysynne*, Leycestre," (29 May, 1414), i, 197; at Lutterworth [Lutterworthy, MS.], (30 May, 1414), i, 197; at Blackawton (25 August, 1414), i, 198^{b}; "Procuratorium Domini pro Convocacione Cleri" (*see* Ovyngham, John), i, 200^{b}.—*See*, also, i, 206, 209^{b}, 210, 321^{b}; ii, 118. —Hunden, who became Chancellor, 27 Jan., 1407-8 (ii, 231), retained his Canonry till his death (ii, 175); but exchanged his Archdeaconry for a Canonry and the Prebend of Holy Cross in Lincoln Cathedral, and the R. of Crawley Magna in that Diocese (ii, 164^{b}); for his Will, see i, 324^{b}.

Hunne, John, and Agnes Dabernon,—

Commission to enquire as to certain reports about them (23 May, 1412), ii, 246^{b}. Dispensation for their marriage, notwithstanding affinity in the fourth degree, by reason of the said Agnes being related in that degree to one Agnes Hertecote, with whom the said John had formerly committed fornication (7 Oct., 1412), i, 169.

Hunte, Robert, *see* St. Illogan.
Huntingdon, John Holland, (1) Earl of, patron of Calstock, R., ii, 6^{b}; his presentation to Brixham, V., disputed, ii, 258^{b}.

[1] Cheden, MS.

[2] He was Archdeacon of Rochester, and received a Dispensation from the Pope enabling him (as the annual value thereof was only seventy marks) to hold *beneficia incompatibilia* in plurality. *See*, ii, 101.

Huntingdon, John Holland (2) Earl of, patron of Broad Clyst, ii, 200b.

Huntingdon, John, collated to the Wardenship of St. Laurence's Hospital, Crediton, ii, 187.

Huntyngford, John (*see* Lifton), ii, 265.

Huntsham [Hunsham and Hunsam, MS.], John [Wyllesdon, *alias*, Jordan], R. of, a Penitentiary in the Deanery of Tiverton, i, 50, 94, 115, 143, 173b, 194, 207b, 216b, 237b; licensed to celebrate in the chapel of St. James at Stallynche in that parish (16 July, 1410), i. 100b.

Hurde, Richard, instituted to Brendon, R., ii, 147b.

This Rector, together with William Sampson (receiver and occupier of the revenues of Monkleigh) and Thomas Davy (receiver, etc., etc., of Lapford) having been excommunicated for refusing to pay what was due to the Abbot of Forde (collector of the *una decima* granted by Convocation, 1 Henry V.), and being contumacious, are handed over by the Bishop to the secular arm (6 Oct., 1414), i, 202b.

Hurdewyk, William, and Mabel, relict of John Skynner,—

Dispensation of Pope Boniface IX., for their re-marriage,—"oblate nobis pro parte Willelmi Hurdewyk, laici, et Mabille, relicte quondam Johannis Skynner, laici, mulieris, Exoniensis Diocesis, peticionis series continebat quod cum olim, dicto Johanne tunc in humanis agente, prefatus Willelmus eandem Mabillam carnaliter cognovisset, idem Willelmus cum dicta Mabilla, in casu[1] quo dictum Johannem decedere contingeret, contraxit per verba de futuro quamvis de facto, et deinde, predicto Johanne vita functo, cum iidem Willelmus et Mabilla matrimonium hujusmodi licet tamen clandestine et eciam de facto solemnizassent, matrimonium ipsum extitit auctoritate ordinaria divorciatum ipseque Willelmus eandem Mabillam abjuravit. Cum autem, sicut eadem peticio subjungebat, prefatus Willelmus perantea eciam quandam aliam mulierem, eidem Mabille tertio et quarto consanguinitatis gradu conjunctam, cognoverit, prolem ex ea procreando, ipsique Willelmus et Mabilla, ad obviandum scandalis et periculis que exinde inter ipsos, amicos, et consanguineos sunt exorta et exoriri[2] forundantur, matrimonium invicem de novo contrahere proponant, si ad id Apostolice Sedis accederet assensus......... Nos, igitur, qui salutem querimus singulorum, et scandalis Christifidelium libenter, in quantum possumus, obviamus, hujusmodi supplicacionibus inclinati, Fraternitati tue per Apostolica scripta mandamus quatinus, si est ita, dictaque Mabilla alias propter hoc rapta non fuerit, eosdem Willelmum et Mabillam ab excommunicacionis et aliis sentenciis atque penis quas propter premissa incurrerunt, auctoritate nostra absolvas, hac vice dumtaxat, in forma Ecclesie consueta; injunctis eis inter alia, sub pena juramenti per eos prestandi, quod de cetero similia non committant, nec ea committentibus dabunt auxilium, consilium, vel favorem, et pro modo culpe penitencia salutari: et nichilominus cum eisdem Willelmo et Mabilla ut, premissis non obstantibus, matrimonium invicem de novo contrahere et in eo postquam contractum fuerit remanere libere et licite valeant, eadem auctoritate dispenses, prolem ex hujusmodi matrimonio suscipiendam legitimam numerando."—The Bishop, having enquired into the circumstances, and found that they had been truly represented, granted Dispensation accordingly (10 April, 1403), i, 63b.

---

[1] Causu, MS., on an erasure. [2] Exorriri, MS.

Hurdyng, Thomas, i, 330b.

Hurn, Adam, *see* atte Hurn, ii, 75b.

Hurte, John, V., of Nether Lyme, exchanges for Salcombe [Regis], V., ii, 163b.

Hurte, Robert and Rose (relict of William) Loppethorne,—

Their marriage was unlawful because they were related in the fourth degree of affinity. Dispensation granted 4 Jan., 1409-10, i, 92b.

Hurst, Juliana, wife of John, i, 315.

Hurst, Rd., R. of Exbourne (deceased), ii, 132b; his Will, i, 315.

Hurst, Thomas, of Apuldram, ii, 293b.

Hurst, Walter, i, 315.

Husey, John, instituted to Broadhembury, V., ii, 90; exchanges for Combe Raleigh, R., ii, 161b.

Husten (or Hustyn), in St. Breoke, i, 80b.

Husy, Nicholas, chaplain (of Chivelston), i, 330b; ii, 261.

Hyde, John, R. of Loxbeare, i, 39b. *See* atte Hyde.

Hyde, William, instituted to Great Torrington, R., ii, 52; his death, ii, 153b.

Hydon, Richard and William, i, 301.—William was co-patron of Huxham, R., ii, 200.

Hyeonysc, William, instituted to Stoke Fleming, R., ii, 202.

Hykdon, William, V. of St. Colan (deceased), ii, 94.

Hykedon, John, V. of Tavistock (deceased), ii, 15b.

Hykke, John: a Commission was directed, 4 March, 1410-11, to John Waryng, V. of Liskeard—

"Ad audiendum, cognoscendum, et procedendum, in quadam causa matrimoniali, que coram Officiali nostre Peculiaris Jurisdiccionis, et nostro Commissario Generali in Devonia, inter Aliciam Kateryn, mulierem, relictam Johannis Hykke, partem actricem, ex parte una, et Johannem Payn, virum, nostre Diocesis, partem ream, ex altera, aliquamdiu vertebatur, et adhuc pendet indecisa."—No further particulars are given; neither is there any record of the result.

Hylle, Joan, wife of John, i, 323b.

Hulle, Joan, *see* Trevarthian, Otho, i, 128.

Hulle, John (of Exeter), *see* Ringmore (*Institutions*).

Hulle (or Hille), Sir John, knt., presents to Pillaton, R., ii, 45b; with Robert Hull, senior, presents to Dittisham, R., ii, 53; (with Robert, his son), co-patron of West Putford, R., ii, 82; does homage to the Bishop for lands in Talaton, part of the Manor of Crediton (12 April, 1407), ii, 310b; *see* also, i, 329; ii, 315b.

Hulle, John (son of Sir John), does homage to the Bishop at

Clyst, for lands in the parish of Talaton (Manor of Crediton, 13 May, 1416), ii, 311 ; *see*, also, i, 300b, 308b.

Hylle, John, a minor, and Agnes, daughter of William Rynell, of Ugborough, i, 172b.

Hylle, John, instituted to Harberton, V., ii, 9b ; exchanges for Musbury, R., ii, 67.

Hulle, John, instituted to Colyton, V., ii, 147b ; chaplain of the perpetual Chantry of Whyteford (in that parish), ii, 268 ; *see*, also, i, 320b.

Hulle, John (scholar),—*Dispensacio super defectu natalium* (29 May, 1414), i, 196b ; and again (3 Oct., 1414), i, 201b.

Hille, Nicholas, i, 325.

Hylle, Peter, ii, 360.

Hulle, Robert, senior ; patron of the Chantry Chapel in the cemetery of Ermington, ii, 9b, 32, 32b, 102 ; presents to Dittisham, R., ii, 106b (and *see* Hulle, Sir John) ; to Truro ; R., ii, 140b, 245 ; nominates to Poundstock, V., ii, 180.

Hull, Robert [of Spaxton], and Isabella his wife, daughter and heir of Sir Thomas Fychett, knight,—

They complained to the Bishop that some person, or persons, unknown, had carried off certain deeds and documents affecting her inheritance, and the Bishop excommunicated the robbers (1 July, 1399), i, 28b : he was patron of Spaxton (Dioc. of Bath and Wells), ii, 43— Robert Hylle, as lord of Halton, presented to St. Dominick, R., ii, 193b.—On 14th Dec., 1415, the King's writ was issued for the administration of the oath as Escheator in Devon to Robert Hill, of Spaxton, ii, 354b ; *see*, also, i, 329, 329b, 335b.

Hulle, Robert (junior, of Churchstow), ii, 291.

Hille, Vincent, V. of Luppit, exchanges for Chudleigh, ii, 65.

Hulle (*or* atte Hulle), Walter, inst. to Cheldon, ii, 5 ; resigns, ii, 68 ; resigns Moreleigh, R., ii, 159b, having been instituted to Goodleigh, R., ii, 158b, 253b, 349 ; [resigns, and] is instituted to Cheriton Fitzpaine, R., ii, 191.

Hulle, William, of St. Petrock's, Exeter, and Agnes Mychel, of St. Kieran's, made petition to the Bishop as follows,—

They had contracted to marry, and had ordered their banns to be published on three solemn days, viz., on two Sundays and on the Day of the Conversion of St. Paul. They desired to be married "citra Septuagesimam", but the interval was not sufficient for the banns. The Bishop, considering the inconvenience of postponing their marriage till after Easter, gave licence to the Rector of either parish to marry them on any day before the beginning of Lent, if no impediment were alleged (26 Jan., 1412), i, 142b.

Hull, William, i, 320.

Hull, William, instituted to Dean [Prior], ii, 98 ; resigns, ii, 99.

Hyllary, Roger, Judge, ii, 342.

Hynde, William, instituted to Mariansleigh, V., ii, 105.

Hytte, John, junior, i, 333.

I.

Iddesleigh [Edwyslegh, MS.], William Badecok, R. of, ii, 303.

Ide, Archdn. Lydeford's bequests to this parish, i, 310.

Ideford [Yddeford, MS.], Holridge, in the parish of, i, 246.

Idrych, William, of Apuldram, ii, 293^{b}.

Ikelyngton, John, instituted to St. Columb-major, R., ii, 131^{b}; exchanges for St. Mary's R., Southampton, ii, 137^{b}.

Ilchester, the "White Hall[1]" at, i, 311, 311^{b}; the Friars of, i, 311, 320^{b}.

Ilfracombe [Ilfredecombe, *also* Ilfridecombe *alias* Ilfardecombe, MS.], Thomas Barton, R. of, *see* Barton, Thomas,—

Commission of enquiry on the presentation of Hugh Herle, chaplain, by Sir John Herle, knt. (19 March, 1415-16), ii, 258.—Hugh Herle, R. of, licensed to celebrate in the Chapels of St. Nicholas the Confessor, and St. Windred,[2] the Virgin, at Legh [*or* Lee], on their Festivals, for one year only, from 24 July, 1416, i, 223.—Commission as to "dilapidations," on the complaint of Herle against Barton (10 Oct., 1416), ii, 260; licence of non-residence for a year, from 12 Feb., 1416-17, i, 230^{b}.

Ilond, John, chaplain, i, 332.

Ilsington [Hylstyncton, MS.], Thomas, V. of, a Penitentiary in the Deanery of Moreton, i, 50.

Illogan, *see* St. Illogan.

Ingram, Nigel, of the parish of Colyton, and Joan, relict of Ralph Laplode, intending to marry, the Bishop issued a licence, directed to William, V. of Sidbury (18 Jan., 1412-13), i, 174^{b}.

Innocent ("alias Nocent"), John, i, 309^{b}.

INSTITUTIONS, COLLATIONS, AND EXCHANGES.

ABBOTSHAM [Abbotysham, MS.], Vicars of—

John Bullok; on whose resignation was instituted, 17 March, 1400-1,
John Downe, chaplain; patrons, the Abbot and Convent of Tavistock, ii, 17.

AFFETON (now merged in West Worlington—*see* p. 1, *note*) Rectors of,—

Roger Puttenham. This Rector exchanged (26 Oct., 1400) with
John Fyssher (R. of Danbury, Dioc. of London, patrons, the Prior and Convent of St. Bartholomew's, Smithfield); patron, Thomas Affeton, domicellus, ii, 51^{b}. There is no record of his death or resignation, but
Walter Tokere, priest, was inst., 26 Oct. 1409; patron, John Botriaux, ii, 107^{b}.

---

[1] "Aulbe Sale de Ivelchestre."

[2] This was the Chapel called elsewhere "Sancti Nicholai supra portum maria," since converted into a lighthouse.

William Morys, chaplain, succeeded (on Toker's resignation), 13 Jan., 1416-17, patron, John Botreaux, Esquire, ii, 181b.
Thomas Bowryng, chaplain, was inst. on the resignation of Morys, 25 July, 1419; the same patron, ii, 201.

ALPHINGTON [Alfyngton and Alvyngton[1], MS.], Rectors of—
Reginald Moun; on whose death was inst. (3 Dec., 1398),
Roger Sare, priest; patron (for that turn), Robert Cary, ii, 10.
William Trendelbeare, chaplain, succeeded: there is no record of his institution; but on his death
Richard Courtenay, LL.B[2]., was inst., 7 May, 1403 (proxy—John Kyck, chaplain); patron, Sir Peter Courtenay, knt., ii, 67.
John Pleystowe, chaplain, succeeded, on Courtenay's resignation, 28 Dec., 1403; the same patron, ii, 74.
Geoffrey Barger, chaplain, was inst. on the death of Playstowe *(sic)*, 5 July, 1415; patron, Edward, Earl of Devon, ii, 166.—Commission of enquiry as to the vacancy and right to present (25 June, 1415), ii, 256b. This Rector exchanged with
John Mathu (V. of Broadclyst), 6 July, 1419; the same patron, ii, 200b.—Commission of enquiry, etc. (30 June, 1419), ii, 267b.

ALVERDISCOTT [Alvardiscote, Alverdyscote, MS.], Rectors of—
John Seward; on whose death a difficulty arose as to the patronage. On the 16th of June, 1401, the Vicar-General inst., in the Cathedral,
John Juvenel, chaplain, to the vacant benefice; "ad quam per nobilem virum dominum Jacobum de Chuddelegh, militem, racione cujusdem litere attornamenti sibi per nobilem virum, dominum Thomam Flemmyng, militem, extra regnum Anglie existentem et degentem, in hac parte sub sigillo suo consignate, specialiter facte, et concesse, verum ipsius ecclesie hac vice patronum, eidem Vicario extitit presentatus; et ipsum Rectorem instituit canonice in eadem . . . . et, prestita canonica obediencia per eundem, mandatum fuit Archidiacono Barumensi, seu ejus Officiali, pro ipsius induccione," ii, 19b. On the very next day, however (17 June), the Bishop inst. ("in hospicio nostro Londonie")—
Henry Charer, chaplain, "in artibus inceptorem, ad ecclesiam parochialem de Alverdyscote, Exoniensis Diocesis, vacantem; ad quam per dilectum sibi in Christo Johannem Flemmyng, filium Thome Flemmyng, verum ipsius ecclesie patronum, jure dicti Thome Flemmyng, qui advocacionem prefate ecclesie predicto Johanni Flemmyng ista vice dumtaxat per literas suas patentes concessit, eidem Domino extitit presentatus; et ipsum Rectorem instituit canonice in eadem, etc, ii, 54.

ALWINGTON, Rectors of—
Thomas Was; on whose death was inst. 23 Feb., 1407-8,
John Harry, chaplain, (proxy, Richard Graynevyll, LL.B.); patron, John Hankeford, domicellus, ii, 100. Herry *(sic)* exchanged with
John Fayrwode, LL.B. (Warden of St. David's Hospital, Swansea), 18 March, 1410-11; the same patron, ii, 131. This Rector exchanged with
John Cokworthy (R. of Rudbaxton, Dioc. of St. David's), 26 Sept., 1416; the same patron, ii, 179.

ALWINGTON, Chantry of St. Andrew in the Church of—
William Hals; after whose resignation the Bishop collated, *by lapse*,
Henry Hokisylle, chaplain, 23 Feb., 1397-8 (proxy, Robert Dobbe), ii, 36b. This Chantry became vacant shortly afterwards, probably on the resignation

[1] ii, 166; and at ii, 200b "Alfyngton *alias* Alvyngton."
[2] Eldest son of Sir Philip Courtenay, and nephew of William, Archbishop of Canterbury. He died Bishop of Norwich.

of Hokisylle, who 5 July, 1401, was inst. to the Chantry at Beaford, ii, 19b. The Bishop issued a Commission of Enquiry, 2 Dec., 1398, as to Sir William Hankeforde's claim to present (ii, 221b); and 14 Feb., 1398-9, the said claim having been established,

Richard Colbrugg, priest, was inst., (ii, 10b); on whose resignation

John Nouns, priest, was inst., 19 Sept., 1399; the same patron, ii, 13.—There is no record of his resignation; but he was inst. to Meeth, R., 25 Sept., 1410, ii, 123b, and probably resigned this Chantry soon afterwards, for

Thomas Eweny, chaplain, was inst.[1] 23 Sept., 1411: the same patron, ii, 135b.

ANGERSLEIGH [Angerlegh, MS.]; *see* HORWOOD, R.

ANTONY [Sancti Jacobi de Anton in Cornubia, MS.], Vicars:

Adam Tregonet; on whose death

William Mey, clerk, "cum quo in hac parte per Sedem Apostolicam dispensatum existit," was inst., 15 Nov., 1405; patron, for that turn, King Henry IV, ii, 87. On Mey's resignation

William Pyers, chaplain, was inst., 8 Feb., 1407-8: patrons, the Abbot and Convent of Tavistock, ii, 99b.

ARLINGTON [Alryngton, MS.], Rector of,—

Walter Laneman; on whose death was inst., 7 Dec., 1396,

John Durden, priest; patron, Lady Elizabeth Paulet, in right of the Manor, part of the lands of her late husband, John Ralegh, assigned to her as dowry, ii, 6b.

ARRETON R., Diocese of Winchester, *see* BRIDESTOWE, R.

ASHBRITTLE, R., Diocese of Bath and Wells, *see* CHITTLEHAMPTON, V.

ASHBURTON [Aysschperton, MS.], Vicars of,—

John Otery, who exchanged, 7 May, 1397, with

Peter Duk (V. of St. Mary Church), patrons of both benefices, the Dean and Chapter of Exeter, ii, 34. He exchanged 20 March, 1401-2, with

Richard Madeforde (V. of Widecombe-in-the-Moor), (proxy for Madeforde—Ralph Dollebeare), ii, 57. On whose death

William Hayford, chaplain, was inst., 5 May, 1405, ii, 84.

ASHBURY[2] ["Sancte Marie de Ayschbyry" MS.], Rectors of,—

John Myleton; on whose death was inst., 8 Jan., 1416-17;

John Schere, chaplain, patrons, the Prior and Convent of Launceston, ii, 181b.

ASHCOMBE [Aysshcomb and Ayssheecomb, MS.], Rectors of,—

William Lyght; on whose death was inst., 15 March, 1412-13,

John Leyman, chaplain (proxy—John Wolston, clerk); patrons, the Prior and Convent of Merton, ii, 148. On Leyman's resignation

Henry More, chaplain, was inst., 16 Sept., 1415; ii, 169.

ASHFORD [Ayssceford, MS.], Vicars of,—

William Dounyng; on whose death was inst., 4 Dec., 1413,

John Clerk, chaplain; patrons, the Prior and Convent of Pilton, ii, 154.

ASHREIGNEY [Esse Regny, MS.], Rectors of,—

William Smyth; on whose resignation was inst., 27 Feb., 1413-14,

John Dayell, chaplain; patrons, Giles de Esse, Joceus de Trobrygge, Thomas Reymound, and Thomas de Trobrygge, ii, 156. On the resignation of Dayhulle (*sic*),

Robert Doget, chaplain, was inst., 18 July, 1416 (proxy—Roger Blakehay); patrons, the same, ii, 177b.

---

[1] "Collated"—margin; a clerical error. [2] Now united with North Lew, R.

ASHTON [Asschiston, Ayschirton, Asshirton, MS.], Rectors of,—
Richard Brugg ; on whose death was inst., 16 Feb., 1399-1400,
William Benet, priest ; patron, Sir James Chuddelegh, knt, ii, 14b. He exchanged with
William Hawkyn (V. of Coombe Keynes, Dioc. of Salisbury ; patrons, the Prior and Convent of Merton), 26 Aug., 1403 (proxy—William Cleve, chaplain) ; patron, John Courtenay, domicellus, ii, 68b. Haukyn (*sic*) exchanged with
Robert Belet (R. of Cheddington—Dioc. of Salisbury ; patrons, Thos. Bolour and William Gust, domicelli), 27 May, 1404 ; patron, the same, ii, 75b.

ASHWATER [Essewater and Aysshewater, MS.], Rectors of,—
John Lugans ; on whose death was inst., 24 April, 1404,
John Tone, clerk (proxy—John Heynstekot, literate) ; patrons, the Prior and Convent of Frithelstock, ii, 75b. On Tone's death
Edward Dauntesey was inst., 25 Aug., 1406, ii, 91b. He exchanged with
John Jerbard, R. of Roborough, 23 March, 1412-13 ; ii, 148.

ATHERINGTON[1] [Aderyngton, MS.], Rectors of,—
Simon Hoke ; on whose resignation was inst., 3 Feb., 1397-8,
Walter Bullok ; patron, King Richard II, ii, 36b. On whose[2] death
Thomas Shepey, clerk, was inst., 7 Sept., 1406, patron, King Henry IV., ii, 91b.

AVETON GIFFARD, Rectors of,—
John Juhelfyete ; on whose death was inst., 13 June, 1403,
Thomas Tremayn, LL.B. ; patrons, Richard Hankeford, William Burleston, Henry Foleford, Nicholas Tremayn, and John Lacche, ii, 67.

AVETON GIFFARD, the Chantry "de Lyneton" in the parish Church there,—
Thomas Leuedeston, chaplain, was inst., 23 Sept., 1406 ; patrons, Rd. Hankeford, Hy. Folyford, Nicholas Tremayn, and Jno. Lacche, ii, 91b.

AXMINSTER, Vicars of,—
William Rothewell. He exchanged 20 Sept., 1395, with
John Whattecomb (or *Watcombe*), for Hemyock, R., inst. by proxy—William Langton ; patrons, Thomas de la Ware and Nicholas Slak, Canons of York and Prebendaries of Grendale and Warthill, ii, 27b.
Henry Pake, chaplain, was inst. on Whattecomb's resignation, 2 June, 1401 ; patrons, Walter Cook and Thomas de Weston, Prebendaries of Axminster, ii, 19. Whattecomb resigned, 20 May, and the Commission therein was dated 12 May. *See* ii, 17b. On Pake's death
John Worthyn, chaplain, was inst., 29 July, 1413 ; patrons, Walter Cook and Richard Pittes, Canons of York, and Prebendaries of Grendale and Warthull therein, ii, 151b. He exchanged with
John Mathew (Warden of St. Laurence's Hospital, Crediton), 21 Sept., 1417 ; patrons, Walter Cook and Thomas Grenewode, Canons of York and Prebendaries etc., ii, 187.

AXMINSTER ; Prebend of Grendale in the Cathedral Church of York and the "portion" thereto annexed in this Church,—
Robert Nevill, clerk, son of Ralph, Earl of Westmoreland (referred to as "adhuc impuberis"): the Archbishop of York writes to Bishop Stafford on his behalf ; and he was inst., 7 Aug., 1414, ii, 160b, 161.

AXMOUTH, Vicars of,—
William Slade ; on whose resignation (to be Warden of Ottery),

[1] For the Chantry Chapel of Umberleigh in this parish, *see* Umberleigh.

[2] Here called John—a clerical error.

John Coterell, priest, who had resigned the said Wardenship, was inst., 2 Feb., 1397-8; patron, King Richard II (the temporalities of the Priory of Lodres in Dorset (a cell to the Benedictine Abbey of St. Mary of Montburg, Dioc. of Coutances, Normandy), being in his hand, ii, 212.

AYLESBEARE [Ayllisbeare, MS.], Vicars of,—

Adam atte Hurn; on whose death

Robert Pym, chaplain, was inst., 22 April, 1404; patrons, the Prioress and Convent of Polslo, ii, 75b. On Pym's death

John Bycote, chaplain, was inst., 30 May, 1407; ii, 96b; on whose death

Thomas Trevet, chaplain, was inst., 31 July, 1410; ii, 121.

BAGBOROUGH, R. (Diocese of B. and W.), *see* UPLOMAN, R.

BAMPTON, V. (Diocese of Lincoln) *see* HEAVITREE, V.

BAMPTON [Baunton, MS.], Rectors of,—

John Michel; on whose death was inst., 7 March, 1397-8,

Edward Dokeworthy, priest: patrons, John, Prior, and the Convent of the Cathedral Church of Bath, ii, 8. On his death

Thomas Warde, sub-deacon, LL.B., was inst., 24 May, 1418 (proxy—John Lane, clerk); ii, 192. Commission of Enquiry issued 12 Feb., 1417-18, ii, 264. He exchanged with

Matthew Doune (R. of Whimple); instituted by proxy—John Lane, clerk, 17 June, 1418; ii, 192. The Commission of Enquiry herein (in which Sir Hugh Courtenay, senior, is called the patron) was issued 15 Feb., 1417-18, ii, 264.

BAMPTON, the Chantry of Forde,[1]—

Elias Ramysham, who exchanged, 6 Feb., 1396-7, with

John Neweton (R. of Skilgate, Dioc. of B. and W.—patron, Simon Barnabe); patron, Sir Hugh Courtenay, knt., ii, 32b. On Neweton's death

Geoffrey Veale, chaplain, was inst., 7 Aug., 1417: patron, Sir Hugh Courtenay, *senior*, knt., ii, 186b. On Veale's resignation

Thomas Pay, chaplain, was inst., 6 Aug., 1419; the same patron (described as Lord of Bampton), ii, 201b.

BATHEASTON, V. (Dioc. of Bath and Wells), *see* HOCKWORTHY, V.

BARNSTAPLE [Barnestapol and Barnestapolia, MS.], the Archdeaconry of—

Robert Rugge or *Rygge*; whose successor

Richard Aldryngton (alias Colcomb), was collated 22 Aug., 1400, ii, 50. On 17 of Oct., in the same year, a Commission was directed to Robert Rygge (then Chancellor of the Cathedral), to receive his resignation; and

John Orum, S.T.B., was collated 1st Nov. following, ii, 15b.

BARNSTAPLE [Barnastapol], Priory of St. Mary Magdalen at,—

Henry Sutton; on whose death was inst., 3 Sept., 1398,

Simon Oclee, Monk of Bermondsey, priest. This Priory depended on the Abbey of St. Martin-in-the-Fields, Paris: and Oclee was presented by Roger, Archbishop of Canterbury, John, Prior of St. Mary at Thetford, and John, Prior of Bermondsey (on account of the Schism). The Letter-Apostolical of Pope Boniface is quoted at length,—ii, 39.

BARNSTAPLE [Barnataspolia, MS.], Vicars of,—

John Fereste; on whose death was inst., 17 Feb., 1396-7,

[1] The Chapel was in the Churchyard and dedicated, probably, to the Blessed Virgin: at ii, 201b, it is described, simply as "in Manerio"; but in Bishop Lacy's Register it is referred to, in 1437, as "libera Capella de Forde *infra cemeterium* ecclesie parochialis de Bampton."

William Knyght, Bachelor in Degrees (proxy—Richard Palmer, R. of St. Clement Danes, London); patron, King Richard II, ii, 33. He exchanged with
John Lemman (R. of Kilkhampton), 12 Dec., 1403; patrons, the Prior and Convent of St. Mary's Priory, Barnstaple, ii, 71. On Lemman's death
William Pilton, chaplain, was inst. (proxy—Adam Bacon, chaplain), 23 Jan., 1411-12; the same patrons; ii, 139.

BARNSTAPLE [Barnestaple, MS.], Chantry of S. Salphinus in the Castle,—
Thomas Haywode, chaplain, was inst., 27 Feb., 1408-9; patron, King Henry IV., ii, 104b.

BARNSTAPLE, Chantry of St. Thomas, "juxta pontem ville de Barnestaple,"—
Adam Abraham; on whose death was inst., 28 Dec., 1412,
William Mille, chaplain; patron for that turn, King Henry IV., ii, 147b.

BEAFORD [Beauforde, MS.], Rectors of—
Robert Amyet; on whose resignation, was inst., 28 May, 1404,
William Speccote, chaplain; patron, William de Beaumount, domicellus, ii, 76. There is no mention made here of Speccote's predecessor; but Amyet must have *resigned*, for it is recorded elsewhere (ii, 75b), that he was inst. to the R. of Shirwell, 6 May, 1404.

BEAFORD [Beauford, MS.] Chantry in the Chapel of the Holy Trinity at—
Alexander Vyel; on whose death
Henry Hokeshill, chaplain, was inst., 5 July, 1401; patron, King Henry IV., ii, 19b. On the death of Hokeshill,
John Walhop, chaplain, was inst., 27 March, 1402; patron the same, ii, 57b.

BEAWORTHY [Beworthy, MS.] Rectors of—
Richard Madek; this Rector exchanged, 14 Nov., 1403, with
John Avery (V. of St. Andrew's, Launcells); patrons, the Prior and Convent of Launceston, ii, 69b.

BEERFERRERS [Byrferrers, MS.], Archpriests of—
Richard Monk; on whose death was inst., 17 Feb., 1416-17,
Roger Monk, chaplain; patrons, Sir John Corneweyll, knight, and Alexander Champernoun and Thomas Bonevyle, Esquires, ii, 182.—The Commission of Enquiry as to patronage, etc., was dated 16 Jan.; ii, 260b. On Roger's resignation
John Monk was inst., 16 June, 1417; patrons the same, ii, 186.—Commission of Enquiry dated 16 May, 1417, ii, 261.

BELSTON, Rectors of—
Walter Umfray; on whose death was inst., 14 Jan., 1417-18,
Adam Hay, chaplain; patron, Henry Foleford, Esquire, ii, 189.

BERKS, the Archdeaconry of, in the Cathedral Church of Salisbury, was exchanged, 21 Dec., 1404, by
Simon Sydenham, LL.B., with
Walter Medeford for the Archdeaconry of Salisbury and his Canonry and Prebend of West Sampford in the Church of Crediton (Thomas Byldesthorp, clerk, proxy for Sydenham, and Edmund Hildesle for Medeford); ii, 81.

BERRY POMEROY [Bury Pomeray, MS.], Vicars of—
John Stakforde; on whose death was inst., 29 May, 1399,
Walter Dommewyll, priest; patrons, Robert, Prior, and the Convent of St. Mary at Merton (Dioc. of Winchester), ii, 12. On the death of Dounewell *(sic)*,

William Cloneburgh, chaplain, was inst., 13 May, 1414; patrons, the same, ii, 158b.

BICKLEIGH [Bykelegh], Rectors of—

Thomas Pontyngdon; on whose death was inst., 8 Feb., 1397-8,

John Langh, priest; patrons, William Colmton, clerk, Hugh Waleys, Walter Raynald, Nicholas Hele, Gregory Miriet, and Alexander Clyvedon, by virtue of a feoffment in their favour made by William, own brother and heir of John Pontyngdon of Bicklegh, ii, 8. Lange *(sic)* exchanged with

John Lodre (V. of Stogumber, Dioc. of B. & W.), 26 Nov., 1405; patron, Sir Philip Courtenay, knight, ii, 87b. This R. exchanged with

John Hoper (V. of East Coker, Dioc. of B. & W.), 14 Oct., 1406; patrons, Sir Edw. Courtenay, knight (son of Edward, Earl of Devon). Robert Cary, Oger Buryn, Robert Wey (R. of Powderham), and Gilbert Byschop, ii, 92b. This R. exchanged with

John Loveton (V. of Dulverton, Dioc. of B. and W.), 10 March, 1416-17; patron, Nicholas Pontyngdon, ii, 182.

BICKLEIGH [Byclegh and Byckelegh, MS.], Vicars of—

Richard Underdoune; on whose death was inst., 23 Sept., 1411,

Augustine Strode, priest, LL.B.; patrons, the Abbot and Convent of Buckland, ii, 136. Commission of Enquiry dated, 22 Sept.; ii, 243b. On Strode's resignation

Alfred Gyst, chaplain, was inst., 13 Sept., 1412, ii, 144. On whose death

Michael Robert, chaplain, was inst., 20 April, 1416; ii, 176.

BICTON [Buketon, MS.], Rectors of—

Walter Wyne; on whose death was inst., 28 Dec., 1395,

John Wolfe, priest; patron, Ralph Sachevile, in right of his wife as Lady of the Manor of Bicton with the advowson thereof. The Vicar-General had, first (17 July, 1395), issued a Commission to Richard Wykyslond, LL.B., to investigate this claim to present, ii, 2b.

John Aubrey, priest, was inst. on the death of Wolff *(sic)*, 14 Sept., 1396; patron, Joan Hampton. relict of Ralph Sachevile, ii, 6. He exchanged with

John Scorch (V. of Harpford), 10 March, 1398-9; patron, Wm. Knyght, ii, 11; Commission (dated 3 Feb.) ii, 223. On whose death was inst.

John Trille, priest, 8 Nov., 1399; patron, Wm. Knyȝth, ii, 14.

Robert Martyn, chaplain, succeeded on the death of Trylle, 13 Oct., 1402; patron, Wm. Knyght; ii, 23. On whose death

Geoffrey Cornyseche, chaplain, was inst., 22 March, 1404-5, patron the same, ii, 83.

BIGBURY [Bykebury, MS.], Rectors of—

William Poundestok [Canon of Exeter]; on whose death was inst., 10 June, 1414,

John Bykebury, clerk; patron, Wm. Bykebury, domicellus; ii, 159.

BISHOP'S NYMPTON, Vicars of—

John Schute (q.v.) There is no record of his resignation, but he was succeeded by

Nicholas Whyte, alias *Quythe*, chaplain, collated 19 July, 1407; ii, 97.

BISHOP'S TAWTON, Vicars of—

John Mark; on whose death was inst. (21 Oct., 1411),

John Forst, chaplain; patron, Ralph Tregrisiow, Dean of Exeter, "racione Decanatus predicti"; ii, 136.

BITTADON [Byttedene, MS.], Rectors of—

John Stoke; on whose resignation, was inst., 1 May, 1397,

Stephen Taillour, priest (proxy—Thos. Wyet, clerk); patron, John Loueryng; ii, 7; on whose death

John Bruwere, priest, was inst., 15 June, 1399 (proxy—Thomas Wyot *(sic)*; patron, John Loueryng; ii, 12b.

BLACKAWTON [Blakaueton and Blakeaueton, MS.] Rectors of,—

William Piers; on whose death was inst. (4 July, 1401),
Roger Bolter, clerk; patrons, the Prior and Convent of Plympton, ii, 19b.
Henry Gardiner, chaplain, succeeded, on Bolter's resignation, 22 April, 1419 (proxy—John Pral, chaplain), ii, 198. On whose death was inst. (3 Sept., 1419)
John Birkhede, chaplain (proxy—Thos. Seys, clerk) ii, 204b.

BLACKBOROUGH [Blakeburgh, MS.], Rectors of—

William Porter, chaplain, inst., 27 Feb., 1402-3; patron, John Wyke, Esq., ii, 25.
John Beke succeeded: his institution is not recorded; but on his death
Thomas Toffe was inst., 2 June, 1405; patron, John Wyke "de Nenhide,"[1] domicellus, ii, 85. On the death of Tofte *(sic)*
John Heanok, chaplain, was inst., 15 July, 1413; patrons, John Blakelake, clerk, Roger Tremayl, and Wm. Newton, ii, 151b. On whose death
John Forster, chaplain, was collated *by lapse*, 25 Feb., 1413-14; ii, 156.

BLACK TORRINGTON, Rectors of—

John Wyndout, who exchanged, 14 Jan., 1404-5, with
David Loueryng (R. of St. Mary-Steps, Exeter); patron, Ela, relict of Sir Rd. de St. Maur, knt., ii, 81b.

BLISLAND [Blyston, MS.], Rectors of—

John Laurence; this R. exchanged, 25 Nov., 1396, with
John Balsham (R. of Gransden-Parva, Dioc. of Ely), patron, K. Ric. II.; ii, 32. On whose death[2] was inst. (24 Nov., 1410),
John Bailly, clerk, M.A. (proxy—John Thorp); patron, Henry, Prince of Wales, ii, 124. On whose resignation
Thomas Kardowe, chaplain, was inst., 17 Dec., 1411; patron, the same, ii, 138b.

BOCONNOC [Boconnok, MS.], Rectors of—

Walter Raynald; on whose resignation was inst., 25 Feb., 1417-18,
John Houper, chaplain, patrons, Elizabeth and Anna Mountagu, daughters of John, Earl of Salisbury, deceased, ii, 190. Commission of Enquiry, dated 8 Feb., 1417-18; ii, 264.

BODMIN (St. Petrock's), Vicars of—

Robert Northwode; on whose death was inst., 12 Aug., 1400,
John Stephyn, chaplain; patron, the Prior and Convent of Bodmin, ii, 49b. On Stephyn's death
Laurence Velaw, chaplain, was inst., 11 May, 1417, ii, 183.

BODMIN PRIORY, Priors of—

William Carnellov; on whose death
Alan Kenegy succeeded, 22 Dec., 1403; ii, 73.

BONDLEIGH [Bonlegh, MS.], Rectors of—

John Hopere; on whose death was inst., 18 Sept., 1403,
Thomas Gambon, chaplain; patron, Walter Gambon, domicellus, ii, 69.

BOSHAM, the Collegiate Church of; Collations, etc.—

John Wykham, M.A., collated, 25 Jan., 1396-7, to the Prebend of Walton, *vice*

---

[1] *Hodie* Ninehead Court.

[2] A brass to his memory remains in the chancel of Blisland Church, from which we learn the day of his death; it represents him fully vested, with this inscription at the foot:—"Orate pro anima Johannis Balsam quondam Rectoris istius ecclesie, qui obiit die Michaelis Septembris Anno Domini MCCCC decimo" *(Maclean.)*

Nicholas Wykham, resigned, ii, 32b. He exchanged, for the Prebend of Thorp in the Cathedral Church of York with the said

Nicholas Wykham (Canon of Howden in that Diocese) 25 May, 1397; ii, 34. Commission of Enquiry dated 2 Feb., 1396-7; ii, 211b.

William Langeton collated, 24 July, 1398, to a Canonry and the Prebend of Apuldram [Appeldurham, MS.], *vice* Thomas Cook, resigned (proxy—William Walton), ii, 38b.

Richard Deen (V. of Hackington [Hakynton, MS.], Dioc. of Canterbury, exchanged with Peter de Carsfeld, and was collated, 16 June, 1399, to his office of Sacristan (with a Canonry and a Prebend annexed thereto), ii, 41b.

Laurence Haukyn, chaplain, collated 9 Jan., 1319-1400, to a Canonry and the Prebend of Funtington, *vice* Nicholas Braybrok, deceased; ii, 45.

Ralph Waterman, collated, 20 July, 1400, to the Office of Sacristan, *vice* Richard Deen, resigned, ii, 48b.

Richard Hals exchanged his R. of Warbleton (Dioc. of Chichester) with the above-named William Langeton for his Canonry and Prebend of Apuldram, 20 Nov., 1400; and 25 Nov., Hals resigned, and Langeton was again collated, ii, 52.

Thomas Ayschperton, chaplain, collated, 15 June, 1401, to a Canonry and the Prebend of Westbrook, *vice* Richard Courtenay, resigned, ii, 54. On his resignation thereof

Matthew Doune, chaplain, succeeded, 30 Oct., 1406. It is stated that the Bishop collated him "*ante prandium*," ii, 92b. Doune exchanged this preferment, on the very same day, with

Nicholas Bodeway (R. of Bratton [Clovelly]), *ibid.* There is no record of Bodeway's resignation or death; but

Richard Tyttesbury, LL.B., was collated to this Prebend, 16 Nov., 1406; ii, 93.

John Macworth, chaplain, collated (proxy—William Kays, literate), to the above-named Prebend of Funtington, on the resignation (proxy—William Brounyng, chaplain), of Laurence Haukyn, 28 April, 1407; ii, 96; and the said

Laurence Haukyn was collated, on the same day, to the above-named Prebend of Walton, *vice* Nicholas Wykham, deceased, ii, 96b.

William Langeton was collated to the Prebend of Westbrook, 22 July, 1407, in exchange with

Richard Tyttesbury, who was collated to the Prebend of Apuldram (ii, 97), and, 23 Sept., 1407, exchanged this preferment for a Prebend in the Church of Saint Teath with

William Sutton, ii, 98.

John Lamburn, chaplain, collated, 22 Feb., 1407-8, to the office of Sacristan, *vice* Ralph Waterman, resigned, ii, 100.

Richard Gabriell (Prebendary of Penylles in the Church of Chulmleigh), exchanged with *Thomas Barton* (whose proxy was John Olveston), and was collated to his Canonry and the parochial Prebend in Bosham, 10 May, 1408; ii, 101b.

John Stone, clerk, collated, 25 March, 1410, to a Canonry and the Prebend of Funtington, *vice* John Makworth (*sic*), resigned, ii, 109.

Robert (son of John) *de Gunwardby* (V. of Stapleford, Dioc. of Ely—patrons the Prior and Chapter of Ely), exchanged with John Lamburne (whose proxy was William Whitman), and was collated, 4 May, 1410, to his office of sacristan, ii, 109b. On Gunwardby's death

Robert Tremylet, succeeded, 11 Dec., 1412; ii, 147.

Michael Lercedekne, clerk, LL.B., collated 1 May, 1414, to a Canonry and the Prebend of Westbrook, *vice* William Langeton, deceased, ii, 158b.

John Leyman, chaplain, collated 28 Aug., 1415, to the office of Sacristan, *vice* Robert Tremylet, deceased, ii, 168.

Roger Bolter, chaplain, collated 10 June, 1416, to a Canonry and the Prebend of Apuldram, *vice* William Sutton, deceased, ii, 176b.

William Rayner, chaplain, collated, 22 Feb., 1417-18, to a Canonry and the Prebend of Westbrook, *vice* Michael Lercedekne, resigned, ii, 189b.

William Kelyngmersh, collated, 12 May, 1418, to a Canonry and the Prebend of Walton, *vice* Laurence Haukyn, deceased, ii, 191.
Martin Lercedekne, chaplain, collated, 24 July, 1418, to a Canonry and the Prebend of Apuldram, *vice* Roger Bolter, resigned, ii, 193.
Nicholas Dygon, chaplain, collated, 8 May, 1419, to a Canonry and the Prebend of Apuldram, *vice* Martin Lercedekne, resigned, ii, 198.
Nicholas Pycot (V. of West Dean, Dioc. of Chichester), exchanged with John Leyman, and was collated, 20 May, 1419, to his office of Sacristan, ii, 199.
Robert Allerton, clerk, collated 12 June, 1419, to a Canonry and the Prebend of Funtington, *vice* John Stone, deceased, ii, 199b.
Michael Lercedekne, chaplain, collated, 2 Aug., 1419, to a Canonry and the Parochial Prebend, *vice* Richard Gabriell, deceased, ii, 201b.

BOVEY TRACY, St. Peter and St. Paul [Boveytracy, MS.], Vicars of—
John atte Mille : on whose death was inst., 5 Sept., 1401,
William Pollok, chaplain, ; patron, William Pathulle, Master of the Hospital of St. John Baptist, Bridgewater, ii, 20.

BOW, *see* NYMET TRACY.

BRADFORD, Rectors of—
Robert Lang; on whose death was inst., 10 Jan., 1411-12,
Richard Pends, LL.B., patron, Isolda, widow of Walter Denys of Bradford, ii, 139; *see*, also, ii, 244. On his resignation,
John Wolston, chaplain, was inst., 15 July, 1416; patron Isolda Wybbury, widow of Walter Denys, ii, 177b. On his resignation,
James Carslegh, clerk, LL.B., was inst., 24 May, 1418; patron, Isolda Wybbury, formerly wife of Walter Denys, deceased, ii, 191b. He exchanged with
Geoffrey Veale, for his Chantry of Ford in the parish of Bampton, 2 Aug., 1419; the same patron, ii, 201b.

BRADNINCH [Bradenyng *alias* Bradenassch, MS.], Rectors of—
John Bampton alias *Chapman*; this R. (by his proxy Thomas Randolf), exchanged, 15 July, 1395, with
John Wendovere (proxy—John Gardiner) for his Archdeaconry of Lewes (Dioc. of Chichester): patron, Sir Philip Courtenay, knt., ii, 27.

BRADSTONE, Rectors of,—
Richard Burneman; who exchanged 27 Oct., 1418, with
John Warde (R. of Moorlinch [Merlynch, MS.], Dioc. of B. and W), ii, 195.

BRADWORTHY[1], Vicars of,—
John Dalkyn; on whose death was inst., 25 Feb., 1405-6,
John Yurd, chaplain; patrons, the Abbot and Convent of Torre, ii, 88b. On the resignation of Yerde (*sic*),
Nicholas Botteburgh, chaplain, was inst., 27 Sept., 1413; ii, 152b.

BRAMPFORD SPEKE [Bramforde, MS.], Vicars of,—
John Rok; who exchanged, 18 March, 1403-4, with
John York, patrons, the Prior and Convent of St. Nicholas, Exeter, ii, 75. On York's resignation
John Stonyng, chaplain, was inst. 15 Dec., 1417; ii, 188b.

BRANSCOMBE, Vicars of,—
Robert Hamond; on whose death was inst., 31 May, 1401,

---

[1] At fol. 49, vol. i, a space is left between 18 and 21 Sept., 1400. In the margin is written "Dedicacio Ecclesie de Bradeworthy," but the blank was never filled in. This Church was destroyed by lightning in 1395, and was rebuilt and enlarged; see i, 7b.

John Taylour, chaplain ; patrons, the Dean and Chapter of Exeter, ii, 18b.

BRATTON [CLOVELLY], Rectors of,—

Reginald Bryta ; he exchanged, 30 Oct., 1406, with

Nicholas Bodeway (R. of Bridestowe). The Bishop was patron of both benefices. On the same day, Bodeway exchanged with

Matthew Doune, Canon and Prebendary of Westbrook in Bosham, ii, 92b. On whose resignation

Stephen Anstewell, chaplain, was collated 29 June, 1409; ii, 106. He exchanged 9 June, 1417, with

William Derwent (R. of Shobrook), ii, 186 ; and Derwent exchanged, 8 July following, with

William Causey (R. of South Perrott—Dioc. of Salisbury), ii, 186b.

BRATTON "in Archidiaconatu Barum," i.e. BRATTON FLEMING, Rectors of,—

Walter Galway ; on whose death was inst., 28 March, 1410,

John Hermane, chaplain ; patron, Sir Thomas Flemmyng, knt., ii, 109.

BRENDON, Rectors of,—

Baldwin Kymbuscumque ; on whose resignation was inst., 23 May, 1409,

John Cole, chaplain ; patron, Walter Grendon (Prior of the Hospital of St. John of Jerusalem in England), ii, 105b. On Cole's resignation

Richard Hurde, chaplain, was inst., 15 Dec., 1412, ii, 147b.

BRENT [Brenta, MS.], Vicars of,—

Robert Knygth ; on whose death was inst., 11 Feb., 1406-7,

John Junne, M.A., chaplain ; patrons, the Abbot and Conv. of Buckfast, ii, 94b.

BRIDESTOWE (Brystowe and Brydstow MS.), Rectors of,—

Robert Wantynge, who exchanged, 14 May, 1397, with

Nicholas Bodeway (R. of Arreton, Dioc. of Winchester—patron, Richard II), ii, 34. He exchanged, 30 Oct., 1406, with

Reginald Bryta (R. of Bratton Clovelly, the Bishop being patron of both benefices), ii, 92b. Bryta exchanged, 30 Sept. 1409, both this Rectory and, also, his Canonry etc. in Ottery St. Mary, with

John Prate (R. of Dittisham), ii, 106.b Prata (*sic*) exchanged, 24 May, 1413, both Bridestowe and the said Canonry with

John Wykyngton (R. of St. Pancras in the City of London—patron, the Archbishop of Canterbury), ii, 150b. This Rector exchanged, 23 July, 1415, with

William Weston (R. of Deene, Dioc. of Lincoln), ii, 166b ; on whose resignation

John Fosse, chaplain, was collated 26 Nov., 1416, ii, 180.

BRIDFORD [Bredeforde, MS.], Rectors of,—

William Gore, on whose resignation was inst., 25 Sept., 1399,

Richard Veysy, priest : patron, Sir Richard Champernoun, knt., ii, 13.

BRIDGERULE [Bryggeruwell, MS.], Vicars of,—

Thomas Skede ; who exchanged, 25 Feb., 1407-8, with

Robert Ballard, chaplain, for his Chantry at Morthoe. The Prior and Convent of Launceston were patrons of Bridgerule ; ii, 100b.

BRIMPTON REGIS (Dioc. of B. and W.), *See* LITTLEHAM, V., ii, 87.

BRISTOL [Brystow], St. Michael's, R., *See* COTLEIGH, R., ii, 64 ; also, SEATON, V., ii. 84b.

BRITHLEGH, the Chantry of,—

Richard Poghemylle, inst., 28 March, 1401 ; patron, Edward, Earl of Devon, ii, 17.

BRIXHAM, Vicars of,—

Richard Holrygge ; on whose death was inst., 22 May, 1416,
Walter Wadham ; patron, Sir Edward Courtenay, Knt., son of Edward, Earl of Devon, ii, 176b.

BROAD CHALK, V. (Dioc. Sarum.), *See* CHERITON BISHOP, ii, 30.

BROAD CLYST [Brodeclyst *and* "Clyston *alias* Brodeclyst" MS.], Vicars of,—
Nigel Brode ; on whose death was inst., 15 Sept., 1413,
John Matheu, chaplain ; patron, for that turn, the Prior and Convent of Totnes. ii, 152. Commission of Enquiry dated 8 Aug., 1413, ii, 252. Mathu (*sic*) exchanged, 6 July, 1419, with
Geoffrey Barger (R. of Alphington), patron, Sir John Huntyndon (*sic*), E. of Huntingdon, ii, 200b—Commission, dated 30 June, 1419 ; ii, 267b.

BROADHEMBURY, Vicars of,—
Roger Stanlegh ; on whose death was inst., 24 July, 1406,
John Husey, chaplain ; patrons, the Dean and Chapter of Exeter, ii, 90. He exchanged, 22 Sept., 1414, with
Gilbert Deneman (R. of Combe Raleigh), ii, 161b.

BROADOAK or BRADDOCK [Brodoke and Brodeoke, MS.], Rectors of,—
William Serll ; on whose death was inst., 21 July, 1403,
John Bondon, chaplain ; patron, Richard Prydeaus, domicellus, ii, 68. On the resignation of Bunden (*sic*),
William Torryngton, chaplain, was inst., 16 March, 1413-14 ; patron, John Prydeaux, senior, ii, 157.

BROAD NYMET [Brodenymyt, MS.], Rectors of,—
John Bradeford ; on whose death was inst., 25 Sept., 1416,
John Baudyn, chaplain ; patron, John Mulys, senior, ii, 179. On whose resignation
John Cornu, chaplain, was inst., 19 Oct., 1418 ; patrons, Robert Cary, domicellus, Robert Waye, clerk, and Gilbert Bysshop, ii, 195.—Commission of Enquiry, dated 25 Aug., 1418, ii, 266.

BROAD SYDLING [Brodesydelyng, MS.], Dioc. of Salisbury, *See* COMBE RALEIGH, R.

BROADWOOD WIDGER [Brodewodewygger, MS.], Vicars of,—
John Knyght ; who exchanged, 7 March, 1406-7, with
Thomas Launcel (V. of Honeychurch) ; patrons, the Prior and Convent of Frithelstock, ii, 95.

BRUSHFORD [Bryshford. MS.], (Dioc. of B. and W.) *See* WASHFIELD *and* NORTH LEW.

BUCKFAST ABBEY,—
William Paderstow, . . Sept., 1395 ; ii, 210b.
[*William Slade*.]
William Beaghe ; confirmed 8 Sept., 1415 ; ii. 169.

BUCKERELL [Bokerel and Bokerell, MS.], Vicars of,—
John Brystowe ; on whose death was inst., 28 Oct., 1401 ; patrons, the Dean and Chapter of Exeter,
Thomas Hicks, chaplain, ii, 20b. On his death
Thomas Henford, chaplain, was inst., 15 Oct., 1405, ii, 86b ; on whose death
John Gyffard, deacon, was inst., 6 May, 1409 ; ii, 105.

BUCKFASTLEIGH [Bokfastlegh MS.], Vicars of,—
John Fardell ; on whose death was inst., 26 Aug., 1406,

David Hugh, chaplain ; patrons, the Abbot and Convent of Buckfast, ii, 91b. On the death of Hughe (*sic*),
Roger Goslay, chaplain, was inst., 30 June, 1414 ; ii, 160. On the death of Gosley (*sic*),
Richard Profete, priest, was inst., 2 Dec., 1415 ; ii, 173b. On the resignation of Prophet (*sic*),
Henry Baudyn, chaplain, was inst., 22 Dec., 1416 ; ii, 181b.

BUCKLAND ABBAS, V. (Dioc. of Salisbury), *See* ST. IVE.

BUCKLAND BREWER [Bokelond Brywer, MS.], Vicars of,—
John Copehill ; on whose death was inst., 18 July, 1405,
Richard Dunste, chaplain ; patrons, the Abbot and Convent of Torre ; ii, 85b.

BUCKLAND FILLEIGH [Bokelond Fyllegh, MS.], Rectors of,—
John Castell, clerk, was collated 24 Jan., 1399-1400 ; ii, 45.
John Gyffard, chaplain, was collated 28 Nov., 1408, ii, 103b. The date of his resignation (or death) is not recorded ; but he was one of the witnesses to a "dispensation," granted 24 Feb., 1408-9 (i, 84). He seems to have been succeeded by
John Bowode, who is described as Rector of this parish [Boklond Fylly, MS.] in a licence of non-residence for one year granted 12 July, 1410 (i, 100b) ; but I can find no record of his collation.

BUCKLAND [Boklond, MS.] MONACHORUM, Vicars of,—
Thomas Wappelegh ; who exchanged, 4 Aug., 1398, with
William Grim (R. of Lamorran), and was inst. (proxy—Ralph Dolbeare) ; patrons, the Abbot and Convent of Buckland, ii, 40. On the resignation of Grym (*sic*), a Commission (dated 15 July, 1400), was directed to John, Prior of Plympton, to admit
Gilbert Baker, chaplain ; ii, 228. On Baker's death
Thomas Braddegh, clerk, was inst., 4 Feb., 1405-6 ; ii, 88b.

BUDLEIGH [Buddelegh, MS.], Vicars of,—
Richard Sonde alias *Waltham* ; on whose death was inst., 13 May, 1402.
Hugh Hokere, chaplain ; patrons, the Prioress and Convent of Polslo, ii, 21b.

BURLESCOMBE, Vicars of—
John Loteby ; on whose death was inst., 24 July, 1413,
William Baunton, chaplain ; patrons, the Abbess and Convent of Canonsleigh, ii, 151b.

BURRINGTON [Boryngton, MS.], Vicars of—
Roger Cole ; who exchanged, 12 June, 1411, with
Thomas Bost, for his Chantry at Charleton Adam (Dioc. of B. and W.; patrons, the Abbot and Convent of Tavistock, ii, 133.

BUTTERLEIGH [Boterlegh, MS.], Rectors of—
Robert Vyet ; on whose death was inst., 23 Sept., 1402,
John Stretton (alias *Oliver*), chaplain ; patrons, the Prior and Convent of St. Nicholas, Exeter, ii, 23.

CADELEIGH, Rectors of—
William Oke ; on whose resignation was inst., 3 June, 1407,
John Symons, chaplain ; patron, Richard Courtenay, clerk, ii, 96b.

CALSTOCK [Calestok, MS.], Rectors of—
Thomas Wygtouht ; on whose death was inst. (proxy—William Smale), 4 Jan., 1396-7,
Thomas Malesouers, priest ; patron, John Holland, Earl of Huntingdon. He was *inducted* by Benedict Canterbury, R. of Camborne, ii, 6b. On the death of Malsore (*sic*)
John Malewayn, clerk, was inst., 14 Jan., 1402-3 ; patron, Sir John Cornewaylle, knt., ii, 23b.

CAMELEY [Camlee, MS.], Dioc. of B. and W., *see* YARCOMBE, V.

CANONSLEIGH PRIORY [Canonlegh, MS.], Prioresses of—
Lucy Warre; on whose death,
Mary Beauchamp was elected; confirmed, 12 Dec., 1410, ii, 128b.

CARDYNHAM [Cardynan, MS.], Rectors of—
Thomas Aumarle; on whose death was inst., 23 March, 1401-2,
John Pole, junior, clerk (proxy—John Rodberd, clerk); patrons, James Aumarle, John Pole, senior, Robert Maynard, Thomas Hertescote, and John Bole. The Commission for his institution was directed to John Westecote, R. of St. Petrock's, Exeter, ii, 21. On Pole's death,
John Halsanger, chaplain, was inst., 27 Oct., 1413; patrons, Robert Maynard and Thomas Hertescote, by concession to the said Robert and Thomas, and also to James Aumarl, John Pole, and John Bole, by Sir John Dynham, knt., of his Manor of Cardynham and the advowson of the Church, for life, and to the survivors of them. Of these Aumarl was dead, and Pole and Bole had conceded all their rights in the said Manor to the said Robert and Thomas, ii, 153. Commission of enquiry dated 22 Oct., 1413, ii, 252b. Halsaungre (*sic*) exchanged with
John Waryn (R. of Grittleton, Dioc. of Salisbury), 2 Jan., 1413-14; patrons, the aforesaid Robert and Thomas; ii, 154b.

CARSWELL or CRESSWELL[1] ["Carssewell *alias* Cressewell," M.S], Prebendaries of—
Richard Danyell; on whose resignation was inst., 16 July, 1418,
Robert God; patron, Edward, Earl of Devon and of the lordship of Okehampton, ii, 193.

CHAGFORD [Chaggeford, MS.], Rectors of—
John Dypphull (also Canon of Chichester). He exchanged . . . . April,[2] 1397, with
Laurence Haukyn (R. of Charing, Dioc. of Canterbury), ii, 33b; who was instituted to Chagford, 11 July, 1397; patrons, John Newethorp, William Croisere, and William Wymbelden, ii, 34b. On Haukyn's resignation John Lydeford, junior, was inst. (proxy—Hervey Wyket), 9 Nov., 1397; patrons, the same, ii, 35b.

CHALBURY [Chaulburgh, MS.], Dioc. of Salisbury, *see* JACOBSTOWE (Devon), ii, 142b.

CHALLACOMBE [Choldecomb and Chaudecomb, MS.], Rectors:
William White; on whose death was inst., 14 Dec., 1399,
John Neue, priest; patron, Sir William Talbot, knt., ii, 14b; *see*, ii, 265b
Neve (*sic*) exchanged with
William Haukyn (R. of Cheddington, Diocese of Salisbury; patron, James Hornesbowe); instituted (proxy—Richard Sprynggold), 16 Nov., 1405); patron, William Beaumound, domicellus, ii, 87. Haukyn exchanged with
John Gruys (V. of Haselbury, Dioc. of B. & W.), 11 June, 1409; patron, John Chechester, domicellus, ii, 105b.

CHARDLINCH [Cherdelynche, MS.], (Dioc. of B. & W.), R., *see* REWE, R., ii, 21b, and also UPLOMAN, R., ii, 93.

CHARING (Dioc. of Canterbury), *see* CHAGFORD, ii, 34b.

CHARLES [Charlys, MS.]. Rectors of—

[1] One of the four Prebends in the Church of St. Mary within the Castle of Exeter.

[2] A blank in the MS.; it was either the 27th or 28th.

John Vele; who exchanged, 7 July, 1400, with
Thomas Passewar (V. Over-Stowey, Dioc. of B. & W.); patron, King Henry IV. ii, 48b. Passewarre *(sic)* exchanged, 27 Oct., 1407, with
Thomas Hernyngeston (V. of Halse, Dioc. of B. & W.); patron, Thomas Kyngeslond, ii, 98b. On the resignation of Herynggeston *(sic)*,
Peter Major, chaplain, was inst., 3 July, 1409, patron, Thomas Kynggyslond (*sic*), ii, 106. On Major's death
Thomas Horlok, chaplain, was inst., 31 March, 1418; patron, Thomas Kyngeslond *(sic)*, ii, 190.

CHARLETON ["ad ecclesiam parochialem de Charleton in Southammes"], Rectors of—
Laurence Allerthop, chaplain, inst., 13 April, 1396; patron, Thomas de Berkeley, Lord of Berkeley, ii, 30. Allerthorp *(sic)* exchanged, 27 April, 1397, with
John Syggeston (R. of Brantingham, Dioc. of York); patron, the same throughout), ii, 33. On Syggeston's death
John Came, chaplain, was inst., 3 Aug., 1402, ii, 63b. On the death of Camme *(sic)*
John Wynterburne, chaplain, was inst., 18 Oct., 1408; ii, 103.

CHARLETON ADAM, *see* BURRINGTON.

CHAWLEIGH [Chalvelegh, MS.], Rectors of—
John Poyns, who exchanged 2 Feb., 1413-14, with
Matthew Wonston (R. of Maperton, Dioc. of B. & W.); patron, Edward, Earl of Devon, ii, 155.

CHEDDON [Cheden, MS.], Dioc. of B. & W., *see* WEST ALVINGTON, ii, 49b.

CHEDDINGTON (Dioc. of Salisbury), *see* ST. JOHN IN CORNWALL, R. (ii, 56b); ASHTON, R. (ii, 75b); and CHALLACOMBE, R. (ii, 87).

CHELDON [Chedyldon and Chedeldon, MS.], Rectors of—
Thomas Miere, on whose resignation was inst., 21 April, 1396,
Walter atte Hulle, priest, patron, Edmund Caylleways, ii, 5. On the resignation of Walter Hulle *(sic)*, chaplain,
Oliver Radysworthy, chaplain, was inst., 16 July, 1403; patron, Edmund Kayleway *(sic)*, domicellus, i, 68. On the death of Radysworth *(sic)*
John Rynel, chaplain, was inst., 22 Dec., 1411; patron, Edmund Kaylleway *(sic)* domicellus, ii, 138b.

CHELMSFORD, St. Margaret's Chapel at, *see* ST. PROBUS (preb.), ii, 46.

CHERITON BISHOP [Churyton Episcopi, MS.], Rectors of—
John Boun, who exchanged, 4 May, 1396, with
John Taylour (V. of Broadchalk—patron, William Waltham, as Prebendary of Chalke in the Conventual Church of Wilton), 4 May, 1396; patron, the Bishop, ii, 30. Taylour exchanged, 24 Nov., 1401, with
John Lane (R. of Hemington, Dioc. of B. & W.); ii, 56. On his resignation
Lewis Busshbyry was collated 6 Oct., 1410, ii, 123b.

CHERITON FITZPAINE, Rectors of—
Richard Weynman; on whose death was inst., 9 May, 1418,
Walter Hylle, chaplain, patron, John Copleston, senior, ii, 191.

CHEVEREL-PARVA, Chantry at (Dioc. of Salisbury), *see* JACOBSTOW (Devon), R., ii, 177.

CHICHESTER CATHEDRAL, Canonry and Prebend of Thorney;

Laurence Haukyn, chaplain, was collated thereto, 8 Nov., 1397, by the Bishop of Exeter (under the authority of a Commission issued by Robert, Bishop of Chichester), in the room of *John Lydeford*, senior, resigned ; ii, 35b.—*See* EXETER, Archdeaconry of, ii, 109.

CHIDDINGFOLD [Chydyngfold MS.], Dioc. of Winchester, *see* COMBMARTIN, ii, 167.

CHITTLEHAMPTON [Chetelampton, Chitelhampton, and Chetelhampton, MS.], Vicars of—

Philip Hokke ; who exchanged, 21 Jan., 1395-6, with

Walter Salterne (R. of Ashbrittle, Dioc. of B. and W.—patron, Anselm Swan) ; patrons, the Abbot and Convent of Tewkesbury, ii, 3.—Commission of Enquiry dated 22 Dec., 1395, ii, 210b. He exchanged, 16 Oct., 1405, with

John Marnhull (R. of "Shafton St. Rumbold"—patrons, the Abbess and Convent of Shaftesbury) ; ii, 86b. Marnull (*sic*) exchanged, 3 Aug., 1409, with

John Wynsham (V. of Combe St. Nicholas, Dioc. of B. and W.) ; ii, 106b.

CHRISTOW [Cristow MS.], Vicars of—

Thomas Paulyn ; on whose death was inst., 9 Dec., 1411,

William Gyle, chaplain ; patron, Joan, the Queen, ii, 138. Commission of Enquiry dated 18 Nov., 1411, ii, 244. On Gyle's death

William Wethy, chaplain, was inst., 4 May, 1416 ; patron, K. Henry V., ii, 176.

CHUDLEIGH [Chuddelegh, MS.]. Vicars of—

John Basynghan de Melton exchanged with

Vincent Hille, 22 Jan., 1402-3, for his Vicarage of Luppit, ii, 65.

CHULMLEIGH [Chulmelegh, MS.], Rectors of—

William Halyett ; who exchanged, 20 Dec., 1404, with

William Lane (R. of Roseash) ; patron, Edward, Earl of Devon, ii, 80b.

Institutions to Prebends in this Church (patron, Edward, Earl of Devon) :—

William Typ, clerk, vice *William de Ledes*, deceased, 1 July, 1396, ii, 5b.

John Candelesby, clerk, vice *William Typp* (*sic*), resigned, 7 Nov., 1397, ii, 35b.

William Typ, clerk, vice *Roger Payn*, deceased, 22 Nov., 1399, ii, 14.

Richard Gabriell, clerk, vice *Robert del Skyres*, resigned, 16 March, 1407-8, ii, 101.

Thomas Barton (in exchange[1] with *Richard Gabriell*, 25 March, 1410). *See* Bosham, ii, 101b.

William Floyer, clerk, vice *John Candelesby*, deceased, 12 Nov., 1415, ii, 173b.

Thomas Colyns, clerk, vice *Thomas Barton* [Berton, MS.], deceased, 31 March, 1416, ii, 175b.

John Wendover, chaplain, to the Prebend of Netherhayne : proxy—Thomas Newhall, clerk ; vice *Richard Bruton*, deceased, 1 Dec., 1417, ii, 188b.

CHURCHSTANTON [Cherystaunton, MS.], Rectors of,—

John Wyllys, on whose death was inst., 31 May, 1396,

Thomas Modeslegh, priest ; patron, Sir William Bonevile, Knt., ii, 5b.

CLANNABOROUGH [Cloneneburgh, MS.], Rectors of—

Robert Doget. *See* Blackhay, Roger.

John Thomma was collated, 23 Jan., 1416-17, "jure devoluto," ii, 182.—Nothing is said (in the record of Thomma's collation) of his predecessor's resignation or death. Robert Doget, however, occurs as Rector in 1410 (*see* i, 100b) ; and it will be seen, on referring to ASHREIGNEY, that he was instituted to that parish, 18 July, 1416, when, evidently, he resigned Clannaborough ; and on 26 July the Bishop issued a Commission of Enquiry as to the patronage : the Church would have been vacant for six months on the 18th of Jan., and on the 23rd the Bishop collated by lapse.

---

[1] Prebend of Penylles.

CLAYHIDON [Hydon, MS.], Rectors of—
John Achard; on whose death was inst., 15 Jan., 1404-5,
Peter Byschop, chaplain; patrons, Jas. Aumarle, John Pole, Robert Maynard, Thos. Hertyscote, and John Bole, ii, 81b.

CLOVELLY [Clovely MS.], Rectors of—
Walter Crabbe; on whose death was inst., 16 Jan., 1396-7,
Richard Loman, priest; patron, William Caru, ii, 7.
William Penwonan. There is no record of his institution, but his name occurs as Rector, 6 Sept., 1407 (i, 82b); and it is stated that on his death
Richard Planya (or *Plenya*), priest, was inst., 31 May, 1411; patron, Thomasia, relict of William Cary, ii, 133.

CLYST FOMISON [Fomson, MS.], *alias* Clyst St. Michael, Rectors of—
Philip Newenton; on whose resignation was collated, 2 July, 1396,
Richard Hoper, who exchanged 26 Oct., 1400, with
John Orum (R. of Theynton, Dioc. of Lincoln), ii, 51. On Orum's resignation (*which took place on the same day*),
John Hethen, chaplain, was collated, ii, 51. Hethen soon resigned, and
John Barell, chaplain, was collated, 14 Aug., 1401, ii, 54. There is no record of Barell's resignation; but (ii, 74b) he was inst. to St. Illogan, R., 26 Feb., 1403-4; and was succeeded, 6 April, 1404, by
Thomas Morton, chaplain (ii, 75), who exchanged, 29 Nov., 1404, with
John Beef (R. of Charlton, Dioc. of Rochester—patron, Guy, Bishop of St. David's); ii, 80b.

CLYST HYDON, Rectors of—
Walter Dodyngton, who exchanged, 8 June, 1399, with
John Hele (R. of Clyst St. Laurence—patron, John Vautard, domicellus); proxy—William Bremelcombe: patron, Otho Chambernoun, domicellus, ii, 41. Hele exchanged, 20 March, 1408-9, with
Roger Ferrour, V. of Yarcombe; patron, the same, ii, 104b.

CLYST ST. GABRIEL, Wardens of the Chapel of—
John Aller (R. of Clyst St. George); on whose death was collated, 2 May, 1407,
John Bef (or Beef, R. of Clyst Fomison), ii, 96b.

CLYST ST. GEORGE, Rectors of—
John Aller, on whose resignation was inst., 10 Aug., 1406,
John Burell, clerk (proxy—John Kenok, V. of Dawlish); patron, the Prior and Convent of Merton (Dioc. Winchester), ii, 90b. On his resignation
William ȝoksale, chaplain, was inst. (proxy—John Yoksale, literate), 13 June, 1410; ii, 115. On the resignation of Yoxhal *(sic)*
Thomas Twyford, clerk, was inst., 4 April, 1411; ii, 132. Twyforde *(sic)* exchanged, 23 March, 1412-13, with
Thomas Polton (proxy—William Sandel), for his R. of Lucoombe (Dioc. of B. & W.); ii, 148b. On whose resignation
William Knyght, chaplain, was inst. (proxy—Walter Boway, chaplain), 25 Sept., 1416; ii, 179.

CLYST ST. LAURENCE, Rectors of—
John atte Wille; on whose death was inst., 17 Dec., 1395,
John Hele, priest; patron, John Vautard, domicellus, ii, 2. He exchanged, 8 June, 1399, for Clyst Hydon, R., with
Walter Dodyngton; patron, the same; ii, 41; on whose death was inst., 23 Dec., 1403,
John Blakalake, chaplain; patron, John Hele, R. of Clyst Hydon, ii, 74. He exchanged, 7 July, 1405, with

John Yvery (R. of Stoodleigh) ; patron, the same, ii, 85. Ivery *(sic)* exchanged 4 Sept., 1408, with
William Bedmond (R. of Clutton, Dioc. of Wells) ; patron, the same, ii, 102ᵇ. On the death of Bedeman *(sic)*
John Olyver, chaplain, was inst., 27 June, 1419 ; patron, the same, ii, 200.

CLYST ST. MARY, Rectors of—
Henry Patows (or *Pattows*) ; who exchanged, 8 May, 1401, with
William Grene (V. of Honington, Lincolnshire—patrons, the Prioress and Convent of Stixwold) ; patron, John Tylle, ii, 53ᵇ. He exchanged with
John Newerk (R. of Stratford-juxta Glemham, Dioc. of Norwich ; patron, John Glemham), and was inst. (proxy—John Gaynysborugh, clerk), 15 Aug., 1406 ; patron, King Henry II., ii, 91.

CLUTTON [Clotton, MS.], R. Dioc. of Wells, *see* CLYST ST. LAURENCE, ii, 102ᵇ.

COATES [Cotes, MS.], R. (Dioc. of Ely), *see* COMBMARTIN, ii, 82ᵇ.

COLATON RALEIGH [Coleton Ralegh, MS.], Vicars of—
Nicholas Sachevile ; on whose death was inst., 19 Jan., 1395-6.
Stephen Reaker, priest, patron, the Dean of Exeter, ii, 8. Reskyer (*sic*) exchanged 11 June, 1399, with
John Midderhille (V. of St. Cubert) ; patron, Ralph Tregrisiou, Dean of Exeter, ii, 41. Mydderhull (*sic*) exchanged, 26 May, 1401 (*see* fol. 228), with
William Lake (R. of Rowington, Dioc. of B. and W.) ; certificates concerning the said exchange, ii, 18.

COLCOMBE, Chantry of St. John-the-Evangelist in the Manor of—
Stephen Smyth, chaplain : he exchanged, 30 Nov., 1397, with
William Wythye (V. of Stogumber, Dioc. of B. and W. ; patron, Thomas Bokkyng, Canon of Wells), proxy, William Slade (Smyth's proxy being Robert Alkebarowe) ; patron, Edward, Earl of Devon, ii, 30. On the resignation of Wythy *(sic)*
William Dagfen, priest, was inst., 31 July, 1399 ; patron, the same, ii, 13.

COLEBROOKE [Colbrok, MS.], Vicars of—
Andrew Hude ; on whose death was inst., 3 Jan., 1415-16,
William Kelwa, priest ; patrons, the Dean and Chapter of Exeter, ii, 174.

COLERIDGE [Colrygge, MS.], Vicars of—
Thomas Sprot ; on whose death was collated, 8 March, 1408-9,
Robert Feld, chaplain ; patron, the Bishop, ii, 104ᵇ. On Feld's resignation
Thomas Hoper, chaplain, was collated 20 Feb., 1411-12 ; ii, 140.

COLLUMPTON [Colmpton, MS.], Vicars of—
John Burnel ; on whose death was inst., 10 July, 1411,
William Sechevyll, chaplain ; patrons, the Prior and Convent of St. Nicholas, Exeter, ii, 134. Sechevile (*sic*) exchanged, 24 March, 1415-16, with
Edward Fysshacre (R. of Shirwell) ; ii, 175ᵇ.

COLYFORD—Chantry of St. Edmund-by-the-bridge ; Colyton.
John Tweta, chaplain, was collated, *by lapse*, 23 Sept., 1411, ii, 135ᵇ. On the resignation of Twyta (*sic*)
William Clerk, chaplain, was inst., 1 June, 1416 ; patron, Thomas Stowford ii, 176ᵇ.

COLYTON, Vicars of—
Richard Wykeslonde ; on whose death was inst., 17 Jan. 1410-11,
John Potyngdon, chaplain ; patrons, the Dean and Chapter of Exeter, ii, 130 On whose death
John Hulle, chaplain, was inst., 20 Dec., 1412 ; ii, 147ᵇ.

COMBE-IN-TEIGNHEAD [Comyngteynhede, MS.], Rectors of—

On 1 March, 1417-18 a Commission was directed to the Archdeacon of Exeter, or his Official, to enquire, in full Chapter of the Deanery, concerning the vacancy and right of patronage, John Prediaux having presented Richard Halswill, chaplain (ii, 264b). There is no record of his institution; but on the 25th July, 1418, the Bishop collated

Geoffrey Hough, clerk, "jure devoluto," ii, 193.

COMBE ST. NICHOLAS (Dioc. of B. and W.), *See* CHITTLEHAMPTON, ii, 106b.

COMBMARTIN, Rectors of—

Richard Noreys; this Rector exchanged, 20 Oct., 1402, with

Nicholas Stoke (R. of Hampton Meysy, Dioc. of Worcester); patron, K. Henry IV, ii, 64. Stoke exchanged (proxy—Thomas Weston, clerk), 16 March, 1404-5, with

William Goldyng (R. of Coates, Dioc. of Ely; patrons, John Abbot, John Eyer, and John Fryngg), who was inst. by proxy—William Broun, chaplain, ii, 82b. On Goldyng's resignation

Philip Pope, chaplain, was inst., 29 Oct., 1405; ii, 87. Pope exchanged, 29 July, 1415, with

Robert Wantynge (R. of Chiddingfold, Dioc. of Winchester); inst. by proxy—Ralph Clerk; ii, 167. Wantyng (*sic*) exchanged, 16 Dec., 1416, with

John Langle (R. of Westmill, Dioc. of Lincoln); ii, 181.

COMBE RALEIGH, Rectors of—

John Whitoun: who exchanged, 3 Dec., 1398, with

Thomas Hichecok (V. of Broad Sydling, Dioc. of Salisbury—patrons, the Abbot and Convent of Middelton); inst. by proxy—William Bremelcombe; patron, Thomas Pomeray, domicellus; ii, 40b. Commission of Enquiry dated 11 Nov., 1398 (in which his name is spelt "Hygecok"), ii, 220b. He exchanged by proxy—John Warde, chaplain, 16 Dec., 1403, with

Robert Box (V. of East Coker, Dioc. of B. and W.); patron, Sir Thomas Pomeray, Knt., ii, 71. On the death of Box

Gilbert Deneman, chaplain, was inst. (proxy—William Ryder), 31 July, 1407; ii, 97b. Deneman exchanged 22 Sept., 1414, with

John Husey (V. of Broadhembury); ii, 161b.

COMBPYNE [Combpyn, MS.], Rectors of,—

William Langerygg; on whose death was inst., 9 Jan., 1411-12

John Knowston, chaplain; patron, Edmund Pyn (*sic*), domicellus, ii, 138b. On the death of Knoweston (*sic*),

Walter Lebet, chaplain, was inst., 21 July, 1419; patron, Edmund Pyne, ii, 200b.

COOMBE-KEYNES [Combe Kaynes, MS.], (Dioc. of Salisbury), *see* ASHTON, ii, 68b.

CORNWALL, Archdeaconry of (and Prebend in GLASNEY thereto annexed),

Nicholas Brabroyk; on whose resignation was collated, 14[1] July, 1397,

Edward Dauntesey, Doctor of Decrees, ii, 35. He was consecrated Bishop of Meath ("*Episcopus Medensis*"), having resigned his Archdeaconry, etc., (by proxy, John Leman, chaplain); and his successor[2],

[1] "13 July, 1396" in Oliver's List, but in error.

[2] Oliver inserts here "John Orum," simply stating that his name "occurs in 1411"; but Orum was, at that time, Archdeacon of *Barnstaple*, and the Register states distinctly that Bremour succeeded when Dauntesey resigned.

John Bremor was collated, 3 April, 1413; ii, 149. On the death of Bremour (*sic*)
Richard Penels, chaplain, was collated, 15 Sept., 1418[1]; ii, 193b; on whose death
William Fylham, chaplain, was collated 29 May, 1419 (proxy, Benedict Drew, clerk), ii, 199.

CORNWOOD, Vicars of—
William Pykesleygh; who exchanged, 4 Dec., 1405, with
Robert Offcote (V. of Queen Camel, Dioc. of B. and W.); patron, Guy, Bp. of St. David's, ii, 87b.

CORNWORTHY PRIORY, Prioresses of—
Joan Lucy; on whose death succeeded
Eleanora Blake, preferred by the Bishop (by lapse), 28 Feb., 1411-12; ii, 140.

CORSTON, R. (Dioc. of B. and W.), *see* Hemyock, ii, 195b.

COTLEIGH [Cottelegh and Cortelegh, MS.], Rectors of,—
John Hokrr; who exchanged, 14 Oct, 1402, with
John Chamburleyn, chaplain (R. of St. Michael's, Bristol); patrons, Jas. Armarle (*sic*), John Pole, Robert Maynard, Thos. Hurtyschote, and John Bole, ii, 64. Chamberleyn (*sic*), exchanged, 26 March, 1407, with
Henry Thomas (R. of Knightslegh, Dioc. of B. and W.); patrons, Jas. Aumarle, John Pole, Robert Maynard and Thos. Hertescote, ii, 95b. This R. exchanged, 30 March, 1414, with
Augustine Strood (V. of Lamerton); patrons, Robert Maynard and Thomas Hertescote, ii, 157b.

COWICK [Cowyk, MS.], Priors of—
William Estrepeny; on whose resignation was inst., 29 May, 1398,
John Bourgeauuill, monk of Bec. He was presented by Robert, Bishop of London, and William, Prior of Okebourne (Diocese of Salisbury), because of the Schism, ii, 37.—In Oliver's *Monasticon* the name of this Prior is spelt Bourgeanyll: the letters 'n' and 'u' are of course indistinguishable in antient MSS., but at i, 73b it is spelt "Burgeawyll," and at i, 80, Burgeavyll: it is here, therefore, "uu (w)," and not "nn," as Oliver seems to have thought.

CRANTOCK [Sancti Karentoci, MS.], the Collegiate Church of—
Deans:—
Thomas Hendeman, chaplain, S. T. P. He exchanged (proxy—William Clyve, R. of Whitestone), 25 Feb., 1409-10, with
John Soor (for his Chantry of St. Michael in the Cemetery of St. Austell); patron, the Bishop; ii, 108b. On Soor's resignation,
John Waryn, chaplain, was collated, 27 July, 1414; ii, 160b. On whose resignation
William Talkarn, chaplain, was collated, 11 May, 1418, ii, 191.
Collations to *Canonries* in this Church.:—
William Langton, vice *John Martyn*, deceased, 18 Aug., 1395, ii, 27b.
Edmund Weston, clerk, vice *William Langeton*, resigned, 13 July, 1396; ii, 31.
Hervey Wyket, clerk, vice *William Ledes*, deceased, 18 July, 1396; ii, 31.
John Kyngton; also, Canon of St. Mary's Colleg. Church, Shrewsbury and Preb. of the Altar of St. Michael therein; he exchanged all his preferments for a Canonry in St. Paul's, London, and the Prebend of "Eeldstrete" therein, with
Thomas Aston, collated, 17 Oct., 1399 (proxy—William Tanfeld), ii, 43.—Commission directed to Richard Bromley, Dean of St. Mary's, Shrewsbury, 10 Oct., 1399; ii, 226.
Richard Aldryngton, chaplain, vice *Nicholas Braybrok*, deceased, 9 Jan., 1399-1400: ii, 45.

---

[1] This date is omitted in Oliver's List.

Simon de Melborne, clerk, vice *Roger Hampton*, resigned, 9 Feb., 1400-1 ; ii, 52ᵇ.
John Cole, LL.B., vice *Stephen Vaggescomb*, resigned (proxies Hugh, Bishop of Derry, and the said John Cole), 18 Nov., 1402 ; ii, 64ᵇ.
Thomas Aston exchanged with
Roger Hampton, Warden of the Chapel of St. Helen, Ingelby (patron, Thomas Gra, of York), 4 July, 1400 ; ii, 47ᵇ.
Simon Fraunceys, clerk, vice *Edmund Weston*, clerk, deceased, 20 Nov., 1403 ; ii, 70. He was collated, also, 14 June, 1414, to the Canonry resigned by *John Wylle*, ii, 159ᵇ.
Thomas Clifford: he exchanged with
Laurence Haukyn, Canon of Exeter, 23 Aug., 1414 ; ii, 161.
Elias Stoke, vice *Hugh Hyckelyng*, deceased, 31 Jan., 1415-16 ; ii, 174ᵇ.
Roger Bolter, chaplain, vice *Baldwin Shyllyngford*, deceased, 21 Feb., 1417-18 ; ii, 189ᵇ. He was collated, also, 24 April, 1418, to the Canonry vacated by *Laurence Haukyn*, deceased (ii, 190ᵇ), and resigned his first Canonry, to which
John Waryn, chaplain, was collated, 3 May, 1418 ; ii, 191.
John Arondell, alias *Hylle*, clerk, vice *Richard Aldryngton*, resigned (proxy—John Harry, chaplain), 12 Jan., 1418-19 ; ii, 196ᵇ.
Thomas Redman, chaplain, vice John Waryn, resigned, 24 June, 1419 ; ii, 200.

CRAWLEY MAGNA, R. (Dioc. of Lincoln), *see* TOTNES, Archdeaconry of, ii, 164ᵇ.

CREACOMBE [Crewcomb, MS.], Rectors of—
John Yeate ; on whose death was inst., 15 Oct., 1399,
Oliver Radysworthy, priest ; patron, William Hautysforde, domicellus, ii, 13ᵇ.
[On whose appointment to Cheldon (ii, 68), and subsequent resignation]
John Legh, chaplain, was inst., 7 Aug., 1403 ; patron, the same, ii, 68ᵇ.

CREDITON [Criditon, MS.], the Collegiate Church of the Holy Cross—
Deans :—
William Trey ; on whose death was collated, 22 April, 1412,
Thomas Estbroke, LL.B., ii, 141ᵇ. On Estbroke's resignation
William Fylham, chaplain, was collated, 20 Sept., 1417 ; ii, 187. On whose resignation
John Saunder, chaplain, was collated, 24 Feb., 1418-19, ii, 197.
Precentors :—
John Whytewyll ; on whose death
Robert Alkebarowe, chaplain, was collated, 24 July, 1407, ii, 97ᵇ ; on whose resignation
William Quirley, chaplain, was collated, 8 May, 1418 ; ii, 191.
Collations of *Canons* and *Prebendaries* :—
John Prophet, clerk, to a Canonry and the Preb. of Wodelond, vice *John Wendelynburgh*, senior, deceased ; 12 Sept., 1395 ; ii, 27ᵇ.
Richard Hals, clerk, to a Canonry and the Preb. of Crida, *alias Estcridia* ; he exchanged, 27 Nov., 1395, with
William Sutton, also a Canon there and Preb. of Carswill therein (John Hals proxy for Richard Hals, and Richard Tyttesbury for William Sutton,) ii, 29.
William Langeton to the Preb. of Prustecomb, vice *William Ledes*, deceased, 26 June, 1396 ; ii, 31.
Richard Aldryngton, clerk, to a Canonry and the Preb. of Rigge, vice *William Baunton*, deceased ; 8 Oct., 1396 ; ii, 32. He is described as the Bishop's "commensalis."
John Park, clerk, to a Canonry and the Preb. of Wodeland, collated 12 Dec., 1397 ; ii, 36ᵇ.
Richard Hoper, priest, to a Canonry and one of the [six] Bursal Prebends, vice *John Northwode*, deceased, 8 April, 1398, ii, 37.

William Asthill, clerk, to a Canonry and one of the six Bursal Prebends, vice *Henry Maupas*, resigned, 12 July, 1398, ii, 38.

Laurence Haukyn, chaplain, to a Canonry and the Preb. of Crosse, vice *Roger Payn*, deceased, 20 Nov., 1399 ; ii, 44b.

John Prophet, chaplain, to a Canonry and the Preb. of West Sampford, vice *John Dodyngton*, deceased, 17 July, 1400 ; ii, 48b. He resigned in favour of *Walter Medeford*, clerk, 4 Oct., 1402 ; ii, 64.

Stephen Anstywill, to a Canonry and Bursal Preb., in exchange with *John Snape* (V. of Hurstbourne Priors, Dioc. of Winchester), 9 April, 1407 ; ii, 95b.

Nicholas de Rysheton, son of Henry de Rysheton, clerk (of the Dioc. of Lichfield), to a Canonry and the Preb. "de Pole," vice *Nicholas de Rysheton*, LL.D., 20 April, 1410 ; ii, 109b.

William Trevell, LL.B., to a Canonry and the Preb. of "Rugge," in exchange with *Richard Aldryngton* (who was collated to Trevell's canonry, etc., in Glasney), 21 July, 1411 ; ii, 134b.

Reginald Bryta, chaplain, to a Bursal Preb., vice *Stephen Oryse*, deceased ; 23 Jan., 1411-12 ; ii, 139.

Hervey Wyket, to a Canonry and the Preb. of "Rugge," in exchange with *William Trevell*, LL.B., who was inst. to Wyket's Rectory of St. Mawgan-in-Pydar, 4 July, 1411 ; ii, 139b.

Hugh Hyckelyng (proxy—Robert Hyckelyng), to a Canonry and Bursal Preb., in exchange with *Reginald Bryta*, who was collated to his Canonry and the Preb. of Combe-prima in Wells Cathedral, 23 Sept., 1413 ; ii, 152.

Roger Bolter, chaplain, to a Canonry and the Preb., of Prustecomb, vice *William Langeton*, deceased ; 30 Jan., 1413-14 ; ii, 155.

Major Parys, priest (proxy, Richard Talbot), to a Canonry and the Preb. of Henstyll, vice *Ralph Tregrisiow*, deceased, 25 July, 1415 ; ii, 167.

Richard Penels, to a Canonry and Bursal Preb., vice *Hugh Hyckelyng*, deceased, 30 Jan., 1415-16 ; ii, 174b.

Richard Palmer, chaplain, to a Canonry and the Preb. of Stowford, vice *Thomas Barton*, deceased, 18 March, 1415-16 ; ii, 175.

Richard Penels, chaplain, to the Canonry and the Preb. of Cridia *alias* Estcridia, vice *William Sutton*, deceased, 18 March, 1415-16 ; ii, 175.

William Knyght, chaplain, to a Canonry and Bursal Preb., vice *Richard Penels*, resigned, 22 March, 1415-16, ii, 175b.

Michael Lercedekne, chaplain, to a Canonry and the Preb. of Karswell, vice *Richard Hals*, deceased, 25 May, 1417, ii, 186.

Richard Gabryell, chaplain, to a Canonry and the Preb. of Crosse, vice *Laurence Haukyn*, deceased, 11 April, 1418, ii, 190b.

William More, chaplain, to a Canonry and Bursal Preb., vice *Richard Weyneman*, deceased, 23 May, 1418 ; ii, 191b.

John Schute, chaplain, to a Canonry and the Preb. of Cridia *alias* Est Cridia, vice *Richard Penels*, deceased, 11 Jan., 1418-19 ; ii, 196b.

Thomas Welyn, chaplain, to a Canonry and Bursal Preb., vice *Robert Wyghale*, deceased, 11 Feb., 1418-19, ii, 197.

Martin Lercedekne, to a Canonry and the Preb. of Stowford, vice *Richard Palmer*, deceased, 25 April, 1419 ; ii, 198.

John Cobethorn, LL.B., to a Canonry and the Preb. of Crosse, vice *Richard Gabriell*, deceased, 1 Aug., 1419, ii, 201.

Martin Lercedekne, to a Canonry and Prebend of Karswelle [vice *Michael Lercedekne* ; *see* ii, 186], 3 Sept., 1419 ; ii, 205.—The Bishop was in harness to the last ; earlier in the day he had instituted John Birkhede to Blackawton, R., and this collation of Martin Lercedekne was his last official act. This interesting entry must be transcribed in full :—" Item, eisdem die et loco [Clyst], dominus contulit,[1] intuitu caritatis, magistro Michaeli

[1] In our modern phrase the Bishop collates the clerk to the Benefice ; in the Register, always, he collates the Benefice to the Clerk.

Lercedekne, Exoniensis Diocesis capellano, canonicatum in Ecclesia Collegiata Sancte Crucis Criditonensi et Prebendam de Karswelle in eadem, ipsius domini patronatus et Diocesis, vacantes, et äd ipsius Domini collacionem pleno jure spectantes, et ipsum canonicum et prebendarium instituit et investivit canonice in eisdem cum suis juribus et pertinenciis universis, juribus, etc. Et, prestita canonica obediencia domino per eundem, mandatum fuit Precentori dicte ecclesie pro ipsius induccione, etc., et optinuit literas, etc.

1419.

Et eodem die dominus Edmundus, Exoniensis Episcopus, diem suum clausit extremum, cujus anime propicietur Deus, Amen.
videlicet anno Domini 1419.[1]"

CREDITON, Chapel of St. Laurence, Wardens of—
John Peuesey; on whose death was collated 2 Feb., 1396-7,
John Loundon (of the Convent of the Holy Trinity, Hounslow), ii, 32b, on whose death
John Mathew, chaplain, was collated, 17 July, 1410 (Mandate for his induction directed to Richard Palmer, R. of Ugborough), ii, 121. He exchanged, 21 Sept., 1417, with
John Worthyn (V. of Axminster), ii, 187. Worthyn, however, resigned immediately, and the Bishop, on the same day, collated
John Huntyngdon, chaplain, a Cistercian monk; *ibid.*

CREED [Sancte Cride, MS.], Rectors of—
John Grey; who exchanged, 18 Nov., 1395, with
Ralph Rudruth, S.T.P. (R. of Grittleton, Dioc. of Salisbury); proxy—Nicholas Herry, M.A.; patron, King Richard II.; ii, 28b. Rudruth (who was also Canon and Preb. of Glasney) exchanged, 6 July, 1399, with
John Fecos (R. of St. Columb-major); patron King Richard II., John Tregois proxy for Rudruth; Hervey Wyket for Fecos; ii, 42. Fecos exchanged, 31 July, in the same year, with
Matthew Bodrygy (R. of St. Gerrans), William Toket, proxy for Fecos, ii, 42.

CREWKERNE [Crokhorn, MS.], Dioc. of B. and W., *see* ST. PROBUS, ii, 47.

CREWKERNE, Chantry Chapel of St. Mary *see* JACOBSTOWE, ii, 86.

CROWAN [Sancte Crewenne, MS.], Vicars of—
Paschasius Penbro; on whose death was inst., 23 Oct., 1403,
Luke Trenewyth, chaplain; patrons, the Abbot and Convent of St. Mary, Tewkesbury, ii, 69b; on his death
Thomas Rosuyk was inst., 21 June, 1414, ii, 159b. On the resignation of Roeuwyk (*sic*)
John Symon, chaplain, was inst., 26 July, 1415; ii, 167.

CRUWYS MORCHARD [Morchard Cruwys, MS.], Rectors of—
Walter (i, 50).
Matthew Doune, chaplain, was inst. 9 March, 1408-9; patron, Walter Robert, clerk, ii, 104b. He exchanged, 1 Oct., 1418, with
John Knyght, deacon (of Farringdon); proxy (for Doune) John Lane, clerk: patrons, Thomas Bratton, John Keynes, Robert Cruwys, clerk, and John Prous of Doderygg, ii, 194b.

CUTTON, the Preb. of, in St. Mary's Prebendal Church within the Castle of Exeter: Prebendaries—
Thomas Kerdyngton; on whose resignation was inst. 20 May, 1400,

---

[1] Videlicet etc., in a later hand.

John Radeclyf, chaplain; patron, Edward, Earl of Devon, ii, 46b; Radeclyff (*sic*), exchanged, 2 August, 1406, with
Walter Robert, R. of Tiverton (2nd Portion); patrons, the same (and of both Benefices); Laurence Haukyn, Canon of Exeter, was Radeclyff's proxy; ii, 90b. Soon afterwards Robert resigned, and Thos. Kerdyngton, here called
Thomas de Kerdyngton was again inst., 11 Feb., 1407-8, ii, 99b; on whose death
Richard Donscombe, chaplain, was inst., 1 Aug., 1419; ii, 201.

DANBURY, R., the Mediety of, *see* AFFETON, R., ii, 51b.

DARTINGTON [Dertyngton, MS.], Rectors of—
Peter Overton; on whose death was inst., 27 Jan., 1413-14,
Ralph Walwayn; patron, Sir John Cornewaill, knt., ii, 155. On the death of Wallewyn (*sic*)
John Bowden, clerk, was inst., 7 July, 1418; patron, Sir John Cornewayll, knt.: Commission dated 11 June, 1418; ii, 265b.

DAVIDSTOWE [Dewstow and Deustowe, MS.], Vicars of—
Thomas Barnard; on whose death was inst., 16 March, 1407-8,
John Compton, chaplain; patrons, William Patehulle, Master, and the brethren of the Hosp. of St. John Bapt., Bridgewater, ii, 101. On whose resignation,
John Colnwayn, chaplain, was inst., 15 Dec., 1412, ii, 147.

DAWLISH [Dowlysch[1], MS.], Vicars of—
John Caynok[1]; on whose death was inst., 10 Feb., 1410-11,
Thomas Fayrforde, chaplain; patrons, the Dean and Chapter of Exeter, ii, 130.

DEAN PRIOR [Dene, MS.], Vicars of—
William Hull, chaplain, was inst., 17 Sept., 1407; patrons, the Prior and Convent of Plympton, ii, 98; on whose resignation,
John Russel, chaplain, was inst., 24 Nov., in the same year; ii, 99.

DEENE [Deen, MS.], R., Dioc. of Lincoln, *see* BRIDESTOWE, R., ii, 166b.

DENBURY [Devenebury, MS.], Rectors of—
Luke Godecote; on whose death was inst., 20 Dec., 1409,
Richard Gabriell, clerk (proxy—William Amadas, literate); patron, the Abbot and Convent of Tavistock, ii, 108. Gabriell appears to have resigned in the following year, though the fact is not recorded; but
Thomas Lowedon, clerk, was inst. (proxy—Reymund Cressy, clerk), 20 May, 1410; ii, 110b.
Richard Gabriell (described as a "chaplain," and apparently the same person), was inst. again, 9 Aug., 1414; ii, 161. On whose resignation
John Batyn, clerk, was inst., 30 April, 1418; ii, 191.

DITTISHAM [Dydesham, MS.], Rectors of—
William Underwode; on whose resignation was inst., 7 Feb., 1395-6,
Thomas Whithed, chaplain; patron, Sir William Coggushale, knt., ii, 29b. On Whythed's resignation
William Underwode, chaplain, was inst., 13 March, 1395-6; patron, the same, ii, 30. He exchanged, 19 Feb., 1400-1, with
John Prata (R. of St. John Zachary, London,); patrons, Sir John Hulle, knt., and Robert Hulle, senior, ii, 53. Prata exchanged, 30 Sept., 1409, with
Reginald Bryta (R. of Bridestowe, and Canon and 7th Preb. of Ottery St. Mary), patron Robert Hulle, domicellus; ii, 106b.

DODBROOKE [Dodebrok and Dodebroke, MS.], Rectors of—
Thomas Swan; on whose death was inst., 4 April, 1403,

[1] "Daulyssh" & "Kenok," MS., ii, 90b.

John Thomas; patron, Sir Richard Champernoun, knt., ii, 65b. His resignation is not recorded: but it appears, elsewhere (ii, 84b), that he was promoted to Portlemouth, 22 May, 1405.

Thomas Quenyllon, chaplain, was inst., 17 June, 1405; patron, the same, ii, 85. On this Rector's death

Thomas Helys, priest, was inst., 6 Nov., 1409; patron, the same, ii, 107b. On whose death

Richard Tryby, was inst., 7 Nov., 1410; patron, the same; ii, 124b. On Tryby's resignation

John Offord, chaplain, was inst., 23 March, 1418-19; patron, Richard Champernoun, Esquire, ii, 197b. Commission dated 9 March, 1418-19; ii, 267.

DODDISCOMBSLEIGH *alias* LEGH PEVERELL [Dodyscomblegh, MS.], Rectors of—

John de Bykelegh; on whose resignation, was inst., 22 Jan., 1395-6,

Baldwin Levenaunt, priest; patron, William Amadas, in right of Katherine, his wife, ii, 3b. On Levenaunt's death

Simon Nywenham was inst., 10 Oct., 1399; patron, John de Nywenham, ii, 13b.

DOLTON [Dowelton, MS.], Rectors of—

William Carvell; on whose death was inst., 9 Aug., 1410,

William Downe, chaplain; patron, Edward, Earl of Devon, ii, 122b.

DOWNE ST. MARY, Rectors of—

Matthew Rolond, alias *Doune*; on whose death was inst., 14 Oct., 1412,

John Gyst, priest; (proxy—William Julyan, R. of Little Hempston); patrons, the Abbot and Convent of Buckfast, ii, 145.—Commission, dated 24 Sept., 1412, ii, 248. On the death of Gyst,

John Horygg, chaplain, was inst., 22 April, 1416; ii, 176.

DREWSTEIGNTON [Teynton Drewe, MS.], Rector of—

Robert Lyner, priest, 14 Nov., 1395; patron, Stephen Durneforde, of Plymouth, ii, 1b.

DULOE [Dulo and Duloo, MS.], Vicars of—

Roger Denys, chaplain, inst., 29 Nov., 1398; patrons, John Colshull, domicellus, and Thomas Lanrak,[1] R. of Duloe, ii, 40. On the death of Denys

Thomas Estebrok, chaplain, LL.B., was inst., 5 Aug., 1400; patrons, John Colshull, Lord of Tremethert, and Thomas Lanrak, R. of Duloe, ii, 49. On the resignation of Estbroke (*sic*)

Robert Ousthorpe, chaplain, was inst., 11 June, 1412; patron, John Colshull, domicellus, and Thomas Lanrak, R. of Duloe. A Commission had been issued to ascertain the facts as to this vacancy, under which Henry Wynnegode, LL.B. (the Bishop's Official Peculiar in Cornwall), had certified, 9 June, in St. Mary's Chapel, at Looe, the result of their enquiry, ii, 141b.

DULVERTON (Dioc. of B. and W.), *see* BICKLEIGH, R., ii, 182.

DUNCHIDEOCK [Donsshidioke, MS.], Rectors of—

John Langge; on whose death was inst., 9 Jan., 1410-11,

John Prouȝ (elder son of John Prouȝ, of Chagford), clerk; patron, William Buddockysyde, domicellus, ii, 130.—Commission dated 24 Dec., 1410; ii, 236b. On whose resignation

John Prouz, clerk (younger son of John Prouz of Chagford), was inst., 25 June, 1411; patron, the same, ii, 134. On the death of Prous (*sic*)

John Tapyn, chaplain, was inst., 17 June, 1419; patron, William Bottokysyde (*sic*), ii, 199b.—Commission dated 31 May, 1419; ii, 267b.

DUNKESWELL ABBEY [Donkeswyll, MS.], Abbots of—

---

[1] The name *may* be Laurak; but it is almost certainly Lanrak; "Landrake," a parish near Duloe, is written in the same way in the MS., ii, 10b.

Alexander Burlescombe,—Commission to Henry [Nony], Bishop of Ardagh, for his Benediction as Abbot; 25 Aug., 1397, ii, 212b.

Richard Lamport, monk,—Commission to Henry [Nony] Bishop of Ardagh, for his Benediction as Abbot, 17 July, 1399, ii, 225b.

John Bokelonde,[1] monk,—Commission to William, Bishop of Caithness, for his Benediction as Abbot, 10 June, 1419, ii, 267b.

DUNTERTON [Donterton, MS.], Rectors of—

Thomas Moyseben; on whose death was inst., 11 Jan., 1410-11,

John Halsangre, chaplain, (proxy—Henry Webbere); patrons, Jas. Aumarle, Thos. Hertescote, and Robt. Maynard, ii, 130.—Commission, dated 10 Dec., 1410; ii, 236b. On the resignation of Halsanger (*sic*)

John Mathew, chaplain, was inst., 23 Dec., 1413; patrons, Robt. Maynard and Thos. Hertescote, ii, 154b.—Commission dated 23 Nov., 1413; ii, 253.

EAST ALLINGTON [Alyngton, MS.], Rectors of—

Roger Langeman; who exchanged, 6 Nov., 1407, with

Richard Olyver ("Minister" in Ottery St. Mary); patron, Richard Prydeaux, domicellus, ii, 98b.

EAST ANSTY [Ansteycrues, MS.], Rectors of—

Robert Ryre; on whose death was inst., 2 Sept., 1406,

Roger Polford, chaplain; patron, William Wylford, domicellus, ii, 91b.

EAST BUCKLAND [Estbokelond, MS.], Rectors of—

Thomas Broun; on whose death was inst., 14 March, 1395-6,

William Caucey, priest; patron, Isabella de Fillegh, ii, 4b. On the resignation of Cauay (*sic*)

John Tuderyngton, chaplain, was inst., 6 Nov., 1400; patron, John Fyllegh, domicellus, ii, 16.

EAST COKER (Dioc. of B. and W.), V., *see* COMBE RALEIGH, R., ii, 71; and BICKLEIGH, R., ii, 92b.

EAST DOWNE [Estdoune, MS.], Rectors of—

John Dene; on whose death was inst., 17 Feb., 1409-10,

John Cook, chaplain (proxy—Thomas Wyot, literate); patron, Matilda Brent, *alias* Damesele, ii, 108b.

EAST LYDFORD (Dioc. of B. and W,), *see* HUXHAM, R., ii, 74b.

EAST OGWELL [Estwogwyll, MS.] Rectors of—

Thomas Ferrers; who exchanged, 18 Aug., 1411, with

John Lane, Cantor in Ottery St. Mary; patron, Walter Reynald, ii, 135. Lane exchanged, 12 May, 1419, with

John Wille, alias *Scryvener* (R. of Studland, Dioc. of Salisbury); patron, Walter Reynell (*sic*), Esquire, ii, 198b.

EAST WORLINGTON [Wolryngton and Est Wolryngton, MS.], Rectors of—

John Kylyngton; on whose death was inst., 10 March, 1399-1400,

John Richard alias *Woborn*, clerk; patron, Thomas Affeton, domicellus, ii, 14b. On Richard's resignation (or death) apparently,—but the register is silent on the point,—

Robert Forde, chaplain, was inst., 3 April, 1407; patron, Thomas Affeton, domicellus, ii, 95b. On Forde's death

William Morys, chaplain, was inst., 20 May, 1419; patron, John Botreaux, Esquire, ii, 198b.

---

[1] Oliver has placed him, also (by mistake) among the Abbots of *Ford* (*Monasticon*, p. 340.)

EGG BUCKLAND [Eckebokelond, MS.], Vicars of—
John Tappyng; on whose death was inst., 7 Dec., 1402,
John Wode, chaplain; patrons, the Prior and Convent of Plympton, ii, 23b.

EGLOSHAYLE [Egloshayl *and* Egloshayll, MS.], Vicars of—
William Cornewayll, who exchanged, 8 Feb., 1400-1, with
Richard Coventre (V. of Batheaston, Dioc. of B. and W.); patron, the Bishop, ii, 52b. On the death of Coventre
John Mychel, chaplain, was collated, 27 June, 1403, ii, 68.

ELINGDON [Elyndon, MS.], i.e., WROUGHTON, R. (Dioc. of Salisbury), *see* SUTTON juxta PLYMOUTH, V., ii, 105b.

ERMINGTON, the Mediety of the Church of; Rectors—
William Falewell; on whose death was inst., 11 July, 1397,
Richard Tyttesbury, chaplain; patron, King Richard II., ii, 34b. On Tyttesbury's death
Henry Maupas, chaplain, was inst. (proxy—John Sherlond), 7 June, 1409; patron, King Henry IV., ii, 105b. He exchanged, 16 July, 1410, with
Thomas Redman, R. of Stanford-on-Avon (Dioc. of Lincoln), proxy—John Noble, clerk; patron, King Henry IV.; ii, 120b. He was also Rector of Kenn, i, 100b.

ERMINGTON, Vicars of—
John Langebrok; on whose death was inst., 28 Sept., 1400,
Thomas Row, chaplain; patrons, Francis, Prior, and the Convent of Montacute (Dioc. of B. and W.), ii, 51.

ERMINGTON, Chantry-chapel of the B. V. M., in the Cemetery—
Robert Saunder, chaplain; he exchanged, 23 Nov., 1396, with
Richard Penwyn (R. of Stoke-Gabriel); patron, Robert Hull; ii, 32. On Penwyn's resignation
Walter Bollok (or *Bullok*), LL.B., was inst., 27 Nov., 1396; patron, the same, ii, 32b. On Bollok's resignation (of which there is no record, but it is stated, elsewhere (ii, 36b), that he was instituted to Atherington, R., 3 Feb., 1397-8),
John Sprydell, chaplain, was inst., 26 July, 1398; patron, Robert Hulle, senior, ii, 9b.
Robert Keyl, chaplain, was inst., 20 Aug., 1408; patron, the same, ii. 102b.

EXBOURNE [Ekysbourn, MS.], Rectors of—
Richard Hurst; on whose death was inst., 20 May, 1411.
John Bornebury, clerk; patron, Thomas Prouse, of Ekysbourn, ii, 132b.—Commission dated 28 April, 1411; ii, 241b.

EXETER, the Cathedral Church of—
Deans:—
Ralph Tregrisiow; *Stephen Payn*; *John Cobethorne*, (*q.v.*)
Precentors:—
Hugh Hyckelyng; on whose death was collated, 30 Jan., 1415-16,
Laurence Haukyn, chaplain, ii, 174b; on whose death
Roger Bolter, chaplain, was collated, 11 April, 1418, ii, 190.
Chancellors:—
Robert Bosoun; on whose death
Robert Rugge, S.T.P., was collated, 30 Jan., 1399-1400; ii, 45b. On the death of Rygge (*sic*),
Richard Snetesham, chaplain, S.T.B., was collated, 12 April, 1410; on whose death
Thomas Hendeman, chaplain, S.T.P., was collated, 19 Jan., 1416-17; ii, 181b.
Treasurers:—
William Trevellys; on whose death

John Dodyngton, chaplain, was collated, 26 Sept.,[1] 1399; ii, 42b. On whose death

Richard Hals (chancellor), was collated, 27 Sept., 1400; ii, 50b. On the death of Hals

Roger Bolter, chaplain, was collated, 25 May, 1417; ii, 186b. He resigned (on becoming Precentor, 11 April, 1418; *See* ii, 190), and was succeeded by

Michael Lercedekne, who was collated, 23 April, 1418; ii, 190b.

Archdeacons of EXETER:—

Philip de Alençon, who died in 1397. (*See* ii, 214).

Walter Cook, collated, 21 Oct.,[2] 1399; ii, 43b.

Angelus, Bishop of Ostia, and a Cardinal; he died 31 May, 1408.

The name of this Archdeacon is not given in either Oliver's or Le Neve's List, and I find no record of the date of his collation. The fact of his having held the office evidently escaped notice because it is found recorded not among the collations, &c., but among the *Commissions*, in a separate part of the Register. The document containing it, then, being of exceptional interest, may well be given *in extenso*:—"*Commissio Officialis, Archidiaconatu Exoniensi vacante.*—Edmundus, miseracione divina Exoniensis Episcopus, dilecto in Christo filio, Magistro Ricardo Wykeslond, in legibus bacallario, salutem, graciam, et benediccionem. Cum reverendissimus in Christo pater et dominus, dominus Angelus, Ostiensis Episcopus, sacrosancte ecclesie Romane, dum vixit, Cardinalis, Archidiaconus Exoniensis in ecclesia nostra Exoniensi, ultimo die mensis Maii proxime preteriti extremum clauserit diem suum, fructusque redditus, et proventus quicumque et omnis et omnimoda jurisdiccio Archidiaconalis ejusdem Archidiaconatus, durante vacacione ejusdem, ad nos de jure pertinere dinoscantur; ad exigendum, igitur, colligendum, et recipiendum fructus, redditus, proventus, et obvenciones quoscumque predictos, crimina eciam et defectus subditorum quorumcumque ipsius Archidiaconatus corrigendum, puniendum, et canonice reformandum, jurisdiccionemque Archidiaconalem ibidem integraliter excercendum, omniaque alia et singula faciendum, excercendum, et expediendum que circa premissa necessaria fuerint et quomodolibet oportuna, et que ad Archidiaconum ipsius Archidiaconatus pertineret si esset ibidem Archidiaconus, vobis committimus vices nostras et, hujusmodi vacacione durante, plenariam potestatem. In cujus rei testimonium sigillum nostrum presentibus est appensum. Datum in Manerio nostro Criditonensi, ix die mensis Julii, Anno Domini Millesimo cccc viij, et nostre consecracionis anno quartodecimo."—ii, 232.

William Pilton;[3] he exchanged,[4] 28 Feb., 1409-10, with

Thomas Hendeman, S.T.P. (Canon and Prebendary of Colworth in Chichester Cathedral (proxy—William Clyve, R. of Whitstone), ii, 109. On Hendeman's resignation, ii, 182.

Roger Bolter, chaplain, was collated, 25 Jan., 1416-17; on whose resignation

John Schute, chaplain, was collated, 21 Sept., 1417; ii, 187b.

Archdeacons of CORNWALL, TOTNES, *and* BARNSTAPLE, *see* S.V.—

Sub-deans:—

John Puddesdon (Sub-dean and Penitentiary); on whose death

Thomas Noell, LL.B., was collated, 9 Oct., 1399; ii, 43. On Noell's death

Thomas Estbroke, LL.B., chaplain, was collated, 18 Sept., 1417; ii, 187.

Canons and Prebendaries:—

---

[1] Not August, as in Oliver's List.

[2] Not 16 Oct., as in Oliver.

[3] I find no record of the date of his collation, and his name is omitted altogether from Oliver's List.

[4] The exchange and its date are both omitted by Oliver, who merely states that Thomas Hendeman "occurs [as Archdeacon], 23rd Nov., 1411."

Roger Walden; on whose resignation
Walter Gybbes, was collated (proxy—Rd. Guy, clerk), 25 Jan., 1396; ii, 29b.
John Exeestre exchanged with
Walter Trote (R. of Ipplepen), and was collated 15 Sept., 1396 (proxy—Hervey Wyket), ii, 31b.
William Baunton; on whose death
Michael Cergeaux was collated, 1 Nov., 1396, ii, 32; on whose death
William Langeton was collated, 28 Aug., 1397; ii, 35.
John Michel; on whose death
Laurence Haukyn, chaplain, was collated, 20 Sept., 1397, ii, 35.
Thomas Redman, clerk, was collated, on the resignation of *William Langeton*, 27 July, 1398; ii, 38b.
Henry Blakeborne; on whose death
Nicholas Bubbewyth, chaplain, was collated, 5 Sept., 1399; ii, 42b.
Rd. Courtenay, clerk, 3 Oct., 1399, vice *Wm. Trevellys*, deceased, ii, 42b.
Nicholas Braybrok; on whose death
Richard Hals, clerk, was collated, 9 Jan., 1399-1400, ii, 45.
Robert Bosoun; on whose death
John Park, clerk, was collated, 30 Jan., 1399-1400, ii, 45b.
John Dodyngton; on whose death
Robert Hallum was collated, 11 Aug., 1400; ii, 49b.
Walter Columpton; on whose death
Richard Aldryngton, chaplain, was collated, 20 March, 1400-1; ii, 53.
William Pyers; on whose death
Richard Broun, M.D. and S.T.B. was collated, 1 July, 1401; ii, 54.
Richard Tyttesbury, LL.B., chaplain, was collated, on the death of *Walter Trote*, 31 March, 1404; ii, 75.
John Lugans; on whose death
John Schillyngford, LL.D., chaplain, was collated, 27 July, 1404; ii, 78.
Walter Levenant; on whose death
William Ekerton, chaplain, was collated, 1 Nov. 1404; ii, 80.
John Haget, chaplain, was collated, 15 Aug., 1406; ii, 91.
William Pylton was collated, on the death of *John Shillyngford*, 25 Sept., 1406; ii, 92.
John Ixworth, LL.D. (1406—month omitted), on the death of *Robert Hallum*, ii, 93.
John Cheyne; on whose death
Thomas Hendeman was collated, 18 Jan., 1406-7; ii, 94.
William Hunden, chaplain, was collated, on the death of *Richard Tyttesbury*, 11 June, 1409; ii, 105b.
Robert Rygge; on whose death
Roger Bolter, chaplain, was collated, 29 March, 1410; ii, 109b.
John Haget; he exchanged with
Thomas Teynton, canon of Salisbury, and Preb. of the Principal Altar (otherwise called "Major Pars," therein); ii, 150.
Walter Gybbys; on whose death
John Westecote, chaplain, S.T.B., was collated (proxy—Roger Bolter, clerk), 24 May, 1413; ii, 150b.
Richard Courtenay; on whose resignation
Stephen Payn, chaplain, was collated, 28 Aug., 1413; ii, 152.
John Stevenys, chaplain, was collated (proxy—Roger Bolter, clerk), on the death of *William Ekerdon*, 18 Dec., 1413; ii, 154.
John Westecote, S.T.B., was collated, on the death of *William Langeton*, 5 Feb., 1413-14; ii, 155b. On his resignation
Richard Gabriell, chaplain, was collated (proxy—Roger Bolter), 11 Feb., 1413-14; ii, 156.
John Orum, chaplain, S.T.P., was collated, on the death of *Richard Broun*, 29 March, 1414; ii, 157.
William Poundestoke; on whose death
John Staforde, chaplain, LL.D., was collated, 10 April, 1414; ii, 158.
Thomas Clyfford; he exchanged his canonry in Crantock with Canon *Laurence Haukyn*, 23 Aug., 1414; ii, 161.

John Hody, chaplain, on the death of *Thomas Teynton* ; collated (proxy—Michael Lercedekne), 25 May, and inducted 4 June, 1415 ; ii, 165.
Lawrence Haukyn, chaplain, was collated, on the death of *Ralph Tregrisiow* ; 25 July, 1415, ii, 166b.
Hugh Hyckelyng ; on whose death
Richard Snetesham, chaplain, was collated, 30 Jan., 1415-16 ; ii, 174b.
Richard Penels, chaplain, collated, on the death of *William Hunden*, 21 Feb., 1415-16 ; ii, 174b.
Thomas Barton ; on whose death
Thomas Stephyn, chaplain, was collated, 24 March, 1415-16 ; ii, 175b.
Michael Lercedekne collated, 25 Jan., 1416-17, on the death of *Richard Snetesham* ; ii, 182.
John Schute, chaplain, collated, on the death of *Richard Hals*, 25 May, 1417 ; ii, 185b.
Baldwin Shyllyngford ; on whose death
Thomas Tremayn, chaplain, was collated, 23 Feb., 1417-18 ; ii, 189b. He afterwards resigned his Canonry for that of *Laurence Haukyn*, deceased ; collated, 13 April, 1418, having been succeeded by
John Holond, who was collated (proxy—Canon Richard Palmer), 8 May, 1418, ii, 190b, 191.
Matthew Doune, collated, on the death of *John Westecote*, 27 June, 1418 ; ii, 192.
John Cobethorn, chaplain, collated, on the death of *Richard Penels*, 11 Jan., 1418-19 ; ii, 196b.
William Fylham, chaplain, collated, on the death *Thomas Clyfforde*, 1 Feb., 1418-19 ; ii, 196b.
Robert Allerton, clerk, collated (proxy—Thomas Redman, clerk), on the death of *Richard Palmer* ; 11 May, 1419 ; ii, 198b.
Richard Graynevyll, chaplain, was collated on the death of *John Holond*, 12 April, 1419, ii, 197b.
John Waryn, chaplain (proxy—Michael Lercedekne, Treasurer, collated on the death of *Stephen Payn*, 23 June, 1419, ii, 199b.
William Lyndewode, LL.D., chaplain ; collated, vice *Rd. Gabriell*, deceased, 2 Aug., 1419 ; ii, 201b.

Vicars Choral, collated by lapse[1] :—

John Cade, for Canon Laurence Haukyn, 1 May, 1401, i, 56.
John Soor for Canon Richard Courtenay, 26 May, 1401, i, 56b.
Thomas Wobbrok, priest, for Canon Laurence Hawkyn, 30 May, 1410, i, 97.
Henry Demalt, priest for Canon William Langton, 16 Jan., 1412-13 ; i, 173b.
Robert Trevyne[2], for Canon Richard Palmer, 25 May, 1413 ; i, 180b.
John Hauk[3], chaplain, for Canon Martin Lercedekne, 20 Dec., 1413 ; i, 190.
Alexander Beare, for Canon William Langeton, 17 March, 1413-14 ; i, 195.
Thomas Devenish, for Canon John Orum, 10 Aug., 1414, i, 198.
Richard Thomma, chaplain, for Canon John Park, 9 July, 1415 ; i, 211b.
John More, chaplain, for Canon William Pylton, 27 Sept., 1416 ; i, 226.
Richard Brouuste, chaplain, for Canon John Park, 3 Oct., 1417 ; i, 234b.
Robert Langhman, for Canon John Stafford, 17 Dec., 1418 ; i, 244.
Thomas Fyllecombe, chaplain, for Canon Steph. Payn, 10 Jan., 1418-19, i, 244b.
John Frenssh, chaplain, for Canon Michael Lercedekne, 10 April, 1419 ; i, 246b.

---

[1] When, on a vacancy, the Canon failed to appoint his Vicar, the nomination lapsed to the Dean after one month, and from him, after eight days to the Bishop.

[2] The Bishop ordered his admission (which had been unduly delayed), 23 Aug., 1413 ; i, 183.

[3] Here (and elsewhere) it is stated that the Bishop, after diligent and personal examination, had found his nominee "modulandi instrumentum habere et cantus scienciam congruentem."

EXETER—Chantry in the West Chapel, without the west door of the Cathedral, in which the body of John de Grandisson, formerly Bishop of Exeter, of blessed memory, lies entombed, lately founded for the sake of his soul—

Thomas Hogge, chaplain, collated 28 Feb., 1402-3 ; ii, 65.

ST. JAMES'S PRIORY, Priors of—

[*Ralph Legh*, to whom succeeded]

John Thetford, inst., 30 Oct., 1399 ; patrons, during the Schism—*see* Barnstaple, Priory of ST. MARY MAGDALENE, ii, 43b.

ST. NICHOLAS'S PRIORY, Priors of—

Robert Bregg : on whose death

Thomas Haukherst, monk of Battle, was inst., 23 May, 1396 ; patrons, John, Abbot, and the Convent of Battle, ii, 5b. On whose resignation

William Mershe, monk of Battle, was inst., 3 June, 1400 ; patrons, the same ii. 46b. He [became Abbot of Battle, 23 July, 1404, and] was succeeded by

William Bekett, monk of Battle, inst. 21 Feb., 1404-5 ; patrons, the same, ii, 82. On Bekett's death

John Underdoune, monk of Battle, was inst., 7 June, 1414 ; patrons, the same, ii, 158b. On whose death

John Dalyngton, monk of Battle, was inst., 9 March, 1418-19 ; patrons, the same, ii, 197.

EXETER, Parishes of—

ALL HALLOWS, GOLDSMITH STREET ["Omnium Sanctorum in Aurifabria," MS.], Rectors of—

John Frake, on whose death was inst., 6 Feb., 1407-8,

John Pruet, chaplain ; patron, Edward, Earl of Devon, ii, 100.

ALL HALLOWS-ON-THE-WALLS, Rectors of—

Willam Wyt ; on whose death was inst., 26 Dec., 1399.

Edward Piers, chaplain ; patrons, the Dean and Chapter of Exeter, ii, 44b. On whose resignation

John Osborn, clerk, was inst., 25 Aug., 1400[1] (proxy—Henry Drenek, chaplain, substitute for John Lugans, Canon of Exeter, his original proxy), ii, 50. He exchanged, 20 Sept., 1400, with

Richard Hals, of St. Ive ; ii, 50b. Four days later Hals resigned, and

Edward Pyers, chaplain, was again inst., 24 Sept., 1400 ; ii, 50b. On whose resignation

William Hoper, chaplain, was inst., 21 June, 1403 ; ii, 67b. There is no record of his death or resignation ; but it would seem that his successor was

Hugh Smert, clerk, LL.B., who was inst., 24 Sept., 1407 ; ii, 98b. On Smert's death

Robert Dunnyng, clerk, was inst., 23 Aug., 1411 ; ii, 135b. On whose resignation

John Wyche, chaplain, was inst., 5 May, 1416, ii, 176. He exchanged with

William More (R. of Beynton Dioc. of Salisbury), who was inst., 21 July, 1419, by the Bishop of Salisbury, on behalf[2] of the Bishop of Exeter ;

---

[1] "Et subsequenter, eisdem die et loco, prestita canonica obediencia per eundem Henricum substitutum nomine quo supra, mandatum fuit Magistris Johanni Lydeford, juniori, et Johanni Dyght, Commissariis Domini in Archidiaconatu Exoniensi, visitacione ipsius Domini ibidem inexpleta pendente, pro ipsius Johannis Osborn induccione."

[2] "Nos, variis et arduis prepediti negociis quominus hujusmodi permutacionis expedicioni ad presens intendere valeamus," . . . . paternitati vestre reverende vices nostras committimus per presentes. [Dated at Clyst, 15 July, 1419.]

EXETER, Parishes of—

patrons, on this occasion, the *President* of the Chapter and the Chapter, ii, 200b.

ST. EDMUND on Exe Bridge, without the Westgate, Rectors of—

John Hembery ; on whose death was inst., 27 July, 1413,
Thomas Placy ; patrons, the Mayor, &c., of Exeter, ii, 151b.

St. GEORGE, Rectors of—

John Doget ; on whose death was collated, *by lapse*, 2 May, 1411,
Walter Symon, chaplain, ii, 132b. But see the next institution, and also the four Commissions of Enquiry, ii, 234b, 235 ; for on the 19th Aug., 1411,
Richard Mannyng, clerk, was inst. as successor to Doget ; proxy, John Burgon, R. of St. Olave's ; patron, K. Henry IV, ii, 135. On Mannyng's death
William Normanton, clerk, was inst., 7 Dec., 1414 ; patron, K. Henry V, ii, 162b. He exchanged, 11 Dec., 1418, with
Thomas Greyston (R. of Thorney, Dioc. of Chichester) ; patron, the same ; ii, 196.

ST. KERRIAN [Sancti Kyerani, MS.], Rectors of—

John Lusquyt ; on whose death was inst., 14 Dec., 1398,
Walter Trote, priest ; patrons, the Dean and Chapter of Exeter, ii, 10b. On Trote's death
Henry Wade, chaplain, was inst., 4 March, 1403-4, ii, 74b. On Wade's death
Thomas Cook, chaplain, was inst., 10 Sept., 1408, ii, 103.

ST. LAURENCE, Rectors of—

John Avery ; he exchanged, 16 March, 1402-3, with
Richard Doty (V. of St. Andrew's, Launcells) ; patrons, the Prior and Convent of Merton), ii, 26. Doty exchanged, 28 Nov., 1403, with
Nicholas Cole (V. of Staverton), ii, 70b.

ST. MARTIN, Rectors of—

John Beaumound ; on whose death was inst., 12 April, 1407,
Richard Marke, M.A. ; patrons, the Dean and Chapter of Exeter, ii, 96.

ST. MARY STEPS, Rectors of—

Nicholas Crese ; on whose death was inst., 1 June, 1398,
David Loueryng, priest ; patron, Baldwin de Shillyngforde, ii, 9. He exchanged 14 Jan., 1404-5, with
John Wyndout (R. of Black Torrington) ; ii, 81b ; and Wyndout, also, exchanged, 11 Nov., 1410, with
Robert Mareschall, V. of Widecombe-[in-the-Moor] ; ii, 124b. Marescall (*sic*) exchanged, 31 March, 1412, with
Elias Stoke (R. of Greinton, Dioc. of B. aud W.) ; ii, 140b.

ST. OLAVE, Rectors of—

William Aller ; on whose death was inst., 6 Jan., 1403-4,
John Burgoun, clerk ; patrons, the Prior and Convent of St. Nicholas, Exeter ; ii, 74. On Burgoun's resignation
Walter Cade, chaplain, was inst., 17 July, 1415 ; ii, 166.

ST. PANCRAS, Rector of—

Holond, John, priest, was inst., 4 Dec., 1395 ; patron, Stephen Durneforde, of Plymouth ; ii, 2.

ST. PAUL, Rectors of—

Robert Kerdewille, on whose resignation was inst., 8 June, 1398,
Roger Bernard ; patrons, the Dean and Chapter of Exeter ; ii, 9. On Bernard's death was instituted
William Nycol, chaplain, 14 Sept., 1411 ; patron, the Bishop, by special grant ; ii, 135b. Commission dated 4 March, 1410, to inquire as to the presentation, by the Dean and Chapter, of Reginald Russell ; ii, 239.

EXETER, Parishes of—

ST. PETROCK, Rectors of—

John Westecote; on whose death was inst., 11 July, 1418,

John Rysbi, clerk; patrons, the *President* of the Chapter and the Chapter of Exeter; ii, 193.

ST. STEPHEN, Rectors of—

John More; on whose resignation was collated, 8 Nov., 1404,

John Dyght, clerk; ii, 80. On Dyght's death

Henry Alkebarowe, clerk, was collated, 19 Dec., 1405; ii, 87b. He shortly afterwards resigned (though it is not so stated), on his institution to the V. of Modbury (*see* ii, 93b), and

William Brounyng, subdeacon, was collated, 24 Dec., 1406, ii, 94. Brounyng exchanged, 3 March, 1406-7, for Modbury, with the above-named

Henry Alkebarowe, chaplain; ii, 94b; on whose resignation (on his institution to the V. of Fremington; *see* ii, 96b),

John Adam, clerk, was collated, 29 June, 1407; ii, 97. There is no record of Adam's resignation, or death; but

Robert Colyn, chapl., was collated to the vacant Benefice, 4 July, 1408; ii, 102.

ST. THOMAS-THE-MARTYR ("de Cowyk juxta Exoniam"), Vicars of—

Peter Monk; on whose death was inst., 24 July, 1405,

John Alkebarwe, chaplain; patron, K. Henry IV., ii, 85b. On the death of Alkebarw (*sic*)

Walter Batyn, chaplain, was inst., 27 Sept., 1414; patron, K. Henry V., ii, 161b.—Commission of Enquiry, dated 18 Sept., 1414, ii, 255b.

HOLY TRINITY, Rectors of—

Rogere Harpere; on whose death was inst., 18 Nov., 1402,

John Govys (alias *Donk or Douk*), chaplain; patrons, the Dean and Chapter of Exeter, ii, 23. On the death of Govys

Robert Dunnyng, chaplain, was instituted, 14 April, 1416; patrons, the *President*, &c., ii, 176.

EXMINSTER, Rectors of—

John Chamberleyn; on whose death was inst., 8 Jan., 1396-7,

John Gardyner, priest; patrons, the Prior and Convent of Plympton, ii, 6b. On whose death

Henry Gardyner was inst. (proxy—Richard Skinner, chaplain) 8 June, 1400; ii, 47. He exchanged, 9 Jan., 1405-6, with

Roger Smyth (R. of Yate, Dioc. of Worcester); proxies—Robert Raulyn and William Dene, chaplain, ii, 88.

FARINGDON, R. (Dioc. of Winc.), *see* MARHAMCHURCH, ii, 45b.

FARRINGDON [Farendon, MS.], Rectors of—

Thomas Tredowargh, LL.B., collated, 30 April, 1397, ii, 34. On whose resignation was collated 19 Dec., 1410,

John Wortham, clerk, ii, 129. On the 28th of the same month, Worthyn (*sic*) exchanged with

Thomas Berty (R. of St. Endellion), ii, 129b. On whose death

Thomas Greyston, chaplain, was collated, 27 April, 1415, ii, 164b. On whose resignation

John Knyght, clerk, was collated, 1 Jan., 1417-18; ii, 189. Knyght exchanged, 1 Oct., 1418, with

Matthew Doune (R. of Cruwys Morchard), ii, 194b.

FARWAY [Fareweye *and* Fareway, MS.], Rectors of—

Philip Boghelegh; on whose resignation was inst., 23 Dec., 1410,

John Boghelegh, chaplain; patron, Edward, Earl of Devon, ii, 129b. He exchanged, 26 Oct., 1412, with

Thomas Hendeman (V. of Widecombe[-in-the-Moor]); ii, 145b. On whose resignation

John Podryngheye, chaplain, was inst., 13 April, 1415; ii, 164.

FENITON [Fyneton MS.], Rectors of—

John Byttylegate; on whose death was inst., 6 Aug., 1404,

John Bone, chaplain; patron, William Frye, ii, 78b.

FILLEIGH, Rectors of—

Edmund Stone; on whose death was inst., 17 Aug., 1399,

William Prydeaux, priest; patron, John Fillegh, domicellus, ii, 13.

FORDE, the Chantry of; *see* BAMPTON.

FOWEY [*also*, Fowy, *and* "Sancti Fimbarri" MS.], Vicars of—

John Hemburgh; on whose death was inst., 24 Aug., 1411,

William Cave, chaplain (proxy—Robert Treyage, senior, literate); patron, K. Henry IV, ii, 135b. There were two Commissions of Enquiry in this case; one dated 2 April, 1411, ii, 240; the other, 24 July, 1411, ii, 242b. On Cave's resignation

John Fuller, chaplain, was inst., 14 April, 1412; patron the same, ii, 143. On whose death

Richard Udan, chaplain, was inst., 18 June, 1416; patrons, the Prior and Convent of Tywardreath, ii, 177.

FREMINGTON, Vicar of—

Henry Alkebarowe, chaplain, inst. 9 June, 1407; patrons, the Abbot and Convent of Hartland, on the nomination of K. Henry IV, by reason of the minority of the son and heir of Sir John Holond, Knt.; ii, 96b. *See*, also, i, 141b.

FRITHELSTOCK [Frythelestok, MS.] PRIORY, Priors of—

John Pynnok; on whose death

Thomas Rede was elected, and confirmed 18 May, 1417; ii, 183.

FUGGLESTON [Fogheleston, MS.], with BEMERTON [Bymerton, MS.], *see* KING'S NYMPTON, ii, 103b.

GEORGENYMPTON, *see* NYMET ST. GEORGE.

GITTISHAM [Gydesham, MS.], Rectors of—

Thomas Hert; on whose death was inst., 13 Feb., 1408-9,

Walter Shinke, chaplain; patrons, Thos. Beaumount, John Wolfe, Henry Crosse, and Wm. Squyer, ii, 104.

GLASNEY; the Collegiate Church of St. Thomas of Canterbury:—[1]

Sacristans,—

Geoffrey Carreu; on whose death

Nicholas Harry, chaplain, was collated, 28 March, 1401; ii, 53.

Canons and Prebendaries,—

Benedict Canterbury, priest, in succession to *Simon Wythiel*; inst. (proxy—Robert Lywer), 13 Dec., 1395; patron, the King (during the vacancy of the See), ii, 2.

Ralph Rudruth, S.T.P., collated on the resignation of *John Grey* (proxy—

[1] The Provosts during the Episcopate of Bishop Stafford were Thomas Yorkflete, who "occurs .... July 31" and *William Cullyng* (who outlived Stafford, but his collation is not recorded).

Michael Cergeaux), 22 Dec., 1395; Nicholas Herry was Grey's proxy; ii, 29b.
Thomas Welyn, chaplain, on the death of *John Vincent*, collated 19 Sept., 1396; ii, 31b.
Richard Hals, clerk, on the death of *John Bray*; collated 12 April, 1399; ii, 41, 42.
John Fecos, on the resignation (by exchange) of *Ralph Rudruth*, 6 July, 1399, ii, 42.
Matthew Bodrygy, on the resignation (by exchange) of *John Fecos*, 31 July, 1399, ii, 42.
Richard Norys, chaplain, on the resignation of the said *Richard Hals*; collated 31 Jan., 1399-1400; ii, 45b.
Nicholas Stoke; he exchanged his Canonry and his R. of Withiel, with
Thomas Chapman (R. of Hampton-Meisy, Dioc. of Worcester), 1 June, 1402, ii, 58.
Nicholas Bury, chaplain, on the resignation of *Richard Norys*; collated, 23 Nov., 1402; ii, 65.
William Styward, on the death of *John Rauf*; collated, 28 May, 1403; ii, 67.
Richard Tyttesbury, chaplain, on the death of *William Styward*; collated 17 Nov., 1403; ii, 70. *William Rayner*, chaplain, on Tyttesbury's resignation; collated, 31 March, 1404; ii, 75.
Clement Wylde, chaplain, on the resignation of *Matthew Bodrygy*; collated, 2 July, 1409; ii, 106.
John Barell, chaplain, on the death of *William Somerford*; collated 29 March, 1410; ii, 109b.
Walter Robert, LL.B., on the death of Walter Estcolmp; collated, 6 Oct., 1410; ii, 123b.
Richard Olyver, priest, on the death of *Nicholas Byry (sic)*; collated, 22 April, 1411; ii, 132.
William Trevell, LL.B., clerk, on the resignation of *William Rayner*; collated 18 July, 1411; ii, 134. Trevell exchanged, 21 July, 1411, with
Richard Aldryngton (Canon and Prebendary of Rugge, in Crediton), ii, 134b. He was succeeded by the said *William Trevell*, 12 Aug., 1411; *ibid.*
William Noe; he was Preb. of St. Probus, and exchanged with *Clement Wylle*, 8 Oct., 1412; ii, 145.
John atte Water; he was Canon and 7th Prebendary in the Church of Ottery, and exchanged with *Walter Robert*, 14 June, 1414; ii, 159.
Henry Wynnegode, chaplain; he was a Preb. of St. Probus, and exchanged with *John atte Water*, 9 May, 1417; ii, 182b.
Martin Lercedekne, chaplain, on the resignation of *William Reyner (sic)* collated, 23 Feb., 1417-18; ii, 189b.

GLASNEY, the Chantry of Beaupre in—
John Lyndeseye, chaplain, was succeeded by
John Treloscan, priest, collated "hac vice, jure nobis in ea parte legitime devoluto," 6 Oct., 1411; ii, 136. It appears that
John Nanskylly, chaplain, held this Chantry at some subsequent date,—"quam nuper et immediate optinuit,"—1 July, 1415, when the Bishop, (*see* ii, 166), issued his mandate to the Provost of Glasney for the admission of
Robert Trewolge alias Stephyn, as his successor. But there is no record of his collation; and Treloscan seems to have been still in possession some two years later, when the Bishop issued a similar mandate (30 Sept., 1417), for the admission of
Richard Opus, priest, *in Treloscan's room*, and on his decease:—"ad cantariam perpetuam, quam nuper et immediate optinuit dominus Johannes Treloscan, capellanus . . . per mortem ejusdem vacantem." Probably Nanskylly held the benefice for a short time in the interval, Treloscan being appointed again; but there is no record of the transaction: ii, 187b.

GLASNEY, the Chantry (or Portion) "de Ponte" in—
Alan Trelees; on whose death was inst., 29 May, 1410;
John Dawe, chaplain; patrons, William Cullyng, provost, and Nicholas Herry, Sacristan, ii, 111. On Dawe's resignation
John Godegrave, chaplain, was inst. (proxy—Henry Wynnegode, clerk), 22 Dec., 1414; ii, 163.

GOODLEIGH [Godelegh, MS.], Rectors of—
Walter Baret; on whose death was inst., 30 May, 1414,
Walter Hulle, chaplain (proxy—John Wolston, clerk); patron, Thomas Denys, ii, 158b.—Commission of Enquiry, on the presentation of James Frankchayny by Richard Foldhay, dated 7 Feb., 1413-14; also, a second Commission, dated 20 Feb., 1413-14; ii, 253b. There is no record of Hulle's resignation; but he was instituted to Cheriton-Fitzpaine, 9 May, 1418 (*see* ii, 191), and on the 4th of June following
Nicholas Toker was inst. to Goodleigh; patron, Roger Waye, ii, 192.

GRADE [ecclesia parochialis Sancte Crucis, *alias* Grade, in Decanatu de Keryer, MS.], Rectors of—
Thomas Tresawel; on whose death was inst., 4 Dec., 1409,
Michael Lercedekne, priest, LL.B.; patrons, Richard and Thomas Trevanyon, ii, 107b. He resigned a few days later; and
John Polglas, chaplain, was inst., 18 Dec., 1409; patrons, the same; ii, 107b.

GREINTON [Graynton, MS.], Dioc. of B. and W., *see* EXETER, ST. MARY STEPS, ii, 140b.

GRENDALE, Prebend of, in York Minster, collation of Richard Pyttes to, ii, 107.

GRITTLETON [Grydlington, MS.], Dioc. of Salisbury, *see* LISKEARD, ii, 149b. and CARDYNHAM, ii, 154b.

GULVAL [Lanestley, MS.], Vicars of—
John Vorn; on whose death was inst., 16 March, 1395-6,
John Profyt, priest; patrons, the Prior and Convent of St. German's, ii, 4b.
John Proues; I find no record of his institution, but on his death
Nicholas Stryke, chaplain, was inst., 20 Nov., 1413, "ad vicariam perpetuam ecclesie parochialis Sancte Gwelvele, *alias* Wolvele, de Lanesely"; ii, 153b.

GWENNAP [Sancte Wenneppe, MS.], Vicars of—
Richard Bolham; he exchanged, 7 Aug., 1404, with
John Colyn (R. of Landewednack), proxy for Colyn—William Penfern, clerk; patrons, the Dean and Chapter of Exeter, ii, 78. He exchanged 19 Sept., 1418, with
Thomas Gerweys, R. of Ludgvan (proxy, John Wolston, chaplain); patrons, the *President* and Chapter of Exeter, ii, 194.

HACCOMBE [" ecclesie parochialis sive Archipresbitatus Sancti Blasii de Haccombe"]; Archpriests of—
Henry Bole; on whose death was inst., 30 July, 1400,
Michael Lercedekne, clerk; patron, Sir Warine Lercedekne, knt, ii, 49.
Michael Lercedekne, chaplain, LL.B., was inst., 14 Dec., 1409; patron, Sir Hugh Courtenay, senior, knt., ii, 107b. On his resignation
Edward Legh, chaplain, was inst., 1 April, 1413; patron, Sir Hugh Courtenay de Haccombe, knt., ii, 149.

HACKINGTON [Hakynton, MS.], V., Dioc. of Canterbury, *see* BOSHAM, ii, 41b.

HALFORD, R. (Dioc. of B. and W.), *see* WILLAND, R., ii, 31.

HALSE, V. (Dioc. of Wells), *see* MARTINHOE, R., ii, 56 ; also, CHARLES, R., ii, 98b.

HALWELL [Hallewell, MS.], Rectors of—

Hugh Pestur ; on whose death was inst., 17 May, 1399,

John Godefray, priest ; patron, Robert Normanton (locumtenens of the Prior of the Hospital of St. John of Jerusalem in England, while in foreign parts) ; ii, 12.

HAMPTON MEISY, R. (Dioc. of Worcester), *see* GLASNEY and WITHIEL, ii, 58 ; also COMBEMARTIN, ii, 64.

HARBERTON [Hurberton, MS.], Vicars of—

Gervase Combe ; on whose death was inst., 18 May, 1398,

Robert Kerdewille, priest ; Commission directed to Robert Lywer, R. of Drewsteignton ; patrons, the Dean and Chapter of Exeter, ii, 8b. On Kerdewille's death

John Hille, priest, was inst., 2 Oct., 1398, ii, 9b. He exchanged 15 May, 1403, with

Robert Mareschall (R. of Musbury), ii, 67.

HARPFORD [Herpeford, MS.], Vicars of—

John Scorch ; he exchanged, 10 March, 1398-9, with

John Aubrey (R. of Bicton) ; patron, the King, by reason of the temporalities of Otterton Priory being in his hands, ii, 11, 223. This Vicar exchanged, 16 Nov., 1417, with

Thomas Spreth (R. of Wambrook, Dioc. of Salisbury) ; patron, William Kenolmersah, ii, 188. Commission of Enquiry, dated 3 Nov., 1417, ii, 263. He exchanged, 28 June, 1418, with

Walter Bury (R. of Lazarton, Dioc. of Salisbury) ; patron, the same, ii, 192b ; who exchanged, 10 Feb., 1418-19, with

John Grede (R. of Poughill) ; patron, the same[1], ii, 197.

HASELBEARE, V. (Dioc. of Wells), *see* PINHOE, ii, 92.

HASELBURY [Haselbere, MS.], V., Dioc. of B. and W., *see* CHALLACOMBE, ii, 105b ; also, JACOBSTOWE (Devon), ii, 157b.

HATHERLEIGH, Vicars of—

Roger Trefrew ; on whose death was inst., 3 July, 1417,

Robert Herward, chaplain ; patrons, Peter, Abbot, and the Convent of Tavistock, ii, 186.

HEANTON PUNCHARDON [Heaunton-Ponchardon, MS.], Rectors of—

William Belmyslond ; on whose death was inst., 4 March, 1396-7,

John Stoke, priest ; patron, William Beaumount, ii, 7. On Stoke's death

Richard Knyght, chaplain, was inst., 17 Nov., 1412 ; patron, K. Henry IV. (by reason of the minority of Thomas, son and heir of William Beaumont), ii, 146.

HEANTON PUNCHARDON, Chantry of St. Mary at—

Richard Admot ; on whose death was inst., 5 April, 1413,

John Polsave, chaplain (proxy—William Rew, clerk) ; patron, the King (and for the same reason), ii, 149.

HEATHFIELD [Hethfeld, MS.], R., Dioc. of B. and W., *see* THORVERTON, ii, 165b ; also, WEST DOWNE, ii, 40b.

[1] Kynwolmersh, MS.

HEAVITREE [Hevytre, MS.], Vicars of—

John Lile; on whose death was inst., 9 Sept., 1396,
Thomas Plymmewode, priest; (patrons, the Dean and Chapter of Exeter), ii, 6. This Vicar exchanged, 28 Oct., 1401, with
John Wydelond (successor to John Holrig, as V. of Bampton, Dioc. of Lincoln), ii, 55b.

HEDDINGTON, R., Dioc. of Salisbury, *see* WASHFIELD, ii, 167b.

HELLAND [Hellond, MS.], Rectors of—

Robert Michel; on whose death was inst., 16 Jan., 1415-16,
John Wyllet, priest; patron, Thomas Colyn de Hellond, ii, 174b.

HEMINGTON, R. (Dioc. of B. & W.), *see* CHERITON BISHOP, ii, 56.

HEMYOCK, Rectors of—

John Whattecomb (or *Watcombe*): he exchanged, 20 Sept., 1395, with
William Rothewell (V. of Axminster); proxy—William Langton; patron, Sir William Hasthorp, knt., ii, 27b.

HEMYOCK, Chantry in the Chapel of St. Katherine at—

Richard Mychell; on whose death was collated, *by lapse*, 11 April, 1415,
John Marschall, chaplain, ii, 164. He exchanged, 26 Nov., 1418, with
Robert Daldych (R. of Corston; Dioc. of B. and W.); instituted by proxy—John Reynold; and, also, inducted by proxy—John Andrew: patron, Sir John Dynham, knt., ii, 195b. On his resignation
John Berne, chaplain, was inst., 11 May, 1419; patrons, Robert Maynard and Thos. Hurtyscote, ii, 198b. Commission of Enquiry, dated 25 April, 1419; ii, 267b.

HENNOCK [Hanok, MS.], Vicars of—

John Smyth; on whose death was inst., 2 Nov., 1399,
John Cok, priest; patrons, the Abbot and Convent of Torre, ii, 14. On John's death
William Cok, deacon, was inst., 10 April, 1413; ii, 149b.

HEREFORD CATHEDRAL, Canonry and Prebend of Pratum-min.,

John Gorwell, clerk, of the Dioc. of Exeter, was collated thereto in succession to *Walter Trote* (who resigned by proxy—Richard Hals, Treasurer of Exeter Cathedral), 11 June, 1401; ii, 53b.

HERNE [Hierne, MS,], Dioc. of Canterbury, Chapel of the Blessed Virgin Mary at; *see* POUGHILL, R., ii, 65b.

HEYES (*alias* HEGGES) in the Prebendal Church of St. Mary, within the Castle of Exeter, Prebendaries of—

Nicholas Bubbewyt, clerk, inst., 21[1] June, 1396; patron, K. Richard II, ii, 30b. On the resignation of Bubbewyth (*sic*),
Richard Courtenay, LL.B., was inst., 3 July, 1403, proxy—William Everard, clerk; patron, Edward, Earl of Devon, ii, 67b. On the resignation of this Prebendary (on his promotion to the see of Norwich),
Thomas Hendeman,[2] S.T.P., was inst., 3 Sept., 1413, and was inducted by proxy—Richard Penall; ii, 152.

HEYTESBURY [Heghtredesbury, MS.], Dioc. of Salisbury, *see* ST. PROBUS, ii, 200.

HIGHAMPTON [Heghaunton *and* Hyghamton, MS.], Rectors of—

Walter Rede; on whose death was inst., 9 Jan., 1406-7,

---

[1] Not 16 June, as in *Oliver*; this Prebendary afterwards became Bishop of London and of Salisbury.

[2] Not Henderman, as in Oliver's List.

John Bele, chaplain ; patron, Robert Cary, domicellus ; ii, 94. On the death of Beel (*sic*),

John Hendy was inst., 17 April, 1412, patron, for that turn, Richard Boyton. A Commission was issued, and it was reported to the Bishop that Robert Cary was patron, "jure hereditario," for two out of three turns, and the said Richard Boyton for one turn (by right of Margaret his wife) ; ii, 141.

HIGH BICKINGTON [Heybukynton *and* Heybukyngton, MS.], Rectors of—

William[1] *Credy* ; on whose death was inst., 17[2] Aug., 1406,

Roger Wodehele, clerk (proxy—Thomas Racheford, chaplain) ; patron, K. Henry IV, ii, 91. This Rector was succeeded by

John Clerk de Codeford, chaplain, inst., 13 March, 1406-7 ; ii, 95.

HIGH BRAY [Heghbray, MS.], Rectors of—

Thomas Langrom ; on whose resignation was inst., 14 May, 1418,

John Cruse ; patron, Sir Thomas Flemmyng, knt., ii, 191b. Commission of Enquiry, 14 April, 1418, ii, 265.

HITTISLEIGH [Hytteneslegh *and* Hitteslegh, MS.], Rectors of—

Robert Cok, chaplain, collated *by lapse*, 17 Sept., 1400, ii, 50. The Bishop was at Launceston Priory ; and the Mandate for the induction was directed to John Lydeford, junior, and John Dyght, "commissariis Domini in Archi diaconatu Exoniensi, Visitacione ipsius Domini ibidem inexpleta pendente." On Coke's *(sic)* death

John Goorde, chaplain, was inst., 15 Nov., 1417 ; patron, John Cole, of Nithewey, Esquire, ii, 187b.

HOCKWORTHY, Vicars of—

Richard Covyntre ; who exchanged, 9 Nov., 1399, with

William Redhode (V. of Batheaston, Dioc. of B. and W.) ; patron, Lucy Werre (or Warre), Abbess of Canonsleigh, ii, 44. On Redhode's death

Thomas Whytyng, priest, was inst., 18 Feb., 1399-1400 ; ii, 14b.

HOLBETON [Holbogeton, MS.], Vicars of—

Thomas Pykenet ; on whose death was inst., 6 Jan., 1396-7,

John Grym, priest ; patrons, the Prioress and Convent of Polslo, ii, 6b.

HOLCOMBE ROGUS [Holecomb Rogis, MS.], Vicars of—

Henry Portioye ; who exchanged, 4 Oct., 1399, with

John Pyke (R. of Spaxton, Dioc. of B. and W. ; patron, Robert Hylle) ; John Elmede, proxy for Pyke, and Laurence Haukyn for Portioye ; patron, K. Henry IV., ii, 42b.

HOLCOMBE BURNELL [Holecombe Burnel, MS.], Vicars of—

Richard Warmyscombe ; on whose resignation was inst., 5 Oct., 1418,

Robert Rynald, chaplain ; patron, John Orum, Canon of Wells, and Preb. of Holcombe Burnell therein ; ii, 194b.

HOLNE, V.—*Ralph Dollebeare* seems to have held this Benefice in Stafford's time ; but there appears to be no record of any institution between 1364 and 1443, in which year Dollebeare was succeeded by *John Colle*.

HOLLACOMBE [Holecombe, MS.], Rectors of—

John Neel : who exchanged, 28 July, 1403, with

Robert Pytman (R. of Huish) ; patron, the Prior and Convent of Bodmin, ii, 68b. On whose death

---

[1] Thomas, MS.—a clerical error.

[2] The day on which his predecessor's Will was proved ; *see* i, 308.

John Retyn, chaplain, was inst. "ad ecclesiam parochialem Sancti Petroci de Holecombe," 14 Oct., 1418; ii, 194b.

HOLSWORTHY, Chantry of Trewen, in the Church of;—

Thomas Row, chaplain, collated by lapse, 6 July, 1400, the preferment having been claimed by John Lyer, chaplain, ii, 48. This claim seems to have been successful; for Row shortly afterwards resigned, and the said

John Leyer (sic) was inst., 16 Nov., 1400; patron, John Denys, domicellus, ii, 51b. On Leyer's death

John Wyndegrynde, chaplain, was inst., 17 Sept., 1412; patron, "hac vice," Richard Peperell, senior, domicellus, ii, 144b. Commission of Enquiry, dated 18 Aug., 1412, ii, 248.

HONEYCHURCH [Honychurche, MS.], Rectors of—

Thomas Launcell (or Launcel), chaplain, was collated *by lapse*, 25 Oct., 1402 (Roger Cobbelond, proxy), ii, 64. He exchanged 7 March, 1406-7, with

John Knyght (V. of Broadwoodwidger); patron, "hac vice," John Sleghe, (proxy—Walter Robert), ii, 95. He appears to have been succeeded by

John Reue (or *Reve*), whose institution is not recorded; but on his death

John Ramfray, chaplain, was inst., 1 May, 1408; patron, "hac vice," Nicholas Bromford, domicellus, ii, 101. On Ramfray's death

John Were, chaplain, was inst., 14 June, 1414; patron, "hac vice," Nicholas Fitz-Herbert, ii, 159.

HONINGTON, V. (Dioc. of Lincoln), *see* CLYST ST. MARY, ii, 53b.

HONITON (*alias* HONYNGTON), Rectors of—

Richard Madeford; who exchanged, 25 Jan., 1399-1400, with

Edward Fysch (V. of Widecombe[-in-the-Moor]); patron, Sir Philip Courtenay, knt., ii, 45. This Rector (here called *Fyshacre*), exchanged, 27 Nov., 1408, with

Robert Fynour (R. of Shirwell),; patron, Richard Courtenay, clerk; ii, 103. On Fynour's death

John Sneynton, chaplain, was inst., 15 Feb., 1412-13; patron, the same; ii, 148.

HOPE MANSEL [Maylosell, MS.], Dioc. of Hereford, *see* LOXBEARE, ii, 168b.

HORWOOD [Horwode, MS.], Rectors of—

Nicholas; on whose death, was inst., 31 July, 1395,

John Noble, priest; patron, "hac vice," Simon Passelewe; ii, 1b. A Commission of Enquiry was issued 20 Jan., 1398-9, as to a proposed exchange between Noble and William Cantelo, R. of Angersleigh [Angerlegh, MS.], Dioc. of B. and W.; and, also, as to the right of presenting to Horwood, to which Simon Passelewe had laid claim; ii, 222. There appears to be no record of the exchange having been effected or of Noble's resignation; but 24 Oct., 1404,

John Deyman, chaplain, was inst., "ad ecclesiam parochialem de CHURCHHOREWODE . . . . vacantem;" patron, John Paslew (*sic*), ii, 79b.

HUISH [described in the MS. as "Hywyssh juxta Merton"; *also* Hywych], Rectors of—

Robert Pytman, who exchanged, 28 July, 1403, with

John Neel (R. of Hollacombe); patron, Margaret, relict of Andrew Reede; ii, 68b. I find no record of Neel's resignation or death; but

John Fenton, chaplain, was inst., 28 Nov., 1404; patron, "hac vice," Sir Thomas Pomeray, knt., ii, 80b.

HUNTSHAM [Hunsham, MS.], Rectors of—

John Wylledon alias *Jordan*; on whose death was inst., 8 Nov., 1418,

Walter Chyterwell, chaplain; patron, "hac vice," Robert Bere, ii, 195b. Commission of Enquiry, dated 18 Oct., 1418; ii, 266b.

HUNTSHAW [Hunshawe, MS.], Rectors of—

John Colrygg; on whose death was inst., 30 Nov., 1399,

John Wyche, clerk; patron, K. Henry IV, ii, 44b. He exchanged, 17 Aug., 1400, with

William atte Kyrke (V. of Cadeby, Dioc. of Lincoln); ii, 49b.

HURSTBOURNE PRIOR'S [Husbourne Prioris, MS.], *see* CREDITON, ii, 95b.

HUTTON [Hoton, MS.], *see* ST. AUSTELL, ii, 52b.

HUXHAM [Hoxham, MS.], Rectors of—

John Knyghton; who exchanged, 3 Feb., 1403-4, with

Richard Salman (R. of E. Lydford, Dioc. of B. and W).); patron, Thomas Baunfilde, domicellus; ii, 74b. He exchanged, 24 Sept. following, with

William Lychfyld (V. of Lamerton); patron, the same, ii, 79. On whose death

Thomas Gybbys, chaplain, was inst., 7 June, 1410; patron, John Bampfyld, domicellus, ii, 115. On the resignation of Gybbe (*sic*),

John Beere, clerk, was inst., 2 July, 1419; patrons, Roger Bolter, Wm. Hydon, Richard Bamfeld, Esquire, Thos. Gybbe, and John Mathu, clerks, ii, 200.

ICKLESHAM [Ilesham, MS.], *see* ST. CLEER, ii, 51.

IDEFORD [Yddeforde, MS.], Rectors of—

David Ralle; on whose death was inst., 27 Feb., 1402-3,

John Duyn, chaplain; patron, "hac vice," Gilbert Burton, ii, 25.

ILFRACOMBE [Ilfridecombe, *alias* Ilfardecombe, MS.] Rectors;—

Thomas Barton; on whose death was inst., 28 March, 1416,

Hugh Herle, chaplain; patron, "hac vice," Sir John Herle, knt., ii, 175b.

INGELBY, Chapel of St. Helen at, *see* CRANTOCK, ii, 47b.

INSTOW [Yenstowe, MS.], Rectors of—

Richard Wynter; on whose death was inst., 2 May, 1406,

Thomas Lange clerk (proxy—John Dabernon); patrons, Sir William Hankeford, knt., and Richard and John Hankeford; ii, 89. On Lange's death

Alexander Courteys, chaplain, was inst., 19 Sept., 1412; ii, 144b. Commission of Enquiry dated 7 Sept., 1412; ii, 248b.

INWARDLEIGH, Rectors of—

Richard Traunce; who exchanged, 27 Jan, 1402-3, with,

John Flemmyng; patrons, Thos. Rytherdon, Rd. Burdon, John Culley, Matthew White, John Fordeman, and Robert Ouger, ii, 24b. On Flemmyng's resignation was inst., 17 Jan., 1409-10,

Thomas Schere, chaplain; patrons, Ivo Credy, Esquire, Adam Credy, Ralph Credy, Thos. Ryderdon, John Cullegh, John Fordeman, Matthew Whyte, and Augerus Vyell; ii, 108b.

IPPLEPEN [Ippelpenne, MS.], Rectors of—

Walter Trote; who exchanged, 15 Sept., 1396, with

John Excestre, Canon of Exeter (Hervey Wyket, clerk, being Trote's proxy); patron, K. Richard II., ii, 31b. There is no record of his death or resignation, but he was succeeded by

John de Spryngthorp, chaplain (proxy—Thomas Haselee), 25 Oct., 1400; patron, K. Henry IV., ii, 51. He exchanged, 21 Nov., 1402, with

John Morehay (R. of West Keal, Dioc. of Lincoln); patron, K. Henry IV., ii, 64b. He exchanged, 11 May, 1410, with

Richard Gabriell (Canon and Preb. of Warminster, *alias* Luxvyle, in Wells Cathedral); patron the same, ii, 110b.

JACOBSTOW [Stawe Sancti Jacobi, MS.] Devon, Rectors of—

William Clerk; this Rector exchanged, 6 Sept., 1405, with

John Harcombe, chaplain (Chantry-Priest of St. Mary's Altar in the Church of Crewkerne, Dioc. of B. and W.); patron, Nicholas Bromford, domicellus, ii, 86. Harkecomb (*sic*) exchanged, 3 Aug., 1412, with

John Botuler (R. of Charlbury, Dioc. of Salisbury); ii, 142b. Boteller (*sic*) exchanged, 6 April, 1414, with

Richard Batte (V. of Haslebury, Dioc. of B. and W.); ii, 157b. He exchanged 19 Oct., 1414, with

John Corbyn (V. of Toller Porcorum, Dioc. of Salisbury); ii, 162; who exchanged, 10 July, 1416, with

John Iveray (for his Chantry of Cheverel Parva, Dioc. of Salisbury); patron John, son and heir of the said Nicholas Bromford, ii, 177.

KEA [Landege, MS.], Vicars of—

John Rychowe; on whose death was collated, 21 Dec., 1412,

Otho Betty, chaplain; ii, 147b. Commission as to dilapidations, dated 12 Feb., 1412-13, ii, 250b.

KENTISBEARE, Rectors of—

John Whattelegh; on whose death was inst., 22 March, 1406-7,

William Reche, chaplain; patron, Richard Clopton, ii, 95. On Reche's death

Walter Symon, chaplain, was inst., 10 Dec., 1412; patron, William Stevenes, chaplain (to whom the right of presentation had devolved from Richard Clopton, being annexed to the manor of Kentisbeare), ii, 147. Commissions of Enquiry herein, ii. 248b, 249. On the death of Symond (*sic*)

William Legh, chaplain, was inst., 2 July, 1415; patron, "hac vice" Sir Edward Courtenay, son and heir of Edward, Earl of Devon, ii, 166.

KENTISBURY, Rectors of—

Philip Pym; on whose resignation

Thomas Baker, chaplain, was inst., 3 July, 1409; patron, John Wolff, ii, 106.

KENTON, Vicars of,—

William Rammeslond: on whose death was inst., 12 Dec., 1399,

Richard Mey (proxy—John Cheyne); patrons, the Dean and Chapter of Salisbury, ii, 14b. There appears to be no record of his resignation or death, or of the institution of—

Adam Lylborn or *Lyllebourne* his successor; whose Will, however, is to be seen, i, 307; and on whose death

Thomas Upton, was inst., 6 Nov., 1406; ii, 93.

KILKHAMPTON, Rectors of—

John Lemman; who exchanged, 12 Dec., 1403, with

William Knygh[1] (V. of Barnstaple); patron, Sir John Greynevill, knt., ii, 71.

KILVE [Culve, MS.], R., Dioc. of B. and W., *see* STOODLEIGH, R., ii, 130b.

KINGSBURY, V., Dioc. of B. and W., *see* SUTCOMBE, R., ii, 102b.

KINGSTON, V., Dioc. of B. and W., *see* PARRACOMBE, R., ii, 79b.

KINGSTON RUSSELL, Dioc. of Salisbury, *see* ST. IVE, R., ii, 54.

KING'S NYMPTON, Rectors of—

John Haget (or *Hacket*—*see* i, 6b); on whose resignation was inst., 24 April, 1407,

Thomas Barton, chaplain; patron, Richard Corneweyl, domicellus, ii, 96. But, 21 Feb., 1407-8, Barton having resigned,

John Haget was again inst. (proxy—Richard Wayneman); patron, the same, ii, 100. Both were Canons of Exeter, and Barton held other valuable pre-

[1] *Sic*; elsewhere "Knyght."

ferment in the Diocese. This Rector exchanged, 30 Nov., 1408 (proxy—Laurence Haukyn, chaplain), with
William Southam (R. of Fuggleston *with* Bemerton, Dioc. of Salisbury; patron, Joan, Abbess of Wilton); proxy—Richard Weyneman *(sic)*; patrons, Richard Cornewayle and Alice, his wife, ii, 103b. On Southam's death
Philip Staunton, chaplain, was inst.,[1] 5 Dec., 1412; patron, Richard Cornewayl, ii, 146. A Commission of Enquiry (in which is added "and Cecilia, his wife,") was issued, 30 Nov., 1412, ii, 249b.

KINGSTEIGNTON, Vicars of—
Roger Castelgof; on whose resignation was inst., 13 March, 1401-2,
John Bokepound, chaplain; patron, Thomas Feriby, Canon of Salisbury Cath., and Preb. of Teignton therein, ii, 57. On his resignation
Roger Horewell, chaplain, was inst., 12 March, 1415-16; ii, 175.

KNYGHTESLEGH, R. (Dioc. of B. and W.), *see* COTLEIGH, R., ii, 95b.

LADOCK [Sancte Ladoce, MS.], Rectors of—
Nicholas Kelly; on whose death was inst., 11 June 1414,
Renaldus Tretherf, clerk, (proxy—John Wolston, clerk); patron, John Tretherf, ii, 159. Commission of Enquiry, dated 31 May, 1414, ii, 254.

LAMERTON, Vicars of—
William Lychfyld: who exchanged, 24 Sept., 1404, with
Richard Salman (R. of Huxham); patrons, the Abbot and Convent of Tavistock, ii, 79. On the death of Selman *(sic)*
Augustin Strod, chaplain, was inst., 6 Sept., 1412; ii, 144. Strood *(sic)* exchanged, 30 March, 1414, with
Henry Thomas (R. of Cotleigh); ii, 157b. On whose death
William Floyer, chaplain, was inst., 17 Aug., 1414, ii, 161.

LAMORRAN [Lamoren, MS.], Rectors of—
William Grym: who exchanged, 4 Aug., 1398, with
Thomas Wappelegh (V. of Buckland-Monachorum); patron, John Trevenour, Esquire, ii, 40. On his death
John Tresagnow, chaplain, was inst., 23 Oct., 1410; ii, 124.

LANDCROSS [Langcars, *also* Langkars *and* Lankars, MS.], Rectors of—
John Roys; on whose death was inst., 6 Dec., 1398,
John Drewe, priest; patron, Sir James Chuddlegh, knt., ii, 10. On his death
John Juvenel, priest, was inst., 16 May, 1399; patron, the same, ii, 12. On Juvenel's resignation,
John Dolbiry, chaplain, was instituted, 14 July, 1401; patron the same,[2] ii, 20. It is not stated that Dolbiry resigned; but he did so on his presentation to Totnes V., to which he was inst., 3 March, 1406-7; and on 4 April, in the same year, this Rectory being vacant,
John Cook, chaplain, was inst.; patrons, Thomas Beaumount, John Bury, Thomas Pyllond, and John Syntabyn de Lobbe, ii, 95b.

LANDWEDNACK [Sancti Winwolay[3] de Landewynnek, MS.], Rectors of—
John Colyn; who exchanged, 7 Aug., 1404, with
Richard Bolham (V. of Gwennap), proxy for Colyn, William Penfern, clerk); patrons, John Trethewy and John Skewys, ii, 78.

---

[1] To "Nymynton," MS., here.
[2] Sir James de Chuddelegh, MS.
[3] The "y" is dotted, and was sounded separately as an "i": at fol. 175 it is "Sancti Wynwolai."

Nicholas Bolham succeeded, on the resignation of *Richard*, 28 Feb., 1415-16; patron, Sir Otho Trevarthyan, knt., ii, 175.

LANDRAKE [Lanrak, MS.], Vicar of—
Richard Lannire, priest, inst., 22 Jan., 1398-9; patrons, the Prior and Convent of St. Germans, ii, 10b.

LANGTREE, Rectors of—
John Cornewale; on whose death was inst., 13 May, 1411,
Walter Cook, chaplain; patron, Constance de Spenser, ii, 132b. Commission of Enquiry, dated 15 March, 1410-11, ii, 239b.

LANLIVERY, Vicars of—
William Bonok; on whose resignation was inst., 18 June, 1416,
Robert Chamberleyn, chaplain; patrons, the Prior and Convent of Tywardreath, ii, 177.

LANREATH [Lanreythyow, MS.], Rectors of—
William Somerford; on whose death was inst., 13 June, 1410,
Henry Rychard, clerk; patron, William Swynborne, ii, 115.

LANSALLOS [Lansalewes, MS.], Rectors of—
Guy Blaunkmonster; on whose death was inst., 20 Feb., 1404-5,
Ralph Colyn, clerk; patron, John Colshull, domicellus. The Mandate for his Induction was directed to Robert Estebrok, V. of Duloe, "absente Archidiacono Cornubiensi," ii, 82.

LANTEGLOS [BY CAMELFORD], Rectors of—
Thomas Clyfford; who exchanged, 28 Feb., 1401-2, with
Richard Aldryngton alias *Colcombe* (R. of Stoke-in-Teignhead); proxy—John Matheu; patron, K. Henry IV.; ii, 57. He exchanged, 27 July, 1416, with
William Trebel (R. of St. Mawgan-in-Pyder); proxy—John Whitewaye, clerk; patron, K. Henry V.; ii, 178.

LANTEGLOS [BY FOWEY], Vicars of—
John Hoper, on whose death was inst., 30 Nov., 1412,
John Compton, chaplain; patrons, the Master and Brethren of the Hospital of St. John Bapt., Bridgewater, ii, 146.

LAUNCELLS, St. Andrew's, Vicars of—
Richard Doty; who exchanged, 16 March, 1402-3, with
John Avery (R. of St. Laurence's, Exeter); patrons, the Abbot and Convent of Hartland, ii, 26. He exchanged, 14 Nov., 1403, with
Richard Madek (R. of Beaworthy): ii, 69b.

LAUNCESTON, St. Stephen's Priory, Priors of—
Stephen Tredydan, who was succeeded by
Roger Combrygge; on whose death (18 June, 1410; ii, 115b),
John Honylond, was elected, and confirmed 5 July, 1410; ii, 119b.

LAWHITTON, Rectors of—
Peter Lamoren; who exchanged, 20 April, 1419, with
John Germen (R. of Poltimore); proxy for Lamoren, John Edward, sub-deacon; patron, the Bishop, ii, 197b.

LELANT [Lananta, MS.], Vicars of—
John Clerk; on whose death was collated, 10 June, 1416,
John Bryt, chaplain, ii, 176b.

LEWES, Archdeaconry of, *see* BRADNINCH; ii, 27.

LEW TRENCHARD [Lywtranchard, MS.], Rectors of—
Geoffrey Paccheshulle; on whose death was inst., 2 May, 1399,
Roger Eustas, priest; patron, "hac vice," John Wyse, domicellus, ii, 12.

LEZANT [Lausant *and* Lausante, MS.], Rectors of—

Patrick Wode (or *atte Wode*), chaplain, collated 12 March, 1396-7; ii, 33; on whose death

Henry Wynnegode, clerk, was collated, 25 Jan., 1413-14, the Mandate for his induction being directed to John Colman, V. of South Petherwin: ii, 155. He exchanged, 11 Jan., 1415-16, with

John Burgoun, chaplain, (R. of St. Erme), the Mandate for his induction being directed to Richard Kyttow, chaplain, ii, 174b. On his resignation

John Wolston, chaplain, was collated, 23 May, 1418; ii, 191b.

LIMPSFIELD [Lymnesfelde, MS.], R., Dioc. of Winchester, *see* ST. PROBUS, ii, 193b.

LINCOLN CATHEDRAL, Canonry and Prebend of Bedford therein, *see* ST. PROBUS, ii, 56b.—Canon and Prebend of Holy Cross in, *see* TOTNES, Archdeaconry of, ii, 164b.

LINKINHORNE [Lankenhorn, MS.], Vicars of—

Nicholas Donyell was V. 18 Nov., 1400 (*see* i, 50), when he was licensed to celebrate in his manse, probably on account of illness, for he died soon after, and

Thomas Raylecomb, chaplain, was collated, *by lapse*, 10 Sept., 1401; ii, 54b. There is no record of his cession, but he seems to have been succeeded by

Richard Peryn, on whose death[1]

John Clerk, chaplain, was inst., 2 April, 1411; patrons, the Prior and Convent of Launceston, ii, 132. On Clerk's death

Andrew Anstysmyll, chaplain, was inst. (to the Church "Sancti Melori de Lankynhorn"), 6 Aug., 1419; patrons the same, ii, 201b.

LISKEARD [Leskyret *and* Leskyrd, MS.]. St. Martin's; Vicars—

Henry Frend resigned 29 Jan., 1398-9; *see* ii, 222. The V. was then suffered to lapse, and the Abp. of Canterbury presented John Waryn. A question arose whether the right to present had not rather lapsed to the Bp. of Exeter, who, accordingly, ordered Richard Olyver, clerk, to make inquisition thereupon. The result was to confirm the right of the Abp., by reason of the long lapse of time, and certificate was made therein, accordingly, 19 Jan., 1400-1:

John Waryn had been duly collated the day before; ii, 54b. He exchanged, 15 April, 1413, with

Thomas Speke (R. of Grittleton, Dioc. of Salisbury); the Prior and Convent of Launceston were patrons of Liskeard, ii, 149b. On the death of Spek (*sic*)

John Aysch, priest, was inst., 5 Oct., 1415; ii, 169b.

LITTLEHAM [Lytelham, MS.], St. Swithin's, near Bideford, Rectors of—

Thomas . . . . . .

John Pers, priest, inst., 19 Sept., 1399; patron, John de la Beer, ii, 13. On the death of Piers (*sic*)

Richard Covyan, chaplain, was inst., 10 Aug., 1402; patron the same, ii, 22b.

LITTLEHAM near Exmouth, Vicars of—

William Drewe; who exchanged, 22 Oct., 1405, with

John Morchard (V. of Brimpton Regis, Dioc. of B. and W.); patrons, the Dean and Chapter of Exeter, ii, 87. On Morchard's resignation

John Puttes, chaplain, was inst., 20 April, 1407; ii, 96.

---

[1] He was treacherously murdered in March, 1411, while riding near his parish-church (i, 136).

LODDISWELL [Lodeswell *and* Lodeswyll, MS.], Rectors of—
John Whytloff; on whose death was inst., 16 April, 1405,
Thomas la Zouche, clerk (proxy—John Selow); patrons, Henry Scrop, knt., and Robert Love (*sic*), domicellus, ii, 83ᵇ. On this Rector's death
Peter Holdych, chaplain, was inst., 26 March, 1411; patron, Robert Lovell, ii, 131ᵇ. Two Commissions of Enquiry as to the right of presentation were issued, 3 Feb., and 18 Feb. in the same year; ii, 238ᵇ. During this Rector's incumbency the Rectory was appropriated to Slapton College, and Peter Holdych, having resigned the same, was inst. as the first Vicar, 22 Oct., 1413: patrons the Rector, etc., of the said College, ii, 153.

LONDON, ST. AUGUSTINE'S "ad portam," *see* MARHAMCHURCH ii, 122.—ST. PANCRAS, R., *see* BRIDESTOWE, ii, 150ᵇ.

LOXBEARE [Lokkysbere and Lockesbere, MS.], Rectors of—
John atte Hyde [Hyde MS., i, 39ᵇ]; on whose resignation was inst. 23 Dec., 1401,
John Walwyn, chaplain; patron, John Avenel, lord of "Lokkesbeare," ii, 20ᵇ. He exchanged 22 Aug., 1412, with
John Smyth (R. of Stanton-on-the-Wold, Dioc. of York); patron the same, ii, 143ᵇ. On whose cession
John Lodeford appears to have succeeded; but the date of his institution is not recorded: he exchanged 7 Sept., 1415, with
John Herward, clerk (R. of Hope Mansell, Dioc. of Hereford); patron, John Avenel, domicellus, ii, 168ᵇ.

LOXHORE [Lokkyshore, MS.], Rectors of—
Thomas Yo; on whose death was inst., 17 July, 1406,
William Fedde, chaplain (proxy—Thomas Wyot, clerk); patron, "hac vice" William Beaumount, domicellus, ii, 90.

LUCCOMBE, R. (Dioc. of B. and W.), *see* CLYST ST. GEORGE, ii, 148ᵇ.

LUDGVAN [Sancti Luduoni, MS.], Rectors of—
Thomas Gerweys; who exchanged, 19 Sept., 1418, with
John Colyn (V. of Gwennap); patron, Lady Elizabeth, relict of Sir John de Haryngton, knt. (proxy for Gerweys, John Wolston, chaplain), ii, 194.

LUFFINCOTT [Loghyngcote *and* Logyncote, MS.], Rectors of—
John Lucas; on whose death was inst., 14 Nov., 1398,
John Godefray, priest; patron, Nicholas Loghyncote, ii, 10. On his resignation
Richard Aylmere was inst., 20 June, 1399; ii, 12ᵇ.

LUPPIT [Louepit, MS.], Vicars of—
Vincent Hille; who exchanged, 22 Jan., 1402-3, with
John Basyngham de Melton (V. of Chudleigh); patrons, the Abbot and Convent of Newenham; ii, 65. He exchanged, 22 Dec., 1403, with
John Vyan (V. of Westbury, Dioc. of B. and W.); ii, 71. On Vyan's death
William Stephenes, chaplain, was inst., 23 Nov., 1416; ii, 180.

LUSTLEIGH, Rectors of—
John Affeton; on whose death was inst., 15 Feb., 1400-1401.
John Etewell, chaplain; patron, John Wybbery (or Wybbury), domicellus, ii, 17. On the resignation of Ettewell (*sic*),—proxy, John Hals, literate,
John Burlegh, chaplain, was inst., 17 Dec., 1406; ii, 93ᵇ.

LYMPSTON [Limeston, MS.], Rectors of
Henry Andreu; on whose resignation was inst., 13 April, 1407,
John Holout, priest; patron, Sir William Bonevyll, knt., ii 96.

MAKER [Macre, MS.], Vicars of—

John Prund ; on whose resignation was inst., 6 Oct., 1405,

John Stybbe, chaplain ; patrons, the Prior and Convent of Plympton, ii, 86. On whose resignation

John Motelegh, chaplain, was inst., 30 July, 1406 ; ii, 90. On the resignation of Mottelegh (*sic*),

John Pral was inst., 7 July, 1410 ; ii, 120.

MAMHEAD [Mammehede, MS.], Rectors of—

William Hoghe ; on whose death was inst., 9 April, 1400,

John Chapel, chaplain ; patrons, Sir William Bonevyle, knt., John Strech, John Prestecote and John Uggeburgh, chaplain, ii, 45b. On his death

John Colyn, chaplain, was inst., 14 Oct., 1410 ; patron, Thomas, Baron de Carrew ; ii, 124. Colyn exchanged, 23 Dec., 1417, with

John Tomme (V. of Rattery) ; patron, Sir Thomas Carrew, knt., Baron de Carrew ; ii, 189.

MANACCAN [Managhan, MS.], Vicars of—

John Nans ; on whose resignation was inst., 30 Aug., 1395,

John Oppy, priest ; patron, the King (during the Vacancy of the See), ii, 1b.

MANSTON, R., Dioc. of Salisbury. *See* YARCOMBE, V., ii, 156b.

MAPERTON, R., Dioc. of B. and W.) *See* Chawleigh, R., ii, 155.

MARHAMCHURCH [Marwenchurch *alias* Sancte Merwenne, *also* Marwynchurch, MS.], Rectors of—

Simon Lynam ; who exchanged, 12 April, 1400, with

Robert Alkebarwe (R. of Faringdon. Dioc. of Winchester) : patron, Sir John Herle, knt., (proxy for Lynam, John Barell), ii, 45b. On the resignation of Alkebarowe (*sic*),

Robert Burstede, chaplain, was inst., 24 July, 1407 ; ii, 97b. He exchanged, 3 Aug., 1410, with

John Schirford (R. of St. Augustine's "ad portam," in the City of London) ; ii, 122. On the death of Shyrfford (*sic*),

James Dyrehyll, chaplain, was inst., 30 Nov., 1417 ; ii, 188. Commission of Enquiry, 3 Nov., 1417 ; ii, 263b.

MARIANSLEIGH [Marnelegh, Maryneslegh, Maryonlegh, MS.], Vicars of—

Robert Tregaria ; on whose death was inst., 15 May, 1396,

John Wytteney, priest ; patrons, Robert, Prior, and the Convent of Belrygge (*sic*), ii, 5.

John Wynchestre ; whose institution is not recorded, but on whose resignation

Robert Feld, chaplain, was inst., 22 Nov., 1401 ; patrons, the Prior and Convent of Herlynch, ii, 56.—Feld's resignation is not recorded, but it must have occurred about the 8th of March, 1408-9, when he was inst. to Coleridge, V.

William Hynde, chaplain, succeeded, 21 March, 1408-9 ; ii, 105.

MARISTOW [Stowe Sancte Marie], Vicar of—

John Piers, chaplain, inst., 30 May, 1406 ; patrons, the Prior and Convent of Plympton, ii, 89b.

MARSH, R., Dioc. of Lincoln, *see* *Witheridge*, R., ii, 30

MARTINHOE [Martyngho *and* Matyngho, MS.], Rectors of—

Thomas Heryngeston : he exchanged, 16 Dec., 1401, with

John Brent (V. of Halse, Dioc. of B. and W.) ; proxy—Hugh Bremham ; patron, John ap Roppard, domicellus ; ii, 56. He was, probably, succeeded by *John Baker*, whose institution is not recorded, but on whose death

William Percevale, clerk, was inst., 23 Oct., 1418 (proxy—Matthew Percevale, literate) : patron, Philip Percevale, ii, 195. Commission of Enquiry, dated 30 Sept., 1418 ; ii, 266b.

MARWOOD [Merwode and Merewode (i, 12), MS.], Rectors of—
Hamund Brereton ; on whose death was inst., 4 Dec., 1403,
John Kyngton (proxy—Nicholas Hemyngford) ; patron, K. Henry IV., ii, 70b. He exchanged, 2 April, 1406, with
Thomas Chauntrell (Canon and Preb. in St. Martin's, London) ; patron, the same, ii, 89.

MAYFIELD [Maghfeld, MS.], V., in the jurisdiction of the Abp. of Canterbury ; *see* SEATON, ii, 82.

MEAVY [Mewy, MS.], Rectors of—
William Newenham ; on whose death was inst., 1 May, 1396,
Henry Gardiner, clerk (proxy—Richard Skynner, priest) ; patron, the Prior and Convent of Plympton, ii, 5. On whose resignation
John Schute, clerk, was inst., 26 Sept., 1400 ; ii, 50b. On whose resignation
John Dygon, chaplain, was inst., 19 Sept., 1407 (proxy—William Brounyng, chaplain) ; ii, 98. On Dygon's resignation
Richard Toker, chaplain, was inst., 22 July, 1410 ; ii, 121. On whose death
Richard Lyle, chaplain, was inst., 14 March, 1416-17 ; ii, 182b. On Lyle's resignation
John Cole, chaplain, was inst., 25 Oct., 1417 ; ii, 187b.

MEETH [Methe, MS.], Rectors of—
John Gome : who was succeeded by
Robert Gyffard ; patron, King Richard II.—*See* the Commission, dated 1 Dec., 1398, to promote an exchange between Gome and the said Robert Gyffard, R. of Thorne Coffin, Dioc. of B. and W. ; ii, 221. On Gyffard's death
John Nouns, chaplain, was inst., 25 Sept., 1410 ; patron, Thomas Deneys, ii, 123b.

MENHENYOT [Mahenyet *and* Mahynyet, MS.], Rectors of—
John Philypp ; on whose death was inst., 12 Dec., 1411,
John Waryn, clerk ; patrons, Henry, Prince of Wales (guardian of the heir of the late John Carmynow), Sir Wm. Talbot, knt., and Wm. Milford ; ii, 138.

MERTON, Rectors of—
John Monke ; on whose death was inst., 7 Dec., 1412,
Thomas Wyllyng, chaplain ; patrons, Sir John de la Pomeray and Sir Thos. Stawell, knights, and Robert Cornu. Sir John Fitzth Waryn, knt., had presented John Monke ; and, as to the three others named above, a Commission of Enquiry had been issued, 29 Nov., 1412, and the Bishop was certified that the advowson was annexed to the Manor of Merton : that Sir John de la Pomeray presented in the right of his wife, Joan, daughter and co-heir of Richard de Merton, deceased ; that Sir Thomas Stawell presented by hereditary right, as son and heir of Elinor, wife of Matthew Stawell, deceased, a daughter of the said Richard de Merton, and sister and co-heir of Joan de la Pomeray ; and that Robert Cornu presented in right of Isabella, his wife, daughter and heir of Agnes, wife of John Brythlegh, deceased, daughter and heir of the said Richard de Merton, and sister and co-heir of the said Joan and Elinor ; ii, 146b, 249b.

MESHAW [Meweschathe, MS.], Rectors of—
John Elias ; on whose resignation was inst., 1 April, 1398,
John Nottecleve, priest ; patron, Thomas de Affeton, ii, 8b.

MICHAELSTOW [Myghelstowe, MS.], Rectors of—
Simon Barton ; on whose death was inst., 25 Aug., 1404,
Robert Bulle, chaplain ; patron, Henry, Prince of Wales, etc., ii, 78b. On the death of Bole *(sic)*
John Nowers, clerk, was inst., 7 Dec., 1407 ; ii, 99.

MILTON [Middelton, MS.], R., Dioc. of B. and W., *See* UPLYME, ii, 37

MILTON [ABBOT], Vicars of—

Roger Wille; on whose death was inst., 23 May, 1411,
Hugh Clerk, chaplain; patrons, the Abbot and Convent of Tavistock, ii, 132b.
Roger Sturt, deacon, was inst., on Clerk's death, 4 Dec., 1416; ii, 180b.

MILTON DAMAREL, Rectors of—

John Sergent; on whose death was inst., 27 April, 1411,
Walter Robert, priest: patron, Edward, Earl of Devon, ii, 132b. Commissions of Enquiry, ii, 237b, 238. On Robert's resignation
Walter Colle, clerk, was inst.. 6 May, 1413; ii, 150b. On whose resignation
William Copleston, clerk, was inst., 1 Oct., 1415; ii, 169b. On Copleston's death
John Phylyp, chaplain, was inst., 5 Dec., 1415; ii, 173b. On Phylyp's resignation
Ralph Respryn, clerk, was instituted, 7 April, 1418; ii, 190.

MINSTER [" Talkern," MS.], Rector of—

Reginald Wellesleigh, clerk, was inst., 16 June, 1408; patron, Henry, Prince of Wales, etc., ii, 102.—He appears to have been the first "Rector," of this parish, succeeding John de Stratton, the last Prior of this alien Priory (*Maclean*).

MODBURY PRIORY—

(dependent on the Benedictine Abbey of "Sancta Maria de Sancto Petro super Divam" (S. Pierre sur Dive, in the Diocese of Seez, Normandy). By Commission from the Bishop, who was at Daventry, the Vicar-General, Dean Tregrisiou, inst. (at Tregrisiou, in Cornwall)—in the room of
John Michel, who had resigned—
John Rogger, monk of the said Abbey, 7 March, 1398-9; patron, Sir Richard de Campo Arnulphi [Champernoune], knt., on the nomination of K. Henry IV., ii, 10b. On Rogger's resignation,—he became Prior of Tywardreath.—
Richard Leycestre, monk of Battle, was inst., 27 Feb., 1406-7; patron, etc., the same, ii, 94b. On the death of Richard de Leycestrya (*sic*)
William Fauchilon, monk, was inst., 9 Jan., 1415-16, having been nominated to K. Henry V. by Sir Richard de Champernoun, the true patron, ii, 174b.

MODBURY, Vicars of—

Henry Alkebarowe, chaplain, inst. 7 Dec., 1406; patron, K. Henry IV., ii, 93b. He exchanged, 3 March, 1406-7, with
William Brounyng, deacon (R. of St. Stephen's, Exeter); ii, 94b.

MONKLEIGH, Vicars of—

John Trunket; on whose death was inst., 26 April, 1410,
John Borre, chaplain; patrons, William Cryche (Prior) and the Convent of Montacute, ii, 109b.

MONKOKEHAMPTON, Rectors of—

Robert Culleigh, chaplain, inst., 15 Dec., 1404; patron, William Holte, ii, 80b. On whose death
John Bavdyn (in the Commission *Bawedyn*), chaplain, was inst., 3 July, 1418; patron, "hac vice" Ralph Fycon, esquire, ii, 192b. Commission of Enquiry, dated 28 June, 1418, ii, 266.

MORCHARD BISHOP, Rectors of—

Walter Nywaton; on whose death was collated 14 Nov., 1401,
William Rayner, chaplain, ii, 56.

MOREBATH [Morbathe, MS.]. Vicars of—

Robert Dyghere; on whose resignation was inst., 7 July, 1405,
Richard Bogheway, chaplain; patrons, Robert (Prior) and the Convent of Berlinch (Dioc. of B. and W.), ii, 85b.

MOORLINCH [Merlynch, MS.], Dioc. of B. and W. *See* BRADSTONE, R., ii. 195.

MORELEIGH [Morlegh, MS.], Rectors of—

Alan Benet (*see* i, 21b, 49b); he appears to have been succeeded by

Walter Hyll; on whose resignation was inst., 15 June, 1414,

William Smyth, chaplain; patrons, Joan, daughter of Martin de Fyschacre, and John Uffiyt, ii, 159b.

MORETON-HAMPSTEAD [Morton, MS.], Rectors of—

Henry Broklond; on whose death was inst., 14 July, 1404,

William Bruter, chaplain; patron, Sir Peter Courtenay, knt., ii, 78. He exchanged, 13 Aug., 1416, with

Richard Penels (V. of Paignton); patron, K. Henry V., ii, 178b. On whose death

Thomas Bryd, chaplain, was inst., 22 April, 1419 (proxy—Richard Chechestre, clerk); patron the same, ii, 198.

MORTHOE [Mortho *and* Morteho, MS.], Vicars of—

Richard Hopkyn; on whose death was inst., 10 July, 1419,

Stephen Pakyn, chaplain; patrons, the *President* and Chapter of Exeter, ii, 200b.

MORTHOE, Chantry[1] in the Church of; Incumbents—

William Dagfen; on whose resignation was inst., 31 July, 1399,

William Wythy, priest; patron, Elizabeth Lancastre, Duchess of Exeter and Countess of Huntingdon, by a concession granted to her by her husband, John, Duke of Exeter, ii, 13. On Wythye's (*sic*) resignation

Robert Ballerd, chaplain, was inst., 17 Sept., 1402 (proxy—Richard Noreys, chaplain), patron, K. Hen. IV.; ii, 63b. Ballard (*sic*) exchanged, 25 Feb., 1407-8, with

Thomas Skede (V. of Bridgerule), patron, the same ii, 100b. Skydye (*sic*) exchanged, 3 Dec., 1411, with

Robert Trybbe (for his Chantry of St. Leonard's, Raleigh); patron, the same, ii, 137.

MORVAL, Vicars of—

Godfrey Tullok; on whose resignation was inst., 25 Jan., 1403-4,

Peter Clastek, chaplain; patron, the Prior and Convent of St. German's, ii, 74.

MORWENSTOWE [Morewenstowe, MS.], Vicars of—

Walter Vox; on whose death was collated, 23 Feb., 1407-8,

Robert Tayllour, chaplain; the Mandate for his Induction was directed to the Archdeacon of *Totnes*; ii, 100.

MULLION [Sancti Melani], Vicars of—

Robert Bolham; on whose death was inst., 19 Dec., 1417.

William Caam, chaplain; patrons, the *President* and Chapter of Exetor, ii, 188b.

MUSBURY [Mousbury, MS.], Rectors of

Robert Mareschall; who exchanged, 15 May, 1403, with

John Hylle (V. of Harberton); patron, Edward, Earl of Devon, ii, 67.

MYLOR [Sancti Meloris], Vicars of—

Ralph Frankeleyn; on whose death was inst., 16 March, 1401-2,

Richard Treles, chaplain; patron, William Cullyng, Provost of Glasney, ii. 21.

NEWENHAM ABBEY [Nywcham, MS.],—

Nicholas Wysbech; confirmed, 29 Oct., 1413; ii, 153b.

NEWTON FERRERS [Nywaton, MS.], Rectors of—

Henry Blakborne; on whose death was inst., 29 July, 1399,

---

[1] This Chantry was dedicated to St. Katherine and St. Mary Magdalene, *see* ii, 137.

John Andrew, priest ; patron, Martin Ferrers, ii, 12b. On Andrew's death was inst., 18 Feb., 1418-19,

Richard Tryby, chaplain ; patron, "hac vice," Alexander Champernoun, Esquire, ii, 197. Commissions of Enquiry (1) dated 27 Sept., 1418, ii, 266b ; (2) on the presentation of John Thomas, chaplain, by Sir John Cornewaylle, knt., dated 18 Nov., 1418, *ibid.*

NORTHAM, Vicars of—

Brian Sloman ; on whose death was inst., 1 Feb., 1405-6,

Christopher Jacob, chaplain ; patron, the Warden and Canons of Ottery, ii, 88. On Jacob's death

Henry Clement, chaplain, was inst., 22 June, 1419 ; ii, 199b.

NORTH BOVEY, Rectors of—

Richard Hale ; on whose resignation was inst., 11 April, 1396,

Ralph Peryn de Polmargh, priest ; patron, "hac vice" Osbert Hamely, ii, 5. He exchanged, 12 July, 1398, with

William Donscombe (V. of St. Merryn) ; patron, Thomas de Berkeley, Lord of Berkeley, ii, 38. On the death of Dunscumb (*sic*)

Robert Kyngewyll, chaplain, was inst., 8 Feb., 1417-18 ; patrons, Thomas Criave and John Throkmorton, Esquires, and John Baisham, clerk, ii, 189. Commission of Enquiry, 28 Jan., 1417-18, ii, 264.

NORTH HUISH [Hywysch, Northywysch *and* Northȝhywysch, MS.], Rectors of—

William Robyn ; on whose death was inst., 29 March, 1398,

Thomas Tremayn, clerk ; patron, Isabella Daumarle, ii, 8b. On whose institution to Aveton Giffard, 3 June, 1403, and consequent resignation,

John Combe, chaplain, was inst. 27 June, 1403 (proxy—Arnulph Langryg) ; patron, Isabella, relict of Sir John Daumarle, knt., ii, 67b. On Combe's death

Thomas Tremayn, priest, was again inst., 18 Sept., 1412 (proxy—Nicholas Tremayn) ; patrons, "hac vice," William Fokeray and Richard Brouste, chaplain, ii, 144b. Within six years, Tremayn again resigned this benefice, and

Robert Alkebarowe, chaplain, was inst., 24 Feb., 1417-18; patrons, the same, ii, 189b.

NORTHILL [Northull, MS.], Rectors of—

John Redeclyf ; on whose death was inst., 7 Dec., 1407,

Walter Robert, LL.B. ; patron, Edward, Earl of Devon, ii, 99. On Robert's death

Richard Donscomb, chaplain, was inst., 10 Sept., 1415, ii, 169.

NORTHLEIGH, Rectors of—

Stephen Josep ; on whose resignation was inst., 28 March, 1401,

Robert Julyan, chaplain ; patrons, Lucy Warre (Abbess) and the Convent of Canonsleigh, ii, 17.

NORTH LEW [Northlyw, MS.], Rectors of—

Richard atte Yate ; who exchanged, 8 March, 1395-6, with

Richard More (R. of Brushford, Dioc. of B. and W., patron, Sir Robert Cornu, knt.) ; patron, "hac vice" John Holland, Earl of Huntingdon, ii, 4. Commission dated 7 Sept., 1395 ; ii, 211.

NORTH MOLTON, Rectors of—

Richard Raundes ; on whose death was collated, *by lapse*, 27 Sept., 1400,

Laurence Haukyn, chaplain ; ii, 50b. He exchanged, 23 June, 1406, with his nephew,

Richard More (R. of St. Columb-major) *See* i, 333 ; patrons, the Warden and Canons of St. George's, Windsor, ii, 89b.

NORTH TAWTON [*alias* Chepyngtauton, MS.], Rectors of—

John Northwode; on whose death was inst., 29 Jan., 1397-8,

John Buure, priest: patron, Richard Hankeford, "hac vice," in right of his wife Thomasia, daughter and heir of Sir Richard Stapilton, knt., Lord of Estyngton, in the said parish, ii, 8.

NORTH TIDWORTH [North Tudworth Meeles, MS.], *see* OTTERY, ii, 136b.

NORTON, Prebend in the church of (Dioc. of Durham), *see* OTTERY, ii, 100b.

NYMET ROWLAND [Rolond, MS.], Rectors of—

Robert Forde; who exchanged, 1 March, 1402-3, with

John Gyffard (for his Chantry of Umberleigh); patron, John Copleston, ii, 25b. It is not stated that Gyffard resigned; but he was collated to Buckland Filleigh, 28 Nov., 1408 (*see* ii, 103b), and 5 Dec., in the same year,

William Cook, chaplain, was inst.; patron, the same, ii, 104. On the death of Coke (*sic*)

Roger Blakhay, chaplain, was inst., 22 Dec., 1417; patron, John Copleston, *senior*, ii, 189.

NYMET ST. GEORGE, Rectors of—

Robert Byngham; on whose resignation was inst., 12 Nov., 1407,

Robert Holewny, chaplain; patrons, Matthew Doune, chaplain, and John Westcomb, ii, 99.

NYMET TRACEY [i.e. Bow], Rector of—

William Bremelcombe, clerk, inst., 23 Aug., 1399; patron, K. Richard II., ii, 42b.

OAKE [Oke, MS.], Dioc. of B. and W., *see* STOODLEIGH, ii, 83b.

OARE [Are, MS.], R., Dioc. of B. and W., *see* RALEGH, ii, 64b.

OCKENDON [Wokyngton, MS.], South, *see* OTTERY, ii, 139b.

OKEFORD [*also* Okford, MS.], Rectors of—

Edward Gyst; on whose death was inst., 19 Dec., 1409,

Nicholas Hertecombe, chaplain; patron, Matilda, Countess of Salisbury, ii, 108. On the death of Hyrtecombe (*sic*)

Humphrey Bonyour, chaplain, was inst., 5 Dec., 1412 (proxy—Alan Aspe; ii, 146b.—A Commission of Enquiry had been issued 18 Nov., 1412, ii, 249b. On the death of Bonyour ["Bungent," MS.],

Thomas Durnell, chaplain, was inst., 25 Sept., 1416 (proxy—Richard Palmer, chaplain); ii, 179.—Commission of Enquiry, dated 31 Aug., 1416, ii, 259b.

OKEHAMPTON [Okhampton, MS.], Vicars of—

Richard Yestebrok; on whose death was inst., 17 Dec. 1413,

John Newecum, chaplain; patron, K. Henry V., ii, 154.

OTTERTON PRIORY [Otritonia *alias* Oterton, MS.]—

[*Thomas Pagu*; admitted 19 Aug., 1393], was succeeded by

Robert Magne, monk of St. Michael's "in periculo maris," who was collated "jure libere devoluto" 30 Sept., 1403; ii, 69b. [He appears to have been the last Prior: the Priory, with the manor and church of Sidmouth, was annexed by Henry V., 20 April, 1415, to his foundation of Sion House, Middlesex (Oliver's *Monast.* p. 248)].

OTTERTON [Oterton, MS.], Vicars of—

Walter Caprygg; on whose death was inst., 25 April, 1416,

Nicholas Broke, chaplain; patrons, Sir Henry Fitz Hugh and Sir John Rodevale, knights, and Robert Morton, Esquire, ii, 176.

OTTERY ST. MARY, the Collegiate Church of—

Wardens :—

John Coterell "occurs as Warden (according to *Oliver*) in 1387." He resigned and was inst. to Axmouth, V., Feb., 1397.

William Slade succeeded, having resigned Axmouth, ii, 212.

John Bokelond, chaplain, succeeded, on the death of Slade, 28 Sept., and was collated, 17 Oct., 1399 : i, 29 ; ii, 43. He exchanged with

John Typet (R. of South Ockendon [Wokyngton, MS.], Dioc. of London ; patron, Maurice Bruyn, domicellus), and was collated, 3 Feb., 1411-12 ; ii, 139b. On Typet's death

John Sarger, priest, M.A., and Scholar in Theology, was collated, 28 Jan., 1414-15 ; ii, 163b.

Ministers :—

John Langelegh ; on whose death was collated, 21 Dec., 1404,

Richard Olyver, deacon, ii, 81b. He exchanged 6 Nov., 1407, with

Roger Langeman (R. of East Allington), ii, 98b ; on whose death

Robert Wantyng, chaplain, was collated, 30 Nov., 1408, ii, 103b. He exchanged, 1 Dec., 1411, with

John Goldeney (R. of North Tidworth, Dioc. of Salisbury), ii, 136b.

Precentors :—

John Bryver ; on whose death

Walter Robert, LL.B., was collated, 21 Feb., 1408-9 ; ii, 104b. He resigned, and

John Lane, chaplain, succeeded, 6 Oct., 1410 ; ii, 123b. Lane exchanged, 18 Aug., 1411, with

Thomas Ferrers (R. of East Ogwell), ii, 135.

Sacristans :—

Roger Perer ; on whose resignation

John Hamound, chaplain, was collated, 24 Oct., 1395 ; (proxy—Robert Alkebarowe), ii, 28.

Canons, Collations of :—

John Candelesby, clerk (Dioc. of Lincoln), to a Canonry and the 8th Prebend, on the resignation of

John de Garton ; 5 July, 1395, ii, 27.

Thomas Hereford, clerk, to a Canonry and Prebend (on the resignation of *Robert Alkebarwe*, 22 Oct., 1401 ; ii, 55b.

William Rayner, chaplain (R. of Rodmerton, Dioc. of Worcester), by exchange with the above-named *Thomas Hereford*, 13 Nov., 1401 ; ii, 55b.

Robert Alkebarow, chaplain, again, to a Canonry and the 7th Prebend (lately held by *John Vincent*), 14 Nov., 1401 ; ii, 56.

Walter Gybbes (proxy—Thomas Redeman, chaplain), to a Canonry and the 6th Prebend (on the death of John Byttellysgate), 14 Sept., 1404 ; ii, 78b.

Reginald Bryta, chaplain, to a Canonry and the 7th Prebend (on the resignation of Robert Alkebarowe), 2 Aug., 1407 ; ii, 97b. He exchanged 27 Feb., 1407-8, with

William de Wyke, clerk (Prebendary in the church of Norton, Dioc. of Durham), ii, 100b. But he resigned, 3 March, and

Reginald Bryta was again collated to the same Prebend, ii, 100b ; but soon after exchanged it (together with his R. of Bridestowe) with

John Prata (R. of Dittisham), 30 Sept., 1409 ; ii, 106b. *Prata* exchanged both preferments, 24 May, 1413, with

John Wykyngston (R. of St. Pancras, London), ii, 150b.

Roger Hampton, chaplain, to a Canonry and the 8th Prebend, (on the resignation of the above-named *John Candelesby*) 29 June, 1413 ; ii, 151b.

Henry Blakemore, chaplain, to a Canonry and the 6th Prebend (on the death of *William Langeton*), 9 Feb., 1413-14, ii, 155b.

John Watere was collated, 20 Feb., 1413-14 (proxy—John Lauerence), to a Canonry and the 7th Prebend, by exchange with *John Wykyngston* above-named, for his Minor Canonry in St. Paul's Cathedral and his Chantry,

founded therein for the souls of Robert Drayton and John Chishull; ii, 155b.
This Canon (here called "atte Water"), exchanged, 14 June, 1414, with
Walter Robert (Canon and Preb. in Glasney) ii, 159; who died shortly afterwards, and was succeeded by
John Schute, chaplain, 28 Oct., 1415; ii, 173b. On whose resignation
John Podynghaye was collated, 25 May, 1417; ii, 186.

OVER STOWEY, V. (Dioc. of B. and W.), *see* CHARLES, R., ii, 48b.

PADSTOW [Padrystow, MS.], Vicars of—
John Stephyn; on whose resignation was inst., 16 Nov., 1400,
Laurence Merther, chaplain; patrons, the Prior and Convent of Bodmin, ii, 51b.

PAIGNTON [Peyngton, MS.], Vicars of—
Thomas Ayesschperton; on whose death was collated, 22 Feb., 1406-7,
John Schute, chaplain, ii, 94b. On his collation to a Canonry in Ottery (28 Oct., 1415; see ii, 173b), Schute resigned, and
Richard Pendels, chaplain, was collated, 15 July, 1416, ii, 177b. This Vicar exchanged, 18 Aug., in the same year, with
William Bruter, (R. of Moreton Hampstead); proxy—John Schute, chaplain, ii, 178b. On Bruter's death
John Cobethorn, chaplain, was collated, 1 Jan., 1417-18; ii, 189. Cobethorn exchanged, 17 May, 1418, with
Nicholas Lovecok (R. of St. Ive), ii, 191b.

PARKHAM—
John Fairforde; on whose death was inst., 5 April, 1398,
John Radeclyff, priest; patrons, Sir John Wadham, knt., William Hankeforde, Thomas Beaumond, John Bydewille, and Henry Crosse, by virtue of a feoffment of the manor and advowson of Parkham to them made by Wm., son and heir of Sir John Beaumond, knt., ii, 8b. On Radeclyf's (*sic*) resignation
John Fouk, clerk, was inst., 17 June, 1399; patrons, Roger Beaumount, R. of Bideford, John Stoke, R. of Heanton [Punchardon], and William Schute, R. of Tedburn; by virtue of a feoffment of the said manor and advowson to them made by the above-named Sir John Wadham, knt., Thomas Beaumount, William Hankeforde, John Bydewyll, and Henry Crosse, ii, 12b. On Fouke's death
Richard Graynevyll, LL.B., was inst., 7 Oct., 1406: patrons, William Durneford and Alice his wife, ii, 92.

PARLEY, R. (Dioc. of Salisbury), *see* WASHFIELD, R., ii, 142.

PAUL [Sancti Pauli, MS.] Vicars of—
Odo Bost; on whose resignation was inst., 26 Feb., 1417-18,
John Patry, chaplain; patrons, the Abbot and Convent of Hales, ii, 190. Commission of Enquiry, dated 10 Feb., 1417-18; ii, 264.

PARRACOMBE [Parrecomb, MS.], Rectors of—
John Wynsham; on whose resignation, was inst., 17 Jan., 1397-8,
Matthew Doune, priest; patron, Philip Fitzwaryn, ii, 7b. On the resignation of Downe (*sic*),
Thomas Galon de Fayreford, was inst., 10 Sept., 1400; patron, the same, ii, 50. This Rector exchanged, 8 Oct., 1404, with
Thomas Dygon (V. of Kingston, Dioc. of B. and W.); patron, John Seyntabyn, domicellus, ii, 79b. On whose resignation
John Lyngdon, chaplain, was inst., 30 Oct., 1413; patron, Robert Whytefeylde de Parracombe, ii, 153b.

PAYHEMBURY, Vicars of—
Richard Lauerans; on whose death was inst., 20 April, 1413,
Thomas Rondoulf, chaplain; patrons, the Abbot and Convent of Forde, ii, 150.

PELYNT [Pleuynt *or* Plenynt, MS.], Vicars of—

Robert Herry; on whose death was inst., 26 Dec., 1395,

Robert Walter, priest; patron, Sir John Herle, knt. (the Manor and Rectory of Pelynt having been farmed to him by the Abbot and Convent of Newenham), ii, 2. On Walter's resignation

John Bele, chaplain, was inst., 11 Oct., 1414; patron, the Abbot of Newenham. The Bishop assigned to Robert Walter, "senio confractum et impotentem," 8 marks *per annum*, in quarterly payments, "pro victu et vestitu. . . . . durante ipsius vita."

PELYNT, Chantry-Chapel of St. Nun [Sancte Nynnine,],—

John Bele, afterwards V. of Pelynt, chaplain, was collated *by lapse*, 18 June, 1409; ii, 106.

PENNE, R. (Dioc. of B and W.), *see* WARKLEIGH, R., ii, 54^{b}.

PENRYN, *see* ST. GLUVIAS.

PERRAN-UTHNO [Uthenow, MS.] Rectors of—

William Mayhow; on whose death was inst., 10 Nov., 1414,

Hugh Sperke, chaplain; patron, John Whalysbrow, domicellus, ii, 162^{b}.

PETER TAVY [Tavy Sancti Petri, MS.], Rectors of—

Paschasius Rogger; on whose death was collated, 1 June, 1401,

John Hethen, chaplain: ii, 53^{b}. On whose resignation (for Talaton, R.),

John Franke was collated, 11 July, 1404; ii, 77^{b}.

PETROCKSTOWE, Rectors of—

John Gaylard; on whose death was inst., 26 May, 1413,

John Herward, chaplain; patrons of Gaylard, the Abbot and Convent of Buckfast, true patrons; patron of Herward (by their concession) for one turn, John Martyn, ii, 151. Commission of Enquiry, dated 22 April, 1413, ii, 251^{b}.

PHILLACK [Sancte Felicitatis, MS.], Rectors of—

William Selby (*see* i, 62, 76^{b}); who seems to have been succeeded by

William Pylton, who was inst., 15 July, 1408; (proxy—Henry Wyngode, LL.B.); patron, Sir John Arundell, knt., ii, 102^{b}. On whose resignation (proxy—Adam Bacon),

John Munford alias *Burybrygg*, chaplain, was inst., 24 July, 1409; ii, 106^{b}. On the resignation of "Mundeford *alias* Burghbrygg" *(sic)*,

Nicholas Bildeston, clerk, was inst. 9 March, 1410-11; ii, 131.

PILLATON [Pylaton, MS.], Rector of—

Major Parys, chaplain, inst., 27 Feb., 1399-1400; patron, Sir John Hulle, knt., ii, 45^{b}.

PILTON PRIORY, Priors of—

William Charlton; on whose death was inst., 4 Jan., 1412-13,

Richard Kengeswode, monk of Malmesbury, patron, the Abbot and Convent of Malmesbury, ii, 147^{b}.

PINHOE [Pynne *and* Pinhoo, MS.], Vicars of—

William Syward; who exchanged, 17 Oct., 1395, with

John Grouse or *Grose* (for his Chantry of St. James in the church of St. Pancras, London, founded for the soul of William Causton); patron, the Prior and Convent of St. Nicholas Priory, Exeter, ii, 27^{b}.—Commission, dated 12 Oct., 1395; ii, 210^{b}. Gruse (*sic*) exchanged, 16 Sept., 1406, with *Stephen Progmer* (V. of Haselbeare—Dioc. of Wells); ii, 92. On his resignation *Thomas Crystow*, chaplain, was inst., 18 May, 1417; ii, 183.

PITMINSTER, V., Dioc. of B. and W., *see* STOODLEIGH, R, ii, 97.

PLYMOUTH, SUTTON juxta, *see* SUTTON.

PLYMTREE, Rectors of—

John Tregenewylle (*also*, Tregrenewyll *and* Grenwyll); on whose death was inst. 17 Dec., 1417.

Thomas Job, clerk, (proxy—Nicholas Bokelly, literate), patron, Margaret Peverel, ii, 188b.

POLSLO PRIORY, Prioresses of—

Christina de Seton; on whose death

Matilda Talbot, was elected, 25 June, and confirmed, 2 July, 1404, ii, 77.

POLTIMORE [Poltemore *and* Poltymor, MS.], Rectors of—

John Smyth; on whose death was inst., 14 March, 1402-3,

John Matthu, chaplain; patron, Thomas de Bampfylde, ii, 26b. On the resignation of Mathu *(sic)*

William Trebele, clerk, LL.B., was inst., 23 June, 1411; patron, John Bampfylde, Lord of Poltimore, ii, 134. About two months later he resigned, and

John Mathu was inst. again, 11 Aug., 1411; patron, the same, ii, 134b.

Richard Aldryngton, chaplain, succeeded, on the resignation of Mathu, 2 Dec., 1413; patron, the same, ii, 152b, 154. On whose resignation was inst., 14 Sept., 1416,

John Germen; patron, the same, ii, 179. This Rector exchanged, 20 April, 1419, with

Peter Lamoren (R. of Lawhitton); patrons, Roger Bolter, clerk, William Hydon, Richard Bamfeld, Thomas Gybbe (R. of Huxham), and John Mathu (who had become V. of Broadclyst, 15 Sept., 1413), ii, 197b. On the death of Lamoren

Thomas Gybbe, chaplain, was inst., 16 June, 1419; patrons, the same (omitting Thomas Gybbe himself), ii, 199b.

PORTLEMOUTH [Portelemouth, MS.], Rectors of—

John Belamyslond; on whose death was inst., 13 Sept., 1399,

William Gore, priest; patron, Sir Richard Champernoun, knt., ii, 13. On Gore's death

John Thomas, deacon, was inst., 22 May, 1405; patron, the same, ii, 84b.

POUGHILL [Rectoria sive Porcio de Poghille, MS.], Prebendaries of—

John Wyllyngham; on whose death was *collated*, 5 Oct., 1408,

Thomas Sprotburgh, clerk; ii, 103. There seems to have been some doubt as to the right of presentation. The Prebend is here described as "vacantem, et ad ipsius Domini collacionem *pleno jure* spectantem," and nothing is said about lapse. But, within three years, the Prebend is again described as vacant; and the same incumbent is not collated, but instituted on the presentation of a private patron,—"Item, secundo die mensis Junii [1411], ibidem [*at Crediton*], dominus admisit Thomam Sprotburgh, clericum, ad Prebendam, sive Porcionem decimarum, de POGHYLLE, alias dictam COLETON PRAL, in parochia capelle curate de Malleburgh, ab ecclesia parochiali de Alvyngton-juxta-Kyngesbrygg dependentis [*i.e.* Malborough, a daughter parish to West Alvington, near Kingsbridge], Exoniensis Diocesis, vacantem; ad quam per dilectum in Christo filium, Johannem Govys, verum ipsius Prebende, sive Porcionis, pattronum, eidem Domino extitit presentatus; et ipsum Prebendarium, sive Porcionarium, instituit canonice in eadem, cum suis juribus et pertinenciis universis," ii, 133.

POUGHILL [Poghwyll, MS.], St. Olave's, in Cornwall, Vicars of—

Walter Copan; on whose death was inst., 24 June, 1417,

William Carter; patrons, the Prior and Convent of Launceston, ii, 186.

POUGHILL [Poghull *and* Poghhulle, MS.], in Devon, Rectors of—

Richard Hopere; on whose resignation was inst., 5 July, 1396,

John Milnere, clerk (proxy—Philip Neweton); patrons, the Prior and Convent of St. Nicholas, Exeter ; ii, 31. Mylnere (*sic*) resigned, and

William Maii, priest, was inst., 16 Oct., 1397 ; ii, 7^{b}. He exchanged, 6 April, 1403 (proxy—Henry Bawdyn) with

Thomas Elys, chaplain, for his Chantry of St. Mary of Herne, Dioc. of Canterbury, ii, 65^{b}. On whose resignation

John Grede, chaplain, was inst., 7 Jan., 1412-13; ii, 147^{b}. He exchanged with *Walter Bury* (V. of Harpford), 10 Feb., 1418-19 ; ii, 197.

POUNDSTOCK, Vicars of—

Benedict Whalysbrow, chaplain, collated, *by lapse*, 7 March, 1402-3, ii, 65^{b}. Commission dated 18 June, 1402, ii, 229. On the death of Whalesbrow (*sic*) was inst., 25 March, 1415,

Richard Trevelyan, chaplain ; patrons, the Rector, etc., of the Coll. Chantry of Slapton, ii, 164. Trevylyan (*sic*) exchanged, 14 Nov., 1416, with

Thomas Haywode (R. of Stoke Rivers) ; patrons, the same, but on the nomination of Robert Hulle, senior, ii, 180.

POWDERHAM, Rectors of—

John Hamound ; on whose resignation was inst., 24 Oct., 1395,

Roger Perer, chaplain (proxy—Thomas Abyngdon) ; patron, Sir Philip Courtenay knt., ii, 28^{b}. On Perer's death

Robert Weye, chaplain, was inst., 3 Aug., 1400 ; ii, 49.

PUDDINGTON [Podynton, MS.], Rectors of—

Gregory Nywelond ; on whose death was inst., 25 Feb., 1397-8,

William Stokhay, priest ; patron, K. Richard II., "occasione forisfacture" of Sir John Cary, knt., ii, 8.

PYWORTHY [Peworth *alias* Pyeworth, MS.], Rectors of—

John Flemmyng ; this Rector (who, after an Inquisition, had been found sound in mind, etc.), exchanged, 27 Jan., 1402-3, with

Richard Traunce (R. of Inwardleigh) ; patron, K. Henry IV., ii, 24^{b}. Commission, ii, 228^{b}. On whose death

Richard Gabriell, clerk, was inst., 5 March, 1404-5. ii, 82^{b}. He resigned and *John Cowyk* was inst., 10 May, 1408 ; proxy—John Olveston, ii, 101^{b}.

QUEEN CAMEL [Quene Cammell, MS.], Dioc. of B. and W. ; *see* CORNWOOD, V., ii, 87^{b}.

QUENNINGTON, R. (Dioc. of Worcester), *see* ST. CLEER, V., ii, 89.

QUETHIOCK [Sancti Hugonis de Quedek, MS.], Vicar of—

John Rogger, chaplain, collated 30 April, 1399, ii, 41.

RACKENFORD [Rackerneforde, MS.], Rectors of—

Robert Alkebarowe ; on whose resignation was inst., 16 June, 1396,

John Croke or *Crooke*, priest ; patron, "hac vice," Matthew Hordelegh, ii, 5^{b}. On whose death

Robert Cruwes, chaplain, was inst., 19 May, 1413 (proxy—Richard Reymound) ; patrons, Matthew Hordelegh and Juliana, his wife (formerly wife of Alexander Creuwes), ii, 150^{b}. Commissions of Enquiry (6 March and 24 March 1412-13, and 20 April, 1413), ii, 250^{b}, 251^{b}.

RALEIGH, Chantry of St. Leonard's, in the parish of Pilton—

John Neue or *Neve*, on whose resignation was inst., 12 March, 1399-1400,

Thomas Prydel or *Prydew*, chaplain, ii, 15. He exchanged, 3 Nov., 1402, with

Robert Trybbe (R. of Oare [Are, MS.], Dioc. of B. and W.) ; patron, Sir William Talbot, knt, ii, 64^{b}. Trybbe exchanged, 3 Dec., 1411, with

Thomas Skydye (for his Chantry of St. Katherine and St. Mary Magd., in the Church of Morthoe) ; patrons, John Chechester, Richard Hankeford, and Henry Foleford, ii, 137. On the resignation of Skydye

John Parle, chaplain, was inst., 30 March, 1417 ; patrons, the same, ii, 182b. On whose resignation

Thomas John, de Helleston, chaplain, was inst., 2 May, 1418 ; patrons, the same, ii, 191.

RATTERY [Rattrew, MS.], Vicars of—

John Tomme ; who exchanged, 23 Dec., 1417, with

John Colyn (R. of Mamhead) ; patrons, the Abbot and Convent of St. Mary and St. Dogmael in Kemeys, ii, 189.

REWE, Rectors of—

John Carmynel ; on whose death was inst., 13 Feb., 1400-1,

Thomas Warre, clerk ; patron, John Chuselden, ii, 52b. He exchanged, 15 April, 1402, with

John Pytte (R. of Chardlynch, Dioc. of B. and W.) ; patron, John Chiseldon (*sic*), ii, 21b. He exchanged, 5 Aug., 1402, with

Thomas Vesey (R. of Warkleigh) ; patron, the same, ii, 22b.

RINGMORE [Rydemore, MS.], Rectors of—

John Mayn ; on whose death was inst., 17 June, 1396,

John Stancomb ; patrons, Sir James Chuddelegh, knt., John Hulle (of Exeter), and James Durburgh ; by virtue of a feofment which had been made to them by the true patron, Nicholas Kyrkham, domicellus (deceased), ii, 5b.

ROBOROUGH [Rowburgh, MS.], Rectors of—

John Wayssehbourne ; on whose death was inst., 21 March, 1398-9,

Richard Colebrugg, priest ; patron, Richard Hankeforde, by right of his wife Thomasia, daughter and heir of Sir Richard Stapeldon, knt., ii, 12. On the death of Colebrygge (*sic*)

John Gorewyll, jun., clerk, LL.B., was inst. (proxy—Henry Wade, priest) ; patron the same, ii, 25b. There is no record of his resignation ; but he was inst. to Wyke St. Mary, 5 Aug., 1406 (*see* ii, 90b). and

Richard Graynevyll, LL.B., was inst. to this parish, 23 Aug. ; ii, 91b. On whose resignation, 30 Nov., 1409 (i, 91),

John Jarberd, clerk, was inst., 5 Feb., 1409-10 ; ii, 108b. Jerbard (*sic*) exchanged, 23 March, 1412-13, with

Edward Dauntesey (R. of Ashwater) ; ii, 148. Within a month Dauntesey was consecrated Bishop of Meath, and resigned Roborough ; and

John Fayrest, chaplain, was instituted, 10 April, 1413 ; ii, 149.

ROCHE, Rectors of—

John Rede, chaplain, inst., 20 Feb., 1396-7 ; patron, Sir John Dynham, knt., ii, 33. On whose resignation when instituted to South Pool,

John Shyrley, clerk, was inst., 3 May, 1398 ; (proxy—John Whytewaye, clerk) ; ii, 8b. On whose resignation

Walter Peion, clerk, was inst., 13 June, 1399 ; (by proxy—John Whytewaye, clerk), ii, 12b. Peion soon resigned, and

John Shirley was again inst. (same proxy), 17 Nov., 1400 ; ii, 51b.

John Beare, chaplain, followed : he was instituted 27 March, 1402—"pro eo quod quidam Johannes Shirley, ultimus ipsius ecclesie Rector, infra annum a tempore commissi sibi regiminis prefate ecclesie et pacifice possessionis ejusdem assecute numerandum, ad sacerdocium, juxta canonicas sancciones, justo impedimento cessante, se fecit minime promoveri." Beare's patrons were James Daumarle, John Pole, Robert Maynard, Thomas Hertescote, and John Bole—ii, 57b.

ROCKBEARE [Rokebeare *and* Rokebear, MS.], Vicars of—

John Pyllegh ; on whose resignation was collated 23 Feb., 1405-6,

Hugh Germyn, chaplain, ii, 88b.

John Belde, chaplain, was collated 22 April, 1418, ii, 190b.

RODMERTON, R., Dioc. of Worcester, *see* OTTERY, ii, 55b.

ROMANSLEIGH [Romoundeslegh, MS.], Rectors of—

Nicholas Joye; on whose death was inst., 10 May, 1416,

John Dayhyll, chaplain; patron, John, son and heir of Robert Haeche, ii, 176b.

ROSEASH [Aysch Raff *and* Esserauf, MS.], Rectors of—

William Lane; who exchanged, 20 Dec., 1404, with

William Halyett alias *Hamme* (*see* i, 5), R. of Chulmleigh; patrons, John Bury, William de Wyllemere, Thomas Colyn, Andrew de Gyffard and William Langedon; ii, 80b. On the death of Halyet *(sic)*

Richard Reve (or *Reue*), chaplain, was inst. (proxy—Richard Welfare, chaplain), 15 May, 1406; patrons, John Bury and Thomas Colyn, domicelli, ii. 89b.

ROTHERFIELD [Retherfeld, MS.], Dioc. of Chichester; *see* UGBOROUGH, R., ii, 84.

ROUSDON [Rous Down *alias* Ralph Down; "Sancti Pancracii-juxta-Axemouth"; "Sancti Pancracii de Doun, juxta Lyme," MS.], Rectors of—

Robert Loudeney; on whose death was inst., 18 April, 1407,

John Wattys, chaplain; patron, K. Henry IV, ii, 96. On the resignation of Wattes *(sic)*

Roger Whytyng, chaplain, was inst., 11 June, 1408; ii, 102. On Whytyng's death

Nicholas Schaldon, chaplain, was inst., 7 July, 1410; ii, 120; and 28 June, 1414,

Hugh Lyne, chaplain, was inst.; patron, K. Henry V, ii, 160.

[RUAN-] LANYHORNE, Rectors of—

John Bradwyll; on whose death was inst., 16 May, 1414,

Thomas Harry, chaplain; patron, Thomas Arundell, of Cornwall, ii, 158b.

RUAN-MAJOR [Sancti Rumoni magni, MS.], Rectors of—

John Peuleyn, on whose death was inst., 6 Dec., 1398,

Stephen Gerveys, clerk (proxy—Robert Lywer, R. of Drewsteignton); patron, John Trevarthyou *(sic)*, domicellus, ii, 10. On whose death

Thomas Jacka (*alias* Jowydavy, *see*, i, 181), chaplain, was inst., 27 Aug., 1400; patron, Sir John Trevarthyan, knt., ii, 50.

RUDBAXTON [Rudpaxton, MS.], R. (Dioc. of St. David's), *see* Alwington, R., ii, 179.

ST. ANTONY-IN-KERRIER [Sancti Antonii, *sive* Antonini, in Kerrier, MS.], Vicars of—

John Dyre; on whose resignation was inst., 18 April, 1415,

Thomas Orian, chaplain; patron, K. Henry V. (the temporalities of Tywardreath Priory being in his hands, during the war with France), ii, 164b. On the death of Orion *(sic)*

John Oppy, chaplain, was inst., 24 May, 1418; patrons, the Prior and Convent of Tywardreath, ii, 191b. Commission, dated 30 April, 1418, ii, 265.

ST. AUSTELL [de Sancto Austolo, MS.], Vicars of—

John Juyll; on whose death was inst., 11 Dec., 1414,

Vivian Codan, chaplain; patron, K. Henry V, ii, 162b.

ST. AUSTELL [Sancti Austoli, MS.], Chantry Chapel of St. Michael in the Cemetery of (to which was annexed the R. of St. Clether)—

Henry Stonton; he exchanged, 10 Feb., 1400-1401, with

William Markowe (V. of Hutton, Dioc. of London; patrons, the Dean and Chapter of St. Paul's); patrons, the Prior and Convent of Tywardreath, ii, 52b. I find no record of Markowe's resignation or death; but, 20 Oct., 1408,

John Soor, chaplain, was inst., patron, K. Henry IV, ii, 103. He exchanged 25 Feb., 1409-10, with
Thomas Hendeman, chaplain, S.T.P., Dean of Crantock (proxy—William Clyve, R. of Whitstone); ii, 108b. On Hendeman's resignation,
John Sutton, chaplain, LL.B., was inst., 22 Aug., 1411; patron, the same, ii, 135.

ST. BREAGE [Sancte Breace, MS.], Vicars of—
John Ude; on whose death was inst., 8 Sept., 1403,
William Pensans, chaplain; patrons, the Abbot and Convent of Hales (Dioc. of Worcester), ii, 69.

ST. BREOKE [Pouton, *alias* Nansant, MS.], Rectors of—
William Sutton; on whose death was collated, 21 March, 1415-16,
John Schute, chaplain; ii, 175. On whose resignation
John Worthyn, was collated, 21 Sept., 1417; ii, 187b.

ST. BREWARD [Sancti Brueredi, MS.], Vicars of—
John Hoky; on whose death was inst., 1 April, 1419,
Reginald Russell, chaplain; patrons, the *President* and Chapter of Exeter, ii, 197b.

ST. CLEER, Vicars of—
Roger Tredynec; on whose death was inst., 23 July, 1400,
William Hopkyn, chaplain; patron [Robert Normanton, for] the Prior of the Hospital of St. John of Jerusalem, in England, ii, 49. He exchanged, 5 Oct., 1400, with
William Wryght (R. of Icklesham [Ilesham, MS.], Dioc. of Chichester); patrons, the same, ii, 51.
Walter Lambard, chaplain, succeeded, 29 May, 1405 (proxy—Thomas Cook, chaplain); patron, Walter Grendon, Prior of the said Hospital, ii, 84b. Lambard exchanged, 8 March, 1405-6, with
John Chaundeler (R. of Quennington, Dioc. of Worcester, proxy—Robert Hopkyns), ii, 88b. On the death of Chandeler *(sic)*
Stephen Stokes, chaplain, was inst., 15 Jan., 1406-7; ii, 94. On whose death
William Dawe, chaplain, was inst., 7 March, 1412-13; ii, 148.

ST. CLEMENT'S[1] [Lamorek, MS.], Vicars of—
William Bealde; on whose death was inst., 23 July, 1400,
Thomas Nahillyn, chaplain; patrons, the Provost and Chapter of Glasney, ii, 48b. On Nahyllyn's death
John Lamledyr, chaplain, was inst., 18 Oct., 1400; patrons, the same, but on the nomination of William Bodrygan, ii, 15b. I find no mention of his death or resignation; but apparently
Walter Fraunces, inst. 26 March, 1409, was his immediate successor; patron, the Prior of St. Michael's Mount, ii, 105.

ST. CLETHER [Sancti Clederi, MS., *also* "de Sancto Cledero"], Vicars of—
Richard Bray; on whose death was inst., 21 May, 1397.
John Carwargh, priest; patron, Henry Staunton, R. of St. Clether, ii, 7. His resignation is not recorded; but he was instituted to St. Mary Church in the autumn of 1403 (though the exact date has not been preserved) and
John Hauk, chaplain, succeeded him, 18 Nov., 1403; patron, K. Henry IV. (as holding the temporalities of the alien Priory of Tywardreath, during the war with France). ii, 70. On Hauk's resignation
William Wille, chaplain, was inst., 27 Feb., 1413-14; patron, John Sutton, chaplain of St. Michael's in the Cemetery of St. Austell; ii, 156b. Commission, dated 10 Jan., 1413-14, ii, 253.

---

[1] Near Truro.—the Manor of "Moreak," called the parish "de Moreak," at ii, 105.

ST. COLAN [Sancte Colani, MS.], Vicars of—
William Hykdon; on whose death was collated, 7 Jan., 1406-7,
John Tewyn, chaplain; ii, 94. On whose death
Thomas Harry, chaplain, was collated, 5 June, 1411; ii, 133. On whose resignation
Richard Wyllyam, chaplain, was collated, 29 July, 1412; ii, 142b. This Vicar exchanged with
Stephen Reskyr (V. of St. Cubert), who was collated, 18 Oct., 1412; (proxy—Henry Wynnegode); ii, 145.

ST. COLUMB-MAJOR [Sancte Columbe majoris, MS.], Rectors of—
John Bray; on whose death was inst., 11 March, 1398-9,
John Fecos, priest; patron, John Aroundell, domicellus, ii, 11b. He exchanged, 6 July, 1399, with
Ralph Rudruth (S.T.P., see ii, 28b), R. of Creed (John Tregois being proxy for Rudruth, and Hervey Wyket for Fecos): patron, the same, ii, 42. On Rudruth's death
Richard More, clerk, was inst., 25 June, 1404; patron (and to the end of the period), Sir John Arundell, knt., ii, 76b. More exchanged, 23 June, 1406, with
Laurence Haukyn (R. of North Molton); ii, 89b. His resignation is not recorded; but
John Ikelyngton, chaplain, apparently his immediate successor, was instituted (proxy—John Foughler, clerk), 31 March, 1411; ii, 131b. He exchanged 8 Dec., 1411, with
Peter de Alcobass (R. of St. Mary's, Southampton—patron, the Bishop of Winchester); his proxy being Richard Palmer, and for Alcobass, John Foughler; ii, 137b. On his resignation
Hervey Wyket, clerk, was inst., 14 Aug., 1416; ii, 178b. On Wyket's resignation
John Bremor, chaplain, was inst., 16 Sept., 1417; ii, 187. On whose death
Richard Aldryngton, alias *Colcombe*, chaplain, succeeded 27 Nov., 1418; ii, 195b.

St. CUBERT [Sancti Cuthberti *and* Cutberti, MS.], Vicars of—
John Midderhille: he exchanged, 11 June, 1399, with
Stephen Reskyer (V. of Colaton Raleigh), Ralph Dollebeare being proxy for Reskyer, and Hervey Wyket for Midderhille; patron, the Prior and Convent of Bodmin, ii, 41. Resker (*sic*) exchanged, 18 Oct., 1412, with
Richard Wyllyam (V. of St. Colan); proxy—Henry Wynnegode; ii, 145b.

ST. DOMINICK [Sancte Dominice, MS.], Rectors of—
John Ernam; on whose resignation was inst., 19 Dec., 1397,
Roger Waterman, priest: patron, Sir William Coggeshale, knt., ii, 7b. On Waterman's death
Thomas Coulyng, chaplain, was inst., "ad ecclesiam parochialem Sancte Dominice *de Halton*," 4 Aug., 1418; patron, Robert Hylle, lord of Halton, ii, 193b.

ST. ENDELLION [Sancte Endeliente, MS.], Rectors of—
Roger Masek; on whose death was inst., 20 March, 1402-3,
John Harry, chaplain; patron, the Prior and Convent of Bodmin, ii, 26 "Harry" (*sic*) exchanged 19 March, 1404-5, with
Thomas Berty (V. of St. Gwinear), proxy—William Redenerth; ii, 83. "Thomas Albon" occurs as Rector, 8 Oct., 1410;[1] but there is no record of

[1] Item dictis die et loco [Crediton 8 Oct., 1410], emanavit litera compulsoria pro domino Thomas Albon, Rectore ecclesie parochialis Sancte Endeliente, Exoniensis Diocesis, licenciato de non residendo per dominum Edmundum, Exoniensem Episcopum predictum, directa Magistro Johanni Coulyng, Vicario perpetuo Ecclesie parochialis Sancte Minerve (*sic*) ac

his institution. It is possible that "Albon" was an *alias* of Thomas Berty; at any rate it was Berty, who 28 Dec., 1410, exchanged this Benefice with *John Worthyn* or *Wortham* (R. of Farringdon); ii, 129b. There is no record of Worthyn's resignation or death; but the parish must have been vacant for not less than six months when, 6 April, 1414, the Bishop collated *John Wolston*, clerk, *by lapse*, ii, 158. His successor, *William Gorteboos*, clerk, was inst., 3 Aug., 1418; patron, the Prior and Convent of Bodmin (as before), ii, 178b.

ST. ENDELLION, "Bodmin" Prebend in the Church of,—*Prebendaries*—

Richard Bruton; on whose death was inst., 27 Dec., 1417, *John Arundell*, alias *Hylle* (proxy—Andrew Lanvyan, clerk); ii, 189.

ST. ENDELLION, [Trehaverock] Prebend in the Church of—*Prebendaries*—

Matthew Bodrygy; on whose resignation was inst., 3 June, 1400, *Hervey Wyket*, clerk; patron, Sir John Aroundell, knt.. by grant of the turn from Elizabeth, relict of William Bray, of Treworlas; ii, 46b.

ST. ENODER [Sancti Enodori, MS.], Vicars of—

Peter Gerveys; on whose resignation was inst., 26 May, 1396, *Richard Osmond*, chaplain; ii, 30b.

ST. ERME [Sancti Heremitis, MS.], Rectors of—

John Tregek; on whose death was inst., 9 March, 1405, *William Kylyow*, chaplain; patron, "hac vice," Guy Sentabyn, domicellus, ii, 82b.—There can be no doubt that "ecclesia parochialis Sancti Heremitis" means, here, the Church and parish near Truro, now called "St. Erme," for I find, from Bishop Lacy's Register, that, on the death of William Kylyow, Thomas Markanut was inst., 2 May, 1432; patrons, Nicholas Thorley and Alice, his wife; and in the same Register (ii, 152) this benefice is described as "Ecclesia Sancti Ermetis *juxta Truru*," the patrons being the same. But there was *another* ST. ERME [Sancti Ermetis, MS.], R., to which the Bishop collated, and which is described as "ad ipsius Domini collacionem pleno jure spectantem." On the death of *John Mark*, *John Burgoun*, chaplain, was collated 16 July, 1415; ii, 166; and 11 Jan., 1415-16, this Rector exchanged with *Henry Wynnegode*, clerk (R. of Lezant), the Bishop being patron of both benefices, ii, 174b. Is ST. ERVAN intended? Oliver states (Monasticon p. 438) that the Church there was dedicated to "St. Hermes."

ST. ERTH [Sancti Erci, MS.], Vicars of—

Ralph Godman; on whose death was inst., 17 Dec., 1395, *William Talcarne*, priest; patrons, the Dean and Chapter of Exeter, ii, 2.

ST. EWE Rector of—*John Preston* (q. v.)

Domino Thome Cook, capellano, dicte Exoniensis Diocesis, ad compellendum dominum Walterum Maysmere, capellanum, ad deserviendum cure domini Thome Albon, ecclesie parochialis Sancte Endeliente rectoris predicti, necnon primo, secundo, et tercio. ac peremptorie monendum, et efficaciter inducendum ac requirendum prefatum dominum Walterum, quem dictus dominus Edmundus, Exoniensis Episcopus, requisivit et monuit, quod cure predicte deserviat, sub pena suspensionis ab officio in Constitucione Provinciali bone memorie domini Simonis, quondam Cantuariensis Archiepiscopi, in hac parte rite edite et publice promulgate, quem, si hujusmodi monicionibus et requisicionibus infra viginti dierum spacium a tempore monicionum premissorum, cessatis causis legitimis, de quibus causis in litera precedente plenius apparet, non paruerit, eo ipso se noscat incursurum, etc." Vol. i, fol. 107b.

ST. GENNYS [Sancti Genisii, MS.], Vicars of—

Adam Thomas; who exchanged, 21 April, 1412, with

John Lavyngton (V. of St. Andrew's, Yarnscombe); patrons, the Prior and Convent of Launceston, ii, 141b.

ST. GERMAN'S PRIORY, Priors of—

John Averay, on whose death (8 Sept., 1404),

John Pyper was elected (23 Sept.), ii, 78b.

ST. GERRANS [Sancti Gerendi, MS.], Rectors of—

Matthew Bodrygy; who exchanged, 31 July, 1399, with

John Fecos (R. of Creed and Canon and Preb. in Glasney); proxy—William Toket; patron, the Bishop, ii. 42. On the death of Fecos

Walter Bowny, clerk, was collated, 29 June, 1414; ii, 160, but exchanged immediately, viz., 1 July, with

Thomas Watkyn (R of St. John in Cornwall) *ibid.*

ST. GLUVIAS ["Sancti Gluviaci de Penryn," MS.], Vicars of—

John Wryter: on whose death was collated, 23 April, 1414,

Thomas Treedves, chaplain; ii, 158.

ST. GORAN [Sancti Goroni, MS.], Vicars of—

John Noo; on whose death a Commission was directed to Dean Tregrisiow, 26 Oct., 1399, for the collation of

John Quynterell, chaplain (ii, 226), which took place 22 Dec.; ii, 44b.

ST. GWINEAR [Sancti Winneri, MS.], Vicars of—

Thomas Berty; who exchanged, 19 March, 1404-5, with

John Harry (R. of St. Endellion); patron, the Bishop, ii, 83.

ST. HILARY [ecclesia de Sancto Hillario, MS.], Vicars of—

Henry Bray; on whose death was inst., 24 Dec., 1403,

Alan Lannystly, chaplain; patron, K. Henry IV., "racione temporalium Prioratus Sancti Michaelis in Cornubia alienigeni in manu sua occasione guerre inter ipsum et illos de Francia mote existencium;" ii, 74.

ST. ILLOGAN ["Sancti Illogani de Logan" and "Sancti Illogani *alias* Illugani," MS.], Rectors of—

Thomas Colteford (or *Cotford*) occurs as Rector, i, 12; also, ii, 316. After his death

William Styward, chaplain, was inst., 28 April, 1397; patron, "hac vice," K. Richard II., ii. 33b. On Styward's death

John Barell, chaplain, was inst., 26 Feb., 1403-4; patron, K. Henry IV., ii, 74b; but this appointment having been irregularly made (*see* St. Illogan [*Breve Regium*] in the *General Index*), the Church was declared to be vacant and the right of presentation lapsed to the Bishop; who, however, collated the said John Barell, 28 May, 1404; ii, 76.

ST. IVE [Sancti Ivonis, MS.], Rectors of—

Richard Hals; who exchanged, 20 Sept., 1400, with

John Osborn (R. of All Hallows-on-the-Walls, Exeter); patron, Robert Normanton, for the Prior of the Hospital of St. John of Jerusalem, in England, ii, 50b. Osborn exchanged, 8 Aug., 1401, with

William Dyber, chaplain (Warden of the Free Chapel of Kingston-Russell, Dioc. of Salisbury—patron, Sir Maurice Russell, knt.); patron, Walter Grendon, Prior of the aforesaid Hospital, ii, 54. Dyber exchanged, 16 Dec., 1408, with

Nicholas Lovecok (V. of Buckland-Abbas, Dioc. of Salisbury); patron, the same, ii, 104. Lovecok exchanged 17 May, 1418, with

John Cobethorn (V. of Paignton); patron, John Brympston, deputy of William Hulles, Prior of the Order of St. John of Jerusalem, in England, ii, 191b.

ST. JOHN [Sancti Johannis (*also* Sancti Johannis Baptiste) in Cornubia, MS.], Rectors of—

Thomas Tyso; on whose death
Robert Belet, priest, was inst., 9 March, 1398-9; patron, Edward, Earl of Devon, ii, 11. Belet exchanged, 24 Feb., 1401-2, with
John Mychel (R. of Chedington, Dioc. of Salisbury), patron, James Hornesbogh, domicellus); patron, the same; ii, 56^b. On Mychel's resignation
Thomas Watkyn, clerk, was inst., 18 July, 1403; patron, the same, ii, 68. He exchanged, 1 July, 1414, with
Walter Boway, clerk (R. of St. Gerran's); patron, Sir Hugh Courtenay, knt., son of Edward, Earl of Devon, ii, 160. Boway exchanged, 20 Dec., 1416, with
Thomas Ralegh (R. of Sutcombe), (proxy—John Lane, clerk); patron, the same, ii, 181.

ST. JUST-IN-PENWITH, Vicar of—

Nicholas Harry; his institution is not recorded; but he was presented by the Provost and Chapter of Glasney, being one of their number, and died in 1427.

ST. KEYNE [Sancte Keyne, MS.], Rectors of—

Thomas Hawley, clerk, *collated*, by lapse, 1 Nov., 1396, ii, 32. On whose [Hawlegh, MS.] resignation
Nicholas Vesy, priest, was inst., 19 Sept., 1398; patron, John Hawlegh, domicellus, ii, 9^b.

ST. KEVERNE [Sancti Kyerani, MS.], Vicars of—

Thomas Wythe; on whose death was inst., 23 Feb., 1405-6,
William Bray, deacon; patron, Robert Scherleton, of Bishop's Cleeve, Co. Gloucester, ii, 88^b.

ST. MABYN [Sancte Mabene, MS.], Rectors of—

John Restowrek (or *Rescowrek*); on whose resignation was inst., 13 April, 1415,
Thomas Hendeman, priest, S.T.P.; patron, Thomas Beaumont, Esquire, ii, 164.

ST. MADRON [Sancti Maderni, MS.], Vicars of—

Laurence Trewythgy; on whose death was inst., 17 Jan., 1407-8,
John Burdett, chaplain; patron, Walter Grendon, Prior of the Order of St. John of Jerusalem, in England: ii, 99^b.

S. MARTIN'S-BY-LOOE [Sancti Martini juxta Loo, MS.] Rectors of—

Michael Cergeaux; who exchanged, 18 June, 1396, with
John Gyles (Preb. of Merston in the Coll. Church of St. Mary, Stafford); patron, John Rayle, domicellus, ii, 30^b. On this Rector's resignation
John Cergeaux, was inst., 12 July, 1397; patron, John Raly (*sic*), domicellus, ii, 35.

ST. MARY CHURCH [Seyntmarichurch, MS.], Vicars of—

Peter Duk; who exchanged, 7 May, 1397, with
John Otery (V. of Ashburton); patrons, the Dean and Chapter of Exeter, ii, 34. He was succeeded by
John Carvargh [*Carwargh*, also "*Carvargh* alias *Carbargh*," MS.], the date of whose institution is not recorded; but it was most probably about 18 Nov., 1403, when he was succeeded by John Hauk, as V. of Clether (ii, 7, 70.) On his resignation
John Alvethecote, chaplain, was inst., 22 June, 1415, ii, 165.

ST. MAWGAN IN PYDAR [Sancti Maugani in Pydre, MS.], Rectors of—

William Hendre, on whose death, was inst., 25 July, 1410,

Hervey Wyket, clerk; patron, Sir John Arundell, knt., ii, 121. He exchanged, 24 July, 1411, with

W. Trebell, LL.B. (Canon and Preb. of Rugge, in the Church of Crediton); ii, 139b. [This entry had been accidentally omitted, and there is a contemporaneous memorandum in the margin, stating that it should have been registered five folios back.] Trebel (*sic*) exchanged, 27 July, 1416, with

Richard Aldryngton, alias *Colcomb*, (R. of Lanteglos-by-Camelford); proxy—John Whytewaye, clerk; patron, the same, ii, 178b.

ST. MAWNAN [Seynt Maunan, MS.], Rectors of—

Benedict Whalesbrewe, whose name is not mentioned among the Institutions; but *see* i, 18. He was succeeded by

Richard Gabriell, clerk; instituted, 17 Nov., 1398, patron, Richard II., ii, 40. Gabriell's resignation is not recorded; but he was inst. to Pyworthy, 5 Mar., 1404-5 (*see* ii, 82b), and 8 Ap. (following) served as proxy for his successor,

Thomas Pytyngton, clerk, collated by reason of *lapse*; ii, 83b. This Rector exchanged, 22 July, 1416, with

Richard Beauchamp (R. of Whitechapel-without-Algate, City of London—patron, Robert Rothebury, R. of Stepney [Stebbenhith, MS.]); patron, John Whalesbrewe esquire; ii, 178.

ST. MELLION [Sancti Melani, MS.], Rectors of—

Baldwin Schylyngford; on whose death was inst., 16 March, 1417-18,

John Smyth, chaplain; patron, William Frye de Fyneton; ii, 190.—Commission dated 4 March, 1417-18; ii, 264b.

ST. MERRYN [Sancte Marine, MS.], Vicars of—

Richard Hopere; he exchanged, 9 Nov., 1395, with

William Dunscombe (R. of Poughill); patron, the Bishop, ii, 28b. Donscombe (*sic*) exchanged with

Ralph Peryn de Polmargh (R. of North Bovey); collated 12 July, 1398; ii, 38.

ST. MEWAN [Sancti Mewani, MS.], Rectors of—

Henry Gathell; on whose death was inst., 1 Feb., 1403-4,

John Cok; patron, Sir Wm. Talbot, knt., ii, 74.

ST. MICHAEL'S MOUNT, Priors of—

Richard Auncell [Monk of Tavistock; ii, 338b]; on whose death was inst., 21 Oct., 1410,

William Lambert, monk of Tutbury [the last Prior]; patron, Henry, Prince of Wales, etc., ii, 124.

ST. MINVER [Sancte Menefrede, MS.], Vicars of—

William Rede; on whose resignation was inst., 7 April, 1407,

John Cowlyng, M.A.; patrons, the Prior and Convent of Bodmin; ii, 95b.

ST. PANCRAS JUXTA AXEMOUTH, R., *see* ROUSDON.

ST. PETROCK MINOR "in Nansfeynton," Rectors of—

John Coke; on whose death was collated, 12 April, 1398,

John Nansmolken, priest; patron, the Bishop, ii, 37.

ST. PINNOCK [Sancti Pinnoci, MS.], Rectors of—

Walter Lyewer (or *Lewer*; see ii, 351, 352); on whose resignation

John Stephyn, chaplain, was inst., 25 Sept., 1410; patron, "hac vice," Michael Langaker, ii, 123. A Commission was directed to the Archdeacon of Cornwall, 22 July, 1419, as to the vacancy and patronage of this Church, *Richard Knockya*, chaplain, having been presented by Sir Wm. Botreaux, knt., ii, 268. This was little more than a month before the Bishop's death, and the result is not recorded in his Register.

ST. PROBUS, Vicars of—

William Noe; he exchanged, 8 Oct., 1412, with

Clement Wylle (Canon and Preb. of Glasney); patron, the Bishop, ii, 145.

ST. PROBUS, Prebendaries (or Portioners) in the Church of—

Robert Martyn, chaplain; collated 24 May, 1396, on the resignation of *Thomas Tuggel* (proxy—Richard Tyttesbury); ii, 30b.

Adam de Mottrum (also, Archdeacon of Ely and Canon and Preb. of Fenton, in York Cathedral), exchanged, 27 Oct., 1397, with

John Welbourne, Precentor of Salisbury, and Canon and Preb. of Burbage and Husburn therein, ii, 35.

Richard Bray (proxy—Hervey Wyket), exchanged, 14 April, 1400, with

Roger Smith, Warden of the Free-Chapel of St. Margaret at Chelmsford (patron, the Bishop of London), ii, 46.

John Welbourne, exchanged, 23 June, 1400, with

Adam de Mottrum (R. of Crewkerne, 2nd Portion—Dioc. of B. and W.), ii, 47; on whose resignation (proxy—John Constable, clerk),

William Mottrum was collated, on the same day; ii, 47b.

John de Candelesby (or *Candlesby*), clerk, was on the resignation of *John Kyrby* (28 Feb., 1400-1401), ii, 53.

William Norton, chaplain, was collated, 10 Oct., 1401, on the resignation (proxy—Robert Opy, clerk), of *Thomas Lavyngton*, ii, 55b. Norton exchanged (25 Feb., 1401-2), with

John Fyfide (Canon and Preb. of Bedford-minor in Lincoln Cathedral), ii, 56b. The above-named

Thomas Lavyngton, chaplain, was collated, 18 April, 1402 (proxy—John Hexham, clerk), on the resignation (proxy—John Wath), of the said *John Fyfide*, ii, 57b.

Roger Smyth, clerk, exchanged, 30 May, 1402, with

Edward Dauntesey (R. of Yate, Dioc. of Worcester), ii, 57b.

Fulke de Stafford, clerk; collated, 14 Nov., 1404, on the death of the above-named *Robert Martyn*, ii, 80.

Richard Bolham, chaplain; collated, 15 May, 1405, on the resignation of the above-named *Edward Dauntesey* (proxy—William Penfern, clerk), ii, 84b. On whose resignation (proxy—the same).

Nicholas Bolham, chaplain, was collated, 16 May, 1408; ii, 102.

Roger Bolter, chaplain; collated, 13 Feb., 1412-13, on the death of *Fulke de Stafford*, ii, 148.

William Mottrum exchanged, 26 Dec., 1414, with

John Chitterne (Preb. of Goodworth in the Conventual church of Wherwell, Dioc. of Winchester; patron, the Abbess and Convent of Wherwell) Richard Wylles, proxy for Chitterne; ii, 162b. On Chitterne's resignation,

William Swyft, chaplain, was collated, 30 Aug., 1415; (proxy—William Wylleadon, clerk); ii. 168b.

Richard Penels, chaplain, collated, 28 Oct., 1415, on the death of *John Candelesby*, ii, 173b.

Henry Wynnegode, chaplain; collated, 28 Feb., 1415-16, on the resignation of *Nicholas Bolham*, ii, 175.

John Westcote, chaplain, collated, 10 June, 1416, on the resignation of *Richard Penels*, ii, 176b. *Henry Wynnegode* aforesaid exchanged, 9 May, 1417, with

John atte Water (Canon and Preb. of Glasney); ii, 182b.

Michael Lercedekne; collated, 21 Feb., 1417-18, on the resignation of *Roger Bolter*, ii, 189b. He soon resigned, and was succeeded by

Richard Penels, chaplain, 25 April, 1418; ii, 190b.

William Frye, clerk, collated, 23 July, 1418 (proxy—Robert Frye, literate), on the death of *John Westcote*, ii, 193. And 28 July *John atte Water* exchanged with

John Bernyngham, clerk; R. of Limpsfield, Dioc. of Winchester (John Lane, proxy), ii, 193b.

William Swyft exchanged, 27 June, 1419, with

John Saunders, Canon of the Colleg. Church of Heytesbury and Preb. of Titherington and Horningham therein (John Hender, proxy); ii, 200.

ST. SITHNEY [Sancti Sythnini, MS.], Vicars of—
John Kembel; on whose death was collated, 17 Nov., 1403,
Richard Peryn, chaplain; patron, the Bishop, ii, 70.

ST. STEPHEN'S-BY-SALTASH [Sancti Stephani de Saltasshe, MS.], Vicars of—
John Drake; on whose resignation was inst., 30 March, 1398,
John Orukern, chaplain; patron, the Dean (or Warden) and the College of Windsor, ii, 36b. He resigned, and
William Yonge, chaplain, was inst., 8 July, 1408; ii, 102.

ST. STEPHEN'S IN BRANNEL [Sancti Stephani de Branell, MS.], Rectors of—
Thomas Cornewayle exchanged, 29 Nov., 1416, with
Michael Lercedekne (R. of Thorney, Dioc. of Chichester)—(proxy for Cornewayle, Philip Swete; for Lercedekne, John Froden), patron, Thomas Hendour, Esquire; ii, 180b. On whose resignation
John Burgoun, chaplain, was inst., 24 April, 1418; patron, the same, ii, 190b.

ST. STEPHEN'S IN BRANNEL, Vicars of—
John Treverbyn, chaplain; inst., 21 Nov., 1398; patron, King Richard II., ii, 40. Commission of Enquiry as to the patronage, 25 Nov., 1398; ii, 221. On whose death
Thomas Herry, chaplain, was inst., 12 March, 1413-14; patron, Thomas Hendour, esquire, ii, 157. On the resignation of Harry (*sic*).
John Chiwarton, junior, chaplain, was inst., 15 June, 1414; patron, the same; ii, 159b.

ST. STITHIAN'S [Sancte Stediane, MS.], Vicars of—
Thomas Penfern; on whose death was inst., 1 Dec., 1413,
William Raff, chaplain (proxy—John Betty, chaplain); patron, the Abbot of Rewley [de Regali loco juxta Oxoniam, MS.], ii, 153b. On Raff's resignation (on his institution to St. Wendron)
John Dayow, chaplain, was inst., 1 March, 1416-17; ii, 182.

ST. TEATH [Sancte Tethe, MS.], Vicars of—
John Kelly; on whose resignation was collated, 19 Oct., 1411,
John Colle, chaplain; patron, the Bishop, ii, 136.

ST. TEATH, Prebendaries in the Church of—
William Cergeaux; whose successor
William Sutton, exchanged 23 Sept., 1407, with
Richard Tyttesbury, Canon and Preb. of Apuldram in the Church of Bosham, ii, 98.

ST. WINNOW [Sancti Winnoci, MS.], Vicars of—
Philip Bole; on whose death was inst., 21 Nov., 1404,
Walter Galy, chaplain (proxy—William Brounyng, clerk); patrons, the Dean and Chapter of Exeter, ii, 80. On Galy's death
Thomas Hendeman, chaplain, was inst., 2 Jan., 1411-12 (proxy—William Clyve, R. of Whitstone). Mandate for his Induction, directed to the Official-Peculiar of the Dean and Chapter in Cornwall, or to John Colyn, V. of St. Vepe; ii, 138b. His resignation is not recorded; but it clearly took place on his appointment to Widecombe-in-the-Moor (to which V. he was inst., 26 Oct., 1412). *See* ii, 145b.
John Gylle, chaplain, succeeded; inst., 15 Sept., 1412, ii, 144.

SALCOMBE-REGIS [Saltecomb *and* Saltcomb, MS.], Vicars of—
John Robert; on whose death was inst., 16 May, 1410,
Thomas Schapelegh, chaplain; patron, the Dean and Chapter of Exeter, ii, 110b. Shaplegh (*sic*) exchanged, 20 Feb., 1414-15, with
John Hurte, (V. of Nether Lyme, Dioc. of Salisbury), ii, 163b.

SALISBURY Cathedral, Prebendaries of Kingsteignton and Yealmpton therein,—
William Waltham; he exchanged, 17 June, 1398 (proxy—John de Feriby), with
Thomas de Feriby, chaplain (Preb. of St. Martin's Altar in Beverley Colleg. Church), ii, 37b.

SALISBURY, Archdeaconry of, *see* BERKS, Archdeaconry of—

SALTASH, *see* St. Stephens-by-Saltash.

SAMPFORD COURTENAY [Samforde Courtenay, MS.], Rectors of—
John Passenham; on whose resignation was inst., 14 July, 1402,
Walter Robert, chaplain; patron, Edward, Earl of Devon, ii, 22b. On Robert's resignation
Thomas Hendeman, S.T.P., was inst., 12 March, 1403-4 (proxy, John Walle, clerk), ii, 74b. On whose resignation
Laurence Smyth, clerk, was inst., 4 June, 1410; ii, 114b. On Smyth's death
Henry Huchyn, chaplain, was inst., 25 Aug., 1419; ii, 201b.

SANCREED [Sancti Sancredi, MS.], Vicars of—
John Mychel: on whose death was inst., 6 Nov., 1410,
Richard Talvargh, chaplain; patron, the Dean and Chapter of Exeter, ii, 124.

SATTERLEIGH [Saterlegh], Rectors of—
William Whyte, on whose death was inst., 21 April, 1396,
Thomas Torner, priest; patron, "hac vice," Thomas Saterlegh, ii, 5. On Torner's death
John atte Ya, chaplain, was inst., 15 March, 1416-17; ii, 182b. Commission of Enquiry, dated 22 Feb., 1416-17; ii, 261.

SEATON [Seton, MS.], Vicars of—
Roger Danyel; on whose death was inst., 16 April, 1400,
Richard Manyngford, chaplain; patrons, the Abbot and Convent of Sherborne; ii, 46. He exchanged 2 March, 1404-5 (proxy—John Speek, clerk), with
John Scoy " de Louthorp (V. of Mayfield in the Jurisdiction of the Abp. of Canterbury); ii, 82. This Vicar exchanged, 17 May, 1405, with
John Hoker (R. of St. Michael's, Bristol); ii, 84b. On whose death
John Flesshewere, chaplain, was inst., 6 July, 1418, ii, 193.—Commission of Enquiry, dated 13 June, 1418, ii, 265b.

SHAFTESBURY, St. Rumbald's [" Sancti Rowaldi Shafton, MS.]
See CHITTLEHAMPTON, V., ii, 86b.

SHEBBEAR [Schefbeare, MS.], Vicars of—
John Wayte; on whose death was inst., 15 Sept., 1401,
John Harry, chaplain; patrons, the Abbot and Convent of Torre, ii, 20.

SHEVIOKE [Schevyok, MS.], Rectors of—
Benedict Grysby; on whose death was inst., 23 March. 1404-5,
John Godwyn, chaplain; patron, Edward, Earl of Devon; ii, 83b. On Godwyn's death
Richard Donscombe, clerk, was inst. 31 Dec., 1406; patron, the same, ii, 94. On whose resignation
John Walle, chaplain, was inst., 13 Sept., 1415; patron, Sir Hugh Courtenay, son of Edward, Earl of Devon, ii, 169.

SHILLINGFORD, Church of St. George, Rectors of—
David Loveryng; on whose resignation was inst., 15 June, 1398,
John Tailour, priest; patron, Baldwin de Shillyngforde, ii. 9b. On the resignation of Taylour (*sic*)
Richard Skydemore, clerk, was inst., 6 June, 1401; patron, Baldwin Shillyngford, ii, 19b.

SHIRWELL [Schyrwyll *and* Shyrwyll, MS.], Rectors of—

Baldwin Beaumuont (*sic*); on whose death was inst., 6 May, 1404,

Robert Amyet, chaplain; patron, William Beaumuont (*sic*), ii, 75b. On Amyet's death

Robert Fynour, chaplain, was inst., 13 May, 1407; patrons, Thos. Beaumound John Bury, Thos. Pyllond, and John Syntabyn de Lobbe, ii, 96b. He exchanged, 27 Nov., 1408, with

Edward Fyschacre (R. of Shirwell); patrons, Thos. de Beaumount, John Byry, and Thos. Pyllond, ii, 103. Fyschacre (*sic*) exchanged, 24 March, 1415-16, with

William Secheville (V. of Collumpton); patron, King Henry V, ii, 175b.

SHOBROOKE [Schokebroke *and* Schokbroke, MS.], Rectors of—

John Isaak; who exchanged, 22 Jan., 1400-1401, with

William de Humberston (R. of the Chapel of Legh, *alias* "le Mote," Dioc. of Chichester); proxy—William Bradenham; patron, the Bishop; ii, 52. Humberston (proxy—William Bradenham, again), exchanged 26 Oct., 1404, with

William Derwent (V. of Tenterden, Dioc. of Canterbury); (proxy—Robert Lyster, chaplain); patrons, the Abbot and Convent of St. Augustine, Canterbury, ii, 79b. He exchanged, 8 July, 1417, with

William Causey (R. of South Perrott, Dioc. of Salisbury), ii, 186.

SIDMOUTH [Sydemouth, MS.], Vicars of—

Henry Oustyn; on whose death was inst., 23 May, 1402,

John Corvet, chaplain; patrons, "hac vice," Sir Peter Courtenay, knt., Rd. Amys, Prior of Stoke Courcy, John Kyrchill, and Richard Bacwylle, clerks, ii, 22.

SIDBURY, Vicars of—

Thomas Rawlyn; on whose death was inst., 26 Sept., 1401,

William Broun; patrons, the Dean and Chapter of Exeter, ii, 20b.

SILVERTON [Silferton, MS.], Rectors of—

William Oterhampton; on whose death was *collated*, "jure devoluto," 17 April, 1415,

Richard Hoper, chaplain (proxy—Reginald Bryta, R. of Dittisham); ii, 164b.

SKILGATE, R. (Dioc. of B. and W.), *see* BAMPTON, Chantry of FORDE, ii, 32b.

SLAPTON; Rectory of the Colleg. Chantry of the B.V.M. (within the Manor of Slapton; commonly called the Chantry of Guy de Bryene, senior), Rectors of—

Robert Hawkesworth; whose successor was

Walter Danyel, chaplain, *collated* 14 May, 1400; patron, "hac vice," the Bishop, ii, 46b. He died 16 March, 1409-10, and

John Bouryng was inst., 3 June, 1410; ii, 111.

SLAPTON, P.C. annexed to the Chantry of St. Mary there; "Ministers"—

[*John Combe* is mentioned in the will of *Walter Trote* (Canon of Exeter, and, from 1375 to 1381, Rector of the Collegiate Chantry), dated 4 Nov., 1399, as "ministrum in perpetuo officio ministeriatus parochianorum ecclesie parochialis de Slapton, perpetue cantarie de Slapton noviter fundate, i, 302b.]

Peter Holdych, chaplain, inst. 12 July, 1403; patron, Walter Danyell, R. of the College of St. Mary at Slapton, ii, 68.

William Cote, chaplain, inst. 16 April, 1411; patrons, the Community of Slapton, ii, 132.

SOMERLEGH ; Prebend in the Cathedral Church of Chichester—

John Pomfret resigned (proxy—Thomas Weston), and

John Dypphull, chaplain, was collated (proxy—Robert Penaanaz), by the Bishop of Exeter on behalf of the Bishop of Chichester, . . . April, 1397 (the *day* of the month, is omitted) ; ii, 33b.

SOUTHAMPTON, St. Mary's, R., *see* ST. COLUMB-MAJOR, ii, 137b.

SOUTHLEIGH, Rectors of—

John Taylour, chaplain, inst., 15 June, 1414 ; patron, Alice Bonevile, Lady of Southleigh, ii, 159b. On whose resignation

William Lane, chaplain, was inst., 20 August, 1415, ii, 168.

SOUTHMOLTON, Rectors of—

John Harche ; on whose death was inst., 12 Jan., 1406-7,

William Peion, chaplain ; patron "hac vice," Sir John Cornewaill, knt., ii, 94. He exchanged, 10 Sept., 1410, with

John Park (R. of Whittington, Dioc. of Worcester), patron, the same ; ii, 122b.

SOUTH PERROTT [South Perot, MS.], R., *see* BRATTON [CLOVELLY] R., ii, 186b.

SOUTH PETHERWIN [Pyderwyn, MS.], Vicars of—

Thomas Trelynow alias *Godok* ; on whose resignation was inst., 7 Oct., 1410,

John Colman, chaplain ; patrons, the Prior and Convent of St. German's, ii, 123b.

SOUTH POOL [South Pole, MS.], Rectors of—

Edward Patryngg ; on whose death was inst., 28 March, 1398,

John Reed, priest ; patron, Sir John Dynham, knt., ii, 8. On the death of Rede (*sic*),

John Aller, chaplain, was inst., 10 Aug., 1406 ; patrons, Jas. Aumarle, John Pole, Robert Maynard, Thos. Hertescote, and John Bole, ii, 90b. On Aller's death

William Langeton was inst., 24 June, 1407 ; patrons, the same, ii, 97. On whose death

John Carvargh, chaplain, was inst., 19 Feb., 1413-14 ; patrons, Robert Maynard and Thomas Hertescote, ii, 155b.

SOUTH TAWTON, Vicars of—

Geoffrey Lange ; on whose death was inst., 20 Dec., 1411,

Richard Man, chaplain ; patrons, the Warden and College of Windsor, ii, 138. On Man's resignation

John Hegneh, chaplain, was inst., 15 July, 1416 ; ii, 177b.

SOWTON, R., *see* CLYST FOMISON.

SPAXTON, R. (Dioc. of B. and W.), *see* HOLCOMBE ROGUS, V., ii, 42b.

SPREYTON [Sprayton, MS.], Vicars of—

Peter Dyne ; on whose resignation was inst., 8 Jan., 1405-6,

John Gyffard, chaplain ; patron, King Henry IV, ii, 88.

STANFORD-ON-AVON [-super-Avene, MS.], R. (Dioc. of Lincoln), *see* ERMINGTON, R., ii, 120b.

STAPLEFORD [Stapilforthe, MS.], R., *see* BOSHAM, ii, 109b.

STAVERTON, Vicars of—

Nicholas Cole ; who exchanged, 28 Nov., 1403, with

Richard Doty (R. of St. Laurence, Exeter) ; patrons, the Dean and Chapter of Exeter, ii, 70b.

P

STICKLEPATH [Stikilepath *and* Stikelpath, MS.], Chantry Chapel of—

Nicholas Bubbewyth; on whose resignation was inst., 27 Sept., 1396,
Patrick Wode, priest; proxy—Henry Peek, priest; patron, Edward, Earl of Devon, ii, 6. On Wode's resignation, the said
Henry Peke (*sic*), was inst., 21 May, 1397; ii, 7.

STOCKLEIGH ENGLISH [Stokkelegh Englyssch, MS.], Rectors of—

Roger Batyn; on whose death was inst., 16 Sept., 1396,
William Herle, clerk; patron, Sir John Herle, knt., ii, 6.

STOCKLEIGH POMEROY [Stokeleigh Pomeray, MS.], Rectors of—

Robert Wyghale; on whose death was collated, 8 Feb., 1418-19,
John Peake, chaplain; ii, 197.

STOGUMBER [Stokegommere *and* Stokegummur, MS.], (Dioc. of B. and W.) *see* COLCOMBE, Chantry of, ii, 36; and BICKLEIGH R., ii, 87b.

STOKECLIMSLAND [Stoke-in-Clymmeslond, MS.], Rectors of—

Richard Prentys: on whose resignation was inst., 3 Dec., 1397,
Walter Westney, clerk (proxy—Robert Bristowe); patron, K. Richard II., ii, 36b. Commission of Enquiry, ii, 213b. On Westney's resignation
Nicholas Stoke, priest, was inst., 15 June, 1398; patron, the same, ii, 9b. He *exchanged*, 4 Nov., 1399, with
Thomas Welyn [*alias* Abyngdon], (Canon and Preb. of Glasney and R. of Withiel); but the latter was not *instituted* till the 18th of November; patron, K. Henry IV., ii, 43b.

STOKE DAMAREL [Stoke Damarle, MS.], Rectors of—

Walter Estcolm; on whose death was inst., 1 Sept., 1410,
John Walle, chaplain; patron, Edward, Earl of Devon, ii, 122b. On Walle's resignation
Richard Lemmonesworth, chaplain, was inst., 20 Sept., 1415; patron, Sir Edward de Courtenay, ii, 169.

STOKE FLEMING [Sancti Ermundi (*sic*) de Stoke Flemmyng, MS.], Rectors of—

Walter Colmpton; on whose death was inst., 1 March, 1400-1,
Stephen Josep, chaplain; patrons, Sir William Bonevyle, knt., John Strech, John Prestecote, and John Uggeburgh (chaplain); ii, 17. On the death of Joseph (*sic*).
William Hyeonyse, chaplain, was inst., 2 Sept., 1419; patron, Sir Thomas de Carrew, knt., ii, 202.

STOKE GABRIEL [Stok Sancti Gabrielis, MS.], Vicars of—

Richard Penwyn; who exchanged, 23 Nov., 1396, with
Robert Saunder, chaplain (for his Chapelry of the B.V.M. in the Cemetery of Ermington), ii, 32. On whose resignation
John Harry, chaplain, was collated, 6 Oct., 1417; ii, 187b.

STOKE-IN-TEIGNHEAD [-in-Tynhyde, MS.], Rectors of—

Thomas Tugel; on whose death was collated, 10 Nov., 1397,
Richard Aldryngton (alias *Colcomb*), clerk; ii, 35b; *and again*, 25 Nov., 1400, ii, 52. He exchanged, 28 Feb., 1401-2, with
Thomas Clyfforde (R. of Lanteglos-by-Camelford), ii, 57. On whose death
William Fylham, chaplain, was collated, 1 Feb., 1418-19; ii, 196b. On whose resignation
James Carselegh, LL.B., chaplain, was collated, 2 Aug., 1419; ii, 201b.

STOKE RIVERS [Stokerevers, MS.], Rectors of—
John Alkeburgh, chaplain ; on whose death was inst., 4 May, 1403,
John Jukys, chaplain ; patron, Wm. de Beaumount, domicellus, ii, 66. On whose resignation
Thomas Haywode, chaplain, was inst., 23 Dec., 1410 ; patrons, Thos. Beaumount, John Wolf, Henry Crosse, and Wm. Squyer, ii, 129b. He exchanged, 14 Nov., 1416, with
Richard Trevylyan (V. of Poundstock), patrons, the same, ii, 180.

STOKENHAM, Rectors of—
Henry Blakeborn, on whose death was inst., 22 July, 1399,
Thomas Montagu (proxy—John Wytymer) ; patron, John Montacute, Earl of Salisbury, ii, 42. On whose death
Richard Prentys, chaplain, was inst., 14 July, 1404 (proxy—Edward Prentys, clerk) ; patron, K. Henry IV., ii, 77b. On whose death a dispute arose as to the patronage, and Thomas de Montacute, Earl of Salisbury, and Lord Monthermer presented, and the Bishop admitted and instituted, 28 Oct., 1416 (proxy—Laurence Haukyn, Canon of Exeter,)—
Edward Prentys, chaplain, ii, 179b. Matilda, Countess of Salisbury, had meanwhile appealed to the Judges at Westminster, who decided in her favour, and the said institution was quashed ; her presentee
Adam Davenport, clerk, being inst., 10 May, 1417 ; (proxy—John Shyllyngford) ; ii, 183. *See* Stokenham in the General Index.

STOKENHAM [Stokynham, MS.], Vicars of—
William Clyfton ; on whose death was inst., 14 Jan., 1395-6,
John Ulveston priest ; patron, the Rev. Henry Blakeborn, R. of Stokenham, ii, 2. On the death of Ulston *(sic)*,
James Frankecheny, chaplain, was inst., 31 May, 1418 ; patron, Adam Davenport, R. of Stokenham, ii, 192. Commission of Enquiry, dated 13 May, 1418 ; ii, 265.

STOODLEIGH [Stodelegh *and* Stodelygh, MS.], Rectors of—
John Batyn, who exchanged, 16 April, 1405, with
John Ivercy (R. of Oake, Dioc. of B. and W.) ; patron, Elinor Fitzpayn, ii, 83b. Yvery (*sic*) exchanged, 7 July, 1405, with
John Blakelake (R. of Clyst St. Lawrence) ; patron, Thomas Hornhay, domicellus, and Alice his wife, ii, 85. This R. exchanged, 8 July, 1407, with
John Fenton (V. of Pitminster, Dioc. of B. and W.) ; patron, Eleanora Fitz Payn ; ii, 97. Fenton exchanged, 1 Aug., 1410, with
John Corbyn (R. of Wittenham Rowley, Dioc. of Salisbury) ; patron, Alienora de Fypeyn : ii, 121b. He exchanged, 3 March, 1410-11, with
Thomas Caux ("Minister sive Rector de Culve" (*i.e.*, Kilve), Dioc. of B. and W.) ; patron, the same, ii, 130b.

STOWFORD [Stouford, MS.], Rectors of—
Roger Lompe ; on whose death was inst., 10 April, 1409,
Thomas Greyston, chaplain ; patron, John Colshull [esquire], ii, 105. On whose resignation
William Copleston, clerk, was inst., 6 May, 1415 ; patron, the same, ii, 164b. On whose resignation
John Laury, chaplain, was inst., 18 Oct., 1415 ; patron, Sir John Colshull, knt., ii, 169b.

STRATFORD-JUXTA-GLEMHAM, Dioc. of Norwich, R., *see* CLYST ST. MARY, R., ii, 91.

STUDLAND [Stodland, MS.], R. (Dioc. of Salisbury), *see* EAST OGWELL, ii, 198b.

SUTCOMBE [Suttacombe, MS.], Rectors of—

Roger Rome; on whose death was inst., 11 Feb., 1404-5,
John Drayton, chaplain; patron, Sir Ivo Fitz-Waryn, knt., ii, 82. This R. [described, here, as "*alias* Bonde"], exchanged 20 Aug., 1403, with
Thomas Rale (V. of Kingsbury, Dioc. of B. and W.); patron, Sir John Fitz-Wareyn, knt., ii, 102b. Ralegh (*sic*) exchanged, 20 Dec., 1416 (proxy—John Lane, clerk), with
Walter Boway (R. of St. John-in-Cornwall), patron, Sir Thos. Stawell, knt., and Robert Cornu, esquire; ii, 181.

SUTTON-juxta-Plymouth [Plymmouth, MS.], Vicars of—
Michael Cergeaux; on whose resignation was inst., 12 July, 1397,
John Gyles, M.A., patron, the Prior and Convent of Plympton, ii, 35. "Master Gyles" exchanged, 8 May, 1409, with
Thomas Guldesfelde (R. of Elingdon, Dioc. of Salisbury); proxy—William Karlee, literate; ii, 105b.

SWANSEA [Sweynesey, MS.], Hospital of St. David at, *see* Alwington, R. ii, 131.

TADYPORT (Chantry in the Chapel of St. Mary Magdalene)—
Thomas Verlegh, priest; inst., 13 April, 1396; patron, John Hankeford, in right of the lands of Joan, his wife, ii, 5.

TALATON [Taleton, MS.], Rectors of—
[*William Warre*: there is no record of his death, or resignation; but the Church was vacant for some time, as]
John Hethen, chaplain, was collated *by lapse*, 10 July, 1404; ii, 77b. On Hethen's death
Nicholas Ayscherygh, chaplain, was inst., 18 Aug., 1405; patron, "hac vice" Thomas Brythlegh, domicellus, ii, 85b.

TALKERN, R., *i.e.*, MINSTER, q.v.

TALLAND [Tallan, MS.], Vicars of—
Walter Racan; on whose death
John Trethewy, priest, was instituted, 13 July, 1396; patrons, Stephen (Prior) and the Convent of Launceston, ii, 6.

TAMERTON, Vicars of—
Simon Nywenham; on whose resignation was inst., 8 Nov., 1399,
Thomas Moene, priest; patrons, the Prior and Convent of Plympton, ii, 14. On the resignation of "Thomas Baker, *alias* Meone" (*sic*),
Thomas Forde, chaplain, was inst., 27 Oct., 1403; ii, 153.

TAUNTON (Chantry of St. Andrew in the Church of St. Mary Magd.), *see* UPOTTERY, V., ii, 69.

TAVISTOCK ABBEY, Abbots of—
Thomas Cullyng; on whose death
John Mey was elected, and confirmed 30 July, 1402; ii, 63b.

TAVISTOCK, Vicars of—
John Hykedon; on whose death was inst., 17 Oct., 1400,
John Lucas, chaplain; patron, Thomas (Abbot) and the Convent of Tavistock, ii, 15b. On whose death
Roger Sturt, deacon, was inst., 17 Oct., 1416; ii, 179b. On whose resignation
John Borneslo, chaplain, was inst., 6 Dec., 1416; ii, 181.

TAWSTOCK [Taustoke *alias dicta* Toustoke, MS.], Rectors of—
[*Walter Gybbes*: his name is not mentioned among the Institutions; but he had been R. since 1390, was Canon of Exeter, and seems to have resigned Tawstock about three months before his collation to a Canonry in Ottery St. Mary, 14 Sep., 1404.]

William de Pilton, succeeded him, being inst, 10 June, 1404 ; patron, K. Henry, IV., ii, 76.

TEDBURN [St. Mary,—Tettebourne, MS.], Rectors of—

William Schute ; on whose death was inst., 29 Jan., 1418-19,

Thomas Coffyn, chaplain ; patron, Sir Wm. Esturmy, knt. ; ii, 196ᵇ.—Commission of Enquiry, dated 17 Jan., 1418-19 ; ii, 267.

TEIGN BREWER [TENG BRUWER—the antient name of TEIGNGRACE,—" Ecclesia parochialis Apostolorum Petri et Pauli], Rectors of—

Thomas Whyte ; on whose death was inst., 4 Jan., 1409-10,

Peter Wynkeleigh, chaplain ; patron, John Prestecote, ii, 108. On whose death

Richard Parker, chaplain, was inst., 23 Nov., 1412 ; patron, "hac vice," Margery, relict of John Prestecote, ii, 146. On whose death

William Come, chaplain, was inst., 5 April, 1414 ; patron, the same ; ii, 157ᵇ.

TEIGNGRACE, *i.q.*, TEIGN BREWER, q.v.

TENTERDEN (Dioc. of Canterbury), *see* SHOBROOKE, R., ii. 79ᵇ.

THEYNTON, R. (Dioc. of Lincoln), *see* CLYST FOMISON, ii, 51.

THORNBURY, Rectors of—

Walter Trenylen : on whose resignation was inst., 31 March, 1404,

John Dygon, Canon of Plympton Priory ; patron, Henry Cornu, domicellus. A pension of £10 *per annum* was reserved to the said Henry Trenylen, for the necessaries of life, lest he should disgrace the clergy by begging ; also a chamber in the Rectory manse, to be chosen by himself, so that he did not choose the principal chamber, ii, 75. On Dygon's resignation[1]

Richard Bere, chaplain, was inst., 15 Jan., 1411-12 ; patron, Walter Cornu, domicellus, ii, 139.

THORNE COFFIN, R. (Dioc. of B. and W.), *see* MEETH, R., ii, 221.

THORNEY, R. (Dioc. of Chichester), *see* ST. STEPHEN'S-IN-BRANNEL, R., ii, 180ᵇ; also, ST. GEORGE'S, EXETER, ii, 196.

THORVERTON [Thurverton, MS.]. Vicars of—

Andrew Stoke ; on whose resignation was inst., 18 Aug., 1405,

William Dene, chaplain ; patrons, the Dean and Chapter of Exeter, ii, 86. This Rector exchanged, 23 June, 1415, with

William Mogrygge (R. of Heathfield Durburgh, Dioc. of B. & W.) ; ii, 165ᵇ.

THURLESTON, Rectors of—

Robert Benet ; on whose death was inst., 13 Jan., 1418-19,

John Somayster, Canon of Torre Abbey ; patron, William Ferrers de Churcheton, Esquire, ii, 196ᵇ.

TINTAGEL [Boscynny-juxta-Tyndagell, *also* "juxta Bossyny," MS.], Vicars of—

Stephen Goof ; on whose death was inst., 6 May, 1400,

Peter Rous, chaplain ; patron, K. Henry IV. (the temporalities of the Abbey of Fontevrault being in his hands during the war with France); ii, 46. On the death of Rous

John Kelly, junior, chaplain, was inst. 25 Sept. 1407 ; (proxy—Warin Kelly); patron, the same ; ii, 98ᵇ.

---

[1] This resignation is separately recorded ; it took place by proxy—Richard Penels, and was witnessed by Thomas Burnel, notary-publick.

TIVERTON, the Principal (or Pitt) Portion, Rectors of—

William Smyth de Colmpton; on whose resignation was inst., 6 May, 1413,
Walter Robert; patron, Edward, Earl of Devon, ii, 150^{b}. On Robert's death
Walter Colle, deacon, was inst., 27 Sept., 1415; ii, 169^{b}.

TIVERTON, the Second (or Clare) Portion, Rectors of—

Richard Gurney; on whose death was inst., 11 Dec., 1398,
Thomas Hendeman, priest; ii, 10. On whose resignation
Walter Robert, LL.B., was inst., 12 March, 1403-4; (proxy—John Walle, clerk), ii, 74^{b}. He exchanged, 2 Aug., 1406, with
John Radeclyff (Preb. of Cutton); proxy—Laurence Haukyn, Canon of Exeter; ii, 90^{b}. On the death of Redeclyf (*sic*)
James Frankcheyne, clerk, was inst., 12 Dec., 1407; ii, 99.

TIVERTON, the Third (or Tydcombe) Portion, Rectors of—

John Colyer; on whose death was inst., 17 Jan., 1402-3,
Alan Benet, priest, ii, 23^{b}.

TOLLER PORCORUM, V. (Dioc. of Salisbury), *see* JACOBSTOW, R. (Devon), ii, 162.

TORBRIAN [Torrebryan, MS.], Rectors of—

Nicholas Wake; on whose death was inst., 24 April, 1405,
William Peion, chaplain, (proxy—Thomas Peion, literate); patron, Sir John Chaundos, knt., ii, 83^{b}. [On Peion's resignation—*see* South Molton],
John Gentylman, chaplain, was inst., 11 March, 1406-7; (proxy—Philip Pope, chaplain); ii, 95.

TORRE ABBEY, Abbots of—

[*William Norton*, to whom succeeded]
Matthew Yerd, 19 July, 1412; ii, 142^{b}.
William Mychel succeeded, 18 March ["eodem die"—not "March 19" as in Oliver's *Monasticon*], 1413-14; ii, 157

TORRINGTON [*i.e.*, S. Michael's, Great Torrington; also called in the MS. Chepyng Toryton], Rectors of—

Laurence Bryghtlegh; on whose death was inst., 10 Jan., 1400-1,
William Hyde, chaplain; patron, Sir Robert Chalons, knt., ii, 52. On this Rector's death
Stephen Payn, chaplain, was inst., 12 Nov., 1413 (proxy—Philip Marschall): patron, the same; ii, 153^{b}. On Payn's election to the Deanery of Exeter,
William, Bishop of Solubria, was inst., 19 Dec., 1415; patron, "ea vice," John Copleston, junior. A Commission of Enquiry herein had been directed (10 Dec.) to the Dean of the Deanery of Torrington, and to Thos. R. of Torrington-Parva, John Knyght, and William Alyn, notaries; who found that all things were regular, and certified the Bishop accordingly on the said 19th Dec.; ii, 173^{b}. On the death of "William Yeurde" (*sic*)
Henry Trethewy, chaplain, was inst., 24 April, 1418; (proxy—Thomas Greyston, chaplain); patron, Sir Robert Chalouns, knt., ii, 190^{b}. Commission of Enquiry, dated 18 April, 1418; ii, 265.
William Alyn, clerk, was inst., 16 Dec. following; patron the same, ii, 196^{b}.

TORRINGTON; the Rectory or Chapel of St. James in the Castle of Chepyngtoryton, Rectors of—

Thomas Peyngtour; on whose death
John Carter, chaplain, was inst., 15 Sept., 1401; patron, "hac vice," Sir Ivo Fytzwaryn, knt., ii, 20. On Carter's death
Stephen Potter, chaplain, succeeded, 1 June, 1405; patron, Sir Robert Chalouns, knt., ii, 85.

TOTNES, Archdeacons of—

John Lydeford, senior; on whose death was collated, 21 Jan., 1407-8 [not 26 Jan., 1408; as in Oliver's List].

William Hunden, who exchanged, 29 May, 1415, with

William Barton (Canon and Preb. of Holy Cross in Lincoln Cathedral and R. of Crawley-magna); proxy—Richard Barton; ii, 164[b].

TOTNES PRIORY, Priors of—

Thomas Swynforde, after whose resignation, 24 March, 1406-7 (ii, 349[b]),

John Southam, monk of the said Priory, was inst., 11 June, 1407; patron, William la Zouche de Haryngworth, on the nomination of K. Henry IV. (on account of the war with France), ii, 96[b].

TOTNES, [Tottonia, MS.], Vicars of—

John Sabyn; on whose death was inst., 3 March, 1406-7,

John Dolbiry, chaplain; patrons, the Prior and Convent of Totnes, ii, 95.

TOTNES, the Chantry Chapel of the Holy Ghost, at Warlond, Wardens—

Thomas Persoun; on whose death was collated, 8 April, 1401,

Hugh Heynys, friar of Hounslow[1], ii, 53.

TOWNSTAL [Tounstalle *and* Tunstall, MS.], Vicars of—

Matthew Yurd; on whose resignation was inst., 9 Dec., 1396,

Nicholas de Cherleton, Canon of Torre Abbey; patrons, the Abbot and Convent of Torre, ii, 6[b]. His successor,

Richard Bradeworthy, monk of Torre Abbey, was inst., 26 Sept., 1400; ii, 50[b]. On whose death

William Mychell, Canon of Torre, was inst., 9 Oct., 1406; ii, 92. His resignation is not recorded; but he became Abbot in March, 1413-14 (*see* ii, 157), and his successor,

John Burgh, Canon of Torre, was inst., 24 April, 1414 (proxy—John Lane, clerk), ii, 158.

TREGONY, Vicar of—

John Wolrele, chaplain; inst., 6 Dec., 1395; patrons, the Prior and Convent of Merton (Dioc. of Winchester), ii, 29.

TRENEGLOS, Vicars of—

Reginald Foter; on whose death was inst., 14 July, 1409,

Thomas Hendre, chaplain, patron, K. Henry IV., ii, 106[b].

TRENTISHOE [Trendysho, MS.], Rectors of—

John Skynner; he exchanged, 9 Dec., 1417, with

Simon Tovy (V. of Westleigh); proxy—Thomas Whyot, clerk; patron, Walter Harry de Trendysho; ii, 188[b].

TREVALGA, St. Petrock's, Rectors of—

John Mayow: he exchanged, 23 Oct., 1399, with

Robert Seek (R. of Perran-Uthno); proxy—John Chiket; patrons, the Dean and Chapter of Exeter, ii, 13[b]. Commission, dated 5 August, 1398; ii, 220 [Mayow is called *William* therein]. On the death of Robert Seke (*sic*)

Walter Twyneow, chaplain, was inst., 16 July, 1406; ii, 90.

TRING [Trenge, MS.], (Dioc. of Lincoln), *see* UFFCULME, ii, 44[b].

---

[1] "Fratri domus sive monasterii de Houndyslowe, Ordinis Sancte Trinitatis et redempcionis captivorum, Londoniensis Diocesis, eundem Ordinem expresse professo, custodiam Capelle Sancti Spiritus de Warlond, juxta villam Tottonie . . . . per mortem fratris Thome Persoun, ultimi ipsius Capelle Custodis, vacantem."

TRURO [Beate Marie de Treurev, and in the margin "Truru" MS.], Rectors of—

Thomas Wille; on whose death was inst., 18 March, 1411-12,

Nicholas Treberveth; patron, "hac vice," Robert Hulle, senior, domicellus, ii, 140b, 245.

TYWARDREATH PRIORY [Trewerdrayth, MS.], Priors of—

William de la Haye; on whose death was inst., 9 Dec., 1399,

John Maslyn, monk of the Monastery of St. Mary and St. Peter "super Dynam"; patron, K. Henry IV. (in whose hand the temporalities of the Monastery of St. Sergius and St. Bacchus then were), ii, 44b. On the death of Maslyn

John Rogger was inst., 14 Dec., 1406; patron, Henry, Prince of Wales, ii, 93b.

TYWARDREATH, Vicars of—

Thomas Jordan; on whose resignation was inst., 29 March, 1409,

Robert Hood, chaplain; patron, K. Henry IV., ii, 105.

UFFCULME, Rectors of—

Peter Pykeryng: who exchanged, 30 Dec., 1399, with

John Luk (R. of Tring, Dioc. of Lincoln); patron, John, Prior of the Cathedral Church of Bath, ii, 44b.

UGBOROUGH [Uggeburgh, MS.], Rectors of—

John Cheyne: who exchanged 13 May. 1405, (proxy—William Brounyng, clerk), with

John Schillyngford, R. of Rotherfield, Dioc. of Chichester (proxy—Richard Skydmore, chaplain); patrons, the Prior and Convent of Plympton, ii, 84. On the death of Shillyngford (*sic*)

Richard Palmer, chaplain, was inst., 19 Dec., 1406; ii, 93b. On whose death

Roger Bolter, chaplain, was inst., 21 April, 1419; ii, 198.

UMBERLEIGH [Womberley, Womberlegh *and* Wumberlegh, MS.], in the parish of Atherington, Chantry-priests of—

Henry Lovelak; on whose resignation was inst., 27 Jan., 1400-1401,

John Doune, chaplain, patron, K. Henry IV., ii, 52b. His resignation is not recorded; but he was inst. to Abbotsham, V., 17 March, 1401 (*see* ii, 17), and on the 28th of the same month

John Gyffard, chaplain, was inst. to this Chantry, ii, 17b. Gyffard exchanged, 1 March, 1402-3, with

Robert Forde (R. of Nymet Rowland); ii, 25b. His resignation is not recorded, but he was inst. to East Worlington, R., 3 April, 1407 (*see* ii, 95b): and on May x . . . . [a blank left to be filled in, and never attended to], in the same year,

Walter Yonge, chaplain, was instituted ii, 96b. On the death of Yonge,

William Hele, chaplain, was inst., 2 Aug., 1410; ii, 122.

UPLOMAN [Lomen *and* de Lomena, *also* "Wellyngton Lamon," MS.], Rectors of—

Robert Scheterne; on whose resignation was inst., 12 Dec., 1397,

John Bisschop, priest; patron, K. Richard II. (John Wrothe, son and heir of Sir John Wrothe, knt., the true patron, being at the time, a minor). ii, 7b. Byschope (*sic*) exchanged, 6 Aug., 1402, with

Richard Forste (R. of Bagborough, Dioc. of B. and W.); patron, K. Henry IV. ii, 63b. Forst (*sic*) exchanged, 7 Nov., 1406, with

Thomas Warre (R. of Chardlinch, Dioc. of B. and W.); patron, K. Henry IV., during the minority of [John], son and heir of Margaret, widow of Sir John de Wroth, knt.[1]; ii, 93. On the resignation of Warr (*sic*),

[1] "racione minoris etatis filii et heredis Margarete, que fuit uxor Domini Johannis de Wroth, militis, in sua custodia existentia."

Robert Baret was inst., 12 Nov. 1411, patron, Henry IV. (as above), ii, 136b.—[There can be no doubt that Uploman is meant by "Wellyngton Lamon," though the fact is not very apparent at first sight; and it may be well, perhaps, to quote the entry at length :—

"Item, duodecimo die mensis Novembris, Dominus, in Manerio suo Criditonensi, admisit dominum Robertum Baret, capellanum, ad Ecclesiam Parochialem de Wellyngton Lamon, Exoniensis Diocesis, per liberam resignacionem domini Thome Warr, ultimi ipsius Ecclesie Rectoris, in manibus ejusdem Domini factam et per ipsum admissam, vacantem. Ad quam per excellentissimum in Christo Principem et Dominum, Dominum Henricum, Dei gracia Regem Anglie et Francie illustrem et Dominum Hybernie, verum ipsius Ecclesie, hac vice, patronum, racione custodie terre et heredis Johannis Wroth, militis, defuncti, in manibus suis existencium, eidem Domino extitit presentatus; et ipsum Rectorem instituit canonice in eadem cum suis juribus et pertinenciis universis : *Curam animarum*, etc. : *Juribus*, etc. Et, prestita canonica obediencia per eundem, mandatum fuit Archidiacono Exoniensi, seu ejus Officiali, pro ipsius Induccione ; et obtinuit literas Institucionis et Induccionis." [1]

UPLYME, Rectors of—

Stephen Eyr, on whose death was inst., 14 July, 1397,

John Parys, clerk ; patrons. John (Abbot) and the Convent of Glastonbury, ii, 7b. He exchanged, 8 May, 1398, with

Richard de Skelton (R. of Middleton, Dioc. of B. and W.) ; ii, 37. On the death of Richard Skelton (*sic*)

Nicholas Wilton, clerk, was inst., 13 April, 1399 ; ii, 12.

William Musket, chaplain, succeeded, 29 July, 1400 ; ii, 49.

UPOTTERY [Upotray, MS.], Vicars of—

John Custa ; he exchanged, 20 Sept., 1403, with

William Plusche (for his Chantry of St. Andrew, in the Church of St. Mary

---

[1] In Pole's *Collections* I find, under "Lomen or Uplomen" (p. 212), that it "was ye enheritanc of a famyly of yt name . . . . in Kinge Henry 2 tyme, Willm de Lomen, or Lumine ; Willm de Lomen, Kt, his sonne ; Sr Richard, sonne of Sr Willm ; and Sr Richard de Lomen, the last ; after whom followed Sr John de *Willington*." He makes no mention, in this place, of the Wroths ; but, under Aderington (p. 422), I find that "Jordan de Chambernun" of Umberlegh in that parish, "had issue William, wch by Eva his wief had issue the Lady Jone, wife of Sir Ralph de Willington . . . . shee had issue Sr Ralph de Williuton (*sic*)" who "by Julian (wch I take to bee daughter and heire of Sr Richard de Lomene, for all the lands of Lomen descended in her issue) had issue Sr John," whose descent is given, through several generations, to "Margaret, wief of John, son of Sr John Wrothe, and Isabell, wief of Willm Beaumont. John Wrothe," he adds, "by ye said Margaret had issue Elizabeth wief of Sr Willm Palton, by whom hee had Umberlegh : Sr Willm, sonne of Sr William and Elizabeth, had issue Sr Wm Palton, of Umberlegh, which maried Anne, daughter of Sr Phillip Courtenay, and died wthout issue, by wch meanes Umberlegh, and the rest of Willington's lands fell unto Sr Thomas Beamont, sonne of Willm Beamont and Isabell Willington." It will be observed that Pole makes no mention of John, the minor referred to in the Register, as (in 1397) the son and heir of Sir John Wrothe, and afterwards (in 1406) as the son and hair of Margaret his widow. He died a minor, and without issue, when all the lands passed in the female line to the Beaumonts of Shirwell (Esq. 13 H. IV No. 25). Thus it is plain to see how the parish of 'Lomen' came to be called "Wellyngton Lamon" in 1411 ; a fact which I have not seen stated, however, in any book of reference to which I have access.

Magd., Taunton); patrons, the Dean and Chapter of Exeter, ii, 69. On whose death
John Noble, chaplain, was inst., 27 June, 1416; ii, 176b.

UPTON HELLIONS [Uppeton Hylyon, MS.], Rectors of—
Richard Pyther; on whose death was inst., 27 Sept., 1416,
John Payn; patron, John Watton, esquire, ii, 179b.

VERYAN [Elerky, MS.], Vicars of—
Walter Levenaunt; on whose resignation was inst., 22 Jan., 1395-6,
John de Bykelegh, priest; patrons, the Dean and Chapter of Exeter, ii, 3b. On whose death
William Ayshecote, chaplain, was inst., 13 Nov., 1402; ii, 23b.

VIRGINSTOWE [Virgenystow, MS.], Rectors of—
John Osborne; on whose death was inst., 13 June, 1410,
Alfred Gyst, chaplain; patrons, the Abbot and Convent of Tavistock, ii, 115. On Gyst's resignation
Robert Sturt, clerk, was inst., 13 Sept., 1412; ii, 144 On Sturt's resignation
Walter Crewys, accolite, was inst., 23 Oct., 1416 (proxy—Thomas Burnell, clerk), ii, 179b.

WALKHAMPTON [Walkampton, MS.], Vicars of—
John Lange; on whose death was inst., 14 Jan., 1405-6,
William Tregodok, chaplain; patrons, the Abbot and Convent of Buckland, ii, 88.

WAMBROOK, R. (Dioc. of Salisbury), *see* HARPFORD, ii, 188, 263.

WARBLETON [Warbylton, MS.], R. (Dioc. of Chichester), *see* BOSHAM, ii, 52.

WARKLEIGH [Warkelegh *and* Warkele, MS.], Rectors of—
Laurence Whyteley; who exchanged, 20 Aug., 1401, with
Thomas Veysy (R. of Penne, Dioc. of B. and W.—patron, John Cheselden, esquire); patron, K. Henry IV., as Custos of the lands of Fulk Fitzwaryn (heir of Sir Fulk Fitzwaryn, knt.), a minor; ii, 54b. He exchanged, 5 Aug., 1402, with
John Pytte (R. of Rewe); patron, "hac vice"—K. Henr. IV., ii, 22b.

WASHBOURNE [Whasseborne *and* Waysshebourne, MS.], in the parish of Harberton, Chantry Chapel of—
Geoffrey Wyngkelegh, chaplain, was inst., 6 April, 1403; patron, Sir John Hauley, senior, ii, 65b. On the death of Wynkele (*sic*)
Thomas Perell, chaplain, was inst., 23 March, 1418-9, patron, John Hauley, Esquire, ii, 197b.

WASHFIELD [Wayssbfeld, Wayschfeld, *and* Wayschefeld, MS.], Rectors of—
William Wodeborne; who exchanged, 11 Jan., 1409-10, with
John Halys alias *Sparwe* (R. of Brushford, Dioc. of B. and W.); patrons, Thomas Werthe, Simon Bernevyle, and Richard Delyngton, ii, 108. Halys exchanged, 13 July, 1412, with
William Walyssch, (R. of Parley, Dioc. of Salisbury); patrons, the same, ii, 142. Walsche (*sic*) exchanged, 18 Aug., 1415, with
Robert Blake (R. of Heddington, Dioc. of Salisbury); patrons, Simon Bernevyle, John Dynyngton (*sic*), Wm. Walrond, Wm. Werthe, Wm. Hugelyng, and Nicholas Trelawny, ii 167b. On Blake's resignation
Robert Gervays, chaplain, was inst., 12 November, 1416; patron, "hac vice," Alice, widow of Richard Wolff, ii, 180.

WEEK (*or* WYKE) ST. MARY, Rectors of—

William Hals, chaplain, was inst., 26 July, 1404 (proxy—William Gorewell literate); patron, K. Henry IV., ii, 78. On whose death
John Gorewell, junior, LL.B., was inst., 5 Aug., 1406 (proxy—William Gorewell, literate); patron, K. Henry IV., ii, 90b.

WELLS CATHEDRAL; Canonry and Prebend of WARMINSTER *alias* LUXVYLE; *see* IPPLEPEN, ii, 110b. Also, Canonry and Prebend of COMBE PRIMA: *see* CREDITON, ii, 152.

WENDRON [Sancte Wendrone, MS.], Vicars of—
Simon Body; on whose death was inst., 8 Feb., 1416-17,
William Raff, chaplain; patrons, the Abbot and Convent of Rewley, Oxon, ii, 182.

WEST ALVINGTON [the "West" omitted in MS.], Vicars of—
John Gordray; who exchanged, 2 Feb., 1395-6 (proxy—John Wolf), with
John Hullyng (R. of Sutton-juxta-Bygenhurne [*i.e.*, Bignor], Dioc. of Chichester; patrons, the Prior and Convent of Lewes); patrons, the Dean and Chapter of Salisbury, ii, 29b. He exchanged, 12 Aug., 1400, with
John Baylebeyn (R. of Cheddon [Cheden, MS.], Dioc. of B. and W.); ii, 49b. On whose death
Simon Pawle, chaplain, was inst., 16 June, 1405; ii, 85.

WEST ANSTY, Vicars of—
John Port; on whose death was inst., 12 Nov., 1415,
William Speare, chaplain; patrons, the Dean and Chapter of Exeter, ii, 173b.

WESTBURY, V. (Dioc. of B. and W.), *see* LUPPIT, ii, 71b.

WEST DEAN (Dioc. of Chichester), *see* BOSHAM, ii, 199.

WEST DOWN, Vicars of—
William Moggarygh; who exchanged, 7 April, 1399, with
Thomas Lange (R. of Heathfield, Dioc. of B. and W.; patron, Robert Normanton, *locum tenens* of the Prior of the Hospital of St. John of Jerusalem in England); patron, the Bishop; ii, 40b.

WEST KEAL [Westerkele, MS.], R. (Dioc. of Lincoln), *see* IPPLEPEN, ii, 64b.

WESTLEIGH [Wesley, MS. (in the margin)], Vicars of—
Simon Tovy; he exchanged, 9 Dec., 1417, with
John Skynner (R. of Trentishoe); patrons, the Dean and Chapter of Exeter, ii, 188b. On Skynner's death
Ralph Kyngysford, chaplain, was inst., 28 Sept., 1418; ii, 194b.

WESTMILL (Dioc. of Lincoln), R., *see* COMBMARTIN, R., ii, 181.

WEST PUTFORD [Putteford, MS.], R., Rectors of—
John Boghedon; on whose death was inst., 11 Feb., 1404-5,
Stephen Gyffard, clerk; patrons, "hac vice" Sir John Hulle, Sir John Wadham, and Sir Wm. Hankeford, knights, and Robert, son of the said John Hulle; ii, 82.

WHERWELL, Prebend of Goodworth in the Conventual Church of (Dioc. of Winchester), *see* St. Probus, ii, 162b.

WHIMPLE [Whympell *and* Whympel, MS.] Rectors of
John Drake; he exchanged 22 Sept., 1407 (proxy—Walter Robert) with
Matthew Doune, for his Rectory or Portion "de la Grene" in the Church of Wodesdon, Dioc. of Lincoln, and Wardenship of the Free Chapel of Crofton, Dioc. of Salisbury); patron, K. Henry IV., ii, 98. Doune exchanged, 17 June, 1418, with
Thomas Warde, LL.B. (R. of Bampton); patron, K. Henry V., ii, 192.

WHITCHURCH, Vicars of—

Henry Smyth; on whose death was inst., 25 May, 1398,
John Raddych, priest; patron, K. Richard II. (in whose hands were the temporalities of the Abbey of Tavistock), ii, 9.

WHITECHAPEL extra Aldgate (Dioc. and City of London), *see* ST. MAWNAN, R., ii, 178.

WHITSTONE (in Devon), Rectors of—

William Clyve was instituted by Bishop Brantingham, on the resignation of *John Clebury*, in 1392; patron, Sir Philip Courtenay, knt. He is thrice mentioned in Stafford's Register (as "Rector ecclesie parochialis de Whytston"), and survived that Bishop; ii, 108ᵇ, 109, 138ᵇ.

WHITSTONE [Whytston, MS.], (in Cornwall), Rectors of—

Thomas Bardolf; on whose death was inst., 30 Aug., 1410,
David Sauly, chaplain; patron, Sir John Arundell, knt., ii, 121.

WHITTINGTON [Wythyndon, MS.] R. (Dioc. of Worcester), *see* SOUTH MOLTON, R., ii, 122ᵇ.

WIDECOMBE[-IN-THE-MOOR—Wydecombe, MS.], Vicars of—

Edward Fysch, who exchanged, 25 Jan., 1399-1400, with
Richard Madeford (R. of Honiton); patrons, the Dean and Chapter of Exeter, ii, 45. He exchanged, 20 March, 1401-2 (proxy—Ralph Dollebeare), with
Peter Duk (V. of Ashburton); ii, 57. Duk exchanged, 13 Oct., 1405, with
Robert Mareschall (V. of Harberton); ii, 86. This Vicar exchanged, 11 Nov., 1410, with
John Wyndout (R. of St. Mary Steps, Exeter); ii, 124ᵇ. On whose death
Thomas Hendeman, chaplain, was inst., 27 Aug., 1412; ii, 143ᵇ. He exchanged, 26 Oct. following, with
John Boghelegh (R. of Farway); ii, 145ᵇ.

WILLAND [Wyldelonde *and* Wildelond, MS.], Rectors of—

Thomas Brunyng; he exchanged, 8 Aug., 1396, with
Peter Bryd (R. of Holdford, [Holeford, MS.], Dioc. of B. and W.); proxy—John Touker; patrons, the Prior and Convent of Taunton; ii, 31. On the death of this Rector, called in the MS., "Peter Holford," *i.e.* apparently "Peter Bryd de Holford,"
John Bourne, chaplain, was inst., 21 Jan., 1401-2: ii, 21.

WINKLEIGH, Vicars of—

Richard Troubrigge: on whose death was inst., 16 June, 1403,
Edward Pyers, chaplain; patron, the Dean and Chapter of Exeter, ii, 67ᵇ. On whose death
Hugh Hendeston, chaplain, was inst., 21 Oct., 1413; ii, 153.

WITHERIDGE [Wytherygg, MS.], Rectors of—

William Vexford; he exchanged, 14 May, 1396, with
John Luffewyk (R. of Marsh [Mersseh, MS.], Dioc. of Lincoln—patron, Richard de Pole); patron, the Prioress and Convent of Cannington, Dioc. of B. and W., ii, 30.

WITHIEL, Rectors of—

Thomas Welyn [*alias* Abyngdon]: he exchanged, 4 Nov., 1399, with
Nicholas Stoke (R. of Stokeclimsland), patrons, the Prior and Convent of Bodmin; ii, 43ᵇ. Stoke exchanged, 1 June, 1402, with
Thomas Chapman (R. of Hampton Meisy, Dioc. of Worcester); ii, 58.

WITTENHAM ROWLEY, R., Dioc. of Salisbury, *see* STOODLEIGH, R., ii, 121ᵇ.

WOODLEIGH, [Wodelegh MS.] Rectors of—

William Chamburnoun; on whose death was inst., 20 Dec., 1406,
William Breerlegh, M.A., chaplain ; patron, Edward, Earl of Devon, ii, 93b.

WOOLFARDISWORTHY [Wolferdysworthy Spenser, MS.], Rectors of—
John York : who exchanged, 18 March, 1403-4, with
John Rok (V. of Brampford-Speke) ; patron, John Ufflete, domicellus, ii, 75.

YARCOMBE [Yartecombe, Yartcombe, Yardecombe, *and* Yeartecombe, MS.], Vicars of—
Roger Ferrour ; he exchanged, 20 March, 1408-9, with
John Hele (R. of Clyst Hydon); patron, Joan, Queen of England, ii, 104b. Hele exchanged, 8 March, 1413-14, with
Richard Tanton (R. of Manston, Dioc. of Salisbury) ; patron, K. Henry V., ii, 156b. Taunton *(sic)* exchanged, 2 Sept., 1418, with
Thomas Calf (R. of Cameley, Dioc. of B. and W.) ; patron, William Kenolmersh, ii, 194. On the death of Calfe *(sic)*
John Matthew, chaplain, was inst., 14 July, 1419 ; patron, the same, ii, 200b.

YARNSCOMBE, St. Andrew's [Ernyscombe *and* Ernescombe, MS.], Vicars of—
Geoffrey Palmer ; on whose resignation was inst., 6 July, 1409,
John Lavyngton, chaplain ; patrons, the Master and Brethren of the Hospital of St. John Baptist, Exeter, ii, 106. This Vicar exchanged, 21 April, 1412, with
Adam Thomas (V. of St. Gennys) ; ii, 141b. On whose resignation
John Davy, chaplain, was inst., 12 July, 1415 ; ii, 166.

YATE, R. (Dioc. of Worcester), *see* ST. PROBUS, ii, 58 ; also, EXMINSTER, ii, 88.

YEALMPTON [Yealhampton, MS.], Vicars of—
John Play ; on whose death was inst., 7 Aug., 1415,
Hugh Maunsell, chaplain ; patron, Thomas Feriby, Canon of Salisbury, and Preb. of Kingsteignton and of Yealmpton therein, ii, 167b.

ZEAL [MS. SELE] MONACHORUM, Rectors of—
Walter Beare ; on whose death was inst., 13 Oct., 1398,
John Tyrell, clerk ; patrons, the Abbot and Convent of Buckfast, ii, 10. On Tyrell's death
John Sprydell, chaplain, was inst., 28 June, 1408 ; ii, 102.

ZENNOR [Sancte Senare, MS.], Vicars of—
John Wylla, chaplain, was collated, 24 June, 1400, ii, 47b. And on the death "Johannis, ultimi Vicarii,"
Nicholas Jory, chaplain, was collated, 12 Jan., 1416-17, ii, 181b.

Instow, Huish in the parish of, i, 73b.—

Thomas Lauge (subdeacon), R. of this parish, obtained a dispensation (to study at Oxford) for one year, from 22 April, 1407, i, 81.—He seems not to have returned to his benefice ; for, 22 Jan., 1410-11, the Bishop wrote thus to the Archdn. of Barnstaple—"ad nostrum pervenit auditum quod quidam Thomas Langge, Rector ecclesie parochialis de Yenstow . . . absque causa racionabili, seu licencia nostra aut alia legitima quacumque, ab ecclesia sua prefata per tempora diuturna se absentatus, gregemque proprium deserens curam animarum sibi commissam, hospitalitatem eciam, ac cetera que ad ipsum de jure et consuetudine pertinent, effectualiter observare et tenere negligit et omittit, in anime suo grande periculum ac aliorum perniciosum exemplum." The Bishop declares that he cannot, with a safe conscience, wink at such misconduct any longer, and directs the Archdn. to admonish the offender personally (if he can find him, and if not, then anyone who may act as his proxy), in the parish-church, before the principal parishioners and their friends, once, twice, and thrice, to enter within six months from that day, into residence, or failing therein to appear within twenty days before the Bishop at Exeter; i, 111b.

Commissions of Enquiry as to the right of patronage, (1) directed to the Archdn. of Barnstaple (11 Aug., 1410), ii, 233b.—(2) To the like effect (6 Oct., 1410) on behalf of John Fayreste, chaplain, presented by Sir William, and by Richard and John, Hankeford[1] (6 Oct., 1410), ii, 234.

Alexander Courteys, R., was licensed as a Publick-Preacher, (3 Oct., 1412), i, 168b; and 22 June, 1414, he was again so licensed within the Deanery of Trigg-major, i, 197. He was a Penitentiary in the Deanery of Barnstaple, 194b; 207b, 217, 231, 237b, 245b.

Insworth [Innyswerk, MS.], Sir Rd. Champernoun's Manor of, i. 119.

Inwardleigh, John Gedefray (R. of Halwell), appointed "Curator" to John Flemmyng, R., i, 74.

Ipplepen, John Excestre, R. of—

He made complaint to the Bishop that certain disgraceful persons, unknown, had broken a window and thereby effected an entrance into his Rectory-House, and had carried off a number of important deeds, etc., therein preserved in a chest; the Bishop ordered the offenders to be denounced publickly and threatened with excommunication unless restitution were made (15 June, 1398), i, 20.

(*Breve Regium*, 27 Sept., 1400), Prohibition to admit to this Rectory, then vacant, pending the settlement of the dispute as to the patronage between the King and Sir Almaric[2] de St. Amand. But it turned out that there was no such case before the Judges after all[3]; and the King, in a second Writ (dated 21 Oct.), nominated John de Spryngthorp, who was instituted on 25 Oct., ii, 312b; 51.—He was licensed to hear the Confessions of his parishioners (8 March, 1401-2), i, 55.

Isaak (or Ysak), John R. of Shobrooke, exchanges for the Chapel of Legh, or "le Mote" (Dioc. of Chichester), ii, 52.

Iverey (or Iveray[4]), John, R. of Oake (Dioc. of Bath and Wells, exchanges for Stoodleigh, R., ii, 83b; exchanges Stoodleigh for Clyst St. Laurence, R., ii, 85, and again exchanges for Clutton, R. (Dioc. of Wells), ii, 102b. A John Iveray exchanged his Chantry of Cheverel-parva (Dioc. of Salisbury), for Jacobstow, R. (Devon), ii, 177.

Ivybridge [Brigg, MS.], in Ermington, i, 60b; [Yvebrygg, MS.], 112.

---

[1] The date of Thomas Lange's death cannot now be ascertained; but nearly two years later than this Sir William (with Richard and John) Hankeford presented Alexander Courteys *on the death of Lange*, and he was instituted 19 Sept., 1412. There had been a Commission of Enquiry on the 7th of September; ii, 144b, 248b.

[2] "Almaricum de Sancto Amando, chivaler," here; and in the second writ, "Adomarum de Sancto, etc."

[3] "Quia tamen nulla contencio, in eadem Curia nostra, inter nos et prefatum Adomarum, de advocacione predicta, tempore confeccionis dicte Prohibicionis nostre, mota fuit nec adhuc existit, vobis significamus quod, etc."

[4] "Yuery," at ii, 85.

Ixworth, John, collated to a Canonry in Exeter Cathedral, ii, 93. *See* Ovyngham, John, i, 138b, 200b.

J.

Jacka, Thomas, instituted to Ruan-major, R., ii, 50; *see* i, 181.

Jacob, Christopher, instituted to Northam V., ii, 88; his death, ii, 199b.

Jacob, John, accused of polluting the cemetery of Barnstaple, ii, 241b; *see*, also, i, 324b.

Jacobstowe (Cornwall), John Hesyll, R. of—

He obtained licence of non-residence for one year, from 26 Oct., 1398, on condition of his residing in the College of Glasney (of which he was Canon), i, 21b; also, a similar licence, for two years (7 Oct[1]., 1405), i, 76b; and again with no condition attached, for one year, from 27 June, 1410, i, 99.

Jacobstow (Devon), John Harecombe, R.; licence of non-residence from 28 March to Michaelmas 1409, i, 88b.—Thomas Body, parochial chaplain, i, 99b.

Jakkeiowy, Robert and William (*see* Luxulyan), i, 160b; ii, 247[2].

Jakys, John, i, 24b[3],; instituted to Stoke Rivers, R., ii, 66; resigns, ii, 129b.

James, Edmund, i, 320b.

Janet, Margaret, i, 329.

Janinus (in Thomas Reymound's Will), i, 332.

Jarberd, John, instituted to Roborough, R., ii, 108b; exchanges for Ashwater, R., ii, 148.

Jaunte, Englesia, of Barnstaple, *see* Landkey, i, 108b.

Jele, Thomas (*alias* Boterworth), *see* Widecombe, i, 180b.

Jelle, Richard, of Harberton, assaults John Wolhay, chaplain, ii, 226b.

Jernemuth, John, saddler, of Norwich—

Demand for the restitution of his corpse, which had been unjustly buried "in ecclesia sive capella de Feld" in that city: case of appeal, 5 Id. May, 1398, ii, 218b, 219.

Jew (or Jewe), William, of Canonsleigh, i, 319, 329b.

Jew's Bridge, i, 306b.

Joan, Queen of England, presents to Yarcombe, V., ii, 105; to Christow, V., ii, 138, 244.

---

[1] Apparently; but there is a little confusion of *months* at this place.

[2] Here Jakkejowy. MS.

[3] With the Bishop at St. Frideswide's, Oxford.

Job, Thomas, instituted to Plymtree, R., ii, 188^{b}.

Joce, or Yoce[1], a Friar, a Penitentiary in the Deanery of East, i, 115^{b}, 143^{b}, 174, 194^{b}, 207^{b}, 217, 231, 238.

Jodel, Walter, chaplain, licensed to preach in the parish church of Clovelly (19 Feb., 1411-12), i, 145.

John, Thomas (de Helleston), instituted to the Chantry of Raleigh, ii, 191.

Joliblode, Thomas, proxy for Thomas Greyston, ii, 196^{b}.

Jordan (*alias* Wyllesdon), John, R. of Huntsham (deceased), ii, 195^{b}.

Jordan, Thomas, V. of Tywardreath, resigns, ii, 105.

Jory, Nicholas, collated to Zennor, V., ii, 181^{b}.

Josep, Stephen (or Joseph), R. of Northleigh, resigns, and is instituted to Stoke Fleming, R., ii, 17; i, 138, 173; ii, 245^{b}; his death, ii, 202.

Jowydavy (*alias* Jacka), Thomas, R. of Ruan-major, *see* Jacka.

Joye, Nicholas, R. of Romansleigh (deceased), ii, 176^{b}. And *see* Wembworthy.

Judde, John and Walter, i, 332.

Juhelfȝete [also, Juhelȝete, MS.], John, R. of Aveton-Giffard (deceased), ii, 67. *See*, also Wolhay, John, ii, 226^{b}.

Jul, Alice and Walter, i, 332.

Jul (or Juyl), John, Vicar of St. Austell:

This Vicar, and several other offenders (*see* Clok, Richard) refused to appear before the Consistory Court, for which they were excommunicated; and, being contumacious—"cum Sancta Mater Ecclesia ultra non habeat quid faciat"—the Bishop hands them over to the Secular arm for punishment (4 Jan., 1398-9), i, 24.—Juyl seems to have determined to appeal forthwith to the Pope; for we find the Bishop, on the 31st of August, addressing his Vicar-General in the following terms:—"Exposuit nobis dilectus filius dominus Johannes Juyl, perpetuus Vicarius Ecclesie parochialis Sancti Austoli, in Cornubia, nostre Diocesis, quod ex certis causis justis et necessariis ipsum ad hoc moventibus, quas sue consciencie relinquimus, voluit limina Apostolorum et Dominum nostrum Summum Pontificem pro salute ipsius anime visitare. Unde nos, suis devotis in hac parte nobis porrectis peticionibus inclinati, vobis et vestrum cuilibet mandamus quatinus eundem dominum Johannem a dicta Vicaria ex causis premissis se absentantem occasione absencie sue hujusmodi usque ad Festum Pasche proxime futurum non molestetis sive gravetis quovismodo."—i, 28^{b}.—His death, ii, 162^{b}.

Julyan, Nicholas, Canon of St. German's, i, 48.

Julyan, Robert, instituted to Northleigh, R., ii, 17.

---

[1] Called in one place (i, 115^{b}) "Custos de Tymbyg," and elsewhere "Custos de Trebighe."

Julyan, William, R. of Little Hempston, ii, 145.

Junne, John, instituted to Brent, V., ii, 94[b].

Jurdan, Roger, clerk, of Exminster, i, 301[b].

Juvenel, John, instituted to Landcross, R., ii, 12; resigns, ii, 20; instituted to Alverdiscott, R., ii, 19[b].

Juyll, Roger, clerk,—*Dispensacio super defectu natalium* (23 Sept., 1413), i, 184[b].

Juyll, William; *see* Atherington, i, 207; ii, 256.

K.

Kamok, W.; *see* Chudleigh, i, 239.

Kardowe, Thomas, instituted to Blisland, R., ii, 138[b]; i, 173.

Kardlyngton, Thomas, Prebendary of Cutton [Cotton, MS.]—
Mandate requiring him to appear at Westminster, and shew cause why he should not pay to Thomas Hendeman, Preb. of Heyes [Heyghes, MS.], the sum of 6s. 8d., an annual rent in arrear (*Breve Regium*, 30 Nov., 1413), ii, 347[b].

Kayleway, Edmund, presents to Cheldon, R., ii, 68, 138[b].

Kaynysham, John, cousin to Sir Rd. Champernoun, knt., i, 333[b].

Kays, William, proxy for John Macworth, ii, 96.

Kederowe, John, Sheriff of Cornwall, ii, 351[b].

Kellesnylle, Richard de, Judge, ii, 342.

Kelly, John, scholar,—*Dispensacio super defectu natalium*; "de *presbitero* et soluta genitus" (12 June, 1400), i, 42: and again (24 May, 1415), i, 210.

Kelly, John, junior, instituted to Tintagel, V., ii, 98[b].

Kelly, John, resigns St. Teath, V., ii, 136.

Kelly, Nicholas, R. of Ladock (deceased), ii, 159; *see* Ladock.

Kelly, Warin, proxy for John Kelly, ii, 98[b].

Kelwa, William (notary-publick), i, 38, 79[b], 327[b]; ii, 16[b].—Wm. Kelwa was inst. to Colebrook, (3 Jan., 1415-16), ii, 174.

Kelyngmersh, William, collated to a Canonry and the Prebend of Waleton in Bosham, ii, 191.

Kembell, John, V. of St. Sithney—
Licence to celebrate in the Chapels of St. Mary Magdalen, St. Elvin, and St. Gelvin (22 May, 1398), i, 18. [In the margin are the words—"non habuit effectum"]; his death, ii, 70.

Kemell, in the parish of Stoke, *see* Bryt (*Oratories*).

Kemeys, the Abbot and Convent of St. Mary and St. Dogmael in, present to Rattery V., ii, 189.

Kemp, John, ii, 256.—Kempe, John (*see* Oldcastel), i, 192[b].

Kenn; Thomas Redeman, R.; licence of non-residence for a year, from 2 Feb., 1397-8; i, 15; and from 25 July, 1410 (from his R. of Ermington likewise), i, 100^{b}. He was also Canon of Exeter, i, 239^{b}.

Kendale, Richard, *see* Luxulyan, i, 160^{b}; ii, 247.

Kene, John (of Devon), *see* St. Feock, i, 161.

Kenegy, Alan, Prior of Bodmin, i, 75; his election, ii, 72.

Kengeswode, Richard, instituted Prior of Pilton, ii, 147^{b}.

Kennerleigh (in Crediton—Kynwarlegh, MS.), *see* Dynham, Sir John, ii, 310^{b}.

Kenok, John, V. of Dawlish, proxy for John Burell, ii, 90^{b}.

Kenolmerssh *or* Kynwolmerssh, William, presents to Harpford, V., ii, 188, 192^{b}, 197, 263; to Yarcombe, V., ii, 194, 200^{b}.

Kentisbeare, Wood, in the parish of, i, 83.—John Whateley (or Whatteley, subdeacon), R., i, 8; (deacon, M.A.), Dispensation (to study at Oxford) for a year, from 14 March, 1395-6, i, 8^{b}.

Commissions of Enquiry as to the patronage:—(1) On the presentation by John Crokern "de Childehay," of Walter Symon, priest (1 Oct., 1412), ii, 248^{b}.—(2) by John Blaklake and Henry Tournour, clerks, and Walter Aldebury of Peter Soot, priest (19 Oct., 1412), ii, 249.—(3) by Rd. Courtenay, clerk, of James Frankcheyny, priest (31 Oct., 1412), ii, 249.—(4) by Wm. Stevenes, chaplain, of Walter Symon, chaplain (4 Nov., 1412), *ibid.*

[*Breve Regium*, 4 Oct., 1412]: Prohibition to admit, pending the settlement of the dispute as to the patronage between John Blakelake, clerk, Henry Turnour, clerk, and Walter Aldebury and Ralph Maloysell, John Crokern, Thomas Brokhampton, William Myryden, and Edward Brydham, ii, 345.—Suspension of the Prohibition (28 Nov., 1412), ii, 345^{b}.

Commissions of Enquiry:—On the presentation (1) of William Stevyn, chaplain, by Sir Edward Courtenay, knt., eldest son and heir of Edward, Earl of Devon (15 May, 1415), ii, 256^{b}. (2) Of William Legh, chaplain, by Joan, relict of Ralph Maloysell (17 May, 1415), *ibid.* (3) Of the same William Legh, by Edward Courtenay, son and heir of Edward, Earl of Devon (30 June, 1415), *ibid.*—(4) As to dilapidations, against Walter Symond, the late R., on the complaint of William Legh, R. (18 July, 1415), ii, 257.—Licence of non-residence was granted to Legh from 14 Feb., 1415-16, to Michaelmas, 1416; i, 216.

Kentisbury [Kyntysbyry *and* Kyntysbery, MS.], Philip Pym, R., licenced to celebrate in the Chapel of St. John Baptist (25 May, 1400), i, 39.—Thomas [Baker], R., licence of non-residence for a year, from 17 July, 1410; i, 100^{b}; *see* also, i, 123^{b}, 327^{b}.

Kenton; William Slegh, of, i, 318.—Adam Lylborn, V., his Will, i, 307.—Thomas Uppeton, V., a Penitentiary in the Deanery of Kenn, i, 94, 115, 143, 173^{b}, 194, 207^{b}, 216^{b}, 231, 237^{b}, 245.

Kenwyn [Kenwen, MS.], a Chapel in St. Kea, i, 228.

Kenylyon, John, chaplain to Sir John Champernoun, knt., i, 333ᵇ.

Kenyngton, the King's Manor of, i, 191ᵇ.

Kerdewille, Robert, resigns St. Paul's, Exeter, ii, 9; instituted to Harberton V., ii, 8ᵇ; his death, ii, 9ᵇ.

Kerdyngton (*or* de Kerdyngton), Thos., Preb. of Cutton, resigns, ii, 46ᵇ; is again inst. thereto, ii, 99ᵇ; his death, ii, 201.

Kestell, Henry (of Cornwall), ii, 351ᵇ.

Kewrig, Richard (a layman), excommunicate and contumacious (27 Nov., 1395), i, 7.

Keych, Henry, chaplain, i, 320ᵇ.

Keyl, Robert, instituted to the Chantry in the Cemetery of Ermington, ii, 102ᵇ.

Keynedon [Kynaden, MS.], in the parish of Stokenham, i, 90ᵇ.

Keynes, John, co-patron of Cruwys Morchard, R., ii, 194ᵇ.

Kiffyn, Howell, *see* Oldcastel, i, 192ᵇ.

Kilkhampton, William and Thomasia Greynevyle of, i, 186.—William Knyght, R., i, 84; a Penitentiary in the Deanery of Trigg-major, i, 93ᵇ, 115ᵇ, 143ᵇ, 174, 194ᵇ, 207ᵇ, 217, 231, 238, 245ᵇ; *see*, also, ii, 244ᵇ, 257, 261ᵇ.

Kingsbridge, John Prestecote's tenement in, i, 318ᵇ.

Andrew Blakhalle, of this town, having been accused of assaulting Philip Cradele, a priest, some asserting that he merely put his hand on him and in a lawful manner, whereas the Curate of the place abstained from communion with him and refused to celebrate in his presence, the Bishop commands Richard Olyver, President of his Consistory Court, to make enquiry and deal with the case (1 April, 1411), ii, 240ᵇ.—Meeting of the Chapter of the Deanery of Woodleigh there, to enquire as to the vacancy and patronage of the R. of Stokenham, and report to the Bishop, ii, 357.

The Bishop's Ordinacio between the R. of Churchstow and the parishioners of Kingsbridge on the dedication of their Chapel and Cemetery:—

Referring to a petition from Roger Saunder, John Veel and Wm. Surmound and others, parishrs. of Kingsbridge, setting forth (1) that their Chapel of St. Edmund, K. and Martyr, had been built long ago, and on a magnificent scale; (2) that they had always been exempt from all liabilities as to the Mother-Church, but were bound to maintain their own Chapel and also the Chancel thereof, and the books and necessary ornaments (because it had been granted to them for their own sole convenience), though they were not charged with the support of their Chaplain, or with the provision of bread and wine for the Eucharist, which burdens fell on Roger Bacheler, Rector of Churchstow, who was also bound, as his predecessors had been, to provide for all sacraments and sacramentals in the said Chapel, save only for the burial of their dead, which only could take place at the Mother-Church at Churchstow, a fee of one denarius being payable for the same; (3) that the said Chapel stood in a valley near the sea-shore, and a long way from the said parish church, which was built on the top of a lofty mountain [*in cacumine montis excelsi*], the road to it, along which funerals had to pass, being by a long and tedious ascent of the said mountain, both dangerous and difficult; (4) that they, the said parishrs. of Kingsbridge, were some of them sailors or shipmasters, while some were tradesmen and merchants, and others artificers and mechanicks, making a living by the labour of their hands, and devoting themselves to works of publick utility, so that they could with difficulty attend to even the burial of the dead, when so long and tedious a journey was necessary; and supplicating the Bishop to consecrate their Chapel and its Cemetery, and to grant them rights of interment therein; the Bishop declares that he had looked into the whole matter carefully, consulting the Abbot and Convent of Buckfast, on whose land the said Chapel and Cemetery stood, as well as Roger Bacheler, the Rector of Churchstow, and certain of his parishioners there, viz., Robt. Hulle, junr., John Hacche, Robt. and John Holdyche, John Wordell and Walter Legh, and also the Dean and Chapter of Exeter; and had found that all the statements in the said petition were true; and that, accordingly, he was prepared to consecrate the said Chapel and Cemetery, reserving all the rights of the mother Church intact, and subject to certain conditions as follows—(1) Every adult parishioner of Kingsbridge, being married and a householder, was to hear Mass every year, on the local Feast Day, viz., the Assumption of Blessed Virgin Mary, in the Mother-Church, and for himself and family to make an offering of one denarius to the R. (2) Every unmarried parishioner, male or female, being a householder, was to do the same, and pay one obolus; and on the Day of the Dedication of the said Mother-Church (Sept. 5), all such were bound to attend their own Chapel and keep the Day as a Double Feast, abstaining from servile work, as well as on the Day of the Dedication of the said Chapel, viz., St. Edmund's Day, and to make an offering of one obolus there, for the use of the said Rector. (3) The executors or friends of any person buried there were to pay one denarius to the R., as if the interment had taken place at Churchstow. (4) Every innkeeper or brewer of beer for sale, was to pay the sum of one denarius in lieu of the flagon of ale which, after the manner of tithes in kind, the Rector had been accustomed to receive *pro qualibet pandoxacione:* (5) And whereas there are always some who, from avarice and malice, are wont to defraud the Church and the Clergy, using at funerals the lights commonly called *fraternalia*, and, against the will of the Curates, erecting lofty tombs of stone, all men were forbidden so to employ the tapers belonging to any fraternity, in the said Chapel or its Cemetery, unless they first indemnified the Rector by paying him two denarii, or to set up such great monuments of stone therein without first paying him six denarii; but modest tombs, level with the ground and offering no obstacle to passengers, erected solely in memory of respectable men and women, and inviting prayers for their souls, were in no wise prohibited; but in both cases the said Rector was to be consulted. And as to other lights, not "fraternalia," those that were carried, with the bodies of the dead, into the Cemetery were to be given to the said Rector for his own use; but those that were only used outside the Cemetery were to remain, as formerly, at the disposal of the executors and friends. (6) The trees and the herbage (or grass) in the said Cemetery were to belong to the said Rector. (7) In case of any resistance to these provisions or violations of them, if the majority of the adult parishioners were to blame, and after eight days' notice, given on a Sunday during Mass, they remained rebellious, all right of sepulture in the Chapel and Cemetery would be forfeited, and would return to Churchstow until their submission; but if the minority or any individual parishioner were in fault, the Rector was to proceed according to law, in the usual manner.

The Chapel was dedicated by Bishop Stafford on 26 Aug., 1414, and the Cemetery on the following day; and he signed and sealed the Ordinacio at Chudleigh on the 30th of August. The Dean and Chapter of Exeter had done so on the 20th of July, in their Chapter-House; the Abbot of Buckfast, in the Chapter-House there, on July 23; Roger Bacheler, the Rector, using the seal of the President of the Consistory Court of Exeter, at Churchstow, on the 22 July; the above-named parishioners of Churchstow, using the seal of the Dean of Woodleigh, at Kingsbridge, on July 24; and Roger Saunder, John Veel, John Torryng, Wm. Surmound, Andrew Blakhall, John Redewyll, Rd. Lockyngton, Roger Dyer, Thos. Lever, Robt. Bold, David Ryder, Robt. Blake, Thos. O'yver, and others, parishioners of Kingsbridge, using the seal of the Town [*sigillum nostrum et dicti Burgi de Kyngysbrygge*], at Kingsbridge, on 25 July; all in 1414 : ii, 290b—292b.

Kings Nympton, John Haket, R., licence of non-residence (to study at Oxford), for a year, from 14 Nov., 1395, i, 6b.—*John*[1] Southam, R., for two years, from 12 Feb., 1411-12, i, 145.

A Commission of Enquiry as to the dilapidations here, through the neglect of the late R., William Southam, was issued 9 Dec., 1412, on the complaint of his successor, Philip Staunton, ii, 250. This R. obtained licence of non-residence from 12 Jan., 1413-14 to St. John Baptist's Day, 1414; i, 190b.

Kingsteignton and Yealmpton, Prebend of, in Salisbury Cathedral, ii, 37b.

Kingston, a daughter Church to Ermington:

Ordinacio touching the Chapel and the new Cemetery there; in which Richard Hals, Treasurer and Official Principal, sets forth that Pope Boniface IX. had lately conceded to the inhabitants of this village or hamlet the right of sepulture in the said Chapel, dedicated to St. James the Apostle, and in a cemetery annexed thereto as soon as dedicated, and he quotes the Letters Apostolick at large. They had complained that the bodies of the dead had to be carried all the way to Ermington, at great inconvenience, although their children had been baptized, and the Sacraments and all Sacramental rites administered in their said Chapel, from old time. Accordingly permission was granted for the enclosure of a cemetery, and for its dedication, the rights of the Mother-Church being saved.—[Dat. at Rome, at St. Peter's, iij Non. Febr., ann. Pontificat. XII.] Subsequently, on 10 May, 1402, the parties appeared before the said Rd. Hals in the Consistory Court, at Exeter, viz., Richard Tyttesbury, R. of the Mediety of Ermington, represented by Ralph Dolbeare, literate, and the parishioners of Ermington by Rd. Pyperell and John Dymmok, together with Thos. Row, Vicar of Ermington, on the one part, and the inhabitants of Kingston, represented by Thos. Cotemor and Thos. Whyteway, their proctors, on the other—and settled the terms of an agreement herein, thus:—The inhabitants of Kingston were to resort, as before, to the Mother-Church on the Day of the Dedication thereof, viz., 5 Feb., and on the local Feast Day, viz., the Feast of SS. Peter and Paul, every year, observing both after the manner of Double Feasts, but not of necessity bound to pay the accustomed dues: their Chaplain, also, was not to say Mass in their Chapel, on the said Feast of Dedication, unless there were a corpse there to be buried the same day. They were bound for ever to contribute to the renewal and repair of the nave of the Mother-Church, and the books, vestments, ornaments, and other burdens belonging to the parishioners, whenever the parishioners should will to make a levy for the said purpose; they were to have a vote in the matter, being represented by two of their members, with appeal to the Bishop in case of disagreement; but in the absence of their representatives the parishioners of Ermington could proceed without them, and enforce payment. They were bound also to keep up, at their own cost, part of the cemetery at Ermington as of old, viz., the part on the S. and E. of the church between the two stiles (*scansilia*), measuring in length 12 rods and 10 feet. Also they were to pay yearly, on the Feast of St. Nicholas the Bishop, twelvepence, to maintain two processional candles in the Church of

---

[1] A clerical error apparently; he is elsewhere called William.

Ermington, to be paid to the wardens of the said Church of St. Peter, according to immemorial custom; but whenever they brought their dead to Ermington to be buried, they were to have the use of the said candles (without requiring to ask permission of the parishioners of Ermington), to be lighted as soon as the body is brought into the Church, and kept burning till it is carried forth to the burying. The parishioners of Ermington were to have quiet possession of the lands, tenements, &c., called "Peterysloude at Hacche" (situate within the parish of the said Chapel) for the use and service of the Mother-Church, as from time immemorial. And as their Chapel was built and is continued for their convenience, they were to keep it in repair, not the nave only, but the chancel also, with all books and ornaments whatsoever; but the V. was to provide and maintain a fit chaplain to minister therein. Also the parishioners of Kingston were to give yearly, on the Feast of the Dedication of their Chapel, to the Vicar of Ermington one *lagena* of wine, or the estimated value thereof, in acknowledgment of their liberty of sepulture therein, and to the R. and V. thereof their tithes, great and small, as aforetime, together with all dues and offerings, under certain pains and penalties in case of default. This Ordinacio was duly ratified, &c., &c., in the presence of Rd. Wykeslond, Rd. Talbot, John Lydeford, junr., and Thomas Tredowar, advocates, and Wm. Knyght and Wm. Combe, proctors, on the day and in the year above-named.

The names of the parishioners of Ermington who appeared, by proxy (as above), in this case were—Walter Pruston, John Mayovu, John Holewyll, Henry Schetcote, and Andrew Baker. Their *procuratorium* was dated 6 May, 1401.

The names of the parishioners of Kingston were John Hacche, Roger Edmund, John Broun, Thos. Carswyll, Wm. Coppe, Walter Yurl, and Ambrose Palmer [Dated at Kyngeston, and sealed by the Dean of Plympton], 6 Jan., 1401-2; ii, 275-278.

A Commission was directed, 22 July, 1402, to "Episcopus Soltaniensis[-in Media,"—John Greenlaw] to consecrate this Chapel and cemetery, ii, 229ᵇ.

Kitton [Keton, MS.], in Holcombe Rogus, i, 226.

Knokya, Richard, chaplain, presented to St. Pinnock, ii, 268.

Knolle, Richard, a parishioner of Linkinhorne, i, 116.

Knowston (*or* Knoweston), John, instituted to Combpyne, R., ii, 138ᵇ; i, 142; his death, ii, 200ᵇ, 268.

Knyf, John, chaplain, i, 332.

Knyght, John, V. of Broadwoodwidger, clerk, exchanges for Honeychurch, R., ii, 95;—

He was a notary-publick, ii, 174; Commissioned as Registrar of the Consistory Court of Exeter (15 Sept., 1416), ii, 259ᵇ; collated to Farringdon, R., ii, 189; exchanged for Cruwys Morchard, R., ii, 194ᵇ, when still in deacon's orders; and a Commission was issued for his ordination as Priest, ii, 266ᵇ.

Knyght, John, of Bridport, ii, 313.

Knyght, Richard, presented to Heanton-Punchardon, R., ii, 247; instituted thereto, ii, 146.

Knyght, William, patron of Bicton, R., ii, 11ᵇ, 14, 23, 83.

Knyght, William; his Commission as Official-Peculiar in Devon (10 Aug., 1395), ii, 210; *see* i, 35ᵇ; inst. to Barnstaple, ii, 33; 50, 50ᵇ; exchanges for Kilkhampton, ii, 71; i, 84; ii, 257; collated to a Canonry in Crediton, ii, 175ᵇ; 261ᵇ.

A Commission was directed to him (5 Feb., 1411-12), for proving the Will of Sir John Greynevyll, knt., ii, 244ᵇ.—William Knyght, R. of Clyst St. George (probably the same person); his institution, ii, 179.

Knygth, John, i, 319.

Knygth, Robert, V. of Brent (deceased), ii, 94ᵇ.

Knyghton, John, R. of Huxham, exchanges for East Lydford (Dioc. of Bath and Wells), ii, 74ᵇ.

Knyghtiston, John, does homage to the Bishop, at Crediton for lands at Knyghtiston in Bishop's Morchard (10 July, 1418), ii, 311ᵇ.

Kye, John, i, 304.

Kyck, John, proxy for Richard Courtenay, *see* Alphington, ii 67.—John Kykke, probably the same, was R. of Offwell [Uffewyll, MS.], in 1410, i, 103ᵇ.

Kyldreynek, John, *see* St. Pinnock, ii, 351.

Kylryngton, John, R. of East Worlington (deceased), ii, 14ᵇ.

Kylyow, William, instituted to St. Erme, R., ii, 82ᵇ.

Kymbuscumque, Baldwin, R. of Brendon, resigns, ii, 105ᵇ.

Kyng, John—

Licensed to serve the Chapel at Whytefeld, in Marwood, pending a suit between the inhabitants of that hamlet and Thomas Chaunterell, R. of Marwood (10 April, 1419), i, 246ᵇ.

Kyngdon, Roger, does homage to the Bishop, at Crediton, for lands in Lawhitton (29 April, 1411), ii, 310ᵇ.

Kyngford, Richard de, of Prancraswyke, i, 69.

Kyngeslond, Thomas, presents to Charles, R., ii, 98ᵇ, 106, 190.

Kyngewyll, Robert, instituted to North Bovey, R., ii, 189ᵇ, 264.

Kynggeston, Richard, Dean of Windsor, ii, 89.

Kyngton, John, Canon and Prebendary of Crantock, etc., ii, 43, 226; instituted to Marwood, R., ii, 70ᵇ; exchanges for a Canonry and Prebend in Great St. Martin's, London, ii, 89.

Kyngton, in Devon, ii, 310.

Kyngysford, Ralph, deacon—

His petition; setting forth that formerly, when he was a simple clerk, only fourteen years old, he and a fellow clerk, one Robert Hoper, of the same age, were playing *cum quadam mirica, sive scopa facta de miricis*, when, quite by accident, he struck the said Robert on the eye, and entirely destroyed the sight. Later on he proceeded, without scruple, to the Orders of subdeacon and deacon; but when, in due course, he desired to take priest's Orders, and was prepared to make ample reparation to the mutilated clerk, the said Robert refused to come to terms, and Ralph appealed for a remedy to the Holy See. His prayer was granted, and Letters Apostolick were addressed to the Bishop; whereupon a Commission was directed to Ralph Morwyll, William Payn, and William Andrew, to cause the said Robert to appear before the Bishop, in his manor of Clyst, and shew cause, etc. (24

May, 1412), i, 149b. In the end, the said Robert Hoper having refused to take the sum of 40s offered by way of reparation for the injury, and continuing contumacious, a full Dispensation was granted to Kyngysford (20 Sept., 1412), i, 171b. Six years later he was presented to Westleigh, R. by the Dean and Chapter, ii, 194b.

Kyrby, John, Prebendary of St. Probus, resigns, ii, 53.

Kyrchill, John, co-patron of Sidmouth, V., ii, 22.

Kyrkham, Nicholas, patron of Ringmore, R., ii, 5b.

Kyrke, Wm., *see* atte Kyrke, ii, 49b.

Kyte, John, a parishioner of Cowick, ii, 287.

Kyttow, Richard, chaplain, ii, 174b.

L.

Lacche, John, co-patron of Aveton-Giffard, R., ii, 67b; and of the Chantry "de Lyneton" therein, ii, 91b.

Ladock (or St. Ladock)—

A licence to Nicholas [Kelly], R., to celebrate in his own manse, and also in the Chapel of St. John, in St. Erme (30 April, 1411), i, 123b. –Renaldus Tretherf, R., i, 203; (sub-deacon) dispensation (to study at Oxford), for two years from 3 March, 1418-19, i, 245b.

A Commission of Enquiry as to Dilapidations was issued (22 June, 1414) on the complaint of Tretherf against his predecessor, ii, 245b.

Lake, John, and Joan Paes, Dispensation in favour of ;—

They had contracted marriage in ignorance of the existence of any impediment thereto, and had afterwards discovered that they were related in the fourth degree of consanguinity (22 Sept., 1406). John Lake, of Linkinhorne, occurs at i, 113b; *see*, also, i, 316b, ii, 213.

Lambard, Walter, instituted to St. Cleer, V., ii, 84b; exchanges for Quennington, R. (Dioc. of Worcester), ii, 89.

Lambert, William, presented to the Priory of St. Michael's Mount, by Henry, Prince of Wales; Commission of Enquiry as to the patronage (31 July, 1410), ii, 233; his institution, ii, 124, 338b, 349.

Lamburn (*or* Lambourne), John, collated Sacristan of Bosham, ii, 100; 280, 281; exchanges for Stapleford, V. (Dioc. of Ely), ii, 109b.

Lambroke, Katherine, i, 329.

Lamerton; Augustine Strode, V., ii, 254—

Commission of Enquiry as to the patronage, the Abbot and Convent of Tavistock having presented Augustine Strode, chaplain (23 June, 1412), ii, 247b.

Commission of Enquiry as to Dilapidations, on the complaint of William Floyer, V., against Henry Thomas, his predecessor (11 Jan., 1414-15), ii, 256; *see*, also, ii, 355.

Lamledyr, John, inst. to St. Clement's (Lamorek, MS.), ii, 15b.

Lammanva, Petronilla (*see* "Oratories") i, 84.

Lamoren, Peter, R. of Lawhitton, ii, 209b, 265b; exchanges for Poltimore, R., ii, 197b; his death, ii, 199b.

Lamorran [Lammoran, MS.], Thomas Hoppeley (or Wappelegh *see*, ii, 40, 124), R., licence of non-residence for a year, from 19 May, 1400 (*contemplacione Willelmi Bentley, de Plymmouth*), i, 38.

Lamport, Richard, Abbot of Dunkeswell, ii, 225b.

Lancaster, John de, Provincial of the Dominicans in England, i, 101b.

Lancastre, Elizabeth, Duchess of Exeter, ii, 13.

Lancastre, John, Duke of, *ibid.*

Landcross [Lancars, MS.], John Badecok and Richard Scotte of, *see* Badecok; i, 163.

Landew, Chapel of St. Bridget at, in Lezant, i, 238.

Landkey [Laundekey, MS.], "capella parochialis et curata"—

The Bishop writes to the Dean of Barnstaple, the V. of Bishop's Tawton, and the other Clergy of the Deanery, removing the Interdict which had been laid on this Church by reason of a clandestine marriage between John Godecherle, baker, and Englisia (*alias* Engge) Jaunte, of the parish of Barnstaple, which had been celebrated by an Augustinian Friar of Bristol (as was alleged), "contemplacione Johannis Mulys, predicte capelle curate et parochialis de Laundekey parochiani" (5 Nov., 1410), i, 108b.

Lane, John, R., of Hemington (Dioc. of Bath and Wells), exchanges for Cheriton Bishop. ii, 56; resigns, and is collated Precentor of Ottery, ii, 123b; exchanges for East Ogwell, R., ii, 135; proxy for John Burgh, ii, 158; for Thomas Raleigh, ii, 181b; for Thomas Warde, ii, 192; for John Bernyngham, ii, 193b; for Matthew Downe, ii, 194b; exchanges East Ogwell for Studland, R. (Dioc. of Salisbury), ii, 198b; *see*, also, i, 333.

Lane, William, R. of Roseash, exchanges for Chulmleigh, R., ii, 80b; i, 82b, 217, 231, 238, 245b; is instituted to Southleigh, R., ii, 168; i, 221; *see Oratories*, i, 39.

Laneman, Walter, R. of Arlington (deceased), ii, 6b.

Langaker, Michael, presents to St. Pinnock, R., ii, 123; *see*, also, ii, 350b, 351b.

Lange, Geoffrey, V. of South Tawton (deceased), ii, 138.

Langh or Lange, John, instituted to Bickleigh, R., ii, 8; exchanges for Stogumber, (Dioc. of Bath and Wells), ii, 87b—

A John Lange was V. of Walkhampton (deceased), ii, 88; also, one John Langge was R. of Dunchideock, (deceased), ii, 130; and *see*, i, 19b.

Langge, Oliver, *see* Rychard, Robert, ii, 235b.

Langh (or Langeman), Roger, R. of Bradford, i, 82[1], 87, 97; (deceased), ii, 139.

Langge, Thomas, R. of Heathfield (Dioc. of Bath and Wells), ii, 40^b; instituted (probably the same), to Instow, R., ii, 89; i, 81, 111^b; his death, ii, 144^b; *see*, also, i, 315.

Lange, Walter, *see* Bridgewater; i, 96.

Langebrok, John, V. of Ermington (deceased), ii, 51.

Langdon, Geoffrey, i, 327^b, 328.

Langedon, Joan, wife of Wm. (of South Petherwyn), ii, 263^b.

Langedon, John, does homage to the Bishop, in London, for lands in Lawhitton (20 May, 1397), ii, 310.

Langedon, William, co-patron of Roseash, ii, 80^b; i, 237.

Langeford, Thomas, i, 306^b.

Langelegh, John, "minister" of Ottery; his Will, i, 303^b; also, John Langelegh (brother of the said John), and Juliana, and Sibella Langelegh, i, 304.

Langeton, Wm., (Dioc. of Norwich), together with John Rochewell, (Dioc. of York), clerks; witnesses to the Dispensation in favour of Walter and Emma Vyel (*q.v.*), i, 14;—

Collated to a Canonry in Crantock, ii, 27^b; resigns, and is collated to the Prebend of Prustecombe in Crediton, ii, 31, 58^b; i, 40, 40^b, 42^b, 51^b, 64, collated to a Canonry in Exeter Cathedral, ii, 35; i, 78^b, 79, 89, 100, 116, 117, 127, 129, 137, 137^b, 147^b, 162, 166^b, 167, 175^b, 182, 184, 195, 305^b, 313^b, 321; appointed proxy in Convocation for the Bishop (24 Feb., 1397-8), i, 15; resigns his Canonry of Exeter and is collated to a Canonry and the Prebend of Apuldram in Bosham, ii, 38^b; exchanges the same for Warbleton, R. (Dioc. of Chichester), and eight days later is collated to the same Canonry and Prebend again, ii, 52 (*see* ii, 280, 281); exchanges with Richard Tyttesbury for another Canonry and Prebend [Westbrook] in Bosham, ii, 97; is instituted to South Pool, R., *ibid*; his death, ii, 155, 155^b, 158^b; his Will, i, 322. Langeton died Canon of Crediton, Bosham, Ottery, and Exeter: he is stated to have resigned the last in 1398, and to have been succeeded by Thomas Redman (ii, 38^b): I find no record of his collation to the Canonry in the Cathedral to which John Westecote, or to the sixth Preb. in Ottery to which Henry Blakemore, succeeded on Langeton's death, ii, 155^b.

Langley [Langelegh, MS.], in High Bickington, *see* Pollard (*Oratories*), i, 208^b.

Langelegh, John, "Minister" and Canon and Prebendary of Ottery (deceased), ii, 81^b.

Langle, John, R. of West Mill (Dioc. of Lincoln), exchanges for Combmartin, R., ii, 181; i, 230^b.

Langman, John, i, 310.

Langman, Robert, a deacon—

Ordained sub-deacon and deacon by alien Bishops, without licence: a Dispensation was granted in his favour (5 Nov., 1410), i, 227^b; *see*, also, (R. L. "junior," chaplain), i, 244, 310.

---

[1] John, here—a clerical error, MS.

Langeman, Roger, R. of East Allington; he exchanged for the office of "Minister" in Ottery St. Mary, ii, 98b; his death, ii, 103b.

Langewylle, Chapel of Our Lady of, in Dodbrooke, ii, 244b.

*Langrom, Thomas, R. of High Bray (resigns), ii, 191b.

Langryg [*and* Langarygge, MS.], Arnulph, proxy for John Combe, ii, 67b; clerk, of Slapton Collegiate Chantry, ii, 111.

Langerygg, William, R. of Combpyne (deceased), ii, 138b.

Langston, John, *see* Blisland, ii, 245.

Langtree, R. [*Breve Regium*]—

(1) Prohibition to admit to this Benefice, pending settlement of the dispute between the King and Constance le Despenser (17 March, 1410-11), ii, 338.

(2) Suspension of the Prohibition (4 May, 1411), ii, 339b.—There had been a Commission of Enquiry, 15 March, 1410-11 (ii, 239b): in the event, Constance le Despenser's presentation of Walter Cook was held to be good, and he was instituted 13 May; ii, 132b. To this Rector a licence was granted, 25 Oct., 1412, to celebrate in the Chapel of St. Nicholas at Stowford [Stauford, MS.], in this parish; i, 171b.

Langunnett [Langonet, MS.], *see* Derneforde (*Oratories*), i, 209b.

Lanhergy, John, a layman, excommunicate and contumacious—

(1) *Litera super inquisicione Domini facta Judicibus Secularibus, ut excommunicatus repellatur ab agendo* (19 Jan., 1396-7), i, 11.

(2) *Significavit* (dated 23 Jan.), *ibid.*

Lanivet [Lannyvet *and* Lanyveth, MS.], Alfred Gyffard, R.; licence of non-residence (to study at Oxford), for two years, from 28 April, 1396, i, 8b; also, for a year, from 4 June, 1398, i, 18b; from 19 July, 1399, i, 28b; and from 5 Jan., 1402-3, i, 62b.

Licence was granted to him (17 June, 1411), to celebrate in St. Benet's Chapel in this parish—"in capella in honore Sancti Benedicti infra parochiam predictam constructa et situata;" i, 126b. [There are still considerable remains of the antient Chapel and of a house to which it was attached: it stands near the parish-church, and has been the subject of much misapprehension. Dr. Oliver had to explain his reasons for omitting it from his *Monasticon* of the Diocese. "As to St. Bennet's," he writes (Pref., p. v.) "in the parish of Lanivet in Cornwall, asserted to have been a nunnery subordinate to some foreign monastery in Italy, in France, or elsewhere (for various places have been named), it was nothing more than a Chapel of Special Devotion, as is proved by a document, dated May 6, 1535, in vol. ii, of Bishop Veysey's Register."]

Lankynhorne, Roger de, a parishioner of Linkinhorne, i, 116.

Lanlawren [Lanlawarn, MS.], in the parish of Lanteglos-by Fowey, (q.v.) i, 80.

Lanlivery, Michael Robert, parochial-chaplain of, i, 50; William Bonnok, V., *see* Bonnok, *ibid.*—Pylle, in the parish of, i, 75.

Commission of Enquiry as to the patronage on the presentation of Robert Chamberleyn, priest, by the Prior and Convent of Tywardreath (13 June, 1416), ii, 259.—Lostwithiel; a Chapelry dependent on "Lanlyveray," i, 220b; a "capella curata" in the said parish, ii, 260b.

Lannire, Richard, instituted to Landrake, V., ii, 10[b].

Lannysely, Alan, instituted to St. Hilary, V., ii, 74.

Lanow, i.e. St. Kew (q.v.)

Lanrak, John, chaplain, i, 301[b]. Thomas Lanrak; *see* Duloe.

Lanreath [Lanratow, Lanrethowe, Lanraythiow, *and* Lanraythow, MS.]; William Somerford, R., Canon of Glasney; licence of non-residence (to reside in that College), for a year, from 13 Nov., 1405, i, 77.—Henry Rychard, R., for a year, from 27 June, 1410, i, 99; also, from 15 Nov., 1411, to Michaelmas, 1412; i, 139: also from 22 Oct., 1412, to Michaelmas, 1413; i, 170; also, for one year, from 22 June, 1414; i, 197[b]; and for two years, from 7 Oct., 1417, i, 235; *see*, also, i, 181[b].—Trefraudewell, in this parish, i, 77.

Lansallos [Lansalwys *alias* Lansalawys, MS.], Chapel of St. Peter at Porthpyre [*hodie* Polperro], in—

Licence to the inhabitants of this village to cause Divine Service to be celebrated in the said Chapel except on the Feasts of Christmas, Easter, the Purification, St. Katherine, and All Saints (20 May, 1400), i, 38.

Commission of Enquiry as to the alleged pollution of the Church during a quarrel between John Trenarrak (*alias* Lawry) and Agnes, relict of Hervey Eyr, with bloodshed (12 Jan., 1413-14), ii, 253[b].

Lanteglos [by Camelford], Thomas [Clyfford], R.—

Licensed to celebrate in the Chapel of the Blessed Virgin Mary in Camelford (31 Jan., 1396-7), i, 11. He had licence of non-residence for two years, from 8 April, 1399, i, 26.

Richard Aldrington, R.—

Licensed to serve the Chapel of St. Thomas-the-Martyr, in Camelford (25 May, 1405), i, 75.—On the petition of this R., relaxation was granted of the Interdict under which the Church lay through the fault of Richard Welyngton, R. of St. Tudy (11 June, 1412), i, 161[b].

William Trebell (sub-deacon), R.; dispensation (to study at Oxford), for one year, from 27 Aug., 1417, i, 233[b]; *see*, also, i, 242[b].

Lanteglos [by Fowey], "juxta Polrywan" (i.e. Polruan), MS.—

Licence to the inhabitants of Boedynnek (*hodie* Bodinnick), for their Chapel of St. John Baptist (22 Oct., 1406), i, 80. There was a Chapel, also, at "Lanlawarn *alias* Pensiden," *see* Bonefas (*Oratories*); *ibid.*

John Hoper, V., a Penitentiary in the Deanery of West, i, 143[b].—John Compton, V., ditto, i, 174, 194[b], 207[b], 217, 231[b], 238, 245[b].

Lanvyan, Andrew, clerk, *Dispensacio super defectu natalium* (1 May, 1419), i, 247.

Lapford, the R. of (mentioned 5 Sept., 1410), i, 105[b].—

His name is not given; but I suppose *Thomas de Bukenarle* is meant, who was instituted in 1382 by Bishop Bruntingham: no institution to Lapford, by Bishop Stafford, is recorded.—See Hurde, Richard, i, 202[b].

Laployd[1], Chapel of St. Katherine, *see* Bridford, i, 90[b].

Laplode, Joan, relict of Ralph, *see* Ingram, Nigel, i, 174[b].

Larkbeare, in the parish of St. Leonard's, Exeter, i, 223.

Latymer, Alienora, i, 329[b]; Elizabeth [Hulle, step]-daughter of Matilda Latymer, a Sister of Buckland, i, 329; John and Ralph [Hulle], sons of Matilda, *ibid*; Margaret [Hulle, step]-daughter of Matilda, *ibid*: Matilda Latymer's Will, i, 329.

Launcell, Thomas, collated *by lapse* to Honeychurch, R., ii, 64; exchanges for Broadwoodwidger, V., ii, 95.

Launcells [Launcell, *and* Launcelys MS.], Rd. Doty, R., licensed to celebrate in all chapels and oratories in his parish (21 May, 1400), i, 38[b].—Thorlebeare, in this parish, i, 212.

Lancels, John, Canon of St. Stephen's, Launceston, ii, 117.

Launceston, the Priory of St. Stephen's at—

The Prior having represented to the Bishop that the Feast Day of the Priory Church (a Feast of the Second Rank) occured in the Octave of the Assumption, a Double Feast; other Feasts also coinciding, viz., those of SS. Agapetus, Magnus, Philibertus, Timotheus, Symphorianus, Audoenus and Genesius, so that their full services could not be properly celebrated, the Bishop transferred the Feast of Dedication to Oct. 22 (18 June, 1401), i, 56[b]

Licence of non-residence from 12 Sept., 1401, granted to John Waryn, Vicar of Liskeard, to enable him to remain at Rome until the settlement of the dispute—*super jure et possessione ejusdem Vicarie*—between this Priory and himself, i, 58.

Stephen [Tredydan], Prior of, ii, 313[b].—On the death of this Prior, 8 Dec., 1403, the Bishop granted his licence (12 Dec.), for the election of a successor, appointing the Subprior and Noel Patreda, steward of his lands in Cornwall, to be the guardians thereof in the interval, ii, 72. Roger Combrygge was elected. I find no record of the fact; only of his death, which occurred, 18 June, 1410. The Bishop was informed thereof, at Crediton, on the 20th, by John Honylond, one of the Canons, the bearer of a letter from the Community, dated 19 June, requesting the Bishop, as Patron, to grant his licence to proceed to an election. It was granted; and on the same day the Bishop appointed David Treludek, sub-prior, and Richard Reppryn (his steward in Cornwall) to have charge of the goods of the Priory during the vacancy; the spiritual charge being committed to the former alone. On the 30th John Wylle was deputed to inform the Bishop of the election (on the 28th), of John Honylond, by David Treludek (sub-prior), and all the other members of the community; viz., Robert Hervy, Thomas Tredak, John Batyn, John Cleve, Thomas Osburne, Simon Anstyswylle, John Wylkyn, John Cade, John Lancels, John Honnylond, John Thomme, and William Frengy, all priests, in the presence of John Sutton, clerk, notary-publick, William Hunden and Richard Penels. A Mandate was issued to the Dean of Trigg-major, and to John Bylker and John Clerk, priests, to publish the election in the usual manner; and the election was in due course confirmed, 5 July, and the Mandate for the new Prior's induction and installation directed to Laurence Bodeman, R. of Lifton: ii, 115-120.

Licence was granted to Prior Honnylond, 17 July, 1410, to celebrate within the several Manors and Mansions belonging to the Priory—"cum vos ad hujusmodi maneria . . . . . causa recreacionis vel alia legitima declinare

[1] Lapflote, MS.: "Laplywood" in the old Parish Registers.

contigerit" ; i, 101. Shortly afterwards the Priory was declared to be n arrears for three years (1408-10), to the Pope's Collector (10 Sept, 1410), i, 105. One Simon, sub-prior, is mentioned as a Penitentiary in the Deanery of Trigg-major, i, 231, 238, 245b.—The Prior and Convent presented to Talland, V., ii, 6 ; to Beaworthy, R., ii, 69b ; to Bridgerule, V., ii, 100b ; to Linkinhorne, V., ii, 132, 201b ; to St. Gennys, V., ii, 141b ; to Liskeard, V. ii, 149b, 169b ; to Ashbury, R., ii, 181b ; to Poughill (Cornwall), ii, 186 ; *see*, also, i, 324.

Launceston, Walter Trethewy, licensed as a Publick-Preacher in the parish of (22 March, 1414-15), i, 209.

Laurence, John, R. of Blisland, exchanges for Gransden-parva (Dioc. of Ely), ii, 32. A John Lauerence is mentioned as proxy for John Watere, ii, 156.

Lauerans, Richard, V., of Payhembury (deceased), ii, 150.

Laurence, Thomas, i, 300b.

Laury, Joan, a Canoness of Canonsleigh, ii, 125.

Laury, John, instituted to Stowford, R., ii, 169b.

Laverde, John, clerk—*Dispensacio super defectu natalium* (31 May, 1409), i, 89.

Lavoy, Alice, i, 333b.

Lavyngton, John, instituted to Yarnscombe, R., ii, 106 ; exchanges for St. Gennys, V., ii, 141b.

Lavyngton, Thomas, Preb. of St. Probus (resigns), ii, 55b ; is again collated to a Prebend there, ii, 57b.

Lawhitton; Peter [Lamoren], R., licensed to hear confessions (28 Feb., 1395-6), i, 8 ; licensed to celebrate in his Rectory house (3 April, 1414), i, 195b—

By the inscrutable judgment of God this R. was smitten with blindness, and so overcome with infirmities that he was quite unable to discharge his duties : and yet he had wasted, and continued to waste the profits of his Living, and was suffering the buildings thereof to fall into ruin. The Bishop, therefore, desiring to obviate this danger to the souls of the parishioners, directed a Commission to James Carslegh (Official of his Peculiar Jurisdiction in Cornwall), empowering him to appoint a fit person as coadjutor-priest, with sole charge of the parish, reserving a sufficient maintenance for the said Peter, and requiring the coadjutor to render a true account to the Bishop (19 June, 1418), ii, 265b ; *see*, also, Langedon, John (ii, 310) ; Bodulget, Stephen (ii, 310b ; and Kyngdon, Roger (*ibid*) ; also, i, 46b ; ii, 209b.

Lawys, Roger, *see* Symon, John, ii, 332b.

Leardecrune, Michael, clerk,—*Dispensacio super defectu natalium* (27 Feb., 1397-8), i, 15b.

Lebet, Walter, instituted to Combpyne, R., ii, 200b, 268.

Leche, John, "*alias dictus* Wade," *see* Lewannick.

Leche, John, sub-prior of Plympton, i, 94, 115b.

Lecture, by the Chancellor in the Cathedral, *see* Bosom, Robert, i, 6.

Ledes (*or* de Ledes), William, dies Preb. of Chulmleigh, and Canon of Crediton and of Crantock, ii, 5b, 31.

Lee Bridge [Leghbrygge, MS.]—

This still important bridge (which is described as "juxta Cholounslegh [*hodie* Challonsleigh], a villa de Plimpton ultra aquam de Yalme ad Civitatem Exoniensem directe ducentia," having been almost destroyed by floods; the approaches to the said bridge being, moreover, very muddy in winter and even dangerous to travellers, and funds for its repair and improvement falling short, the Bishop promises an Indulgence to the Faithful contributing to so necessary a work (10 April, 1414), i, 195b.

Leedes Castle, in Kent, ii, 27.

Legh, *see* Denys (*Oratories*), i, 38b.

Legh, Edward, instituted Arch-priest of Haccombe, ii, 149.

Legh, John, instituted to Creacombe, R., ii, 68b.

Legh, Nicholas, i, 38b.

Legh, Walter, of Churchstow, ii, 291.

Legh, William, instituted to Kentisbeare, R., ii, 166; 256b, 257; i, 216.

Leicester, the Parliament held at, 2 Henry V.—

Statutes ordained therein, concerning "Hospitals," "the Estate of Labourers," "Murders, treason, etc."; against the Lollards; against riotous assemblies, insurrections, and the like, ii, 324.

Leke, William, R. of Rowington (Dioc. of Bath and Wells), exchanges for Colaton Raleigh, V., ii, 18, 228.

Lelant (St. Uny)[1], the parish of—

Chapel of St. Mary Magdalene at Brunnion[2], i, 20b; chapel of Porthya[3], i, 39b; Trembethow, i, 240b.

Chapels of St. Towennoc[4] the Confessor, and St. Ya the Virgin[3]: Peter Pencors, William Stubba, James Tregethes, John Guvan, and other parishioners of the said chapelries, complained that they lived, for the most part, four, three, or (at least) two miles from the Mother-Church of Lelant, the roads being mountainous and rocky, and liable, in winter, to sudden inundations, so that they could not safely attend Divine Service, or send their children to be baptized, their wives to be purified, or their dead to be buried; the children often went unbaptized, and the sick were deprived of the last Sacraments. They stated that they had built the two Chapels above-named at their own expense and had enclosed suitable cemeteries, to be sufficiently endowed for two priests to serve therein, and they prayed the Bishop to consecrate the same; who, accordingly commissioned Richard Hals and John Gorewyll to meet all the parties (including, specially, the Vicar of Lelant, John Clerk), and to enquire and report (27 Sept., 1409), ii, 232b.

Bulls of Pope Alexander V. and of Pope John XXIII, for the Dedication of the dependent chapels of St. Tewinnoc and St. Ya; presented to the Bishop, in the Chapel of his Palace at Exeter, 8 Sept., 1411, by two parishioners thereof, viz., Peter Pencors and John Guvan, who asked him to give effect

[1] Sancti Eunii, MS.; *also*, Sancti Ewnini de Lananta, and Ecclesia Sancti Eunyny.

[2] Breynyon, MS.

[3] i.e. St. Ives.

[4] *hodie* Towednack.

thereto. They told him of the difficulties above recited, complaining that they were obliged to repair to their parish Church for the baptism of their children, to receive the Sacraments, and to bury their dead; that occasionally some of them were unable to undertake such a journey, and some were left to die without confession and the last Rites of the Church, to the great loss of their souls. Accordingly, they desired that fonts should be placed in these Chapels and the Sacraments administered therein; also that the cemeteries should be licensed for interments. Inquiry was ordered; the Petition to be granted, if the result were satisfactory. Both Bulls are given in full; and in the second, reference is made to a contention between these parishioners and John, the Vicar of Lelant. The Bishop forthwith directed the Precentor and the Chapter of Crediton, who were Rectors of Lelant, and John [Clerk], the said Vicar, to appear before him personally (together with any others concerned), in the Church of Crediton (12 Sept., 1411), i, 133b. The Bishop shortly afterwards went into Cornwall: we find him at Penryn on the 5th of Oct., at Helston on the 7th, and on the 9th at "Lananta," on which day he granted his licence to celebrate Divine offices in the said Chapels, i, 135b.

John Bryt, V. of Lelant, is mentioned ii, 264: *see*, also, the Will of John Wythewyll, Precentor of Crediton, i, 309b.

Lelow, John, proxy for Thomas la Zouche, ii, 83b.

Leman, John, proxy for John Bremor, ii, 149.

Lemman, John, R. of Kilkhampton, exchanges for Barnstaple, V, ii, 71; his death, ii, 139.

Lemmonesworth, Robert, instituted to Stoke Damerel, R., ii, 169; i, 215b.

Lene, John, a parishioner of Linkinhorne, i, 116.

Lepe, Elias, a chaplain, i, 105b.

Lercedekne, Elizabeth (relict of Sir Warin), i, 58; her Will, i, 309.

Lercedekne, Martin, R. of St. Mawgan-in-Kerrier, i, 97.

He was Canon of Exeter, i, 190, 234b; collated to a Canonry in Glasney, ii, 189b; also, in Bosham, ii, 193; which he resigned, and was collated to a Canonry in Crediton, ii, 198.

Lercedekne, Michael, clerk, instituted to Haccombe, 30 July, 1400, ii, 49.

There is no record of his cession; but Michael Lercedekne, chaplain, LL.B. (whom Oliver seems to regard as a distinct person) was instituted, 14 Dec., 1409: ii, 107b (having, just before, been instituted to Grade R., which he *immediately* resigned, *ibid.*) *See* i, 56b, 60b, 147b, 162, 166b, 167b, 172b, 176, 178. He resigned Haccombe early in 1413, and appears soon afterwards as R. of Thorney (Dioc. of Chichester), ii, 151b, 153; and *see* i, 186b, 200, 201b, 202, 210, 213, 215, 217b, 321. He was then collated to a Canonry and the Prebend of Westbrook in Bosham, ii, 158b; i, 212, and is mentioned as proxy for John Hody, ii, 165. Having exchanged Thorney for St. Stephen's in Brannel, R. (ii, 180b, and *see* i, 225, 225b, 230b), he was collated to a Canonry in Exeter Cathedral, ii, 182; i, 232b, 233b, 234, 235, 240; also, to a Canonry and the Prebend of Kerswell in Crediton, ii, 186, and (on his resignation of his Canonry in Bosham), to a Prebend in St. Probus (ii, 189b), which he soon resigned, together with St. Stephen's in Brannel, on his collation to be Treasurer of Exeter Cathedral, ii, 190b. *See*, also, i, 243b, 244, 245b, 246b, 247, 248. A little later, he was again collated to a

Canonry in Bosham, ii, 201 ; 294. While Treasurer he obtained licence of non-residence for one year, from 9 Sept., 1418 ; ii, 242b.

Lercedekne, Sir Warine, knt., presents to Haccombe, ii, 49.

Lercevesque, John de, V. of St. Hilary, ii, 348b.

Lessness Abbey (Dioc. of Rochester), i, 325.

Lesteuder (*hodie* Lestowder) in St. Keverne, i, 64b.

Leuedeston, Thomas, inst., to the Chantry " de Lyneton," in the Church of Aveton Giffard, ii, 91b.

Levenaunt, Baldwin, inst. to Doddiscombsleigh, ii, 3b ; his death, ii, 13b.

Levenaunt, Walter, Canon of Exeter, i, 19b ; V. of Elerky (i.e. Veryan), resigns, ii, 4 ; his death, ii, 80.

Lever, Thomas, of Kingsbridge, ii, 292.

Lewannick [Lawanek, MS.], see Trethak, Thomas, i, 145.—Thomas Bray, V. of, and others[1] ; their excommunication (3 March, 1398-9), i, 26.

Lewes, Archdeacon of, *see* Wendovere, James.

Lewes Priory presents to Sutton (Dioc. of Chich.), ii, 29b.

Lew Trenchard [Liewetrenchard, MS.]—*Breve Regium* :—

Mandamus to the Bishop to admit the nominee of John Wyse, who had recovered the right of nomination against John Monk, clerk (24 April, 1399), ii, 309. Roger Eustas was, accordingly, instituted, 2 May, ii, 12.

Ley, Richard, *see* Beamound, Joan, i, 161b.

Leye, John, a parishioner of Linkinhorne, i, 116.

Leycestre, Rd., inst. to Modbury Priory, ii, 94b ; (decd.) ii, 174b.

Leyer (*or* Lyer), John, inst. to the Chantry of Trewen (Holsworthy), ii, 51b ; his death, ii, 144b.

Leyman, John, inst. to Ashcombe, ii, 148, resigns, ii, 169 ; is collated Sacristan of Bosham, ii, 168 ; 294 ; exchanges from West Dean (Dioc. of Chichester), ii, 199.

Lezant [Lausante, MS.], Trecarrel in, i, 74b.—Chapel of St. Bridget of Landew, i, 238.

Commission of Enquiry as to the dilapidations left by Patrick atte Wode, R. (22 June, 1414), ii, 254b.—Henry Wynnegode, R., i, 196b, ii, 254.

Lifton ; mansion of the Miletons, at Westwick, i, 125b.—Chapel of St. Peter (licensed, 16 Oct., 1399), i, 31.—Laurence Stevyn, *alias* Bedeman (or Bedmond), R., licence of non-residence for one year, from 22 Nov., 1397 ; a Penitentiary in the Deanery of Tavistock, i, 50, 94, 115b,

---

[1] viz., William Smale, chaplain, Martin de Doboner, V. of St. Feock, John Wade, *alias* Leche, and Joan Penryn.

Deanery of Ipplepen, i, 50, 237ᵇ, 245; proxy for John Gyst, ii, 145.

Little Modbury [Lytelmodbury, MS.], licence granted to William Brounyng, Vicar of Modbury, to celebrate in the Chapel of St. Leonard there (27 Dec., 1407), i, 82ᵇ.

Little Torrington, Thomas [Dunham (*see* ii, 341ᵇ)], V. of, a Penitentiary in the Deanery of Torrington, i, 50, 143ᵇ, 174, 194ᵇ, 207ᵇ, 217, 231, 238, 245ᵇ.—Manor of Woodland, i, 226.

Lobbe, Thomas, i, 325.

Lockyngton, Richard, of Kingsbridge, ii, 292.

Loddeford (in Shebbear) *see* Hankeford, ("*Oratories*"), i, 78.

Loddiswell [Lodeswyll *and* Lodeswell, MS.], John Wytloff, R. (deceased), ii, 83ᵇ; his Will, i, 305ᵇ.—Thomas la Zouche (sub-deacon), R., dispensation (to study at Oxford) for four years, from 17 March, 1405-6, i, 77ᵇ; also, for three years, from 6 Feb., 1409-10, i, 94 (but he died in 1410-11):—

[*Breve Regium*]. Prohibition to admit to this Benefice pending the dispute between the King and Sir William la Zouche, knt. (30 Jan., 1410-11), ii, 338. This Prohibition was suspended, 18 March, 1410-11, ii, 338ᵇ. On 3 Feb. a Commission had been issued, on behalf of Stephen Noble, who had been presented by the King, ii, 238ᵇ; also a second like Commission on 18 Feb., *ibid*. Peter Holdyche, V., was licensed to celebrate in his Vicarage House, 16 Feb., 1413-14, i, 194. *See*, also, ii, 357ᵇ.

Appropriation to the College of Slapton of this Rectory—The Bishop states that he had received Letters Apostolick from Pope John XXIII. on behalf of the Rector and College of Slapton; which he recites at large. The Pope had received a petition from the College, setting forth that, formerly, the Church of Loddiswell, of which they were Patrons, had been assigned to them (on the strength of a Letter from P. Boniface VIII.), for the support of the Rector, 6 priests and 4 clerks (the number then; since much increased), a suitable Portion being reserved for the Vicar thereof; but that the said Pope, on xi Kal. Jan. Anno Pontif. XIV., had quashed all appropriations made by himself which had not already taken effect—[See fol. 284ᵇ. *ad finem*]. They pleaded, however, for an exception in this case, as the income of the College was insufficient for its maintenance, not exceeding 160 marks, while the revenue of Loddiswell did not exceed 60 marks; and the Pope granted their request, reserving for the Vicar who should serve the said Church a competent stipend [Dat. at Rome, at St. Peter's, xiiij Kal. Feb., in the 3rd year of his Pontificate—i.e. 1413]. The Bishop, accordingly, proceeded to assign the said Vicar's portion, having summoned to appear before him all parties interested, and especially Sir Peter Holdyche, Rector of Loddiswell; and after obtaining a return of the fruits and profits of the benefice, and of the glebe lands, buildings and enclosures, and also of the Episcopal dues, and of all burdens ordinary and extraordinary, he made division between the College and the Vicars, as follows:—The College was to have all the great tithes of the whole parish, that is to say "decimas garbarum sive granorum frumenti, ordei, siliginis, avenarum, fabarum, pisarum, vescarum et omnium aliorum bladorum sive segetum cujuscumque generis fuerint aut nature," from all fields, meadows, &c., under cultivation, and from the gardens of the parishioners; while the great tithes arising from the Sanctuary (*de Sanctuario*) of the said Church were reserved for the Vicars, whether they kept it in hand or no. Moreover the College was to hold, for the storing of their crops, and for the accommodation of themselves, their agents, and their beasts, whenever they might need to be there, the barn lately built there, "una cum area et parietibus suis," where, lately, were cattle houses, commonly called "boveria," and other buildings, recently pulled down (just outside the wall or enclosure of the inner manse of the Rector), which had been constructed to shelter the cattle and other beasts, and which the College was to rebuild, in the antient or in another form, as might seem best, at their own cost. They were to have also a certain "park" commonly called "Movhay," together with a certain close, on the west side of the said barn, commonly called "Fursepark," with free ingress and egress to and fro—"ad ea et ab hiis"—for ever. But the hedges and banks of the said close "of Fursepark," with the trees and plants growing therein, the College was to have and keep up on the side where the pool or ditch—"alveus, fossa, sive fossata"—adjoins "Fursepark," whereas on the side where it adjoins the Sanctuary and glebe lands the Vicar was to maintain them. To provide against loss and injury befalling himself or his successors, in consequence of this transaction, the Bishop assigned an annual pension of 20s., to be paid by the College, at the Palace at Exeter, every year, on Michaelmas Day from the date of the cession, or decease, of the present Rector, and their entering on quiet possession. Moreover, to augment the Vicar's stipend the College was to pay him annually xl *s.* in four quarterly payments on the Quarter Days; and for the relief of poor parishioners, according to statute, x *s.*, on the Feast of the Translation of St. Thomas the Martyr of Canterbury, to be distributed in the Church of Loddiswell, year by year, as long as this appropriation should endure. Further the Bishop decreed, as to the right of presentation to the vicarage, that, on the cession or decease of Sir Peter Holdyche, the Rector of Loddiswell, the College should be bound to present to the Bishop, within six months, a suitable parson; and he confirmed this right of presentation to the College for ever, on the understanding that the Vicar's portion and the lands, etc., of the Church of Loddiswell, "which, in the Diocese of Exeter we call *vulgariter* the Sanctuary," be secured to him, and the tithes of the said Sanctuary, and the whole altilage and the tithe *feni*, and all the small tithes of the parish, and all emoluments pertaining to the Church, and the pension of xl *s.*, together with the hall, chambers, kitchen, and all other buildings, enclosures, etc., belonging to the Church, save only the great tithes and the barn, the court, and its fences, and the Movhay and Fursepark, above-mentioned. To prevent disputes, such as are apt to rise between appropriators and vicars as to the apportionment of tithes in cases of change in the mode of cultivation of meadows and orchards, the Bishop ordered that notwithstanding any change of culture, such as converting arable land into pasture or garden ground, or *vice versa*, there should be no change in the tithes on that account, as to the mode of dealing with them; but all great tithes, howsoever arising, should belong to the College, and all tithes *feni*, or other small tithes to the Vicar. Rules were prescribed touching the *onera* to be borne by both parties; and with regard to the Vicars, in order to prevent mistakes and disputes in the future, the Bishop thought it expedient to decree that over and above the entire cure of the souls of the parishioners, the Vicar should be bound to maintain in proper order and repair, and to renew when necessary, the whole Chancel with its windows, and the *celatura* over the High Altar, the Office books also, and one Psalter; also, to pay the tenths—payable to the King or any other, and a pension of 6s. 8d. paid by the said Church, from antient times, to the Prior and Convent of Totnes, and all Synodals, &c., and all dues payable to episcopal legates and nuncios of the Apostolick See, to the Archbishop, the Bishop, and their Officers and Commissaries; and to the Archdeacon; –viz., procurations, subsidies, and the like—and he was to serve as Dean-Rural in his turn—"ac eciam Decani-Ruralis officii excercicium cum acciderit." He was to provide, also, incense and lights for the Chancel, and in short all *onera* whatsoever (save only the three pensions of *xxs. xls.* and *xs.* aforesaid, and those which pertain to the parishioners) and this, on the ground that the Bishop had assigned, not only a sufficient, but even a superabundant portion to the said Vicar. And the Bishop specially reserved to himself and his successors the power of summary sequestration *absque strepitu et figura judicii*, in case the vicar should give any trouble to the College herein, or interfere with their rights as laid down by these presents.—Executed by the Bishop at Clyst, 19 Oct., 1413,—by the Rector, Priests and Clerks of the College, in their Chapter House at Slapton, on the 15th February, 1413-14—and by Peter Holdyche, (hitherto Rector, but from that time) Vicar of Loddiswell, on the 12th day of the same month, in the Bishop's presence, at Clyst, using the seal of Wm. Hunden, Archdeacon of Totnes; ii, 288-290^{b}.

Lodeford, John, R. of Loxbeare, exchanges for Hope Mansell, R. (Dioc. of Hereford), ii, 168^{b}.

Lodre, John, V. of Stogumber (Dioc. of B. and W.), exchanges for Bickleigh, R., ii, 87^{b}; for East Coker (Dioc. of B. and W.), ii, 92^{b}.

Lodres, Priory of (Dioc. of Salisbury), i, 9^{b}.

Loghyngcote, Nicholas, patron of Luffincott, ii, 10, 12^{b}.

Lollards,—

(1) The Bishop's Mandate for the publication of the *Breve Regium* against the Lollards, addressed to the Official Principal and President of his Consistorial Court (24 July, 1413), i, 182; also, to the four Archdeacons on the same day, i, 182^{b}. (2) A Copy of the "Constitucio Provincialis contra Lollardos," ii, 318. (3) "Commissio contra Lollardos," directed to the Bishop of Exeter (23 March, anno primo), ii, 321; and (4) to the Sheriff of Devon (21 Aug., anno primo), *ibid.* (5) "Statutum Regium contra Lollardos," ii, 322.

Loman, Richard, instituted to Clovelly, ii, 17.

Lome, John—father and son, and Robert Lome; i, 312.

London, Robert de Braybroke, Bishop of,—

He was consecrator of Bishop Stafford, i, 1.—His letter on behalf of Katherine Brokas (q.v.), i, 7^{b}. His letter to Bishop Stafford, with the Archbishop's Mandate for a general Intercession on Michaelmas Day, 1397, for the King and the Realm, i, 13. *See*, also, ii, 278.

Hospital of St. Anthony; Indulgence to the Faithful contributing to its support (1 May, 1399), i, 26^{b}; repeated 12 June, 1399, i, 27—"ad sustentacionem fratrum et pauperum infirmorum Domus Sancti Antonii Londonie, a Monasterio Sancti Antonii, Ordinis Sancti Augustini, Viennensis Diocesis, dependentis, ac pauperum et infirmorum ad dictam Domum confluencium."

Longbridge [Deverill], (Dioc. of Salisbury), i, 320.

Longfield (Dioc. of Rochester), i, 325.

Looe [Loo, MS.]—

Indulgence to the Faithful contributing to the cost of a new Bridge in course of erection over the tidal river of Looe, between the towns of East and West Looe [Estlo—Westlo, MS.], which was of great importance to travellers between the towns of Plymouth and Fowey (22 Oct., 1411), i, 137^{b}.—This Bridge was still unfinished some four years later, and a second Indulgence was published, 6 June, 1415; ii, 210^{b}. But funds again failing short, a third Indulgence was granted, 16 June, 1418; i, 240^{b}.—Chapel of St. Mary at Looe, ii, 141^{b}.

Loppeham, Dionysius, ii, 305.

Loppethorne, William, *see* Hurte, Robert, i, 92ᵇ.

Losquyt, Thomas, a chaplain, i, 303.

Lostwithiel ("capella curata" in the parish of Lanlivery)—
Commission of Enquiry as to its pollution by William Staynour and John Gylle of Lostwithiel (directed to John Sutton, LL.B., 28 Jan. 1416-17), ii, 260ᵇ. The case was found to have been exaggerated; there had been no bloodshed and no pollution; and the Bishop ordered Divine Service to be at once resumed (5 Feb., 1416-17), i, 229ᵇ.

Loteby, John, V. of Burlescombe (deceased), ii, 151ᵇ.

Loteby, Thomas, V. of Dunsford (q.v.)

Loudenay, Robert, R. of St. Pancras (Rousdon), deceased, ii, 96.

Loueryng *or* Loveryng, David, R. of Shillingford (resigns), ii, 9ᵇ; inst. to St. Mary Steps, Exeter, ii, 9, exchanges for Black Torrington, ii, 81ᵇ; i, 76, 330ᵇ.

Loueryng, John, patron of Bittadon, ii, 7; of Roche, ii, 12ᵇ.

Loundon, John, collated Warden of the Chapel of St. Laurence, Crediton, ii, 32ᵇ; his death, ii, 121.

Love (*or* Lovell), Robert, co-patron of Loddiswell, R., ii, 83ᵇ; in right of his wife (Elizabeth, grandaughter of Guy de Bryan), patron of Slapton Collegiate Chantry, ii, 111ᵇ; presents to Loddiswell; ii, 131ᵇ.

Lovecok, Nicholas, V. of Buckland Abbas (Dioc. of Salisbury), exchanges for St. Ive, ii, 104; again exchanges for Paignton, ii, 191ᵇ; i, 245.

Lovecote, Nicholas de; R. of Stokenham, ii, 358.

Lovelak, Henry, Chantry priest of Umberleigh (resigns), ii, 52ᵇ.

Lovelane, Margery and Alice (deceased), i, 331ᵇ.

Loveton, John, V. of Dulverton, exch. for Bickleigh, R., ii, 182.

Loveworth, Edward, Vicar-Choral, i, 310, 310ᵇ.

Loweden, Thos., inst. to Denbury, ii, 110ᵇ; i, 148, 183; resigns, ii, 161.

Loxbeare [Lokkysbeare, MS.], John Hyde, R.; licence of non-residence from 1 June, 1400—"licenciam ...... ad beneplacitum domini tantummodo duraturam," i, 39ᵇ.—John[3] [Walwyn] R., *see* Say, Agnes, i, 121ᵇ.

Loxhore [Lookkyssore, MS.], William Vedde (*or* Fedde), R. *See* Goodleigh, i, 190ᵇ.

Lucas, John, R. of St. George's, Exeter, ii, 336ᵇ.

[3] The date is 1411; John Walwyn exchanged with John Smyth in 1412.

Lucas, John, R. of Luffincott (deceased), ii, 10.

Lucas, John, inst. to Tavistock, ii, 15[b]; his death, ii, 179[b].

Lucas, John, and Joan Hetteway—

They had gone through the ceremony of marriage, not knowing that the said Joan was related, in the 2nd and 3rd degrees of consanguinity to Joan Lucas, the said John's first wife; and they appealed for a Dispensation to Pope Innocent VII, which eventually was granted by Pope Boniface IX, although the said John had perjured himself by cohabiting with the said Joan after discovering their position and swearing on the Holy Gospels to remain apart (5 May, 1408), i, 85.

Lucy, Joan, Prioress of Cornworthy (deceased), ii, 140.

Ludbrook [Lodebrok, MS.], in Modbury; licence to William Brounyng, Vicar, to celebrate in the Chapel of the B.V.M. there (27 Dec., 1407), i, 82[b].

Luerne, Robert, clerk, of Littleham i, 32[b].

Luffewyk (*or* Lovewyke), John, R. of Marsh (Dioc. of Lincoln), exchanges for Witheridge, ii, 30; i, 73.

Lugans, John, Canon of Exeter, ii, 50, 226; and R. of Ashwater (deceased), ii, 75[b], 78.

Luk, John, R. of Tring, exchanges for Uffculme, R., ii, 44[b]—

He was S. T. B., and was licensed as a Publick Preacher (17 April, 1411), i, 122[b]

Luky, Joan, *see* Ruan-major, i, 181.

Lump [*also* Lumbb, Lompe, *and* Lumppe, MS.], Roger, R. of Stowford (q.v.), i, 7, 18[b], 56[b]; his death, ii, 105.

Luppit [Leuepit, MS.], Vincent [Hille, V.] de, a Penitentiary in the Deanery of Dunkeswell, i, 50.

The Cemetery here having been polluted by John Vyenne, V., who had laid violent hands on one William Alon therein, and shed his blood, the Bishop directed a Commission to the Archdeacon of Exeter, to make enquiry, and if the alleged facts were established to close the Cemetery till it should be reconciled (16 April, 1411), ii, 241.

Lustleigh Church, i, 308[b],—John Burlegh, R., *see* Carslegh, Simon, i, 191; a Penitentiary in the Deanery of Moreton, i, 143, 174, 194[b], 207[b], 217, 231, 237[b], 245.

Lusquyt, John, R. of St. Kerrian's, Exeter (deceased), ii, 10[b].

Lutrell, Richard, i, 307[b].

Luxulyan [Sanctorum Ciricii et Julitte de Lossulyan]—

Commissions: (1) for the absolution of Robert and William Jakkeiowy, Robert Trewbys, and Richard Kendale, excommunicated for committing a violent assault on Wm. Coulyn in the Cemetery of the said Church, i, 160[b]. (2) for the Reconciliation of the Cemetery, ii, 246[b].—Both Commissions were issued 1 June, 1412.

Lychfyld, Wm., V. of Lamerton, exchanges for Huxham, ii, 79; his death, ii, 115,—spelt here "Hyccheafylde"—cler. error.

Lydeford, Edward (of Exeter), i, 319[b].

Lydeford, John (senior), Canon of Thorney in Chichester

Cathedral (resigns), ii, 35b; Canon of Exeter, ii, 79; Archdeacon of Totnes, ii, 212b; his death, ii, 99b; his Will, i, 309b; *see*, also, ii, 49, 50b.

Lydeford, John (junior), LL.B., instituted to Chagford, ii, 35b; *see*, also, ii, 47, 47b, 50.

Lydeford, John, and Alice his wife, i, 329, 332b.

Lydford, Henry, Rector of, i, 214.

Lydiard St. Laurence, ii, 18b.

Lye, John (Friar Min.), licensed to hear confessions (13 April, 1401), i, 56.

Lyghfote, John, a Vicar in the Church of Crediton, ii, 255.

Lyghtfote, John, *see* Sutton, William, ii, 353.

Lyght, William, R. of Ashcombe (deceased), ii, 148.

Lyle, R., chaplain, i, 331b; inst. to Meavy, ii, 182b; resigns, ii, 187b; presented by Margaret, Countess of Somerset, to St. George's, Exeter, but not admitted, ii, 235b.

Lyle, Thomas, i, 332.

Lyllebourne, Adam, V. of Kenton (deceased), ii, 93; his Will, i, 307.

Lymington, i, 311b; John Reue (or Reve) of, i, 312.

Lympston [Limeston, Limston, *and* Leveneston, MS.]—

The parish-church, having been rebuilt, was dedicated 24 Sept., 1409, in honour of the Nativity of the Blessed Virgin Mary, i, 90b. Henry Andrew, R. appointed a Penitentiary in the Deanery of Aylesbeare, i, 50. Early in 1407, becoming old and infirm and unable to do his duty, he resigned and applied for a pension. The Bishop accepted his resignation; and the patron, Sir William Bonevyll, knt., having appointed John Holcot, chaplain, he was instituted [13 April, 1407], and at the request of the said patron and with the new Rector's consent, the Bishop assigned to Andrew a pension of £10 for life, to be paid yearly on St. John Baptist's Day, by Holcot and his successors (16 April, 1407), i, 81.—Holcot seems to have been almost continuously non-resident. Within two years of his institution he obtained licence of non-residence for one year, from 4 Dec., 1408 (i, 87b); and, after a short interval, for a like period, year after year; viz., from 1 Aug., 1410 (i, 101); from 24 July, 1411 (i, 129b); from 4 Aug., 1412 (i, 163); from 17 Sept., 1413 (i, 183b); from 2 Oct., 1414 (i, 201b); from 23 Jan., 1415-16, to Michaelmas, 1416 (i, 215b); from 25 Jan., 1416-17, to Michaelmas, 1417 (i, 229); from 27 Jan., 1417-18, (i, 237b), and from 21 July, 1419 (i, 247b).

Lynde, John, chaplain, of Bodmin, i, 77b.

Lyndeseye, John, Chantry-Priest of Beaupre, in Glasney, ii, 136.

Lyndestan, Anna, *see* Derlyng, Thomas, i, 229.

Lyndewode, Wm., collated Canon of Exeter Cathedral, ii, 201b.

Lyne, Hugh, inst. to Rousdon, ii, 160; i, 208b.

Lyneton, the Chantry of, *see* Aveton-Giffard (*Institutions*).

Lyngdon, John, inst. to Parracombe, ii, 153b.

Lyngham, Robert, R. of St. Mary-Major, Exeter, i, 310, 310b, 322, 326, 326b, 331, 332b.

Lynnam, Simon, R. of Marhamchurch, exchanges for Faringdon (Dioc. of Winchester), ii, 45b.

Lynton; the Chapel of the B. V. M. and of SS. John-Baptist, Dennis, and Ruman,—licence to celebrate on the Feasts of those Saints (14 April, 1402), i, 60b.

Lypton (or Lupton), William and Joan Cole of, i, 34.

Lyster, Robert, proxy for William Derwent, ii, 79b.

Lytelton, Robert, does homage to the Bishop for Cumtun pole, in the parish of Paignton, ii, 310.

Lywer, Robert, clerk, i, 47b, 86b: R. of St. Pancras, Exeter; his Commission as Registrar to Dean Tregresiou, Vic. Gen., 6 Sept., 1395, ii, 210; inst. to Drewsteignton, ii, 1b; proxy for Benedict Canterbury, ii, 2; proxy for Stephen Gerveys, ii, 10; appointed co-adjutor to the Rector of Roborough, ii, 23.

Lyewer *or* Lewer, Walter, exchanges Cold Ashton (Dioc. of Worcester) for St. Pinnock, ii, 351, 352; resigns, ii, 123.

Lyȝe, Walter, i, 329b.

M.

Macworth (*or* Makworth), John, collated Canon and Preb. of Funtington, Bosham; ii, 96, 280, 281, 281b; resigns, ii, 109.

Madeford, Richard, R. of Honiton, exchanges for Widecombe, ii, 45; for Ashburton, ii, 57; his death, ii, 84.

Madek, Richard, exchanges Beaworthy for Launcells, ii, 69b.

Magne, Robert, collated to the Priory of Otterton, ii, 69b.

Maiden-Newton, the Church of, i, 320b.

Major, Peter, inst. to Charles, R., ii, 106; his death, ii, 190.

Maker [Macre, MS.]; Taxation of the Vicarage:—

The Bishop searched the Registers of Walter I. (i.e. Bishop Bronescombe), and, found therein that the said Bishop, on the Saturday after the Feast of the Assumption, 1269, being then at St. Breward, taxed this V. and assigned to the V. thereof the whole altilage, together with the tithe of pease, with one house of residence and 8 acres of the Sanctuary, "cum una marcata in decimis garbarum in loco competenti;" and he was to discharge all burdens (30 July, 1418), i, 241b.

Malborough; Preb. of Poghylle in; *See* "Institutions."

Malesouers, Thos., inst. to Calstock, ii, 6b; his death, ii, 23b.

Malewayn, John, inst. to Calstock, ii, 23b; i, 64, 68, 125b.

Malmesbury, the Abbot and Convent of, present to Pilton Priory, ii, 147b.

Maloysell, Joan, relict of William, ii, 256b.

Maloysell, Ralph, *see* Kentisbeare, ii, 345b.

Malston, in the parish of Charleton, i, 173.

Mamhead [Mammehed, MS.], John [Colyn], R., i, 122—

Commissions of Enquiry; (1) directed to the Archdeacon of Exeter, on behalf of John Colyn, chaplain, presented by Thomas, Baron de Carrew (9 Oct., 1410), ii, 234b.—(2) to the same Archdeacon, 8 Nov., 1410, on Colyn's complaint as to the dilapidations caused by his predecessor, John Chapel, ii, 235.—This R. obtained licence of non-residence for a year, from 21 Sept., 1411; i, 135: also, from 28 Oct., 1412, till Michaelmas, 1413, i, 171b; from 12 Jan., 1413-14, to Michaelmas, 1414, i, 173; and for one year, from 14 Oct., 1416, i, 226b. *See*, also, ii, 241. [At i, 135 and 171b he is called 'Thomas,' by clerical error].

Man, Richard, inst. to South Tawton, ii, 138; resigns, ii, 177b.

Manaton [Maneton, MS.], William Trendelbeare, R.; licence of non-residence for a year (except a week at Passion-tide), from 24 Jan., 1395-6; also, for 2 years, from 6 Nov., 1401, i, 58b.

Mannyng, Richard, R. of St. George's, Exeter (i, 161),—

He was presented by King Henry IV. (but not, at first, admitted) ii, 235. *See*, also, ii, 135; his institution, *ibid*; his death, ii, 162b.

Manston, Walter, priest, i, 321.

Mantyngho, Gencian, Canon of Hartland, ii, 183b.

Manyngford, Richard, inst. to Seaton, ii, 46; exchanges for Mayfield, ii, 82.

Manuel [Palæologus], Emperor of Constantinople, ii, 312b.

Mapilton, Robert de, clerk (Dioc. of York), ii, 27.

Marazion [Marghasyow, *and* Marchyou, MS.],—

The Chapel of St. Ervetus, here, was licensed 16 June, 1397, i, 12b.—The House of William Tregilliowe in this place is twice mentioned: he seems to have entertained the Bishop, i, 88b, 137.

Marchant, John, a chaplain in Devon:—

Being excommunicate and contumacious, he is handed over by the Bishop to the Secular Arm, (4 Jan., 1398-9), i, 24.

Marche, Thomas, chaplain, ii, 168b.

Marhamchurch [Marwenchurche *alias* Sancte Marwenne, MS.], Whalesburgh (i, 42) and Bere (i, 43), in this parish, Simon Lynnam, R.; licence of non-residence[1] for 2 years, from 31 Jan., 1396-7, i, 11; also, for one year from 16 April, 1398,[2] i, 17.

[1] Contemplacione nobilis viri Comitis Arundell, si in ipsius obsequiis dicto tempore steterit.

[2] Contemplacione Reverendi in Christo Patris . . . . Guydonis, Menevensis Episcopi, si, &c.

One Cecilia Moys, desiring to lead the contemplative life of an anchorite in a certain House in the Cemetery of Marhamchurch, the Bishop, 4 May, 1403, commissioned Philip, Abbot of Hartland, and Walter Dollebeare, R. of Southill, to place her there under proper protection, assigning her till Christmas as a time of probation, i, 64.—Licence to choose confessors was granted, 10 Oct., 1405, to *Lucie* Moys, anchorite of Marhamchurch, i, 76ᵇ. *See* i, 313.

Robert Alkebarowe, R., i, 78ᵇ.—John Shirford, R.

The Bishop writes to the Dean of Trigg-major, and to Benedict [Whalysbrow], V. of Poundstock, on behalf of the said John Shirford, informing them that whereas Walter Deneys, the said John's proctor herein, had arranged with Peter Symon, chaplain, to serve at Marhamchurch for that year, the said Peter had broken his contract : the Bishop ordered him to be admonished and compelled to keep his engagement (8 Oct., 1410), i, 107.—On the complaint of the patron, Sir John Herle, knt., that John Schirford R., had allowed the Chancel, books, and buildings of his benefice to fall into grievous disrepair—"que suorum precessorum et predecessorum magnificencia construxerat"—issued a Commission of Enquiry (11 Nov., 1412), ii, 249. He was still only a subdeacon, and letters dimissory for his ordination as deacon and priest were granted 17 March, 1412-13, i, 178. On 6 Sept. following he was granted licence of non-residence for one year, i, 183ᵇ.—Commissions :—(1) of Enquiry as to dilapidations, on behalf of James Dyrehell, R., against John Shyrford, his predecessor, 12 Dec., 1417, ii, 263ᵇ ; (2) To sequestrate (amount estimated £55 10s. 0d.), 20 Jan., 1417-18, *ibid.*

Marisco, St. Mary de, a cell (near Exeter) dependent on Plympton Priory, i, 89ᵇ.

Maristow [Morestow, MS.]; Northleigh in this parish, i, 226.

Mark, John, V. of Bishop's Tawton (deceased), ii, 136.

Mark, John, R. of St. Ervan (?) (deceased), ii, 166.

Mark, Ralph, cousin of Richard, i, 332ᵇ.

Mark (*or* Marke), Richard, inst., to St. Martin's, Exeter, ii, 96; licensed as a Publick Preacher (5 Jan., 1409-10), i, 92ᵇ; *see*, also, i, 306ᵇ, 310, 311, 327ᵇ, 332ᵇ, 333ᵇ.

Markedene, Roger, clerk, i, 313, 313ᵇ.

Marker, Richard, clerk,—*Dispensacio super defectu natalium* (27 Sept., 1417), i, 234.

Marker, Walter, chaplain, i, 303ᵇ.

Markowe, William, V. of Hutton (Dioc. of London), exchanges for the Chantry of St. Michael in the Cemetery of St. Austell, ii, 52ᵇ.

Marland [Peter's] R., appropr. to Cornworthy Priory, ii, 359ᵇ.

Marnhull (or Marnull), John, R. of St. Rumbald's, Shaftesbury, exchanges for Chittlehampton, ii, 86ᵇ ; for Combe St. Nicholas (Dioc. of B. and W.) ii, 106ᵇ.

Marschel, John, chaplain, a Penitentiary in the Deanery of Aylesbeare, i, 94, 115.

A John Marschall was collated [1] to the Chantry of St. Katherine at Hemyock, ii, 164; which he exchanged for Corston (Dioc. of Bath and Wells), ii, 195b.

Marschall, Philip, proxy for Stephen Payne, ii, 153b.

Marschell, Richard, a chaplain, i, 310.

Marscall, *or* Mareschall, Robert, R. of Musbury, exchanges for Harberton, ii, 67; for Widecombe, ii, 86; for St. Mary-Steps, ii, 124b; for Greinton, (Dioc. of B. and W.), ii, 140b.

Martinhoe, William Percevale, R., i, 246b,—

Commission of Enquiry as to dilapidations caused by the neglect of John Baker, on the complaint of the said William Percevale (22 Dec., 1418), ii, 266b.—Licence of non-residence from 30 May to Michaelmas, 1419, i, 247b.

Marton, Thomas, i, 300b.

Martyn, John, Canon of Crantock (deceased), ii, 27b; i, 303.

Martyn, Philip, i, 307b.

Martyn, Robert, inst. to Bicton, ii, 23; collated to a Preb. in St. Probus, ii, 30b; his death, ii, 80, 83.

Martyn, Robert, *see* Beamound, Joan, i, 161b.

Martyn, William, presents to Petrockstowe, ii, 151, 251b.

Marwood [Merwode *and* Merewode, MS.], *see* "*Oratories*" (Marwood, Walter), i, 40.—Hamund Brereton, R., licence of non-residence for one year, from 7 April, 1397, i, 12.

Pending an action in the Consistorial Court, when Thomas Chaunterel was Rector, between the said R. and the inhabitants of the village of Whytefeld, in the said parish, as to finding a chaplain to serve the Chapel there, the said villagers refused to attend the Mother-Church, and Chaunterel refused to serve the said Chapel; whereupon the Bishop directed Richard Mychel, chaplain, to hear confessions, and to officiate in the said chapel on the Easter-Day then ensuing, and to administer the Sacrament (*Sacramentum Eucaristie*), but without stipend from the R., whose dues, etc., at Whytefeld were reserved to him (7 March, 1410-11), i, 117b. This licence was renewed, 26 March, 1412, i, 146; also, 31 March, 1413, i, 179; also, 10 March, 1413-14, i, 194b; also, 4 April, 1416, i, 220; also, 1 April, 1417, i, 232; and again (in favour of John Kyng, chaplain), 10 April, 1419, i, 246b. Thomas Chaunterel occurs as Penitentiary in the Deanery of Shirwell, i, 143b, 174, 194b, 207b, 217, 231, 238, 245b.

Mary Tavy [Tavymarie, MS.],—Roger Damarl, priest, R. of—

He was excommunicated because, not being ignorant of just impediment, he had taken part in the clandestine marriage of Robert Martyn and Englesia, daughter of John Toker, celebrated in the church of Milton Abbot by Geoffrey Aleyn, chaplain of Brentor: absolved on submission, 21 Jan., 1412-13, i, 175. *See* i, 161b.

Mascal, John, i, 312.

Masek, Roger, R. of St. Endellion (deceased), ii, 26.

Maslyn, John, inst. to Tywardreath Priory, ii, 44b; (decd.), ii, 93b.

Mason, John, *see* Brixham, ii, 258b.

---

[1] "vacantem, et ad ipsius Domini collacionem, juxta ipsius cantarie fundacionem, jure sibi devoluto, illa vice, spectantem.

Massingham, John, i, 300^{b}.

Matford (*or* Metford), John, i, 314.

Matheu [Matthu, Mathu *and* Matthew, MS.], chaplain, i, 305.

He was commissioned *ad vendicandum clericos super felonia coram judicibus convictos*, 20 Nov., 1399, and was licensed, the same day, to the Chantry in the Palace at Exeter, ii, 44;—instituted to Poltimore R., ii, 25^{b}; proxy for Thomas Clyfford, ii, 57; collated Warden of the Chapel of St. Laurence, Crediton, ii, 121; i, 112^{b}; resigns Poltimore, ii, 134; is again inst. thereto, ii, 134^{b}; again resigns, ii, 152^{b}, 153, 154; having been inst. to Broad Clyst, ii, 152, 252; i, 327^{b}; is inst. to Dunterton, ii, 154^{b}; exchanges St. Laurence, Crediton, for Axminster, ii, 187, and Broad Clyst for Alphington, ii, 200^{b}, 267^{b}; is inst. to Yarcombe, ii, 200^{b}.—Co-patron of Huxham, ii, 200.

Maundevyll, William, *see* Bosham, i, 25^{b}.

Maunsell, Hugh, inst. to Yealmpton, ii, 167^{b}.

Maupas, Henry, Canon and Bursal Preb. of Crediton, resigns, ii, 38; inst. to Ermington, R., ii, 105^{b}; exchanges for Stanford-on-Avon (Dioc. of Lincoln), ii, 120^{b}.

May, Walter, of Littleham, i, 32.

Maii (*or* May), William, inst. to Poughill (Devon), ii, 7^{b}; exchanges for the Chantry of St. Mary at Herne (Dioc. of Canterbury), ii, 65^{b}.

Maydenhych (*or* Maydenhith), John de, Canon of Wells, ii, 18; Official Principal—Dioc. of Salisbury, ii, 28^{b}: mentioned, ii, 47, 48^{b}, 49^{b}, 52^{b}.

Mayn, John, R. of Ringmore (deceased), ii, 5^{b}.

Maynard, Robert (with Margaret his wife), licensed to choose confessors (18 Aug., 1401), i, 58.

He was co-patron of Roche, ii, 57^{b}; of Cotleigh, ii, 64, 95^{b}, 157^{b}; of South Pool, ii, 90^{b}, 97, 155^{b}; of [Clay] hydon, ii, 81^{b}; of Dunterton, ii, 130 (and 236^{b}), 154^{b} (and 253); of Cardynham, ii, 153 (and 252^{b}), 154^{b} (and 253); of St. Katherine's Chantry, Hemyock, ii, 198^{b} (and 267^{b}).

Mayovu, John, of Ermington, ii, 277.

Mayowe, John, clerk.—*Dispensacio super defectu natalium* (20 May, 1411), i, 124.

Mayow [John] (called *William* in the Commission of Enquiry, ii, 220, and elsewhere in the Reg.), inst. to Perran-Uthno, ii, 13^{b}, licensed to celebrate in the Chapel of St. James near Petrys met (28 June, 1403), i, 67; his death, ii, 162^{b}.

Maysmere, Walter, chaplain, *see* St. Endellion, i, 107^{b}.

Mayster, Alice, i, 306^{b}.

Meavy [Mewy, MS.], Henry Gardiner, R.; dispensation (to study at Oxford) for 3 years, from 18 Dec., 1396, i, 10^{b}; John Shute (or Schute), R.; ditto for 3 years, from 22 April, 1401, i, 56; also for one year, from 27 March, 1405, i, 74; and from 19 Sept., 1406, i, 79.

Meddon, in the parish of Hartland, St. Martin's Chapel, i, 38^b.

Medeford (*or* Medford), Walter, collated to a Canonry in Crediton, ii, 64.

He was also Archdeacon of Salisbury and exchanged for the Archdeaconry of Berks, ii, 81. Walter Medford occurs as Dean of Wells,—"domini nostri Pape Nuncio, ac ejusdem et Sedis Apostolice in regno Anglie Collectori,"—11 July, 1418, in a "Certificatorium pro Collectore Domini Pape."—The Appropriation of Loddiswell to the Chantry of Slapton is mentioned in the Postscript, and a List of Arrears is appended; i, 240^b.

Meeth [Methe, MS.], John Nouns, R. of—

On his presentation by Thomas Deneys (on the death of Robert Gyffard), a Commission of Enquiry was directed to the Archdeacon of Barnstaple, ii, 233^b. A licence of non-residence was granted to this R., from 26 Oct., 1410, to Michaelmas, 1411, i, 111.

Melborne, Simon de, collated to a Canonry in Crantock, ii, 52^b.

Menevia (St. David's), Guy [de Mona], Bishop of, i, 17, 60^b, 62.

Menhenyot, Padirda in, i, 35^b, 240^b; Trencruke in, i, 9^b.

John Philypp, R., Penitentiary in the Deanery of East, i, 49^b; his death, ii, 138; 227.

In compliance with the prayer of this Rector and the parishioners, the Bishop altered the Feast of the Dedication of this Church from 8 March to 2 Oct. (21 May, 1405), i, 74^b.

Commissions of Enquiry as to the patronage,—(1) when Sir Wm. Talbot and Wm. Milford had presented Richard Milford (30 Oct., 1411), ii, 243^b; (2) when John Waryn had been presented by the Prince of Wales (12 Nov., 1411), ii, 244. In the end Waryn was admitted, and being only "primam tonsuram habens," Letters Dimissory were granted for his Ordination (20 Dec., 1411), i, 140^b; from which time he was almost continuously non-resident for years, (1) for a year from the said 20 Dec., *ibid.*; (2) by dispensation (to study at Oxford) for 2 years, from 13 Feb., 1411-12, i, 145; (3) ditto, for a year (with licence for Divine Service in his Rectory House), from 1 April, 1414, i, 195^b; (4) ditto, for a year, from 20 Sept., 1415, i, 212^b; (5) licence of non-residence from 11 May to All Saints' Day, 1417, i, 232.—He was once Penitentiary in the Deanery of East, i, 245^b.

Merle, Alexander, i, 328.

Merriott (Dioc. of Bath and Wells), i, 311^b.

Merashe, William, monk of Battle, inst. to St. Nicholas Priory, Exeter, ii, 46^b.

Merther, Laurence, inst. to Padstow, ii, 51^b.

Merton, the Priory of (Dioc. of Winchester), i, 323^b—

The Prior and Convent were patrons of Berry-Pomeroy, ii, 12, 158^b; of St. Laurence, Exeter, ii, 26, 70^b; of Tregony, ii, 29; of Combekeynes (Dioc of B. & W.), ii, 69; of Clyst St. George, ii, 90^b, 115, 132, 148^b, 179; of Ashcombe, ii, 148, 169.

Merton, Richard de, lord of the Manor of Merton, ii, 146^b.

Merton, *see* Monk (*Oratories*), i, 149^b; Dynsbeare in, i, 71; Chapel of St. Mary at Speccote in, i, 38^b.—John Frouke of, i, 40.—John [Monke], R. of, a Penitentiary in the Deanery of Torrington, i, 50; on whose death—

A Commission of Enquiry was issued, 25 June, 1412, on the presentation of Richard Penels, chaplain, by Sir John de la Pomeray, knt., ii, 247b.—A second Commission was issued, 29 Nov., 1412; and in the end Thomas Wyllyng was admitted on the presentation of the said Sir John, Sir Thomas Stawell, and Robert Cornu, ii, 146b, 249b. Willyng was inst., 7 Dec., and on the same day obtained a licence of non-residence till Michaelmas, 1413, i, 173; this was repeated for a year, from 5 Aug., 1414, i, 198; and again from 5 Nov., 1416, i, 227b.

Merwode, Henry, does homage to the Bishop, at Crediton, for lands in Ashburton (2 May, 1412), ii, 311.

Meryk, John, a chaplain, i, 305b.

Metshole, *see* Mitchell.

Metton, John, i, 304b.

Mey, John, monk of Tavistock; elected Abbot, ii, 58, 59.

Mey, Richard, inst. to Kenton, ii, 14b.

Mey, William, inst. to Antony, ii, 87; resigns, ii, 99b.

Michaelstow [Stowe Sancti Michaelis, MS.], Simon Barton, R.

He obtained licence of non-residence for two years, from 22 Aug., 1400, to make a pilgrimage to Jerusalem and the Holy Sepulchre; the Bishop permitting him to retain the income of his benefice, if he provided for the due performance of the duties, and made up for the injury caused by his absence by giving alms to his poor parishioners; the Bishop to fix the amount, i, 45. *See* Barton, Simon—John Nowers, R., obtained licence of non-residence for three years, from 6 Feb., 1416-17: i, 230.

Micham, Simon (deceased), i, 331.

Midderhille, John, V. of Cubert, exch. for Colaton Raleigh, ii, 41.

Middleton, the Abbot and Convent of, present to Broad Sydling, ii, 40b, 220b.

Miere, Thomas, R. of Cheldon, resigns, ii, 5.

Milforde, Henry, i, 303b.

Milford, Richard, clerk, presented to Menhenyot, but not admitted, ii, 243b.—William Milford was co-patron of Menhenyot, ii, 138, 243b.

Milforde, in the parish of Hartland; Chapel of St. James, i, 38b.

Mill [Mulle, MS.], in the parish of Thorverton, i, 88.

Millbrook, Sir Richard Champernoun's manor of, i, 119.

Mille, John, *see* atte Mille, ii, 20.

Mille, Katherine de, i, 315; Richard, i, 329b.

Mille, Wm., inst., to the Chapel of St. Thomas-by-the-Bridge, Barnstaple; ii, 147b.

Milnere, John, inst. to Poughill, R., ii, 31; resigns, ii, 7b.

Milton, in the parish of Morwenstowe, i, 40, 84.

Milton [Abbot], marriage of Robert Martyn and Alicia

Wyllyam of, *see* Beamound, Joan, i, 162, 175b.—Roger Wylle, V.; ii, 58b, 60b, 61b.

A Commission of Enquiry as to the dilapidations left by Roger Wylle, predecessor of Hugh Clerk, was issued 8 Aug., 1411, ii, 243.

Milton Damarel [Damarle *and* Daumarle, MS.], John [Sergent], R.; a Penitentiary in the Deanery of Holsworthy, i, 50.

He was appointed to investigate a charge against one Richard Trengere of having assaulted Thos. Smyth, clerk (1 Aug., 1400), *see* Bideford, i, 44b; appointed to the charge of Pyworthy, ii, 22, 228b; his death, ii, 132b.

Walter Robert, R., ii. 246b.

A Commission was issued, 1 Feb., 1410-11, on the presentation of Robert Osanne, clerk, by Richard Courtenay, Lord of Milton Damarel, ii, 237b; and a second like Commission on the next day, ii, 238.—[*Breve Regium.*]—Edward, Earl of Devon, having presented Walter Robert, clerk, the Bishop was commanded to certify the King as to the circumstances (6 July, 1411), ii, 341. [*Breve Regium.*]—

The Bishop, in accordance with the King's Mandate, sends the official Letter of the Archdeacon of Totnes, shewing that he had convened the Clergy of the Deanery, viz., Edw. Daundesey, John Grymestone, David Loveryng, Roger Lang, Stephen Andrew, Thos. Raly, Robt. Pytman, and John Cowyk, Rectors of Ashwater, Holsworthy, Black Torrington, Bradford, Putford, Sutcombe, Holcombe, and Pyworthy, and also other neighbouring clerks, who knew the facts, viz., Laurence [Bedeman], Wm. Badecok, Thos. Dunham, Rectors of Lifton, Iddesleigh, and Torrington-parva, and John Yerde, Roger Treuerew, and Thos. Launcell, vicars of Bradworthy, Hatherleigh, and Broadwoodwidger—who testified that John Sergent, the last R., died 27 Jan., 1411—that Edw., Earl of Devon, and Sir John Arundell, knt., were the true patrons at that time; the former presenting 2 turns successively, and the latter the 3rd turn. At the last vacancy, Sir Rd. Stapyldon, knt., on the death of Walter Wollecomb, immediate predecessor of John Sergent, presented the said John Sergent, and because the said Sir Rd. was an outlaw at the time, on the suit of Sir Peter Veel, knt., K. Richard presented William Orbyry, clerk, and thereupon issued a writ of *Quare impedit* against Richard Stapyldon and John Sergent, and forthwith the said outlawry terminating, the said Richard Stapyldon recovered his right to present. But meanwhile the Living had lapsed to the Bishop (Brantingham); who, however, "graciously" collated Stapyldon's nominee, the said John Sergent. The right to present now belonged to Edw., Earl of Devon, for his 1st turn, by virtue of a settlement under the great Seal, the terms of which are recited at length. "Michaelmas, 15 Edw. III., K. of England, and 2 Edw. III., as K. of France [1341.]"—Before Roger Hyllary, Wm. Basset, Thos. de Heppescotes, and Rd. de Kelleshylle, Judges,—between Hugh de Courtenay, Earl of Devon, and Margaret his wife, and Wm. Chebeseye, chaplain, and John Horncastell, chaplain, concerning the Manors of Cadelegh, Nuneham Courtenay, Whitewell and Huntbear, and certain rents in Milton Damarel, and the advowsons of Woodleigh, Stoke Damarel, Milton Damarel, and St. Leonard's in the suburbs of Exeter, in Devonshire; the Manor of Hull in Dorset, and a mediety of the Manor of Crewkerne in Somersetshire.—The Earl acknowledged the rights herein of the said Wm. and John, and they, in their turn, conceded the same to the Earl and Margaret his wife (the manors, rent, and mediety to the Earl and the said Margaret and to his heirs whatsoever, and the advowson to the Earl and the said Margaret and their heirs; to have and to hold of the King and his heirs, by customary service for ever. Moreover, the said Wm. and John granted the said Manor of Hull, which Clarice, wife of Sir Rob. de Hull held at the time of her death, and which ought to have reverted to the said Wm. and John, to remain to the said Earl and Margaret and the heirs of their bodies in like manner. Provided that, if the said Earl and Margaret should leave no heir, the said manor of Hull and the said advowson should remain to the direct heirs of the said Earl for ever. This settlement was made by the King's command, and they say that Edward Courtenay is the heir of the said Hugh and Margaret, being son of Sir Edw. de Courtenay, knt., who was son and heir of the said Hugh and Margaret, to whom accordingly belongs the right of presentation to Milton Damarel for this turn.—The living was free from pensions, portions, &c.—and was taxed at xx marks,—the Clerk presented was of good repute, and in every way fit; in priest's orders, and over 40 years old. He was R. of the Parish of Northill, and Preb. of Glasney. Richard Courtenay had presented one Rob. Osan, clerk, but on investigation it was decided that the said Richard had no right to present, as indeed Osan had himself confessed. [Dated in the parish-church of Holsworthy [Hollysworth, MS.], 22 April, 1411], ii, 341.

Walter Colle, R.; licence of non-residence (to study at Oxford), for 3 years, from 16 Oct., 1413, i, 186.

Commission of Enquiry as to dilapidations, on the complaint of William Copleston, R., against Walter Colle, his predecessor (21 Nov., 1415), ii, 257b. Copleston died immediately after institution (ii, 173b), and a second Commission was issued on the complaint of John Phylyppe, against the same Walter Colle (30 April, 1416), ii, 258b. Phylyp (*sic*) obtained licence of non-residence from 18 Feb., 1416-17, till the F. of St. Andrew, 1417, i, 230b.

Ralph Respryn (sub-deacon), R.; dispensation (to study at Oxford), for 3 years, from 25 Sept., 1418; he was to take deacon's Orders within the first year; i, 242b.

This R. complained to the Bishop of a certain chaplain, John Forde, residing at Bradworthy, with no cure of souls, who refused to serve in his Church of Milton Damarel, although he had been offered a competent salary. The Bishop ordered the Dean-Rural to take the necessary steps to compel him (10 Jan., 1418-19), i, 244b.

Minster, *see* Boscastle; also, Ferres, Richard, ii, 311.

Minster Priory; John Stratton, Prior; he allowed the buildings to become ruinous, not caring to restore them: the Bishop sequestrates the revenues (16 June, 1402), i, 61.

Miriet, Gregory, *see* Bickleigh, R.

Mitchell [Metshole, MS.],—

Licence granted for a year to the inhabitants of this village for the Chapel of St. Francis there: they had pleaded that they resided, partly in the parish of St. Newlyn, partly in St. Enoder, and at a great distance from the parish-church in either case; moreover, the main road through the County passed through the place, which was much frequented by travellers who desired to use the said Chapel (24 Nov., 1398) i, 22b. On 24 Oct., 1399, the licence was renewed for another year, i, 31. On 13 Sept, 1400, it was renewed during pleasure, i, 47b. And finally, a perpetual[1] licence was granted, 3 Jan., 1413-14, i, 190b.

Modbury Priory, Mandate for its Visitation, 14 May 1400, i, 36b.

Commission therein (2 July, 1400), ii, 227. Mandate to the Prior, the Visitation

[1] The chapel has perished (and the perpetual licence with it), though it is (or should be), as much wanted as ever. This little place returned two members to Parliament from 1552 to 1832.

having been postponed to 10 July, i, 43. [John Rogger], Prior, licence of non-residence (3 Feb,, 1401-2) i, 54^b. [Richard Leycester] Prior, in arrears of procurations due to the Pope's collector, i, 105.

Modbury, the parish-church of, i, 302.—
William Brounyng V. was appointed the second (*see* Bishop's Nympton), of the eight chaplains of the Bishop, who dispensed with his residence at Modbury when required to serve in that capacity, permitting him to retain the revenues of his Vicarage intact, provided the work of the parish were properly attended to (21 March, 1406-7) i, 80^b.—Licensed, 20 Feb., 1412-13, to hear the confessions of his parishioners, i, 176^b.—For the manor of Modbury, *see* i, 119; Orcherton, i, 172^b; Whympston, i, 109; the chapel of the B.V.M. at Ludbrook, and St. Leonard's at Little Modbury, i, 82^b.

Modeslegh, Thomas, clerk, i, 312; inst. to Churchstanton, ii, 5^b.

Moene, Thomas, inst. to Tamerton, ii, 14.

Moggarygh (*or* Mogrygge), William, V. of West Doune, exchanges for Heathfield Durburgh (Dioc. of B. and W.), ii, 40^b; for Thorverton, ii, 165^b.

Mohun, *or* Moun, Reginald, R. of Alphington (deceased), ii, 10.

Moune, John, *see* Cornu, Matilda (*Oratories*), i, 76.

Moun, Thomas, *see* Eyr, Magota (*Oratories*), i, 240^b.

Mokeworthy, John, of Holsworthy, i, 332.

Mol, Nicholas (deceased), i, 331^b.

Molland [Bottreaux]—the Feast of Dedication, changed from 8 Sept. to 3 Oct. (11 Aug., 1405) i, 76.

Mols, Joan, daughter of Geoffrey, i, 161.
Being excommunicate and contumacious, she is handed over to the secular arm by the Bishop (at Leicester), 14 May, 1414, i, 196.

Molton, Robert de, R. of Clannaborough, ii, 359.

Molyngey, in St. Austell, *see* Chayndyt (*Oratories*), i, 49.

Monk, John, *see* Lew Trenchard, ii, 309.

Monk, John, R. of Merton (deceased), ii, 146^b.

Monk, John, inst. Archpriest of Beer Ferris, ii, 186, 261.

Monk, Peter, V. of Cowick (deceased), ii, 85^b.

Monk, Rd., Archpriest of Beer Ferris; licensed to celebrate in his manse there (19 Aug., 1416), i, 226; his death, ii, 182.

Monk, Roger, chaplain, inst. Archpriest of Beer Ferris, ii, 182, 260^b; resigns, ii, 186. *See* i, 309.

Monk, Thomas, of St. Sidwell's, Exeter, i, 320.

Monkleigh [Munkelegh, MS.], Sarah Chope of, i, 99^b.—*See* Hurde, Richard, i, 202^b;—*also*, Ermington, ii, 339.

Montacute Priory (Dioc. of Wells), i, 138; patrons of Ermington, ii, 51.
A Commission was issued, 2 Feb., 1397-8, to investigate complaints of certain injuries inflicted on the said Priory, ii, 212.—*See* Stoke Fleming, ii, 245^b.

Mountagu, Elizabeth and Anna, daughters of the late John, Earl of Salisbury, present to Boconnoc, ii, 190, 264.

Montagu (*or* de Montacute), Thomas, inst. to Stokenham, R., ii, 42; his death, ii, 77[b]. *See* Blakebourne, Henry; i, 30[b].

Montfort, John Symon, *see* Clok, Richard, i, 24.

Monthermer, Sir Ralph de, knt., presents to Stokenham, ii, 358.

Moorstone, in the parish of Halberton, *see* Moryston, i, 77.

Morchard, John, V. of Brimpton Regis (Dioc. of B. and W.), exchanges for Littleham, V., ii, 87; resigns, ii, 96.

Morchard Episcopi, the parish-church of, i, 319[b].

William Reynald (*or* Rayner, q.v.), R., complained to the Bishop that, although there were many chaplains in Devonshire, not beneficed, fit to undertake the cure of souls, and bound to do so when required by proper authority, he had found it impossible to find one to serve his parish. He had offered a good stipend to one of them, Elias Lepe, who refused the offer. The Bishop commissioned the Dean of Crediton Collegiate Church, and the R. of Lapford, to admonish the said Elias, and inform him that, unless he entered on his appointed duties within ten days, he was to appear before the Bishop at Crediton, and be dealt with accordingly (5 Sept., 1410), i, 105[b]. This William Rayner (*sic*) was licensed to choose a Confessor, 29 Nov., 1416, i, 228. *See*, also, Knyghtiston, John, ii, 311[b].

More, Joan, Canoness of Canonsleigh, ii, 125.

More, Joan, of Hartland, i, 313.

More, John, R. of St. Stephen's, Exeter (deceased), ii, 80; *see*, i, 323, 327[b].

More, Henry, inst. to Ashcombe, ii, 169.

More, Richard, inst. to North Lew, ii, 4, 211. Richard More, (I suppose the same) was inst. to St. Columb-major, ii, 76[b], and exchanged for North Molton, ii, 89[b]; i, 149[b]. He nephew to Precentor Haukyn, i, 333.

More, William, collated to a Canonry in Crediton, ii, 191[b]; he was R. of Beynton (Dioc. of Salisbury), and exchanged for All Hallows-on-the-Walls, Exeter, ii, 200[b].

Morebath [Morbath, MS.], Chapel at Estcort in, i, 60.

Morgan, Philip, *see* Oldcastel, i, 192[b].

Morehay, John, R. of West Keal (Dioc. of Lincoln), exchanges for Ipplepen, ii, 64[b]; for a Canonry and the Prebend of Warminster in Wells Cathedral, ii, 110[b].

Moreleigh [Morlegh *and* Morley, MS.], Alan Benet, R.; licence of non-residence for one year from 18 Oct., 1398, i, 21[b]; and from 28 Sept., 1400, i, 49[b].—William Smyth, R.; licence of non-residence from 16 Feb., 1414-15, to Michaelmas, 1415, i, 208[b]; also from 11 Nov., 1415 to Michaelmas, 1416, i, 215.

Morley [in *Walsingham* "Murlee"], Sir Robert, keeper of the Tower, i, 192.

Moreton [Hampstead], Henry [Brokelond], R., a Penitentiary in the Deanery of Moreton, i, 50; his Will, i, 303.—William Bruter, R., a Penitentiary in the same Deanery, i, 94, 115; the new tower of the parish church, i, 332b.

Morrish, in Wyke St. Mary, *see* Mares (*Oratories*), i, 191.

Morton, a manor of the Fulfords, i, 61b.

Morton, Robert, esquire, co-patron of Otterton, ii, 176.

Morton, Thomas, collated to Clyst Fomison, ii, 75b; exchanges for Charlton (Dioc. of Rochester), ii, 80b.

Morwenstowe [Morestawe *and* Morewenstowe, MS.]—
Licence to celebrate in the Chapel of St. Mary at Milton in, (22 Sept., 1400), granted to Walter Vox, V., i, 49; and again to Robert Taylour, 20 March, 1407-8; i, 84.

Morwyll, Ralph, clerk, i, 149b.

Morys, Wm., inst. to Affeton, ii, 181b; resigns, ii, 201; inst. to East Worlington, ii, 198b.

Moryston; *see* Gambon (*Oratories*), i, 77.

Mottelegh (*or* Motelegh), John, chaplain, coadjutor to John Tappyng, V. of Egg Buckland, ii, 23; inst. to Maker, ii, 90; resigns, ii, 120.

Mottrum, Adam de, ii, 35; R. of Crewkerne (2nd Portion); exch. for a Preb. in St. Probus, and resigns it at once, ii, 47.

Mottrum, Wm., collated to a Preb. in St. Probus, ii, 47b; exchanges for the Preb. of Goodworth in the Conventual Church of Wherwell, (Dioc. of Winchester) ii, 162b.

Mouns, Thomas, of St. Gennys, ii, 261b, 262.

Mountenay, Sir Theobald, knt., *see* Ottery, ii, 278b.

Mousehole [Mosal, MS.], Chapel of the Blessed Virgin Mary, —
It had been ruinated by the sea; and, as it had long been a useful landmark (to the saving of many lives) for vessels entering the narrow harbour, and money to rebuild it was not forthcoming, the Bishop granted an Indulgence to the Faithful who should contribute to the work (17 Oct., 1414), i, 202b.

Mouelond (*or*, perhaps, Monelond), Roger, i, 315b.

Moys, Cecilia and Lucy, recluses of Marhamchurch (q.v.)

Moyseben, Thomas, R. of Dunterton (deceased), ii, 130.

Mullion [ecclesia Sancti Melani, MS.]—
The Bishop issued a Monition, 29 July, 1411, against certain persons who had prevented the collecting and taking away of the great tithes, appropriated to the Dean and Chapter of Exeter; it was directed to the Deans of Kerrier and Penwith and to Robert Bolham, vicar of Mullion, i, 130.—Bolham was frequently a Penitentiary in the Deanery of Kerrier, i, 49b, 143b, 174, 194b, 207b, 217, 231.

Mulsow, William de, i, 304^{b}.

Mulys, John, i, 111, 323^{b}—
A John Mulys was patron of Broadnymet, ii, 179.—*See* Landkey, i, 108.

Munford (*or* Mundeford), *alias* Burgbrygg (or Burghbrygg), John, inst. to Phillack, ii, 106^{b}; resigns, ii, 131.

Musbury [Mosebury *and* Mousbery, MS.], Robert Marscall (*or* Marchall), R.; licence of non-residence for a year, from 28 June, 1397, i, 12^{b}; and from 8 Dec., 1397, i, 14.

Musket, William, inst. to Uplyme, ii, 49.

Mychel, Agnes, of St. Petrock's, Exeter, *see* Hulle [Hylle], Wm., i, 142^{b}.

Mychel, John, R. of Bampton (deceased), ii, 8.

Mychel, John, Prior of Modbury, resigns, ii, 10^{b}.

Mychel, John, Canon of Exeter, i, 31; his death, ii, 35—
The Bishop granted an Indulgence, 25 Oct., 1399, to the Faithful who should pray for the soul of this Canon, who was buried in the south aisle of the Cathedral, before the image of St. Michael the Archangel, i, 31^{b}.

Mychel, John, R. of Cheddington (Dioc. of Salisbury), exchanges for St. John-in-Cornwall, ii, 56^{b}; i, 63; resigns, and is collated to Egloshayle, ii, 68.
A John Michel occurs as V. of Sancreed, i, 16^{b}: he died in 1410, i, 124; another John Michel, chaplain, was appointed by the Bp. "Curator" of Thos. Noel, subdean, who was aged and infirm (27 July, 1417), ii, 262. See i, 325, 325^{b}.

Mychell, Richard, chaplain; *see* Marwood;—
He was licensed to hear the confessions of the inhabitants of Whytefeld in the parish of Marwood, 21 March, 1414-15, i, 209.

Mychell, Richard, Chantry priest of St. Katherine's in Hemyock Church (deceased), ii, 164.

Mychel, Robert, R. of Helland (deceased), ii, 174^{b}.

Mychell, Wm., inst. to Townstal, ii, 92; elected Abbot of Torre, ii, 157.

Mydderhille, Robert, and Isabella Waryn—Commission of Enquiry (17 June, 1411), ii, 242.

Mydderhull, John, V. of Colaton Raleigh, exchanges for Rowington (Dioc. of B. and W.), ii, 228.

Myleton, John, R. of Ashbury (deceased), ii, 181^{b}.

Myldebyry, John, priest, of Slapton Colleg. Chantry, ii, 111.

Myllynse, Chapel of St. Mary at; *see* Petyt (*Oratories*), i. 56.

Mylor; manor of the Bodrugans, at Restranget, i, 145. *See* Bodrugan (*Oratories*).

Myryden, William, *see* Kentisbeare, ii, 345^{b}.

N.

Nahyllyn, Thos., inst. to St. Clement's (Truro), ii, 48b; his death, ii, 15b.

Nanfan [Nanvan, MS.], in Cury (St. Breage), i, 237b.

Nans, John, V. of Manaccan, resigns, ii, 1b.

Nanseglos, Thomas—

[*Breve Regium*]—The Bishop was commanded to make enquiry concerning a rape said to have been committed on Elizabeth, the wife of the said Thomas, by Thomas Ude, of Pengelly, and John Pope, of London, *skinner*, by whom it was pretended that the said Thomas and Elizabeth had not been married, whereas they declared that they were married at Holcombe, in the parish-church there; (28 Nov., 1409), ii, 332.—The Bishop's Return (dated 31 Jan. 1409-10) shews that they *were* married at Holcombe, ii, 332b.

Nanskelly, Henry and John, *see* St. Issey; ii, 227b. John was Chantry-priest of Beaupre in Glasney, ii, 166.

Nansmolken, John, collated to St. Petrock-minor "in Nansfeynton," ii, 37.

Nansou [*hodie* "Nansough"], Manor of Oliver Wyse, i, 202b.

Nansumer, Henry, priest—

He had obtained admission to full Orders while under age, and a Dispensation was granted in his favour (18 Sept., 1400), i, 48b. To Henry Nansumer, chaplain, probably the same person, the Bishop directed his Letter in the matter of the sequestration of the revenues of Minster Priory (q.v.), i, 61.

Nappe, John, of Apuldram, ii, 293b.

Naynow, John, i, 315.

Neel, John, R. of Hollacombe, exchanges for Huish, ii, 68b.

Nelond, John, of Apuldram, ii, 293b.

Neue (or Neve), John, Chantry-priest of Ralegh, resigns, ii, 15; inst. to Challacombe, ii, 14b; i, 60b; exchanges for Cheddington (Dioc. of Salisbury), ii, 87.

Nevill, Robert, son of Ralph, Earl of Westmoreland, inst. to the Portion in Axminster annexed to the Preb. of Grendale, in York Cathedral, ii, 160b, 161.

Newecum, John, inst. to Okehampton, ii, 154; 292b; and *see* i, 194b, 207b, 217, 231, 237b.

Newenham Abbey, i, 318; burial-place of Sir Wm. Bonevyll, knt., i, 311; the Abbot of, in arrears of procurations due to the Pope's Collector, i, 105, 110; the Abbot and Convent present to Luppit, ii, 65, 71b, 180; to Pelynt, ii, 161b.

Newenham, William, R. of Meavy (deceased), ii, 5.

Newenton, Philip, R. of Clyst Fomison, resigns, ii, 31.

Newerk, John, R. of Stratford-juxta-Glemham (Dioc. of Norwich); exchanges for Clyst St. Mary, ii, 91.

Newethorp, John, co-patron of Chagford, ii, 33^b, 34^b, 35^b.

Neweton, John, R. of Skilgate (Dioc. of B. and W.), exch. for the Chantry of Forde (Bampton), ii, 32^b; his death, ii, 186^b.

Neweton, Philip, proxy for John Milnere, ii, 31.

Newton, Wm., co-patron of Blackborough, ii, 151^b.

Newnham [Nywenham, MS.], in Plympton St. Mary, i, 88.

Nywehous, Joan, *see* Calwelegh, John, i, 73.

Newhouse, Hugh, Abbot of (Dioc. of Lincoln), ii, 47^b.

Newport, William, chaplain, of Ipswich, ii, 213^b.

Newton [Nywaton, MS.], in the parish of Churchstow, i, 4, 85^b.

Newton, mansion of Richard Trevaga, i, 37^b.

Newton, in the parish of St. Mellion, i, 238^b.

Newton Abbot [Nyweton Abbatis], mansion of Gilbert Smyth in, i, 246^b.

Newton Ferrers [Nywaton, Nyweton, Newaton Ferys MS.], Puslinch in, i, 76.—John Andrew, R., licence of non-residence for a year, from 29 April, 1405, i, 74; from 20 Oct. to Michaelmas, 1406, i, 80; licensed to celebrate in his manse, 27 Oct., 1412, i, 171^b.—Richard Tryby, R., i, 245^b, 334.

[*Breve Regium*]—Prohibition to admit to this Benefice, pending the settlement of the dispute between Sir John Cornewaill, knt., and Alexander Champernoun, Esquire (20 Nov., 1418), ii, 363^b. [*Breve Regium*]—The said Alexander Champernoun having recovered his right to present, for this turn, against Thos. Bonevyll and John Seton, clerk; Mandate to the Bishop to proceed accordingly (4 Feb., 1418-19), *ibid.* Also, against Sir John Cornewaill (12 Feb.), ii, 364.

Newton St. Cyres [Nywaton Sancti Ciricii *and* Neuton Sancti Cirici, MS.]—

Mandate directed to the Archdeacon of Exeter for the visitation of his Archdeaconry: he was to appear before the Bishop, 12 May, in the Church of this parish (dated 5 April, 1400), i, 35.

Nithewey, John Cole of, *see* Hittisleigh (*Institutions*), ii, 187^b.

Noble, John, inst. to Horwood, ii, 1^b, 222. A John Noble was instituted to Upottery, ii, 176^b.

Noble, Robert le, i, 319^b.

Noble, Stephen, presented by Henry IV. to Loddiswell, R., but not admitted, ii, 238^b.

Noe, Wm., V. of St. Probus, exch. for a Canonry in Glasney, ii, 145; licensed as Publick Preacher, 27 March, 1413, i, 178^b.

Noel, Thomas, Sub-dean and Penitentiary of Exeter; *see* Wytbery, John, i, 133^b; ii, 262, 263; his death, ii, 187.

Non-residence of the Clergy,—

Commissions of Enquiry touching this matter, directed to the four Archdeacons (22 Dec., 1397), ii, 214.—Also, general monition against the same, by the

Metropolitan and his Suffragans (14 March, 1409-10), i, 96b.—Mandate to cite non-resident incumbents, directed to the four Archdeacons (18 June, 1410), i, 98. Similar Mandates for the Sequestration of the Benefices of offenders (4 Aug., 1410), i, 102.—Like Mandates were issued, 23 April, 1411, i, 123; also, 19 Oct., 1412 (requiring to be certified as to their names), i, 170; 18 Sept., 1413, i, 183b; and 15 Sept., 1414, i, 198b.

Nony, Henry, Bishop of Ardagh (q.v.); *see*, also, ii, 225b.

Noo, John, V. of St. Goran (deceased), ii, 226.

Nores [*also* Norys *and* Noreys, MS.], Rd., R. of Combmartin, i, 7b; collated to a Preb. in Glasney, ii, 45b; proxy for Rob. Ballerd, ii, 63b; exchanges Combmartin for Hampton-Meysy (Dioc. of Worcester), ii, 64; resigns his Canonry, ii, 65.

Noreys (*or* Norys), Thomas, i, 309, 332, 332b.

Normand, John, excommunicate and contumacious; the Bishop certifies for his arrest (17 Oct., 1398), i, 21b.

Normanton, Robert, patron (as *locum-tenens* of the Prior of St. John of Jerusalem), presents to Halwell, ii, 12; to Heathfield (Dioc. of B. and W.), ii, 40b; to St. Cleer, ii, 49, 51; to St. Ive, ii, 50b.

Normanton, William, inst. to St. George's, Exeter, ii, 162b; 350; i, 210; exchanges for Thorney (Dioc. of Chichester), ii, 196.

North Allington (*hodie* "East Allington"), parish of, i, 318.

North Huish, the Church of, i, 308b.

Thomas Tremayn, R., was a Penitentiary in the Deanery of Totnes, i, 50; *see*, also, Butterford, i, 37.—John Combe, R., *see* Butterford, i, 67b; licence of non-residence for 2 years from 24 Sept., 1405, i, 76b. *See*, also, ii, 112b, 247b; his death, ii, 144b; his Will, i, 317b.

Thomas Tremayn, priest, was again inst., after Combe's death, 18 Sept., 1412. The Bishop issued a Commission herein, and the Official of the Archdeacon of Totnes certified, 14 Sept., that Isabella, relict of Sir John Damarle, knt., was patron of this Church at the last vacancy, but that for this turn Wm. Fokeray, and Rd. Brouste, chaplain, were patrons, having acquired the manor of North Huish, with the advowson of the Church, ii, 144b, 248b. Tremayn obtained licence of non-residence, with permission to farm out the revenues of his benefice from 12 April to Michaelmas, 1414, i, 196.

North Lew [*and* Northlyw, MS.], *see* Bele, John, i, 73b.—Richard More, R.; licence of non-residence (to study at Oxford) for 2 years, from 22 Jan., 1398-9 [written "Lorthlew"—a clerical error].

Obtained licence of non-residence for two years, from 28 Sept., 1407, *dummodo medio tempore in obsequio famuliari* (sic) *Domine Regine steterit*, i, 82b.

North Molton, Richard Raundes (*or* de Raundes), R.—

He obtained licence of non-residence for 3 years, from 25 April, 1396, *contemplacione nobilis viri Ducis Gloucestrie*, i, 8b; for his Will, *see*, i, 300.—[*Breve Regium*]—For the Abbot of Lilleshull, to give him quiet possession of this Church, 28 June, 1419, ii, 364.—*See*, also, i, 14, 149b.

North Pool (in the parish of South Pool), John Cole of, i, 319.

North Tawton, Matthew Chapman of, i, 140b;

[*Breve Regium*—8 June, 1410]—Mandate to the Bishop, to enquire as to the right of patronage claimed by Richard Haukeford, who (many years previously) had presented John Boure,[1] clerk ; ii, 333b.—On 8 Oct. following, the Bishop certified as follows : Diligent search had been made in the Diocesan Registry, and it was found that Ralph Tregrysiou, Dean of Exeter and Vicar-General, had been deputed to make enquiry as to the patronage of North Tawton (*alias* Chepyngtauton). This was done through the Archdeacon of Barnstaple. The said Richard Hankeford had presented the said John Boure; and the Archdeacon was to report the facts, as ascertained, to the said Vicar-General; (16 Jan., 1397-8). For this purpose he summoned John [Hopere] de Bonelegh, John [Poyns] de Chalvelegh, Thomas [de Bukenarle] de Lappeford, Roger [Yurd] de Wemmaunthy, Robert [Forde] de Nymet Roland, Walter [Beare] de Sele-monachorum (in the person of John Gyffard, chaplain)—all Rectors ; and these Vicars, viz., Roger [Cole] de Burryngton, and Thomas [Sprot] de Colrych, all of the Deanery of Chulmleigh, in full Chapter assembled; who said that the Church of North Tawton had become vacant by the death of John Northwode, 10 Jan. [1397-8], and that Rd. Hankford was the true patron, in right of his wife Thomasia, daughter and heir of Sir Richard Stapylton, knt., Lord of Estyngton, in the said parish ; her grandfather, also a Sir Richard Stapylton, had last presented. They reported further that there was a pension of two marks, payable to St. Nicholas' Priory, Exeter, which had been withheld for the three years last past ; also, that all had been done regularly in the case of this presentation (28 Jan., 1397-8) : ii, 333b.—[*Breve Regium*, 1 Nov., 1413]—To certify the King as to an earlier Enquiry, made in the time of Walter [de Stapledon], the late Bishop, as to the vacancy and right of patronage.—[*Breve Regium*] ; The Bishop's certificate therein, to the effect that the Archdeacon of Barnstaple had then reported, to the said Bishop Walter de Stapledon, that he had convened the Dean of the place (*loci Decanum*), viz., Henry, R. of Wembworthy, and other neighbouring Clergymen, who were not satisfied as to the vacancy, not having been able to prove that Richard de Wellyngton, the last Rector, was dead, or that he had resigned, or been deprived ; they found, however, that Sir Richard de Stapledon was the true patron, having bought the glebe and the advowson of Hugh de Walletort *(sic)*, 9 March, 1317 ; ii, 348.—This John Boure (*or* Bowre), R. ; obtained licence of non-residence for a year, 9 July, 1398, *contemplacione honorabilis viri, Willelmi Hankeford, Justiciarii Domini nostri Regis*, i, 20b : a Penitentiary in the Deanery of Chulmleigh, i, 94, 115b, 143b, 174, 194b, 207b ; Overseer of the Will of Rd. Hurst, R. of Exbourne, i, 315. *See*, also, ii, 333b, 334.

Northcote, Walter, i, 318b.

Northhale, Robert, ii, 313.

Northam, *see* atte Yeo, Henry, i, 138. Appropriation of this Church, ii, 278b.—Chapel of St. John in this parish [Northham, MS.], licensed 26 July, 1400, i, 44b.

Northill [Northulle, MS.]; John Redeclyf, R.; licence of non-residence for a year, from 4 Dec., 1397, i, 14 ; also, for 3 years, from 3 Oct., 1402 (*see* page 37, note (5)).—Walter Robert, R., Preb. of Glasney, presented to Milton Damarel, ii, 341, 342.

[*Breve Regium*, 7 Oct., 1415], Mandate to the Bishop to search the Registers and prepare a List of Clerks inst. to this parish, from the death of Bishop Thomas Bitton : ii, 354.—Bequests to the Church and the parish, i, 324.

---

[1] *See* Bome (p. 28) and p. 38, Note 2.

Northleigh [Northlegh *and* Northleghe, MS.], Stephen [Joseph] R.; licence of non-residence (with relaxation of sequestration, etc.), for one year, from 1 Nov., 1397, i, 18; also, from 28 Feb., 1398-9, to 1 Nov., 1400 (*contemplacione honorabilis viri domini Nicholai Caru militis*), i, 26.

Northleigh, manor of, in the parish of Maristow, i, 226.

Northmore, Richard, i, 308b.

Northwode, John, R. of North Tawton, ii, 334; and Canon of Crediton (deceased), ii, 8, 37.

Northwode, Robert, V. of Bodmin (deceased), ii, 49b.

Norton [-Fizwarren], juxta Taunton, i, 306; ii, 359(?).

Norton, in the parish of Broadwoodwidger, i, 230.

Norton, Henry, of the parish of St. Paul's, Exeter, i, 314b.

Norton, William, Canon of Lincoln, *see* St. Probus, ii, 55b, 56b.

Noss [" villam de Nasse (*sic*) in parochia de Yalmpton," MS.]—
Special licence granted to the inhabitants for Divine Service in their Chapel of St. John Baptist, on his Feast, and on ferial days, at their own charges, and saving the rights of the Mother Church, to which they were to resort on Sundays and other Festivals (16 May, 1400), i, 37.

Nottecleve, John, inst. to Meshaw, ii, 8b.

Nouns, John, inst. to the Chantry in the Church of Alwington, ii, 13; resigns, and is inst. to Meeth ii, 123b; i, 111.

Nowers, John, inst. to Michaelstow, ii, 99; i, 230.

Noy, David, of the parish of St. German's, chaplain, a Penitentiary in the Deanery of East, i, 217, 231, 238, 245b.

Nycol, William, chaplain, i, 325b; collated to St. Paul's, Exeter, ii, 135b; i, 330.

Nytheway, Nicholas, i, 332.

Nywelond, Gregory, R. of Puddington (deceased), ii, 8

Nywenham, John de, patron of Doddiscombsleigh, ii, 13b.

Nywenham, Simon, inst. to Doddiscombsleigh (*alias* Legh Peverel), ii, 13b; resigns Tamerton, ii, 14.

Nymet, Alice, of the parish of St. Paul's, Exeter, i, 314b.

Nymet Rowland, William Cook[1] (*or* Coke), R.; licence of non-residence for a year, from 25 July, 1410, i, 101.

Nymet Tracy [i.e., Bow], William Bremelcombe, R. (accolite)—
Dispensation (to study at Oxford) for three years from 15 Oct., 1399, i, 31; licensed (25 May, 1400), to celebrate in the Chapel "Sancti Martini de Bowe," on Ascension Day and on the Feast of St. Martin, i, 39; (subdeacon) dispensation (to study at Oxford) for 4 years, from 5 Oct., 1403, i, 61b; a

[1] *Not* William Smyth, R. of Ashreigney (note 5 page 7). The MS. has been corrected and is a little obscure; Smyth was *not*, also, R. of Nymet Rowland.

Penitentiary in the Deanery of Chulmleigh, i, 143^{b}, 174, 194^{b}, 207^{b}, 217, 231, 237^{b}, 245^{b}.—*See* ii, 268.

Nynson, Thomas, R. of Stokenham, ii, 358.

Nywaton, Walter, R. of Morchard Bishop (deceased), ii, 56.

Nywecombe, Thomas, *see* atte Nywecombe, i, 332.

O.

Oby, Nicholas, R. of St. Euny, *see* Redruth, i, 48, 49^{b}, 74^{b}.

Oby, Robert, i, 332.

Oclee, Simon, inst. to Barnstaple Priory, ii, 39.

Odetrof, William, a parishioner of Linkinhorne, i, 116.

Officote, Robt., V. of Queen-Camel (Dioc. of B. and W.), exchanges for Cornwood, ii, 87^{b}; i, 238^{b}, 247^{b}.

Offord, John, inst. to Dodbrooke, ii, 197^{b}, 267.

Offwell [Uffewyll, MS.], John Kykke, R.; the sequestration imposed for non-residence taken off (16 Aug., 1410), i, 103^{b}.

Ogle, Robert, i, 305; Katherine, wife of Robert, i, 305^{b}.

Ogwell, East [Estwoggewyll, MS.], John Lane, R.; a Penitentiary in the Deanery of Kenn, i, 143, 173^{b}, 194, 207^{b}, 216^{b}, 231, 237^{b}.

Oke, William, R. of Cadeleigh (resigns), ii, 96^{b}.

Okeford, Nicholas Hertecomb, R.; licence of non-residence for a year, from 18 Sept., 1410, i, 105; ditto, from 10 June, 1412 i, 161; Thos. Durnell, R., ditto, from 11 March, 1416-17, i, 231^{b}; and for 2 years, from 13 July, 1418, i, 241^{b}.

Okehampton Castle, the Chapel in, ii, 293.

Okehampton, Richard [Estebrok], V.; Penitentiary in Deanery of Okehampton, i, 50; his Will, i, 321.—John Newcombe, V., ii, 292^{b}; Penitentiary, i, 194^{b}, 207^{b}, 217, 231, 237^{b}.

Okehampton and Cowick, Ordinacio concerning, by Bishop Stafford—The Bishop sets forth that between the Prior and Monks of Cowick, appropriators of the Parish-Church of Okehampton [Okhampton, *alias* Okementon], on the one part, and John Newcomb, Vicar, thereof, on the other part, grave differences had lately arisen, touching the repairs of the Chancel and the provision of office-books therein, and that the said Prior, &c., by their proxy, John Hethfeld, chaplain, and the said Vicar in person had appeared before him at Clyst, 3 June, 1417, and had stated their case, the former alleging that by Bishop Briwere's Ordinacio, and by custom, the Vicar was liable, and the said Vicar maintaining the contrary view. With the consent of both parties, the Bishop settled their differences thus :—"The said Vicar and his successors were to keep up both the Chancel and the office-books; and by way of compensation it was agreed that in the case of any subsidy to be paid by the Vicar, and in the case of procurations payable by him on account of Archiepiscopal and Episcopal visitations, the Prior, &c., should pay one entire moiety of the same. Also the Prior and Convent agreed to remit 6s. 8d. per annum out of an annual pension of two marks payable to them by the Vicar, reducing the said pension to 20s. per annum. This settlement the Bishop declared to be just and fair, and he confirmed the same accordingly. Bishop Briwere's Ordinacio, mentioned above, is quoted in full, granting to the Prior and Convent of Cowick the Church of "Okementon" and the Chapel in the Castle there, with the consent of Courtenay [*de consensu de Curtenay, veri patroni*], reserving to the Vicar all the obventions of both, the glebe [*sanctuarium*] and the court and buildings thereon, and the tithes, great and small, therefrom; save that the Convent was to enjoy the tithes *garbarum* both of the whole parish and of the tenants of the glebe, together with a suitable space adjoining the Vicar's court, and a barn; with two silver marks yearly at Michaelmas. The Vicar was to be liable for *omnia onera debita et consueta Episcopalia, etiam Archidiaconalia, dictam ecclesiam et dictam capellam contingencia* [these were the disputed words], and to provide for Divine service daily in the said Chapel. It was dated at Exeter, die Martis, in Easter week, 1239.—The date of this Ordinacio was as given above, "at Clyst, &c." The Prior, &c.. signed it on 7 June, in their Chapter House; the Vicar, at Clyst, on the same day, ii, 292^{b}, 293^{b}.

Okenbury [Wokynbury, MS.], in the parish of Ringmore; John Stancombe, R., licensed to celebrate in the Chapel of St. Katherine there (14 Nov., 1410), i, 109.

Okinforda, Meliora, *celeraria* of Canonsleigh Abbey, ii, 125.

Oldcastel, Sir John: Certificatorium super execucione Literarum Domini Cantuariensis contra Dominum Johannem Oldcastel.—Certain charges of heresy had been brought against Sir John in Convocation, and it was determined to make representation thereon to the King; at whose instance further proceedings were stayed for a time, that he might be induced to recant his errors. The King's efforts proving of no avail, the Archbishop attempted to cite him by means of one John Boteler, who proceeded to his castle of Coulyng for that purpose; but Oldcastel declined to be served. The Archbishop accordingly caused him to be publickly cited to appear before him on Sept. 11th, in his Castle of Ledys, and as he failed to appear, he declared him contumacious and excommunicate. He was again cited to appear, on the Saturday next after St. Matthew's Day (Sept. 23), on which day, having been apprehended, he was brought before the Archbishop and the Bishops of London and Winchester, in St. Paul's Cathedral, in custody of Sir Robert de Morley, knt., Keeper of the Tower. The Archbishop declared to him the charges alleged against him and told him that he had been pronounced excommunicate for contumacy; but he refused absolution, and, taking from his bosom a certain Indenture containing the profession of his faith, he read it aloud, and then handed it to the Archbishop, as follows:—

"I, Johan Oldcastell, knyght, Lord of Cobham, wole that alle Cristen men wyte and vndirstonde that I clepe Almyghti God in to witnesse that it hath ben, now is, and ever with the help of God schal be myn entent and my wille to bileve feithfully and fully alle the sacraments that ever God ordeyned to be do in holichurche, and more over for to declare me in these foure poyntis. I bileve that the most wurschupfull sacrament of the auter is Cristys body in fourme of breed, the same body that was born of the blessid Virgyne oure Lady Seinte Marie, doon on the cros, deed ant bured, the thridde day roos for deeth to lyf, the whiche body is now glorified in Hevene. Also, as for the sacrament of penance, I bileve that it is nedefull to everyman that schal be saved to forsake synne and do duhe penaunce for synne bifore doon, with trewe confession, veray contricion, and duhe satisfacion, as Goddis lawe limyteth and techeth, and ellys may he not be saved; which penance I desire alle men to doo. And as of ymages Y undirstonde that they be not of bileve, but that they were ordeyned syth the bileve was ȝive of Crist, by sufferance of the churche, to be kalenders to lewed men, tho represente and brynge to mynde the passion of oure Lord Ihu Crist, ant martirdoom and good lyvyng of other seyntes; ant that who so it be that doth the wurschup to dede ymages that is duhe to God, or putteth feith, hope, or trust in help of hem, as he schulde doo to God, or hath affeccion in oon more than in an other, he doth yn that the grete synne of Mawmetria. Also, I suppose this fully that every man in this erthe is a pilgrym toward blisse or toward peyne; and that he that knoweth not, ne wole not knowe ne kepe, the holy commandements of God in his lyvynge here, al be it that he goo on pilgremage to all the world and he dye so, he schal be dampned, and he that knoweth the holy commaundements of God and kepeth em to his ende, he schal be saved, though he never in his lif go on pilgremage, as men use now, to Canturbury or to Rome, or to any other place."

The Archbishop acknowledged that this profession contained many things which were both good and Catholick, but further questioned him on certain points. He refused to answer further, and was warned by the Archbishop that if he persisted in refusing, he would be condemned as a heretick; and he expounded to Sir John the doctrine of the Church on the points at issue, the latter replying that he believed what the Church taught and God's word declared, but not what the Pope and Cardinals and Prelates of the Church maintained. The Archbishop, pitying him, gave him the following statement of doctrine, in English, that he might consider it with greater deliberation, and appointed the following Monday (Sept. 25) for his final answer:

"The faith and the determinacion of holichurche touchyng the blisful sacrament of the auter is this, that after the sacramental wordis ben sayd by a prest in his masse the materiel bred that was bifore is turned into Cristes veray Body and the materiel wyn that was bifor is turned in to Crystes verray Blood, and so ther leveth in the auter no material breed ne material wyn, the whiche were there bifore the seyinge of the Sacramental wordis. How lyve ȝe this article? Holichurche hath determyned that every cristene man lyvynge here bodilich in erthe oughte to be schryve to a prest ordred by the Churche, if he may come to hym. How feele ȝe this articule? Criste ordeyned Seynt Petir the apostell to ben his vicaire here in erthe, whos see is the churche of Rome, ordeynyng and grauntyng the same power that he ȝaf to Petir schulde succede to alle Peters successours, the whiche we callen now Popes of Rome: by whos power in churches particuler special ben ordeyned prelatis as Archebischopis, bischopis, curatis, and other degrees to whom cristen men oughte to obbeye after lawes of the Churche of Rome. This is the terminacion of holychurche. How feele ȝe this article? Holichur (*sic*) hath determyned that it is needefull to a cristen man to goo a pilgremage to holy places, and there specially to wurschupe holy reliqes of seyntes, apostelys, martirs, confessours, and alle seyntes approved by the Church of Rome: how feele ȝe this article." On the day appointed the same Prelates sat again, with the addition of Benedict, Bishop of Bangor and certain others, viz., Henry Ware, the Archbishop's Official, Philip Morgan, Howel Kiffyn, John Kempe, Wm. Carleton, John Wyttnam, Thomas Palmere, Rt. Wombewelle, John Whitheed, Robert Chamburlayn, Rd. Dodyngton, Thomas Walden; and Jas. Cole, and John Stevenys, notaries public. Oldcastel was again brought before the tribunal, by Sir Robert de Morley; but he refused to ask for absolution except from God; and, having been invited to say what answer he could give as to the points which had been submitted to him, he made a full statement of his opinion as to the Holy Eucharist, the Sacrament of Penance, the adoration of the Cross, and the Power of the Keys, concluding by warning the bystanders in a loud voice against his Judges, who were deceiving both them and their own selves. Again the Archbishop exhorted him; but, as he refused to give way, he solemnly and in the Name of God adjudged him guilty of heresy, and directed the Bishop of London, and through him all the Suffragans of the Province of Canterbury, to provide for publishing the sentence in every church "in a loud and intelligible voice, and in the mother tongue." His letter was dated at Maidstone, 10 Oct., 1413, and the Bishop of London's to Bishop Stafford, in accordance therewith, and containing a copy thereof, at Hadham, on 23 Oct., following; i, 191-193b.

Olveston, John, proxy for Thos. Barton, and John Cowyk, ii, 101b.

Olyver, John, inst. to Clyst St. Laurence, ii, 200; *see* Stretton.

Olyver, Richard, LL.B., i, 47, 73b, ii, 24b, 48b, 50, 50b.

Richard Olyver was collated Minister of Ottery, ii, 81b; exchanged for [East] Allington, ii, 98b; 112b, 127, 357; i, 143, 174, 194b, 207b, 186b; collated to a Canonry in Glasney, ii, 132, 244b, 245b; i, 238; notary-publick, ii, 171; *see* Crowan, ii, 222; appointed President of the Consistorial Court (23 Feb., 1407-8), ii, 231.—*See* Liskeard (*Institutions*), ii, 54b.

Oppy, John, inst. to Manaccan, ii, 1b; to St. Anthony-in-Meneage, ii, 191b, 265.

John Oppy, clerk, obtained a dispensation *super defectu natalium*, 10 Feb., 1416-17, i, 230b.

Opy, Robert, proxy for William Norton, ii, 55b.

Opton, Thomas, i, 324b.

Opus, Rd., collated to the Chantry of Beaupre, Glasney, ii, 187.b

ORATORIES: *Licence to celebrate Divine Service in Domestick Chapels or Oratories, granted to*—

ALDRYNGTON, RICHARD, Canon of Exeter, in his house in the Close (21 Oct., 1416), i, 226b.

ALMYSCOMB, WILLIAM, in the Chapel of St. Thomas the Apostle, in his mansion of Prestecote (*hodie* Prescot), Culmstock (23 Sept., 1414), i, 200b.

ALVECOTE, AGNES, in the Chapel of St. Stephen in her mansion of Alvecote, Shebbear (24 Dec., 1409), i, 92b.

AMADAS, WILLIAM, and MARGARET his wife (28 Aug., 1400); i, 46. Here (and in all other cases where the name of the manor is not mentioned), the licence is in general terms, thus—"ut in Capellis et Oratoriis, ac aliis quibuscumque locis honestis, cultui divino dispositis, infra Civitatem et Diocesim Exoniensem ubilibet constitutis, divina possint in sua et eorum alterius, necnon liberorum suorum presencia, per presbiteros ydoneos facere celebrari."

ANDREW, JOHN, R. of Newton-Ferrers [Newaton Ferys, MS.], in the Oratory within his rectory-house (27 Oct., 1412), i, 171b.

ARNALD, EDMUND, and JOAN his wife, in their mansion at Dartmouth, in the parish of Townstal (26 March, 1412), i, 146.

ARUNDELL, SIR JOHN, knt., and ANNORA his wife (17 Feb., 1399-1400), i, 33. Also, JOHN ARUNDELL of Trerice [Treryz, MS.], esquire, Joan, his wife, and Nicholas, their son, in their Manor of Effard [*hodie* Efford—in the parish of Stratton] (2 Dec., 1413), i, 190; also, in their manor of Thor-le-beare [*hodie* Thurlebeer], in Launcells [Launcelys, MS.], (18 August, 1415), i, 212.—Also to NICHOLAS ARUNDELL, domicellus, and ELIZABETH his wife; and to PETRONILLA LAMMANVA (11 March, 1407-8), i, 84.—[Lammanva (*hodie* Lamanver), is in the parish of Budock: Thomas de Lamanva was inst. to St. Just-in-Penwith in 1393.]—Also to THOMAS ARUNDELL, domicellus, and MARGERY his wife, in all their mansions in Cornwall (26 Feb., 1414-15), i, 208b.

ATTEFFORDE (*alias* WYBBERY), ISOLDA, relict of GILBERT; also, to WALTER BUREL and ALICE his wife; in their manor of Wodelond (*hodie* Woodland), Ermington (27 March, 1414), i, 195b.

AYSSH, WALTER, and ELIZABETH his wife, in their mansion of Farleigh, in the parish of Tiverton (30 Sept., 1406), i, 80.

BASSET, JOHN, and AGNES his wife, in their manor of Tehidy [Thehudy, MS.], in St. Illogan (28 May, 1402), i, 61.—Also, to JOHN BASSET, domicellus, in all his mansions within the Diocese (30 Aug., 1407), i, 82[b].

BAWCOMB, ALICE, relict of EDMUND; also to JAMES BAWCOMB and ISABELLA his wife, in their mansion of Bawcombe [*hodie* Bowoombe], in Ugborough (28 June, 1400), i, 43.

BEAUCHAMB (*sic*) JOHN, and MARGARET his wife, of Boswyns (22 Aug., 1395), i, 4[b].—Also, to ROGER BEAUCHAMP, of Boswyns in Plymouth, and MARGARET his wife (16 Nov., 1395), i, 7.—Also, licence was granted, 21 March, 1414-15, to JOHN BEAUCHAMP and JOAN his wife, for their mansion of Bennerton [*hodie* Binnerton], in St. Crowan. It was specially provided that all other parishioners were to be excluded on Sundays and Festivals; that the celebrations might be "cum clericis"; and that service was not to be celebrated in the Chapel of St. Augustine, near their said residence, on the strength of this licence.—i, 209.

BELE, JOHN, *see* CARY ROBERT, i, 73[b].

BERYE, CLARICIA, relict of JOHN BERYE, domicellus, in her mansion of Aveton-Gyffard (6 July, 1403), i, 67[b].

BEVYLE, RALPH, *see* TRETHERF, Reginald, i, 47.

BODMIN [ALAN KENEGY], PRIOR of, in the Chapel of St. Nicholas, in his demesne of Pendevy [*hodie* Pendavey], Egloshayle (15 Feb., 1403-4), i, 69[b].

BODRUGAN, WILLIAM, and JOAN his wife, in their manor of Restranget [*hodie* Restronguet], in Mylor (18 Feb., 1411-12), i, 145. Also, to the said William and Joan, and their sons, William, Otho, and Thomas, in all their manors or mansions in Cornwall (4 Dec., 1412), i, 172[b].

BOKELLY, NICHOLAS, and ALICE his wife, in their mansion of Bokelly, in St. Kew ["in parochia *Sancti Doquini*"], (15 Sept., 1400), i, 48.

BONEFAS, ROBERT, and CONSTANCE his wife, in the chapel of the Blessed Virgin Mary, at Lanlawarn *alias* Pensiden, in Lanteglos [-by-Fowey], (22 Oct., 1406), i, 80.

BONEVYLE, SIR WILLIAM, knt.:—Licence to John Govys, R. of Holy Trinity, Exeter, "ut *in aula* infra mansum domini Willelmi Bonevyle, militis, infra parochiam dicte ecclesie Sancte Trinitatis situatum, divina possis celebrare, ac per presbiteros ydoneos facere celebrari, necnon parochianis tuis quibuscumque Sacramenta et Sacramentalia conferre et ministrare valeas" (17 April, 1404), i, 70[b]. His parish-church was being rebuilt at the time, and was licensed by the Bishop on the 27th of September following, having been "de novo erecta et constructa," i, 72.

BONEYTHON [*hodie* "Bonython"] SIMON, and EURINUS his son (5 June, 1397), i, 12[b].—On the 15th of Nov., 1402, licence was granted to the said Eurinus and Sarah his wife, for all their mansions in the Diocese, i, 62.

BOSON, EDMUND, and MABEL his wife, and JOHANNA FALEWELL, "mulieri," in the mansion of the said Edmund at Hele [i.e. Bosumahele] (28 April, 1396), i, 8[b].—On the 5th of September, 1408, a licence was granted to JOHN BOȜON, domicellus, and ALINORA his wife, "necnon JOHANNE FALEWYLL," for the Chapel of St. John Baptist within the manor of "Boȝon Hele" in Dittisham, i, 86[b].—To ROBERT BOSOM, Chancellor of Exeter Cathedral, a general licence was granted, 16 Oct., 1395, i, 6.

BOTTREAUX, ELIZABETH, "mulieri," in the Chapel of St. Mary Magdalene, at Boswithgny (1 March, 1395-6), i, 8[b].—This licence was renewed 20 July, 1398; the Chapel being described as "Boswythgy infra parochiam Sancti Ercii in Cornubia" i.e. in St. Erth, probably the estate now called "Bosworgey"; i, 21.—On 24 Nov., 1399, a general licence was granted to WILLIAM, son of SIR WILLIAM BOTREAUX, knt., and to SIR RALPH BOTREAUX, knt., and John and Anna, children of the said Sir William, i, 32[b]. Also, 27 June, 1410, a like general licence was granted to WILLIAM, lord of Botraux (*sic*), his wife, and their sons and daughters, i, 99. And 15 July, 1411, to JOHN BOTREAUX and ELIZABETH his wife, for all their manors and mansions in the Diocese, i, 128[b].

BOWEDON, NICHOLAS, in his mansion at Lerkebeare [*hodie* Larkbeare], in the parish of St. Leonard's, Exeter, for one year only (18 July, 1416), i, 223.

BRAKLEE, JOHN, and THOMASIA, his wife, in their mansions of Plympton and "Westhoobray" (8 Dec., 1407), i, 82b.

BROOK, THOMAS, esquire, and JOAN his wife, in their manor or mansion, at Wycroft [*hodie* Weycroft], in the parish of Axminster (29 Nov., 1417), i, 237.

BRYT, GUY, and ISABELLA his wife and their children (10 Aug., 1395), i, 4.—To this Guy Brit (*sic*) a licence was granted, 26 July, 1400, for his mansion of "Kemell" in the parish of Stoke [Damarel], i, 44b.—Also, 27 Sept., 1408, to William Bryt and Joan his wife, and to Thomas Collan, in the Chapel of the B.V.M. at "Bossym in parochia Sancti Corentini" [*hodie* Bochym, in the parish of Cury], i, 87.

BRYGHTLEGH, LAURENCE, R. of Great Torrington (8 April, 1400), i, 35b. To THOMAS BRYGHTLEGH, domicellus, a general licence was granted, 11 Dec., 1400, i, 51b.

BRYTHBRYTHTYSTON, JOHN, and CECILIA his wife, in their dwelling-house at "Downe Thommas," in the parish of Plympton (15 Dec., 1417), i, 237.

BUREL, WALTER and ALICE, *see* ATTEFORDE.

BURGEAWYLL (*or* BURGEAVYLL), JOHN, Prior of Cowick, in his manor of Crystowe, in the parish of Crystowe [*hodie* Christow] (2 March, 1404-5), i, 73b. This licence was renewed, with the addition of the words "singulisque monachis dicti Prioratus existentibus et futuris" (21 Oct., 1406), i, 80.

BURLESTON, WILLIAM, and ELIZABETH his wife, and their children (22 April, 1402), i, 60b. To ELIZABETH BURLESTON, JOHN CHUDDERLEGH and MARGARET his wife, and WILLIAM and JOHN BURLESTON, the said Elizabeth's lawful issue, a licence was granted, 18 Sept., 1410, for the said Elizabeth's manor of Yungeston, in the parish of Harberton. This manor was long ago merged in other estates, and its identity destroyed; its very existence was forgotten until, in consequence of my enquiry, some traces thereof were found in the name of a field, and the memory of an old barn which formerly stood therein.

BUTTE, JOHN, and JOAN, his wife, in all their mansions in the Diocese (25 Oct., 1408), i, 87. This licence was renewed for all their mansions throughout the County of Cornwall (17 March, 1412-13), i, 178; and again (1 Jan., 1415-16), i, 215b.

BYDEWYLL, ISABELLA, relict of JOHN, in her mansion in the parish of Barnstaple (5 Dec., 1402), i, 62b.

BYKEBURY, WILLIAM, domicellus, and JOAN, his wife [of Bykebury—*hodie* Bigbury (29 April, 1410), i, 95b.—This licence was renewed, for all their mansions and manors in the Diocese (14 April, 1411), i, 122b.

CADE, JOHN, and ALICE, his wife, in their mansion of Blagdon [Blakedon, MS.] (27 Oct., 1395), i, 6b. This licence was renewed, 2 Dec., 1396, for their mansions both of Blagdon and Ashcombe [Ayssachcomb, MS.], i, 9b.

CARMENOWE, WILLIAM, and MARGARET, his wife, in their manor of Boconnoc [Bokoenek, MS.] (28 May, 1397), i, 12.

CAREU, Sir THOMAS, and ELIZABETH, his wife, with their children (16 Nov., 1400), i, 49b.

CARVEK, ISABELLA (11 June, 1397), i, 12b; also to WILLIAM CARVEK, R. of Dolton, within his rectory house (8 July, 1400), i, 43b.

CARSLAKE, WILLIAM, and JOAN, his wife, in their mansion of Harston "in parochia de Bryxston ab ecclesia parochiali Sancte Marie de Plympton dependente" (29 Dec., 1408), i, 87b; *see*, also, STYLVERLOK.

CARY, ROBERT, and MARGARET his wife, in their mansion at Holeway, in North Lew (22 Feb., 1404-5), i, 73b. On the same day (not 26 Feb., as misprinted at page 19), John Bele, chaplain, was licensed to serve the chapel on this manor, *ibid.* On 19 Oct., 1410, licence was granted to the said Robert, during pleasure, for all his manors, etc., throughout the Diocese, i, 108; and on the 23rd it was renewed—"ad tempus infirmitatis vestre qua nunc detinemini tantummodo duraturam, *ibid.*

CAYLEWAY, EDMUND, and JOAN, his wife, in the Chapel of the Blessed Mary and St. Giles, within their mansion of Chenyston [*hodie* Chenstone], in Chawleigh (26 Aug., 1400), i, 45b.

CHALOUNS, RALPH, domicellus, "tam infra mansione set maneria vestra quam extra, ubi vos moram trahere seu ad tempus declinare contigerit" (17 Jan., 1410-11), i, 111b.

CHAMBERLEYN, THOMAS, chaplain, and Vicar-Choral at Glasney—"infra clausum dicti Collegii . . . gravi infirmitate detentus, ita quod ad ecclesiam hujusmodi non poterit comode accedere" (7 Aug., 1403), i, 67b.

CHAMPERNOUN, ISABELLA, wife of RICHARD CHAMPERNOUN, junior, esquire, within the residence of Sir Richard Champernoun, knt., "ubi nunc inhabitat," from 13 Jan., 1418-19, till the Nativity of St. John Baptist next ensuing, i, 244b.

CHAYNDYT, JOHN, and EBOTA his wife, in the Chapel of the Blessed Mary, within their mansion of Myllynsa [*hodie* Molingey], in the parish of St. Austell (22 Sept., 1400), i, 49.

CHEYNE, SIR WILLIAM, knt., and CECILIA his wife, in their manor of Pynho (27 Jan., 1401-2), i, 54b.

CHOULYNG, RICHARD, *see* HELYGAN.

CHUDDERLEGH, JOHN, domicellus, in his mansion of Chudderlegh [*hodie* Chedderleigh], in the parish of Bickleigh [E] (11 April, 1408), i, 85; *see*, also, BURLESTON. On 1 April, 1412, licence was granted to John Chudderlegh and Margaret his wife, for their manors of Chudderlegh and Halberton, in the parishes of Bickleigh and Halberton, i, 147.

CHYDEWODE, JOAN—"mulieri" (24 Sept., 1400), i, 49.

CLERK, WILLIAM, of Dartmouth, in his mansion "de Dertemovth" (4 Dec., 1396, i, 10. On 7 June, 1408, licence was granted to William Clerk, senior, of Dartmouth, for his mansion "de Derthemouth." i, 86.

CLOTEWORTHY, WALTER, *see* HACCHE, RICHARD, i, 8b.

CLYFFORD, ALICE, wife of WILLIAM (1 Aug., 1410), i, 101.—On 5 Sept, 1415, a like licence was granted to THOMAS CLYFFORD, Canon of Exeter, i, 212b.

CODEMORE, THOMAS, and RICHARD HYLLYNG (18 Dec., 1405), i, 77.

COLE, JOHN, domicellus, and BLANCHE his wife (7 Feb., 1395-6), i, 8.—On 5 April, 1400, licence was granted to JOAN, relict of WILLIAM COLE, of Plymouth, in her mansions at Plymouth and Lypton i, 34.

COLSHULLE, JOHN, domicellus, and ANNA his wife, and their family, within their mansions of Tremethert [*hodie* Tremadart—in Duloe] and Dename, in Cornwall (10 Dec., 1414), i, 205.

COLYER, JOHN, R. of Tiverton (3rd Portion), in his mansion at "Tytecombe" (2 July, 1400), i, 43.

COLYN, ALICE, relict of JOHN; also to THOMAS RAYSCHELEGH and JOAN his wife, in their mansion of Hole, in Georgeham [Hamme Sancti Georgii, MS.] (30 Nov., 1402), i, 62.

COPELSTON, JOHN, domicellus, and ALICE his wife, in their mansion of Copelston (27 Oct., 1395), i, 6b.

CORK, JOHN, and KATHERINE his wife, in their manor of Paderda in Menhenyot [Mahenyet, MS.] (28 June, 1418), i, 240b.

CORNU, MATILDA, relict of HENRY; also to JOHN MOUNE and JOAN his wife, in their mansion of Poslyuche [*hodie* Puslinch], in Newton Ferrers [Nyweton Ferys, MS.] (11 Aug., 1405), i, 76.—Licence was granted, 29 March, 1403, to WALTER CORNU, domicellus, i, 63; and again, 22 Nov., 1408, to WALTER CORNU and CONSTANCE his wife, and to ROBERT CORNU, their son, and ISABELLA his wife, i, 87.—Also, 7 Oct., 1405, to JOHN and JOAN DYNMOK together with WALTER CORNU and ELIZABETH his wife, i, 76b. [According to Pole, this Elizabeth, daughter of Ralph Rous, of Little Modbury, married (1) Roger Peperell, (2) William Dymock, (3) Walter Cornu: John Dymock was her son by her second husband. *See* DYMMOK.]

COURTENAY, SIR HUGH, knt., and PHILIPPA his wife, i, 85.—On 20 May, 1408, a general licence was granted to SIR EDWARD COURTENAY, knt., son of the

Earl of Devon, i, 86.—Also, 11 Sept., 1418, to MATILDA, wife of HUGH COURTENAY, senior, knt., i, 242b.
CROKKER, JOHN, and ALICE his wife, 5 April, 1400, i, 34.
CRYDIA, ELIZABETH, in her manor or mansion of Orlegh, in Buckland Brewer [Boklond Bruerre] (6 March, 1416-17), i, 231b.
CURTEYS, THOMAS, and MATILDA his wife, in their mansion of Pylle [*hodie* Pill], in Lanlivery [Lanuyvery, MS.] (6 June, 1405), i, 75.
DAUNEY, JOHN, domicellus, and JOAN his wife (15 July, 1405), i, 75b.
DENCLYF, JOHN, and ALICE his wife (3 May, 1407), i, 81b.
DENE, JOHN, chaplain (for one year only, from 26 Sept., 1413), i, 185.
DENYS, JOHN, and ALICE his wife, in their mansions of Ghydecote and Legh, both in the parish of Thornbury (21 May, 1400), i, 38b.
DEVERELL, JOHN, and ALICE his wife, in their mansion of Deverell in St. Gwinear, 20 Feb., 1413-14, i, 194.
DOGET, ROBERT, chaplain, within the residence of the Vicars of the Colleg. Ch. of Crediton (27 April, 1419), i, 246b.
DONYELL, NICHOLAS, V. of Linkinhorne [Laukynhorn, MS.], in his Vicarage house (18 Nov., 1400), i, 50.
DOTY, RICHARD, V. of Launcells, in all oratories, etc., within the said parish (21 May, 1400), i, 38b.—He exchanged for St. Laurence's, Exeter, and afterwards for Staverton, where, 27 May, 1412, he obtained licence to celebrate within his Vicarage house, i, 160b.
DOUNE, HUGH, and ISABELLA his wife, in their mansion of Wyke, in the parish of Axminster (8 Dec., 1407), i, 82b.
DOURYSCH, ALICE, *see* SPENCER, RICHARD, i, 212b.
DURNEFORDE, STEPHEN, and RADEGUND his wife, in their mansion of East Stonehouse, in the parish of Plymouth (28 Sept., 1414), i, 200b.—The said Stephen and Radegund, 16 April, 1415, obtained a licence for their mansion of Langonet [*hodie*, Langunnet], in St. Veep, i, 209b. And licence was granted 9 Feb., 1416-17, to ALICE DURNEFORD, "apud Norton, infra parochiam de Brodewode Wyger . . . commoranti . . . infra manerium suum de Norton predictum," i, 230.
DYGON, JOHN, Canon of Plympton (27 March, 1402), i, 60b.
DYMMOK, JOHN, and JOAN his wife, in their mansion of Brygg [*hodie* Ivybridge], Ermington (6 May, 1402), i, 60b. *See* CORNU, WALTER.
DYNCLEVE, STEPHEN, and ELIZABETH his wife (30 Jan., 1402-3), i, 59.
DYNHAM, SIR JOHN, knt., and MATILDA his wife (26 Nov., 1396), i, 9b.
DYRWYN, JOAN, in her mansion of Foleford [now Shobrooke Park], in the parish of Crediton, 29 Sept., 1413, i, 185.
EGGECOMB, PETER, and ELIZABETH his wife, in their mansion in the parish of Calstock (12 May, 1411), i, 123b.
EMAT, WALTER, *see* HELYGAN.
ESSE, GILES DE, and JOAN his wife, in their mansion of Esse Boleyne, in the parish of Crediton (2 June, 1407), i, 82.
EYR, MAGOTA; also to THOMAS MOUN and ISABELLA his wife, in their manors of Trevlesyk (*hodie* Trelissick) in St. Erth, and Trembethow in St. Uny Lelant [Sancti Ewnini de Lananta, MS.] (28 June, 1418), i, 240b.—*See* MAHUN, THOMAS.
FALEWYLL, JOAN, *see* BOSON.
FECOS, JOHN, R. of St. Gerrans [Sancti Gerendi, MS.], in the manse of his Rectory (10 Feb., 1410-11), i, 115b.
FYȜTPAYN, ELINORA DE; also THOMAS HORSEY and ALICE his wife (20 June, 1400), i, 42b. A similar licence was granted, 28 April, 1404, to ELINORA, relict of SIR JOHN FYȜTPAYN, knt., i, 71.
FYȜWARYN, THOMASIA, relict of WALTER; also, to ALMERIC FYȜTWARYN and MARGARET his wife, in the Chapel of St. Katherine within their mansion of Totele (*hodie* Totley), in Black-Torrington (8 July, 1401), i, 57b.
FLAMMAK, RICHARD, and MARGARET his wife (5 Dec., 1406), i, 80b.
FOLEFORD, HENRY, and WILHELMINA his wife, in their mansions of Foleford [*hodie* Fulford, in Dunsford] and Morton (8 July, 1402), i, 61.

FOLLE, EMMOTA, "mulieri,"—"infra Decanatum de Trygg minor" (16 Sept., 1400; i, 48.

FORTESCU, WILLIAM, and MARGERY his wife, in their mansion of Combe [Come MS.], in Holbeton (15 May, 1400), i, 37.—Licence was granted, 17 Nov., 1410, to WILLIAM FORTESCU, senior, and ELIZABETH his wife; also, to WILLIAM FORTESCU, junior, and MATILDA, *alias* MABILLA, his wife, for the mansion of the said William (senior), at Wymedeston, *alias* Wymeston [*hodie* Whympston], in the parish of Modbury, i, 109.—Also, 8 May, 1412, licence was granted to JOHN FORTESCU and CLARICE his wife, for their aforesaid manor of Combe in Holbeton, i, 149b.

FOUKE, WILLIAM, domicellus, in his mansion of Pylle [*hodie*, Pill], in Bishops-Tawton (6 April, 1400), i, 35b.

FRAUNCEYS, ALICE; also JOHN FRAUNCEYS and ALIANORA his wife, in their mansions of Hele and Chyvethorn [*hodie*, Chevithorne], in Bradninch and Tiverton (27 May, 1416), i, 221b.

FROUKE, JOHN, in the Chapel of the Holy Trinity, within his mansion in the parish of Merton (8 June, 1400), i, 40.

FURSDON, JAMES DE, and JOHN his son, within their mansion of Fursdon (23 June, 1400), i, 42b.—Licence was granted, 2 Sept., 1400, to JOHN FURSDON and JOAN his wife, for their mansion of Fursdon, in the parish of Liskeard, i, 46b.

FYLHAM, PETER DE, and ANNINA his wife, in the Chapel of St. Andrew within their mansion of Fylham, in Ugborough (14 Dec., 1400), i, 51b.

GAMBON, JOHN, domicellus, and IDENIA his wife, within their mansion of Morystón [*hodie* Moorstone], in Halberton (23 Jan., 1405-6), i, 77.

GEBAY, WILLIAM, *see* HELYGAN.

GERVEYS, JAMES, and ISABELLA his wife, in their mansions of Banadlak [*hodie*, Benallack] and Trervell [? Trerule] (29 April, 1400), i, 36b.—*See* TREGOS—A general licence was granted, 6 May, 1404, to PETER GERVEYS, V. of Constantine, for his said parish, i, 71.

GLYVEAN, RICHARD, and JOAN his wife (27 March, 1397), i, 11b.—This licence was renewed, 22 Nov., 1398, i, 22b.

GORWELL, JOHN, Canon of Exeter (7 June, 1401), i, 56b.

GOVYS, JOHN, domicellus, and AGNES his wife, and JOHN and RICHARD their sons; also to MARGERY WYMOND: in the Chapel of B.V.M. within their mansion of Kynaden [*hodie*, Keynedon], in Stokenham (11 Oct., 1409), i, 90b.—*See*, also, BONEVYLL.

GRAUNT, WILLIAM, and MARGARET his wife, and JOAN (their daughter), in their manor of Stepheneston, [*hodie* Stevenstone] in Great Torrington (18 Feb., 1411-12), i, 145.

GRAYNEVYLL, RICHARD, LL.B., R. of Parkham (21 May, 1407), i, 82.

GREYNEVYLL, SIR JOHN, knt., MARGARET his wife, and JOAN their daughter (22 May, 1400), i, 38b.—Licence was granted, 5 October, 1413, to WILLIAM GREYNEVYLE and THOMASIA his wife, for their mansions in the parish of Kilkhampton, i, 186.

GREYNDON, RICARDA—"mulieri," in her residence in St. Petrocks, Exeter (8 Nov., 1414), i, 203.

GRYLLESTON, WILLIAM, and ELIZABETH his wife (18 Feb., 1401-2), i, 60b. This licence was renewed for WILLIAM GRYLLESTON and JOAN his wife, 22 Dec., 1408, i, 87b.—William Grilleston was of Grilleston [*hodie*, Grilstone], in the parish of Bishop's Nympton, 13 Ric. II. (*Pole*). *See* Vautard (*General Index*.)

GURLYN, HENRY, and MARGARET his wife (6 Dec., 1406), i, 80b.

GYBBES, WALTER, R. of Tawstock [Toustok, MS.] (23 Aug., 1396), i, 9.—This licence was renewed to him as Canon of Exeter, 3 Dec., 1397, i, 14.

GYFFARD, GEOFFREY, and EMMA his wife, in their mansion of Yoe [*hodie* Yeo, MS.], in the parish of Alwington,[1] 26 March, 1408.

---

[1] In North Devon; not West Alvington in South Devon, where Pole erroneously placed Yeo.

HACCHE, JOHN, R. of South Molton; a general license for his whole parish (25 May, 1400), i, 39. To RICHARD HACCHE and WALTER CLOTEWORTHY licence was granted, 26 April, 1396, for the Chapel of St. James and St. Bartholomew in the said parish: i, 8b.

HAISENDE, WILLIAM, *see* SCHALDON, JOAN.

HALAP, JOAN, relict of LAURENCE; also, to JAMES HALAP and MATILDA his wife, in their manor of Tregonyon in [St. Michael] Penkevel (10 Dec., 1415), i, 215b.

HALS, JOHN, within all his manors, etc., in the Diocese (2 Oct., 1416), i, 226.

HANKEFORD, RICHARD and THOMASIA his wife, in their mansion of Huish in the parish of Instow (26 Feb., 1404-5), i, 73b.—To JOHN HANKEFORD and JOAN his wife licence was granted, 4 Aug., 1406, for their mansion of Loddeford, in Shebbear [Scheftbeare, MS], i, 78.

HAWKLEY, JOHN, of Dartmouth, and JOHN his son (*per biennium duntaxat duraturam*—from 18 April, 1397), i, 12.—A general licence was granted (12 Nov., 1408), to JOHN HAULEY, domicellus, and MARGARET his wife, i, 87. It was renewed in favour of the same persons, 7 April, 1417: i, 232.

HELE, NICHOLAS, and ALICE his wife (22 Oct., 1402), i, 62.

HELIGAN, JOHN, and ELIZABETH his wife, in their mansion of Trencruk [*hodie*, Trencreek], in Menhenyot (25 Nov., 1396), i, 9b. To JOHN HELYGAN, domicellus, and ELIZABETH his wife, licence was granted 8 May, 1401, for their mansion of Helygan, in the parish of St. Mabyn [Sancti Mabani, MS.], i, 56.—Also, to NICHOLAS HELYGAN and EMMOTA his wife, for all their Oratories in Cornwall (18 Sept., 1400), i, 48.—The Chapel "Sancti Aldelmi de Ammel in parochia de Lannov" [*hodie* Chapel-Amble, in St. Kew], was licensed 24 May, 1405, in favour of the said NICHOLAS and EMMOTA and ROGER and NICHOLAS the sons of the said Nicholas; also, of RICHARD CHOULYNG, EDMUND SMYTH and ISOTA his wife, NICHOLAS SOBY and JOAN his wife, RICHARD WATTY and JULIANA his wife, WALTER EMAT and MARGARET his wife, and WILLIAM GEDAV and his wife, i, 75.—Also, to JOHN HELYGAN and ISABELLA his wife, a licence was granted, 24 Sept., 1411, for their manor of Trencruk, i, 135; and this licence was renewed to the said John and Isabella "ac familiaribus eorundem" (12 Oct., 1411,) i, 135b.

HERLE, SIR JOHN, knt., and MARGARET his wife, (16 Feb., 1396-7), i, 11b. This licence was renewed to the said John and Margaret, (23 Aug., 1400), i, 45.

HEYE, ROBERT, and ISABELLA his wife, in their mansion of Heye [*hodie*, Hay], in St. Ive (2 Nov., 1403), i, 68.

HICKELYNG, HUGH, Precentor of Exeter, for one year only (1 Aug., 1395), i, 4.

HOLEMORE, RICHARD, and EDITH his wife, in their residences in the parishes of Frithelstock [Frethelystoke, MS.], and Alwington (28 March, 1419), i, 246.

HOLDYCHE, PETER, V. of Loddiswell [Lodeswyll, MS.], in his Vicarage-house (16 Feb., 1413-14), i, 194.

HONNYLOND, JOHN, Prior of St. Stephen's, Launceston, in all his manors and residences (17 July, 1410), i, 101.

HORSEY, THOMAS, and ALICE his wife (24 Sept., 1400), i, 49.—*See*, also, FYȜPAYN, ELINORA DE, i, 42b.

HUGH, DAVID, V. of Buckfastleigh, in his vicarage-house (30 Dec., 1407), i, 83.

HULLE, ROBERT, MABILLA his wife, and their children (4 Dec., 1395), i, 7. A general licence was granted 16 June, 1398, to ROBERT HULLE, junior, and ISABELLA his wife, i, 20b.

HYLLE, JOHN—"nobili viro ... Domini Regis Justiciario"—and Matilda his wife, "in ipsorum et eorum alterius, necnon liberorum et familiarium suorum presencia" (1 Oct., 1397), i, 13b.

HURDEWYKE, ROBERT, and JOAN his wife, in their mansion of Bere [*hodie* Beer], in Marhamchurch (28 June, 1400), i, 43.

HYDE, WILLIAM, R. of Great Torrington, in his rectory-house (6 March, 1403-4), i, 70.—Renewed to William Hyde (then "in Decretis Bacullario"), and extended to any suitable oratory in the parish, 6 July, 1408, i, 86.

HYLLYNG, RICHARD, *see* CODEMORE, THOMAS.

KELLY, THOMAS, and MARGARET his wife, in their house at Southwyke, in Germansweek (7 July, 1411), i, 128b; "volumus autem quod diebus Dominicis et festivis ad ecclesiam vestram parochialem predictam, pro divinis inibi audiendis, personaliter cum comode poteritis, accedatis." A licence was granted, 30 April, 1411, to NICHOLAS KELLY, R. of St. Ladock, for his rectory-house; also, for the Chapel of St. John, in St. Erme, i, 123b.

KELWA, WILLIAM, and MARINA his wife (22 June, 1401), i, 57b.

KENEBEARE, JOAN, her son JOHN, and his wife ALICE, in their mansion of Trefalford [*hodie* (?) Trevollard], in the parish of Saltash (11 July, 1407), i, 82.

KEYNES, JOHN, domicellus, JOAN his wife, and their children (17 Oct., 1409), i, 90b.

KYRKHAM, ROBERT, and AGNES his wife, in their mansion of Blakedon [*hodie* Blagdon] Kyrkham, in the parish of Paignton (14 Feb., 1410-11), i, 115b.

KENDALE, JOHN, and JOAN his wife, in their mansion of Treworgy, in the parish of "Reprenne" (2 Sept., 1400), i, 46b. *See* Treworgy.

LAMBRUN, SIR WILLIAM, knt., and SIBILLA his wife (7 July, 1400), i, 43b.

LAMMANTA, PETRONILLA, *see* ARUNDELL.

[LAMORKEN], PETER, R. of Lawhitton, in his rectory-house (3 April, 1414), i, 195b.

LANE, WALTER, and THOMASIA his wife, in the oratories "infra mansum Rectoris de Rowesassche [i.e. Roseash] ac mansum ipsius Walteri in parochia Barumensi" (25 May, 1400), i, 39. The said Rector was William Lane, a member of the family.

LANDAWARNEH, JOHN, and JOAN his wife, in the Chapel of the B. V. M. "atte Hille" [*hodie*, Hill], in Duloe (28 Aug., 1402), i, 61b. There is an estate in this parish called "Lanwarnick."

LANHEROY, JOHN, and JOAN his wife, and their children, in their mansion of Pengelly in St. Brooke [Sancti Brioci *alias* Pouton, MS.] (28 June, 1400), i, 43.

LEGH, NICHOLAS, and MATILDA his wife, in the Chapel of St. Mary of Legh, in their mansion of Legh [*hodie* Ley], in Beerferris (21 May, 1400), i, 38b.

LERCEDEKNE, the LADY ELIZABETH, relict of SIR WARIN LERCEDEKNE, knt., "in sua et familiarium suorum presencia" (23 July, 1401), i, 58.

LOTEBY, THOMAS, V. of Dunsford, in his Vicarage-house (21 Sept., 1411), i, 135.

LYNDE, JOHN, chaplain, in chapels, oratories, &c., within the parish of Bodmin (15 Feb., 1405-6), i, 77b.

MAHUN, THOMAS, and ISABELLA his wife, MICHAEL TRENUYD, and MARGERY EYR (*see* EYR, MAGOTA). This licence was granted for a year, 17 June, 1398, for the Chapel of the B. V. M. at Breynyon [*hodie* Brunnion], in the parish of St. Uny Lelant [Sancti Eunii in Cornubia, MS.]; but in the margin are the words—"non habuit effectum," i, 20b.

MALEBONS, JOHN, R. Calstock (q.v.), i, 49.

MALKWAYN, JOHN, R. of Calstock (q.v.), i, 74.

MARES, JOHN, and JOAN his wife, in their house of Mares [*hodie* Marries], in Wyke St. Mary (18 Jan., 1413-14), i, 191.

MATTEFORDE, JOAN, "mulieri," for one year only (10 Nov., 1395), i, 6b. This licence was renewed "during pleasure," 28 June, 1400, i, 43.

MAYNARD, ROBERT (domicellus), for three years (15 Feb., 1401-2), i, 60.

MERWODE, WALTER, and JOAN his wife, in their mansion of Merwode [*hodie*, Marwood], in Marwood (7 June, 1400), i, 40.

MEWY, RICHARD, and MATILDA his wife, in their mansion of Walradan, in Whitchurch (26 Nov., 1401), i, 58b.

[MYCHEL, JOHN], Prior of Modbury, in the Chapel of St. Margaret, within his manor of Penquit, on St. Margaret's day (22 June, 1397), i, 12b.

MICHEL, SIMON, and JOAN his wife, in their house of "Dewdon" (14 June, 1398), i, 20.

MILETON, GILBERT, and JOAN his wife (1 May, 1396), i, 8b. To RICHARD MILETON and EMMOTA his wife, licence was granted, 10 June, 1411, for their house of Westwyke [*hodie* Westwick] in the parish of Lifton, i, 125b. *See*, also, Ashbury, JOHN MILETON, R. of; i, 11b.

MONK, WILLIAM, domicellus, and JOAN his wife, in their mansion of Poderyg [*hodie*, Potheridge, in Merton] (18 Oct., 1395), i, 6b. Licence was granted, 11 May, 1412, to WILLIAM MONK alone, "infra mansum suum de Poderugg, infra parochiam de Merton," i, 149b.

MONK, RICHARD, Archpriest of Beerferris [Bereferes, MS.], in his manse there (19 Aug., 1416), i, 226.

MOUNR, JOHN, *see* CORNU, MATILDA, i, 76.

MOYLYS, JOHN, and . . . . . . his wife, in the Chapel of St. Martin, near their mansion of . . . . . . , in the parish of St. Winnow (22 Sept., 1400), i, 49.—The blanks indicated above are left in the MS., and were never filled in. We learn, however, from Bishop Brantingham's Register that he licensed this Chapel of St. Martin, in 1389, "quam Johannes Moyle sumptibus suis construxit apud Bodivalgan."

MULLE, THOMAS, and JULIANA his wife, with their children, and Joan, mother of the said Thomas, in their mansion of Mulle [*hodie* Mill], in Thorverton (1 Feb., 1408-9), i, 88.

NANVAN, JAMES, and MARGARET his wife, in their mansions of Nanvan [*hodie*, Nanfan] and Bonython, in St. Breage (6 Jan., 1417-18), i, 237b.

NEUE [*or* NEVE], JOHN, R. of Challacombe, in his rectory-house (13 April, 1402), i, 60b.

NORTHCOTE, WALTER, and ALIANORA his wife, in their mansion of Hackworthy, in Tedburn St. Mary [Tettebourne, MS.] (2 Sept., 1415), i, 212b.

NORTHWODE, WILLIAM, in his mansion in the parish of Were [*hodie* Wear Giffard] (16 April, 1411), i, 122b.

OFFECOTE, ROBERT, R. of Cornwood, in his rectory-house (19 Dec., 1410), i, 110b.

OLYVER, RICHARD, LL.B., and JOHN WARYN, LL.B., in the Chancellor's house in the Close (5 March, 1411-12), i, 145b.

ORTHAM, WILLIAM, and ELINORA his wife, in the Chapel of St. Peter, in Lifton (16 Oct., 1399), i, 31.

OTERHAMPTON, WILLIAM, R. of Silverton, in his rectory house (20 March, 1412-13), i, 178b.

OVERTON, PETER, R. of Dartington, in his rectory-house (2 June, 1407), i, 82.

PADIRDA, NOEL, and THOMAS his son, their wives and their children, in their mansions at Padirda, in the parish of Menhenyot (6 April, 1400), i, 35b.

PASSENHAM, JOHN, R. of Sampford [Saunford, MS.] Courtenay, and ELENA his sister, in his rectory-house (30 June, 1397), i, 13.

PAYLE [*hodie* "Pawley"], SIMON, V. of [W.] Alvington (30 May, 1408), i, 86.

PENELLYS, ELIAS, and MARGARET his wife, in the Chapel of St. Katherine, in their mansion in the parish of Brixham (19 Dec., 1409), i, 92b. Elias Peniles was "of Luckton [*hodie* Lupton] in the parish of Brixham" (*Pole*, p. 283.

PENGERSEK, JOHN, and JOAN his wife, in their mansion of . . . . . . in the parish of . . . . . . (6 Sept., 1400), i, 47. The blanks were not filled in: Pengersick is in the parish of St. Breage.

PENROSE, JOHN, and CONSTANCE his wife (1 Dec., 1395), i, 7. A licence was granted, 6 Sept., 1400, to JOCEUS PENROS and JOAN his wife, for their mansions in Cornwall, i, 47; also, 14 May, 1405, to SIR VIVIAN PENROS, knt., and MARGERY his wife, for their mansions throughout the Diocese, i, 74b.

PENTYRE, RICHARD, and JOAN his wife, in their mansions throughout the Diocese (8 May, 1405), i, 74b.

PETYT, JOHN, and MARGARET his wife, in the Chapels of St. Mary the Virgin, within their mansions of Predennek [*hodie* Pradannack, in the parish of Mullyon], Rostek and Myllynse (6 May, 1401), i, 56.

PEVERELL, THOMAS, domicellus, and MARGARET his wife (18 Oct., 1395), i, 6.

POLLARD, WALTER, and ELIZABETH his wife (3 Oct., 1408), i, 87.—Licence was granted 2 Sept., 1410, to JOHN POLLARD and EMMA his wife, for their house in the parish of St. Giles [-in-the-Wood], i, 104.—Also, 15 March,

1414-15, to Richard Pollard and Thomasia his wife, and to John their son, for their house at Langelegh [*hodie* Langley], in High Bickington [Bukyngton, MS.], i, 208b.

Polmorva, John, domicellus (31 Dec., 1406), i, 80b.—This was a general licence for the City and Diocese : and on the same day the Bishop granted a special licence to the said John and Elizabeth his wife, and their children ; also, to Thomas Tremere, for their mansion of Husten in the parish of Fauton [*hodie* Hurston, in the parish of St. Breoke], *ibid.*

Polsave, Thomas, Margaret his wife, and Joan their daughter (17 Nov., 1395), i, 7.—A like licence was granted, 12 July, 1398, to the said Thomas and Margaret, and to their daughters Joan, Elizabeth, and Katherine. The terms were very general—" in capellis, oratoriis, sive aliis quibuscumque locis honestis, ubi te Thomam, Margaretam, Johannam, Elizabetham, vel Katerinam, in Diocesi Exoniensi, morari et larem fovere contigerit " ; i, 20b.

Pomeray, Sir, John de la, knt., and Joan his wife (18 Oct., 1395), i, 6b. Also, Sir Thomas Pomeray, knt., and Joan his wife (3 May, 1407), i, 81b.

Prouse, Thomas, and Joan his wife, for two years, from 12 July, 1401, i, 57b.

Prydeaux, Sir John, knt., and Elizabeth his wife (14 Nov., 1395), i, 6b.—The Bishop granted a general licence, 21 Sept., 1403, for all their mansions in the City and Diocese, to Richard Prydeaux, domicellus, and Joan his wife, i, 67b.—Also, 22 Nov., 1412, to John Prydeaux and Elinora his wife, for the Chapel within their manor of Orcheton, in Modbury [Modbyry, MS.], i, 172b.

Puddesdon, John, sub-dean of Exeter (24 Aug., 1395), i, 5.

Pyllond, Thomas, and Isabella his wife, in their mansion of Pyllond, in Pilton (6 May, 1403), i, 64b.

Pyn, Edmund, domicellus, and Alice his wife, in their mansion of Pyn [*hodie* Pynes], in Upton Pyne [Upton Pyn, MS.] (13 April, 1400), i, 36b.

Pyper, John, Prior of St German's, in the manors and residences belonging to his Priory (5 Oct., 1411), i, 135.

Pyperell, Richard, and Alice his wife, and their children, in their house at Ermington (14 May, 1400), i, 37. A general licence was granted, 10 June, 1405, to Richard Pyperell, Joan his wife, and their children, i, 75.—Also, 24 Feb., 1411-12, to Richard Pyperell, junior, and Christina his wife, for their chapel of St. John Baptist in their manor of Pynesford [i.e. Penesford], in the parish of Ashprington, i, 145b (*see* Wolhaye).

Ralegh, John, domicellus, and Elinora his wife, their children and family (18 Oct., 1395), i, 6.—A general licence was granted, 31 Oct., 1402, to John Ralegh and Elizabeth his wife, i, 62.

Raybchelegh, Thomas, and Joan his wife, *see* Colyn.

Reskarek, Thomas, domicellus, and Agnes his wife ; also, Walter Reskarek, his brother (29 Sept., 1403), i, 67b.

Reskymer, Ralph, and Idonea his wife, in their manor of Reskymer, in the parish of . . . . [left blank in the MS. ; this manor is in St. Mawgan-in-Meneage] (27 Sept., 1408), i, 86b.

Respresa, Richard, and Joan his wife (24 May, 1402), i, 61.

Reymond, Thomas, and Joan his wife, and Richard their son, in their manor of Symeston [*hodie* Simpson], in the parish of Holsworthy [Hallysworthy, MS.] (4 Oct., 1413), i, 185b.

Reynald, Walter, domicellus (12 Jan., 1412-13), i, 173.—In this licence the name of the priest who is to serve under its authority is inserted ; it was granted " Stephano Joseph, presbitero, Rectori ecclesie parochialis de Stokeflemyng, Exoniensis Diocesis, ut in Capella, sive oratorio, infra manerium sive mansionem Walteri Reynald, domicelli, apud Malston, infra parochiam de Charlaton [*hodie* Charleton], dicte Exoniensis Diocesis, situatum, divina possit in dicti Walteri presencia celebrare . . . . per unum annum tantummodo duraturum."

Rome, Roger, R. of Sutcombe in his Rectory-house (21 Sept., 1400), i, 49.

Rosmaren, John, and Elizabeth his wife, in their mansion of Rosmaren [*hodie* Rosemerrin], in St. Budock (6 May, 1404), i, 71.

Row, John, Canon of Glasney, for a year (3 Feb. 1398-9), i, 25.

Row, Richard, in his mansion in the parish of Plymouth (11 May, 1411), i. 123^{b}.

Rudruth, Ralph, R. of St. Columb-major; a general licence within his said parish (15 Sept., 1400), i. 48.

Rynsy, John, of Godolghan [*hodie* Godolphin], and Elianora his wife, in their manors of Godolghan and Rynsy in St. Breage (2 Dec., 1398), i, 23^{b}.—It was stipulated that on Sundays, and other Feasts, they should resort to their parish-church, whenever they could conveniently do so.

Schaldon, Joan; also, to William Hausende and Christina his wife, in their mansion of Kyntebury in the parish of Plymouth (10 Dec., 1410), i, 110^{b}.—At the end are added the words: "Et habet licenciam, omissa clausula *volumus*, etc." This clause contained the stipulation referred to above, under Rynsy: "Volumus autem quod diebus Dominicis et aliis Festivis ad ecclesiam vestram parochialem predictam, pro Divinis inibi audiendis, cum commode poteritis, personaliter accedatis."

Schapwyk, John, and Christina his wife, in the Chapel of the Holy Trinity, within their residence at Boghedon [*hodie* Bowden], in the parish of Totnes (14 Dec., 1417), i, 237.

Seint Aubyn, Geoffrey, and Elizabeth his wife, and their children (26 Oct., 1399), i, 31^{b}.

St. Maur ["domino de Sancto Mauro et Ele ejus uxori ...... necnon liberorum suorum et familie sue presencia," MS.], in their mansion at Northmolton (26 Nov., 1397), i, 14.

Selman, John, and Elizabeth his wife, and their children and family, in their mansion of Nywenham [*hodie* Newnham], in Plympton St. Mary (1 Feb., 1408-9), i, 88.

Serokaux, Richard, domicellus (28 Jan., 1395-6), i, 7^{b}.

Setebuegh, William, and Emmota his wife, in their mansion of Seteburgh, in Parkham (7 Jan., 1404-5), i, 72^{b}.

Smyth, Edmund, and Isota his wife, *see* Heligan.

Smyth, Gilbert, and Isabella his wife, in their house at Newton Abbot in Wolborough ["infra mansum sive habitacionem suam in villa de Nywcton Abbatis, in parochia de Wolleburgh"] (1 May, 1419), i, 246^{b}.

Soby, Nicholas, and Joan his wife, *see* Heligan.

Soor, Ralph, and Margaret his wife, in their mansion of Talvern [*hodie* Tolverne], in Philleigh [Sancti Filii, MS.] (6 Sept., 1400), i, 47.

Speccote, Margaret, relict of Richard; also, Nicholas Speccote and Isabella his wife, in the Chapel of St. Mary within their mansion of Speccote, in Merton (23 May, 1400), i, 38^{b}.

Spencer, Richard, and Constantina his wife, and also, to Alice Dourysch, "mulieri," in their house at Spenceryscome [*hodie*, I suppose, "Spence Combe"], in the parish of Crediton (2 Sept., 1415), i, 212^{b}.

Stoke, John, R. of Heanton Punchardon,[1] in his Rectory-house (19 April, 1412), i, 148.

Stowford, Thomas, and Joan his wife, in their house at Stowford, in the parish of Dolton [Duelton, MS.] (17 Jan., 1414-15), i, 207.—To this Thomas and Joan licence was granted, 6 June, 1418, for their manor or mansion, of Gadcombe [*hodie*, Gatcombe] in the parish of Colyton (6 June, 1418), i, 240.

Strache, John, and Joan his wife (18 Oct., 1395), i, 6^{b}.

Strete, William, Prior of Berlinch (Dioc. of B. and W.), in his manor of Estcort in Morebath [Morbath, MS.] (15 Feb., 1401-2), i, 60.

Stybbe, John, chaplain, within the parish of Ermington (11 April, 1408), i, 85.

---

[1] "domino Johanni Stoke, Rectori ecclesie parochialis de Yaunton."—It is difficult to recognize "Heanton" under this guise, and I took it for Yealmpton at first; but there can be no doubt about the fact. He died shortly after the licence.

SYLVERLOK, JOHN, and ALICE his wife, and WILLIAM CARSLAK, in the Chapel of St. Martin, within their mansion of Hareston in the parish of Plympton; for three years (25 June, 1399), i, 28.—This licence was renewed—"during pleasure,"—26 April, 1403, i, 64.

SYRESTON, JOHN, JOAN his wife, and JOAN the mother of the said Joan Syreston, in their mansion of Trevarthyan in St. Newlyn (23 June, 1400), i, 42[b]. Licence was granted, 2 Oct., 1407, to the said John and Joan Syreston, and to Thomas and Henry their sons, for their mansions of Trevarthan (*sic*), Cracamtallan [? Crackington, in the parish of St. Gennys], Thurlebeare, and Whytheleye [Whiteley is the name of a farm in the neighbouring parish of Wyke St. Mary], i, 82[b].

TALBOT, WILLIAM, domicellus, and THOMASIA his wife (12 Feb., 1396-7), i, 11[b]. This licence was "during pleasure;" and it was renewed for two years in favour of the said William and Thomasia, (26 April, 1399), i, 26[b]. On 22 Dec., 1403, licence was granted to HENRY TALBOT and KATHERINE his wife, for their mansion of Pytwyll, in Georgeham, i, 69[b]. On 25 May, 1400, a general licence was granted to SIR WILLIAM TALBOT, knt., and THOMASIA his wife, and their children, i, 39. And 10 Oct., 1410, a general licence for all their mansions and manors in the Diocese was granted to SIR WILLIAM and his then wife ELINOR; also, to Thomas, William, John, Walter, and Richard *filiis*, and to Juliana, *filie—naturalibus et legitimis dicti Domini Willelmi et Thomasie uxoris sue defuncte*, i, 108.—On the 3 June, 1407, licence was granted to Matilda Talbot, prioress of Polslo, within her said Priory, i, 82.

THORNE, ELIZABETH, relict of HENRY, and her children, in her mansion of THORNE [in the parish of Holsworthy] (21 Sept., 1400), i, 49.

TOPCLYFF, THOMAS, and MARGARET his wife, in their mansion of Worthyhele [*hodie*, Worthele], in Ermington (2 Feb., 1417-18), i, 238.

TRECARL, ROBERT; also to CHRISTINA, relict of HENRY TRECARL, and JOAN, wife of the said Robert, in the Chapel of the Blessed Mary Magdalene, within their mansion of Trecarl [*hodie*, Trecarrel], in Lezant (8 May, 1405), i, 74[b].

TREGARY, WALTER, and BLANCHE his wife, in the Chapel, "sive *privato* oratorio," in their mansion of Hacche in South Molton (25 Nov., 1409), i, 91.

TREGONEN, WILLIAM, and JOAN his wife, in their Chapel "sive *privato* oratorio," in their mansion [of Tregonen or Tregonan] in St. Ewe" (15 Jan., 1409-10), i, 93[b].

TREGOS, WILLIAM, and ELIZABETH his wife; also, to ISABELLA, relict of JAMES GERVEYS, in their mansions in St. Anthony [-in-Meneage] (6 May, 1404), i, 71.

TREGOYS, DAVID, and MARGARET his wife, in the Chapel of the B. V. M, at Tregoys (5 June, 1397), i, 12[b].

TRELOUNY (*sic*), JOHN, and MATILDA his wife, in their mansions of Wolleston [*hodie*, Woolston], Trelouny [i.e. Trelawny, in the parish of Alternon], and Tregarrek [*hodie*, Tregarrick] (18 May, 1400), i, 37[b].

TREMAYLLE, ROGER, and MARGARET his wife, in their house at Oversonde [*hodie*, Over-Sand], in the parish of Sidbury (25 Jan., 1418-19), i, 245.

TREMAYN, JOHN, and RICHARD his brother, "in capella sive oratorio infra villam de Tremayn" (3 June, 1400), i, 39[b].

TREMERE, THOMAS, *see* POLMARVA.

TRENCRUK, RALPH, domicellus, in his mansion of Trefraudewell [Trefraul], in Lanreath (19 Nov., 1405), i, 77.

TRENEWYTH, RALPH, and JOAN his wife, in their mansion of Trenewyth [*hodie* Trenowth], and in the Chapels of the Holy Trinity and of the B.V.M. within their said demesne of Trenewyth in St. Probus (8 Jan., 1404-5), i, 72[b].

TRENOWYTH, STEPHEN, and MARGARET his wife, in their mansion of Erte [*hodie* Erth], in St. Stephen's-by-Saltash (8 Oct., 1413), i, 186.

TRENUYD, MICHAEL, see MAHUN, THOMAS.—He belonged, no doubt, to the family of Trenwith, of Trenwith, in the parish of St. Ives.

TRETHERF, REGINALD, and Launia,[1] his wife; also, to RALPH BEVYLE (11 Sept., 1400), i, 47.

TREVANYON, THOMAS DE, and MARGARET his wife, in their mansions of Trereys [*hodie* Trerice], Tregoos, and Trevanyon, in Cornwall (14 Dec., 1410), i, 110b.

TREVAGA, RICHARD, and MARGARET his wife, in their houses of Trevaga [*hodie* Trevage, in Alternon], Trevelle, and Nyweton [*hodie* Newton] (18 May, 1400), i, 37b.—To John Trevaga, senior, and Margery his wife, a licence was granted, 13 March, 1417-18, for their house at Neweton [*hodie* Newton Ferrers] in St. Mellion [Sancti Melani, MS.], i, 235b.

TREVERTHIAN, JOHN, domicellus (4 Dec., 1395), i, 7.—To Sir JOHN TREVARTHIAN, knt., and JOAN his wife, a general licence was granted, 15 Sept., 1400, i, 48.

TREVENOUR, JOHN, JOAN his wife and their children (19 Nov., 1401), i, 58b.

TREWALWARD, MARGARET, in her mansion of Trewalward in St. Stephen's-by-Saltash (for two years only—21 March, 1396-7), i, 11b.

TREWETHENEK, ROGER, JOAN his wife, and RICHARD their son (15 Nov., 1406), i, 80.

TREWOYEF, JOHN, senior, and MAGOTA his wife, John, their son, and Isabella his wife in their house [*hodie* Trewoof], in St. Buryan [Sancte Beriane, MS.] (9 May, 1413), i, 180b.

TREWYȜTHOROP, JOHN, a Canon of Bodmin Priory, within the said Priory (18 Nov., 1400), i, 50.

TYTTESBURY, RICHARD, R. of the Mediety of Ermington (10 April, 1400), i, 36.

VALEWYLL, JOHN, and AGNES his wife, in their house [*hodie* Velwell] in Rattery [Rattre, MS.] (31 March, 1417), i, 232.

WALLEROND, WILLIAM, and JULIANA his wife (for one year only—28 Feb., 1395-6), i, 8.

WARRE, LUCY, Abbess of Canonsleigh, within her monastery (25 July, 1410), i, 101.—To JOHN WARRE and JOAN his wife, licence was granted 2 Aug., 1416, for their house at Keton [*hodie* Kitton], in Holcombe Rogus [Holcombe Rogys, MS.], i, 226.

WARYN, JOHN, LL.B., see OLYVER.—I find, also, that licence was granted, 1 April, 1414, to JOHN WARYN, R. of Menhenyot, for his Rectory-house, i, 195b.

WATTY, RICHARD, and JULIANA, his wife, see HELIGAN.

WERTHE, WILLIAM, and ELIZABETH his wife, in their house at Holryg in Ideford [Yddeforde, MS.] (7 April, 1419), i, 246.

WESTECOTE, JOHN, Canon of Exeter (17 April, 1414), i, 196.

WHALESBURGH, JOHN, domicellus, JOAN his wife, and William their son, in the Chapel at Whalesburgh, in Marhamchurch, and in all other their mansions throughout the Diocese (11 June, 1400), i, 42.

WHITELEGH, RICHARD, ISMANNA his wife, and Rich. their son, in their manor of Nywaton [*hodie* Osborn Newton], in Churchstow [Churstawe, MS.] (18 July, 1395), i, 4. On 14 May, 1408, the Bishop, being at Kingsbridge, close by, granted a licence to RICHARD WHYTELEGH, domicellus, and JOAN his wife, for their said mansion of Nywaton; i, 85b.

WHYTYNG, JOHN, domicellus, and Alice his wife, in their mansion of Woda [*hodie*, Wood], in Kentisbeare (6 Jan., 1407-8), i, 83.

WOLF, RICHARD and ALICE his wife, in their house at Schyllyngham, in St. Stephen's-by-Saltash [Sancti Stephani de Aysch, MS.], (26 May, 1412), i, 160.

WOLHAYE, JOHN, and JOAN his wife, in the Chapel of St. John, within their mansion of Pensford [Pynford, MS.], in Ashprington (13 May, 1400), i, 37.

[1] ? Lavinia: the MS. is obscure here.

WONARD, JOHN, and ISABELLA his wife, and RICHARD their son (8 April, 1403), i, 63b.

WOTTON, JOHN, domicellus, and ENGLESA (*sic*) his wife, in their mansion of Wytheworthy, in Widworthy (8 March, 1408), i, 84.

WYBBURY, GILBERT, and ISOTA his wife, in their Chapel at Wollegh, in Beaford (23 May, 1400), i, 39.—A licence was granted 31 July, 1416, to JOHN WYBBURY, for his manors, or mansions, of Wodelond, in Little Torrington, and Northleigh in Maristow [Morestowe, MS.], i, 226. *See* ATTEFFORDE.

WYKE, JOEL, and NICHOLA his wife, in the Chapel of St. James within their mansion of Flambertyswyke, in Chawleigh [Chalvelegh, MS.], on the Feast of St. James (12 June, 1400); i, 42b.

WYLLYSFORDE, ISOTA, relict of ROBERT, within her mansion in St. Petrock's, Exeter (13 April, 1404), i, 70b.

WYMOND, MARGERY, *see* GOVYS, JOHN.

WYSE, OLIVER, and MARGARET his wife, in their manors or mansions of Beusewyn, Nansov, and Greyston, in Cornwall (9 Oct., 1414), i, 202b.

YEO, ROBERT, and JOAN his wife, in their mansion of Heampton Sachevyle [*hodie*, Heanton Sachville], in the parish of Petrockstow [Patrikstawe, MS.], (17 Oct., 1401), i, 58b.

Orcheton, the manor of, in the parish of Modbury, i, 172b.

Orian, Thos., inst. to St. Anthony in Kerrier, ii, 164b; his death, ii, 191b.

Orlegh, in the parish of Buckland-Brewer, i, 231b.

Orum, John, S.T.B. i, 24b, 47b.

He was Archdeacon of Barnstaple; collation, ii, 15b; exchanged his R. of Theynton (Dioc. of Lincoln) for Clyst Fomison, and immediately resigned, ii, 51; was collated to a Canonry of Exeter, ii, 157; i, 198; and, as Canon of Wells and Prebendary of Holcombe-Burnell therein, presented to the V. thereof, ii, 194b.

Osanne, Robert, presented to Milton Damarel, but not admitted, ii, 237b.

Osborn, John, inst. to All Hallows-on-the-Walls, Exeter, ii, 50; exchanges for St. Ive, ii, 50b; i, 49b; exchanges for the Chapelry of Kingston-Russell (Dioc. of Salisbury), ii, 54.

Osborne, John, R. of Virginstow (deceased), ii, 115.

Osburne, Thomas, Canon of St. Stephen's, Launceston, ii, 117.

Osmond, Richard, collated to St. Enoder, ii, 30b.

Osmund, Peter, clerk,—*Dispensacio super defectu natalium* (14 March, 1404-5), i, 73b.

Ostia, Angelus, Bishop of, Archdeacon of *Exeter* (q.v.).

Oterford, Nicholas, i, 304b.

Oterhampton, Wm., R. of Silverton, ii, 257b; his death, ii, 164b.

Otery, John, V. of Ashburton, exch. for St. Mary Church, ii, 34.

Otterton [Robert Mayne], Prior, in arrear of procurations due to the Pope's collector, i, 105.

Ottery St. Mary, i, 327.

Commission directed to Dean Tregrisiou and Rd. Aldryngton, Canon of Crediton, to confer on John Bokelond the office of Warden (28 Sept., 1399), i, 29.

The Bishop's Mandate for the Visitation, 21 June, 1400 ; i, 39b.

Henry, a chaplain of this parish, was a Penitentiary in the Deanery of Aylesbeare, i, 50.

Robert, Bishop of London, and Bishop Stafford, to the Warden and College of,—" Ordinacio " concerning certain rents in the City of London, bequeathed to the College for pious purposes. -Sir William Thyrnyng, knt., Sir Gerard Braybrok, knt., Thos. Stowe, clerk, Edmund Hampdene, esq., John Wyke, clerk, John Skystelyng, clerk, and Roger Albryghton, clerk, with the King's licence, had assigned to the College for ever a certain messuage called Blosmysyn, with a shop on the north side thereof, in the parish of St. Laurence, Old Jewry, and a garden in the parish of All Saints' Hony Lane thereto adjoining ; also, a messuage called *Warehous* annexed thereto, and a certain yearly rent of 26s. 8d. arising out of certain tenements hard by, formerly belonging to Walter Cavendysh, citizen and mercer of London, and William Gore, citizen and foundour of the said city. The Bishops appropriate the proceeds thus :—

(1) To each of the 8 canons, if in residence, 2s. 6d.
(2) „ the Parochial Chaplain, 15d.
(3) „ the Master of the School. 10d.
(4) „ each of the 2 clerici aquebajuli, 10d., quarterly.
(5) „ „ 8 vicars and 2 priests [appropriation of the R. of Northam] and the morning chaplain, 12d.
(6) To each of the 8 clerks called Secundarii, and the clerk of Our Lady's Chapel, 8d.
(7) To each of the 2 clerks called " clerici ecclesie," 8d.
(8) „ „ 8 choristers, 4d., every month, counting 13 months in the year
(9) To the canons, priests, and clerks, for the obit of Nicholas Braybrok and Sir Thomas Mountenay, knt. (on second day after the F. of the Epiphany) 10s. among them, and
(10) 3s. 4d. to be given to the poor—for their souls.
(11) to four of the clerks, viz., the 2 clerici ecclesie and the 2 aquebajuli, 8d. yearly, in the future, *pro classico in dicto obitu faciendo.*
(12) and (for repairing their houses)—to the Vicars, 3s. 4d. ; to the secundarii, 16d. ; to the schoolmaster and the choristers, 2s.
(13) to the receivers of the rents, &c., 13s. 4d. for their labour, over and above all costs for repairs.
(14) to a chaplain, to serve in the West Chapel, without the door of the Cathedral (wherein the body of John de Grandisson, the late Bishop, rests), for his food and clothing, 8 marks a year in quarterly payments of 26s. 8d., on condition of continual residence ; and if the receivers were in arrear of such payments for a month at the end of any quarter, they were to pay the chaplain 40d. in compensation, out of their own allowance.

The said chaplain was to be removed if he alienated in any manner the books, missal, and other ornaments of the Chantry ; the College to provide all things necessary for the service, and to renew and repair the same, and to receive from these rents 6s. 8d. yearly for the same.

The Receivers were to see to the due observance of the obit of Nicholas Braybrok, *in the Cathedral*, on the same 2nd day after the Epiphany, and to remunerate the priests and clerks. They were to provide a strong chest, to be kept in the Treasury at Ottery, for the safe keeping of all moneys, each of the two receivers to hold a key. If any of the beneficiaries were non-resident, except on College business, or being resident absented himself from his duties, unless sick, he should forfeit his allowance.

The election of Receivers was to take place annually on the vigil of St. Michael the Archangel, one Canon and one Vicar being chosen by the College. Rules were laid down for their guidance. Provision was made for prayers on behalf of the above-named Bishops (of London and Exeter) in life and after death, for ever; and power was reserved to the Bishops of Exeter to vary all these provisions at their discretion, if necessary.—Dat. London, 22 Feb. 1402-3; and accepted by the Coll. 5 April 1404, ii, 278, 279b. *See* Oliver's *Monasticon*, pp. 275-7.

John Hamond, Sacristan, accused of certain grave offences, appeared before the Bishop's commissaries, and was convicted. The Bishop decided that, forasmuch as the said Sacristan was, by reason of old age, quite incapacitated for duty, a coadjutor was necessary; and he appointed Henry Clement, priest, and chaplain of the parish—"virum utique providum et circumspectum"—to serve in this capacity during pleasure, with an annual stipend of 30s.; requiring Walter Robert, Precentor, and Robert Wantyng, Minister, to see to the due carrying out of the arrangement (12 Nov., 1409), i, 90.—Certain grave charges were also brought before the Bishop against the Canons; who were accused of quarrelling, disobeying the statutes, neglecting the Divine offices, and other scandalous conduct: so the Bishop descended upon the place, 20 June, 1408, to see and hear for himself. The Warden, etc., appeared before him and asked him to deal with the case summarily. But the Bishop ordered a formal enquiry to be made, and directed a Commission to the Treasurer, Richard Hals, and to William Hunden, Archdeacon of Totnes, for the settlement of the matter, in his own necessary absence (2 July, 1408), ii, 231b.

John Sarger, chaplain, was licenced to preach in the Deaneries of Aylesbeare, Honiton, Dunkeswell, and Plymtree (7 Dec., 1416), i, 228.—John, Warden of Ottery, was a Penitentiary in the Deanery of Aylesbeare, i, 245.—John Langelegh, minister; his will, i, 304.—Thomas Ferrers, Precentor, i, 319. Bequests to the College by John Prestecote, i, 318; by Canon William Langeton, i, 322b.—The Wardens and Canons present to Northam, ii, 88, 199b.

Ouger, Richard, co-patron of Inwardleigh, ii, 24b.

Ousthorp, Robert, presented to Duloe, V., ii, 246; instituted, ii, 141b.

Oustyn, Henry, V. of Sidmouth, resigns, ii, 22.

Overby, William, chaplain, ii, 313.

Oversand [Oversonde, MS.], in the parish of Sidbury, i, 245.

Overton, Peter, R. of Dartington, i, 82; his death, ii, 155.

Ovyngham, John, LL.D., and John Ixworth, LL.D.,—
They were appointed by the Bishop his Proctors in Convocation, 14 Nov., 1411, i, 138b; and again, with Wm. Hunden, 26 Sept., 1414, i, 200b.

Owlyscomb, William de (i.e., William Davy, V. of Awliscombe), a Penitentiary in the Deanery of Honiton, i, 50.

Oxford, Canon Wm. Ekerdon's bequest to poor clerks at, i, 320b; Stapyldon Hall in, i, 327.

P.

Packe, Edwold, and Joan his wife, i, 320b.

Paccheshulle, Geoffrey, R. of Lew Trenchard, ii, 12.

Padirda, manor of, in the parish of Menhenyot, i, 35b, 240b.

Paderstow, William, Abbot of Buckfast, ii, 210^{b}.

Padstow [Padystow, MS.]; Laurence Merthere, V., a Penitentiary in the Deanery of Pyder, i, 93^{b}, 115^{b}, 143^{b}, 174, 207^{b}, 217, 231, 238, 245^{b}.

Merthere was licensed to celebrate in the Chapels of Holy Trinity, St. Michael, St. Petrock, St. German, and St. Wethenye, in the parish of St. Petrock of Padistow (28 Sept., 1415), i, 213^{b}.

Paes, Joan, *see* Lake, John.

Page (*alias* Skelly), Bernard, a Canon of St. German's, i, 48.

Page, John, i, 300^{b}, 310.

Paignton [Peyngton, MS.]; Blagdon Kyrkham in, i, 115^{b}.—Compton [Cumtunpole, MS.], ii, 310; lands of Stantor in, *ibid.*—John Schute, V.; i, 86^{b}, 169^{b}, 172^{b}, 176, 201^{b}, 202, 322^{b}; ii, 111, 160^{b}; licensed as Publick Preacher in the Diocese (21 Jan., 1412-13), i, 175.—William [Bruter], V., a Penitentiary in the Deanery of Ipplepen, i, 231.—John Cobbethorne, V., a Penitentiary in the same Deanery, i, 237^{b}.—Nicholas Lovecok, V., a Penitentiary in the same Deanery, i, 245.—Margery, daughter of John Baron of; licence for her marriage with John Harry of Brixham (15 Jan., 1417-18, i, 237^{b}.—Hugh de Hyckelyng's bequests to the poor of, i, 326, 326^{b}.

Pake, Henry, Vicar of Axminster—

He was admitted by the Bishop, in London, 12 May, 1401, ii, 17^{b}; and instituted later on, ii, 19; his death, ii, 151^{b}.

Pakwode, John, i, 314.

Pakyn, Stephen, instituted to Morthoe, V., ii, 200^{b}.

Palmer, Ambrose, of Kingston (parish of Ermington), ii, 277^{b}.

Palmer, Geoffrey, R. of Yarnscombe, resigns, ii, 106.

Palmer, John, brother of Canon Richard Palmer, i, 334.

Palmer, Richard, R. of St. Clement-Danes, London.

He is mentioned very frequently; first, as proxy for William Knyght, ii, 33; inst. to Ugborough, ii, 93^{b}; i, 81, 83^{b}, 87^{b}, 91; ii, 121; proxy for John Ikelyngton, ii, 137^{b}; for Thos. Durnell, ii. 179; for John Holond, ii, 191. He was Canon of Exeter, ii. 160^{b}, 191; i, 116, 117, 125, 137^{b}, 149, 167^{b}, 169^{b}, 172^{b}, 178^{b}, 180^{b}, 182, 184^{b}, 185, 185^{b}, 200, 201^{b}, 206, 208, 209^{b}, 212, 229, 230^{b}, 243^{b}, 244, 313^{b}, 314, 321, 325; collated to a Can. and the Preb. of Stowford in Crediton, ii, 175: he died holding both Canonries, with his R. of Ugborough, ii, 198, 198^{b}. He was in attendance on the Bishop at Lutterworth, i, 197; and at Blackawton, i, 198^{b}.—Precentor Haukyn's bequests to, i, 333; his Will, i, 334.

Palmer, Robert, V. of St. Perran [Zabulo]—

[*Breve Regium*]—To appear at Westminster and shew cause why he should not pay to the Dean and Chapter of Exeter the sum of £16, arrears of an annual payment of £4 (4 July, 1395), ii, 303^{b}.

Palmer, Thomas, i, 192^{b}.—Palmer, William, i, 305.

Pancraswyke, the "Ordinacio" of the Chapel—"Sancti Pancracii de Prankardeswyke (*sic*),"—

The Bishop having been informed by the parishioners of this Chapelry (which was attached to Bradworthy, belonging to Torre Abbey), that it was a separate parish as to population and boundaries, possessing its own baptistery, and all things pertaining to a parish except the right of sepulture; that the roads and streams between them and the Mother-Church were dangerous for funerals, and therefore they prayed the Bishop to dedicate the said Chapel, and the adjacent ground for a Cemetery; he issued a Commission, directed to the Religious of Torre Abbey and to John Dalkyn, V. of Bradworthy, to make enquiry as to the facts. The result being favourable to their petition, the Bishop summoned the Abbot of Torre and the Vicar, on the one part, and the parishioners, by their proxies, Robert atte Wode and Richard Heyne, on the other part, to appear before him at Chudleigh, 8 Nov., 1403, for the determination of this business. The prayer of the parishioners was granted, saving the rights of the Mother-Church; to which they were all bound to repair once a year (on the Sunday next after the Feast of St. Pancras), and offer one *obolus*; but they were to make their oblations at their own Chapel on all Saints' Days and at Christmas and Easter; the chaplain to be withdrawn to the Mother-Church in case of default or attempt to evade these conditions (8 Nov., 1403), i, 68.

Parfay, John, i, 328^b.

Park, John, R. of Whittington (Diocese of Worcester),—

He was collated to a Canonry and the Preb. of Wodelond in Crediton, ii, 36^b; and to a Canonry in Exeter Cathedral, ii, 45^b; i, 211^b; exchanged Whittington for South Molton, ii, 122^b; *see* i, 234^b, ii, 234: licensed to confess his parishioners of South Molton (10 April, 1416), i, 220.

Park, John and Joan, cousins of William Hunden, i, 325.—John Parke occurs, i, 328^b.

Parker, Richard, priest, i, 318^b; inst. to Teignbrewer, ii, 146; his death, ii, 157^b.—Parker, Robert, i, 333^b.

Parkere, Elizabeth, wife of John (a daughter of Wm. Wilford), i, 319^b, 320.

Parkham, Seteburgh in the parish of, i, 72^b.

[*Breve Regium*]—Prohibition to admit pending the settlement of the dispute as to the patronage between Wm. Durneford and Alice his wife, and Thomas Beaumont, John Bydewyll, Henry Crosse, and John Foke (dated at Bristol, 12 March, 1397-8), ii, 307^b. The said John Fouk (*sic*) was inst. 17 June following (ii, 12^b); he was only in subdeacon's orders, and within a year (17 April, 1400), obtained a dispensation (to study at Oxford) for *seven* years; i, 30^b. He did not live so long, but died in 1406, ii, 92. Letters Dimissary had been granted to him, 21 Jan., 1402-3, to enable him to proceed to deacon and priest's orders, i, 62^b. Richard Graynevyll, LL.B., his successor, was inst. 7 Oct., 1406 (ii, 92); and, 21 April, 1407, was licensed to celebrate in all chapels and oratories in the Diocese, i, 82. But, as with his predecessor, his parishioners did not see much of him: on 3 June, 1410, he obtained licence of non-residence for one year, i, 97; also, from 22 Oct., 1411, i, 137^b; from 31 Oct., 1413, to Michaelmas, 1414, i, 187^b; from 18 Oct., 1414, to Michaelmas, 1415, i, 203; from 20 Oct., 1415, to Michaelmas, 1416, i, 213^b; from 7 Oct., 1416, to Michaelmas, 1417, i, 226^b; from 10 Dec., 1417, to Michaelmas, 1418, i, 237; and for a year from 10 Oct., 1418, i, 243; *see*, also, ii, 236.

Parle, Jno., inst. to the Chantry, Raleigh, ii, 182^b; resigns, ii, 191.

Parliament and Convocation—

De veniendo ad Parliamentum (*Breve Regium*), (30 Nov., 1396), ii, 303^{b}. Ditto, 18 July, 1397, ii, 306^{b}. Ditto; Chester, 19 Aug., 1399; the Bishop's mandate herein; London, 2 Sept., 1399, ii, 309^{b}. Ditto, Westm., 19 June, 1402, ii, 314. Ditto, Westm, 26 Oct., 1409, ii, 332; and 18 Dec., 1409, ii, 332^{b}. Ditto, Westm., 21 Sept., 1411, ii, 342^{b} [John Wakeryng and John Rome appointed, by the Bishop, his proctors, 24 Oct., 1411, i, 138^{b}]. Ditto, Westm., 1 Dec., 1412, ii, 346; and 22 March, 1412-13, ii, 346^{b}. Ditto, Westm., 1 Dec. (also, again, 21 Dec.), 1413, ii, 348 The Bishop's *Procuratorium* on behalf of John Wakeryng, Keeper of the Rolls, and John Rome, Clerk of Parliament, is dated 6 Jan., 1413-14, i, 190^{b}]. Ditto, Westm., 26 Sept., 1414, ii, 349^{b}. Ditto, Westm., 12 Aug., 1415, ii, 353 (prorogued 29 Sept., 1415, *ibid*). Ditto, Westm., 21 Jan., 1415-16, ii, 354^{b} [*Procuratorium* on behalf of John Wakeryng, Keeper of the Privy Seal, 7 March, 1415-16, i, 217]. Ditto, "apud Sandewicum," 3 Sept., 1416, ii, 356^{b} [*Procuratorium*—Simon Gaunstede, Keeper of the Rolls, and Richard Gabryell, Canon of Exeter, 3 Oct., 1416, i, 226^{b}. Ditto, Westm., 5 Oct., 1417, ii, 361. [*Procuratorium*: Henry Ware, Keeper of the Privy Seal, and Canon Richard Gabriell, 17 Oct., 1417, i, 235.

Parracombe, Thomas Dygon, R.; licence of non-residence for two years, from 3 Feb., 1404-5, provided he gave one mark each year to his poor parishioners, i, 73; also for one year, from 3 Feb., 1407-8, i, 83^{b}; and from 29 Sept., 1409, *usque ad finem Pasche*, 1410.

He exceeded the term of his licence, the consequence being a sequestration, "occasione non residencie et absencie ejusdem domini Thome ab eadem, per ipsum aut, auctoritate sua, per ministros." This had, evidently, the desired effect, for it was taken off, 3 Sept., 1410; i, 106^{b}.

Parys, John, inst. to Uplyme, ii, 7^{b}; exchanges for Middleton (Dioc. of B. and W.), ii, 37.

Parys, Major, inst. to Pillaton, ii, 45^{b}; collated to a Canonry in Crediton, ii, 167. He is called "Mauger" Parys in Archdeacon Lydeford's Will, i, 310.

Pascow, Elena (of Cornwall), i, 161, 181.

Passclewe (*or* Paslew), Simon, patron of Horwood, ii, 1^{b}, 222;

Paslew, John, patron of Horwood, ii, 79^{b}.

Passenham, John, R. of Sampford Courtenay, resigns, ii, 22^{b}.

Passer, Walter, i, 306^{b}.

Passewar, Thomas, V. of Over Stowey (Dioc. of B. and W.), exch. for Charles, ii, 48^{b}; for Halse (Dioc. of B. and W.), ii, 98^{b}.

Paston, Benedict de, *see* Chudleigh, ii, 239.

Patchole, in the parish of Kentisbury, *see* Baker, Thos., i, 123^{b}.

Pathulle (*or* Patehulle), Master of the Hosp. of St. John Bapt., Bridgewater, i, 307^{b}; presents to Bovey Tracy, ii, 20; 101.

Patreda, Noel, Steward of the Bishop's Lands in Cornwall, ii, 71^{b}, 72; *see* St. German's, ii, 78^{b}.

Patry, John, instituted to Paul, V., ii, 190, 264.

Patryngg, Edward, R. of South Pool (deceased), ii, 8.

Pattows, Henry, R. of Clyst St. Mary, exchanges for Honington (Dioc. of Lincoln), ii, 53b.

Paulet (*or* Poulet), **Lady Elizabeth**, patron of Arlington, ii, 6b. She was sister of William Credy, i, 307b, 308.

Paulet, Thomas, i, 307b, 308.

Paulyn, John (junior), i, 332.

Paulyn, Thomas, V. of Christow (deceased), ii, 138.

Pawle, Simon, instituted to West Alvington, ii, 85; 357b; i, 86.

Pay, Thomas, inst. to the Chantry of Forde, Bampton, ii, 201b.

Paye, Wm., does homage to the Bishop for lands in Farringdon (3 Feb., 1412-13), ii, 311.

Payn, John, instituted to Upton Hellions, ii, 179b.

Payn, John, a layman; *See* Hykke, ii, 239b.

Payn, Roger, Preb. of Chulmleigh, and Canon and Preb. of of Crosse, in Crediton (deceased), ii, 14, 44b.

Payn, Stephen, collated to a Canonry in the Cathedral, ii, 152; i, 244b; inst. to Great Torrington, ii, 153b; i, 195b, 203b:

Dean Tregrisiow being dead, the Chapter deputed two Canons, viz., Thos. Hendeman, Archdeacon of Exeter, and Thomas Redman, to apply to the Bishop, 9 August, 1415, for licence to elect a successor, which the Bishop granted, the same day; ii, 167b. On 28 Oct., the Bishop being at Chudleigh, Redman presented to him the decree of the election of Stephen Payn. The document is in the name of the Precentor, Hugh Hickelyng (President of the Chapter), and sets forth that Tregrysiow died 25 July, and was buried 19 Aug. (*sic*); that the licence to elect a successor was received 23 Aug.; that 18 Sept. and following days were fixed for the said election; that, the Chapter being summoned, there attended the said Precentor, Archdeacon Hendeman (*Exon*), Archdeacon Orum (*Barum*), Baldwin de Schillyngforde, Martin Lercedekne, John Gorewill, Thos. Redman, John Parke, Rd. Aldryngton, Rd. Palmer, John Stafforde, Roger Bolter, John Westecote, Rd. Gabriell, Thos. Clyfforde, and Laurence Havkyn (all Canons); also Rd. Hals, Treasurer; John Stephen, by proxy—Roger Bolter; and John Hody, by proxy—Thos. Redman; that John Ikesworth, Wm. Hundene, Thos. Barton, Wm. Pylton, and Stephen Payn, were absent; and Martin Lercedekne left before the election took place, when the choice of all fell upon Stephen Payn, B.A. John Waryn notary-publick was present; also Rd. Olyver, Rob. Lingham, and Rob. Dunnyng, notaries-publick of the Dioceses of Exeter and Wells. The formal documents relating to this election, the proclamation thereof, etc., are set forth at length, ii, 169b—173b. Payn forthwith resigned Great Torrington, ii, 174. He is mentioned, in two writs "de venire facias," dated 20 June, and 12 July, 1418, as the King's Almoner, in the matter of the goods and chattels of Rd. Bishop of Norwich, deceased, ii, 362b. His death is mentioned, ii, 199b. Thereupon the Chapter applied to the Bishop, through Martin Lercedekne and Thos. Redman, for licence to elect a successor, which was granted (1 June, 1419), *ibid.*

Payn, William, clerk, i, 149b.

Payon, John—

He was son and heir of William Payon and Elizabeth (daughter of John Porth collam), his wife, both deceased, and complained to the Bishop that some person or persons unknown had abstracted the title deeds of his lands in Bodmin and in the village of Bodellek in the Bishop's domain of Pawton [St. Breoke]; the Bishop declared the offenders excommunicate and directed the Deans of Trigg-major and minor to proclaim the sentence in all the Churches of those Deaneries (23 August, 1400), i, 45.

Payton, Isabella, widow of Vincent Wryght, i, 324b.

Peake, John, collated to Stockleigh-Pomeroy, ii, 197.

Peatte, John (Deanery of East), ii, 336b.

Peawtermaker, John, i, 21b.

Peion, Walter, inst. to Roche, ii, 12b; resigns, ii, 51b.

Peion, William, i, 76b; inst. (by proxy—Thos. Peion), to Torbrian, ii, 83b; [resigns, and is] inst. to Southmolton, ii, 94; i, 80b, 88; exch. for Whittington (Dioc. of Worcester), ii, 122b; "dilapidations" at South Molton, ii, 234.

Peke (Pek *or* Peek), Henry, chaplain, i, 315.

He was proxy for Patrick Wode, on his institution to the Chantry of Sticklepath, ii, 6; and was soon after himself instit. thereto, ii, 7; a Penitentiary in the the. Deanery of Okehampton, i, 143, 174, 194b, 207b.

Pelynt [Pleuynt *and* Pleuynte, MS.], Robert Walter, V.:—

He was licensed to hear the confessions of his parishioners from 6 Feb., 1408-9, to Trinity Sunday following, i, 94b; and again, 19 Jan., 1411-12; i, 141b.—On 26 Sept., 1412, he was licensed to put out to farm the revenues of his Benefice, for 3 years, i, 168.

Penbegil (*or* Penbigell), William; i, 24b; *Dispensacio super defectu natalium* (31 Dec., 1407), i, 83.

Penbro, Paschasius, V. of Crowan (deceased), ii, 69b.

Pencors, Peter, a parishioner of Lelant, i, 133b, ii, 232b.

Pendevy, in Egloshayle; *see* Bodmin (*Oratories*), i, 69b.

Penegrogov [*hodie* Penny Crocker], in St. Gennys [St. Juliot], ii, 261b, 262.

Penels, Nicholas, Thomas, and Joan, i, 332b.

Penels, Richard, i, 325, 325b, 327b; ii, 118.

Instituted to Bradford, ii, 139; proxy for John Dygon, *ibid.*; mentioned, i, 213, 215; ii, 252; collated to a Preb. in St. Probus, ii, 173b; to a Canonry and two Prebends in Crediton, ii, 174b; to a Canonry of Exeter, *ibid*, i, 222b, 225, 225b, 232b, 234; ii, 263: resigns his Canonry and Bursal Prebend in Crediton, ii, 175b; also his Prebend in St. Probus, ii, 176b; resigns Bradford, and is inst. to Paignton, ii, 177b; exchanges Paignton for Moreton [Hampstead], ii, 178b; again collated to a Preb. in St. Probus, ii, 190b; and to the Archdeaconry of Cornwall (and the Prebend in Glasney annexed), ii, 193b; his death, ii, 196b, 198, 199; his Will, i, 332b.—He was presented, by Sir John de la Pomeray, knt., to Merton, in 1412, but not admitted thereto, ii, 247b.—His name [Penell] occurs as an Advocate in the Consistorial Court, ii, 239, 241; and 24 July, 1415, he was commissioned to preside in that Court, ii, 257.—Wm. Penels, brother of Richard, i, 333.

Penalugan, Isabella (*see* St. Pinnock), ii, 350b, 351b.

Penfern, Thomas, V. of St. Stithian's (deceased), ii, 153b.

Penfern, William, proxy for John Colyn, ii, 78 ; for Edward Dauntesey, ii, 84^{b} ; for Richard Bolham, ii, 102.

Pengelly, in St. Breoke, mansion of John Lanhergy, i, 43.—Thomas Ude, of Pengelly, ii, 332.

Pengelly, Henry and John, parishioners of Linkinhorne, i, 116.

Pengelly, John, Canon of St. German's, i, 48.

Penhall, Rd., inducts Thos. Hendeman to the Preb. of Heyghes, ii, 152.

Richard Penels, R. of Bradford, etc., etc., appears as "Penall," ii, 252 ; perhaps the same man is intended here.

Penhalow, John, see St. Germoe, ii, 264.

Penkryg [*also* Penkerygg, MS.], Wm., chapl. of Uffculme, i, 160^{b} ; licensed as Confessor at Canonsleigh (25 May, 1417), i, 232.

Penpel, Stephen, uncle to Dean Tregrisiow, i, 323^{b}.

Penpons, Richard, clerk, i, 120^{b}.

Penquit, a manor of the Prior of Modbury, i, 12^{b}.

Penryn, Joan, *see* Lewannick, (*note*) i, 26.

Penryn, *see* Fareway, John, ii, 310^{b}.

Penzance [Pensansȝ, MS.], Chapel of St. Mary (licensed 15 June, 1397), i, 12^{b}.

Pensans (*alias* Talwart), Michael, scholar—

Dispensacio super defectu natalium (dated in the House of Wm. Tregilliowe, at Marchyow [i.e., Marazion], 7 Oct., 1411), i, 136^{b}, 138.

Pensansȝ, Robert, *see* Somerlegh, Prebend of, ii, 33^{b}.

Pensans, William, instituted to St. Breage, ii, 69 ; 264^{b}.

Pensford, in Ashprington, *see* Pyperell *and* Wolhaye (*Oratories*).

Penwonam, Wm., R. of Clovelly, i, 82^{b} ; (deceased) ii, 133.

Peperell, Richard, presents to the Chantry of Trewen-juxta-Holsworthy, i, 144^{b}.

Percevale, Matthew, Philip, and William, *see* Martinhoe (*Institutions*) ; *also* i, 247^{b}.

Perch, John, ii, 256.

Perer, Richard, collated, *by lapse*, to the Priory of St. Michael's Mount, ii, 338^{b}, 348^{b}.

Perer, Roger, Sacristan of Ottery, resigns, ii, 28 ; inst. to Powderham, ii, 28^{b} ; his death, ii, 49.

Perell, Thomas, inst. to the Chantry of Washbourne, ii, 197^{b}.

Perkyn, John, ii, 338.

Pers, John, instituted to Littleham, R., ii, 13 ; i, 32.

Persey, Joan, i, 312^{b}.

Persones, John (*alias* Appuldore), i, 306.

Persoun, Thos., Chantry-priest of Warlond, near Totnes, ii, 53.

Peryn, John (*alias* Golepyn), of St. Kew—

(which is called in the MS. "Nowe," i.e., Lanow). Having been convicted at the instance of William Clyfforde, in a case of perjury and breach of faith, he is excommunicated, and, refusing to submit, is handed over, by the Bishop, to the Secular Arm (6 May, 1416, i, 221).

Peryn de Polmargh, Ralph, inst. to North Bovey, ii, 5; exchanges for St. Merryn, ii, 38.

Peryn, Richard, collated to St. Sithney, ii, 70.

Peryn, Richard, V. of Linkinhorne, his death, i, 136; ii, 132.

Pestur, Hugh, R. of Halwell (deceased), ii, 12.

Peter Tavy, John Frank, R. of; licence of non-residence for 3 years, from Michaelmas, 1406 (dated 23 Aug.), i, 78; a Penitentiary in the Deanery of Tamerton, i, 174, 194b, 207b, 217, 231, 237b, 245.

Peteryslonde *alias* Hacche, in the parish of Kingston, ii, 277.

Petheler, Walter, i, 321.

Petrockstowe [Patrickstawe, MS.]; Chapel at Heanton Sachville, *see* Yeo (*Oratories*), i, 58b—

John Herward, parson of, ii, 351b. This R. obtained a licence of non-residence from 14 Dec., 1413 to Michaelmas, 1414, except during Lent, when he was to reside and serve his Church laudably, i, 190.—[*Breve Regium de venire facias*]: in the case of the debt of the said John Herward to the Abbot of Buckfast (21 Oct., 1415), ii, 354.

Petyt, John and, also, Stephen—in each case *Dispensacio super defectu natalium* (6 Sept., 1400), i, 47.

Peuesey, John, Warden of St. Laurence's, Crediton, ii, 32b.

Peuleyn, John, R. of Ruan-major (deceased), ii, 10.

Peuwyn (or Penwyn), Rd., a chaplain, i, 83; V. of Stoke Gabriel, which he exchanged for the Chapel of the B. V. M. in the Cemetery of Ermington, ii, 32; resigns, ii, 32b.

Peverell, Thos. (domicellus), and Margaret his wife, i, 6; Thos. (domicellus), i, 26b; Margaret, i, 83b, 93, 107 (*see* South Pool); she presents to Plymtree, ii, 188b.

Peyngtour, Thomas, R. of St. James' Chapel in the Castle of Chepyngtoryton (deceased), ii, 20.

Peyt, Reginald, chaplain of the "capella curata" of Shute [Schete, MS.], ii, 268.

Phelipp, John, *see* Preston, John, ii, 351b.

Philipp, Cecilia, i, 301b.

Philips, Richard, a priest, *see* Hakeworthy, Roger, i, 97b.

Phillack, Wm. Selby, R.—

He obtained licence of non-residence for a year, from 30 Nov., 1402; i, 62; ditto, from 12 Oct., 1405, i, 76b.—John [Munford *alias* Burgbrygg (*see*, ii, 106b)], R.; the sequestration taken off his Benefice, and licence of non-residence granted for a year, from 7 Aug., 1410, i, 102b.—Nicholas Bildeston (prim. tonsur.), R.; Letters Dimissory granted to him and a Dispensation (to study at Oxford) for 3 years, from 17 March, 1410-11, i, 121.

Philleigh [Sancti Filii, *and* "Eglosros," MS.], Talvern, mansion of Ralph Soor in, i, 47; Wm. Tregos, R. of "Eglosros" and Canon of Glasney—licence of non-residence (but to reside at Glasney), for one year, from 13 Nov., 1405, i, 77.

Philipp, John, R., of Menhenyot, i, 74b; ii, 227; decd., ii, 138.

Phylyp, John, inst. to Milton Damarel, ii, 173b, 258b; i, 230b; resigns, ii, 190.

Phylyp, John, chaplain in the Deanery of Holsworthy, i, 244b.

Phylep (*or* Phylp), Richard, i, 301, 315.

Piers, Edward, inst. to All-Hallows-on-the-Walls, Exeter, ii, 44b; resigns, ii, 50; inst. again, ii, 50b; resigns again, ii, 67b; inst. to Winkleigh, *ibid.*; his death, ii, 153.

Piers, John, R. of Littleham (deceased), ii, 22b.

Piers, John, inst. to Maristow, ii, 89b. *See*, i, 305.

Piers, Wm., Can. of Exeter; R. of Blackawton (decd.), ii, 19b, 54.

Pyers, William, inst. to Antony, ii, 99b; i, 86.

Pill [Pylle, MS.], in Lanlivery, Thomas Curteys of, i, 75.

Pillaton, Major Parys, R. of; licence of non-residence for one year from 8 Oct., 1405, i, 76b.

He was twice the Bishop's proctor "super visitacione Liminum Apostolorum," 28 April, 1410 (i, 98); and 9 May, 1413 (i, 182b); *see*, also, i, 203b, 238.

Pillisdon, Katherine, of Polsloe, ii, 76b.

Pilton, Pyllond, in the parish of, i, 64b.

On 27 Oct., 1410, the Bishop granted an Indulgence to the Faithful who should contribute to the support of St. Margaret's Hospital for lepers and infirm folk in this parish, i, 108b.

An Interdict under which the Church and Cemetery had been laid, because a certain unlicensed chaplain had been suffered to preach therein, was taken off, 13 May, 1412; i, 149b.

Pilton Priory; Mandate for its visitation on 28 May, 1400, i, 36b; anticipated for 24 May, i, 37.—[Wm. Charlton], Prior, was a Penitentiary in the Deanery of Barnstaple, i, 94, 115b, 143b; also, Rd. [Kengeswode], Prior, i, 174. The said William was found in arrears of the procurations due to the Pope's Collector for three years, 1408-10, i, 105, 110. A Commission was directed to the Prior in the matter of the alleged pollution of the Church and Churchyard of Barnstaple, ii, 240b; *see*, also, i, 198. The Prior and Convent present to Ashford, ii, 154.

Pilton, William de, instituted to Tawstock, R. ii, 76.

He was afterwards collated to a Canonry at Exeter, ii, 92; i, 226.—A Clerk of the same name was inst. to Phillack, ii, 102b, and soon resigned it, ii, 106b. A little later, a Wm. Pylton was inst. to Barnstaple, ii, 139—perhaps the same person. Becoming Archdeacon of Exeter, sometime in 1408,—the date is not recorded,—he presently exchanged that Preferment for a Canonry and the preb. of Colworth in Chichester Cathedral, ii, 109.

Pinhoe, William Cheyne of, i, 54b.

Pyperell, Richard, of Ermington, i, 37; ii, 275.

He was Sheriff of Devon: (*Breve Regium*) Mandate to the Bishop, dated 10 Dec., 1411, to administer the oath to him; which was done at Stockleigh Pomeroy, 18 Jan., 1411-12, ii, 344.

Pytyngton (*or* Pytyng), Thomas, collated *by lapse* to St. Mawnan, ii, 83b; i, 75b, 78, 80b, 105,—

Letters-Dimissory were granted to him ("primam tonsuram habenti") 1 July, 1405; certificate thereof, on a scrutiny of the Register, 3 Jan., 1412-13, i, 173.

Pyttes, Richard, Canon of Wells, ii, 63b, 64b, 71, 83b, 87b.

He became Chancellor of York; and on his collation to a Canonry and the Prebend of Grendale in York Minster, the Archbishop wrote to the Bishop of Exeter, requesting that he should be inducted to the "porcio" in the Church of Axminster, part of the endowment of the said Prebend: the Bishop issued his Mandate accordingly, directed to the Archdeacon of Exeter, on behalf of Henry Gelys, R. of St. Leonard's, Berwick, bearer of the Archbishop's Letter, and proxy for Pyttes (25 Oct., 1409), ii, 107.—See, ii, 151b.

Placy, Thomas, inst. to St. Edmund's, Exeter, ii, 151b.

Planya (*or* Plenya), Rd., inst. to Clovelly, ii, 133; i, 233.

Play, John, V. of Yealmpton (deceased), ii, 167b.

Playstowe (*or* Pleystowe), John, inst. to Alphington, ii, 74; i, 84b; his death, ii, 166.

Platek, Richard, ii, 360.

Plusche, Wm., chantry-priest of St. Andrew, in St. Mary Magd., Taunton, exch. for Upottery, ii, 69; his death, ii, 176b.

Plymmeswode, Thos., inst. to Heavitree, ii, 6; i, 55b; 295b, 296; exchanges for Bampton (Dioc. of Lincoln), ii, 55b; i, 322.

While V. of Bampton, he was licensed as a Publick Preacher in the Cathedral and the City of Exeter, 5 June, 1411, i, 127b.

Plymouth [Plymmouth, MS.], *see* "Oratories" for Steph. Durneforde, of, ii, 1b, 2.—John and Roger Beuchamp, of, i, 4b 7.—William and Joan Cole, of, i, 34.—Kyntebury, *see* Schaldon (*Oratories*), i, 110b.—Rd. Row, of, i, 123b; and ten others, inhabitants of Plym.,—*see* Cergeaux, Mich., ii, 219.—

An Indulgence was granted, 22 Aug., 1410, to the Faithful contributing to the repair of the road from Tamerton to Plymouth, which was in a very bad state—via profunda et lutosa, perigrinantibus et laborantibus per eandem nimis nociva et periculosa—i, 103b.—Also, for the repair of three bad roads in the neighbourhood (1) near Challonsleigh, leading from Plympton to Ivybridge; (2) a lane near Plympton, called "Lynchlane"; (3) the road leading from Plymouth to Smapolemille 26 Jan., 1410-11, i, 112.—The road from Plymouth to Fowey, *see* Looe, i, 137b.

The Lazar House at, i, 306b, 331b; the Carmelites of, i, 301b; the Friars Minors of, i, 309.—The fortifications,—

The Mayor and Burgesses proposed to reconstruct two towers and a causeway which had been all but destroyed by the Bretons,—"cum itaque Maior et Burgenses ville de Plymmouth, nostre Diocesis, duas turres, cum uno calceto, apud eandem villam jam tarde per inimicos nostros de Britannia in non modica sui parte combustam et destructam pro defensione non solum ejusdem ville set eciam patrie circumiacentis, ac salva navium custodia ibidem applicancium, cum Dei adiutorio construere et de novo edificare proponant; quorum constrvccio et edificacio ad tantos et tam graves sumptus et expensas veraciter, ut credimus, se extendent quod iidem Maior et Burgenses opus hujusmodi ex suis bonis perficere non valebunt,"—the Bishop granted an Indulgence to the Faithful who should help them (20 Jan., 1416-17), i, 228ᵇ.

The parish-church (commonly called "Sutton-juxta-Plymmouth"),—

Wm. Grene, chaplain thereof, a Penitentiary in the Deanery of Plympton, i, 217, 220, 237ᵇ, 245.—Thomas Gyldyfold (i, 138), [*also*, Guldesfelde, MS.], Vicar; licensed to hear the confessions of his parishioners (8 March, 1411-12), i, 145ᵇ. He had been excommunicated for refusing to pay the "Secunda medietas decime" to the King's collector; but on giving full satisfaction therein, he was formally absolved, 12 March, in the same year, i, 146.—The Chapel of St. Katherine on the Hoe [Howe, MS.] built for God's honour, (and commonly attended by large numbers of people), having fallen into a dilapidated state, the Bishop granted an Indulgence to the Faithful who should contribute to its repair; the concession to extend over five years (22 Nov., 1413), i, 190.

Plympton, John Brakler of, *see* Brakler (*Oratories*), i, 82ᵇ.—John Wylle, of (q.v.), i, 247.—John Sylverlok and Wm. Carslake, of Hareston, *see* Sylverlok (*Oratories*), i, 28, 64; 87ᵇ.—John Selman, of Newnham, *see* Selman (*Oratories*), i, 88.—John Brythrythtyston, of (*see Oratories*), i, 237.—The Tamerton road, *see* Plymouth, i, 103ᵇ; "Lynchlane," i, 112; Lee Bridge, i, 195ᵇ.—Down Thomas, i, 237.—The Lazar-House, i, 306ᵇ, 309, 318ᵇ, 331ᵇ. The Priory,—

Mandate for its visitation 15 May, 1400, i, 36ᵇ.—The Prior and Convent present to Meavy, ii, 5, 50, 98, 121, 182ᵇ, 187ᵇ; to Exminster, ii, 6ᵇ, 47, 88; to Tamerton, ii, 14, 153; to Blackawton, ii, 19ᵇ, 198, 204ᵇ; to Eggbuckland, ii, 23ᵇ; to "Sutton-juxta-Plymmouth," ii, 35, 105ᵇ; to Ugborough, ii, 84, 93ᵇ, 198; to Maker, ii, 86, 90, 120; to Maristow, ii, 89ᵇ; to Dean Prior, ii, 98, 99.—The Prior in arrears of procurations due to the Pope's Collector, for 2 years, 1409-10, i, 105.—*See*, also, i, 333; also, Wykyngston, John, ii, 351ᵇ.—John Leche, Sub-prior, was a Penitentiary in the Deanery of Plympton, i, 94, 115ᵇ; also, Robert Symon, a canon, i, 143, 174, 194ᵇ, 207ᵇ, 217, 231; also, Nicholas Selman, Sub-prior, i, 245.

Plymtree, John Tregreuewyll *or* Grenwyll, R.—

His licenses of non-residence were almost continuous:—(1) for a year, from 16 Feb., 1397-8, "contemplacione dilecte filie, Margarete Peverell, i, 15; (2) for a year, from 1 May, 1399, "contemplacione Thome Peverel, domicelli," i, 26ᵇ; (3) for 2 years from 17 Feb., 1407-8, "contemplacione Margarete Peverel," i, 83ᵇ; (4) for 2 years, from 10 Jan., 1409-10, "contemplacione Margarete Peverell," i, 93; which licence was renewed for one year, 19 Aug., 1410; i, 103ᵇ; (5) for 2 years, from 16 Oct., 1411, i, 136; (6) for one year, from 24 Feb., 1413-14, ii, 194; (7) for one year, from 15 Feb., 1414-15, i, 208ᵇ; (8) for one year, from 17 Feb., 1416-17, i, 230ᵇ. Thomas Job, R., obtained a dispensation (to study at Oxford) for 3 years, from 8 April, 1418, i, 239.

Poghemylle, Rd. inst. to the Chantry of Brythlegh, ii, 17.

Poghylle (*alias* Coleton Pral), Prebend of, *see* Malborough.

Pole, John, senior, *see* Cardynham.

He was co-patron of, Roche, ii, 57^b; of Cotleigh, ii, 64, 95^b; of [Clay]-hydon, ii, 81^b; and of South Pool, ii, 90^b, 97^b.—John Pole, junior, clerk, instituted to Cardynham; ii, 21; 254; his death, ii, 153.

Pole, Rd. de, presents to Marsh (Dioc. of Lincoln), ii, 30.

Pole, William, i, 322^b.

Polford, John, and Roger [Polfford, MS.], i, 331—

Roger was inst. to E. Anstey, called antiently and in this Register "Ansteycrues," ii, 91^b.

Polglas, John, inst. to Grade, ii, 107^b.

Pollard, Isabella, i, 315.

Polmogh, Richard, chaplain; *see* Cury, i, 4.

Polperro, *see* Porthpyre.—Polruan, *see* Lanteglos-by-Fowey.

Polsave, John, inst. to the Chantry of the B.V.M., Heanton Punchardon, ii, 149; 251^b.

Polslo Priory, Mandate for its Visitation (1400), i, 36.—John Grym, priest, appointed Penitentiary, i, 4^b.

Christina de Seton, Prioress, licensed to appoint a Confessor for her House, 1 March, 1395-6, i, 8^b; licence renewed, 9 Jan., 1396-7, i, 10^b.—On her death the Bishop wrote to John Westecote, R. of St. Petrock's, Exeter, and John Prestecote, domicellus, appointing them guardians of the temporalities of the Priory. Also, on the same day, to the sub-prioress and Convent, with licence to elect a successor (4 June, 1404), ii, 76.—Matilda Talbot was elected, 25 June; and, the fact having been duly notified to the Bishop by John Bycote, chaplain, John Westcote was commissioned to proclaim the same, and to certify the Bishop thereof, ii, 76^b.—Election confirmed, 2 July, 1404, ii, 77.—She was licensed to choose a Confessor, 29 July, 1411, i, 129^b.

This Priory was patron of Holbeton, ii, 6^b; of Budleigh, ii, 21^b; of Aylesbeare, ii, 75^b, 96^b, 121. Churches appropriated to the Priory, ii, 359^b.—Grendon's bequests to the Priory, i, 316; Thos. Reymound's, i, 331^b.—*See*, also i, 303, 318, 319^b, 323^b.

Polton, Thomas, Archdeacon of Taunton, ii, 69; —

He exch. Luccombe (Dio. of B. and W.), for Clyst St. George, ii, 148^b: resigned, ii, 179.

Pomeray, Sir John de la, knt., co-patron of Merton, ii, 146^b, 247^b; *see* Duk, Peter, ii, 260;—

He did homage to the Bishop, in London, for Kyngton in Devon and Treflouan in Cornwall, 21 Sept., 1397, ii, 310.—Licensed, with Joan his wife, to choose Confessors (14 Nov., 1410), i, 109.

Pomeray, Sir Thos. knt., patron of Combe Raleigh, i, 82, ii, 40^b; 220^b, 71, 161^b; presents to Huish, ii, 80^b.

Sheriff of Devon: Mandate to the Bishop to administer the oath to him (*Breve Regium*—29 Nov., 1410), ii, 337, 8; and again, 18 Nov., 1413, ii, 347^b.

Pomfret, John, see Somerlegh, Prebend of, ii, 33^b.

Pontyngdon, Nicholas, presents to Bickleigh, R., ii, 182.

Pontyngdon, Thomas, R. of Bickleigh, (deceased) ii, 8.

Pope's, the, Nuncio and Collector in England; his Mandate,

and the Bishop's Letter thereupon to the D. and C. of Exeter and the four Archdeacons (17 Sept., 1410), i, 104b.

Pope, John, of London, *skinner*, ii, 332.

Pope, Philip, inst. to Combmartin, ii, 87 ; proxy for John Gentylman, ii, 95 ; exchanges for Chiddingfold (Dioc. of Winchester), ii, 167.

Pope, Roger, a monk of Tavistock, ii, 59.

Popham, Henry, domicellus, does homage to the Bishop, at Salisbury, for lands in Faryngdon, in Hampshire (13 Aug., 1408), ii, 310b.

Port, John, V. of West Anstey (deceased), ii, 173b.

Porter, Robert, of Apuldram, ii, 293b.

Porter, William, instituted to Blackborough, ii, 25.

Porteworthy, Thomas, i, 329.

Portey, *alias* Grantelond, William, i, 305.

Porthcollam, Elizabeth, *see* Payon, John, i, 45.

Porthpyghan, *i.e.* the Manor of Port Looe, in Talland.

Licence granted to the inhabitants of this hamlet to have Divine Service, at their own charges, in the Chapel of St. Nicholas there (23 June, 1400), i, 42b.

Porthpyre [*hodie* Polperro], in Lansallos [Lansalwys, MS.],—

Licence granted to the inhabitants to have Divine Service, at their own charges, in their Chapel of St. Peter, on all days except Christmas-Day and Easter Day, and the Feasts of the Purification, St. Katherine, and All Saints ; (21 May, 1400), i, 38.

Portioye, Henry, V. of Holcombe-Rogus, exchanges for Spaxton (Dioc. of B. and W.), ii, 42b.

Portlemouth, John Thomas (deacon), R. of ; dispensation (to study at Oxford) for 4 years, from 22 Sept., 1405, i, 76 ; a Penitentiary in the Deanery of Woodleigh, i, 143, 174, 194b, 207b, 217, 231, 237b, 245.

Portour, William, i, 322b.

Potheridge ; *see* Monk (*Oratories*), i, 6b, 149b.

Pott, Stephen (Torrington), ii, 265b.

Potter, John, his house in St. Edmund's, Exeter, i, 122b.

Potter, Stephen, inst. to the Chapel of St. James in the Castle, Torrington, ii, 85.

Pottok, William, instituted to Bovey Tracy, ii, 20.

Poughill, Thomas [Elys], R., a Penitentiary in the Deanery of Cadbury, i, 94, 115.—John Grede, R. ; licence of non-residence for one year, from 25 Sept., 1415, i, 213.

Pound, Robert, of Tiverton, i, 183b.

Poundestoke, William, R. of Bigbury, and Canon of Exeter (decd.), ii, 158, 159; his Will, i, 321^{b}; *see*, also, i, 6, 95^{b}.

Poundstock, Richard, V. of, a Penitentiary in the Deanery of Trigg-major, (16 Nov. 1400) i, 49^{b}.

A Commission was directed (18 June, 1402), to Robert Rygge, Chancellor, and Rd. Hals, Treasurer, to investigate the right of Joan, relict of Sir John Trevarthian, to present Edward Dauntesey to this Benefice. They were to call the Rector, etc., of the Collegiate Chantry of Slapton to give evidence; ii, 229. The Bishop collated Benedict Whalysbrow, *by lapse*, 7 March, 1402-3; ii, 65^{b}. This V. is mentioned, i, 107 (*see* Marhamchurch).

Powton (i.e. St. Breoke); Wm. Sony of, i, 239; *see*, also, ii, 310.

Powderham, the Church of, i, 307; Robert Wey, R., co-patron of Bickleigh R., ii, 92^{b}.

Poyns, John, R. of Chawleigh, exchanges for Maperton (Dioc. of B. and W.), ii, 155; i, 78.

Pral, Jno., inst. to Maker, ii, 120; proxy for Hy. Gardiner, ii, 198.

Prata, John, R. of St. John Zachary (London), exchanges for Dittisham, ii, 53; for Bridestowe, and a Canonry etc., at Ottery, ii, 106^{b}; for St. Pancras (London), ii, 150^{b}.

Pratte, John, farms the revenues of Cruwys-Morchard, i, 138.

Prauncard, John, i, 320^{b}.

Pradannack *see* Petyt, John (*Oratories*), i, 56.

Preachers, unlicensed—

The Bishop's Mandate to Henry Wynnegode, his Official-Peculiar in Cornwall, to make Enquiry as to all preaching in Cornwall contrary to the Provincial Constitution therein lately made and provided; 8 July, 1412, i, 162^{b}.

Preachers, Friars; concerning the right and privileges of the Order, which had been invaded (31 Oct., 1397), ii, 213^{b}: case of appeal (2 Jan., 1397-8), ii, 214^{b}, 215.

Prentys, Edward, proxy for Richard Prentys, ii, 77^{b}; presented to Stokenham R. by Thomas de Montacute, Earl of Salisbury, ii, 357; inst., ii, 179^{b}.

Prentys, John, i, 307^{b}.

Prentys, Richard, R. of Stoke Climsland, resigns, ii, 36^{b}; inst. to Stokenham, ii, 77^{b}; 261, 357^{b}, 358; his death, ii, 179^{b}.

Prescot [Prestecote], in the parish of Culmstock, i, 200^{b}.

Prestecote, John, and Margaret his wife, licensed to choose Confessors (2 Sept., 1410), i, 104: Joan and Margery, his wives, and Joan, his dau., i, 317^{b}, 318^{b}; his Will, i, 317^{b}.

He was co-patron of Mamhead, ii, 45^{b}; and of Stoke Fleming, ii, 17; and presented to Teign Brewer, ii, 108. He was a Commissioner in the election of the Prioress of Polsloe, ii, 76. Margery Prestcote, his widow, presented twice to Teign Brewer, ii, 146, 157^{b}.

Prestecote, William, father of John, i, 317^{b}.

Preston [" Pruteston juxta Loddiswell," MS.], ii, 358.

Preston, John, R. of St. Ewe, i, 8, 31^b—

[*Breve Regium—de venire facias*]—John Preston, chaplain, probably this R. of St. Ewe; to appear before the Barons of the Exchequer, "ad respondendum et satisfaciendum" concerning "33 libr. de precio cccc bidentium," the property of Robert Tresilian, temp. Ric. II., viz., 17 Nov., A° Regni VI. (i.e. 1382), and received by the said John Preston from one John Phelipp, for the use and profit of the said Rob. Tresilian (20 Feb., 1414-15), ii, 351^b.

Processions—*Certificatorium Cantuariensi Episcopo de processionibus faciendis* (12 June, 1415), i, 211.

Prode, Adam, Canon of Frithelstock, i, 53^b.

Prophet, John, Dean of Hereford, ii, 27; collated to a Can. and the Preb. of Wodelond in Crediton, ii, 27^b; to another Can. therein, ii, 48^b: which he soon resigned, ii, 64.

He complained of the state in which he found the Wodelond Prebendal buildings, through the neglect of John Wendlyngburgh, his predecessor; and the Bishop ordered an enquiry (16 Sept., 1395), i, 5^b.

He appears to have been Canon of Abergwili (Dioc. of St. David's) and Prebendary of Llandogy therein, which he exchanged with Richard Wynchcomb, also Canon therein and Prebendary of "Royll" (proxy—Robert Fry), 3 Dec., 1395, ii, 29.—John *Profyt*, possibly this pluralist, was inst. about this time (16 March, 1395-6) to Gulval and held it for a short time; ii, 4^b.

Profete, Rd., inst. to Buckfastleigh, ii, 173^b; resigns, ii, 181^b.

Prous, Agnes, wife of William, i, 323.

Prous, John, "of Doderygg," co-patron of Cruwys-Morchard, ii, 194^b.

Prouȝ, John (elder son of John Prouȝ, of Chagford), inst. to Dunchideock, ii, 130, 236^b; dies, and is succeeded by John, younger son of John Prousȝ, ii, 134: his death, ii, 199^b.

Proues, John, V. of Gulval (deceased), ii, 153^b.

Prousz, Thomas, of "Ekysbourn," presents to Exbourne, ii, 132^b.

Provincial Constitution as to jurisdiction by married or bigamous clerks, etc.,—

"Certificatorium super execucione Constitucionis Provincialis de Registrariis conjugatis" (10 Dec., 1414), i, 205.

Provisors,—"Statuti contra Provisores editi modificacio"; 30 March, 1399, ii, 223^b. *See*, also, ii, 230.

Pruet, John, chaplain and priest, i, 303^b, 318^b, 319; inst. to All-Hallows, Goldsmith-street, Exeter, ii, 100.

Pruston, Walter, of Ermington, ii, 277.

Prydeaux, Sir John, knt., Elizabeth, his wife, and Thomasia his daughter, *see*, his Will, i, 302.

The name is variously spelt: Richard Prydeausȝ presented to Broadoak, ii, 68^b; and to East Allington, ii, 99; John Prydeaux, senior, presented to Broadoak, ii, 157; John Prediaux to Combe-in-Teignhead, ii, 264^b. Wm. Prydeaux was instituted to Filleigh, ii, 13; and Thos. Prydel (or Prydew) to the Chantry of Ralegh, ii, 15; which he subsequently exchanged for Oare (Dioc. of B. and W.), ii, 64^b.

Prynsȝ, Walter (and his wife), i, 332.

Puddesdon, John, Sub-Dean of Exeter (*see Oratories*), 5.

Puddington Church, i, 319ᵇ.—William [Stokhay], R., i, 203ᵇ.

Pult, Roger, of Apuldram, ii, 293ᵇ.

Pulter, Walter, i, 305.

Puslinch in Newton-Ferrers ; *see* Cornu (*Oratories*) i, 76.

Putford [West], Stephen [Gyffard], R., a Penitentiary in the Deanery of Holsworthy, i, 143, 174, 194ᵇ, 207ᵇ, 217, 231, 237ᵇ, 245ᵇ.

Puttenham, Roger, R. of Affeton, exchanges for Danbury (Dioc. of London), ii, 51ᵇ.

Puttes, John, instituted to Littleham, V. ii, 96.

Pyak, John, i, 329ᵇ.

Pycot, Nicholas, V. of West Dean (Dioc. of Chichester), exchanges with the Sacristan of Bosham, ii, 199.

Pygeslegh (*or* Pykkeslegh), William, V. of Cornwood, exchanges for Queen Camel (Dioc. of B. and W.), ii, 87ᵇ.

Pyke, John, R. of Spaxton (Dioc. of B. and W.), exchanges for Holcombe-Rogus, ii, 42ᵇ.

Pykenet, Thomas, V. of Holbeton (deceased), ii, 6ᵇ.

Pykenyng, Peter, R. of Uffculme, exchanges for Tring (Dioc. of Lincoln), ii, 44ᵇ.

Pyle, Robert, clerk, i, 331ᵇ.

Pylle, in Bishop's Tawton ; *see* Fouke (*Oratories*), i, 35ᵇ.

Pyllegh, John, V. of Rockbeare, resigns, ii, 88ᵇ.

Pyllond, in the parish of Pilton ; see *Oratories*, i, 64ᵇ.

Pyllond, Thos., co-patron of Landcross, ii, 95ᵇ ; of Shirwell, ii, 96ᵇ, 103ᵇ.

Pylton, Wm., Archdn. of Exeter, exch. with Thos. Hendeman, ii, 109.

Pym, Philip, R. of Kentisbury i, 39; resigns, ii 106.

Pym, Robert, inst. to Aylesbeare, ii, 75ᵇ ; his death, ii, 96ᵇ,

Pyn in Upton Pyn (*sic*) ; *see Oratories*, i, 36ᵇ.

Pyne [*or* Pyn, MS.], Edm., presents to Combpyne, ii, 138ᵇ, 200ᵇ,

Pynnok, John, Prior of Frithelstock, i, 53 ; his death, ii, 183.

Pyper, John, Prior of St. German's (q.v.)—

Pyther, Richard, R. of Upton-Hellions (deceased), ii, 179ᵇ.

Pytman, John, *see* Barnstaple, i, 198ᵇ. *See*, also, ii, 255.

Pytman, Rob., R. of Huish, exchanges for Hollacombe, ii, 68b; his death, ii, 194b.

Pytte, John, senior, i, 316b.

Pytte, John, instituted to Rewe, ii, 21b; exchanges for Warkleigh, ii, 22b.

Pytwyll, in the parish of Georgeham, i, 69b.

Pyworthy [Pyworth, MS.], John Flemmyng, R.—

It had been represented to the Bishop that he was notoriously unfit to discharge his duties, being weak of body and enfeebled in mind; he was also, nearly blind. The Bishop accordingly appointed John Sergeaunt, R. of Milton Damarel, to take care of both Flemmyng and his parish, and Flemmyng consented to the arrangement; but the Bishop reserved to him an allowance for victuals and clothing, and made due provision for the services in the parish-church, and for the repair and maintenance of the Rectory House and the other buildings; and he stipulated that the afflicted Rector's convenience should be consulted in every way, and all annoyance to him avoided; requiring, moreover, that to him, or his assigns, a due account should be rendered (27 June, 1402), ii, 22.—Nevertheless, in the following year, Flemmyng was permitted to exchange this Benefice for Inwardleigh, having been found, after an inquisition, to be sound in mind and body (27 Jan., 1402-3), ii, 228b. He lived for some years, resigning in 1409; ii, 108b. But *see* Inwardleigh, i, 74. John Cowyk, R.; licence of non-residence for a year, from 16 July, 1410, i, 100b; also, from 5 Feb., 1411-12, to Michaelmas, 1412, i, 144; and from 18 April, to Michaelmas, 1417, i, 232. *See* i, 327b.

Q.

Quenyllon, Thomas, inst. to Dodbrooke, ii, 85; decd. ii, 107b.

Querley, Wm. collated Precentor of Crediton, ii, 191; i, 245.

Quethiock,—"Sancti Hugonis de Quedek," *see* "Institutions," ii, 41.

Quyddyssh, Walter, i, 332.

Quyntrel, John, clerk,—*Dispensacio super defectu natalium* (15 April, 1409):

He is described as *de presbitero genitus et soluta*, i, 88b. A John Quynterell was collated to St. Gorran, 22 Dec., 1399; ii, 44b.

Quythe, Nicholas, *see* Whyte, Nicholas, ii, 97.

R.

Racan, Walter, V. of Talland (deceased), ii, 6.

Racheford, Thomas, proxy for Roger Wodehele, ii, 91.

Rackenford, the Church of, i, 319b.—Robert Alkebarowe, R.; licence to choose a Confessor (1 Sept., 1395), i, 5; *see*

Alkebarowe, Robert.—John Crooke, R., i, 138.—Commission of Enquiry as to the patronage,—

(1) on the presentation of Geoffrey Barger, chaplain, by Edward, Earl of Devon, as patron, during the minority of Humphrey, son and heir of Robert Cruwys (6 March, 1412-13), ii, 250b.—(2) On the presentation of Robert Crewys, chaplain, by Humphrey Crewys (24 March, 1412-13), ii, 251.b—(3) On the presentation of Robert Cruwes, chaplain, by Matthew Hordelegh and Juliana his wife (20 April, 1413), *ibid*; he was inst. 19 May; ii, 150b; and obtained licence of non-residence, 22 Dec., 1414, till Michaelmas, 1415; i, 205b.

Raddych, John, inst. to Whitchurch, ii, 9.

Radener, John, citizen of London, *see* Frenssh, Katherine.

Radeslo, William, chaplain at Gittisham, i, 312b.

Radestok, John, i, 312.

Radwyll, William, i, 307b.

Raddington, Gregory, R. of (Dio. of B. & W.), *see* Canonsleigh, i, 62b.

Radysworthy, Oliver, inst. to Creacombe, ii, 13b; resigns and is inst. to Cheldon, ii, 68; (decd.), ii, 138b; his Will, i, 315b.

Raff (*or* Rauf), John, Can. of Glasney, i, 65b, 66; his death, ii, 67.

Raff, Wm. inst. to St. Stithians, ii, 153b; resigns, and is inst. to St. Wendron, ii, 182.

Ragger, John, *see* Derlyng, Thomas, i, 229.

Rake, the Manor of [near Kingsbridge], i, 318b.

Ralegh, St. Leonard's Chantry at, *see* "Institutions."

Ralegh, John, formerly husband of Lady Elizabeth Paulet, ii, 6b.

Ralegh, Sir John de, of Beaudeport (A.D. 1347, *see* Exeter, St. George's), ii, 336.

Ralegh, John, of Fardell, i, 302,—

[*Breve Regium*]—"pro recipiendo sacramentum Escetoris in Comitatibus Devonie et Cornubie ["Ralee," MS.], 8 Nov., 1409, ii, 332.

Rale, Thos., V. of Kingsbury (Dioc. of B. and W.), exch. for Sutcombe, ii, 102b; for St. John in Cornwall, ii, 181; i, 238b.

Ralle, David, R. of Ideford (deceased), ii, 25.

Raly, (*or* Rayle), John, patron of St. Martin's-by-Looe, ii, 30b, 35.

Rame, John Dawny, R.; licensed to celebrate in St. Michael's Chapel in that parish (2 Feb., 1396-7), i, 11b.

Ramfray (*or* Ramfrey), John, inst. to Honeychurch, ii, 101; i, 146; his death, ii, 159.

Rampisham (Dioc. of Salisbury), the Church of, i, 306.

Ramysham, Elias, exchanges the Chantry of Forde for Skilgate (Dioc. of B. and W.), ii, 32b.

Ramyslond, Wm., Vicar of Kenton, i, 307; his death, ii, 14b.

Randolf, Thomas, proxy for John Bampton, R. of Bradninch, on his collation to the Archdeaconry of Lewes, ii, 27.

Thomas Rondoulf, I suppose the same, was instituted to Payhembury, ii, 150.

Rattery [Rattre, MS.]. John and Agnes Valewyll, of, i, 232.

Raulyn, Robert, proxy for Roger Smyth, ii, 88.

Rawlyn, Thomas, V. of Sidbury, i, 318; his death, ii, 20b.

A *Dispensacio super defectu natalium*, in favour of Thomas Raulyn, clerk, was granted 8 Oct., 1417, i, 235.

Raundes (*or* de Raundes), Rd., R. of North Molton and Canon of Windsor; his death, ii, 50b; his Will, i, 300. The Church of Raunds, *ibid.*—Matilda de, *ibid.*

Rawe, John, priest, Canon, etc., of Glasney (q.v.)

Rawe, (*or* Rewe), William,—

Mandate, directed to Benedict Caunterbyry, against the said William, a married clerk, pretending to act as official of the Archdeacon of Cornwall, and to exercise spiritual and ecclesiastical juridiction in Cornwall, not only over laymen but over the Clergy also (13 March, 1403-4), i, 70.

Rawston [Raveston, MS.], see Holeway, Wm., ii, 311.

Raylecomb, Thomas, collated, *by lapse*, to Linkinhorne, ii, 54b.

Raynold, Nich., excommunicate and contumacious, is handed over by the Bishop to the secular arm (17 July, 1411), i, 129b.

Raynald, Walter, *see* Bickleigh, R. (*Institutions*).

Raynald, Walter, R. of Boconnoc, resigns, ii, 190.

Rayner, William, chaplain, i, 314;

He was R. of Rodmerton (Dioc. of Worcester), which he exchanged (ii, 55b), for a Canonry and Prebend in Ottery St. Mary, and forthwith was collated to Morchard Bishop, ii, 56. His name is written "Reynald," i, 105b, and "Reyner," ii, 189b.—Subsequently he was collated to a Canonry in Glasney ii, 75; which he resigned, on his collation to another Canonry therein, ii 134b; again resigning, he was collated to a Canonry in Bosham, ii, 189b.

Rayschelegh, John, chaplain, licensed to serve the Chapel of St. Edmund the Bp. in the Manor of Coleton in the parish of Chulmleigh (29 Sept., 1413), i, 185. Thomas Rayschelegh; see *Oratories*, i, 62.

Realm, the;—*Mandatum pro pace et tranquillitate Regni*,—

This document is not dated; but it comes between the 4th and the 8th of June, 1398, i, 18b. A like mandate was dated 3 Nov., 1399, i, 31b. Again 25 April, 1418, the Bishop enforces the King's Mandate for arraying and arming all persons whatsoever, ecclesiastical, religious, and secular, exempt and not exempt, for the defence of the Realm and Church against the French and Spaniards, and their allies, who were threatening invasion *cum magna classe navium et galearum, in multitudine copiosa hominum bellatorum* (25 April, 1418), i, 239b.—The Bishop replies (17 Aug., 1418), that, with the least possible delay, he had caused to be armed and in readiness for any emergency, 204 men of his Diocese, besides 1,201 archers; i, 241b.—*See*, also, Henry IV. and Henry V.

Reche, Rd., chaplain, licensed to serve the Chapel of St. Morwetha [*hodie* Morvah], in St. Madern (17 April, 1409), i, 89.

Reche, Wm., inst. to Kentisbeare, ii, 95; (decd.), ii, 147.—*See* i, 301.

Reconciliation of polluted Churches and Cemeteries—

Bull of Pope John [xxiii] authorizing the Bishop to reconcile the same by the ministry of any fit priest, dated at St. Peter's, viii Kalend. Marcii Pontificatus Anno Secundo i, 166.

Reda, Roger, a parishioner of Linkinhorne, i, 116.

Reed (*or* Rede), John, R. of Roche, resigns, ii, 8^b; inst. to South Pool, ii, 8; his death, ii, 90^b.

Rede, Rosa, wife of John Rede, of Dartmouth, i, 330^b.

Rede, Thos., Can. of Frithelstock, i, 53^b, 54; elected Prior, ii, 183.

Rede, Walter, R. of Highampton (deceased), ii, 94.

Rede, William, V. of St. Minver, resigns, ii, 95^b.

Reede, Margaret, relict of Andrew, presents to Huish, ii, 68^b.

Redeclyf (*or* Radeclyff), Jno. (R. of Northill), inst. to Parkham, ii, 8^b; resigns, ii, 12^b; inst. to the Preb. of Cutton, ii, 46^b; exch. for Tiverton (2nd Portion), ii, 90^b; (decd.), ii, 99.

Redenerth, William, proxy for John Harry, ii, 83.

Redeness, Walter de, i, 327^b.

Redewyll, John, of Kingsbridge, ii, 292.

Redhode, Wm., V. of Batheaston, exchanges for Hockworthy, ii, 44; his death, ii, 160^b.

Reeke, William, farmer of the revenues of Denbury, i, 138.

Redeman, Thomas, R., of Kenn, etc.—

Collated to a Canonry in Exeter Cathedral, ii, 38^b; i, 239^b; exch. Stanford-on-Avon, (Dioc. of Lincoln) for Ermington, R., ii, 120^b: proxy for Walter Gybbes, ii, 78^b; for Rd. Allerton, ii, 198^b.—Thos. Redman (I presume the same) was, subsequently, collated to a Canonry in Crantock, ii, 200.

Redruth [Rudruth, MS.], Nicholas [Oby], R., a Penitentiary in the Deanery of Penwith, i, 49^b.

License was granted 14 Sept., 1400, to Nicholas Oby, R. of the Church "Sancti Ewnini," for the Chapels of SS. Christopher and Ruman in that parish, i, 48. Renewed 18 May, 1405, "ut in capella Sancti Rumani in villa sive hameletta de *Redruth* infra parochiam Sancti Eunini, in Cornubia, Exoniensis Diocesis, situata, presbiteri itinerantes, et alii quicunque presbiteri ydonei, in presencia extraneorum itinerancium sive perigrinorum, divina valeant celebrare, dummodo per hoc ecclesie matrici loci hujusmodi nullum fiat prejudicium, et Rector loci ad invencionem alicujus presbiteri, ibidem de cetero celebraturi, ex consuetudine, vel alio modo, artetur, seu quoviamodo obligetur: ad beneplacitum domini duraturam," i, 74^b.

Remyngton, James (of London), chaplain, i, 331.

Rendy, Nicholas, i, 332.

Reprena, Thomas, scholar—*Dispensacio super defectu natalium* (18 Sept., 1417), i, 233^b.

Reppryn, Rd., the Bishop's Steward in Cornwall, ii, 116.

Richard Reprenne, John Arundell, John Grenevyll, Wm. Stourton, and Roger Trewethenek took the oath as Justices of the Peace for Cornwall (*Breve Regium*, 12 Oct., 1410), ii, 335b.

Reprenne, "the parish of"; *see* Kendale, (*Oratories*), i, 46b.

Residence in Benefices, Mandate as to (18 June, 1399), ii, 224b.

Resker (*or* Reskyer), Stephen, inst. to Colaton Raleigh, ii, 3; exchanges for St. Cubert, ii, 41; for St. Colan, ii, 145b.

Reskemner, Ralph, i, 323b.—Alice Reskimer, *ibid. See* also, i, 86b.

Respryn, Ralph, inst. to Milton Damarel, ii, 190; i, 242b, 244b.

Ressere, in Lawhitton; *see* Clovter, Thomas, ii, 311.

Restalek, Ralph de, inst. to St. Hilary, 18 Jan., 1342-3; ii, 349.

Restaurek, John, R. of St. Mabyn, a Penitentiary in the Deanery of Trigg-major, i, 93b, 115b, 143b, 174, 194b, 207b; a Commissioner for the election of the Prior of Bodmin, ii, 72; his resignation [Restowrek, MS.], ii, 164.

Restronget, *see* Bodrugan (*Oratories*), i, 145.

Retyn, John, inst. to Hollacombe, ii, 194b.

Reue (*or* Reve), John, of Lymington, i, 312.

Reue (*or* Reve), John, R. of Honeychurch (deceased), ii, 101.

Reue (*or* Reve), Richard, inst. to Roseash, ii, 89b; i, 328.

Revel, John, and John Rogeer, deacons; Dispensation in favour of (23 Sept., 1402)—

They had been ordained deacons "ab alieno Episcopo," viz., by Nicholas, Episcopus Christopolitanus [Suffragan of Wells]: i, 61b.

Rew, William, proxy for John Polsave, ii, 149.

Rewe; Thomas Warre, R.—

He obtained a licence of non-residence (to study at Oxford) for 4 years from 14 Feb., 1401-2; he was to proceed to sub-deacon's Orders within a year, i, 54b; with Letters-Dimissory to any English Bishop, i, 55.—Thomas Vesy, R.; licence of non-residence for a year, from 15 Oct., 1402, i, 62.

Rewley, the Abbot and Convent of, present to St. Stithian's, ii, 153b 182; to St. Wendron, ii, 182.

Reymound, Joan, wife of Thomas, i, 332, 332b; John, and Sibil his wife, i, 331b; Richard and Thomas, i, 320.

Richard was proxy for Robert Cruwes, ii, 150b; Thomas was co-patron of Ashreigney, ii, 156, 177b.—The Will of Thos. Reymound, i, 331b; and *see* i, 319.

Reynell (*or* Reynald), Walter, presents to E. Ogwell, ii, 135, 198b.

Reynold, John, proxy for Robert Daldych, ii, 195b.

Rynald, Robert, inst. to Holcombe-Burnell, ii, 194b.

Richard II. presents to Stoke Climsland, ii, 9b, 36b.

Also to the Preb. of Heyes, ii, 31; to Halford (Dioc. of B. and W.), and to

Ipplepen, ii, 31^{b}; to Blisland, ii, 32; to St. Illogan, and to Arreton (Dioc. of Winchester), ii, 34; to Ermington, R., ii, 34^{b}; to Atherington, ii, 36^{b}; to St. Mawnan and to St. Stephen's in Brannel, ii, 40; to Creed, ii, 42; to Nymet Tracy, ii, 42^{b}; to Meath, ii, 221; to the Priory of St. Michael's Mount (on account of the war with France), ii, 338^{b}, 349.

Richard (*alias* Woborn), John, inst. to E. Worlington, ii, 14^{b}; i, 45.

Richard, Henry, *see* Symon, John, ii, 332^{b}.

Ringmore [Rydemour, *and* Rydmore, MS.]; John Stancombe, accolite, R., i, 12^{b}; dispensation (to study at Oxford) for 2 years, from 1 Dec., 1397, i, 14.

This dispensation was renewed, before its expiration, viz., 30 Oct., 1398, in favour of John Stoncombe (*sic*), sub-deacon, with permission to enjoy all the revenues of his benefice: i, 21^{b}. He was licensed to celebrate on St. Katherine's Day, in the Chapel which had been built at Okenbury in honour of that Saint (14 Nov., 1410), i, 109.[1]—Licence of non-residence, for a year, from 2 Dec., 1410, i, 110; for 2 years, from 29 Jan., 1411-12, i, 142^{b}; for 2 years, from 15 April, 1414, i, 196; for a year, from 29 April, 1417; i, 232.

Rinsy, Manor of, *see* Rynsy (*Oratories*), i, 23^{b}.

Robert, Joan, sister of Walter; also, John Robert, i, 324.

Robert, John, V. of Salcombe [Regis] (deceased), ii, 110^{b}.

Robert, John, and John Robert "de Clompit," parishioners of Linkinhorne, i, 116.

Robert, Michael, instituted to Bickleigh V., ii, 176.

Robert, Walter, LL.B., i, 73^{b}, 315^{b}—

He was instituted to Sampford Courtenay, ii, 22^{b}; and, on resigning it, to Tiverton (2nd Portion), ii, 74^{b}; this he exchanged for the Preb. of Cutton, ii, 90^{b}; which he soon after resigned (ii, 99^{b}), and was inst. to Northill, ii, 99. He was then collated Precentor of Ottery, ii, 104^{b}; i, 90; but soon resigned, and was collated to a Canonry in Glasney, ii, 123^{b}; i, 133^{b}; a little later he was inst. to Milton Damarel, ii, 132^{b}, 238, 246^{b}, 341; but resigned on his institution to Tiverton (1st Portion), ii, 150^{b}; i, 183^{b}, 194, 207^{b}; soon after which he exchanged his Canonry in Glasney for a Canonry and the 7th Prebend in Ottery, ii, 159. This pluralist died R. of Northill and of Tiverton, as well as Canon of Ottery, ii, 169, 169^{b}, 173^{b}; his Will, i, 324. He occurs as proxy for Matthew Downe, ii, 98; and as presenting to Cruwys-Morchard, ii, 104^{b}.—On 4 Aug., 1412, a Commission of Enquiry was issued, on his complaint as Canon of Glasney, as to the dilapidations left by his predecessor, Walter Estcolmp, in his manse of residence, ii, 248.

Roborough [Roweburgh, MS.]; Richard Colebrugg, R.,—

Rob. Lywer, R. of Drewsteignton, appointed his co-adjutor, ii, 23.—John Gorewyll, jun., R., subdeacon: dispensation (to study at Oxford) for 3 years, from 1 Feb., 1403-4, i, 69^{b}.—Richard Graynevyll, R.; his resignation, 30 Nov., 1409, i, 91.—John Jerbard, R.; dispensation (to study at Oxford) for 2 years, from 26 Jan., 1410-11, i, 117^{b}; licence of non-residence for a year, from 13 Feb., 1412-13, i, 176^{b}. John Fayryste, R.; licence of non-residence from 20 March, 1418-19, to Michaelmas, 1419, i, 246.

---

[1] This Chapel stood in the court-yard, near the mansion, and was destroyed within living memory, having been used as a pigeon-house. A small endowment, now commuted at £6, being part of the Rectorial tithes of the adjoining parish of Kingston, is still enjoyed by Stancombe's successors.

Robyn, William, R. of North Huish (deceased), ii, 8b.

Roche, John Beare, R.,—

He obtained licence of non-residence for a year, from 20 Sept., 1402, "dummodo interim domos et edificia Rectorie sue faciat competenter reparari," i, 61b. He was licensed to celebrate on St. Michael's Day, in the Chapel of St. Michael in his parish — "licenciam ... post illum diem minime duraturam" (16 Sept., 1409), i, 90b. Renewed "ad beneplacitum," 15 July, 1410, with no limitation of days, but saving the rights of the Mother-Church, i, 100b.

Rochester, the Archdeaconry of, i, 324b.

Rochewell, John, *see* Langeton, William, i, 14.

Rockbeare, R., appropriated to Canonsleigh, ii, 359b.

Rodberd, John, clerk, *see* Cardynham ; ii, 21.

Rodevale, Sir John, knt., co-patron of Otterton, ii, 176.

Rodenay, Alice [*absolucio Alicie Rodenay, post mortem, etc.*] :

"Edmundus, miseracione Divina Exoniensis Episcopus, dilecto in Christo filio, domino Johanni [Southam], Priori Prioratus Tottoniensis, nostre Diocesis salutem, graciam, et benediccionem.—Ex parte Thome Rodenay, mariti Alicie Bastard, nuper uxoris sue, nunc defuncte, nostre Diocesis, cum humili insinuacione nobis extitit insinuatum quod cum nos, officium nostrum exequentes pastorale, eandem Aliciam, nobis et officio nostro delatam super eo quod a marito suo legitimo predicto, et ipsius consorcio maritali, absque judicio Ecclesie, temere divertebat, et eidem adherere contempsit, minus juste, propter ipsius contumaciam pariter et rebellionem in non comparendo coram nobis, certis die et loco, ad quos extiterat legitime evocata, super premissis responsura, contractam, excommunicari et ipsam sic excommunicatam publice nunciari fecerimus, et decreverimus, justicia id poscente ; eadem tamen Alicia eandem excommunicacionem, licet postea ad maritum suum rediens antedictum, sustinuit per dies non modicos, animo indurato ; tandem, languens in extremis et morsum habens consciencie ante ipsius mortem signa et indicia penitencie de premissis, ut asseritur, habuit manifesta, et sic finivit dies suos : unde ex parte ejusdem de absolucionis beneficio in hac parte impendendo nobis extitit supplicatum.—Nos, igitur, attendentes quod Ecclesia nulli claudit gremium set aperit redeunti, vobis committimus et mandamus quatinus super premissis diligenter veritatem inquiratis ; et si, per inquisicionem eandem, inveneritis dictam Aliciam ante ipsius mortem signa penitencie et indicia de excommunicacione predicta, ut premittitur, habuisse, et sic decessisse—super quibus vestram conscienciam intendimus onerare—tunc, et non aliter, eidem beneficium absolucionis in forma juris impendatis, et ejus corpus, si aliud canonicum non obsistat, in sacra Sepultura sepeliri, ut convenit, faciatis. Ad que facienda vobis committimus vices nostras : in cujus testimonium sigillum nostrum presentibus est appensum. Datum in Manerio nostro Criditonensi, vicesimo tercio die mensis Marcii, Anno Domini Millesimo CCCCmo decimo (1410-11), et nostre consecracionis anno sexto decimo," i, 121b.

Rodewyll (*or* Rothewell), Wm., R. of Hemyock, exchanges for Axminster, ii, 27b ; i, 207b.

Roges, Christina, sub-prioress of Canonsleigh, ii, 125.

Rogger, John, inst. to Modbury Priory, ii, 10b, 11 ; resigns and is inst. to Tywardreath Priory, ii, 93b.

John Rogeer [*margin* Rogger], *see* Revel, John, i, 61b.—*See* Quethiock (*Inst.*)

Roger, Paschasius, R. of Peter Tavy (deceased), ii, 53b.

Rok, John, V. of Brampford Speke, exch. for Woolfardisworthy R., ii, 75.

Rok, Thomas, priest, LL.B.,—

Letters Dimissory were granted him, 14 Sept., 1395, for ordination "a quocunque Catholico Episcopo infra Regnum Anglie intitulato," i, 5. He was afterwards ordained priest, however, "ab *alieno* Episcopo, videlicet Willelmo Basiliensi Episcopo" (Suffragan of London); dispensation granted, 18 April, 1398, i, 17.

Rokeby (Dioc. of Coventry and Lichfield), i, 322^b,

Rolond *alias* Doune, Matth., R. of Down St. Mary (decd.), ii, 145.

Romansleigh [Rommodyslegh, MS.], Nicholas [Joye], R.; *see* Wembworthy.

Commission of Enquiry on the presentation of John Dayhyll, chaplain, by John son and heir of Robert Hacche (10 April, 1416), ii, 258°.

Rome; Hosp. of the Holy Trinity and St. Tho. of Canterbury,—

The Bishop's Letter—addressed to the four Archdeacons, the Deans Rural, and the parochial Clergy—on behalf of this Hospital for poor and infirm English folk; directing them to receive and assist the representatives of the said Hospital seeking alms; and conceding an Indulgence to the Faithful who should contribute to its maintenance (30 Nov., 1398), i, 22^b. The collections for the Cathedral, however, were not to suffer;—"volumus autem quod questores fabrice Ecclesie nostre Exoniensis tempore Quadragesimali, questibus aliis tunc cessantibus, privilegio gaudeant singulari presentibus, per biennium a dato earundem tantummodo duraturo."—The following extract from the Schedule appended to this document will be read with interest:—"In primis utique in eodem Hospitali pauperes cujuscumque status Nacionis Anglicane benigne recipiuntur, esurientes pascuntur, mortui sepeliuntur, mulieres pregnantes recipiuntur donec purificentur, ceteraque opera misericordie in eodem fiunt continue et excercentur; ubi ante ipsius Hospitalis fundacionem pauperes debiles et infirmi, ac eciam peregrini nostre Nacionis Anglicane per viam depredati et paupertate depressi, propter inopiam nudi sub Divo, ab aliis Hospitalibus et locis inhumaniter jacti, in dicta urbe Romana pernoctabant; unde quidam, propter frigus quod paciebantur, perpetuam incurrebant infirmitatem; quidam vero, a lupis vulnerati, fere devorabantur: cujus quidem Hospitalis fundacionem, construccionem et dotacionem Sanctissimus in Christo Pater et Dominus, Dominus Gregorius, Divina Providencia Papa xj^us, auctoritate Apostolica confirmavit. Set quia Hospitale hujusmodi nondum competenter constructum existit (*sic*) et construccione indigeat non modicum sumptuosa, ac Christi pauperes et infirmi ad istud confluentes et in eo degentes, quasi nichil habeant unde vivant nisi de elemosinis que ipsis pia largicione Fidelium de Anglia transmittuntur, Sanctissimus in Christo Pater et Dominus, Dominus Bonifacius, Divina Providencia Papa IX, hec pie et sancte prospiciens, universis Christi Fidelibus, de penitentibus et confessis, qui ad premissa manus porrexerint adjutrices, septem annos et totidem Quadragenas—Symon et Willelmus Archiepiscopi Cantuarienses, Rogerus Cantuariensis Episcopus modernus, Alexander Ebor., Willelmus London., Willelmus Wynton., Thomas Exoniensis, Thomas Dunolmensis, Thomas Eliensis, Johannes Lincoln., Johannes Bathoniensis et Wellensis, Edmundus Exoniensis, Willelmus Cicestrensis, Henricus Norwycensis, Thomas Roffensis, Radulphus Sarisburiensis, Henricus Wygornensis, Episcopi singuli eorum singulos quadraginta dies de injunctis eis penitenciis misericorditer relaxarunt. Item, ex statuto dicti Hospitalis, quilibet Sacerdos infra dictum Hospitale pernoctans, unam Missam qualibet ebdomeda pro fratribus et sororibus, vivis et defunctis, cantabit. Alii vero literati unum Psalterium in ebdomeda dicent. Laici vero qualibet ebdomeda totum circulum pro dictis fratribus et sororibus ibunt, cujus circuli magnas indulgencias et remissiones nemo novit dinumerare, nec potest, nisi solus Deus. Item, in eodem Hospitali plures Misse, singulis diebus, pro fratribus et sororibus ac benefactoribus dicti Hospitalis celebrantur. Et omnes qui dederunt anulum, firmaculum,[1] aurum, vel argentum, aut aliquod aliud bonum sibi a Deo collatum, erunt participes omnium Missarum, perigrinacionum, et aliorum bonorum spiritualium que in dicto Hospitali fiunt et fient imperpetuum."—A like Indulgence was granted 10 Oct., 1412, i, 169^b.

Procuratorium ad visitandum Limina Apostolorum—Appointment, by the Bishop, of Major Parys, Canon of Crediton and R. of Pillaton, 8 July, 1417, i, 233; and again, 24 Nov., 1417, i, 238.

Rome, John, "clericus Parliamenti," i, 138^b, 190^b.

Rome, Richard, of Pancraswyke, i, 69.

Rome, Roger, R. of Sutcombe, *see Oratories*, i, 49; decd., ii, 82

Rondoulf, Thos., *see* Randolf.

Rooch—John, and Agnes his wife; Walter, Robert, and Joan i, 323.

Roppard, John ap, domicellus, presents to Martinhoe, ii, 56^b.

Roseash [Rowesassche, MS.]—

A Chapel in the Manse of [William Lane], R. of this parish, was licensed, 25 May, 1400, for the use of Walter Lane and Thomasia his wife (*see Oratories*), i, 39.—William Halyet, R. (deceased), i, 324.

Rosemerrin, in the parish of St. Budock (*see Oratories*), i, 71.

Rostek, Chapel of St. Mary, *see* Petyt (*Oratories*), i, 56.

Rosuwyk, Thomas, inst. to Crowan, ii, 159^b; resigns, ii, 167.

Rote, Alice, i, 312.

Rothebury, Rob., R. of Stepney, presents to Whitechapel, ii, 178.

Rous, Peter, inst. to Tintagel, ii, 46; his death, ii, 98^b.

Rousdon; John Wattys, R.; licence of non-residence for a year, from 28 July, 1407, his buildings to be put in repair meanwhile, i, 82.—Nicholas Schaldon, R.; ditto, from 9 Jan., 1412-13, till Michaelmas, 1413, i, 173.—Hugh Lyne, R.; ditto, from 15 Feb., 1414-15, till Michaelmas, 1415, i, 208^b.

Row, John and Joan, i, 331; *see*, also, i, 321.

Row, Matthew, of Tiverton, ii, 268^b.

Row, Richard, of Plymouth, *see* Cergeaux, Michael, i, 123^b, ii, 219.

Row, Robert, and Joan Smyth—

Commission of Enquiry as to certain reports about them (5 July, 1419), ii. 268. It seems that formerly, not being aware of any impediment, they had contracted marriage, *per verba, legitime . . . . . non tamen in facie Ecclesie, secundum morem patrie.* Afterwards, they found that they were related in the 4th degree of consanguinity: dispensation granted (31 July, 1419), i, 247^b.

[1] I. q. fibula, fibulatorium; *agrafe, boucle, broche*; olim *fermail* (*D'Arnis.*)

Rowe, Robert, i, 309ᵇ.

Row, *alias* Ford, Thomas, *see* Ford; i, 167.

Row, Thomas, collated *by lapse* to the Chantry of Trewen, Holsworthy, ii, 48; resigns (ii, 51ᵇ), on institution to Ermington, V., ii, 51, 276; i, 56, 313.

Rowe, William, R. of Sampford Peverell, i, 179ᵇ, 190ᵇ.

Rowington, R. (Dioc. of B. and W.), ii, 18, 228.

[Ruan] Lanyhorne; John Bradewell, R.; licence of non-residence for a year, from 17 Nov., 1395, i, 7; ditto, from 28 March, 1397, i, 12; ditto, from 29 Nov., 1398, i, 22ᵇ; ditto, from 10 March, 1405-6, i, 77ᵇ; ditto, for 2 years, from 3 Feb., 1408-9, i, 88; ditto, for a year, from 15 Sept., 1410, i, 104ᵇ; ditto, from 8 Sept., 1411, i, 133ᵇ; ditto, from 17 Sept., 1412, i, 166.—Thomas Harry, R., ii, 264ᵇ.

Ruan-major, Thomas Jowydavy (*alias* Jacka), R. of,—

With five others, viz., Geoffrey Goff, Matilda, wife of Wm. Fycook, Elena Pascow, Joan Luky, and Margaret Bolpyth, excommunicated and contumacious, are handed over to the secular arm (3 June, 1413), i, 181.

Rudruth, Ralph, S.T.P., R. of Grittleton (Dioc. of Salisbury), inst. to Creed, ii, 29; collated Canon of Glasney, ii, 29ᵇ, 225.

He was licensed to confess his parishioners (24 March, 1395-6), i, 8ᵇ; exchanged for St. Columb-major, ii, 42; i, 48; his death, ii, 76ᵇ.

Rugge, David (a Friar Minor), chaplain, i, 227ᵇ.

Rural Dean, the office of,—

In the "Ordinacio et Taxacio Vicarie de Tunstalle" [Townstal, Dartmouth], it was provided that the Vicars should not refuse to serve in this office when the turn of the parish came round:—"Subeant eciam dicti Vicarii .... Officium Decani Ruralis quociens pro dicta Ecclesia juste fuerit subeundum," i, 75ᵇ.—*See*, also, Loddiswell, p. 244, *ad finem*.

Russell, David, Dominican Friar, of Dublin; licence of incorporation at the Dominican Convent, Exeter (4 Aug., 1410), i, 101ᵇ.

Russel, John, inst. to Dean [Prior], ii, 99; 355.

Russell, Sir Maurice, presents to the Chapelry of Kingeston-Russell, ii, 54.

Russell, Reginald, inst. to St. Breward, ii, 197ᵇ.—*See* Houper, John, ii, 213.—Robert Russell occurs i, 332.

Rychard, Henry, instituted to Lanreath, ii, 115.—Robert, *see* Filleigh, i, 110ᵇ; ii, 235ᵇ.—William, i, 111.

Rychowe, John, V. of St. Kea (deceased), ii, 147ᵇ; 250ᵇ.

Ryder, David, of Kingsbridge, ii, 292.

Ryder, Wm., proxy for Rectors of Combe Raleigh, i, 82, ii, 97ᵇ.

Ryderdon, Thomas, co-patron of Inwardleigh, ii, 108ᵇ.

Rydon, Andrew, i, 312; Robert, i, 327b.

Rygge (*or* Rugge), Rob., Archdn. of Barnstaple, S.T.P., i, 19b, 301.

He was Commissioned, together with John Schillyngford, LL.D., 11 July, 1396, to deal with a case of reparation, between Walter Dollebeare, Canon of Glasney, and his predecessor, Thos. Walkyngton, ii, 211.—He became Chancellor of the Cathedral, ii, 45b; 58b, 60b, 62, 213, 228b, 229. Appointed Vicar-General (27 Sept., 1400), ii, 15b. On the 24th June, 1402, the Bishop sent to him the King's Letter, under the Privy Seal, concerning the complaint of poverty, etc., made by the Doctors and other Graduates of Oxford and Cambridge, "pur ce qils ne purroient accepter benefices par provision de nostre tresseint Pere le Pope come ils soleient, et ce par encheson de le statut encontre provisours fait:" a remedy to be sought through Convocation and Parliament, and certain returns as to benefices to be made, ii, 230. He was appointed proctor for the Bishop in Convocation, together with Richard Tyttesbury, LL.B. (6 April, 1404), i, 70b.—His death, ii, 109b.

Rykkyll, William, *see* Smale, John.

Rynel, John, instituted to Cheldon, ii, 138b.

Rynell, Agnes, daughter of William, i, 172b.

Rysbi, John, inst. to St. Petrock's, Exeter, ii, 193; i, 242b, 331.

Rysdon, John, presented to Clannaborough, ii, 259b.

Ryssheton, Nicholas de, LL.D., Canon of Crediton, resigns, ii, 109b.—Nicholas, son of Henry de Ryssheton, collated to a Canonry in Crediton, *ibid.*

Rytherdon, Thos., co-patron of Inwardleigh, ii, 24b.—John, i, 332.

Ryve, Robert, R. of East Anstey (deceased), ii, 91b.

S.

Saberton, Robert, i, 100.

Sabyn, John, V. of Totnes (deceased), ii, 95.

Sachevile, Nicholas, V. of Colaton Raleigh (deceased), ii, 3.

Sachevile, Ralph, patron of Bicton, ii, 2b.

Sechevyll, Wm., inst. to Collumpton, ii, 134; i, 207; exchanges for Shirwell, ii, 175b.

William Sechevill (*or* Sachevyll) was presented to St. George's, Exeter (q.v.), but not admitted, ii, 234b; *see*, also, ii, 335b, 341.

St. Amand, Sir Almeric (*or* Adomar) de, *see* Ipplepen, ii, 312b.

St. Antony, Hosp. of, in London,—

It was dependent on the Augustinian Monastery of St. Antony, Diocese of Vienna. Indulgence granted to the Faithful contributing to its support, 1 May, (i, 26b) and renewed 12 June, 1399, i, 27.—At the end is a list of Indulgences, etc., granted in favour of this Hosp. by Alexander IV., Urban IV., Clement VI. (*sic*), John XXII., Urban VI., and Boniface IX. The inmates are thus described: "quorum quidam igne infernali sic torquentur et cremantur quod ipsi, quasi membrorum omni officio destituti, monstra horribilia pocius quam homines esse videntur," i, 27ᵇ.

St. Anthony-in-Meneage, *see* Tregos (*Oratories*), i, 71.

Sentabyn [*hodie*, St. Aubyn], Guy, presents to St. Erme, ii, 82ᵇ.

Seyntabyn, John, presents to Parracombe, ii, 79ᵇ.—John Syntabyn de Lobbe was co-patron of Landcross, ii, 95ᵇ; of Shirwell, ii, 96ᵇ.

St. Austell; John Jul (*or* Juyl), V., *see* Jul.—Chantry-Chapel in the Cemetery;—John Sutton, chaplain, a Penitentiary in the Deanery of Powder, i, 231ᵇ, 238, 245ᵇ; as Rector he presents to the Vicarage of St. Clether, ii, 156ᵇ, 253. *See* Chayndyt (*Oratories*), i, 49.

St. Breage, Wm. Pensans, V., ii, 264ᵇ.—Manors of Rinsy and Godolphin [*see Oratories*), i, 23ᵇ.—Nanfan and Bonython [in Cury], i, 237ᵇ.

St. Breoke (*alias* Pawton *and* Nansant), Wm. Sutton (sub-dea.) R.

He was continually non-resident by licence—from 28 Aug., 1395 (to study at Oxford) one year, i, 5; from 13 Dec., 1398 i, 24: from 18 Dec., 1400, i, 51ᵇ; from 6 Nov., 1402, i, 62; from 21 July, 1410, i, 100ᵇ; from 23 Nov., 1411, i, 140ᵇ; from 7 Oct., 1412, i, 168ᵇ—all for one year; also from 6 Nov., 1412, to Michaelmas, 1413, i, 187ᵇ.—Commission issued 4 May, 1416, on a complaint as to dilapidations, ii, 258ᵇ.—For Pengelly (i, 43), and Hustem (i, 80ᵇ), *see* Lanhergy and Polmorva (*Oratories*); Bodellek, i, 45ᵇ.

St. Breward [Sanctus Bruueredus, MS.], *see* Maker, i, 241ᵇ.

St. Budock; *see* Rosmaren (*Oratories*), i, 71.

The Chancel—roof and walls—being ruinous, it was dangerous to hold service therein. Commission, 25 June, 1399, directed to Thos. Noel and Rd. Olyver, to enquire as to the liability for repair and maintenance, and the neglect of the Provost and Canons of Glasney and John Wryter, Vicar; ii, 225.

St. Buryan [Sancte Beriane, MS.], *see* Trewoyef (*Oratories*).

St. Cleer [Sancti Clari, MS.], William Dawe, V. of—

He was licensed by the Pope to be non-resident for *ten years*, due provision being made for the cure of souls [Dated at Constance, viii Kal. Marcii, Pontificat. Aº 5º] (25 March, 1415), i, 228.—On 19 April, 1417, he was licensed to celebrate, *once*, by a fit priest, in the Chapel of St. Wynwalo at Craddock in this parish, i, 232. *See* the Will of Wm. Trenowyth, i, 301ᵇ.

St. Clement's V.; Rob. de Talvargh, inst. (A.D. 1329), ii, 348ᵇ.

St. Clether, R., annexed to St. Michael's Chantry in the Cemetery of St. Austell, ii, 52ᵇ.

St. Columb-major; John Bray, R., licensed to hear the confessions of his parishioners (9 Nov., 1398), i, 22.—Ralph Rudruth, R., *see Oratories*, i, 48; a Penitentiary in the Deanery of Pyder, i, 49ᵇ.—Laurence Haukyn, R., i, 102.

Commission of Enquiry as to dilapidations, issued 24 April, 1419, on the complaint of Rd. Aldryngton, R., against his predecessor, John Bremour, ii, 267b.

St. Columb-minor, *see* Crantock.

St. Creed, Ralph Rudruth, R.—

Licensed to hear confessions (24 March, 1395-6), i, 8b; to choose confessors (1 April, 1396), *ibid.*—Matth. Bodrigy, R. (Can. of Glasney); licence of non-residence, for a year (to reside at Glasney), from 13 Nov., 1405, i, 77; also, for a year, from 27 Sept., 1409 [Botrigy, MS.], i, 90b.

St. David's, Guy, Bishop of [Menevia], presents to Charlton (Dioc. of Rochester). ii, 80b; to Cornwood, ii, 87b.

St. Dominick; Roger Waterman, R,—

He obtained licence for St. Etheldrid's Chapel therein (9 April, 1405), i, 74; and Thomas Cowlyng, R., for the Chapel of St. Ildract the Confessor (6 March, 1418-9); i, 245b.

St. Endellion; *see* Cook, Thos., i, 48; Maysmere, Walter, i, 107b; Aleyn, Wm., chaplain, ii, 264b.

Commission of Enquiry as to the patronage, issued, 24 July, 1416, on the presentation of Wm. Gorteboos, clerk, by the Prior and Convent of Bodmin, ii, 259b.—This R. obtained a dispensation (to study at Oxford), for 3 years, from 8 Oct., 1416, not being bound to proceed meanwhile to higher Orders, i, 226b.—Commission of Enquiry as to dilapidations in the Prebendal House of John Arundell, *alias* Hylle, successor to Richard Bruton; issued, 6 Jan., 1417-8, ii, 263b. Sequestration for the amount (£26 10s. 8d.), 2 March following, ii, 264b.

St. Erme, Chapel of St. John in the parish of, i, 123b.

St. Erth; *see* Botreaux (*Oratories*), i, 8b, 21.—Wm. Talkarn, V., a Penitentiary in the Deanery of Penwith, i, 49b, 93b, 115b, 143b, 174, 194b, 207b, 217, 231, 238, 245b.

At i, 135b, he is referred to as "Willelmo Talkarn, *seniori*, . . . in Artibus Magistro et Scolari in Theologia" (licensed to preach—9 Oct., 1411). Wm. Talkarn, *junior* (also, M.A. and Sch. in Theolog.), was on the same day licensed to preach. He was licensed, 15 Feb., 1403-4, to celebrate "in capella Sancti Erci predicti, in parochia Sancti Erci antedicta, juxta Trefussa situata . . semel in anno, videlicet in crastino Pasche," ii, 69b.—Treliasick [Trevlesyk, MS.], *see* Eyr (*Oratories*), i, 240b.

St. Ewe [Sancta Ewa, MS.]; John Preston, R.,—

He obtained licence of non-residence for a year, from 7 Feb., 1395-6—"et dimittendi fructus redditus et proventus ipsius ecclesie, dicto tempore, ad firmam"; i, 8.—Also, from 1 Nov., 1399, to Michaelmas, 1400; his Rectory-house to be properly repaired in the meanwhile, i, 31b.—*See* Tregonen (*Oratories*), i, 93b.

St. Ewny, i.e., Redruth, q.v.

St. Feock; Martin de Doboner, V., and others[1].—

Certificatorium pro excommunicatis capiendis—3 March, 1398, i, 26.

A similar document occurs, i, 161, dated 8 June, 1412. The offending persons in this case are Martin de Boner (*sic*), V. of St. Feock, Rd. Dygon, chaplain, Elena Pascow,[2] Rosa Trehures, Joan, daughter of Geoffrey Mols,

---

[1] viz., Wm. Smale, chaplain; Thos. Bray, V. of Lewannick; John Wade, *alias* Leche, and Joan Penryn.

[2] Elena Pascow occurs again, in a similar document (dated 3 June, 1413), i, 181.—*See* Ruan-major.

John Clement, Wm. Cook, Philip Baker, Rosa Wexmaker (all of Cornwall); and Nicholas Gay, John Kene, and John Breton (of Devon).

St. German's Priory, John Averay (Aneray, *Oliver*), Prior of,—

The Bp. visited St. German's in this Prior's time, 3 Sept., 1400, and found that John Pengelly, Nicholas Julyan, John Brystowe, and Burnard Page (*alias* Skelly), canons, had been guilty of scandalous and immoral conduct. He commanded each of them to be put to open penance. Pengelly was to sit on the floor in the middle of the Refectory, at meal time, and have nothing but bread and water, once in the day, every Friday for seven weeks; for a whole year he was to confine himself strictly to the choir and cloister, and not to walk about the nave or speak to any women (whether of doubtful character or not), unless he had a trustworthy Brother in his company: he was not to undertake any manner of office within the said Priory throughout the year: and he was to forfeit out of his allowance for clothing one noble, to be expended on the fabrick of the Church: should he rebel, the Prior was to shut him up *in ergastulo ipsius Prioratus* for eight days, and allow him no flesh meat. Julyan was also condemned to sit on the floor of the Refectory "duabus sextis feriis, inchoando die Veneris proximo post festum Sancti Michaelis Archangeli," and to have only bread and water once in the day; for a quarter of a year "a festo Sancte Fidis;" he was to be confined to the cloister and choir; and to forfeit 40*d.* out of his allowance for clothing, to be applied to the fabrick of the Church; moreover, he was to sleep in the common dormitory. The same penance was assigned to Brystowe; and Page was to abstain from fish and wine for two successive Fridays, and contribute 40*d.* to the fabrick-fund. The Bishop wrote to the Prior (from Launceston Priory), 18 September, requiring him to see to the execution of the sentence in each case, "in virtute obediencie nobis prestite," i, 48.

This Prior was collector in Cornwall of the moneys granted, 2 March, 1397-8, by Convocation to the King: the Bishop threatened the contumacious with excommunication (3 Feb., 1398-9), ii, 222b.

The Priory being vacant, by Averay's death, 8 Sept., 1404, the Sub-prior and Convent, on the 11th, obtained the Bishop's licence to elect a successor. Noel Patreda, the Bishop's steward in Cornwall was made guardian of the Temporalities; and on the 23rd John Pyper, one of the Canons was elected. John Waryn, V. of Liskeard, was commissioned to proclaim the election in due form and to certify accordingly on the 27th. Pyper had been accused of adultery, and was required to attend, and purge himself from the said charge, in the Cathedral, on the 1st Oct., before Hugh Hyckelyng, Precentor, Rob. Rigg, Chancellor, and John Lideford and John Schillyngford, canons; this he did, and his election was confirmed at Coventry,[1] ii, 78b. Six years later (2 July, 1410), a Commission was directed to Archdeacon Hunden, Chancellor of the Diocese, to receive him in Liskeard Church, that he might purge himself from certain charges brought against him, ii, 232b.—On 17 Sept., 1410, he was found in heavy arrears to the Pope's Collector, i, 105.—Licensed, 5 Oct., 1411, to celebrate in private oratories, within all manors etc. belonging to the Priory, i, 135.

David Noy, chaplain, of this Priory, was a Penitentiary in the Deanery of East, i, 217, 238, 245b.

The Prior and Convent presented to Gulval, ii, 4b, 158b; to Landrake, ii, 10b; to Morval, ii, 74; and to South Petherwin, ii, 123b.

St. Germoe ["capella curata et parochialis Sancti Girmoci in Cornubia"],—

Commission directed 3 Feb., 1417-18, to John Bryt (V. of Lelant), to enquire as

[1] Not dated: but the Bishop was at Coventry on the 8th Oct., and for several days afterwards, ii, 79b, i, 72.

to the pollution of the cemetery there, with bloodshed, by Ralph Collurian and John Ewty, a minor, on the one part, and John Penhalow on the other, ii, 264. On 3 March, a commission was directed to Bryt, and to Wm. Penans (V. of St. Breage), to reconcile the same. In the latter the names are Ralph Collurian, John Wyse, John Ewty de Margaiov [? Market-Jew—Marazion], Warin, a servant of the said Ralph, and John Penhalow; ii, 264ᵇ. *See*, i, 314ᵇ.

St. Gerrans [Sancti Gerendi, MS.], John Fecos, R., *see Oratories*, i, 115ᵇ—Thomas Watkyn, R., i, 217ᵇ, 233ᵇ.

St. Giles [-in-the-Wood], *see* Pollard (*Oratories*), i, 104.

St. Goran, John [Noo], R.: a Penitentiary in the Deanery of Powder, i, 49ᵇ.

St. Gwinear, *see* Harry, John, i, 135ᵇ.

St. Hilary, the "Ordinacio" of the Vicarage of, extracted from Bishop Walter de Stapledon's Register; ii, 348ᵇ.

In this document three Vicars are mentioned, viz., Matthias de Skewyhek, John de Lercevesque, and Ralph de Restalek.—*See* Marazion: *also*, the Will of Wm. Bachyler, i, 314ᵇ.

St. Illogan, Wm. Styward, R.;—

Inquisition as to dilapidations caused by his predecessor, Thos. Cotteford (30 April, 1397), i, 12; ii, 316.—John Barell, R., i, 88ᵇ; ii, 125.

This R. complained to the Bp. that, (although the right of appointment to the office of *aquebajulus* pertains to the R. or V. of a Church), on his appointing one Thos. Tresculerd, clerk, to the said office at St. Illogan, when he had enjoyed the same peaceably for a month and more, certain persons, to wit Thos. and Ralph Carnarthur, Rob. Hunte, and Rd. Bre, had not only removed the said Thomas from his benefice but also had intruded one John Carnarthur into the same. The Bishop satisfied himself as to the facts, and wrote to the Dean of Penwith, to John Chyvarton and John Hoggekyn, chaplains, and to Rd. Penpons, clerk, directing them to warn the offenders, and the intruder also, to desist from their wrong-doing, and not to molest Tresculerd, under pain of excommunication (16 March, 1410-11), i, 120ᵇ.

Brev. Reg.—(1.) Prohibition to admit, pending settlement of the dispute as to the patronage between John Basset *and* the Bishop, Henry, Prince of Wales, Sir John Arundell, and John Barell, clerk, 28 Sept.: 1403, ii, 314ᵇ.—Also (2) [MS. here, "Seynt Lugans], 12 Oct., 1403; ii, 315.—(3.) Prohibition suspended, 10 Nov., 1403, ii, 315ᵇ. (4.) Forbidding the Bishop to present by lapse "jure ordinario," 12 Feb., 1403-4; *ibid.*—(5.) John Basset had appeared at Westminster, in Hilary Term; and it was alleged, on the King's behalf, that Sir Wm. Basset, 'chivaler,' was seized of Tehidy [Tihidy, MS.]—to which the advowson of this Church belonged—and held the same of K. Richard II., as of the Duchy of Cornwall, by military service; that he presented one Thos. Cotford to the said Church, who was inst. in time of peace, in K. Richard's time; and that, later on, the said Wm. Basset conceded the said Manor, but not the said advowson, to Thos. Chambernon, Otho Bodrigan, John Colyn, Thos. Cotford, and Jas. Gervays, for the term of their natural lives, with reversion to Wm. Basset—his heirs, &c.; that the said Wm. Basset died, and so the reversionary right on the death of the persons above-named, together with the advowson, had descended to John, the said William's son, a minor; so that the King [Richard II] was seized both of the body of the said minor and of the said advowson during his minority; that, afterwards, the Church became vacant, on the death of Thos. Cotford, while John Basset was still a minor, and the King thereupon presented Wm. Styward, who was duly inst.; that, soon after, Styward also died, and the right to present was claimed by the King [Henry IV.] John Basset traversed these pleas on various grounds, and claimed judgment in his favour (8 May, 1404), i, 315b.—*See* "Institutions."

St. Issey:

This parish was antiently called "Egloscruc;" by which Oliver supposed that the parish of "Egloskerry" was meant (*Monasticon*, p. 438); and he identified "Eglosroe" with St. Issey in one place (p. 438), and with Philleigh in another (p. 439); whereas it is, undoubtedly, the antient name of the latter parish, which is, in "Roseland," and of that only. The references which he gives from the Registers of Brantingham, Stafford, and Vesey, belong—not to Egloskerry but to St. Issey; and so, of course, does the Dedication "Sanctorum Ide et Lyddy de Egloscruc," or, simply, "Sancta Ida."—It may be expedient, therefore, to give in full the two documents referring to this parish which are found in Bishop Stafford's Register:—

I. "INDULGENCIA":—"Universis Sancte Matris Ecclesiæ filiis, ad quos presentes litere pervenerint, Edmundus, miseracione divina Exoniensis Episcopus, salutem in Eo per Quem fit remissio peccatorum. Mortuorum memoria eo cunctis prestancior esse dinoscitur quo magis cedit vivis ad meritum et prestat suffragia resolutis. Volentes, igitur, mentes Fidelium ad orandum pro defunctis per allectiva Indulgenciarium munera propensius excitare de Dei Omnipotentis immensa misericordia, et gloriosissime Virginis Marie, Genetricis Ejusdem, ac Beatorum Apostolorum Petri et Pauli, patronorum nostrorum, Omniumque Sanctorum meritis et precibus confidentes, omnibus parochianis nostris, et aliis quorum Diocesani hanc nostram Indulgenciam ratam habuerint pariter et acceptam, de peccatis suis vere penitentibus et confessis, qui pro anima Domine Matildis Chyverston, cujus corpus in Ecclesia Sanctorum Idi et Lidi, Martirorum, in Cornubia requiescit humatum, et pro animabus omnium Fidelium defunctorum, Oracionem Dominicam cum Salutacione Angelica, dixerint mente pia, quadraginta dies Indulgencie tociens quociens concedimus per presentes. In cujus rei testimonium sigillum nostrum cum impressione signeti nostri in dorso presentibus est appensum. Datum in Hospicio nostro London ensi, xviij° die mensis Octobris, Anno Domini Millmo CCCmo nonagesimo nono, et nostre Consecracionis Anno Quinto.—i, 31.

II. Edmundus, miseracione Divina Exoniensis Episcopus, dilecto in Christo filio, Magistro Benedicto Canterbury, Officiali nostre Peculiaris Jurisdiccionis in Cornubia, salutem, graciam, et benediccionem. Quia dilecti nostri in Christo filii, Decanus et Capitulum Ecclesie nostre Cathedralis, per suas literas patentes, vobis cum presentibus exhibendas, dilectum nobis Dominum Henricum Nanskelly, capellanum, ad perpetuam vicariam Ecclesie parochialis Sancte Ide, alias Egloscruk, in Cornubia, nostre Diocesis, per resignacionem Domini Johannis Nanskelly, ultimi ipsius vicarie Vicarii, ut asseritur, vacantem, presentarunt. Nos, vero, attendentes quod nulla racio verisimile reddit ut quisquam beneficium multis forte expensis et laboribus adquisitum, quo sustentari debet, precipue cum nullum habeat aliud beneficium, facile, sine magna causa, sponte resignet, vobis, igitur, committimus et mandamus quatinus dicto Domino Johanni Nanskelly, in vestra presencia personaliter constituto, de causis resignacionis hujusmodi ob quas videlicet prefatam vicariam suam resignare et dimittere intendit, et de rei veritate earundem, necnon si pacto aliquo illicito vel simoniaca pravitate intercedente, seu dolo, fraude, metu, aut oppressione aliqua inductus seu coactus resignacionem hujusmodi fecit aut interposuit, et an in eadem voluntate resignandi et dimittendi beneficium suum hujusmodi adhuc perseveret, ac ceteris in ea parte de jure requisitis inquiratis et vos informetis. Et in eventum quo per inquisicionem et informacionem hujusmodi inveneritis resignacionem hujusmodi fore liberam, spontaneam, et in omnibus licitam et canonicam, Ad admittendam et recipiendam in forma juris resignacionem hujusmodi, dummodo de sufficienti et congrua sustentacione eidem Domino Johanni quam diu vixerit ministranda de qua contentari ... [a blank is left here], super quo vestram consciencium oneramus, coram vobis fiat fides et ydonee caveatur; ac dictum Dominum Henricum ad eandem vicariam Sancte Ide, alias Egloscruk, cum residendi inibi onere, secundum formam Constitucionum Dominorum Othonis et Octoboni, quondam Apostolice Sedis in Anglia legatorum in hac parte editorum juratum, ac jure presentantis et meritis presentati ad eandem ac ceteris articulis et circumstanciis universis in hac parte de jure necessariis et opportunis vobis constiterit ad plenum, nichilque in ea parte obviaverit de canonicis institutis in forma juris admittendi ipsumque Vicarium perpetuum instituendi canonice in eadem cum suis juribus et pertinenciis universis; juramentum quoque canonice obediencie in forma solita ab eodem Domino Henrico nomine nostro recipiendi, ipsumque in corporalem possessionem dicte vicarie juriumque et pertinenciarum universorum ejusdem inducendi seu induci mandandi et faciendi, ceteraque omnia et singula faciendi, exercendi, et expediendi que in premissis et circa ea necessaria fuerint seu quomodolibet oportuna—Vobis, de cujus fidelitate et industria plene confidimus, committimus vices nostras et plenariam in Domino potestatem. Et quid in premissis feceritis nos hujusmodi negocio expedito debite certificatis, per literas vestras patentes, harum ac tocius processus vestri in hac parte habendi seriem, sigillo vestri officii consignatas.—Dat. in Manerio nostro Criditonensi xvto die mensis Julii, Anno Domini Millmo Quadringentesimo, et nostre Consecracionis Anno Sexto.—ii, 227b.

There is no record of his institution, but it seems that it was accidentally omitted; for at ii, 48b, in the margin, I find the following memorandum:—"Hic deficit Institucio Vicarii de Egloscruk."[1] The date must have been 23 July, 1400; and Henry Nanskelly was, doubtless, intended; but he is not mentioned by name. John Nanskelly, the resigning Vicar, was instituted, by Bishop Brantingham, 26 April, 1382; he was V. of Launcells, and exchanged with Rd. Doty, who is described as Vicar of the Church "Sanctorum Ide et Lydi de Egloscruk."

St. Ive [" Sancti Ivonis, MS.], John Osborn, R., i, 49b.

Wm. Dybere, R., had licence of non-residence for a year (*contemplacione nobilis viri domini Humfridi Stafford, militis, dummodo interim in ipsius steterit obsequiis*), from 3 July, 1402; i, 61.—Rob. Heye, of Heye, *see* "Oratories," i, 68.

St. Ives [Saucte Ye, Virginis, MS.]—

Licence was granted, 3 May, 1400, "habitatoribus ville de Porthya" for their Chapel "de Porthya, infra parochiam de Lananta situata," i, 89b.—*See* Lelant, i, 133b; ii, 232b.—John Stephyn, "de Porthia," i, 14, 14b.

St. John of Jerusalem, Hospital of,—

The Bishop addresses the Archdeacons, Deans-Rural, and Clergy generally, concerning the Letters of Pope Alexander V. on behalf of the said Hospital; granting an Indulgence to the Faithful who should contribute to its support (10 March, 1410-11), i, 117b. And again, 16 March, 1410-11), i, 120b.

St. John-in-Cornwall, Walter Boway, R., i, 334.—

To John Michel, R.; licence of non-residence was granted for two years (*contemplacione nobilis viri domini Edwardi Courtenay Comitis Devonie*"), and a sequestration relaxed, 4 April, 1403, i, 63.—Thos. Ralegh, R., obtained licence of non-residence from 5 March, 1417-18, to Michaelmas, 1418; i, 238b.—Thos. Wattekyn, R., ii, 153.

St. Just-in-Penwith; [Nicholas Harry (?)], V., i, 103.

St. Kea [Landege, MS.]—

A question arose as to the taxation of the Vicarage of this Church, and the Bishop caused the Register of Walter I. (i.e. Bronescombe) to be examined:

---

[1] It is curious that the next entry (ii, fol. 228) is the subject of a like accidental omission in the regular Record of Institutions.—"Item, eisdem die et loco, emanavit consimilis Commissio Johanni, Priori Prioratus de Plympton directa, ad admittendum Gilbertum Baker, capellanum ad perpetuam vicariam ecclesie parochialis de Bokelond, Exoniensis Diocesis, per liberam resignacionem Domini Willelmi Grym, ultimi Vicarii ejusdem; ad presentacionem Religiosorum virorum Abbatis et Conventus de Bokelond, Cisterciensis Ordinis, ut in forma superius annotatur." But at fol. 49 I find only, in the margin, "Hic deficit Institucio Vicarii de Bokelond."

it was found that that Prelate "die Jovis post Festum Assumpcionis Beate Marie, 1270," assigned to the V. the whole altilage of the Mother-Church, and of the Chapels of Kenwen [*hodie* Kenwyn] and Tregeufedon [Tregavethan ?], "exceptis decimis fabarum et pisorum in campis crescencium." He was, also, to have all the buildings, with the whole "sanctuary," pertaining to the said church and chapels; to pay £3 yearly to the Canons of Glasney, and to bear all burdens whatsoever (10 Nov., 1416), i, 228.

St. Keverne [Sancti Kierani, MS.]—

The Bishop licensed (13 May, 1403), the Chapel of St. John Bapt. at Lesteuder [*hodie* Lestowder], for celebrations on the Feasts of that Saint's Nativity and Decollation, i, 64[b]. [*Breve Regium*—12 Feb., 1416-17].—Wm. Bray, V.; Mandate to appear before the Barons of the Exchequer at Westminster, to make answer concerning certain goods and chattels of his—viz., 1 *portiforium*, worth 40s.; 2 horses, worth 10 marks; 3 beds "cum capitalibus," worth 30s.; 3 pairs of "blankettes," worth 20s.; 4 pairs of sheets (*listhiaminum*), worth 26s. 8d.; 3 togas, worth 60s.; 2 *basilardi harnesiati* in silver, worth 5 marks; 2 silver belts, worth 40s.; 3 bankers; 6 cushions (*quyssons*), worth 13s. 4d.; 2 tables (*tabule mensales*), and 2 pairs of trestles (*trestularum*), worth 10s.; 3 forms with one chair (*cathedra*), worth 5s.; 3 table-cloths (*mappe mensales*), and 3 napkins (*manutergia*), worth 20s.; 2 washbasins (*lavatoria*) with 2 ewers (*pelves*), worth 10s.; 3 brazen pots (*olle*) and 3 small dishes (*patelle*), worth 30s.; 20 plates of tin, worth 6s. 8d.; 1 silver cup (*ciphus*), worth 20s.; 12 silver spoons (*cocliaria*), worth 26s. 8d.; 3 chests, worth 13s. 4d.; and other goods and chattels and divers utensils for household use to the value of £10, all forfeit to the King, the said Wm. having been outlawed 29 Sept., 7 Henry IV. (1405), at the suit of the Abbot of Beaulieu. Also, concerning all the revenues of the Vicarage from the said 29 Sept., ii, 360[b]. [*Breve Regium*—28 April, 1417]—Mandate to the Bishop, to relax the sequestration of the said goods and chattels, *ibid.*

St. Kew [Lanou and Lannow; *also* "Sancti Doquini"[1] (i, 48), MS.]—Nicholas [Tresulgan][2], V., a Penitentiary in the Deanery of Trigg-Minor, i. 49[b], 217, 231, 238, 245[b].

Commission to enquire as to the interdict laid on this church and on that of St. Neot's certain persons having been permitted to preach therein, who had no authority or licence from the Bishop (17 May, 1412), ii, 246. It appears (i, 161[b]) that John Burgh, chaplain, was the irregular preacher at St. Kew, and (i, 161) Walter Treyngoff, M.A., at St. Neot's: both interdicts were relaxed, 11 June, 1412.—*See* Bokelly *and* Helygan (*Oratories*).

St. Keyne [Sancte Keyne, MS.]; Thomas Haweley, R., licence of non-residence for a year from 18 April, 1397, i, 12.

Commission directed to Rd. Hals (25 Aug., 1397); sequestration of the revenues for waste and dilapidation, ii, 213.—[*Breve Regium*—14 May, 1396]; Prohibition to admit to [Seynt Kayne, MS.], pending litigation as to the patronage between John Hauley and Thos. Spencer; ii, 303[b].

---

[1] This is very curious. A Sanctus Docwinus founded a Monastery in Llandaff (*See* Rees' Welsh Saints, 183, and Index), and these Welsh Saints frequently appear in Cornwall. Another name of St. Kew is Landoho or Lanehoc (*Domesday*) or Lantloho, i.e. Lan-doc (Docwinus), softened afterwards into Lannow. Rees identifies Docwinus with Cyngar, and says that his church in Glamorganshire is Llandoch. In Prynne's Records, iii, 718, "S. Landoco" actually occurs. —C.W.B., Ex. Coll. Oxon.

[2] He was V. in 1388 (as we learn from Bishop Brantingham's Register), and was living as late as 1418-19 (i, 245[b]); only his Christian name is given in Stafford's Register.

St. Leonard's, Exeter; Matthew Stoke, R., i, 106^{b}.—The Anchorite of, i, 301.

St. Mabyn, John Restaurek, R., a Penitentiary in the Deanery of Trigg-minor, i, 93^{b}, 115^{b}, 143^{b}, 174, 194^{b}, 207^{b}; *see* ii, 72.—Helygan; *see Oratories*, i, 56.

St. Madron [Sancti Maderni, MS.]—

Chapel of St. Bridget, licensed 22 Sept., 1400, i, 49; Chapel of St. Morwetha, licensed [the Bishop was staying at the time "in domo habitacionis Willelmi Tregilliowe apud Marchiow (Marazion)"]; for Rd. Reche, chaplain, "absque prejudicio matricis ecclesie, dum tamen eorum quorum interest accedat consensus ...... proviso quod parochianis dicte vicarie Sacramenta et Sacramentalia sine licencia vicarii, sive procuratoris sui, nullo modo in eadem capella ministret," 17 April, 1409), i, 89.—Questions having arisen as to the taxation of this Vicarage, the Bishop caused the Register of Walter de Stapeldon to be searched. It was found that Nicholas Arthur, of Tintagel, had been presented to the said Vicarage by W. de Tothale, Prior of the Hospital of St. John of Jerusalem in England, and that he had been duly admitted and instituted. That Bishop, at the same time, determined the Vicar's portion; giving him the entire Sanctuary, with the house of residence thereon, and also the whole altilage *cum decima piscarie*. He was to entertain in the said house the Prior, and any of the Brethren who might visit the parish; but at their own expense. The Vicars were to pay procurations and Synodals, and keep up the books, vestments, and other ornaments of the Church pertaining to the Rectory thereof, as well as the glass of the windows in the chancel and the chancel roof, after they had once for all been put in thorough order by the said Religious, who were to bear all other ordinary and extraordinary burdens in connection with the said chancel. At Pentecost and at All Saints, the Vicar was to pay, yearly, to the said Religious in the said parish-church a pension of four marks, in equal sums; the Vicar above-mentioned having sworn, after his institution, that he would faithfully pay the said pension. The Bishop reserved to himself and his successors the right to augment, diminish, or vary the Vicar's portion, at discretion. This Taxation is dated London, 3 Id. Marcii, 1309; and Bishop Stafford's "Scrutinium," 12 March, 1414-15; i, 208^{b}.

St. Martin's-by-Looe; John Gyles, R.,—

He obtained a dispensation (to study at Oxford), for 2 years, from 5 Aug., 1396; i, 9.—John Cergeaux, R: the like dispensation, from 3 Oct., 1397 (with Letters Dimissory, granted on the same day, i, 13^{b}; and repeated, 13 Jan., 1397-8; i, 14^{b}. He obtained the like dispensation (when sub-deacon), 4 Oct., 1399, i, 31: also, 3 Oct., 1401, i, 58; and again (but for one year), 18 Oct, 1403, by which time he was LL.B., but still a sub-deacon, i, 68.

St. Mary Church; Hugh de Hyckelyng. *See* his Will, i, 326.

St. Matthias, the Apostle, Feast of,—

The Bishop's certificate to the Archbishop as to the publication of his Mandate for the due observance, throughout the Province, of the vigil thereof (14 March, 1410-11), i, 119^{b}.

St. Maur, Ela, presents to Black Torrington, ii, 81^{b}.

St. Mawgan-in-Kirier; Martin Lercedekne, R. (Canon of Exeter),—

He was licensed as a Publick Preacher (2 June, 1410), and on the same day obtained licence of non-residence for a year; but he was to reside at Exeter, as Canon, i, 97.

St. Mawgan-in-Pydar [" de Lanherne," ii, 333],—
The Bishop having been informed of serious dilapidations in the chancel of the parish church, the buildings, and enclosures, through the neglect of Wm. Hendre, the late R., directed a Commission to Benedict Canterbury, R. of Camborne, to ascertain what moneys Wm. Hendre had received from his predecessor, how they had been laid out, and the extent of the existing dilapidations; also, the estimated cost of repairs, etc., and who was liable for the same (1 Aug., 1410), ii, 233.—Wm. Trebell, sub-deacon, R., obtained a dispensation (to study at Oxford), for 3 years, from 6 Feb., 1411-12, i, 144; and for 2 years, from 18 June, 1415, i, 210b.—Licensed, 2 Dec., 1413, to celebrate in the Chapel of St. Blaise on Christmas Day, at Easter, and on St. Blaise's day; and in the Chapel of St. James the Apostle on St. James's day: both chapels were in this parish, i, 190.

St. Mawnan [Seynt Maunan, MS.], Benedict Walesbru, R., relaxation of sequestration for non-residence (4 May, 1398), i, 18.—Rd. Gabriell, R., i, 32b.—Thos. Pytyngdon, R., i, 75b.
[*Breve Regium*]—Prohibition to admit, pending dispute between the King and John Whalesbrew (12 June, 1405), ii, 318b.—Suspended, 1 March, 1405-6; *ibid.* Meanwhile the Bishop had collated by lapse (*see* " Institutions ").
This R. [Pytyngton, MS.], obtained a dispensation, 7 July, 1406 (to study at Oxford), for one year, i, 78; and, again, 27 Aug., 1408, for *five* years, i, 86b. Before these dispensations were granted he seems to have suffered sequestration of the revenues of his benefice " occasione non residencie et absencie," which was not formally taken off till 26 Sept., 1410; i, 105.

St. Mellion [Sancti Melani, MS.],—
Baldwin Schyllyngford, R.; licence of non-residence for a year, from 30 May, 1410 (but he was to reside at Exeter, as Canon), i, 97.
Commission as to dilapidations caused by the said Baldwin, on the complaint of John Smyth, R. (28 April, 1418); ii, 265.—
Chapel of St. John Baptist. The Bishop grants an Indulgence to those who should attend there on the F. of that Saint's Nativity, and contribute to the maintenance of the fabrick (4 Nov. 1409), i, 90b. Newton [Ferrers] in. *See* Trevaga (" Oratories ") i, 238b.

St. Mewan; Henry [Gathell], R.; *see* Clok, Rd., *note*.

St. Michael Carhayes [Caryhayes, MS.],—Rd. Clok, **chaplain**, *see* Clok, Rd., *note*.

St. Michael Penkevil ["parochia de Penkevel," MS.], **Tregonyon**, *see* Halap (*Oratories*), i, 215b.

St. Michael " in periculo Maris," the Abbot of, patron of St. Michael's Mount, Cornwall, ii, 338b, 348b.

St. Michael's Mount, the Prior in arrear of Procuration to the Pope's collector for 3 years, 1408—1410; i, 105, 110.
Commission, directed to the Archdn. of Cornwall (31 July, 1410), to enquire as to the patronage of this Priory; Henry, Prince of Wales, had presented Wm. Lambert, monk, ii, 233,—
[*Breve Regium*—Sancti Michaelis de Monte Tumba in Cornubia," MS.]—The King requires the Bishop to certify him as to the names, etc., of all Priors inst. there from the time of Edw, [I], son of Henry [III]; 5 Feb. 1410-11; ii, 338.—The Bishop received it 20 March, and certified, 9 April,

as follows :—He had caused the Register to be searched for the period indicated, and had found (I.), in the Reg. of Walter I [i.e. Bp. Bronescombe], that on the day of St. Thomas Apost. [21 Dec.], 1266, in London, that Bishop admitted *Ralph de Cartaret*, on the presentation of the Abbot of St. Michael's-in-periculo-maris ; also, that 3 Id. Apr. [11 April], 1275, at Flokeston, he collated *Rd. Perer*, monk of St. Michael's-in-periculo-maris, *by lapse.* (II.) in the Reg. of Walter II [i.e. Bp. Stapledon], 12 Sept., 1316, at Paignton, Brother *Peter de Cara Villa*, monk of St. Michael's-in-periculo-maris, was admitted on the resignation of Brother *Geoffrey de Gernon*, [who had been inst. 9 July, 1283 (patron, the same)] ; also (III.) in the Reg. of Bishop Grandisson, that, 3 Oct., 1349, at Clyst, that Prelate admitted Brother *John Hardy*, priest, monk of St. Michael's-in-periculo-maris, patron, the same ; and 24 April, at Chudleigh, Brother *John de Volant*, monk and priest, on the death of Brother John Hard *(sic)*, patrons the same ; (IV.) In the Reg. of Thos. Brantingham, that 7 Dec., 1385, in London, that Bishop admitted Brother *Rd. Auncell*, monk of Tavistock, on the presentation of K. Richard II., on account of the war with France : (V.) in Stafford's own Register that, 21 Oct., 1410, at [Bishop's] Tawton, he had admitted Brother *Wm. Lambert*, monk of Tutbury (Dioc. of Lichfield), on Auncell's death ; K. Henry IV. presenting.—ii, 338ᵇ. [Two Priors are omitted in this List, viz., Nicholas Isabel, inst. 24 Sept., 1312, and Rd. Harepath (see Brantingham's Reg., ii, 91).]

[*Breve Regium.*—24 Nov., 1413] ; the King to be certified, as to the Priory being "conventualis necne," ii, 347ᵇ.—The Bishop's Certificate to the King :—He had caused diligent search to be made in the Registers of his predecessors. with the following result :—(I.) Reg. of Walter I. ; on 3 Id. (i.e. 11) Apr. 1265 (*sic*), at Flokeston, the Bishop collated by *lapse*, Rd. Perer, monk of &c.—(II.) Register of Peter [Quivil] ; on 7 Id. (i.e. 9) Jul., 1283, at Legh Canonicorum, he admitted Geoffrey de Sernon *(sic)*, on the presentation of the Abbot, &c. of St. M.-in-peric.-maris.—(III.) Register of Walter II. ; there was found therein an "Ordinacio" of the Vicarage of St. Hilary, appropriated to St. Michael's Mount (which is recited at large)—(IV.) Register of John de Grandisson ; wherein is recorded that 7 *Non.* Dec. *(sic)*, 1329, at Chudleigh, Robert de Talvargh was admitted to the V. of St. Clement de Moresk, on the presentation of the Prior of St. Michael's Mount ; also that 18 Jan., 1342-3, that Bishop admitted Ralph de Restalek, priest to St. Hilary V. ; patrons, the same.—(V.) Register of Thos. Brantyngham ; wherein it was recorded that, in London, 7 Dec., 1385, was admitted Brother Rd. Auncell, monk of Tavistock, on the presentation of K. Rich. II. (because of the war with France). (VI.) Bishop Stafford himself admitted, at [Bishop's] Tawton, 21 Oct., 1400, Brother Wm. Lambert, monk of Tutbury, on Auncell's death. [17 March, 1413-14] ; ii, 348ᵇ. *See*, ii, 105.—Bequest to the Chapel on the Mount, i, 314ᵇ.

St. Minver [Sancte Minerve, MS.], John Coulyng or Cowlyng, V., i, 107ᵇ ; a Penitentiary in the Deanery of Trigg-minor [Sancte Minfrede, MS.], i, 143ᵇ, 174, 194ᵇ, 207ᵇ, 217, 231, 238, 245ᵇ.

St. Morwetha, Chapel of [Morvah], *see* St. Madron, i, 89.

St. Neot's [Sancti Nioti, MS.], *see* St. Kew, i, 161 ; ii, 246 ; *see*, also, Ermington, ii, 339.—John Treyngoff, V., i, 161.

St. Newlyn, Trevarthyan in, *see* Syreston (*Oratories*), i, 42ᵇ.

St. Nicholas Priory, Exeter ; the Bishop's Mandate for its Visitation (28 April, 1400)—dated 5 April ; i, 34ᵇ.

St. Pancras, London, Causton's Chantry in the Church of, ii, 28, 210ᵇ.

St. Paul's, London, the Dean and Chapter of, present to Hutton, ii, 52^b, and St. John-Zachary, ii, 53.

St. Perran-Uthno[1] [simply "Sancti Perani," MS.], Chapel of St. James ;—

Licence to John Andrew, a layman, to erect the same with an Indulgence to the faithful who should assist in the work (12 Sept., 1400), i, 47.—Licence was granted, 28 June, 1403, to Wm. Mayov, R. "de Udno Peryn," to celebrate, during pleasure, "in capella Sancti Jacobi juxta Petrys met infra parochiam de Udno," i, 67.—Renewed for 2 years only, "Rectori ecclesie parochialis Sancti Pirani" (17 April, 1409), i, 89.

St. Perran-[Zabulo] "ecclesia Sancti Pyrani,"

The Bishop had occasion to examine the Register of his predecessor, Walter Bronescombe, as to this Benefice, and found that die Martis next after the Feast of St. Laurence, 1269, being at St. Newlyn, that prelate had collated thereto, *by lapse*, one Drocus, described as *de eadem* [ecclesia] *presbiter*, assigning to him all the altilage of the Mother Church and of the Chapel, as well as all *obvenciones de turnis reliquiarum provenientes*; the said Vicar to pay 6 marks annually to the Dean and Chapter of Exeter, and undertake all burdens (15 March, 1413-14), i, 195.

St. Petrock's, Exeter, John Westecote, R.; Commissioner in the election of Matilda Talbot, Prioress of Polslo, ii, 76.

St. Pinnock, R.—

[*Breve Regium*]—In the suit, pending and undecided between K. Henry V. and Rd. Trevaga, Thos. Treȝethyan, Thos. Colyn, Michael Langakre, Isabella Penalugan, and John Stephyn, chaplain, the King requires the Bishop to examine the Registers and certify him whether Walter Lewer, clerk, temp. Ric. II, was inst. on the presentation of Sir Wm. Botreaux, knt. (as Thos. Covele, on the King's part, asserted), or not; 12 Nov., 1414; ii, 350^b.—The Bp. certified that he had examined the Register, and found that Henry Bishop of Worcester, at Whethyngdon, 21 May, 1389, commissioned thereto by Thos., late Bishop of Exeter, admitted Walter Lewer to the said R., void by the resignation of Thos. Elwel, in a case of exchange with the said Walter Lewer, R. of Cold Aiston (Dioc. of Worcester), the patrons of St. Pinnock, on that occasion, being Sir Wm. Botriaux, knt., John Kyldreynek, John Bury, Rd. Trevaga, Thos. Trethyan, Thos. Colyn, and John Churchehulle (12 Jan., 1414-15), ii, 351.—[*Breve Regium de quare impedit*—16 April, 1415], in the same case, ii, 351^b; and the Bishop's certificate (30 April, 1415) to the same effect, ii, 352.—Later on, the Bishop issued a Commission of Enquiry on the presentation of Rd. Knokya, chaplain, by Sir Wm. Botreaux, knt. (22 July, 1419), ii, 268.

St. Probus, Wm. Noe, V., a Penitentiary in the Deanery of Powder, i, 49^b, 93^b, 115^b, 143^b.—Clement Wylle, V., the same, i, 174, 194^b, 207^b.—Roger Smyth, Preb. of, i, 56^b.—*See* Trenewyth (*Oratories*), i, 72^b.

St. Ruan [Sancti Romoni, MS.], Stephen Gerveys, R.; licence of non-residence, for 2 years, from 29 Jan., 1398-9, i, 24^b.

St. Sancreed, *or* Sancreed [Sancti Sancredi, MS.]—

A special licence of non-residence was granted, 29 March, 1398, to John

---

[1] Almost certainly not "Zabulo," as suggested at p. 5 *antea*; *see* Andrew, John (who was a *layman*), and *for* "celebrate" *read* "build."

Mychel, V., for one year (to study at Oxford.) He was admitted to this benefice, "absque juramento de personaliter residendo"; and he was permitted to enjoy the entire revenues thereof, due provision being made for the cure of souls and for largess to the poor; i, 16b.

St. Sidwell's, Exeter, i, 320; and *see* Heavitree.

St. Sithney; *see* Kembell, John, i, 18.

St. Stephen's-in-Brannel [Sancti Stephani de Branell, MS.],—Thos. Cornevayll, LL.B., R.; licence of non-residence for a year, from 9 July, 1408, i, 86: also [Sancti Stephani in *Burnall*, MS.], from 14 Aug., 1409, i, 89b.

The Bishop writes (3 Oct., 1410), to the Dean of Powder and to all Curates in that Deanery, with reference to the complaint of this Rector that, whereas his Chancel was in a very dilapidated State—in ipsius coopertura defectus paciatur enormes—and he was responsible for its repair, and had hired workmen and procured materials for the purpose, certain iniquitous persons, chiefly layfolk, who had no legal right to interfere, had threatened both himself and his workmen, preventing their bringing ladders and other necessary implements into the cemetery, and effectually putting a stop to the work. The Bishop ordered the offenders to be warned that they desist from their unlawful proceedings on pain of excommunication, i, 106; and 28 Nov., he granted to Thos. Cornewayll licence of non-residence till the ensuing Michaelmas—"dum tamen cancellum ecclesie tue predicte interim in coopertura et meremio de novo construes, seu construi, ac in muris ejusdem, fenestris, et ceteris suis defectibus, competenter eundem repares, aut facias reparari," i, 109b. This licence was renewed for a year, 21 Sept., 1411; i, 135.—His successor, John Treverbyn, was a Penitentiary in the Deanery, i, 143b, 174, 194b.

St. Stephen's-by-Launceston, *see* Launceston.

St. Stephen's-by-Saltash; Erth, *see* Trenowyth (*Oratories*), i, 186; Trewalward, *see Oratories*; i, 11b.

John Crukern was inst. to this V., 30 March, 1398 (ii, 36b); on 7 Nov., the Bishop commissioned Dean Tregrisiow to enquire "an Johannes Crukern intrusit se in vicaria de Saltasch;" ii, 220b. The result is not recorded; but he held the benefice till 1408, in which year he resigned. At i, 33, I find the following document:—"Reverendo in Christo Patri ac Domino, Domino Lodowico, Dei et Apostolice Sedis Gracia Episcopo Wlteranensi, ejusdemque Sedis Nuncio et Collectori in Anglia, Edmundus, Ejusdem miseracione Episcopus Exoniensis, salutem et fraternam in Domino caritatem. Quia dilectus nobis in Christo filius, Dominus Johannes Crukern, perpetuus Vicarius ecclesie parochialis de Saltasch, nostre Diocesis, in quodam negocio perjurii et fidei lesionis ex officio vestro et ad promocionem Domini Thome Butiller Decani, sive Custodis Collegii, sive libere Capelle Regie, infra Castrum de Wyndesore, Sarumensis Diocesis, situati, ac Collegii predicti, prefate ecclesie de Saltasch proprietariorum, contra eundem Dominum Johannem Crukern, vicarium antedictum, coram vobis mota et indiscussa pendente; vestram in ea parte jurisdiccionem sua mera, libera, et spontanea voluntate, ut intelleximus, prorogavit,—Nos hujusmodi prorogacioni, quatenus de jure possumus, nostrum prebemus assensum, ipsamque prorogacionem prout ad nos attinet ratificamus, et tenore presencium approbamus, corona, dignitate et juribus regiis in omnibus semper salvis. In cujus rei testimonium sigillum nostrum presentibus est appensum. Datum in hospicio nostro Londoniensi, xxvto die mensis Novembris, Anno Domini Millesimo CCCmo, nonagesimo nono, et nostre Consecracionis Anno Quinto." —Wm. Yonge was inst., on Crukern's resignation, 8 July, 1408 (ii, 102), and seems to have, shortly afterwards, committed an outrage against his predecessor, who contined, apparently, to reside in the parish. [*Breve de venire facias*, 20 Nov., 1410]; Mandamus to the Bishop,—William Yong, chaplain, to appear before the Judges at Westminster, in the Octave of St. Hilary, to shew cause why he, and several others with him, to wit Rd. Sheborne, chaplain, John Smyth of Saltash, John Sampson, Thos. Thyngden, Wm. Buttesyde, Thos. Everell, Peter Salomon, Roger Hervy "de Aysah," Wm. Pyers, Simon Marcheford, chaplain, and Rd. Baker of Saltash, did "vi et armis" break into the closes and houses of John Crukern, clerk, at St. Stephen's and at Saltash, and at St. Stephen's did assault and beat him (treating him so shamefully that he despaired even of life), and carried off 2 horses, 5 steers, 3 pigs, and 30 sheep, his property, worth 18*l*, as well as 30 geese and 30 capons worth 40*s*., and goods and chattels to the value of 20*l*., besides committing other enormities and inflicting on him serious loss. ii, 336.—The "execucio Brevis" was committed to the Dean and the Curates of East and to Walter Dollebeare, Apparitor-General, and John Peatte (24 Dec., 1410), ii, 336b.

St Stithian's [Sancte Stediane, MS.]. Thos. [Penfern], V.; a Penitentiary in the Deanery of Kerrier, i, 49b.

St. Tudy [Sancti Tudii, MS.], *John* Welyngton, R., licence of non-residence for a year, from 15 March, 1402-3, i, 63.

He is called "John" here—a clerical error; for he is called "Richard" elsewhere in this Register, and also in the Registers of Brantingham and Lacy. His institution was not recorded; but he is mentioned, as R. of St. Tudy, as early as 1380, and as late as 1424, when he appears to have resigned (*Maclean.*) His benefice was under sequestration on account of his non-residence without authority, in 1410, on 14 Oct., in which year the sequestration was taken off, i, 108.—On 16 June, 1412, Rd. Aldryngton, R. of Lanteglos-by-Camelford, obtained a relaxation of an interdict under which his Church had been placed in consequence of Rd. Welyngton, R. of St. Tudy, having preached therein without licence, i, 161b. He was frequently appointed a Penitentiary in the Deanery of Trigg-minor, i, 243b, 174, 194b, 207b, 217, 231, 238.

St. Vepe [Sancti Vepi, MS.], Jno. Colyn, V., ii, 138b.—Langunnet in, i, 209b.

St. Veryan [Sancti Elerky, MS.]; *see* Clok, Rd., i, 24.

St. Wenn, Benedict Bollegh, V., a Penitentiary in the Deanery of Pydar, i, 207b, 217, 231, 238, 245b.

St. Winnow, *see* Moylys, John (*Oratories*).

Salcombe [Regis], bequest to the Church of, i, 312b.

Salcombe (in the Deanery of Woodleigh),—

Licence (granted 30 Jan., 1401-2), "ut in quadam Capella, in villa sive hameletta de Salcomb infra parochiam de Alvyngton [i.e., West Alvington] .... situata, *de novo erecta et constructa*, divina per quoscumque presbiteros ydoneos, sumptibus hujusmodi ville .... de Salcomb inhabitancium conducendos, absque prejudicio matricis ecclesie, valeant celebrari; dummodo ad hoc accesserit concensus (*sic*) Vicarii de Alvyngton antedicta,—per unum annum duraturam,"—i, 59. On 6 May, in the same year, this licence was renewed, "ad beneplacitum"; i, 60b.

Salisbury, John [Waltham], Bp. of, one of the consecrators of Bp. Stafford, i, 1.—*See* i, 83b; *also*, Constance, i, 203b.—Thomas Southam, Canon of, *see* Barton, Simon, i, 12.—The Friars of, i, 311.

The Dean and Chapter were patrons of Kenton, ii, 14^b, 93 ; and of West Alvington, ii, 29^b, 49^b, 85.

Salisbury, John Montacute, Earl of ; patron of Stokenham, R., ii, 42, 358.

Salisbury, Matilda, Countess of (widow of John).
She recovered her right of presentation to Stokenham R., against Thos., E. of Salisbury, and Edward Prentys, his nominee, ii, 360^b.—*See*, ii, 183, 260^b, 357^b, 358.—She presented to Okeford, ii, 108 ; 146^b, 249^b ; 179, 259^b.

Salle, William, i, 308^b.

Salman, Rd., R. of E. Lydford (Dioc. of B. and W.), exchanges for Huxham, ii, 74^b ; for Lamerton, ii, 79.

Salterne, Walter, V. (by exchange) of Chittlehampton (ii, 3, 210^b), exchanges for St. Rumbald's, Shaftesbury, ii, 86^b.

Sampford Courtenay ; Laurence Smyth, clerk, R., licence of non-residence for a year, from 6 July, 1410 ; i, 100^b ; from 21 Dec., 1411, to Michaelmas, 1412 ; i, 140^b ; a Penitentiary in the Deanery of Okehampton, i, 245^b.—*See* Passenham (*Oratories*).

Sampford Peverell ; Wm. Rowe, R., licence of non-residence for a year, from 7 April, 1413 ; i, 179^b ; for 2 years, from 12 Jan., 1413-14 ; i, 190^b.

Sampson, Wm., *see* Hurde, Rd., i, 202^b.

Sare, Roger, instituted to Alphington, ii, 10.

Sarger, John, M.A., chaplain, i, 332^b; collated Warden of Ottery, ii, 163^b ; i, 228 ; licensed as Publick-Preacher in the Diocese, 17 March, 1417-18 ; i, 238^b.

Saterlegh, Thos., patron of Satterleigh, ii, 5 (" hac vice "); 182^b (" verum patronum ") ; 261.

Sauly, David, inst. to Whitstone (Cornwall), ii, 121.

Saunder, John, monk of Tavistock, ii, 59.—John Saunder occurs as Dean of Crediton (his collation), ii, 197.

Saunder, Robert, V. of Stoke Gabriel (resigns), ii, 187^b.

Saunder, Roger, of Kingsbridge, ii, 290^b, 292.

Saunder, Thomas, i, 312.

Saunders, John, Canon in the Colleg. Ch. of Heytesbury, and Preb. of Titherington and Horningham therein (Dioc. of Salisbury), exchanges for a Preb. in St. Probus, ii, 200.

Sauplers, Robert, of York, *see* Bard, Robert, i, 17^b.

Say, Agnes, of Washfield, i, 121^b.

Sayer, John, of Canterbury, i, 20^b.
Indulgence granted for his relief (16 July, 1398). He had served the Kings of England in the wars, and having lost all his property in a fire he became inpoverished.

Scarburgh, John, *see* Washfield; ii, 259^{b}.

Schaldon, Nicholas, inst. to St. Pancras-juxta-Axmouth, ii, 120.

Schanke, Walter, i, 324^{b}; inst. to Gittisham, ii, 104.

Schapplegh, John, i, 328.—Schaple, Mabel (wife of John), i, 318^{b}.

Schaplegh, Roger, i, 327^{b}.

Schapelegh, Thos., inst. to Salcombe [Regis], ii, 110^{b}; exchanges for Nether-Lyme, ii, 163^{b}.

Schavyshylle, Peter, chaplain, i, 315.

Scheldrake, Alice, John, and William, i, 325.

Schepey, Thos. (sub-deacon), inst. to Atherington, R., q.v.; ii, 91^{b}; i, 94^{b}, 205^{b}, 212, 235.

Schephurd, Henry, i, 308^{b}.

Schephurde, Roger, literate—*Dispensacio super defectu natalium* (13 June, 1400), i, 42^{b}.

Schere, John, chaplain, i, 48^{b}; inst. to Ashbury, ii, 181^{b}.

Schere, Thos., clerk—*Dispensacio super defectu natalium* (14 Sept,, 1400), i, 48^{b}; inst. to Inwardleigh, ii, 108^{b}.

Scherleton, Robert, *see* St. Keverne (*Institutions*), ii, 88^{b}.

Schetcote, Henry, of Ermington, ii, 277.

Scheterne, Robert, R. of Uploman, resigns, ii, 7^{b}.

Schirford, John, R. of St. Augustine's "ad portam" (London), exchanges for Marhamchurch, ii, 122; i, 107, 178; his death [Shyrfford, MS.], ii, 188, 263^{b}.

Schirrigg, Thos. de, R. of Stokenham, ii, 358.

Schute, John, chaplain, i, 313^{b}, 332^{b}, 333, 334:—

He was V. of Bishop's Nympton, i, 78^{b}; inst. to Meavy, ii, 50^{b}; i, 56, 74, 79; collated to Paignton, ii, 94^{b}; i, 86^{b}, 169^{b}, 172^{b}, 175, 176, 201^{b}, 202, 322^{b}; ii, 111, 160^{b}; resigns Meavy, ii, 98; collated to a Canonry in Ottery, ii, 173^{b}; also to St. Breoke, ii, 175, 258^{b}; resigns Paignton, ii, 177^{b}; collated to a Canonry in the Cathedral, ii, 185^{b}; resigns his Canonry and seventh Preb. in Ottery, ii, 186; resigns St. Breoke, and is collated to the Archdeaconry of Exeter, ii, 187^{b}; i, 235, 243^{b}, 244, 247, 248; collated to a Canonry in Crediton, ii, 196^{b}.

Schute, William, R. of Tedburn St. Mary (deceased), ii, 196^{b}.

Schypwaysch, John, *see* Tankert, John, i, 127.

Scobehill, Robert, i, 309.

Scoche, Wm. *see* Heanton Punchardon, ii, 251^{b}.

Scodier, Thos., clerk—

Breve Regium (25 Jan., 1395); in compliance with which the Bishop (25 June) granted an annual pension of two-and-a-half marks to the said Thos., on the occasion of his own then recent elevation to the See of Exeter; ii, 303.

Scorch, John, V. of Harpford, exchanges for Bicton, ii, 11, 223; his death, ii, 14.

Scos, Wm., and Rosa his wife, de Loperygg (*hodie* Lupridge),—
[*Breve Regium*—26 May, 1397]; "de inquirendo an Rosa, uxor Willelmi Scos, fuerat matrimonialiter copulata Johanni Herewodeshore."—Peter, son and heir of John Whitlegh, denied that they had been married; but Wm. and Rosa deposed to the fact that they were married at the door of Hilberton (*sic*) Church, and undertook to prove the same, when, where, and as, the Court should determine. The King commanded the Bp. to make inquisition and report the result to the Judges at Westminster, in the Octave of St. Michael. So the Bishop directed Rd. Hals, clerk, to enquire and certify, which he did, 10 Oct., to the effect that he had clearly ascertained that the said John and Rosa were married in the Church of Ugborough [Ugeburgh, MS.], the said John being less than 8 years old, and that they lived together till he was in his 13th year, when he died; but that as to the consummation of the marriage there was no proof either way:—ii, 305

Scotte, Rd. of Landcross, *see* Badecock, John, i, 163.

Scoy, John, "de Louthorp," V. of Mayfield, exchanges for Seaton, ii, 82; for St. Michael's, Bristol, ii, 84ᵇ.

Scrop, Sir Henry, knt., co-patron of Loddiswell, R., ii, 83ᵇ.

Scryven, John, literate,—*Dispensacio super defectu natalium* (3 April, 1400), i, 34;—"tecum qui, ut asseris, milicie ascribi desideras clericali, auctoritate nostra ordinaria misericorditer dispensamus."

Scryvener, John, *see* Wille, John, ii, 198ᵇ.

Seaton; John [Hoker], V.; a Penitentiary in the Deanery of Honiton, i, 94, 115, 143, 173ᵇ, 194, 207ᵇ, 216ᵇ, 231, 237ᵇ; his Will, i, 331ᵇ.

Segrom, Robert, of Apuldram, ii, 293ᵇ.

Seke, Richard, priest,—
Without the Bishop's licence, he had been ordained deacon by the Bp. of Pisa, and priest by the Bp. of Winchester,—Dispensation in his favour (5 Sept., 1406), i, 78ᵇ.

Seek (*or* Seke), Rob., inst. to Trevalga, ii, 13ᵇ; his death, ii, 90.

Selby, Wm., R. of Phillack, i, 62, 76ᵇ.

Selman, Nicholas, chaplain,—
He was Canon of Plympton Priory, and was licensed as Publick-Preacher in the Deaneries of Totnes, Plympton, Tavistock, and Tamerton (22 Sept., 1414), i, 199ᵇ; sub-prior of Plympton, i, 245.

Selman, Richard, V. of Lamerton (deceased), ii, 144.

Sergeant, John, R. of Milton Damarel, ii, 22, 341ᵇ; his death, ii, 132ᵇ, 238.

Serle, John and William (brothers), i, 307ᵇ.

Serll, Wm., R. of Broadoak (deceased), ii, 68ᵇ.

Seteburgh, in the parish of Parkham, i, 72ᵇ.

Seton, Christina, Prioress of Polslo (deceased), ii, 76.

Seton, John, clerk, *see* Newton Ferrers, ii, 363ᵇ.

Seward, John, R. of Alverdiscott (resigns), ii, 19ᵇ.

Seymere, John, chaplain, i, 332[b].

Seyncler, Raulyn, i, 312.

Seys, John, chaplain, i, 306.

Sharshull, John de, Precentor of the Cathedral, i, 239.

Shaftesbury, St. Rumbald's, ii, 86[b].

Shaldon, Nicholas, R. of St. Pancras, Exeter, i, 173.

Shebbear [Scheftbeare *and* Schebbere, MS.], *see Oratories*,—Hankeford, i, 78; and Alvecote, i, 92[b]. *See*, also, Holand, John, i, 207.

Sheepwash [Schepwasch, MS.], *see* Holand, John, *ibid.*

Schene, Monastery of St. Bridget at,—

Margaret, an anchorite near Bodmin licensed to migrate to (10 March, 1415-16), i, 218.

Shepton, the Chapel at, i, 312[b].

Sherborne [Schirborn, MS.], the Abbot and Convent of, present to Seaton, ii, 82[b], 84[b], 193, 265[b].—*See*, also, i, 320[b].

Sherford [" Schyreford, infra fines et limites ecclesie parochialis de Stokenham "],—

John Hals and Agnes (relict of John) Govys, of this parish, intending to marry, their banns were published once, and the Bishop granted a special license to John Dene, the parochial chaplain of Sherford, to celebrate the marriage at once, having first, on the same day published the banns for the second time (6 Oct., 1412), i, 168[b].—*See*, also, Bokete, Nicholas, ii, 261; also, i, 330[b].

Sherlond, John, proxy for Henry Maupas, ii, 105[b].

Shevioke [Schevyok, MS.], John Godwyn, R.: license of non-residence for two years (*see* Bridestowe, *note* ([b]), i, 76[b].—Richard [Donscombe], R.; for a year, from 25 July, 1410, i, 101; from 9 Jan., 1412-13 to Michaelmas, 1413, i, 173.

Shillingford, Rd. Skydemore, R.; i, 58[b].

Shillingford [*also*, Schyllyngford, etc., MS.], Baldwin de, clerk: i, 308;—

He was patron of St. Mary Arches, Exeter, ii, 9; of Shillingford, ii, 9[b], 19[b]; of St. Mary-Steps, ii, 81[b], 124[b], 140[b]; R. of St. Mellion, i, 97; he died Canon of Crantock and of Exeter, ii, 189[b], 190, 265; his Will, i, 330.—John, his brother (LL.D.), was Official-Principal (Commission dated 20 June, 1395), ii, 209; *see* Rugge, Robert, ii, 211; collated to a Canonry in the Cathedral, ii, 78, 79; exchanged his R. of Rotherfield (Dioc. of Chichester) for Ugborough, ii, 84; i, 76, 77; his death, ii, 92, 93[b]; his Will, i, 308. He was proxy for Adam Davenport, ii, 183. *See*, also, i, 330[b].

Shillingham, in St. Stephen's-by-Saltash, *see* Wolf (*Oratories*).

Shiplegh, John, *see* Dean Prior, ii, 355.

Shirley, John, inst. to Roche, ii, 8[b]; resigns, ii, 12[b], inst. again, ii, 51[b]; deprived, ii, 57[b].

Shirwell [Shyrwyll, MS.],—

Commission as to dilapidations on the complaint of Wm. Seshevyle against Edw. Fysshacre, his predecessor (2 April, 1416), ii, 258^{b}.

Shobrooke [Schokbrok, MS.]; John Isaak, R.; licence of non-residence for a year from 24 Aug., 1395, i, 5; and [Ysak, MS.], from 22 Oct., 1399, i, 32^{b}.—Wm. Humberston, R. [Schokebrok, MS.]; for 2 years, from 12 June, 1401, i, 56^{b}; for one year from 3 Dec., 1403, i, 69^{b}.—Wm. Derwent, R., for one year, from[1] ... March, 1407-8, i, 84.

Shogger, Rob., and Joan his wife (of Crediton), i, 305^{b}; Walter, and Joan his wife, i, 305.

Shordich, Thos., *see* Brixham, ii, 258^{b}.

Shrewsbury Colleg. Ch. of, *see* Crantock (*Institutions, &c.*), ii, 43.

Shuppe, Wm. of Apuldram, ii, 293^{b}.

Shute, near Axminster, i, 311^{b}.

Sidbury; Thos. Rawlyn, V., i, 318. — Wm. Brown, V., a Penitentiary in the Deanery of Aylesbeare, i, 94, 115, 143, 173^{b}, 194, 207^{b}, 216^{b}, 231, 237^{b}, 245.—*See* Ingram, Nigel, i, 174^{b}; *also*, i, 326^{b}, 328^{b}, 329.—Robert Wonard, of Sidbury [Sydebyry, MS.], *see* Wonard, i, 229.

Silverton; Wm. Oterhampton, R.,—

He obtained licence of non-residence for a year from 9 July, 1396, i, 9; also [Sulferton, MS.], for 2 years from 1 May, 1399, (*contemplacione nobilis viri domini Mathei Gornay, militis*), i, 26^{b}; also, for 3 years from 4 July, 1401; (*dummodo in obsequiis nobilis viri Mathei Gournay, militis, steterit, ac domos et edificia Rectorie sue medio tempore faciat competenter reparari*), i, 57^{b}; and again, for 3 years from 23 Sept., 1405 (*dummodo in obsequiis, etc.*, as before), i, 76^{b}. He appears to have neglected the required repairs; for, 13 Sept., 1408, licence of non-residence for 2 years was granted to him on condition that they should be properly carried out, i, 86^{b}. Also [Sylferton, MS.], from 21 Aug. to Michaelmas, 1410, and from Michaelmas to the Feast of St. Matthew next following, i, 103^{b}.—Commissions, (1) Inquisition as to dilapidations, on the complaint of R. Hoper, R., against Oterhampton (16 Jan., 1415-16), ii, 257^{b}.—(2) For sequestration of effects (22 Jan., 1415-16), *ibid.*

[*Breve Regium*—14 Oct., 1414];—Prohibition to admit, pending settlement of the dispute as to the patronage between Sir John Tiptoft, knt., and Rob. Cary, Esquire; ii, 349^{b}.

[*Breve Regium*—19 Oct., 1414];—Prohibition, etc., pending settlement of dispute between John Wadham and Sir John Tiptoft, knt. and his wife Philippa; ii, 350.—*See*, also, Oterhampton (*Oratories*), i, 178^{b}.

Skardevyle, William, of Funtington, ii, 280, 281^{b}.

Skede [*or* Skydye], Thos., V. of Bridgerule, exchanges for the Chantry at Morthoe, ii, 100^{b}; for the Chantry at Raleigh, ii, 137; resigns, ii, 182^{b}.

Skelton, Richard, R. of Uplyme, ii, 12.

---

[1] "Item, ... die mensis Marcii," MS.; this entry comes between 24 Feb. and 8 March.

Skewyhek, Matthias de, V. of St. Hilary (circa 1260), ii, 348b.

Skewys, John, co-patron of Landewednack, ii, 78.

Skydemore, Rd., inst. to Shillingford, ii, 19b; i, 58b; proxy for John Schillyngford, ii, 84.

Skynner, John, R. of Trentishoe, exch. for Westleigh, ii, 188b; his death, ii, 194b.

Skynner, Rd. (chaplain), i, 302; (clerk), i, 326, 326b, 328b; (priest), ii, 5.

Skynner, Thomas, and Margaret, dau. of John, i, 330b.

Skyrdon, William and Joan his wife, i, 304.

Skyres, Robert del, Preb. of Chulmleigh, resigns, ii, 101.

Skystelyng, John, clerk; *see* Ottery, ii, 278.

Slade, Wm., V. of Axmouth, i, 9b; proxy for Wm. Wythie, ii, 36; resigns, and becomes Warden of Ottery, ii, 212.

Slapton, the Collegiate Chantry and Parish-Church of—

Mandate for the Visitation (on 14 May, 1400), i, 36b; i, 317b, 332b.—Appropriation thereto of the Rectory of Loddiswell, ii, 288-290b.—Patrons of Loddiswell V., ii, 153; of Poundstock (on the nomination of Rob. Hulle, senior), ii, 164, 180.—John Combe, *Minister* of, i, 302b.—Wm. Cote, *Minister*, ii, 357b.—Canon Trote's Legacies to, i, 302b; John Ulveston's, i, 330b.

Election of Rector: It was notified to the Bishop, at Crediton, 22 May, 1410, (by John Schete, V. of Paignton, one of three proxies herein—the others being Peter Holdych, Minister of the said Chantry, and Wm. Floyer, chaplain, on behalf of Wm. Coote, Sacristan, Thomas Ferrour, senior, John Myldebyry, priests, Arnulph Langarygge, Thomas Ferrour, junior, Richard Champarnon, and Thomas Taylour, clerks, all of the said Chantry), that John Bouryng, priest, had been elected. Walter Danyel, the late R., died 16 March, 1409-10, and was buried the day following. The patron, Robert Lovel (Lord of the Manor, by right of his wife, Elizabeth, grand-daughter of Guy de Bryan), having given the Community licence to elect, they met in the Chapter-House, 2 May, 1410, and appointed the 5th for the election, which took place accordingly, in the presence of John Twyford, notary-publick, and other witnesses, to wit, Rd. Olyver, R. of [East] Allington (who presided), and John Comb, R. of [North] Huish. The Bishop's Mandate for the proclamation (dated at Crediton, 23 May), was directed to the said John Comb and to John Ulveston, V. of Stokenham, who complied therewith on Sunday, 1 June, in the Chapel of the said College, and in the parish-church and village of Slapton, and certified the Bishop to that effect on the day following. The election was confirmed, and the Bishop's Mandate for Induction and Installation issued, 3 June, 1410: ii, 111—114b.—*See* Bouryng, John, i, 131, 132. He was a Penitentiary in the Deanery of Woodleigh, i, 245.

Sleghe, John, presents to Honeychurch, ii, 95.

Sleghe, William, of Kenton, i, 318.

Slocok, Thomas, i, 325.

Sloman, Brian, V. of Northam (deceased), ii, 88.

Smale, John, i, 332.—

A Commission was directed (1 Oct., 1396) to Dean Tregrosiow and Chancellor Bosoun, in the matter of John (son of Nicholas) Smale, clerk. He had been, it seems, maliciously indicted, before Wm. Rykhyll and Wm. Brynchele, Judges, for that, having been imprisoned on account of a certain alleged felony, he had feloniously broken out of gaol, by night, on the Feast of the Epiphany, 18 Ric. II., and made good his escape. "Unde idem Johannes, occasione cujusdam Inquisicionis juratorum laicorum, per prefatos Justiciarios tanquam reus criminis predicti dampnatus, *privilegio clericali* se protegens juxta Ecclesiasticam libertatem et Regni Anglie consuetudinem, nobis et carceri nostro Exoniensi extiterat liberatus." It was asserted that he was innocent, and on his humble petition that he might be permitted to clear himself of the charge the Bishop issued this Commission. Full enquiry was made, both in the neighbourhood, the prison, and at his birthplace; and trustworthy persons, who knew him well, testified that from the day of his birth, and especially at the very time when he had been charged with the said offence and thrown into prison, his life and reputation, his manners, and his conduct, were and had been uniformly good, and the Commissioners pronounced him innocent, "juxta modum et formam canonice purgacionis," and certified the Bishop accordingly (28 Oct., 1396); i, 10b.

Smale, Wm., chaplain, *see* St. Feock (note), i, 26.

One Wm. Smale, perhaps the same, was proxy for Thos. Malesouers, R. of Calstock, ii, 6b.—Walter Smale occurs, i, 331.

Smert, Hugh, inst. to All-Hallows-on-the-Walls, Exeter, ii, 98b; his death, ii, 135b.

Smithfield [Smethfeld, MS.], the Prior and Convent of St. Bartholomew's, present to Danbury (Dioc. of London), ii, 51b.

Smyth, Benet, of Northleigh, i, 312.

Smith, Edmund, *see* Helygan (*Oratories*).—Smyth, Gilbert, i, 309.

Smyth, Henry, V. of Whitchurch, ii, 9.

Smyth, Joan, *see* Row, Robert, ii, 268.

Smyth, John, V. of Hennock (deceased—1399), ii, 14.

Smyth, John, R. of Poltimore (deceased—1402-3), ii, 25b.

Smyth, John, R. of Stanton-on-the-Wold (Dioc. of York), exchanges for Loxbeare, ii, 143b.

Smyth, John, inst. to St. Mellion, ii, 190, 264b, 265.

Smyth, John, i, 304b: ii, 351b.—And *see* Throwleigh.

Smyth, Laurence, inst. to Sampford Courtenay, ii, 114b; i, 100b; his death, ii, 201b.

[*Breve Regium—de venire facias*]: Laurence Smyth, Collector of Customs and Subsidies for the late King, in the Port of Exeter, a clerk, and beneficed in the Diocese, to render (together with John Horewode, lately also a Collector of Customs) an account of the duties remaining unpaid on all wool, hides, skins, woollen goods, and other merchandise shipped (*de omnibus lanis, coriis, pellibus, lanutis, ac aliis mercandisis . . . in navibus seu vasis in portu predicto carcatis*) by home or foreign merchants in the said Port, or exported thence to foreign parts, or conveyed to places within the Realm (12 Nov., 1414), ii, 351.

Smyth, Margery, wife of John, of Cornworthy, i, 330b.

Smyth, Roger, Warden of St. Margaret's, Chelmsford—

He exchanged for a Prebend in St. Probus, ii, 46; i, 56b; for Yate (Dioc. of Worcester), ii, 58; and, lastly, for Exminster, ii, 88.

Smyth, Stephen ; *see* Colcombe (*Institutions*) ii, 36.

Smyth, Thomas, chaplain, i, 329b.

Commission directed to Roger Beaumount, R. of Bideford, and John Sergeaunt, R. of Milton Damarel (1 Aug., 1400).—The Bishop had been informed that one Rd. Trengere had shamefully assaulted Thos. Smyth, chaplain. The Commissioners were to make inquiry, and (if necessary) inspect the wound or other injuries inflicted on the said Thos., and report to the Bishop, i, 44b.

Smyth, Wm., R. of Ashreigney (i, 49b, 101) ; resigns, ii, 156.

[*See* page 7, *note* 5 ; where it is stated, in error, that "he was also, R. of Nymet Rowland" ; there is an erasure, and the MS. is obscure]. A Wm. Smyth was Vicar in Crediton Colleg. Ch., i, 316b.—Also, a Wm. Smyth was R. of Moreleigh, ii, 159b ; i, 208b, 215 ; *see*, also, i, 314.—And Wm. Smyth "de Colmpton" was R. of Tiverton (Principal Portion) ; resigned, ii, 150b.

Snape [*or* Snap], John, i, 325.

Cousin to Can. Henry Brokelond, i, 303, 303b.—A John Snape, exch. his Can. in Crediton for Hurstbourne Priors (Dioc. of Winchester), ii, 95b.

Snelland, John, i, 332.

Snetesham, Rd., S.T.B., collated Chancellor of the Cathedral, ii, 109b ; also, Canon of Exeter, ii, 174b ; his death, ii, 181b, 182. Licensed as a Publick-Preacher in the Diocese (18 Feb., 1413-14), i, 194.

Sneynton, John, inst. to Honiton, ii, 148; i, 181b, 211b ; ii, 252.

Snowblonche, William, i, 331.

Soby, Nicholas, *see* Helygan (*Oratories*).

Sock, Dennis, i, 311b.—Socke, John, clerk, i, 312.

Solubriensis Episcopus, inst. to Torrington, ii, 174.

[Wm. Yeurde, Suffragan of Sarum, 1409-1417 ; Exon., 1415-16, Winton, 1407-17 (*Stubbs*).]—He was commissioned (4 May, 1416) to confirm, etc., in the Diocese, ii, 259, 262b.

Soltoniensis Episcopus [John Greenlaw],—

Commissioned (generally) to confirm, dedicate, consecrate, etc. (19 June, 1402), ii, 229b.—Also (specially), 22 July, 1402, to dedicate the Chapel of St. James and its cemetery, at Kingston (Ermington), *See* Kingston, ii, 229b.

Somayster, John, inst. to Thurleston, ii, 196b.

Somer, Cecilia, wife of John ; also, Walter Somer, i, 330b.

Somerford, Wm., R. of Lanreath and Canon of Glasney, i, 77 ; (deceased), ii, 109b, 115.

Somerset and Devon, Sir Wm. Bonevyll's bequests for the repair of the bridges on his demesnes in, i, 311b.

Somerset, Margaret, Countess of, presents to St. George's, Exeter, ii, 235b.

Sonde (*alias* Waltham), Rd., V. of Budleigh (deceased), ii, 21b.

Sony, Wm., born on the Bishop's Manor of Powton ; his Manumission : directed to the D. and Ch. of Exeter (5 April), and by them accepted and sealed (8 April, 1418), i, 239.

Soor, John, priest-vicar in the Cathedral, collated (*by lapse*) i, 56b.

He is mentioned as proxy for John Waryn (V. of Liskeard), ii, 55b; inst. to the Chantry in the Cemetery of St. Austell, ii, 103; exchanged with the Dean of Crantock, ii, 108b; resigned the Deanery, ii, 160b.

Sourapeldore, Magota, i, 303b.

Sourton (Bridestowe), Wm. Hawke, chaplain of, i, 214.

Southampton, i, 96; ii, 137b.

Southam, John, Prior of Totnes, i, 197b; his institution, ii, 96b; 254b, 349, 349b; i, 197b.

Southam, Thomas, Canon of Salisbury, i, 12.

Southam, Wm., R. of Fuggleston *w.* Bemerton, exchanges for King's Nympton, ii, 103b; i, 145; his death, ii, 146, 250.

Southecomb, Hamon, i, 332.

Southill [Southulle, MS.], Walter Dollebeare, R.,—

He was a Penitentiary in the Deanery of East, i, 49b.—See Marhamchurch, i, 64.—Relaxation of the Sequestration imposed on account of non-residence, and licence of non-residence for a year, from 12 Sept., 1410; i, 104.—*See*, also, Fresell, Walter, i, 197b; and ii, 54b, 227.

Southole, Chapel of the Holy Cross at; *see* Hartland, i, 38b.

Southleigh, Wm. Lane, R.; licence of non-residence from 6 May to Michaelmas, 1416, i, 221.

Southmolton; John Hacche, R., licence of non-residence for a year, from 14 July, 1395, i, 4; a Penitentiary in the Deanery of Molton, i, 50; *see* "*Oratories*," i, 39.—Wm. Peyon, R., licence of non-residence for 2 years, from 17 Jan., 1406-7, i, 80b; for 2 years, from 31 Jan., 1408-9, i, 88. John Park, R.—

On the 4th of Oct., 1410, the Bishop issued a Commission of Enquiry directed to the Archdeacon of Barnstaple, on the complaint of this R. as to the grievous dilapidation of the chancel, books, etc., etc., caused by the neglect of Wm. Peion, his predecessor; ii, 234.

On 5 Oct., 1410, the Bishop wrote to the Dean of Molton and the Curates of that Deanery, and to Matthew Stoke (R. of St. Leonard's by Exeter), on behalf of this R., setting forth that whereas all ecclesiastical property is, by law, protected against waste and depreciation, and offenders are liable to the greater excommunication, "quidam iniquitatis filii, quorum nomina ignorantur pariter et persone, sepes et fossas clausurarum, necnon ostium cujusdam columbaris Rectorie predicte ingressi temere et dolose, cuniculosque in eisdem clausuris ac columbas in columbari predictis, in multitudine copiosa ex consuetudine existentes, firmato primitus per eosdem et cooperto foramine ex parte superiori ejusdem columbaris, per quod columbe ejusdem evolare et revolare consueverant, ceperunt, occiderunt, asportarunt, et destruxerunt; mansum insuper et domos Rectorie predicte intrarunt, trestelloque et tabulas, cistamque pro panibus conservandis, situlam, ac alias res diversas per Rectores quondam Rectorie predicte, dum in rebus agebant humanis, successoribus suis quibuscumque canonice intrantibus donatas, legatas, et eisdem successive sine alienacione perpetuo remansuras, abstulerunt, contrectarunt, occuparuntque injuste, et occupant in presenti, preter et contra voluntatem Rectorum Ecclesie predicte qui pro tempore fuerant, et magistri Johannis Park, ecclesie predicte nunc

Rectoris aut suorum procuratorum, seu aliorum qui, vacante ecclesia predicta, per nos seu ministros nostros, seu aliter, eadem plena, hujusmodi rerum custodiis fuerant deputati; in animarum suarum grande periculum, ecclesieque predicte Rectorum pro tempore et nunc existencium ac nostrum prejudicium non modicum et gravamen." The Bishop directs their excommunication to be publickly proclaimed in Southmolton church, and in all churches in the neighbourhood, and that enquiries should be instituted with a view to their detection, i, 106b.—A licence to hear the confessions of his parishioners was granted 10 April, 1416, to John Park; then, also, Canon of Exeter, i, 220.

The Chapels of St. James and St. Bartholomew in this parish were licensed, 26 April, 1396, for Rd. Hacche and Walter Cloteworthy, i, 8b.—Hacche, in this parish, *see* Tregary (*Oratories*), i, 91.—Penance of Robert Rychard, of Chittlehampton, in the market-place of Southmolton, *see* Filleigh, i, 110b.—Marriage licence of Rob. Wonard, of Sidbury, and Blonchia Frenachton, of Southmolton (23 Jan., 1416-17), i, 229. [*See* Frenachton (page 107), where "of Sidbury" should be "of Southmolton"].

The parishioners having represented to the Bishop that their parish-church had been dedicated on the 2nd Sunday in Lent, and consequently that it often happened that the Feast of Dedication could not have its proper Services, he acceded to their request that the Feast might be transferred to October 10, and granted an Indulgence to the parishioners who should frequent the services on the new Feast Day (27 Sept., 1417), i, 234b.

South Petherwin [Southpyderwyn, MS.], Jno. Colman, V. ii, 155. —

Walter Trethewy, chaplain, licensed to preach in the parish-church (22 March, 1414-15), i, 209.—The Bishop was informed that the Church had been polluted by bloodshed in a quarrel between Joan, wife of Wm. Langedon, and Elinore, wife of Robert Tremayle, and caused enquiry to be made; subsequently he issued a declaration that no pollution had taken place, and that the Church was to be used again for Divine Service immediately (29 Nov., 1417), i, 237.—The Commission herein was dated 19 Nov.; ii, 263b.

South Pool [Pole, MS.]; relaxation of an Interdict:—

The Bishop wrote to the Dean of Woodleigh and to the Curate of the parish, and the chaplains serving in the parish-church (8 Oct., 1410), to the effect that, whereas the said Church lay under an Interdict, on account of a sermon having been preached therein by a certain secular chaplain, name unknown, who had no cure of souls there, but had been brought in by certain of the parishioners (not out of contempt, but in ignorance), though he had neither mission nor licence from the Bishop, the said Interdict was taken off, the Bishop desiring to temper rigour with mercy, and, also, to comply with the desire of the noble Lady, Margaret Peverel (a parishioner), and the Bishop directed proclamation of the said Relaxation to be made in South Pool Church, and in the neighbouring churches; i, 107.—Canon Wm. Langeton's bequests to this parish, i, 322b.

Southweek, in Germansweek; *see* Kelly (*Oratories*), i, 128b.

Sparke, Richard, of Woodbury, i, 312.

Sparnen, John, clerk,—*Dispensacio super defectu natalium* (15 April, 1412), i, 147.

John Sparnen, accolite, had been ordained by an alien Bishop, and a dispensation in his favour was granted, 27 May, 1413; i, 174b.

Spernon, John, Canon of Bodmin, ii, 72.

Speare, Wm., instituted to West Anstey, ii, 173b.

Speccote; parish of Merton; *see* Speccote (*Oratories*), i, 38b.

Speccote, Wm., inst. to Beaford, ii, 76.

Speek, John, proxy for John Scoy, ii, 82^b.

Speke, John (junior), Joan, relict of, and daughter and heir of Martin Fyschakre, ii, 234^b.

Speeke, Thos., R. of Grittleton (Dioc. of Salisbury), exchanges for Liskeard, ii, 149^b; his death, ii, 169^b.

Spence Combe, *see* Spencer (*Oratories*), i, 212^b.

Spencer, Gilbert, chaplain, i, 320^b.

Spencer, Thos., *see* St. Keyne, ii, 303^b.

Sperke, Hugh, inst. to [St. Perran] Uthno, ii, 162^b, 255^b.

Spore, Thos., i, 301.

Spreth, Thos., R. of Wambrook (Dioc. Sarum.), exch. for Harpford, ii, 188, 263; for Laȝarton (Dioc. Sarum.), ii, 192^b.

Sprot, Thomas, V. of Coleridge (deceased), ii, 104^b.

Sprotburgh, Thos., Preb. of Poughill *see* "Institutions."

Sprydell, *or* **Spredell, John**, inst. to the Chantry at Ermington, ii, 9^b; to Zeal Monachorum, ii, 102. *See* i, 138.

Spryg, John (son of Richard), ii, 254.

Spryngotte (*or* **Spryngold**), **Rd.**, chaplain, i, 301; proxy for Wm. Haukyn, ii, 87.

Spryngthorp *or* **Spryngthorn, John de**, inst. to Ipplepen, ii, 51, 312^b; i, 55; exch. for W. Keal (Dioc. of Lincoln), ii, 64^b.

Spycer, John, of Exeter, i, 318.

Spygernell, Thos., of Apuldram, ii, 293^b.

Spyrewey, Rd., and Alice Styl,—

Commission of Enquiry as to certain reports about them (9 Feb., 1411-12), ii, 245.—Dispensation to enable them to marry, being within the 4th degree of consanguinity (dated xiiij Kal. Jan. [i.e., 19 Dec., 1411], the 1st year of Pope John xxiij, i, 148; *and* 26 April, 1412), i, 148^b.

Squyer, Wm., co-patron of Gittisham, ii, 104: of Stoke-Rivers, ii, 129^b, 180.

Squyer, Simon, R. of St. George's, Exeter, ii, 336^b.

Stabba, Wm., a parishioner of Lelant, ii, 232^b.

Stacy, John, i, 315.

Stafford; Thos. Granger's lands in that County, i, 308^b.

Stafford; Rd. Caurs (Warden of St. Leonard's Hosp. there), *v.* John Hauberk [Case of Appeal], 8 May, 1398; ii, 218.

STAFFORD, EDMUND, BISHOP OF EXETER,—

His Consecration at Lambeth, i, 1.—Oath of Allegiance to the Apostolick See, i, 3.—Letter to Pope Boniface IX concerning his Consecration, &c., i, 14.—Letter appointing as proxies to visit Rome, John Franseys, Walter Cook, and Rd. Tyttesbury, i, 15.—Letter appointing Wm. Laugeton, Can. of

Exeter his proxy in Convocation, i, 15.—Letters to his Vicar-General, and the four Archdeacons, enforcing the Archbishop's Mandate as to observing the Festivals of SS David and Chad, Bishops and Confessors; Winifred, Virgin, and Thomas of Canterbury, i, 15b.—His Mandate to proceed against non-resident clerks in the Archdeaconry of Exeter, i, 16b.—Archdn. Hunden's bequests to, i, 325; Precentor Haukyn's ditto, i, 333.

The "Ordinacio" of his Chantry in the Cathedral:

The Bishop addressing all sons of Holy Mother Church to whom these presents should come, refers to the uncertainty of life, and to his desire to prepare for the last days of his pilgrimage. King Henry IV., by his Letters Patent had granted a special licence to William Ekerdon and Edmund Elyot, clerks, and to Robert Grey, enabling them to convey to the Dean and Chapter of Exeter the Manors of Wynterborn Wast, Bokhampton, and Swanwych, in the County of Dorset, and the advowson of the Church of Winterborn, to find 3 chaplains to celebrate daily in the Cath. Church for the King himself and his sons in life, and for their souls after death, and also for the Bp. himself, and Sir Humphrey de Stafford, knt. his kinsman, and for all the faithful departed. Subsequently, the said Wm. Ekerdon, Edmund Elyot and Rt. Gray, conveyed the said estates accordingly; and the Bishop proceeded to this ordinacio—which provided (1) that the Dean and Chapter with the revenues of these estates (which he had purchased "*in rei veritate nostris industria et laboribus mediantibus, de et cum bonis patrimonialibus et de peculio nostro ad utilitatem nostram*") should provide 2 fit priests to be called the *annivellarii* of Edmd. Stafford, Bishop, who should hold no other benefice or receive other stipend, and should serve continually at the altar of St. John Evan., adjoining the Lady-Chapel, for the Bishop himself, and for Sir Humphrey de Stafford and Elizabeth his wife; also for Sir Rd. de Stafford, knt. and Isabella Stafford, the Bishop's father and mother, and for his uncle Ralph de Stafford, Earl of Stafford; and, lastly, for King Henry IV.,—for all these whether living or departed, and for all the faithful departed; the said priests to do their duty well, or be punished for their negligence. They were to be subject to the Dean and Chapter. Rules were laid down to provide for vacancies. Each priest was to receive annually 100s. in quarterly payments and a share in the obits. The Dean and Chapter were to find and keep up the missals, chalice, vestments, and the ornaments of the altar; also bread and wine and lights; except in the first instance, when the Bishop himself would provide what was necessary; and the priests, at their admission, were to give security for the safe keeping of all such things. Having regard to the fact that in his Cathedral Church of Exeter there were fewer obits kept about the time of the Feast of St. Lambert than at other times, he ordered that these obits should be kept on that day. He ordered that the Dean and Chapter should pay to every Canon who should be present thereat the sum of 12d.; to every vicar, 6d; to every annuellar priest, 3d.; to every chorister boy, 2d.; and like sums to sundry other officials; to the Treasurer, also, for wax candles and other lights, 8d. It was further provided that during the lifetime of the Bishop and others named above who were still alive, a Mass of the Holy Trinity should be said on St. Lambert's Day, and the same payments made to those who should assist as in the case of the obits. The Dean and Chapter were to be held harmless in case of losses from any cause except their own negligence. The Bishop states that the advowson of the Church of Winterborn Wast had been purchased by Sir Humphrey de Stafford, and he decreed that as soon as the Dean and Chapter came into quiet possession of the revenues thereof, they should, after paying a competent stipend to the vicar, provide a third chaplain, to be called Humphrey de Stafford's, and to serve at the same altar, in like manner, for the whole state (living or departed) of the Bp. himself and of the said Humphrey and of the Bp.'s relatives, Ralph and Hugh de Stafford, formerly Earls of Stafford, and of Sir John and Margaret de Stafford the parents of the said Humphrey; for the king, and for all the faithful departed — and payments were to be made, as above, to those who should assist at these obits. The Treasurer was to provide two lights for the tomb of Sir Humphrey, if he were buried in the Cathedral, if otherwise, then *circa formulam* (covered with a pall), to be placed on the pavement near the Bishop's tomb, in his memory. In case the said revenues from the Church should fail no deduction was to be made from the stipends of the two former priests for the benefit of the third. The priests were to have a copy of this "ordinacio" to be written on the fly-leaf at the beginning or end of the missal. Three copies were also to be made for (1) the Dean and Chapter; (2) the Bishops of Exeter; and (3) Bishop Stafford's heirs. Dated at Crediton—1 Oct., 1408; ii, 281^b-284.

Stafford, Fulke de, collated to a Preb. in St. Probus, ii, 80; his death, ii, 148.

Stafford, Sir Hugh de, Earl of Stafford, ii, 282.—Sir Humphrey knt., i, 61; (*and* Elizabeth his wife), ii, 282. Sir John and Margaret his wife, *ibid.*

Stafford, Matilda, wife of Sir Richard, ii, 228^b.—Sir Ralph, Earl of Stafford, ii, 282—Sir Rd., father of the Bishop, ii, 228^b, and Isabella his wife, ii, 282 *et seqq.*

Stafforde, John, collated Can. of Exeter, ii, 158; i, 244.

Stakforde, John, V. of Berry Pomeroy, ii, 12.

Stalleworth [Stalworth; *also* Stalworthy *and* Stalworde MS.], Walter, chaplain, i, 318^b, 329; ii, 127.

Licensed as Publick-Preacher in the Archdeaconry of Exeter (15 Jan., 1409-10), i, 93^b; a Penitentiary in the Deanery of Tiverton, i, 94, 115; also in the Deanery of Plymtree, i, 143, 173^b, 194, 207^b, 216^b, 231; licensed (4 March, 1411-12), Confessor at Canonsleigh, i, 145^b.

Stallynche, in Huntsham; Chapel of St. James (licensed 16 July, 1410), i, 100^b.

Stancombe, John, inst. to Ringmore, ii, 5^b.

Stanlegh, Roger, V. of Broadhembury (deceased), ii, 90.

Stantor, John, does homage to the Bp., in London, for lands in Paignton (26 Sept., 1397), ii, 310.

Stapyl, in Normandy, i, 96.

Stapylton, i, 311^b.

Stapuldon, John, i, 326^b.

Stapylton (*or* Stapyldon), Sir Rd., knt., Lord of Estyngton (in No. Tawton), and Sir Rd., his father, ii, 334; presents to Milton Damarel, ii, 341^b; patron of No. Tawton, i, 348.—Thomasia, his dau., wife of Rd. Hankeford, ii, 8, 334.

Stapeldon, John, Prior of Abingdon, i, 310^b.

Stapulforde, John de, nephew to Hugh de Hyckelyng, i, 326^b.

Staunton, Hy., R. of St. Clether, presents to the V. thereof, ii, 7.

Staunton, Philip, inst. to Kingsnympton, ii, 146, 250.

Staverton, John Ulveston's bequests to the Church of, i, 330b: Rd. Doty, V., *see Oratories*, i, 160b.—The Bridge, i, 330b.

This Bridge over the Dart [still standing and quite perfect—and a most interesting building], being notoriously in a ruinous condition, so that it could neither be rebuilt, nor even repaired unless the Faithful would contribute to the cost, the Bishop wrote to the Archd. of Totnes and the Incumbents of the Deaneries of Ipplepen, Moreton, and Totnes, directing them to collect the alms of their parishioners, and promising an Indulgence of 40 days (18 Jan., 1412-13), i, 174b.

Stawell, Sir Thos., knt., co-patron of Merton, ii, 146b; of Sutcombe, ii, 181.

Staynour, Wm., *see* Lostwithiel, i, 229b; ii, 260b.

Sterlyng, Rd., successor to Hugh de Hyckelyng, i, 326b.

Stephenes, Wm., inst. to Luppit, ii, 180.

Wm. Stevenes is mentioned as presenting to Kentisbeare, ii, 147, 249.

Stephyn, John, of Porthia (i.e, St. Ives), accolite, i, 14, 14b, 15b.

A John Stephyn was V. of Padstow, and resigned (ii, 51b), on his inst. to Bodmin, ii, 49b; 72. He died V. of St. Petrock's Church there, ii, 183.—A John Stephyn was inst. to St. Pinnock, ii, 123, 350b, 351b.

Stevenys, John, Notary-Publick, i, 192b;—

He was collated to a Can. in the Cathedral, ii, 154; licensed to choose a Confessor (21 July, 1415), i, 211b.

Stevyn, *alias* Bedeman, Laurence, R. of Lifton (q. v.), i, 14.

Stephyn, Thos., collated Can. of Exeter, ii, 175b; *see*, also, i, 214b, 219, 227b, 236.

Stephyn, William (chaplain), ii, 256b.

Stevenstone in Great Torrington; *see* Graunt (*Oratories*), i, 145.

Sticklepath, Henry Pek, Chantry-priest, a Penitentiary in the Deanery of Okehampton, i, 143, 174, 194b, 207b.

Stixwold [Stykeswold]; Prioress presents to Honington, ii, 53b.

Stockleigh-English [Soklegh (*sic*) Englysch, MS.]; Wm. Herle (sub-deacon), R., Dispensation (to study at Oxford) for a year, from 9 May, 1397, i, 12; 15b.

Stockleigh-Pomeroy [Stokele Pomeray, MS.]; Rob. Wyghale, R.

He had licence of non-residence for 2 years ("et insistere studio literarum in Universitate Oxoniensi") from 18 Dec., 1400, i, 51b; also [Stokelypomeroy, MS.], for a year, from 25 July, 1410, i, 101.—*See* Piperell, Rd., ii, 344.

Stockwell, ii, 359.

Stoke, Andrew, V. of Thorverton (resigns), ii, 86.

Stoke, St. Nectan [Hartland], the Church of, i, 313b.

Stoke, Elias, i, 327b, 333b.—

He was R. of Greinton (Dioc. of B. and W.), and exch. for St. Mary Steps, Exeter, ii, 140b; collated Can. of Crantock, ii, 174b.

Stoke, John, i, 333b; R. of Bittadon, ii, 7; inst. to Heanton Punchardon, *ibid*; i, 148; his death, ii, 146.

Stoke, Matthew, *see* Dunchideock, i, 19b.

A Matthew Stoke occurs as R. of St. Leonard's, Exeter, in 1410; i, 106b.—*See*, also, i, 301, 310, 328b, 333b. He was Preb. of Thorney in Chichester Cathedral, ii, 35b; proxy for John Park, ii, 123.

Stoke, Nicholas, inst. to Stokeclimsland, ii, 9b.

He exchanges for Withiel and a Can. in Glasney, ii, 43b; for Hampton Meisy (Dioc. of Worcester), ii, 58; for Combmartin, ii, 64; for Coates (Dioc. of Ely), ii, 82b. He was accused to the Bishop of cutting down timber in the woods pertaining to his Preb. in Glasney, without real necessity, and the Bp. wrote to Benedict Canterbury, Preb. of the said Colleg. Church, directing him to inhibit Nicholas, publickly, from continuing this waste, and to take steps for preventing the like offence for the future (19 Nov., 1400), i, 50b.

Stoke [*or* Stokes], Steph., inst. to St. Cleer, ii, 94; (decd.), ii, 148.

Stokeclimsland [Stokeinclymeslond, MS.], Thos. Abyngdon [alias Welyn], R., i, 78b, 187b, 325; licensed to put out the revenues of his benefice, for 3 years, to be farmed (12 Aug., 1411), i, 131.

Stoke Damarel; Robert Lemmonesworth, R.; licence of non-residence from 25 Nov., 1415, to Michaelmas, 1416, i, 215b.

Stokenham; John [Ulveston], V.

He was executor of the Will of Henry Blakbourne, i, 30b; his own Will, i, 330b: *See* Slapton, ii, 112b.—Henry Blakbourne, R; *see* Blakebourne.—Thomas de Montacute, R. (case of dilapidations), i, 30b.

Commission of Enquiry on the presentation of Adam Davenport to this R., by Matilda, Countess of Salisbury (15 Oct., 1416), ii, 260b. *Breve Regium* ["Stokenham, Stoke in Hamme. *alias* Stoken in Hammes," MS.) :—The Bishop to certify the King as to the tenour of an Inquisition held at Kingsbridge touching the last vacancy and the patronage (20 Nov., 1416) ii, 356b.

Breve Regium,—The Bishop to examine the Registers from 1199 (*sic*) and certify the King as to all presentations thereto; 20 Nov., 1416, ii, 357.—A similar *Breve Regium*, dated 24 Nov., 1416, *ib.*—The Bp's. certificate, as follows:—He recites the report of the Inquisition at Kingsbridge (by the Archdeacon of Totnes), to whom he had written, informing him that Thos. de Montacute, Earl of Salisbury and Lord of Monthermer, had presented Edw. Prentys, clerk, and requiring him to convene the Chapter and certify in the usual way [Dat. Clyst, 14 Oct., 1416]. The Archdeacon, etc., met in full Chapter, in the Chapel of St. Edmund the K., Kingsbridge, and on the 26th day of October, inst.; present—*Rectors*: Rd. Olyver of Alyngton [i.e., East Allington]; Thos. Tremayn, of Aveton Giffard; Wm. Breyrlegh, of Woodleigh; John Wynterborne, of Charleton; John Carwarch, of Pole [So. Pool]; Roger Bacheler, of Chyrstow; Rd. Tryby, of Dodebroke; Rob. Benet, of Thurleston; John Bykebery, of Bykebery [Bigbury]; *Vicars*: Wm. Cote, *minister* of Slapton; John Wolston, of Stokenham; Simon Paule, of Alwyngton [West Alvington]; and Peter Holdyche, of Loddiswell. Evidence having been taken, it appeared that the Church of Stokenham became vacant, 1 Oct., 1416, by the death of Rd. Prentys; the true patron was Thos. de Montacute, Earl of Salisbury; but on the last occasion King Henry IV. presented: the right belonged to the said Earl for this turn, and was hereditary: two presentations had been made, (1) by the said Earl, (2) by Matilda, Countess of Salisbury; apart from which there was no legal question involved. No pension or portion was charged on the living. It was taxed at £33 6s. 8d. The said Edw. Prentys was fit in every way, in priest's orders, and more than 40 years old, and well beneficed elsewhere, being Archdeacon of Essex [Estsex] in the Cathed. Church of St. Paul's, London. Nothing was known against patron or nominee.—Here follows a copy of the Bishop's letter to the Archdeacon, dated Clyst, 15 Oct., 1416, informing him of the presentation of Adam Davenport, clerk, by the Countess of Salisbury, and demanding enquiry and report. This, also, was laid before the Chapter at the same time. The Chapter found that the true patron was Thos. Montacute, Earl of Salisbury, by hereditary right, etc., etc., the said Adam Davenport was in priest's orders and over 60 years old, and (as was said) with no other benefice. He was not himself objected to, but it was objected that Matilda, the said Countess, was not the true patron. The inquisition, duly sealed, was dated in the said Chapel of St. Edmund, on the said 26 Oct., ii, 357. (5) The Bishop's certificate as to the examination of the Registers. He had found that Walter de Stapledon, 6 Idus July, 1315, i.e. 10 July (at Pruteston, i.e., Preston, juxta Loddiswell), admitted Thos. Nynsom, priest, by R. de Coleton, his official and commissary, on the resignation of Nicholas de Lovecote, and on the presentation of Sir Ralph de Monthermer.—Also, that Bishop Grandisson, 6 Idus (i.e., 8th) Sept., 1328, at Chudleigh, admitted Thos. de Schirrigg, clerk; patron, Sir Thos. de Monthermer, and that on 6 Dec., 1357, the same Bishop collated at Chudleigh, Henry Blakebourne, priest (by lapse), and that he had himself, 22 July, 1399 [in MS., 1499], admitted, at Wallingford, Thos. Montagu, on Blakeborn's death, patron, John de Montacute, Earl of Salisbury, and on 14 July, 1404, at Clyst, he admitted, on Montagu's death, Rd. Prentys, chaplain, patron, King Henry IV., for that turn; and 28 Oct., 1416, at Clyst, Edward Prentys, on the death of Rd. Prentys, on the presentation of Sir Thos. de Montacute, Earl of Salisbury, and Lord of Monthermer.—Dated Clyst, 14 Dec., 1416, ii, 358.

Breve Regium—Matilda, widow of John de Montacute, Earl of Salisbury, having recovered the right of presentation before the Judges at Westminster, against Thomas Montacute, Earl of Salisbury, and Edward Prentys, by default, Maudate to the Bishop to admit her clerk (28 April, 1417), ii, 360ᵇ.—Commission of Enquiry as to dilapidations on the complaint of Adam Davenport, R., against his predecessor, Rd. Prentys (15 May, 1417), ii, 261. Commission for sequestration, directed 31 May, 1417, to John Wolston (i. q. Ulveston), V. of Stokenham, Nicholas Husy, chaplain, of Chivelston, and Nicholas Bokete, chaplain of Sherford; the dilapidations referred to above having been assessed by the Archd. of Totnes in the sum of £50 at least, which had not been paid, ii, 261.—Davenport obtained licence of non-residence from 1 Aug., to All Saints' Day, 1419; i, 247ᵇ.—*See* Sherford, i, 168ᵇ.

Stoke Fleming; Steph. Joseph, R.; i, 113, 138. *See*, Reynald (*Oratories*), i, 173.

Commission for the absolution of this R., who had been excommunicated because he failed to pay to the Prior of Montacute the 2nd moiety of a certain Subsidy (24 March, 1411-12), ii, 245ᵇ.

Stoke Gabriel; Robert [Saunder], V., a Penitentiary in the Deanery of Ipplepen, i, 143, 174, 194ᵇ, 207ᵇ, 217.

Stokeinteignhead [St. Andrew's], Thomas Clyfford, R.; his licence of non-residence for a year, from 13 Sept., 1411; i, 133ᵇ.—*See* i, 333ᵇ.

Stoke Rivers, John Jakys, R.; licence of non-residence, from 21 July to Michaelmas, 1410; i, 100ᵇ.

Stokhay, Wm., inst. to Puddington, ii, 8.

Stokker, William, chaplain, i, 316ᵇ.

Stokys, William, i, 320ᵇ.

Stone, Edmund, R. of Filleigh (deceased), ii, 13.

Stone, Gilbert de, Canon of Hereford, ii, 58.

Stone, John, collated Can. and Preb. of Funtington in Bosham, ii, 109, 294; his death, ii, 199b.

Stone, Rob., ii, 351b.—For Wm. Stone, *see* atte Stone.

Stonehouse, East [Est Stonhouse, MS.], Stephen Durneforde of (*see Oratories*), i, 200b.

Stonton, Henry, Chantry-priest of St. Michael's in the Cemetery of St. Austell, exch. for Hutton (Dioc. of London), ii, 52b.

Stonyng, John, inst. to Brampford Speke, ii, 188b.

Stoodleigh; John Blakelake, R.—

He obtained licence of non-residence from 16 Dec., to Michaelmas, 1406, "cum relaxacione sequestri in fructibus dicte ecclesie occasione non residencie sue retroacte interpositi," i, 80b.

Stourton, Wm., takes the oath as J. P. for Cornwall, ii, 335b.

Stowe, Thos., clerk, *see* Ottery, ii, 278.

Stowford, Thos., presents to St. Edmund's Chantry, "juxta pontem" at Colyford, ii, 176b.

Stowford, Roger Lumpp[1], R.—

Licence of non-residence for a year, from 14 Nov., 1395, his Rectory-house to be properly repaired meanwhile, i, 7. This licence was renewed (30 May, 1398) "ut per unum annum, a dato presencium cotidie numerandum, insistendo in parochia et villa de Yakesley, Lincolnensis Diocesis, super cura, custodia et subvencione parentum tuorum, ut asseris paraliticorum et decrepitorum, ibidem degencium, te a dicta ecclesia tua, etc.;" i, 18b.—This licence was renewed for a year, 18 June, 1399, and for the same cause, i, 28. Licence of non-residence was again granted to him for a year from 31 May, 1401, i, 56b.—Thos. Greyston, R., had licence of non-residence for a year, from 16 Oct., 1409; i, 90b.

Stowford [Stoford, MS.], in Harford; licence to Simon Elys, R., for the Chap. of St. Nicholas there (14 Dec., 1400), i, 51b.

Stowford [Stauford, MS.], in Langtree [Langetre, MS.],—

Licence to Walter Cook, R., for the Chapel of St. Nicholas there (25 Oct., 1412) i, 171b.

Strange, William, i, 308b.

Stratton; Walter Cryk, V.; *see* Bude, i, 45.

Stratton, John, Prior of Minster, i, 61.

Strecch (or Strech), John, i, 312; co-patron of Mamhead, ii, 45b; of Stoke Fleming, ii, 17.

Stretton (*alias* Oliver), John, inst. to Butterleigh, ii, 23.

Strode [*or* Strood MS.], Augustine, inst. to Bickleigh, V., ii, 136, 243b; resigns for Lamerton, ii, 144, 247b, 254; exch. for Cotleigh, ii, 157b; a Penitentiary in the Deanery of Tamerton, i, 94, 115b, 143.

---

[1] also Lumpe *and* Lumppe, MS.

Strozis, Marcellus de, LL.D., Papal Nuncio and Collector in England, i, 104b, 110;

Certificatorium pro,—(6 Feb., 1411-12), i, 144 : ditto (20 Feb., 1412-13, and 5 May, 1413), i, 180 : his acquittance of the Bp. from whom he had received £9 5s. 0d.—"Peter's Pence," for 1412 (5 June, 1413), i, 181b.—*Certificatorium pro*—(11 Feb., 1413-14), *ibid.*

Stryke, Nicholas, inst. to Gulval, ii, 153b.

Stryla, Walter, a parishioner of Linkinhorne, i, 116.

Sture, Joan, wife of William—

She complained to the Bp. that she had been falsely and maliciously accused of adultery with one John Colard, chaplain ; and, having purged herself of this charge, the Bp. directed his Mandate to Wm. Trey, Dean of Crediton, to denounce the false accusers, publickly, and proclaim their excommunication, in his Collegiate Church (14 June, 1411), i, 126.

Sturt, Roger, inst. to Virginstow, ii, 144 ; i, 170, 213b ; resigns, and is inst. to Tavistock, ii, 179b; resigns, and is inst. to Milton Abbot, ii, 180b, 181.—Peter Sturt, occurs, i, 316b, 320.

Sturte, John (a parishioner of Taunton), and Agnes, dau. of Rob. Pound of Tiverton : special licence for their marriage in Tiverton Church (5 Sept., 1413), i, 183b.

Stybbe, John, *see Oratories*, i, 85. A John Stybbe was inst. to Maker, ii, 86 ; resigned, ii, 90.

Stykerygge, John, i, 324.

Styl, Alice, *see* Spyrewey, i, 148, 148b ; ii, 245 ; John, i, 332.

Styward, Wm., inst. to St. Illogan, ii, 33b, 316 ; i, 12 ; collated Canon of Glasney, ii, 67 ; his death, ii, 70, 74b.

Subsidies, etc. :—

For the expenses of Nuncios Apostolick and Prelates proceeding to the Council of Constance—"*Certificatorium de nominibus collectorum cujusdam Subsidii* (15 Nov., 1414) ; i, 204. To be collected in the Diocese of Exeter, and paid, in London, to John Kempe and John Perch (or one of them) : Commission directed to Thos. Hendeman, Archd. of Exeter, and the other Archdeacons, as to the collection and payment thereof (15 Nov., 1414), ii, 256.

Declaration as to the concession of a Subsidy, and Certificate by the Bishop (4 Jan., 1414-15), i, 206.—*Certificatorium factum Archiepiscopo Cantuariensi super concessione quatuor denariorum de libra* (11 April, 1416), i, 220b.—*Certificatorium factum Archiep. Cantuariensi super concessione duorum denariorum de libra* (22 June, 1416), i, 221b.—Acquittance (by John Estcourt, LL.B.), on payment on account made by John Batyn, clerk, viz., £26 17s 8d ob., for taxed benefices in the 3 Archdeaconries of Devonshire, and for untaxed benefices therein £5 14s 9d (5 July, 1416), i, 222b ; also, in the Archdeaconry of Cornwall, £3 3s 8d ob. in full payment for untaxed, and £5 7s 11d in part payment for taxed benefices (5 July, 1416), i, 223 ; also from the Bishop, £3 16s 11d ob. et quadr. (5 July, 1416, *ibid.*—*Commissio Archiepiscopi Cantuariensis ad levandam medietatem unius decime* (6 April, 1397 ; published in the Dioc. of Exeter, 20 April), ii, 305.—*Breve Regium, de levando medietatem unius decime* (30 Nov., 1397) ; Certificate (6 May, 1398), ii, 307.—*Breve Regium, de levando unam decimam et medietatem unius decime* (24 July, 1398) ; The Bishop's Commissions to the Collectors, dated 28 Sept., 1398, and 10 March, 1398-9, ii, 309.—*Breve Regium, de levando decimam et medietatem unius decime* (12 April, 1401); the Bishop's acknowledgement (7 May, 1401), ii, 313.—*Breve Regium*, demanding a return as to certain possessions of St. John's Hosp., Exeter, Cornworthy Priory, and sundry other Religious Houses in the Diocese, at the time of the recent grant of Convocation of the "*decima et medietas unius decime*" (12 June, 1402), ii, 314.—*Breve Regium, de levando decimam et medietatem decime* (2 Feb., 1402-3), ii, 314^{b}.—Ditto (12 Oct., 1403), ii, 315.—*Breve Regium, de levando subsidium et decimam* (17 May, 1404), ii, 316.—*Breve Regium, de levando unam decimam cum dimidia* (6 Dec., 1404), ii, 317^{b}.—*Breve Regium*, (1) *pro decima et dimidio levanda* (1 Oct., 1410), and, subsequently, *ad levandum primum dimidium*, ii, 334^{b}; certificate returned, 10 Oct., 1410; ii, 335.—*Breve Regium, ad levandum secundum dimidium decime* (14 April, 1411), ii, 339.—*Breve Regium, pro secundo dimidio decime levando* (2 May, 1411), ii, 339.—Certificate herein (14 April, 1411), ii, 340. *Breve Regium de levando decimam etc.*,—The Bishop to certify as to the Incumbents of certain parishes in the Diocese, on 21 April, 1404 (10 July, 1411), ii, 340^{b}.—The Bishop's Return (23 Sept., 1411), ii, 342^{b}.—*Breve Regium*, for the names of the Collectors (1 Oct., 1411), ii, 343^{b}.—Commission, *pro tertio dimidio decime colligendo in Comitatu Devonie* (14 Nov., 1411), ii, 343^{b}. Certificate (14 Nov., 1411), *ibid.*—*Breve Regium, pro dimidio decime levando* (2 June, 1412), ii, 344^{b}.—The Bishop's Commission therein (24 July, 1412), *ibid.*—His Certificate (24 July, 1412), ii, 345.—*Breve Regium, pro una decima levanda* (27 Sept., 1413), ii, 346^{b}.—Commission (21 Oct., 1413), ii, 347.—Certificate (24 Oct., 1413), *ibid.*—*Breve Regium*), *pro una decima levanda* (14 Nov., 1414), ii, 350.—Commissions (12 and 13 Dec., 1414), ii, 350^{b}.—Certificate (12 Dec., 1414), *ibid.*—(*Breve Regium*, Commission issued by the Bishop *pro secunda decima in Comitatu Devonie colligenda* (29 Oct., 1415), ii, 353^{b}; *in Comitatu Cornubie*, ii, 354.—Certificate (8 Nov., 1415), *ibid.*—*Breve Regium, pro duabus decimis levandis*, (10 June, 1416), ii, 355.—The Bishop's Commission—*pro una decima*, in Devon (11 July, 1416), ii, 355^{b}; in Cornwall (11 July, 1416), ii, 356.—Certificate (14 July, 1416), *ibid.*—*Breve Regium, pro duabis decimis levandis, &c.* (28 Nov., 1416), ii, 358.—Commission *pro una decima et dimidis* (26 Dec., 1416), ii, 358^{b}.—Certificate (26 Dec., 1416), *ibid.*—Commission *pro dimidio decime levando* (21 Feb., 1416-17), ii, 360.—Commission *pro decima levanda* (14 Nov., 1418), ii, 363.—Certificate (same date), ii, 363^{b}.—*Breve Regium, de decima, etc.*, Royal Prohibition in the case of Vivian Auger, Peter Hylle, and Richard Platek, in the Consistory Court (5 Feb., 1416-17), ii, 360.—*Breve Regium, pro duabis decimis levandis* (22 Dec., 1417), ii, 361.—Commission: for Devon (2 Jan., 1417-18), ii, 361^{b}: for Cornwall (same date), ii, 362;—Certificate (1 Jan., 1418), *ibid.*

Sudden, Joan, wife of John, i, 330^{b}.

Sully, Sir John, knt., buried at Crediton, i, 327^{b}.

Surmound, Wm., of Kingsbridge, ii, 290^{b}, 292.

Sutcombe [Suttecombe, MS.], Roger Rome, R., (*see Oratories*) i, 49.—John Drayton, R., licence of non-residence from 12 Feb., 1404-5, to Michaelmas, 1405, i, 73^{b}; for a year from 13 Oct., 1405, i, 76^{b}.

Commission of Enquiry as to the alleged pollution of the cemetery by Rd. Theobald, and Henry atte Wode, in a quarrel with Thomas Glanvyle (21 June, 1417), ii, 261^{b}. The Bishop found that there had been no pollution, and ordered that the dead should be buried therein as usual (14 Aug., 1417), i, 233. Walter Boway, R., licensed to celebrate in the Chapel of St. Leonard (17 Oct, 1417), i, 235^{b}.

Sutton, Henry, Prior of St. Mary Magdalene, Barnstaple, ii, 39

Sutton, John, inst. to the Chantry in the Cemetery of St. Austell, ii, 135; 156^{b}, 253; a Penitentiary in the Deanery of Powder, i, 217, 231^{b}, 238, 245^{b}. He was Preb. of Crediton, i, 332^{b}; and a Notary Publick, ii, 118.—Robert Sutton occurs, i, 326^{b}.

Sutton, Wm., R. of St. Breoke; ii, 358^{b};—

He was Can. of Crediton and Preb. of Carswell, which he exch. for that of Crida therein, ii, 29.—Also, Preb. of St. Teath, which he exchanged for a Can. in Bosham, ii, 98, 280, 281.—[*Breve Regium, de venire facias*]; Wm. Sutton, of Crediton, clerk; to shew cause why he assaulted John Lyghtfote, clerk, at Crediton; beating, and wounding, and otherwise evil-entreating him (11 July, 1415), ii, 255, 353.—His death, ii, 175, 176^{b}.

"Sutton,"—cook to Archdeacon Lydeford, i, 310.

John Sutton was "cocus" of the cell of St. Mary-in-the-Marsh, by Exeter, i, 89^{b}.

Swan, Anselm, patr. of Ashbrittle (Dio. of B. and W.), ii, 3^{b}, 210^{b}.

Swan, Richard, ii, 342^{b}.

Swan, Thomas, R. of Dodbroke (deceased), ii, 65^{b}.

Swanage [Swanwych, MS.], in Dorsetshire, ii, 281^{b} *et seqq.*

Swathele, Sarah, i, 332.

Swayne, Ralph, layman, and Agnes, relict of Rob. Wyndouth;—

Dispensacio super affinitate, Apostolica auctoritate; they had married (though not ignorant of the fact that Robert "de sacro fonte lavaverat (*sic*)" a son of the said Ralph)—"per verba legitime de presenti carnali tamen copula minime subsecuta." They were permitted to marry "de novo" (5 June, 1400), i, 39^{b}.—John Swayn, i, 325, 325^{b}.

Swete, Philip, proxy for Thomas Cornewayle, ii, 180^{b}.

Swillington, Sir Roger de, Knt., presents to Stanton-in-the-Wold (Dioc. of York), ii, 143^{b}.

Swyft, Wm., collated Preb. of St. Probus, ii, 168^{b}; exch. for a Can. and the 2nd Preb. in the Coll. Ch. of Heytesbury (Dioc. of Salisbury), ii, 200.

Swynborne, Wm., presents to Lanreath, ii, 115.

Swynflete, Wm., i, 328.

Swynford, Thomas, i, 197^{b}; ii, 254^{b}.

Breve Regium (1 Aug., 1414),—The King to be certified as to his resignation of Totnes Priory and the admission of John Southam, monk, ii, 349.—The Bishop certified (19 Sept.), that Swynford resigned, 24 March, 1406-7; that the resignation was confirmed, 11 June following; on which day Southam was admitted on the presentation of Wm. la Zouche of Haryngworth, on the nomination of K. Henry IV., ii, 349^{b}.

Sydenham-Damarel, the Church of, i, 308^{b}.

Sydenham, Simon, Archdn. of Berks, exch. for the Archdeaconry of Salisbury and a Canonry in Crediton, ii, 81.

Sydewyne, Robert de, R. of Clannaborough, ii, 359.

Sygelond, Sybil, i, 307.

Syggeston, John, R. of Charleton, ii, 33; i, 13; (decd.) ii, 63^b.

Symeston, in Holsworthy, *see* Reymond (*Oratories*), i, 185^b; also, i, 332. Richard Symston, *ibid*; also, Wm. and Sarah his wife, i, 331^b.

Symme, John (of Littleham), i, 32; 32^b.

Symon, John, inst. to Crowan, ii, 167.—*See* i, 305.

Symons, John, inst. to Cadeleigh, ii, 96^b.

Symon, John [*Breve Regium*—5 Feb., 1409-10];—

In the case (pending in the Consistorial Court at Exeter) of John Symon, natural son and the heir of Roger Lawys (surviving) and Margaret, *alias* Margarie, Symon (the late wife of the said Roger)? *and* John Folle, a child, and Henry Richard, his guardian,—a case of legitimization,—the Bishop to certify the King (5 Feb.), ii, 332^b,—again (8 Feb., 1409-10), ii, 333. The Bishop made return that, after enquiry, he had ascertained that Wm. Hendre, R. of "St. Maugan de Lanherne," and Thos. Estbrok, V. of Duloe, Commissaries of the Official-Principal of the said Consistory-Court, gave sentence in this case: Thos. Wythyel, clerk, appeared on behalf of John Symon; but John Folle and Henry Richard were contumaciously absent: it was decided that Symon had proved his case, and that the action was vexatious; Folle and Richard were condemned in the costs (£20): ii, 333.

Symon, Peter, chaplain, of Marhamchurch, i, 107.

Symon, Rob. Can. of Plympton, a Penitentiary in the Deanery of Plympton, i, 143, 174, 194^b, 207^b, 217, 231.

Symon, Walter, collated (*by lapse*) to St. George's, Exeter, ii, 132^b; inst. to Kentisbeare, ii, 147, 249; his death [Symond, MS.], ii, 166.

Syngham, John, *see* Widecombe, i, 180^b.

Syrjonhykk, Wm., scholar,—*Dispensacio super defectu natalium* (29 June, 1416), i, 222.

Syward, Wm., V. of Pinhoe, exch. for the Chantry of St. Pancras, London, ii, 28, 210^b.

T.

Taillour, Stephen, inst. to Bittadon, ii, 7; his death, ii, 12^b.

Talaton [Taleton, MS.], John [Hethen], R. of, i, 73.

Breve Regium.—Prohibition to admit, pending settlement of the dispute as to patronage between Oliver Cervyngton and Sir John Hille (20 April, 1404), ii, 315^b. Prohibition suspended, 8 May, 1404 (the name of Wm. Morhay taking the place of that of Sir John Hille), *ibid*.—*See*, also, ii, 310^b, 311.

Talbot, John (of St. Paul's, Exeter), i, 314^b.

Talbot, Matilda, elected Prioress of Polslo, ii, 76^b, 77; i, 331.

Talbot, Rd, (clerk; chaplain), i, 32^b, 315; ii, 24^b, 46^b, 49, 49^b, 50, 50^b; proxy for Major Parys, ii, 167.

Talbot, Sir Wm., knt., patron of Challacombe, ii, 14^b; presents to the Chantry of Raleigh, ii, 64^b; to St. Mewan, ii, 74; to Menhenyot, ii, 243^b; co-patron of Menhenyot, ii, 138, 243^b.

Breve Regium,—To administer the oath to him, as Sheriff of Devon (30 Nov., 1416), ii, 359 (Administered 11 Jan., 1416-17; *ibid*).

Talcarne [*also* Talkarn, MS.], Wm., inst. to St. Erth, ii, 2; collated Dean of Crantock, ii, 191.

Talkern, i.e. Minster; Reginald Welleslegh, R., dispensation (to study at Oxford), for 2 years, from 7 Aug., 1408, i, 86.

Talland [Tallan *and* Tallam, MS.]

The chapel of St. Nicholas "de Porthpyghan" [Looe], licensed (23 June, 1400), i, 42.—John Trethewy, V., a Penitentiary in the Deanery of West, i, 49^b.—Walter Trethewy, chaplain, licensed to preach in the parish-church (22 March, 1414-15), i, 209.

Talvargh, John, clerk,—*Dispensacio super defectu natalium* (11 April, 1410), i, 95.

Talvargh, Richard, inst. to Sancreed, ii, 124.

Talvargh, Rob. de, inst. to St. Clements (Dec., 1329), ii, 348^b.

Talvern, in Philleigh; *see* Soor (*Oratories*), i, 47.

Talwart *alias* Pensans, Michael, scholar, *Dispensacio super defectu natalium* (7 Oct., 1411), i, 136^b.

Tambroke, Katherine, *see* Canonsleigh, p. 49; ii, 125.

Tamerton; Thos. [Moene], V., a Penitentiary in the Deanery of Tamerton, i, 50.—See Plymouth, i, 103^b.

Tanfeld, Wm., proxy for Thos. Aston, ii, 43, 226.

Tankert *alias* Schypwaysch, clerk—*Dispensacio super defectu natalium* (17 June, 1411), i, 127.

Tappyng, John, V. of Egg Buckland, ii, 23; his death, ii, 23^b.

Tapyn, John, inst. to Dunchideock, ii, 199^b, 267^b.

Taunton Priory, i, 318.—Patrons of Clannaborough, ii, 259^b, 356, 359; of Willand, ii, 21, 31^b.

Taunton, Robert Hereward, Archdeacon of, i, 310^b.

Taunton, John, *see* Bridgewater, i, 90.

Taunton (*or* Tanton), Rd., R. of Manston (Dioc. Sarum), exch. for Yarcombe, ii, 156^b; for Cameley (Dioc. B. and W.), ii, 194.

Taverner, Thos., clerk (son of Thos. Taverner, of Fowey), i, 315.

Tavistock, Chap. of St. Mary Magd., licensed 18 Sept., 1400, i, 48; the Lazar House, i, 306^b, 331^b.

An Indulgence was granted, 25 July, 1410, to the Faithful who should contribute to the support of this Hospital, i, 100^b.

Tavistock Abbey,—

John May, elected Abbot (12 July, 1402), ii, 58; confirmed (20 July), ii, 62^b; mandate for his Installation, *ibid*.

Mandate for its Visitation, 18 May, 1400, i, 36^b.—Thos. Cullyng, Abbot, in arrears of Procurations due to the Pope's Collector, for 3 years (1408-10), i, 105, 110.—The Abbot and Conv. presented to Whitchurch, ii, 9; to

Tavistock, ii, 15b, 179b, 181 ; to Abbotsham, ii, 17 ; to Antony, ii, 99b ; to Denbury, ii, 108, 110b, 161, 191 ; to Lamerton, 79, 144, 157b, 161, 247b ; to Virginstowe, ii, 115, 144, 179b ; to Burrington, ii, 133b ; to Milton-Abbot, ii, 132b, 180b ; to Hatherleigh, ii, 186.—*See* Burrington. Also, ii, 303b.

Tavistock, John [Lucas], V. of; a Penitentiary in the Deanery of, i, 50, 94, 115b, 143, 174, 194b, 207, 217, 231, 237b, 245b.

Tavy, Ecclesia de (*see* the Will of Isabel Daumarle), i, 308b.

Tawstock [Toustok, MS.]—

The Chapel of St. Laurence licensed, 3 Aug., 1400, i, 45.—Walter Gybbes, R., licensed to choose a Confessor (23 Aug., 1396), i, 9. *See* Gybbes, Walter.

Tawt, Richard, i, 331b.

Tawton (Bishop's), q. v.: Pylle, in this parish, *see* Fouke (*Oratories*), i, 35b.—Rd. Westecote of, *see* Westecote, i, 149.—Walter Beare of, *see* Beare, ii, 310.—Beare, in this parish, *see* Halle, Wm., ii, 310b.

Taylor, John, clerk,—*Dispensacio super defectu natalium* (25 Aug., 1414), i, 198b.

Taylour, Andrew, i, 332b.

Taylour (*or* Tayllour, John), i, 315, 324b ; inst. to Shillingford, ii, 9b ; resigns, ii, 19b ; inst. to Branscombe, ii, 18b, 19.

John Taylour, V. of Broad Chalk (Sarum), exch. for Cheriton-Bishop, ii, 30 ; for Hemington (B. and W.), ii, 56.—John Taylour inst. to Southleigh, ii, 159b ; resigns, ii, 168.

Taylour, Rob., collated to Morwenstow, ii, 100 ; i, 84.

Taylour, Thos., scholar,—*Dispensacio super defectu natalium* (2 May, 1409), i, 89.

Thos. Taylour, clerk (of Slapton Colleg. Chantry), i, 317b ; ii, 111.

Tedburn St. Mary, Hackworthy in, *see* Northcote (*Oratories*).

Tehidy [Tihidy, MS.], ii, 316 ; *see* Basset (*Oratories*), i, 61.

Teignbridge, i, 318.

Terrers, Nicholas, *see* Exeter, St. George's, ii, 336b.

Tetcott [Tettecote, MS.], Rob., R. of, a Penitentiary in the Deanery of Holsworthy [Haldesworthy, MS.], i, 50.

Tewkesbury Abbey ; patrons of Chittlehampton, ii, 3b (210b), 86b, 106b ; of Crowan, ii, 69b, 159b, 167 ; *see* ii, 303.

Tewyn, John, collated to St. Colan, ii, 94 ; his death, ii, 133.

Teynton (*or* Teyngton), Thos., Can. of Salisbury, exch. for a Can. in Exeter Cathedral, ii, 150 ; *see* Constance, i, 203b ; his death, ii, 165.

Themot, Laurence, his manumission,—

"manumisimus et relaxavimus Laurencium Themot, nativum nostrum de manerio nostro de Tauton, ipsumque pro bono servicio suo hactenus nobis impenso et imposterum impendendo, cum tota sequela sua, a jugo et onere quibuscumque nativitatis, villenagii, et servitutis, cum omnibus bonis et catallis suis habitis et habendis, liberavimus per presentes" (Crediton, 20 April, 1405) i, 75.

Thetford Priory, ii, 39.

Thetford, John, inst. Prior of St. James's Priory, Exeter, ii, 43ᵇ.

Thomas, Adam, V. of St. Gennys, exch. for Yarnscombe, ii, 141ᵇ; resigns, ii, 166.

Thomas, Henry, R. of Knightsleigh (Dioc. of B. and W.) exch. for Cotleigh, ii, 95ᵇ: for Lamerton, ii, 157ᵇ; 256; his death, ii, 161.

Thomas, John, inst. to Dodbrooke, ii, 65ᵇ; i, 64ᵇ; [resigns and is] inst. to Portlemouth, ii, 84ᵇ; i, 76.

Thomma, John, collated to Clannaborough, ii, 182.—John Thoma (*or* Thome) Can. of Launceston, occurs, ii, 117.

Thorlethorp, John, ii, 362ᵇ.

Thornbury; Walter Trenylen, R.,—

He resigned, having represented to the Bp. that he was "senio confractus, viribus corporis sui ad regimen ecclesiarum destitutus." The patron for that turn, Henry Cornu, domicellus, appointed John Dygon, Can. of Plympton Priory; and the Bp. assigned to Trenylen an annual pension of £10 to be paid quarterly, with a choice of a chamber in the Rectory-House, the chief chamber excepted (31 July, 1404), i, 71ᵇ.—Dygon was inst. (ii, 74); and, 7 Jan., 1404-5, obtained licence of non-residence for 2 years, i, 72ᵇ; for a year, from 10 May, 1408, i, 85ᵇ; and again from 16 July, 1410, i, 100ᵇ.

Thorndon, John, canon-regular of St. Peter's, Ipswich, ii, 213ᵇ.

Thorne, Wm. (St. Pancras, Exeter), i, 319ᵇ.

Thornecombe [in Dorsetshire], R.—

The parish-church and the Chap. of St. Melorus in the said parish, having been placed under an Interdict, the Bishop granted relaxation of the same, 29 Jan., 1411-12; i, 144.

Thorney (Dioc. of Chichester), Michael Lercedekne, R., i, 321. *See* Haccombe, i, 178ᵇ.

Thorp, John, proxy for John Bailly, ii, 124ᵇ.—Wm. Thorp, i, 305.

Thorverton; the Bridge, i, 327ᵇ: *see* Mulle, Thos. (*Oratories*), i, 88.—Andrew [Stoke], V., a Penitentiary in the Deanery of Cadbury, i, 50.

Throkmorton, John, co-patron of North Bovey, ii, 189ᵇ, 264.

Throwleigh, John Smyth, R.—

He was licensed to celebrate in the Chap. of St. Mary "atte Wallyn" (7 April, 1400), i, 35ᵇ; a Penitentiary in the Deanery of Dunsford, i, 50.

Thorlebeare, in Launcells, *see* Arundell (*Oratories*), i, 212.

For Thurlebeare, *see* Syreston (*Oratories*), i, 82ᵇ. Alice Hoggeȝ of Thurlbeare, i, 312. And *see* i, 311ᵇ.

Thurleston; Rob. Benet, R., *see* Stokenham, ii, 357ᵇ. John Wytloff's bequest to the Church, i, 306.

Thyrnyng, Sir Wm., *see* Ottery St. Mary, ii, 278; *also*, ii, 303.

Tin, the tithe of,—

"Noverint universi per presentes nos Edmundum, miseracione divina Episcopum

Exoniensem, recepisse de Johanne de Waterton, Receptore denariorum Domini Principis in Comitatibus Cornubie et Devonie, sexdecim libras, tresdecim solidos, et quatuor denarios sterlingorum, nomine decime de Coignagio Stannarum, in Comitatibus predictis, provenientis, nobis et ecclesie nostre debite ad Festum Sancti Michaelis proxime preteritum ante datum presencium, pro anno tunc proxime elapso ; unde pro decima stannarum in comitatu Cornubie sex libras, tresdecim solidos et quatuor denarios, et Devonie decem libras. E quibus quidem sextedecim (*sic*) libris, tresdecim solidis, et quatuor denariis fatemur nos fore solutum et predictum Receptorem inde quietum, sigillo nostro presentibus signato. Datum apud Clyst, vicesimo tercio die mensis Novembris, anno Regis Henrici Quarti post Conquestum Anglie duodecimo" (1410).—In the margin :—"*Acquietancia xvj. lib. xiijs. et iiijd. pro decima stagnarum in Com. Cornubie et Devonie pro anno Regis undecimo*," i, 109b.

A similar acquittance, and for the same amounts in both counties, was given by the Bishop to John de Waterton, at Chudleigh, 23 Nov., 1411, i, 140b ; and again, 22 Oct., 1412, i, 172b.—Also, to John Wylcotys, 25 Oct., 1413, i, 187 ; 14 Oct., 1414, i, 202b ; 4 Oct., 1415, i, 213b ; pro decima *cunnagii*, 3 Oct., 1416, i, 226b ; 4 Oct., 1417, i, 235b ; 18 Oct., 1418, i, 244.

Tintagel; Chap. of St. Dionisius, Trevena, licd. 11 July, 1400; i, 43b.

Tiptoft, Philippa, wife of Sir John, ii, 350 ; *see* Silverton.

Tiverton, parish of—

Several Chapels in this parish were licensed 2 July, 1400.

Dr. Oliver (Eccles. Antiq., ii, 109), describes them as "the Chapel of St. Thomas, at Chetescombe Bolham, of St. James on the Loman, and St. Katherine's, East Bradleigh ;" and he adds that, "the Chapel of *St. Thomas at Chetscombe* is again mentioned by Bp. Lacy, 28 Aug., 1442."—But the entry in the Register is as follows—"in capellis de Chetescombe Bolham Sancti Thome in villa de Tyverton, Sancti Jacobi de Lompne et Sancte Katerine de Estbradlegh in parochia de Tyverton ;" i, 43.—Licence was granted (22 Nov., 1408) to James Frankcheyne, R. of the Second Portion, for the Chapels of St. Luke, St. Stephen, and St. Katherine in this parish ; i, 87. —Farleigh ; *see* Ayssh (*Oratories*), i, 80.—Chevithorne [Chyvethorn, MS.], *see* Fraunceys (*Oratories*), i, 221b.—Mandate for an Enquiry as to dilapidation in the parish church (6 Sept., 1412), i, 165b.—An Indulgence of 40 days "per biennium," granted to the Faithful who should contribute to the maintenance of a priest to serve "ad altare alte crucis in ecclesia parochiali de Tyverton" (16 May, 1416), i, 221b.

Commission of Enquiry (directed to Walter Coke, LLB., R.), as to the pollution of the Cemetery by Matthew Row and John Barstaple (10 Aug., 1419), ii, 268b.—Commission to reconcile (23 Aug., 1419) *ibid.*—Bequest to the poor of Tiverton by Canon Henry Brokelond, i, 303.

Rectors of Tiverton :—(1st Portion), Walter Robert, i, 183b ; a Penitentiary in the Deanery of Tiverton, i, 194, 207b ; his Will, i, 324 ; Walter Colle ; Dispensation (to study at Oxford) for a year, from 31 Oct., 1415, i, 214 ; licence of non-residence for a year, from 3 Oct., 1416, i, 226 ; and from 21 April to the F. of All Saints, 1418, i, 239.—(2nd Portion), James Frankcheyne, licence of non-residence from 10 Nov., 1412, to Michaelmas, 1413, i, 171b.—(3rd Portion), John [Colyer], a Penitentiary in the Deanery of Tiverton, i, 50.—Alan Benet ; licence of non-residence for a year, from 25 July, 1410, i, 101 ; a Penitentiary in the Deanery of Tiverton, i, 216b ; 231, 237b, 245.

Toffe (or Tofte), Thos., inst. to Blackborough, ii, 85 ; i, 77, 103 ; his death, ii, 151b.

Toker, Adam, i, 321.

Toker, Englisia ; *see* Beaumound, Joan, i, 161b, 175b.

Toker, Nicholas, inst. to Goodleigh, ii, 192 ; i, 245.

Toker, Rd., inst. to Meavy, ii, 121 ; his death, ii, 182b.

Tokere, Walter, inst. to Affeton, ii, 107b ; resigns, ii, 181b.

Toker (Tokere *or* Thoker) Wm., chaplain, a Penitentiary for the Deanery of Ipplepen, i, 94, 115, 143, 174, 194b, 207b, 217, 231, 237b, 245.

Toket, William, proxy for John Fecos, ii, 42.

Tolke, Walter (*cissor*) and Isabella de Tottonia,—

They had married in ignorance of all impediments, and afterwards discovered that Reynald Beek, who had had illicit intercourse with Isabella, was related to Walter in the 3rd degree of consanguinity. Dispensation granted 31 July, 1416, i, 225b.

Tomme, John, V. of Rattery, exch. for Mamhead, ii, 189.

Tone, John, inst. to Ashwater, ii, 75b, i, 71, 72; decd. ii, 91b.

Tone, Philip, Abbot of Hartland, ii, 183b.

Torbrian; Nich. Wake, R., executor of Walter Trote's Will, i, 303.—Wm. Peyon, R., licence of non-residence for a year, from 17 Oct., 1405, i, 76b.—John Gentylman, R.,—

He obtained no fewer than eight licences of non-residence—(1) for a year, from 1 Feb., 1408-9, i, 88 ; (2) for a year, from 30 Sept., 1410 (and a sequestration taken off), i, 105b; (3) from 21 Jan., 1411-12, to Michaelmas, 1412, i, 142 ; (4) for a year, from 20 Sept., 1413, i, 184 ; (5) from 15 March, 1414-15, to Michaelmas, 1415, i, 208b ; (6) from 15 Jan., 1415-16, to Michaelmas, 1416, 215b ; (7) from 16 Dec., 1416, to Michaelmas, 1417, i, 228 ; (8) for a year, from 1 March, 1418-19, i. 245b.

Torner, Thomas, inst. to Satterleigh, ii, 5 ; his death, ii, 182b.

Torre Abbey, i, 15b, 75b, 318.

William [Norton] Abbot, i, 30 ; in arrears of procurations due to the Pope's collector (1410), i, 105. — Matthew Yerde, elected Abbot ; Letter of John, Abbot of Welbeck and the Abbot of Hales on his behalf ; he does homage to the Bishop in the Chapel at Clyst (21 July, 1412), ii, 142b.—Wm. Mychel, Abbot-Elect ; his "Obediencia" (18 March, 1413-14), ii,157.—John Dowelton, Monk of Torre, ii, 252.—The Abbot and Conv. presented to Townstal, ii, 6b, 50b. 92, 158 ; Hennock, ii, 14, 149b ; Shebbear, ii, 20 ; Bradworthy, ii, 88b, 152b (*see* i, 68) ; Buckland Brewer, ii, 85b.

Torridge [Toryg, MS.], the river, *see* Woodford Bridge, i, 25b.

Torrington (Great); Almshouse rebuilt, *see* Colyn, Rd., i. 5 ; the Lazar-House at, 331b.—

Laurence Bryghtlegh, R., was licensed to celebrate in private Oratories (8 April, 1400), i, 35b.—Wm. Hyde, R. ; to celebrate in St. Saviour's Chapel, in this parish (10 Feb., 1401-2), i, 54b ; also (on the same day) to hear the Confessions of his parishioners, for one year only, *ibid.* ; also 6 (March, 1403-4), to celebrate in his Rectory-House ; and (on the same day), to be non-resident, and study in Oxford, for a year, i, 70 : also, 6 July, 1408 (he was then "Bachelor in Decrees"), to celebrate in a certain chapel in this parish, i, 86.—Stephen Payn, R., was licensed to celebrate in St. Saviour's Chapel (27 March, 1414), i, 195b ; 203b ;—Wm. Alyn, R. (i, 246), obtained a dispensation (to study at Oxford) for 3 years, from 2 Aug., 1419, i, 247b.

Commissions :—(1) directed to Henry Trethewy, R., as to dilapidations caused by the neglect of Wm. Yeurde, the late R., (27 May, 1418), ii, 265. (2) directed to Steph. Pott, chaplain, Wm. Blanche, and Wm. Alyn, clerk, on the petition of the said Henry Trethewy : the amount due was at least £43 6s 8d, and sequestration of Yurde's (*sic*) effects was ordered, 10 June, 1418, ii, 265^{b}.—Manor of Stevenstone, *see* Graunt (*Oratories*), i, 145.—*See*, also, Wyger, John, i, 203^{b}.

Torryngton, William, inst. to Broadoak, R., ii, 157.

Tothale, W. de, Prior of the Hosp. of St. John of Jerusalem, i, 208^{b}.

Totley [Totele, MS.]. in Black Torrington; Chapel of St. Katherine ; *see* Fyȝtwaryn (*Oratories*), i, 57^{b}.

Totnes ; the Bridge, i, 306^{b}, 318, 330^{b}.—Lazar-house at, i, 306^{b}, 309, 318^{b}, 331^{b}.

Totnes Priory,—

Mandate for its visitation, 13 May, 1400, i, 36 : in arrear of the procurations due to the Pope's Collector for one year (1410), i, 105 : Thos. Swynford, Prior, resigns, and John Southam is admitted, ii, 349, 349^{b}.—*See*, also, Rodenay, i, 121^{b}.—The Priory presents to Totnes, ii, 95 ; to Broad Clyst, ii, 152, 252.

Totnes, parish of ; Bowden, *see* Schapwyk (*Oratories*), i, 237 ;

Commissions of Enquiry (1) as to the alleged pollution of the Church in a quarrel between John Southam and Thos. Swynford, Prior of Totnes, and others their abettors, about the rights of the Priory of Totnes (21 June, 1414), ii, 254^{b}.—The quarrel occurred 18 June, and as it was said that blood was shed, the Vicar and parishioners had since refrained from using the Church. The Bishop, finding that the matter had been exaggerated, and that there was no blood shed or very serious quarrel, directed the Vicar (23 June) to resume its use immediately ; i, 197^{b}.—(2) As to the pollution of the cemetery, in a quarrel, with bloodshed, between Steph. Bellegh and Wm. Brydon (28 Jan., 1418-19), ii, 267.—The Bp. found that there was no pollution, and ordered the dead to be buried as before (31 Jan.), i, 245. John [Dolbiry], V., Penitentiary in the Deanery of Totnes, i, 217, 231, 237^{b}, 245.

Totnes, Archdeaconry of,—

Mandate for its Visitation (A.D. 1400), i, 35^{b}.—John de Lydeford, Archd., his Will, i, 309^{b}.—Can. William Hunden's bequest for the repairs of roads and bridges in this Archdeaconry, i, 324^{b}.—Can. Rd. Penels bequeaths 40 marks for the poor and sick therein ; 2 marks to be reserved for the poor of Brixham, i, 332^{b}.

Tottonia, Isabella de, *see* Tolke, Walter, i, 225^{b}.

Touker, John, proxy for Peter Bryd, ii, 31^{b}.

Townstal [Tunstalle, MS.], the "Ordinacio" of the Vicarage,—

The Rectory was appropriated to Torre Abbey ; and the Bishop, with the consent of the Abbot and of Rd. Bradeworthy, V , made order as to the endowment of the Vicarage as follows :—The V. and his successors to be paid 20 marks annually, in quarterly payments (under a penalty of forfeiting 20s. to the Bishop, in case of default for 15 days after each quarter-day), and to have, by way of manse, the houses, garden, and curtilage in his occupation at the time, and so used time out of mind ; also, from the funeral offerings one penny (only) for every burial in Townstal parish-church and in the Chapel at Dartmouth thereto depending, or in the cemeteries thereunto annexed ; and the same on every anniversary ; also, the tithe *casei, butiri, et lactis, aucarum, et porcellorum.* The Vicars were to be liable for the repair of the desks in the Chancel and the office-books (as if they were Rectors), and to serve the office of Dean-Rural in their turn [*ac officium Decani Ruralis quociens pro dicta ecclesia juste fuerit subeundum*] ; they were to pay the procurations canonically due to the Archdeacon, also synodals, etc., and "Peter's Pence" [*Sinodaticum et cathedraticum, cum denariis Sancti Petri*]. But for all other like burdens the Abbey was to be liable. Dated at Crediton, 4 July, 1405. Signed and sealed by the Abbot, 27 July; by the Dean and Chapter of Exeter, 31 July; and by the Vicar (who used the seal of the Bishop's Official-Peculiar in Devon—*quia sigillum meum pluribus est incognitum*), i, 75b.

John Burgh, V., was licensed (13 Feb., 1414-15) to hear the confessions of his parishioners, i. 208; a Penitentiary in the Deanery of Totnes; i, 217, 231, 237, 245.—In his time the executors of Sir John Daubryggecourt, knt., represented to the Bishop that, whereas the deceased had directed in his Will that his body should be buried in the Conventual Church of Dale, in the Dioc. of Coventry and Lichfield, the Vicar, not being aware of the fact, had buried him in the Chapel of the Holy Trinity at Dartmouth, where—a stranger to the place—the said knight happened to die. The Bishop issued his Mandate, requiring the V. to cause the body to be exhumed and delivered over to the executors (23 Oct., 1416), i, 226b; Arnald, Edmund (*see Oratories*), i, 146.

Tournere, Stephen, i, 324.

Tovy, Simon, V. of Westleigh, exch. for Trentishoe, ii, 188b.

Towednack, *see* Lelant, i, 133b; ii, 232b.

Tracy, Thomasia, a Canoness of Canonsleigh, ii, 125.

Trae, William, clerk, i, 309b.

Wm. Tray (*or* Trey) was Dean of Crediton; *see* Sture, Wm., i, 126; his Will, i, 316b; his death, ii, 141b.—To a Wm. Treye (*alias* Stocker), clerk "de presbitero genito et soluta," a Dispensation *super defectu natalium* was granted, 26 Feb., 1408-9, i, 88.

Traunce, Rd., inst. to Pyworthy, ii, 24b; his death, ii, 82b.

Trebel, Wm., LL.B., coll. Can. of Glasney, ii, 134; exch. for Can. in Crediton, ii, 134b; and again for R. of St. Mawgan-in-Pyder, ii, 139b; exch. for Lanteglos-by-Camelford, ii, 178. He was R. of Poltimore in 1411, ii, 134.

Treberveth, Nich., is presented to Truro, ii, 245; his complaint as to dilapidations, ii, 246b; his inst., ii, 140b.

Trecarrel, in Lezant, *see Oratories*, i, 74b.

Tredak, Thos., Canon of Launceston Priory, ii, 117.

Tredewy, Henry, chaplain, licensed as Publick Preacher in the Archdeaconries of Barnstaple and Cornwall (14 Jan., 1409-10), i, 93b.

Tredewy (*or* Trethewy), Wm., recluse and anchorite of Great Torrington, a Penitentiary in the Deanery of Torrington, i, 94, 115b, 143b, 174, 194b, 207b, 217, 231, 238, 245b.

Tredowargh, Thos., collated to Farringdon, ii, 34; resigns, ii, 129; *see* i, 33, 55.

Tredydan, Stephen, Prior of Launceston (deceased), ii, 72.

Tredynec, Roger, V. of St. Cleer (deceased), ii, 49.

Trefalford, *see Oratories*, i, 82.

Treflouan, in Cornwall, *see* Pomeray, John de la, ii, 310.

Trefraudewell, *see* Trencruk (*Oratories*), i, 77.

Trefrew [Treuerew, MS., ii, 341b]; Roger, V. of Hatherleigh (deceased), ii, 186.

Trefruff, William, Bachelor in Decrees, i, 89.

Trefussa, in St. Erth, i, 70.

Tregaria, Robert, V. of Mariansleigh, ii, 5.

Tregarrek, *see* Trelouny (*Oratories*), i, 37b.

Tregek, John, R. of St. Erme (deceased), ii, 82b.

Tregethes, James, a parishioner of Lelant, ii, 232b.

Tregeufedon [? Tregavethan], Chapel in St. Kea, i, 228.

Tregilliowe, Wm., of Marazion, i, 88b, 136b.

Tregodok, Wm., inst. to Walkhampton, ii, 88.

Tregodynov, John, clerk,—
Dispensacio super defectu natalium (? 17 Dec.), ". . . . . . septima die," MS., 1397), i, 14.

Tregois, John, proxy for Ralph Rudruth, ii, 42.

Tregonet, Adam, V. of Antony (deceased), ii, 87.

Tregonyon, *see* Halap (*Oratories*), i, 215b.

Tregonnen, William, ii, 351b.

Tregony, *see* Trevarrek, Rd., 209b; the Ch. of St. James, i, 323b.

Tregoos, *see* Trevanyon (*Oratories*), i, 110b.

Tregos, Wm., R. of "Eglosros," i.e., Philleigh,—
He was Can. of Glasney, and had licence of non-residence for a year, from 13 Nov., 1405 (to reside at Glasney), i, 77; John Godegrave, sub-deacon, was collated, by lapse, to be his Vicar at Glasney, 7 Aug., 1410, i, 102b.

Tregower, William (senior), i, 314b.

Tregoys, Chapel of St. Mary at, *see* Tregoys (*Oratories*), i, 12b.

Tregrenewylle, John, R. of Plymtree (deceased), ii, 188b.

Tregrisiou, Ralph, LL.D., Dean of Exeter, V. G. of the Diocese, etc.; his Commission (20 June, 1395), i, 1; ii, 209; *see*, also, i, 4, 5b, 9, 10b, 19b, 30.
Commission, directed (24 May, 1397), to John Lideford, Archd. of Totnes, and Walter Gybbes, Can. of Exeter, as to the detention, by Can. Walter[1] Colompton and others, of the revenues belonging to the said Ralph; ii, 212b.—He died 25 July, 1415 (being Can., also, of Crediton, ii, 166b, 167); and the Bp. issued a Commission (20 Aug.), directed to Wm. Knyght, R. of Kilkhampton, to collect and hold certain of the revenues of the Deanery, ii. 257.—As Dean, he presented to Colaton Raleigh, ii, 41b; to Bishop's Tawton, ii, 136.—His Will, i, 323.—Tregrisiou, in Cornwall; Dean Tregrisiou there; ii, 7, 9b.

[1] *Not* "John," as at page 64 (an *erratum*).

Trehage, Robert, *see* Crantock, ii, 262.

Trehures, Rosa, *see* St. Feock, i, 161.

Trelaba, Thomas, a parishioner of Linkinhorne, i, 116.

Trelawny, *see* Trelouny (*Oratories*), i, 37[b].

Trelawny, Nich., co-patron of Washfield, ii, 168; 342[b].

Trelaunay (*sic*), Roger, son of Nicholas, i, 315.

Trelees, Alan, Chantry-priest, "de Ponte," in Glasney (deceased), ii, 111; *see*, also, i, 66.

Treles, Richard, inst. to Mylor, ii, 21.

Trelissick [Treulesyk, MS.], in St. Erth, i, 240[b].

Trelong, in Trekeyr, lands of Arundell, ii, 311.

Treloscan, John, *see* Glasney, Chantry of Beaupre, ii, 136; his death, ii, 187[b].

Treludek, David, sub-prior of St. Stephen's, Launceston, ii, 116.

Trelynow (*alias* Godok), Thos., V. So. Petherwyn (resigns), ii, 123[b].

Tremadert, *see* Colshull (*Oratories*), i, 205, ii, 49.

Tremayle, Elinor (wife of Rob.) of So. Petherwyn, ii, 263[b]; i, 237.

Tremayle, Roger, co-patron of Blackborough, ii, 151[b]; i, 312.

Tremayn, Nich., co-patron of Aveton-Giffard, ii, 67[b]; and of the Chantry "de Lyneton," therein, ii, 91[b]. *See*, also, ii, 144[b].

Tremayne, Rd., clerk,—*Dispensacio super defectu natalium* (5 Aug., 1417), i, 233.

Tremayne, Thos., inst. to No. Huish, ii, 8[b]; resigns, ii, 67[b]; inst. to Aveton-Gifford, ii, 67; again to No. Huish, ii, 144[b], 248[b]; *see*, i, 94, 115[b], 196, 217, 231, 237[b], 309; ii, 357.

He was collated to a Can. in the Cathedral, and thereupon resigned No. Huish, ii, 189[b]; resigned this Canonry, ii, 191, having been collated to that held by Laurence Haukyn, deceased, ii, 190[b].—*See* Butterford, i, 37.

Tremayn, *see* *Oratories*, i, 39[b].

Trembethow, in St. Uny Lelant, i, 240[b].

Tremylet, Rob., collat. Sacristan of Bosham, ii, 147; his death, ii, 168.

Trencruke (Menhenyot), *see* Heligan (*Oratories*), i, 9[b], 135.

Trendelbeare, Wm., R., of Manaton, i, 7[b], 58[b]; his death, ii, 67.

Trendelove, Wm., R. of Clannaborough (in 1330), ii, 359.

Treneglos, Reginald [Foter], V.; a Penitentiary in the Deanery of Trigg-Major, i, 49[b].

Treneglos, Michael, clerk,—*Dispensacio super defectu natalium* (22 Dec., 1414), i, 205[b].

Trenewyth, in St. Probus, *see* Trenewyth (*Oratories*), i, 72.[b]

Trenewyth, Luke, inst. to Crowan, ii, 69[b]; his death, ii, 159[b].

Trenowyth, Wm., his Will, i, 301b; Udelina, his sister, *ibid.*

Trenylen, Walter, R. of Thornbury, i, 71b; resigns, ii, 75.

Trerice, *see* Trevanion *and* Arundell (*Oratories*), i, 110b, 190, 212; ii, 311.

Trervell, mansion of James Gerveys (*see Oratories*), i, 36b.

Tresagnow, John, inst. to Lamorran, ii, 124.

Tresawel, Thos., R. of Grade, deceased, ii, 107b.

Tresculerd, Thos., *aquebajulus* at St. Illogan, i, 120b.

Tresilian, Robert, *see* Preston, John, ii, 351b.

Treskere, Reginald, i, 48b.

Trethak, Thomas, Canon of Launceston,—

Licensed (22 Feb., 1411-12), to hear the confessions of the parishioners of St. Stephen's-by-Launceston, Linkinhorne, Lewannick, and St. Gennys, in the Deanery of Trigg-Major; i, 145.

Tretherf, Jno. presents Renaldus Tretherf to Ladock, ii, 159, 254.

This Renaldus, "scholar," obtained a Dispensation *super defectu natalium*, (30 May, 1414, i, 197; also, a Dispensation (to study at Oxford), for 4 years from 12 Nov., 1414, i, 203. *See*, also, i, 245b.

Trethewy, Henry, inst. to Great Torrington, ii, 190b, 265; 265b.

Trethewy, John, inst. to Talland, ii, 6; i, 49b.

To John Trethewy, clerk, *de presbitero genito et soluta*, was granted, 24 Feb., 1407-8, a Dispensation *super defectu natalium*, i, 84. A like Dispensation was granted, 23 Sept., 1412, to John Trethewy, scholar, who is described as *de soluto genitus et soluta*, i, 166b.

Trethewy, Walter, clerk,—*Dispensacio super defectu natalium* (9 Feb., 1400-1), ii, 16b.

He was afterwards licensed to preach in the churches and chapels of the town of Launceston, and in the parishes of Talland and South Petherwin (22 March, 1414-15), i, 209.

Treȝethyan (*or* Trethyan), *see* St. Pinnock, ii, 350b, 351, 351b, 352. Also, Trevaga, Richard; *ibidem.*

Trevaga, *see* "*Oratories,*" i, 37b.

Trevalga; Walter Tyneov, R.; licence of non-residence for 3 years, from 6 Jan., 1408-9, i, 88; also [Tynyow, MS.], from 14 Jan., 1412-13, to Michaelmas, 1413, i, 173b; and for a year, from 16 Feb., i, 1414-15, i, 208b.

Trevanyon, *see Oratories*, i, 110b.

Trevanyon, Rd. and Thos., present to Grade, ii, 107b.

Trevarrak, John, *see* Lansallos, ii, 253b.

Trevarrek (*or* Trewarrek), Richard, of Tregony.—

He was excommunicated for refusing to pay £19 due to the Dean and Chapter of Exeter, and, continuing contumacious, was handed over by the Bp. to the secular arm, 3 Dec., 1414; i, 205. Upon this he seems to have paid all but £6 6s 8d, which he refused to meet, and he was finally handed over to the secular arm, 18 April, 1415; i, 209b.

Trevarthyan, in St. Newlyn, *see* Syreston (*Oratories*).

Trevarthyon (*sic*), John, patron of St. Ruan-major, ii, 10; Sir John Trevarthyan, knt., presents to the R., ii, 50; Joan, relict of Sir John Trevarthian, ii, 229.

Trevarthian, Otho, and Joan Hulle,—
They desired to marry, their parents and friends consenting, but required a Dispensation, being within the 4th degree of consanguinity. Dispensation granted, 22 June, 1411, i, 128.—Sir Otho Trevarthyan, knt., was patron of Landewednack, ii, 175.

Trevelle, *see* Trevaga (*Oratories*), i, 37b.

Trevellys,[1] Wm., Treasurer of the Cathedral, ii, 217b; his death, i, 329b; ii, 42b.

Trevelyan, John (M.A., and Scholar in Theology), licensed a Publick Preacher in the Archdeaconry of Cornwall, 9 Oct., 1411, i, 135b.

Trevelyan, Rd., inst. to Poundstock, ii, 164; exch.[2] for Stoke Rivers, ii, 180.

Trevelyan, Wm., chaplain, a Penitentiary in the Deanery of Penwith, i, 143b, 194b, 207b, 217, 231, 238, 245b.

Trevelves, Thos., collated to St. Gluvias "de Penryn," ii, 158.
A chaplain; and a Penitentiary in the Deanery of Pydar, i, 143b, 174, 194b.

Trevena, Chapel of St Dionysius, (*see* Tintagel.) i, 43b.

Trevenour, John, presents to Lamorran, ii, 124.
He did homage to the Bishop, in London, for lands in Cornwall, 20th Sept., 1397, ii, 310.

Treverbyn, John, inst. to St. Stephen's-in-Brannel, V., ii, 40; i, 143b, 174, 194b; his death, ii, 157.

Treverbyn Bridge,—
It carried the road from Liskeard to Bodmin over the Fowey, and being ruinous, the Bishop wrote to the Archdn. of Cornwall, ordering collections to be made throughout the Archdeaconry, and promising an Indulgence to the Faithful who should contribute (21 Jan., 1412-13), i, 174b.

Trevet, Thomas, inst. to Aylesbeare, i, 121.

Treveysek, John, chaplain; *see* Aller, John.

Trevysek, Thomas, of St. Gennys, ii, 261b, 262.

Trevugy, Robert, a chaplain, ii, 48.

Trevyda, Joceus, clerk,—*Dispensacio super defectu natalium* (7 March, 1415-16), i, 217b.

Trewalward, *see Oratories*, i, 11b.

Trewarnene (in Cornwall), ii, 348.

---

[1] Not "Trenellys," as in *Oliver's* List. [2] Trevylyan, MS.

Trewbys, Rob., *see* Luxulyan, i, 160b, ii, 247.

Trewen, Chantry of ; *see* Holsworthy.

Trewen, Sampson, chaplain ; *see* Widecombe, i, 180b.

Trewethenek, Roger, takes the oath as J.P. for Cornwall, ii, 335b.

Trewolge (*alias* Stephyn), Rob., *see* Glasney; Chantry of Beaupre, ii, 166.

Treworgy, *see* Kendall (*Oratories*). This place is described as "in parochia de Reprenne"—i.e., St. Winnow ; but it is in the neighbouring parish of Duloe.

Trewoyef, John (senior and junior), *see Oratories*, i, 180b.

Trewreff, John and Margaret (*alias* Mage), his wife,—

Dispensation granted, confirming their marriage, although they were related in the 4th degree of affinity (17 April, 1409), i, 88b.

Trewynt, John, *see* Blisland, ii, 245.

Trewythgy, Laurence, V. of St. Madron (deceased), ii, 99b.

Treyage, Rob., senior, proxy for Wm. Cave, ii, 135b.

Treyngoff, Walter, clerk,—*Dispensacio super defectu natalium* (23 July, 1411), i, 129.—*See* St. Neot's, i, 161.—John Treyngoff was V. of St. Neot's, i, 161b.

Trigal, Sampson, Prior of Lodres, i, 9b.

Trille, John, inst. to Bicton, ii, 14 ; his death, ii, 23.

Trobrygge, Joceus and Thos. de, co-patrons of Ashreigney, ii, 156, 177b.

Joceus Trobrugge (*sic*) did homage to the Bp. at Crediton, for lands at Trobrugge within the demesne of Crediton (16 Sept., 1411), ii, 310b.

Troubrygge, Rd., V. of Winkleigh (deceased), ii, 67b.

Trote, Walter, inst. to St. Kerrian's, Exeter, ii, 10b ; exch. Ipplepen for a Can. in the Cathedral, ii, 31b ; resigns his Can. and Preb. of Pratum min. in Hereford Cath., ii, 53b ; his death, ii, 74b, 75 ; his Will, i, 302b.

Trugge, John, a parishioner of Linkinhorne, i, 116.

Trunket, John, V. of Monkleigh (decd.), ii, 109b; *see* also, i, 320b.

Truro [Truru, Treurev and Trurw, MS.], the Friars of, i, 301b.

Thomas Welle, R., was licensed to hear confessions, 16 May, 1400, i, 37 ; a Penitentiary in the Deanery of Powder (*pro* "*secunda parte*"), i, 49b, 93b, 115b ; licensed[1] to choose Confessors (27 May, 1410), i, 96. Commissions of Enquiry :—(1) to the right of presentation ; Rob. Hylle, senior, having presented Nich. Treberveth, chaplain (12 March, 1411-12), ii, 246 ; (2) as to the dilapidations in the Chancel, etc., on the complaint of the said Nicholas against Thos. Wille (24 May, 1412), ii, 246b.—Treberveth was a Penitentiary in the Deanery of Powder, i, 245b.

---

[1] *John* Wylle, MS. ; a clerical error.

Trybbe, Rob., R. of Oare (Dioc. of B. and W.), exch. for the Chantry of Raleigh, ii, 64ᵇ; for that of SS. Katherine and Mary Magd., Morthoe, ii, 137.

Tryby, Rd., inst. to Dodbrooke, ii, 124ᵇ; resigns, for Newton Ferrers, ii, 197, 197ᵇ, 266ᵇ; *see* i, 245,ᵇ 334; ii, 357ᵇ.

Tuderyngton, John, inst. to East Buckland, ii, 16.

Tugel, Thos. R. of Stokeinteignhead (deceased), ii, 35ᵇ.
A Thomas Tuggel was Preb. of St. Probus; (resigned), ii, 30ᵇ.

Tullok, Godfrey, V. of Morval (deceased), ii, 74.

Tunerton (*perhaps* Tuverton, i.q. "Tiverton"), Thomas, i, 319ᵇ.

Turks, the,—

The Bishop writes to the King [Henry IV.], acknowledging receipt of a *Breve Regium*, dated Westminster, 11 Jan., 1400-1, in which—referring to the danger of Constantinople being taken by Bajazet, and to the Indulgences granted by the Pope to those who should help the Emperor Manuel—he commanded the Bp. to certify him as to the names of the Commissioners and their Deputies in his Diocese; also of all who held keys of the chests and coffers which contained the contributions of the Faithful, and of the places where such chests, etc., were kept. The Bp. replied that there was one such chest or coffer in Exeter Cathedral, of which Wm. Overby, chaplain, held the key, who, with Rob. Northale, of the Dioc. of Norwich, and John Knyght, of Bridport, had gone round the Diocese collecting money, which they still had in their keeping. They had left the Diocese; and he could not answer for their readiness to obey the summons to appear in the Court of Chancery at Exeter.—Dated 12 April, 1401, ii, 312ᵇ.

Turnour, Henry, *see* Kentisbeare, ii, 249, 345, 345ᵇ.

Tutbury [Tuttebury, MS.], Wm. Lambert, monk of, ii, 124.

Tweta (*or* Twyta), John, *see* Colyford, ii, 135ᵇ, 176ᵇ.

Twyford, Alice, wife of John, i, 304.

Twyford, John, a notary-publick, ii, 112, 126; proxy for John Typet, ii, 139ᵇ.—*See*, also, i. 164.

Twyford, Thos., inst. to Clyst S. George, ii, 132; i, 141ᵇ; exch. for Luccombe (Dioc. of B. and W.), ii, 148ᵇ.

Twyneow, Walter, inst. to Trevalga, ii, 90.

Twywil, Baldwin de,—

Dispensation for his marriage with Isabella, relict of Baldwin de Eggecombe, granted by the Pope. Her late husband and Baldwin de Twywil were related in the 4th degree of consanguinity; knowing which they had, nevertheless, come together and had had issue; but their petition was granted, and their children declared legitimate (27 Aug., 1400), i, 45ᵇ.

Tycon, John, Gittisham, i, 312ᵇ.

Tylby, Thomas, of Apuldram, ii, 293ᵇ.

Tylle, John, priest, presented to Clyst St. Mary, ii, 53ᵇ.

Tyly, Richard, i, 331ᵇ.

Tymbyg, *see* Yocc, i, 93ᵇ.

Tynten, John, does homage to the Bishop, in London, for lands in Powton—i.e. St. Breoke (12 July, 1397), ii, 310.

Typet, John, R. of So. Ockendon (Dioc. London), exch. for the Wardenship of Ottery St. Mary, ii, 139^b; his death, ii, 163^b.

Typ (*or* Typp), Wm., inst. to a Preb. in Chulmleigh, ii, 5^b; resigns ii, 35^b ; is inst. to another Preb. there, ii, 14.

Tyre, John, *see* Fraunceys, John, i, 63.

Tyrell, John, inst. to Zeal Monachorum, ii, 10; i, 24; decd. ii, 102.

Tyrry, John, i, 318^b.

Tyso, Thos., R. of St. John-in-Cornwall, ii, 11.

Tyttesbury, Baldwin ; Margaret, his wife ; Edmund, his son ; Katherine and Isabella, his daughters, i, 313.—Isabella, sister of Canon Rd. Tyttesbury, *ibid.*—John Tittysbery was the first husband of Emma (*alias* Emmota) Vyel, i, 13^b.

Tyttesbury, Rd., Registrar and Notary-Pub., i, 13^b, 14^b, 15, 38, 39, 40, 40^b, 41^b, 42^b, 44^b, 46^b, 47, 47^b, 48^b, 51^b, 64, 70^b,[1] 71, 73, 73^b, 78, 78^b, 79, 79^b, 81, 83, 83^b, 84, 85, 87^b, 88, 88^b, 89.

Proxy for Wm. Sutton, ii, 29 ; for Rob. Martyn, ii, 30^b ; inst. to Ermington, R., ii, 34^b, 275 ; i, 36 ; collated to a Can. in Glasney, ii, 70 ; resigns it and is collated to a Can. in the Cath., ii, 75 ; also to a Can. and the Preb. of Westbrook, in Bosham, ii, 93, which he exch. (with Wm. Langeton) for another Can. and Preb. therein, ii, 97 ; again exch. for a Preb. in St. Teath, ii, 98 ; his death, ii. 105^b ; his Will, i, 313.—Thos. Tyttesbury, nephew of the above, *ibid.*

Tywardreath, [John Masseline], Prior ; licence of non-residence from 3 Feb., 1401-2, to Michaelmas, 1402, i, 54^b. —[John Rogers], Prior ; in arrear of procurations due to the Pope's Collector, i, 105.

This Priory presented to the Chantry of St. Michael in the Cemetery of St. Austell, ii, 53 ; to St. Anthony-in-Meneage, ii, 191^b, 265 ; to Lanlivery, ii, 177, 259 ; to Fowey, ii, 177, 259.

U.

Uda, John, V. of St. Breage (deceased), ii, 69.

Uda, Thos., clerk,—*Dispensacio super defectu natalium* (12 Oct., 1411), i, 187.—Thos. Uda, "of Pengelly," ii, 332.

Udan, Rd., is presented to Fowey, ii, 259 ; inst. thereto, ii, 177.

Uffculme [Ufcolme, Uffecolm, Uffecolump, Ufcolmp, MS.].—

The Rectors of this parish were continually non-resident ; Peter Pykeryng, obtaining licence for a year, from 1 Aug., 1395, i, 4 ; and again from 15 May, 1396, for three years, *contemplacione Reverendi Patris* ...... *Tidemanni*,

---

[1] LL.B., Can. of Exeter, Bishop's Proctor in Convocation, 1403.

Dei gracia Wygornensis Episcopi, i, 9; also, for a year, from 19 July, 1399, with the proviso, *in loco honesto interim commorando*, i, 28b.—John Luk, succeeded; and forthwith, obtained a dispensation (to study at Oxford), for 2 years, from 9 Feb., 1399-1400, i, 33; also, licence for the same purpose, for 2 years, from 18 June, 1402, i, 61; also, for 2 years, from 31 Jan., 1407-8, *contemplacione......Roberti, Dei gracia Sarumensis Episcopi*, i, 83b; also, for 2 years, from 4 Feb., 1409-10, i, 94. Having taken the degree of S.T.B., Luk was licensed as a Publick Preacher, 17 April, 1411, i, 122b; and, 13 April, 1412, obtained licence of non-residence for 3 years, i, 147. On 18 May, 1413, he obtained licence to put out his benefice to farm for 3 years i, 180b; and, on the next day, licence of non-residence for the same period, *ibid.* Finally, he obtained licence of non-residence from 22 April, to All-Saints' Day, 1418, i, 239.—The Bishop issued (1 June, 1412), his Mandate for an inquisition as to the alleged pollution of the Cemetery in a quarrel, with effusion of blood, by two parishioners, John Domet and Wm. Warde, i, 160b; and, 11 June, a Commission for its Reconciliation, ii, 247.

Ufflete, John, presents to Woolfardisworthy, ii, 75.

He was co-patron [Ufflyt, MS.], of Moreleigh, ii, 159b, and presented Wm. Sechevill to St. George's, Exeter, but was found not to be the true patron; ii, 234b.—*See*, also, ii, 335b, 341, 349b, 350.

Ugborough, Nicholas Fox, a poor scholar of, i, 313b.—Bowcombe in, i, 43; and Filham, i, 51b (*see Oratories*).

John de Shillyngford, R., LL.D., i, 308: license to choose a confessor, 28 Aug., 1405, i, 76; and 13 Jan., 1405-6, to hear the confessions of his parishioners, i, 77.—Rd. Palmer, R., i, 81, 83b, 87b, 91; inducts John Mathew to St. Lawrence's chapel, Crediton, ii, 121. He was Can. of Exeter; *see* his Will, i, 334.—The Bishop granted a special licence to John Wylle, chaplain of this Church, for the marriage of John Hylle, a minor, and Agnes, dau. of Wm. Rynell, though their banns had been published but once, i, 172b.—Reference to the marriage of John and Rose Herewordeshore in this church, ii, 306.

Uggeburgh, John, co-patron of Mamhead, ii, 45b, *see* Stoke Fleming (*Institutions*).

Ugbrooke, i, 326b.

Ulveston, Elena, sister of John, i, 330b.

Ulveston, John, inst. to Stokenham, V., ii, 2b; 112b; decd., ii, 192; his Will, i, 330.b—Thos., his brother, *ibid.*

Umfray (or Umfrey), Walter, R. of Belston, i, 6, 12, 183b, 202b; his death, ii, 189.

Underdoune, John, inst. to St. Nicholas Priory, Exeter, ii, 158b, his death, ii, 197b.

Underdoune, Richard, V. of Bickleigh (deceased), ii, 136.

Underwode, Wm. resigns Dittisham, ii, 29b; inst. again thereto, ii, 30; exch. for R. of St. John-Zachary (London), ii, 53.

Uploman; bequests to the Church, i, 312b; *see* Bysschop, John.—Thos. Warre, R. (i, 80) obtained licence of non-residence for a year, 11 Oct., 1410, i, 108.

Uplyme (*also* Uppelym, MS.); John Parys, R.—

Dispensation (to study at Oxford) for 3 years, from 27 Sept., 1397, i, 13b.—Wm. Musket, R.[1]; licence of non-residence for 2 years, from 1 May, 1408, i, 85; relaxation of sequestration, and licence for a year, from 1 Oct., 1410, i, 106.

Upottery, John [Noble], V., a Penitentiary in the Deanery of Dunkeswell, i, 216b.

Uppecote, John, *see* Burrington, i, 165.

Upton, *or* Uppeton, Thos., inst. to Kenton, ii, 93 ; i, 146b.

Upton-Hellions [Uppeton Helyon, MS.]—
Consecration of the High Altar, in honour of the Assumption of the B. V. M. (15 Sept., 1409), i, 90b : the F. of the Dedication changed from 7 to 10 Dec. (6 Dec., 1409), i, 92.—[Pyther], R.[1] ; licence of non-residence for a year, from 21 July, 1410 ; i, 100b.

Upton Pyne [Vpton Pyn. MS.], *see* Pyn (*Oratories*), i, 36b.

Uscher, John, ii, 213.

V.

Vaggescomb, Stephen, Can. of Crantock (resigns), ii, 64b.

Valdryan, Eustace, *see* Brixham, ii, 258b.

Valewyll, John, of Rattery ; John Gwynne, V. of Brent, licensed as his confessor from 31 March, 1417, till the following Easter [11 April], i, 232.

Valletort [Walletort, MS.], Hugh de, ii. 348.

Vautard, Jno., patron of Clyst St. Laurence, ii, 2, 41, 85, 102b, 200.

Vautard, Joan (daughter of John), i, 307b.
A special licence was granted, 23 Jan., 1414-15, for the marriage of John Vawtard (*sic*), jun., of Clyst St. Laurence, and Joan, dau. of Wm. Grylleston, of Collumpton ; also of Rob. Grylleston, of Collumpton, and Emmota, dau. of John Vawtard, sen., i, 207.

Vayron, John, i, 319.

Vays (*alias* Hegheden), Rob. ; *Dispensacio super defectu natalium* (17 June, 1411), i, 126b.

Veale, Geoffrey, inst. to the Chantry of Forde (Bampton), ii, 186b ; exch. for Bradford, ii, 201b.

Vedde, Wm., R. of Loxhore [Lookkyssore, MS.], i, 190b.

Veel, John, of Kingsbridge, ii, 290b, 292.—A John Vele was R. of Charles, and exch. for Over-Stowey (Dio. of B. and W.), ii, 48b.—Rob. Veel occurs i, 320b.

Velaw, Laurence, inst. to St. Petrock's, Bodmin, ii, 183.

Vendover (*or* Wendover), John, R. of Bradninch (q. v.)

Verlegh, Thos., inst. to the Chantry of Tadyport, ii, 5.

Veryan, Wm. [Aysshecote], V., a Penitentiary in the Deanery of Powder, i, 143b, 174, 194b, 207b, 231b, 238, 245b.

---

[1] Vpton Hylyon, MS.

Vexford, Wm., R. of Witheridge, exch. for Marsh (Dioc. of Lincoln), ii, 30.

Vesy, Nicholas, inst. to St. Keyne, ii, 9^b.

Veysy, Thomas, inst. to Rewe, ii, 22^b; i, 62.

Veysy, Rd., inst. to Bridford, ii, 13; *see*, also, i, 334.

Veysy, Thos., R. of Penne (Dio. of B. and W.), exch. for Warkleigh, ii, 54^b.

Vienna, *see* St. Antony, Hospital of, i, 26^b, 27, 27^b.

Vincent, John, late Can. of Ottery, ii, 56; of Glasney, ii, 31^b.

Vincent, Richard, clerk; *Dispensacio super defectu natalium* (2 Nov., 1418), i, 243.

Virginstowe [Vyrgenystowe, MS.],—

Roger (*see* Errata) Sturt, accolite, R.; dispensation (to study at Oxford) for 3 years, from 11 Oct., 1412, i, 170; for 3 years, from 9 Oct., 1415, i, 213^b.—Walter Crewys, accolite, R.; dispensation (to study at Oxford) for 2 years (but to take sub-deacon's orders in the first year), 9 Feb., 1416-17, ii, 230^b.

Visitation (Episcopal),—

Commission directed to John Lydeford, Archd. of Totnes, and Walter Levenaunt, Can. of Exeter: the Churches named are St. Sidwell's, Clyst Honiton, Stoke, Branscombe, Colyton, Sidbury, Salcombe [Regis], Topsham, Ide, Dawlish, St. Mary Church, Staverton, Ashburton, Colebrooke, Littleham, St. Piran, and St. Winnow (30 April, 1400), ii, 226^b.

Volant, John de, inst. Prior of St. Michael's Mount, ii, 338^b.

Vorn (*or* Vorum ?), V. of Gulval (deceased), ii, 4^b.

Vox, Walter, V. of Morwenstow, licensed to celebrate in the Chapel of St. Mary, at Milton, i, 49; (deceased), ii, 100.

Vyan, John, V. of Westbury (Dioc. of B. and W.), exch. for Luppit, ii, 71^b; his death, ii, 180.

This John Vyenne (*sic*) polluted the cemetery of Luppit, by assaulting Wm. Alon therein, ii, 241.—A John Vyen, clerk, obtained a dispensation *super defectu natalium* (13 Sept., 1400), i, 47^b.

Vyel, Alexander, Chantry-priest of Beaford (deceased), ii, 19^b.

Vyell, Augerus, co-patron of Inwardleigh, ii, 108^b.—Rd. Vyell, i, 332.

Vyel, Walter, and Emma (*or* Emmota), his wife,—

They were married in ignorance of the fact that John Tyttesbury, her first husband, was related to the said Walter in the 3rd degree of consanguinity. Dispensation granted, 16 Oct., 1397; i, 18^b.

Vyet, Robert, R. of Butterleigh (deceased), ii, 23.

W.

Wace, Robert, *see* Bridgewater, i, 96.

Waddon, Thos., clerk, i, 334; *Dispensacio super defectu natalium* (2 Nov., 1418), i, 243^b.

Wade, Henry, clerk,—*Dispensacio super defectu natalium* (13 Dec., 1398), i, 24.

Henry Wade occurs as proxy for John Gorewyll, ii, 25^{b} ; inst. to St. Kerrian's, Exeter, ii, 74^{b} ; deceased, ii, 103.

Wade, *alias* Leche, John, *see* St. Feock (*note*), i, 26.

Wadeton, in Paignton, *see* Holeway, Wm., ii, 311.

Wadham, Sir John, co-patron of W. Putford, ii, 82, *see* Parkham ; *also* Silverton.

Wadham, Walter, inst. to Brixham, ii, 176^{b} ; 258^{b}.

Wake, Nicholas, R. of Torbrian, i, 303 ; his death, ii, 83^{b}.

Wakeryng, Sir John, " Custos Rotulorum," i, 138^{b}, 190^{b}.

Procuratorium pro Parliamento Domini Regis (24 Oct., 1414), i, 203 ; *pro Concilio Regis* (8 April, 1415), i, 209^{b} ; *pro Parliamento* (7 Oct., 1415), i, 213^{b} ; Keeper of the Privy Seal, i, 217, 219.

Walden, Roger, Canon of Exeter, resigns, ii, 29^{b}.

Walden, Thomas, *see* Oldcastel, i, 192^{b}.

Waldryan (*or* Valdryan) Eustace, *see* Brixham, ii, 355.

Waleys, Hugh, *see* Bickleigh, R.

Waleys, Rd. does homage to the Bishop, at Clyst, for lands at Colebrook, Crediton (17 June, 1418), ii, 311.

Walhop, John, inst. to the Chantry of Beaford, ii, 57^{b}.

Walkyngton, Thos., *see* Rugge, Robert, ii, 211.

Walle, John, chaplain, i, 71.

John Walle, clerk, occurs as proxy for Walter Robert and for Thomas Hendeman, ii, 74^{b}. He was inst. to Stoke Damarel, ii, 122^{b} ; resigned and was inst. to Shevioke, ii, 169.

Wallebeare, Thos., clerk,—*Dispensacio super defectu natalium* (24 Sept., 1408), i, 86^{b}.

Wallyn (" atte Wallyn "), in Throwleigh, ii, 35^{b}.

Walreddon [Walradon, MS.], in Whitchurch, *see* Mewy (*Oratories*), i, 58^{b}.

Walrond, Nich., chaplain, *see* Washfield, i, 121^{b}.

Walrande, William, i, 319.—*See* Washfield, ii, 168.

Walshe, Stephen, John, and Elizabeth, i, 312^{b}.

Walyssch (Wallyssh *and* Walsche), Wm., R. of Parley (Dio. of Salisbury), exch. for Washfield, ii, 142 ; i, 173, 194^{b} ; exch. for Hedington, (Dio. of Salisbury), ii, 167^{b}.

Walter, Laurence, *see* Cullyng, William.

Walter, Rob., inst. to Pelynt, ii, 2 ; i, 94^{b}, 141^{b}, 168 ; resigns, ii, 161^{b}.

Walter, Thomas, i, 310.

Walter, William, clerk,—*Dispensacio super defectu natalium* (20 Sept. 1415), i, 212^{b}.

Waltham, Richard, *alias* Sonde (q.v.), ii, 21^{b}.

Waltham, Wm., Preb. of Kingsteignton and Yealmpton in Salisbury Cathedral, ii, 37^{b}; Preb. of Chalke, in the Conventual Church of Wilton, ii, 30.

Walwayn, Ralph, inst. to Dartington, ii, 155; i, 193^{b}, 209^{b}, 221^{b}, 233; his death [Wallewyn, MS.], ii, 193.

Walwyn, John, R. of Loxbeare, exch. for Stanton-on-the-Wold, (Dio. Ebor), ii, 143^{b}.

Wanel, Henry, ii, 346.

Wantynge, Rob., R. of Bridestowe, exch. for Arreton (Dioc. Winton), ii, 34.

Robt. Wantynge, R. of Chiddingfold (Dio. Winton), exch. for Combmartin, ii, 167; i, 212, 221^{b}; for Westmill, (Dio. Lincoln), ii, 181. Rob. Wantyng was collated "Minister" of Ottery of Mary, ii, 103^{b}; i, 90; and exch. for North Tidworth (Dio. Sarum), ii, 136^{b}.

Wappelegh, Thos., V. of Buckland Monachorum, exch. for Lamorran, ii, 40; his death, ii, 124.

Warbleton, the Church of, i, 322^{b}.

Warbstow [Warbystowe, MS.], V., *see* Bernard, John, i, 58^{b}.

Warda, John, a parishioner of Linkinhorne, i, 116.

Warde, John, i, 305;—

A John Warde was proxy for Thos. Hichecok, ii, 71; and John Warde, R. of Moorlinch (Dio. of B. and W.) exch. for Bradstone, ii, 195.

Warde, Thos., inst. to Bampton, R., and exch. for Whimple, ii, 192, 264. *See* i, 246^{b}.

Ward (*or* Warde), Wm., of Uffculme, i, 160^{b}; ii, 247.

Warde, Wm. (deceased), i, 331^{b}.

Ware, John, inst. to Honeychurch, ii, 159.

Ware, Henry, Official of the Abp. of Canterbury, i, 192^{b}.

Warlond, *see* Totnes, ii, 53.

Warmyscombe, Rd., V. of Holcombe Burnell, resigns, ii, 194^{b}.

Warre (*or* Werre), Geoffrey, i, 304.

Warre, Lucy, Abbess of Canonsleigh, i, 62^{b}; ii, 14^{b}, 17, 44.

Warre, Thos., inst. to Rewe, ii, 52^{b}; i, 54^{b}, 55; exch. for Chardlinch (Dio. of B. and W.), ii, 21^{b}; for Uploman, ii, 93; i, 108; resigns, ii, 136^{b}.

Waryn, Isabella, *see* Mydderhille, Rob., ii, 242.

Waryn, John, collated to Liskeard, ii, 55; 79; 239^{b}, 340^{b}, 342^{b}; *also*, i, 58, 64.

He exch. for Grittleton (Dio. of Salisbury), ii, 149b; for Cardynham, ii, 154b; 254; i, 226b, 243; was inst. to Menhenyot, ii, 138, 244; i, 145, 195b, 212b, 232, 245b; appointed Registrar of the Consist. Court (22 Sept., 1409), ii, 232; collated Dean of Crantock, ii, 160b, 172; Commissioned (10 June, 1415) *ad terminandum causas, etc.*, in the Consist. Court, ii, 256b; resigned the Deanery of Crantock, and was collated to a Can. therein, ii, 191; resigned it, ii, 200, and was collated Can. of Exeter, ii, 199b. *See*, also, ii, 262, and Olyver, Rd., i, 145b.—A John Waryn occurs as farming the revenues of Bampton, i, 138.

Waryn, Thos., clerk,—*Dispensacio super defectu natalium* (12 Aug., 1412), i, 164.

Was, Thos., R. of Alwington,—

He is described as "senio confractus et mentis discrecione privatus," and quite unequal to the discharge of his duties; the cure of souls was neglected, the goods of the church wasted, the groves (*nemora*) pertaining thereto cut down, and everything falling into dilapidation. So the Bp. appointed Henry Harri, chaplain, his "coadjutorem sive curatorem" (2 Jan., 1404-5), i, 72.—His death, ii, 100.

Washbourne, Chantry of; Geoffrey Wynkelegh, chaplain; licence of non-residence from 8 May to Michaelmas, 1416; i, 221b.

Washfield, John Halys, *alias* Sparwe, R., and Curate of the dependent Chapel of Hederlond,—

He had been convicted of incontinency with Agnes Say, his servant; and, refusing to perform the moderate penance assigned to him (viz., to go afoot to to the Cathedral and there offer, for the fabrick thereof, the sum of 6s. 8d., proceeding thence to the Colleg. Ch. of Crediton and making the like offering), he was excommunicated. Continuing impenitent, he was inhibited from serving his churches, and the parishioners were forbidden to hold communion with him. John [Walwyn], R. of Loxbeare and Nich. Walrond, chaplain, were commissioned by the Bp. to see to this matter, and also to confess such of the parishioners as came to them, and to administer to them the Eucharist and the other Sacraments and Sacramentals (26 March, 1411), i, 121b.—Wm. Wallyssh, R.; licence of non-residence from 20 Dec., to Michaelmas, 1412; i, 173; also, for a year (and to farm out his benefice), from 1 March, 1413-14; i, 194b.—Rob. Blake, R., licence of non-residence from 30 March, to Michaelmas, 1416, i, 219b.—Commissions of Enquiry:—(1) on the presentation of John Scarburgh, chaplain, by Thos. Worthe, Simon Bernevyle, and Matilda Dylyngton (1 Sept., 1416), ii, 259b.—(2) On the presentation of Rd. Gerveys, chaplain, by Rd. Wolfe (4 Sept., 1416), *ibid.* (3) By Alice, widow of Rd. Wolfe (2 Oct., 1416), ii, 260.

[*Breve Regium*];—Prohibition to admit pending settlement of the dispute as to the patronage between Thos. Werthe, Simon Barneville, and Matilda, lately wife of Wm. Dylyngton, on the one part, and Alice (lately wife of Rd. Wolf), and Rd. Gerveys, clerk, on the other part (26 Sept., 1416), ii, 356b.—Suspension of this Prohibition (7 Nov., 1416), *ibid.*

Washford, John Gode, R.; licence of non-residence for a year, from 15 June, 1396, i, 9.

Wassche, Joan, *see* atte Wassche.

Wastel, Nicholas,—

This person being at the time in the house of John Potter, of St. Edmund's, Exeter, laid violent hands, in the month of March [1411], on John Goorde, clerk; for which he was excommunicated; and the Bishop issued his

Mandate to the Dean of Christianity and the Curates of that Deanery, for the proclamation thereof (22 April, 1411), i, 122^{b}.—*His absolution* (18 May, 1411), i, 123^{b}.

Watelyngton, Roger, of Exeter, his Will, i, 317; Joan (his wife) and John (his son), *ibid.*

Watere, John, a minor-canon and chantry-priest, of St. Paul's, London, exch. for a Can. and the 7th Preb. in Ottery, ii, 155^{b}.—*See* atte Water.

Waterman, Ralph, collated Sacristan of Bosham, ii, 48^{b}, 228; resigns, ii, 100.

Waterman, Roger, inst. to St. Dominick, ii, 7^{b}; i, 74; his death, ii, 193^{b}.

Waterton, John de, Receiver for the Prince in Cornwall, i, 109^{b}. *See* Tin, the Tithe of; i, 140^{b}, 172^{b}.

Wath, John, proxy for John Fyfide, ii, 57^{b}.

Watkyn, Thos., clerk (Diocese of London), i, 44^{b}.

A Thos. Watkyn *or* Wattekyn, was inst. to St. John-in-Cornwall, ii, 68, 153; exch. for St. Gerran's, ii, 160; i, 217^{b}, 233^{b}.

Watte, John, i, 315.

Watty, Richard, *see* Helygan, Nicholas.

Wattys [*or* Wattes], John, inst. to St. Pancras-juxta-Axemouth [Rousdon], ii, 96; i, 82; resigns, ii, 102.

Waye, Roger, presents to Goodleigh, ii, 192.

Waye, Rob., co-patron of Broadnymet, ii, 195.

Weye, Rob., inst. to Powderham, ii, 49.—A Rob. Wey was co-patron of Bickleigh, R., ii, 92^{b}.—*See* i, 307.

Weye, William, i, 315^{b}.

Wayne, Florence, i, 306^{b}.

Waysschbourne, John, R. of Roborough (deceased), ii, 12.

Wayte, John, V. of Shebbear (deceased), ii, 20.

Wear Giffard ["Were," MS.]; John, R. of, a Penitentiary in the Deanery of Hartland, i, 174, 194^{b}, 207^{b}, 217, 231, 238, 245^{b}.

Webbe, Thos., *see* Widecombe, i, 180^{b}.

Webber, Elys, and John, i, 308^{b}.—Hy. Webbre, i, 332^{b}; ii, 130.

Welbeck, Jno. "Dei paciencia" Abbot of, ii, 142^{b}.

Welbourne, Jno., Preb. of St. Probus, by exch. with Adam de Mottrum, ii, 35; exch. for Crewkerne (2nd Portion), ii, 47.

Welfare, Rd., proxy for Rd. Reve, ii, 89^{b}.

Welleslegh, Reginald, scholar, *Dispensacio super defectu natalium* (14 Feb., 1401-2), i, 54^{b}; inst. to Talkern (i.e. Minster), ii, 102.

Wellington (Somerset), i, 319.

Wells, Walter Medford, Dean of, Papal Nuncio, etc., i, 240^{b}.

Wells (near Walsingham—Dio. of Norwich), i, 322^{b}.

Wellysford, Matilda Latimer's Manor of, i, 329.

Welyn, Thos. (*alias* Abyngdon), R. of Withiel, i, 5; collated Canon of Glasney, ii, 31^{b}; exch. his R. and Can. for Stoke Climsland, ii, 43^{b}; i, 131; collated Canon of Crediton, ii, 197.

Welyngton, Rd., R. of St. Tudy, i, 63 (here called "John" by mistake); i, 108, 161^{b}.

A Rd. Welyngton is referred to as having been R. of North Tawton, ii, 348.

Welywort, John, and Margaret, i, 332.

Wembworthy [Wemmaworthy, MS.],—

Roger [Yurd], R. of, and others, excommunicate and contumacious; the Bishop writes to the king for their arrest (8 June, 1396), i, 9.—Henry, R. of Wemmaworth (*sic*), and Dean Rural, ii, 348.

Wendlyngburgh [*also* Wendelynburgh *and* Wendyngburgh, MS.], senior; Canon of Crediton (q.v.), i, 5^{b}; his death, i, 331; ii, 27^{b}.

Wendovere, John (Archd. of Lewes), exch. for Bradninch, ii, 27; a Penitentiary in the Deanery of Plymtree, i, 94, 115, 143, 173^{b}, 194, 207^{b}, 216^{b}, 231, 237^{b}, 245; inst. Preb. of Netherhayne in Chulmleigh, ii, 188^{b}.

Wenelok, John, accolite,—

Ordained (by Bp. Brantingham) sub-deacon, at Crediton, 24 Sept., 1390; title, Tavistock Abbey; deacon, at Chudleigh, 20 May, 1391; title, the same; priest, at Chudleigh, 23 Sept., 1391, title the same (Scrutiny of Brantingham's Register, made 20 July, 1414), i, 197^{b}.

Weryng, John, chaplain, i, 321.—John and Rob., i, 326^{b}.—Richard, i, 324^{b}.

West, John, i, 326^{b}.—Richard West, chaplain, i, 325^{b}.

[West] Alvington; John [Baylebeyn], V., a Penitentiary in the Deanery of Woodleigh, i, 50.—Simon Paule, V., i, 86; ii, 357^{b}.—Bequest to the Church-Wardens, i, 318.—Salcombe in, i, 59, 60^{b}.

West Putford, Steph. Gyffard, sub-deacon, R.; Dispensation (to study at Oxford), for 2 years, from 13 Oct., 1405, i, 77.

West Worlington, ii, 51.

Westcomb, John, co-patron of Georgenympton, ii, 99.

Westecote, John, S.T.B., R. of St. Petrock's; Exeter; i, 51, 92^{b}, 142^{b}, 316^{b}, 319^{b}, 320; ii, 21, 76.

He was Can. of Exeter, ii, 150^{b}; and licensed to celebrate in any of his residences in the Diocese (17 April, 1414), i, 196; resigned his Canonry (4 Feb., 1413-14), and was collated (5 Feb.), to another, ii, 155^{b}; resigned again, ii, 156; collated to a Preb. in St. Probus, ii, 176^{b}; his death, ii, 192^{b}, 193; his Will, i, 331.

Westecote, Richard—" nativum nostrum de manerio nostro de Tauton ;" his Manumission (1 *and* 23 April, 1412), i, 149.

Westhoobray, *see* Brakler (*Oratories*), i, 82ᵇ.

Westney, Walter, inst. to Stokeclimsland, ii, 36ᵇ ; resigns, ii, 9ᵇ.

Weston, Edmund, collated Preb. of Crantock, ii, 31 ; (decd.) ii, 70ᵇ.

Weston, Thos. de, Preb. of Axminster, ii, 17ᵇ, 19ᵇ.—*See* Somerlegh, ii, 33ᵇ.—Proxy for Nicholas Stoke, ii, 83.

Weston, Wm., R. of Deene (Dio. of Lincoln), exch. for Bridestowe, ii, 166ᵇ ; i, 214 ; resigns, ii, 180.

Westwick, in Lifton, *see* Mileton (*Oratories*), i, 125ᵇ.

Wethy, Wm., inst. to Christow, ii, 176.

Wexmaker, Rosa, of Cornwall ; *see* St. Feock, i, 161.

Weycroft [Wycroft, MS.], in Axminster, i, 237.

Weyneman (also Weneman, Wenman, Wayneman), Rd., chaplain, ii, 50ᵇ.

He was R. of Cheriton Fitzpaine, i, 79ᵇ ; a Penitentiary in the Deanery of Cadbury, i, 143, 173ᵇ, 194, 207ᵇ, 216ᵇ, 231, 237ᵇ ; proxy for John Haget, ii, 100 ; for Wm. Southam, ii, 103ᵇ ; dies, R. of Cheriton (ii, 191), and Can. of Crediton (ii, 191ᵇ).

Whalysbrow (*also*, Whalesbrow and Walesbru), Benedict, R. of St. Mawnan, i, 18 ; collated to Poundstock, ii, 65ᵇ ; his death, ii, 164.

Whalesbrewe (*or* Walesbreu), John, presents to St. Perran-Uthno, ii, 13ᵇ, 162ᵇ ; 255ᵇ ; to St. Mawnan, ii, 178. *See*, ii, 318.

Whateley (*or* Whattlegh), John, R. of Kentisbeare, i, 8, 8ᵇ ; his death, ii, 95.

Whattecomb, John, V. of Axminster, resigns, ii, 17ᵇ, 19ᵇ.

Wherwell, the Abbess and Conv. present to the Preb. of Goodworth in their Conventual Church, ii, 162ᵇ.—Anneys Bonevyll, a nun of, i, 311ᵇ.

Whimple (*and* Wympel, MS.),—

John Drake, R. ; had licence of non-residence for 2 years, from 23 Oct., 1402—*contemplacione Reverendi in Christo Patris ... Guidonis, Dei gracia Menevensis Episcopi*, i, 62 : also for one year, from 28 Nov., 1404, i, 72.—Thos. Warde, R., i, 242ᵇ ; licence of non-residence from 20 April to Michaelmas, 1419, i, 246ᵇ.

Whitchurch [Whitechurche, MS.], Walreddon in, i, 58ᵇ.

White, John, a Friar Minor of Exeter,—

He was licensed to hear Confessions from 27 Feb., 1395-6 till the Oct. of Easter, i, 8 ; also, 1 Oct., 1397, i, 13ᵇ ; also (for a year), ... Feb., 1398, i, 25ᵇ ; also, from 25 March till the Oct. of Pentecost, 1399, i, 34 ; also, 17 Feb., 1401, i, 55.—*See*, also, i, 302ᵇ.

White, Matthew, co-patron of Inwardleigh, ii, 24ᵇ, 108ᵇ.

Whithed, Thos. R. of Dittisham, inst. and resigns, ii, 30.

Whitheed, John, *see* Oldcastel, i, 192b.

Whitelegh, Peter (s. & h. of John), ii, 305b (*see Oratories*).

Whitman, Wm., proxy for John Lamburne, ii, 110.

Whitoun, John, R. of Combe Raleigh, exch. for Broad Sydling (Dio. of Salisbury), ii, 40b, 220b.

Whitstone [Devon], Wm. Clyve, R., proxy for Thos. Hendeman, ii, 108b, 109.

Whitstone [Cornwall], David [Sauly], R., a Penitentiary in the Deanery of Trigg-major, i, 143b, 174, 194b, 207b, 217, 231, 238, 245b.

Commission directed to the Archdn. of Cornwall, in a case of dilapidations against Thos. Bardolf, the late R. (7 Aug., 1410), ii, 233b.

Whympston, *see* Fortescue (*Oratories*), i, 109.

Whytbe, Walter, Canon of Frithelstock, ii, 183b.

Whyte, Wm., R. of Satterleigh (deceased 1396), ii, 5.—Another Wm. White was R. of Challacombe (deceased, 1399), ii, 14b.

Whyte, *alias* Quythe, Nicholas, collated to Bishop's Nympton, ii, 97; *see*, i, 315.

Whyte, Thos., R. of Teignbrewer (deceased), ii, 108.

Whytefeld, chapel of, in the parish of Marwood (q.v.)

Whytefeylde, Rob., presents to Parracombe, ii, 153b.

Whyteley, Laurence, R. of Warkleigh, exch. for Penne (Dioc. of B. and W.), ii, 54b.

Whyteway, John, notary-publick, i, 324b, 332b; ii, 16b; proxy for John Shirley, ii, 52; for Rd. Aldryngton, ii, 178b.

Whyteway, Thos., *see* Kingston, ii, 276.

Whytewyll, John, Precentor of Crediton (deceased), ii, 97b.

Whytheleye (*or* Witheley), i, 76, 82b.

Whytyng, Henry, i, 312b.—Roger was inst. to St. Pancras [Rousdon], ii, 102; deceased, ii, 120.—Thomas was inst. to Hockworthy, ii, 14b.—William was a monk of Sherborne, i, 320b.

Widecombe [-in-the-Moor], i, 308,—

John Boghelegh, V., and nine others, excommunicated and contumacious (viz. Thos. Jele *alias* Boterworth, Robert Honychurch, and John Syngham (all of Devon), and Sampson Trewen, chaplain, Thos. Deynsell, John Caru, John Hunte, Thos. Webbe, and Wm. Hogg (all of Cornwall), are handed over, by the Bishop, to the secular arm (3 June, 1418), i, 180b.

Widelegh, Robert, i, 328b.

Wigwar, John, i, 328.

Wilford, John, i, 320. Margaret, wife of William, i, 319b, 320.

Wilford, Rob., son of William (of Exeter), i, 319^b, 320; Rob. and Elizabeth (deceased), i, 331.—William Wilford, citizen of Exeter, i, 316^b; his Will, i, 319^b.

There was a Commission to prove this will, in which he is described as "nostras, dum vixit, robas gerentis" (26 Sept., 1413), ii, 252^b.

Willand; John Bourne, R., Penitentiary in the Deanery of Tiverton, i, 245.

Wilton, Preb. of Chalke in the Conventual Ch. of, ii, 30; the Abbess and Conv. present to Fuggleston *w.* Bemerton, ii, 104.

Wilton, Nicholas, inst. to Uplyme, ii, 12.

Winchester, William [of Wykeham], Bp. of, i, 17^b, 79; St. Swithin's Priory, i, 33^b; Thomas, R., of St. Maurice, i, 310^b.

Windout, Thos., monk of Tavistock, ii, 59.

Windsor Castle, i, 300.

Thos. Butiller, Dean of Windsor, i, 33.—Rd. Kynggeston, Dean, ii, 89.—Wm. Falewell and Rd. de Raundes, Canons, i, 300. The Dean (or Warden) and College present to St. Steph.-by-Saltash, ii, 36^b, 102; to No. Molton, ii, 89^b; to So. Tawton, ii, 138, 177^b.

Wisborough (Diocese of Chichester), i, 322^b.

Witheridge, John Luffewyk [also Lovewyke, MS.], R.,—

He complained to the Bishop that, his parish-church having been dedicated 4 March, it was often impossible to keep the F. of Ded. with its proper services: the Bp. changed the day to July 16 (11 Feb., 1403-4), i, 73. He was often Penitentiary for the Deanery of Molton, i, 94, 115^b, 143^b, 174, 194^b, 207^b, 217, 231, 238, 245^b.

Withiel [Whythiell, MS.], Thos. Welyn [*alias* Abyngdon], R.,—

Licensed to choose Confessors (2 Sept., 1395), i, 5.—Thos. Chepman, R., and Can. of Glasney, had licence of non-residence (to reside in the College), for a year, from 13 Nov., 1405, i, 77.

Wobbrok, Thos., collated a Priest-Vicar in the Cathedral (*by lapse*), i, 97.

Woborn, John, *see* Richard, John.—He was Rector of East Worlington, i, 72.

Wode, John, inst. to Egg-Buckland, ii, 23^b.

Wode, Patrick, inst. to the Chapelry of Sticklepath, ii, 6; collated to Lezant, ii, 33.—*See* atte Wode.

Wodeborne, Wm., R. of Washfield, exch. for Brushford (Dio. of B. and W.), ii, 108.

Wodecroft, Alexander, i, 314.

Wodehele, Roger, inst. to High Bickington, ii, 91.

Wodelond, John, of Apuldram, ii, 293^b.

Wolborough [Wolleburgh, MS.], Newton-Abbot in, i, 246^b.

Wolff, Alice (widow of Rd.), *see* Washfield, ii, 180, 356^b.

Wolf, Beatrix (widow of John), *see* Carslegh, Simon, i, 191.

Wolfe, John, inst. to Bicton, ii, 2b, 6.
John Wolf was proxy for John Gordray, V. of W. Alvington, ii, 29b.—A John Wolfe was co-patron of Gittisham, ii, 104; and of Stoke Rivers, ii, 129b, 180; presented to Kentisbury, ii, 106.—For Richard Wolff, *see* Washfield, ii, 259b.

Wolhay, John, chaplain;—
He had been grievously assaulted by one Richard Jelle, of Harberton; and the Bishop commissioned John Juhelȝete, R. of Aveton-Giffard, to enquire and report (16 April, 1400), ii, 226b.

Wolston, John (chaplain), i, 327b, 333.
He was proxy for John Leyman, ii, 148; for Walter Hulle, ii, 158b; for Renaldus Tretherf, ii, 159; for Thos. Gerweys, ii, 194: collated, *jure devoluto*, to St Endellion, ii, 158; inst. to Bradford, ii, 177b; resigned Bradford, and was collated to Lezant, ii, 191b.—A John Wolston (or Ulveston), was V. of Stokenham, ii, 261, 357b.

Woleston, *see* Trelouny (*Oratories*), i, 37b.

Wolvele, John, inst. to Tregony, ii, 29.

Wombewelle, Thos. *see* Oldcastel, i, 192b.

Wonston, Matthew, R. of Maperton (Dio. of B. and W.), exch. for Chawleigh, ii, 155.

Wood, in Kentisbeare, *see* Whytyng (*Oratories*), i, 83.

Woodbury [Wodebury, MS.]; the parish-church, i, 311, 311b.
On 23 Sept., 1409, "dominus dedicavit ecclesiam parochialem de Wodebury, de novo constructam, in honore Sancti Swythini, Confessoris, i, 90b.—Luke Busch, of Woodbury, i, 312.

Woodford Bridge,—
An Indulgence was granted, 4 Feb., 1398-9, to the Faithful contributing "ad construccionem et reparacionem pontis vulgariter nuncupati Wodeford Brygge, ducentis ultra aquam de Toryg inter Toryton Magnam et Launceston ... ruinam notorie minantis"; i, 25b.

Wodham, Wm., "serviens Episcopi," i, 314.

Womberley, mentioned in the Will of Wm. Credy, i, 308.

Wonard, Rob. (of Sidbury), and Blonchia, dau. of Wm. Frenschton (of Southmolton, decd.); special marriage-license granted (23 Jan., 1416-17), i, 229.

Woodland [Wodelond, MS.],—
There was a Manor of this name in Ermington, i, 195b; also, in Little Torrington, i, 226.—For Wodelond in Bishop's Tawton, *see* Holeway, Wm., ii, 311. There was a Prebend of "Wodelond" in the Colleg. Ch. of Crediton, i, 5b.

Woodleigh, John Wytloff's, bequest to the Church, i, 306.
Wm. Breerlegh (*also* Breelegh, MS., i, 105b, and Breyrlegh, ii, 357b), R., was a Penitentiary in the Deanery of Woodleigh, i, 50; licence of non-residence for a year, from 11 June, 1409, i, 89; and again (with relaxation of sequestration), from 28 Sept., 1410; i, 105b.—*See* Derlyng, Thos., i, 229.

Woolfardisworthy, John York, R.; licensed to celebrate in the Chapel of St. James (17 July, 1400), i, 44.

Woolleigh [Wollegh, MS.], *see* Wybbury (*Oratories*), i, 39; *also*, Amyet, Robert, *ibid.*

Wordell, John, of Churchstow, ii, 291.

Werthe, Alice, i, 309,—

She was a nun of Cornworthy, and obtained licence to migrate to Canonsleigh (14 March, 1415-16), i, 218.

Werthe, Tho., co-patron of Washfield, ii, 108, 142, 168, 259ᵇ, 356ᵇ.

Wortham [*or* Worthyn], John, collated to Farringdon, ii, 129; exch. for St. Endellion, ii, 129ᵇ; i, 131.

John Worthyn, chaplain, was inst. to Axminster, ii, 151ᵇ; and soon afterwards the Bishop appointed him the 3rd of his chaplains, and dispensed with his residence at Axminster, or any other Benefice which might be conferred on him; he was to make ample provision for the cure of souls (18 Sept., 1413), ii, 187. He exchanged Axminster to be Warden of St. Laurence's Hospital, Crediton, and immediately resigning the same (ii, 187), was collated to St. Breoke, ii, 187ᵇ.—*See*, also, i, 332, 333.

Worthele [Worthyhele, MS.], in Ermington, i, 238.

Wotton, John, presents to Upton Hellions, ii, 179ᵇ.—Richard, i, 327ᵇ.

Wrest, Wm., of Apuldram, ii, 293ᵇ.

Wrothe (*or* Wroth), John, son and heir of Sir John.—*See* Uploman (*Institutions*).

Wryght, Vincent, *see* Payton, Isabella, i, 324ᵇ.

Wryght, Wm., R. of Icklesham, exch. for St. Cleer, ii, 51.

Wryter, John, V. of St. Gluvias (deceased), ii, 158; mentioned as V. of St. Budock (the dau. Church), ii, 225.

Wybbury,[1] Isolda, widow of Walter Denys, presents to Bradford, ii, 177ᵇ.—*See* atte Forde (*Oratories*(.

Wybbery, John, patron of Lustleigh, ii, 17, 93ᵇ.

Wyburgh, Agneta, daughter of Wm.; *see* Bragge, Roger, i, 224ᵇ.

Wyche, John, inst. to Huntshaw, ii, 44ᵇ; exch. for Cadeley (Dioc. of Lincoln), ii, 49ᵇ; inst. to All-Hallows-on-the-Walls, Exeter, ii, 176; exch. for Beynton (Sarum), ii, 200ᵇ.

Wydeslond, John, V. of Bampton (Dioc. of Lincoln), exch. for Heavitree, ii, 55ᵇ; i, 327ᵇ.—John Wyddyslond, *ibid.*—*See* i, 322 [Wythyslond, MS.]

Wydeslond, Robert, V. of Colyton, i, 312.

Wydesworthy, Thomas, and Agnes his wife, i, 319.

Wyger, John, a chaplain without employment,—

He refused to serve in the Church of Great Torrington (which was wholly destitute of a Chaplain), although he had been offered a competent stipend by the R., Stephen Payne, who asked the Bp. to interfere; Wyger was ordered to submit on pain of suspension, etc. (15 Nov., 1414), i, 203ᵇ.

Wyghale, Rob., R. of Stockleigh Pomeroy (i, 51ᵇ, 101), and Canon of Crediton, his death, ii, 197.

---

[1] Called elsewhere "Isolda, relicta Gilberti atte Forde, *alias* Wybbery" (27 March, 1415), i, 195ᵇ.

Wygtought, Thomas, R. of Calstock, i, 8b; ii, 6b.

Wyke St. Mary; William Hals, R.; his Will, i, 306.

John Gorewyll, R., was licensed to celebrate in the Chap. of St. Laurence in this parish (5 Aug., 1400), i, 45: licence of non-residence for a year, from 17 Oct., 1407,—*Johanni Gorewell, juniori, in Legibus Bacalario ... dummodo medio tempore steterit in Universitate Oxoniensi*; i, 82b.—[*Breve Regium*], Mandamus to the Bishop to admit a fit Clerk, on the King's presentation, on his recovery of the right to present, against John Colshull and Emma his wife (22 June, 1404).—Prohibition to admit, *pendente lite* (13 Oct., 1404).—*See* Mares, John, i, 191 (*Oratories*).

Wyke, in the parish of Axminster, i, 82b.

Wyke, Edith, wife, and John, son of Robert, i, 321.

Wyke, John, Esquire ["de Nenhide"], presents to Blackborough, ii, 25, 85.—*See* i, 328.—For John Wyke, clerk, *see* Ottery St. Mary, ii, 278.

Wyke, Wm. de, Preb. in the parish-church of Norton (Dio. of Durham), exch. for a Can. and [the 7th] Preb. in Ottery St. Mary, and then resigns, ii, 100b.—*See* i, 305b.

Wykeley, Peter,—a Friar Minor,—

He was admitted as a Confessor in the Diocese—*ad quod ministerium exequendum per fratrem Willelmum, Fratrum Minorum Provincie Anglicane ministrum, juxta formam Capituli* super Cathedram, *Domino extitit presentatus* (8 March, 1410-11), i, 119b.

Wykes, Wm., and John Castell (clerks, of the Dioc. of York and of Coventry and Lichfield), appointed by the Bp. his Proctors, etc. (9 June, 1400), i, 40.

Wyket, Hervey, clerk, i, 222b;—

Collated to a Preb. in Crantock, ii, 31; inst. to the Preb. of Trehaverock in St. Endellion, ii, 46b; to St. Mawgan-in-Pydar, ii, 121; which he exch. for a Can. and the Preb. of Rugge in Crediton, ii, 139b; inst. to St. Columb-major, ii, 178b; resigned, ii, 187. He was proxy for Rd. Bray, John Fecos, John Midderhille, Rd. Peryn de Polmargh, and Walter Trote [q.v.]

Wykham (*or* Wykeham), John; collated to the Preb. of Walton, in Bosham, ii, 32b.

Wykeham [*also* Wykham, MS.], Nicholas, Can. of Howden, *see* Bosham; resigned his Preb. of Walton, in Bosham, ii, 32b; his death, ii, 96b.

Wykelond, Richard, i, 307b; perhaps the same as Richard Wykeslond, LL.B., notary-publick, i, 16b, 324; ii, 11b, 37, 37b, 41, 41b, 43, 49b, 60b, 61.

Commission, as President of the Consist. Court, etc. (20 March, 1397-8), ii, 216; (6 Jan., 1398-9), ii, 222; Official, during the vacancy of the Archdeaconry of Exeter (9 July, 1408), ii, 232; proxy for John Otery, ii, 34; V. of Colyton, his death, ii, 130; Commission directed to Rd. Hals and Rd. Talbot, to prove his Will (7 Jan., 1410-11), ii, 237: and *see* i, 315b. Richard "Wekyslond" (deceased) is referred to, i, 331.

Wykyngston, John, R. of St. Pancras, London—

He exch. for Bridestowe, and a Can. and the 7th Preb. in Ottery St. Mary, ii, 150^b; i, 201^b; exch. his Can., etc., for a minor-Canonry and Drayton's Chantry in St. Paul's, London, ii, 155^b; and Bridestowe for Deene (Dio Linc.), ii, 166^b (here called "Wygyngton").—[*Breve Regium, de venire facias*]—John Wykyngston, R. of Bridestowe, to appear at Westminster and shew cause why he should not pay to John, Prior of Plympton, £10 being arrears of an annual rent of 10 marks, 8 Feb., 1414-15; ii, 351, 351^b.

Wilcotys, Jno., the King's Receiver in Devon and Cornwall; *see* "Tin."

Wylde, Clement, collated to a Canonry in Glasney, ii, 106.

Wylde, Henry, i, 305.

Wylkyn, John, *see* Lanbrobys, John, i, 196^b.—John Wylkyn, Can. of St. Stephen's, Launceston, occurs ii, 117.

Wylle, Clement, Can. of Glasney and V. of St. Probus, i, 174, 194,^{b}, 207^b; ii, 145.

The name occurs somewhat frequently:—John Wylle, Can. of Launceston, was thrice appointed a Penitentiary in the Deanery of Trigg-major, i, 143^b, 174, 194^b.—John Wylle, chaplain of the parish-church of Ugborough, i, 172^b; and *see*, i, 312, 322^b.—John Will, a poor clerk, of Oxford, i, 328.—John Wylle, of the par. of Plympton, excommunicated and contumacious, was handed over by the Bishop to the secular arm (8 May, 1419), i, 247.—John Wylla, collated to Zennor, ii, 47^b.—John Wille, *alias* Scryvener, R. of Studland (Dio. of Salisbury), exch. for E. Ogwell, ii, 198^b.—John Wylle, Can. of Crantock, resigned, ii, 159^b.—See atte Wille *and* atte Wylle.

Wylle, Nycoll, i, 312.

Wylle, Roger, V. of Milton [Abbot], ii, 58^b, 60^b, 61^b; his death, ii, 132^b, 243.

Wille, Thos. R. of Truro, ii, 246^b; i, 93^b, 96, 115^b: his death, ii, 140^b.

Wille, William, inst. to St. Clether, ii, 156^b, 253.

Wyllemere, William de, co-patron of Roseash, ii, 81.

Wyllesdon, John (*alias* Jordan), R. of Huntshan (decd.), ii, 195^b.

Wyllesdon, Richard, proxy for John Chitterne, ii, 162^b.

Wyllesdon, William, proxy for William Swyft, ii, 168^b.

Wyllet, John, inst. to Helland, ii, 174^b; i, 240.

Wylyam, Hervey, clerk.—*Dispensacio super defectu natalium* (17 Oct., 1413), i, 186^b [afterwards V. of St. Issey; *see* Lacy, Reg. ii, 212].

Wyllyam, Rd., coll. to St. Colan, ii, 142; exch. for St. Cubert, ii, 145^b.

Wyllym, Marista, of Lagham, i, 306.

Wyllyng, John, i, 301.

Wyllyng, Thomas, inst. to Merton, ii, 146^b; i, 173, 198, 227^b.

Wyllyngham, John, R. of Poughill (deceased), ii, 103.

Wyllys, John, R. of Churchstanton (deceased), ii, 5^b.

Wymbeldon, Wm., co-patron of Chagford, ii, 33^b, 34^b, 35^b.

Wymond, John, clerk, i, 222^b.

Wynchcombe, Rd., *see* Prophet, John, Can. of Abergwyly, ii, 20.

Wynchestre, John, V. of Mariansleigh, resigns, ii, 56.

Wyndegrynde, John, inst. to Trewen Chantry, Holsworthy, ii, 144^b, 248.

Wyndout, John, R. of Black Torrington, exch. for St. Mary Steps, Exeter, ii, 81^b; for Widecombe, ii, 124^b; his death, ii, 143^b.

Wyndouth, Rob. and Agnes, *see* Swayne, Rd., i, 39^b.

Wyndesore, Richard, i, 306^b.

Wyne, Walter, R. of Bicton (deceased), ii, 2^b.

Wynkankton, John, i, 332.

Wyngkelegh, Geoffrey, inst. to the Chantry of Washbourne, ii, 65^b; i, 221 [Wynkelegh]; his death [Wynkele], ii, 197^b.

Wynkelegh, Peter, inst. to Teignbrewer, ii, 108; decd., ii, 146.

Wyngode [*also* Wynnegode, MS.], Henry, LL.B., ii, 141^b—

Proxy for Wm. Pylton, ii, 102^b, for Stephen Reaker, ii, 145^b; collated to Lezant, ii, 155. Proxy for John Godegrave, ii, 163.—A Commission was directed to him (3 March, 1413-14) *ad petendum et recipiendum clericos convictos ... in Cornubia*, ii, 254; and with Augustine Strode, V. of Lamerton), to enquire as to the dilapidations of Cardynham, *ibid.*—He exch. Lezant for St. Ervan (?), ii, 174^b; and was collated to a Preb. in St. Probus, ii, 175; which he exch. for a Can. in Glasney, ii, 182^b—Official-Peculiar in Cornwall, i, 161^b, etc.

Wynsham, John, R. of Parracombe (resigns), ii, 7^b.

John Wynsham, V. of Combe St. Nicholas (Dio. of B. and W.), exch. for Chittlehampton, ii, 106^b.

Wynter, Richard, R. of Instow (deceased), ii, 89^b.

Wynterburne [*also*, Wynterborne *and* Wynterbourne], John, inst. to Charleton, ii, 103, 357^b.—Roger was Prior of the Friars Preachers, of Bristol, i, 306.

Wynterborn-Wast, Manor and advowson of (Co. Dorset), ii, 281^b, *et seqq.*

Wyet [*or* Wyot], Thos., proxy for Stephen Taillour, ii, 7; for John Bruere, ii, 12^b; for Wm. Fedde, ii, 90; for John Cook, ii, 108^b; for John Hermane, ii, 109; for Simon Tovy, ii, 188^b [Whyot, MS.].

Wysbech, Nicholas, Abbot of Newenham, ii, 153^b.

Wyse, John, clerk,—*Dispensacio super defectu natalium* (21 July, 1403), i, 67^b; and again, 24 Aug., 1406; i, 78.

A John Wyse occurs as patron of Lew Trenchard, ii, 12; 309; and *see* St. Germoe ii, 264^b.

Wyssynton, Wm., and Agnes Dunneworth,—
They were married in ignorance of impediment, viz. consanguinity in the 4th degree; Dispensation granted, 4 Oct., 1413; i, 185b.

Wyt, Wm., R. of All Hallows-on-the-Walls, Exeter (deceased), ii, 44b.

Wytbery, Henry—
Eldest son of John Wytbery, jun., when a child, under 11 years, had been handed over against his will to the Friars Minors at Exeter, by his father, in order (as was supposed) to exclude him from succeeding to his inheritance; and, fearing his father's threats, he had actually assumed the habit and tonsure before his 11th birthday. The Friars themeselves were in some difficulty, fearing that he might escape to his friends; so they kept moving him about "like a vagabond" for six months or more, and at length conveyed him into Wales to their house at Carmarthen. Here he told his story to the Superior, and begged to have his ordinary clothes returned to him, with permission to return to the world, even though he went naked. But the Superior was angry, and shut him up closely till the end of his year of probation. Then the said Superior summoned him to his presence, and endeavoured to persuade him to profess, when he declined to do so, and again begged for leave to return to the world. But the Superior threatened to punish him with the utmost severity if he deserted the Order, and kept him shut up more closely than ever, not delaying to put his threats into execution, and at last resorting to a stratagem to effect his purpose. Henry did not understand Latin, and the Superior, knowing this, gave him the "Profession" written in Latin to read, and compelled him to do so, though he was most unwilling. On the strength of this device they announced that he was a professed Minorite, and when he was in his 15th year, by threats of imprisonment and by bodily tortures, they forced him to take the Order of Sub-Deacon against his will. Nevertheless, Henry never ceased to protest against the treatment that he had received, and to declare that he would seize the first opportunity of returning to the world. This he at last succeeded in doing, and petitioned the Pope for redress and remedy. The Bull of Alexander V., reciting the above facts, is given at length; therein the Pope commands strict enquiry to be made into the circumstances, and that Henry, if his story turned out to be true, should be permitted to return to the world, and also to marry if he pleased. This is followed by a copy of a 2nd Bull, of the next Pope, John XXIII., reciting the 1st Bull, and stating that (in consequence of the death of Alexander) the latter had never been executed. Henry, however, had renewed his petition, and Pope John granted his request. He appeared in person before the Bishop, at Crediton, on 20 August, 1411, and presented both Bulls, and on August 25, Stafford issued a Commission to the Archdeacon of Exeter, to Thos. Noel, LL.B., Sub-Dean in his Cathedral Church, Rd. Olyver, Judge of the Consistory Court, and Walter Robert, Canon of Glasney, to make inquisition in the matter, and to act accordingly with his authority, in consequence of his own absence on urgent business making it impossible for him to do so.—i, 131b.

Wythewyll, John, Precentor of Crediton (his Will), i, 309.

Wythe, Thomas, V. of St. Keverne (deceased), ii, 88b.

Wythiell, Simon, Canon of Glasney, ii, 2.

Wythye, Wm., V. of Stogumber, exch. for the Chantry of Colcombe, ii, 36; resigns, and is inst. to the Chantry of Morthoe, ii, 13; resigns, ii, 63b.—*See* Colebrook), ii, 249b.

Wytloff, John, R. of Loddiswell (decd.), ii, 83b; his Will, i, 305b.

Wytteney, John, inst. to Mariansleigh, ii, 5.
Wyttnam, John, see Oldcastel, i, 192.b
Wytymer, John, proxy for Thomas Montagu, ii, 42.

Y.

Ya, John, *see* atte Ya.
Yarcombe; John Hele, V., a Penitentiary in the Deanery of Dunkeswell, i, 94, 115, 143, 173b, 194.
Yarnscombe, appropr. to the Hosp. of St. John, Exeter, ii, 360.
Yate, Joan and Richard, *see* atte Yate.
Yaxley [Yakesley *and* Yakysley, MS.], i, 18b, 28.
Yealmpton, Noss Mayo in, i, 37.—John [Play], V., a Penitentiary in the Deanery of Plympton, i, 50.
Yeate, John, R. of Creacombe (deceased), ii, 13b.
Yeo [Yoe, MS], in the parish of Alwington, i, 84.
Yeo, Walter and William, i, 308b.
Yestebrok, Richard, V. of Okehampton (deceased), ii, 154.
Yeurde [*also* Yurde, MS.], Wm., R. of Great Torrington, ii, 265, 265b; his death, ii, 190b.
Ynngeston, in Harberton, *see* Burleston (*Oratories*), i, 105.
Yoce,—"fratrem Michaelem Yoce, custodem de Tymbyg," ii, 93b.
Yonge (*or* Young), John, perpetual Vicar of Bosham, ii, 147, 168b, 280, 281, 294.
Yonge, Walter, inst. to Umberleigh, ii, 96b; his death, ii, 122.
Yonge, Wm. inst. to St. Stephen's-by-Saltash, ii, 102, 336, 338.
Yoksale, or Yoxhal, Wm., inst. to Clyst St. George, ii, 115; resigns, ii, 132.
York, Edw., Duke of, Patron of Canonsleigh Abbey; *see* le Despenser, ii, 125b.
York, John, R. of Woolfardisworthy, i, 44; exch. for Brampford Speke, ii, 75; resigns, ii, 188b.
Yoxsale, John, i, 305.
Yul, Robert, i, 306b.
Yurd, John, inst. to Bradworthy, ii, 88b; [Yerde, MS.], resigns, ii, 152b.
Yurd, Matthew, V. of Townstal, ii, 6b; ["Yerde, MS.], Abbot Elect of Torre, his "Obediencia," ii, 142b.

Yurd, Roger, R. of Wembworthy, i, 9.

Yurl, Walter, of Kingston (q.v.), ii, 277[b].

Yuse [Hughes ?], Hugh, i, 314.

Z.

Zeal Monachorum; Walter Beare, R.; licence of non-residence for a year, from 28 May, 1396, i, 9; also,[1] for a year, from 4 June, 1397, i, 12.—John Spredell, R., i, 138.

Zennor [John Wylla], V. of, i, 103.

Zouche, Thos. la, inst., to Loddiswell, R., ii, 83[b]; i, 77[b], 94; his death, ii, 131[b]. Sir William was patron of Loddiswell, ii, 338.

Zouche, Wm. la (of Haryngworth), presents to Totnes Priory, ii, 96[b], *see*, also, ii, 349.[b]

ȝeake, John, i, 331[b].

ȝeo, Henry, *see* atte ȝeo.

ȝokshale, *see* Yokshale.

---

[1] He is here called "Robert"—a clerical error.

WILLS.

I. WM. FALEWELL, Rector of the Mediety of the Church of Ermington; Canon of Windsor. i, 300.

Executors: John Bremesgrave and John Busch, chaplains.

Proved 30 May, 1397, before the Bishop.—[The will itself is not given.]

II. RD. DE RAUNDES, R. of Northmolton; Canon of Windsor.

Dated at Windsor Castle, in testator's house there, 23 March, 1398-9. i, 300.

He commends his soul to Almighty God, Blessed Mary, and All Saints, and orders his body to be buried in the Church of St. John Baptist, Windsor, if it can be done conveniently; and if not, then in the church of the parish where he may happen to die. For the fabrick of the nave of such church he leaves 20s.; and for masses for two years, to be said therein for his soul, and for his parents and benefactors, £10 13s. 3d.; also for 4 *trigintalia*[1] for his own soul, 10s. For the poor, on the day of his funeral, 40s.; for prisoners, 20s.; for poor bed-ridden folk, unable to make their living, 20s.; for all other expenses on the occasion, 40s. Not more than five wax lights to be burnt around his body. To the nave of Northmolton Church he leaves 40s: and believing, on his conscience, that, after all he had laid out on the repairs of his church and manse, the sum of £10 ought to content his successor, especially as he had not received a penny from his own predecessor on account of dilapidations, he leaves that sum to the next Rector, but solely on condition that he gives a full discharge therein to his executors, and makes no further claim upon them. To the poor of Northmolton he leaves 40d. To the ministers of All Saints', Derby (to keep his exequies), 20s. To his sister Matilda 40s, and one of his best garments. For the fabrick of the nave of Raunds Church, 40s. For the poor there, 40s. To Thomas Aynho 20s. The residue of his estate, after paying his debts, to be devoted to pious uses.

Executors:—Thos. Marton; John Massyngham; and Thos. Laurence (to each of whom he leaves 40s. over and above their necessary expenses).—*Witnesses:*—The said executors ["Lorence" here in MS.], and John Page, John Chiselet, John Hull, and others.—*Proved* 8 February, 1399-1400, before the Dean of Windsor, in the Chapter House there; registered at Clyst, 14 April, 1400. The Bishop's seal was affixed, at Crediton, 19 August.

III. JOHN DE DODYNGTON, R. of Crewkerne, Can. of Exeter and Preb. of Crediton.

Dated 26 March, 1400. i, 301.

He commends his soul to God, the Blessed Mary, the Blessed Apostles Peter and Paul, and St. Bartholomew (his patrons), and to All Saints; and directs his body to be buried in the Cathedral, before the altar of St. John, by the side of Canon William Dounebryge—"*magistri mei, dum vixit.*" He leaves 1d to every poor person asking an alms in God's name, on the day of his burial; and for the funeral rites and his obit £26 13s. 4d.—To his mother, should she survive him, £20. To the Bishop his large Missal (if his other effects sufficed to pay his debts and legacies without selling it).—To each of his two sisters, 100s. To Otho Chambernon the gilt cup, (*ciphum*) which the Bp. had given him, and 40s. To the said Otho's wife, for the good of testator's soul, and the soul of Rd. Hydon, her former husband—"*secundum velle suum*"—100s. To Master Rob. Rygge, a cup "*de testa ovis vocate* Gripe."[2] To Laurence Haukyn, his little Missal and one Antiphonar, on the condition already stipulated. To each of his servants, "*commoranti in hospicio meo, portanti vestem armigerorum sive clericorum ejusdem secte,*" 40s., and to each valet, 30s. To each serving-man, 10s. To Wm. Clyve, 60s.; to John Beston, 100s.; to his sister Agnes, 100s.; to his sister Amisia, 40s. To Nicholas Fitz Herbert a silver cup worth 40s. and his second-best horse. To Wm. Hydon his best horse and 20s. To the Anchorite of St. Leonard's, 40s. (to pray

---

[1] "Officium 30 Missarum."—*D'Arnis.*

[2] Is *ovis* a clerical error for *avis*?

for their souls). To Thos. Spore, 40s.; to Geoffrey Boterell, 20s.; to Thos. Cook, 20s.; to Matthew Stoke, a cup with its cover, formerly the property of one Stephen, a recluse.—To each of his executors, accepting administration, 5 marks.

He directed that his obit and that of William Dounebryg, should be observed at Exeter for 20 years, and that two chaplains should say mass for his soul, and for Margaret de Courtenay, William, the late Archbishop, William Dounebryg, Stephen the recluse, and Henry Blakeborne, at the discretion of his executors, with any residue derived from the proceeds of his benefices. His best vestment and his large manual to be given to the church of Crewkerne, if testator were R. at the time of his death.

Executors :—Laurence Haukyn, Nich. Fitʒ Herbert and Wm. Clyve; Rob. Rygge and Otho Chambernon to be overseers. They were to pay all his debts, a list of which he left in his own handwriting.

At the end the following legacies are added :—

To Wm. Hayford three *tricennalia*;[1] to John Dene, the same; to Richard Philep, two *tricennalia*; to Wm. Reche, 13s. 4d.; to John Wyllyng, 10s.; to Rd. Spryngolte, 10s.; to John Crede, 6s. 8d.; to the Hosp. of St. John, Exeter, 20s.; to Friar John Gryndel, for his own use, 6s. 8d.; and to the Friars, Preachers and Minors, at Exeter, *de panibus meis canonicalibus*, at the discretion of his executors.

Proved, 20 April, 1400, before the Bishop, at Clyst.

IV. William Trenowyth; of St. Cleer, Cornwall.

Dated, 15 April, 1400. i, 301b.

He commends his soul to God, and his body to holy burial.

He leaves to the V. of St. Cleer, 12d. for tithes forgotten. To John Lanrek, chaplain (for his soul), 2s. To the Friars of Truro [Truru, MS.], 2s. 6d. To John Grene, chaplain, 2s. 6d. To the store (*stauro*) of St. Cleer, 3 sheep. To the Friars of Bodmin, 2s. 6d.; to the Carmelites of Plymouth, 2s. 6d. To the store (*instauro*) of St. Mary, in St. Cleer Church, 2 sheep; to the store of the Holy Cross therein, 1 sheep, and the same to the store of St. James. To Udelina, his sister, 1 cow and 12 sheep. To Cecilia Philipp, 1 brazen pot.

The residue to his executors, for his funeral rites and for the good of his soul; they were to reimburse themselves, in reason, for their trouble and expenses.

Executors :—Rd. Bray and Wm. Bray, his sons. *Proved*, during the Bishop's Visitation of the Archdeaconry of Cornwall, before Rd. Hals, his Commissary, at Clyst, 24 April, 1400.

V.—John Gardyner, R. of St. Martin's, Exminster.

Dated, 20 May, 1400. i, 301b.

He commends his soul to God Almighty, and directs his body to be buried, near his father, in Exminster Church. He leaves to the Hosp. of St. John, Exeter, 13s. 4d. To the Friars Minors of Exeter, 13s. 4d. To John Brugyth, priest of the parish-church thereof, [Exminster] 3s. 4d. To Joan, his sister, 13s. 4d. To Rd. Drake, clerk, *si velit scolas exercere*, 13s. 4d. For the maintenance of the fabrick of his said parish-church, 3s. 4d. To Roger Jurdan, his clerk, 26s. 8d.; also, one bed with furniture complete, one mattrass, and his best horse. The residue of his estate he leaves to his executors to be spent for the good of his soul.

Executors :—Henry Gardiner, his brother, and Rd. Skynner (chaplains); and Roger Jurdan, clerk.

Proved, 31 May, 1400, by Rd. Hals (Canon and Chancellor of the Cathedral) in the Consistory Court there.

VI.—Sir John Prydeaux, Knight.

Dated, 5 June, 1403. i, 302.

---

[1] Officium 30 Missarum ... vel obventiones quæ obveniunt sacerdotibus ratione ejusdem Officii.—*D'Arnis.*

He was moved to make his Will on finding himself in imminent danger of death. He commends his soul to God, and directs that his body be buried "in ala Beati Petri de Modbury."[1]

He leaves 100s. towards certain works in progress in Modbury Church, on condition that the parishioners either buy (or engage to buy within two years) a complete set of vestments; otherwise the money was to be applied to the *tabula* recently bought for the High Altar there. He leaves to his wife, Elizabeth, a horse, called *Bayerd*; and to his daughter Thomasia all his pearls. The residue of his estate he directs his executors to use for the good of his soul.

Executors:—His wife, Elizabeth; his daughter, Thomasia; John Copleston; John Ralegh, of Fardell [Furdell, MS.]; John Dyghte; and Roger Berd, chaplain. *Proved*, 7 Aug., 1403, before the Bishop, at Crediton.

VII.—Walter Trote, Can. of Exeter, and R. of St. Kerrian

Dated, 4 November, 1399. i, 302b.

He commends his soul to God, Blessed Mary, and All Saints; his body to be buried in the Cathedral. He leaves to every Canon present at his funeral 2s. To every Vicar, 12d. To every Annuellar priest, 6d. To each of the Secondaries, and to each chorister, in like manner 3d. He orders six torches to be burnt when his body is carried into the Cathedral, on the night of his exequies and on the day of his funeral; each weighing 13 pounds of wax and 6 pounds "*de Rosyn*," with the wicks thereto (*cum lichinis ad eosdem*). To 6 poor men to carry the said torches, a cloak apiece (made of grey cloth, with hood); and for the good of his soul he orders 1d. to be given to every poor person attending his funeral. To the chaplains of St. Mary's Chapel in the Chantry at Slapton, 3s. 4d. each, to say and sing *Placebo* and *Diryge* on the night of his exequies, and Mass on the day of his burial. To two secondaries in the said Chapel, 2s. each. To two boys, 12d. each. To the said Chapel a missal and an antiphonar; and, for the use of the chaplains there, 24 silver spoons and 6 silver cups, with the arms of Sir Guy Bryan, knight, thereon, to remain for the store of the chaplains for ever. To the Hosp. of St. John Baptist, Exeter, 13s. 4d.; to each poor scholar thereof, 12d.; to the poor men therein 3s. 4d. To be distributed among the poorer tenants of the Manor of Slapton 15s. To the prisoners in the King's prison at Exeter, and in the Lord Bishop's 4d. each. To the Friars Preachers of Exeter, 6s. 8d. To the Friars Minors there, 6s. 8d. To the men and women in the Leper's House of St. Mary Magd. by the West Gate, Exeter, 3s. 4d.; to the Leper's House at Barnstaple, 12d. To every man or woman lying *in novo redditu Simonis Grendon*[2] over against testator's house, 3d. For Barnstaple Bridge, 10s. For Bideford Bridge, 13s. 4d. For Cowley [Covlegh, MS.] Bridge, near Exeter, 3s. 4d. To his Ch. of St. Kieran he leaves a gradual, and for its High Altar one *tualla*, with a green frontal, and a frontal of the same colour to hang above the Altar, with two curtains to match, and one frontal of the same colour to hang before the Altar, also a chasuble with its parures.[3] To John Whyte he leaves 5 marks. To Andrew, his servant, 13s. 4d. To Rd. Anslade, 13s. 4d. To Walter Cook, lately his servant, 10s. The residue to his executors, to be devoted to pious uses, for the good of his soul.

Executors:—John Combe, Minister of the Parish Church of Slapton, in the Chantry recently founded there; Nicholas Wake, R. of Torbrian; and Thos. Losquyt, chaplain.—*Proved*, 12 March, 1403-4, before the Bishop, at Clyst.

---

[1] The (north) transept, is still called the "Orcherton aisle." In its north wall the mutilated effigies of Sir John Prydeaux and Elizabeth his wife repose under a very beautiful canopy, which has recently been restored at the cost of Mr. Prideaux-Brune, of Prideaux Place, Cornwall (under the direction of the R. of Ringmore.) It is the custom, now, to call the church "St. George's," but wrongly: it was dedicated to St. Peter.

[2] *See* Grendon's Will, *infra*, No. XXXII.

[3] *cum paruris*.—Halliwell quotes *Test. Vetust.* p. 267,—"with the aubes and *parures*."

VIII. Henry Brckelond, Can. of Exeter and R. of Moreton.

Dated, 15 January, 1403-4. i, 303.

He commends his soul to God, and his body to sacred sepulture. He leaves £20 for his funeral expenses, and for the poor who should attend; also 20s. for his poor parishioners at Moreton, and the same for the poor of Tiverton on the same day. To Moreton Church he bequeaths a set of vestments, a chalice, a corporal and *tuallum*, with a frontal displaying the arms of the late Countess [of Devon]; also a super-altar, with two cruets (*phiolis*) from his Chapel at Exeter. To the Hosp of St. John Bapt. at Exeter, 20s. To the Cathedral a new large Psalter, not quite complete (but to be completed by his executors, and chained to his own stall in the choir); also a Manual. To the Church of Crediton he leaves his Missal; his cousin, John Snape, to have the use of it, whenever he pleases, within the said Church, but not to carry it out; also, his second Psalter. To the Prioress of Polslo, a small chest (*ypent'*)[1] for her use, and that of her successors for ever. To the Cathedral aforesaid, a great coffer, *cofferam de Flaundris*, to keep vestments in. To the Convents of Polslo, Canonsleigh, and Cornworthy, 6s. 8d. each. To the Friars Preachers of Exeter, 6s. 8d., and the same to the Friars Minors there. To sick men at St. Mary Magdalen's, near Exeter, 3s. 4d.

To John Snape, his cousin, he leaves a Breviary (given him by one John Martyn, who desired his prayers); but Snape was not to sell it, but leave it to some good priest, who would pray for testator and for the said John Martyn. Another Breviary that he had lent him is to be given up to his executors; and he leaves him a book containing the matins of the B. V. M., *Placebo* and *Dirige*, and the visitation of the sick; also, an old set of Decretals, and another book of Decretals; also, 2 beds complete, with one pair of bed-curtains (*Redelles*), crimson; also, 1 *par pellium de latyn* which testator had from the Countess, and a large chest which belonged to his father; also, two silver cups, given him by Snape's father, and twelve silver spoons, six of which were already in his keeping; also, two coats, trimmed with rich fur (*furratas cum pellour*—" pelury"), and two hangings (*dorsers*) of tapestry, six cushions, and three bench coverings (*bankers*) to match. To Walter Marker, chaplain, he leaves 6s. 8d. To Rob. Colyn, chaplain, the small Breviary, *quod est in sacello positum*. To John Pruet, chaplain, the Breviary in John Snape's possession and 20s. To Magota Sourapeldore 20s. and an old cloak, (*armilausam-duplicatam de rubeo et bockehorne*). To Joan, wife of Thomas Cornwale, 5s. and a cupboard (*unum almary*) already in her possession. To Henry Milforde, his servant, 20s. To John Boldebury, another servant, his third best bed, with all its furniture, (*cum toto apparatu sive Rydellis*) also, two small-sized brazen pots and two brazen dishes, one of the better sort; also 40s. To another servannt, Thomas Ellomede, 10s. To Wm. Boldebury, 13s. 4d.; and a book of the matins of the B. V. M. To John Batyn, another servant, goods to the value of one mark. To Thomas Estmond, another servant, 40d. To another servant, Rd. Favel, 40d. As to the legacies in money, those who so wished might select any of his movable goods of the same value, at the prices assigned in his Inventory. The residue he leaves to his executors, to be used for the repose of his soul.

Executors:—John Snape, Rob. Colyn, and John Pruet, priests. They were to administer jointly, and none of them separately without the consent of his colleagues; but all together and with one mind. *Proved* 10 July, 1404, before the Bishop at Clyst.

IX.—John Langelegh, Minister of the Collegiate Church of St. Mary at Ottery.

Dated, 17 July, 1404. i, 304.

He commends his soul to God, and orders his body to be buried in the cemetery there, outside the west door, before the image of Blessed Mary. He leaves to every Canon attending his funeral (unless engaged in duty elsewhere in the Church), 8d.; to a hundred poor persons 100d., or bread to the same value, if

---

[1] I-paynned; ornamented (A.S.) *Halliwell*.

his goods admit. To John Langelegh, his brother, six silver spoons. To Henry Clement a Breviary and a manual; requiring him to pray for his soul as long as he lived, and to bequeath the books to another priest, so that they might never be sold. To the Vicars, among them, for thirty Masses (for the rest of his soul, and for Wm. Slade), 2s. 6d. To Geoffrey Warre, a book containing the Common of Saints. To Wm. Skyrdon, a cloak *coloris de Storion*,[1] with a hood of the same colour. To Joan Skyrdon, his wife, *unam jupam blodii coloris mixti penullatam cum pedibus agnorum nigri coloris*. To Juliana, testator's sister, a dress of red colour, *cum una pellicia* [*pellisse*] and its hood. To Sibella, his stepmother, a dress of red colours, mixed, trimmed with fur, with its hood. To the daughters of the said Sibella, 12d. each. To her sons, after the girls (*post illas*) 4d. each. To Wm. atte Stone a short doublet. To the sons of his sister Juliana, 4d. each; to Magota, her daughter, 12d. To Joan, wife of John Redclyf, a dress of green colours, mixed, with hood; and 11d. to pay for the making. To Wm. Cotyn and his wife 3s. 4d. To the Church of Ottery *unum quaternum optimum de organis'*. To Alice, wife of his servant John, a crimson dress trimmed with white. To John Kye, an oak table *et unum kerchef pro amictu suo*. To Alice, wife of John Twyford, two wine-skins, each containing *quartam lagene*. To Thos. Bateman, 3s. 4d.

Executors:—Henry Clement and Geoffrey Ware (*sic*), who were to dispose of the residue of his estate for the good of his soul, with leave to buy any article not bequeathed, if they paid as much as any other person would have to pay, so as not to defraud his soul. *Witnesses*:—Rob. Alkebourn, Nicholas Oterford, John Metton, John Smyth, and John Coke. *Proved*, 19 July, 1404, before the Bishop at Clyst.

X.—Maurice Burgh, "Domini dum vixit familiaris."

Dated, 2 Jan., 1404-5, in the town of Crediton. i, 304b.

He commends his soul to his Creator and to Blessed Mary, His Glorious Mother, and all the saints, directing his body to be buried in the parish where he may happen to die. He leaves 5s. among sixty priests to say sixty Masses on the day of his burial (if it can be managed), or as soon as possible afterwards; of these Masses 15 were to be of the Holy Trinity, 15 of the Holy Ghost, 15 of the Holy Cross, and 15 of Blessed Mary, Mother of God; for his soul and for all the faithful departed. Also, £30 to two chaplains to say divine service and celebrate daily, in the church of St. Mary at Clyst, for the three years immediately following his death, for his soul, and for Edw. III., the late King; also, for Wm. de Mulsow, for his parents, for their benefactors, and for all the faithful dead; every chaplain to receive yearly, for his service 100s. Also, he leaves his chasuble of white and crimson silks, an alb, an amice of white linen, a stole, a maniple (*phanonem*), and apparels to match (or of other like material, as near as possible in colour to the chasuble), for perpetual use in the said church, to be worn by the aforesaid chaplains while discharging the above-mentioned duties. And if they celebrate elsewhere, his executors are to provide a chasuble, alb, amice, stole, and maniple, and all necessary apparels, made of good materials, at their discretion. At the end of the three years these vestments to be given to the Church in which the Masses were said, to remain therein for ever. To the church of St. Michael, at Clyst, he leaves a chasuble (to be provided by his executors) of silk, embroidered with dogs, birds, and waves (*undis*) in divers colours, and, to wear with it, an alb, an amice of fine linen a stole, a maniple, and apparels to match the chasuble, or as nearly as possible of the same colour. To the sick and bed-ridden, and other indigent people, he leaves 100s., to be distributed immediately after his death: and 5 marks on the day of his exequies, every poor person attending to have 1d., and to pray for his soul, &c. To the Friars Minors, the Friars Preachers, and the House of St. John, in Exeter, he leaves 6s. 8d. each. To Walter Shoggere and Joan his wife, if he should happen to die in their house, 6s. 8d. each. To John Palmer, Wm. *de coquina*, John Warde, John Piers, John Yoxsale, John Clyston, Rd. Baron, John Derby, Wm. Thorp,

---

[1] "Storinus.—color *sturni* [a starling], qui Italice *stornello* dicitur"—*D'Arnis*.

and Walter Pulter, servants of the Lord Bishop, 3s. 4d. each. To Henry Wilde, 20s. and a gown, [*unam gounam*] made of green cloth, embroidered on the left sleeve with leaves of white cloth, sewn on. To Rob. Ogle, his chest called a 'Shipcoffre,' standing in the Bishop's manor-house at Clyst, and a gown of freize (*frise*) cloth, called "*Mouster Villers*," bought at Coventry. To John Gylbert 3s. 4d. and a gown of green cloth, with facings of black cloth. To Philip "*de coquina*" of the Lord Bishop 3s. 4d., his bench [*sellam*] and "brig,"[1] and a gown of worsted "particoloured in shades of crimson colour, *gounam de worstede motteley partitam blodii et sanguinei coloris*, and a doublet of worsted, striped in crimson and lead-colour, (*barre blodii et plonketi coloris*). To Joan Gardiner, then staying at Crediton, 6s. 8d., and a gown of scarlet cloth, with white serge, (*gounam de skarleto cum blanketo duplicatam*). All these bequests were subject to conditions which the testator proposed to convey to his executors by word of mouth. To William Grantelond (alias Portey), a gown of *ray*[2] *sendre*, the gift of the Lord Bishop, bordered with crimson cloth, (*partitam cum panno blodio mixto, cum agnellis albis furruratam*. To Thomas de la Chambere, a gown of green *ray*, (*de Ray viridi cum panno de plunket partitam*) To any poor bed-ridden or indigent person, one of his bed-quilts, of divers colours of wool-work, and one of his blankets; and to some other poor person a tester of the same suit (*testeram de secta dicti lecti*) as the said bed, and one of his woollen blankets. Also, to Colkyn (*sic*), living with the Lord Bishop, a gown, his Lordship's last summer gift (*de liberata ultima estivali dicti Domini mei Exoniensis*). To Rob. Alkebarowe and John Matheu, chaplains, 20s. each, that they may be willing to administer. His two silver-mounted daggers [*baselardi*], and his three silver girdles he orders to be sold to the best advantage, and the money expended on works of piety for the good of his soul, &c., as well as all legacies which might lapse by reason of death. The residue to be divided among the chaplains, who should say the masses for his soul, among the poor and wretched, and in other like works of piety.

Executors:—Rob. de Alkebarowe and John Matheu, above-mentioned.

Witnesses:—John Simon, Rob. Shogger, (of Crediton), Wm. de Wyke and others.

It is added that testator, after this will was made and sealed, bequeathed certain goods to certain persons, by name, as follows:—First to the Guild or Fraternity of the B.V.M. recently established (*inchoate*), in the Ch. of the Holy Cross at Crediton, 26s. 8d.; towards reglazing a window (*in adjutorium operis unius fenistre* (*sic*) *de novo vitriande*) in the said Church, 40s.; to "Arwehedmaker," of Exeter, 13s. 4d.; to Philip, in the Lord Bishop's kitchen, all his shirts, breeches, boots and shoes (*camisias, braccas, calciamenta, et sotulares*; to Katherine, wife of Rob. Ogle, 3 cups *de Warre*; to master Wm. de Langeton a girdle; to the said Rob. Ogle a small knife, called a "Wodeknyf"; to Joan, wife of Rob. Shogger, a mattrass (*unum materasium de carde*). Also he left 4 ells of material to make 2 *towalia*, one for the Church of St. Mary at Clyst, and one for the Church of St. Michael at Clyst; to Stephen, chaplain of the aforesaid Guild, a small knife, with a handle of maple, ornamented with silver, in a sheath with a silver hooke (*chape*); to Wm. Fyssh *1 quaternum pergameni de Curie*. The provision made in his will (*ubi testamentum canit quod voluit*) that two chaplains should say masses for his soul in the Church of St. Mary Clyst, he changed in this codicil, directing them to celebrate, instead, at the altar of the aforesaid guild, in Crediton Church.

Proved with the codicil, 29 April, 1405, before the Bishop, at Crediton.

XI. JOHN WYTLOFF, R. of Loddiswell. i, 305b.

He commends his soul to Almighty God, his Creator, to Blessed Mary, Glorious Virgin, and to All Saints, and orders his body to be buried in the church of the Friars Preachers at Bristol.

---

[1] brigam meam.—I suppose, a "brig," *i.e.* "a utensil used in brewing," etc. "A kind of iron set over the fire."—*Halliwell*.

[2] *ray*—"striped cloth:" *sendre*—sendrus, i.e. cinereus; or perhaps "sendal," i.q. "cendal," a rich thin silken stuff.

He leaves to John Meryk, chaplain, his Breviary, and his girdle of silk with silver clasp; also 100s., to pray for his soul. To the Convent of the Friars Preachers at Bristol, for the work on their church, 40s. To Roger Wynterborne, Prior of the said Convent, 40s. To the Convents of the Minorites, Carmelites, and Augustinians, at Bristol, £3; viz., 20s. to each.—To the Church of Rampisham [Ramsham, MS.], 20s., and to the Church of Frome St. Quintin [Frome Quyntyn, MS.], 20s. To his poor parishioners he leaves 10 marks, to be expended in bread and for shoes (*sotularibus*) or paid in money. To Mariota Wyllym, of Lagham, 13s. 4d. To the works in progress in the churches of Woodleigh, Churchstow, Dodbrooke, Thurleston, Bigbury, and Aveton-Giffard, £6 (20s. to each). To John Bruere, his servant, 100s. To John Appuldore (otherwise called Persones) 100s. To Matilda Denys, widow, his silver cup, with cover. To Rob. Frenche his wine-bottles (*utres*), a silver cup (and cover) to drink wine in, and 100s. to buy himself wine, because testator could no longer drink wine with him (unless God should so will); and he asks him to help his executors, when they came into Devonshire to realize his estate. To the R. of St. Michael's, Bristol, 20s. The residue of his estate, after payment of his debts, to be devoted to works of charity and to masses for his soul, for John Seys, chaplain; and for all to whom he was bound by any special tie, and all the faithful departed.

Dated at Bristol, 6 March, 1404-5.

Executors:—Roger Wyntyrborne, afore-mentioned; and John Meryk, chaplain.

Proved 5 April, 1405, before the Bishop, at Crediton.

XII. William Hals, Rector of Wyke St. Mary.

Dated, 30 September, 1405. i, 306.

He commends his soul to God, Blessed Mary, and All Saints, and his body to sacred sepulture in the Chancel of the Church of Norton-by-Taunton, to which Church he leaves 26s. 8d. for a new chalice. To the monks of Cleeve Abbey 20d. each, to pray for his soul; and the same to John Gay, chaplain. To William Hele, chaplain, for his soul and for that of Henry Hokehyll, a Breviary for his lifetime; to be sold after his death, and the proceeds applied by testator's executors for the same end. To his godsons (*cuilibet filiolo meo*) 12d. each. To Florence Wayne 100s., and his second-best brass pot, one of his best dishes, a small iron spit and all his clothes. To John Dabernoun, a saddle (*cellam*), a pair of travelling-boxes (*trussyngcofferys*), and a wallet (*mantica*). He leaves 12s. 6d. for 5 trentals, for the souls of his father and mother, his brother David, and Matilda, his said brother's wife; and 15s. for 6 trentals for his own soul. To Thos. Langeford *1 jupam ferid'*[1] *duplicatam cum carde*. To his executors, for their trouble, 20s. each. The residue to be disposed of for the good of his soul.

Executors:—John Dabernoun and Walter Passer.

Proved 15 June, 1406, before the Bishop, at Crediton.

XIII.—John Fardel, V. of Buckfastleigh.

Dated, 12 September, 1406. i, 306b.

He commends his soul to God, and directs that he be buried in Buckfastleigh Church, near his parents. He leaves to the said Church 26s. 8d., to buy an "Ordinal," for use therein; but nothing more is to be claimed of himself, or his executors. To Buckfast Abbey, 13s. 4d., that they may pray for him there. To a chaplain to say Mass for him in Buckfastleigh Church, for a year, 100s. To the Lepers' Houses at Totnes, Plympton, Plymouth, Tavistock, Barnstaple and Exeter, 12d. each. To the Bridge at Totnes; to Jews' Bridge [*ponti Iudeorum*], and Dart Bridge, 12d. each. To everyone whose godfather he was [*compater, videlicet in Fonte sacro*] 4d. To Roger Gosley, chaplain, 13s. 4d. To Andrew Cook 4 bushels of wheat and 8 of barley. To Robert Yul 2 bushels of barley, a coat, and a hood. To John Beare, smith, 4 bushels of wheat and 8 of barley, a coat, and a hood. To John Beare, clerk, a bed complete, and a Breviary. To Laurence Fox 1 cow and 2 calves. To Is[abella][2] Cook a dress. To Richard Mark, chaplain, to pray

[1] "Furred"(?)—*See* "Ferdegews" (Halliwell's *Glossary*. The MS. is obscure; perhaps "sericam" was intended.

[2] Perhaps "Isolda," or "Isota."

for him, 20s. To Richard Harpere 40s. and a bed. To Ralph Dollebeare, that he may help to collect what is due to testator, 20s. To Alice Maÿster a bed. To Alice Harpere 20s.—To John Harpere 20s. To Alice Mayster, 20 pounds of wool. To Richard Wyndesore, 20s.

Executors :—The said Richard Wyndesore and Richard Mark.

Proved, 23 September, 1406, before the Bishop, at Clyst.

XIV. ADAM LYLBORN, V. of Kenton i, 307.

He commends his soul to God Almighty, Blessed Mary, and All Saints, and orders his body to be buried near the tomb of Wm. Ramyslond. He leaves a Manual, two Processional books, a surplice, and 40s. (to buy a cope), to his Church of Kenton. To Powderham Church a Processional Book. To the poor 20s., and the same amount *inter pauperes domesticos*. To John, the chaplain there, 3s. 4d. To John, a servant, 4s. 4d. To Sybil Sygelond 20s. and his best brass pot. To maintain a respectable chaplain to pray for his soul for a year: [the amount of this bequest is omitted]. To each priest attending his obsequies and Mass on the day of his funeral, 12d.

Executors :—Rob. Weye (a chaplain), and John Buryknoll.

Dated, at Kenton, 10 September, and

Proved 16 September, 1406, before the Bishop, at Clyst.

XV. JOHN CHEPMAN, of Honiton. i, 307.

Dated on the Monday next before the Feast of St. Peter ad Vincula [*i.e.* 26 July, in] 1406.

He commends his soul to God, and orders his body to be buried in St. Michael's Church, Honiton, before the Great Cross.

He leaves to Edward [Fysch (or Fishacre)], R. of Honiton, on account of tithes forgotten, 20s. He bequeaths the whole rent derived from a certain croft (*crofta terre*), called "le ʒethfeld," to be amortized[1] for a chaplain, to celebrate in the Chapel of All Saints, Honiton, at the altar of St. John Baptist, for the souls of himself, his wife, his sons, and all others for whom he is bound to pray. To the works at the parish-church he leaves 2 marks. For the roofing of the Chapel of All Saints £10, if the parishioners are willing to cover it with lead; if not his executors are to dispose of this sum at their discretion. To every priest taking part in his exequies, and in the Mass on the morrow, 12d. To his godchildren, 12d. each. To three blind men, viz., Rd. Helyer, John Bocher, and Andrew Braggher, 40d. each. For the repair of divers bridges,[2] 40s. To Rob. Crocker, chaplain, 6s. 8d. To Richard Helyer, clerk of Honiton, 12d. To Joan, dau. of John Vautard, 40s. To his servant, Isabella, 40s. To the Friars Minors of Exeter and the Friars Preachers there, 6s. 8d. to each. To repair the Chapel of St. Thomas, at Honiton, 20s. To Thos. Clement, chaplain, 40d. The residue for the good of his soul.

Executors :—His son John and John Prentys, with Laurence Haukyn and Rd. Wykeslond for overseers.

Witnesses :—Rob. Crocker and Rd. Lutrell.

Proved, 13 August, 1406, before the Bishop at Clyst.

XVI.—WILLIAM CREDY, R. of [High] Bickington.

Dated, 1 August, 1406. i, 307b.

He commends his soul to God; his body to be buried in the cemetery of St. John Baptist, Bridgwater, between the two gates, viz., the gate of Thomas Caudel and the gate of the antient infirmary of the Church.[3]

He leaves to Wm. Patehill, Master of the said House, 40s.; and to each of the brethren there, 20s. To the said House one set of Decretals and one *Sextus Liber cum Clementinis*: and to every one serving in his office there, 2s. To Wm

---

[1] totum redditum meum . . . . . ad mortificandum uni capellano. "Mortificare" i.q. "Amortizare."

[2] "diversorum poncium:" they are not mentioned by name.

[3] "ostium antique ecclesie firmarie." *See* below, "Item lego cuilibet pauperi *in firmaria* predicta xijd."

Radwyll a surplice and his cloak.[1] To Philip Martyn a book of sermons, a green coat, with hood, and 40d. To each poor person in the infirmary aforesaid, 12d. To Edith Chepstowe, 12d. To the Master of the said Hospital a priest's set of vestments (*par vestimentorum sacerdotale*). To the Lady Elizabeth Poulet, his sister, a missal, and a chalice with two cruets (*cruetis*) of silver; also a ciborium[2] and a reliquary. To Wm. Halswyll *omnia arma mea* at Bridgewater, *cum brekendariis*. To Philip Martyn 2 sheets. To Rob. Halswyll a Manual and a Book called *Maria Egiptiaca*. To Thos. Paulet a bed called *broydit bed*. To Joan Halwyll (*sic*) 40s., a silver bowl and 6 spoons. To Rob. Halswyll, 2 spoons and a silver bowl. To John Alexander, 13s. 4d. To John Byke his greaves and spurs, a cloak, a coat of russet cloth, and a hood of scarlet cloth, a saddle and bridle;[3] 13s. 4d., and a doublet. To Agnes, dau. of Thos. Credy, a bed with tapestry. To Joan, dau. of Adam Crydy (*sic*), one of his best beds, with 2 sheets and 2 blankets (the Lady Elizabeth to choose a bed for herself first); also 40s. To Wm. Serle and to John, his brother, 40d. each. To Wm. Halswyll *unum scrinium longum*. To Joan atte Yeate, 6s. 8d. and 4 yards of cloth (*quatuor virgas de panno*). To Wm. Credy 20 marks. To Joan Halswyll an ewer and wash-basin. To Adam Credy, his brother, he leaves a hanging (*doser*), with a bench-cover (*banker*) and 6 cushions (*cussynys*); also 12 new plates of tin. To Dionisia Braunscombe 20s. To Wm. Halswyll a long coat of worsted. To the Lady Elizabeth Poulet he bequeaths a mare (*unum jumentum*). To Thos. Poulet a colt out of the said mare (*unum pullum equinum ejusdem jumenti.*) To his brother, Adam Crydy (*sic*), his colt, then at Womberley, and a chaldron (*unum cacabum*). To the Lady Elizabeth, his sister, a wagon, bound with iron. To Ralph Crydy (*sic*) a cup, with cover. To Adam Credy all his lands and tenements, rents, reversions, etc., in Devon, belonging to him by hereditary right after the death of Wm. Credy, his father, and Thos. Credy, his brother; to have and to hold, to the said Adam, and his heirs of his body, so that if he should die without an heir of his body, all the said lands, tenements, &c., should devolve on his sister, the Lady Elizabeth Poulet for the term of her life—after her death they were to pass to testator's nephew, Thos., son of Elizabeth Paulet (*sic*), and the heirs of his body; failing which they were to pass to the direct heirs of his said sister, Elizabeth.

Executors:—Adam Credy, Ralph Credy, and Henry Crosse; who are to act under the Lady Elizabeth, his sister.

Proved, 17 August, 1406, before the Bishop at Crediton.

XVII. John de Shillyngford, Can. of Exeter and R. of Ugborough. i. 308.

He commends his soul to God, and orders his body to be buried, if it can be arranged conveniently, in St. Katherine's chapel in the parish-church of Widecombe[-in-the-Moor], by the side of his mother; that, to quote the testator's own touching words—"*ubi habui primum* salve *ibi recipiam ultimum meum* vale." And, as it had been his wont to spend too much time on the disposition of his worldly affairs, he bequeaths all that he is possessed of to his most dear and faithful brother, Baldwin de Shyllyngford, leaving him everything; and if he should see fit to devote any portion thereof for the good of testator's soul and the souls of his parents, he was to do so in the way he thought best. And he makes the said Baldwin his sole executor.

Dated, in London, on the day after the Feast of the Annunciation, 1388.

Proved 16 October, 1406, before the Bishop, at Clyst.

XVIII. Thos. Granger, "Domini, dum vixit, famuliaris." i, 308b.

He commends his soul to God Almighty, and orders his body to be buried in

---

[1] or, perhaps (in this connection), chasuble,—"Cum mantello meo;"—"mantellus," i. q. "vestis ecclesiastica, casula, *chasuble*."—*D'Arnis*.

[2] So the context seems to suggest: the words are "reportorium" and "scrinium."

[3] "cellam (i.e., sellam) cum freno."

the Chapel of St. Gabriel, at Clyst. He leaves to John Graunger (*sic*) his son, all his lands and tenements in the county of Stafford and 13s. 4d. To the High Altar of the aforesaid Chapel, 6s. 8d. The residue of his estate he bequeaths to Alice, his wife; but she was to pay all his debts.

Executors:—Alice, his wife, and John Caulee. *Dated*, at Clyst, 31 October, 1406. On 24 February, 1406-7, the said John Caulee and Wm. Salle, *husband of the said Alice*, in her name, appeared before the Bishop, at Clyst, and refused to administer. The Bp. appointed Rob. Wastell "tanquam ab intestato," in their stead.

XIX. Isabella Daumarle.

Dated, 19 June, 1407. i, 308b.

She commends her soul to God Almighty and the glorious Virgin Mary, and orders her body to be buried in the Church of Aveton Giffard, to which church she bequeaths 100s. and her best set of vestments: to the church of Holbeton she leaves 100s.; to [North] Huish 20s.; and the like sum to the churches of Sydenham [Damarel], "Tavy," Lustleigh, and Gidleigh; also to the Friars Minors and Preachers of Exeter; and to the Carmelites of Plymouth: to the Minorites there she leaves 13s. 4d.; to Cornworthy Priory 2 marks; and to each of the houses for lepers in the county of Devon outside of Exeter, 13s. 4d.

For her funeral expenses, and for obits and trentals, to be observed for a year, she leaves £50; and £100 for the hire of two chaplains to serve for ten years, after her death. To John Grym, V. of Holbeton, and Rd. Brouste she leaves 40s. each. To Thos. Cook, Elys Webber, John Hyll, Thos. Gay, and Henry Schephurd, 20s. each. To Wm. Yeo and John Webber, 40d. each. To Walter Yeo and Rd. Northmore 6s. 8d. each. To William Gayne 40d. To Joan Gay 6s. 8d. For the repair of bridges £10. To Nicholas, her son, she bequeaths her Missal; to her son Thos., her cloaks of "gris" (*penulas meas de grisio*); to her two daughters, Joan and Margaret, her other cloaks; to her son James 50 marks. To Wm. Strange 10s. To Rd. Halswyll 40s. The residue of her estate she leaves to her sons Nicholas, Thos. and James in equal shares.

Executors:—Her said three sons. *Witnesses*:—John Grym, V. of Holbeton, Rd. Halswyll, and Roger Monk, chaplain. *Proved* 11 July, 1407, before the Bishop at Crediton, by Thos. Tremayn, one of the executors named therein.

XX. Elizabeth Lercedekne, ("*in pura viduetate mea.*")

Dated at Haccombe, 12 December, 1406. i, 309.

She commends her soul to God her Almighty Creator, the Blessed Virgin Mary, His Mother, and all His Saints in Heaven, directing her body to be buried in the choir of the Church of the Friars Preachers nearest to the place of her decease; to whom she leaves 100s. that they may pray for her soul, and because of her burial in their church. Also, to the Friars Minors of Exeter, 13s. 4d., and to those of Plymouth, 6s. 8d.; to pray for her soul. To the Lepers' Houses at Plympton, and at Exeter; 3s. 4d. each. To the Hospital of St. John, Exeter, 6s. 8d. To the Lepers' House, at Totnes, 3s. 4d. To the High Altar of the Church of St. Blaise at Haccombe, in compensation for tithes and oblations forgotten, or kept back, 6s. 8d. She directs her executors to procure two priests, to celebrate for her soul and for all the faithful dead, continuously, in the said church of Haccombe, and to pay them as they may jointly determine. To Rob. Cary she leaves a silver-gilt cup, with cover, *gravatum cum ressents ypounsed cum rolles*. To the Lady Alice Werthe 2 marks sterling, "*de Corneworthy*." The residue, after payment of her debts and execution of her Will, she bequeaths to her servants, to be divided among them all.

Executors:—Rob. Scobehill, Thos. Norys, and Gilbert Smyth.

Proved, 7 August, 1406, before the Bishop, at Crediton.

XXI. John Wythewyll, Precentor of Crediton.

Dated, 13 July, 1407. i, 309.

He commends his soul to God, and his body to holy sepulchure in the Lady-Chapel at Crediton. He bequeaths to the Vicars of the said Church a "portion," due to him from the Church of Lelant [Lanaunt MS.; *i.e.* St. Uny Lelant, in

Cornwall], and retained by John Innocent, *alias* "*Nocent*."[1] The residue he leaves to his executors, to spend for the good of his soul.

Executors:—Rd. Aldryngton, Canon of Exeter, Wm. Trae, and John Bowode, clerks; and Rob. Rowe.

Proved, 2 September, 1407, before the Bishop, at Crediton.

XXII.—John de Lydeford, Archdeacon of Totnes.

Dated on the Feast of St. Gregory, Pope (i.e., 12 March), 1406. i, 309b.

He commends his soul to God, his Maker and Saviour, beseeching Him Who bought his soul and the souls of all the faithful with His Precious Blood, to deal with it according to His Mercy, when it should have passed from this vale of misery, of His exceeding great kindness and goodness ineffable. He orders his body to be buried in the Cathedral, on the north side of the Choir, in a place selected by himself, and lately assigned to him by the Dean and Chapter. He leaves £20 for his anniversary, to be observed for 20 years continuously after his decease; the money (which he desires should be kept in the Treasury of the Cathedral, or other safe place) to be distributed on each occasion among the canons, vicars, annuellars, secondaries, and chorister-boys, who shall join in saying *Placebo* and *Dirige* at night, and the Mass of *Requiem* on the morrow; viz., to each Canon 4d.; to each Vicar and Annuellar 2d.; to each Secondary 1d.; and to each chorister-boy *ob.*; the clerk of the Treasury, each year, to have 4d. for his trouble in the distribution. If any portion of the sum allotted for the year remained over it was to be replaced, except some ten, eight, or six pence, to be reserved for the poor and needy mendicants present in the Church. Every canon and other priest, sharing in this distribution, to perform strictly the stipulated services. If any preferred to commemorate testator at their own Masses, they were to do so on the day of their proper turn, or on the nearest possible day. If his rules were infringed by the Stewards of the Treasury, or by any other person, the anniversaries were to be suspended, and the £20 applied to other pious uses. Immediately after his death, his executors were to engage two priests, of good conversation and reputation, and pay them a sufficient salary, to say Mass daily (apart from lawful impediment), for a year, for testator's soul, and for Rob. Herward and Edw. Loveworth, at the altar of St. John the Evangelist, on the north side of the Lady Chapel (with the sanction of the Dean and Chapter), and also the service for the dead, *Placebo* and *Dirige*, with the usual commendations. He leaves four trentals (*trentella*), for four priests, with the like intent. To the Church of Ide he bequeaths his chalice, gilt within and without (which he had been accustomed to use in his own chapel at Exeter); also his beautiful large noted Breviary, to remain there for ever, for the use of the parish presbyters and the parishioners; the officiating presbyter and the parishioners, on Sundays and other Feasts, to make special mention of his name in the Mass among the benefactors; also, his third set of vestments, with a chasuble of crimson cloth *de Blodio stragulato*; on condition that the executors are, first, promised that testator's condition will be fulfilled. To the poorer parishioners and his tenants there, he leaves 40s., to be divided at the discretion of his executors; and to Matthew Stoke the same sum, and his new long crimson coat, furred with pelury (*cum pellura furratam*), and a large hood of the same suit, well furred. To James Carialegh, his clerk, £10 to help him in his scholastick studies. To John Holeway, his clerk, 12 marks, and a bed suitable to his station, viz., the bed with tapestry which testator bought of Robert, his Vicar. To Sutton, his cook [*coco meo*] 60s.; to Thos. Walter, 60s.; to Wm. Carislegh, 40s.; to John Page, 40s.; to John Langman, 20s.; to his dear friends, John Gorewyll, LL.D., and his brother, John the younger, Mauger Parys, Rd. Mark, Rob. Lyngham (R. of St. Mary [Major] at Exeter), John Holond (R. of St. Pancras), John Govys, Rob. Langman (his Vicar), Rd. Marschell (his chaplain), Peter Hopere, Wm. Hayford, John Deyman, and John Beawfys (chaplains), 20s. each; entreating

[1] Under "Nocent" (*i.e.* "a wicked man"), Halliwell quotes (Hall, 1548, *Henr.* IV. f. 14)—"An innocent with a *nocent*; a man ungylty with a gylty; was pondered in an egale balaunce."

them all to remember him in their Masses, etc., and trusting in God to deliver him more speedily and easily from Purgatory by reason of their prayers and merits. To the Friars Preachers of Exeter (to which Order he had himself been admitted), 40s. To the Friars Minors (to whom also he belonged), he leaves no money, but simply refers them to the engagement to pray for his soul and keep his anniversary, into which they had entered, according to their custom, when he was admitted: his executors to attend to the matter immediately after his death. To Rob. Lyngham, before mentioned, 20s. in addition to the former legacy, and his black cup of maple (*de maserio note nuncupatum*) gilt, with a cover silver-gilt (wherefrom testator had drunk much good wine); entreating him to pray for him, and to assist his executors. The residue, after paying his debts (*que pauca sunt, ut spero*) his executors were to bestow on his poor relations and other indigent persons; and he desires that their names should be ascertained diligently; also, that poor penniless people, bedridden, and confined to their huts and cottages (*in lectis et tugurriis et casis suis cubantes*), unless they were really able to work, should be remembered; and that frequent Masses should be said for his soul, by chaplains of good repute, and for his parents and friends, especially for Rob. Hereward (formerly Archdn. of Taunton), John Stapeldon (late Prior of Abingdon), and Edw. Loveworth (formerly a Vicar in the Cathedral), Nicholas, Rector of Crawley, and Thos. Rector of St. Maurice, Winchester; and for all the faithful dead, specially those who had done him service. He leaves £10 for the repair of the more necessary bridges and roads near Exeter. As to his funeral expenses, he charges his executors to do their utmost to keep them within reasonable bounds, avoiding superfluity and pomp and every kind of excess; and he absolutely prohibits all banqueting on the occasion, on the part of the Canons and other Ministers; only his executors and those actually engaged in the necessary work of burying him, and a goodly number of the very poor, chosen by his executors, were to be feasted; all customs to the contrary, when Canons of Exeter depart this life, notwithstanding; but he desires that priests attending his funeral, and celebrating then, or on the following day, shall have a repast and the sum of 3d. and no more. His executors were not to allow any exchanges, or re-arrangements of his legacies; but distribution was to be made as he had directed. He leaves to the poor and sick inmates of the Hosp. of St. John, Exeter, half a mark, and the same amount to poor scholars and clerks therein, to be faithfully divided by the Prior; and each of them is to say *unum Psalterium* [" *Spalterium, MS.*"] for his soul.

Executors:—The afore-mentioned Rd. Mark, John Holond, and John Govys: to the first of whom he leaves 40s., besides his legacy of 20s.; also his fair Bible, and a silver cup *de les plat pycys*,[1] with cover; a long table cloth of Parisian work (*de opere Parisius*) and a long *tuallum*. To John Holond he gives 40s., in addition to the former 20s., his fair, new, *Legenda Sanctorum et Temporalis* in two volumes, and a silver cup *de les plat pycys*.[1] To John Govys he gives his red bed, embroidered, with tapestry, and canopy, and three curtains to match, in addition to the 20s. mentioned above, and a silver-cup *de les plat pycys*,[1] and its cover; also a table-cloth and a *tuallum* of Parisian work, in middling condition, not his best; also six spoons of the small set and pattern, and a dozen (*unum dosyne*) new vessels of tin, *garneysy*. He hoped there would be no contention or quarrelling [*briga*] between them, but that they would do their best to carry out his Will and certain directions written on a separate sheet of parchment for their guidance. He concludes with an Anathema on those who should change or hinder his directions, and Benediction for those who fulfil them.

Proved, 13 December, 1407, before the Bishop at Crediton.

XXIII. Sir William Bonevylle, knt.

[It has been suggested that it would be expedient to print this interesting Will in full. The various readings marked L are from the Lambeth MS., kindly collated for me by Mr. Greenfield.] i. 311.

---

[1] *See* Will No. xxxvii.—" Ciphum argenteum *flat* cum cooperculo."

En noun de Dieux, Amen.—Ieo, William Bonevylle, chiualer, deuys moun testament en ma bone memorie samadie proschein deuaunt le feste de lassumpcoun de nostre Dame, lan del Incarnacoun de nostre Seigneur ichus M^{l}ccccvij^{o}, en cest manere que suit. Primerement ieo deuise malme a Dieux et a sa douce Mere, et a toutz lez seintz de Parais, et moun corps destre enterre deuaunt le haut croys de lesglise de Nywenham. Ensement ieo deuise a mesme lesglise de Nywenham pour gysaunce de moy et de mes compaignes illeoqes, et pour prier pour noz almes, xl li. de money. Ensement ieo deuise a feiere et reperarailler lesglise et le clocher de Wodebury xx marcz. Ensement ieo deuise al hospitalle de seynt Johan dexestre ls. Ensement al heremyte de Stetth[1] pour prier pour moy xxs. Ensement ieo deuise as ffreres de Iuelchestre cs. Ensement as nonaynes de Aulbe Sale[2] en mesme la ville x li. Ensement ieo deuise as ffreres menours de Bryggewater cs. Ensement as ffrerez de Dorchestre ls. Ensement as ffrerez prechers dexestre cs. Ensement as ffreres menours dexestre cs. Ensement ieo deuise as ffrerez menours et precheurs de Saresbirs cs., come a chescun ordre ls. Ensement ieo deuise as ffrerez Austyns precheurs et menours de Bristuit vijli. xs., come a chescun ordre ls. Ensement ieo deuise a ceut pourez chapeleyns pour celebre trentalez messez pour malme xij li., xs. come a chescun deaux ijs. vjd. Ensement ieo deuise a diversez pluys pourez prestez pour celebrer x^{ml} messez pour malme et de toutz cristientz xli li. xiijs iiijd, en tout le hast apres ma morte come il bonement pourra estre feit. Ensement ieo deuise a sink centz pourez hommez et femmes pour lour vesture et chausure, pur prier pour malme, c li.; cestasauoir a chescun deaux iiijs Ensement ieo deuise a aultre poure people venant al jour de lenterement de moun corps x li., cestasauoir a chescun qi vient 1d. Ensement ieo deuise a labbe et couent de Glastingbirs, en eide del susteignaunce de lour froyter,[3] xl li. Ensement ieo deuise a iiij prestez annuellez pour celebrer pour malme et de toutz cristienz per ij annez apres ma mort xl li., a chescun cs. per an, cestasauoir A Shete j, A Meriet un aultre, a Wodebury le tierce, et en aulbe sale de Iuelchestre le quarte. Ensement ieo deuise as nonaignez de Cornworth v. marcz. Ensement ieo deuise a lez pontez et voyes que sount feblez et perfondez deinx mez Seigneuries en les countez du Deuens' et Somerset en eide de lour feire et reparaillier c marcz. Ensement ieo deuise a mez pluys pourez tenauntz en bondage de Stapultoun xx marcz et xx quarters du furment de ma grange illeoqes. Ensement a mez tenantz en bondage de Lymyngtoun xx marcz et xx quarters de furment destier prys de ma grange de Socke. Ensement a mez tenantz de Meriet xij quarters de furment illeoqes. Ensement a mez pluis pourez tenauntz de Thurlebere x quarters de furment illeoques. Ensement a mez tenauntz de Wodebury xx marcz. Ensement a mez pourez tenauntz de Chiristaunton x marcz. Ensement a mez pourez tenauntz de Shete x marcz. Ensement ieo deuise a gaigner licence du Roy pour amorteiser l marcz du terre et de rent per an, a vn meisoun Dieu fait a exestre en Combestrete, pour xij pourez hommes et femmez y estre herbegez a toutz iours, ccc marcz. Ensement ieo deuise a la dit meisoun Dieu en honour de Dieux, et pour la dite meisoun susteigner et lez avauntditz pourez hommes et femmes, tout moun Rente deinx la citee dexestre fforprys moun hostiel illoeqes nadgairs a Monsieur Daudeley quelle suslite hostiell ieo deuise a Alice ma compaigne a terme de sa vie. Et apres soun deces a mes heyers madles de moun corps engendrez, et pour defaute de tiel issue a mez droitz heiers

[1] In the Lambeth MS. "alermytage de Stathe;" i.e. Saint Teath in Cornwall. The MS. is obscure, but there can be no doubt as to what is meant. *Maclean* ("Trigg-Minor, iii, 129) states "that Wm. Carminow, son of Sir Walter Carminow, and Alice Tinten, granted the manor of Newhall, in St. Teath, to Alice, relict of his brother Ralph, for her life, in the name of dower," and that "this lady, by her charter, released it, with the manor of Polrode and others, to John Carminow, son and heir of the aforesaid William, for the purpose of securing an annuity of 100 marks *per annum to Sir Wm. Bonville, whom she afterwards married.*"

[2] "del Aube Sale," L.

[3] The Frater-house, as in Bale's Kynge-Johan (p. 27), quoted by Halliwell.—"Fratter," L.

en fee. Ensement ieo deuise a ma dite compaigne c marcz de money, la moite de tout moun vessellea dargent forsprys moun vessellea nadgairs a monsieur Maiheu de Gurney, et le vessell de meistre Ricard Courtenay sil soitz forfetz.[1] Ensement ieo deuise a dite compaigne toutz mez libres vestimentz ouec aultre appareill a ma chapell regardantz, forpris un missall le pluys petit quelle ieo deuise a leaglise de Socke Denys [Sock Dennis.] Ensement ieo deuise a ma dite compaigne toutz maners necessariez appourteignauntz a ma sale, chambre, Panetrie, Botelrie,[2] Cusyne, et pestrine deinx moun maner de Shete. Ensement, oue tout moun estor viff et mort en mez ditz manoirs de Shete, Whiscombe, Douylesheies, Uppeheies, Southlegh, Tateworth, et Pokyngtoun a temps de ma mort esteantz davoir lauaundit estor a terme de sa vie, et apres soun desez tout le vesselle dargent a la deuise oue lestor auauntdit soit vendu et distribuit pour noz almez, Margarete iadis ma compaigne et de noz auncestrez et amys. Ensement ieo deuise a dame Anneys Bonevylle ma soere, nonaigne de Wherewell, x marcz de money, un hanapp,[3] ovec un couercle dargent et ma meillour hoppelond,[4] ouec le furrure. Ensement ieo deuise a William moun fitz cc marcz de money en eide de luy marier. Ensement ieo deuise ieo deuise (*sic*) a Thomas ffitz du Johan Bonevylle, qi Dieux assoile, xx li. de money. Ensement ieo deuise a Johan, fitz de Thomas Bonevylle, qi Dieux assoile, en eide de luy marier, c marcz, sur condicioun que lauauntdite money atteindra en lez maynez de mez executours tanque al temps que couenablez mariagez pour les auauntditz enfauntez soyent ordeignez par lours pluys proschemz amys iesqes al temps que les enfauntz auauntditz veignent a lour pleine age qils pourount estre mariez par descrescoun de lour mesmez. Et si aueigne qe les ditz enfantz ou ascun deux deuyent deuant qils soient mariez, ou deuaunt qils veignent a lour pleyne age, qadonqe ieo voille et deuise qe la somme dargent a celuy qi soit mort deuise soit ordeigne et done a pourez gentz, pour malme et de toutz cristiens. Ensement ieo deuise a ma ffile, Dame Katerine Cobbeham, xx li. Ensement a ma file, Dame Elizabet Carrew, xx li. Ensement ieo deuise a Raulyn Seyncler pour acchater un corrodie pour luy a terme de vie, et ceo par disposicoun et ordinaunce de mez executours, xx li. Ensement ieo deuise a William ffiton[5] pour luy acchater, et ceo par ordinaunce de mez executours, xx li. Ensement ieo deuise a Thomas Balle pour luy acchater un corrodie par disposicion et ordinaunce de mez executours, x marcz. Ensement ieo deuise a Richard Sparke de Wodebury x marcz. Ensement ieo deuise a Johan Streech[6] xx li. A Johan Churchhulle[7] x marcz ; a Andreu Rydoun x li. ; a Rogier Tremayll x marz, et a Margarete sa femme xls. Ensement ieo deuise a Thomas Saundre[8] x marcz ; a Johan Holcot,[9] clerc, cs. ; a Johan Radestoke, clerc, cs. ; a Johan Socke,[10] clerc, cs. ; a Johan Mascal,[11] ls. ; a Robert Cokesden lxs. ; A Edward Dyer lxs. ; A Wylliam Gylle[12] xxs. ; a Robert Lome xxs. ; A Johan Reue de Lymyngtoun, xiijs. iiijd. ; a Johan Lome le fitz vjs. viijd. ; a Nycol Colyer,[13] Baker, vj.s. viijd. ; a Johan Durke vjs. viijd. : a Alice[14] Hoggez de Thurlebere x marcz ; a Luce Aumarle xxvjs. viijd. Ensement ieo deuise a le vicary de Colytoun cs. A mez pourez tenauntz de Axemynstre cs., a Johan Lome, le piere, xs. a Nycol Wylle x marcz, a Johan Wylle cs., a Benet Smyth de Nortlegh lxvjs. viijd. Ensement ieo deuise a labbe et covent de fforde xx quarters de furment. Ensement ieo deuise qe vjs. de money soient distribuitz pour lalme du Alice[15] Rote, vjs. en money pour lalme dun Cordewener iadis demurraunt a Londrez, et xs. de money pour lalme dun Lucas Bussh de Wodebury. Ensement ieo deuise qe toutz mez debtez soient duement et pleinement payez. Et si ascunz offencez ou extorsions depar moy soient faitez as ascuns persounz ieo voille et deuise qe lour soit restorez solanc la quantite de loffence et ceo per ordinauncz dez mez surueyours et executours. Ensement ieo deuise qe moun hostiell et ma meyny soient enterement tenuz ensemble per j quarter dun an apres ma mort. Et ieo voille qe nulle enterement pour moy soit feit, mesqe

---

[1] "Sil soit forfeittz," L.
[2] "Butlerye," L.
[3] A drinking-cup.
[4] A great coat.
[5] "ffitton," L.
[6] "Strech," L.
[7] "Chirchehill," L.
[8] "Sander," L.
[9] "Holkot," L.
[10] "Soke," L.
[11] "Mascall," L.
[12] "Gyll," L.
[13] "Colier," L.
[14] "Alis," L.

xxiiij torches de cere et xxiiij pourez hommes vestuitz le iour de lenterement de moun corps. Ensement ieo voille et deuise qe tout le residue de toutz mes biens et chateux pardesuis nient deuisez, soient vendutz, ordeignez, et distribuitz pour malme, mez auncestrez, et de toutz cristienx, et ceo par ordinauncez de mez executours, si come ils voillent respondre ent deuaunt Dieux al iour de Jugement. Et dycell moun testament loialment ferre et acompler ieo face et ordeigne tielx mes executours desoubz escriptz, cestasauoir Alice, ma compaigne, William Ekerdoun, clerc, Thomas Modeslegh,[1] clerc, Andreu Rydoun, Johan Socke, clerc, Johan Holcot, clerc, et Rogier Tremaille, ensemblement ove la souruewe de monsieur Thomas Brooke et de Johan Streech,[2] qe ma ordinaunce suisdicte depar mes executours soit pleinement a compliz, et qe nulle chose soit fait sanz consaylle et assent dez ditz sourueyours. En tesmoignnaunce du qelle chose aycest moun testament oue mez proprez mayns iay mys moun seal. Done iour et an suisdictes. Ensement ieo deuise a la femme recluse a seint Leonard, pres a la cite dexestre la. Done come desuis. Ensement ieo deuise a synquant pluis pourez hommez et femmes eiantz jeofuez enfauntz l vaches.

Probatum fuit suprascriptum testamentum et insinuatum coram Domino in Manerio suo Criditonensi, xxiiijto die mensis Marcii,[3] Anno Domini Millesimo cccc^{mo} octavo [*i.e.* 1408-9[4]], ac pro vero testamento dicti defuncti libere pronunciatum; commissaque fuit administracio omnium bonorum dictum testamentum concernencium, ubicunque infra Diocesim Exoniensem existencium, discretis viris Domino Johanni Holcot, capellano, et Andree Rydon, executoribus in eodem testamento nominatis, prestito primitus ab eisdem, ad Sancta Dei Evangelia juramento corporali de fideli inventario omnium bonorum dicti defuncti conficiendo, ac bona hujusmodi juxta ipsius defuncti ultimam Voluntatem fideliter administranda; necnon de vero compoto Domino inde reddendo cum fuerint ex parte Domini predicti requisiti. Reservata Domino potestate committendi hujusmodi administracionem ceteris executoribus in eodem testamento nominatis, cum venerint eam in forma juris admissuri. Et postea idem Dominus Episcopus commisit potestatem Magistro Roberto Rygge, ecclesie Cathedralis Exoniensis Cancellario, committendi administracionem bonorum hujusmodi ceteris executoribus in eodem testamento nominatis—ut in forma.

XXIV. THOMAS HERT, Rector of Gittisham.

Dated, 9 May, 1407. i, 312^{b}.

He commends his soul to God, and his body to be buried as God disposes.

He bequeaths to Gittisham Church a cow, to keep a wax light burning continually before the image of St. Michael there; and another cow, to keep up his obit year by year; the said cows to remain in charge of the Churchwardens. To the Chapel at Shepton, for prayers for his soul, 6s. 8d.; to Uploman Church, 6s. 8d.; to the Church of Salcombe [Regis], 6s. 8d. To each of his sons spiritual he bequeaths 12d. To Gittisham Church he gives a Breviary, to remain and be used therein in perpetuity. To the Friars Preachers of Exeter, and the Friars Minors there, 13s. 4d. each. To the Hospital of St. John, there, 6s. 8d.; to each poor person in the said Hospital, and in East Gate (*in porta de Esteyete*), 12d. For distribution among

---

[1] "Modesley," L.

[2] "Streche," L.

[3] "Marcii" is written *on an erasure.*—*Note* by B. W. Greenfield, Esq. (4 Cranbury Terrace, Southampton):—"As Probate of this Will was—by virtue of a Commission from Abp. Arundel—granted, at Exeter, under the seal of the Archdn. of Barnstaple, on 18 April, 1408, and registered, accordingly, at Lambeth [Arundel, I. 253], it is probable that the Probate taken before the Bp. of Exeter was the prior act of the two; in which case its precise date would correspond with 24 March, 1407-8, if the month is correctly given."

[4] Oliver (*Monasticon*, page 404) adopts this later date, without question. I suspect that the scribe, when he corrected the *month* forgot to correct the *year*.

the poor on the day of his death, 20s. To buy a new bell for Gittisham Church, 40s. To John Tycon, his servant, he leaves a cow. To Alice, wife of John Forneauxe, a heifer worth 6s. 8d. To Wm. Radeslo, his chaplain, 8 marks, to say Mass for his soul, wherever he pleases. To Elizabeth Walshe, a heifer, worth 8s. To Stephen Walshe, 3s. 4d. To John Walshe, 3s. 4d. To John Gobe, his servant, 6s. 8d. To Joan Persey, 3s. 4d. To John Beseys two[1] [?] To his executors, for their trouble, he leaves 40s. each; and they are to dispose of the residue for the good of his soul.

Executors:—Wm. Radeslo, chaplain, and Henry Whytyng.—[There is no memorandum of this Will having been proved.]

XXV. RICHARD TYTTESBURY, Can. of Exeter, and R. of the Mediety of the Church of Ermington, "in pura siquidem sinceritate Fidei Catholice existens." i, 313.

He commends his soul to God, his Creator, Who redeemed it with His Precious Blood, with the utmost intensity of devotion and with all his desire: his body to be buried wherever his executors, or one of them, direct. He leaves 40s. to be given to prisoners and other poor people within two days, and a further sum of 100s. to be dealt with in like manner within eight days, after his death. To Baldwin Tyttesbury, his brother, he leaves 100s., part of a sum already received by him, for which testator held his written and sealed acknowledgment. To Edmund, the said Baldwin's son, 40s.; to Katherine, his daughter, 20s.; to Isabella, his daughter, 20s.; to Margaret, his wife, one of testator's coats, without the fur, and 20s. To Isabella, testator's sister, 13s. 4d.; to Thos. Tyttesbury, his nephew, *in partem exhibicionis sue ad jura regalia singulis annis ad tempus sex annorum*, seven marks, as long as he shall so continue (unless testator, in his life time, should otherwise dispose thereof); and if within the said six years, he should inherit, or acquire by marriage, a good and sufficient fortune, or should die in the interim, the legacy was to lapse, and be devoted to pious uses for the good of testator's soul. To the same Thomas, he leaves all emoluments etc., arising from his own lands and tenements, held by testator as his guardian, from testator's death until the said Thomas's majority; the said Thomas to marry at his own discretion, without interference from his executors. To Alice, daughter of Thos. Hodysford, he leaves one of his coats, with the fur upon it. To his parishioners at Ermington, and especially those employed in agriculture, 10 marks. To the poor parishioners at Faringdon, Dioc. Winton, 10s. To the poor parishioners of Westbeare, Cantuar. Dioc., 10s. To the Anchorites of St. Leonards, near Exeter, of Marham Church, and of Bodmin, 40d. each. To Richard Graynevyll, for life, the use of the book called *Pupilla Oculi*, in the said Richard's own handwriting; to go, after his death, to Ermington Church for ever, to be used by the ministers of the Church for their learning, and never to be sold by the parishioners; and he leaves him the 24s. that he owed testator. To Wm. Brounyng, his clerk and executor, he bequeaths a book of Decretals, beginning (on the second folio) "*juxta quod iste testatur*," with the Sixth Book bound up in the same volume; also *meum nigrum Quaternum*; and the use, for six years, of his Books on Civil Law, with the exception of Cinus;[2] due security for their return being given to his executors. Edmund Tyttesbury to have them afterwards (or their value, to buy a *Corpus Juris Civilis*, if he addicted himself to the study of the same), for his life time; then to be sold for the good of testator's soul. To Roger Markedene, his clerk, 40s., and his little girdle of black silk with silver mounts; and, should the said Roger attain the priesthood, he is to be preferred to all others to say Mass for testator's soul, the executors to pay him a reasonable salary, notwithstanding the fact that he is an executor himself. To Thos. Rowe, V. of Ermington, he leaves his best girdle. To Joan More, of Hartland, 20s.

[1] The MS. is obscure here—"ij ou' m̄." Possibly "Oves Masculos" may be intended: *see* p. 399, *line* 22,—"oves utriusque sexus."

[2] Cinus (or Cino), an eminent Canonist of Pistoia, died at Bologna, in 1336.

To John Rowe, a poor clerk of St. John's Hosp., Exeter, 8s. 4d. a year, to provide clothing, as long as he remains there; and when his time is completed, the executors are to send him to a grammar-school for a year. To every poor scholar in the said Hospital (the said John included), 12d.; and to the Prior and Brethren there, being priests, 13s. 4d., to be equally divided among them. To his Church of Ermington he bequeaths his Ordinal and a chalice worth 40s. (or more, at the discretion of his executors). To Rd. Palmer, his Book called "*Raymound.*" To Alice, dau. of Thos. Hodysford, 6s. 8d. To Nicholas Fox, a poor scholar of the parish of Ugborough, 13s. 4d., by way of exhibition to grammar-schools. To the store of the Church of Stoke St. Nectan, 6s. 8d. The residue of his estate to be disposed of by his executors for the good of his soul.

Executors:—Rob. Alkebarowe and John Barell, chaplains, and Wm. Brounyng and Roger Markeden, his clerks; each to receive for his trouble 20s., and all reasonable expenses incurred. To Rob. Alkebarowe he gives for life, his Breviary (which begins on the second folio—*Dominus noster*).

Witnesses:—Reginald Bryta, R. of Brattou [Clovelly], John Schute, chaplain, and Henry Alkebarowe, clerk, R. of St. Stephen's, Exeter.

Dated at the Bishop's Manor of Clyst, 24 February, 1405-6.

Proved 7 June, 1409, before the Bishop, at Crediton.

XXVI. Thomas Bullok, "serviens ... Episcopi."

Dated at Crediton, 16 December, 1409. i, 313b.

He commends his soul to God, &c., and directs that he be buried in the Church of Crediton. To the Bishop he bequeaths *par precum de auro cum uno monili* containing a jewel called "a dyamaund." To Wm. Langton, chaplain, *par precum de rubio lambour*. To Wm. Rayner, chaplain, his best gold ring; to John Barell, chaplain, one of his gold rings; to Rd. Palmer, chaplain, the same; to Reginald Bryta, chaplain, the same; the same, also, to Laurence Haukyn, chaplain. To the Guild in the parish-church of Crediton, to maintain a chaplain and the Ornaments thereof, 40s. To the parishioners of Crediton, 20s., to buy a chalice, or other Ornament of the Altar; to renew a glass window in the said church, 20s.; to all the Vicars there, in equal shares, 20s.; for the statue, or image, of the Holy Cross there, *unum par precum de Get cum Gaudes de auro cum uno monili de auro*; to Wm., the Dean, 6s. 8d.; to Wm. Allerton, parish chaplain there, 6s. 8d.; to Steph. Drake, chaplain of the Guild, 6s. 8d.; to some priest, to celebrate for his soul in the said Church for two years, £10; to ten poor men unfit for labour, 3s. 4d., to be equally divided; to every poor person attending his funeral, 1d.

To Wm. Wodham, an attendant of the Bishop, and to Lewis Busshebury, clerk, of the Bishop's household, 13s. 4d. each. To Roger Chamberlen, a silver dagger (*baslardum*). To John Pakwode, a silk girdle. To Wm., the senior, and Wm., the junior, attendants [*puero seniori . . . puero juniori*] of the Bishop's chamber, each 40d. To Wm. Cook, chaplain, 13s. 4d. To his sister, Alice Bullok, 40s., and a silver girdle (*unam zonam argenteam de coreo*). Four torches to be burnt at his funeral, during the Service; after which two of them were to be given to the altar of the Guild; two to the Parochial Altar at Crediton. Of five wax lights, four were to be used and dealt with after the same manner; the fifth to go to the altar of St. Nicholas therein. To Alexander Wodecroft he leaves 3s. 4d.; to Hugh Yuse, 20s.; and to John Matford, 20s.; the residue for the repose of his soul.

Executors:—Hugh Yuse and John Metford (*sic*).

Witnesses:—John Bowode, Wm. Cook, John Barell, Steph. Drake, and Wm. Smyth, chaplains.

Proved 14 June, 1410, before the Bishop, at Crediton.

Summa bonorum, £45 8s. 2d. *ob*.

XXVII. William Bachyler.

Dated at Crediton, 14 September, 1410. i, 314b.

He commends his soul to God: his body to the Cemetery at Crediton.

He bequeaths to the V. of St. Hilary, Cornwall, for tithes forgotten, 2s. 10d. To his three sons £10, in equal shares; to his dau. Nichola, £5; and to his dau. Joan,

£5. To John Gelow, 6s. 8d. To each priest attending his exequies, 6d. To John Collard, chaplain (to pray for his soul), 20d. For the fabrick of the Chapel at St. Michael's Mount in Cornwall, 12d. For the fabrick of the Church of St. Hilary, 12d.; of the Chapel of St. Germoe [Sci. Girmow, MS.], 12d.; of the Chapel of the Holy Trinity, 12d.; of the Church of St. Gulval [Sancte Golvele, MS.], 12d. To a chaplain, appointed by his executors, to say Mass for his soul for a year, 7 marks. To Joan Bacheler (*sic*), his wife, all the utensils in his house "portionem meam attingentia." To John Holle, 11s. To Roger Bacheler (*sic*), his brother, a green coat, with his best hood. The residue of his estate he gives to Wm. Tregower, senior, for the rest of his soul, and appoints him Executor.

Proved 15 September, 1410, before the Bishop, at Crediton.

XXVIII. ROGER BERNARD, R. of St, Paul's, Exeter, and a Vicar in the Cathedral.

Dated 9 August, 1410. i, 314b.

He commends his soul to God and his body to sacred sepulture. To every parishioner, rich or poor, being a householder [*larem foventi*] he leaves 4d. To those present in the Cathedral on the day of his funeral—to every Canon, 8d.; to every Vicar, 4d.; to every Annuellar, 4d.; to every Secundary, 3d.; to every chorister, 2d.; to every priest, 4d.; and to the sacristans 4d. each.

He bequeaths his super-altar (*superaltare meum cum una tuella benedicta*) to the altar of St. John Baptist in the Church of St. David of Dewstow [*i.e.* Davidstow], in Cornwall. To the Friars Preachers of the City of Exeter, present within their enclosure, 4d. each. To the Friars Minors in like manner, 4d. each. To seven boys, chanting the Psalms, 4d. each. His messuage, with the appurtenance thereof, in the village of St. Paul's, Exeter (which came to him by the gift and feofment of Alice Nymet, but formerly belonged to Henry Norton), situated between the cottages (*cotagia*) once belonging to Leonard Carrew (now the property of John Talbot) in the said village on the east side thereof, and the cottages formerly belonging to Hugh Ferrour, on the west side—in width; and extending lengthwise from the garden of John Talbot on the south side, to the village of St. Paul's aforesaid on the [a word has been omitted here] side—he orders his executors to sell, and dispose of for the good of his soul, and for his parents, benefactors, and friends.

Executors:—Rd. Talbot; Thos. Greystoun, chaplain; and Roger Batyn, citizen of Exeter; to each of whom he leaves 6s. 8d. They are to pay his debts, and if necessary for that purpose, to diminish the above amounts.

Also, he leaves to Rob. Cruwys, R. Phylp, John Fotergay, John Burlegh, Henry Haynok, Peter Schavyshylle, and John Gylle, all chaplains (except Burlegh), 12d. each; and to Thos. Taverner, clerk, born at Fowey [Foway MS.], son of John Taverner, 6s. 8d. (if it can be done). To John Holond, chaplain, 6s. 8d., to pray for his soul, and that he may be to him a prudent and good friend. To John Boeyn, son of Rd. Boeyn, citizen of Exeter, 40d. To Roger, son of Nich. Trelaunay, 20d.

Proved, 24 February, 1410-11, before the Bishop, at Crediton.

Summa bonorum in Inventario, £13 17s. 11d.

XXIX. RICHARD HURST, Clerk, Rector of Exbourne.

Dated at Exbourne, 5 March, 1410-11. i, 315.

He commends his soul to God, the B.V.M., and All Saints, and orders his body to be buried in his Church of Exbourne. To the store of St. Mary therein he bequeaths two oxen and two cows; and to the store of St. Saviour one cow. To Juliana, wife of John Hurst, he bequeaths a cow that he had from her *nomine mortuarii*. To Thos. Langge, an ox and a cow, and half a quarter of wheat. To John Watte, a cow, a steer, and half a quarter of wheat; also a crimson coat. To Rd. Bordevylle, his red cow, and half a quarter of wheat. To John Taylour, a coat *de sturgyn*, and half a quarter of wheat. To John Stacy, Isabella Pollard, Rd. Godefray, John Naynow, John Courteys, Henry Bodde, Katherine de Mille, and Nich. Whyte, he leaves two bushels of wheat apiece. He bequeaths six and a half marks for the salary of a chaplain to celebrate, for a year, for his soul. To Joan, dau. of Nich. Bromforde, his god-daughter (*filiole mee*), 6s. 8d. To every priest attending his exequies and the Mass the day after, 12d. To Henry Peke, chaplain, to pray for his soul, 3s. 4d.

Executors :—Walter Hurst, his brother, with John Boure, R. of North Tawton, as overseer, to whom he leaves 20s., for his trouble.

Proved, 10 March, 1410-11,[1] before the Bishop at Crediton.

Summa bonorum, £28 14s. 9d.

XXX.—Oliver Radysworthy, Rector of Cheldon.

Dated 1 May, 1411. i, 315b.

He commends his soul to God and Blessed Mary, and orders his body to be buried before the door of his parish-church.—He leaves to Robert atte Forde, to celebrate for his soul, 3s. 4d.; also to Wm. Weye, Roger Monelond, and John Bloy, 3s. 4d. each. The residue of his estate, after paying his debts in full, he leaves to John Bloy, "junior" *(predicto.)*

Executor :—The said John Bloy, with Wm. Weye and Roger Monelond as overseers.

Proved, 22 August, 1411, before the Bishop, at Crediton.

Summa bonorum, £7 10s. 10d.

XXXI.—Simon Grendon, citizen of Exeter.

Dated, 30 July, 1411. i, 315b.

He commends his soul to God and All Saints, and directs his body to be buried in the Cathedral under the north tower, before the image of the Blessed Mary. A thousand Masses to be said for his soul, immediately after his death, wherever priests can be found. Fifty poor persons to be clothed by his executors on the day of his burial, twelve to carry torches of ten pounds' weight; the others torches of a pound weight: fifty other poor persons to be clothed in like manner. On the day of his funeral, and for his obit in the Cathedral, they were to give to each Canon present at the Mass 12d.; to each Vicar present 8d.; to each Annuellar 6d.; to each Secondary 4d.; to each chorister 2d.; and he left £20 to be distributed "generaliter." To the Friars Preachers at Exeter, the Friars minors, and the Hospital of St. John Baptist there, the nuns of Polslo, and the nuns of Cornworthy he gives, in each case, 6s. 8d. To every Curate in Exeter 6s. 8d.; but the V. of Heavitree was to have 6s. 8d., and the parish priest of St. Sidwell's 3s. 4d. He leaves £20 for a new conduit, to carry the water *ad Quadruvium*[2] *Civitatis Exoniensis*, and to other parts of the city, at the discretion of the Mayor and his executors, and others whom they may consult; the work to be completed within four years from his death. To the Church of Grendon (Dioc. Lichf.), he leaves a set of vestments of *Baudekyn* and a chalice worth 30s. To the Church of Butterton [Boterdon, MS.]. (in the same Dioc.) a set of vestments *de Baudekyn*, and a chalice of the same value. To the Hosp. of St. Mary Magdalene, Exeter, he leaves 6s. 8d.; to the Priory of St. Nicholas there, 6s. 8d. (to pray for his soul); to Cowick Priory 6s. 8d.; to every priest celebrating at St. Petrock's, Exeter, at his death, 2s.

He also leaves £10, to buy twenty cows[3] for as many poor people; his executors to take care that each person had the full value of 10s. To his nine god-sons, all called "Simon," he leaves 60s. His executors were to sell all his lands, tenements, rents, reversions, &c., in the city of Exeter and in its suburbs, and apply the proceeds to the relief of the poor and for other charitable purposes, for the good of testator's soul. To John Frensch he leaves five marks and a cloak; to Peter Furber 40s. and a cloak; the whole residue of his estate to be dealt with by his executors for the good of his soul.

Executors :—Ricarda, his wife; Wm. Wylford, Peter Sturt, and John Lake;

---

[1] There is a memorandum, at the end of this Will, referring to the Will of Rd. Wykeslond which had been proved before Rd. Hals, the Bishop's Commissary. The Bishop (at Crediton) granted letters of administration 15 Feb. [1410-11], to the executors, Roger Bolter and Walter Robert.

[2] So "Carfax," at Oxford.

[3] *See* page 393, line 16.

and, as overseer, John Westecote, R. of St. Petrock's aforesaid; to each of whom he bequeaths five marks.

Proved, 2 Sept., 1411, before Roger Bolter (Canon of Exeter and Commissary of the Bishop herein), in St. Petrock's Church.

XXXII. William Tray, Vicar in the Collegiate and Parochial Church of the Holy Cross, Crediton, and Dean of Crediton.

Dated 20 January, 1411-12. i. 316b.

He commends his soul to God, and directs his body to be buried in the Church of Crediton. To Wm. Smyth, Vicar therein, he leaves his habit, to wit his surplice, hood, and cope. To Wm., his chaplain, a black silk girdle, with silver clasp; and a dagger (*basilardum*), with two knives (*cultellis*), silver mounted; also a bed-cover with crimson tapestry and four sheets; 2 brazen pots, 1 saucepan (*unum chafcur*); 1 dish, and 1 little pot [*possenet*]. To John, his servant, a brass pot in a fragile state; also a double coat of crimson colour; and a cloak of green colour, the one in poorish condition (*armilausam debiliorem*). To the Vicars of Crediton he leaves 40d. To John Pytte, senior, a bed, of crimson colour. If his executors desired to buy any portion of his remaining goods, they were to have the preference at a fair price; the residue to be applied for his soul's weal.

Executors:—Wm. Stokker, his chaplain, and John Pytte, senior.

Proved 16 February, 1411-12, before the Bishop, at Crediton.

Summa bonorum, £16 2s. 9d.

XXXIII. Roger de Watelyngton i, 317.

Dated in the house of Richard Boson, citizen of Exeter, 23 March, 1411-12.

He commends his soul to Almighty God, Who redeemed it with His Precious Blood, and his body to sacred sepulture; and leaves to two priests[1] to say Mass for his soul, for a year, £10. To the R. of St. John "de Arcubus" (*curato meo*), he leaves 20d. To the Friars Minors and Friars Preachers of Exeter, to pray for his soul, 40d. to each. To the Prior, &c., of St. John Baptist at Exeter, 6s. 8d. For the fabrick of the Church of the Holy Cross, Crediton, 40s. To the Church of St. Thomas-the-Martyr, Cowick, 40d. To the Church of St. John "de Arcubus," Exeter, 20s.

Executors:—Joan, his wife, and John, his son, to whom he leaves the residue; Rd. Boson to be overseer, with a legacy of 13s. 4d. for his trouble.

Proved 7 May, 1412, before the Bishop, at Crediton.

Summa bonorum, £84 0s. 10d.

XXXIV. John Combe, Rector of North Huish.

Dated at Slapton, 9 November, 1411. i, 317b.

He commends his soul to God; his body to be buried in the parish-Church of St. James, Slapton, before the image of the B. V. M., *que vocatur* Pyte.[2]

He bequeaths to Thos. Taylour, clerk of the Chantry of the B. V. M., within the Manor of Slapton, 100s., to be paid by his executor to the said Thos, if he proceeded to the Order of Priesthood, and submitted himself meanwhile to the said executor; otherwise the legacy was to lapse. The residue of his estate he bequeaths to the Chantry of Slapton.

Executor:—John Bowryng, Rector of the said Chantry.

Proved 17 August, 1412, before the Bishop, at Clyst.

Summa bonorum, £356 16s. 4d.

XXXV. John Prestecote [Testamentum Johannis Prestecote *nuper defuncti.*—Margin].

Dated, 25 January, 1411-12. i, 317b.

---

[1] He thus describes, with singular minuteness, the *sort* of priests he wanted—"presbiteris habilibus et honestis, ac bone conversacionis et honeste vite, necnon bone fame."

[2] Nicholas Morton, R. of this Collegiate Chantry, in his Will, dated 26 August, 1534, leaves 3s. 4d. "unto our Lady of *Pitie*."

He commends his soul to God, and his body to be buried in the Chapel of the Blessed Mary at Culmstock[1]; to which Chapel he bequeaths a set of vestments *de plonket*[2] and an old Missal, there to remain for ever; that they might pray for his soul, the souls of Wm. Prestecote, his father, and Joan, his mother, and for all the faithful dead. To the Church of Culmstock, he leaves his best set of vestments of red silk, and his large tablet of alabaster (*alabaustre*, MS.) to stand over the altar of the B.V.M. there, that they may pray for his soul, and for the souls of his wives, Joan and Margery, and all to whom he is bound. Also, to Culmstock Ch. he leaves two images of angels, with their brackets, to stand in the Chancel near the High Altar; also, his new Missal, to remain at Prestecote, for use in the Chapel, as long as his wife Margery resided there; after her death, or her departure therefrom, to be taken to Culmstock Church, to which he, moreover, bequeaths his Gradual, his Ordinal, and a book called a Manual; also a book called "Synod." To the Churchwardens of Culmstock he leaves 13s. 4d., for the soul of Thos. Rawlyn (late V. of Sidbury), towards the cost of the bells to be provided there; also 20s., to provide an oil lamp, to hang in the Chancel and be lighted every Sunday, and on all Double Feasts for ever, at Mattins and at High Mass (for his soul and his parents'); also his new gilt cross, to be carried to the church on the day of his burial, before his body, and then placed on the High Altar, there to remain on all Double (but not on other) Feasts. To the keepers of the store of the said Church he leaves two oxen, two cows, and twenty sheep "utriusque sexus," with 13s. 4d., to maintain his anniversary and those of Joan and Margery, his wives, and of Wm. Prestecote and Joan his wife, on one day, yearly, for ever, and to pay one penny yearly, for the said souls, aforesaid, at the Mass of St. John (*ad Collectum Sancti Johannis.*) He, further leaves £23 6s. 8d. for a chaplain, to say Mass, for five years after his death, in the Chap. of the Blessed Mary at Culmstock, for his own soul, and for Joan, his late wife; for John de Chivereston, knight, John Spycer (of Exeter), Wm. Sleghe (of Kenton), John Boys (of Halberton), and all the faithful dead; the said chaplain to receive seven marks yearly for his services. To the Churchwardens of Northalynton [*hodie* East Allington] he leaves an ox, six sheep, and also 6s. 8d., to keep the anniversary of John Boys atte Wode, there, for ever. To the Churchwardens of [West] Alvyngton an ox, a cow, and 13s. 4d., to maintain his anniversary and that of Joan his late wife. To the V. of Culmstock, for tithes forgotten, 13s. 4d. To the Canons, Vicars, and other Ministers of the Cathedral, 20s. for *Placebo* and *Dirige*, on the day of his funeral, before the Mass of Requiem. And in like manner, to the Canons, etc., at Ottery, 20s. To the Prior of Taunton, 6s. 8d., and to every Canon there 2s. To the Abbot of Torre, 6s. 8d., and to every Canon there, 12d. To the Abbot of Dunkeswell [Dounekeswyl, MS.], 10s., and to every monk there, 12d.; to the Abbot of Newenham, 6s. 8d., and to every monk there, 12d.; the same to the Prior and monks of St. Nicholas', Exeter; to the Prior, etc., of the Hosp. of St. John, Exeter, 13s. 4d.; to the Prioress of Polslo, his best silver cup—with cover, called "*Franceys*," to remain in that House for ever, and be called "*Prestecote*," in his memory; also, 10s., and to each nun, 2s.; for his soul and for his two wives: to the Abbess of Canonsleigh, 6s. 8d., and to each nun, 12d.; and the like sum to the Prioress and Nuns of Cornworthy. To each of the chaplains at Polslo, Canonsleigh, and Cornworthy, at the time of his death, 8d. To the Friars Minors of Exeter, 40s., and to the Friars Preachers there, 13s. 4d. For the repair of the Bridge at Totnes, he leaves 3s. 4d.; for the maintenance of the Bridge at Teignbridge [Tyngbrygg, MS.] 3s. 4d.; and for the repair of the Bridge at Culmstock, 20s. To the V. of Culmstock, for two trentals of masses for his soul, immediately after his death, 5s.; and to the Vicars of Burlescombe and Halberton, Walter Stalworthy, chaplain, and John Pruet, for the like service, the same sum to each. To the Lazar-houses at Exeter, Totnes, Plympton, and Honiton, 3s. 4d. each. To his wife Margery he leaves the remainder of his term in a certain tenement (which he bought of the Earl of Devon), in the town of Kingsbridge; the same to be sold if

---

[1] Colmpstoke throughout, MS.

[2] plunket—a coarse woollen cloth.

she died before the term expired, and the proceeds devoted to pious uses for their souls. To his dau. Joan, he leaves two oxen, two cows, and forty sheep of both sexes; also, a bed suitable to her rank, with tapestry; also his third best brass pot, a dish, a ewer and wash-basin, his best cloak of scarlet cloth with fur, and 40s. To John Tyrry, his valet (*garcioni meo*), one robe *de liberatis meis*, a brass pot, and 10s. To Walter Northecote all his books on the Law of Land, all his steel armour (except his sword), and his second best colt (*unum pullum secundum meliorem*). To his tenants at Presteoote 12d. each. To John Almyaheghys, his servant, 13s. 4d. and a cow. To all others in his service at the time of his death, 40d. each. To Wm. Almyscumb, his best silver girdle, and to Joan his wife, a crimson dress with fur: also to the said Joan and to John their son (testator's godson) he bequeaths his ewer and wash-basin from his house at Exeter. To Rd. Parker 5s. to celebrate for his soul. To Clarice, his servant, for her long service, 20s. and a bed suitable to her condition. The old Missal in his Chapel at Prestecote, and the old vestments, with all the furniture of the Altar, and his chalice in use there, to remain there for the life of Margery, his wife, and then to be given to the Ch. of Culmstock, for use in the Chapel of the Blessed Virgin; the afore-mentioned vestments, etc., to remain for Wm. Almiscumb and his heirs, in the Chapel at Prestecote. He leaves to his executors his interest in the Manors of Rake and Elston[1], the proceeds to be applied to the payment of his debts and legacies: to each executor accepting administration he leaves 40s.; also, he bequeaths to them, to be sold, one press at Rake, for making cider (*unum torculare apud Rake pro cisare faciendo*). To Mabel, wife of John Schaple, he leaves a gold ring, with "Hoc Nomine IHC." engraved thereon. Three hundred Masses to be said for his soul, immediately after his death, and before his burial. After his death a woollen pall of black cloth, with a Cross of white linen in the midst, was to be placed upon his body; and two round wax lights, and no more, to be set, one at his head and the other at his feet, each to contain eight pounds of wax; also six wax torches, each of the same weight, were to be provided; his executors, and the men carrying the said torches, to be clad in black cloth. After his burial, two of the said torches to be deposited in the Ch. of Culmstock at the High Altar, a third in the Chapel of the B.V.M. there, to be burnt at the Elevation of the Sacrament: the fourth to be placed in the Chap. of Prestecote, for the same purpose, as also the fifth, which was to be given to Burlescombe Ch., and the sixth, to the Chapel at Culm Davy.[2] Every chaplain present at his funeral to have 6d.; every poor person, 1d., and any that were blind, 2d. His gifts to his servants to be distributed at the time of his death. All his goods and chattels, after payment of his debts and legacies, to be sold and applied to pious uses, for his soul, and for the souls of his wives, etc.

Executors:—Margery, his wife; Thos. Reymond; Wm. Jew, of Canonsleigh; John Pruet, chaplain; Wm. Almyscumb, and John Cole of North Pool [Northpole, MS.]

On 29 October, 1412, testator added a *Codicil* to his Will, bequeathing to the Church of Culmstock a further sum of 60s. towards the bell (*in subsidium collecte campane ibidem*), also to John Vayron, John Knygth, John Broke, and John Burneman, 20s. each; and to Wm. Almyscumb, his clock (*orilogium meum, alias dictum clokke*). Ten marks were to be paid to Thos. Ferrers, Precentor of Ottery, to put Wm. Walrande, his cousin, (son of Wm. Walrande, junior), to school, for four years after testator's death. To Wm. Almyscumb, and Joan his wife, he grants a moiety of the rent and service of Rob. Fourbour and of Agnes his wife, and the reversion of a moiety of a new tenement, with appurtenances, in the town of Wellington, a garden, and a parcel of land adjacent, which the said Robert and Agnes hold for life, by testator's concession, and that of John Brycon, senior; also, a moiety of the rent and service of Thos. Wydesworthy and Agnes his wife, and the reversion of a moiety of a certain tenement, a garden, a dovecot, and a parcel of ground in the same town, which they held for life by grant from the same persons.

---

[1] Alwyston, MS,—"Aileston" in *Pole's Devon*: in the parish of Churchstow.

[2] Comb Davy, MS. This chapelry is in the parish of Hemyock.

Proved 23 November, 1412, before the Bishop at Clyst. The testator is here referred to as "dicti defuncti robas, dum vixit, ipsius Domini gerentis."

Summa bonorum :—£295 0s. 1d. ob. q.

XXXVI. William Wilford, citizen of Exeter.

Dated, 30 June, 1413. i, 319b.

He commends his soul to God and All Saints, and his body to holy sepulture in the Cathedral, or in the cemetery thereof, as his executors shall determine; they are, also at their discretion, to make distribution to the poor at his funeral. Two wax lights, each weighing six pounds, to be set, the one at the head, the other at the foot of his body; and twelve torches, each weighing ten pounds, of which one is to be offered at every altar in his parish church of St. Petrock; one for the Church of Morchard, one for Rackenford, one for E. Anstey, one for Puddington [Poutyngton, MS.], and the other four as the executors might please.

He bequeaths to the Friars Preachers at Exeter and to the Friars Minors there, 13s. 4d. to each; to the Hospital of St. John Baptist there, 20s.; to the Prioress and Convent of Polslo 20s.; and to all of these four flagons of wine apiece. To the Priory of Cowick, 13s. 4d. and four flagons of wine. To the lepers of St. Mary Magd., Exeter, 6s. 8d. To Thomas Tunerton [perhaps "Tuverton"] enough cloth to make a cope. To every priest celebrating, at the time of his death, in St. Petrock's Church, 20d. To John Westecote, Rector there, 4 marks, for tithes forgotten. The bed-ridden poor to be remembered.

He leaves £10, to make a conduit in the City of Exeter, assigning his croft without the South Gate for the erection and maintenance thereof. To his dau. Elizabeth, wife of John Parkere, he leaves the reversion of a tenement in the north suburb of Exeter, which once belonged to Rob. le Noble, and passed to testator's wife, Margaret, for her life; if the said Elizabeth died without heirs of her body, the tenement to be sold, and the money applied to pious uses. To Wm. Thorne, his servant, he leaves one of his shops in the parish of St. Pancras, for life; to go on his death to testator's son Robert, and his heirs; if Robert died without issue, the shop was to be sold and the proceeds applied to pious uses. His house, near St. Petrock's Ch., of which Edw. Lydeford was tenant, he directs to be sold: part of the proceeds (viz., 20s. yearly, for fifty-eight years), to be divided between the Rector, priests, and other ministers, serving God in that Church, to sing an antiphon of St. Mary therein, before her image in the new aisle. But if the said Edward, or any other person, were willing, by concession of the executors, and paying a rent of 25s. a year, to rebuild the said house, he might keep it for the term aforesaid, and testator would grant and bequeath to him all his timber at Southernhay (*totum meremium meum quod est apud Southynghay*), towards the said rebuilding; the reversion of the said house to be sold at the end of the said term, and the proceeds devoted to keeping up the singing of the said Antiphon, daily, year after year. But if the said Edward would neither accept the said term, nor rebuild the house, the proceeds of the eventual sale of the fee simple thereof were to be applied to keeping up the said Antiphon for ever.

All his interest in the messuages, lands, etc., in the parish of St. Sidwell, which testator had recently acquired by grant from Thos. Monk, he leaves to remunerate his servants and attendants. And all those messuages, etc., in the City of Exeter and its suburbs, which had come to him by purchase or bequest, in fee simple, he leaves to his executors in trust for his son Robert, a minor, together with the lands, &c., in Exeter and its suburbs bequeathed to testator by Rob. Wilford, his father; all rents, etc., to be kept in a chest with four keys, one for each executor, and applied to the maintenance of his said son till he should come of age; any residue meanwhile accruing to be applied annually to the support of two Chaplains, to say Mass for testator's soul, year by year, in St. Petrock's Ch., and for the relief of the poor; reserving, however, for the said Robert, on his attaining his majority, a hundred marks for his immediate needs. Then he was to come into absolute possession of the said lands: but if he should first die, leaving no heir of his body, the property was to be sold, and the proceeds applied to pious uses. To Wm. Hull, and to John Parkere (husband of testator's daughter, Elizabeth) he bequeaths all that his part or share in the ship, or barge, called '*le*

Marie de Exemoth," which Rd. Crese and testator held in common. To Rd. Reymond he leaves 100s. To John Wilford a jewel worth four marks, to be selected by the executors. All his domestick servants to be remunerated (*remunerentur et habeant rewardum*). To Margaret, his wife, and Robert, his son, (when the latter should come of age), he leaves, in equal shares, all his household utensils belonging to the chamber, hall, pantry, kitchen, and buttery, for daily use: the silver cups, salt cellars, spoons, and other silver plate, to be divided in equal portions, according to custom, "*inter me, et uxorem meam et dictum Robertum filium meum—prout moris est.*" The residue to be applied for his soul's health.

Executors:—Margaret, his wife; Thos. Reymond; Henry Hull, testator's brother, and Peter Sturt; with John Westecote for overseer; to each of whom he bequeaths 5 marks for his trouble.

Proved, 2 October, in the Church of St. Petrock, Exeter, before Roger Bolter, Canon of Exeter, the Bishop's Commissary therein; and certified accordingly, 3 October, 1413, by the Bishop at Clyst.

Summa bonorum:—£228 6s. 9d.

XXXVII.—William Ekerdon, Canon of Exeter and R. of Longbredy [Langebridie, MS.] (Dioc. of Salisbury).

Dated at Colyton, 8 November, 1413. i, 320b.

He commends his soul to God and his body to sacred sepulture, next to Dodyngton (*juxta Dodyngton*) in the south tower of the Cathedral.

To the fabrick of the Church of Salisbury he leaves 6s. 8d.; to St. Peter's at Exeter 40s.; for the nave of the Church of Maiden-Newton 6s. 8d., and for the light there before the image of St. John Baptist, 20s. To the Friars of Dorchester 13s. 4d.; to those of Ilchester 10s.; to the Friars Preachers of Exeter, 10s.; to the Friars Minors there, 10s. To find four chaplains to celebrate for him, the year after his death; two in the Church of Longbredy [Langebrydy, MS.], and two in Exeter Cathedral: he bequeaths £22, for their stipends, and for wax, wine, and other necessaries. To Edmund Elyot, clerk, he leaves 40s.; to Wm. Whytyng, a monk enclosed at Sherborne, 6s. 8d.; to John Prauncard 6s. 8d.; to Wm. Dyber 40s.; to the abbot and monks of Abbotsbury and of Cerne, 20s. in each case. For the poor on the day of his burial he bequeaths such sum as his executors may think fit to spend; and they were also to provide for a thousand Masses, to be said immediately after his death. To John Brode he leaves 100s., part of the money that he owed testator. To Walter Hanecok, his young page (*pagetto meo*), he leaves five marks; to Wm. Flay 5 marks; to John Ekerdon 100s.; to Wm. Felde 100s.; to John Horsman 13s. 4d.; to Wm. Holme 6s. 8d.; to Reginald, his chorister, 6s. 8d.; to Thos. Bolworth, his late chorister, 13s. 4d.; to John Trunket 10s. For his obit, in the choir of his Cathedral, for a month from the date of his death, £4 12s. 2d. He leaves his doublet, *de corrodio Exoniensis Episcopi*, together with the fur, to Hugh, his Vicar. To Matilda, mother of Walter, his page, he leaves 6s. 8d. and a single skirt; to Edm. James 6s. 8d.; to Rob. Veel a silver cup, flat, with cover, (*ciphum argenteum flat cum cooperculo*—*See* p. 390, *note*); to Robert Grey a silver cup, perforated (*pounsett*), the cover marked with St. Andrew's cross. To the Church of Longbredy he leaves a book called "*Willelmus de Montibus*;" also, a Gradual, an Antiphonar, an Ordinal, a Missal, a chalice gilt, an apparel of silk for the altar (*unum apparatum de cerico pro altari*), and a set of vestments; for keeping his obit, yearly, and to pray for his soul, every Sunday in the pulpit: also, a Breviary [bound in] red (*portiforium rubium*) to be lent to a certain poor priest, and so handed from priest to priest as long as it should last; and in like manner a Breviary bound in silk. He leaves to John Hull the Breviary already in his possession.—To John Byncombe 13s. 4d.—For four poor clerks to be sent to the schools at Oxford, for two years, fifty marks in equal shares. He orders the sum of £20 to be deposited in a chest in the [Cathedral] Treasury, for his obit for twenty years, to be bestowed on those present, at the rate of 20s. a year.—He leaves to John Hull, his executor, five marks for his trouble, and the same sum to John Brode, Rob. Dunnyng, and Gilbert Spencer.—To John Gilbert, to say for his soul thirty masses of St. Gregory (*trentale Sancti Gregorii*), ten marks.—To Henry Keyche, chaplain, 40s.—To Edwold Packe 20s., and to Joan his wife a skirt, furred (*penulatam*). The residue of his estate to be disposed of by his executors, for the good of his soul.

Executors :—John Hull, V. of Colyton; Rob. Dunnyng, of Exeter; Gilbert Spencer, chaplain; and John Brode, his valet [*meum valectum*].

Proved 4 December, 1413, before the Bishop, at Clyst, in the presence of Wm. Langton and Rd. Palmer, Canons of Exeter, and Michael Lercedekne, R. of Thorney.

Summa bonorum :—£372 17s. 1d., ob. q.

XXXVIII.—Richard Estebrok, Vicar of Okehampton.

Dated, 5 December, 1413. i, 321.

He commends his soul to God, and his body to ecclesiastical sepulture.—To Walter Manston, to celebrate in Okehampton church for three years for the health of his soul, and for his exequies daily, he bequeaths thirteen pounds of silver; and to the principal store of the said church 20s., that his anniversary may be kept for ever. On the day of his burial the sum of 40s. was to be given to the poor. To Walter Manston, chaplain he leaves 20s. and his second best doublet.—To Thos. Estebrok, his best girdle with silver clasp, a silver cup and cover, and his best doublet.—To Joan Hore his second best girdle[1] with silver clasp.—To Edith, wife of Rob. Wyke, his two other girdles, with silver clasps, and a quarter of wheat.—To Rob. Wyke the two cows already in his keeping.—To every priest taking part in his exequies, and present and celebrating for his soul on the day of his funeral, 12d., and to each priest only celebrating on the day of his burial 6d.—To Joan, dau. of Wm. Hore, to Matilda (another dau.), to John, son of Rob. Wyke, and to Walter Petheler, he leaves a cow each.—To Adam Toker a cow and half a quarter of wheat.—To John Row, his servant, a heifer.—To John Gavet, his servant, 6s. 8d. To John Weryng, chaplain, his third-best doublet and 6s. 8d.—To Thos. Estebrok, Joan Hore, and Edith, wife of Rob. Wyke, three brass pots and a saucepan,[2] viz., to Thomas his best pot, to Joan his second best, and to Edith his third-best and a saucepan[2]—if the residue sufficed to pay his debts and legacies; if not, the articles were to be sold.—To each executor who should act, he leaves 20s.

Executors :—Thos. Estebrok, and Walter Manston; and he orders them to distribute 40 measures[3] of wheat among his poor parishioners.

Proved, 11 January, 1413-14, before Wm. Hunden, Canon of Exeter and Commissary of the Bishop, in the Chapel of St. Gabriel at Clyst.

XXXIX.—William Poundestoke, R. of Bigbury and Canon of Exeter.

Dated at Exeter, 9 May, 1414. i, 321[b].

He commends his soul to his Creator and his body to holy sepulture.

He leaves to the store of the church of St. Laurence of Bigbury, 40s.; also, the better of his two Breviaries there, for use on the north side of the choir for ever, never to be otherwise used or alienated; also, a large dossal embroidered with the birds called *popardys*, to spread before the High Altar[4] on Feast-day.—To the store of the chapel of St. Michael-de-la-Burgh,[5] he leaves 20s.; and to the store of the Chapel of St. Milburga,[6] 13s. 4d. For distribution among

---

[1] "Sonam," *i.q.*, "zona"; the word is so spelt throughout this Will.

[2] Schafer.—*See* "Chafer" and "Chaufere" in Halliwell's Dictionary.

[3] Modius—"mensura constans 16 sextariis."

[4] Dorsorium largum, operatum volucribus vocatis *popardys*, ad sternendum coram Summo Altari. There is a difficulty about "popardys." "Popinjay" is a parrot; "popeler"—I quote Halliwell—"a kind of bird explained by *populus* in the Prompt. Parv."; and he elsewhere gives "popler"—evidently the same word—as "a sea-gull." Nominale MS.

[5] On an island now called "Burgh-Island."

[6] Known, locally, as "Millbourne," and quite recently destroyed.

his poor parishioners, as soon as possible after his death, he leaves 40s., for the good of his soul, &c.—To the Cathedral he leaves 40s., to defend the rights of the said cathedral church; also, for its fabrick, 40s.; also, a *Legenda de Temporali*, and another *de Sanctis*.—To John Holecombe, chaplain (or to some other fit priest, if the said John be unable, or unwilling, to undertake the duty), he leaves £4 13s. 4d., yearly, for four years, to say Mass for his soul, and for his parents, and next-of-kin;—also, for Sir Wm. de Bykebury, his progenitors and descendants, —in the Church of Bigbury and in the chapel de-la-Burghe afore-mentioned: and twice a week, at least, in the said chapel.—Also 20s., to be divided among the priests who should say *Placebo* and *Dirige* and Masses, at the time of his decease, or as quickly as possible afterwards; and 10s. among Christ's poor, on the same day, that they might pray for him. He directs that the dignity and customs of the Cathedral of Exeter, as to exequies, singing the Psalter, and the whole manner of sepulture, be observed.—He leaves £20 in money (which will be due to his estate after his death, on account of residence), to keep his anniversary in the Cathedral as long as the money lasts; directing that every year, on the day of his obit, 13s. 4d., part thereof, be distributed among the Canons, Vicars, and other Ministers of the Cathedral, according to their degree and the custom of the church; also to the two clerks of the Treasury he leaves 13s. 4d.—To the parish-church of Poundstock he leaves his new Missal, and, if the parishioners are willing, 20s., to maintain his anniversary, and that of his parents, &c., for ever; if not, the Missal to be sold, and (with the 20s.) applied to pious uses.—To the Priory of St. John, in Exeter, he leaves 13s. 4d.—To the Friars Preachers there, 6s. 8d.; and weekly, "post tricennalem diem quatuor panes canonicales de residencia mea post mortem meam debendos." He leaves the like bequest to the Friars Minors of Exeter.

Executors:—Roger Bolter, Can. of Exeter; Thos. de Plymmeswode, V. in the Ch. of Bampton (Dioc. of Lichfield); Rob. Lyngham, R. of St. Mary-Major, Exeter, and John Wythyslond, V. of Heavitree; to each of whom he leaves 40s. and a silver cup with cover. Any residue, after payment of his debts and funeral expenses to be applied to pious uses, and works of charity, especially among the poor tenants of the Dean and Chapter of Exeter, and his own parishioners of Bigbury—for the souls of himself, Sir Wm. Bykebury, knt., his parents, &c.: but subject to the fulfilment of further instructions in a Codicil (which is not given in the Register).

Proved 8 February, 1413-14, by all the executors except Thos. de Plymmeswode; who appeared before the Bishop, separately, at Clyst, 17 February, together with John Bykebury, his surety in the sum of 100s.; the said Thomas belonging to "an alien Diocese."

XL. William Langeton, Canon of Exeter.

Dated at the Bishop's Manor of Clyst, 29 January, 1413-14. i, 322.

He commends his soul to God, His Almighty Creator; and desires to be buried in the Cathedral, either on the right, or to the left of the tomb of Bishop Stafford [erected by the Bishop in his lifetime.]

He leaves to the Cathedral his *Corpus Juris Civilis*, in five books, given him by Thos. Stafford, to be placed in the Library, and secured by a chain; there to remain for ever. To the Church of Wells [Wellys, MS.], near Walsingham (Dioc. of Norwich), he leaves a Missal, an Ordinal, and a copy of the *Pupilla Oculi*; also, a set of vestments, for priest, deacon, and subdeacon, with a cope to match—all to be bought by his executors at a cost of £10. To the Church of Rokeby (Dioc. of Coventry and Lichfield), he leaves a set of vestments for the priest only, to cost 40s.; and the like to the Churches of Warbleton [Warbylton, MS.], Bosham, and Wisborough [Wysbergh, MS.], all in the Dioc. of Chichester; and, also, to the Church of Ottery, if his executors are not asked to provide the cope required by the statutes on account of his Prebend therein. For the fabrick of the nave of the Collegiate Church of Crediton—"jam fere ad terram prostrate"—he leaves all rents, profits, &c., coming to him at the time of his death, on account of his Prebend of Prustecomb therein, over and above anything due to the said College, according to the statutes, on account of his said Prebend. To the Church of South Pool he leaves a set of vestments for the priest and a cope, to cost 66s. 8d. To the poor at Wells, 66s. 8d.; to those at Wisborough, 20s.; at Westbrook (his Prebend), 20s.; at Apuldram (formerly his Prebend), 20s.; at Warbleton, 20s.; at South Pool, 20s. To Wm. Pole he bequeaths a silver cup with its cover, having three feet fashioned after the similitude of lions. To John Wylle, chaplain, to pray for his soul and for all the faithful departed, 20s.; also a doublet with hood. To the chaplains, clerks, and boys of the Bishop's Chapel at Exeter, 100s. To the other members of the Bishop's household, 100s. To John Arderne a silver cup and cover, with testator's arms engraved on the top of the cover. To Margaret, wife of John Arderne, a scarlet robe, with its fur.

The residue he leaves to his executors, directing them, first, to send Wm. Portour, his godson [*filiolo meo*], to school for two or three years, and to apply the remainder to pious uses, for his soul.

Executors:—John Schute, V. of Paignton; and John Arderne, Esquire.

Proved, 17 February, 1413-14, before the Bishop, at Clyst.

Summa bonorum:—£211 11s. 6d. ob. q.

XLI. Joan, widow of—*que fui uxor*—Robert Dyrwyn.

Dated at Foleforde,[1] in the parish of Crediton, 2 September, 1391. i, 323.

She commends her soul to God, and requests to be buried in Crediton Church in the place "ubi Magister meus jacet."

To the Precentor, Canons, and other Ministers of the said church she leaves 13s. 4d. for *Placebo* and *Dirige*, Commendation, and Mass, on the day of her burial. To the Dean of Crediton, 10s., viz. 5s. of the goods of her "Master," and 5s. of her own goods; to pray for their souls. To each Vicar, 8d.; to each Annuellar 6d. To her sister Margery she bequeaths goods worth 40s.; to her son William her best silver cup, her best goblet (*maser*), and half her vessels of brass, pewter, and wood, the cups excepted. To Agnes, wife of Wm. Prous, she leaves her horse, viz. *Amelere*,[2] or his value in money. To each of John More's boys, living at the time of her death, 20d. To each *Aquebajulus* in the Church of Crediton 2d. To all her servants at the time of her death, 2s. to be distributed among them. To Agnes Rooch, 20d. To John Rooch and Agnes his wife, 20d. To Walter, Robert, and Joan Rooch, 12d. each. To Nicholas Aleyn, 12d. The residue of her estate she leaves to such poor persons as are most in need of help, and for priests willing to say Mass for her "Master" and herself.

Executors:—William, her son; Wm. Prous; and her sister Margery; to each of whom she leaves 5s.

Proved, 5 April (and 18 June), 1415, before the Bishop at Clyst.

Summa bonorum—£60 and 20d.

XLII. Ralph Tregrisiow, Dean of Exeter.[3] i, 323.

He commends his soul to God and to Blessed Mary His Mother; his body to be buried in the Cathedral, should he happen to go the way of all flesh in the County of Devon [*si in Comitatu Devonie humanitus mihi contingat*;] but should he die in Cornwall, then either in the Church of St. Crida the Virgin [i.e. Creed], or in that of St. Kyby, Duloe. If he happened to die in any other County, his executors were to bury him in the Church of the parish where death met him, unless they had just cause for not doing so—a matter which he leaves to them.

To the fabrick of the Cathedral he bequeaths 100s.; to that of Crediton Church 100s.; to that of Creed—"ubi fui oriendus"—40s., to buy a store [*instaurum*] for the said Church; the parishioners to undertake that prayers should be said for his soul, &c. every Sunday, for ever. He, also, leaves to Creed a silver cup (*cupam*) and cover, with the arms of the See (*cum armis Petri et Pauli*) engraved thereon.—To the

---

[1] Voleforde, MS.—Now Shobrooke Park.

[2] I suppose, the horse's name: "*Ambler*"?

[3] considerans quod in hunc mundum veni, et de hoc mundo exiam; advertens etiam quod nil cercius morte et nil incercius hora mortis, de terrenis bonis meis volens disponere, condo testamentum meum."

fabrick of Duloe Church he leaves 100s., to buy a store for the use of the said Church, on the like conditions as to prayers for his soul. To the Vicars of the Cathedral he leaves 20s. to pray for his soul and for that of Steph. Penpel. He leaves £40 for the poor on the day of his burial, and orders that his funeral expenses shall, on no account, exceed £10. He desires to be buried within three days of his death, or on the morning of the fourth day, at latest; and, after his burial, his executors were to distribute alms, as their conscience should dictate, for his soul and that of his uncle, Step. Penpel. To Rd. Drayton he leaves ten marks, and the like sum to Benedict Caunterbery. His "*Corpus Juris Civilis et Juris Canonici cum eorum Doctoribus*," he leaves to clerks and scholars—"de cognacione mea, vel de cognacione predicti Magistri Stephani"—but on condition that none of them should alienate, sell, or pledge the same, but that they should always so remain: and if no such clerks could be found, then the books to were be lent to fit scholars or clerks in the county of Cornwall, for a time. To Ralph Reskemner he bequeaths his best ewer and silver basin; his best silver drinking-cup (*potellum*), and six of his best silver spoons; his best bed, with canopy and curtains of red materials; his best set of vestments; and six more of his best silver spoons; making a dozen in all. To Benedict Canterbery he leaves a silver cup, and cover with his arms. To Isabella, relict of James Gerwes a silver cup and his best robe with fur of vair (*cum foruris de variis*). To Joan de Hellond a silver cup. To Joan, wife of John Hylle, his second-best robe, also with fur of vair, and a silver cup.—To the Ch. of St. James, Tregony [de Tregonia] his large Missal; formerly the property of his said uncle, the Dean of Wells. To Ida, wife of Belion,[1] he leaves his third best robe, with fur of vair, and a silver cup. To Thos. Gvynov his small Breviary, the gift of his uncle, the Dean of Wells. To Dame Alice Reskimer ("*sorori de Bokelond*"), his cousin, 20s. To the convent of Polslo, 20s. To the Canons of the Cathedral attending his funeral, 6s. 8d. each; to every Vicar so attending 40d.; to every Annuellar 20d.; and to every Secondary 12d. To each of his executors, consenting to serve, 100s. To John Canon, baker, 20s. The residue of his estate to be devoted to pious uses for the soul of testator, the above-named Stephen, and his parents and heirs, his benefactors, and all others who in any way had benefited him.

Executors:—John Mulys and James Halap; and they were charged to treat and agree with the Prior and Conv. of Merton for the Rectory of the Church of Tregony, in Cornwall, and all other their possessions near Tregony, for a certain sum of money, with a view, to buying certain possessions near Merton, in exchange for those of the said Prior and Convent near Tregony. Also, his executors were to keep his anniversary in the Cathedral for 40 years, and to pay 6d. to each Canon present at *Placebo*, *Dirige*, the Commendations and the Mass; 3d. to each Vicar; 2d. to each Annuellar; to each Secondary 1d.

Dated in testator's house in Exeter, 16 June, 1411.

Proved 26 July, 1415, before the Bishop, at Clyst.

XLIII. Walter Robert, Rector of the Principal (*i.e.* Pitt) Portion in the Church of Tiverton.

Dated, 12 July, 1414. i, 324.

He commends his soul to God and his body to holy sepulture.

To the Church of Northill he leaves the Breviary which he received from his "Master," William Colmpton, for the use of the R. of Northill alone, the parishioners to have no right to the same. Poor parishioners there, who owed him very small sums on account of tithes, were to be relieved from payment thereof, in part or altogether, at the discretion of his executors. To the Prior and Convent of Launceston he bequeaths 20s., to pray for him and for his benefactors. For the fabrick (or repair) of the church of Tiverton 20s. To his mother he leaves 3d. a week, so long as she survives him, *pro potu recenti sibi providendo*. To his sister Joan his best robe, with hood and fur; also 6 of his small silver spoons,

[1] "Item Ide uxori belion."

and a silver cup[1] which she had in her possession; also a table-cloth and a towel of second best quality, and one pair of sheets; also the silver girdle which she had in keeping. To a young[2] and respectable chaplain he leaves 8 marks, to celebrate in Tiverton Church (and not elsewhere) for testator's soul, and for the souls of Rd. Wykeslond, Wm. Halyet, late R. of Roseash,[3] and John Stykerygge, and for the good estate of Wm. Colmpton, his "Master," or (if deceased) for his soul. To John Robert and his wife he leaves half a mark, and remits all the debt that they owed him; also he leaves them one pair of sheets. To Thomas Frist, of Morchard Cruwys, he bequeaths 13s. 4d. and forgives him a debt.

And whereas, a little time ago, testator brought an action at law against Stephen Tournere, and recovered from him 10 marks, and perhaps went beyond the bounds of moderation and made haste to revenge himself in the said action; and because the said Stephen is a poor man,—"although he brought a false charge against me,—and that he did so God knoweth,—nevertheless, as in the fear of God, I leave him 20s.; but, then, he must give up the rancour he nourishes towards me in his heart, and keep a decent tongue in his head for the future, a thing which he has never been accustomed to do, or, at any rate, rarely."

To Joan, his brother's daughter, he leaves a single robe with hood, at the discretion of the executors; and he gives her 40d., and remits the sum she owed him. To Richard, his brother's son, he leaves 6 marks, to keep him at school, the money to be advanced to him, as he requires it, by Walter Colle. To Walter Haydurer, chaplain, to pray for his soul, he leaves 10s. Also to John Fax half a mark; to Rd. Weryng, 20s.; and to "Little[4] Walter," his servant, 40d. To his successor in his Portion at Tiverton he bequeaths a large-sized brass pot, and one of his best dishes; also a mortar and a good iron spit, the chaldron (*caldarium*) which stands in the kitchen, 4 pipes and 2 hogsheads[5]—empty, and the vessels used for brewing;[6] also 6 silver spoons, and a silver cup and cover[7] in the keeping of John Fax; also, a surplice with an amice of black cloth furred with gris;[8] subject to this condition, that he personally reside on his benefice, and settle quietly any claim he may have on the executors on account of repairs at Tiverton; else he was to have none of these things.

And, whereas Thomas Hendeman owed testator 10 marks, he was willing, if he paid the executors 5 marks without giving any trouble, to remit the rest; but he was to do so within fifteen days after demand or be made to pay the whole. To Margery, his brother's daughter, he leaves half a mark. And all the the residue of his estate (except the legacies mentioned above or in a codicil), he leaves to Walter Colle, his sister's son, to be applied to pious uses, and specially in providing food and necessaries for testator's "Master," William Colmpton, as long as he lived, and to bury him decently; and to provide, if necessary, for his brother, Wm. Colle.

Executors:—The aforesaid Walter Colle; Matthew Doune; and John Whyteway, notary-publick. To Matthew Doune, for his trouble, he bequeaths all his utensils at Morchard-Cruwys, and remits the money due to him for things which the said Matthew had bought of him from time to time. To John Whyteway he leaves 20s.

Memorandum at the end of the Will:—"Isabella Payton owes me, for debts incurred by Vincent Wryght, her husband, 10s. and two marks: also six marks on her own account, and 9s. 11d., of which sums if she pay my executors the 6 marks which she borrowed of me to buy wine with, after her said husband's

---

[1] peciam argenti ("a piece of silver")—"pecia = Vas, calix"—*Ducange*: any "piece of plate." In the (English) Will of Nicholas Morton, R. of the Colleg. Ch. of Slapton, he leaves to the College "a peace of sylver in valew of 20s." *Oliver's Monasticon*, p. 322. *See* note 7 below.

[2] uni capellano *juveni* et honesto.

[3] Rawysaysch, MS.

[4] item lego parvo Waltero, famulo meo.

[5] pipas—hogeshedys.

[6] vasa ad pandoxandum ordinata.

[7] peciam argenti cum coopertorio.

[8] superpellicium cum almicio de panno nigro furrato de grisio.

death, I give her up the remainder; otherwise she must pay the whole. Also my Lord, the Earl of Devon, owes me £20 (as John Gunne well knows), but if the said Earl means to be a good Lord etc. (*sit eis bonus Dominus etc.*) to my executors, and not give them trouble in the execution of my Will, I remit the whole debt, as well as 5 marks which the Lady Matilda, his Countess, owes me: otherwise I hold him accountable before the Most High God.—Also, Walter Schanke owes me 6 marks, and I have a *Catholicon* and a Book of Brito[1] in pledge; let him pay, and the books be restored. Also he owes me 8 marks (a loan), and one mark: and I have in pledge a silver cup, now in Exeter. Also he owes, for his expenses in the case of John Jacob, I know not how much. I remit the 8 marks, the 1 mark, and the said expenses; and, over and above this, I leave him 5 marks, in recompense for a large book of Mattins, which he gave me *gratis*. Also I leave him the Breviary which he has in his possession. And my will is that his silver cup, which I have in Exeter, be restored to him."

Proved, 20 September, 1415, before the Bishop, at Clyst.

XLIV. William Hunden,[2] clerk, Archdeacon of Totnes, Canon of Exeter, etc.

Dated, at the Archdeacon's House, in the Close; 27 January, 1415-16. i, 324b.

He commends his soul to God, Blessed Mary and All Saints; his body to holy sepulture, where God shall please.

He leaves to poor decrepit persons and to prisoners £10, and more if necessary, at the discretion of his executors. Also, to mend the publick roads and bridges in the Archdeaconry of Totnes, 40s.; and the like amount for the same purposes in the Archdeaconry of Rochester. To three chaplains, for a year (or to one chaplain for three years, if three cannot be procured), £20, viz. 10 marks each per annum, to say Mass daily for his soul, and for John and Joeta, his parents, Thos. Opton, John Dangy, John Tayllour, Edith Foot, John Snape, and Wm. Brydbrok. To the Abbot and Convent of Lessness [Lesenes, MS.—Dioc. of Rochester], a pair of gilded ewers (weighing 10 lib. de troy 8 oz. and over—never to be sold or alienated); for the Canons there to say a collect at Mass, every day, for ever, for his soul, and to keep up his anniversary. To the Ch. of Longfield [Langefelde, MS.] in the same Diocese, a vestment of cloth of gold *de luca*.—To John Hunden, his brother, a bed, draped with red *worstede*, with curtains, and everything to match for a bedchamber; also one of his best suits, to wit a tunic (*collobium*), trimmed with fur of *menyvere* (i.e. *de menu vair*), with fur hood; also another tunic; also a set in green and red *worstede* for the hall; one best pair of sheets, 6 silver cups called *Gobelettes*, one bowl (*maser*) gilt, with cover, and 12 silver spoons parcel-gilt (*deaurata in parte*); also *pixidem deauratam pro pulvere*;[3] one of his best table-cloths, a towel, and 2 hand-napkins (*sauenapys*); and he gives up to the same John £20 which he had borrowed. To Margery, his sister, a pallet-bed (*unum lectum palet*) of white, green, and red *worstede*, with three curtains, complete, for her bed-chamber; 2 silver cups, on the cover of one of which was engraved—"Ihc est Amor meus;" a robe furred, hood, and a second double robe; also a tunic (*collobium*) with fur *de Grey*, a table-cloth, a towel, and 2 hand-napkins. To Wm. Scheldrake £10, to put him to school; and to his cousin Alice, dau. of John Scheldrake, £10, to enable her to marry. To

---

1 "*Catholicon* et Librum Britonis."—"Brito super Vocabula Biblie" appears among the books in "Tercius descus" in the Cathedral Inventory of 1506.—William Brito was a Friar: he is mentioned by Leland as well known for his Lexicon of the Bible.—*Oliver*. There was, also, a copy of "Catholicon" in the same "descus."

2 "Sanus mente et corpore, desiderans, dum in membris vigor viget corporis et racio regit mentem—quam quidem, racionem sepe adeo languor obnubilat ut non solum temporalium rerum verum eciam sui ipsius cogit ipsa languioris (*sic*) vehemencia oblivisci condicionis humane inevitabile debitum prevenire—condo testamentum meum in hunc modum."

3 A spice box?—"Dust"—pounded spice. *Palgrave* (quoted by *Halliwell*).

his cousin Joan Park, £20; 2 silver cups, one with a cover, not engraved; 12 silver spoons; a bed of red and white *worstede*, with three curtains, one pair of *blankettys*, and 2 pairs of sheets. To the Bishop of Exeter, his "Johannes de Liniano *super antiquis*," in 2 volumes.[1] To the University of Cambridge, "Johannes in Novella, *super antiquis et Sexto Libro*, in 3 volumes, to remain for ever in the New Library there, for the use of graduates and scholars in residence. To Laurence Haukyn a book called "*Pollicronicon*." To Rd. Palmer his Bible. To Roger Bolter a book called "*Kalendarium sive Inventarium Juris*;" to Thos. Abyndon his "*Legenda Sanctorum*," and a book "*De taxis ecclesiarum*." To Rd. Penels, "*Cinus*[2] *super Codicem*," and "*Lapus super Sexto Libro et Clementinis*," with divers others, all in one book; also "*Johannes in Addicionibus*."[3] To John Swayn, a silver cup called a Bowl (*bolle*—a tankard), with cover, which testator had been accustomed to use in his chamber; also "*Johannes de Atona*,"[4] and "*Constitutiones Provinciales*;" and all his papers and little books—"*de formis instrumentorum et aliarum materiarum diversarum de practica*." To John Park, his brother, he forgives a debt of £50. He gives the use of his Breviary, *quod incipit, in secundo folio*, "Suscipere voluisti Domini," to John Forde, chaplain, for life, and after his death to some other poor chaplain chosen by the said John; the said Breviary to descend from priest to priest, as long as it should hold together.—To Thos. Slocok he gives the use of another Breviary, *quod incipit in secundo folio* 'Nos [miseros[5]]' To John Mychel a "*Sextus Liber cum tribus Doctoribus*" *qui incipit, in secundo folio*, "fuit quare hoc dixerunt." To the Cathedral he leaves his Henry Bohic *in suis Distineccionibus* (in two volumes), to remain for ever in the new Library,[6] for the use of the Canons and others who resort to the Library with the Canons' leave.—To the Church of Crawley (Dioc. of Lincoln), he leaves £5, for a tabernacle to be painted, or for some other ornament, for the image of St. Firmin, patron of the Church. To the Church of Hadstoke (Dioc. of London), his vestment *de panno aureo de Cyper*. To the Church of Rokyslegh (Dioc. of Rochester), a vestment *de Bordalysaunder* for ferial days. To John Hunden, his brother, a Missal, beginning on the 2nd folio, "*ad principale altare*;" also 2 silver ewers, engraved with images of Peter and Paul; two silver lavers, a chalice gilt, two silver jugs (*urciolos*), a pax silvered, a vessel for salt, and a bell gilded, a set of green hangings for an altar, and a vestment to match: also two towels for use at the same altar. To Nich. Hille he remits 26s. 8d., and leaves him 40s. To Rd. Godeman, 40s. To Thos. Lobbe 40s. To Wm. Dygher 40s. To Thos. Chesterton 20s. To Janyn *de coquina* 6s. 8d. To his brother John all his lands, tenements, &c., in the County of Suffolk, as by hereditary right and by no other title, for life; to revert afterwards to Wm. Scheldrake, his cousin, and his issue; failing which, to John Scheldrake, his brother, and his heirs; failing whom to his next-of-kin in perpetuity. If his said brother, in contempt of his Will, should sell the property, he was to forfeit all the above-mentioned legacies; neither was he to have them till he had given

---

[1] The "Sextus descus" in the Inventory of 1506, contained "Prima (and Secunda) pars Johannis de Lyniano," and also a copy of the book next mentioned—"Johannes in Novella." The "Policronicus" was in "Quintus descus."

[2] This book was in "Quintus descus" in the Inventory of 1506.—See p. 394 (*note* 2).

[3] There was a copy in "Secundus descus"—Inventory of 1506.

[4] He was Bishop of Vercelli, circ. 960. His book was in the "Secundus descus" in 1506.

[5] Apparently; but the MS. is defective here.

[6] Henry Boyck, LL.D., flourished in Lower Brittany about the year 1390 (*Oliver*.) It is interesting to see the names of these two volumes "Prima Pars Henrici Bowyck" and "Secunda Pars," in the Inventory of this Library made in 1506 ("Secundus Descus," and another copy in "Sextus Descus.") Only nineteen out of the whole number (359), Dr. Oliver tells us, remained in 1752!

at least the security of his oath not to alienate the said property. The executors were to sell all his lands, etc., in "Tyrtyscleve," in the County of Kent, the proceeds to be paid to Joan Park, his cousin, for a marriage portion. To Wm. Barton and his successors, Archdeacons of Totnes, he leaves *omnia lecta de tabulis ac formulas tabulas pro vestimentis conservandis in eisdem*, that may be found in any chambers in the Archdeacon's house in Exeter; also, *tabulam principalem secundariam cum trestallis et scabellis omnibus in eadem aula existentibus cum uno novo scryne et copborde* erected therein; also the tables, etc., used in the buttery, and all tables and treatles in the kitchen; also, all the timber prepared for the construction of the hall-roof on the garden side. But the said Wm. Barton and his successors were not to alienate any of these things: and the roof was to be put up within a reasonable number of years, or the executors were to sell the whole, and apply the money to pious uses. The residue he bequeaths to his brother John, Rd. Penels, John Swayn and John Mychel, chaplain, to be used for the good of his soul; and he appoints them his executors.

Witnesses: Rob. Dunnyng, clerk, of the Diocese of Bath and Wells, notary-publick; Wm. Nicol, and Rd. West, chaplains.

Proved 10 March, 1415-16, before the Bishop, at Clyst.

Summa Bonorum:—£362 14s. 11d.

XLV.—Hugh de Hyckelyng, Precentor of Exeter.

Dated in the Precentor's Manse in the Close, 8 August, 1415. i, 325[b].

He commends his soul to God, his Creator and Redeemer; his body to be buried in the Cathedral, near the altar of the Chantry of Thomas [Brantingham] the late Bishop. To the fabrick of the Cathedral he leaves 100s. As to his funeral rites, he desires everything to be done with due regard to the honour of the Church, but without any herse (*absque hercia*), or any general feasting save only for the Canons and Ministers of the Cathedral taking part in the ceremonies; avoiding excessive expenses, *que magis tendunt ad pompam mundi quam ad salutem anime*. To every Canon present at his funeral he leaves 40d.; to every Vicar 20d.; to every Annuellar 12d.; to every Secondary 6d.; to every Chorister 4d. The Canons present *in die tricennali*, at *Placebo* and *Dirige*, Commendation and Mass, were to have 20d. each; the Vicars 12d.; the Annuellars, 8d.; the Secondaries, 4d.; the Choristers, 3d. He leaves £27 to maintain his obit in the Cathedral for 20 years from his burial, viz., 27s. on each day of his obits in the 20 years, according to the use of the said Cathedral; each Canon to receive at least, 4d., if present at *Placebo* and *Dirige*, and the same for Commendation and Mass; the Vicars and Annuellars, 2d. each; and each Secondary and Chorister 1d. The bellringers to be paid according to the custom of the said Church. If any part of the 27s. were not spent, the money was to be added to the fund. He leaves for distribution on each of these days, among poor, lame, and infirm people, unable to work, 5s. Also £16 for three worthy priests, to say Mass for his soul, and for his parents, friends, etc., in the Cathedral Church, at the altar of the tomb of Thos. Brantingham, the late Bp., for the year immediately following testator's death; each to receive eight marks; and also 13s. 4d. to provide a light, and wine and bread, during the year. Moreover each of these priests was to say *Placebo*, *Dirige*, and the Commendations daily throughout the year. He leaves also, 40s., for 16 trentals, to be said immediately after his death. To the fabrick of the Colleg. Ch. of Glasney (where he had been Canon), he leaves 40s. To each Vicar and Annuellar in the Cathedral, taking part in his exequies on the day of his burial, 6s. 8d., to pray for his soul, etc., specially, for a year after his death, every day, when they say Mass and use other prayers and suffrages. To the Friars Minors of Exeter, the Friars Preachers there, and the Hosp. of St. John, 20s. to each; and to the poor infirm folk of St. Mary Magd., near Exeter, 13s. 4d. To John Boterel, chaplain, he bequeaths £6 13s. 4d., a large Breviary and an Ordinal. To the Ch. of Crediton 20s. for his obit there, within a month of his death. The rest of his goods his executors were to dispose of, for the good of his soul, among the parishioners of Paignton, Chudleigh, and Saint Mary Church, and other poor persons, especially parishioners and tenants of the Dean and Chapter.

His executors desiring to acquire any of his goods, at a just value, to have preference over outsiders, and each who consented to act, 13s. 4d. for his trouble.

Executors: Laurence Haukyn, clerk; Henry Foleford; Rob. Lyngham, clerk; Rd. Skynner, clerk; Rob. Dunnyng, clerk; and Rob. Hyckelyng, Esquire.

If any of the legatees mentioned in this Will, or in the Codicil thereto, should resort to litigation, their legacies to be forfeited. All the legatees, on receipt of their said legacies, to give the executors full discharge. The executors were on no account to lend any portion of the testator's goods to anyone, but to distribute the same immediately.

The Codicil, dated 8 August, 1415:— Testator's best robe of scarlet cloth, or another in good condition, with all its fur, to be sold, and the money spent in purchasing a comely vestment for the Lady-Chapel in the Cathedral, to remain therein while it lasts. To Alice, his sister, he leaves £6 13s. 4d. To John de Stapulforde, his nephew, 100s. To Rob. de Hyckelyng, his cousin (*cognato*), 40s., a bed, and the cup of silver gilt which testator bought of Robert's mother, together with its cover. To John, son of Wm. Hickelyng, for a marriage portion, £26 13s. 4d. To his servant John Stapuldon (after repaying the 40s. which he owes) £13 6s. 8d. To his servant, Wm. Stokys, £6 13s. 4d., and two oxen. He desires his executors to return (paying all expenses) to the Prior and Convent of Haltemprice [Hautemprys MS.], Dioc. of Ebor. two books which they lent him in his youth,[1] to wit *Digestum Vetus* and *Inforciatum*: he leaves them 40s., to pray for his soul. To his servant, Rob. Weryng, 20s., an ox, and 20 sheep, then at Ugbrooke. To his servant, John Weryng, an ox and 20s. To Rd. Skynner, chaplain, 100s., a book called *Pars oculi*, and a robe trimmed with fur; that he may remember him in his prayers; also, a Breviary. To Wm. Broun, V. of Sidbury, 13s. 4d. He bequeaths some tapestry (*novum doser meum de opere tappesterie*), for the High Altar of the Cathedral: and two side-hangings (*costres*) to match, for the Lady-Chapel. To his poor tenants, *et nativis pauperibus* at Paignton he leaves £3 6s. 8d., to pray for him; and 60s. to his poor parishioners there; the same at Chudleigh. To Edw. Galbrygg, his servant, 40s.; to John Harry, another servant, 26s. 8d.; to Rob. Sutton, another, 26s. 8d.; to John Chamberleyn, another, 20s. To Rd. Sterlyng, his succentor, 40s. over and above his fees. To Hugh, son of Rob. Hyckelyng, his godson, £10. To John West, his secondary, 20s. To Benedict, his cup-bearer (*servienti pincerne*), 20s. To Walter, cousin of John Boterell, 20s. To Thos. Dyrell, his chorister, 20s.[2] To the Prioress and Nuns of Polslo, for his soul, 40s. To Rob. Lyngham, R. of St. Mary-Major, Exeter, his new Psalter.

Proved, in the parish-church of St. Leonards without the South Gate, 28 March, 1416, before Roger Bolter, Can. of Exeter, the Bishop's Commissary. Sealed, at Clyst, 30 March. The inventory was produced, at Clyst, 6 April.

Summa Bonorum, £334 19s. 10d.

XLVI. Thos. Barton, Can. of Exeter, R. of Ilfracombe, etc.

Dated, at Exeter, 27 June, 1415. i, 327.

He commends his soul to God, His Mother the Glorious Virgin Mary, and All Saints; his body to holy sepulture in the Cathedral, near the tomb or oratory of Thomas [Brantingham] the late Bishop, on its south side, under a marble slab. One half of the Vicars, Annuellars, Secondaries and Choristers to celebrate *Placebo* and *Dirige*, daily, in turns, while his body lay at his house; each Vicar and Annuellar to receive 2d., each Secondary 1d., each chorister a halfpenny. Two wax lights, each weighing three pounds, to burn at his head and feet, while his body remained in the choir. Sixteen poor men, clothed in black cloth or russet, to carry four torches, each of 7 or 8 pounds of wax, and 7 tapers, each weighing 2 pounds of wax. And twelve poor persons, wearing black cloth, were to carry 12 wax-lights, not burning, each weighing 1 pound, for the 12 Altars in the Church, to be lighted on the said altars at the time of his exequies. Also 20 torches, each weighing about 7 or 8 pounds, were to be provided for 20 churches, or chapels-in-charge, in Exeter and

---

[1] Robert de Hicklyng was the 8th Prior (14 Dec. 1362).

[2] "Item Thome, choriste meo, vis., Dyrell."

the suburbs, to be lighted daily at the elevation of Christ's Body, while they lasted. and every clerk belonging to the said churches and chapels, vested in his surplice was to carry a lighted torch before the corpse, from testator's house, and through the midst of the town, to the Broad Gate of the Close, and from thence to carry it extinguished, each to his own church, for rendering this service. His funeral expenses to be regulated by the executors, at their discretion; but no Canon or citizen was to be invited except such as had actually to assist at the service: and 200 poor persons were to be fed. the same day, in a suitable manner, on baked meats and roast (*de coctis et assatis*) with spiced drink (*cum potu subtili*), not more than enough for poor men of that sort; lest they should gorge themselves. His Ordinale, according to the use of Sarum, and his large Breviary, bought of the executors of the late Bishop, to be chained with iron chains to the table to which the *Catholicon*, and *Lira Super Quatuor Evangelistas* are chained: the clergy generally[1] to have all reasonable access thereto. His exequies to be celebrated in the choir; each Canon present to have 2s., each Vicar 12d., each Annuellar 6d., each Secondary 4d., each Chorister 2d., and the same on the 30th day with payments to about the same amounts; also in the Churches of Crediton and Ottery; in St. Mary-Major, by the clergy of the City; and in the Priory Churches of St. Nicholas, St. John, Cowick, &c., with like payment in each case. On the day before his funeral, or on the day itself, there was to be a general distribution of alms to beggars and indigent people—1d. to each; but to the decrepit the blind, and the helpless, unable to make a living, in Exeter, Crediton and Ilfracombe [Ilford, MS.], 4d. each. His exequies were to be kept in Ilfracombe Ch., on some convenient day after his funeral, and 40s. distributed among poor parishioners. Also, he makes provision for the celebration thereof for an octave after his death, by the Fellows of the Hall in Oxford called "Stapyldon Halle" and they were to divide 40s. among them; those that were priests to say Mass, the others the Psalter. The Friars-Preachers of Exeter were to keep his anniversary for a year, and to receive 5 marks. A fit priest was to say Mass in Ilfracombe Ch., after his death, for 7 years. Another priest was to celebrate, and pray, at Bishop Brantingham's altar, for 7 years, for testator's soul and the Bishop's, and for all their benefactors. The sum of £26 13s. 4d., English money (due after his death on account of residence), to be placed in safe keeping in the Treasury, for distribution, year by year amongst those present at his obit. And the sum of £20, in gold, was to be deposited in the Archives of the Church of Crediton, to maintain the late Bishop's anniversary, and his own. To the Priory of Cornworthy, on account of its extreme poverty (*pauperima* domus), he leaves 20s., each nun to have 12d. to celebrate his exequies, and every priest there 8d.; the rest to go to the nuns in common.

For the construction of a new window, the raising of the walls,[2] and for timber for the roof of the north transept (*gabuli borealis*) of Crediton Church, in which John Sully, knt., lies, he leaves £20, if other Canons, or the parishioners, are willing to contribute to the same, so that it may be completed to correspond with the other transept; else, the money was to be spent about the High Altar, to enclose the presbytery and the walls with columns in comely fashion, and to provide 2 small tablets of alabaster, decently painted, for the two small side-altars in the choir (*pro altaribus parvis in choro collateralibus*). He leaves 100s. for the construction of a bridge adjoining the mill called "New Mill" [Nyewemylle, MS.], near Crediton, with 2 arches of stone, if the inhabitants are willing to contribute, and complete the work within a year; else the money is to be given to the poor, or laid out on the roads, where most wanted. Also, he leaves £10 towards rebuilding the bridge at Thorverton, with arches of stone, if the inhabitants set about the work in earnest within a year, and persevere with it; otherwise the money to be devoted to pious purposes. To each of his executors he leaves 40s., besides their legacies and expenses. The residue, whether in possession or owing, to be expended on works of piety, or according to the directions in a Codicil.

---

1 "Vulgus clericale," i.e. I suppose, "the inferior clergy!"

2 "murorum," *not* "minorum," as Dr. Oliver read it.

Executors :—Rd. Gabryell, Rd. Penels, John More, John Wyddyslond, and John Cutvyn.

Witnesses :—Wm. Kelwa, notary-publick ; John Cowyk, R. of Pyworthy ; Wm. Fraunceys ; Geoffrey Langdon ; Roger Schaplegh ; Rob. Rydon ; Rd. Wotton ; and others.

Codicil :—To Laurence Hawkyn, he leaves a pair of rosaries, etc. (*unum par oraculorum nigrorum cum gaudiis de auro, et anulum aureum cum signaculo vertibili de petra blodia ex parte una, et aquila cum duobus capitibus ex altera, et botellum de argento semiplenum de balsamo puro*). To Rd. Gabryell, besides a girdle already given to him, he leaves his purse, called a *Gipsier*, and a ring of silver-gilt. To Rd. Penels he leaves his girdle of black silk, with buckle and ornaments of silver gilt, a baslard, *et unum par oraculorum de Ambre* with a gilt cross, and a buckle with an image of St. Katherine. To John More his large bed, *de rubio Werstede, videlicet coopertorium tapetis cum dimidia celatura et 3 Ridellis* ; also, his *portiforium plenarium* according to the use of Sarum (on fol. ii, *Veni, Domine*), directing him to give it, when about to die, to a worthy priest, who will use it and hand it on to another ; and so on as long as it lasts. To John Duffelde a small round goblet (*maser*) and a silver cup worth about 30s. To Elias Stoke his overcoat (*supertunicam*) of green cloth, with a cloak and hood of green *Tartaryn*. To Rd. Mark an overcoat with hood *de horegrene* ; and a book of sermons, bound in red leather (already in his possession), subject to the same conditions as the other books. To John Mathew, V. of Broadclyst, a pamphlet (*pamfilium*), of the late Bishop's, entitled *Lucidarium*, with sermons and other good treatises and discourses ; that he may pray for the Bishop's soul. To Thos. Baker, R. of Kentisbury, his bed *de blodio worstede cum tapete, dimidia celatura de odium*,[1] *et* iij^bus^ *Ridellis de blodio carde*[2] ; he was also to have some jewel of silver if he were diligent in getting in the money owed to testator at Ilfracombe. To John Wolston a silver cup (*peciam*) and cover, worth about 26s. 8d. To John Cutvyne a long scarlet robe *fibulatum cum una furrura grisia de Scache*: (in check fashion ?), and a small book called "Raymond." To John Wydeslond, V. of Heavitree, *unam supertunicam de nigro blodio, furratam de bise, cum capicio duplicato de eadem* ; also a small goblet (*maser*), black, bound with silver and gilt. To Wm. Baker (who was with the Bishop of Bath), a silver cup, not engraved, worth about 20s. To John Holond a cloak of violet (*clamidem de violet*) without fur, and an overcoat of the larger size, with hood to match. To John Cowyk, some of his utensils at Ilfracombe, viz., 2 iron spits, 2 ranges (*rackeʒ*) of iron, 2 brass pots, one brass chaldron (*cacabum*), one of his better dishes, the cooking vessels of tin, and a table-cloth of Parisian work ; also a Breviary, once the property of Walter de Redeness, on the same conditions as the other books. To Thos. Horelock, his priest at Ilfracombe, he leaves other of his utensils there, to the value of 26s. 8d., a proper valuation having first been made. To John Copleston, junior, he bequeaths his long silver-gilt cup, standing on 3 lions, with a cover enamelled on the knob (*cum cooperculo aymelato in pomello*), which had been bequeathed to testator by Alexander Merle ; hoping that he would stand by his executors, and assist and protect them in every way in his power. To John Wille, a poor clerk, 40s., if he continue in the schools at Oxford. To Geoffrey Langdon 66s. 8d. To John Wyke, certain utensils worth 20s. To Elias Bear the cup of maser-wood, bound with silver, not already bequeathed, and 20s., or the value thereof. To the anchorite enclosed at St. Leonard's a robe of black cloth or russet, and 20s. towards his maintenance. His servants, at the time of his death, to be continued in their service for 30 days, and rewarded according to length of service and diligence in work, at the discretion of the executors. If Rd. Gabriell remained in testator's house, or elsewhere within the Close, he was to have the tapestry embroidered with figures of men (*aulam* [i. q. aulaeum] *enbrowdeatam cum hominibus*), which belonged to the late Bishop ; also testator's mirror,[3] and his new table ; but the money left him in the Will testator

---

[1] *Sic* MS., *or* "odem": I suspect a clerical error for "eodem."

[2] *Carde*—"panni species videtur." (*Du Cange*).

[3] speram meam—i e. *speculum* ; or, perhaps, "*sphere*," *a globe*.

withdraws, as he does not need money. All his personal attire (*vestimenta mea pro corpore*), except his garments of scarlet cloth, of great value and trimmed with fur, testator bequeaths to respectable and poor Rectors, Vicars, and priests, in the city of Exeter and the neighbourhood, especially those belonging to St. Gabriel's Chapel at Clyst. To the Hosp. of St. John Baptist, Exeter, he leaves 20 marks for the support of one priest, to say mass for two years, in their Church, if it please them, for the souls of the late Bp. Brantingham, Robert his brother, and Henry Blakeburne. To St Mary's Chapel at Crediton he leaves 2 curtains (*ridelli*) and a frontal of crimson silk (*frontale de rubio et blodio tartarin*) with the Crucifix and Mary and John embroidered thereon. He orders a chasuble to be made of cloth of gold, red, *cum orfreis de precioso auro*,[1] *velluet, et aliis peciis remanentibus in Capella mea*, and given to the Church of Bampton : if any materials were left they were to be made into receptacles for corporals (*repositoria pro corporalibus*), and given, by way of charity, to poor churches. In like manner towels, made of different kinds of materials, were to be given to the poorer Churches appropriated to the Dean and Chapter of Exeter. To Rd. Reve, R. of Roseash, [Ease Ravff, MS.], he leaves an overcoat and hood, which he bought of the wife of John Schapplegh ; and to J. Wigwar his larger overcoat with hood to match. All his coverlets (*lodices*) or blankets, and sheets, (*linthiamina usitata de canvass*), at Exeter or at Ilfracombe, he gives to the decrepit and the bedridden, to prisoners, and to infirm and poor persons not remembered in his Will. To the altar of St. Michael in the Church of Crediton he leaves his alabaster tablet, beautifully painted ; unless the parishioners of Ilfracombe are willing to contribute 40s., over and above the sums in the hands of Thos. Baker, collected from the executors of persons buried in the nave of their Church. To Thos. Barnard, his godson, (*filio meo levato de sacro fonte*) he leaves 26s. 8d., if he continue to attend school. His larger silver-gilt chalice, and his sheets *de panno de Reynes*, he orders to be sold, and the money laid out for the repose of the soul of Wm. Swynflete, his cousin. The aforementioned John Cowyk to have 2 round cups of silver, called bowls (*bollys*), a purse (*gipcier*), a silver ring, and 6 small silver spoons. None of his goods to be delivered up, lent, or alienated in any way whatsoever, till they had been properly valued, and the price paid to the executors. All legacies to lapse unless the legatees survived him. His executors might purchase any articles at a fair and duly attested price. He expresses an anxious wish that the gold deposited with the Prior of St. John Baptist, Exeter, and the proceeds of the sale of his goods and the recovery of debts, be distributed among the parishes of Devon and Cornwall, at the rate of 6s. 8d. each, any residue to be reserved for priests at Exeter, Oxford, and Ilfracombe willing to say Mass for the souls of his benefactors ; for poor clerks of Devonshire studying at Exeter (*Exonie scolatizantibus*) ; and for other works of piety. Directions are given for distributing among the Canons, &c., of the Cathedral present at his anniversary the forty marks laid up for that purpose in the Cathedral Treasury ; and for the distribution of the £20 laid up in the Archives at Crediton for the anniversaries of Bishop Brantingham and of testator. An iron-bound chest of the late Bishop's, in the keeping of the Precentor, to be given up to the Cathedral-Treasury, and used for the safe keeping of moneys devoted to the obits of Canons, etc. ; and another similar chest, and an iron coffer, (*cathedra* [i.e. 'arca']) in the possession of testator, to be delivered over to the Church of Crediton. He leaves to Glasney some tapestry of the late Bishop's, worked with Katherine's wheels and swans (*tapetum Domini defuncti cum rotis Katerine et cingnis contextum*), to be spread before the High Altar on the greater Festivals; the late Bishop's *parysii* [the "pavise" was a large shield], and his brass gun to be handed over to the Cathedral Treasury. The missal, chalice, and other 'ornaments,' which belonged to Henry Blakburne, to be sold for the said Henry's soul, as also ij *salices argentee cum procellis deauratis*.[2]

---

[1] Perhaps "bullion;" the MS. is obscure and doubtful.

[2] Sic MS.—I suppose 'calices' was intended, and 'parcellis'—"two chalices of silver, parcel gilt."

Proved 31 March, 1416, before the Bishop at Clyst.
Summa bonorum :—£51 11s. 2d.

XLVII.—John Govys, R. of Holy Trinity, Exeter; a Vicar in the Cathedral Church.

Dated 31 March, 1416. i, 328b.

He commends his soul to Almighty God, his Creator, Who redeemed it with His precious blood; his body to holy sepulture in the Cathedral cemetery. A hundred Masses were to be said for his soul within two days after his death. To the Canons he leaves 12d. each, to the Vicars 10d., to the Annuellars 8d., to the secondaries 4d., to the choristers 2d., if present at his obit. To each Rector in the city, present in his surplice and preceding his corpse to the Cathedral, 6d.; to every other priest present, 4d. To the Prior and Brethren of the Hospital of St. John within the East-gate, 6s. 8d.; to the poor boys serving God there, 12d., and the same to the poor men. To the Friars Preachers of Exeter 6s. 8d.; the same to the Friars Minors. All were to wear surplices at his exequies, and to say the service simultaneously, finishing it at about the same time; proceeding and afterwards, in their habits and surplices, before his corpse, to the Cathedral, devoutly chanting.

To Robert Lyngham, R. of St. Mary Major, he bequeaths his small cup, bound with silver, and gilt, called *lytelmaser*, together with its cover. To Wm. Brown, V. of Sidbury, his best cup of maple silver-bound, with its cover, and 6s. 8d.—For the fabrick of the Cathedral Church 6s. 8d. To John Parke 6s. 8d. To Matth. Stoke 3s. 4d. To John Parfay 20d. To Rob. Widelegh 20d. To Rd. Skynnere 20d. To the Wardens of Holy Trinity Church all that tenement, with garden adjacent thereto, situate at the South gate of the city of Exeter, near the said Church, and lately granted to testator by the Mayor and Community of Exeter for a fixed term of years (as by Indenture appeared); to have and to hold from the date of his death to the end of the said term, on condition that the said Wardens and their successors should maintain his anniversary in the said Church, year by year, throughout the term, employing the Rector and clerk of the said Church, and four others, annuellar priests, belonging to the city, and paying the said Rector 4d., the clerk 2d., and the other priests 2d. each, for their services; also 12d. for the light, and for bread, etc., 2s.; taking 6d. for their trouble in the matter. Any residue to be used for the advantage of the said Church. To John Lydeford and Alice his wife he leaves 6s. 8d. To Juliana, wife of John Forchull, 6s. 8d. All his parishioners, old as well as young, to be feasted on the day of his burial, and pray for his soul. Those who were nursing him in his sickness were to be remunerated well and not grudgingly, according to their deserts. Thos. Freman, chaplain, was to receive 106s. 8d. annually, from an annual rent of eight pounds granted to testator by the Warden and College of Vicars-choral of Exeter, to say Mass for his soul, &c.; he was to be paid from that source as long as it lasted; and 4 marks were to be laid out for testator's soul, to the best of his executors' discretion: if the said Thomas died or was promoted before the termination of this payment, some other priest was to take his place. To Thos. Porteworthy he leaves 20d. To each executor 13s. 8d. for his trouble. The residue to be distributed, for the good of his soul, etc., among poor priests and clerks and other needy persons as soon after his death as possible.

Executors :—Wm. Broun, V. of Sidbury; and Thos. Freman, chaplain.
Proved, 15 April, 1416, before the Bishop, at Clyst.

XLVIII.—Matilda Latymer.

Dated "die Martis in Septimana Pasche," 1416. i, 329.

She commends her soul to God, to Blessed Mary His Mother and to All Saints; her body to holy sepulture in the Ch. of St. John's Priory, Exeter, near the grave of Sir John Hulle, knight, her late husband. To the said Priory she leaves £10, and all animals—horses, oxen, etc. (*omnia annimalia, videlicet affros et averia*), at the time of her death, on her land, near Exeter, held of Rob. Hulle. She leaves also, £10, to find two chaplains to say Mass for her soul for two years.—To her daughter Elizabeth, a sister at Buckland, 100s., and a silver cup, '*flat*,' gilt, with cover (*See* pp. 390 (note), 402); also a set of coral beads (*Bedys de corall*). To the

Convent of Buckland 40s. To her son John, all her store on her manor of Wellysford; and to her son Ralph all her store on her manor of Bickleigh (Bykele, MS.) To the Church of Holcombe [Rogus] 40s.; and 20s. to be distributed on the day of her funeral, among the lame, blind, and infirm of that parish. To her son John, and all her children, she leaves the Benediction of God Almighty and her own. To the said John she, also, bequeaths £40, and a red bed, with canopy complete (*lectum rubeum cum integro Sele*),[1] 3 curtains (*courtynes*), 3 side-hangings (*costers textis toutdys en ioye*), 3 cushions (*quissones*), '*cum columbellis*,' 1 canvass (*canefas*), 1 mattrass, 2 blankets, 2 pairs of sheets, viz., 1 pair *de quatuor foliis* and another pair *de tribus foliis tele de raynes*, one ewer and laver of silver gilt, one "coupe" (a cup; a vat.—*Halliwell*), silver gilt, *cum j pomello blodio*; 2 chargers, 12 plates of one set, and 6 saucers. To her son Ralph she leaves £40, and a bed, white and green, *de Norfolk*, with white roses, 1 canvass, 1 mattrass, 2 blankets, 2 pairs of sheets *de iij foliis tele Cornubiensis*, half-a-dozen silver platters (*platerys*); half-a-dozen dishes; half-a-dozen saucers, and a silver cup and cover with 3 crescents on the top (*de iij cressantis supra*). To her daughter Margaret she leaves 100s.; a girdle with trefoils (*cum trifoliis*); also, j *cameram integram, rubeam et nigram pavele*; a primer bound in silk, and half her pearls.[2] To Thos. Daubenay 100s. To her "sister Chambernon" a dress of green colour, and her mantles furred with ermine.[3] To Isabella Hull a set of long beads of gold with large beads of coral, and a necklace of gold (*de longe bedys auri cum gaudeis de Corall, et 1 nouche auri*). To Rob. Hulle a signet of gold, with a lamb thereon. To Margaret Janet 20s. and a dress furred with *grys*. To her servants, 60s. among them. To her chambermaid a dress of russet, *furratam cum agnis nigris*. To Katherine Lambroke, 20s. and a silver cup, cum ђ & t. To the Sisters of Cornworthy 40s. To the V. of Holcombe [Rogus] 13s. 4d. To the V. of Hockworthy 6s. 8d. To Walter Stalleworth 20s. To Rd. Mille a silver cup with a nettle (*urtica*) on the cover. To Wm. Jewe 40s. All her kerchiefs (*keuerchiefs*) to be distributed among the females in attendance around her death-bed. The rest of her clothes to be given to those who, in the judgment of her executors, needed them most. To Alienora Latymer 60s. To Edith Gunny 20d. and a russet dress, furred with *grys*. To the poor 20d., that they might pray for her soul. To Rob. Hulle a silver cup, with gilt cover, *in uno casu*. The rest of her jewels to be divided among her children.

Executors:—John Hulle, her son; Rob. Hulle; Wm. Jewe.

Proved, 13 May, 1416, before the Bishop, at Clyst.

XLIX.—Richard Holrygge, Vicar of Brixham.

Dated 4 April, 1416. i, 329b.

He commends his soul to God, and his body to holy burial.

To Richard Herygawde, chaplain, he leaves a book called "Pars oculi." To Thos. Smyth, chaplain, *unam togam penulatam cum Crestygrey*. To John Pyak a coat of crimson cloth. To the Nuns of Cornworthy a silver cup and cover, and to each of them one spoon, and 20s. among them. To the Friars Minors of Exeter 20s. To the Friars Preachers there 13s. 4d. To a chaplain, to say Mass for his soul in Brixham Church, for a year, 8 marks. To each of his executors 13s. 4d. 20 marks to be spent on his funeral expenses.

Executors:—Rd. Herygawde; Walter Lyȝe; and Thos. Dollynge.

Proved, 4 May, 1416, before the Bishop, at Clyst.

Summa bonorum:—£54 13s. 4d.

L.—Richard Hals, Treasurer of the Cathedral.

Dated, at his house in Exeter, 1 May, 1417. i, 329b.

He commends his soul to God, the Blessed Virgin Mary, St. Katherine, Saint Peter, Prince of the Apostles, his Guardian Angel (*Angelo michi commisso*), and to

---

[1] This word, I suppose, is the same as "Cele"—a canopy (Rutland Papers, pp. 7-10; quoted by Halliwell.)

[2] "Medietatem omnium perleum meorum vocatorum *perlys*."

[3] "*Manticas* furratas cum ermyn."

All Saints, desiring to be buried in the Cathedral beside of the tomb of Wm. Trevellys, late Treasurer, at the foot of his grave, at the entrance to the choir on the north side, if he should happen to die in the County of Devon, or in the parts adjacent thereto: if otherwise, then in the Church of the parish where he might die, or other suitable place at the discretion of his executors.

To his mother, Matilda, he leaves a silver cup, plain, with cover, worth 38s. by weight, and, towards her maintenance, 2 marks per annum, in quarterly payments as long as she lived ; if this sum, in addition to the rents and properties which she enjoyed in her own right, did not suffice, the executors were to give her as much of the residue of his estate as might be necessary. To the Hosp. of St. John, Exeter, he leaves 20s., and the same to the Friars Preachers and the Friars Minors. To the lepers ('*leprosariis' in Hospitali ... habitantibus*) of St. Mary Magdalene's Hospital 6s. 8d. All these were to pray for his soul. Poor people attending his funeral and asking alms were to have 1d. each ; every Canon of the Cathedral taking part in the service, 40d. There was to be no stated feast on the occasion, except for the officiating Ministers and testator's relations and friends ; also for the poor, decrepit, and infirm. To the Custos and Vicars Choral he leaves 40s., to pray for his soul, &c. With the residue his executors were to pay his debts, and apply the balance to pious purposes, according to instructions which he had given them ; and—he adds significantly—"prout et sicut varietates temporum secundum rotam fortune et vires facultatum mearum postulabunt et mortis sufficient in tempore."

Executors :—John Hals, his brother ; Roger Bolter, Archd. of Exeter ; and Wm Nycol, R. of St. Paul's, Exeter.

Proved, 25 May, 1417, before the Bishop at Clyst.

Summa bonorum :—£289 10s. 2d., ob.

LI.—Baldwin de Schyllyngford, Canon of Exeter.

Dated at Exeter, 1 March, 1417. i, 330.

He commends his soul to Almighty God, and his body to holy sepulture where his executors may determine.

To the fabrick of the Cathedral he leaves 100s. To the Cathedral Treasury[1] £6 13s. 4d. Whatever his executors did in the administration of his property was to be done unanimously, without controversy. They were to devote any residue to pious uses, for the welfare of the souls of sundry relations and benefactors, and of all the faithful dead.

Executors :—David Lovryng, R. of Black Torrington ; and John de Schyllyngford, his brother.

Proved, 23 February, 1417-18, before the Bishop, at Clyst.

LII.—John Ulveston, Vicar of Stokenham.

Dated, 14 March, 1417-18. i, 330b.

He commends his soul to God : his body to be buried in the chancel at Stokenham. For the maintenance of each light in the Church he leaves 3s. 4d., and to the store of St. Hubert, therein, 2s. For the maintenance of the lights in Staverton Church 6s. 8d., to be divided among them equally. A priest to be paid to say Mass for his soul in Staverton Church for six consecutive years. To Buckfast Abbey he leaves 40s. To the House of St. John, Exeter, 13s. 4d. To the Friars Preachers there, 6s. 8d. To the Prioress and Nuns of Cornworthy, 3s. 4d. To the store of the Chapel of Chivelston, 3s. 4d. ; to that of the Chapel of Sherford, 3s. 4d. Immediately after his death his executors were to distribute 20s. among the poor of Stokenham.

To his sister, Joan atte Wassche, he leaves 6s. 8d. To Joan, wife of John Suddon, 20s. To Cecilia, wife of John Somer, 6s. 8d. To Rosa, wife of John Rede, of Dartmouth, 40s. To Elena, his sister, a silver girdle and a goblet (*maser*) To Thos. Hurdyng, his servant, 16s. and a bed ; to John Godefray 10s. ; to Walter Somer 20s. ; to Thos. Skynner, 20s. ; to Agnes wife of Alexander

[1] ad excrescencias Scacarii. "Excrescentia" — Fortuita clericorum obventio—*casuel du Clergé* (Rym).

Gerard, 20s. ; to John, son of the said Alexander, 3s. 4d. ; to Thomas, another son, 20d. ; to Philip, another son, 20d. ; to Margery, daughter of the said Alexander, 3s. 4d. ; to Margery, wife of John Smyth, of Cornworthy, 20s. To the College (or Chapel) of the Blessed Mary within the Manor of Slapton 6s. 8d., to every priest of the said College 12d. ; and they were to say the office of the dead for his soul. To each of his God-children 4d. For the bridge at Aveton Giffard 6s. 8d. ; for Staverton bridge 3s. 4d. ; for Totnes bridge 3s. 4d. To Margaret, daughter of John Skynner, 3s. 4d. and the same to her brother John. The residue of his property after paying his funeral expenses and his debts, he leaves to Thos. Ulveston, his brother, and to John Ulveston, whom also he appoints his executors, with Nich. Husy and Nich. Buckyeth, chaplains, for overseers ; each of the latter to have 40s. for his trouble.

Proved, 11 May, 1418, before the Bishop, at Clyst.

Summa bonorum :—£210 3s. 3d., ob.

LIII.—John Westcote, Canon of the Cathedral, and R. of St. Petrock's.

Dated at Exeter, 20 July, 1411. i, 331.

He commends his soul to God, Blessed Mary, and All Saints ; his body to be buried in the Cathedral, near the tomb of Wm. Cok, then recently made. He leaves 5 marks for Masses to be said, after his death, wherever priests can be found ; and 10 marks for the poor, but he would have no general distribution on the day of his funeral. For that day, and for his obit in the said Church, he leaves to each of the Canons *pro tunc in villa presenti*, 12d. ; to every Vicar 6d. ; to every Annuellar 4d. ; to every Secondary 2d. ; to every Chorister 1d. ; to each Rector or Curate in the city, at the principal exequies in St. Petrock's Church, 12d. To each parish-clerk, 4d., and 2s. in addition to the parish-clerk of St. Petrock's. To the Prior, etc., of St. John's, Exeter, 40s. ; and to the Friars Preachers and Minors, 10s. to each. To the poor of the Infirmary (*pauperibus infirmarie*) 3s. 4d. ; to the poor of St. Mary Magdalene, Exeter, 2s. ; to every infirm poor person, and to every prisoner in Exeter, 4d. ; to the poor scholars in the House of St. John, Exeter, to pay for their victuals next Lent, 3s. 4d. To Rob. Lyngham a book, entitled *De veritate Theologie*, with many other contents, as appeared inscribed on the outside of the book, *et sub cornu scriptum* ; also, for his trouble as an executor, 20s. To Wm. Broun 13s. 4d. and his black girdle. To Hugh Hoker (to pray for his soul) 13s. 4d. To Roger Polford six of his best cushions (*quissones*), his best dorser and bankar,[1] and his best pair of sheets. To John Row a flat silver cup (*unum flat pecium argenteum*),[2] and to John Row 13s. 4d. To Rob. Lyngham a book *De exposicionibus Epistolarum et Evangeliorum Dominicalium*, qui incipit—"Benedictum Lignum per quod fit Justitia," et incipit in exposicione—"Cum Sancta Mater Ecclesia."—To every priest hired to say Mass for a year, in testator's Church, for his soul, 2s. To Matilda Talbot, Prioress of Polslo, 20s. ; to every Nun there 2s. To Walter Smale his red bed, of *worstede*, with curtains (*cum ridellis*), his best mattrass, a pair of blankets, and a pair of sheets ; also 20s. To John Rysby 100s. and a red bed *cum gallis*, with tapestry ; his second-best mattrass, one pair of his best blankets and 2 pairs of his second-best sheets ; a ewer and basin, a brass pot, a dish, and six tin plates "ygarneschit," one table cloth of Flemish work (*de opere Flandrino*), and 2 towels of Cornish material (*de panno Cornubico*). To Wm. Snowblonche 40s. and two coats with hoods, *de meis usitatis* ; also, *unum supellicium*, one pair of blankets, and one pair of sheets, and two vests, together with testator's linen garments ; also, a brass pot and a dish. For the fabrick, or the ornamentation of his Church of St. Petrock, 40s. To John Polfford, his servant, 20s., *cum una veste et capucio*. He leaves £10 to a priest to say Mass for his soul, for the souls of his parents, for Rob. Wilford and Elizabeth his wife, Simon Grendon, Rd. Wekyalond, and all his parishioners and benefactors. To John Rysby he bequeaths 11 volumes (to pray for the souls of

---

[1] "cum dorsorio . . . et bankario."

[2] *See* Will No. xxii., p. 390, *ad fin.* "pecium" i.q. "pecia" (*D'Arnis.*)

Simon Micham, and John Wendynburgh); these books were never to be alienated, but to go to his successor, and so on, from hand to hand, for ever. His Missal, noted, he bequeaths to the Church of St. Creed, in Cornwall, for the use of the parish-priest there for ever; also 20s. To Jas. Remyngton, chaplain, of London (to say Mass for his soul), he leaves 20s.

Executors:—Rob. Lyngham; Roger Polfford, Walter Smale, and John Rysby; to whom he leaves all the residue to deal with according to their discretion.

Proved, 23 June, 1418, before the Bishop, at Clyst.

Summa bonorum:—£210 6s. 1d.

LIV.—JOHN HOKERE, Vicar of Seaton.

Dated, at Seaton, 5 June, 1418. i, 331b.

He commends his soul to God; his body to be buried in the Chancel at Seaton. To John Bradefford, chaplain, he leaves his Breviary (*portiforium meum vocatum Jurnale*) a ewer and laver; also 8 marks (to say Mass for his soul, and for his parents for a year after his death). To his brother William the best of his two horses, his sword, and his bow and arrows. To Rd. Hokere, his cousin a silver girdle, and a sword silver-mounted (*unam spatam argento harnesiatam*). To Rd. Tawt, his servant, a horse. To Rd. Tyly a half share (*dimidietatem*) in a cow; and a like half share to Wm. Burnard. To John ȝeake a present (*unum donatum*). The residue to his brother William and John Bradefforde (*sic*), chaplain; whom he names his executors.

Proved, 11 July, 1418, before the Bishop, at Crediton.

Summa bonorum:—£30 10s.

LV.—THOMAS REYMOUND.

Dated, 8 June, examined and signed by testator, 3 Aug., 1418. i, 331b.

He commends his soul to God; his body to holy sepulture.

He leaves to the R. of Holsworthy, for tithes forgotten, 20s. To the Abbot, etc., of Tavistock, of Buckland, and of Forde, 20s. each; the same to Glasney: also, to the Prioress, etc., of Polslo, with the "*Liber Gestorum Karoli, Regis Francie.*" To the Prior, etc., of Frithelstock 13s. 4d. To the Prioress, etc., of Cornworthy 20s. To the Prior, etc., of Cowick he remits what they owed him on account of his pension. To the House of St. John Baptist, Exeter, 13s. 4d., and the deed (*cartam*) by which John Bolle gave to Rob. Pyle, clerk, the vacant plot of ground (*placeam*) on which the said Prior, etc., erected their new building. To St. Andrew's, Colebrook, 20s. He directs *Placebo* and *Dirige*, the Commendation, and a solemn Mass of Requiem, to be said in the choir of Crediton Church on, or before, the day of his burial, and distribution to be made to the Precentor, the Dean, the Canons, Vicars, and other Ministers then present, with ringing of the bells. To the Vicars he gives 8 marks; one of them to say Mass, daily, for two years, for K. Edward III. and K. Richard II.; also for Wm. Hody, Wm. Warde, Margery and Alice Lovelane, and Nich. Mol; for his benefactors, and for all whose goods he had in his possession, whether justly or unjustly, and all to whom he had ever done an injury. To the said Vicars he also leaves 20s. To the Friars Preachers and Friars Minors of Exeter, 13s. 4d. each. To the Leper Houses at Barnstaple and at Totnes, 4s. 1d. each, and to those at Exeter, Honiton, Plympton, Plymouth, Tavistock, and Torrington, 40d. each. To the store of St. Peter of Holsworthy, 43s. 4d., to provide there yearly, for ever, two wax lights of three pounds' weight, to be burnt before the Sepulchre at Easter. To the store of St. Katherine, of Holsworthy, two bullocks, two cows, and 12 sheep, to maintain his own obit, and those of Joan his wife, and their sons and daughters, of John Reymound and Sibil his wife, and of Wm. Symston and Sarah his wife; and to keep their names on the Roll of Intercessions for every Sunday in the year. To John Heysyll and Rd. Lyle, chaplain, 13s. 4d. each. To Thos. Cole, chaplain, 13s. 4d., and his *Agnus Dei*, set in silver. To John Knyf and John Dyre, chaplains, 6s. 8d. each. And, whereas John Copleston, senior, owed him, under a bond, 100s., he leaves him 40s., part thereof. To Thomas Noreys, who owed him the same sum (also under a bond), he leaves 20s., his *Nova Statuta de Lege*, and a book of *Placebo et Dirige*. To Thos. Copleston 6s. 8d. To Thos. Deneys 20s., and 10s. for a horse, all of which he owed testator. To every boy born of Katherine his sister, by her husband Wm. Hamptefforde,

13s. 4d. To Walter Quyddyssh 20s. To Rd. Symston 20s. and a coat with hood. To John Styl 20s. and a coat with hood, 2 doublets (*dobletes*) and a pair of shoes (j *par caligarum*). To Sarah Swathele 6s. 8d. To Rob. atte Wode 40s. and his crimson coat, furred with calaber (*cum calabre*), with hood of scarlet (*cum rubeo capicio de skarlet*); also an old jerkin (*unum Jakke antiquum*), a silver cup (*cifum*) called a little bow (*bolle*); the horse atte Wode was accustomed to ride, and testator's black girdle silver-mounted. To Rob. Russell 6s. 8d., and a coat with hood. To John Drake 5s. and a coat with hood. To Thos. Doune 40d. and a coat with hood. To John Snellard 40d. To Walter Jul 40d. or a young bullock. To Nicholas Nytheway 40d. To John Smale 40d. To John Welywort (to enable him to marry), 40s. in money; chattels to the value of seven marks; a bed, with two counterpanes (*lodicibus*) and two sheets; a pot, a dish, 4 platters of pewter (*platres de peautre*) 6 plates, and 2 salt cellars of the same. To Isolda Cole 5s. and a cow. To Alice Cole a young bullock. To Joan Bryan a heifer. To Joan and Alice Fabyan 20s. each; and to each of them a young bullock (*borectum*) and a heifer. To John Mokeworthy, of Holsworthy, 6s. 8d., a coat with hood, and a young bullock. To John Paulyn, junior, 5s. a coat with hood, and a cow. To Janinus (*Item lego Janino*), 40d. To Walter Judde 40d. and a heifer. To Roger Godman a young bullock three years old. To John Rytherdon, John Cotell, Hamon Southecomb, Thos. atte Nywecourte, and John Worthem, all the debt they owed testator for wheat bought of him. To Walter Hakker a young bullock. To Richd. Vyell 20d. To John Fayreby 20d. To Walter Prynsȝ, and his wife, 40d. To Rob. Oby 20d. To John Judde 40d. and a riding-coat. To Alice Jul a young bullock. To Nich. Rendy a cow. To Rob. Denyas a young bullock. To the prisoners (*prisonibus*) in the Bishop's gaol 5s. To the prisoners in the King's gaol 10s. To the chaplain of the lepers at Crediton 6s. 8d. To Margaret Welywort 40d. To Joan, his wife he bequeaths all his gold rings, and (for her lifetime) his best Missal and chalice, with the vestments, cruets (*fiolis*), and bell; to go after her death to Holsworthy Ch., that the parishioners might maintain their obits and those of their parents, and keep their names on the Roll of Intercessions for every Sunday in the year. Also, all his interest in his house at Exeter, called "Kellyysynne," with remainder to John Copleston junior, if she died before the determination thereof; also all his growing corn (*blada mea*) and hay for the year at Symston Lake and Wallen. To John Hacche 20s. and *Tercios meos de Lege*, formerly the property of John Wynkankton; also his best bow. To Robert [Pytman], Parson (*persone*) of the Church of Hollacombe, for tithes forgotten, 40d. To Walter Colyn a bullock. Four priests were to be found, to say Mass, at Holsworthy, for his soul, for two years after his death. To Roger Horne he leaves 3 sheep. To John Hond, chaplain, his worsted coat. To Thos. Lyle a heifer. To John Holand, Parson (*persone*) of St. Pancras' Ch., on account of oblations forgotten, 40d. To the store of St. Pancras' Ch., 40d. Any residue to be devoted to works of piety.

Executors:—John Grymston, Parson (*personam*) of Holsworthy; Joan, testator's wife; John Copleston, junior; Thos. Noreys; and Robert atte Wode; each to receive 40s. for his trouble.

Proved 24 August, 1418, before the Bishop, at Clyst.

Summa bonorum:—£419 5s. 4d.

LVI.—Richard Penels, Canon of Exeter.

Dated in the Close, Exeter, 28 December, 1418. i, 332b.

He commends his soul to the Most High and Undivided Trinity—Father, Son, and Holy Ghost, beseeching the Son of the Most Glorious Virgin Mary that, even as with His Precious Blood He redeemed it on the Altar of the Cross, so He would vouchsafe to keep, and defend, and save it from every spirit of evil. He desires that his body may be buried in the Cathedral; and to every Canon present on the occasion he leaves 20d.; to every Vicar 12d.; to every Annuellar 8d.; to every Secondary 6d.; to every Chorister 3d. For the Nave of Crediton Ch. he leaves £20; for the bridge at Chudleigh, 100s., on condition that the piers are built of stone; and for the new campanile of the Church of Moreton [Hampstead] 100s. His poor parishioners there to have 100s. to pray for his soul. Should the Bishop confer testator's Prebend of Crydy on John Schute, the said John was to have an antient chalice, and a small brass pot, which testator had, himself, received by the gift of John Sutton. To every poor priest in the Hospital of St. Gabriel at Clyst he leaves a coat. Forty marks to be divided among blind, lame, infirm, and poor persons in the Archdeaconry of Totnes, and that with all possible speed, employing trusty persons at testator's cost; he appropriates two marks thereof to the poor of Brixham. To the executors of Rd. Holrygge, late V. of Brixham 20s., for tithes due to them. Immediately after his death a thousand Masses to be said for his soul, &c., as quickly as possible, with the Collect *Deus Cui proprium major.* To Henry Webber 14 marks, to say Mass for his soul, (if he be promoted to the priesthood within the three terms of the year next after testator's death), and 20s. for the expenses of his Ordination; also, "*Sextum meum Decretalium cum uno Doctore; Innocencium meum; et antiquiora mea Decreta;*" also, the use of his Breviary, which was not to be alienated, but bequeathed to some poor priest, who would pass it on in like manner. To Rich. Chichestre his *Digestum vetus*, a small volume, et *Codicem meum* (and, as the said "Codex" [Justinian] was of small value, his executors were to buy another, suitable for the use of a scholar); also, "*Decretales meos;*" and he left him 100s., so that for three years he might have five nobles a year, and more if the executors saw fit and he continued in the schools. To his elder brother, Nicholas, testator leaves his second-best silver cup with the cover, the better of his two brass pots, and a dozen of his tin vessels. To his brother Thomas his third cup with its cover, and the 20s. which he owed. To his sister Joan his best cup and cover, 6 silver spoons, his red bed, with its curtains, —the last that he bought,—also 2 blankets, a pair of sheets (of those in good condition), a mattrass, and a *canevas*; also, five marks in money, and two small pots, his new ones of brass. To Rd. Marke, for tithes forgotten, and to pray for his soul, 13s. 4d. To Helias Stoke and Rob. Lyngham, 6s. 8d. each, to pray for his soul. To the Prior, &c., of the Hosp. of St. John, 13s. 4d. To the lepers (*leprosariis*) of St. Mary Magd. 6s. 8d.; to the poor boys of the Hosp. of St. John 6s. 8d. To John Sarger, chaplain, 3s. 4d. To Ralph, cousin of Rd. Mark, Thos. Hogge and John Cabyn, 3s. 4d. each. To the Prioress of Cornworthy two marks, viz., 13s. 4d. for herself, and 13s. 4d. among the nuns. To the R. of the Chapel of the Blessed Mary of Slapton 6s. 8d., and to the Brethren there 13s. 4d. among them, according to their rank. To John Hoper, chaplain, 40s., and the coat which testator bought against next Christmas—to pray for his soul. To John Seymere, chaplain, 13s. 4d. To John Whyteway 26s. 8d. To John Lydeford and his wife 6s. 8d. To Andrew Taylour 3s. 4d. To John Schute his silver salt-cellar and cover. To Thos., his Vicar-Choral, his cope (*capam*). To Roger Bolter his *Liber Decretorum* (if he consented to be overseer to his estate and to assist his executors.) To Wm. Trebel 6 silver spoons and a book called "Jon Aton," and his executors were not to demand the money that was between them, but the said William was to give it, himself, to the poor. To John Hytte, junior, and Wm. Dygher, he leaves 3s. 4d. each. To each boy of the Bishop's Chapel 12d. To John Bele the coat and hood which testator had of the livery of the Prior of Plympton (*quem habui, isto anno, de liberata Prioris Plymptonie*) and 6s. 8d. To John Bele his brown riding coat (*jupam equitalem brunei coloris*). To William, senior in the Bishop's kitchen 6s. 8d.

Executors:—His brother William (with 40s. and his two old silver cups, worth by weight 40s., for his trouble), and John Lane (to whom he leaves four marks.)

Proved, 23 January, 1418-19, before the Bishop, at Clyst.

LVII.—Laurence Haukyn, Precentor of the Cathedral, &c.

Dated at the Bishop's Manor of Clyst, 6 April, 1418. i, 333.

He commends his soul to his Creator, Who redeemed it with His Precious Blood; his body to sacred sepulture where God might please, i.e. near the place where he chanced to die; if in the Diocese, then in the midst of the Choir at Crediton, in the space between the choir-stalls; but if beyond the Diocese, as his executors, or any one of them, being present there, might determine, or as his friends should arrange. His funeral expenses were not, through worldly vain-glory, to exceed the bounds of moderation.

To his well-beloved lord, Edmund, Bishop of Exeter, he leaves his white satin vestment with corporal to match, and all the furniture of the altar, to wit 2 frontals, and 2 curtains of silk (*Tartaryn*), red and white, 2 consecrated towels of white linen: also a tablet (*Tabelletam*) of gold with the image of St. Peter. To Roger Bolter a silver cup called *le Brendelle Kow* (a legacy from Wm. Broun); also his best silver salt-cellar and cover. To Rd. Palmer an Antiphonar, quod incipit in secundo folio, "*Periculis*;" to be used by himself as long he pleased, and then handed on to other worthy priests, as long as it lasted; also a silver cup and cover—*cum cooperculo batere; cum stellis et aymelato cum* I. & P. *in summitate cooperculi*; also a pair of rosaries of coral (*par precularum de Coraill*), with a gold ring enamelled all round with divers images (*cum uno anulo circum diversis ymaginibus aymelato*). To Rd. More, his nephew, a silver cup, the cover engraved with a vine; his best *mazer*;[1] 12 of his best silver spoons; his *Legenda Aurea*, que incipit in secundo folio, "*De Festivitate*," to use till his death, the book to be passed on to other worthy priests, as long as it lasted; and he was to pray for the soul of John Clive[2] and for testator. To Sir Edw. Courtenay, knight, eldest son of the Earl of Devon, he leaves six silver goblets, with covers. To John Shute a Breviary, quod incipit in secundo folio "*peccato nos custodire*;" to use for life, and pass on as in the other cases; also a great silver bowl (*bolle*) and cover, with a silver pix (*cum una pixide vocata Powder Box*). To John Worthyn a silver cup and cover, with *Benedictus Deus* inscribed round the latter, and 12 of his second-best silver spoons. To John Arderne, Esquire, 100s. To John Wolston, clerk, 100s. His executors were to remunerate his servants at their discretion, according to grade and length of service, and the residue was to be disposed of for pious purposes as they should see fit.

Executors:—John Shute, clerk; John Arderne, Esquire, and John Wolston, clerk: with Roger Bolter and Rd. Palmer as *Overseers*.

Proved 3 February, 1418-19, before the Bishop at Clyst.

LVIII.—Thomas Clyfford, Canon of Exeter.

Dated on the Sunday next after the F. of St. Lucy the Virgin, i.e. 18 December 1418. i, 333b.

He commends his soul to Almighty God; his body to be buried in the Cathedral.

To St. Andrew's, Stokeinteignhead, he leaves a set of vestments of red velvet (*felwet*). To Rd. Clyfford a silver cup, with a cover having a small *bolle* on the top. To Matth. Stoke a silver cup, with a knop (*knappe.*) To John Clyfford, his brother, the fellow to the same (*sociam ejusdem pecii.*) To Wm. Clyfford, his brother, 20s. To Alice Lavoy a silver salt-cellar and cover; his best brass pot; and an iron spit (*broche de ferro.*) To Alice Clyfford, his sister, his best robe; to the aforesaid Alice Lavoy, his second-best; and to Isabella Bremely, his third and fourth. To Gunneta Gybbys, his fifth. To Rob. Parker, 40d. To Rd. Holever, 6s. 8d. To Rd. Marke, 6s. 8d. To the Sub-Dean of Exeter, 6s. 8d. To Wm. Bere, 2s. To Thos. Clyfford, his second brass pot. To John Stoke, 5s. The residue, after paying his debts, to be devoted to pious uses.

Executors:—John Clyfford, his brother; and Matthew Stoke.

Proved 28 February, 1418-19, before the Bishop, at Clyst.

LIX.—Sir Richard Champernoun, Knight.

Dated 26 February, 1418-19. i, 333b.

He commends his soul to God, and his body to sacred sepulture in his parish-church of Dodbrooke, by the side of the body of Katherine, his wife.

To his son Richard he leaves a plough, with eight oxen and all appurtenances thereof in Dodbrooke, and the half of all his sheep on the said Manor; also, a bed, one of his best silver cups, with cover, twelve of his best spoons, and a fourth part

---

[1] Meam *murram*; i.e., his cup made of *maple*, i.q., "mazer."

[2] The MS. is obscure: the name may be "Elme."

of his pots, dishes, and all his other utensils in London, stored in a certain cask or casks (*utensilium Londonie in quadam pipa sive in pipis existencium.*) To his son John he leaves another plough, with eight oxen, and all appurtenances at Innesworth, and half his sheep on that Manor; also another bed, and the third part of all his pots, dishes, and other utensils in London (as above). To the Wardens of his parish-church of St. Thomas of Dodbrooke he bequeaths a set of red vestments, of good quality, complete; also, a red cope; the parishioners of Dodbrooke to pray for his soul, for his wives and sons, and for all benefactors; also, his best Breviary. To John Kaynysham, his cousin, 20s. To John Kenylyon, his chaplain, 20s. To Wm. Colver 6s. 8d. The residue, after paying his debts, to be given to a priest, or priests, to say Mass in Dodbrooke Church, and receive for their stipend eight marks a year, provided that Mass were always said for his anchorite, giving herself continually to prayer, (*Anacorite mee continuo oratrici*), and that his servants were remembered according to their deserts and length of service.

Executors:—Rd. Champernoun, his son; Rd. Vaysy, R. of Bridford; Rd. Tryby, R. of Newton Ferrers; and Henry Drewe.

Proved, 3 April, 1419, before the Bishop, at Clyst.

Summa bonorum: £200 4s. 2d. ob.

LX.—Richard Palmer, Canon of Exeter, and R. of Ugborough.

Dated at Clyst Episcopi, 2 May, 1415. i, 334.

He commends his soul to God Almighty, Who redeemed it with His Precious Blood; his body to sacred burial. To his parish-church of Ugborough he leaves a new Missal, a new Gradual, and another of some age; also, a new Manual, a book called *Pars Oculi*, a *Legenda Sanctorum*, and two Processionals, to be kept in the Church, for use in Divine Worship, as long as they should last. To John Palmer, his brother, residing in the parish of Clyfton (Dioc. of Lichfield), he bequeaths 100s. To Thos. Waddon, his clerk, 40s. To each executor, if willing to serve, six marks; and they were to devote to pious uses any residue.

Executors:—Roger Bolter, and John Schute, chaplains.

Witnesses:—Walter Boway, notary-publick, R. of St. John-in-Cornwall; Thos. Greyston, R. of Farringdon; and Robert atte Wylle, clerk.

Proved, 17 April, 1419, before the Bishop, at Clyst.

ADDITIONAL NOTES TO THE WILLS:—

No. III., p. 379 (note 2).—It is possible that 'ovis' is a clerical error for 'ovi' (in which case vocat' would, of course, stand for 'vocati'). Mr. Greenfield sends me the following extract from the Will of John Hille, of Spaxton, dated 21 Oct., 1434:—"Item, Johanni, filio et heredi meo, unum ciphum de uno ovo vocato *a Grypeseg*, cum coopertorio de argento et deaurato."

No. IX., p. 383.—"*unum quaternum optimum de organis*'." This is obscure. Perhaps it means "an excellent quire of Organ-musick." I find "Liber Organicus" in the Inventory of 1506.

No. X., p. 384, line 5.—"*vnam govnam de frise vocat*' Mouster Villers." This word appears as 'musterdevyllys' in the will of Wm. Holcombe (Redmayne's Registr. fol. 27), quoted by Oliver; who states, in a note, that it "sometimes takes the grotesque form of *mustard-devils*, and is said to be a corruption of *moitié-develours*." "It has been plausibly derived," he adds, "from Montivilliers in Normandy (called Moustier Villiers in the 15th Century), the seat of a supposed manufactory" (*Monasticon*, p. 278, *note*). Line 21—"*de liberata*," i.e. "of the livery" (*see* p. 400, *line* 5, and p. 421, *ad finem*). Line 40—"*de carde*"; *see* p. 418, *note* 2. Line 44—"*de Curie*," i.e. "on Cookery." (W. D. M.)

No. XLII., p. 405.—"volo quod faciant me sepeliri infra triduum post mortem meam, vel quarto die de mane, ad ultimum." It is singular that Tregrisiow, who alone of our Testators gives instructions in his Will for a speedy burial, should be the only person of whom it is recorded in this Register that he was suffered to remain unburied for an unprecedented length of time. He died 25 July, 1415 (ii, 167b, 257)—"defuncto . . . . mensis Julii die vicesima quinta ; ipsiusque corpore *decimo nonc die mensis Augusti* ex tunc proximo sequenti reverenter ecclesiastice tradito sepulture" (ii, 169b). Apparently "*decimo* nono" is a mistake for "*nono*," on which day (*see* ii, 167b) the petition for the Election of a Dean was presented to the Bishop and granted ; and the above record proceeds thus—"licenciaque *postmodum* eligendi Decanum . . . . *petita et obtenta*, subsequenter, vicesimo tercio die ejusdem mensis Augusti"—the Chapter proceeded to the Election. Even then the interval would be a fortnight !

No. XLIV., p. 409, *ad finem*—"*Item Janyn de coquina* ; cf. p. 420, *line* 18.

No. XLVIII., p. 416, line 8—*toutdys en ioye* ; perhaps these words were worked on the hangings—a kind of motto, "always happy." Line 18.—"*Pavele* is perhaps a mis-spelling of *paille*, which in old French is sometimes spelt *paele* (W. D. M.) Line 33.—For *casu* read *cas*' ; perhaps. "*in uno castula*."—This Testator was a daughter of Sir Giles Daubeney, knt., of Baryngton, Somerset, who died 24 June, 1386. She was thrice married : 1st to Sir Wm. Percehay of Kyton, in the parish of Holcombe-Rogus, son and heir of Sir Henry Percehay, knt., one of the Justices of the Court of Common Pleas. She was his second wife, and he died, s.p., between Feb., 1383-4, and Feb., 1386-7 ; 2nd, before April, 1390, to Sir John Hulle, knt., one of the Justices of the Court of C. P., by whom she had issue two sons and a daughter. She was his 2nd wife, and he died 24 June, 1408 ; 3rd, before Sept., 1412, to Sir Rob. Latimer, knt., of Duntish, Dorset, as his second wife, by whom she had no issue. Her 'sister Chambernon' was Katherine, who married Sir Rd. Champernowne, of Modbury.—Rd. Mille was one of the feoffees of Sir Rob. Latimer of his manors of Dewlish and Child-Okford, on his marriage with Matilda, to hold to their joint issue, with remainder to his right heirs.—Wm. Jewe, of Canonlegh, Devon, was an executor of the will of Sir John Hulle, Matilda's former husband, who settled on her the manors of Wellysford and Bickleigh (B. W. G.)

No. LIV., p. 419, *line* 19—*unum donatum* : perhaps 'a Donatus,' the popular Latin Grammar (W. D. M.)

ORDINATIONS.

REGISTR., VOL. I. FF. CCXLIX—CCLXXXIX.

1. Per Fratrem Henricum, Ennachdunensem Episcopum, in Ecclesia Beate Marie majori, Civitatis Exoniensis (18 Sept., 1395); fol.[1] 249.—Per Dominum[1] in Ecclesia de Horseley (18 March, 1395-6), 249ᵇ.—**3.** In Capella Manerii sui de Horseley (1 April, 1396), *ibid.*—**4.** In Capella Hospicii sui Londonie (26 May, 1396), 250.—**5.** Per Fratrem Henricum Nony, Ardakanensem Episcopum, in Ecclesie B.M. majori (23 Dec., 1396), 250ᵇ.—**6.** Per eundem, in Ecclesia B.M. majori (22 Dec., 1397), 251.—**7.** Per Fratrem Henricum, Ennachdunensem Episcopum, in Ecclesia B.M. majori (21 Sept., 1398), 252.—**8.** In Capella Hospicii sui Londonie (15 March, 1398-9), 252ᵇ.—**9.** Ibidem (20 Sept., 1399), *ibid.*—**9a.** Ibidem (16 Nov., 1399), 253.—**10.** In Capella Manerii sui de Clyst (3 April, 1400), *ibid.*—**11.** Ibidem (17 April, 1400), 253ᵇ.—**12.** Apud Tottoniam (13 May, 1400), 254.—**13.** Apud Slapton (14 May, 1400), *ibid.*—**14.** Apud Modbury (15 May, 1400), *ibid.*—**15.** Apud Plympton (16 May, 1400), *ibid.*—**16.** Ibidem (17 May, 1400), *ibid.*—**17.** Apud Tavystoke (18 May, 1400), *ibid.*—**18.** Apud Holdesworthy (19 May, 1400), *ibid.*—**19.** Apud Hertylond (20 May, 1400), *ibid.*—**20.** Apud Frytelstoke (21 May, 1400), 254ᵇ.—**21.** Apud Tauton (22 May, 1400), *ibid.*—**22.** Apud Pylton (23 May, 1400), *ibid.*—**23.** In Eccles. sua Colleg. Criditonensi (12 June, 1400), *ibid.*—**23a.** Apud Criditon (24 Aug., 1400), 255.—**24.** In Prioratu Sancti Germani (30 Aug., 1400), *ibid.*—**25.** Apud Leskyrd (1 Sept., 1400), *ibid.*—**26.** Apud Trewardrayth (2 Sept., 1400), *ibid.*—**27.** Apud Grampount (3 Sept., 1400), *ibid.*—**28.** Apud Penryn (4 Sept., 1400), *ibid.*—**29.** Apud Carmynow (7 Sept., 1400), *ibid.*—**30.** In Prioratu Sancti Michaelis (8 Sept., 1400), 255ᵇ.—**31.** In Prioratu predicto (9 Sept., 1400), *ibid.*—**32.** Apud Sanctum Carentocum (10 Sept., 1400), *ibid.*—**33.** Apud Powton [St. Breoke] (12 Sept., 1400), *ibid.*—**34.** Apud Botreaux Castel (16 Sept., 1400), *ibid.*—**35.** In Prioratu Lancestonensi (18 Sept., 1400), *ibid.*—**36.** Apud Bradeworthy (19 Sept., 1400), 256.—**37.** Apud Hatherlegh (20 Sept., 1400), *ibid.*—**38.** In Capella Manerii sui de Chuddelegh (18 Dec., 1400), *ibid.*—**39.** In Capella Hospicii sui Londonie (28 May, 1401), 256ᵇ.—**40.** Ibidem (20 May, 1402), *ibid.*—**41.** Ibidem (23 Sept., 1402), *ibid.*—**42.** Ibidem (23 Dec., 1402), 257.—**43.** Ibidem (10 March, 1402-3), *ibid.*—**44.** In Capella Manerii sui de Clyst (31 March, 1403), 258.—**45.** In Eccles. Colleg. Criditonensi (22 Sept., 1403), *ibid.*—**46.** In Capella Manerii sui de Chuddelegh (22 Dec., 1403), 259.—**47.** In Capella Manerii sui de Clyst (23 Feb., 1403-4), 259ᵇ.—**48.** Ibidem (15 March, 1403-4), 260.—**49.** Ibidem (19 March, 1403-4), 260ᵇ.—**50.** Ibidem (24 May, 1404), *ibid.*—**51.** Apud Holdesworthy (18 June, 1404), 261.—**52.** Apud Toryton (24 June, 1404), *ibid.*—**53.** Apud Tauton (25 June, 1404), *ibid.*—**54.** Apud North Molton (26 June, 1404), *ibid.*—**55.** Apud Clyst (14 Aug., 1404), *ibid.*—**56.** Apud Ayschperton (23 Aug., 1404), *ibid.*—**57.** Apud Peyngton (25 Aug., 1404), *ibid.*—**58.** Apud Kynggesbrygge (27 Aug., 1404), *ibid.*—**59.** Apud Plympton (28 Aug., 1404), *ibid.*—**60.** Apud Tavystoke (30 Aug., 1404), 261ᵇ.—**61.** In Capella Manerii sui de Clyst (20 Sept., 1404), *ibid.*—**62.** In Capella Manerii sui de Criditon (20 Dec., 1404), 262. **63.** Ibidem (14 March, 1404-5), *ibid.*—**64.** Ibidem (18 April, 1405), 262ᵇ.—**65.** Apud Lawhytton (8 May, 1405), 263.—**66.** Apud Cuttyngbeke (10 May, 1405), *ibid.*—**67.** Apud Lostwythyel (12 May, 1405), *ibid.*—**68.** Apud Grampound (13 May, 1405), *ibid.*—**69.** Apud Penryn (14 May, 1405), *ibid.*—**70.** Ibidem (15 May, 1405), *ibid.*—**71.** Apud Marcasyow [Market-Jew—Marazion] (16 May, 1405), 263ᵇ.—**72.** Apud Sanctam Neulinam (19 May, 1405), *ibid.*—**73.** In Manerio suo de Pauton [in St. Breoke] (21 May, 1405), *ibid.*—**74.** Apud Bodmyn (23 May, 1405), 264.—**75.** Apud Lanteglos (24 May, 1405), *ibid.*—**76.** Apud Lawhytton (26 May

[1] The words 'fol.' and 'Per Dominum' will not be repeated throughout; all the Ordinations are by the Bishop of the Diocese unless otherwise expressly stated.

1405), *ibid.*—**77**. Apud Chuddelegh (6 June, 1405), *ibid.*—**78**. In Capella Manerii sui Criditonensis (13 June, 1405), *ibid.*—**79**. Ibidem (19 Sept., 1405), 264^{b}.—**80**. In Capella Manerii sui de Clyst (19 Dec., 1405), 265.—**81**. Ibidem (18 Sept., 1406), *ibid.*—**82**. Ibidem (18 Dec., 1406), 266.—**83**. Ibidem (19 Feb., 1406-7), *ibid.*—**84**. In Ecclea. Colleg. Criditonensi (12 March, 1406-7), 266^{b}.—**84a**. Ibidem (25 March, 1407), *ibid.*—**85**. Ibidem (21 May, 1407), 267.—**86**. Ibidem (24 Sept., 1407), *ibid.*—**87**. Apud Toryton Magnam (7 Oct., 1407), 267^{b}.—**88**. In Ecclea. Colleg. Criditonensi (17 Dec., 1407), 268.—**89**. Ibidem (10 March, 1407-8), 268^{b}.—**90**. Ibidem (31 March 1408), 269.—**91**. Ibidem (9 June, 1408), *ibid.*—**92**. Ibidem (22 Sept., 1408), 270.—**93**. Ibidem (22 Dec., 1408), 270^{b}.—**94**. Ibidem (2 March, 1408-9), *ibid.*—**95**. Ibidem (23 March, 1408-9), 271.—**96**. *Ordinati per Dominum ad primam tonsuram diversis locis et temporibus* [between 23 March, 1408-9, and 1 June, 1409], 271^{b}.—**97**. In Ecclea. Colleg. Criditonensi (1 June, 1409), 272^{b}.—**98**. Ibidem (20 Sept., 1409), 273.—**98a**. Ibidem (6 Dec., 1409), *ibid.*—**99**. Ibidem (21 Dec., 1409), *ibid.*—**100**. Apud Honyton (19 May, 1410), 273^{b}.—**101**. Apud Criditon (14 June, 1410), *ibid.*—**102**. In Palacio suo Exoniensi (26 June, 1410), *ibid.*—**103**. Ibidem (25 July, 1410), *ibid.*—**104**. In Ecclea. Colleg. Criditonensi (20 Sept., 1410), *ibid.*—**105**. Ibidem (23 Sept., 1410), 274.—**106**. Apud Manerium de Tavton Episcopi (18 Oct., 1410), *ibid.*—**107**. Ibidem (19 Oct., 1410), 274^{b}.—**108**. Ibidem (21 Oct., 1410), *ibid.*—**109**. Ibidem (25 Oct., 1410), *ibid.*—**110**. Ibidem (26 Oct., 1410), *ibid.*—**111**. Ibidem (27 Oct., 1410), *ibid.*—**112**. Ibidem (28 Oct., 1410), *ibid.*—**113**. Ibidem (30 Oct., 1410), *ibid.*—**114**. In Ecclea. Colleg. Criditonensi (20 Dec., 1410), 274^{b}.—**115**. Ibidem (7 March, 1410-11), 275.—**116**. In Capella infra Manerium suum Criditonense (28 March, 1411), 276.—**117**. Apud Ayschperton (5 May, 1411), 276^{b}.—**118**. In Capella sua de Peyngton (6 May, 1411), *ibid.*—**119**. Ibidem (7 May, 1411), *ibid.*—**120**. Ibidem (8 May, 1411), *ibid.*—**121**. Apud Kyng (*sic*) ["Kingsbridge"] (9 May, 1411), *ibid.*—**122**. Apud Plympton (10 May, 1411), *ibid.*—**123**. Apud Tottoniam (7 May (*sic*), 1411), *ibid.*—**124**. Apud Plymmouth (11 May, 1411), 277.—**125**. Apud Tavystok (12 May, 1411), *ibid.*—**126**. Apud Hall [i.e., Holsworthy] (13 May, 1411), *ibid.*—**127**. Apud Hertlond (14 May, 1411), *ibid.*—**128**. Apud Haterlegh (15 May, 1411), *ibid.*—**129**. In Ecclea. Colleg. Criditonensi (6 June, 1411), *ibid.*—**130**. Apud Criditon (22 Aug., 1411), 277^{b}.—**131**. Ibidem (19 Sept. 1411), *ibid.*—**132**. In Manerio suo de Codynbeke [Cuddenbeak] (29 Sept., 1411), 278.—**133**. Ibidem (30 Sept., 1411), *ibid.*—**134**. Apud Lyskert (1 Oct., 1411), *ibid.*—**135**. Apud Lostwythyel (2 Oct., 1411), *ibid.*—**136**. Apud Grampond (3 Oct., 1411), *ibid.*—**137**. Apud Trewrew (3 Oct., 1411), *ibid.*—**138**. In Manerio suo de Penryn (4 Oct., 1411), 278^{b}.—**139**. Ibidem (5 Oct., 1411), *ibid.*—**140**. Apud Marvysiow [Market-Jew] (8 Oct., 1411), *ibid.*—**141**. Apud Lananta [Lelant] (9 Oct., 1411), *ibid.*—**142**. Apud Redruth (10 Oct., 1411), *ibid.*—**143**. In Capella Sancti Francisci apud Medschole [Mitchell] (11 Oct., 1411), *ibid.*—**144**. In Manerio suo de Pavton (12 Oct., 1411), *ibid.*—**145**. Apud Bodmyn (14 Oct., 1411), *ibid.*—**146**. Apud Lanteglys (15 Oct., 1411), 279.—**147**. Apud Lawhytton (19 Oct., 1411), *ibid.*—**148**. In Ecclea. Colleg. de Otery Sancte Marie (15 Dec., 1411), *ibid.*—**149**. In Capella infra Manerium suum Criditonense (19 Dec., 1411), *ibid.*—**150**. In Manerio suo de Peyngton (27 Feb., 1411-12), 279^{b}.—**151**. In Capella infra Manerium suum Criditonense (19 March, 1411-12), *ibid.*—**152**. In Capella infra Manerium suum de Clyst (28 May, 1412), 280.—**153**. Ibidem (13 July, 1412), 280^{b}.—**154**. Ibidem (24 Sept., 1412), *ibid.*—**155**. Ibidem (13 Dec., 1412), 281^{b}.—**156**. Ibidem (17 Dec., 1412), *ibid.*—**157**. Ibidem (19 Jan., 1412-13), 282.—**158**. In Palacio suo Exoniensi (22 Aug., 1413), *ibid.*—**159**. In Capella infra Manerium suum de Clyst (23 Sept., 1413), *ibid.*—**160**. Ibidem (20 Dec., 1413), 282^{b}.—**161**. Apud Chuddelegh (26 Jan., 1413-14) 283.—**162**. Apud Clyst (16 Feb., 1413-14), *ibid.*—**163**. Ibidem (3 March, 1413-14), *ibid.*—**164**. Ibidem (24 March, 1413-14), 283^{b}.—**165**. Ibidem (25 June, 1414), 284.—**166**. Apud Blakesueton (25 Sept. 1414), *ibid.*—**167**. Apud Kyngysbrygge (26 Sept., 1414), *ibid.* **168**. Ibidem (27 Sept., 1414), *ibid.*

169. Apud Barum Dominus Willelmus Salobriensis (*sic*) Episcopus ac Suffraganeus Domini ordinavit (22 Aug., 1414), *ibid.*

Idem Suffraganeus ordinavit :—
170. Apud Criditon (24 Aug.)—**171**. Apud Plympton (28 Aug.)—**172**. Apud Tavystoke (30 Aug.)—**173**. Apud Launceston (31 Aug.)—**174**. Apud Calyngton (31 Aug.)—**175**. Apud Sanctum Germanum (1 Sept.)—**176**. Apud Loswythyel (2 Sept.)—**177**. Apud Grampond (3 Sept.)—**178**. Apud Treurew (3 Sept.)—**179**. Apud Penryn (4 Sept.)—**180**. Apud Markysyow [Market-Jew] (5 Sept.)—**181**. Apud Metschole [Mitchell], (6 Sept.)—**182**. Apud Sanctam Columbam (7 Sept.)—all in 1414, and on fol. 284ᵇ.
Also, **183**. Apud Padystow (7 Sept.)—**184**. Apud Bodman (8 Sept.)—**185**. Ibidem (9 Sept.)—**186**. Apud Camelford (10 Sept.)—**187**. Apud Wyke Sancte Marie (10 Sept.)—**188**. Apud Hollysworthy (12 Sept.) **189**. Apud Hertland (13 Sept.)—**190**. Apud Toryton (14 Sept.)—**191**. Apud Okampton (15 Sept.)—**192**. Apud Criditon (17 Sept.)—all in 1414; fol. 285. Per Dominum :—
193. In Capella infra Manerium suum de Clyst (22 Sept. 1414), 285.—**194**. Ibidem (23 Sept., 1414), 286.—**195**. Ibidem (16 Nov., 1414), *ibid.*—**196**. Ibidem (23 Nov., 1414), *ibid.*—**197**. Ibidem (22 Dec., 1414), *ibid.*—**198**. Ibidem (23 Feb., 1414-15), 286ᵇ.—**199**. Ibidem (16 March, 1414-15), 287ᵇ.—**200**. Ibidem (15 April, 1415.)—**201**. Ibidem (4 May, 1415), 288.—**202**. Ibidem (25 May, 1415), *ibid.*—**203**. Ibidem (13 July, 1415), 288ᵇ.—**204**. Ibidem (7 Aug., 1415), *ibid.*—**205**. Ibidem (21 Sept., 1415), *ibid.*
206. Ibidem (21 Dec., 1415)—per Willelmum Solubriensem Episcopum, 289.
207. Ibidem (2 April, 1416), 289ᵇ [per Dominum].
208. Ibidem (4 April, 1416), per Willelmum Solubriensem Episcopum, *ibid.*
Also, per eundem Suffraganeum :—**209**. Ibidem (5 April)—**210**. Ibidem (6 April)—**211**. Apud Morton (5 May.)—**212**. Apud Bukfastlegh (7 May.)—**213**. Apud Tottoniam (8 May.)—**214**. Apud Kynggesbrygge (10 May.)—**215**. Apud Plympton (11 May.)—**216**. Apud Plymmouth (12 May.)—all in 1416; fol. 289ᵇ.
217. Apud Tavystoke (13 May.)—**218**. Apud Launceston (14 May.)—**219**. Apud Loskyrek (16 May.)—**220**. Apud Lostwythyell (18 May.)—**221**. Apud Grampont (19 May.)—**222**. Apud Penryn (20 May.)—**223**. Apud Helston (21 May.)—**224**. Apud Markesyew (22 May.)—all in 1416, fol. 290.
Also per eundem,—**225**. Apud Rudruthe (23 May.)—**226**. Apud Medschole [Mitchell] (24 May.)—**227**. Apud Sanctam Columbam (24 May.)—**228**. Apud Bodmyn (25 May.)—**229**. Apud Camelford (26 May.)—**230**. Apud Wyke [*i.e.*, Wyke-St.-Mary], (27 May.)—**231**. Apud Hallysworthy (28 May,)—**232**. Apud Hertylond (29 May.)—**233**. Apud Toryton (30 May.)—**234**. Apud Barum (31 May.)—**235**. Apud Southmolton (1 June.)—**236**. Apud Hatherlegh (2 June.)—**237**. Apud Okampton (3 June.)—**238**. Apud Criditon (4 June.)—**239**. Apud Bradenynch (8 June.)—**240**. Apud Colmpton (10 June.)—all in 1416, and on fol. 290ᵇ.
241. In Capella infra Manerium de Clyst (13 June, 1416), per eundem Suffraganeum; 291.
242. Ibidem (19 Sept., 1416), 291ᵇ [per Dominum].
243. Ibidem (19 Dec., 1416), per eundem Suffraganeum, *ibid.*
[Per Dominum] :—**244**. Ibidem (6 March, 1416-17), 292. **245**. Ibidem (5 June, 1417), *ibid.* **246**. Ibidem (30 June, 1417), *ibid.* **247**. Ibidem (30 Aug., 1417), *ibid.*
248. Ibidem (18 Sept., 1417) per Dominum Ricardum, Catenensem Episcopum, *ibid.* Also in 1417, per eundem Suffraganeum :—
249. Apud Morton (21 Sept.)—**250**. Apud Ayschperton (23 Sept.)—**251**. Apud Kynggesbrygge (26 Sept.)—**252**. Apud Plymmouth (28 Sept.)—**253**. Apud Tavystoke (29 Sept.)—**254**. Apud Launston (1 Oct.)—**255**. Apud Sanctum Germanum (2 Oct.)—**256**. Apud Lyskyrek (3 Oct.)—**257**. Apud Lostwythyell (4 Oct.)—**258**. In Eccles. Sancti Austoli (5 Oct.)—**259**. Apud Truru (7 Oct.)—**260**. Apud Penryn (8 Oct.)—**261**. Apud Markysyow (9 Oct.)—**262**. Apud Rudruth (10 Oct.)—**263**. In Eccles. Sancte Columbe (11 Oct.)—**264**. Apud Bodmyn (12 Oct.)—**265**. Apud Camylford (13 Oct.)—**266**. Apud Hallysworthy (15 Oct.)—**267**. Apud Hertylond (16 Oct.)—all in 1417, and on fol. 293ᵇ.
Also **268**. Apud Barstapul (17 Oct.)—**269**. Apud Haterlegh (20 Oct.)—**270**. In Eccles. Colleg., Criditonensi (22 Oct.)—**271**. Apud Tuverton (24 Oct.)—all in 1417, and on fol. 294.

272. Apud Clyst (18 Dec., 1417,) *ibid.* [per Dominum].
273. Ibidem (19 Feb., 1417-18,) per eundem Suffraganeum, *ibid.*
[Per Dominum] :—**274** Ibidem. (28 April, 1418,) 295. **275.** Ibidem (24 May 1418), *ibid.* **276.** Ibidem (25 May, 1418), *ibid.* **277.** Ibidem (31 May, 1418), *ibid.*
278. Ibidem (24 Sept., 1418), per eundem Suffraganeum, *ibid.* **279.** In Capella Beate Marie, in parte Orientali infra Ecclesiam Cathedralem Exoniensem situata (26 Sept., 1418),—per eundem Suffraganeum, 295b.
280. Apud Clyst (16 Dec., 1418), *ibid.* [per Dominum].
281. In Eccles. Conventuali Monasterii de Forde (17 Dec., 1418.) *ibid.*—**282.** Apud Clyst (11 March, 1418-19), *ibid.* [per eundem Suffraganeum].
283. Apud Axmynstre (20 April.)—**284.** Apud Otery Sancte Marie (22 April.) **285.** Apud Ayschpertou (26 April.)—**286.** Apud Villam Tottoniam (28 April)—all in 1419, per Willelmum, Catenensem Episcopum ; 296b.
287. Apud Derthemouth (29 April.)—**288.** Apud Kyngysbrygge (30 April.)—**289.** Apud Modbyry (2 May)—**290.** Apud Plympton (3 May.)—**291.** Apud Plymmouth (4 May.)—**292.** Apud Tavystoke (5 May).—**293.** Apud Launceston (6 May.)—**294.** Apud Villam Sancti Germani (9 May.)—**295.** Apud Leskyret 10 May.)—**296.** Apud Lostwythyel (11 May.)—**297.** Apud Sanctum Austolum (11 May.)—**298.** Apud Villam de Tregony (12 May.)—**299.** Apud Truru (13[1] May.)—**300.** Apud Penryn (14 May.)—**301.** Apud Helston (15 May.) —**302.** Apud Markesyew (17 May.)—all in 1419, per eundem Suffraganeum ; fol. 297.
303. Apud Ruddruth (18 May.)—**304.** Apud Sanctam Columbam (19 May.) **305.** Apud Bodmyn (20 May.)—**306.** Apud Camylford (21 May.)—**307.** Apud Hallysworthy (23 May.)—**308.** Apud Hertylond (25 May.)—**309.** Apud Toryton (26 May.)—**310.** Ibidem (28 May.)—**311.** Apud Barum (29 May.)—**312.** Apud Southmolton (29 May.)—**313.** Apud Chylmelegh (30 May.)—**314.** Apud Hatherlegh (31 May).—**315.** Apud Samford Courtenay (2 June.[2])—**316.** Apud Criditon (4 June.)—**317.** Apud Tuverton (8 June.)—**318.** Ibidem (9 June.)—all in 1419, per eundem Suffraganeum, fol. 297b.
319. Apud Clyst (10 June, 1419), per Ricardum, Catenensem Episcopum, 298.

LISTS OF PERSONS ORDAINED.

The figures correspond with the numbers in the above List.

Where more references than one are given, it must be understood that two or more persons bearing the same name are mentioned once ; not the same person more than once ; e.g., "Smyth, John," with *ten* references, stands for ten persons called "John Smyth," who were admitted *ad primam tonsuram* by Bishop Stafford, and at different times.—An asterisk signifies "*Illegitimus*, cum quo Dominus dispensavit."—"L. D."—Letters Dimissory.

I. TONSURATI.

Abbas, John, 70 ; Hy., 96.—Abbot,* Dirlingus, 46 ; Walter, 122.—Abda, Rd. 136.—Abraham, Rd., 205.—Achov, Rd., 74.—Achym, Simon, 96.—Adam, Michael, 185, 288 ; Thos., 215 ; Wm., 282.—Adelerd, Rd., 238.—Adow, John, 96.—Affeton, John, 1.—Alas, Thos., 33.—Alchon, Rd., 28.—Ales, Rd., 96.—Alger, John, 122.—Aller, Thos., 99.—Alot, John, 140.—Alrede, John, 121.—Alsewyll, Rd., 14.—Alva, Rd., 306.—Aly, John, 13.—Alyn, Baldwin, 19 ; Wm., 13.—Alynlugh, John, 222.—Ambros, John, 171.—Amdow, Wm., 138.—Amys, John, 302.—Anderton, Nich. 231.—Andru (or Andrew). Andrew, 38 ; John, 193 ; Peter, 304 ; Rd., 253 ; Robert, 96 ; Simon, 279 ; Wm.,* 96.—Antron, John, 96 ; Wm., 140.—Anwan, John, 73.—Apuldur, Wm., 309.—Archer,* John, 70.—Aredon, John, 14.—Arundell, Wm., 177.—Atkin, John, 276.—atte Beare, John, 7.—atte Cleve, Steph. 108.—atte Feelde, Dioc. Lond. (L. D.), 162.—atte Hole, John, 210.—atte More, John, 23 ; Henry, 10.—atte Roke, Thos., 217.—atte Wode, John, 241 ; Thos. 99.—atte Wylle, Alexander, 108 ; John, 89, 91, 122, 167, 316 ; Thos., 248 ; Wm.

[1] 3 May (Cler. Error) in MS. [2] July (Cler. Error) in MS.

114.—Atteyeo, John, 88.—Avdeley, John, 234.—Auger, John, 75.—Autred, Thos., 184.—Avery, Gervase, 91 ; Rob., 97 ; Thos., 231 ; Walter, 231.—Ayer, John, 129.—Aylword, John, 10.—Ayre, John, 51.—Aysch (or Aysach), Edw., 307 ; John, 1, 12, 231 ; Thos., 310.—Ayschelegh, John, 58.—Aysschecote, John, 36 ; Ayscote, Rd., 137.—Ayscherygge, Wm., 205.—Ayschslake, Roger, 85.—Aysse,* Robert, 87.

Bacheler, John, 121, 253 ; Ralph, 140.—Bacun, Wm., 234.—Badelham, Wm., 25.—Badeworthy, Nich., 52.—Bagge, Thos., 91.—Bagruge, Matth., 80 ; Bahow, Thos., 29.—Bake, Rob., 96 ; Roger, 294 ; Walter, 235.—Bakere, John, 15, 53, 82, 124, 206 ; Nich., 121 ; Rd. 22, 154 ; Thos., 122, 279.—Baker, Wm., 85, 129.—Bakyn, John, 173.—Balle, Edw., 317 ; John, 231.—Baly, Thos., 34.—Banewyll, Wm., 160.—Bapton, John, 97.—Bara, John, 179.—Barbour, John, 120 ; Steph., 23.—Barlebyen, John, 114.—Barlych, John, 12.—Barnehous, Thos., 193.—Baron, Hy., 302 ; Roger, 77.—Barre, John, 310.—Barry, John, 53 ; Wm., 86.—Barstaple,* John, 127.—Bastard, John, 285 ; Rd., 149.—Bata, John, 91.—Batyn, Hugh, 87 ; John, 290, 319 ; Walter, 63.—Baudon, John, 26.—Baudyn, John, 96 ; Thos., 7.—Bavnton, John, 98 ; Rd., 198.—Bayly,* John, 156 ; Nich., 91.—Bay, John, 222.—Bayvyn, John, 10.—Beachym, Peter, 96.—Beaforde, Wm., 104.—Bean, Michael, 73 ; Thos., 71 ; Bedyll, John, 222.—Bele, John, 10 ; Rd., 241.—Belleworthy, Thos., 61.—Beuet, John, 145 ; Thos., 137 ; Wm., 55, 298.—Benny, John, 96.—Benny*, Walter, 96 ; Wm.,* 96.—Bem, Thos., 219.—Berbal, John, 65.—Berd, Wm., 125.—Bere, *or* Beare, Baldwin, 234 ; John, 10. 38, 74, 75, 313 ; Rd., 25. 184 ; Thos., 76 ; Wm., 149, 193, 279.—Berewyk, Udo, 298.—Bermesdon, John, 266 ; Nich., 266.—Bern, John, 127.—Bernard, Wm., 255, 273.—Bertlot, John, 184.—Bertumstede, John, 66.—Berwyk, John, 96.—Beste, Thos., 171.—Beton. John, 218.—Betty, John, 228.—Beverdy, Thos., 311.—Bikelake, Wm., 91.—Bircomb, Rd., 155.—Blachaller, *or* Blacaller, Hy., 66 ; Rd., 132.—Blake, John, 122 ; Wm., 122.—Blakehall, *or* Blakhall, John, 122, 214 ; Wm. 12.—Blakehay, Wm., 246.—Blaklonde, *or* Blakelond, John, 197 ; Wm., 148.—Blewethe, John, 228.—Bluet, John, 7.—Bleyndene, Roger, 73.—Bloke, Rob., 228.—Bloye, Wm., 98.—Blyȝghe, John, 173.—Bochyn, Nich., 273.—Bockebure, Rd., 235.—Boddych, John, 16.—Bodegoode, John, 218.—Botrygan, Otho, 182.—Bodrygan, Wm., 56, 139.—Bodrygy, John, 273 ; Matth.,* 96—Bodulget, Wm., 300.—Body, John, 96, 219 ; Tho., 226.—Bodyn, John, 96.—Bodystou, John, 23.—Bogewaye, Nich., 11.—Boggebrok, John, 80.—Boghedon, John, 97.—Bogheton, Rd., 75 ; Roger, 1.—Boghelegh, Thos., 250.—Bokelly, John, 173.—Bokelond, John, 122, 148.—Bokeram, Steph., 122.—Bokynham, Rd., 236.—Boldebury, Wm., 23.—Bole,* John, 200.—Bolegh, Nich., 228.—Bolepyt, Wm., 76.—Boleven, John, 13.—Bolham, Rd., 180 ; Thos., 91 ; Bollam, John, 29, 312.—Bolter, John, 160 ; Thos., 213.—Bonde, Hy., 310 ; John, 83, 243 ; Roger, 51.—Bonok, Wm., 176.—Bonsta, John, 18.—Bont, Rob., 219.—Borage, John, 115.—Borlase, Andr., 73.—Borsdone, Rob., 191.—Boryton, John, 273.—Bosantwyth, Ralph, 140.—Boscawen, John, 96.—Bosfrawell, John, 223.—Boskenen, Hy., 261.—Bosoun, Ralph, 149 ; Wm., 194.—Bosset, Peter 226.—Bost, Wm., 71.—Bosvetheke, Peter, 222.—Boswarnan, John, 224.—Boswarnek, Thos., 232.—Boswarweth, John, 71.—Boswaye, John, 179.—Boswegow, John, 226.—Boteler, Rob., 61 ; Wm., 91.—Botelwrth, Rd., 231.—Boterel, John, 60 ; Wm., 299.—Botryavx, Wm., 227.—Botrywyly, John, 96.—Botston, John, 152.—Bovy, John, 24, 305 ; Roger, 140 ; Thos., 71.—Bowe, John, 212.—Bowedon, John, 87 ; Bowdon, John, 205.—Bowode, Wm., 121.—Bowre, Wm., 236.—Bowryng, John, 251 ; Wm., 251.—Boys, Rob., 58, 122 ; Walter, 96 ; Wm., 193.—Braas, Walter, 190.—Brabon, John, 28 ; Reginald, 305.—Brace, John, 294.—Braddele, Roger, 216.—Brademore, Wm., 120.—Brag, John, 18.—Bras, John, 257.—Bray, John, 26 ; Reginald, 275 ; Rd., 295 ; Thos., 96, 139,* 245 ; Nich.,* 25.—Brays, John, 74.—Bre, Hy., 223 ; John, 96.—Breand, Wm,, 96.—Brece, Ralph, 71.—Bree, Edw., 71 ; Rd., 96.—Bremelegh, Rd., 92.—Brendon, John, 310.—Brenwoȝe, John, 233.—Brether, John, 211.—Briton, Wm., 260 ; John, 36, 307.—Brode, Rd., 231, 286.—Broke, Hy., 129.—Bromboyt, John, 96.—Bromhouse, John, 54.—Bronde, Jas., 51.—Brond, Thos., 17.—Broun, Hamund, 152 ; Thos., 59.—Browne, John, 218, 256.—Brownwyche, Thos., 235.—Brounyng, *or* Brownyng, John, 63 ; Simon, 147 ; Thos., 233 ; Wm., 96, 99.—Browne, *or* Broun, John, 264,

85 ;* Ralph, 180 ; Thos., 91.—Brownebody, John, 220.—Bruer, John, 96.—Brugeman, Walter, 87.—Brugge, John, 121.—Brygge, Reginald, 129.—Brune, Wm., 9.—Bryan, Reginald, 96 ; Steph., 44.—Bryce, Ralph, 318.—Bryden, *or* Brydden, Rd., 91 ; Martin, 234.—Brydescombe, Rd., 79 ; Bryddyscomb, John, 202.—Brydon, John, 290.—Brygand, Wm., 197.—Brygges, John, 108.—Brygman, Roger, 269.—Brys, Rd., 52.—Brystow, John, 122.—Budde, John, 86, 168 ; Walter, 282.—Buf, John, 85.—Bulsy, John, 279 ; Rd., 132.—Burd, Steph., 243.—Burgan, Thos., 129 ; Wm., 279.—Burges, John, 193 ; Thos., 96.—Burgeys, Thos., 282.—Burgh, Walter, 160.—Burlegh, John, 10.—Burle, Roger, 13.—Burnard, Rd., 66.—Burnet, John, 18.—Bury, Walter, 91.—Busse, Thos., 61.—Bussow, Steph., 141.—Butde, Geoffrey, 222 ; Butte, John, 52.—Byen, Ralph, 154.—Bykebyry, Rd., 184.—Byle, Rob., 291.—Byllowse, John, 144.—Byrche, John, 88.—Byry, Rd., 309.—Byssop, Wm., 57 ; Busschop, Rd., 18.

Cade, John, 173.—Cady, John, 312.—Calaway, David, 265.—Calow, Thos., 260.—Calwe, Thos., 172.—Came,* Rd., 142.—Canon, John, 91.—Canteryll, Wm., 200.—Cambern, Roger, 91.—Camela, Gervase, 74.—Capell, John, 216 ; Peter, 176.—Carbous, Alan, 140 ; Hy. 140.—Carbulek, Simon, 301.—Carburra, Thos., 145.—Carbury, Wm., 74.—Carbure, Wm., 305.—Cardeny, John, 180.—Carklond, Rd., 52.—Carleton, Rob., 97 ; Steph., 278.—Carlyov, John, 68.—Carnel,* John, 69.—Carnelles, Rd., 224.—Carpinter, John, 91.—Carrogen, John, 151.—Carrow, Thos., 265.—Carter, John, 96, 286.—Carthartheo, John, 145.—Carthev, John, 180.—Caru, Thos., 96.—Carutsuyov, John, 69.—Carwen, John, 305.—Carwennek, John, 117.—Carwynnok, Rd., 248.—Cary, Wm., 118.—Caryche, John, 215.—Caryn, David, 301.—Castel, John, [Dioc. Lichf., L. D.], 9a.—Caucy, John, 319.—Cawell, Rd., 231.—Cergeaux, Hy., 75.—Cerger, John, 97.—Certayn, John, 96 ; William, 196.—Certyn, Wm., 148.—Chaaghesti, Arnulph, 231 ; Chakestey, John, 188.—Chagesty, Thos., 18.—Chakeforde, Rd., 238.—Chaldon, Andrew, 205.—Chalons, Rob., 169.—Chamberleyn, John, 69.—Champe, Ralph, 287 ; Thos., 287.—Chapelayn, Wm., 147.—Chapyl, John, 122.—Chapell,* Wm., 137.—Chappelegh, John, 61.—Chavnterell, John, 108.—Chedeley, Simon, 159.—Chedeldon, John, 1.—Chekket, Rd., 305.—Chelest, John, 173.—Chenalus, John, 96.—Chepper, John, 20.—Chepman, Rd., 44 ; Walter, 308 ; Wm., 98.—Cheryton, Wm., 91.—Chyryton, Rd., 206.—Chester, Walter, 91.—Chierne, Ralph, 261.—Cholwyn, John, 184.—Chomberum, Thos., 91.—Chopyn, Thos., 91.—Chosgaran, John, 70.—Chosh, Wm., 91.—Chovythda, Jas., 70.—Chuddelegh, John, 102.—Chyket, John, 66 ; Rd., 132.—Chynals, John, 224.—Chynall, Thos., 252.—Chyrston, Hy., 96 ; Thos., 96 ; Wm., 96.—Chyvethorne, Jas., 273.—Chywarton, Thos., 71.—Clambyle, John, 111.—Clark,* John, 102.—Clauton,* Robt., 60.—Claysse, Thos., 236.—Cleg, Wm., 73.—Clement, John, 169, 278.—Clerk, John, 28, 197, 305 ; Rd., 79 ; Rob., 98 ; Wm., 188.—Cleve, Walter, 128.—Cley, Rob., 121.—Clyet, John, 22.—Clyette, Gregory, 234.—Clyfford,* Rd., 118a.—Clyk, Thos., 21.—Clymmow, Rd., 140.—Clyvere, Walter, 112.—Clywerdon, John, 231.—Cobbe, John, 262.—Cobbelond, John, 52.—Coblond, Hy., 206.—Cody, Baldwin, 71.—Codyng, Wm., 52.—Cok, Jas., 67 ; John, 67, 204 ; Rd., 99, 220, 302 ; Rob. 163 ; Thos., 135, 305 ; Wm., 96.—Coke, Hy., 96 ; Wm., 121.—Cokeworthy, John, 52 ; Rd., 102.—Col, Rd., 121.—Colle, Rd., 69 ; Wm., 162.—Colan, Wm., 206.—Colbeare, John, 108.—Cole, Adam, 193 ; John, 88, 116, 197, 313 ; Hy., 7, 96 ; Rd., 86, 103 ; Rob., 15 ; Thos., 44 ; Walter, 175.—Coleford, Steph., 13.—Colforde, John, 251.—Coleton, John, 286.—Colhay, John, 238.—Collegh, Rd., 20.—Collond, Rob., 97.—Coly, David, 31 ; Oliver, 264.—Colybeare, Rob., 273.—Colyn, John, 122, 232, 313 ; Rd., 51 ; Rob.,* 96 ; Roger, 278 ; Thos., 248.—Colyng, Wm., 234.—Combe, John, 152 ; Wm., 129.—Come, Ralph, 240 ; Rob., 240.—Comben, Wm., 167.—Compton, John, 176.—Cons, John, 189.—Constans, Rd., 96.—Cooche, Simon, 114.—Cook, John, 97, 169, 242 ; Nich., 38, 124 ; Rd., 81 ; Thos., 87, 291 ; Wm., 23.—Coper, Thos., 140.—Copleston, Thos., 99.—Corbyn, Thos., 291.—Corche, Reginald, 26.—Cornevale, Walter, 7.—Cornu,* John, 122.—Cornysch, Roger, 96.—Cornyche, Wm., 215.—Corsede, John, 217.—Corvyn, John, 273.—Cosby, John, 286.—Cosgaren, John, 179.—Cosyn, John, 83 ; Wm., 117.—Cote, John, 83.—Cotaler, John, 45.—Cotell, Roger, 87.—Cothyn,

John, 297; Wm., 297.—Cougun, Thos., 218.—Covelegh, John, 1.—Covlecote, John, 35.—Cowlyng,* Walter, 96.—Coykyn,* Thos., 45.—Crabbe, John, 70.—Cranworthy, Thos., 154.—Cref, Steph., 96.—Criour, Ralph, 16.—Crody, Rd., 71.—Croke, Roger, 219.—Crokker, Rd., 150, 169.—Crocker, John, 294.—Cromlogh, John, 179.—Crose, John, 139.—Crosman, Thos., 1; Wm., 98.—Crosse, John, 79; Wm., 96.—Crossyng, Walter, 285.—Crugow, John, 304.—Cruys, John, 172.—Crewys, Roger, 221.—Crydon, Thos., 316.—Crymel, Wm., 243.—Crynham, Rob., 85.—Crypsse, David, 71.—Cryspyn, Peter, 169.—Crystofere,* Thos., 44.—Crustow, John, 305.—Crystow, Roger, 139; Wm., 260.—Cugy, John, 300.—Curnow,* John, 140.—Curteys, Wm., 71.—Courteys, Roger, 163.—Curteyes, Thos., 223.—Cubert, Benedict, 96; Thos., 264.—Curham, John, 282.—Cuscose, Rob., 278.—Cusske, Rd., 96.—Cutvyn, Rob., 7.—Cutfyn, Walter, 91.—Cuvychy, John, 96.

Daber, Rd., 79.—Daberon, Wm., 266.—Dalby, John, 213.—Dalfyn, Rob., 67.—Dalman, Hy., 122.—Damarle, Rob., 124.—Daukyn, Thos., 75.—Daunand, Hugh, 75; Thos., 75.—Daunser, Rob., 193.—David, Thos., 71.—Davy, John, 52, 57, 96,* 129, 319; Laurence, 108; Rob., 52; Simon, 288; Thos., 218; Walter, 12; Wm., 88, 251.—Davyok, Gregory, 74.—Dawe, John, 145; Walter, 96.—Dayhowe, Hy., 181.—Delamayne, John, 258.—Delve, John, 170.—Denbol, Hy., 23.—Deneford, Wm., 241.—Denyngton, John, 97.—Denys,* Geoffrey, 96; John, 266; Rob.,* 110; Roger, 96; Thos., 92, 96.—Denyssl, John, 75.—Denyunke, Thos., 71; Deraunt, John, 96.—Devy,* Ralph, 96.—Devyok,* Rd., 85.—Dewow, Phil., 91.—Deyman, Henry, 91; John, 123.—Dezer, Wm., 86.—Dobbe, John, 110.—Dobyn, Simon, 152; Wm., 52; Doddelyng, Wm., 234; Dokcombe, John, 91.—Dollyng, Wm., 217.—Doly, Walter, 21.—Donstar, Wm., 57.—Dony, John, 96.—Doune, John, 101; Rob., 96; Wm., 91.—Doune Worthy, Rd., 231.—Dove, Rd., 12.—Downyng, Nich., 173.—Dowrysch, John, 115.—Drake, John, 91, 115, 131, 282.—Dreff, Ralph, 261.—Dreneke, Wm., 223.—Drewe, John, 251; Ralph, 222; Thos., 12, 154.—Dreye, John, 213.—Dreyne, Rd., 228.—Drayn, Wm., 72.—Dreynek, Thos., 24.—Drowette, John, 215.—Dry, Rd., 194.—Drynger, John, 1.—Dulok,* John—"Nativus Domini, cum quo dispensavit," 65.—Dun, John, 121.—Dunham,* Jas., 159.—Dunste, John, 123.—Durant, Thos., 139.—Dure, Ralph, 297.—Dyffen, John, 140.—Dyffert, Tho., 279.—Dygher, Nich., 305; Wm., 305.—Dyer, John, 91; Paschasius, 68; Tho., 75.—Dygandawe, John, 96.—Dygondou, Tho., 71.—Dymmok, John, 278.—Dynggell, John, 264.—Dyrwyll, Rob., 91.

Edmond, Jas., 139.—Edward, Gregory, 54; John, 75, 96, 221; Rob., 57; Walter, 96.—Ellecombe, John, 7.—Elynor,* Wm., 71.—Elys, John, 132; Roger, 26; Walter, 273.—Emond, John, 139; Roger, 183.—Enys, Hy., 96.—Eston, John, 290.—Eustas, Rob., 198.—Exebrygge, John, 50.—Eyer, Rd., 30.—Eym, Thos., 310.

Fabyan,* John, 51.—Facy, Thos., 122.—Fale, Wm., 93.—Faryngdon, John, 83, 282.—Faukener, Thos., 38.—Favell, John, 81.—Faynour,* John, 135.—Fayrman, Rd., 169.—Feraunt, John, 127.—Ferer, Rob., 96.—Ferman, Wm., 83.—Ferrers, Ralph and Rd., 300.—Ferud, John, 52.—Feryby, John, 18.—Ferys, John, 139; Wm., 242.—Feyry, Rob., 312.—Fialegh, John, 99.—Flaysmount, Benedict, 60.—Flemyng, Nich., 96.—Flewan, John, 264.—Flogyn, Wm., 52.—Floyer, Wm., 83.—Focher, Alexander, 91.—Focry, John, 121.—Foghell, John, 122.—Foleford,* Wm., 110.—Folygan, Stephen, 17.—Forde, John, 51, 60, 91; Rob., 209; Wm., 96, 121, 197.—Foreste, John, 227.—Forsdon, Thos., 174.—Forste, Walter, 115.—Fortescu, John, 122; Wm., 91.—Forun, John, 241.—Fot, John, 7.—Fowler, John, 96.—Frank, Rob., 1.—Francheny, Jas., 1.—Frankcheny, Thos. and Wm., 282.—Fraunceys, John, 116; Wm., 61.—Frenche, David, 212.—Frensch, John, 122.—Frenche, John, 211.—Frenschip, Peter, 172.—Frere, John, 308.—Frey, Walter, 213.—Frome, Thos., 163.—Frye, Rob., 278; Wm., 206.—Fuchyt, John, 56.—Fuller, Rob., 216.—Fychet, Edm., 91.—Fynell, John, 176.

Gale, John, 91.—Galsore, Wm., 55.—Galy,* Rd., 145; Thos., 96; Wm., 110.—Gantel, Edm., 17; Wm., 135; Garbere,* Rd., 91.—Gardysch, John, 24.—Garlond, Thos., 97.—Garsand, Wm., 140.—Gawmp, Thos. 96—Gay, John, 19, 96; Gilbert, 309; Rob.,* 96; Wm., 19.—Gayer, Walter, 144.—Geddon *or* Gedon, Jno., 218, 231.—

Geffrey, Hy., 74; John, 139, 177; Roger, 91; Wm., 256.—Gyffray, Jas., 96.—Gebel, Rd., 96.—Geleste, Wm., 254.—Genne, Nich., 58.—Genyn, John, 73; Wm., 54.—Genys, Peter, 173.—Gerard, John, 91 177; Thos., 168.—Gerby, John 184—German, John, 61, 75.—Gerveys or Gervys, John, 22; Thos., 206, 303.—Glamfeld, Nich. 171.—Glamvyll, Thos., 80.—Glonwyle, Walter, 87.—Glover, Thos., 176.—God, John, 71.—Gode, John, 74, 171; Walter, 82.—Goddrevy, John, 70.—Goddrus, Reginald, 96.—Godechyll, Thos., 311.—Godeman, John, 52.—Godere, Thos., 96.—Godfree, John, 96.—Godfray, Wm., 239.—Godwyn, Thos., 86.—Godyng, Thos., 294; Wm., 87.—Goffe, Thos., 222.—Gog, John, 67.—Golde, John, 148.—Goldsmyth, Rd., 91; 103.—Gomenere, Matth., 54.—Goran, Hy., 130.—Gorde, John, 91; Thos., 123.—Gorge, John, 96.—Gorecote, Nich., 293.—Goracote, Wm., 35.—Gorlet, John, 71.—Gorlyn,* John, 71.—Gorven, Walter, 248.—Gotelake, John, 61.—Gotholhan, John, 71, 224.—Goyle alias Jeyle, Rd., 218.—Grabbe, Wm., 96.—Grayhood, Hy., 216.—Gregor, John, 71; Rob., 224.—Grygour, Jas., 306.—Gregory, Nich. and Steph., 96.—Grendon, Steph., 236.—Grene, John, 117.—Gresby, John, 216.—Greyston,* John, 82.—Grugawe, John, 299.—Grulles, Hy., 32.—Grybbyll, Walter, 113.—Grysby, John, 24.—Gullow, Wm., 302.—Gunne, Nigel, 248; Roger, 96.—Gurlyn,* Hy., 319.—Gurnard, John, 88.—Gurteboys, Wm., 146.—Gvy, John, 96.—Gy, Rd., 291.—Guynov, Rd., 69.—Gybbe, Gerveus 58; Matth., 119; Rd., 91; Thos., 67; Wm. 56.—Gyffard, John, 96, 270; Rd.,* 319.—Gygbe, John, 24.—Gygner, John, 126; Thos., 169.—Gylbard, Baldwin, 71; John, 69; Michael, 73; Thos., 96.—Gyldespyn, John, 274.—Gylford, John, 140.—Gylle, John, 81, 91; Steph., 87; Wm., 184.—Gylly, Thos., 96.—Gylman, John, 73.—Gynne, John, 288.—Gyst,* John—"Nativum per Comitem Devonie, Dominum suum, ad omnes Ordines manumissum;" Rob., 291.—Gyttysham, John, 96.

Haderlegh, Rob., 52.—Hake, John and Thos., 152.—Haket, Rd., 249.—Hakewell, John, 213.—Hakeworthy, John, 61.—Hals, John, 102, 278; Rd., 158.—Hamely, John, 12, 223, 262.—Hamelyn, Jas., 252; John, 129, 285; Rd., 91; Thos.,* 33, 263; Wm., 124.—Hamond, John, 118; Wm., 106.—Hancok, John, 202.—Hapkyng, John, 148.—Haps, John, 190; Rob., 190.—Hardy, Thos., 311; Wm., 159.—Harl, John, 81.—Harle, John, 252.—Harlysdon, John, 97; Wm., 294.—Harper, Hy., 96; Thos., 313.—Harry, John, 56, 74, 75, 96, 98a, 117, 145, 181, 243, 264, 300, 301; Michael, 261; Nich., 282; Ralph, 72, 180; Rd., 96, 179, 198, 226; Thos., 68, 71, 86, 261; Walter, 71; Wm., 60, 96, 109.—Harter, Walter, 75.—Hauke, Thos., 251.—Haukedon, John, 96.—Haukyn, Baldwin, 96; John, 184; Steph., 96; Peter, 75.—Hay, Thos., 96.—Hayman, Andrew, 188; Rd., 292.—Hayward, John, 99, 160, 172; Thos., 308.—Hedelnte, John, 216.—Headdon, John, 314.—Heddon, John, 23.—Hedon, John, 96; Stephen, 201.—Hedman, Thos., 98.—Hegow, Rd., 96.—Hele, Wm., 202.—Hellsky, Peter, 139.—Helyer, John, 173, 241, 248.—Hendre, Rd., 298.—Hender, Thos., 219.—Hendry,* John, 72.—Hendy, Gilbert, 230; John,* 29.—Henewode, John, 218.—Henry, Matth., 22; Philip, 180; Rd., 71.—Herbert, Wm., 12.—Herelle, John, 211.—Herford, John, 96.—Hermann, Rd., 216.—Herscote, Rd., 126.—Herte, John, 69; Wm., 218.—Hervy, Hy., 73, 96; John, 96, 285; Philip, 176; Rob., 71; Thos., 68; Wm., 96; Hervy Vychyow, John, 224.—Herwy, Rd., 219.—Herward, ... *sic.*, 241; John, 288.—Hyrward, Wm., 61.—Heryngston, John, 21.—Heryngeston,* John, 88.—Hexste, John, 165.—Heye, John, 96; Rd., 96.—Heym, John, 96.—Hike, Andr., 259; Hy., 256.—Hillary, Rob. [Dioc. Sarum, L.D.], 81.—Hillynge, Rob., 215.—Hobbe,* John, 96, 185; Steph., 75; Wm., 92.—Hobelyn, Rd., 60.—Hobkyn, John, 224, 228; Hy., 223.—Hobman, Wm., 159.—Hochim, John, 218.—Hockemore, Nich., 213.—Hudenay, Roger, 256.—Hogekyn, John, 71.—Hoggekyn, John, 71, 73, 96.—Hochekyn, John, 145.—Hoghekyn, Simon, 96.—Hoggeslond, John, 152.—Hogge, Hy., 228; John, 1, 7, 152*; Oliver, 300; Thos., 157, 273, 310; Wm., 221.—Hoggy, Wm., 304.—Hoky, John, 96.—Holbeton, John, 91.—Holdyche, Wm., 167.—Holecomb, Nich., 116.—Holecom, Wm., 233.—Holman, John, 107, 190; Wm., 65.—Holme, Wm., 19.—Honeford, Thos., 119.—Honte, Rob., 67.—Honychurche, John, 292.—Hopere, Alexander, 53; Edw., 254; Hugh, 66; Nich., 87; Thos., 22.—Hoppekyn, Hy., 302.—Hopkyn, John, 61, 68, 71.—

Hoppekyn, John, 154.—Hopkyn, Odo, 70; 96.—Hoppy, Thos., 96.—Hoppyng, Ralph, 159.—Hore, Wm., 66.—Horewyll, Rd., 129.—Horner, John, 96.—Horsman, John, 234.—Horston, John, 215.—Horton, Rob., 53.—Hortop, John, 50.—Hosband, John, 184.—Hoskorne, Walter, 217.—Hoskyn, John, 96.—Hosyer, Wm., 74.—Hough, Geoffrey, 151.—Hovsyng, Wm., 278.—Howeton, Wm., 122.—Hoyller, Michael, 134.—Hoylton, Baldwin, 75.—Hucche, Gregory, 54.—Huchoim, Peter, 1.—Huchon, John, 34.—Huchyn, *see* Lucas, 150; Rob., 44.—Hull, Wm., 91.—Hunte, Hy., 169; John, 89, 279.—Huppekobe, John, 229.—Hurdyng, Rob., 319.—Hurle, John, 96.—Hurte, Gilbert, 161; Wm., 68, 96.—Huwysch, John, 96.—Hwdy, John, 264.—Hwhette, Nich. and Walter, 218.—Hwyte, John, 282.—Huwytt, John, 96.—Hycka, John, 138, 140.—Hycalys,* Rd., 140.—Hycka Alys, Roger, 224.—Hycke, John, 30; Philip and Wm., 96.—Hygow, Reginald, 300.—Hykewode, Roger and Walter, 60.—Hyllyng, Hy., 205.—Hyl, Gilbert, 96; John, 13, 87, 247, 273; Paul, 176; Rd., 308; Roger, 58; Thos., 91; Wm.,* 242, 278.—Hyllyng, Hugh, 149; John, 56.—Hynde, Edm., 45; Rob., 52; Walter, 63.—Hyndeston, Wm., 167.—Hynston, Hugh, 1.—Hyre, John, 297.—Hyrry, John, 243.—Hytte, John, 130; John, "ejus confratrem," 130.

Ylond, John, 87.—Innocent,* Wm., 141.—Yrysch, Thos., 136.—Ysaac, Rd., 159; Wm., 163.

Jacob, John, 89.—Jacow,* Wm., 145.—Jadehay, Thos., 206.—Jagow, Oliver, 28; Rob.,* 96; Michael, 304.—Jackaby, Thos., 297.—Jake, Steph., 228.—Jakewill, John, 222.—Jakjowy, Phil., 184.—Jakys, John, 169.—Jambe, Rd., 100.—Jamys, Ralph, 228; Thos., 24, 96.—Jankyn, David, 140.—Jay, John, 252.—Jewarton, Rob., 142.—Jeyle, *see* Goyle, 218.—Job, Rd., 96; Rob., 73; Thos., 96.—Jodel, John, 96.—Johan, David, 96; John, 69, 71; Laurence,* 96; Rd., 72, 96; Walter, 69.—Jolyff, John, 110; Nich., 30.—Jon, Hy., 180; Martin, 30; Rob., 126; Wm., 61, 140.—Jon Adam, Rd., 222.—Jona, *see* Matthy. 136.—Jone, Wm., 261.—Jongumethe, Wm., 259.—Joute,* John, 121.—Jouute, Geoffrey, 63.—Jope, Jas., 145.—Jory, Mich., 30.—Jouy, John, 35.—Jule, Laurence, 76; Rob., 50; Thos., 52.—Jull, Wm., 168.—June,* John, 91.—Junne, John, 226.—Juyll, John, 91, 136*; Wm., 10, 197, 293.

Kaylewaye, John, 7.—Kelwa, John *and* Rd., 60.—Kelwe, Wm., 141.—Keche, John, 283; Wm., 215.—Kekyll, Thos., 291.—Keleton, Rob., 213.—Kelly, John, 161.—Kelle, Rd., 220.—Kemel, Rob., 172.—Kena, Wm., 207.—Kencrek, Nich., 252.—Kendale,* Rob., 135; Thos., 114.—Kene, Edm., 45; John, 161, 319,* Walter, 96.—Keneby, Thos., 224.—Kenecote, John, 279.—Keneky, Alexander, 71.—Kenryg, Richard, 83.—Kente, John, 220.—Kerkeke, John, 219.—Kerne, John, 226.—Kernek, Steph., 265.—Kerov, Phil., 68.—Kestell, Simon, 139.—Keston, Rd., 139.—Kestyl, Rd., 66.—Ketyng, John, 20.—Keycham, Thos., 147.—Knol, Roger, 53.—Knolle, Thos., 220.—Knovul, David, 243.—Knyfe, John, 278.—Knyght, John, 7, 312; Laurence, 163; Philip, 26; Walter, 310; Wm., 309.—Knythe, Rd., 220.—Knylle, John, 169.—Knytston, John, 54.—Knyȝthton, John, 61.—Koke, John, 228.—Koker, Wm., 215.—Kolton, Thos., 213.—Krwys, John, 278.—Kylcam, Roger, 294.—Kylliov, John, 69, 70; Osbert 70; Peter, 69.—Kylleyow, Reginald, 222.—Kyllyawe, Steph., 185.—Kylyhow, John, 264.—Kymewarry, Rd., 233.—Kymworth, Wm., 169.—Kyng, Andrew, 168; Rd., 37; Rob., 18; Simon, 127; Steph., 75; Thos., 96; Wm. 173.—Kyngge, Wm., 121.—Kyngman, Wm., 75.—Kyngwylle, Rob., 46.—Kyrek, Nich., 96.—Kyrrys,‡ Thos., 96.—Kyrton, John, 122.—Kyrwythy, Wm., 307.—Kys, Roger, 250.—Kytte, Hy., 217.—Kyttow, Nich., 96.

Laca, John, 231.—Lace, Wm., 19.—Ladycourte, Rob., 91.—Lake, John, 152; Rob., 20; Walter, 108.—Lamanva, John, 222.—Lambert, Rd., 268.—Lamleder*, John, 122.—Lancaster, Wm., 215.—Landawarnek, Wm., 91.—Lane, Rd., 97; Walter, 236.—Laneman, Rd., 268.—Lange, John, 305.—Langebrok, John, 17, 96.—Langedon, Ambrose, 12; Rd., 252.—Langerille, John, 17.—Langman, John, 89.—Langhman, Rob., 81.—Lanhergy, Wm., 74.—Lankebrode, Geoffrey, 288.—Lannargh, John, 301.—Lanner, John, 140.—Lasse, John, 228.—Laurens, John, 70, 242; Phil., 302.—Laurens, Rob. 152.—Laury, Baldwin, 71; John, 29; Ralph,

115 ; Rd., 82.—Levynton*, John, 145.—Lawe, John, 177 ; Rd., 148.—Lawyr, Rd. 1.—Lawys, John, 293 ; Wm., 35,146.—Ledeheade, John, 312.—Leg, Wm., 66. 70*.—Legh, John, 98 ; Rd., 121 ; Thos., 152 ; Wm., 61,126.—Lene, Rd., 96.—Lenyger, Simon, 288.—Leor, John, 99.—Lepe, Rd., 13.—Lesse, Wm., 223.—Lewe, John, 91.—Lewys, John, 1 ; Rd., 159 ; Thos., 1.—Ley, Thos., 290.—Leyde, Roger, 234.—Leye, John, 104,159 ; Thos., 60, 202.—Leyhe, Wm. 213, 302.—Leylond, Walter, 96.—Leyot, John, 18.—Libbe, John, 217.—Lishenwore. Thos., 179.—Loke, Wm, 294.—Lokyer, John, 81, 149.—Lolla, Nich., 24.—Londre, John, 152.—Lorymer, Rd., 19.—Loryng, John, 145 ; Nich., 254.—Loueny, Thos., 30.—Louc-putte, Nich., and Wm., 96.—Loueryng*, Roger, 159.—Loveryng, Steph., 1.—Louk, John, 74.—Lovdrun, Rd., 224.—Love, Rd., 221.—Lovetop, Michael, 27.—Loveton, Rd., 91.—Loveworth, Baldwin, 128.—Lovybounde, Geoffrey, 7.—Lowys,* Rob. 96.—Loyman, Wm., 52.—Loyth, John, 278.—Lucas, John, 71; "*alias* Huchyn" 150 ; Rd., 261.—Luccombe, Thos., 52.—Lucow, John, 96.—Luddre, Thos., 70.—Ludevan, Thos., 71.—Ludlow, Rd., 248.—Luky, John, 27, 73 ; Michael 96.—Lukyn, Wm., 97.—Luston, Rob., 16.—Lwlly, Rd.—226.—Lwttun, Rob., 228.—Lyde, John, 223.—Lydeford, Wm., Dioc: Winton [L.D.] 81.—Lydwon, Simon, 150.—Lyffeston, Thos., 15.—Lyndon, Abel. 91.—Lyne, John 91.—Lytelton, Rd., 129, 251.—Lytilione, Rd., 270.—Lyerd, Walter, 96.—Lyle, Rd., 37.—Lyon, Thos. 291.—Lyvedon, Rd., 92.

Mabbe, John, 117.—Machon, Wm., 60.—Macy, Wm., 254.—Maghingha, Thos., 267.—Major, Martin, 180.—Make, Rd., 143.—Malyt, Steph., 96.—March, Wm., 122.—Marchaunt, John, *or* Marchand, 96, 290, 222 ; Thos., 24.—Marke, John, 152, 222 ; Rd., 96.—Martyn, Edm., 251 ; Jas., 185 ; John, 24, 26, 96, 117, 185, 253, 264, 313 ; Rd., 282 ; Thos., 122 ; Wm., 160.—Marschall, John, 91.—Marschell, John, 197 ; Thos., 89, 197.—Maryet, Wm., 10.—Maryn, John, 74.—Marys, John, 297.—Maskell, Roger, 245.—Masly, Thos., 70.—Maslegh, Thos., 305.—Masley, Rob., 301.—Mason, Wm., 96.—Mate, Rob., 202 ; Thos., 139, 289.—Mathew, John, 117.—Matthu, Hugh, 61.—Maththy, Benedict, 304.—Matthy, Hy., 73 ; Jas., 71 ; Laurence, 31.—Matthy,* *alias* Jona, Rd., 136.—Maver, John, 273.—May, John, 319.—Maygge, John, 52.—Mayn, Wm., 1.—Maynert, Wm., 228.—Mayov, John, 52, 160.—Mayȝow, John, 228.—Mayow, Rd., 256.—Mayov,* Roger, 51.—Mayster, Hy., 248.—Maystre,* John, 31.—Mede, John, 91 ; Thos., 251.—Mederus, Rd., 67.—Medros, Thos., 179.—Melbyry, Wm., 160.—Melkesham, Thos., 169.—Mely, John, 265.—Melynsy, Wm., 32.—Mencudell, John, 222.—Menke, Rd., 70.—Meriet, John, 123.—Mersch, John, 52.—Merston, Thos., 239.—Mertherwa, Thos., 51.—Mervyn, John, 143.—Merwode, Wm., 313.—Merymouth, Walter, 113.—Methe, John, 167 ; Rob., 288.—Methlond, John, 314.—Mewy, Ralph, 102.—Mey, Rob., 295 ; Wm., 291.—Meysak, Rd., 179.—Mille, Roger, 98 ; Thos., 276 ; Walter, 230.—Mody, John, 65.—Moggan, John, 96.—Molly, Ralph, 96.—Mollyng, Wm., 74.—Molys, Thos., 80.—Monder, Wm., 91.—Monk, John, 14 ; Roger, 167 ; Wm., 168, 268.—More, John, 66, 150, 159, 213. 240 ; Thos., 126 ; Wm., 310.—Morgan, John, 146.—Morton, Rd., 126.—Morys, John, 171 ; Thos.,* 147 ; Wm., 114.—Motyn, Wm., 24.—Moyl, Walter, 184.—Moys, John, 148.—Mugge, Steph., 117.—Multon,* John, 242.—Mulys, Thos., 52.—Mwstarde, Thos., *and* Wm., 218.—Mychel, *or* Mychell, Jas., 96 ; John, 31, 73, 91, 154, 223, 224, 261, 291, 303 ; Peter,* 71 ; Reginald, 92 ; Rd., 73, 169, 222, 252 ; Rob., 71 ; Roger, 223, 279 ; Thos., 71 ; Wm.,* 71, 214, 278.—Myddelton, Hy., 248.—Myghelstow, Hy. *and* Rd., 279 ; Myghelystaw, Mark, 179.—Mylford, Rd., 82.—Myngos, John, 297.—Myngoys, Thos., 138.—Mynnow, John, 140.—Mynyk, John, 282.—Myrabel, Ralph, 96.—Myryfyld, Rd., 108.—Myryfeld, Wm., 319.—Myry-wether, John, 161.—Mytherhylle, Rd., 285.

Nabostel, Rd., 29.—Nampister, Mich., 215.—Nans, Rob., 180.—Nanskalan, John, 222.—Nanskeily, John, 172.—Nascunwell, John, 227.—Nasquidan, Ralph, 243.—Nawydan, John, 73.—Neell, *or* Nele, John, 112, 285 ; Hy., 52 ; Rd., 273 ; Wm., 51.—Nethe-cote *or* Nethercote, John, 126, 173 ; Neucomb, Rd., 44.—Newhall, John, 61 ; Walter, 26.—Newton, John, 96, 218 ; Peter, 96.—Neweton, John, 273 ; Thomas, 218 ; Neyler, Thos. *and* Rd., 96.—Nyweton, John, 117.—Nicolas, Rd., 227.—Nycholas, Wm., 169.—Node,* John, 152.—Non, Hugh, 96.—Nordon, Thos., 218 ;

Wm., 230.—Norea, Wm., 193.—Norman, Roger, 96.—Northecote, Wm., 272.—Northode, Peter, 150.—Norton, John. 91 ; Rob., 319.—Norys, Rd., 106.—Notte, John, 220.—Notyng, John, 317.—Noyel, John, 115.—Noyll, Hy., 295 ; Paschasius, 74.—Noyell,* Roger, 92.—Nycol, Hy., 52 ; John, 33, 71, 71,* 158, 233, 278, 286 ; Rd., 172 ; Rob.,§ 127 ; Steph., 32 ; Thos., 179 ; Walter, 96 ; Wm., 71, 138 ; Nycoll Wyta, John, 222.—Nyk, Thos., 60.—Nythtyngale, John, 56.

Oger, John, 74.—Oldeman, Elias, 169.—Olyver, John, 188, 304 ; Rd., 150 ; Thos. 68 ; Wm., 214.—Oliwere, Reginald, 255.—Oppy, John, 26 ; Rd., 285.—Oryswan, John, 222.—Osborne, John, 190 ; Rd., 125.—Oxneham, Wm., 63.

Paket, Thos., 96.—Palmer, John, 76, 87 ; Rd., 22 ; Thos., 233 ; Wm., 99.—Papeyay, John, 92.—Pares, John, 282.—Parker, Andrew, 172 ; John, 123 ; Nich., 19 ; Rd., 79 ; Wm.,* 108.—Parys, Rob., 173 ; Walter, 293 ; Parys Trevyrnoy, John, 79.—Paschow, John, 96 ; Wm., 260.—Pascow, John, 125 ; Nich. 305 ; Rd., 141 ; Thos., 81 ; Wm., 141.—Paslew, John, 104.—Pavkyng, Thos., 145.—Paul, Rd. 145.—Paulhylle, John, 179.—Pauly, John, 71.—Paulyn, Rd., 273.—Paulyng, Wm., 241.—Pay, Thos., 81.—Payn, John, 270.—Paytneyn, Rd., 252.—Peche, Steph., 288.—Pedreda, John, 133.—Peke, Simon, 18.—Pellour, Michael, 71.—Pendre, Wm., 71.—Pennans, Jas., 140 ; John 121*, 140 ; Walter, 70.—Penels,* Rob., 276.—Pengelly, Thos., 96.—Penhale, John, 33 ; Wm., 96.—Penhall, Daniel, 31.—Penhalow, Rd., 70.—Penkworthy, Reginald, 91.—Pennalewy,* John, 319.—Pennalune, Oliver, 298.—Pennelune, Vdo, 243.—Penpows, Wm., 180.—Penpaly, John, 74.—Penpons, Rd., 96.—Penquyte, Rd., 67.—Penrous, John, 96.—Pensans, Thos., 302.—Penwaryn,* John, 46.—Penwerne, Thos., 139*, 298.—Penuwyk, Peter, 29.—Penwyk, Thos., 29.—Penywyk, John, 96.—Peny, Roger, 74.—Peperwyth, Wm., 271.—Perche, John, 214.—Percher, John, 258.—Perkyn, Edm., 91 ; John, 29, 96 ; Thos., 45, 140 ; Walter, 91.—Pernell, Wm., 196.—Perowe, Alan, 30.—Pers, Hy., 71 ; John, 71, 223 ; Steph., 71 ; Wm., 71.—Perok, Wm., 71.—Person, John, 1 ; Nich., 216 ; Rd., 219.—Pertarygge, Wm., 110.—Peryn, Rd., 126, 147.—Perys, Rd., 261.—Pethan, Thos., 96.—Petipase, Hy., 63.—Petteryng, John, 87.—Petyt, Jas., 70 ; Michael, 96 ; Thos.,* 70.—Peynde, John, 278.—Philip, John, 35, 223 ; Thos., 188.—Philipp, Nich., 70, 96 ; Ralph, 70 ; Rob.,* *and* Thos., 96.—Phily, Ralph, 74.—Piryn, John, 259.—Placidas, Andr., 52.—Playmark, Walter, 206.—Plommer, Wm., 23.—Plumer, John, 104.—Plummer, John, 273.—Plymmouuth, Hy., 73.—Pocok, Matth., 152.—Pole, John, 278 ; Rd., 96.—Polgruen, John, 71.—Polgrun, Wm., 30.—Polgwest, Rd., 139.—Polkynhorne, Thos., 223.—Pollard, Wm., 223.—Pollow, John, 278.—Polpere,* Thos., 31.—Polrydan, John, 76.—Poltery, John, 227.—Polyford, John, 152.—Ponford, John, 271.—Ponyng, Wm., 79.—Pope, Wm., 21.—Popham, Reginald, 87.—Porter, John, 52.—Poyer, Rd., 91.—Pound, Thos., 100 ; Wm., 197.—Power, Baldwin, 110.—Predeowse, John *and* Thos., 234.—Predon, Rob., 231.—Prenke, John, 184.—Prestekote, John, 216.—Prew, Steph., 63.—Prior, Rob., 51.—Pryor, Thos., 184.—Prous or Prowse, John, 1, 213 ; Rd., 270 ; Thos., 115.—Prust, Andr., 7 ; Thos., 126 ; Wm., 35.—Prydeaux, Roger, 75.—Prydyaux, Thos., 305.—Pryg, John, 83.—Prymer,* John, 70.—Prynce, John, 283.—Pryns, Wm., 159.—Pulstagg, John, 145.—Pultemore, John, 123.—Putte, Wm., 267.—Pye, John, 177.—Pyers, John, 135, 139,* 305 ; Rob., 88 ; Steph., 306.—Pyk, John, 168.—Pykard, Rd., 108.—Pyke, Thos., 231 ; Walter, 91.—Pyleton, John, 188.—Pylaton, Thos., 18 ; Walter, 87.—Pylcorn, John, 82.—Pyle, Wm., 12.—Pyn, Wm., 1.—Pynde, Thos., 198.—Pynhay, John, 242.—Pynnecote, John, 104.—Pyper, Rd., 252 ; Rob., 108 ; Thos., 286.—Pypet, John, 147 ; Rd., 18.—Pytte, John, 91, 96, 98 ; Martin, 282.

Quenterell, Hugh. 222.—Quyntrel*, John, 70.—Quynte*, Wm., 135.

Raddok, Wm., 115.—Raddon, John, 59 ; Wm., 222.—Raddyche, Rd., 292.—Radeford, John, 54.—Ragenys, Thos., 135.—Ragger, Wm., 10.—Rake, John, 288.—Ralegh, Laurence, 317 ; Thos. 63.—Rafe, Thos., 96.—Rauf, Wm. 34.—Raw, John, 279.—Rawe, John, 278.—Raulyn, Edm., 59 ; John, 96 ; Nich., 140 ; Rd., 87.—Reynald, Henry, 96.—Reynold, John, 31.—Raynald,* John, 96.—Raynolde, Rd., 220.—Reynald, Thos., 75.—Raynald, Thos., 245.—Rayschlegh, John, 310.—Reche, Wm., 81.—Reke, John, 292.—Rede, Baldwin, 127 ; John, 32 ; Peter, 58 ; Thos., 169.—Redeclyf, John, 10 ; 286 ; Roger, 123.—Redewyll, John, 166.—Renowdyn,

Benedict, 96.—Renawdyn, Thos., 300.—Randy, John, 91.—Replegh, Thos. 291.—Repryn, Ralph, 122.—Resmoddres, Joceus, 71.—Retyn, Rd. 184.—Rewe, John 168.—Rewlond, John, 38.—Richard Simon, Thos., 259.—Robert, Rd., 105 ; Steph., 228 ; Walter, 228.—Robyn, Hy., 55, 310 ; John, 28, 35 ; Ralph, 96 ; Roger, 137 ; Thos., 96, 190.—Rodde, Wm., 20.—Roderys, John, 118.—Rodyng, Rd., 15.—Rogge, John, 77.—Rogger, Rd., 53,241 ; Rob., 99, 122 ; Thos.,* 68, 91, 110 ; Wm., 98.—Roke, Rob., 58.—Romen, Roger, 305.—Ronel, Wm., 175.—Roos, John, 96, 257.—Rose, Odo, 73.—Roser, John, 44.—Rosewhorn, John, 71.—Rosy, David and Rd., 96.—Roulyn Pascol, John, 221.—Roupe, John, 251.—Row, Gregory, 122.—Rowe, Jas., 71 ; John, 14, 63, 96 ; Rd., 79 ; Walter, 122 ; Wm., 52.—Rowland, Steph. 91.—Rowse, Rd., 261 ; Roger, 115.—Rous, Hy., 102.—Roys, John, 96.—Ruel, Thos., 96.—Rygge, John, 197.—Rugge, Thos., 285.—Ruggeway, John, 97.—Russel, John, 10, 52, 278* ; Roger, 271.—Rychard, Jas., 96 ; John, 71, 140, 177 ; Nich., 137, 217 ; Paul, 96 ; Rychard Smytht, John, 139.—Rycher, John, 159.—Ryder, John, 13.—Rynald, John, 57 ; Rd., 87.—Rynel, John, 68.—Rynold, John, 19.—Ryppelegh, John, 91.—Rys, Rd., 72.—Rysby, John, 7.—Rysdone, John, 188.—Rysiov, Michael, 69.—Ryte, John, 91.

Sadeler, Walter, 21.—Sage, John, 188 ; Walter, 177.—Sakerlegh, Wm., 91.—Salter, John, 288.—Salysbury, Simon, 1.—Samon, John, 154.—Salmon, Rd., *and* Walter, 215.—Sampson,* Wm., 96.—Sandawe, Rob., 185.—Sander, John, 98.—Saunder, John, 100.—Sare, John, 96.—Sangoll, Roger, 219.—Sarger, John, 102.—Sarges, Rd., 122.—Savery John, 12.—Sayer, John, 58.—Sayle, John, 253.—Saynen, Adam, 115.—Sawle, John, 172.—Scarlet, Thos., 24.—Scatpole, Thos., 193.—Schank, Thos., 184.—Schaplegh, Wm., 115.—Schephurd, Rd., 19, 122 ; Thos., 91.—Schepwyke, Rob., 91.—Schepystall, Thos., 298.—Scheve, John, 108.—Schere, John, 173.—Schire, Wm., 35.—Scheter, John, 286.—Schaplegh, Thos., 163.—Schloman, Rd., 52.—Scholder, Thos., 96.—Schordysch, Thos., [Dioc : Winton : L.D.], 88.—Schorterygge, John, 110.—Schute, John, 15.—Schylston, John, 160.—Schyleston, John, 121.—Schypstal, Wm., 177.—Schyreway, Nich., 164.—Scoce, Wm., 195.—Scolmayst, Thos., 91.—Scoos, Thos., 91.—Scottysham, John, 248.—Scrispyn, Thos., 14.—Scryven, John, 10.—Scryvener. Rd., 122.—Secounder,* John, 70.—Sekerlegh, Hugh, 10.—Sele, Rob., 72 ; Wm., 202.—Selman, John, 52.—Semylyon, Rd., 224.—Serle, John, 129 ; Nich., 116.—Serell, Warine, 96.—Seygnour, Wm., 288.—Seyntabyn, Peter, and Geoffrey, 71.—Seyntmelyon, Thos., 96.—Skawyn, Rd., 134.—Skelton, Rob., 96.—Skuys, John, 73.—Skews, Geoffery, 225.—Skybel, Roger, 96.—Skyber, John, 71.—Skydy, Steph., 96.—Skynner, John, 36, 248 ; Rd., 75 ; Thos., 13 ; Wm., [Dioc. B & W. ; L.D.], 61.—Skynoke, Thos., *and* Wm., 218.—Skyttysch, Rob., 283.—Slegh, Rd., 91.—Slogh, Nich., 121.—Sloper, Rd., 91.—Slwg, John, 219.—Slycard, John, 314.—Smale, Geoffrey, 108 ; John,* 279.—Smalecomb, Hy., 96.—Smok, John, 202.—Smort, John, 163.—Smyrte, Rob., 104.—Smyth, John, 96, 113, 149, 190, 193,* 264, 309, 310, 312, 319 ; Rd.,* 51, 251 ; Rob., 315 ; Steph., 10, 229 ; Thos., 96, 115, 153, 273, 319 ; Walter, 63, 230 ; Wm., 96, 230.—Snaps, John, 13.—Snovblanch, Wm., 91.—Snowdon, John, 125.—Snyfmore, John, 239.—Socsowter, John, 260.—Somer, Walter, 52.—Sone, Joceus, 96.—Soper, Elias, 161.—Sosan, Rd., 177.—Southcote, John, 104.—Sowthwode, Thos., 317.—Spergor, Wm., 96.—Speart, John, 121.—Speda, Thos., 66.—Spede, John. 220.—Spenser, Rob., 81.—Sperk, John, 68.—Sperkewyll, Rd., 59.—Spernen,* John *and* Rd., 70.—Spetygow, Thos., 305.—Spore, John, 167.—Spyne, Wm., 13.—Squier, John, 59 ; Thos., 61 ; Wm., 277.—Stabbe, John, 288.—Stacy, or Stacey, Thos., 18, 187 ; Stacy, Wm., 215.—Stake, John, 81.—Stanbury, John, 160.—Stapulton, John, 233.—Staymour, John, 67.—Stede, John, 147.—Stenlake, John, 171.—Stephyn, John, 20, 52, 60, 73, 87, 173, 300 ; Michael, 72.—Nich., 243 ; Rd., 152 ; Rob., 96.—Sterlyng, Rd., 279.—Sterth, Roger, 319.—Stevyn, Roger, 190.—Stevynston, Wm., 308.—Stoddyn, Thos., 122.—Stodelegh, Thos., 291.—Stofford, Hy., 52.—Stokker, Rob., 116.—Stokys,* Wm., 56.—Stone, John, 80, 91, 170 ; Thos., 185 ; Rob., 89, 123.—Stote, John, 121.—Stoter, Thos., 91.—Stoteworthy, Rd., 127.—Stoverlegh, Thos. [Dioc. Lond., L.D.], 4.—Stowford, Rob., *and* Wm., 14.—Stowte, Ralph, 75.—Stoyle Rob., 89.—Strange, John, 58 ; Wm., 149.—Strangman,* John, 124.—Strode

John, 172.—Strongge, Thos., 51.—Stryke, Rd., 66.—Sturgyn, John, 117.—Sturnell, Peter, 234.—Sturre, John, 149.—Stury, John, 169, 234.—Stykeford, John, 28.—Style, John, 91, 284.—Suddon, John, 87.—Sumpter, Walter, 288.—Sutter, Walter, 318.—Swayn, John, 33.—Wm., 166.—Swolwe, Rob., 273.—Solwe, John, 310.—Sybely, John, 125.—Sydenham,* John, 80.—Symon, John, 45, 56, 68, 91, 96; Paschasius, 96; Rob., 96, 175; Thos.,* 96.—Syre, John, 177.

Tallan, Ralph, 67; Wm., 67.—Tallok, Roger, 123.—Talon, Rd., 228.—Talstus, Steph., 225.—Talvargh, John, 305.—Tankert, Rd., 279.—Tantefer, Simon, 129.—Tauntefer, Reginald, 151.—Taverum, Hy., 83.—Tawton, John, 218.—Taylour, John, 63, 91, 97, 127. 159, 162*, 166*, 177, 278; Paschasius, 96; Rd., 53, 81; Roger, 91; Thos.,* 91; Wm., 96, 291.—Telwen, John, 224.—Temyn, John, 192.—Tharop, Wm., 96.—Thom, John, 30.—Thomas, John, 70, 96*, 183, 184.—Tommas, John, 229, 255.—Thomas, Michael, 72; Peter, 13, 96; Reginald, 70; Wm., 222.—Thomas Mattheu, Ralph, 180.—Thomas Boncur, Hy., 178.—Thomlyn, Thos., 71.—Thomma, Hy., 96.—Tomma, Hy., 223.—Thomma, John, 96, 222; Thos., 243; Vivian, 96; Wm., 96.—Tomme, Hy., 261; John, 232.—Thomme, Wm., 124.—Thorn,* Rd., 126.—Thorner, John, 57, 96.—Thornyng, John, 91.—Thorp,* Walter,, 282.—Tobyn, Wm., 87.—Toker, John, 96, 282, 311; Rd., 81; Rob., 220; Thos., 160, 222; Walter, 113; Wm., 107, 317.—Toly, Rd., 91.—Tolvy, Ralph, 180.—Tomelony, Rd., 22.—Tomkyn, John, 223.—Torner, John, 17; Maurice, 45; Rd., 316; Thos., 151.—Tow, Wm., 63.—Towe, Thos., 286.—Towne, Thos., 249.—Tovnesend, Walter, 22.—Trase, Rd., 10.—Trebartha, John, 76.—Trebovlans, Thos., 96.—Trebras, Alexander, *and* Thos., 69.—Treboste, Rd., 223.—Trebuher, Wm., 70.—Trecarl, Hy., 65.—Tredenek, Alex., 96; John, 96.—Trederf,* Reginald, 72.—Tredyrf,* Rob., 129.—Tredevy, John, 96.—Tredewy,* John, 66.—Tredeuuy, Rd., 96.—Tredower, Rob., 179.—Tredydan, Steph., 76.—Tredynan, Otho, 28.—Trefosburgh, Rd., 96.—Trefreef, John, 51.—Trefrosov, Nich., 72.—Trefrysawe, John, 180.—Trefuthon, John, 300.—Tregadow, John, 222.—Tregalwos, Rd., 74.—Tregaron, Jas., 70.—Tregenworra, Wm., 96.—Treglosek, Alex., 71.—Tregodcke, John, *and* Thos., 254.—Tregodynow,* Wm., 140.—Tregonan, Hy., 70; Thos., 10.—Tregony, Thos., 278,—Tregos, Rob., 252; Roger, 184.—Tregurre, Benedict *and* John, 304.—Tregora, John, 71; Michael, 180.—Tregrasek, John, 71.—Tregustok, Jas., 96.—Trehunthel, John, 139.—Traiagow, John, 96.—Trekehorn, John, 71.—Trekeneder, Thos., *and* Wm., 71.—Trekydys, Nich., 300.—Trelauny, John, 96; Rob., 75.—Trelowny, Roger, 115.—Treles, John, 222.—Tremadok, Hillary, 221.—Tremayll, Odo, 296; Rob., 218; Wm., 219.—Tremayn, Edm., 69.—Trembethe, Thos., 96.—Trembras, Rd., 29.—Tremelet, Rob., 104.—Trempelok, John, 310.—Trenans, John, 74.—Trencruke, Rd., 260.—Trenegles, Theobald, 32.—Trenevere, John, 184.—Treneyryn, John, 73.—Trenevedek, John, 297.—Trengere, Wm., 186.—Trenkere, Roger, 147.—Trenowyt, Phil., 139.—Trenowyth, Wm., 302.—Trenyas, John, 227.—Trenyk, Wm., 91.—Trerwgn, John, 227.—Treynwyth, Peter, 140.—Trenewhyth, Thos., 68.—Trenuwyth,* Thos., 71.—Treynwyth, Thos., 140.—Trepennvyn, Michael, 73.—Treponnen, Laurence, 184.—Tresaugnow, Thos., 27.—Tresculard,* Thos., 142.—Tresir,* Rd., 60.—Trespresum, Nich., 69.—Trethewy, Rd. *and* Wm., 74.—Trethygy, Rd., 96.—Treute, John, 160.—Trevaga, Rd., 66.—Trevanyon, Steph., 69.—Trevelek, Thos., 96.—Trevelysek, John 71.—Treverth, Rob., 27.—Treveva, Rob., 304.—Trevorky, Rd., 73.—Trevylyas, John, 96.—Trevyllok, John, 15.—Trevyne,* Nich., 282.—Trevyrgy, John, *senior, and junior,* 303.—Trevythan, Joceus, 96.—Trevyyn, Wm., 81.—Trewak, Rd., 218.—Trewallos, Walter, 96.—Trewarvene, Mich., 96.—Trewartheleke, John, 223.—Trewaythyen, Nich., 34.—Treweythen, Rd., 98.—Treweff, Jas., 261.—Trewef, John, 70; Hy., *and* Thos., 71.—Trewyf, Thos., 96.—Trewergy, John, 223.—Trewervov, Rd., 71.—Trewet, John, 213.—Trewman, John, 20.—Truman, John, 52.—Treworky, Wm., 71.—Treworneke, Rd., 222.—Trewranek, Thos., 141.—Trewronek, John, 72.—Trewranow, Thos., 96.—Trewyke,* Hy., 140.—Trewyn, Rob., 96.—Trewynnard, Mich., 302.—Trewythyan, Thos., 73.—Troite, Thos., 228.—Troot, Hy., 96.—Trop, Hy., 87.—Trote, Bartholomew, *and* Rd., 228.—Trotyng, Alex., 118.—Trubbe, John, 265.—Trule, John, 10.—Trulle, Rd., 183.—Trya, Thos., 38.—Trgyll, Thos., 169.—Tullok, Walter, 96; Wm., 291.—

Turpin, John, 218.—Twyford,* Roger, 91.—Tybaw, John, 133.—Tybot, Baldwin, 51.—Tyeke, John, 223.—Tymet, Wm., 316.—Tyrel, John, 73, 96.—Tyrell, Wm., 302.—Tyraunt, Thos., 115.

Ude, Oliver, 74; Phil., 108; Laurence, 85; Ralph and Rd., 96; Rd., 135; Udy, John, 244; Rob., 96.—Ulf, John, 282.—Umfray, Bricius, 74; John, 73.—Uppecote, Wm., 159.—Uppeton, Elias, 96.—Usscher, Wm., 99.

Vale, Thos., 248.—Varyon, Thos., 140.—Vattecote, Rob., 310.—Vautard, Roger, 282.—Vedde, George, 22.—Vela, George, 214.—Vele, John, 122; Rd., 291; Thos., 12, 13.—Veale, Wm., 283.—Vely, John, 127; Thos., 308.—Veneov, Matth., 31.—Venet, Hy., 301.—Venton, Wm., 163.—Vereman, Paul, 298.—Voel, Rob., 122.—Vokhume, John, 211.—Volanty, John, 72.—Vycery, John, 161.—Vyen, John, 185.—Vyncent, John, 58, 61.—Vynhagh, Thos., 22.—Vyrwych, John, 61.—Vivyan, John, 96.—Vyvyan, Otho., 304; Thos.,* 71.

Wade, Walter, 219.—Waddon, Thos., 1.—Waldecomb, Ralph, 233.—Walke, John, 18.—Walkele, Wm., 248.—Wallen, Thos, 51.—Walsch *or* Walsche, John, 19, 23, 117; Rd., 282; Wm., 51.—Walsyngham, Thos., 4.—Walter, Roger, 219; Thos., 45. Walys, John 56; Thos., 60.—Wanston, Rd., 116.—Warde, John, 98; Wm., 51.—Ware, John 169, 295.—Warham, Wm., 255.—Waryn, John, 173; Walter, 75.—Wat, Steph., 26.—Water, John, 97.—Waterlag, Thos. 156.—Waterlete, John, 67.—Waterslade, Hy., 152.—Watte*, John, 68, 96.—Watty, Nich. *and* Steph., 71.—Watte, Thos., 70.—Waugge, John, 293.—Waysbeare, John, 104.—Webbe, Rd. 176.—Webber, Hy. 18; John, 60; Laurence, 223; Rd., 125; Thos. 193; Wm., 292.—Wege, Thos. 293.—Welle, John, 91.—Wellys, John, 91.—Wellysford, Thos., 126.—Wely, Wm., 87.—Welyworth, Thos., 51.—Weneman, Rd., 38.—Wering, John, 219.—Weryn, John, 71.—Weryng, John, 91; Rd., 215.— West, Adam, 87; John, 241; Thos., 67.—Westecote, Rd., 23; Rob., 127.—Weye, John, 83, 273.—Whympel, John, 160.—Whyalewylle, Nicholas, 88.—Whyta, John, 116; Wm., 129.—Whyte, John, 110; Rd., 198; Thos., 198; Hy., 315; Walter, 86; Wm., 57, 86.—Whytchurch, John, 124.—Whythechurch, Walter, 73.—Whytston*, Peter, 96; Thos., 51.—Wilky, Steph., 265.—Wingrune, John, 214.—Wodde, John, 212; Wm., 233.—Wodebery, John, 7.—Wodeham, John, 91; Walter, 91.—Wodehouse, John, 152.—Woderobe, John, 159.—Wodyngton, John, 317.—Woggewyll, Wm., 91.—Wolf, Wm., 168.—Wolford, John, 88.—Wolly, John, 279.—Wolston, Roger, 216.—Wonston, Geoffrey, 10.—Wormyston, John, 291.—Worner, John, 220.—Worthevale, Steph., 75, 96.—Woryn, Thos., 26.— Wotton,* Thos., 248.—Wratte, Geoffrey, 161.—Wryke, Wm., 234.—Wryter, John, 279; Hy., 81.—Wugger,* Roger, 87.—Wybbury, John, 54.—Wyddebroke, Steph., 215.—Wyde, John, 288.—Wyet, Rd., 10.—Wyker, John, 88.—Wylberdon, Ralph, 122.—Wylet, Thos., 190.—Wylcok, Baldwin, 71.—Wylkok, John, 59, 213, 224.—Wylkoc, Rd., 301.—Wylkok, Thos., 181.—Wylcok, Ralph, 138.—Wylky, Rd., 122.—Wylkyn, John, 69.—Wylkyng, Hy., 74.—Wylle, John, 21, 28, 68, 75, 140, 152, 229; Nich., 87; Ralph, 28, 179; Rd., 222; Thos., 51, 74, 257, 297.—Wille, Walter, 265.—Wylle, Wm., 61.—Wylliam,* Herves, 69.—Wyllyham or Wyllyam, John, 13, 70, 96, 139, 297, 305; Martin, 30; Michael, 139; Nich., 96; Ralph, 140; Reginald, 69; Rob., 290.—Wyllyng, Rd., 289; Rd., 290.—Wyndesore, John, 117, 292.—Wyndesore Thos., 265.—Wynkelegh, Walter, 290.—Wyse, Joachim, 273; John, 152.—Wyte, Wm., 96.—Wythe, Nich., 237.—Wytherygge, Rob., 53.—Wythley, Walter, 252.—Wythy, John, 279.—Whythyel, Wm., 74.—Wythyng, Wm., 96.—Wyty, Nich., 76.

Yalmpton, Wm., 291.—Yea, Rd., 150.—Yecot, Hy., 60.—Yeo, John, 52; Rd., 51.—Yerneway, John (de Honyton), 203.—Yestecote,* Rob., 131.—Yoe, John, 36, 96.—Yonge, Michael, 96.—York, Rob., 88.—Yorl, Simon, 35.—Yorle, John, 117.—Youngelyng, John, 81.—Yule, John, 317.—Yurl, Rob., 202; Wm.,* 206.—Yurld, John, 91.

ȝedelet, John, 252.—ȝerde, Wm., 87.—ȝunge,* John, 86.

II. ACCOLITI.

Abbot, Walter, 282.—Abbotysbury, John, Monk of Newenham, 248.—Abbotysbery, Rd., Monk of Forde, 51.—Abes, Rd., 282.—Adam, John, 61, 278; Adam (*alias* Cole) Walter, 104.—Appelby, Rob., Monk of Dunkeswell 81.—Averey, Rd. 85.—Alan, John, Fr. Preach., of Truro,—"Trurye" M.S.,—319.-Alcok, Thos., 6.—Aleyn, Rd., 5.—Aller, John, 44.—Alvecote, John, 23.—Aly, John, 80.—Alyn, Philip, Monk of Tavistock, 93; Wm., 151.—Alys. Thos., 208.—Andrew, John, [L. D., Dioc. B. & W.] 319.—Anstyswyll, Andrew, 159.—Archedekene, Master Michael, 38.—Argent, John, 319.—Arthur, Thos., 193.—Arysecote, Rd., 248.—Aston, Thos., 45.—atte Water, John, 6.—atte Wylle, Christopher, 248.—atte Yea, Thos., 114.—Aunger, John, "Conventus de Gyldeford," 3.—Axmynstre, Wm., Monk of Newenham, 248.—Ayschlegh, John, 129.—Aysah, Wm., Canon of Plympton, 98.—Ayashyll, John, Monk of Dunkeswell, 81.

Babyngton, John, 197.—Bacheler, Wm., Monk of Buckland, 163.—Baker, John, 154, 319; Nich., 45; Wm., 61.—Balaham, Nich., 50.—Ball, Hugh, 47; Nich., 193.—Baly, Thos., 104; Wm., 97.—Barger, Geoffrey, 115.—Barlych, John, Monk of Buckfast, 89, 95.—Baroun, Andr. St. John's Hosp., Exon., 62.—Barry, Wm., [L.D. Dioc. Winton], 159.—Barton, John, [L.D., from Vic. Gen., Dioc. B. & W.], 273.—Bastard, Nich., 91.—Bate, John, 116; Wm., 163.—Batyn, John, 278; Walter, 82.—Baudyn, Hy., 10; Thos., 163.—Baunton, John, 273.—Bealde, *alias* Baron, Roger, 152.—Beare, Alexander, 6; John, 45, 85; Wm., 154, 248.—Bele, John, 93; Nich., 88; Rd., 95.—Beale, Rob., 35.—Belworthy, Thos., 164.—Benet, John, 152.—Bertelot, John, 82.—Berton, Wm., [L.D., Dioc. Norwic.], 248.—Bery, Wm., 45.—Beste, John, 85.—Beston, John, 97.—Betty, Thos., [L.D.], 42.—Bevyll, Thos., 50.—Bexynton, Ralph, Monk of Forde, 131.—Blacdon, Jas., Fr. Preach., Exon., 115.—Blakeborme, John, Fr. Carmelit. 6.—Blakhill, Wm., 193.—Blatcheford, Thos., 98.—Blondon, Rob., 193.—Bokelond, John, Monk of Dunkeswell, 23.—Bokeryg, Thos., 248.—Bolham, John, 91.—Bole, Alexander. 193.—Bolter, John, 88.—Bonda, Roger, 95.—Bonde, John, 78.—Bone, John, 50.—Bonok, John, 6.—Borlegh, Roger, 154.—Bosent, Wm., 85.—Bosfrawell, Thos., 4.—Boale, Thos., St. John's Hosp., Exon., 91.—Boston, John, 319.—Bosvelek, Ralph, 89.—Boswyne, Rd., 208.—Boswynsols, Wm., 45.—Boterell, Geoffrey, 10; Rd., 278.—Botteburgh, Nich., 45.—Bounbury, John, 129.—Bour, John, 23.—Bovy, John, 129.—Boway, Nich., 80; Walter, 160.—Bowedon, John, 152, 241.—Bowode, John, 88, 91.—Boystok, John, Canon of Plympton, 44.—Bradeford, John, 10.—Bradelegh, Thos., V. of Buckland[-Monach.], 81.—Brampton, John, Fr. Minor, of Bridgewater, 248.—Bray, Thos., 151.—Brays, Walter, 282.—Bremerygge, John, St. John's Hosp., Exon., 93.—Brenta, Benedict, 97.—Brewys, Thos., 88.—Brok, Thos., 7.—Broke, Wm., 6.—Bromptyslegh, Hy., 93.—Brond, Jas., 163; Thos., 152.—Broun, John, 159; Rd., 7; Thos., 206; Walter, 81.—Brounyng, Wm., 10.—Brovste, Rd., 83.—Brune, John, 243.—Bruschford, Walter, 61.—Bryan, Steph., 152.—Brydon, Rd., Canon of Plympton, 278.—Brygge, John, 248.—Brystow, Thos., Fr. Carmelit., Plymouth, 35.—Bryt, John, Fr. Minor, Exon., 79.—Budde, John, Monk of Buckfast, 248; Wm., Monk of Buckfast. 79.—Bugge, Ingrianus, 152.—Buket, Nich., 115.—Bukknoll, Rob., 91.—Burnell, Thos., 159.—Burnerd, Wm., 282.—Burry, Wm., 6.—Busshebury, Lodewic, [L.D. Dioc. Worc.], 95.—Bykebury, John, Fr. Preach., Plymouth, 61; John, R. of Bigbury, 193.—Bykelake, Walter, 1.—Byrcomb, Rd., 202.

Cade, Wm., 50.—Cadya, Rd., 47.—Cadyho, Wm., 163.—Calmady, Hy., 114.—Calwe, John, 38.—Came, John, 273.—Campyng, *alias* Lurk, Rob., 159.—Camyll, Gervase, 243.—Camyl, John, 159.—Cantel (? Gantel, as in *Tonsurati*), Wm., 278.—Canyngton, John, Monk of Dunkeswell, 248.—Carlynton, Rob., 243.—Carpenter, Rd., 278.—Carslegh, Jas., 81.—Carvargh, Nich., 5.—Caskys, Hy., Monk of Dunkeswell, 248.—Castell, John, R. of Buckland Filleigh, 10.—Chalk, Rob., 10.—Chamberleyn, Rob., 81.—Chamberlayne, Thos., 6.—Chapelyn, Wm., 243.—Chapman, Rd., [L.D. (de Rysburgh, jurisd., Cantuar.)], 14.—Chepman, John, Canon of Hartland, 5; Simon, 98.—Charles, John, 91.—Chernemouth, John, Monk of Forde, 104.—

Chester, Walter, Monk of Buckfast, 241.—Choeshe, Wm., 248.—Chuddelegh, John 273.—Churyton, Wm. 114.—Chyterwyll, Walter, 129.—Clar, John, Monk of Cowick, 6.—Clegh, Wm., 197.—Clerk, John, 10, 131; Rob., 28, 243; Wm., Carmelit. de Sutton, *i.e.*, Plymouth, 45.—Cleyse, John, Fr. Preach. of Truro, 319.—Clok, John, 156.—Cloneneburgh, Wm., 81.—Clyk, Thos., 160.—Clyverdon, John, 1.—Coffyn, Edm., Monk of Buckfast, 79.—Cok, Wm., 63.—Coke, John, *and* Rd., 248; Rob., Monk of Buckland, 45; Thos., 206.—Cokyalegh, John, 115.—Colbron, Thos., 248.—Cole, John, 7, 45, 151; Ralph, 154; Rob., Fr. Preach. Exon, 152; Thos., 92; *see* Adam, Walter.—Coleford, Steph., Canon of Plympton, 193.—Colle, John, 5; Rd. *and* Walter, 159; Wm., 193.—Collyt, John, 42.—Colyn, Jas., 23; John, 154.—Colyford, John, 83.—Comb, Thos., 23; Wm., 1, 98.—Constans, John, 38.—Cook, John, 1; Canon of Torre, 6; Walter, 48; Wm., 5.—Copelston, Rob., 6; Wm., R. of Stowford, 202.—Coracote, Simon, 99.—Cork, John, 85.—Cornu, John, 7.—Couheth, John, 6.—Coule, Bernard, 5.—Cowlyng, John, 149.—Covlyng, Thos., 85.—Crabbe, Wm., 319.—Cranebury, John, Canon of Plympton, 81.—Cranmour, Rd., 94.—Crese, John, 156.—Crok, John, 10.—Crokker, Hy., Monk of Tavistock, 86.—Croppe, Adam, 278.—Crosse, Wm., 152.—Crugg, John, 115.—Crull, John, 114.—Cryspyn, Thos., Monk of Tavistock, 98.—Crystow, Thos., 154.—Cunygy, John, 273.—Curteys, John, Fr. Preacher, Exon, 243.—Cutefen, Walter, Monk of Dunkeswell, 278.

Daber, Walter, 6.—Danels, John, 115.—Darkyn, Thos. 149.—Davy, John, 45, 93, 193, ; Thos., 5.—Dawe, John, 89; Wm., 82.—Decam, John, 10.—Denclyve, John, 159.—Dene, John, 88.—Denesell, John, 278.—Denton, Wm., [L. D. Dioc. Lond.], 4.—Denys, Rob., 129.—Deyman, Henry, Canon of Plympton, 278; Wm., 241.—Dollebeare, Wm., 97.—Donscomb, Rd., R. of Shevioke, 84.—Dorset, John, 45.—Doune, Wm., 151.—Dove, Rd., Monk of Buckfast, 95.—Dowe, John, Fr. Preachers, Exon, 6; Rob., Monk of Buckfast, 89.—Doynel, John, 5.—Doyngued, Peter, Fr. Carmelit. Plymouth, 38.—Drake, John, 151; Rd., 10.—Dunham, Jas., 159.—Dunnyngg, Rob., [L. D.; Dioc. B & W.], 114.—Dygher, John, 248.—Dyght, John, R. St. Steph., Exeter, 62.—Dymmok, Walter, 10.—Dynham, Otho, 282.—Dyrell, Jas., 81.—Dyrmol, Hy. 6.

Edmund, Simon, 198.—Edward, John, 243; Rob., 198; Walter, 273.—Elcombe, John, 205.—Elys, John, 114; Thos., 10.—Emyot, Walter, 35.—Esoth, John, 92.—Esse, Wm., 63.—Estbrok, Thos., 1.—Estcote, Reginald, 91.—Eue, John, 163.

Fale, Wm., 248.—Fax, John, 45; Rd., 197.—Fayrwode, John, 116.—Feddys, George, 197.—Focher, Alexander, Canon of Plympton, 193.—Fokeray, John, Canon of Torre, 319—Folygan, Steph., 152.—Forde, Gregory, 104; John, 163; Thos*, 151; Wm. 282.—Foredon, John, 81.—Forthe, Thos., 39.—Fotryngay, John, 6.—Fountenay, Alex., 50.—Fox, Nich., 115.—Frank, Rob., 82.—Frankcheyne, Jas., R. 2nd Portion, Tiverton, 88.—Frend, Hy., 93.—Frensche, John, 159, 205.—Frye, Wm. 319.—Fychet, John, Monk of Buckfast, 152.—Fylcomb, Thos. 205.—Fylp, Nich., 243.

Gambon, John, 5.—Gardyner, Benedict, 81.—Gassy, John, Carmelit. Sutton, 97.—Gay, Rob., 282; Walter, 47.—Gede, ... 152.—Geek, Rd., 6.—Geke, Wm., 243.—Geffrey, Walter, 80.—Genys, John, 152.—Gerant, Adam, 5.—German, Walter, 282.—Gerocote, Wm., 85.—Gervys, John, 99.—Glamvyle, Thos., 45.—Gode, Rob., 159.—Godefray, John, 50.—Godman, Hy., 89.—Godyer, Thos., 241.—Gogwylmore, Rob., 42.—Gorde, John, 104; Walter, 104.—Gorewyll, John, R. of Roborough, 45.—Gorge, John, 241.—Grafton, Thos., [L. D. Dioc. Lincoln], 198.—Graynevyll, Rd., R. of Wydecomb, (Dioc., B. and W.) [L. D.], 42.—Grede, John, 5.—Grendon, Hy., 45.—Grene, John, 159.—Grussy, Peter, [L. D., Dioc. Sarum], 193.—Grys, John, 80.—Gun, Rob., 95.—Gunne, Henry, 94.—Gustum, Ralph, Fr. Preacher, Exon., 6.—Guynov, Thos., 1.—Gybbe, Gervase, 151; John, 104; Thos., 97, 83.—Gyban, Thos., 156.—Gydelegh, Rd., 93; Wm., 38.—Gydesham, John, 248.—Gyffard, John, 45; Steph., R. of W. Putford, 78.—Gyffort, Hugh, 115.—Gyll, Rd., 149.—Gylle, Steph., 205.—Gynne, John, 159.—Gyon, Roger, 278.—Gyst, Wm., Monk of Buckfast, 23.

Hake, John, 243.—Hakeworthy, Wm., 44.—Hall, Edw., 241.—Hamelyn, John, 99.—Harlok, Thos., 88.—Harry, John, 83, 205; Matth. 129; Nich., 47; Rd., 115;

Roger, 159.—Haseley, John, [L. D.], Carmelit Conv. Oxon, 4.—Hatter, Thos. .--Hauk, John, 42.—Haydure, Steph., 131.—Haydurer, Walter, 61.—Hayman Nich., 97.—Haysch, Walter, 50.—Helyer, Rd. 193.—Hemmyng, Wm., R. of Britton Dioc. Sarum, [L. D.], 319.—Hendre, Wm., 92.—Hendy, Rd., 273.—Henry, John 4.—Herbert*, Philip, 10; Rd., 6.—Herle, Wm., 5.—Herlywas, John, 84.—Hervy, Roger, 5.—Herynggeston, John, 99.—Heryngton, Wm., Dioc. Durham L. D.], 4.—Hevyltorr, Rob., 45.—Hobbe, Roger, 152.—Hode, Walter, 83.—Hogeyn, John, 273.—Hogge, Hugh, Monk of Dunkeswell, 88; John, 23.—Holland, Master John, "in utroque Jure Bacc."; R. St. John Bapt., Southampton, 81.—Holdych, Wm., Canon of Plympton, 278.—Holme, Walter, 93.—Hope, John, 6.—Hoppyng, John, 160.—Hornebroke, Wm. 152.—Horygh, Rd., 193.—Hough, Geoffrey, 278.—Howkere, Thos., [L. D. Dioc., Lland.], 149.—Hunte, Roger, 243.—Hugow, John, 7.—Hugou, Nich., [L. D.], "de Skeftlyng," Dioc. Linc., 9a.—Hurde, John, 114; Rd., 42.—Hurste, Rd. 97.—Hurt, Rd., 38.—Husy, John, 45.—Hycke, Wm., 282.—Hylle, John, 1; [Canon of Torre], 6; 45; [L. D. from Vic. Gen., Dioc., B. & W.] 248; [Monk of Buckland], 248; Roger. 115; Wm., 23.—Hyllyng, Hugh, 319.—Hylyne, Laurence, 89.—Hynde, Edmund, 154; Wm., 53.—Hyovese, Wm., 83.—Hyre, John, 243.—Hyskyn, John, 197; Wm., 6.

Ylond, John, 241.—Yrysch, John, 45.—Ysaac, Geoffrey, 149.—Ywan, Benedict, 91

Jagowe, Phil., 6.—Jamys, Thos., 85.—Janne, Nich., 6.—Jolyf, *or* Jolyff, John, , 282.—Jon, John, 115.—Jope, Rob., 163.—Judde, John, 89.—Jull, Rob., 114; Juyll, Roger, 159.

Kadarn, Rd., 160.—Karnec, Steph.. 156.—Kelly, John, 23.—Kelwa, Wm., 63.—Kena, Walter, 7, 278.—Kene, Edm., 115.—Kenelyon, John, 129.—Kent, Rob., 193; Wm., 46.—Kestell, Gregory, Fr. Preach., Exon, 7; Rd., 282.—Knoky, Rd., 278.—Knoll, Roger, 63.—Knyght, Henry, 5; John, 92; Rd., 6; Wm., 92.—Knyȝt, Thos., 6.—Krecov, Wm., 82.—Kylcam, John, Canon of St. German's 241.—Kyllyow, Peter, 273.—Kymaworthy, Thos., 46.—Kyng, John, 43, 159; Rob., 241, 278; Thos., 319; Kyngge, Wm., 93.—Kyngesten, Wm., Monk of Newenham, 248.—Kyngwyll, Rob., 115.—Kynygy, Hy., 243.

Lake, Walter, 115.—Lamport, John, Monk of Newenham, 273.—Lanaman, Wm., 129.—Lanceston, John, 5.—Landawarnak, Wm., Fr. Carmelit., Sutton i.e. Plymouth), 156.—Lane, Thos., 282; Wm., Fr. Preach. Plymouth, 61.—Lang, John, 152.—Lange, John, 91.—Langebroke, John, 98.—Langman, John, 248; Rob., 159.—Langeman, Rob., 42.—Langedon, Stephen, 85.—Langerygg, Arnulph, 91.—Laurens, John, 163.—Lauerance, Thos., 131.—Laury, Edw., 46.—Laverde, John, 97.—Lawe, Rd., 159.—Lawyr, Rd., 5.—Lawys, Thos., 197; Wm., 248.—Leche, Rd., Fr. Carmelit: Plymouth, 23.—Lewton, John, 248.—Leyman, John, 14.—Loddyn, John, Fr. Carmelit. Plymouth, 38.—Lode, Wm., 50.—Lodyston, Thos., 38.—Loman, John, 63.—London, John, 5.—London, *alias* Duckeley [Dioc. Lond., L.D.], 82.—Longley, Thomas [L.D.], R. of St. Alphege, Lond., 4.—Loryng, Thos., 129.—Loscuryon, Walter, 159.—Lovey, Rd., 193.—Loveton, John, 5; Rd., 319.—Loveworthy, Rd., 85.—Lucas, Thos., 89.—Luky, John, 197.—Lurk, *see* Campyng.—Lybet, Walter, 104.—Lydyngton, John, Canon of Hartland, 5.—Lyff, John, 163.—Lyle, Rd., Canon of Plympton, 79.—Lympton, Rd., 95.—Lyne, John, 241.—Lyneston, Thos., 129.—Lynyger, Walter, 6.—Lynrygg, Rd., 202.—Lythyngton, Rd., 197.—Lythȝfot, John, 6.—Lywer, Geoffrey, 116.

Mab, John, 46.—Made, Rob., 243.—Magge, Oliver, 206.—Malewayn, John, R. of Calstock, 45.—Mannyng, Roger, 3.—Marchaunt, Benedict, 23; Roger, Monk of Buckland, 5.—Marke, John, 61.—Marker, Walter, 81.—Marschal, Rd., 15.—Martyn, John, 5, 45, 159, 160; John, Monk of Buckfast, 241; John, 282; Thos., 163, 241; Walter, 38.—Maryot, Wm., 83.—Mathu, John, Monk of Buckfast, 248.—Mathy, John, 273.—Mattyngho, Gencian, Canon of Hartland, 45.—Mayer, John, Fr. Minor, Bodmin, 319.—Mayg, John, 160.—Mayne, Wm., 93.—Mayor, John, 42, 129; Wm., 89.—Mayster, Rd., 278.—Megge, Wm., of Colchester, 1.—Melbyry, John, 10.—Melford, Rd., 152.—Melyngy, Wm., 156.—Metton, John, 63.—Mey, John, 89, 93; Rob., 197.—Milward, Hy., 43; John, 62, 129.—Moggerys, Wm., 99.—Molenz, Thos., 197.—Monder, Wm., 205.—Monk, John, 243.—More, Henry, 89; John, 206; Rd., 50, 85; Thos., 319; Wm., 241.—

Morgan, Rd., Fr. Preach. Exon, 282.—Mortymer, Rob., 10.—Moryaux, John 78.—Morys, John, 156; Nich., 85.—Mouron, Ralph, 5.—Mowyn, Rd., 94.—Moys, John, 50, 243.—Mullyng, Wm., Canon of Bodmin, 154.—Michel, John, 47, 149, 319; Walter, 115; Walter, Fr. Minor, Exon, 273; Mylle, Wm., 1.—Myryfeld, John, Canon of Bodmin, 154.

Nanslouen, John, 243.—Neel, Wm., 114.—Newhale, John, 97.—Newenham, Rob., 278.—Newlyn, Rob., 6.—Newport, John, Monk of Dunkeswell, 23.—Noreys, Rd., 282.—Northwych, Andrew [L.D.] R. of St. Clement's in Candelwych Strete, London, 4.—Northewyche, John, Monk of Dunkeswell, 278.—Noecas, Wm., 114.—Nycoll, John, 81, 85, 149, 319.—Nycol, Hy., 205.—Nythercote, John, 273.—Nytheway, Hy., 61.—Nywecombe, John, 5.

Olyver, Alan, 241; John, 5.—Oppy,* John, 241.—Opys, Rd., 202.—Osanne, Peter, 319.—Osmound, Peter, 63, 114.—Oterforde, Nich., 45.—Oxenean, Wm., 116.

Pagett, John, 6.—Pakyn, Steph, 40.—Parker, John, 63, 243.—Parkham, Wm., Monk of Dunkeswell, 88.—Papeiay, John, 206.—Parll, John, 5.—Parys, John, 61, [Canon of Plympton], 115.—Pascow, John, 248.—Paslew, John, 163.—Patry, John, 151.—Pay, Thos., 197.—Payn, John, 95, 159, 206; Rob., 23, 115; Thos. 129.—Peake, John, 83. Pellyn, John, 208.—Penant, John, 282.—Penwyth, Walter, 6.—Pepat, John, 248.—Perrer, Peter, 63.—Pers, Walter, 23.—Pertrych, John and Wm., 319.—Peryn, John, 159.—Perys, Wm., 319.—Petthen, Thos., 282.—Phylypp, Rob., 241.—Piers, Wm., 88, 99.—Pleder, Geoffrey, 104.—Plympton, Michael, 6; Wm., Fr. Preach., Exon, 152.—Pollard, Walter, 5.—Poltronogov, Ralph, 82.—Pomery, Rd., 94.—Ponflete, Rd., Carmelit. de Sutton i.e. Plymouth, 45.—Pope, Hy. 99.—Porthcolam, Martin, 2.—Pouter, Hy., 5.—Pretor, John, 243.—Prewe, Thos., 1.—Printeys, Master Geoffrey, 46.—Puddyng, John, 163; Rob., 93.—Pura, John, 243.—Pyken, Joceus, 206.—Pylhede, Nich. 104.—Pynt, John, 198.—Pynwyn, Rd., 1.—Pyperd, John, 50.—Pytlond, Rd., Monk of Buckland, 45.—Pytte, Wm., 151.

Quyntrel, John, 202.

Raw, Rd., 282; Wm., 273.—Raulyn, Edm., 241; John, 85, 273.—Rayschlegh, John, 50.—Reawld, Ralph, Fr. Preach., Exon, 282.—Rede, Baldwin, 282; Peter, 104; Wm. 10.—Rem, Hy., 156.—Reprena, Thos., 248.—Repyngton, Wm. [L.D.], R. of Abketilby, Dioc. Linc., 4.—Resprynn, Ralph, 273.—Rewe, Wm., 1.—Resuhorn, John, 319.—Reynald, Gregory, 7.—Raynald, John, 38.—Reynold, John, 91; Raynold, John, 104.—Raynald, Walter, 6.—Reynowdyn, Rd., 163.—Robert, Hy., 197; John, 319; Rd., 273.—Robyn, John, 81; Thos., 36.—Roddon, John, Monk of Buckfast, 241.—Rogeer,* John, 10.—Rogger, Thos., 83.—Rokelond, John, 248.—Rolf, Wm., Monk of Buckland, 35.—Roskasa, John, 46.—Row, John, 202; Rob., 78; Walter, 198; Wm., 50.—Roys, John, 198.—Rychard, Hy., 129; Jas., 248; John, R. of E. Worlington, 10.—Rygge, Thos., 23.—Rynald, John, 91.—Ryppelegh, John, 115.—Rysoy, John, 278.

Sarger, John, 159, 273.—Saunder, Roger, 193.—Sayer, John, 160.—Scambel, Wm., 149.—Schaftis, Ralph, [L.D.] Carmelit. Conv. Oxon, 4.—Schaplegh, John, 205.—Schepehurde, John, 282.—Schere, Hy., 104; Thos., 381; Wm., 104.—Scherpe, John, Carmelit. Sutton, i.e. Plymouth, 97.—Schoche, John, 193.—Schulder, Thos., 278.—Schute, Geoffrey, [L.D.—Dioc., B. & W.], 78.—Schyphurd, Thos., 202.—Scoch, Wm., 45.—Scoce, Wm., 273.—Scosse, John, 61.—Scotard, John, 6.—Scote, Rd., 47.—Sekerlegh, Wm., 319.—Seller, Walter, 62.—Selman, Walter, 282.—Sergeaux, Rd., 282.—Serle, Walter, [L.D., Dioc. B. & W.], 319.—Sertyn, Walter, 248.—Sewragh, Walter, 282.—Skerell, John, 91.—Skewys, John, 206.—Skoch, Thos., Monk of Torre, 98.—Skyllam, John, 241.—Slokok, Thos. 154.—Smale, Wm., 82.—Smert, Master Hugh, R. of All Hallows on the Walls, Ex., 88.—Smyrt, Rob., 241.—Smyth, John, 48, 97, [L.D. Dioc., Lincoln], 98; Lawrence, 104; Walter, 88.—Snowblanche, Wm., 278.—Soby, Rob., 46.—Somerhay, John, [Dioc. B. & W.; L.D. Magistri Joh. Rouland, V.G.], 243.—Somerset, Wm., Monk of Dunkeswell, 88.—Sosun, T., 152.—Southcote, John, 199.—Southwode, John, 45.—Sparke, Hugh, 149.—Spear, Roger, 47; Wm. 98.—Sperman, Gilbert, 248.—Spord, John, Monk of Buckland, 282.—Stacy, Wm., 273.—Stancombe, John, 5.—Staurin, Joh. de, Fr. Minor of Bridgwater, 193.—Stephyn, John, Monk of Tavistock, 248; Nich., 159; Paul, 10; Peter, 4; Rd., 208; Thos., 6; Wm., 83.—Storme,

Simon, 152.—Stoter, Thos., 198.—Stowte, Ralph, 202.—Stowteworthy, Rd., 248.—Stratton, Peter, Fr. Preach., Plymouth, 61.—Stratton, Thos., Monk of Forde, 5.—Strurth, Roger, 82.—Stryke, R., 93.—Stybbe, John, 129.—Sutton, John, 243.—Swerdecote, John, 5.—Symon, John, 46; Paschasius, 282; Peter, [L.D., Dioc. Meneven.], 163; Thos., 151; Wm., 23.—Sypstall, Wm., 319.

Tallan, Thos., 6.—Talwarth, John, 156.—Tunkert, *alias* Schypwash,* John, 129.—Taunt, Rob., 38.—Taylour, John, 6, 243; Ralph, 197; Thos., 241.—Thomas, John, 5, 89, 163, 319; Roger, 114.—Thome, John, 46.—Thommas, John, 202.—Thommа, Hy., 206.—Tomme, John, 114.—Thomme, Rd., 115, 206.—Thornbury, John [L.D. Dioc. Worcest.], 2.—Thornyng, John, 205.—Thurlok, John, "per dominum manumissus," 152.—Toker. John, 10; Roger, 319; Wm. 6, 82, 152.—Toly, John, 61.—Top, Wm., Fr. Preacher, Exon, 6.—Toruer, John, 81, 88; Maurice, 95.—Torryng, Wm., 151.—Toser, Reginald. 129; Roger, 47.—Toune, Rob., Canon of Plympton, 78.—Tovnysende, Walter, 83.—Tras, Rd. 6.—Tredydan, Steph., 115.—Tredynek, John, 159.—Tregansorn, Rd., 197.—Tregelyst, John, 319.—Tregyrthek, Wm., Canon of Bodmin, 154.—Treloywyan, David, 129.—Tremayn, Rd., 248; Thos., 6.—Trembras, Alex., 282.—Tremenhyr, Steph., 86.—Treneglos, Mich., 197.—Trepesek, Ralph, 43.—Tresagher, Mich., 156; Rich., 88.—Tresavsyn, Roger, 116.—Trethevyn, Wm., Fr. Carmelit., Exon, Dioc., 243.—Trethewy, John, 154; Walter, 48.—Trevenek, Ralph, 2.—Trevethen, Ralph, Fr. Preacher, Exon, 23.—Trevlyan, Rd., 5.—Trevman, John, 193.—Trevohan, John, 114.—Trevotre, Thos., 10.—Trevyn, Rob. 82.—Trevyskyn, Nich., 151.—Trewandra, Ralph, Canon of St. German's, 5.—Treye, *alias* Stocker, Wm., 94.—Treyngof, Walter, 131.—Tropp, Hy., 197.—Trote, Nich., 81.—Troyll, John, 91.—Truru, Roger, 62.—Trust, John, 91.—Tryvet, John, 7.—Twykenham, Fr. Wm., 3.—Twyte, John, 63.—Tylle, John, 79; Wm., 5.—Typet Baldwin, 193.—Tyrell, John, 6; John, 206.

Umfray, John, 63.

Veale, Geffrey, 83.—Vele, John, 199.—Velow, Laurence, 149.—Vool, Rob., 202.—Vorst, John, 47.—Vyen, John, 47.

Wade, John, 92, 160.—Waddon, Thos., 282.—Waleys, John, 10.—Wallyng, Thos., 241.—Walop, John, 6.—Walsche, John, 206.—Walter, Thos., 10, 129; Wm., 205; Warde, Rob., 85; Thos., 6; Wm., 151.—Warre, Thos., 88.—Waryn, John, 5; Thos., 154.—Water, Philip, 61.—Watte, Wm., 5; Waty, John, 282.—Wayte, Rd., 2.—Webber, Hy., 159.—Welaffyn, Peter, 45.—Welfare, Rd., 10.—Well, John, 116.—Wellyworth, Thos., 241.—Wenley, John, Fr. Minor of Bridgewater, 205.—Weryng, John, 10.—Wethen, Nich., 159.—Whatty, Laurence, 159.—Whyselwyll, Nich., 15.—Whyte, John, 273; Wm., 282; Whytelond, Rd., Monk of Dunkeswell, 99.—Wilkot, Benedict, 82.—Wylcok, John, 160.—Willelmi, Nicholas, Canon of Torre, 319.—Wobroke, Thos., 62.—Wode, Rob., 7; Thos., 23.—Wodehous, Thos. [L.D., Ebor. Dioc.], 248.—Wodelond, John [L.D., Dioc. B. & W.], 193.—Wodham, John, 10.—Woforde, John, 61.—Wollay, John, 1.—Wolston, John, R. of St. Endellion, 193.—Wone, John, 61.—Wonston, Geoffrey, 151; Matthew, R. of Maperton (Dioc. B. & W.), 86.—Worthyn, John, 116.—Woven, Hy., 197.—Wrykke, Wm., 319.—Wybbury, John, 99.—Wydelegh, Rob., 61.—Wyke, John, 82; Rd., 10.—Wylberton, Ralph, 278.—Wylkyn, John, 156.—Wylle, John, 45, 129, 154, 198; Fr. Ralph, 319; Rob., 159; Thos., 160.—Wyllyam, John, 47, 282; Martin, 193; Thos., 92.—Wyllyng, John, Canon of Plympton, 81.—Wymond, Ralph, 6.—Wyndegrynde, John, 10.—Wynnegode, Hy., 163.—Wyse, John, 81; Wm. 10.—Wyt, Nich., 319.

Yolton, Baldwin, 152.—Yurd, Wm., 282.—Yurl, Rd., Canon of St. Stephen's, Launceston, 115.—Yurll, Simon, 151.

Ȝeylake, Ralph, 45.

III. SUBDIACONI.

T. *signifies the "Title."*

Abbotysbury. John; Monk of Newenham, 273.—Abendon, Peter [L.D., Dioc. Worc.]; T. Torre Abbey, 159.—Adam, John; T. St. German's Priory, 319.—Alby. John, "Frater Ordinis de Monte Carmel., Exon Dioc." 154.—Alcok, Thos., Monk of Tavistock, 23.—Alre, John; T. his R. of Ebryghton, Dioc. Sarum, 83.—Alvethcote, John; T. Frithelstock Priory, 43.—Alyn, Phil., Monk of Tavistock, 99.—Anstyswyll, Andr., ; T. Launceston Priory. 163. —Appilby, Rob.; Monk of Dunkeswell, 82.—Artour, Thos.; T. Bodmin Priory, 243.—Aston, Thos.; T. Newenham Abbey, 47.—atte Beare, Alexander; T. Canonsleigh Abbey, 10.—atte Welle, Rob. [L. D.—Dioc. B. & W.]; T. St. John's Hospital, 50.—Axmenstre, Wm.; Monk of Newenham, 273.—Aylmer, John; T. St. Nich., Priory, Exon, 131.—Austyn, John; T. Buckfast Abbey, 47.—Ayschecote, Wm.; T. St. Nich. Priory, Exon, 5.—Aysech, Wm., Canon of Plympton, 104.—Aryssechote, Rd.; T. Buckland Abbey, 319.—Aysse, Walter; T. Frithelstock Priory, 85.—Aysshill, John; Monk of Dunkeswell 82.

Bacheler, Wm., Monk of Buckland, 197.—Baker, John; T. Margam Abbey, Dioc. Lland, 319.—Baly, Thos.; T. St. Nich., Priory, Exeter, 104; Wm., T. Bodmin Priory, 98.—Barber, Thomas, Canon of Osney, 2.—Barger, Geoffrey; T. Dunkeswell Abbey, 115.—Barlys, John; Monk of Buckfast, 95.—Baron, Andr., St. John's Hosp., Exon, 63.— Barry, Wm. [L.D. Dioc. Winton]; T. St. Nich. Priory, Exon 160.—Batyn, John; T. his R. of Denbury, 278.—Baudyn, John; T. Dunkeswell Abbey, 10; Thos.; T. Bodmin Priory, 164.—Baunton, Wm., T. Torre Abbey, 6.—Bayslegh John; T. Frithelstock Priory, 79.—Bealde, John; T. Torre Abbey, 6; Roger, T. St. German's Priory, 156.—Beare, John; T. Dunkeswell Abbey, 114.—Becent, Wm., T. Launceston Priory, 97.—Beere, Wm.; T. St. Nich. Priory, Exon, 319.—Bele, John; T. Newenham Abbey. 99; Nich.; T. Canonsleigh Abbey, 39; Walter, T. Launceston Priory, 81.—Beneht, Ralph (of Lincl. Dioc.); T. Maiden Bradleigh Priory, 198.—Benet, Roger; T. Bodmin Priory, 43. —Berthelet, John; T. Launceston Priory, 88.—Berty, Thos. [L. D. Linc. Dioc.]; T. St. Nich. Priory, Exon. 48.—Berye, Wm.; T. St. Nich. Priory, Exon, 61.—Bettow, John; T. Totnes Priory, 129.—Bexington, Ralph, Monk of Forde, 131.—Blake, John [L.D. Dioc. Sarum]; T. Abb. "de Bruera," Lincoln Dioc., 154. —Blakebrome, John, Carmelit. de Plymouth, 7.—Blakehay, Roger; T. St. Nich. Priory, Exon, 10.—Blakehille, Wm. T. Launceston Priory, 273.—Blaklond, John; T. St. Nich. Priory, Exon, 5.—Bodily, Rd.; T. Hales Abbey, 273.—Bodman, Thos., Monk of Dunkeswell, 198.—Bokeknoll, Rob.; T. Dunkeswell Abbey, 93.—Bokelond, John; Monk of Dunkeswell, 38.—Bole, John, [L.D. Johannis Roland, Dioc. B. & W., V.G.]; T. Pilton Priory, 248.— Bolham, John; T. Cleeve Abbey (Dioc. B. & W.) 99.—Bonde, Roger; T. Tavistock Abbey 114.—Boryslegh, Thos.; Hosp., of St. John, Exon., 92.—Boscawen, John; Friar Minor of Bristol, 273.—Bosseȝyow, Nich., Friar Preacher of Truro [Trurie, MS.] 78.—Bosvisek, Ralph; T. Bodmin Priory, 91.—Boswyns Wm.; Canon of Bodmin, 46.—Boterel, John; T. the D. & C., Exon., 10.—Botrigam, Wm.; Torre Abbey, 248.—Botston, John; T. the same, 129.—Botteburgh, Nich., of Exeter, 46.—Boun, John, Monk of Buckland, 6.—Boure, John; T. Frithelstock Priory, 47.—Bowden, John; T. his R. of Dartington, 278.—Bowedon, John, junior; T. Barnstaple Priory, 154.—Bowey, Nich.; T. Dunkeswell Abbey, 91.—Boway, Walter; T. his R. of St. John in Cornwall, 193.—Bowode, John; T. Dunkeswell Abbey, 115.—Bradeforde, John; T. Dunkeswell Abbey, 50.—Bradlegh, Thos.; T. his V. of Buckland-Monachorum, 82.—Bray, Wm., M.A.; T. Bodmin Priory, 47.—Bremelcombe, Wm.; T. his R. of Nymet Tracy, 10.—Bremerygg, John; Hosp. St. John, Exon, 129.—Brenta, Benedict; T. Buckfast Abbey, 97.—Brewys, Thos.; T. Launceston Priory, 115.—Brok, Thos.; T. St. German's Priory, 43.—Brond, Jas.; T. Frithelstock Priory, 206.—Bronwon, Ralph; T. Launceston Priory, 241.—Broun, John; T. St. Nich. Priory, Exon, 160.—Brounyng, Wm.; "Ad titulum Domini sibi concessum," 82.—Brouste, Rd.; T. Tavistock Abbey,

5.—Brugys, Thos. ; Friar, Preacher of Guildford, 2.—Brydon, Rd. ; Canon of Plympton Priory, 282.—Brygge, "Dompnus Johannes"; Monk of Newenham, 7.—Bryscheforde, Walter ; T. Berlinch Priory, 104.—Brytte, John ; Friar Minor of Exeter, 81.—Buckeytte, Nich. ; T. Buckfast Abbey, 160.—Budde, John ; Monk of Buckfast, 278 ; Wm., ditto, 81.—Buggh, Ingram ; T. Buckland Abbey, 154.—Bullok, John ; T. Bodmin Priory, 5.—Burdet, Thos., [L.D.] T. his R. of Aston Cantlow, 43.—Burnebury, John ; T. his R. of Exbourne, 131.—Busshebury, Lewis ; [L.D. Dioc., Worc.], "ad titulum Domini," 97.—Byale, Rob. ; T. Frithelstock Priory, 38.—Bykebury, John ; T. his R. of Bigbury, 193.—Byrcomb, Rd. ; T. Dunkeswell Abbey, 243.

Cade, Wm. ; T. Launceston Priory, 79.—Cadia, Rd. ; T. St. German's Priory, 48.—Cadyho, Wm. ; T. Buckfast Abbey, 197.—Calmady, Hy. ; T. Bodmin Priory, 115.—Campyng, (*alias* Lurk), Rob. ; T. Barnstaple Priory, 163.—Camyl, John ; T. Bodmin Priory, 241.—Canyngton, John ; Monk of Dunkeswell, 273.—Carpenter, Rd. ; T. Dunkeswell Abbey, 282.—Carslake, John, *see* Mopill.—Carslegh, James ; T. his R. of Bradford, 278.—Castel, John, [L.D., Dioc. Cov. & Lichf.] ; T. his R. of Buckland Fillegh, 23.—Champyon, Wm. ; T. Littlemore Priory, 43.—Chepman, John, Canon of Hartland, 6.—Chapman, Rd. ; "de Rysburgh, jurisdict. Cantuar." [L.D.], 4.—Chaunberleyn, Rob. ; T. Bodmin Priory, 82.—Chernemouth, John ; Monk of Forde, 104.—Chester, Walter ; Monk of Buckfast, 241.—Chyryton, Wm. ; T. S. Nich. Priory, Exon, 160.—Chyterwyl, Walter ; T. Newenham Abbey, 149.—Clement, Victor ; Friar Preacher, Exon, 243.—Clerk, John ; T. Launceston Priory, 47.—Cloneneburgh, Wm. ; T. Buckfast Abbey, 84.—Clyk, Thos. ; T. Hartland Abbey, 193.—Clyverdon, John ; T. the same, 42.—Cok, Wm. ; T. Torre Abbey, 156.—Coke, John, [L.D., Dioc. B. & W.] ; T. Taunton Priory, 319.—Colard, John ; T. St. Nich. Priory, Exon, 61.—Colbron, Thos. ; T. Tavistock Abbey, 273.—Cole, John ; T. Totnes Priory, 93 ; Ralph ; T. St. Nich. Priory, Exon, 159 ; Thos. ; T. Buckland Abbey, 98.—Coleford, Steph. ; Canon of Plympton Priory, 198.—Colle, John ; T. St. Nich. Priory, Exon, 6 ; Rd. ; T. Bodmin Priory, 198 ; Wm. ; T. St. Nich. Priory, Exon, 197.—Colles, John ; T. the same, 43.—Columpton, John ; T. St. German's Priory, 241.—Coly, Jas., Fr. Preach. of Truruye (Truro) 45.—Colyford, John ; T. Newenham Abbey, 151.—Colyn, Hy. ; T. St. Nich. Priory, Exon, 95 ; John ; T. Osney Abbey, 198 ; Ralph ; T. his R. of Lansallos, 63 ; Rob. ; T. Hartland Abbey, 1.—Combe, Thos. ; T. Frithelstock Priory, 81 ; Wm. ; T. St. Nich Priory, Exon, 40.—Cook, John, Canon of Torre, 23 ; Walter ; T. Torre Abbey, 86.—Cooksone, John ; T. St. Nich. Priory, Exon, 243.—Copfyn, Edm. ; Monk of Buckfast, 81.—Copleston, Wm. ; T. his R. of Stowford, 202.—Cork, John ; T. Tavistock Abbey, 42 ; Cork, *alias dictus* Philipp, John ; T. St. Nich. Priory, Exon, 91.—Cornu, John T. Hartland Abbey, 98.—Coryton, Andr. ; T. his Preb. in Crantock, 9.—Cote, Wm. ; T. St. Nich. Priory, Exon, 10.—Courtenay, Master Rd. ; T. Bosham, his Preb. of Westbrook, 8.—Courteys, John ; Friar Preacher of Exeter, 273.—Curteys, Wm. ; T. Bodmin Priory, 241.—Covlyng, John ; T. St. Nich. Priory, Exon, 243.—Cowyk, John, [L.D. Dioc. Linc], T. Elsham Priory, 79.—Crabbe, Wm. ; T. St. German's Priory, 319.—Crambre, John ; Canon of Plympton, 82.—Crede, John ; [Dioc. of B. & W.], T. Newenham Abbey, 6.—Crekow, Wm. ; T. Newenham Abbey, 89.—Crokker, Hy., Monk of Tavistock, 86.—Crosse, John ; Carmelite of Plymouth, 104.—Croste, John, [L.D. Dioc. of B. & W.] ; T. "Stodeleye" Priory, 154.—Crulle, John ; T. Canonsleigh Abbey, 114.—Crympe, John, [L.D., Dioc. B. & W.] ; T. Berlinch Priory, 86.—Crempe, Wm. ; T. St. German's Priory, 43.—Cryspyn, Thos. ; Monk of Tavistock, 99.—Cunygy, John, T. Bodmin Priory, 319.—Cutteven, Walter ; Monk of Dunkeswell, 282.

Danels, John ; T. St. Nich. Priory, Exon, 115.—David, Wm. [L.D. Dioc. Menev.] ; T. Priory of St. John Evang., Carmarthen [Kermerdyn, MS.], 149.—Davy, John ; T. Forde Abbey, 94.—Dawe, John ; T. Glasney College, 90 ; Wm., T. St. German's Priory, 86.—Dekam, John ; T. Dunkeswell Abbey, 23.—Dene, John, monk of Dunkeswell, 99.—Denys, Rob. ; T. Launceston Priory, 131.—Deyman, Henry ; Canon of Plympton Priory, 282 ; Wm., ; T. St. Nich., Priory, Exon, 243.—Donscomb, Rd. ; T. his R. of Sheviocke, 84.—Donyell, Peter, Carmelite of Sutton, 45.—Dornyng, John ; T. Buckfast Abbey, 282.—Dorsed, John ; T. Tavistock Abbey, 50.—Doulton, John, Canon of Torre, 5.—Dove, Rd. ; monk of Buckfast, 95.—Downe, John, Friar Preacher, Exon, 7 ; Walter ; Friar Preacher. Exon, 154.—Doyngel, John ; T. St. German's Priory, 42.—Drayton, Thos. ; T. his R. of Lydiard-St.-Laurence, Dioc. B, & W. [L.D.], 88.—Dreuek, Hy. ; T. Launceston Priory, 6.—Dukeslee, John, *see* London.—Dunham, John ; Canon of Frithelstock Priory, 163.—Dunnyng, Rob. [L.D. Dioc. B. & W.] ; T. St. Nich. Priory, Exon, 129.—Dygon, John ; T. his R. of Bledewarth, Dioc. Menev., 50.—Dygth, John ; T. his R. of St. Stephen's, Exon, 63.—Dymmok, Ralph ; T. Tavistock Abbey, 5 ; Walter ; T. Frithelstock Priory, 35.—Dyrehyll, Jas. ; T. Launceston Priory, 97.—Dyreward, John ; T. Tavistock Abbey, 6.

Edilston, John [L.D., Dioc. Ebor.] ; T. Launceston Priory, 282.—Edward, Rob. ; T. Buckfast Abbey, 248 ; Walter ; T. Bodmin Priory, 319.—Elyn, John ; T. the same, 94.—Elyot, John ; T. Dunkeswell Abbey, 45.—Erle, John ; T. the same. 273.—Esoth, John ; T. Bodmin Priory, 93.—Estebrok, Master Thos. ; T. St. Nich. Priory, Exon, 6.—Estecote, John ; T. Berlinch Priory, 23.—Ewn, Rob., Canon of Launceston Priory, 115.

Faukys, Wm. (Dioc. Wells) ; T. Bruton Abbey, 5.—Fax, Rd. ; T. St. German's Priory, 198.—Fayrwode, John ; T. his R. of Alwington, 116.—Feddys, Geo. ; T. Frithelstock Priory, 198.—Felaw, Wm. ; T. Newenham Abbey, 319.—Ferys, Rob. ; T. Beaulieu Abbey, 42.—"Hugo, filius Simonis Mawnus, de Toynton superiore ad Titulum Custodis et Confratrum Cantarie de Spillesby, Dioc. Linc.," 8.—Focher. Alexander ; Canon of Plympton Priory, 198.—Fodrymgheye, John ; T. St. Nich. Priory, Exon, 80.—Folde, Walter [L.D., Dioc. Sarum] ; T. Abbotsbury Abbey, 193.—Folygan, Stephen ; T. Launceston Priory, 248.—Forde, Gregory ; T. St. German's Priory, 154 ; Hugh [L.D., Dioc. B. & W.] ; T. Cleeve Abbey, 154 ; John ; T. Dunkeswell Abbey, 86 ; John ; T. St. Nich. Priory, Exon, 193 ; (*alias* Row), Thos. ; T. Launceston Priory, 243.—Fordon, John ; T. Tavistock Abbey. 86.—Forthe, Thos. ; T. Bodmin Priory, 43.—Frankcheyne, Jas. ; T. his (2nd) Portion in the Church of Tiverton, 89.—Fraunces, Nich. ; T. Bodmin Priory, 198.—Frend, Hy. ; T. Pilton Priory, 95.—Frengy, Wm. ; T. Launceston Priory, 5.—Frenssh, John ; T. Buckfast Abbey, 205 ; John ; T. St. Nicholas' Priory, Exon, 206.—Frode. John ; T. Hospital of St. John Bapt., Bridgewater, 92.—Fouke, John ; T. his R. of Parkham, 11.—Fyllecombe, Thos. ; T. St. Nicholas' Priory, Exon, 206.

Gambon, John ; T, Dunkeswell Abbey, 45.—Gassy, John, Carmelite of Plymouth, 104.—Gay, Walter ; T. Frithelstock Priory, 94.—German, Hugh ; T, St. Nich. Priory, Exon, 5.—Glamvyle, Thos., Canon of Plympton, 79.—Gode, Robt. ; T, Tavistock Abbey, 160 ; Wm. ; T, Buckland Abbey, 6.—Godeberre, Hy., [L.D.], Ord. Augustin., London, 4.—Godefray, John ; T, Launceston Priory, 80.—Godman, Hy. ; T. Hartland Abbey, 104.—Godyer, Thos. ; T, Launceston Priory, 282.—Godysloud, John, [L. D., from John Rouland, V.G., Dioc., B. & W. ; T. St. Nich. Priory, Exon., 197.—Golde, Thos., Friar Minor, Exon, 89 ; Gorde, John ; T, Torre Abbey, 159 ; Walter ; T. Hartland Abbey, 159.—Gorecote, Simon ; T, Launceston Priory, 104 ; Wm. ; T, the same, 104.—Gorewyk, Master John, junior ; T, his R. of Roborough 45.—Grafton, Thos., [L. D.,Dioc. Linc.] ; T, Buckland Abbey, 198.—Graunson, John, [Dioc. Sarum,—"Galfridi Crukadan, utriusque juris Inceptoris," V.G.] ; T, Montacute Priory, Dioc. B. & W., 241.—Graynevyll, Rd., ; T his R. of Wydecombe, Dioc., B. & W., [L.D.], 43.—Gregor, Hy. ; T, Bodmin Priory, 5.—Grussy, Peter, [L. D. Sarum] ; T Abbotsbury Abbey, 193.—Gunne, Hy. : T, Hosp. St. John Bapt. Wells, 94.—Gune, Roger ; T, Launceston Priory, 282.—Gybbs, Thos. ; T, Bodmin Priory, 104.—Gybbe, John ; T, St. German's Priory, 197 ; Thos. ; T, Torre Abbey, 89.—Gyddelegh, Wm. ; T, Launceston Priory, 44.—Gyffard, Hugh ; T, the same, 149 ; John ; T, Dunkeswell Abbey, 94 ; Steph ; T his R, of West Putford, 79.—Gylle, Rd., T, St. German's Priory, 149 ; Steph ; T, Frithelstock Priory, 241.—Gynys, John ; T, St. German's Priory, 154.—Gyst, Wm., Monk of Buckfast, 38.

Hakeworth, Wm., T, St. Nich. Priory, Exon., 63.—Halle, John, [L.D. Dioc., B. & W.] ; T, Montacute Priory, 282.—Halswylle, Rd. ; T, St. Nich. Priory, Exon, 1.—Harde, John ; T, the same, 151.—Harry, John ; T, Buckfast Abbey, 94 ; Matth., T. Barnst. Priory, 197.—

Nich. ; T, Bodmin Priory, 193 ; Rd. ; T, St. Nich. Priory, Exon, 131 ; Roger, T, Launceston Priory, 160 ; Thos. ; T, Bodmin Priory, 44.—Hathy, Thos. ; T. Hartland Abbey, 5.—Hauk, John ; T, Littlemore Priory, 43.—Haydur, Stephen ; T, St. Nich. Priory, Exon, 149 ; Walter ; T, the same, 80.—Hayman, Nich. ; T, Buckfast Abbey, 152.—Helyer, Peter ; Monk of Tavistock, "ad presentacionem Fratris Johannis Houche, Monachi professi ejusdem Domus," 6.—Helygan, John, Canon of St. German's, 81.—Helys, Thos. ; T, Dunkeswell Abbey, 44.—Henry, John, Canon of Bodmin, 45 ; John ; T, Bodmin Priory, 95.—Herberd, Philip ; T, Buckfast Abbey, 23.—Herlywas, John ; T, Bodmin Priory, 86.—Hervy, Roger ; T, St. Nich. Priory, Exon, 5.—Hevytorre, Rob. ; T, the same, 46.—Hobbe, Roger ; T, Launceston Priory, 154.—Hode, Walter ; T. Plympton Priory, 94.—Hogge, Hugh ; T, St. Nich. Priory, Exon, 93 ; Thos. ; T, Hartland Abbey, 5.—Holand, Master John, "in utroque jure Bacc" ; T. his R, of St. John Bapt., Southampton, [L. D.], 81.—Holdych, Wm., Canon of Plympton, 282.—Holne, Wm. ; T, Montacute Priory, Dioc. B. & W., 98.—Holrugg, Wm. ; T. Osney Abbey, 4.—Hoppyng, John ; T, Newenham Abbey, 319.—Horlok, Thos. ; T, St. Nich. Priory, Exon, 93.—Hoskyn, John ; T, the same, 319.—Hosye, Nich. ; T, the same, 1.—Hough, Geoffrey ; T his R. of Combe-in-Teign-Head, 278.—Howe, Rd. ; T, Dunkeswell Abbey, 38.—Howkere, Thos., [L.D., Dioc. Lland.], "ad titulum Prioratus Beate Marie Magdalene de Goldelina, dicte Landavensis Diocesis," 163.—Hoyge, John ; T, St. Nich. Priory, Exon, 63.—Hurde, John ; T., D. and Ch. of Exeter, 129 ; Rd., T, Holy Trin. Priory, London, 43.—Husey, John ; T, Dunkeswell Abbey, 46.—Hyeovyse, Wm. ; T. Torre Abbey, 116.—Hylle, John, Canon of Torre Abbey, 193 ; John, Monk of Buckland, 282.—Hille, Roger ; T, St. Nich. Priory, Exon, 116.—Hylyne, Laurence, [L.D., Dioc. Menev.] ; T, the same, 90.—Hyskyn (alias Rov) John ; T, St. German's Priory, 198.—Hyskyn, Wm. ; T, the same, 38.

Ibel, John ; T. Bodmin Priory, 83.—Irysch, John ; T. Totnes Priory, 46.—Isaak, Geoffrey ; T. Buckfast Abbey, 107.

Jakys, John ; "ad Titulum gracie Domini," 4.—James, Wm. ; T. Canonsleigh Abbey, 89.—Janua, Nich. ; T. Bodmin Priory, 44.—Jede, John [L.D. Dioc. B. & W.] ; T. Taunton Priory, 193.—Job, Rob. ; T. Bodmin Priory, 164.—Joce, John ; T. the same, 151.—"Johannes,"... ; T. St. Nich. Priory, Exon, 84.—Jon, John ; T. Frithelstock Priory, 159.—Judde, John ; T. Canonsleigh Abbey, 197.—Junte, Geoffrey ; T. St. Nich. Priory, Exon, 156.—Juyll, Roger ; T. Buckfast Abbey, 163.

Karter, John ; T. Frithelstock Priory, 23.—Kayskeys, Hy. ; Monk of Dunkeswell, 273.—Kelly, John ; T. Frithelstock Priory, 35.—Kelwa, Wm. ; T. Tavistock Abbey, 164.—Kemeworthy, Thos. ; T. Frithelstock Priory, 63.—Kenelyon, John ; T. St. Nich. Priory, Exon, 131.—Kent, Wm. ; T. St. German's Priory, 79.—Kestel, Rd. ; T. Bodmin Priory, 319.—Keuryg, Rd. ; T. Barlinch Priory, 282.—Knygh, Wm. ; T. Torre Abbey, 98.—Knyght, Hy., T. Taunton Priory, 282.—Kylcam, John ; Canon of St. German's Priory, 241.—Kyng, John, Canon of Plympton, 44 ; Rob. ; T. St. German's Priory, 282.—Kyngeston, Wm. ; Monk of Newenham, 273.

Lamleder, John ; T. Bodmin Priory, 5.—Lamport, John ; Monk of Newenham 278.—Lanaman, Wm. ; Canon of Launceston Priory, 159.—Lanbrobys, (*alias* Wylkyn) John ; T. St. Nich. Priory, Exon, 164.—Lane, Wm. ; Friar Preacher of Exeter, 78.—Langa, Reginald ; T. Plympton Priory, 154.—Langadon, Steph., T. St. Nich. Priory, Exon, 88.—Lange, Master Thos. ; T. his R. of Instow, 83 ; —Langebrook, John ; T. Tavistock Abbey, 205.—Langrygh, Arnulph ; T. Buckfast Abbey, 92.—Lannergh, John ; T. Bodmin Priory, 104.—Lanrak, Fr. John ; Ordinis Fratrum Carmelit, 1.—Launston, John ; T. St. Nich. Priory, Exon, 10.—Laurens, John ; T. Bodmin Priory, 248.—Lavyngton, John ; T. Buckfast Abbey, 10.—Lebet, Walter ; T. Cowick Priory, 114.—Leche, Rd. ; Carmelite of Plymouth, 35.—Ledyngton, John ; Canon of Hartland, 6.—Leget, Rd., "de Blyton Linc. Dioc." ; T. Berlinch, 5.—Lercedekne, Master Michael ; T. his Archpresb. (or R.) of Haccombe, 39.—Leuedyston, Thos. ; T. Buckfast Abbey, 50.—Levyghere, Walter ; T. Newenham Abbey, 43.—Leye, John ; Friar Minor of Bristol, 273.—

Leyman, John; T. Dunkeswell Abbey, 89.—Lokett, John, [L.D. Dioc. Sarum]: T. Cerne Abbas Abbey, 319.—Loman, John; T. Hartland Abbey, 92.—Lordon (*alias* Dukeslee) John, [L.D. Dioc. London.]; T. Sherborne Abbey, 163.—Longley, Thos., [L.D.]; R. of St. Alphege, London, 4.—Loryng, Thos.; T. Frithelstock Priory, 154.—Loskuryon, Walter; T. Hartland Abbey, 198.—Loveworthy, Rd.; T. Frithelstock Priory, 89.—Lucas, John; T. Tavistock Abbey, 1; Thos.; T. St. Nich. Priory, Exon., 93.—Lurk, Rob., *see* Campyng.—Lye, Rd., [L.D. Dioc. Lond.]; T. Priorat. Sancte Trinitatis, London, 4.—Lyff, John; T. Dunkeswell Abbey, 197.—Lyghfot, John; T. St. Nich. Priory, Exon, 44.—Lyle, Rd., Canon of Plympton, 81.—Lympton, Rd.; T. Launceston Priory, 114.—Lynyston, Thos.; T. Buckland Abbey, 156.

Magge, John; T. Frithelstock Priory, 206.—Malewayn, John; T. his R. of Calstock, 46.—Mape, John, Canon of Plympton, 98.—Marchaunt, Rob., Monk of Buckland, 5; Roger, Monk of Buckland, "cum caucione plenius exhibendi," 5; Roger, Monk of Buckland, 6.—Marke, John; T. St. Nich. Priory, Exon, 79.—Marschall, Rd.; T. Plympton Priory, 81.—Martyn, John; T. St. Nicholas Priory, Exon. 1; John; T. Buckland Abbey, 50; John, Monk of Buckfast, 241; John; T. Bodmin Priory, 273.—Maryet, Wm.; T. St. Nich. Priory, Exon, 114.—Matheu, John; T. St. German's Priory, 47.—Mathew, John; T. Dunkeswell Abbey, 33: John, Monk of Buckfast, 278.—Mathu, John; T. Dunkeswell Abbey, 92.—Mattyngho, Gencian, Canon of Hartland, 45.—Mayne, Wm.; T. Frithelstock Priory, 98.—Mayov, John; T. Bodmin Priory, 43.—Mayowe, John; T. Launceston Priory, 131.—Melbury, John; T. Torre Abbey, 63.—Mey, John; T. Totnes Priory, 95; John; T. St. Nich. Priory, Exon, 151; Rob.; T. St. German's Priory, 198.—Mille, Wm.; T. Hartland Abbey, 6.—Moggerys, Wm.; T. Canonsleigh Abbey, 104.—Molentz, Thos.; T. St. Nicholas Priory, Exon, 198.—Monk, John; T. Buckfast Abbey, 243.—Mopill (*alias* Carslake), John, T. St. Nich. Priory, Exon, 197.—More, Hy.; T. St. Nich. Priory, Exon, 93; John; T. the same, 208; Ralph; T. Dunkeswell Abbey, 149; Rd.; T. his R. of St. Columb-Major, 61; Rd., T. Dunkeswell Abbey, 89; Wm.; T. St. Nich. Priory, Ex., 241.—Mortymer, Rob.; T. St. Nich. Priory, Exon, 40.—Moryez, Nich.; T. Buckfast Abbey, 116.—Mosse, John, "de Asteley," Dioc. Heref.; T. Anglesey Priory, Dioc. Ely, 4.—Mown, Rd.; T. Dunkeswell Abbey, 131.—Moys, John; T. Launceston Priory, 63.—Mullyng, Wm., Canon of Bodmin Priory, 160.—Mumby, Walter de [L.D., Dioc. Lincl.]; T. Neusham Abbey., 4.—Mychel, John; T. Bodmin Priory, 151: John; T. Tavistock Abbey, 80; John; T. the same, 282; Walter; T. St. Nich. Priory, Exon, 163; Myryfeld, John: Canon of Bodmin Priory, 156.

Newhalle, John; T. Launceston Priory, 149.—Newport, John, Monk of Buckland. 38.—Noreys, Rd.; T. Frithelstock Priory, 319.—Northwych, Andr., R. of St. Clements "in Candelwych-strete," London [L.D.], 4; John; Monk of Buckfast, 62; John; Monk of Dunkeswell, 282.—Noscas, Wm.; T. Bodmin Priory, 115.—Nycol, John; T. Bodmin Priory, 6.

Odbryght, Thos., T. [L.D. Lincoln] Eccles. Convent. de Burcestre, 43.—Olyver, John; T. Holy Trinity Priory, London, 42; Master Rd., Bach. in Decrees "ad Titulum Domini," 61.—Opus, Rd., T. BodminP riory, 243.—Osmunt, Peter T. the same, 79.—Oterforde, Nich.; T. Dunkeswell Abbey, 63.

Pakyn, Steph.; T. Tywardreath Priory, 43.—Papeiay, John; T. Torre Abbey, 241.—Parker John, "ad Titulum...[blank]; 88.—Parkham, Wm., Monk of Dunkeswell, 99.—Parys, John; T. Plympton Priory, 81; John, Canon of Plympton, 116.—Paye, Thos.; T. St. Nich. Priory, Exon, 241.—Payn, John; T. Newenham Abbey, 114; John; T. Bodmin Priory, 163; John, T. Tavistock Abbey, 241.—Peake, John; T. Buckfast Abbey, 88.—Peubethov, Phil; T. St. German's Priory, 46.—Penell, Rd.; T. Plympton Priory, 115.—Penhale, John; T. the same, 282; Osbert; T. Bodmin Priory, 5.—Penneford, John; T. St. Nich. Priory, Exon, 1.—Penwyn, Rd., T. Rewley Abbey, Oxon, 2.—Perrour, Peter; T. Cowick Priory, 151.—Pertenhale, John [L.D. Dioc. of Linc.]; T. Priory "de Byssemade," 4.—Philipp, John, *see* Cork.—Phylipp, Rd.; T. St. Frideswides Priory, Oxon, 43.—Piers, John; T. St. Nich. Priory, Exon, 273; Walter; T. the same, 85; Wm.; T. the same, 104.—Pilheade, Nich.; T. Hartland Abbey, 154.—Pleder, Geoffrey;

T. Tavistock Abbey, 115.—Poddyng, John; T. Hartland Abbey, 193.—Polsave, John; T. St. Nich. Priory, Exon, 5.—Poltronogow, Ralph; T. Bodmin Priory, 35.—Ponfiete, Rd.; Fr. Carmelit. Sutton, 80.—Pope, Hy.; T. St. Nich. Priory, Exon, 114.—Porcollam, Martin; T. Launceston Priory, 6.—Porteworthy, Thos.; T. Dean & Chapt., Exon, 5.—Pralle, John; T. Buckland Abbey, 6.—Prentys, Geoffrey, M.A.; T. Rewly Abbey, 47.—Preston, Fr. Roger, 10.—Promptyslegh, Hy.; T. Plympton Priory, 104.—Pruet, John; T. Buckfast Abbey, 10.—Prust, Rob.; T. Launceston Priory, 40; Puddyng, Rob.; T. St. German's Priory, 159.—Punter, Henry; T. Canonsleigh Abbey, 42.—Puryman, Rd., Monk of Athelney, Dioc. B. & W.; [L.D. Johannis Roland, V.G.], 248.—Pyers, Wm.; T. Bodmin Priory, 91.—Pyken, Joceus; T. Bodmin Priory, 241.—Pynte, John; T. Launceston Priory, 319.

Radeslo, Wm., T. Dunkeswell Abbey, 6.—Radulphi, Rob.; Friar Minor of Bristol, 273.—Ramesey, John [L. D., Dioc. Lond.], T. Priory "de Harewold," 4.—Raw, Walter; T. St. Nich. Priory, Exon, 206.—Rawlyn, Edm.; T. Buckfast Abbey, 282.—Raulyn, John; T. Bodmin Priory, 278.—Raynfray, John; T. Tavistock Abbey, 6.—Reche, Wm.; T. Dunkeswell Abbey, 6.—Rede, Baldwin; T. Barnstaple Priory, 319; John; Fr. Minor of Bridgewater, 248; John; T. Bodmin Priory, 282; Peter; T. Buckfast Abbey, 114; Wm.; Canon of Plympton, 78.—Renawdyn, Rd., T. St. Nich. Priory, Exon, 164.—Rendy, Rd.; T. St. Nich. Priory, Exon, 43.—Reprens, Thos.; T. Bodmin Priory, 273.—Repyngton, Wm., R. of Abketilby Dioc. Linc., 4.—Respryn, Ralph; T. his R. of Milton Damarel, 278.—Revel, John; T. Tavistock Abbey, 23.—Reynald, John; T. Hosp. St. John Bapt., Wells; Dioc. of B. & W., 99; John; T. Bodmin Priory, 114.—Reynel, John; T. Torre Abbey, 115.—Rynald, Rob.; T. Barnstaple Priory, 47.—Robert, Hy.; T. St. Nich. Priory, Exon. 205; Thos., LL.B. (L.D.—Dioc. Cantuar.); T. Michelham Priory, Dioc. Chich., 3.—Robyn, John; T. St. German's Priory, 81; Thos.; T. Torre Abbey, 92.—Roddon, John, Monk of Buckfast, 241.—Rogger, John; T. Bodmin Priory, 282; Thos., T. Buckfast Abbey, 93.—Rolf, Wm., Monk of Buckland, 38.—Rosfrawell, Thos., "ad titulum gracie Domini," 4.—Rov, John, *see* Hyakyn; Row, Thos., *see* Forde.—Rowe, John; T. Buckfast Abbey, 241; Wm.; T. Launceston Priory, 104.—Rychard (*alias* Woborn), John; T. his R. of East Worlington, 23.—Ryppelegh, John; T. Buckfast Abbey, 241.

Sakerlegh, Hugh; T. St. Nich. Priory, Exon, 86.—Saler, Edm., [Dioc. B & W.]; T. Newenham Abbey, 8.—Sarger, John; T. St. Nich. Priory, Exon, 193.—Saunder, Roger; T. Buckfast Abbey, 197.—Schaplegh, John; T. St. Nich. Priory, Exon, 206.—Schere, Thos.; T. St. German's Priory, 43.—Scherpe, John; Carmelite of Plymouth, 104.—Schirborne, John, [L.D.], Carmelite Convent, Oxon, 4.—Schulder, Thos.; T. Tavistock Abbey, 282.—Schypwasch, John, *see* Tankert.—Schyra, Hy.; T. Launceston Priory, 154.—Schyre, Wm.; Canon of Launceston Priory, 159.—Scoce, John; T. Buckfast Abbey, 85.—Sonce, Rd.; T. Tavistock Abbey, 48.—Scoche, John; T. the same, 241; Wm.; T. St. Nich. Priory, Exon, 89.—Seller, Walter; T. Frithelstock Priory, 81.—Shephurd, Thos.; Monk of Tavistock, 273.—Shute, Geoffrey, [L.D. Dioc. Wells]; T. Dunkeswell Abbey, 81.—Schute, John; "ad titulum Domini sibi concessum" 64.—Skewys, John; T. Bodmin Priory, 208.—Skyllam, John; T. St. German's Priory, 273.—Skynner, John; T. Frithelstock Priory, 5.—Slocok, Thos.; T. St. Nich. Priory, Exon, 199.—Smale, Wm.: T. St. Nich. Priory, Exon, 163.—Smert, Master Hugh; T. his R. of All Hallows-on-the-Walls, Exeter, 89.—Smewyn, Thos.; [Dioc. Sarum,]; T. "domus de Maydenebardelegh," 1.—Smyth, John; T. Launceston Priory, 43; John; T. Buckland Abbey, 47; John; T. Dunkeswell Abbey, 82; Laurence; T. his R. of Sampford Courtenay, 104.—Soby, Rob.; T. St. German's Priory, 47.—Somercote, Wm., Monk of Dunkeswell, 99.—Somercotes, Thos. de, R. of All SS. "de Waynflet" [L.D.] 4.—Southcote, John; T. Berlinch Priory, 273.—Southwode, John; T. D. & C. Exon, 89.—Spear, Wm.; T. Frithelstock Priory, 104.—Spenser, Gilbert [L.D. Dioc. Sarum]; T. Abbotsbury Abbey, 99; Roger; Canon of Osney, 2.—Sperke, Hugh; T. Buckfast Abbey, 151.—Spernen, John; T. Berlinch Priory, 152.—Spert, Roger; "admissus est dummodo exhiberet titulum," 10.—Spryngold, Rd.; T. Barnstaple Priory, 5.—Stacy, Wm.; T. Buckland Abbey, 282.—Stapyll, Wm. [L.D. Dioc. of B. & W.]; T. Taunton Priory, 115.—Stephyn, John; Monk of Tavistock 273; Paul; T. St. German's Priory, 38; Wm.; T. Launceston Priory, 95.—Sthorm, Simon; T. Buckland Abbey, 197.—Stoteworthy, Rd.; T. Hartland Abbey, 282.—Stoute, Ralph; T. Buckfast Abbey, 205.—Sturgeon, John; Monk of Buckfast, "presentatus per Wm. Beaghe, sellerarium ibidem," 5.—Stybbe, John; T. Hartland Abbey, 131.—Susan, Thos.; T. Launceston Priory, 154.—Sutte, Walter [L.D. "Johannis Rouland," Dioc. B. & W., V.G.]; T. Maiden Bradleigh Priory, 248.—Sutton, Master John, LL.B.; T. Launceston Priory, 93.—Symon, John; T. St. German's Priory, 62; Peter; T. Launceston Priory, 5.—Sȝeylake, Ralph; T. Dunkeswell Abbey, 46.

Tankert, (alias Schypwasch), John; T, Launceston Priory, 131.—Tannt, Rob.; T, the same, 40.—Taylour, Thos., [L.D., Dioc. Lland.], "ad titulum Domini Johannis Seynt Jhon, Militis, Domini de Westpery," 63.—Tayllour, Thos.; T. Buckfast Abbey, 241.—Thomas, John; T. his R. of Dodbrooke, 45.—Thome, John; T, Bodmin Priory, 47; Rd., T. Launceston Priory, 115.—Thomma, John; T. Bodmin Priory, 91; John; T. the same, 205; Roger; T, St. Nich. Priory, Exon. 115.—Thommas, John; T, the same, 164.—Toker, Wm.; T, Torre Abbey, 48.—Tolye, John; T, St. Nich. Priory, Exon, 86.—Tomlyn, Rd.; T. Dunkeswell Abbey, 197.—Torner, John; T. Dunkeswell Abbey, 83.—Tosere, Reginald; T. St. Nich. Priory, Exon, 273.—Tournour, John; T, the same, 91.—Towenesahende, Walter; T, Hartland Abbey, 91.—Tredydan, Steph.; T, Launceston Priory, 197.—Treganegy, Benedict; T, Bodmin Priory, 83.—Tregodek, Wm.; T, St. German's Priory, 6.—Tregyrthek, Wm.; Canon of Bodmin, 156.—Tremenhire, Steph.; T. Bodmin Priory, 88.—Trepesek, Ralph; T. St. German's Priory, 114.—Tresaher, Rd.; T. Bodmin Priory, 89.—Trethewy, Walter; T. Launceston Priory, 63.—Treveythyn, Ralph; Fr. Preach. of Truro, 38.—Trevougham, John; T. Bodmin Priory, 115.—Trevyn, Rob.; T. St. Nich. Priory, Exon, 114.—Trewandra, Ralph, Canon of St. German's "cum caucione plenius exhibendi," 5; and again, "canonicus expresse professus," 6.—Trewen, John; T. Berlinch Priory, 62.—Treyngoff, Walter; T. St. German's Priory, 131.—Troot, Nich.; T. the same, 93.—Troppe, Hy.; Monk of Hartland, 241.—Tryvet, John; T. Dunkeswell Abbey, 38.—Turgeys, Nich.; Ordinis Fr. Carmelit., 1.—Tuygg, John; T., D. *and* C., Exon, 205.—Twete, John; T. Tavistock Abbey, 85.—Tybot, Baldwin; T. Hartland Abbey, 206.—Tylle, Wm.; T. St. Nich. Priory, Exon, 6.—Tyrel, John; T. Bodmin Priory, 241.

Uda, Thos.; T. the same, 243.—Urban, Rd.; T. Tywardreath Priory, 156.—Ustas, Roger; T. Launceston Priory, 1.

Valetyn, John; T. St. Nich. Priory, Exon, 273.—Veale, Geoffrey; T. Totnes Priory, 115.—Veele, John, T. Buckfast Abbey, 202.—Vele, Thos.; T. the same, 197.—Velon, Laurence; T. Bodmin Priory, 151.—Vian, John; T. the same, 48.—Vyvyan, Wm.; Canon of Bodmin, 45.

Waddon, Thos.; T. The Chapter of Exeter, 319.—Wade, John; T. Bodmin Priory, 104; John; T. St. Nich., Priory, Exon, 198.—Waleys, Rd.; T. Launceston Priory, 63.—Wallyng, Thos.; T. Buckfast Abbey, 273.—Walter, Thos.; T. Abbotsbury Abbey, Dioc. Sarum, 79; Wm.; T. Dunkeswell Abbey, 282.—Wanston, Matth.; T. his R. of Maperton, Dioc. B. & W., 88.—Ward, Rob.; T. Bodmin Priory, 86.—Waryn, John; T. his V. of Liskeard, 46; Thos.; T. Launceston Priory, 160.—Watkyns, Thos. [L.D. London Dioc.], "ad titulum Domini," 42.—Waty, Laurence; T. Bodmin Priory, 163.—Wayte, Rd.; T. Frithelstock Priory, 10.—Webber, Hy.; T. The Chapter of Exeter, 282; Thos.; T. Frithelstock Priory, 6; Thos.; T. St. Nich. Priory, Exon, 10.—Welfare, Rd.; T. Barnstaple Priory, 50.—Weryng, John; T. Tavistock Abbey, 63.—Westbery, Ralph, [L.D.], Ord. Augustin. London, 4.—Westle, John [L.D. Dioc. B. & W.]; "ad titulum Magistri et Confratrum Domus Sancti Marci Bristollensis, Wygorniensis Diocesis," 151.—Whare, Thos.; T. Pilton Priory, 97.—Whatele, John; T. his R. of Kentisbeare, 1.—Whysselwyll, Nich.; T. Buckfast Abbey, 282.—Whyte, John; T. Canonsleigh Abbey, 273.—Whytelond, Rd., Monk of Dunkeswell, 104.—Widelegh, Rob.; T., D. & C., Exon, 79.—Wilberdon, Ralph;

'. Plympton Priory, 282.—Wobbrok, Thos. ; T. St. Nich. Priory, Exon, 79.—Vode, Thos. ; T. Launceston Priory, 50.—Wofford, John ; T. Buckfast Abbey, 3.—Wolston, John ; T. his R. of St. Endellion, 193.—Wolton, Baldwin ; T. Bodmin Priory, 273.—Won, John ; T. the same, 156.—Wonston, Geoffrey ; '. Plympton Priory, 156.—Worthyn, John ; T. his R. of St. Endellion, 116.—Voven, Hy. ; T. Bodmin Priory, 198.—Wyght, Rob. [Dioc. of B. & W.], T. Keynsham Abbey, 5.—Wylkyn, John, *see* Lanbrobys.—Wylle, John ; T. St. Nich. Priory, Exon, 149 ; John ; T. Buckfast Abbey, 146 ; Rob. ; T. Berlinch Priory, 160 ; Thos. ; T. Bodmin Priory, 197.—Wyllet, John ; T. Launceston Priory, 149.—Wyllyam, John ; T. the same, 197 ; Martin ; T. Bodmin Priory, 97.—Wyllyng, John ; Canon of Plympton, 82.—Wymund, Ralph ; T. Torre Abbey, 45.—Wyndegrynde, John ; T. Buckfast Abbey, 81.—Wyngkelegh, Peter ; Friar-Minor, 6.—Wyse, John ; T. Berlinch Priory, 81.

Yurl, Rd., Canon of Launceston Priory, 115.

Zoche, Edm., Monk of Totnes, 63.

IV. DIACONI

Abbotysbury, John, Monk of Newenham, 278.—Abel, Nich., [L.D. Johannis Roland, V.G. Dioc., B. & W.]; T. Athelney Abbey, 248.—Abendon, Peter, [L.D. Dioc., Worc.]; T. Torre Abbey, 160.—Alby, John ; Carmelite of Sutton, 156.—Alcok ... Fr. conventus ...... *sic* ; 35.—Aleyn, John, [L.D. Dioc., Worces.]; T. Priory "de Halywell," Dioc., London, 4.—Alre, John ; T. his R. of "Ebryghton" Dioc. Sarum, 84.—Alyn, Philip ; Monk of Tavistock, 104 ; Wm. ; T. Dunkeswell Abbey, 159 ; Wm. ; T. his R. of Great Torrington, 319.—Amyhet, Walter ; T. Hartland Abbey, 41.—Andrew, Thos. ; Carmelite, 4 ; Thos. ; Carmelite of Cambridge 4.—Appilby, Rob., Monk of Dunkeswell, 83.—Aston, Thos. ; T. Newenham Abbey, 48.—atte Beare, Alexander, T. Canonsleigh Abbey, 38.—Austyn, John ; T. Buckfast Abbey, 61.—Axmenstre, Wm., Monk of Newenham, 278.—Aylmer, John ; T. St. Nich. Priory, Exon, 152.—Aysche, Wm., Canon of Plympton, 114.—Ayssechewell, Thos. ; Carmelite, 4.—Aysse, Walter ; T. Frithelstock Priory, 86.—Ayssehill, John ; Monk of Dunkeswell, 83.

Bacheler, Wm., Monk of Buckland Abbey, 199.—Baker, Matth., [L.D. Galfridi Crukadan, V.G. Dioc. Sarum] ; T. Terrent Abbey, 208.—Bardolf, John, [L.D. Dioc. B. *and* W.] ; T. Montacute Priory, 62.—Barger, Geoffrey ; T. Dunkeswell Abbey, 116.—Barlynch, John ; Monk of Buckfast, 152.—Baroun, Andrew ; Fr. Hosp. St. John, Exon, 64 ; Wm. ; T. St. Nich. Priory, Exon, 10.—Barry, Wm. ; [L.D. Dioc. Winton,] ; T. the same, 163.—Batyn, Walter ; T. the same, 159.—Baudyn, Thos. ; T. Bodmin Priory, 193.—Baunton, Ralph ; Fr. Preach. Exon, 5.—Baylg, Walter, [L.D. Dioc. Sarum] ; T. Cerne Abbey, 273.—Beare, John ; T. Dunkeswell Abbey, 115.—Bede, Wm., Canon of Plympton, 79.—Bele, John ; T. St. Nich. Priory, Exon, 1 ; John ; T. Newenham Abbey, 104 ; Nich. ; T. Canonsleigh Abbey, 91 ; Walter ; T. Launceston Priory, 82.—Beneht, Ralph, [L.D. Dioc. Linc.] ; T. Maiden Bradleigh Priory, 199.—Benet, John, [L.D. Johannis Roland, V.G. Dioc. B. *and* W.] ; T. Montacute Priory, 273.—Berly, John ; Canon of Taunton Priory, 319.—Berne, Walter de ; Monk of Tavistock, 1.—Berthelet, John ; "ad titulum Prioris et Conventus Sancti Stephani, Civitatis Exoniensis, *sic*." 89.—Berton, Wm. ; [L.D. Dioc. Norwic.] ; T. Dunkeswell Abbey, 273.—Berty, Thos., [L.D. Dioc. Linc.] ; T. St. Nich. Priory, Exon, 50.—Bery, Wm., T. the same, 62.—Bettow, John ; T. Totnes priory, 149.—Betty, John ; T. Bodmin Priory, 45.—Bexyngton, Ralph ; Monk of Forde, 152.—Blake, John, [L.D. Dioc. Sarum] ; T. Abbey "de Bruera," Dioc. Lind. 156.—Blakehay, Roger ; T. St. Nich. Priory, Exon, 11.—Blakelond, John ; T. the same, 6.—Blendeyn, Roger ; T. Tywardreath Priory, 282.—Blewe, Master John, LL.D. ; T. his R. of Benhanger, Dioc. of B. *and* W., 81.—Bobeknolle, Rob., Dioc. of B. *and* W. ; T. Bindon Abbey, 193.—Bocent, Wm. ; T. Launceston Priory, 98.—Bodeman, Thos., Monk of Dunkeswell Abbey, 202.—Bokesoll, Rob.; T. Dunkeswell Abbey, 94.—Bolham John; T. Cleeve Abbey, 104.—Bolle, Wm., Monk of Buckland, 45.—Bonde Roger; T. Tavistock Abbey, 115.—Bone, John; T. St. Nich. Priory, Exon, 2.—Boryalegh, Thos.; Hosp. of St. John, Exon, 93.—Boskawen, John; Fr. Minor, Exon, 278.—Boston, John; T. Torre Abbey, 131.—Boswyns, Wm.; Canon of Bodmin, 47.—Boterel, John; T., D. *and* C. of Exeter, 11.—Bottebourgh, Nich.; T. Hartland Abbey, 47.—Boure, John; T. Frithelstock Priory, 48.—Bowey, Walter; T. his R. of St. John-in-Cornwall, 197.—Bowey, Nich.; T. Dunkeswell Abbey, 92.—Bowedon, John, junior; T. Barnstaple Priory, 156.—Bowode, John; T. Dunkeswell Abbey, 116.—Boystok, John, Canon of Plympton, 45.—Bradeford, John; T. Friars Preach., Exon, 80; John; T. Dunkeswell Abbey, 61.—Bradlegh, Thos.; T. his V. of Buckland-Monachorum, 83.—Bray, Master Wm., M.A.; T. Bodmin Priory, 48.—Breit, John, Fr. Min., Exon, 82.—Bremell, Wm., [L.D. Johannis Roland, V.G. Dioc. B. *and* W.]; T. St. Frideswide's, Oxon, 205.—Bremelcomb, Wm.; T. his R. of Nymet-Tracy, 45.—Bremerygh, John, Hosp. St. John, Exon, 131.—Brigge, John; T. Torre Abbey, 273; John, Monk of Newenham, 23.—Brode, John; T. Tywardreath Priory, 2.—Broke, Robert, [L.D., Dioc. Winton,]; T. Romsey Abbey, 208.—Bromford, John, Canon of Torre Abbey, 193.—Brond, James; T. Frithelstock Priory, 208.—Broun, John; T. St. Nich. Priory, Exon, 163.—Brounyng, Wm.; T. his R. of St. George's, Exeter, 83; Wm., [L.D., Dioc. London,]; T. "Sancti Johannis Baptiste de Halywell," 4.—Brouste, Rd.; T. Tavistock Abbey, 86.—Brydon, Rd., Canon of Plympton, 319.—Bryscheforde, Walter; T. Berlinch Priory, 129.—Brystowe, John; Fr. Carmelit. of Plymouth, 104.—Brwys, Thos.; T. St. Nich. Priory, Exon, 116.—Buckeyete, Nich.; T. Buckfast Abbey, 163.—Budde, John, Monk of Buckfast, 282; Wm.; ditto, 86.—Buggh, Ingrianus; T. Buckland Abbey, 156.—Burell, John; T. his R. of Clyst St. George, 83.—Busch, John, [L.D., Dioc. B. *and* W.]; T. Taunton Priory, 282.—Busshbyry, Lewis, [L.D., Dioc. Worc.]; "ad titulum Domini Episcopi Exoniensis," 104.—Bykebury, John; T. his R. of Bigbury, 197.—Byrcomb, Rd.; T. Dunkeswell Abbey, 248.

Cade, Wm.; T. St. Nich. Priory, Exon, 80.—Cadis, Rd.; T. St. German's Priory, 50.—Cadyho, Wm.; T. Buckfast Abbey, 198.—Calmady, Hy.; T. Bodmin Priory, 116.—Campis, Bernard de, Fr. Minor Exon, 205.—Canyngton, John; Monk of Dunkeswell, 278.—Capell, Thos. [L.D. Johannis Roland, V.G. Dioc. B. & W.]; T. Montacute Priory, 273.—Cardrew, Peter; T. St. German's Priory, 282.—Carpenter, Rd.; T. Dunkeswell Abbey, 319.—Caralake, John; *see* Mopyll, 198.—Caralegh, Jas.; T. his R. of Bradford, 282.—Carter, John; T. Frithelstock Priory, 35.—Cartere, John [L.D. Dioc. B. & W.]; T. Middleton Abbey, Dioc. Sarum, 282.—Castel, John; T. his R. of Buckland Filleigh, 38.—Chamberleyn, Rob.; T. Bodmin Priory, 83; Wm.; *see* Sawyer, 62.—Chapman, Matth. [L.D. Dioc. London]; T. Priory "de Berdene," 4.—Chepman, "Dompnus Johannes", Canon of Hartland, 7.—Chaundeler, Wm., de Lynton (Dioc. Ely); T. St. Bartholomew's Hospital, Smithfield, London, [L.D.] 2.—Cherewod, Reginald; Carmelite, Oxon, 4.—Chernemouthe, John, Monk of Forde, 152.—Chester, Walter, Monk of Buckfast, 248.—Cheyny, Wm. [L.D. Dioc. B. & W.]; T. Cleeve Abbey, 4.—Chicheley, Master Henry; T. his R. of St. Stephen's "in Wallebrok," London, 4.—Chynnok, Rob.; Fr. Preach. of Truro, 131.—Chyryton, Wm.; T. St. Nich. Priory, Exon, 163.—Chyterwyll, Walter; T. Newenham Abbey, 151.—Coden, Vivian; T. Bodmin Priory, 85.—Coffin, Edm., Monk of Buckfast, 86.—Coke, Rob., Monk of Buckland, 82.—Colard, John; T. St. German's Priory, 62.—Cole, John; T. Totnes Priory, 94; Thos.; T. Buckland Abbey, 99.—Colle, Rd.; T. Bodmin Priory, 202; Master Walter; T. his R. of Milton Damerel, 205.—Coly, James, Fr. Preacher of Truro, 78.—Columpton, John; T. St. German's Priory, 243.—Colyford, John; T. Newenham Abbey, 152.—Coleforde, Steph., Canon of Plympton, 205.—Colyn, Hy.; T. St. Nich. Priory, Exon, 97; John; T. Osney Abbey, 199; Ralph, T. his R. *of* Lansallos, 78.—Combe, John; [L.D.], Canon of Berlinch Priory, 156; Wm.; T. St. Nich. Priory, Exon, 41.—Cook, John, Monk of Torre Abbey, 38; John; T. Frithelstock Priory, 61; Walter; T. Torre Abbey, 88.—Cork, *alias* Phylipp, John; T. St. Nich. Priory, Exon, 92.—

Cornu, John; T. Hartland Abbey, 99.—Cote, Wm.; T. St. Nich. Priory, Exon, 11.—Cowlyng, Master John, M.A.; T. Bodmin Priory, 81.—Cowyk, John; [L.D. Dioc. Linc.]; T. Elsham Priory, 80.—Clar, Wm., Augustinian, London, 4.—Clegh, Wm.; T. Launceston Priory, 243.—Clement, Victor, Fr. Preach., Exon, 273.—Clerk, John; T. Launceston Priory, 48.—Cloneneburgh, Wm.; T. Buckfast Abbey, 85.—Clyk, Thos.; T. Hartland Abbey, 197.—Clyverdon, John; T. the same, 43.—Cranebery, John, Canon of Plympton, 85.—Crekow, Wm.; T. Newenham Abbey, 91.—Cremp, John [L.D. Dioc. B. & W.]; T. Berlinch Priory, 88.—Crempe, Wm.; T. St. German's Priory, 44.—Criour, Thos.; T. St. Nicholas Priory, Exon, 1.—Crofte, John [L.D. Dioc. B. & W.]; T. Stodelegh Priory, Dioc. Linc., 156.—Crok, John; T. Tavistock Abbey, 48.—Crook, John; T. St. German's Priory, 81.—Crokker, Hy., Monk of Tavistock, 88.—Crulle, John; T. Canonsleigh Abbey, 115.—Cryppyn, Thos., Monk of Tavistock, 104.—Crystow, Thos.; T. St. Nich. Priory, Exon, 160.—Curtays, John [L.D. Johannis Rouland, V.G., Dioc. B. & W.], Canon Regular of Taunton, 198.—Cuttefen, Walter; Monk of Dunkeswell, 319.

Daneis, John; T. St. Nich. Priory, Exon, 116.—Davy, John; T. Forde Abbey, 95.—Dawe, John; T. the Chapter of Glasney, 91.—Dayman, Wm.; T. St. Nich. Priory, Exon, 248.—Deyman, Hy., Canon of Plymton, 319.—Decam, John; T. Dunkeswell Abbey, 38.—Dene, John; a Monk there, 129.—Denys, Rob.; T. Launceston Priory, 151.—Dier, John; [L.D. Dioc. Lond.]; T. Augustinian Abbey, Bristol, 43.—Doll, John; [L.D., Dioc. Sarum]; T. Abbotsbury Abbey, 97.—Donscombe, Rd.; T. his R. of Sheviocke, 86.—Donyell, Peter, Fr. Carmelit. de Sutton, 62.—Dornyng, John; T. Buckfast Abbey, 319.—Dorset, John; T. Buckland Abbey, 61.—Doulton, John, Monk of Torre Abbey, 6.—Dove, Rd., Monk of Buckfast Abbey, 159.—Doyngel, John; T. St. German's Priory, 43.—Drayton, Thos. [L.D., Dioc., B. & W.]; T. his R. of Lydiard St. Lawrence, 90.—Dreyn, Michael; T. Hosp. St. Barthol., Smithfield, 23.—Dunn, John [L.D., Dioc. Sarum]; T. Middleton Abbey, 114.—Dunnyng, Rob.; T. his R. of All Hallows on-the-Walls, Exeter, 131.—Dyghte, John; T. his R. of St. Stephen's, Exeter, 78.—Dymmok, Walter; T. Frithelstock Priory, 38.—Dyrehill, Jas.; T. Launceston Priory, 98.—Dyrward, John; T. Tavistock Abbey, 7.

Edward, Rob.; T. Buckfast Abbey, 273.—Elyn, John; T. Bodmin Priory, 95.—Elyot, John; T. Dunkeswell Abbey, 46.—Esoth, John; T. Bodmin Priory, 94.—Estebrok, Thos.; T. St. Nich., Priory, Exon, 7.—Estecote, John; T. Berlinch Priory, 38.—Ewn, Rob., Canon of Launceston Priory, 116.

Fax, Rd.; T. St. German's Priory, 202.—Fayrewode, John; T. his R. of Alwington, 129.—Feddys, Geo.; T. Frithelstock Priory, 199.—Focher, Alex., Canon of Plympton, 205.—Folygan, Stephen; T. Launceston Priory, 273.—Forde, Gregory; T. St. German's Priory, 156; Hugh [L.D., Dio. B. & W.]; T. Cleeve Abbey, 156; John; T. Dunkeswell Abbey, 88; John; T. St. Nich. Priory, Exon, 197.—Forden, John; T. Tavistock Abbey, 88.—Forst, John; T. the D. & C. of Exeter, 81.—Forthe, Thos. T. Bodmin Priory, 44.—Fowler, John; T. the same, 273.—Frankcheyne, James; T. his R. of Tiverton, 2nd portion, 90.—Fraunces, Nich.; T. Bodmin Priory, 205.—Frend, Hy.; T. Pilton Priory, 97.—Frensh, John; T. Buckfast Abbey, 243.—Frode, John; T. Hosp. of St. John at Bridgewater, 97.—Fychet, John, Monk of Buckfast, 160.—Fyllecomb, Thos.; T. St. Nich. Priory, Exon, 208.—Fylp, Rob.; T. Bodmin Priory, 248.

Gambon, John; T. Dunkeswell Abbey, 46.—Gassy, John, Fr. Carmelit. of Sutton, 114.—Gay, Walter; T. Frithelstock Priory, 95.—Germyn, Hugh; T. St. Nich. Priory, Exon, 6.—Gervays, Nich. [L. D. Johannis Roland, V.G. Dioc. B. & W.]; T. Montacute Priory, 273.—Glamvyll, Thos., Canon of Plympton, 80.—Gode, Rob.; T. Tavistock Abbey, 163.—Godeman, Henry.; Canon of Plympton, 115.—Godewyn, John; Fr. Minor of Bridgewater, 273.—Godyer, Thos.; T. Launceston Priory, 319.—Godyalond, John [L.D. Johannis Rouland, V.G. Dioc. B. & W.]; T. St. Nich. Priory, Exeter, 198.—Gorde, Walter; T. Hartland Abbey, 160.—Gorecote, Simon; T. Launceston Priory, 114; Wm.; T. Launceston Priory, 114.—Gorewyll, Master John, junior; T. his R. of Roborough, 79.—Goulde, Wm. [L.D. Dioc. B. & W.]; T. Montacute Priory,

282.—Grafton, Thos. [L.D. Dioc. Lincl.]; T. Buckland Abbey, 199.—Graynsvyll, Master Rd., L.L.B.; T. his R. of Roborough, 81.—Grene, Walter [L.D. Dioc. B. & W.]; T. Sherborne Abbey, 154.—Gronigh, Meynoldus; Fr. Min. of Bridgewater, 193,—Grussy, Peter [L.D. Dioc. Sarum]; T. Abbotsbury Abbey, 197.—Grynard, Wm.; Canon of Taunton Priory, 319.—Gunne, Hy.; T. Hosp. of St. John Bapt., Wells, 95.—Gybba, Thos.; T. Bodmin Priory, 114.—Gybbe, John; T. St. German's Priory, 198; Thos.; T. Torre Abbey, 91; Thos.; T. Tywardreath Priory, 241.—Gybon, Thos.; "ad titulum Prioris et Conventus novi Hospitalis Beate Marie extra Byssshoppys gate, Londonie, Ordinis Sancti Augustini," 159.—Gyffard, Hugh; T. Launceston Priory, 151; John; T. Dunkeswell Abbey, 95; Steph.; T. his R. of West Putford, 83.—Gynys, John; T. St. German's Priory, 156.

Hakeworthy, Wm.; T. St. Nich. Priory, Exon, 78.—Harry, John; T. Buckfast Abbey, 95.—Herry, Matth.; T. Barnstaple Priory, 198.—Harry, Nich.; T. Bodmin Priory, 197; Richard.; T. St. Nich. Priory, Exon, 149; Roger; T. Launceston Priory, 163.—Harrys, Walter [L.D. Johannis Roland, V.G. Dioc. B. & W.]; T. Mochelneye Abbey, 248.—Hasard, John [L.D., Dioc. Sarum.]; T. Cerne Abbey, 319.—Hasarde, John [L.D. Galfridi Crukadan, V.G." Dioc. Sarum]; T. Abbotsbury Abbey, 202.—Hauk, John; T. Littlemore Priory, Oxon, 44.—Haukyn, Wm. (Dioc. B. & W.); T. Canonsleigh Abbey, 6.—Haydur, Steph.; T. St. Nich. Priory, Exon, 151; Walter; T. the same, 81.—Hayman, Nich.; T. Buckfast Abbey, 154.—Hegneh, John; T. St. Nich. Priory, Exeter, 11.—Henry, John, Canon of Bodmin, 46; John; T. Bodmin Priory, 97.—Herbert, Philip; T. Buckfast Abbey, 35.—Herlywas, John; T. Bodmin Priory, 88.—Hereford, Thos.; T. his R. of Rodmerton [Dioc. Worc., L.D.], 40.—Hertwell, John, Canon of Osney. 2.—Herward, John; [L.D. Dioc. Sarum]; T. his R. of Winterbourne-German, 116.—Hethen, Rd. [L.D. Dioc. Sarum]; T. Abbotsbury Abbey, 149.—Hevyltorr, Rob.; T. St. Nich. Priory, Exon, 47.—Hobbe, Roger; T. Launceston Priory, 159.—Hode, Walter; T. Plympton Priory, 95.—Hogge, Hugh; T. St. Nich. Priory, Exon, 94.—Hokkeday, Rd. [L.D. "Johannis Rouland, V.G. Dioc. B. & W.]; T. Muchelney Abbey. 202.—Holbech, John, Canon of Osney, 2.—Holdych, Wm.; Canon of Plympton, 319.—Holme, Walter; T. Montacute Priory, 99.—Horlok, Thos.; T. St. Nich. Priory, Exon, 94.—Hough, Geoffrey; T. his R. of Combe-in-Teignhead, 282,—Hoyge, John; T. St. Nich. Priory, Exeter, 78.—Howes, Thos., Fr. Preach. Exon, 45.—Hunte, Roger; T. Launceston Priory, 248.—Hurde, John; T., D. & C. of Exeter, 152; Rd.; T. Priory of the Holy Trinity, London, 46.—Husey, John; T. Dunkeswell Abbey, 47.—Hyeovyse, Wm.; T. Torre Abbey, 129.—Hille, John [L.D. Johannis Roland, V.G. Dioc. B. & W.]; T. Dunkeswell Abbey, 273.—Hylle, John, Canon of Torre, 197. [This name was accidentally omitted in the List of Deacons; and I find the following "erratum" at the end of the List of Priests:—"*Memorandum quod hoc nomen infrascriptum deberet inseri inter Diaconos hoc tempore, videlicet* Johannes Hylle, *Canonicus Regularis Monasterii de Torre, Ordinis Sancti Augustini, Exoniensis Diocesis, ipsum Ordinem expresse professus, per literas Abbatis et Conventus Monasterii predicti presentatus.*" i, 286ᵇ, col. 2.]—Hylle, John, Canon of Buckland, 319; Roger; T. St. Nich. Priory, Exon, 129.—Hyskyn (*alias* Rov.) John; T. St. German's Priory, 199.

Ilemystre, Walter, Monk of Forde Abbey, 38.—Ylond, John; T. Tavistock Abbey, 248.—Irysch, John; T. Totnes Priory, 47.—Isaak, Geoffrey; T. Buckfast Abbey, 198.—Ivel, John; T. Bodmin Priory, 84.

James, Wm.; T. Canonsleigh Abbey, 91.—Jay, Peter, [L.D., Dioc. B. *and* W.]; T. Sherborne Abbey, 62.—Jelyan, Rob.; T. St. Nicholas Priory, Exon, 1.—Job, Rob.; T. Bodmin Priory, 193.—Joce, John; T. the same, 152.—Jon, John, T. Frithelstock Priory, 160.—Judde, John; T. Canonsleigh Abbey, 198.—Junte, Geoffrey; T. St. Nich. Priory, Exon, 159.

Kayskys, Henry, Monk of Dunkeswell, 278.—Kelly, John; T. Hartland Abbey, 38.—Kelwa, Wm.; T. Tavistock Abbey, 164; Wm.; T. the same, 193.—Kemeworthy, Thos.; T. Frithelstock Priory, 78.—Kent, Rob., [L.D., "Johannis

Rouland, V.G." Dioc. B. *and* W.]; T. Berlinch Priory, 198; Wm., T. St. German's Priory, 82.—Kenylyon, John; T. S. Nich. Priory, Exon, 149.—Knyght, John; T. his R. of Farringdon, 278; John, [L.D., Dioc. B. *and* W.]; T. Montacute Priory, 282; Rd., T. Buckfast Abbey, 23; Wm.; T. Torre Abbey, 99.—Kylcam, John, Canon of St. German's, 248.—Kyllyow, Peter; T. Bodmin Priory, 282.—Kyng, John, Canon of Plympton, 45; Wm.; T. Dunkeswell Abbey, 241.—Kyngston, Wm.; Monk of Newenham, 278.

Lace, David; [L.D., Dioc. Menev.]; T. "Langenyth" Priory, 208.—Lacy, John, Canon of Torre Abbey, 193.—Lamport, David; [Dioc. B. & W.;] T. Buckfast Abbey, 1; John, Monk of Newenham, 282.—Lanbrobys *alias* Wylkyn, John; T. St. Nich., Priory, Exon, 164.—Laneman, Wm., Canon of Launceston Priory, 163.—Lang, John, [L.D., Johannis Roland, V. G. Dioc., B. & W.]; T. Taunton Priory, 241; Thos.; T. his R. of Instow, 89.—Langebrook, John; T. Tavistock Abbey, 206.—Langedon, Steph.; T. St. Nich. Priory, Exon, 89.—Langhman, Rob.; T. Buckfast Abbey, 81.—Langrygh, Arnulph; T. Torre Abbey, 93.—Lannergh, John; T. Bodmin Priory, 114.—Launston, John; T. St. Nich. Priory, Exon, 23.—Laveryng, Rob.; T. Dunkeswell Abbey, 6.—Lavyngton, John; T. Buckfast Abbey, 11.—Lebet, Walter; T. Cowick Priory, 115.—Leche, Rd.; Fr. Carmelite de Sutton, 45.—Ledyngton, "Dompnus Johannes," Canon of Hartland, 7.—Legh, Wm.; T. Bodmin Priory, 10.—Lenyghere, Walter; T. Newenham Abbey, 44.—Leuedeston, Thos., junior; T. Buckfast Abbey, 61.—Lewys, Thos.; T. Bodmin Priory, 241.—Leyman, John; T. Dunkeswell, Abbey, 91.—London, Rd.; T. Berlinch Priory, 5.—Loryng, Thos.; T. Frithelstock Priory, 156.—Loskuryon, Walter; T. Hartland Abbey, 202.—Loveton, John; T. Cornworthy Priory, 10.—Loveworthy, Rd.; T. Frithelstock Priory, 91.—Lubberty, John, Fr. Minor, of Bridgewater, 205.—Lucas, Thos.; T. St. Nich. Priory, Exon, 94.—Ludvon, Thos.; T. St. German's Priory, 282.—Luk, Master John; T. his R. of Uffculme, 11.—Lyff, John; T. Dunkeswell Abbey, 198.—Lyghtfot, John; T. St. Nich. Priory, Exon, 45—Lyle, Rd., Canon of Plympton, 82.—Lympton, Rd.; T. Bodmin Priory, 115.—Lyne, John; T. Buckfast Abbey, 243.

Magge, John; T. Frithelstock Priory, 241.—Magg, Martin; T. Tywardreath Priory, 10.—Malewayn, John; T. his R. of Calstock, 61.—Manston, Walter; T. St. German's Priory, 1.—Mape, John, Canon of Plympton, 104.—Marchel, Wm. [L.D. Dioc. B. & W.]; T. Montacute Priory, 282.—Marchaunt, Rob., Monk of Buckfast, 23.—Marke, John; T. St. Nich. Priory, Exon, 80.—Marschall, Rd.; T. Plympton Priory, 82.—Martyn, John; T. Buckland Abbey, 61; John, Monk of Buckfast, 248; Walter; T. Bodmin Priory, 129.—Maryet, Wm.; T. St. Nich. Priory, Exon, 115.—Matheu, John, Fr. Minor of Reading, 4; John; T. St. German's Priory, 50; John; T. Dunkeswell Abbey, 84; John, Monk of Buckfast, 282.—Mathu, John; T. Dunkeswell, Abbey, 93.—Mattyngho, Gencian; Monk of Hartland, 46.—Mayn, Wm.; T. Frithelstock Priory, 104.—Mayowe, John; T. Launceston Priory, 149.—Merther, Master Laurence; T. Rewley Abbey, 10.—Mey, John; T. Totnes Priory, 97; John; T. St. Nich. Priory, Exon, 152; Rob.; T. St. German's Priory, 202.—Milward, John; T. Buckfast Abbey, 241.—Mochell, John; T. Tavistock Abbey, 319.—Moggerys, Wm.; T. Canonsleigh Abbey, 114.—Molentz, Thos.; T. St. Nich. Priory, Exon, 199.—Molner, Nich., Fr. Preach., Exon, 131.—Monder, Wm.; T. Canonsleigh Abbey, 241.—Mopyll, *alias* Carslake, John; T. St. Nich. Priory, Exon, 108.—More, Hy.; T. St. Nich. Priory, Exon, 195; John; T. the same, 241; Ralph; T. Dunkeswell Abbey, 151; Rd.; T. his R. of St. Columb-major, 62; Rd.; T. Dunkeswell Abbey, 91; Wm.; "Exoniensis Diocesis subdiaconus," 243.—Morgan, Thos., Canon of Plympton, 5.—Mortymer, Rob.; T. St. Nich. Priory, Exon, 42.—Mown, Rd.; T. Dunkeswell Abbey, 149.—Morys, Nich.; T. Buckfast Abbey, 129.—Moys, John; T. Launceston Priory, 78.—Mullyng, Wm., Canon of Bodmin, 282.—Mychel, Peter; T. Osney Abbey, 10; Walter; T. St. Nich. Priory, Exon, 193; Wm.; Canon of Torre, 5; Wm. [L.D. Dioc. Linc.]; T. Berlinch Priory, 88.—Myryfeld, John; Canon of Bodmin Priory, 159.

Nansumer, Hy.; T. Rewley Abbey, Oxon, 2.—Newhale, John; T. Launceston Priory, 151.—Newman, Hugh [L.D. Dioc. B. & W.]; Rewley Abbey, Oxon, 2.—

Northwych, John, Monk of Buckfast, 78; Norwych, John, Monk of Dunkeswell 319.—Noccas, Wm.; T. Bodmin Priory, 116.—Nuwenham, Rob.; T. St. Nich. Priory, Exon, 278.

Ocoke, Thos. [L.D. Johannis Rouland]; Canon Regular of Taunton Priory, 198.—Odelond, John [L.D. Johannis Rouland, V.G. Dioc. B. & W.]; T. Cleeve Abbey, 198.—Oliver, John; T. Priory of the Holy Trinity, London, 43; Mas' r Rd.; Bachelor in Decrees, "ad titulum Domini, sibi concessum," 62.—Osmunt, Peter; T. Bodmin Priory, 80.—Oterford, Nich.; T. Dunkeswell Abbey, 78.

Pakyn, Steph.; T. St. Nich. Priory, Exon, 44.—Parker, John; T. Bodmin Priory, 89.—Parys, John; T. Plympton Priory, 82; John, Canon of Plympton, 193.—Patry, John; T. Rewley Abbey, 152.—Payne, John; T. Newenham Abbey, 116.—Peake, John; T. Buckfast Abbey, 89.—Penbethov, Phil.; T. St. German's Priory, 47.—Penell, Rd.; T. Plympton Priory, 116.—Penhale, John; T. Plympton Priory, 319.—Penwyn, Rd.; T. Osney Abbey, 3.—Penwyth, Walter; T. Bodmin Priory, 10.—Perkeham, Wm., Monk of Dunkeswell, 104.—Perkyn, John; T. Bodmin Priory, 241.—Perrour, Peter; T. Cowick Priory, 152.—Petri, Baldwin; Fr. Preach. Exon, 115; Robert; ditto, 163.—Phylipp, John; *see* Cork, 92.—Piers, John; [L.D. Dioc. B. & W.]; T. Cleeve Abbey, 104; Wm.; T. Bodmin Priory, 114; Wm.; T. the same, 92.—Planya, Rd.; T. Launceston Priory, 11.—Pleder, Geoffrey; T. Tavistock Abbey, 129.—Poddyng, John; T. Hartland Abbey, 197.—Poltronogow, Ralph; T. Bodmin Priory, 86.—Poole, John; Canon Regular of Taunton Priory [L.D. Johannis Rouland, V.G. Dioc. B. & W.], 198.—Pope, Hy.; T. St. Nich. Priory, Exon, 115.—Portlond, Hy. [L.D. Dioc. Worc.]; T. St. Frideswide's Oxon, 2.—Pounfleta, Rd.; Carmelite of Sutton, 159.—Prentys, Master Geoffrey, M.A.; T. Rewley Abbey, 48.—Promptyslegh, Hy.; T. Pilton Priory, 114.—Pruet, John; T. Buckfast Abbey, 23.—Prust, Rob.; T. Launceston Priory, 41.—Punter, Hy.; T. Canonsleigh Abbey, 43.—Purs, Wm. (Dioc. B. & W.); T. Hosp. St. John Bapt., Wells, 5; Wm.; T. St. Nich. Priory, Exon, 86.—Pytlond, Rd.; Monk of Buckland, 82.—Pylleheade, Nich.; T. Hartland Abbey, 156.

Ray, Wm.; T. Bodmin Priory, 278.—Raynel, John; T. Torre Abbey, 131.—Rayslegh, John; T. Frithelstock Priory, 83.—Rede, Peter, T. Buckfast Abbey, 115.—Renawdyn, Rd.; T. St. Nich. Priory, Exon, 164.—Reynald, John; T. Hosp. St. John Bapt. Wells, 104; John; T. Bodmin Priory, 115.—Raynold, John; T. St. German's Priory, 10.—Rynald, Rob.: T. Barnstaple Priory, 50.—Robert, Hy.; T. St. Nich. Priory, Exon, 206.—Robyn, Thos.; T. Torre Abbey, 93.—Roddon, John, Monk of Buckfast, 248.—Rogger, John; T. Bodmin Priory, 319; Thos.; T. Buckfast Abbey, 94.—Rose, John, "de Grainale, Linc. Dioc."; T. Hosp. St. John Bapt. without the East Gate, Oxon, [L.D.]; 43.—Rov, John, *see* Hyskyn, 199.—Rudon, John; Fr. Minor, Exon, 278.—Ryburgh, Steph. [L.D., Dioc. B. *and* W.]; T. Cleeve Abbey, 90.—Rychard, *alias* Woborn, John; T. his R. of E. Worlington, 38.

Sakerlegh, Hugh; T. St. Nich. Priory, Exon, 88.—Samelyn, Fr. John, 10.—Sarger, John; T. St. Nich. Priory, Exon, 197.—Saunder, Roger; T. Buckfast Abbey, 198.—Sawyer, *alias* Chamberleyn, Wm., [L.D., Dioc. B. *and* W.]; T. Sherborne Abbey, 62.—Saxon, Rob. de; Fr. Minor, Exon, 114.—Schaplegh, John; T. St. Nich. Priory, Exon, 208.—Schephurd, Thos., Monk of Tavistock, 278.—Schepwaysch, John, T. the same, 149.—Scherpe, John; Fr. Carmelite, of Sutton, 114.—Schipton, John, [L.D., Dioc. Heref.]; T. Wenlock Priory, 163.—Schordeche, Thos., L.D. Dioc. Winton,]; T. St. Nich. Priory, Exon, 149.—Schorm, Simon; T. Buckland Abbey, 198.—Schulder, Thos.; T. Tavistock Abbey, 319.—Schyra, Hy.; T. Launceston Priory, 156.—Schyre, Wm., Canon of Launceston Priory, 163.—Sclusia, Indocus de; Carmelit., 4.—Sclyngesby, John, [L.D., Dioc. Lond.]; "ad titulum gracie Domini Episcopi London," 4.—Scoce, John; T. Buckfast Abbey, 86.—Scoch, Wm.; T. St. Nich. Priory, Exon, 91.—Skoch, Thos.; Canon-Regular of Torre, 104.—Score, Henry; a Friar Minor, 1.—Scote, Rd.; T. Tavistock Abbey, 50.—Seller, Walter; T. Frithelstock Priory, 82.—Shute, Geoffrey [L.D. Dioc. B. *and* W.]; T. Dunkeswell Abbey, 82.—Schute, John; "ad titulum Domini, sibi concessum," 78.—Sirman, John; Fr. Preacher

Exon, 48.—Skewys, John; T. Bodmin Priory, 241.—Slocok, Thos.; T. St. Nicholas Priory, Exon, 202.—Smert, Master Hugh, L.L.B.; T. his R. of All Hallows-on-the-Walls, Exeter, 90.—Smyth, John; T. Launceston Priory, 44; John; T. Buckland Abbey, 50; John; T. Dunkeswell Abbey, 83; Laurence, T. his R. of Sampford Courtenay, 114.—Soby, Rob.; T. St. German's Priory, 50.—Sotyngham, John; Fr. Pr. of Guildford, 2.—Southcote, John; T. his R. of "Douelych Wylam" [Dioc. B. & W.]; 5.—Souton, John; "Canonicus Ecclesie Sancti Patricii, ad titulum dicti beneficii sui per literas dimissorias," 39.—Speare Roger; T. the D. and C. of Exeter, 81; Wm.; T. Frithelstock Priory, 114.—Southwode, John; T. the D. & C., of Exeter, 90.—Sperke, Hugh; T. Buckfast Abbey, 152.—Spernen, Gilbert; T. Bodmin Priory, 273; John; T. Berlynch Priory, 154.—Spert, Roger; T. St. Nich., Priory, Exon, 11.—Stacy, Wm.; T. Buckland Abbey, 319.—Stancomb, John; T. his R. of Ringmore, 7.—Stapyll, Wm.; [L.D., Dioc. of B. & W.]; T. Taunton Priory, 131.—Staunton, John; [L. D., Johannis Roland, V.G. Dioc., B. & W]: T. Sherborne Abbey, Dioc. Sarum, 282.—Stephen, John; Monk of Tavistock, 278; Wm.; Launceston Priory; 97; Stoke, Luke; T. Buckfast Abbey, 5.—Storke Thos.; [L.D., Dioc. Sarum]; T. Cerne Abbey, 193.—Stoteworthy, Rd.; T. Hartland Abbey, 319.—Stoute, Ralph; T. Buckfast Abbey, 241.—Sturgyon, John; Monk of Buckfast, 23.—Stybbe, John; T. Hartland Abbey, 149.—Susan, Thos.; T. Launceston Priory, 156.—Sutton, John; Monk of Forde Abbey, 38; Master John L.L.B.; T. Launceston Priory, 94.—Sylvester, Wm., Fr. Min. Bodmin, 7.—Symon, John; T. St. Germans, Priory, 63; Thos.; T. Bodmin Priory, 152.

Talwargh, Rd., T. Rewley Abbey, Oxon, 2.—Taunt, Rob., T. St. German's Priory, 43.—Taylour, John, Dioc. Meneven: T. Buckland Abbey, 7.—Thomas, John; T. his R. of Dodbrooke, 61.—Thommas, John; T. St. Nich. Priory, Exon, 193.—Thomma, John; T. Bodmin Priory, 92; John, T. Bodmin Priory,, 206.—Thome, John; T. Bodmin Priory, 48.—Thomme, John; T. Launceston Priory, 116; Rd.: T. the same, 129; Roger; T. St. Nich. Priory, Exon, 129.—Thurlok, John; T St. German's Priory, 197.—Toker, Wm., T. Torre Abbey, 50.—Toly, John; T. St. Nich. Priory, Exon, 88.—Tone, John; T. his R. of Ashwater, 80.—Tomlyn, Rd.; T. Dunkeswell Abbey, 196.—Top, Wm., Friar Preach., Exon, 23.—Torner, John; T. Dunkeswell Abbey, 84.—Tournour, John; T. St. Nich. Priory, 92.—Toune, Rob.; Canon of Plympton, 79.—Towneshende, Walter; T. Hartland Abbey, 92.—Tredowarth, Master Thos.; T. his R. of Farringdon, 38.—Tredydan, Stephen; T. Launceston Priory, 198.—Tregenegy, Benedict.; T. Bodmin Priory, 84.—Tregerthek, Wm., Canon of Bodmin Priory, 159.—Tremayn, Rd.; T. Bodmin Priory, 273; Thos.; T. his R. of North Huish, 7.—Trembrace, Alex.; T. Bodmin Priory, 319.—Tremenhire, Steph.; T. the same, 39.—Trenewyth, Rd.; T. the same, 2.—Trepesek, Ralph; T. St. German's Priory, 115.—Tresaher, Rd.; T. Bodmin Priory, 91.—Trethewy, Walter; T. Launceston Priory, 78.—Treveythen, Ralph; Fr. Preach of Truro, 45.—Trevoulyn, John; T. Bodmin Priory, 116.—Trevyda, Joseus; T. the same, 241.—Trevyn, Rob.; St. Nicholas Priory, Exon, 115.—Trewen, John; T. Berlinch Priory, 78.—Treyng of, Walter; T. St. Germans Priory, 149.—Troot, Nich.; T. the same, 94.—Troppe, Henry, Monk of Hartland, 248.—Truvet, John, Friar Min. of Reading, 4.—Turner, John [L. D., Dioc. Sarum]; T. Abbotsbury Abbey, 97.—Tuygg, John; T. the D. & Ch. of Exeter, 208.—Twete, John; T. Tavistock Abbey, 86.—Tylle, Wm.; T. St. Nicholas Priory, Exon, 7.—Tyrell, Nicholas; T. Rewley Abbey, Oxon, 2.

Vnderclyfe, Roger, Fr. Min. Exon, 154.—Veale, Geoffrey; T. Totnes Priory, 116.—Veele, John; T. Buckfast Abbey, 205.—Vele, Thos.; T. Buckfast Abbey, 198.—Velon, Lawrence; T. Bodmin Priory, 152.—Vetty, John; T. the same, 50.—Vyan, John; T. the same, 50.—Vyncent, Nicholas, Friar Preach. Exon, 88.—Vyvyan, Wm., Canon of Bodmin, 46.

Wade, John; T. Bodmin Priory, 114; John; T. St. Nich. Priory, Exon, 202.—Waleys, John [L. D. Johannis Roland, V.G. Dioc. B. & W.]; T. Taunton Priory, 273; Rd.; T. Launceston Priory, 79.—Walter, Thos.; T. Abbotsbury Abbey—Dioc. Sarum, 80.—Walyssh, John; T. St. Nicholas Priory, Exon, 241.—Walter, Wm.; Monk of the same, 278.—Warde, Rob.; T. Bodmin Priory,

88.—Waryn, John; T. his V. of Liskeard, 47.—Wareyn, John [L.D. Dioc. B. & W.]; T. Berlinch Priory, 131.—Waryn, Thos.; T. Launceston Priory, 163.—Watkyn, Thos.; T. his R. of St. John in Cornwall, 45.—Watte, Wm.; T. St. German's Priory, 10.—Wayte, Rd.; T. Frithelstock Priory, 11.—Webber, Thos.; T. St. Nich. Priory, Exeter, 11.—Welfare, Rd.; T. Barnstaple Priory, 61.—Weryng, John; T. Buckland Abbey, 78.—Whare, Thos.; T. Pilton Priory, 98.—Whytelond, Rd.; Monk of Dunkeswell, 114.—Williams, John; Friar Preach, Exon, 44.—Wobbrok, Thos.; T. Torre Abbey, 80.—Woborn, John, *see* Rychard, 38.—Wode, Thos.; T. Tavistock Abbey, 63.—Wodham, John; Monk of Tavistock, 44.—Wofford, John; T. Buckfast Abbey, 84.—Wollegh, John; Friar Preacher, 1.—Wolston, John; T. his R. of St. Endellion, 197.—Wonston, Geoffrey; T. Plympton Priory, 159; Matth.; T. his R. of Maperton, Dioc. of B. & W. 63.—Woven, Hy.; T. Bodmin Priory, 199.—Wydelegh, Rob.; T. the D. & C. of Exeter, 80.—Wyke, John; T. St. Nich. Priory, Exon, 85.—Wylle, John; T. Buckfast Abbey, 61; John; T. St. Nich. Priory, Exon, 151.—Wyllett, John; T. Launceston Priory, *ibid.* Rob.; T. Berlinch Priory, 193; Thos.; T. Bodmin Priory, 198.—Wylkyn, John, *see* Lanbrobys.—Wyllyam, John; T. Launceston Priory, 198; Martin; T. Bodmin Priory, 198.—Wyllyng, John; Canon of Plympton, 85.—Wymond, Ralph; T. Torre Abbey, 46.—Wyndegrynde, John; T. Buckfast Abbey, 83.—Wyndesore, John; T. Buckfast Abbey, 23.—Wynnegode, Hy.; T. his R. of Lezant, 193.—Wyse, John; T. Berlinch Priory, 85.—Wythe, Walter; Canon of Frithelstock, 5.

Yolton, Baldwin; T. Bodmin Priory, 278.—Yonge, Thos.; Canon Regular of Taunton Priory, [L.D. Johannnis Rouland, V.G., Dioc. B. & W.], 198.—Yurd, Roger; T., his R. of Wembworthy, 1.—Yurle, John; T. Buckfast Abbey, 282.—Yurl, Rd.; Canon of Launceston Priory, 116.

ȝeylake, Ralph; T. Dunkeswell Abbey, 50.—ȝouche, Edm., Monk of Totnes, 79.

V. PRESBITERI.

Abbotysbyry, John; Monk of Newenham, 282.—Abendon, Peter [L.D. Dioc. Worc.]; T. Torre Abbey, 163.—Akkelane, Thos., Canon of Torre, 5.—Alby, John; Fr. Carmelit. Sutton, 159.—Aleyn, John [L.D. Dioc Sarum]; T. "Tarent." Dioc. Sarum, 319; Philip; Monk of Tavistock, 149.—Alyn, Wm.; T. Dunkeswell Abbey, 160.—Alkebarowe, Hy.; T. his R. of St Stephen's, Exeter, 81.—Alre, John; T. his R. of Ebryȝthon, Dioc. Sarum, 86.—Ambrose, Canon of Plympton, 5.—Amyhet, Walter; T. Hartland Abbey, 42.—Anstyswyll, Andr.; T. Launceston Priory, 193.—Appelby, Rob.; Monk of Dunkeswell 84.—Artour, Thos.; T. Bodmin Priory, 248.—Asshelegh, Nich. [L.D. Dioc. B. & W.]; T. Sherborne Abbey, 154.—Aston, Thos.; T. Newenham Abbey, 50.—atte Gate, Rd. [L.D. Dioc. London]; T. Tortington Priory, Dioc. Chich., 2.—atte Wylle, John; T. Buckfast Abbey. 5.—Austil, John; T. the same, 63.—Aylmer, John; T. St. Nich. Priory, Exon, 154.—Aylefe, John, de Wendover, Dioc. Lincl. [L.D.]; T. St. Mary's Abbey "de Messandene," [Missenden] 4.—Ayase, Walter; T. Frithelstock Priory, 88.—Ayshyll, John; Monk of Dunkeswell, 104.

Bachelor, Wm.; Monk of Buckland, 206.—Baly, Wm.; T. Bodmin Priory, 104.—Barger, Geoffrey; T. Dunkeswell Abbey, 129.—Barlynch, John; Monk of Buckfast, 159.—Barnestaple, Thos.; Monk of Barnstaple Priory, 78.—Baroun, Andr.; Fr. St. John's Hosp., Exon, 185; Wm.; T. St. Nich. Priory, Exon, 11.—Barry, Wm. [L.D. Dioc. Winton]; T. the same, 164.—Barteram, John; Fr. Preach., Exon, 5.—Barton, Thos. (Fellow of Queen's Coll., Oxon); L.D. Dioc. Carl.; T. the Provost and Fellows of his College, 4.—Baskawen, John; Fr. Min. Bristol, 282.—Batyn, Walter; T. St. Nich. Priory, Exon, 160.—Bavdyn, Hy.; T. the D. & Ch. of Exeter, 43; Thos.; T. Bodmin Priory, 197.—Beare, John; T. Buckfast Abbey, 86; John; T. Dunkeswell Abbey, 116; Rd. [L.D. Dioc. Sarum]; T. Abbotsbury Abbey, 97.—Bedeman, Thos.; Monk of Dunkeswell 205.—Bedyl, Wm.; Fr. Preach., Exon, 88.—Bele, John; T. Newenham Abbey, 114; Nich.; T. Canonsleigh Abbey, 92; Walter; T. Launceston Priory, 83.—Beneht, Ralph [L.D. Dioc. Linc.]; T. Maiden Bradley Priory,

202.—Benet, John ; Fr. Augustin., London, 4 ; John ; Monk of Montacute, 68.—Bertelet, John ; T. Launceston Priory, 91.—Berty, Thos. [L.D. Dioc. Linc.] ; T. St. Nich. Priory, Exon, 61.—Bery, Wm. ; T. the same, 63.—Bettow, John ; T. Totnes Priory, 151.—Betty, John ; T. Bodmin Priory, 46.—Bexle, Rd. ; Monk of St. Nich. Priory, Exon, 63.—Blacheford, *alias* Brygg, Thos. ; T. Buckfast Abbey, 104.—Blakehay, Roger ; T. St. Nich. Priory, Exeter, 23.—Blakelond, John ; T. the same, 7.—Blanchard, Wm. [L.D. Dioc. B. & W.] ; T. Stokecourcy Priory, 45.—Bocent, Wm. ; T. Launceston Priory, 99.—Boghelegh, John ; T. Newenham Abbey, 1.—Bokeknoll, Rob. ; T. Dunkeswell Abbey, 95.—Bole, John [L.D. Johannis Roland, V.G., Dioc. B. & W.] ; Pilton Priory, 278.—Bolham, John ; T. Cleeve Abbey, 114.—Bonde, Roger ; T. Tavistock Abbey, 131 ; Thos. ; T. St. Frideswide's, Oxon, 86 ; Thos. [L.D. Joh. Roland, V.G., Dioc. B. & W.] ; T. Montacute Priory, 248.—Bone, John ; T. St. Nich. Priory, Exon, 3.—Boniell, Rob. [L.D. Dioc. Sarum] ; T. Cerne Abbey, 319.—Borneslo, John ; T. Tavistock Abbey, 159.—Bosfrawell, Thos. ; "ad titulum gracie Domini," 5.—Boston, Rob. ; T. Torre Abbey, 154.—Boswyns, Rd. ; Canon of Bodmin, 61.—Boterell, John ; T. the D. & Ch. of Exeter, 23.—Botrigan, Wm. ; T. Torre Abbey, 273.—Botteburgh, Nich. ; T. Hartland Abbey, 49.—Boun, John ; Monk of Buckland, 35.—Boure, John ; T. Frithelstock Priory, 50.—Bouryng, Thos. [L.D. Joh. Roland, V.G., Dioc. B. & W.] ; T. Abbotsbury Abbey, 273.—Bowedon, John ; T. Pilton Priory, 43.—Boway, Walter ; T. his R. of St. John-in-Cornwall, 198.—Bowey, Nich. ; T. Dunkeswell Abbey, 93.—Bowode, John ; T. Dunkeswell Abbey, 129.—Boystok, John ; Canon of Plympton, 80.—Brabanc', Petrus de ; Fr. Min., Bodmin, 319.—Bradeford, John ; T. Dunkeswell Abbey, 62.—Bradlegh, Thos. ; T. his V. of Buckland-Monachorum, 84.—Bremelcombe, Wm. ; T. his R. of Nymet Tracy, 78.—Bremell, Wm. [L.D. Joh. Roland, V.G., etc.] ; T. St. Frideswide's, Oxon, 206.—Bremerygg, John ; Hosp. St. John Bapt., Exon, 152.—Brenta, Benedict, M.A. ; T. Buckfast Abbey, 99.—Brewys, Thos. ; T. St. Nich. Priory, Exon, 129.—Brode, John ; T. Tywardreath Priory, 3.—Bromford, Nich. ; Monk of Torre, 243.—Brond, Jas. ; T. Frithelstock Priory, 241.—Bronwon, Ralph ; T. Launceston Priory, 243.—Broun, John ; T. St. Nich. Priory Exon, 193.—Brounyng, Wm. ; T. his V. of Modbury, 84.—Brouste, Rd. ; T. Tavistock Abbey, 88.—Brugeman, Hy. ; T. Frithelstock Priory, 1.—Bryn, John ; T. Tavistock Abbey, 319.—Bryce, John [L.D. Dioc. Ely] ; T. Icklington Priory, 43.—Bryd, John [L.D. Joh. Roland, V.G., etc.] ; T. Athelney Abbey, 248.—Brydeport, John ; Monk of Newenham, 38.—Brygge, John ; Monk of Torre, 6.—Brygg, Thos. ; *see* Blacheford, 104.—Bryschefordc, Walter ; T. Berlinch Priory, 149.—Brystowe, John ; Fr. Carmelit., Sutton, 114.—Bryt, John ; Fr. Minor, Exon, 83.—Buckeyete, Nich. ; T. Buckfast Abbey, 197.—Budde, Wm. ; Monk of Buckfast, 95.—Burell, John ; T. his R. of Clyst St. George, 84a.—Burgoun, John ; T. his R. of St. Olave's, Exeter, 49.—Burry, Wm. ; T. St. Nich. Priory, Exon, 23.—Burton, John ; Fr. Minor of Bridgewater, 62.—Bykebury, John ; T. his R. of Bigbury, 198.—Byry, John [L.D.] ; Monk of Abbotsbury, 97.

Cade, W. ; T. Launceston Priory, 81.—Cadia, Rd. ; T. St. German's Priory, 61.—Cadyho, Wm. ; T. Buckfast Abbey, 199.—Calmady, Hy. ; T. Bodmin Priory, 129.—Campyng, *alias* Lurk, Rob. ; T. Barnstaple Priory, 193.—Camyll, John ; T. Bodmin Priory, 243 ; Steph. ; Monk of Montacute Priory, 248.—Canyngton, John ; Monk of Dunkeswell, 282.—Carpynter, John [L.D., Dioc. Sarum] ; T. Sherborne Abbey, 282.—Carslake, John, *see* Mopyll, 199.—Carter, Thos., "de Molyngton, Lincolniensis Diocesis" [L.D] ; 43.—Casey, John ; Fr. Carmelit., Sutton, 115.—Castell, John ; T. his R. of Buckland Filleigh, 78.—Cellyng, Wm. ; Monk of St. Nich. Priory, Exon, 154.—Cergeaux, Master John, T. his R. of St. Martin, "juxta Dulo" 64.—Chamberleyn, Rob. ; T. Bodmin Priory, 84.—Champyon, Wm. ; T. Littlemore Priory—Dioc. Lincoln, 45.—Chernemothe, John ; Monk of Forde Abbey, 193.—Chynnok, Rob. ; Fr. Preach. Truro, 156.—Chyryton, Wm. ; T. St. Nich. Priory, Exon., 164.—Chyterwyll, Walter ; T. Newenham Abbey, 152.—Claveryng, John ; Fr. Minor of Bridgewater, 62.—Clement, Thos. ; T. Newenham Abbey, 1.—Clerk,

John; T. Launceston Priory, 50; John; T. Forde Abbey, 152.—Clovenesburgh. Wm.; T. Buckfast Abbey, 86.—Clyk, Thos.; T. Hartland Abbey, 198.—Clyverdon, John; T. Hartland Abbey, 44.—Cobethorn, John; T. Launceston Priory, 248.—Cockys, Thos.; T. St. Nich. Priory, Exon, 81.—Coden, Vivian; T. Bodmin Priory, 86.—Coffyn, Edm., Monk of Buckfast, 95; Thos.; T. Newenham Abbey, 40.—Coke, Rob.; Monk of Buckland, 89.—Cokyn, John; T. Buckland Abbey, 7.—Colard, John; T. St. German's Priory. 63.—Colle. Rd.; T. Bodmin Priory, 205; Walter; T. his R. of Tiverton—1st Portion, 241.—Colman, John; T. Launceston Priory, 5.—Coly, Jas., Fr. Preach., Truro [Truruye, MS.] 98.—Colyford, Steph.; Canon of Plympton Priory, 206.—Colyn, Hy.; T. St. Nich. Priory, Exon, 98; John; T. Oseney Abbey, 202; Ralph; T. his R. of Lansallos, 79; Rob.; T. Hartland Abbey, 5.—Colcestre, Steph. Monk of Colchester, 4; John; Monk of Colchester, 4.—Cole, John; T. Totnes Priory, 95; Rob.; Fr. Preach. Exon, 206.—Combe, John [L.D. Dioc. Wells]; T. St. Mary's Abbey, Keynsham, 50; Thos; T. Frithelstock Priory, 86; Wm.; T. St. Nich. Priory, Exon, 42.—Come, John [L.D. Dioc. B. & W.]: T. Montacute Priory, 149; Thos.; T. Oseney Abbey, 154; Wm.; T. Dunkeswell, Abbey, 160.—Cook, John; Monk of Torre, 47; John; T. Frithelstock Priory, 62; Thos; T. Frithelstock Priory, 248; Walter. *see* Scot, 4; Walter; T. Torre Abbey, 89.—Cork, *alias* Philipp. John; T. St. Nich. Priory, Exon, 93.—Corneys, John [L. D. Dioc. Sarum.]; T. Sherborne Abbey, 282.—Cote, Wm.; T. St. Nich. Priory, Exon, 23.—Courtenay, Magister Ricardus, Cantor Ecclesie Cicestrensis, ac Canonicus et Prebendarius Ecclesie Exoniensis, in vicesimo etatis sue anno, auctoritate Literarum Apostolicarum, quarum tenor infra sequitur, major factus, eisdem die et loco fuerat per eundem Dominum rite in presbiterum ordinatus. Tenor, vero, hujusmodi Literarum, de qua supra fit mencio, sequitur de verbo in verbum, et est talis,—"Bonifacius Episcopus, servus servorum Dei, dilecto filio, Ricardo Courtenay, Cantori Ecclesie Cicestrensis, salutem et Apostolicam benediccionem. Nobilitas generis, vite ac morum honestas, aliaque laudabilia probitatis et virtutum merita, super quibus apud nos fidedigno commendaris testimonio, nos inducunt ut te specialibus favoribus et graciis prosequamur. Tuis, itaque, in hac parte supplicacionibus inclinati, tecum, qui, ut asseris, decimum octavum tue etatis annum excedis et in subdiaconatus ordine constitutus, ac ex utroque parente de nobili genere procreatus existis, ut cum vicesimum hujusmodi tue etatis annum attigeris ad diaconatus et presbiteratus Ordines statutis a jure temporibus promoveri libere et licite valeas, Lugdunensium Conciliorum et quibuscumque Constitucionibus Apostolicis, ac aliis contrariis, nequaquam obstantibus, auctoritate Apostolica, tenore presencium, de specialis dono gracie dispensamus. Nulli, ergo, omnino hominum liceat hanc paginam nostre dispensacionis infringere, vel ei ausu temerario contraire. Si quis, autem, hoc attemptare presumpserit, indignacionem Omnipotentis Dei et Beatorum Petri et Pauli cicius se noverit incursurum. Datum Rome, apud Sanctum Petrum xviij Kal. Januarii, Pontificatus nostri Anno undecimo," 38.—Cowlyng, John; T. the same, 248; Thos.; T. Launceston Priory, 131.—Cranebury. John; Canon of Plympton Priory, 86.—Cremp, John [L.D. Dioc. B. & W.]; T. Berlynch Priory, 89.—Crekow, Wm.; T. Newenham Abbey, 92.—Criour, Thos.; Canon of Plympton, 5.—Crispyn, Thos., Monk of Tavistock, 159.—Crokker, Hy.; ditto, 92.—Crook, John; T. St. German's Priory, 82.—Crugge, John; T. Rewley Abbey, 205.—Crulle, John; T. Canonsleigh Abbey, 116.—Crystow, Thos.; T. St. Nich. Priory, Exon, 193.—Curteys, Wm.; T. Bodmin Priory, 248.

Dawe, John; T. Glasney College, 92.—Davy, John; T. Forde Abbey, 97.—Dayman, Wm.; T. St. Nich. Priory, Exon, 273.—Denclyfe John (junior); T. Frithelstock Priory, 193.—Dene, John; Monk of Dunkeswell Abbey, 152.—Denys, Robert; Launceston Priory; 154.—Doll, John; [L.D. Dioc. Sarum]; T. Abbotsbury Abbey, 98.—Domerham, Oliver, Monk of Abbotsbury, L.D., 278. Donscomb, Rd.; T. his R. of Sheviocke, 88.—Dorset, John; T. Buckland Abbey, 62.—Dove, Rd.; Monk of Buckfast, 160.—Doynel, Peter; Fr. Carmelit., Sutton,

80.—Drayton, Thos. [L.D. Dioc. of B. & W.]; T. his R. of Lydiard, 91.—Drenek, Hy.; T. Launceston Priory, 7.—Dryffeld, John; Monk of Newenham, 248.—Duelton, John; Canon of Torre, 23.—Dun, John [L.D., Dioc. Sarum]; T. Middleton Abbey, 115.—Dunham, John; Canon of Frithelstock, 193.—Dunnyng, Rob.; T. his R. of All-Hallows-on-the-walls, Exeter, 149.—Dyght, John; T. his R. of St. Stephen's, Exeter, 79.—Dyrehille, Jas.; T. Launceston Priory, 90.

Edward, Rob.; T. Buckfast Abbey, 278.—Eliot, John; T. Dunkeswell Abbey, 47.—Elvet, John (Archdn. of Leicester, L.D.), 4.—Elyn, John; T. Bodmin Priory, 97.—Elys, John; T. Dunkeswell Abbey, 160.—Esoth, John; T. the same, 95.—Estecote, John; T. Berlinch Priory, 41.—Evysham, Rd. [L.D.]; Canon of Bicester [Byrcester, MS.], 43.—Ewn, Rob.; Canon of Launceston Priory, 129.

Faukener, Thos.; T. St. Nich. Priory, Exon, 273.—Fax, Rd.; St. German's Priory, 205.—Fayrewode, John; T. his R. of Alwington, 193.—Feddys, Geo.; T. Frithelstock Priory, 202.—Fodringheye, John; T. St. Nich. Priory, Exon. 81.—Folde, Walter [L.D. Dioc. Sarum]; T. Abbotsbury Abbey, 205.—Forde, John; T. Dunkeswell Abbey, 89; John; T. St. Nich. Priory, Exon, 198.—Fordon, John; T. Tavistock Priory, 91.—Forste, John; T. the D. and Ch. of Exeter, 86.—Fouchere, Alex.; Canon of Plympton, 248.—Fouke, John; T. his R. of Parkham, 44.—Frankcheyny, James; T. his R. of Tiverton, 2nd Portion, 91.—Franke, Rob.; T. Canonsleigh Abbey, 159.—Fraunces, Nich.; T. Bodmin Priory, 206.—Fraunceys, Walter; T. Rewley Abbey, 50.—Frend, Henry; T. Pilton Priory, 98.—Frenssh, John; T. Buckfast Abbey, 248.—Frode, John; T. Hosp. St. John Bapt., Bridgewater, 99.—Froggemore, Rd. [L.D. Dioc. B. & W.]; T. Cleeve Abbey, 62.—Frye, Thos. [L.D. Joh. Roland, V.G. Dioc. B. & W.]; T. Muchelnye Abbey, 248.—Fylham, Wm., M.A.; T. Buckfast Abbey, 104.—Fyllecombe, Thos.; T. St. Nich. Priory, Exon, 241.—Fylp, Nich.; T. Bodmin Priory, 248.

Gaddysby, Wm., L.D., Dioc. Lond.; "ad titulum Monasterii Beate Marie de Gracys juxta Turrim Londoniensem," 4.—Gambon, John; T. Dunkeswell Abbey, 47.—Gawnt, Rob.; L.D. Galfridi Crukadan, Utriusque Juris Inceptoris, V.G. Dioc. Sarum; T. Hermitage Priory, 248.—Gay, Walter; T. Frithelstock Priory, 97.—German, Hugh; T. St. Nich. Priory, Exon, 7; John; T. Bodmin Priory, 7.—Glamvyle, Thos.; Canon of Plympton, 81.—Gode, Hugh; T. Buckfast Abbey, 85; Rob.; T. Tavistock Abbey, 164; Wm.; T. Buckland Abbey, 7.—Godefray, John; T. Launceston Priory, 81.—Godegrave, *alias* Godongrave, John; T. Glasney College, 104.—Godeman, Hy., Canon of Plympton, 110.—Godyslond, John, (L.D., Joh. Rowland, V.G. Dioc. B. & W.), 205.—Gordo, John; T. Torre Abbey, 163; Walter; T. Hartland Abbey, 163.—Gorecote, or Corecote, Simon; T. Launceston Priory, 115; Wm.; T. the same, 115.—Gorewell, Master John, junior; T. his R. of Wyke St. Mary, 81.—Grafton, Thos., L.D., Dioc. Lincl.; T. Buckland Abbey, 202.—Gratford, Nich.; Fr. Carmelit. Sutton, 156.—Guynnow, John; Fr. Preacher, Exeter, 93.—Graunson, John, (L.D., Galfridi Crukadan, Utriusque Juris Inceptoris, V.G., Dioc. Sarum); T. Montacute Priory, 248.—Graynevylle, Master Rd., LL.B.; T. his R. of Parkham, 85.—Grede, John; T. Berlinch Priory, 6.—Grene, Wm., M.A.; T. Lyteling Priory, Dioc. of Lincl., 99.—Greyston, Thos.; T. Tavistock Abbey, 7.—Grussy, Peter [L.D. Dioc. Sarum]; T. Abbotsbury Abbey, 198.—Gybbs, Thos.; T. Bodmin Priory, 115.—Gybbe, Thos.; T. Torre Abbey, 92; John; T. St. German's Priory, 199.—Gybon, Thos.; T. Hosp. of the B.M.V. "extra Bysshoppysgate," London, 160.—Gyddelegh, Wm.; T. Launceston Priory, 45.—Gyffard, Hugh; T. the same, 152; John; T. his V. of Buckerell, 97; Steph.; T. his R. of West Putford, 85.—Gylls, Rd.; T. St. German's Priory, 10.—Gylle, Rd.; T. the same, 151; Steph.; T. Frithelstock Priory, 243.—Gyst, Wm.; Monk of Buckfast, 46.

Hakeworthy, Wm.; T. St. Nich. Priory, Exon, 79.—Hapsey, Walter [L.D. Dioc. Sarum]; T. his Chantry of St. Mary in the parish-church of "Halwestoke," 1.—Harde, John; T. St. Nich. Priory, Exon, 152.—Harry, John; Canon of Bodmin, 47; John; T. Buckfast Abbey, 97; John; T. Bodmin Priory, 243; Nich.; T. the same 199; Rd.; T. St. Nich., Priory, Exon, 151; Roger; T.

Launceston Priory, 164; Thos.; T. Bodmin Priory, 45.—Herry, Matth.; T. Barnstaple Priory, 199.—Hasarde, John; [L.D., Joh. Crukadan, Utriusque Juris Inceptoris]; T. Abbotsbury Abbey, 205.—Hathy, Thos.; T. Hartland Abbey, 6.—Haukyn, John, [Dioc. B. & W.]; T. Canonsleigh Abbey, 7.—Hawle, Thos.; T. his R. of St. Keyne, 5.—Heydure, Steph.; T. St. Nich. Priory, Exon, 152, 151; Walter; T. the same, 82.—Hayman, Nich.; T. Buckfast Abbey, 156. Haywode, Thos.; "ad titulum Domus de Poghele, Sarum. Dioc," 2.—Hegneh, John; T. St. Nich. Priory, Exon, 39.—Helyer, Peter; Monk of Tavistock, 7.—Helys, Thos.; T. Dunkeswell Abbey, 45.—Henry, John; T. Bodmin Priory, 98. —Herbert, Philip; T. Buckfast Abbey, 38.—Hereford, Thos.; [L.D.]: T. his R. of Rodmerton, Dioc. Worc., 41.—Herle, Hugh; T. his R. of Llangattok alias Llancaddok, Meneven. Dioc., 206.—Herlywas, John; T. Bodmin Priory, 89.—Hethen, Rd. [L.D. Dioc. Sarum.]; T. Abotsbury Abbey, 152.—Hevyltorre, Rob.; T. St. Nich. Priory, Exon, 48.—Hobbe, Roger; T. Launceston Priory, 160.—Hode, Walter; T. Plympton Priory, 97.—Hogge, Hugh; T. St. Nich., Priory, Exon, 97; Thos.; T. Hartland Abbey, 6.—Hokkeday, Rich., [L.D., Johannis Rouland, V. G., etc.]; T. Muchelney, Abbey, 205.—Holland, John; Monk of Cowick, 104.—Horlok, Thos.; T. St. Nich. Priory, Exon, 95.—Hotwell, Wm., [L.D. Dioc. Sarum.]; "ad titulum Domus, sive Prioratus, Christi Ecclesie de Twynham, Wynton Dioc," 319.—Hough, Geoffrey; T. his R. of Combe in Teignhead, 319.—Howkere, Thos., [L.D. Dioc. Landaven,]; T. "Prioratus, Beate Marie de Goldcliva," 193.—Howkyng, Marcellus; Fr. Preach, Exon, 48.—Hoyge, John; T. St. Nich. Priory, Exon, 79.—Huchun, Hy.; T. Littlemore Priory, 248.—Hurde, John; T. the D. & Ch. Exon, 156; Rd.; T. Convent of the Holy Trinity, London, 46.—Husy, John; T. Dunkeswell, Abbey, 48; Nich.; T. St. Nich Priory, Exon, 5.—Hyeovyse, Wm.; T. Torre Abbey, 31.—Hyllary, Ralph; T. Rewley Abbey, 85.—Hylle, John; Canon of Torre Abbey, 198; John. [L.D. Joh. Roland, V.G.; etc.]; T. Dunkeswell Abbey, 278; Roger; T. St. Nich. Priory, Exon, 131.—Hylyn, Laurence; [L.D. Dioc. Menev.]; T. St. Nich. Priory, Exon, 91.—Hyskyn, *alias* Rov, John; T. St. German's Priory, 292.

Irysch, John; T. Totnes Priory, 48.—Isaak, Geoffrey; T. Buckfast Abbey, 199.

Jakys, John; T. Frithelstock Priory, 5.—James, Wm., T. Canonsleigh Abbey, 92.—Janus, Nich.; T. Bodmin Priory, 45.—Joce, John; T. the same, 154.—Jon, John; T. Frithelstock Priory, 163.—Judde, John; T. Canonsleigh Abbey, 199.—Jvel, John; T. Bodmin Priory, 85.—Juyll, Roger; T. Buckfast Abbey, 193.—Junte, Geoffrey; T. St. Nich. Priory, Exon, 160.—Juvenell, John; T. Frithelstock Priory, 1.

Karter, John; T. Frithelstock Priory, 38.—Kaskys, Hy.; Monk of Dunkeswell, 282.—Kelleseye, Wm. [L.D. from Michael Cergeaux, LL.D., Canon of Chichester, and V.G. Dioc. Sarum.]; R. of Compton, 4.—Kelly, John. T. Hartland Abbey, 39.—Kelwa, Wm.; T. Tavistock Abbey, 197.—Kemeworthy, Thos.; T. Frithelstock Priory, 79.—Kene, Edm.; T. Hartland Abbey, 205.—Kenegy, Hy.; T. Bodmin Priory, 248.—Kent, Rob. [L. D. Joh. Rouland, V. G.]; T. Berlinch Priory, 199; Wm.; T. St. German's Priory, 83.—Kenylyon, John; T. St. Nich. Priory, Exon, 151.—Kestel, Gregory; Fr. Preach. Exon, 44.—Keuryg, Rd.; T. Berlinch Priory, 319.—Knyght, Henry; T. Taunton Priory, 319; John; T. his R. of Cruwys Morchard, 281.; Rd.; T. Buckfast Abbey, 35.—Knython, Joh.; Monk of Forde, 38.—Kylcam, John; Canon of St. German's Priory, 278.—Kyllyow, Peter; T. Bodmin Priory, 319.—Kyng, John; Canon of Plympton, 46; Rob.; T. St. German's Priory, 319.—Kyngesford, Ralph; T. St. Nich. Priory, Exon, 154.—Kyngeston, Wm.; Monk of Newenham, 282.

Lacy, John, Monk of Torre, 243. Lambrobys, *alias* Wylkyn, John: T. St. Nich. Priory, Exon, 193.—Laneman, Wm.; Canon of Launceston Priory, 198.—Lang, Rd.; Fr. Minor of Bridgewater, 154.—Langa, Reginald; T. Plympton Priory, 159.—Langebrook, John; T. Tavistock Abbey, 241.—Langdon, Steph.; T. St. Nich. Priory, Exon, 90.—Langman, Rob.; T. Hosp. of St. John, at Lechelade, Dioc. Worc. 243.—Langhman, Rob.; T. Buckfast Abbey, 83.—Langrygh, Arnulph; T. Buckfast Abbey, 94.—Lannergh, John;

T. Bodmin Priory, 115.—Launston, John ; T. St. Nich. Priory, Exon, 38.—Laurens, John ; T. Bodmin Priory, 273.—Laurans, Thos. ; T. St. Frideswide's Oxon, 193.—Lavyngton, John ; T. Buckfast Abbey, 23.—Lawe, Rd. ; T. Dunkeswell Abbey, 193.—Lebet, Walter ; T. Cowick Priory, 116.—Leche, Rd., Fr. Carmelit. de Sutton juxta Plymmouth, 62.—Legh, Thos. ; T. Buckland Abbey, 1 ; Wm. ; T. St. Nich. Priory, Exon, 11.—Le[illegible]leston, Thos., junior ; T. Buckfast Abbey, 62.—Leyman, John ; T. Dunkeswell Abbey, 92.—London, Rd. ; Fr. Preach London, 4.—Loskuryon, Walter ; Hartland Abbey, 205.—Loveton, John ; T. Cornworthy Priory, 11.—Loveworthy, Rd. ; T. Frithelstock Priory, 92.—Lowys, Thos. ; T. Bodmin Priory, 243.—Lucas, Thos. ; T. St. Nich. Priory, Exon, 95.—Lurk, John ; *see* Campyng, 193.—Lyddon, Wm. [L.D. Dioc. B. & W.] ; T. Cleeve Abbey, 164.—Lydedyngton, John ; Canon of Hartland, 35.—Lyel, Rd. ; Canon of Plympton, 88.—Lyghfot, John ; T. St. Nich. Priory, Exon, 46.—Lyff, John, T. Dunkeswell Abbey, 199.—Lymon, John ; Canon of Taunton Priory [Dioc. of B. & W., L.D.] 89.—Lympton, Rd. ; T. Bodmin Priory, 116.—Lyndon, John ; T. St. Nich. Priory, Exon, 1.—Lynyston, Thos. ; T. Buckland Abbey, 159.—Lypard, John ; Fr. Minor of Bridgwater, 206.

Magge, John ; T. Frithelstock Priory, 243 ; Martin ; T. Tywardreath Priory, 11.—Malewayn, John ; T. his R. of Calstock, 63.—Mape, John ; Canon of Plympton Priory, 114.—Mapovder [L.D. Dioc. B. & W.] ; T. Athelney Abbey, 319.—Marschel, John ; T. St. Nich. Priory, Exon, 5.—Marchall, John [L.D. Dioc. Ebor.] ; T. Cannington Priory, 104.—Marschall, Rd. ; T. Plympton Priory, 83 ; Walter ; T. Tavistock Abbey, 193.—Martyn, "Johannes junior, filius Johannis ;" T. Buckland Abbey, 78 ; John ; T. Bodmin Priory, 278 ; Rob. ; T. Torre Abbey, 1 ; Walter ; T. Bodmin Priory, 131.—Maryet, Wm. ; T. St. Nich. Priory, Exon, 116.—Mason, Rd. ; T. St. German's Priory, 45.—Matheu, John ; T. the same, 62.—Mathew, John ; T. Dunkeswell Abbey, 85.—Mathu, John ; T. the same, 94.—Mathy, John ; T. Bodmin Priory, 278 ; Rd. ; T. Tywardreath Priory, 45.—Mattyngho, Gencian ; Canon of Hartland, 47.—Maunsell, Thos. [L.D. Magistri Galfridi Crukadan, Utriusque Juris Inceptoris, V.G. Dioc. Sarum] ; T. Priory of Longleat [de Longa leta], 202.—Mayn, Wm. ; T. Frithelstock Priory, 114.—Mayow, John ; T. Launceston Priory, 154.—Mede Peter [L.D. Johannis Roland, V.G.] ; T. Taunton Priory, 241.—Melbiry, John; T. Torre Abbey, 78.—Melton, Master Geoffrey ; "R. ecclesie de Landussyll, Menevensis Diocesis, per L.D. Johannis, Episcopi Lincolnensis, sui Diocesani, racione originis," 4.—Merashe, John, Fr. Preach, Exon, 80.—Merther, Master Laurence ; T. Rewley Abbey, 11.—Mewsham, Wm. ; T. St. German's Priory, 152.—Mey, John ; T. Totnes Priory, 98 ; John ; T. St. Nich. Priory, Exon, 154 ; Rob. ; T. St. German's Priory, 205.—Moggerygg, Wm. ; T. Canonleigh Abbey, 115.—Molussch, Wm. ; Fr. Augustin. "de Rye." 4.—Molner, Nich. ; Fr. Preacher, Exon, 159.—Montagu, Thos. ; Monk of Montacute, 63.—Mopyll, *alias* Carslake, John ; T. St. Nich. Priory, Exon, 199.—More, Hy. ; T. St. Nich. Priory, Exon, 98 ; Ralph ; T. Dunkeswell Abbey, 152 ; Rd. ; T. his R. of St. Columb-major, 63 ; Rd. ; T. Dunkeswell Abbey, 98 ; Wm. ; "Exon. Dioc. diaconus," 273.—Morgan, Thos., Canon of Plympton, 6.—Mortymere, Rob. ; T. St. Nich. Priory, Exon, 43.—Moryez, Nich. ; T. Buckfast Abbey, 131.—Mown, Rd. ; T. Dunkeswell Abbey, 151.—Moys, John ; T. Launceston Priory, 79.—Mullyng, Wm. ; Canon of Bodmin Priory, 319.—Mychell, John ; T. Tavistock Abbey, 81 ; John ; T. Bodmin Priory, 152 ; Peter ; T. Osney Abbey, 11 ; Walter ; T. St. Nich. Priory, Exon, 197 ; Wm. ; Monk of Torre, 6 ; Wm. [L.D. Dioc. Lincoln] ; T. Berlynch Priory, 89 ; Wm. ; [L.D. Johannis Roland, V.G. Dioc. B. & W.] ; T. Muchelney Abbey, 248.—Mylle, Wm. ; T. Hartland Abbey, 7.—Mylward, Hy. ; T. St. Frideswide's, Oxon, 85.—Mylyngy, Wm. ; T. Bodmin Priory, 159.—Myryfeld, John ; Canon of Bodmin Priory, 160.

Nanslowen, John ; T. Bodmin Priory, 248.—Nansumer, Hy. ; T. Rewley Abbey, 3.—Neusham, Wm., of Chesterton, Dioc. Linc. ; "ad titulum gracie Domini Episcopi Londoniensis" 4.—Neweman, Hugh, [L.D., Dioc. B. & W.] ; T. Rewley Abbey, 3.—Newhale, John ; T. Launceston Priory, 152.—Noble,

John, [L.D., Dioc. B. & W.]; T. the D. and Ch. of Exeter, 129.—Northwych John; Monk of Buckfast, 159.—Noscas, Wm.; T. Bodmin Priory, 129.—Nywell John; T. St. Nich. Priory, Exon, 86; Hy.; T. Cold Norton Priory, 248.—Nythyrton, Rd.; Fr. Minor, Bristol, 282.

Odelond, John, [L.D., Johannis Rouland, V.G., Dioc. B. & W.]; T. Cleeve Abbey, 199.—Oke, John, [L.D., Dioc. B. & W.]; T. Staverdale Priory, 154.—Olyvere, Master Rd., "Minister" of Ottery St. Mary; T. his Benefice, 63.—Oppy. John; T. St. Nich. Priory, Exon, 248.—Osmond, Peter; T. Bodmin Priory. 159.—Otford, Nich.; T. Dunkeswell Abbey, 79.—Oxenford, John; Carmelit. Oxon., 4.

Papeiay, John; T. Torre Abbey, 243.—Parker, John, T. Bodmin Priory, 91.—Parys, John; John; T. Plympton Priory, 83; John; Canon of Plympton, 198.—Patry, John; T. Rewley Abbey, 154.—Pauli, Noelus, T. Bodmin Priory, 319.—Pay, Thos.; T. "ad titulum Magistri Domus, sive Hospitalis, Beate Marie de Strode, *alias* Newewerke, et ejusdem loci confratrum, Roffensis Diocesis, 241.—Paye, Thos.; T. St. Nich. Priory, Exon, 243.—Payn, John; T. Newenham Abbey, 131; John; T. Bodmin Priory, 193; John; T. Tavistock Abbey, 243; Rob.; T. St. Nich. Priory, Exon, 90; Wm., son of John Payn "de Tyryngham Dioc. Linc.;" ad titulum Sancte Trinitatis, Civitatis Londoniensis, 4.—Peake, John; T. Buckfast Abbey, 97.—Penberthy, Hy.; T. St. Nich. Priory, Exon. 248.—Penbethov, Phil.; T. St. German's Priory, 48.—Penell, Rd.; T. Plympton Priory, 129.—Pennans, John; T. Bodmin Priory, 248.—Pensans, Michael; T. Rewley Abbey, 152.—Penwyn, Rd.; T. Priory of the Holy Trinity, London, 4.—Perrour. Peter; T. Cowick Priory, 154.—Petyt, John; T. Rewley Abbey, 62; Stephen; T. Thame Abbey, Dioc. Lincoln, 50.—Philipp, John, *see* Cork, 93.—Planya, Rd.; T. Launceston Priory, 23.—Pleder, Geoffrey; T. Tavistock Abbey, 131.—Polglas, John; T. Wherwell Abbey, Dioc. Winton, 40.—Polonia, Jasper de; Fr. Preach. Exeter, 154.—Polskoth, Thos.; T. St. German's Priory, 2.—Poltronogow, Ralph; T. Bodmin Priory, 88.—Polyng, Fr. Edward, 10.—Pomflete, Rd., Fr. Carmelit., Sutton. 160.—Pope, Hy.; T. St. Nich. Priory, Exon, 116.—Pral, John; T. Totnes Priory. 7.—Prentys, Master Geoffrey; T. Rewley Abbey, 49.—Preston, Master John; T. his V. of Sowy [?Stowey], Dioc. B. & W., 5.—Promptyslegh, Hy.; T. Pilton Priory, 115.—Prudde, Simon, de Cotesbruke, [L.D., Dioc. Linc.]; T. St. John Baptist, Hosp., Northampton, 2.—Pruet, John; T. Buckfast Abbey, 38.—Puddying, John; T. Hartland Abbey, 198.—Punter, Hy.; T. Canonsleigh Abbey, 44.—Purs, Walter, T. St. Nich. Priory, Exon, 89.—Pycton, Master Thos., [L.D.]; T. his R. of Tenby. [Tynebie, MS.], Dioc. Menev, 4.—Pyers, John, [L.D., Dioc. B. & W.]; T. Cleeve Abbey, 114; Wm.; T. Bodmin Priory, 93; Wm.; T. the same, 115.—Pyker. Joceus; T. the same, 243.—Pylaton, Wm., Dioc. B. & W.; T. Dunkeswell Abbey, 6.—Pytlond, Rd.; Monk of Buckland, 86.

Rauf, Wm.; T. Bodmin Priory, 40.—Rawe, Walter; T. St. Nich. Priory. Exon, 241.—Rawlyn, Edm.; T. Buckfast Abbey, 319.—Rayder, Philip; Fr. Carmelit. Oxon, 4.—Raynald, John; T. St. German's Priory, 23.—Raynfray, John; T. Tavistock Abbey, 7.—Rayslegh, John; T. Frithelstock Priory, 85.—Rede, John; Fr. Minor of Bridgewater, "per Custodem Custodie Bristollie .. missus, 273; John; T. Bodmin Priory, 319; Peter; T. Buckfast Abbey, 129 Wm.; Canon of Plympton, 80.—Rem, Henry; T. Launceston Priory, 241.—Renawden, Rd.; T. St. Nich. Priory, Exon, 193.—Rendy, Rd.; T. St. Nich. Priory, Exeter, 45.—Revel, John; T. Tavistock Abbey, 41.—Reynald, John; T. Hosp. St. John Bapt., Wells, 114; John; T. Bodmin Priory, 116.—Reynel. John; T. Torre Abbey, 149.—Rexynton, Ralph; Monk of Forde Abbey, 193.—Robyn, Thos.; T. Torre Abbey, 94.—Roddon, John; Monk of Buckfast, 232.—Roger, John; T. Buckfast Abbey, 41.—Rogger, Thos.; Monk of Buckfast, 23. Thos.; T. Buckfast Abbey, 95.—Rokke, John; Fr. Minor, Exon, 90.—Rolle. Wm.; Monk of Buckland, 61.—Row, *see* Hyakyn, John, 202.—Rowe, John; T. Buckfast Abbey, 243.—Ruden, John; Fr. Minor, Bristol, 282.—Russell, Wm. T. Tavistock Abbey, 1.—Rychard, *alias* Woborn, John; T. his R. of East Worlington, 41.—Rynald, Rob.; T. Barnstaple Priory, 61.—Ryppelegh, John; T. Buckfast Abbey, 243.

Sakerlegh, Hugh; T. St. Nicholas Priory, Exon, 93.—Sarger, John; T. the same, 198.—Sanly, David; T. Cleeve Abbey, [Dioc. B. & W.], 1.—Saunder, Roger; T. Buckfast Abbey, 199.—Schaplegh, John; T. St. Nich. Priory, Exon, 241.—Scherpe, John; Fr. Carmelit., Sutton, 115.—Schete, Geoffrey [L.D. Dioc. B. & W.]; T. Dunkeswell Abbey, 83; Rob. [L.D. Dioc. B. & W.]; T. Taunton Priory, 198.—Schoche, Thos.; Canon of Torre Abbey, 114.—Schorm, Simon; T. Buckland Abbey, 199.—Schute, John; "ad titulum Domini," 79.—Schyre, John; T. St. German's Priory, 6.—Scoce, John; T. Buckfast Abbey, 88.—Scoch, Wm.; T. St. Nich. Priory, Exon, 92.—Scoche, John; T. Tavistock Abbey, 243.—Scot, *alias* Cook, Walter [L.D. Thome Stowe, V.G., Episc. Lond.]; "ad titulum Domus de Buttellisham," 4.—Scote, Rd.; T. Tavistock Abbey, 61.—Schruave, Jas.; Fr. Minor of Bridgewater, 154.—Schyra, Henry; T. Launceston Priory, 160.—Schyrbourne, Bartholomew: Monk of Montacute Priory, 248.—Schyre, Wm.; T. Launceston Priory, 243.—Seller, Walter; T. Frithelstock Priory, 83.—Sexpenne, Nich. [L.D. Dioc. Sarum]; T. his Free Chapel of Frome Whytefeld, 97.—Shepwaysch, John; T. Launceston Priory, 151.—Skyllam, John; St. German's Priory, 278.—Skynnere, John; T. Frithelstock Priory, 6.—Slock, Thos.; T. St. Nich. Priory, Exon, 205.—Smale, Wm.; T. the same, 193.—Smyrt, Hugh; T. his R. of All-Hallows-on-the Walls, Exeter, 91.—Smyth, John; T. Buckland Abbey, 78; John; T. Dunkeswell Abbey, 84; Laurence; T. his R. of Sampford Courtenay, 115.—Soby, Rob.; T. St. German's Priory, 62.—Southcote, John; T. his R. of Doulysch Wyllam, Dioc. B. & W. 6.—Southwode, John; T., the D. & Ch. of Exeter, 91.—Speare, Roger; T. the same, 82; Wm.; T. Frithelstock Priory, 115.—Spenser, Gilbert [L.D. Dioc. Sarum]; T. Abbotsbury Abbey, 104.—Sperke, Hugh; T. Buckfast Abbey, 154.—Spernen, John; T. Berlinch Priory, 156.—Spert, Roger; T. St. Nich. Priory, Exon, 23.—Stapyl, Wm. [L.D. Dioc. B. & W.]; T. Taunton Priory, 149.—Stephyn, John; Monk of Tavistock, 282.—Stevyn, Wm.; T. Launceston Priory, 98.—Stoke, John; Monk of Montacute—per privilegium dicto Ordini concessum ordinatus, 63; Luke; T. Buckfast Abbey, 6.—Stonard, Rob.; T. Cowick Priory, 278.—Storke, Thos. [L.D. Dioc. Sarum]; T. Cerne Abbey, 197.—Strode, Master Augustine; T. Tavistock Abbey, 85.—Stryke, Nich.; T. St. German's Priory, 5.—Sturt, Roger; T. his V. of Milton [Abbot] 243.—Stybbe, John; T. Hartland Abbey, 151.—Subenicho, Petrus de, "Provincie Romane Frater Ordinis Minorum, Bridgewater, 319.—Sutton, Master John; LL.B.; T. Launceston Priory, 95.—Master Wm.; T. his R. of Powton, *i.e.* St. Breoke, 5.—Swepston, Wm.; [L.D., Dioc. Linc.]; "ad titulum gracie Domini," 4.—Symon, John; T. St. German's Priory, 78; Thos.; T. Bodmin Priory, 154.—Syrman, John; Friar Preacher, Exon, 78.

Tallan, Thos.; T. St. German's Priory, 7.—Talvargh, John; T. Bodmin Priory, 160; Rd.; T. Rewley Abbey, 3.—Tapyn, John; T. Rewley Abbey, 80.—Tayllour, Thos.; T. Buckfast Abbey, 243.; Thos. [L.D., Dioc. Landav.]; "ad titulum Domini Johannis Seynt Johan, militis, Domini de Westpery," Taunt, Rob.; T. St. German's Priory, 44.—Taunton, Alex.; Fr. Carmelit., Oxon, 4.—Thomas, Master John; T. his R. of Portlemouth, 97.—Thommas, John; T. St. Nich. Priory, Exon, 197.—Thomma, John; T. Bodmin, Priory, 93.—Thomme, Rd.; T. Launceston Priory, 131.—Thomma, Rd.; T. Bodmin Priory, 241.—Thome, John; T. the same, 50.—Thomme, John; T. the same, 129; Roger; T. St. Nich. Priory, Exon, 131.—Thorney, Wm.; Fr. Preach, Oxon, 4.—Thurlok, John; T. St. German's Priory, 199.—Toker, Wm.; T. Torre Abbey, 61.—Toly, John; T. St. Nich. Priory, Exon, 89.—Tomlyn, Rd.; T. Dunkeswell Abbey, 199.—Torner, John; T. the same, 85; Tournour, John; T. St. Nich. Priory, Exon, 93.—Torre, John; Canon of Taunton Priory [Dioc. of B. & W. L.D.] 89.—Torryng, Wm.; T. Buckfast Abbey, 159.—Towne, Rob.; Canon of Plympton, 80.—Towneshende, Walter; T. Hartland Abbey, 93.—Traseȝ, Rd.; T. Buckfast Abbey, 7.—Treberveth, Wm.; T. Osney Abbey, 40.—Tredydan, Steph.; T. Launceston Priory, 199.—Tregenegy, Ralph; T. Bodmin Priory, 85.—Tregerthek, Wm.; Canon of Bodmin Priory, 160.—Treiagow, Michael; T. Bodmin Priory, 5.—Tremenhire, Steph.; T. the same, 91.—Trenewyth, Rd.; T. the same, 3.—Trenythen, Ralph; Fr. Preach of Truro [Truruye, M.S.] 98.—Treresek, Ralph; T. St. German's Priory. 116.—Tresner, Rd.; T. Bodmin Priory, 92.—Treyngoff, Walter; T. St. German's Priory, 151.—Trevonham, John; T. Bodmin Priory, 129.—Trevyn Rob.; T. St. Nich. Priory, Exon, 116.—Trewandra, Ralph. Monk of Tavistock, 7.—Trewen, John; T. Berlinch Priory, 79.—Troot, Nich.; T. St. German's. Priory. 95.—Troppe, Hy.; Canon of Hartland Abbey, 278.—Turgeyr, John: Monk of Buckfast, 1.—Turgys, Fr. Nicholaus, 5.—Turner, John [L.D. Dioc. Sarum]: T. Abbotsbury Abbey, 98.—Tuygg, John; T., the D. & Ch. of Exeter. 241.—Twete, John; T. Tavistock Abbey, 88.—Tybot, Baldwin; T. Hartland Abbey, 243.—Tyrell, John; T. Bodmin Priory, 243; Nich.; T. Rewley Abbey. 3.—Tyrry, John; T. St. Nich. Priory, Exon, 1.—Tyttesbury, Rd.; T. his R. of Westbeare—Dioc. of Canterbury: ordained Priest [L.D.] in the Church of Staines [Stanys, MS.], by Bp. Stafford, by Commission from the Bp. of London (dated 17 Sept., 1395), in which Tyttesbury is called "clerico vestro familiari" 1.

Vayme, Wm., [L.D. Dioc. Sarum]; T. Abbotsbury Abbey, 193.—Vayre. Wm.; T. Newenham Abbey, 1.—Veale, Geoffrey; T. Totnes Priory, 131.—Vele, Thos.; T. Buckfast Abbey, 192.—Velon, Laurence; T. Bodmin Priory, 154.—Vetty, John; T. the same, 61.—Vyan, John; T. the same, 61.—Vyncent, Nich.; Fr. Preacher, Exon, 89.—Vyrsdon, John; Fr. Preach., Exon, 278.—Vyvyan, Wm.: Canon of Bodmin, 47.

Wade, John; T. Bodmin Priory, 115; John; T. St. Nicholas Priory. Exon, 205.—Wadham, John; Fr. Carmelit., 4.—Waleys, Rd.; T. Launceston Priory 80.—Walsh, *alias* More, Wm. [L.D. Clonen. Dioc.]; T. Hosp. of St John Baptist, Bridgewater, 94.—Walter, Nich. [L.D. Dioc. of Wells]; "ad titulum Magistri Johannis Orum, Archidiaconi Barumensis, sibi concessum." 89; Wm.; T. Dunkeswell Abbey, 319.—Warde, John; T. St. Nich. Priory. Exon, 6; Rob.; T. Bodmin Priory, 89.—Warey, John [L.D. Dioc. B. & W.]; T. Berlinch Priory, 119.—Warton, John de [L.D. Dioc. Carl.]; "ad titulum patrimonii Magistri Thome de Barton, dicte Karleolensis Diocesis." 2.—Waryn. John; T. his V. of Liskeard, 48; Thos.; T. Launceston Priory, 164.—Watkyn. Thos.; T. his R. of St. John-in-Cornwall, 46.—Watte, Wm.; T. St. German's Priory, 11.—Waty, Laurence; T. Bodmin Priory, 193.—Wayte, Rich.; T. Frithelstock Priory, 23.—Webbe, Ralph; T. Rewley Abbey, 11.—Webber, Hy.: T., the D. & Ch. of Exeter, 319; Thos.; T. St. Nich. Priory, Exon, 35.—Wegge, John [Dioc. B. & W.]; T. Taunton Priory, 5.—Welfare, Rd.: T. Barnstaple, Priory, 62.—Welleslegh, Rd.; T. his R. of Talkern, [i.e. Minster], 114.—Weryng, John; T. Buckland Abbey, 79.—Westle, John [L.D. Dioc. B. & W.]: "ad titulum Magistri et confratrum Domus Sancti Marci Bristolliensis, Wygorn. Dioc.," 152.—Weston, Wm. [L.D. Dioc. B. & W.]; T. Montacute Priory, 46.—Whare, Thos.; T. Pilton Priory, 99.—Whateley, John; T. his R. of Kentisbere. 2.—Whitemere, Wm. [L.D. Dioc. Coventr. & Lichf.]; T. Ederose Priory, 193. —Whysselwyll, Nich.; T. Buckfast Abbey, 319.—Whyte, John; T. Canonsleigh Abbey, 278.—Whytelond, Rd.; T. Dunkeswell Abbey, 115.—Whythe, Walter; Canon of Frithelstock, 6.—Wilberdon, Ralph; T. Plympton Priory, 319.—Wille, Thos.; T. Bodmin Priory, 199.—Willelmi, John; Fr. Preach., Exon, 78.—Woborn, John. *see* Rychard, 41.—Wode, Thos.; T. Tavistock Abbey. 78.—Wodehouse, Rd.; T. Newenham Abbey, 5.—Wodham, John; Monk of Tavistock. 45.—Wofford, John; T. Buckfast Abbey, 85.—Woleston, John; T. his R. of St. Endellion, 198.—Wonston, Geoffrey; T. Plympton Priory, 160.—Woston. Matth.; T. his R. of Maperton, Dioc. B. & W., 94.—Worthyn, John; T. his R. of St. Endellion, 149.—Woven, Hy.; T. Bodmin Priory, 202.—Wyke. John; T. St. Nich. Priory, Exon, 86.—Wylkyn, John; *see* Lambrobye, 193.—Wylle, John; T. Buckfast Abbey, 62; John; T. St. Nich. Priory, Exon, 152.—Rob.; T. Berlinch Priory, 197.—Wyllet, John; T. Launceston Priory, 152.—William, David [L.D. Dioc. Meneven]; T. Cerne Abbey, 97; Hervey; T. Bodmin Priory, 248; John; T. Launceston Priory, 199; Martin; T. Bodmin Priory, 199; Thos.; T. Buckfast Abbey, 97.—Wyllyng, John; Canon of 'lympton Priory, 86.—Wymund, Ralph; T. Torre Abbey, 47.—Wynnegode, Ienry; T. his R. of Lezant, 197.—Wyndegrynde, John; T. Buckfast Abbey, 6.—Wyndesor, John; T. the same, 35.—Wynscote, Rd.; "ad titulum Prioris iarum," 5.—Wyse, John; T. Berlinch Priory, 86.

Yelmestre, Walter; Monk of Forde Abbey, 81.—Yurl, Rd.; Canon of ,aunceston Priory, 129.

ȝeylake, Ralph; T. Dunkeswell Abbey, 62.

VI. LETTERS DIMISSORY.

The letters T, A, S, D and P stand for "Tonsuratus," "Accolitus," "Sub-iaconus," "Diaconus" and "Presbiter" respectively, and refer in each case to he Orders already attained. Unless it be otherwise stated, it will be understood hat the Ordinations might be "a quocumque Episcopo Catholico infra Regnum Anglie intitulato."

Adam, Walter (A), 12 Jan., 1412-13; i, 173.—Ales, John (A), 21 March, 1416-7; i, 231^{b}.—Aleyn, Wm., Clerk (T), 17 June, 1401 (V.G.); ii, 19^{b}.—Alkebarowe, Henry, R. of St. Stephen's, Exeter, (A), 26 March, 1406; i, 77^{b}.—Alkoc, Thos., Monk of Tavistock (D), 6 March, 1402-3 (V.G.); ii, 25^{b}.—Alvethcote, John A), 23 Feb., 1402-3 (V.G.); ii, 25.—Alward, John (T), 2 May, 1416; i, 221.—Alyn, John (A), 14 Oct., 1405; i, 76^{b}; Wm., "de Venn" (A), 17 March, 1412-3; i, 173; Wm., R. of Great Torrington (T), 23 March, 1418-19; i, 246.—Amyet, Walter (A), 19 Sept., 1401 (V.G.); ii, 20^{b}.—Andrew, Wm. (T), 2 Sept., 418: 1, 242.—Antron, Joceus, "omnes minores Ordines a Guillelmo Ep. Basiliensi," 14 March, 1396-7; i, 11^{b}; also (A), 15 March, 1396-7; i, 11^{b}.—Arthur, John (A), 27 May, 1417; i, 232^{b}; (S), 11 Dec., 1417; i, 237; (D), 5 March, 1417-18; i, 238^{b}.—Artour, Thos. (S), 22 March, 1416-17; i, 231^{b}.—atte Beare, Alexander (D), 19 Sept., 1401 (V.G.); ii, 20^{b}.—Austell, Steph. (T), 22 Nov., 1410; i, 109^{b}; repeated 15 Nov., 1411; i, 139.—Aysche, John (T), 5 Jan., 1410-11; i, 114.—Ayssh, John (T), 17 Feb., 1410-11; i, 117.

Bakaller, John, clerk, 20 Feb., 1409-10; i, 94^{b}.—Baly, Wm. (S), 14 Feb., 1409-10; i, 94^{b}.—Barton, John, (S), 7 March, 1415-16; i, 218.—Bate, Wm. (A), 25 Feb., 1416-17; i, 231; (D), 27 May, 1417; i, 232^{b}.—Batyn, Walter (A), 14 June; i, 181^{b}.—Baudyn. Henry (A), 10 June, 1401; i, 56^{b}.; John, clerk, 14 July, 1401; i, 58.—Baumfylde, John, scholar, 30 Jan., 1402-3 (V.G.); ii, 25.—Bawchyn, *alias* Come, Wm., (T), 2 Oct., 1408; i, 87.—Beare, John (A), 9 Jan., 1406-7; i, 80^{b}.—Beaufysȝ, John (A), 22 Dec., 1403, i, 69^{b}.—Bechamp, Rd. (T), 15 Sept., 1410; i, 104^{b}.—Benet, Roger (S), 11 March, 1402-3; i, 62^{b}.—Benny, Peter (T), 15 Dec., 1397; i, 14; (A), 26th Feb., 1397-8; i, 15^{b}.—Betty, John (A), 4 March, 1402-3; i, 62^{b}.—Bety, Odo (T), "ad Titulum Prioratus Bodmin," 22 March, 1398-9; i, 26.—Bevyll, Thos. (A), 26 Oct., 1404; i, 72.—Beynyn, Wm. (A), 11 Dec., 1400; i, 51^{b}.—Bildeston, Nich., "Utriusque Juris Bacallario," R. of Phillack, (T), 17 March, 1410-11; i 121.—Blacheford, *alias* Brygge, Thos. (A), 3 Dec., 1409, i, 91.—Blakehille, Wm. (S), 5 March, 1417-18; i. 238^{b}; (D), 3 May, 1418; i, 240.—Blenden, *or* Blendeyn, Roger (A), 7 Dec., 1418; i, 244; (D), 23 March, 1418-19; i, 246.—Bodeway, John (T), 13 Nov., 1416; i, 228.—Bodyly, Rd. (T), 23 Oct., 1417; i, 235^{b}; (S), 2 March, 1417-18; i, 238; (D), 14 March, 1417-18; i, 238^{b}.—Bole, Alexander (T), 11 Nov., 1412, i, 172^{b}.—Bolham, Nich. (A), 27 Oct., 1404; i, 72.—Bolter, Roger, R. of Blackawton (T), 22 Aug., 1401; i, 58.—Bonde, John, 23 Nov., 1396; i, 9^{b}.—Borlegh, Roger (A), 24 Sept., 1412; i, 166; (D), "ad Titulum...Monasterii de Bukfestre [Buckfast]," 19 April, 1413; i, 179^{b}.—Bornebury, John (S), 13 July, 1415; i, 211^{b}.—Bornealo, John (A), 17 March, 1412-13; i, 178; (S), 14 June, 1413; 1, 181^{b}.—Boryalegh, Thos., Fr. St. John's Hosp., Exon. (D), 16 May, 1410; i, 95^{b}.—Bosfrawell, Thos., 24 May, 1396; i, 9.—Bosvelec, John (T), 15 June, 1397; i, 12^{b}.—Bosvysek, Ralph (S), 10 Jan., 1408-9; i, 88.—Botrygan, Wm. (T), 15 May, 1417; i, 232; (S), 11 Dec., 1417; i, 237.—Bounde, Thos. (T), 21 Oct., 1406; i, 80.—Bouryng, John, clerk, 6 May, 1397; i, 12.—Bovye, John, *see* Morton.—Bowdon, John, R. of Dartington (D), 6 Feb., 1418-19; i, 245.—Bowedon, John, junior (D), "ad Titulum ...

Prioratus ... Barum," 14 June, 1413, i, 181^{b}.—**Bragge**, John (T), 21 Sept. 1400; i, 49.—**Brake**, John (D), 27 May, 1417; i, 232^{b}.—**Bremelcomb**, Wm R. of Nymet Tracy (A), 15 Oct., 1399; i, 31.—**Brenta**, Benedict, M.A. (S), 10 Sept., 1409; i, 89^{b}.—**Brok**, Nich. (T), 7 Feb., 1409-10; i, 94^{b}; Thos. (A), 28 Feb., 1402-3 V.G.); ii, 25.—**Bronwon**, Ralph (T), 31 March, 1416; i, 219^{b}; (S), 12 Sept., 1416; i, 226.—**Broun**, John (A), 21 March, 1416-17; i, 231^{b}; Thos. (T), 12 March, 1409-10; i, 95; Walter (A), 3 July, 1412; i, 162: John (S), 27 May, 1417; i, 232^{b}.—**Brygge**, John (A), 10 Dec., 1417; i, 237; (D), 5 March, 1417-18; i, 238^{b}; Thos. *alias* Blacheford, q.v.—**Buggh**, Ingrianus (D), "ad titulum ... Monasterii de Boklond, 13 June, 1413; i, 181.—**Bullok**, Walter (S), R. of Atherington, 4 Feb. 1397-8; i, 15; (S), 15 Sept., 1398; i, 18.—**Burell**, John, R. of Clyst St. George, 12 Jan., 1406-7; i, 80^{b}.—**Burgoun**, John, R. of St. Olave's, Exeter, (T), 26 Jan., 1403-3; i, 69^{b}.—**Bussbyry**, Lewis, R. of Cheryton Episcopi (D), 29 March, 1418, i, 239.—**Byalle**, Rob. (S), 24 Feb., 1400-1, i, 55.—**Byke**, Reginald (A), 16 July, 1409; i, 89^{b}.—**Byrcomb**, Rd. (D), 10 Dec., 1417; i, 237.—**Byttebeare**, John (A), 1 Dec., 1401; i, 58^{b}; Steph. (S), 6 June, 1397; i, 12^{b}.—**Byttebere**, *alias* Kyrton (T), 22 Oct., 1417; i, 235^{b}.

Calwe, Rd. (A), 23 March, 1399-1400; i, 34.—**Came**, Wm. (T), 27 Oct., 1404; i, 72 (*see* Kaam).—**Camela**, Gervase (A); 25 Sept., 1418; i, 242^{b}; (S), 26 March, 1419; i, 246; (D), 29 May, 1419; i, 247^{b}.—**Camyl**, John (S); 16 Sept., 1416; i, 226.—**Cararthan**, John, 13 Sept., 1411; i, 134^{b}.—**Carbura**, John (A), 26 Nov., 1414; i, 204^{b}.—**Carder**, John (A), 15 March, 1396-7; i, 11^{b}.—**Cardrew**, Peter (D), 23 March, 1418-19; i, 246.—**Cardu**, Thos., 8 March, 1396-7; i, 11^{b}.—**Carnebon**, Michael (T), 22 Jan., 1403-4; i, 69^{b}.—**Carslegh**, James, R. of Bradford (D), 23 March, 1418-19; i, 246.—**Carswyll** *or* Carsewyll, Rob. (T), 30 Oct., 1399; i, 31^{b}; (S), 7 March, 1399-1400; i, 33^{b}.—**Cergeaux**, John, R. of St. Martin's by Looe, 3 Oct., 1397; i, 13^{b}; (repeated) 13 Jan., 1397-8; i, 14^{b}.—**Champyon**, Wm. (S), 11 March, 1402-3; i, 62^{b}.—**Chuger**, John (T), 2 May, 1416; i, 221.—**Clegh**, Wm. (A), 12 Sept., 1416; i, 226; (D), 25 Feb., 1416-17; i, 231.—**Clerk**, John (A), 13 June, 1406; i, 78; John, of Tiverton (A), 21 Sept., 1411; i, 135; John (T), 9 May, 1414; i, 196.—**Clok**, John (A), 10 March, 1412-13; i, 177^{b}; (S), 4 April, 1413; i, 179; (D), 18 April, 1413; i, 179^{b}.—**Cobethorn**, John (T), 8 Jan., 1416-17; i, 228^{b}.—**Cockys**, Thos. (A), 19 March, 1405-6; i, 77^{b}.—**Cocksone**, John (S), 25 Feb., 1416-17; i, 231; (D), 21 March, 1416-17; i, 231^{b}.—**Coffyn**, Thos. (T), 27 Jan., 1400-1; i, 54^{b}.—**Cok**, Wm. (S), "ad titulum ... monasterii de Torre," 7 April, 1413; i, 179^{b}; (D) V. of Hennock (his title) 12 April, 1413; i, 179^{b}.—**Cokworthy**, John (T), 13 Aug., 1412; i, 164.—**Colbron**, Thos. (S), 5 March, 1417-18; i, 238^{b}; (D), 3 May, 1418; i, 240.—**Cole**, John (A), 17 Nov., 1398; i, 22^{b}; Ralph (S), 8 Nov., 1413; i, 187^{b}; Thos., *see* Stephyn; i, 33^{b}; Thos. (D), 14 May, 1410; i, 95^{b}.—**Coll**, John (A), 10 Feb., 1401-2, i, 60.—**Colle**, John, clerk (T), 13 Dec., 1402 (V.G.); ii, 23^{b}; Walter (A), R. of Milton Damarel; 16 Oct., 1413; i, 186; Wm. (S), 23 Dec., 1414; i, 206.—**Collys**, John (A), 17 July, 1399; i, 28^{b}.—**Collyt**, John, clerk (T), 23 Aug., 1402 (V.G.); ii, 22^{b}.—**Columpton**, John (D), 27 May, 1417; i, 232^{b}.—**Colyford**, John (D), "ad titulum ... Monasterii de Newnham," 13 June, 1413; i, 181.—**Come**, Wm. (A), 17 March, 1412-13; i, 178; (S), 21 April, 1413; i, 180, and *see* Bawchym.—**Cook**, John, clerk (T), 15 Feb., 1402-3 (V.G.); ii, 25; Thos. (A), 21 March, 1416-17; i, 231^{b}; (S), 27 May, 1417; i, 232^{b}.—**Cork**, John (D), 21 June, 1402; i, 61.—**Corndon**, John, Clerk, 19 Feb., 1409-10; i, 94^{b}.—**Cornu**, John (D), 14 May, 1410; i, 95^{b}.—**Coryton**, Andrew (A), 17 Sept., 1399; i, 29.—**Cote**, Wm. (T), 17 July, 1399; i, 28^{b}.—**Cowlyng**, John (T), 14 April, 1399; i, 26^{b}; (S), 27 May, 1417; i, 232^{b}; Thos. (A), 22 Sept., 1410; i, 105.—**Cranemour**, Rd. (A), 17 March, 1412-13; i, 178; Rd. (S), 6 April, 1413; i, 179^{b}; (D), 21 April, 1413; i, 179^{b}.—**Crewys**, Walter, R. of Virginstowe (A), 9 Feb., 1416-17; i, 230^{b}.—**Cristow**, Thos. (A), 8 June, 1413; i, 181.—**Crook**, John (A), 3 June, 1406; i, 77^{b}.—**Crugge**, John (A), 26 Sept., 1414; i, 200^{b}.—**Crympe**, Wm. (A), 26 Oct., 1402; i, 62.—**Cuer**, Peter (T), 7 Oct., 1408; i, 87.—**Curteys**, Wm. (T), 31 March, 1416; i, 219^{b}; (S), 12 Sept., 1416; i, 226.

Davy, John (A), 2 June, 1406; i, 77^{b}; (repeated) 23 Dec., 1408; i, 87^{b}: and apparently) again 20 Nov., 1415; i, 215; (S), 1 April, 1416; i, 220; (D), 12 Sept., 1416; i, 226.—Dawe, Wm. (S), 29 Jan., 1407-8; i, 83ᵇ.—Decam, John D), 16 Feb., 1401-2 (V.G.); ii, 17ᵇ.—Dencleff, John, junior (T), 9 Nov., 1411; , 138ᵇ.—Dene, John (A), 15 March, 1396-7; i, 11ᵇ.—Denys Richard., (D), 4 Dec., 1395; i, 7.—Deyman, John, clerk, 21 Nov., 1400; i, 50ᵇ.—Doyngel, Ivo A), 20 Sept., 1401 (V.G.); ii, 20ᵇ.—Drake, John (A), 1 March, 1416-17; i, 231ᵇ.—(S), 22 March, 1416-17; i, 231ᵇ. Dreyn, Michael (T), 9 Dec., 1398; i, 23ᵇ.—Dygnum, Roger (T), 10 April, 1416; i, 220.—Dymmok, Walter (D), 14 March, 1401-2 (V.G.); ii, 17ᵇ.—Dyra, John (T), 23 Feb., 1404-5; i, 73ᵇ.—Dypford, John (T), 24 Feb., 1400; i, 55.—Dyrehyll, Jas. (A), 27 Sept., 1408; , 87.

Eadmound *or* Edmond. John (T), 14 Dec., 1397; i, 14; apparently repeated, 1 April, 1399; i, 26.—Ellecomb, John (A), 25 Feb., 1416-17; i, 231.—Elys, John, (T), 3 Feb., 1400-1; i, 54ᵇ; (A), 17 March, 1412-13; i, 178; (S), ' April, 1413; i, 179ᵇ.—Erle, John (S), 2 March, 1417-18; i, 238; (D), 19 May, 1418; i, 240.—Esoth, John (S), 5 Jan., 1408-9; i, 87ᵇ.—Estecota. John (D), 14 Sept., 1401 (V.G.); ii, 20ᵇ.

Favkener, Thos (A), 27 May, 1417; i, 232ᵇ; (S), 11 Dec., 1417; i, 237.—Fax, John (A), 3 Oct., 1405; i. 76ᵇ; (D), 21 Jan., 1406-7; i, 80ᵇ.—Felaw, Wm. (S), 18 June, 1419; i, 247ᵇ.—Ferreys, Rob. (T), 9 Feb., 1401-2 (V.G.); ii, 17ᵇ.—Fodrynghey, John (S), 3 June, 1406; i, 78.—Folyet, John, 26 Nov., 1397; i, 14.—Forde, Gregory (D), "ad titulum ... Prioratus Sancti Germani," 14 June, 1413; i, 181ᵇ.—Forde, *alias* Row, Thos. (S), 25 Feb., 1416-17; i, 231; (D). 21 March, 1416-17; i, 231ᵇ.—Forste, John (A), 3 June, 1406; i, 77ᵇ.—Fort, John, clerk (T), 11 May, 1402 (V.G.); ii, 21ᵇ.—Forthe, Thos. (D), 7 June, 1403; i, 64ᵇ.—Fouke, John, R. of Parkham (S), 31 Jan., 1402-3; i, 62ᵇ.—Fowler, John (A), 12 Dec., 1417; i, 237; 5 March, 1417-18; i, 238ᵇ.—Frank, Rob. (A), 26 Sept., 1412; i, 168.—Fraunceys, Walter (T), 6 June, 1403-4; i, 69ᵇ.—Frenssh, John (S), 5 March, 1415-16; i, 218.—Fylham, Wm., M.A. (T), 10 Sept., 1409; i, 89ᵇ.—Fylp, Nich. (A), 25 Feb., 1416-17; i, 231; (S), 27 May, 1417; i, 232ᵇ.—Fylp, Rob. (A), 27 May, 1417; i. 232ᵇ; (D), 12 Dec., 1417; i, 237.

Gabryell, Rd., R. of St. Mawnan, 24 Nov., 1399; i, 32ᵇ.—Gambon, John (A), 10 July, 1402; i, 61ᵇ; Thos. (T), 28 Nov., 1398; i, 22ᵇ.—Gebbe, Thos. (A), 31 March, 1416; i, 219ᵇ.—Geek, Rd. (A), 8 Dec. 1402 (V.G.); ii, 23ᵇ.—Gerveys, Steph., R. of Ruan-major; 29 Jan., 1398-9, i, 24ᵇ.—Gode, Hugh (A), 2 Dec.. 1406; i, 80ᵇ.—Godefray, John (S), 2 June, 1406; i, 77ᵇ.—Godegrave, John (T), 25 Sept., 1404; i, 72.—Goden, Vivian (T), 5 Nov., 1406; i, 80.—Gonne, Henry (T), 1 Sept., 1408; i, 86ᵇ.—Gortebos, Wm., R. of St. Endellion (T), 14 Oct., 1416; i, 226ᵇ.—Govys, John (T), 24 March, 1413-14; i, 195.—Grede, John, 21 Sept., 1396; i, 9.—Gregor, Henry (S) *ab Episcopo Basiliensi*, 15 March, 1396-7; i, 11ᵇ.—Grendon, Henry (A), 26 Jan., 1403-4; i, 69ᵇ.—Grene, Wm. (T), 24 Nov., 1407; i, 82ᵇ.—Grype,....(A), 3 Oct., 1408; i, 87.—Grys, Thos. (A), 26 Nov., 1402; i, 62.—Gune, Henry (D), 2 April, 1409; i, 88; Roger (D), 11 March, 1418-19; i. 246.—Gybbe, Thos. (D), 12 Sept., 1416; i, 226.—Gybon, Thos. (A), 18 June, 1413; i, 181.—Gyddelegh, Wm. (S), 6 June, 1403; i, 64ᵇ.—Gydelegh, Rd. (A), 22 Aug., 1413; i, 183.—Gylbert, John (T), 10 Feb., 1415-16; i, 215ᵇ.—Gyles, John (T), 5 March, 1405-6; i, 77ᵇ.—Gylle, Rd. (S), 19 Dec., 1411; i, 140ᵇ; Steph. (S), 12 Sept., 1416; i, 226.—Gynys, John (D), "ad titulum ... Prioratus Sancti Germani," 14 June, 1413; i, 181ᵇ.—Gyst, Fr. Wm. (S), 8 March, 1402-3 (V.G.); ii, 25ᵇ.—Gyston, John (T), 21 May, 1404; i, 71.

Hacche, John (A), 5 Sept., 1397; i, 13.—Halsangere, John (A), 23 Feb., 1399-1400; i, 33ᵇ.—Haly, John (A), 6 Aug., 1408; i, 86.—Harde, John, clerk (T), 29 Feb., 1411-12; i, 145.—Harry, John (A), 7 March, 1415-16; i, 218; (S), 12 Sept., 1416; i, 226; Nich. (D), 28 Feb., 1414-15; i, 208ᵇ; Thos. (S), 7 June, 1403; i, 64ᵇ.—Hauk, John (D), 6 June, 1403; i, 64ᵇ.—Haydere, Steph. (T), 28 Nov., 1410; i, 109ᵇ.—Haye, Geoffrey (A), 10 Dec., 1395; i, 7.—Haywode, Robert (A), 4 Dec., 1395; i, 7; (S), 24 Feb., 1395-6; i, 8—

Heanok, John (A), 6 Dec., 1400 ; i, 51.—Helyer, Rd. (A), 10 Dec., 1417 ; i, 237 ; (D), 25 Feb., 1417-18 ; i, 238.—Helys, Thos. (S), 6 June, 1403 ; i, 64b.—Hende, Wm. (A), 7 March, 1409-10 ; i, 95.—Hendre, Wm. (A), 1 March, 1416-17 ; i, 231b ; (S), 16 March, 1416-17 ; i, 231b ; (D), 14 May, 1417 ; i, 232.—Henforth, Thos. "*ad omnes Minores Ordines, a Guilelmo Episc. Basiliensi*," 14 March, 1396-7, i, 11b ; (A), 15 March, 1396-7 ; i, 11b.—Henry [*Magistro Henrico*], 4 Dec., 1396 ; i, 10b ; John (A), 19 April, 1397 ; i, 12.—Herell, Wm. (S), R. of Stockleigh English, 26 Feb., 1397-8 ; i, 15b.—Hereword, Wm. (T), 25 Nov., 1399 ; i, 33.—Heydere, Thos. (A), 19 May, 1398 ; i, 18.—Hillary, Ralph (T), 16 Oct., 1406 ; i, 80.—Hirreward, Wm., clerk, 26 Jan., 1401-2 ; i, 59.—Hogge, Hugh (S), 6 Jan., 1408-9 ; i, 87b.—Holme, Rd. (D), 14 May, 1410 ; i, 95b.—Holrug, Wm. (S), 30 May, 1396 ; i, 9 ; (S), apparently repeated "*ab Episc. Basiliensi*," 15 March, 1396-7 ; i, 11b.—Hopere, John, *see* Wylle, John.—Hornabroke, Wm. (A), 8 Oct., 1413 ; i, 186.—Hoskyn, John (S), 2 Sept., 1419 ; i, 248.—Howe, Rd. (S), 16 Feb., 1401-2 (V.G.) ; ii, 17b.—Huchyn, Henry (T), 19 April, 1410 ; i, 95b ; (S), 14 May, 1417 ; i, 232.—Huchun, Henry (T), 4 Nov., 1415 ; i, 214b.—Hulle, John (A), 3 April, 1405 ; i, 74 ; (S), 6 May, 1405 ; i, 74b ; (D), 13 Sept., 1405 ; i, 76 ; John (T), 28 May, 1414 ; i, 196b.—Hunte, Roger (A), 27 May, 1417 ; i, 232b ; (D), 12 Dec., 1417 ; i, 237 ; Thos. (A), 4 Dec., 1395 ; i, 7 ; (S), 24 Feb., 1395-6 ; i, 8.—Hurt, Wm. (T), 6 Dec., 1400 ; i, 51b.—Hyll, John (A), 7 May, 1400 ; i, 36b.—Hynde, Edm. (A), 18 Dec., 1414 ; i, 205b.—Hyr *or* Hyre, John (A), 25 Feb, 1416-17 ; i, 231 ; (S), 21 March, 1416-17 ; i, 231b ; (D), 27 May, 1417 ; i, 232b.—Hyskyn, Wm. (S), 16 Feb., 1401-2 (V.G.) ; ii, 17b.

Ylond, John (A), 27 May 1417 ; i, 232b ; (D), 12 Dec., 1417 ; i, 237.

Janus, Nich. (S), 7 June, 1403 ; i, 64b.—Jerbard, John (T), 29 April, 1406 ; i, 77b ; apparently repeated, when he was R. of Roborough (T), 26 April, 1410 ; i, 95b.—Job, Thos., R. of Plymtree, 8 April, 1418 ; i, 239.

Kaam, Wm. (A), 5 Jan., 1405-6 ; i, 77.—Kelly, John, (D), 24 Feb., 1400-1 ; i, 55 ; John (T), 21 March, 1416-17 ; i, 231b ; (A), 21 March, 1416-17 ; i, 231b ; (S), 27 May, 1417 ; i, 232b ; (D), 10 Dec., 1417 ; i, 237.—Kene, Edm. (A), 12 Jan., 1414-15 ; i, 207.—Kenegy, Henry (A), 25 Feb., 1416-17 ; i, 231 ; (S), 27 May, 1417 ; i, 232b.—Keuryg, Rd. (S), 20 March, 1418-19 ; i, 246.—Knouston, John, clerk (T), 7 Jan., 1402-3 (V.G.) ; ii, 23b.—Knyght, John (A), 3 May, 1418 ; i, 240 ; Henry, (S), 26 March, 1419 ; i, 246.—Knyth, Wm. (D), 14 May, 1410 ; i, 95b.—Kyllyow, Peter (A), 18 May, 1418 ; i, 240.—Kyng, John (A), 11 March, 1402-3 ; i, 62b ; John (A), 24 Sept., 1415 ; i, 213 ; (D), 23 March, 1415-16 ; i, 218 ; Rob. (S), 16 March, 1418-19 ; i, 246 ; Wm. (A), 8 Jan., 1415-16 ; i, 215b.—Kyngwyll, Rob. (A), 28 Sept., 1414 ; i, 200b ; (D), 22 Jan., 1414-15 ; i, 207.—Kyngysford, Ralph (T), 10 Sept., 1409 ; i, 89b.—Kyrton, John (T), 19 May, 1418 ; i, 240.

Ladycourt, Rob. (T), 25 Nov., 1417 ; i, 237.—Lake, Edm. (T.), 9 July, 1404 ; i, 71.—Lanbrobys, *alias* Wylkyn, John (S), 28 May, 1414 ; i, 196b.—Langa, Reginald (S), "ad titulum Prioratus Plympton", 12 June, 1413 ; i, 181.—Langhman, Rob. (A), 3 June, 1406 ; i, 77b.—Langeman, Rob. (A), 16 April, 1415 ; i, 209b.—Lanrak, Rd., clerk ; 2 May, 1396 ; i, 9 ; Thos., R. of Duloe (S), 9 May, 1397 ; i, 12.—Lanscoeek, Rd. (T), 26 Oct., 1404 ; i, 72.—Lanystly, Alan (A), *ab Epis. Basiliensi*, 15 March, 1396-7 ; i, 11b.—Lauerence, Thos. (A), 14 Nov., 1413 ; i, 187b.—Laurens, John (S), 12 Dec., 1417 ; i, 237.—Laury, John (A), 12 Feb., 1396-7 ; i, 11b.—Lawe, Rd. (A), 23 Sept., 1413 ; i, 184.—Legh, Edw., (T), 2 July, 1403 ; i, 67 ; Wm. (T), 2 June, 1411 ; i, 124.—Lercedekne, Michael, Archpriest of Haccombe (S), 6 May, 1402 ; i, 60b.—Loman, John (S), 23 Sept., 1408 ; i, 86b.—Loryng, Thos. (D), 17 March, 1412-13 ; i, 178.—Loueryng, Rob., 16 March, 1396-7 ; i, 11b.—Lovecok, Nich. (A), 17 March, 1401-2 (V.G.) ; i, 17b.—Lovytop, Michael (T), 21 March, 1416-17 ; i, 231b.—Lowys, Thos. (A), 31 March, 1416 ; i, 219b.—Luddon, Thos. (D), 19 March, 1418-19 ; i, 246.—Luditon, Thos. (A.), 7 Dec., 1418 ; i, 244.—Luk, John, R. of Uffculme (T), 30 Dec., 1399 ; i, 33.—Lyghtfoot, John (A), 29 Aug., 1401 ; i, 58.—Lyne, John (A), 10 Sept., 1416 ; i, 226 ; (D), 1 March, 1416-17 ; i, 231b.—Lynyston, Thos. (S), "ad titulum...Monasterii de Boklonde," 12 June, 1413; i, 181.—Lywer, Rob. (T), 23 May, 1414; i, 196^{b}.

Mabbe, John, 12 Sept., 1397; i, 13.—Malewayn, John, R. of Calstock (A), 6 Nov. 1403; i, 68.—Man, John (A), 6 Aug., 1408; i, 86.—Mannyng. Rd. (T), 26 Nov., 1411; i, 140^{b}.—Marchaunt, Benedict (T), 9 March, 1398-9; i, 26.—Marchaunt, Fr. Rob. (D), 8 March, 1402-3 (V.G.); ii, 25^{b}.—Marke, John (D), 3 June, 1406; i, 77^{b}.—Marker, Rd., (T), 7 Dec., 1418; i, 244; (S), 1 May, 1419; i, 246^{b}.—Marker, Walter (A), 19 Sept., 1406; i, 79.—Mares, John (T), 16 Dec. 1401; 1, 59.—Marschall, Philip (T), 30 Nov., 1408; i, 87^{b}.—Marshall, Walter (T), 31 May, 1412; i, 160^{b}.—Martin, John (T), 26 Feb., 1397-8; i, 15^{b}.—Martyn, John (S), 3 May, 1418; i, 240.—Martyn, *alias* Smyth, Thos. (A), 14 May, 1419; i, 247^{b}.—Mason, Rd., (A), 16 Feb., 1402-3 (V.G.); ii, 25.—Mathy, John (A), 5 March 1417-18; i, 238^{b}.—(S), 3 May, 1418; i, 240.—Matthu, John (T), 25 May, 1401; ii, 17^{b}.—Matthy, Rd., clerk (T), 18 Feb., 1402-3 (V.G.); ii, 25.—Mayov, John, 2 Jan., 1402-3; 1, 62^{b}.—Merther, Laurence (T), 8 Nov., 1398; i, 22; (A), 14 March, 1398-9; 1, 26.—Mewan, Rd. (T), 39 Dec., 1415; i, 215^{b}.—Mewsham, Wm. (T), 21 Sept., 1410; i, 105.—Michael, Peter (T), 15 Dec., 1399; i, 33.—Milward, Henry (A), 16 May, 1406; i, 77^{b}: (S), 13 Jan., 1406-7; 1, 80^{b}.—Molentz, Thos. (D), 13 June, 1416; i, 221^{b}.—Mondere, Wm. (A), 1 April, 1416; i, 220; (D), 12 Sept., 1416; i, 226.—Monk, John (S), 3 March, 1416-17; 231^{b}; (D), 22 March, 1416-17; i, 231^{b}.—More, John (D), 12 Sept., 1416; i, 226.—Morewyll, Ralph (T), 24 April, 1419; i, 246^{b}.—Morton, *alias* Bovye, John (A), 9 Oct., 1412, i, 169^{b}; (D), 27 May, 1417; i, 232^{b}.—Morys, John (A), 14 March, 1412-13; i, 178; (S), 6 April, 1413; i, 179^{b}; (D), 13 June, 1413; i, 181.—Mungyn, Ralph (A), 7 July, 1400: i, 43: (A), 18 Oct., 1400, i, 49.—Mychell, John (S), 2 June, 1406; i, 77^{b}.—Mychel, John (A), 17 Dec.,1410; 1, 110^{b}.—Mylbury, John (A), 23 Sept., 1404; i, 72.—Mylleward, *or* Mylward, John (A), 1 April, 1416; i, 219^{b}; (D), 12 Sept., 1416; i, 226.—Mylyngy, Wm. (A), 17 March, 1412-13; i, 178; (S), 4 April, 1413; i, 179.

Nanskelly, John (T), 9 Nov., 1407; i, 82^{b}.—Nanslowen *or* Nanslouwen, John (A), 21 March, 1416-17; i, 231^{b}; (S), 27 May, 1417; i, 232^{b}.—Nansmer, Henry, clerk, 16 Dec.. 1395; 1, 7; (A), 24 Feb., 1395-6; i, 7.—Noel, Thos., 17 June, 1396; i, 9; (A), *ab Episc. Basiliensi* 15 March, 1396-7; i, 11^{b}.—Nuwenham, Rob. (A), 7 Dec., 1418; i, 244; (D), 23 March, 1418-19; i, 246.—Nycoll, Henry (A), 21 March, 1416-17; i, 231^{b}; (S), 27 May, 1417; i, 232^{b}; John (A), 22 Nov., 1406; i, 80^{b}.—Nichol, Thos. (A), 30 Jan., 1397-8; i, 14^{b}.—Nywennine, John (A), 15 Sept., 1405; i, 76.

Olyver, Alan (A), 14 May, 1417; i, 232; (D), 27 Oct., 1417; i, 235^{b}; John (D), 19 March, 1402-3; i, 63.—Oppy, John (A), 21 March, 1416-17; i, 231^{b}; (S), 27 May, 1417; i, 232^{b}.—Opus, Rd. (S), 25 Feb., 1416-17; i, 231; (D), 21 March, 1416-17; i, 231^{b}.—Osanne, Peter (A), 20 June, 1419; i, 247^{b}.—Osborn, John, R. of St. Ive (T), 18 Oct., 1400; i, 49; Martin (T), 28 Feb., 1404-5; i, 73^{b}.—Osmond, Peter (A), 5 April, 1413; i, 179^{b}; (S), 19 April, 1413; i, 179^{b}.—Osmunt, Peter (D), 3 June, 1406; i, 77^{b}.

Pakyn, Steph. (D), 7 June, 1403; i, 64^{b}.—Papeiay, John (S), 12 Sept., 1416; i, 226.—Parker, John (T), 9 Sept., 1400; i, 47.—Paslew, John (A), 30 Sept., 1416; i, 226.—Patry, John (A), 20 March, 1411-12; i, 146.—Paul *or* Pauly, Noel (T), 12 Oct., 1418; i, 243; (A), 11 March, 1418-19; i, 246.—Paulyn, Rd. (T), 11 Nov., 1407; i, 82^{b}.—Paye, Thos. (T), 14 Aug., 1414; i, 198; (S), 12 Sept., 1416, i, 226.—Payn, John (S), 12 Sept., 1416; i, 226.—Payne, Rob. (A), 29 Sept., 1407; i, 82^{b}; (D); 17 Feb., 1407-8; i, 83^{b}.—Penbyrthy, Henry (T), 1 March, 1416-17; i, 231^{b}; (A), 21 March, 1416-17; i, 231^{b}; (S), 27 May, 1417; i, 232^{b}.—Penbygyll, Rd. *see* Trevayament.—Penbygyl, Wm., M.A. (T), 10 May, 1408; i, 85^{b}.—Penels, Rd., 12 Dec., 1398; i, 24.—Penhale, John (D), 2 Sept., 1419; i, 248.—Pennans, John (T), 1 March, 1416-17; i, 231^{b}; (A), 22 March, 1416-17; i, 231^{b}; (S), 27 May, 1417; i, 232^{b}.—Penpaly, John (T), 16 Sept., 1416; i, 226; (A), 25 Feb., 1416-17; i, 231; (S), 21 March, 1416-17; i, 231^{b}; (D), 27 May, 1417; i, 232^{b}.—Penaaus, *alias* Talwart, Michael (T), 2 Oct., 1411; i, 138.—Penwyth, Walter (D), 5 July, 1400; i, 43.—Percevale, Wm., R. of

Martinhoe (T), 1 May, 1419; i, 246b.—Perkyn, John (T), 7 March, 1415-16; i, 218; (A), 31 March, 1416; i, 219b; (D), 12 Sept., 1416; i, 226.—Petyt, John (T), 21 Oct., 1400 (V.G.); ii, 16; Steph. (T), 23 Oct., 1403; i, 68.—Peulyn, John (A), 25 Feb., 1416-17; i, 231.—Phylyp, John (T), 22 April, 1413; i, 180; John, (S), 10 May, 1415; i, 210; Rd. (A), 14 June, 1402 (V.G.); ii, 22.—Pilhende, Nich. (D), 17 March, 1412-13; i, 178.—Planya, Rd. (T), 20 Nov., 1399; i, 32b.—Polreden, John (T), 13 Oct., 1418; i, 243.—Prenteys, Geoffrey, M.A. (T), 22 Oct. 1403; i, 68.—Pretor, John (A), 1 March, 1416-17; i, 231b; (S), 21 March, 1416-17; i, 231b; (D), 27 May, 1417; i, 232b.—Prous *or* Prouse, John, R. of Dunchideock (T), 26 Jan., 1411-12; i, 142; (S), 14 Jan., 1418-19; i, 244b.—Prust, Robert (D), 28 Feb., 1405-6; i, 77b.—Puntere, Henry (A), 19 Sept., 1402 (V.G.); ii, 23.—Purs, John (A), 25 Feb., 1416-17; i, 231; (S), 21 March, 1416-17; i, 231b; (D), 15 May, 1417; i, 232.—Pyers, John (T), 11 Dec., 1417; i, 237; (S), 5 March, 1417-18; i, 238b; (D), 3 May, 1418; i, 240; Wm., clerk, 12 Oct., 1397; i, 13b.—Pyken, Joceus (S), 12 Sept., 1416; i, 226.—Pylton, Wm. (T), 3 Dec., 1401; i, 58b—Pytyngton, Thos., R. of St. Mawnan (T), 1 July, 1405; i, 75b.

Quyntrell, John (A), 3 April, 1419; i, 246.

Rav, Thos. (A), 26 March, 1419; i, 246; Wm. (A), 5 March. 1417-18; i. 238b; (D), 7 Dec., 1418; i, 244.—Ravf, Wm. (T), 1 Dec., 1401; i, 58b.—Rauly, John, 4 Dec., 1396; i, 10b.—Raulyn, John (A), *ab Episc. Basiliensi*, 15 March, 1396-7; i, 11b.—Ravlyn, Philip (T), 27 May, 1417; i, 232b.—Rawlyn, Edm. (S), 16 March, 1418-19; i, 246.—Raynold, John (D), 21 Sept., 1410; i, 105.—Rede, Henry (A), 6 Aug., 1408; i, 86; John (T), 7 Dec. 1418; i, 244; (S), 28 March, 1418-19; i, 246.—Rede, Wm. (T), 3 Oct., 1405; i, 76b.—Rem, Henry (A), 25 Sept., 1415; i, 213.—Renawdyn, Rd. (S), 28 May, 1414; i, 196b.—Rendy, Rd. (S), 20 May, 1403; i, 64b.—Reprene, Thos. (A), 10 Nov., 1417; i, 235b; (S), 5 March, 1417-18; i, 238b; (S), 3 May, 1418; i, 240.—Robert, Henry (T), 21 Feb., 1401-2 (V.G.); ii, 17b; John (D), 20 Nov., 1399; i, 32b.—Robet, Henry (D), 2 April, 1416; i, 220.—Robyn, John (S), 19 Sept., 1406; i, 79.—Rogeer, John (A), 23 Sept., 1401; i, 58.—Roke, Thos., LL.B.; 14 Sept., 1395; i, 5.—Roos, John (A), 25 Feb., 1416-17; i, 231; (S) 21 March, 1416-17; i, 231b; (D), 27 May, 1417; i, 232b.—Roser, John (T), 10 Feb., 1415-16; i, 215b.—Rostase, John (A), 22 Dec., 1405; i, 77.—Rowe, John (S), 12 Sept., 1416; i, 226.—Row, Thos., *see* Forde.—Row, Wm. (S), 21 Sept., 1410; i, 105.—Rychard, Henry, R. of Lanreath (A), 22 Oct., 1412; i, 170; (D), 14 June, 1413; i, 181b.—Rydligo, John (T), 5 Dec., 1398; i, 23b.—Ryppelegh, John (S), 12 Sept., 1416; i, 226.—Rysby, John, R. of St. Petrock's, Exeter (A), 4 Oct., 1418; i, 242b.—Ryvel, John (S), 18 Nov., 1401 (V.G.); ii, 20b.

Sagher, Roger; 15 Sept., 1395; i, 5b.—Sayer, John (T), 22 June, 1411; i, 128b.—Saunder, John (T), 21 Nov., 1409; i, 90b; (S), 16 Feb., 1409-10; i, 94b; Roger, (T), 12 March, 1409-10; i, 95.—Scorell, Thos. (T), 11 June, 1397; i, 12b.—Schere, Thos. (A), 23 Feb., 1402-3 (V.G); ii, 25.—Schirford, John, R. of Marham Church (S), 17 March, 1412-13; i. 178.—Schute, John, R. of Meavy (T), 11 Oct., 1400 (V.G.); ii, 16.—Scoche, John (S), 12 Sept., 1416; i, 226.—Seke, Rd. (T), 20 Nov., 1399; i, 32b.—Sele, Rob. (T), 11 March. 1418-19; i, 246; (S), 1 May, 1419; i, 246b.—Skambel, Wm. (T), 24 Nov., 1413; i, 190.—Skewys, John (D), 12 Sept., 1416; i, 226.—Skywys, Nich., clerk, 9 May, 1397; i, 12.—Skydemore, Rd., R. of Shillingford (A), 8 Dec., 1401 (V.G.); ii, 20b; repeated 15 Dec., 1401; i, 58b.—Smale, Walter (T), 27 Sept., 1406; i, 80.—Smyth, John (A), 8 Oct., 1400 (V.G.); ii, 16; John (A), 12 Feb., 1409-10; i, 94b; Roger, Prebendary of St. Probus (A), 3 June, 1401; i, 56b; Thos. *see* Martyn; Walter (A), 27 June, 1413; i, 181b; Wm. (T), 25 Nov., 1408; i, 87b.—Southcote, John (S), 2 March, 1417-18; i, 238; (D), 3 May, 1418; i, 240.—Speare, Roger (A), 3 June, 1406; i, 77b.—Spernen, Gilbert (A), 12 Dec., 1417; i, 237; (D), 5 March, 1417-18; i, 238b.—Stancombe, John, R. of Ringmore (A), 15 June, 1397; i, 12b.—Stephyn, John (T), "de Porthia" (i.e. of St. Ives), 7 Dec., 1397; i, 14;

'A), 26 Feb., 1397-8 ; i, 15b: John (T), 17 April, 1409 ; i, 88b ; Paul (S), 18 March, 1400-1 ; i, 55 ; Peter (A), 21 Feb., 1399-1400 ; i, 33 ; *alias* Cole, Thos., 17 March, 1399-1400 ; i, 33b.—Stevenys, John (A), 1 June, 1406 ; ;, 77b.—Rob., 23 June, 1413 ; i, 181b.—Stonerd, Rob., (T), 23 Nov., 1417 ; , 236b ; (S), 18 May, 1418 ; i, 240.—Stoute, Ralph (D), 12 Sept., 1416 ; i, 226.—Strode, Augustine (T), 18 Nov., 1406 ; i, 80.—Stryke, Rd. (A), 24 Oct., 1413 ; i, 187.—Sturte, Peter (T), 3 Sept., 1419 ; i, 248.—Sturt, Roger, R. of Virginstowe (A), 11 Oct., 1412 ; i, 170.—Sturt, John (D), 25 May, 1401 ; ii, 17b.—Susan, Thos. (D), "ad titulum ......Sancti Stephani, Launceston," 4 April, 1413 ; i, 179.—Sutton, John (A), 9 Jan., 1400-1 ; i, 54b.—Symme, John (T), 20 Nov., 1399 ; i, 32b.—Symon, John (A), 1 Feb., 1401-2 (V.G.) ; ii, 17b ; Matthew (T), 28 Aug., 400 ; i, 46b ; Thos. (A), 19 March, 1411-12 ; i, 146.

Talwargh, John (A), 16 March, 1412-13; i, 178; (S), 5 April, 1413; i, 179.—Rd. (T), 15 Nov., 1395, i, 7.—Tapyn, John (T), 19 Nov., 1404 ; i, 72.—Taunt, Rob. (S), 11 Sept., 1402 (V.G) ; ii, 23.—Taylour, Thos. (S.), 10 Sept., 1416 ; i, 226.—Thomas, Peter (T), 13 Feb., 1409-10 ; i, 94b.—Thomas, Ralph (A), 4 Nov., 1404 ; i, 72 : apparently repeated 12 Feb., 1406-7 ; , 80b.—Thomma, John (D), 31 March, 1416 ; i, 219b.—Richard (A), 5 March, 1415-16 ; i, 218 ; (S), 1 April, 1416, i, 220.—Thomme, John (T), 21 May, 1405 ; i, 75.—Thurlok, John (A), 28 May, 1414 ; i, 196b.—Thyrward, John (T), 14 April, 1412 ; i, 147.—Tone, John, R. of Ashwater (T), 28 May, 1404 ; i, 71.—Torryng, Walter (A), 31 May, 1412 ; i, 160b.—Toser, Reginald (S), 8 March, 1417-18 ; i, 238b ; (D), 19 May, 1418 ; i, 240.—Trebell, Wm., R. of Lanteglos [-by-Camelford] (S), 8 Sept., 1418 ; i, 242b.—Treberweth, Nich. (T), 2 Jan., 1405-6 ; i, 77.—Treberveth, Wm. (T), 26 Nov., 1401 ; i, 58b.—Tredowarth, Thos., R. of Farringdon (D), 24 Feb., 1400-1 ; i, 55.—Treflyghyon, David (A), 17 Oct., 1413 ; i, 186.—Trefrydowe, Wm. (T), 17 Oct., 1417 ; i, 235b.—Tregodynov, John (T), 15 Dec., 1397 ; i. 14 ; (A), 26 Feb., 1397-8 ; i, 15b.—Treher, John (T), 22 Jan., 1403-4 ; i, 69b.—Trelegh, Thos., "*ab Ep. Basiliensi*," 15 March, 1396-7 ; i, 11b ; (A), 15 March, 1396-7 ; , 11b.—Tremayn, Rd. (A), 27 Oct., 1417 ; i, 235b ; (D), 5 March, 1417-18 ; , 238b.—Trembras, Alexander (A), 16 March, 1418-19 ; i, 246.—Tresagher, Michael (A), 10 March, 1412-13 ; i, 177b ; (S), 5 April, 1413 ; i, 179b ; (D), 8 April, 1413 ; i, 179b.—Tretharapp Rd. (T), 5 March, 1414-15 ; i, 208b. Tretherf, Renaldus, R. of St. Ladock (T), 12 Nov. 1414 ; i, 203.—Trethewy, John (T), "a Reverendo Patre in Christo......Edwardo [Dauntesey], Medensi Episcopo;" 20 Sept., 1413 ; i, 184 ; (A), 22 Sept., 1403 ; i, 67b.—Trethewy, Walter (D), 24 Sept., 1405 ; i, 76b.—Trevman, John (A), 7 Oct., 1416 ; i, 226.—Trevaysment, *alias* Penbygyll, Rd. (T), 12 Dec., 1417, i, 237.—Trevenezek, John (S), *ab Ep. Basiliensi*, 15 March, 1396-7 ; i, 11b.—Trevet, John (S), 12 July, 1401 (V.G.) ; ii, 20.—Trevysa, Joceus (T), 7 March, 1415-16 ; i, 218 ; (A), 1 March, 1416 ; i, 219b.—[Trevyda (*sic*)] (D), 12 Sept., 1416 ; i, 226.—Trewoyef, Henry (T), 7 Jan., 1416-17 ; i, 228b.—Treye, *alias* Stoker, Wm. (A), 3 March, 1408-9 ; i, 88.—Treyngoff, Walter (T), 23 July, 1411 ; i, 129.—Tryby, Rd. (A), 26 Nov., 1401 ; i, 58b.—Tryvet, John (S), 30 March, 1401 ; i, 55.—Twyford, Thos. (T), 2 Nov., 1411 ; i, 138b.—Twygg, John (T), 14 June, 1413 ; i, 181b.—Tybot, Baldwin (S), 12 Sept., 1416 ; i, 226.—Tyers, John (A), 19 May, 1413 ; i, 180b.—Tylle, John, clerk (T), 4 Sept., 1402 (V.G.) ; ii, 23.—Tyrell, John, R. of Zeal Monachorum (T), 20 Dec., 1398 ; i, 24.—Tyrel, John (S), 12 Sept., 1416 ; i, 226.—Tyrell, Nich. (T), 15 Nov., 1395 ; i, 7.

Uda, Thos. (T.), 8 Oct., 1400 (V.G.) ; ii, 16 ; Thos. (T.), 16 Sept., 1416 ; i, 226 ; (S.), 25 Feb., 1416-17 ; i, 231.—Vrban, Rd. (S.), 13 March, 1412-13 ; i, 178 ; (D.), "ad titulum...Prioratus de Trywardrayth." 5 April, 1413 ; i, 179.

Valentyn, John (T.), 11 Dec., 1417 ; i, 237 ; (S.), 5 March, 1417-18 ; i, 238b ; (D.), 3 May, 1418 ; i, 240.—Veele, John (D.), 18 May, 1418 ; i, 240.

Wade, Henry, 5 March, 1398-9 ; i, 26.—Wales, John (A.), 4 Dec., 1396 ; i, 10b.—Walys, John (A), 16 Dec., 1401 ; i, 59.—Wallyng, Thos. (S.), 8 March, 1417-18; 238b; (D.), 19 March, 1418 ; i, 240.—Walsche, *or* Walyssh, John (A.), 31 March,

1416 ; i, 219b ; (D.), 12 Sept., 1416 ; i, 226.—Walter, Thos. (D.), 5 March, 1405-6 ; i, 77b ; Wm. (S.), 20 March, 1418-19 ; i, 246.—War, Geoffrey (A.), 24 July, 1400 ; i, 44 ; apparently renewed 25 Feb., 1400-1 ; i, 55.—Warde, Thos., R. of Whimple (D.), 15 Sept., 1418 ; i, 242b.—Warre, Thos., R. of Rewe (T.), 24 Feb., 1400-1 ; i, 55 ; R., of Uploman (S.), 13 Nov., 1406 ; i, 80.—Waryn, John, M.A., R. of Menhenyot (T.), 20 Dec., 1411 ; i, 140b ; (D.), 22 Aug., 1417 ; i, 233b.—Warry, Steph. (T.), 11 Dec., 1417 ; i, 237.—Waye (Wm.), 22 Nov., 1408 ; i, 87.—Wayneman, Rd. (T.), 7 March, 1409-10 ; i, 95.—Wayte, Rd. (A.), 5 Dec., 1399, i, 33.—Webbe, Ralph (A.), 26 Sept., 1399 ; i, 29.—Webber, Henry (S.), 20 March, 1418-19 ; i, 246.—Wellealegh, Reginald, R. of Talkern [i.e. Minster] (T.), 7 Aug., 1408 ; i, 86.—Welyworth, John (A.), 17 Jan., 1415-16 ; i, 215b.—Whateley, John, R. of Kentisbeare (S.), 24 Feb., 1395-6 ; i, 8.—Whyaselwyll, Nich. (S.), 23 March, 1418-19 ; i, 246.—Whythede, Henry, clerk (T.), 19 Feb., 1413-14 ; i, 194 ; (D.), 3 May, 1414 ; i, 196b.—Whyte, John (S.), 18 May, 1418 ; i, 240.—Wilberdon, Ralph (S.), 20 March, 1418-19 ; i, 246.—Wobbruk, Thos (D.), 6 Feb., 1405-6 ; i, 77.—Wodham, John, monk of Tavistock (A.), 6 March, 1402-3 (V.G.) ; ii, 25b.—Wolton, Baldwin (D.), 7 Dec., 1418 ; i, 244.—Wonne, *or* Won, John (T.), 29 Dec., 1405 ; i, 77 ; (S.), 13 March, 1412-13 ; i, 178 ; (D.), 6 April, 1413 ; i, 179b.—Worthyn, John, R. of St. Endellion (S.), 14 Aug., 1411 ; i, 131.—Wydelegh, Rob. (D.), 3 June, 1406 ; i, 77b.—Wylkyn, John, *see* Lanbrobys.—Wylle, *alias* Hoper, John (A.), 17 Oct., 1405 ; i, 76b ; John (D.), 7 March, 1405-6 ; i, 77b.—Wyllyam Hervey (T.), 21 June, 1415 ; i, 211b.—Wyllyam, Thos. (A.), 23 Sept., 1408 ; i, 86. —Wynnegode, Henry, R. of Lezant (A.), 28 May, 1414 ; i, 196b.—Wyse, Wm. (A.), 13 Sept., 1404 ; i, 72.

Yeurl, *or* Yurle, John (T.), 7 April, 1418 ; i, 239 ; (S.), 14 Jan., 1418-19 ; i, 244b ; (D.), 15 March, 1418-19 ; i, 246.—Yurl, Wm. (T.), 27 May, 1417 ; i, 232b.

Index to Parishes in Devon and Cornwall mentioned in the above Ordination Lists.

The references are to the pages of the present Volume.

Alwington, 446, 453, 461.
Ashwater, 457, 473.
Atherington, 468.

Bigbury, 439, 445, 452, 459.
Blackawton, 467.
Bradford, 445, 452, 468.
Buckerell, 461.
Buckland-Filleigh, 439, 445, 452, 459.
Buckland-Monachorum, 439, 444, 452, 459.

Calstock, 441, 448, 455, 463.
Clyst St. George, 452, 459, 468.
Combe-in-Teignhead, 447, 454, 462.
Crantock, 445.
Cruwys-Morchard, 462.

Dartington, 467.
Denbury, 444.
Dodbrooke, 450, 457.
Duloe, 470.
Dunchideock, 472.

East Worlington, 442, 449, 456, 464.
Exbourne, 445.
Exeter, All-Hallows-on-the-Walls, 442, 449, 453, 457, 461, 465.
Exeter, St. George's, 452.
Exeter, St. Stephen's, 440, 446, 453, 458, 461, 467.
Exeter, St. Olaves, 459, 468.
Exeter, St. Petrock's, 472.

Farringdon, 455, 457, 473.

Haccombe, 447, 470.
Hennock, 468.

Instow, 447, 455.

Kentisbeare, 450, 466, 474.

Lanreath, 472.
Lansallos, 445, 452, 460.
Lanteglos-by-Camelford, 473.
Lezant, 458, 467, 474.
Liskeard, 450, 458, 466.

Marhamchurch, 472.

Martinhoe, 472.
Meavy, 472.
Menhenyot, 474.
Milton-Abbot, 465.
Milton-Damarel, 449, 452, 468.
Minster [Talkern], 466, 474.
Modbury, 459.

North Huish, 457.
Nymet-Tracy, 444, 452, 459, 468.

Ottery-St.-Mary, 464.

Parkham, 461 (*bis*).
Phillack, 467.
Plymtree, 470.
Portlemouth, 465.

Rewe, 474.
Ringmore, 457, 472.
Roborough, 440, 446, 453, 454, 470.
Ruan-Major, 469.

St. Breoke, 465.
St. Columb-major, 448, 455, 463.
St. Endellion, 443, 451, 458, 459, 466, (*bis*), 469, 474.
St. Ive, 471.
St. John-in-Cornwall, 444, 452, 458, 466.
St. Keyne, 462.
St. Ladock, 473.
St. Martin's-by-Looe, 459, 468.
St. Mawnan, 469, 472.
St. Probus, 472.
Sampford-Courtenay, 449, 457, 465.
Shevioke, 440, 445, 453, 460.
Shillingford, 472.
Stowford, 445.

Tiverton (1st Portion), 460.
Tiverton (2nd Portion), 440, 446, 461.
Torrington (Great), 451, 467.

Uffculme, 455.
Uploman, 474.

Virginstowe, 468, 473.

West Putford, 440, 446, 461.
Whimple, 474.
Widecombe[-in-the-Moor], 440.
Wyke St. Mary, 461.

Zeal Monachorum, 473.

AN ITINERARY OF BISHOP STAFFORD (1395-1419).

1395.[1]

London[2]—Continuously from June 20 to March 24, except March 18, when the Bishop was at his manor of Horseley, where, apparently, he remained till he returned to London on the 24th.

1396.

London—All the year with rare exceptions; I find him at Horseley April 1; Aug. 8 and 24, and Oct. 8; at "*Calis*," Nov. 1, and again at Horseley on the same day.

1397.

London—All the year, except towards its close, when I find him "apud Salopiam" Jan. 31, and Feb. 2, 3, and 4. The next date is Feb. 16—London: on the 27th he was "in quodam Hospicio Oxonie, *Battysynne* vulgariter nuncupato;" on March 15 in London; and on the 19th and 20th in Bristol.

1398.

London—All the year, with occasional exceptions. He was at Coventry on Sept. 15; at St. Frideswide's Oxford, Jan. 29; at Daventry some time between Feb. 3 and 28 (the day of the month is omitted).

1399.

London—All dates up to July 6.
St. Alban's—July 10.
Oxford—July 17.
Wallingford—July 22—28.[3]
London—July 31.
Oxford—Aug. 23.
London—Sept. 2, 5.
Oxford—Sept. 17.
London—Sept. 18 to Dec. 15.
Faringdon[4]—Dec. 22—31; Jan. 9 31.
London, Feb. 9—23.
Faringdon—Feb. 27 and March 7.
Winchester[5]—March 17.
Salisbury—March 18.
Clyst—March 24.

1400.

Clyst—March 25 to April 3.
Exeter[6]—April 5—7.
Clyst—April 8—12.
Exeter—April 14.
Clyst—April 16, 20.
Exeter—April 29, 30.
Clyst—May 6.
Exeter—May 7,
Chudleigh—May 9.
Totnes—May 13.
Slapton College—May 14.
Modbury—May 15.
Plympton Priory—May 16, 17.
Tavistock Abbey—May 18, 19.
Holsworthy—May 19.
Hartland Abbey—May 20, 21.
Frithelstock Priory—May 21.
Torrington—May 22.
Bishop's Tawton—May 22.
Pilton—May 23.
Bishop's Tawton—May 23—26.
Crediton—May 27 to June 13.
Canonsleigh—June 20.
Crediton—June 23 to Aug. 1; except July 29 and 30, when he was at Clyst.
Clyst—Aug. 3.
Chudleigh—Aug. 3—5.

---

[1] "Old Style" throughout (the year beginning 25 March), as in the Register.

[2] "In Hospicio nostro Londoniensi—in parochia Sancti Clementis Dacorum, extra Barram Novi Templi."

[3] Here, and in all similar cases, the first and the last dates are given; the intervening dates are often numerous, sometimes almost continuous; and there is no *recorded* break of residence.

[4] "Apud manerium suum de Faryngdon."

[5] "In Prioratu Sancte Swythune" (*sic*).

[6] "In Palacio suo"—here and elsewhere

Clyst—Aug. 6—12.
Crediton—Aug. 17—26.
Sydenham—Aug. 27.
Cuttenbeak—Aug. 28.
St. German's—Aug. 30.
Liskeard—Sept. 1.
Tremadert, Liskeard, Tywardreath — Sept. 2.
Grampound—Sept. 3.
Penryn—Sept. 4.
Glasney[1]—Sept. 6.
Carminow—Sept. 7.
St. Michael's Mount—Sept. 8, 9.
Crantock—Sept. 10.
Cargaul—Sept. 11.
Powton—Sept. 12—14.
Bodmin Priory—Sept. 15, 16.
Boscastle—Sept. 16.
Launceston Priory—Sept. 17, 18.
Bradworthy—Sept. 19.
Hatherleigh—Sept. 20.
Crediton—Sept. 21—27.
Honiton—Sept. 27—28.
Stockbridge—Oct. 1.
Faringdon—Oct. 5—26.
Clyst—Nov. 16—25.
Chudleigh—Dec. 3—26 ; Jan. 9, 10.
Clyst—Jan. 20.
London—Jan. 22 to March 24.

1401.

London—March 28 (from which day the dates are almost continuous—there is no *recorded* exception—throughout the year.

1402.

London—March 27 (from which day the dates are almost continuous, as in the preceding year.

1403.

Clyst—March 29 to April 7.
Exeter—April 8.
Clyst—April 10 to May 20.
London—May 28.
Farnham—June 6.
Winchester—June 7.
Clyst—June 13 to July 21.
Tiverton—July 21[2].
Clyst—July 28.
Crediton—Aug. 7—26.
Campden[3]—Sept. 8.
Crediton—Sept. 18—20.
Exeter—Sept. 21.
Crediton—Sept. 22.
Honiton—Sept. 30.
Salisbury—Oct. 18.
Honiton—Oct. 22.
Crediton—Oct. 23.
Chudleigh—Nov. 2 to Jan. 22.
Clyst—Jan. 25 to March 24.

1404.

Clyst—March 31 to June 10.
Torrington—June 24.
Bishop's Tawton—June 25.
Northmolton—June 26.
Clyst—July 3 to Aug. 14.
Ashburton—Aug. 23.
Chudleigh, Paignton — Aug. 25.
Kingsbridge—Aug. 27.
Plympton—Aug. 28.
Tavistock—Aug. 30.
Clyst—Aug. 31 to Sept. 27.
Coventry—Oct. 8 to Nov. 14.
London—Nov. 19—29.
Clyst—Dec. 15.
Crediton—Dec. 20, 21; and Jan. 2 to March 23.

1045.

Exeter—March 27.
Crediton—March 30 to May 6 (but he was at the Palace on the 16th of April.)
Lawhitton—May 8.
Cuttenbeak—May 10.
Lostwithiel—May 12.
Grampound—May 13.
Penryn—May 14, 15.
Marazion—May 16, 17.
St. Gwennap—May 18.
St. Newlyn—May 19.
Pauton—May 21, 22.
Bodmin—May 23.
Lanteglos [by Camelford]—May 24.
Lawhitton—May 25, 26.
Crediton—May 29 to June 1.
Chudleigh—June 2—6.
Crediton—June 6 to July 7.
Clyst—July 15.

---

[1] "in aula Venerabilis Viri, Magistri Benedicti Canterbury, Canonici."

[2] "in Capella Nobilis Viri, Domini Edwardi, Comitis Devoniæ, in Manerio suo de Tyverton."

[3] "Apud Campedene"—? Chipping-Campden.

Crediton—July 18—24; Aug. 18; Sept. 6—24.
Clyst—Oct. 3 to Feb. 23.
Yeovil[1]—Feb. 25.
Salisbury—Feb. 28.
London—March 5—24.

1406.

London—March 25; April 2—29; May 2—30; June 1—13.
Crediton—June 15.
London—June 23—27; July 7.
Clyst—July 16 to Aug. 15.
Crediton—Aug. 17.
Clyst—Aug. 17—26.
Chudleigh—Sept. 2.
Clyst—Sept. 7 to March 3.
Crediton—March 7—24.

1407

Crediton—March 25 to the end of the year continuously, with no recorded break except
Torrington—Oct. 7th.

1408.

Crediton—March 25—April 7.
Exeter—April 11.
Crediton—April 12, 13.
Exeter—April 13.
Crediton—April 18—28.
Exeter—May 1.
Crediton—May 1—10.
Kingsbridge—May 14.
Plympton—May 17.
Crediton—May 20—31; June 7—11.
Cleeve[2]—June 16.
Crediton—June 28 to July 9.
Chard[3]—July 15.
Crediton—Aug. 6—27 (but he was at Salisbury—Aug. 13); Sept. 1 to Oct. 1.
Exeter—Oct. 2.
Crediton—Oct. 3 to Jan. 6.
Winchester—Jan. 10.
London—Jan. 31; Feb. 1.
Crediton—Feb. 13 to March 24.

1409.

Crediton—March 25—29.
Lawhitton—April 10.
Glasney—April 15.
Marazion—April 17.
Crediton—May 2—28; June 1—29; July 2—24; Aug. 3.
Exeter—Sept. 5.
Upton Hellions—Sept. 15.
Crediton—Sept. 16, 20, 22.
Woodbury—Sept. 23.
Lympston—Sept. 24.
Crediton—Sept. 27 to Jan. 31.
London—Feb. 3 to the end of the year.

1410.

London—March 25 to May 11.
Farnham—May 14.
Winchester } May 16.
Shaftesbury }
Honiton—May 19.
Exeter—May 20.
Crediton—May 25 to June 20.
Exeter—June 26.
Crediton—July 2—25.
Exeter—July 25, 26.
Crediton—July 27 to Sept. 28.
Exeter—Sept. 30.
Crediton—Oct. 1—14.
Bishop's Tawton—Oct. 18 to Nov. 5.
Crediton—Nov. 6—8.
Clyst—Nov. 9.
Crediton—Nov. 11—17.
Clyst—Nov. 21—25.
Ottery—Dec. 4.
Clyst—Dec. 10—12.
Crediton—Dec. 12—24.
Torrington—Dec. 26.
Crediton—Dec. 28 to March 24.

1411.

Crediton—March 25 to May 2.
Ashburton—May 5.
Paignton, May 6, 7.
Totnes—May 7.
Paignton—May 8.
Kingsbridge—May 9.
Plympton—May 10.
Plymouth—May 11.
Tavistock—May 12.
Holsworthy—May 13.
Hartland—May 14.
Hatherleigh—May 15.
Crediton—May 18 to July 18.
Exeter—July 21.
Clyst—July 23.
Crediton—July 24.
Clyst—July 28, 29.
Exeter—July 29.
Crediton—Aug. 7—26.
Chudleigh—Aug. 30.
Crediton—Sept. 1—8.
Exeter—Sept. 12.
Crediton—Sept. 14—23.
Cuttenbeak—Sept. 29, 30.

---

[1] "Apud Yevell, Bathoniensis et Wallensis Diocesis."

[2] "Apud Clyve Sancte Marie, B. and W. Dioc."

[3] Churd, MS.

Liskeard—Oct. 1.
Lostwithiel—Oct. 2.
Grampound } Oct. 3.
Truro }
Penryn—Oct. 4—6.
Helston—Oct. 7.
Marazion—Oct. 7, 8.
Lelant—Oct. 9.
Redruth—Oct. 10.
Mitchell—Oct. 10, 11.
Pauton—Oct. 12.
Bodmin—Oct. 14.
Lanteglos [by Camelford]—Oct. 15.
Lawhitton—Oct. 16—19.
Crediton—Oct. 21 to Nov. 15.
Chudleigh—Nov. 15 to Dec. 3.
Crediton—Dec. 8—12.
Ottery—Dec. 15.
Crediton—Dec. 17 to Jan. 15.
Tiverton—Jan. 17.
Stockleigh Pomeroy—Jan. 18.
Crediton—Jan. 19 to Feb. 20.
Paignton—Feb. 27.
Crediton—March 12—24.

1412.

Crediton—March 25 to May 13.
Clyst—May 17 to Aug. 19.
Chudleigh—Aug. 22—27.
Clyst—Sept. 6 to Oct. 3.
Exeter—Oct. 4—7.
Clyst—Oct. 7 to Jan. 23.
Alton[1]—Feb. 3.
London—Feb. 12 to March 24.

1413.

London—March 25 to June 29.
Clyst—July 14 to Aug. 19.
Exeter—Aug. 22.
Crediton—Aug. 23 to Sept. 6.
Clyst—Sept. 15 to Jan. 18.
Chudleigh—Jan. 25—31.
Clyst—Feb. 2 to March 24.

1414.

Clyst—March 25 to April 19.
Ilchester—April 23.
Bruton—April 24.
Chipping-Norton—May 1.
Leicester—May 6—29.
Lutterworth—May 30.
Daventry—May 31.
Warminster—June 7.
Chard—June 10.
Honiton—June 11.
Clyst—June 14 to Aug. 15.
Chudleigh—Aug. 17.
Paignton—Aug. 23.
Blackawton—Aug. 25.
Blackawton—Sept. 25.
Kingsbridge—Sept. 26, 27.
Clyst[2]—Almost continuously, to the end of the year.

1415.

Clyst—March 25 to May 6.
Exeter—May 15.
Clyst—May 16 to Aug. 9.
Exeter—Aug. 18—20.
Crediton—Aug. 22 to Sept. 3.
Clyst—Sept. 5—25.
Chudleigh—Sept. 27 to Oct. 1.
Clyst—Oct. 4.
Chudleigh—Oct. 5—18.
Crediton—Oct. 20.
Chudleigh—Oct. 28.
Clyst—Oct. 29 to March 24.

1416.

Clyst—March 25 to June 29.
London—July 5—8.
Clyst—July 10 to the end of the year.

1417.

Clyst—Without recorded break throughout the year.

1418.

Clyst—March 25 to July 3.
Crediton—July 6 to 16.
Clyst—July 23 to March 24.

1419.

Clyst—March 25 to Sept. 3.

---

[1] "apud Aulton," MS.

[2] He appears to have been at Paignton, 27 Sept. and 11 and 19 Oct.—on 20 Feb. he was in the Palace at Exeter. Clearly his head-quarters were at Clyst, at this time.

APPENDIX.

[I am indebted to Mr. Dymond for access to the following interesting documents, preserved in the Chest of the Parish of St. Kerrian, Exeter (the Church of which has been destroyed). The Will of John Wilford belongs to our period, and he was a brother to William Wilford (or Wilsford), whose Will is given at page 401. The Inventory also belongs to Bp. Stafford's time].

I.

In Dei Nomine, Amen.—Penultimo die Februarii, Anno Domini Millesimo occc^{mo} decimo septimo, Ego, Johannes Wilsford, civis Civitatis Exoniensis, compos mentis, condo testamentum meum in hunc modum. Inprimis lego et commendo animam meam Deo Omnipotenti Qui eam Suo Sanguine precioso redemit, et corpus meum sacre sepulture. Item, do et lego Johanni Melbury et Thome Montegu, custodibus Ecclesie Sancti Kyrany, Exonie, unam acram terre mee cum pertinenciis in Velewill, jacentem extra Portam Borialem Civitatis Exoniensis predicte, in suburbiis ejusdem Civitatis, inter terram nuper Rogeri Askerswille, quam Willelmus Shaplegh tenet, in parte occidentali, et terram nuper Johannis Sleghe in parte orientali, ac terram vocatam Starcombe in parte boriali, et venellam ducentem versus Starcombe in parte australi. Item, do et lego eisdem Johanni Melbury et Thome, custodibus predictis, unum toftum meum cum gardino adjacente cum pertinenciis, super montem Sancti Davidis extra Portam predictam, in suburbiis ejusdem Civitatis, inter tenementum Roberti Hoigge in parte australi, et terram Johannis Lange in parte boriali, et viam regiam ducentem versus Couelegh in parte orientali, habendam et tenendam predictam terram, toftum, et gardinum, cum omnibus arboribus in eisdem terra, tofto, et gardino crescentibus, simul cum omnibus et singulis suis pertinenciis et proficuis, prefatis custodibus, et eorum successoribus qui pro tempore fuerint, a die confeccionis presencium usque ad finem termini nonaginta et novem annorum proximo sequencium complendam, reddendis inde annuatim capitalibus Dominis feodorum illorum redditibus et serviciis que inde debentur; sub tali condicione tamen, quod predicti custodes, et eorum successores qui pro tempore fuerint, teneant anniversarium meum in predicta Ecclesia Sancti Kyrani annuatim semper die Martis proximo ante Festum Kyrani Episcopi, cum Rectore ejusdem Ecclesie et cum quinque aliis presbiteris et duobus clericis: ita quod Rector inde habeat, si presens fuerit tam ad exequias quam ad Missam, iiijd., et quilibet dictorum presbiterorum sic presens iijd; et quilibet dictorum clericorum sic presens ijd.; et pro lumine ibidem ardente iiijd., et quilibet custos dicte Ecclesie ibidem presens pro ejus labore iijd. Et post finem termini predictorum nonaginta et novem annorum volo quod predicta terra toftum et gardinum cum pertinenciis vendantur per custodes dicte Ecclesie qui pro tempore fuerint, et pecunia inde proveniens volo quod ad usum dicte Ecclesie convertatur. Item, do et lego executoribus meis subscriptis omnia residua messuagia terras et tenementa mea cum pertinenciis que habeo in Civitate Exoniensi et in suburbiis ejusdem ad vendendum imperpetuum; et de pecunia inde proveniente volo quod omnia debita mea primo et principaliter sint plenarie persoluta. Et de residuis ejusdem pecunie, postquam predicta debita mea sic fuerint plenarie persoluta, volo quod Walterus Leye habeat inde decem marcas sterlingorum, si tantum adtunc remanserit; et hoc sub condicione sequente, videlicet quod executores Thome Poleworthy,[*Baker*, pro predicta summa decem marcarum totum debitum quod idem Walterus eis debet pro adquisicione illius tenementi nuper predicti Thome Poleworthy, quod de predictis executoribus nuper perquisivit, sibi totaliter condonare et relaxare voluerint infra triginta dies post vendicionem et deliberacionem eorundem messuagii terrarum et tenementorum meorum predictorum. Et si predicti executores Thome Poleworthy hoc facere noluerint, volo quod executores mei infra scripti inter aliud residuum bonorum meorum predictas decem marcas bene et fideliter disponant, prout eis melius videbitur expedire. Residuum vero bonorum meorum superius non legatorum lego executoribus meis ad inveniendum unum presbiterum celebrantem in Ecclesia predicta pro anima mea et animabus illorum quibus teneor, quamdiu dictum residuum durare poterit. Ad istud vero testamentum bene et fideliter exequendum, ordino, facio, et constituo executores meos Thomam Cooke, clericum, et Edwardum Langynow.

[The Bishop's seal, in fair condition, is attached].

In dorso :—

Probatum fuit presens testamentum in plena Curia Civitatis Exoniensis, ibidem tenta die Lune proximo post Festum Sancti Georgii Martiris, anno regni Regis Henrici Quinti post Conquestum sexto [25 April, 1418], coram Johanne Cooke, Maiore ejusdem Civitatis, Johanne Clerk, Willelmo Shaplegh, Nicholao Trelauny, et Stephano Butteford, ballivis dicte Civitatis, per sacramentum Willelmi Shaplegh, Johannis Melbury, et Ricardi Lawe. Et super hoc facta fuit proclamacio generalis quod si aliquis pro se habeat vel dicere sciat contra testamentum predictum, veniat infra annum et diem, jus suum prosecuturus, si voluerit; super quo preceptum est evidenter Curie predicte liberare sacramentum supra legatariorum, salvo jure cujuscumque.

There are two other copies of this Will in the Parish Chest; one, a shorter Will endorsed—"Est aliud probatum"; the other corresponding with the one printed above, and still retaining the seal of the Official of the Archdeacon of Exeter, somewhat mutilated. It is endorsed as follows:—

Sexto die mensis Marcii, Anno Domini Millesimo quadringentesimo decimo septimo [1417-18], probatum fuit presens testamentum coram nobis, Officiali Domini Archidiaconi Exoniensis, in Civitate Exoniensi, in qua quidem Civitate infrascriptus testator decessit, et per nos approbatum, et pro eodem testamento pronunciatum, in quo Thomas Coke, clericus, et Edwardus Langynow sunt executores nominati; et postea, decimo septimo die mensis Aprilis, Anno Domini Millesimo quadringentesimo decimo octavo, dicto Edwardo coram nobis ibidem personaliter comparenti, in forma juris jurato, administracionem bonorum dicti defuncti infra ambitum Archidiaconatus predicti commisimus. In cujus rei testimonium sigillum Officii nostri presentibus apposuimus. Datum supradicto decimo septimo die mensis Aprilis, Anno Domini Millesimo cccc^{mo} decimo octavo.*

II.

[The MS. is a little damaged, and one or two words are consequently illegible. From "Item, j scalam" to the end it is in a different handwriting, and evidently the work of a comparatively illiterate scribe.]

Hec indentura facta Anno Domini Mill^{o} cccc^{o} xvij^{o} inter parochianos parochie

* Sir William Pole includes William Wilford among the "men of best note, and wch have either in warre or peace bine employed in this countye," and tells us (p. 85) that he "made saile into Britaine wth div's ships of Devonshire, and in revenge of the harmes done by the Lord Cassils, hee tooke fortie ships laden wth oyle & wine, beside other exployts done by him, 4 of H. 4." Robert Wilford, his Father, was Mayor of Exeter no less than twelve times in the course of the years 1375—95; and William himself was Mayor in 1401 and four times afterwards. John was never Mayor; but he was one of the four Bailiffs (elected annually with the Mayor) in 1399, 1401, 1404, and 1412. It is curious that in these two contemporaneous Wills the Family Name should be given in two distinct forms—William Wilford—John Wilsford. Izacke, in his Antiquities of Exeter, adopts the latter form. So does Jenkins; but he only copied Izacke. I suppose Izacke must have seen these St. Kerian MSS., in another of which (dated 1384) Robert Wylsford (*sic*) occurs, and in yet another (dated 1398), William Wilsforde (*sic*). In all other instances, so far as I can learn (and the name occurs frequently), it is spelt Wilford. The "s" in these St. Kerian MSS. is exceedingly clearly written; but I cannot help thinking, though Izacke accepted it, that it must have been a clerical error.

Sancti Kyrany, Civitatis Exoniensis, ex una parte, et custodes ejusdem Ecclesie ex altera, testatur quod predicti custodes receperunt conjuntim (*sic*) in suam custodiam omnia ornamenta et jocalia in hac indentura subscripta et intitulata a predictis parochianis, a Festo Omnium Sanctorum usque ad idem Festum proximum sequens. Inprimis predicti custodes receperunt j calicem argenteam, cum patena, deauratam infra et extra, ponderantem xix uncias et j quarterium. Item, j calicem cum patena argentea deauratam infra, ponderantem xj uncias et iij quarteria. Item, j pixidem argenteam pro Eucaristia, ponderantem x uncias. Item, j seruram argenteam pro eadem pixide.* Item, quatuor corporalia cum iij^bus^ repositoriis. Item, j missale novum, quod incipit, in secundo folio, *in Te confido*. Item, aliud missale vetus quod incipit, in secundo folio, *Sancto superveniet*.* Item, j gradale novum quod incipit, in secundo folio, *vias Tuas*. Item, vetus gradale, quod incipit, in secundo folio, *Thare, qui fuit Nachor*. Item, j anthiphonale (*sic*) quod incipit, in secundo folio, *Quatinus eorum precibus*. Item, aliud anthiphonale (*sic*) quod incipit, in secundo folio, *Patri et Filio*. Item tercium antiphonale vetus, quod incipit, in secundo folio, *premia largiatur*. Item, j legendam sanctorum, que incipit, in secundo folio, ... *fices non potuerunt*. Item, aliam legendam temporalem, que incipit, in secundo folio, *postquam autem*. Item, j manuale novum, quod incipit, in secundo folio, *vis glorie Tue*. Item, vetus Manuale, quod incipit, in secundo folio, *Celi enarrant*. Item, j sinodum, que incipit, in secundo folio, *Offerebantur*. Item, j rubium par vestimentorum, contextum cum avibus auri, et cum orfrayys de viridi velwet. Item, j album par vestimentorum, mixtum cum purpera (*sic*) colore. Item, j par viridum vestimentorum, stregulatum, cum orfrayys de rubio tartaron, contextis cum rosis albis. Item, aliud viride par vestimentorum, stregulatum, cum orfrayys de rubio tartaron contextis cum liliis albis. Item, par blodium vestimentorum, cum rubiis orfrayys de tartaron contextis cum rosis albis. Item, j blodium par vestimentorum, cum orfrayys de rubio velwet. Item, rubium par vestimentorum mixtum cum Agnis Sancti Johannis Baptiste. Item, j albam casulam stregulatam de bord helisaunder, cum albis paruris liniis, contextis cum blodiis subligaribus. Item, par vetus vestimentorum de linio checker. Item, j vetus par vestimentorum de albo linio, polimitum cum angelis. Item, j blodiam capam novam de baudekyn, mixtam cum floribus rubiis et albis. Item, aliam veterem capam de bord helysaunder. Item, j superpellicium novum. Item, aliud vetus superpellicium fractum. Item, superpellicium pro aquebajulo. Item, j tuallum de Paris checker pro mensa Domini in die Passe. Item, iij frontella linia, polimita cum Agnis Johannis Baptiste in medio, et iij penula (*sic*) cum iij tuallis de canvas antedicta predictis frontellis pro quolibet altari. Item, j viride frontellum stragulatum, ad deserviendum magno altari in Duplicibus Festis. Item. ij penulas stregulatas, videlicet j viridem et alteram rubiam pro tuallis ad magnum altare pro Duplicibus Festis. Item, j viride frontellum stregulatum, quondam ordinatum supra magnum altare, cum anulis. Item,* ij virides ridellas stragulatas, ordinatas ad coram magni altaris in Festis Principalibus. Item, ix tualla pro altaribus. Item, ij amictus cum paruris, et j sine parura. Item, j pecia serici, videlicet iiij folia. Item, iij folia serici de lesere.

Item, j corporale et repositorium; et dubito de benediccione ejus. Item, j tunicam blodiam serici. Item, j vexillum nigrum pinctum cum clavibus. Item, j ridellum de . . . . . † et blodio tartaron, pendens supra altare. Item, j chalonem de albo et blodio mixtum cum animalibus, ad deserviendum coram summo altari in diebus festivis. Item j coopertarium (*sic*) blodium mixtum cum croceo colore et albo, ad deserviendum coram summo altari in diebus festivis. Item* duo . . . . † aria serica, et ij de borde helisaunder. Item, v fiolas stagneas. Item, j vas stagneum ad aquam benedicendam. Item,* j lucerna. Item, ij asseres pro Pace, cooperti cum vitro, et j asserem stagneum, et j asserem lignium, *et j de playster paris. Item, ij candelebra ferrea pro processionibus. Item, j lectrinum pro Evangelio, et alterum lectrinum pro summo altari. Item turribulum de latyn. Item, j herciam ad Tenebras candelarum Paschalium.

* A pen has been put through this "Item."
† This word has perished.

Item, j crucem de latyn et alteram de cupro. Item, j magnam cistam pro ornamentis Ecclesie, et duas bursas cum reliquiis. Item, ij manutergia pro manibus sacerdotis. Item, j . . . . .†pro corporibus mortuorum. Item, duo tintinabula ad elevacionem Corporis Dominici. *Item, feretrum mortuorum novum. Item, j . . . . . orium cum serura. Item, j superaltare clausum in ligno, et alterum marmoreum sine clausura ligni. Item, j velum linthium pro alta cruce tempore Quadragesimali. Item, cistam pro sepulchro Dominico. Item, j tabellam pictam de Resurreccione Domini. Item, j velum Quadragesimale, cum fune. *Item, parvam ymaginem Trinitatis, de alabastre. Item, parvam ymaginem Beate Marie, de alabastre, vocatam Pyty. Item, j discum cum capite Johannis Baptiste. Item, iij . . . . pila plumbi super altare, ad firmanda tualla. *Item, j scalam, in longitudine xix scallaria. Item, j novum missale, incipiente secundo folio—*tunc vero fiat*, cum clapsis (*sic*) de argento et deauratis. Item, j portiforium, incipiente secundo folio—*concede nos*, cum j cathena ferrea *et cum j registro argenteo.* Item, j vetus superpellicium. Item j par vestimentorum nigrorum, cum orfrays de nigro, cum Crucifixe. Item, j par candelabrorum de latyne magnum. Item, j parvum par Chaundelerium de latyne. Item, j palle de viridi, cum rubiis floribus, duplicatam cum blodio carde. Item, j canope. Item, j ridellum pro magno altari, de nigro, cum j Crucifixe de Blak Wosted, franged with silke. Item, j auter clothe ejusdem secte, cum Jhus. Item, ii Ridellys de Blak sylke, pro magno altari, cum stirres de golde. Item, iij candelebra de latyne. ‡Item . . . . . Item, unum discum stanneum pro cero Paschalli. Item j ymago Sancti Cristoforii, de alabastre. Item, ymago de Marie assumpcione, de alabastre. Item, j. velum pictum, cum ymagine Sancti Michaelis. Item, iij sheftes pro vexillis. Item, j vexillum de rubio Tartaron cum Barrys de auro. Item, j vexillum, cum ymagine Sancti Kierani et cum albis roeys. Item, j cista parva in Cancello juxta altare. Item, ij formulas ligneis (*sic*) in Navi Ecclesie. Item, j ymago Sancti Johannis Baptiste, cum j tabernacle. Item, j ymago Sancte Anne, cum j tabernacle. Item, j tabula, cum ymagine Sancti Erasmus (*sic*). Item, j tabula cum ymagine Sancti Cristofori. Item, iiij Chaundelerys de ferro in Candello (*sic*). Item, iij Chaundelerys de ferro in Navi Ecclesie. Item, j par trestallorum, cum j mensa pro obitibus per annum. Item, j case pro calice, de albis yerdys. Item j par vestimentorum de albo et blodio serico cum offeras (*sic*) de golde. Item, j novum superpellicium. Item, unum vexillum rubium cum ymagine Sancti Kierani. Item, j pixidis (*sic*) cum munimentis Ecclesie. Item, iij tualla de diaperwork.

---

* A pen has been put through this *Item*.
† This word has perished.
‡ Illegible; but a pen has been put through it.

CORRIGENDA.

[As this is a Book of Reference, it is recommended that the more important of the following corrections be indicated (by an asterisk or some other mark), in the Text, before the Book is used.

Page 1 ; under "Abyngdon," *for* 325b *read* 325 ; and *for* Alberton *read* Allerton

" 5 ; Andrew, John ; *see* page 322 (*note*).

" 7 ; *note* (5) ; *see* Smyth, Wm., page 332.

" 9 ; Auger ; *dele* "Precentor of."

" 16 ; Baudyn, John ; *for* 195b *read* 195.

" 19 ; Bele, John ; *for* 26 Feb. *read* 22 Feb.

" 25 ; Bodellek ; *for* 45 *read* 45b.

" 28 ; *for* Bome *read* Boure ; (and *see* note (2), page 33.

" 36 (note 1) : here, and in a few other instances, the Anglo-Saxon character ȝ is improperly used by the scribe to represent the letter z. Where the MS. is quoted, it has been strictly followed, throughout ; and it seems necessary to direct attention to this clerical error.

" 59 (also 155) *for* Clonenburgh *read* Clovenburgh ; the "n" seemed the more probable rendering of the ambiguous character which stands for "n" and "u" indifferently, as bringing the word closer to its modern form Clannaborough, and it was adopted by Dr. Oliver, in his Taxatio of Pope Nicholas IV. In Fox's Register however, I find the word spelt with a "v," which seems to settle the question.

" 62 (note) ; *for* inundencium *read* inundancium.

" 64 ; *dele* Colompton, John, and *add* 212b to the next entry.

" 81 ; line 39 ; *dele* (3)— reference to note.

" 92 (note 2) ; *for* Longbridge *read* Longbredy.

" 93 (three lines from bottom) ; *for* novi *read* non.

" 103, line 14 ; *for* off *read* of.

" 107, line 4 ; *for* Sidbury *read* Southmolton (see p. 334, line 16).

" 121 ; *for* Hakket *read* Hakker.

" 130 ; *for* Hetheway *read* Hetteway.

" 138 ; *for* Hyeonyse *read* Hyeovyse (*see* p. 441, where the "v" in the MS. is distinct. Also (Hykke, John), *for* 4 March *read* 14 March, and add the reference to the MS.,—ii, 239b.

" 149, line 20 ; *for* Robert *read* Roger.

" 157, lines 1, 3, 5 ; *for* the same *read* John Vautard.

" 159, line 2 ; *for* Sept. *read* Aug.

" 161 (line 19) and page 174 (line 30), *for* Trevell *read* Trebell.

" 175, Haccombe ; *for* Archipresbitatus *read* Archipresbiteratus.

" 179, Horwood—*Nicholas* ; *for* 31 *read* 30 (July).

" 183, line 8 ; *for* de *read* le de ; but the "le" is omitted in the Commission.

" 200, St. Endellion ; *for* John Harry *read* John Henry ; and, in the note, *for* Thomas *read* Thoma.

" 201, line 7 ; *for* 1413 *read* 1416.

" 204, line 49 ; *for* Knockys *read* Knokys.—This name still survives in Cornwall, as "Knuckey ;" and in the List of Ordinations (*see* page 441), it is spelt "Knoky."

" 205, line 15 ; *after* "was" *insert* "collated."

" 210, line 11 ; *for* Stokeleigh *read* Stokelegh ; also, line 30, *for* Richard *read* Robert ; and, line 38, *for* Hyeonyse *read* Hyeovyse.

" 218, line 16 ; *for* Robert *read* Roger.

" 232 ; *add* Labe, John, of Linkinhorne. i, 113b ; and, line 24, omit "John ...... 113b." and *add the reference* "i," 79b, after "1406."

„ 236, line 30 ; *for* 11 *read* 16.
„ 248 ; Lyghfote *and* Lyghtfote (John)—the *same* man is referred to.
„ 316, line 10 ; omit the comma after "is." Also, line 63 ; *for* editorum *read* editarum.
„ 337, line 39 ; *for* i, 348 *read* ii, 348.
„ 343, lines 32, 33 ; *for* decimio—dimidi*s* *read* decimi*s*—dimidio (letters transposed) : also for Sudden *read* Suddon (Joan).
„ 356, last line ; *for* Trewarnene *read* Trewarvene.
„ 431 ; *for* Dygondou *read* Dygondone.

ADDENDA ET NOTANDA.

Page 1 ; *add* Abergwili, *see* Prophet, John.—Also, to "Abyngdon, Thos.," *add* "*alias* Welyn" (q.v.)
„ 6 ; Ardagh ; *after* 220 *add* 225b.
„ 8 ; *add* atte Forde, alias Wybbery ; *see* p. 270.
„ 12 ; *add* Bamfeld, Richard ; *see* page 180 (HUXHAM).
„ 13, Barger ; *add* See page 302, line 3.
„ 19 ; *add* Beek, Reynald, *see* Tolke, Walter.
„ 22 ; Black Torrington, *add* See Totley.
„ 23 ; *add* Blake, Adam, *see* Brixham.
„ 27, Bole, John ; *insert* co-patron of Roche, R., ii, 57b.
„ 28, Bolter, Roger ; *add*—He was elected Dean of Exeter, but declined the promotion ; ii, 202b.
„ 35, Bradworthy ; *see* page 149 (*note*) ; *See*, also, the reference to page 149, below.
„ 38, Brixham ; *add*—*See* Harry, John ; also, *add* Brixton, *see* CARSLAKE, page 272.
„ 40, Brounste (or Bronste); *perhaps* Brouuste (or Brouste).
„ 46, Bykelegh, John ; *add*, his death, ii, 23.
„ 91 ; *add* Eggecombe, Baldwin de, *see* Twywil.
„ 115 ; *add* Godok, Thos., *see* Trelynow.
„ 130, Hickelyng, Hugh ; *add*—also, Canon of Glasney (*see* page 410).
„ 148, line 24 ; *after* day *insert* post prandium.
„ 149, note (1) ; the date was 19 Sept. ; *see* page 425, No. 36.
„ 152, line 27 (Gilbert Baker), *see* page 317 (note).
„ 153 (lines 38 and 42), 155 (line 42), 156 (line 52), 164 (lines 17 and 28), 165 (line 20), 171 (line 45), and 175 (line 15) ; *after* patron *insert* "hac vice."
„ 159, line 38 ; *after* 17 July, *add* ante horam Vesperarum illius diei.
„ 171, ST. PANCRAS (Exeter) ; Holond succeeded Rob. Lywer, who had been promoted to Drewsteignton.
„ 194, line 8 ; *add* ii, 161b.—also (PERRAN-UTHNO) ; Mayhow became Rector by exchange with Robert Seek (*see* TREVALGA, page 215).
„ 201, line 36 ; "Is ST. ERVAN intended ?" *Yes.*
„ 201 (*note*) ; *after* monicionum premissorum *add* "(*sic*)."
„ 223, Janinus ; *add*—and in Archdeacon Hunden's Will "Janyn de Coquina," i, 325.
„ 252, line 32 ; *insert* (after 194b) also 21 March, 1414-15 ; i, 209.
„ 268, line 51 ; *after* 'for' (for 'fro') *add* (sic MS.).
„ 365 ; *add* Wastell, Robert, i, 308.b
„ 369, line 25 ; *after* 16b *add* 24b.
„ 382 (*note*) ; perhaps "painted."
„ 429 ; *add* Bevyle,* Thomas, 70.
„ 431, *add* Eustose, Robert, 278.
„ 446, line 21 ; "Hugo . . . . 8." This entry is misplaced ; it belongs to p. 448, line 21.
„ 452, "Chicheley, Master Hy."—It is worthy of note that this Rector of St. Stephen's, Walbrooke, was none other than the famous Founder of All Souls' College, Oxford, Primate of all England.

SUBSCRIBERS TO THIS WORK.

The Lord Arundell of Wardour.
Acland, Prebendary, V. of *Broad Clyst.*
Alexander, R. D., R. of *South Pool.*
Allin, A. T., V. of *Holbeton.*
Amery, J. S., *Druid, Ashburton.*
Anderton, E. D., *Oakroyd, Falmouth.*
Anstiss, G. W., V. of *Ivybridge.*
Attwood, J. S., 7, *Woodbine Terrace, Exeter.*

The Earl Beauchamp.
The Lord Bishop of Bath and Wells.
Bailey, John, *Stretford, Manchester.*
Balkwill, Benjamin, Banker, *Kingsbridge.*
Baring-Gould, S., R. of *Lew Trenchard.*
Barnes, Archdeacon, R. of *Langtree.*
Barnes, (the late) Prebendary, *The Sanctuary, Probus.*
Barnes, Prebendary, V. of *Heavitree.*
Barnes, William, *Great Duryard, Exeter.*
Bartholomew, R., V. of *Harberton.*
Bartlet, J. M. de L. (Rev.), *Ludbrooke Manor, Modbury.*
Bastard, Baldwin J. Pollexfen, *Kitley.*
Batten, John, *Aldon, Yeovil.*
Bennett, E. G., 10, *Woodland Terrace, Plymouth.*
Bennett, J. A., V. of *South Cadbury, Bath.*
Bennet, R. Gully, *Tresillian, House, near St. Columb-Minor.*
Bewes, T. A. (Rev.), *Beaumont, Plymouth.*
Boase, C. W. (Rev.), Fellow of *Exeter College, Oxford.*
Boase, G. C., 15 *Queen Anne's Gate*, S.W.
Bolitho, E. Alverne, *Windsworth, Looe.*
Bolitho, William, *Polwithan, Penzance.*
Bolitho, William, *Ponsandane, Penzance.*
Bone, F. J., V. of *Stratton.*
Borlase, W. C. M.P., *Lariggan, Penzance.*
Boyle (the late) E. M., 14, *Hill Street, W.*
Browne, W. Bevil, (Rev.) *Grafton, Salcombe.*
Buck, R. H. K., R. of *St. Dominick.*
Bull, (Rev.) Thos. Wm., *Paulton House, Bristol.*
Bullen, J. A., V. of *Dawlish.*
Burch, Arthur, *Principal Registry, Exeter.*
Bush, Canon, R. of *Duloe.*

The Lord Archbishop of Canterbury.
The Lord Clinton.
The Lord Coleridge, Lord Chief Justice of England.
Carah, William, *Praze, Camborne.*
Cardell, T. Magor, *Conoarth, St. Columb.*
Carwithen, (the late) J. C., V. of *Stokenham.*
Carlyon, Edmund, *Polkyth, St. Austell.*
Cartwright, Mrs., *Albourne Place, Sussex* (2 copie).

Chater, D. S., V. of *Blackawton*.
Champernowne, R., R. of *Dartington*.
Chilcott, J. Gilbert, *Gwendroc*, *Truro*.
Clarke, Edward, M.P., 37 *Russell Square*, *W.C.*
Cleaver, W. H. (Rev.), *St. Peter's Home*, *Kilburn*, *N.W.*
Clerical Club, *East Cornwall*, (per Canon *Bush*).
Cocks, (the late) Colonel, *Treverbyn Vean*.
Colborne, Hon. Graham, R. of *Dittisham*.
Colby, F. T., D.D., R. of *Litton Cheney*, *Dorchester*.
Coöde, Edward, *Polapit Tamar*, *Launceston*.
Cope, C. H., R. of *Huish*, *Beaford*.
Cornish-Bowden, F. J., *Black Hall*, *Totnes*.
Cornwall, Royal Institution of, *Truro*.
Cotton, W., *No. 2*, *Manston Terrace*, *Exeter*.
Coulson, Canon, V. of *Bramley*, *Guildford*.
Courtenay, Hon. C. L., *Canon of Windsor*, *V. of Bovey Tracy*.
Courtenay, Hon. H. H., *Preb. of Exeter*, *R. of Powderham*.
Courtney, W. Prideaux, *15*, *Queen Anne's Gate*, *S.W.*
Cowie, B. M., D.D., Dean of Exeter.
Cox, J. Mercer, V. of *Plympton St. Mary*.

The Earl of Devon.
Sir John T. B. Duckworth, Bart.
Daniel, Thomas Carew, *Stoodleigh Court*.
Daubuz, J. C., *Killiow*, *Truro*.
Dawson, George, R. of *Woodleigh*.
David, W., R. of *St. Petrock's*, *Exeter*.
Davies-Gilbert, C., *Trelissick*.
Denison, Archdeacon, V. of *East Brent*.
Devon and Exeter Institution, *Exeter*.
Dimond-Churchward, M.D., V. of Northam, *Bideford*.
Dredge, J. Ingle, V. of *Buckland Brewer*, *Bideford*.
Du Boulay, H. H., V. of *St. Newlyn*.
Dunkin, E. H. W., *Kenwyn House*, *Kidbrooke Park*, *Blackheath*.
Dupuis, E. J. G., R. of *Alphington*.
Dymond, Robert, *1*, *St. Leonard's Road*, *Exeter*.

The Lord Bishop of Exeter.
Eady, Mrs., *Combe Royal*, *Kingsbridge* (2 copies).
Earle, Archdeacon, V. of *West Alvington* (2 copies).
Edmonds, Prebendary, R. of *High Bray*.
Ellacombe (the late*) H. T., R. of *Clyst St. George*.
Everett, A. J., V. of *Berry Pomeroy*.
Exeter, the Dean and Chapter of.
Exeter College, Oxford (Library).

The Earl Fortescue.
The Viscount Falmouth (2 copies).
Farrer, Fred., R. of *Bigbury*.
Fellowes, James, *Kingston House*, *Dorchester*.
Ferguson, R. S., *Carlisle*.
Fixsen, J. F., V. of *Bucknell Salop*.
Fleming, John, *Bigadon*.

---

* I cannot refrain from printing this venerable Clergyman's last words to me:—" Dear Friend,—I have much pleasure in subscribing to your forthcoming Volume, for which I enclose my cheque. I wish to *prepay*, as I may not be living when it is issued. Annus Novus sit tibi et tuis faustus, Deo benedicente, et vestro H. T. ELLACOMBE ; nato 15 Maii, 1790,—Domi de die in diem."

Fletcher, A. Chune, 12A, *Charterhouse Square, E.C.*
Flint, S. Raffles, R. of *Ladock.*
Foster, R., *Lanwithan, Lostwithiel.*
Frowde, Captain, *The Hayes, Newent.*
Frowde, Henry, the *Waldrens, Croydon.*
Furneaux (the late) Alan, V. of *St. Germans.*

Gardiner, the Misses, *The Close, Exeter.*
Garratt, John, *Bishop's Court.*
Gidley, Bartholomew, *Hoopern House, Exeter.*
Gill, Alfred, V. of *Harbertonford.*
Glencross, James (Rev), *Luxstow, Liskeard.*
Goodland, J., *Polperro.*
Granville, Roger, R. of *Bideford.*
Greenfield, B. W., 4, *Cranbury Terrace, Southampton.*
Gregory, E. I., V. of *Halberton.*
Grylls, Colonel, *Lewarn, near Liskeard.*

The Lord Bishop of Hereford.
Bishop Hobhouse.
Rev. Sir St. Vincent Hammick, Bart.
Sir J. McGarel Hogg, Bart., M.P.
Haggard, Christopher, R. of *Filleigh, South Molton.*
Halliday, Mrs. *Glenthorne, Lynton.*
Hanbury, Sampson, *Bishopstowe, Torquay.*
Harvey, Canon, V. of *Probus.*
Hawker (the late) Treasurer, R. of *Berry Narbor.*
Hayne, R. J., V. of *Buckland Monachorum.*
Hedgeland, Prebendary, V. of *Penzance.*
Hems, Harry, *Exeter.*
Hennings, Jas., Duncombe Lecturer, *Kingsbridge.*
Hext, F. J., *Tredethy.*
Highton, E., V. of *Bude.*
Hill, George, V. of *St. Winnow.*
Hingston, Dr. C. Albert, *Sussex Terrace, Plymouth.*
Hitchcock, W. H., (late) V. of *St. John's, Torquay.*
Hobhouse, Archdeacon, R. of *St. Ive.*
Hocken, Harry, V. of *Cople.*
Hockin, Canon, R. of *Phillack.*
Hole, H. T., R. of *Plympton St. Maurice.*
Holmes, T S., R. of *Wookey, Wells (Som).*
Hughes, J. B., V. of *Staverton, Totnes.*
Hullah, Thos., R. of *Calstock.*
Hunt, A. A., V. of *Tipton, Ottery.*
Hurrell, J. S., *The Manor House, Kingsbridge.*

The Earl of Iddesleigh.
Ilbert, P. A., R. of *Thurlestone.*

James, J. Harris, *Grampound.*
Jane, John, V. of *Upottery.*
Jones, E. Douglas, V. of *Looe.*

Kekewich, Trehawke, *Peamore, Exeter.*
Kellock, T. C., *Highfield, Totnes.*
Kelly, Reginald, of *Kelly.*
Kelly, Maitland, V. of *Salcombe.*
Kempe, Prebendary, R. of *Merton.*
Kendall, Francis, V. of *Lanlivery.*
Kinsman, Prebendary, V. of *Tintagel.*

Kirkham, Henry, *Ashcombe, Addlestone, Surrey.*

The Lord Bishop of London.
Sir Massey Lopes, Bart.
Lawrence, Arthur, R. of *St. Ewe.*
Lee, Major, *Dorrington, Whitchurch, Salop.*
Lester, E. A., V. of *Bishop's Nympton.*
Liddon, H. J. (Rev.) *South Milton, Kingsbridge.*
Lightfoot, J. Prideaux, D.D., Rector of *Exeter College, Oxford.*
London, the Guildhall Library.

The Earl of Mount Edgcumbe, (2 copies).
The Viscount Molesworth.
Maclean, Sir John, Knt. F.S.A.
Maclean, Henry, V. of *Lanteglos-by-Fowey.*
MacAndrew, J. J., *Lukesland.*
Marrack, Richard, *No. 2, Strangways Terrace, Truro.*
Marshall, G. W., LL.D., *No. 60. Onslow Gardens, London.*
Martin, Canon Richard, *Heath Lodge, Upton-on-Severn* (*Worc.*).
Martyn, H. J., *Seaward Villa, Newquay.*
Martyn, W. W., R. of *Lifton.*
Mann, C. Noel, V. of *St. Issey.*
Maskell, William, *Penzance.*
Metcalfe, James, V. of *West Teignmouth.*
Metcalfe, W. H., V. of *Ottery St. Mary.*
Mildmay, H. B., *Flete* (2 copies).
Mitchell, H., R. of *Loxbeare.*
Moore-Stevens, J. C., *Winscot, Torrington.*
Morcom, W. G., V. of *Braunton.*
Morris, Charles, V. of *Strete, South Devon.*

Northcote, Hon. H. S., M.P., No. 7, *Seamore Place, London.*
Northcote, Hon. A. F., R. of *Washfield.*
Norrington, Charles, *Abbotsfield, Plymouth.*

The Lord Bishop of Oxford.
Oldham, D'Oyly W., R. of *Exbourne.*
Ogle, (the late W. R.), V. of *Bishopsteignton.*

Sir Henry Peek, Bart.
Paul, F. B., R. of *Lanivet.*
Pearson, J. B., D.D., R. of *Whitstone, Exeter.*
Pearson, J. L., 13, *Mansfield Street, W.*
Pentreath, F. R., D.D., *Powderham Terrace, Teignmouth.*
Penzance Public Library.
Peters, W. H., *Harefield.*
Phillpots, Canon, *Porthgwidden.*
Phillpotts Library, *Truro.*
Pigot, Prebendary, R. of *Fremington.*
Piper, G. H., *Court House, Ledbury.*
Pitman, Mrs., *The Rectory, Aveton Giffard.*
Pitts, N. W. P., *Whympston, Modbury.*
Pode, J. D., *Slade Hall, Cornwood.*
Poland, F. W., V. of *Paignton* (2 copies).
Pole-Carew, W. H., *Antony.*
Powell, J. R., R. of *Buckland Filleigh.*
Power, John, V. of *Alternon.*
Powning, Jas., *Dart View, Totnes* (2 copies).
Poynton, F. J., R. of *Kelston, Bath.*
Price, Major W. E., *Hillfield, Gloucester.*

Prideaux-Brune, C. G., *Prideaux Place, Padstow.*
Purcell, W. H. D'Olier, V. of *Exmouth.*
Purey-Cust, A. P., D.D., Dean of York.
Pye, F. W., R. of *Blisland.*

The Lord Robartes (2 copies).
Admiral of the Fleet, Sir Alfred Ryder, K.C.B.
Radford, W. T. A., R. of *Down St. Mary.*
Randolph, Douglas Cater (Rev.), *Orford, Wickham Market.*
Rashleigh, Jonathan, *Menabilly.*
Rashleigh, Stanhope (Rev.), *West Lodge, Wickham (Hants).*
Reibey, J. H., R. of *Denbury.*
Rodd, (the late) Charles, R. of *Northill.*
Rodd, H. Tremayne, V. of *St. Gwinear.*
Roe, H. Farwell, R. of *Revelstoke.*
Rogers, Canon, V. of *Gwennap.*
Rogers, W., R. of *Mawnan.*
Rolleston, Septimus, V. of *St. Minver.*
Ross, C. C., *Morrab House, Penzance.*
Rossall, J. H., *Rock House, Torquay.*
Rowe, J. Brooking, *Plympton Lodge.*
Rundle, W. Dunstan, R. of *Little Hempston.*

The Earl of St. German's.
The Lord Bishop of St. David's.
The Lord Bishop of Salisbury.
Sir John St. Aubyn, Bart.
Lady Prothero Smith.
St. Aubyn, St. Aubyn Hender Molesworth, *Clowance.*
St. Aubyn, Edmund, R. of *Stoke Fleming.*
St. Aubyn, J. Piers, *Lambe Buildings, Temple, E.C.*
Salisbury, E. Lister, V. of *St. Agnes.*
Sanders, Archdeacon, Chancellor of Exeter Cathedral.
Sandford, Prebendary, V. of *Cornwood.*
Scobell, G. R., V. of *Bickleigh.*
Sergeant, Capt. C. E., *St. Benet's, Lanivet.*
Seymour, A. E., V. of *Bromsgrove.*
Shelly, John, 20, *Princess Square, Plymouth.*
Shewell, Frank, V. of *Loddiswell.*
Shuckford, Mrs., *Blistra-Bay House, Newquay.*
Simms, A. H., V. of *Kingsbridge.*
Smith, H. J. E., V. of *Crantock.*
Sorrell, Joseph (Rev.), *St. Bartholomew-the-Great, E.C.*
Southcomb, H. G., R. of *Rosecash.*
Spencer, A., R. of *St. Sidwell's, Exeter.*
Spry, E. G., *Furze-upland, Kenwyn.*
Steinmetz, J. H., *Heathfield, Bushey.*
Stephens, John, 5, *Elm Terrace, St. Austell.*
Strother, J. B., V. of *Shaugh Prior.*
Stubbs, C. W., V. of *Stokenham.*
Surridge, J. E., R. of *Dodbrooke*
Sutton, Meyrick, V. of *St. Keverne.*

The Lord Bishop of Truro.
Bishop Twells.
Tanner, J. Vowler, R. of *Chawleigh.*
Theed, E. R., R. of *Sampford Courtenay*
Thornton, G. W., R. of *Holsworthy.*
Thornton, W. H., R. of *North Bovey.*

Thynne, Canon, R. of *Kilkhampton.*
Tregellas, Walter, *Morlah Lodge, Brompton, S.W.*
Tremayne, J., *Heligan.*
Tremenheere, Hugh Seymour, C.B., 43, *Thurloe Square, S.W.* (2 copies.)
Turner, Miss, *Armidale, Salcombe.*
Twysden, Thos., R. of *Charleton.*

Rev. Sir Vyell Vyvyan, Bart.
Vautier, Canon, R. of *St. Mabyn.*
Venning, J. J. E., *Ker Street, Devonport.*
Ventris, H. L., R. of *St Columb.*
Vivian, Colonel, *Exeter.*
Vyvyan, Herbert F., R. of *Withiel.*
Vyvyan-Robinson, P., R. of *Landewednack.*

The Lord Bishop of Winchester.
The Lord Bishop of Worcester.
Sir John Walrond, Bart.
Admiral of the Fleet, Sir Provo Wallis, G.C.B. (2 copies).
Wainwright, Thos., *Barnstaple.*
Wallas, G. J., R. of *Shobrooke.*
Walrond, W. H., M.P., *11, Beaufort Gardens, London, S.W.*
Waterfield, H. B., V. of *St. Eval.*
Waters, Edmund Chester, *29, The Grove, Hammersmith, W.*
Weaver, F. W., V. of *Milton, Evercreech.*
Wells, the Dean and Chapter of.
Weymouth, T. Wyse, *Wolston House, Kingsbridge.*
Wheeler, Benjamin (Rev.), *South Huish, Kingsbridge.*
Whitaker, Canon, Chancellor of the Cathedral, *Truro.*
Wilkinson, Prebendary, D.D., V. of *Plymouth.*
Williams, Henry, R. of *Ashleworth, Gloucester.*
Williams, Philip, R. of *Rewe.*
Willimott, W., V. of *Quethiock.*
Windeatt, Edward, *Totnes.*
Wise, Canon, *Ladock* (2 copies).
Wolfe, Prebendary, *Torquay.*
Woollcombe, (the late) Archdeacon, *The Close, Exeter.*
Wrey, A. Bourchier, V. of *St. Mary Church.*
Wroth, John, *Combe, Bigbury.*
Wyatt, Mrs., *Corse Vicarage, Gloucester.*
Wyatt, Mrs. Robert, *Lower House, Thursley, Godalming.*